American Casebook Series
Hornbook Series and Basic Legal Texts
Nutshell Series

of

WEST PUBLISHING COMPANY
P.O. Box 3526
St. Paul, Minnesota 55165
June, 1982

ACCOUNTING

Fiflis and Kripke's Teaching Materials on Accounting for Business Lawyers, 2nd Ed., 684 pages, 1977 (Casebook)

ADMINISTRATIVE LAW

Davis' Cases, Text and Problems on Administrative Law, 6th Ed., 683 pages, 1977 (Casebook)

Davis' Basic Text on Administrative Law, 3rd Ed., 617 pages, 1972 (Text)

Davis' Police Discretion, 176 pages, 1975 (Text)

Gellhorn and Boyer's Administrative Law and Process in a Nutshell, 2nd Ed., 445 pages, 1981 (Text)

Mashaw and Merrill's Introduction to the American Public Law System, 1095 pages, 1975, with 1980 Supplement (Casebook)

Robinson, Gellhorn and Bruff's The Administrative Process, 2nd Ed., 959 pages, 1980 (Casebook)

ADMIRALTY

Healy and Sharpe's Cases and Materials on Admiralty, 875 pages, 1974 (Casebook)

AGENCY—PARTNERSHIP

Fessler's Alternatives to Incorporation for Persons in Quest of Profit, 258 pages, 1980 (Casebook)

Henn's Cases and Materials on Agency, Partnership and Other Unincorporated Business Enterprises, 396 pages, 1972 (Casebook)

Reuschlein and Gregory's Hornbook on the Law of Agency and Partnership, 625 pages, 1979, with 1981 pocket part (Text)

AGENCY—PARTNERSHIP—Continued

Seavey's Hornbook on Agency, 329 pages, 1964 (Text)

Seavey and Hall's Cases on Agency, 431 pages, 1956 (Casebook)

Seavey, Reuschlein and Hall's Cases on Agency and Partnership, 599 pages, 1962 (Casebook)

Selected Corporation and Partnership Statutes and Forms, approximately 775 pages, 1982

Steffen and Kerr's Cases and Materials on Agency-Partnership, 4th Ed., 859 pages, 1980 (Casebook)

Steffen's Agency-Partnership in a Nutshell, 364 pages, 1977 (Text)

AMERICAN INDIAN LAW

Canby's American Indian Law in a Nutshell, 288 pages, 1981 (Text)

Getches, Rosenfelt and Wilkinson's Cases on Federal Indian Law, 660 pages, 1979 (Casebook)

ANTITRUST LAW

Gellhorn's Antitrust Law and Economics in a Nutshell, 2nd Ed., 425 pages, 1981 (Text)

Oppenheim, Weston and McCarthy's Cases and Comments on Federal Antitrust Laws, 4th Ed., 1168 pages, 1981 (Casebook)

Posner and Easterbrook's Cases and Economic Notes on Antitrust, 2nd Ed., 1077 pages, 1981 (Casebook)

Sullivan's Hornbook of the Law of Antitrust, 886 pages, 1977 (Text)

See also Regulated Industries, Trade Regulation

LAW SCHOOL PUBLICATIONS—Continued

BANKING LAW

See Regulated Industries

BUSINESS PLANNING

Epstein and Scheinfeld's Teaching Materials on Business Reorganization Under the Bankruptcy Code, 216 pages, 1980 (Casebook)

Painter's Problems and Materials in Business Planning, 791 pages, 1975, with 1982 Supplement (Casebook)

Selected Securities and Business Planning Statutes, Rules and Forms, approximately 490 pages, 1982

CIVIL PROCEDURE

Casad's Res Judicata in a Nutshell, 310 pages, 1976 (text)

Cound, Friedenthal and Miller's Cases and Materials on Civil Procedure, 3rd Ed., 1147 pages, 1980 with 1982 Supplement (Casebook)

Cound, Friedenthal and Miller's Cases on Pleading, Joinder and Discovery, 643 pages, 1968 (Casebook)

Ehrenzweig, Louisell and Hazard's Jurisdiction in a Nutshell, 4th Ed., 232 pages, 1980 (Text)

Federal Rules of Civil-Appellate-Criminal Procedure—West Law School Edition, approximately 350 pages, 1982

Hodges, Jones and Elliott's Cases and Materials on Texas Trial and Appellate Procedure, 2nd Ed., 745 pages, 1974 (Casebook)

Hodges, Jones and Elliott's Cases and Materials on the Judicial Process Prior to Trial in Texas, 2nd Ed., 871 pages, 1977 (Casebook)

Kane's Civil Procedure in a Nutshell, 271 pages, 1979 (Text)

Karlen's Procedure Before Trial in a Nutshell, 258 pages, 1972 (Text)

Karlen and Joiner's Cases and Materials on Trials and Appeals, 536 pages, 1971 (Casebook)

Karlen, Meisenholder, Stevens and Vestal's Cases on Civil Procedure, 923 pages, 1975 (Casebook)

Koffler and Reppy's Hornbook on Common Law Pleading, 663 pages, 1969 (Text)

McBaine's Cases on Introduction to Civil Procedure, 399 pages, 1950 (Casebook)

McCoid's Cases on Civil Procedure, 823 pages, 1974 (Casebook)

Park's Computer-Aided Exercises on Civil Procedure, 118 pages, 1976 (Coursebook)

Shipman's Hornbook on Common-Law Pleading, 3rd Ed., 644 pages, 1923 (Text)

CIVIL PROCEDURE—Continued

Siegel's Hornbook on New York Practice, 1011 pages, 1978 with 1981–82 Pocket Part (Text)

See also Federal Jurisdiction and Procedure

CIVIL RIGHTS

Abernathy's Cases and Materials on Civil Rights, 660 pages, 1980 (Casebook)

Cohen's Cases on the Law of Deprivation of Liberty: A Study in Social Control, 755 pages, 1980 (Casebook)

Lockhart, Kamisar and Choper's Cases on Constitutional Rights and Liberties, 5th Ed., 1298 pages plus Appendix, 1981, with 1982 Supplement (Casebook)—reprint from Lockhart, et al. Cases on Constitutional Law, 5th Ed., 1980

Vieira's Civil Rights in a Nutshell, 279 pages, 1978 (Text)

COMMERCIAL LAW

Bailey's Secured Transactions in a Nutshell, 2nd Ed., 391 pages, 1981 (Text)

Epstein and Martin's Basic Uniform Commercial Code Teaching Materials, 599 pages, 1977 (Casebook)

Henson's Hornbook on Secured Transactions Under the U.C.C., 2nd Ed., 504 pages, 1979 with 1979 P.P. (Text)

Murray's Commercial Law, Problems and Materials, 366 pages, 1975 (Coursebook)

Nordstrom and Clovis' Problems and Materials on Commercial Paper, 458 pages, 1972 (Casebook)

Nordstrom and Lattin's Problems and Materials on Sales and Secured Transactions, 809 pages, 1968 (Casebook)

Nordstrom, Murray and Clovis' Problems and Materials on Sales, 515 pages, 1982 (Casebook)

Nordstrom's Hornbook on Sales, 600 pages, 1970 (Text)

Selected Commercial Statutes, 1367 pages, 1981

Speidel, Summers and White's Teaching Materials on Commercial and Consumer Law, 3rd Ed., 1490 pages, 1981 (Casebook)

Stockton's Sales in a Nutshell, 2nd Ed., 370 pages, 1981 (Text)

Stone's Uniform Commercial Code in a Nutshell, 507 pages, 1975 (Text)

Uniform Commercial Code, Official Text with Comments, 994 pages, 1978

UCC Article 8, 1977 Amendments, 249 pages, 1978

UCC Article 9, Reprint from 1962 Code, 128 pages, 1976

UCC Article 9, 1972 Amendments, 304 pages, 1978

COMMERCIAL LAW—Continued

Weber and Speidel's Commercial Paper in a Nutshell, 3rd Ed., 404 pages, 1982 (Text)

White and Summers' Hornbook on the Uniform Commercial Code, 2nd Ed., 1250 pages, 1980 (Text)

COMMUNITY PROPERTY

Huie's Texas Cases and Materials on Marital Property Rights, 681 pages, 1966 (Casebook)

Mennell's Community Property in a Nutshell, approximately 410 pages, 1982 (Text)

Verrall's Cases and Materials on California Community Property, 3rd Ed., 547 pages, 1977 (Casebook)

COMPARATIVE LAW

Glendon, Gordon, and Osakwe's Comparative Legal Traditions in a Nutshell, 402 pages, 1982 (Text)

Langbein's Comparative Criminal Procedure: Germany, 172 pages, 1977 (Casebook)

CONFLICT OF LAWS

Cramton, Currie and Kay's Cases-Comments-Questions on Conflict of Laws, 3rd Ed., 1026 pages, 1981 (Casebook)

Ehrenzweig's Conflicts in a Nutshell, 3rd Ed., 432 pages, 1974 (Text)

Scoles and Hay's Hornbook on Conflict of Laws, approximately 950 pages, 1982 (Text)

Scoles and Weintraub's Cases and Materials on Conflict of Laws, 2nd Ed., 966 pages, 1972, with 1978 Supplement (Casebook)

Siegel's Conflicts in a Nutshell, 469 pages, 1982 (Text)

CONSTITUTIONAL LAW

Engdahl's Constitutional Power in a Nutshell: Federal and State, 411 pages, 1974 (Text)

Lockhart, Kamisar and Choper's Cases-Comments-Questions on Constitutional Law, 5th Ed., 1705 pages plus Appendix, 1980, with 1982 Supplement (Casebook)

Lockhart, Kamisar and Choper's Cases-Comments-Questions on the American Constitution, 5th Ed., 1185 pages plus Appendix, 1981, with 1982 Supplement (Casebook)—reprint from Lockhart, et al. Cases on Constitutional Law, 5th Ed., 1980

Manning's The Law of Church-State Relations in a Nutshell, 305 pages, 1981 (Text)

Miller's Presidential Power in a Nutshell, 328 pages, 1977 (Text)

CONSTITUTIONAL LAW—Continued

Nowak, Rotunda and Young's Handbook on Constitutional Law, 974 pages, 1978, with 1982 pocket part (Text)

Rotunda's Modern Constitutional Law: Cases and Notes, 1034 pages, 1981, with 1982 Supplement (Casebook)

Williams' Constitutional Analysis in a Nutshell, 388 pages, 1979 (Text)

See also Civil Rights

CONSUMER LAW

Epstein and Nickles' Consumer Law in a Nutshell, 2nd Ed., 418 pages, 1981 (Text)

McCall's Consumer Protection, Cases, Notes and Materials, 594 pages, 1977, with 1977 Statutory Supplement (Casebook)

Schrag's Cases and Materials on Consumer Protection, 2nd Ed., 197 pages, 1973 (Casebook)—reprint from Cooper, et al. Cases on Law and Poverty, 2nd Ed., 1973

Selected Commercial Statutes, 1367 pages, 1981

Spanogle and Rohner's Cases and Materials on Consumer Law, 693 pages, 1979, with 1982 Supplement (Casebook)

See also Commercial Law

CONTRACTS

Calamari & Perillo's Cases and Problems on Contracts, 1061 pages, 1978 (Casebook)

Calamari and Perillo's Hornbook on Contracts, 2nd Ed., 878 pages, 1977 (Text)

Corbin's Text on Contracts, One Volume Student Edition, 1224 pages, 1952 (Text)

Fessler and Loiseaux's Cases and Materials on Contracts, approximately 960 pages, 1982 (Casebook)

Freedman's Cases and Materials on Contracts, 658 pages, 1973 (Casebook)

Friedman's Contract Remedies in a Nutshell, 323 pages, 1981 (Text)

Fuller and Eisenberg's Cases on Basic Contract Law, 4th Ed., 1203 pages, 1981 (Casebook)

Jackson and Bollinger's Cases on Contract Law in Modern Society, 2nd Ed., 1329 pages, 1980 (Casebook)

Keyes' Government Contracts in a Nutshell, 423 pages, 1979 (Text)

Reitz's Cases on Contracts as Basic Commercial Law, 763 pages, 1975 (Casebook)

Schaber and Rohwer's Contracts in a Nutshell, 307 pages, 1975 (Text)

Simpson's Hornbook on Contracts, 2nd Ed., 510 pages, 1965 (Text)

LAW SCHOOL PUBLICATIONS—Continued

COPYRIGHT

Nimmer's Cases and Materials on Copyright and Other Aspects of Law Pertaining to Literary, Musical and Artistic Works, Illustrated, 2nd Ed., 1023 pages, 1979 (Casebook)

See also Patent Law

CORPORATIONS

Hamilton's Cases on Corporations—Including Partnerships and Limited Partnerships, 2nd Ed., 1108 pages, 1981, with 1981 Statutory Supplement (Casebook)

Hamilton's Law of Corporations in a Nutshell, 379 pages, 1980 (Text)

Henn's Cases on Corporations, 1279 pages, 1974, with 1980 Supplement (Casebook)

Henn's Hornbook on Corporations, 2nd Ed., 956 pages, 1970 (Text)

Jennings and Buxbaum's Cases and Materials on Corporations, 5th Ed., 1180 pages, 1979 (Casebook)

Selected Corporation and Partnership Statutes, Regulations and Forms, approximately 775 pages, 1982

Solomon, Stevenson and Schwartz' Materials and Problems on the Law and Policies on Corporations, approximately 1160 pages, 1982 (Casebook)

CORRECTIONS

Krantz's Cases and Materials on the Law of Corrections and Prisoners' Rights, 2nd Ed., 735 pages, 1981, with 1982 Supplement (Casebook)

Krantz's Law of Corrections and Prisoners' Rights in a Nutshell, 353 pages, 1976 (Text)

Model Rules and Regulations on Prisoners' Rights and Responsibilities, 212 pages, 1973

Popper's Post-Conviction Remedies in a Nutshell, 360 pages, 1978 (Text)

Robbins' Cases and Materials on Post Conviction Remedies, 506 pages, 1982 (Casebook)

Rubin's Law of Criminal Corrections, 2nd Ed., 873 pages, 1973, with 1978 Supplement (Text)

CREDITOR'S RIGHTS

Epstein's Debtor-Creditor Law in a Nutshell, 2nd Ed., 324 pages, 1980 (Text)

Epstein and Landers' Debtors and Creditors: Cases and Materials, 2nd Ed., approximately 725 pages, 1982 (Casebook)

Epstein and Sheinfeld's Teaching Materials on Business Reorganization Under the Bankruptcy Code, 216 pages, 1980 (Casebook)

CREDITOR'S RIGHTS—Continued

Riesenfeld's Cases and Materials on Creditors' Remedies and Debtors' Protection, 3rd Ed., 810 pages, 1979 with 1979 Statutory Supplement and 1981 Case Supplement (Casebook)

Selected Bankruptcy Statutes, 351 pages, 1979

CRIMINAL LAW AND CRIMINAL PROCEDURE

Cohen and Gobert's Problems in Criminal Law, 297 pages, 1976 (Problem book)

Davis' Police Discretion, 176 pages, 1975 (Text)

Dix and Sharlot's Cases and Materials on Criminal Law, 2nd Ed., 771 pages, 1979 (Casebook)

Federal Rules of Civil-Appellate-Criminal Procedure—West Law School Edition, approximately 350 pages, 1982

Grano's Problems in Criminal Procedure, 2nd Ed., 176 pages, 1981 (Problem book)

Heymann and Kenety's The Murder Trial of Wilbur Jackson: A Homicide in the Family, 340 pages, 1975 (Case Study)

Israel and LaFave's Criminal Procedure in a Nutshell, 3rd Ed., 438 pages, 1980 (Text)

Johnson's Cases, Materials and Text on Substantive Criminal Law in its Procedural Context, 2nd Ed., 956 pages, 1980 (Casebook)

Kamisar, LaFave and Israel's Cases, Comments and Questions on Modern Criminal Procedure, 5th ed., 1635 pages plus Appendix, 1980 with 1982 Supplement (Casebook)

Kamisar, LaFave and Israel's Cases, Comments and Questions on Basic Criminal Procedure, 5th Ed., 869 pages, 1980 with 1982 Supplement (Casebook)—reprint from Kamisar, et al. Modern Criminal Procedure, 5th ed., 1980

LaFave's Modern Criminal Law: Cases, Comments and Questions, 789 pages, 1978 (Casebook)

LaFave and Scott's Hornbook on Criminal Law, 763 pages, 1972 (Text)

Langbein's Comparative Criminal Procedure: Germany, 172 pages, 1977 (Casebook)

Loewy's Criminal Law in a Nutshell, 302 pages, 1975 (Text)

Saltzburg's American Criminal Procedure, Cases and Commentary, 1253 pages, 1980 with 1982 Supplement (Casebook)

LAW SCHOOL PUBLICATIONS—Continued

CRIMINAL LAW AND CRIMINAL PROCEDURE—Continued

Saltzburg's Introduction to American Criminal Procedure, 702 pages, 1980 with 1982 Supplement (Casebook)—reprint from Saltzburg's American Criminal Procedure, 1980

Uviller's The Processes of Criminal Justice: Investigation and Adjudication, 2nd Ed., 1384 pages, 1979 with 1979 Statutory Supplement and 1980 Update (Casebook)

Uviller's The Processes of Criminal Justice: Adjudication, 2nd Ed., 730 pages, 1979. Soft-cover reprint from Uviller's The Processes of Criminal Justice: Investigation and Adjudication, 2nd Ed. (Casebook)

Uviller's The Processes of Criminal Justice: Investigation, 2nd Ed., 655 pages, 1979. Soft-cover reprint from Uviller's The Processes of Criminal Justice: Investigation and Adjudication, 2nd Ed. (Casebook)

Vorenberg's Cases on Criminal Law and Procedure, 2nd Ed., 1088 pages, 1981 (Casebook)

See also Corrections, Juvenile Justice

DECEDENTS ESTATES

See Trusts and Estates

DOMESTIC RELATIONS

Clark's Cases and Problems on Domestic Relations, 3rd Ed., 1153 pages, 1980 (Casebook)

Clark's Hornbook on Domestic Relations, 754 pages, 1968 (Text)

Krause's Cases and Materials on Family Law, 1132 pages, 1976, with 1978 Supplement (Casebook)

Krause's Family Law in a Nutshell, 400 pages, 1977 (Text)

EDUCATION LAW

Morris' The Constitution and American Education, 2nd Ed., 992 pages, 1980 (Casebook)

EMPLOYMENT DISCRIMINATION

Cooper, Rabb and Rubin's Fair Employment Litigation: Text and Materials for Student and Practitioner, 590 pages, 1975 (Coursebook)

Player's Cases and Materials on Employment Discrimination Law, 878 pages, 1980 with 1982 Supplement (Casebook)

Player's Federal Law of Employment Discrimination in a Nutshell, 2nd Ed., 402 pages, 1981 (Text)

EMPLOYMENT DISCRIMINATION—Continued

Sovern's Cases and Materials on Racial Discrimination in Employment, 2nd Ed., 167 pages, 1973 (Casebook)—reprint from Cooper et al. Cases on Law and Poverty, 2nd Ed., 1973

See also Women and the Law

ENERGY AND NATURAL RESOURCES LAW

Rodgers' Cases and Materials on Energy and Natural Resources Law, 995 pages, 1979 (Casebook)

Selected Environmental Law Statutes, 681 pages, 1981

Tomain's Energy Law in a Nutshell, 338 pages, 1981 (Text)

See also Environmental Law, Oil and Gas, Water Law

ENVIRONMENTAL LAW

Currie's Cases and Materials on Pollution, 715 pages, 1975 (Casebook)

Federal Environmental Law, 1600 pages, 1974 (Text)

Findley and Farber's Cases and Materials on Environmental Law, 738 pages, 1981 (Casebook)

Hanks, Tarlock and Hanks' Cases on Environmental Law and Policy, 1242 pages, 1974, with 1976 Supplement (Casebook)

Rodgers' Hornbook on Environmental Law, 956 pages, 1977 (Text)

Selected Environmental Law Statutes, 681 pages, 1981

See also Energy and Natural Resources Law, Water Law

EQUITY

See Remedies

ESTATES

See Trusts and Estates

ESTATE PLANNING

Casner and Stein's Estate Planning under the Tax Reform Act of 1976, 2nd Ed., 456 pages, 1978 (Coursebook)

Kurtz' Cases, Materials and Problems on Family Estate Planning, approximately 850 pages, 1982 (Casebook)

Lynn's Introduction to Estate Planning, in a Nutshell, 2nd Ed., 378 pages, 1978 (Text)

See also Taxation

EVIDENCE

Broun and Meisenholder's Problems in Evidence, 2nd Ed., 304 pages, 1981 (Problem book)

LAW SCHOOL PUBLICATIONS—Continued

EVIDENCE—Continued

Cleary and Strong's Cases, Materials and Problems on Evidence, 3rd Ed., 1143 pages, 1981 (Casebook)

Federal Rules of Evidence for United States Courts and Magistrates, 325 pages, 1979

Graham's Federal Rules of Evidence in a Nutshell, 429 pages, 1981 (Text)

Kimball's Programmed Materials on Problems in Evidence, 380 pages, 1978 (Problem book)

Lempert and Saltzburg's A Modern Approach to Evidence: Text, Problems, Transcripts and Cases, 2nd Ed., approximately 1240 pages, 1982 (Casebook)

Lilly's Introduction to the Law of Evidence, 486 pages, 1978 (Text)

McCormick, Elliott and Sutton's Cases and Materials on Evidence, 5th Ed., 1212 pages, 1981 (Casebook)

McCormick's Hornbook on Evidence, 2nd Ed., 938 pages, 1972, with 1978 pocket part (Text)

Rothstein's Evidence, State and Federal Rules in a Nutshell, 2nd Ed., 514 pages, 1981 (Text)

Saltzburg's Evidence Supplement: Rules, Statutes, Commentary, 245 pages, 1980 (Casebook Supplement)

FEDERAL JURISDICTION AND PROCEDURE

Currie's Cases and Materials on Federal Courts, 3rd Ed., approximately 1050 pages, 1982 (Casebook)

Currie's Federal Jurisdiction in a Nutshell, 2nd Ed., 258 pages, 1981 (Text)

Federal Rules of Civil-Appellate-Criminal Procedure—West Law School Edition, approximately 350 pages, 1982

Forrester and Moye's Cases and Materials on Federal Jurisdiction and Procedure, 3rd Ed., 917 pages, 1977 with 1981 Supplement (Casebook)

Merrill and Vetri's Problems on Federal Courts and Civil Procedure, 460 pages, 1974 (Problem book)

Wright's Hornbook on Federal Courts, 3rd Ed., 818 pages, 1976 (Text)

FUTURE INTERESTS

See Trusts and Estates

HOUSING AND URBAN DEVELOPMENT

Berger's Cases and Materials on Housing, 2nd Ed., 254 pages, 1973 (Casebook)—reprint from Cooper et al. Cases on Law and Poverty, 2nd Ed., 1973

See also Land Use

INDIAN LAW

See American Indian Law

INSURANCE

Dobbyn's Insurance Law in a Nutshell, 281 pages, 1981 (Text)

Keeton's Cases on Basic Insurance Law, 2nd Ed., 1086 pages, 1977

Keeton's Basic Text on Insurance Law, 712 pages, 1971 (Text)

Keeton's Case Supplement to Keeton's Basic Text on Insurance Law, 334 pages, 1978 (Casebook)

Keeton's Programmed Problems in Insurance Law, 243 pages, 1972 (Text Supplement)

York and Whelan's Cases, Materials and Problems on Insurance Law, aproximately 780 pages, 1982 (Casebook)

INTERNATIONAL LAW

Henkin, Pugh, Schachter and Smit's Cases and Materials on International Law, 2nd Ed., 1152 pages, 1980, with Documents Supplement (Casebook)

Jackson's Legal Problems of International Economic Relations, 1097 pages, 1977, with Documents Supplement (Casebook)

Kirgis' International Organizations in Their Legal Setting, 1016 pages, 1977, with 1981 Supplement (Casebook)

Weston, Falk and D'Amato's International Law and World Order—A Problem Oriented Coursebook 1195 pages, 1980, with Documents Supplement (Casebook)

Wilson's International Business Transactions in a Nutshell, 393 pages, 1981 (Text)

INTRODUCTION TO LAW

Dobbyn's So You Want to go to Law School, Revised First Edition, 206 pages, 1976 (Text)

Kinyon's Introduction to Law Study and Law Examinations in a Nutshell, 389 pages, 1971 (Text)

See also Legal Method and Legal System

JUDICIAL ADMINISTRATION

Carrington, Meador and Rosenberg's Justice on Appeal, 263 pages, 1976 (Casebook)

Leflar's Appellate Judicial Opinions, 343 pages, 1974 (Text)

Nelson's Cases and Materials on Judicial Administration and the Administration of Justice, 1032 pages, 1974 (Casebook)

JURISPRUDENCE

Christie's Text and Readings on Jurisprudence—The Philosophy of Law, 1056 pages, 1973 (Casebook)

LAW SCHOOL PUBLICATIONS—Continued

JUVENILE JUSTICE

Fox's Cases and Materials on Modern Juvenile Justice, 2nd Ed., 960 pages, 1981 (Casebook)

Fox's Juvenile Courts in a Nutshell, 2nd Ed., 275 pages, 1977 (Text)

LABOR LAW

Gorman's Basic Text on Labor Law-Unionization and Collective Bargaining, 914 pages, 1976 (Text)

Leslie's Labor Law in a Nutshell, 403 pages, 1979 (Text)

Nolan's Labor Arbitration Law and Practice in a Nutshell, 358 pages, 1979 (Text)

Oberer, Hanslowe and Andersen's Cases and Materials on Labor Law—Collective Bargaining in a Free Society, 2nd Ed., 1168 pages, 1979, with 1979 Statutory Supplement and 1982 Case Supplement (Casebook)

See also Employment Discrimination, Social Legislation

LAND FINANCE

See Real Estate Transactions

LAND USE

Hagman's Cases on Public Planning and Control of Urban and Land Development, 2nd Ed., 1301 pages, 1980 (Casebook)

Hagman's Hornbook on Urban Planning and Land Development Control Law, 706 pages, 1971 (Text)

Wright and Gitelman's Cases and Materials on Land Use, 3rd Ed., 1300 pages, 1982 (Casebook)

Wright and Webber's Land Use in a Nutshell, 316 pages, 1978 (Text)

See also Housing and Urban Development

LAW AND ECONOMICS

Manne's The Economics of Legal Relationships—Readings in the Theory of Property Rights, 660 pages, 1975 (Text)

See also Antitrust, Regulated Industries

LAW AND MEDICINE—PSYCHIATRY

Cohen's Cases and Materials on the Law of Deprivation of Liberty: A Study in Social Control, 755 pages, 1980 (Casebook)

King's The Law of Medical Malpractice in a Nutshell, 340 pages, 1977 (Text)

Shapiro and Spece's Problems, Cases and Materials on Bioethics and Law, 892 pages, 1981 (Casebook)

Sharpe, Fiscina and Head's Cases on Law and Medicine, 882 pages, 1978 (Casebook)

LEGAL CLINICS

See Office Practice

LEGAL HISTORY

Presser and Zainaldin's Cases on Law and American History, 855 pages, 1980 (Casebook)

See also Legal Method and Legal System

LEGAL METHOD AND LEGAL SYSTEM

Aldisert's Readings, Materials and Cases in the Judicial Process, 948 pages, 1976 (Casebook)

Bodenheimer, Oakley and Love's Readings and Cases on an Introduction to the Anglo-American Legal System, 161 pages, 1980 (Casebook)

Davies and Lawry's Institutions and Methods of the Law—Introductory Teaching Materials, 547 pages, 1982 (Casebook)

Dvorkin, Himmelstein and Lesnick's Becoming a Lawyer: A Humanistic Perspective on Legal Education and Professionalism, 211 pages, 1981 (Text)

Fryer and Orentlicher's Cases and Materials on Legal Method and Legal System, 1043 pages, 1967 (Casebook)

Greenberg's Judicial Process and Social Change, 666 pages, 1977 (Coursebook)

Kempin's Historical Introduction to Anglo-American Law in a Nutshell, 2nd Ed., 280 pages, 1973 (Text)

Kimball's Historical Introduction to the Legal System, 610 pages, 1966 (Casebook)

Mashaw and Merrill's Introduction to the American Public Law System, 1095 pages, 1975, with 1980 Supplement (Casebook)

Murphy's Cases and Materials on Introduction to Law—Legal Process and Procedure, 772 pages, 1977 (Casebook)

Reynolds' Judicial Process in a Nutshell, 292 pages, 1980 (Text)

See also Legal Research and Writing

LEGAL PROFESSION

Aronson's Problems in Professional Responsibility, 280 pages, 1978 (Problem book)

Aronson and Weckstein's Professional Responsibility in a Nutshell, 399 pages, 1980 (Text)

Mellinkoff's The Conscience of a Lawyer, 304 pages, 1973 (Text)

Mellinkoff's Lawyers and the System of Justice, 983 pages, 1976 (Casebook)

Pirsig and Kirwin's Cases and Materials on Professional Responsibility, 3rd Ed., 667 pages, 1976, with 1981 Supplement (Casebook)

LAW SCHOOL PUBLICATIONS—Continued

LEGAL PROFESSION—Continued

Smith's Preventing Legal Malpractice, 142 pages, 1981 (Text)

LEGAL RESEARCH AND WRITING

Cohen's Legal Research in a Nutshell, 3rd Ed., 415 pages, 1978 (Text)

Dickerson's Materials on Legal Drafting, 425 pages, 1981 (Casebook)

Felsenfeld and Siegel's Writing Contracts in Plain English, 290 pages, 1981 (Text)

Gopen's Writing From a Legal Perspective, 225 pages, 1981 (Text)

How to Find the Law With Special Chapters on Legal Writing, 7th Ed., 542 pages, 1976. Problem book available (Coursebook)

Mellinkoff's Legal Writing Sense and Nonsense, 242 pages, 1982 (Text)

Rombauer's Legal Problem Solving—Analysis, Research and Writing, 3rd Ed., 352 pages, 1978 (Coursebook)

Squires and Rombauer's Legal Writing in a Nutshell, 294 pages, 1982 (Text)

Statsky's Legal Research, Writing and Analysis, 2nd Ed., 167 pages, 1982 (Coursebook)

Statsky's Legislative Analysis: How to Use Statutes and Regulations, 216 pages, 1975 (Text)

Statsky and Wernet's Case Analysis and Fundamentals of Legal Writing, 576 pages, 1977 (Text)

Teply's Programmed Materials on Legal Research and Citation, 334 pages, 1982. Student Library Exercises available (Coursebook)

Weihofen's Legal Writing Style, 2nd Ed., 332 pages, 1980 (Text)

LEGISLATION

Davies' Legislative Law and Process in a Nutshell, 279 pages, 1975 (Text)

Nutting and Dickerson's Cases and Materials on Legislation, 5th Ed., 744 pages, 1978 (Casebook)

Statsky's Legislative Analysis: How to Use Statutes and Regulations, 216 pages, 1975 (Text)

LOCAL GOVERNMENT

McCarthy's Local Government Law in a Nutshell, 386 pages, 1975 (Text)

Michelman and Sandalow's Cases-Comments-Questions on Government in Urban Areas, 1216 pages, 1970, with 1972 Supplement (Casebook)

Reynolds' Hornbook on Local Government Law, approximately 780 pages, 1982 (Text)

Stason and Kauper's Cases and Materials on Municipal Corporations, 3rd Ed., 692 pages, 1959 (Casebook)

LOCAL GOVERNMENT—Continued

Valente's Cases and Materials on Local Government Law, 2nd Ed., 980 pages, 1980 with 1982 Supplement (Casebook)

MASS COMMUNICATION LAW

Gillmor and Barron's Cases and Comment on Mass Communication Law, 3rd Ed., 1008 pages, 1979 (Casebook)

Ginsburg's Regulation of Broadcasting: Law and Policy Towards Radio, Television and Cable Communications, 741 pages, 1979 (Casebook)

Zuckman and Gayne's Mass Communications Law in a Nutshell, 431 pages, 1977 (Text)

MILITARY LAW

Shanor and Terrell's Military Law in a Nutshell, 378 pages, 1980 (Text)

MORTGAGES

See Real Estate Transactions

NATURAL RESOURCES LAW

See Energy and Natural Resources Law, Environmental Law, Oil and Gas, Water Law

OFFICE PRACTICE

Binder and Price's Legal Interviewing and Counseling: A Client-Centered Approach, 232 pages, 1977 (Text)

Edwards and White's Problems, Readings and Materials on the Lawyer as a Negotiator, 484 pages, 1977 (Casebook)

Hegland's Trial and Practice Skills in a Nutshell, 346 pages, 1978 (Text)

Shaffer's Legal Interviewing and Counseling in a Nutshell, 353 pages, 1976 (Text)

Strong and Clark's Law Office Management, 424 pages, 1974 (Casebook)

Williams' Legal Negotiation and Settlement, approximately 207 pages, 1982 (Coursebook)

OIL AND GAS

Hemingway's Hornbook on Oil and Gas, 486 pages, 1971, with 1979 pocket part (Text)

Huie, Woodward and Smith's Cases and Materials on Oil and Gas, 2nd Ed., 955 pages, 1972 (Casebook)

See also Energy and Natural Resources Law

PARTNERSHIP

See Agency—Partnership

LAW SCHOOL PUBLICATIONS—Continued

PATENT LAW

Choate and Francis' Cases and Materials on Patent Law, 2nd Ed., 1110 pages, 1981 (Casebook)

See also Copyright

POVERTY LAW

Brudno's Poverty, Inequality, and the Law: Cases-Commentary-Analysis, 934 pages, 1976 (Casebook)

Cooper, Dodyk, Berger, Paulsen, Schrag and Sovern's Cases and Materials on Law and Poverty, 2nd Ed., 1208 pages, 1973 (Casebook)

LaFrance, Schroeder, Bennett and Boyd's Hornbook on Law of the Poor, 558 pages, 1973 (Text)

See also Social Legislation

PRODUCTS LIABILITY

Noel and Phillips' Cases on Products Liability, 2nd Ed., 821 pages, 1982 (Casebook)

Noel and Phillips' Products Liability in a Nutshell, 2nd Ed., 341 pages, 1981 (Text)

PROPERTY

Aigler, Smith and Tefft's Cases on Property, 2 volumes, 1339 pages, 1960 (Casebook)

Bernhardt's Real Property in a Nutshell, 2nd Ed., 448 pages, 1981 (Text)

Boyer's Survey of the Law of Property, 766 pages, 1981 (Text)

Browder, Cunningham, Julin and Smith's Cases on Basic Property Law, 3rd Ed., 1447 pages, 1979 (Casebook)

Burby's Hornbook on Real Property, 3rd Ed., 490 pages, 1965 (Text)

Chused's A Modern Approach to Property: Cases-Notes-Materials, 1069 pages, 1978 with 1980 Supplement (Casebook)

Cohen's Materials for a Basic Course in Property, 526 pages, 1978 (Casebook)

Donahue, Kauper and Martin's Cases on Property, 1501 pages, 1974 (Casebook)

Hill's Landlord and Tenant Law in a Nutshell, 319 pages, 1979 (Text)

Moynihan's Introduction to Real Property, 254 pages, 1962 (Text)

Phipps' Titles in a Nutshell, 277 pages, 1968 (Text)

Uniform Land Transactions Act, Uniform Simplification of Land Transfers Act, Uniform Condominium Act, 1977 Official Text with Comments, 462 pages, 1978

See also Housing and Urban Development, Real Estate Transactions, Land Use

REAL ESTATE TRANSACTIONS

Bruce's Real Estate Finance in a Nutshell, 292 pages, 1979 (Text)

Maxwell, Riesenfeld, Hetland and Warren's Cases on California Security Transactions in Land, 2nd Ed., 584 pages, 1975 (Casebook)

Nelson and Whitman's Cases on Real Estate Transfer, Finance and Development, 2nd Ed., 1114 pages, 1981 (Casebook)

Osborne's Cases and Materials on Secured Transactions, 559 pages, 1967 (Casebook)

Osborne, Nelson and Whitman's Hornbook on Real Estate Finance Law, 3rd Ed., 885 pages, 1979 (Text)

REGULATED INDUSTRIES

Gellhorn and Pierce's Regulated Industries in a Nutshell, 394 pages, 1982 (Text)

Morgan's Cases and Materials on Economic Regulation of Business, 830 pages, 1976, with 1978 Supplement (Casebook)

Pozen's Financial Institutions: Cases, Materials and Problems on Investment Management, 844 pages, 1978 (Casebook)

White's Teaching Materials on Banking Law, 1058 pages, 1976, with 1980 Case and Statutory Supplement (Casebook)

See also Mass Communication Law

REMEDIES

Cribbet's Cases and Materials on Judicial Remedies, 762 pages, 1954 (Casebook)

Dobbs' Hornbook on Remedies, 1067 pages, 1973 (Text)

Dobbs' Problems in Remedies, 137 pages, 1974 (Problem book)

Dobbyn's Injunctions in a Nutshell, 264 pages, 1974 (Text)

Friedman's Contract Remedies in a Nutshell, 323 pages, 1981 (Text)

Leavell, Love and Nelson's Cases and Materials on Equitable Remedies and Restitution, 3rd Ed., 704 pages, 1980 (Casebook)

McCormick's Hornbook on Damages, 811 pages, 1935 (Text)

O'Connell's Remedies in a Nutshell, 364 pages, 1977 (Text)

York and Bauman's Cases and Materials on Remedies, 3rd Ed., 1250 pages, 1979 (Casebook)

REVIEW MATERIALS

Ballantine's Problems

Black Letter Series

LAW SCHOOL PUBLICATIONS—Continued

REVIEW MATERIALS—Continued

Smith's Review Series

West's Review Covering Multistate Subjects

SECURITIES REGULATION

Ratner's Securities Regulation: Materials for a Basic Course, 2nd Ed., 1050 pages, 1980 with 1982 Supplement (Casebook)

Ratner's Securities Regulation in a Nutshell, 300 pages, 1978 (Text)

Selected Securities and Business Planning Statutes, Rules and Forms, approximately 490 pages, 1982

SOCIAL LEGISLATION

Brudno's Income Redistribution Theories and Programs: Cases-Commentary-Analyses, 480 pages, 1977 (Casebook)—reprint from Brudno's Poverty, Inequality and the Law, 1976

LaFrance's Welfare Law: Structure and Entitlement in a Nutshell, 455 pages, 1979 (Text)

Malone, Plant and Little's Cases on Workers' Compensation and Employment Rights, 2nd Ed., 951 pages, 1980 (Casebook)

See also Poverty Law

TAXATION

Chommie's Hornbook on Federal Income Taxation, 2nd Ed., 1051 pages, 1973 (Text)

Dodge's Federal Taxation of Estates, Trusts and Gifts: Principles and Planning, 771 pages, 1981 with 1982 Supplement (Casebook)

Garbis and Struntz' Cases and Materials on Tax Procedure and Tax Fraud, 829 pages, 1982 (Casebook)

Gunn's Cases and Materials on Federal Income Taxation of Individuals, 785 pages, 1981 (Casebook)

Hellerstein and Hellerstein's Cases on State and Local Taxation, 4th Ed., 1041 pages, 1978 with 1982 Supplement (Casebook)

Kahn's Handbook on Basic Corporate Taxation, 3rd Ed., Student Ed., 614 pages, 1981 with 1982 Supplement (Text)

Kahn and Gann's Corporate Taxation and Taxation of Partnerships and Partners, 1107 pages, 1979, with 1981 Supplement (Casebook)

Kragen and McNulty's Cases and Materials on Federal Income Taxation, Vol. I: Taxation of Individuals, 3rd Ed., 1283 pages, 1979 with 1982 Supplement (Casebook)

TAXATION—Continued

Kragen and McNulty's Cases and Materials on Federal Income Taxation, Vol. II: Taxation of Corporations, Shareholders, Partnerships and Partners, 3rd Ed., 989 pages, 1981 with 1982 Supplement (Casebook)

Kramer and McCord's Problems for Federal Estate and Gift Taxes, 206 pages, 1976 (Problem book)

Lowndes, Kramer and McCord's Hornbook on Federal Estate and Gift Taxes, 3rd Ed., 1099 pages, 1974 (Text)

McCord's 1976 Estate and Gift Tax Reform-Analysis, Explanation and Commentary, 377 pages, 1977 (Text)

McNulty's Federal Estate and Gift Taxation in a Nutshell, 2nd Ed., 488 pages, 1979 (Text)

McNulty's Federal Income Taxation of Individuals in a Nutshell, 2nd Ed., 422 pages, 1978 (Text)

Rice's Problems and Materials in Federal Estate and Gift Taxation, 3rd Ed., 474 pages, 1978 (Casebook)

Rice and Solomon's Problems and Materials in Federal Income Taxation, 3rd Ed., 670 pages, 1979 (Casebook)

Rose and Raskind's Advanced Federal Income Taxation: Corporate Transactions—Cases, Materials and Problems, 955 pages, 1978 (Casebook)

Selected Federal Taxation Statutes and Regulations, approximately 1350 pages, 1982

Soboleff and Weidenbruch's Federal Income Taxation of Corporations and Stockholders in a Nutshell, 362 pages, 1981 (Text)

TORTS

Green, Pedrick, Rahl, Thode, Hawkins, Smith and Treece's Cases and Materials on Torts, 2nd Ed., 1360 pages, 1977 (Casebook)

Green, Pedrick, Rahl, Thode, Hawkins, Smith, and Treece's Advanced Torts: Injuries to Business, Political and Family Interests, 2nd Ed., 544 pages, 1977 (Casebook)—reprint from Green, et al. Cases and Materials on Torts, 2nd Ed., 1977

Keeton's Computer-Aided and Workbook Exercises on Tort Law, 164 pages, 1976 (Coursebook)

Keeton and Keeton's Cases and Materials on Torts, 2nd Ed., 1200 pages, 1977, with 1981 Supplement (Casebook)

Kionka's Torts in a Nutshell: Injuries to Persons and Property, 434 pages, 1977 (Text)

Malone's Torts in a Nutshell: Injuries to Family, Social and Trade Relations, 358 pages, 1979 (Text)

LAW SCHOOL PUBLICATIONS—Continued

TORTS—Continued

Prosser's Hornbook on Torts, 4th Ed., 1208 pages, 1971 (Text)

Shapo's Cases on Tort and Compensation Law, 1244 pages, 1976 (Casebook)

See also Products Liability

TRADE REGULATION

McManis' Unfair Trade Practices in a Nutshell, approximately 400 pages, 1982 (Text)

Oppenheim and Weston's Cases and Materials on Unfair Trade Practices and Consumer Protection, 3rd Ed., 1065 pages, 1974, with 1981 Supplement (Casebook)

See also Antitrust, Regulated Industries

TRIAL AND APPELLATE ADVOCACY

Appellate Advocacy, Handbook of, 249 pages, 1980 (Text)

Bergman's Trial Advocacy in a Nutshell, 402 pages, 1979 (Text)

Goldberg's The First Trial (Where Do I Sit?) (What Do I Say?) in a Nutshell, 396 pages, 1982 (Text)

Hegland's Trial and Practice Skills in a Nutshell, 346 pages, 1978 (Text)

Jeans' Handbook on Trial Advocacy, Student Ed., 473 pages, 1975 (Text)

McElhaney's Effective Litigation, 457 pages, 1974 (Casebook)

Nolan's Cases and Materials on Trial Practice, 518 pages, 1981 (Casebook)

Parnell and Shellhaas' Cases, Exercises and Problems for Trial Advocacy, 171 pages, 1982 (Coursebook)

TRUSTS AND ESTATES

Atkinson's Hornbook on Wills, 2nd Ed., 975 pages, 1953 (Text)

Averill's Uniform Probate Code in a Nutshell, 425 pages, 1978 (Text)

Bogert's Hornbook on Trusts, 5th Ed., 726 pages, 1973 (Text)

Clark, Lusky and Murphy's Cases and Materials on Gratuitous Transfers, 2nd Ed., 1102 pages, 1977 (Casebook)

Gulliver's Cases and Materials on Future Interests, 624 pages, 1959 (Casebook)

TRUSTS AND ESTATES—Continued

Gulliver's Introduction to the Law of Future Interests, 87 pages, 1959 (Casebook)—reprint from Gulliver's Cases and Materials on Future Interests, 1959

Halbach (Editor)—Death, Taxes, and Family Property: Essays and American Assembly Report, 189 pages, 1977 (Text)

McGovern's Cases and Materials on Wills, Trusts and Future Interests: An Introduction to Estate Planning, approximately 750 pages, 1982 (Casebook)

Mennell's Cases and Materials on California Decedent's Estates, 566 pages, 1973 (Casebook)

Mennell's Wills and Trusts in a Nutshell, 392 pages, 1979 (Text)

Powell's The Law of Future Interests in California, 91 pages, 1980 (Text)

Simes' Hornbook on Future Interests, 2nd Ed., 355 pages, 1966 (Text)

Turrentine's Cases and Text on Wills and Administration, 2nd Ed., 483 pages, 1962 (Casebook)

Uniform Probate Code, 5th Ed., Official Text With Comments, 384 pages, 1977

Waggoner's Future Interests in a Nutshell, 361 pages, 1981 (Text)

WATER LAW

Trelease's Cases and Materials on Water Law, 3rd Ed., 833 pages, 1979 (Casebook)

See also Energy and Natural Resources Law, Environmental Law

WILLS

See Trusts and Estates

WOMEN AND THE LAW

Kay's Text, Cases and Materials on Sex-Based Discrimination, 2nd Ed., 1045 pages, 1981 (Casebook)

Thomas' Sex Discrimination in a Nutshell, 399 pages, 1982 (Text)

See also Employment Discrimination

WORKMEN'S COMPENSATION

See Social Legislation

LAW AND AMERICAN HISTORY

CASES AND MATERIALS

By

STEPHEN B. PRESSER

Professor of Law, Northwestern University

JAMIL S. ZAINALDIN

Assistant Professor of History and Lecturer in Law,
Case Western Reserve University

AMERICAN CASEBOOK SERIES

ST. PAUL, MINN.
WEST PUBLISHING CO.
1980

Library of Congress Cataloging in Publication Data

Presser, Stephen B. 1946–
  Law and American history.

  (American casebook series)
  Includes index.
    1. Law—United States—History and criticism.   2.
Law—United States—Cases.   I. Zainaldin, Jamil S.,
  1948-   joint author. II. Title. III. Series.
KF352.A7P73   349.73   80–15905

ISBN 0-8299-2094-3

  P. & Z. Cs. Law & Am.History ACB

  1st Reprint—1982

To Carole and to Isabelle

*

PREFACE

One hundred years ago, Christopher Columbus Langdell published the second edition of his Casebook on contracts, in which he attempted to regularize and summarize what he believed to be the few sensible and important doctrines of that field. Later that year, he was blasted by Oliver Wendell Holmes, Jr. for his "theological" views, and for his insistence that legal rules be analyzed simply in terms of logic, instead of the "feelings * * * which have actually shaped the substance of the law." As did Langdell in his *first* edition, we are attempting to provide a new set of classroom materials, what we believe to be this generation's first commercially-published comprehensive casebook treatment of the history of America law. Like Langdell, and perhaps somewhat atavistically, we believe that there is no more exciting or rewarding teaching method than to provide students with primary sources and to require them to analyze, criticize, and evaluate them for themselves. Like Langdell too, we believe that an enlightened use of the Socratic method can help in this endeavor, at least where the questioner, like Plato's Socrates, can use the method with some compassion, irony, and wit, and with the understanding that on most important philosophical and legal issues there are no clear or easy answers. In the notes and questions which follow most of the readings we have suggested some approaches to this kind of Socratic dialogue. Still, with regard to our understanding of the nature of American law, like nearly everyone laboring in the vineyards of legal history or jurisprudence today, we owe much to Holmes. Our primary concern in this casebook, then, is to provide some sense of the changing *substance* of American law and the varied uses to which it has been put.

We believe that American law—both constitutional and private —has been central to the development of American society, that American law mirrors the social values of our culture, and that at any given time American law can also be seen to reflect the economic preferences or the political ideology of particular groups in the polity. A second aim of these materials, then, is to explore the *functioning* of legal institutions in the context of the American republic. It appears that courts were the principal lawmakers throughout much of America's history, and our attention will most often be directed to the courts, but we will also attempt some systematic study of legislatures, executives, and administrative agencies. Particularly in the early materials, we will be concerned with the workings of lower courts and juries, an area of study that has received insufficient attention in American legal history. No matter which legal agency makes the pronouncement of a rule of law, however, we think that such a pronouncement can profitably be studied as an expression of what is then perceived to be the appropriate distribution of wealth and power in American society. Accordingly, the choices made by courts and legislatures between and among alternate policies and rules, the conditions which have influenced lawmakers, and the ultimate meanings that can be attributed to their decisions will be here examined.

A third goal of these materials, related to the second, is to explore the rather unique and sensitive *role of American lawyers*. We have sought to limn the tensions produced by American lawyers' delicate position as they have attempted to respond to conflicting demands of clients, courts, and the sovereign people. To the degree that lawyers select issues to be tried by courts, frame arguments, and articulate the policies and the concepts of law, they too are lawmakers and worthy of study in an introductory survey course. Thus, we have attempted to furnish some material on the political dimensions of professional advocacy, and, because it is somewhat similar in these respects to professional advocacy, of professional legal scholarship.

While these materials stress the variable nature of the substance of American law, and while we have sought to examine the working of the law at several different levels, we think that there are several transcendent values expressed in our law, which lend some thematic unity to our presentation, and which perhaps make it possible to speak coherently of an identifiable "American" legal history. We have emphasized four such values. The first two are not unique to this country, but were of paramount importance during our colonial and revolutionary period and figure prominently in our English heritage. These are the ideas (1) that there ought to be some *restraints on arbitrary power*, and, accordingly, that power should only be exercised pursuant to the rule of law, and (2) that the ultimate political principle ought to be *popular sovereignty*—that the people themselves should be responsible for the content of the rules of law, and that the legal system should inure to the benefit of all the people.

The third and fourth values seem, in modern times at least, to have reached their fullest expression in America. They appeared most prominently in our history following the War for Independence, and are the ideas (3) that a primary purpose of the law should be the furtherance of *economic progress and social mobility*, and that the maintenance of such progress and mobility is the best means for implementing democratic theory, and (4) that the law ought to construct and maintain a large area for the functioning of *private enterprise* relatively immune from the incursions of public power. We think that a rough consensus has existed in our history about the need to implement these four values, but we think that the opinions regarding the primacy to be accorded to individual values, the appropriate means of attaining them, and their inherent contradictions have been a source of great conflict. Chapter by chapter, we have sought to explore these issues of conflict and consensus in the following manner.

The *Prologue*, beginning with an analysis of Sir Edward Coke's confrontation with James I, and concluding with a description of the Trial of the Seven Bishops for seditious libel in 1688, presents the conflict between advocates of the King's prerogatives and those of the "rule of law's" restraints on such power, against the background of political and legal turmoil in seventeenth-century England. At issue also is the deeper question of who should make and determine the content of the law—King, Judges, or Parliament? The issue of the source of law is pursued in *Chapter 1*, which treats the colonial and Revolutionary eras in American history. The opening sections explore the application by lawyers and juries of the theory of the primacy of the "popular will" in colonial legal disputes. The closing sections review the conflict between the colonies and Parliament, culminating in the development of a full-blown American theory of popular sovereignty, as indebted to contemporary philosophical notions of the social contract and natural rights as it is to the experience of the English Parliament. *Chapter 2* portrays the ideological ferment in the early years of the American republic, especially between the "Federalists" and "Republicans," as the implications of the Revolutionary theory of popular sovereignty were worked out in a series of politically-charged trials in the Federal District Courts. This Chapter concludes with the election of Thomas Jefferson as President and the impeachment trial of Justice Samuel Chase, and offers, in cameo form, a temporary resolution of the debate over who ought to make and determine law in a republic.

Chapter 3 takes us into the Age of Jackson. It is concerned with the extent to which democratic ideology and ideas about economic progress and social mobility are involved in the development of tort, contract, and property law. We will examine the political implications of the growth of judicial policy-making in those years, and the concomitant limitations on popular jury power in a period of rapid economic growth. The final section, on the law of business corporations, offers a glimpse into the social divisions that may have followed economic development and legal change; through the judicial process, a protected sphere of private property rights begins to triumph over public legislative power. *Chapter 4* begins with an analysis of *Swift v. Tyson* (1842), but approaches it from a somewhat unconventional angle. Using *Swift* as a symbol of mid-century jurisprudence, the question the materials address is whether judicial policy-making and the private law developments reviewed in *Chapter 3* served the interests of particular economic groups or of the community generally. The readings following *Swift*, on codification, the popular election of judges, and the law of slavery, are offered as evidence of the emerging political conflict over the distribution of law-making power and private wealth that may have ultimately resulted in the American Civil War—a clash which probably reflected a fundamental lack of ideological consensus on the means of modernizing and industrializing America.

Chapter 5 presents an opportunity for relating all that has been read with what is to come. This Chapter takes a somewhat narrower focus than the others, in an effort to evaluate judicial attitudes toward capital aggrandizement and labor organization from the early nineteenth to the early twentieth centuries. Issues of arbitrary power (as they involved unions and business corporations), abuses of judicial discretion (implicit in the conspiracy doctrine), private property rights (involved in the threat to business posed by union coercion), liberty (invoked in the theory of free competitive enterprise), and equality (concerning the appropriate status for workers in the polity) weave in and out of the early nineteenth-century decisions. The rulings of Chief Justice Shaw at the middle of the century are presented as illustrating the compromise reached: the contract paradigm is employed by Shaw in an attempt to correct a perceived imbalance of power, and to maintain a model of free competitive enterprise. This balance, the materials proceed to show, is upset toward the end of the century with the rise of large-scale corporate organization, and the resurgence of anti-union judicial activism that seems to legalize the growing inequalities in the industrial marketplace. The state activism of the Progressive Era, the subject of a concluding section on the rise of workmen's compensation legislation in the early twentieth-century, suggests the outlines of a new compromise: legislatures begin replacing courts as the chief policy-makers, bureaucratic and managerial structures eclipse private dispute resolution in the courts, individual security and popular equality are placed above entrepreneurial risk and economic libertarianism as guiding policy values. In short, a social theory of the collective public interest which reworks old ideas about popular sovereignty begins to overshadow the nineteenth-century contractarian individualism which had ostensibly promoted economic progress and social mobility.

Chapter 6, like *Chapters 1* and *2*, is concerned with broader jurisprudential issues. It attempts to trace the changes in legal philosophy in the late nineteenth and early twentieth centuries which accompanied the changes in the law presented in the latter sections of *Chapter 5*. The first part of the chapter is concerned with the ideas of "legal science" expounded by Field, Langdell, and Holmes. In Holmes' work particularly, it can be seen that the contradictions and seeming arbitrariness of late nineteenth-century judicial behavior, evident in the materials on workingmen and corporations, had provoked a fundamental re-examination of the nature of law. Other materials in *Chapter 6* suggest further substantive legal developments: the intransigence of the "Nine Old Men," and the so-called "Constitutional Revolution" of 1937. These developments forced still further jurisprudential exegesis, including the work of the "legal realists" in the 'thirties, and of their disciples in the 'forties and 'fifties. We think that the exposure of the great ambit of judicial discretion by the legal realists had much to do with the constitutional jurisprudence of the Warren Court, whose path-breaking opinions in *Brown v. Board of Education* and other cases involving the constitutional rights of minorities (and majorities) in turn led to two new branches of jurisprudence, which we treat as the "neutral principles" school of Herbert Wechsler, and the "liberal" juris-prudence of J. Skelly Wright. In *Chapter 6*, we study how the policies behind nineteenth- and early twentieth-century constitutional law, which supposedly implemented democratic values, were questioned, and gave way in the middle twentieth-century to a new theory of the activist state which emphasizes central planning by executives, admin-istrative regulation, and other means to promote equality of access to the marketplace and the political process. Still, we suggest, in some excerpts and in the notes, that twentieth-century legal theoreticians seemed uneasy about abandoning many traditional aspects of the American rule of law, and while they were able to expose inequities in the old jurisprudence, they often seemed unable or unwilling to offer clear notions of the appropriate values to be implemented in the juris-prudence they proposed.

The uncertain nature of constitutional jurisprudence explored in *Chapter 6* gives way in *Chapter 7* to an examination of the influence of this constitutional jurisprudence on Private Law. As did *Chapter 3*, *Chapter 7* briefly surveys developments in contracts, torts, and proper-ty. This time, however, the nineteenth-century values and principles which were justified as promoting economic progress and social mobili-ty seem to be coming into conflict with new doctrines such as reliance, unconscionability, and unjust enrichment in contracts and enterprise liability in torts, all of which emphasize adherence to communitarian standards of fairness. These "new" doctrines, while resting on dif-ferent theoretical foundations, seem to harken back to some of the tenets of seventeenth and eighteenth-century jurisprudence which the doctrines examined in *Chapter 3* supplanted, and these "new" legal developments appear to have the potential ultimately to obliterate the nineteenth century's carefully constructed distinction between the pub-lic and private spheres of law. The chapter and the casebook close with some occasionally whimsical, but occasionally profound, comments on the appropriate behavior for late twentieth-century lawyers.

It should be evident by now that we have followed a somewhat idiosyncratic method of selection of documents and materials to il-lustrate American legal history. We were aware of two excellent models for emulation. One is the casebook, *The Legal Process: An Introduction To Decision-Making By Judicial, Legislative, Executive, and Administrative Agencies* (1961) edited by James Willard Hurst, Lloyd K. Garrison, Carl A. Auerbach, and Samuel Mermin, which presents an overview of American legal history by concentrating on legal developments relating to a single problem, the appropriate treatment of industrial accidents. The other is the narrative treatment, *A History of American Law* (1973) by Lawrence M. Friedman, which attempts some coverage of nearly every topic in American law. Like good Aristotelians, we have attempted an approach somewhere in the middle; we have been rather selective of the subjects covered in order systematically to illuminate the historiographical issues which we felt to be important, but we have also tried to consider a sufficient number of topics in both public and private spheres so that we might be able to speak generally about the "law." Some readers and teachers may be particularly disappointed that we have not included more on the history of criminal and family law, two areas just now blossoming in legal historical research. If the book is able to go into a second edition, we may be able to expand our treatment of these important areas. The paucity of our allusions to the legal implications of race and sex in American society may also be questioned. We felt that these topics are adequately treated in Constitutional law courses, but we *have* sought to include some materials, *e. g.*, on the nineteenth-century slavery debates and the early twentieth-century cases on the working conditions of women, which individual instructors might expand to explore related issues. Finally, we have made only the briefest and most oblique references to developments in the economic analysis of law or the theory of social choice, which seem to hold promise for late twentieth-century jurisprudence. Here too, individual instructors and students may wish to supplement our treatment.

All of the materials have been abridged, with deletions indicated by * * *. Most footnotes have been omitted; those that remain have their original numbering. Asterisk footnotes have been added. Because most of the secondary readings which we have included are the most important work in particular areas, we encourage students to return to the originals for fuller development of each piece's ideas, and for a fuller understanding of the general development of American legal history. Each excerpt from a copyrighted work carries its own acknowledgment, but it is appropriate here to express our gratitude generally to our colleagues and others who graciously permitted us to use their work. One, Robert Ireland, was even kind enough to allow us to print part of an unpublished manuscript.

We have a special intellectual debt to two men: Stephen Presser studied with Professor Morton J. Horwitz of the Harvard Law School; Jamil Zainaldin studied with Professor Stanley N. Katz, then at the

PREFACE

University of Chicago, now at Princeton and the University of Pennsylvania School of Law. By their scholarship and their unfailing encouragement they have not only sparked our interests and sustained our labors, but they have given substantial shape and content to the field of American legal history, a small part of which is reflected here. Other obvious intellectual influences have come from the writing and personal communications of many others in our field, including J. Willard Hurst, a towering figure, Grant Gilmore, Lawrence M. Friedman, John Reid, William E. Nelson, David H. Flaherty, G. Edward White, Mark Tushnet, Robert W. Gordon, Charles W. McCurdy, Wythe Holt, and Dennis Hutchinson. Professor Thomas A. Green of the University of Michigan Law School has a special responsibility for this project, for which we are grateful, and Professor Katz, in an extraordinary gesture of collegiality, reviewed the manuscript before publication. Many others have offered advice and support along the way. We are unable to thank each individually, but Bernard Bailyn, the Honorable Malcolm Richard Wilkey, Marshall Shapo, Leonard Barkan, Timothy Breen, and Daniel D. Polsby deserve particular mention. Judges Collins J. Seitz, Edward M. Dumbauld, Albert Maris, and John Gibbons helped shape the materials that derive from Presser's work on the Third Circuit history.

Northwestern University Law School's Dean, David S. Ruder, its Director of Research, Professor Robert W. Bennett, and Professor Clinton W. Francis cooperated to permit Presser to devote seven uninterrupted months to the preparation of this manuscript, a debt which he can never repay. A succession of dedicated Northwestern University Law Students served as research assistants for the project; Karen V. Kole, Denison H. Hatch, Cynthia Sopata, Mark C. Amador, and Christopher W. Garrett. While all these were valuable, our two most recent assistants were completely indispensible: Barbara Ziegler, who, in addition to research duties, supervised the securing of permissions and compiled the index, and Kenneth S. GoodSmith, who toiled full-time during the Summer of 1979, and came out of retirement at Christmas to oversee the completion of the manuscript. The manuscript was typed principally by three long-suffering but unfailingly courteous and helpful secretaries, Jane Perpich, Diana Yee, and Elizabeth Quintos. The illustrations are from the Collection of the Library of Congress, and are all in the public domain. We thank Leroy Bellamy of the Library's Prints and Photographs Division for his assistance in making the selections.

PREFACE

As is usual, we acknowledge that what is good in the book is likely to be due to the contributions of others, but we take full responsibility for its failings. In an undertaking of this nature, one's reach must exceed one's grasp. Any suggestions for improvement will be gratefully received.

STEPHEN B. PRESSER

JAMIL S. ZAINALDIN

Chicago, Illinois
Cleveland, Ohio
June, 1980

SUMMARY OF CONTENTS

*

TABLE OF CONTENTS

TABLE OF CONTENTS

TABLE OF CONTENTS

TABLE OF CONTENTS

TABLE OF CONTENTS

TABLE OF AUTHORITIES

References are to Pages

TABLE OF AUTHORITIES

TABLE OF AUTHORITIES

TABLE OF AUTHORITIES

TABLE OF AUTHORITIES

*

TABLE OF CASES

The principal cases are in italic type. Cases cited or discussed are in roman type. References are to Pages.

TABLE OF CASES

*

Engraved by J. Pofselwhite

COKE.

LAW AND AMERICAN HISTORY

Prologue

THE ENGLISH HERITAGE

SECTION A. THE KING AND THE CHIEF JUSTICE: JAMES I AND SIR EDWARD COKE

CATHERINE DRINKER BOWEN, THE LION
AND THE THRONE *

Chapter Twenty-Two, * * * Common Law versus the Prerogative
* * *, 291–306 (1956).

* * *

Only three steps from courtroom floor to bench, yet Edward Coke became, almost overnight, another man. "The most offensive of Attorney Generals," wrote Francis Bacon's biographer, "transformed into the most admired and venerated of Judges." When advocates turn judge, the world expects them to be worthy of the occasion; the bench would seem to lift the spirit as well as the body of a lawyer. But with Coke the breach is not merely noticeable, it is startling and from a distance of centuries, hard at first to credit. A sharp road cuts between the countries of this life; Coke's farewell at Norwich carried a symbolism deeper than he knew. Attorney General Coke, sharp driving tool of crown authority, put on the robes of judgeship and became to all appearances the champion of another cause. "There is a maxim," he told the Lower House: *"The common law hath admeasured the King's prerogative.* It is not I, Edward Coke, that speaks it but the records that speak it." "The King," he advised James, "cannot take any cause out of any of his courts and give judgment upon it himself." "No person," he wrote in the *Second Institute,* "ought in any ecclesiastical court to be examined upon the cogitation of his heart or what he thinketh."

* Reprinted with the permission of the publisher, copyright ©, 1956, 1957, By Catherine Drinker Bowen, Published by Little, Brown & Co. in association with the Atlantic Monthly Press.

Such pronouncements, had they come from England's Attorney General, would have been near to treason. As Elizabeth's servant moreover, Coke could hardly have shaped the words; his mind was turned another way. But spoken by Chief Justice Coke, the words were to come as natural evolvement, behind them the long affirmation of Coke's years as scholar, judge and Commons man. Times had changed, the scene was ready.

* * *

Coke's change of direction was logical: Stuart England was not Tudor England; a man could with honesty uphold Elizabeth's prerogative and cry down James's. Not only had Elizabeth her country's welfare at heart, with skill and strength to sustain it, but the situation around her had been different. Tudor England suffered under continual threat from the Continental Catholic powers. "War-and-no-war," Ralegh had called it in 1593, begging for fighting ships against the Spaniard. To a growing nation, unity is above all essential, a strong central government, discipline throughout the realm. A succession of armadas, then as now, can blow away the very breath of civil liberties. Elizabeth, like her father before her, was careful not to let such questions come to full public issue; when they reared their heads, as with the brothers Wentworth, she put the talker in the Tower. Her Commons were too inexperienced for effective protest, her judges of common law had not yet seen the need for independent action.

James came to the throne, and for a brief year or two the issue and the antagonists seemed to remain the same; in the Gunpowder trials it was Rome, Spain, a foreign enemy that Coke, Attorney General, continued to fight. Yet by the year 1607, James had revealed himself to those with eyes to see. This good-natured prince, fond of theological disputation and the deer hunt, desired to rule England as he had ruled Scotland, above the state and above the law. Parliaments were a trial laid on recurrently, like God's plagues on Pharaoh. There were kings, James wrote blandly, "before any Parliaments were holden, or laws made"—a statement which to Coke's mind was as unEnglish as the tasseled crown of Don Velasco's hat. Squarely behind James stood Lord Chancellor Ellesmere, served by Masters in Chancery, Clerks in Chancery and a battery of civilians learned in Roman law. At Ellesmere's side Archbishop Bancroft exercised the wide legal powers of the Anglican Established Chuch. "*Rex est lex loquens,*" said Ellesmere. "The King is the law speaking." "It is clear by the word of God in the Scripture," said Bancroft, "that judges are but delegates under the King." "The twelve Judges of the realm," said Francis Bacon, "are as the twelve lions under Solomon's Throne. They must be lions, but yet lions under the throne, being circumspect that they do not check or oppose any points of sovereignty." Edward Coke did not agree. "The King is under God and the law!" he said.

The pronouncements clashed, ringing discordant like bells of state whose voices would not mix. Each voice represented a theory of government. Bacon, later to be Chancery's greatest champion, as yet had scarcely entered the arena. Ellesmere and Coke as chief antagonists were well matched, superficially similar. Both men despised disorder, remaining convinced that England should be ruled by "the better sort," which meant gentlemen with a substantial yearly income from land and manor. Both were strikingly handsome. If spectators came to Chancery for a sight of the old lord presiding whitehaired in his robes (Ellesmere was sixty-seven), Coke had an added attraction, the dramatic quality of the unexpected. To the end of his official life no one knew what Coke might say or do; the quality of outrageousness remained.

Coke's first point of attack was not Chancery (that would come later) but Archbishop Bancroft's disciplinary body, the Ecclesiastical High Commission. This was a group of men, led by Bishops and Privy Councilors, who in 1559 had been authorized by Act of Parliament to keep order within the Established Church, discipline the clergy and punish such lay offenses as were included in the ecclesiastical jurisdiction—at the time, a necessary and useful body. Toward the end of Elizabeth's reign, however, the Commission began to extend its powers; already in the 1590's there had been murmurs against it, mostly from Puritans and Nonconformists. Since James's accession the Commission had grown larger; it numbered nearly eighty and called itself a court—the *Court of High Commission*—encroaching, Coke noted with concern, on common-law jurisdiction.

Against this encroachment there was but one recourse. If cases already on trial by the High Commission could be proven to be lay cases rather than ecclesiastical, trial might be summarily stopped by a writ of prohibition.* The distinction between "lay" and "ecclesiastical" was not, however, easy to come at, the Church authority being wide and reaching far beyond theological or clerical matters. Since time immemorial—in the lawyers' phrase, "time out of mind"—the Church had regulated family affairs. Marriage and divorce, baptism, burial and the making of wills were under ecclesiastical jurisdiction. Church courts were empowered to punish perjury, defamation, drunkenness, breaches of faith, mistreatment of wives by husbands, incontinence and crimes of sexual behavior not covered by the common law.
* * *

Elizabeth, as head of the Established Church, quite naturally upheld this ecclesiastical jurisdiction, exercised once by Rome and transferred to Episcopal Canterbury only by long and bitter struggle. To Coke as to Elizabeth the transfer meant national independence, an

---

* A "Writ of Prohibition" was an order from Coke's court of "Common Pleas" or from the "Court of King's Bench" ("common law" courts) to a "prerogative" or "ecclesiastical" court forbidding either of the latter courts from hearing a matter in which the common law courts had exclusive jurisdiction.

English Church authority rather than a Roman one. Why should they not uphold it? When, in the House of Commons, James Morrice in 1593 opposed the High Commission and the oath ex officio which governed its procedure, Speaker Coke did not defend him.

But times and rulers change. Elizabeth had never called herself "a little God to rule over men," nor said, as James did: "General laws, made publicly in Parliament, may by the King's authority be suspended upon causes known only to him." Above the horizon a cloud loomed; Coke saw it darken England's sky. Archbishop Bancroft presented complaints * * * in the form of twenty-five elaborate articles of grievances against the common-law courts. * * * In 1607 a new law dictionary appeared in London, entitled The Interpreter, dedicated to Bancroft, much read and talked of. Under the word "king" was to be found the following: "He is above the law by his absolute power; he may alter or suspend any particular law that seemeth hurtful to the publick estate. Thus much in short because I have heard some to be of opinion that the laws be above the King." Dr. Cowell, the author, served as Professor of Civil Law at Oxford; there was little doubt as to what circumstances had fed his fire.

* * *

During these months, when Coke and Parliament together challenged Archbishop Bancroft, there ran in the courts a notorious suit, very pertinent to the point at issue. Fuller's Case, it was called, after the barrister who defended it. Nicholas Fuller, a Parliament man (member for London) had been much employed by Puritans in their troubles with the ecclesiastical discipline.* Voluble, active, indiscreet, Fuller was given to protesting subsidy bills in Parliament and saying unkind things about the Scots. "Nick Fuller," they called him in the Lower House. At the moment he had in tow no less than twenty Puritan clients, most of whom were trying to escape fines for nonconformity. Two of these—Lad, a Norfolkman, and Mansell, a preacher—had been imprisoned for contempt because at their trial before the High Commission they refused the oath ex officio. Fuller, in defense of his clients, over-reached himself and insulted the bishops in open court. High Commission procedure, said he, was "popish, under jurisdiction not of Christ but anti-Christ"; the oath ex officio led "to the damnation of their souls that take it"; he had heard said that bishops embezzled the fines of poor nonconformist preachers instead of paying them properly into Exchequer.

Fuller, upon this, found himself in custody for contempt. ("Nicholas Fuller," it was said, "pleaded so boldly for the enlargement of his

* The English "Puritans" were Protestants who opposed many "Popish" practices of the Established Church of England and of the ecclesiastical courts. In particular they protested the use of the oath ex officio, a proceeding whereby the ecclesiastical courts could question a man on his beliefs and impose punishment if these beliefs did not accord with orthodoxy.

clients that he procured his own confinement.") The two clients were forgotten; to this day, no one knows what became of Lad and Mansell. But for nearly nineteen months, Fuller's Case rocked back and forth between King's Bench and High Commission—directed largely by Fuller himself from the White Tavern in Southwark, where Archbishop Bancroft had locked him in. King's Bench defended its prohibition on grounds that a barrister's conduct in court was a lay matter, to be tried at common law. Archbishop Bancroft declared otherwise. In the end, after two arraignments, Fuller was convicted, fined two hundred pounds and put in Fleet Prison. The charge was slander, schism, heresy, impious error, and the holding of pernicious opinions.

Coke, technically, had not been concerned beyond acting as mediator between King's Bench and Archbishop Bancroft. Yet for the common law it was a notable defeat, the case having been badly managed not only by Fuller, who talked too much in court, but by Judges Fenner and Croke of King's Bench, who issued their prohibition during the summer vacation when the other judges were away. Putting Fuller in jail only heightened popular feeling and emphasized the point at issue: Was the High Commission a court of record, with power to imprison and to fine? Bancroft, Ellesmere and James said *Yes;* the common law said *No.* London visitors wrote home to their counties about Nicholas Fuller and his case, Parliament discussed it. The Lower House took Fuller's side. King James showed agitation. By Elizabeth's Act of Supremacy (1559) James was monarch over Church as well as state; who impugned ecclesiastical authority impugned the sovereign. "I pray you," he wrote to Sir Robert Cecil, "forget not Fuller's matter. I prophecy unto you that when soever the ecclesiastical dignity together with the King's government thereof shall be turned into contempt and vanish in this kingdom, the kings hereof shall not longer prosper in their government and the monarchy shall fall to ruin."

Dr. Cowell had been right; it was high time for an authoritative definition of the word "king." Lord Chancellor Ellesmere was ready to add a definition of his own. When the public conscience got out of order, the Lord Chancellor must set it in line by public rebuke delivered from Star Chamber or such official platform as was available. During Fuller's troubles a magnificent forum presented itself. Calvin's Case came to court in a blaze of fame and dignity. It was a test case to determine if a man born in Scotland after James's accession could call himself an English subject and inherit English lands—in a sense, James's own suit, brought largely at his instigation. Parliament had defeated the royal plan of union with Scotland; James hoped to salvage at least the rights of citizenship for his onetime countrymen. Fourteen judges, drawn from all three courts, tried Calvin's Case in Exchequer Chamber; each judge, during several days of trial, gave an oral opinion before a crowded courtroom. Ellesmere spoke last; the gist of his oration centered upon neither Calvin nor Scotland.

It was a heavy salvo directed at loose talkers who during the past months had expressed themselves too vividly concerning the oath *ex officio,* bishops in general and the royal prerogative in particular. Certain new-risen philosophers, said Ellesmere scornfully, looked upon the common law as above the monarch, even daring to declare that "kings have no more power than the people from whom they take their temporal jurisdiction!" Such persons called upon the law of nature, asking "if kings or people did first make laws?" Near treason! said Ellesmere warmly. "The monarch is the law. *Rex est lex loquens,* the king is the law speaking."

In his place nearby, Coke must have heard it with gloom and revulsion. "Our constitution," Ellesmere went on indignantly, "is to be obeyed and reverenced," not bandied by persons walking in Paul's aisle or sitting in ordinaries "drowned with drink, blown away with a whiff of tobacco!" Such "busy questionists" cited Plato and Aristotle on the framing of states and commonwealths. In Ellesmere's opinion, Plato and Aristotle were men "lacking knowledge of God, born in popular states, mislikers of monarchies" and no more fit to give laws "than Sir Thomas More's *Utopia* and such pamphlets as we have at every mart."

It was a typical expression of a point of view. And the Lord Chancellor, without referring openly to the court of Common Pleas, had employed the oratorical trick of classifying thoughtful, purposeful men all in one lump with popular demagogues—and, by the use of More's name, with "popery" too. Ellesmere added a three-column definition of the English common law that must have well-nigh curdled Coke's blood. Pronouncing the word *moreover* like an ejaculation, he fired a parting shot: "Moreover! Had Calvin's Case proven difficult, his Majesty himself should have decided it—the most religious, learned and judicious king that ever this kingdom or island had!"

Such a statement, made officially in an English courtroom—and by the Lord Chancellor himself—was a slap in the face of Edward Coke and all who held his ideas on government. "It is not customary," the great Chief Justice Fortescue once had said, "for the kings of England to sit in court or pronounce judgment themselves." Every English lawyer knew it, a maxim bred in the bone. Against it the Chief Justice of Common Pleas had but one official recourse: to withdraw suits from prerogative courts whenever and however he could, narrow down the Roman law jurisdiction and starve it to bones. By siege or by assault, Coke's weapons were slight. Mere legal quibbles, some called them—prohibitions, for instance. Yet giants still were vulnerable if pebbles could be found.

During the year following Fuller's imprisonment and Ellesmere's oration, prohibitions flowed out from Common Pleas under Coke's seal. Fuller's friends meanwhile distributed pamphlets, designed to get him out of jail, eloquent with Fuller's previous courtroom arguments, many of which were clever and some of which were sound. Coke, defending his own position, even borrowed certain of the phrases—unless, indeed, Coke had inspired it in the first place. In an icy January of 1608, Fuller, having "kist the rod and made his submission," was freed, romping out of jail "very frolick," wrote a Londoner, "and so joyfull that he would not lose so much time as to go about (by London Bridge) but would needs passe over the river on foot. His owne weakness and want of judgment hath ben his greatest enemie."

Archbishop Bancroft watched the prohibitions roll from Common Pleas in term time and was alarmed. He appealed to James, advised him of the danger. Let his Majesty summon Coke and his brethren, tell them they overstepped.

* * *

The Privy Council met customarily on Sunday morning at Whitehall Palace. * * * On Sunday, November 6, 1608, common-law judges and ecclesiastics were summoned to Whitehall. The two sides, said James, might give their reasons and cite authorities; he would act as arbitrator to decide if the disputed prohibitions were valid. It was a role James fancied, being quick at disputation; next to running down a deer he loved to track the argument to its undefended lair. Actually, decision on this Sunday morning would hang not upon individual suits prohibited but on a final interpretation of Elizabeth's original patent authorizing the Court of High Commission—several long skins of parchment, to Bancroft perfectly explicit and clear. Coke thought differently. Could the patent be proven faulty, High Commission was ruined. Bancroft was prepared to defend it, Coke to destroy it.

Yet as the meeting progressed, no valid arguments were produced. Opponents stood sullen, merely denying each other's statements. James, impatient, demanded if the patent were too long a document— the judges too busy to read it?—and adjourned the meeting until the following Sunday, when "he hoped both sides would be better prepared. All the courts were under one King, one God, one country; he had excellent expectation of them all." But Coke, before the churchmen could reach the door, burst out with a long, disagreeable speech, repeating, among other insults, Nicholas Fuller's charge that commissioners had embezzled their fines. Archbishop Bancroft retorted indignantly. James interrupted, warned the two, "Take heed of heat in this business!" adding that he intended to make note of those who disregarded his wishes.

Next Sunday, Bishops and Judges reconvened. James sat in his chair, the disputants remained standing before him. Sir Julius Caesar, a Doctor of Roman Law, took notes. The King opened the meeting by remarking shortly that he had come neither to hear nor to make orations. Coke, as spokesman for the judges, this time was well prepared. ("Questions short," wrote Caesar; "deliberations long, conclusions pithy.") Ecclesiastical courts, said Coke, had undoubted authority to proceed, so long as no temporal matters were involved. But let a temporal issue enter the case, and it must be transferred to the common-law courts—even in causes of clearly ecclesiastical nature. Drawing on statutes of Edward II, III, VI, Coke acknowledged that civil lawyers construed these statutes otherwise. * * *

The King broke in. Common-law judges, he said, were like papists who quoted Scripture and then put upon it their own interpretation, to be received unquestioned. Just so, "judges allege statutes, reserving the exposition thereof to themselves." At this point some one, probably Bancroft, brought up the touchy matter of James's own powers. Coke's *Report* gives the statement unidentified:

"In cases where there is not express authority in law, the King may himself decide it in his royal person; the Judges are but delegates of the King, and the King may take what causes he shall please from the determination of the Judges and may determine them himself. And the Archbishop said: that this was clear in divinity, that such authority belongs to the King by the Word of God in the Scripture. To which it was answered by me: that the King in his own person cannot adjudge any case, either criminal—as treason, felony, &c., or betwixt party and party; but this ought to be determined and adjudged in some court of justice, according to the Law and Custom of England. * * * And it was greatly marvelled [Coke adds in comment] that the Archbishop durst inform the King that such absolute power and authority, as is aforesaid, belonged to the King by the Word of God."

The sovereign, Coke told James, might sit in Star Chamber, "and this appears in our books." But only to consult with the judges, not *in judicio.*

(In Star Chamber was a chair of state, emblazoned with the royal arms. For thirty years Coke had seen it empty; Elizabeth never claimed her right to sit. There were powers a wise sovereign did not put to public test.) "And it appears by Act of Parliament," Coke went on, addressing the King, "that neither by the Great Seal nor by the Little Seal, justice shall be delayed; *ergo,* the King cannot take any cause out of any courts and give judgment upon it himself. * * *"

Here the record becomes confused and it is difficult—as always in Coke's *Reports*—to separate what was said at the moment from what may have been added later. It is unlikely that James would have endured without interruption so long and violent a speech. From Sir Julius Caesar and various newsletters, it appears that at some point James broke in, told Coke he "spoke foolishly." Himself, the King, as supreme head of justice, would defend to the death his prerogative of calling judges before him to decide disputes of jurisdiction. Moreover, he would "ever protect the common law."

"The common law," Coke interjected, "protecteth the King."

"A traitorous speech!" James shouted. "The King protecteth the law, and not the law the King! The King maketh judges and bishops. If the judges interpret the laws themselves and suffer none else to interpret, they may easily make, of the laws, shipmen's hose!"

At this point James shook his fist and Sir Julius Caesar, after one brief sentence, stopped taking notes. Coke's *Report* picks up the story. "Then the King said that he thought the Law was founded upon Reason, and that he and others had Reason as well as the Judges. To which it was answered by me, that true it was that God had endowed his Majesty with excellent science and great endowments of Nature. But his Majesty was not learned in the Laws of his Realm of England; and Causes which concern the Life, or Inheritance, or Goods, or Fortunes of his Subjects are not to be decided by natural Reason but by the artificial Reason and Judgment of Law, which requires long Study and Experience before that a man can attain to the cognizance of it; and that the Law was the golden Metwand and Measure to try Causes of the Subjects, which protected his Majesty in safety and Peace: With which the King was greatly offended, and said that then he should be under the Law, which was treason to affirm (as he said). To which I said, that Bracton saith, *Quod Rex non debet esse sub homine, sed sub Deo et Lege*—that the King should not be under man, but under God and the Laws."

Sir Rafe Boswell to Dr. Milborne

" * * * the Lord Coke humbly prayed the king to have respect to the Common Lawes of his land &c. He prayed his Majesty to consider that the Ecclesiastical Jurisdiction was forren. After which his Majesty fell into that high indignation as the like was never knowne in him, looking and speaking fiercely with bended fist, offering to strike him, &c. Which the Lo. Cooke perceaving fell flatt on all fower; humbly beseeching his Majestie to take compassion on him and to pardon him if he thought zeale had gone beyond his dutie and allegiance. His Majestie not herewith contented, continued his indignation. Whereuppon the Lo. Treasurer [Robert Cecil] the Lo. Cooke's unckle by marriage, kneeled down before his Majestie and prayed him to be favourable. To whom his Majestie replied saying, What hast thou to doe to intreat for him? He answered, In regard he hath married my neerest kinswoman, &c."

There is another account of this Sunday meeting, written within a fortnight by one John Hercy to the Earl of Shrewsbury and postmarked Westminster Hall at 10 in the forenoon: "The Lord Cooke amongst other offensive speech should say to his Majestie that his Highnes was defended by his lawes. At which his Majestie was very much offended, & told him he spake foolishly and said that he was not defended by his lawes but by God; and so gave the Lord Cooke in other words a very sharp reprehension both for that & other things." Nothing is said here about Coke's falling on all fours, though the writer adds that if Cecil, "most humbly on his knee," had not interposed "to pacify his Majesty," it would have gone hard with Coke. Whatever happened, it was a tremendous scene: a king's fist raised against a judge, the small pale hunchback throwing himself between. "My little great Lord," they called Cecil now; he carried more power and more care than any man in England, and after his father's example he remained faithful to his friends.

Very likely, Coke did fall on his face. It was that or a cell in the Tower. The Chief Justice of Common Pleas knelt, and rose, and went out into November city streets. King James, having disposed of these vexing questions, as it seemed in one brief forenoon, turned his face again to Royston where the red deer ran.

Next morning a new prohibition, under Coke's seal, went out to High Commission from the Court of Common Pleas.

NOTES AND QUESTIONS

1. Few figures in Anglo-American legal history are as imposing as Sir Edward Coke. At one time or another he held practically every position of political and legal importance: High Steward of Cambridge University (1575), Solicitor-General (1592), Speaker of the House of Commons (1593), Attorney-General (1594), and Chief Justice of both the Court of Common Pleas (1606) and King's Bench (1613). Early in Coke's career he began to publish his thirteen-volume series of Reports which interspersed descriptions of cases with Coke's own analysis. Later in his life he turned to a more extensive investigation of law, publishing the four-volume Institutes of the Laws of England; commentaries on the English law relating to real property (First Institute, Coke on Littleton (1628)), statutes of Parliament (Second Institute (1642)), Criminal Law (Third Institute (1644)), and the jurisdiction and history of the various English courts (Fourth Institute (1644)). Until well into the nineteenth century these works of Edward Coke were still frequently cited as authoritative in American courtrooms. See, e. g., T. Plucknett, A Concise History of the Common Law 281–284 (5th ed. 1956).

2. Probably as important as Coke's writing, however, was his prolonged struggle with James I and James's officers over the limits of the King's prerogative, with which this excerpt is primarily concerned. How could James I maintain that he was not subject to English Law? Note that Ellesmere, in defending the King's prerogative, seems to make a special effort to impeach Plato and Aristotle's teachings. What does this have to do with the issue at hand? Why does Ellesmere think that Plato and Aristotle are suspect because they lived in "popular states?"

3. You will remember that when Coke was explicating "the statutes of Edward II, III, VI" to demonstrate that Ecclesiastical courts had no authority in cases involving temporal matters, Coke conceded that "civil

lawyers construed these statutes otherwise * * *" immediately there-after James broke in and stated that Common law judges "were like papists who quoted Scripture and then put upon it their own interpretation * * *" James stated also that "judges allege statutes, reserving the exposition thereof to themselves." What point was James trying to make? How could anyone suggest that the interpretation of statutes was not best done by judges? Does James's later suggestion that "If the judges interpret the laws themselves and suffer none else to interpret, they may easily make, of the laws, shipmen's hose!" have any bearing on this? On the other hand, what did Coke mean when he told James I that legal cases "are not to be decided by natural Reason but by the artificial Reason and Judgement of Law * * * which requires long Study and Experience before that a man can attain to the cognizance of it * * *"?

4. James appears to have won this round with Coke, at least if Coke's falling on the floor can be regarded as capitulation. Why did Coke capitulate? Or did he? You will have noted that Coke did not immediately cease issuing prohibitions. After some years of judicial contests between Coke and the prerogative courts, however, Coke was first "kicked upstairs" from the Court of Common Pleas to the Court of King's Bench (where he could do less damage), and was eventually dismissed from the bench completely. Coke was temporarily restored to the King's good graces, and was even made a Privy Councilor by James. Still later, however, Coke began once again to oppose the Royal Prerogative, as a member of the English Parliament, where he clashed with both James and James's son and successor, Charles I. For the full story see, in addition to the book by Catherine Drinker Bowen from which this excerpt has been taken, Stephen D. White, Sir Edward Coke and the "Grievances of the Commonwealth" 1621–1628 (1979), and on the conflict between the Chancellors and Coke, see Catherine Drinker Bowen, The Temper of a Man: Francis Bacon 133–74 (1963).

5. In 1649 Charles I was beheaded following a dispute with Parliament during the English Civil Wars of 1642–1660. What do you suppose this dispute between the Stuart Kings and Parliament had to do with the debate you have just read between Coke and James I? During the period between the end of Charles's reign and the restoration of the monarchy, in the person of Charles's son, Charles II, in 1660, England was governed by the military, led initially by the famous Puritan, Oliver Cromwell, self-styled Lord Protector. Following the death of Cromwell, the Puritan dictatorship proved too much for the English, and the monarchy's re-establishment was greeted with much enthusiasm and introduced a period of political quiescence. This serenity came to an end during the reign of Charles II's brother, James II, to whom we now turn.

SECTION B. THE TRIAL OF THE SEVEN BISHOPS

LADY TREVELYAN, ED., II THE WORKS OF LORD MACAULAY *

39–41, 145–147, 150–152, 153–156, 157–160, 164–167, 168–178, 182–184 (1866).

[These excerpts begin with a discussion of the First Declaration of Indulgence, issued by James II, a Catholic, on April 4, 1687].

In this Declaration the King avowed that it was his earnest wish to see his people members of that Church to which he himself belonged. But, since that could not be, he announced his intention to protect them in the free exercise of their religion. * * * He had long been convinced, he said, that conscience was not to be forced, that persecution was unfavourable to population and to trade, and that it never attained the ends which persecutors had in view. He repeated his promise, already often repeated and often violated, that he would protect the Established Church in the enjoyment of her legal rights. He then proceeded to annul, by his own sole authority, a long series of statutes. He suspended all penal laws against all classes of Nonconformists. He authorised both Roman Catholics and Protestant Dissenters to perform their worship publicly. He forbade his subjects, on pain of his highest displeasure, to molest any religious assembly. He also abrogated all those Acts which imposed any religious test as a qualification for any civil or military office.

That the Declaration of Indulgence was unconstitutional is a point on which both the great English parties have always been entirely agreed. Every person capable of reasoning on a political question must perceive that a monarch who is competent to issue such a Declaration is nothing less than an absolute monarch. Nor is it possible to urge in defence of this act of James those pleas by which many arbitrary acts of the Stuarts have been vindicated or excused. It cannot be said that he mistook the bounds of his prerogative because they had not been accurately ascertained. For the truth is that he trespassed with a recent landmark full in his view. Fifteen years before that time, a Declaration of Indulgence had been put forth by his brother. * * * That Declaration, when compared with the Declaration of James, might be called modest and cautious. The Declaration of Charles dispensed only with penal laws. The Declaration of James dispensed also with all religious tests. The Declaration of Charles permitted the Roman Catholics to celebrate their worship in private dwellings only. Under the Declaration of James they might build and decorate temples, and even walk in procession along Fleet Street with crosses, images, and censers. Yet the Declaration of Charles had been

---

* These excerpts are taken from the masterwork of Thomas Babington Macaulay, 1st Baron Macaulay, The History of England from the Accession of James the Second (5 vols 1849–61). As you will see, the work can hardly be called objective, but many have believed it profound.

pronounced illegal in the most formal manner. The Commons had resolved that the King had no power to dispense with statutes in matters ecclesiastical. Charles had ordered the obnoxious instrument to be cancelled in his presence, had torn off the seal with his own hand, and had, both by message under his sign manual, and with his own lips from his throne in full Parliament, distinctly promised the two Houses that the step which had given so much offence should never be drawn into precedent.

* * *

On the twenty-seventh of April 1688, the King put forth a second Declaration of Indulgence. In this paper he recited at length the Declaration of the preceding April. His past life, he said, ought to have convinced his people that he was not a person who could easily be induced to depart from any resolution which he had formed. * * * He announced that he meant to hold a Parliament in November at the latest; and he exhorted his subjects to choose representatives who would assist him in the great work which he had undertaken.

On the fourth of May, * * * he made an Order in Council that his Declaration of the preceding week should be read, on two successive Sundays, at the time of divine service, by the officiating ministers of all the churches and chapels of the kingdom. In London and in the suburbs the reading was to take place on the twentieth and twenty-seventh of May, in other parts of England on the third and tenth of June. The Bishops were directed to distribute copies of the Declaration through their respective dioceses.

When it is considered that the clergy of the Established Church, with scarcely an exception, regarded the Indulgence as a violation of the laws of the realm, as a breach of the plighted faith of the King, and as a fatal blow levelled at the interest and dignity of their own profession, it will scarcely admit of doubt that the Order in Council was intended to be felt by them as a cruel affront. It was popularly believed that Petre * had avowed this intention in a coarse metaphor borrowed from the rhetoric of the East. He would, he said, make them eat dirt, the vilest and most loathsome of all dirt. But tyrannical and malignant as the mandate was, would the Anglican priesthood refuse to obey? The King's temper was arbitrary and severe. The precedings of the Ecclesiastical Commission were as summary as those of a court martial. Whoever ventured to resist might in a week be ejected from his parsonage, deprived of his whole income, pronounced incapable of holding any other spiritual preferment, and left to beg from door to door. * * * It might also well be apprehended that, if the clergy refused to read the Declaration, the Protestant Dissenters would misinterpret the refusal, would despair of obtaining

---

* Father Edward Petre, a Jesuit extremist, had been James's confidential adviser since 1678.

any toleration from the members of the Church of England, and would throw their whole weight into the scale of the Court.

The clergy therefore hesitated.   *   *   *

*   *   *

On the eighteenth a meeting of prelates and of other eminent divines was held at Lambeth.   *   *   *   After long deliberation, a petition embodying the general sense was written by the Archbishop with his own hand. It was not drawn up with much felicity of style. Indeed, the cumbrous and inelegant structure of the sentences brought on Sancroft * some raillery   *   *   *   But in substance nothing could be more skilfully framed than this memorable document. All disloyalty, all intolerance, was earnestly disclaimed. The King was assured that the Church still was, as she had ever been, faithful to the throne. He was assured also that the Bishops would, in proper place and time, as Lords of Parliament and members of the Upper House of Convocation, show that they by no means wanted tenderness for the conscientious scruples of Dissenters. But Parliament had, both in the late and in the present reign, pronounced that the sovereign was not constitutionally competent to dispense with statutes in matters ecclesiastical. The Declaration was therefore illegal; and the petitioners could not, in prudence, honour, or conscience, be parties to the solemn publishing of an illegal Declaration in the house of God, and during the time of divine service.

This paper was signed by the Archbishop and by six of his suffragans, Lloyd of Saint Asaph, Turner of Ely, Lake of Chichester, Ken of Bath and Wells, White of Peterborough, and Trelawney of Bristol. The Bishop of London, being under suspension, did not sign.

It was now late on Friday evening; and on Sunday morning the Declaration was to be read in the churches of London. It was necessary to put the paper into the King's hands without delay. The six Bishops crossed the river to Whitehall. The Archbishop, who had long been forbidden the Court, did not accompany them.   *   *   * James directed that the Bishops should be admitted. He had heard from his tool Cartwright that they were disposed to obey the royal mandate, but that they wished for some little modifications in form, and that they meant to present a humble request to that effect. His Majesty was therefore in very good humour. When they knelt before him, he graciously told them to rise   *   *   *. James read the petition: he folded it up; and his countenance grew dark. "This," he said, "is a great surprise to me. I did not expect this from your Church, especially from some of you. This is a standard of rebellion." The Bishops broke out into passionate professions of loyalty: but the King, as usual, repeated the same words over and over. "I tell you, this is a standard of rebellion." "Rebellion!" cried Trelawney, falling

---

* William Sancroft, Archbishop of Canterbury, and thus leading prelate of the Established Church (Anglican Protestants).

on his knees. "For God's sake, sir, do not say so hard a thing of us. No Trelawney can be a rebel. Remember that my family has fought for the crown. Remember how I served Your Majesty when Monmouth was in the West." "We put down the last rebellion," said Lake: "we shall not raise another." "We rebel!" exclaimed Turner; "we are ready to die at your Majesty's feet." "Sir," said Ken, in a more manly tone, "I hope that you will grant to us that liberty of conscience which you grant to all mankind." Still James went on. "This is rebellion. This is a standard of rebellion. Did ever a good Churchman question the dispensing power before? Have not some of you preached for it and written for it? It is a standard of rebellion. I will have my Declaration published." "We have two duties to perform," answered Ken, "our duty to God, and our duty to Your Majesty. We honour you: but we fear God." "Have I deserved this?" said the King, more and more angry: "I who have been such a friend to your Church? I did not expect this from some of you. I will be obeyed. My Declaration shall be published. You are trumpeters of sedition. What do you do here? Go to your dioceses; and see that I am obeyed. I will keep this paper. I will not part with it. I will remember you that have signed it." "God's will be done," said Ken. "God has given me the dispensing power," said the King, "and I will maintain it." * * * The Bishops respectfully retired. That very evening the document which they had put into the hands of the King appeared word for word in print, was laid on the tables of all the coffeehouses, and was cried about the streets. * * * How the petition got abroad is still a mystery. Sancroft declared that he had taken every precaution against publication, and that he knew of no copy except that which he had himself written, and which James had taken * * *. The veracity of the Archbishop is beyond all suspicion. But it is by no means improbable that some of the divines who assisted in framing the petition may have remembered so short a composition accurately, and may have sent it to the press. The prevailing opinion, however, was that some person about the King had been indiscreet or treacherous.

In the City and Liberties of London were about a hundred parish churches. In only four of these was the Order in Council obeyed. * * * Even in the chapel of Saint James's Palace the officiating minister had the courage to disobey the order. The Westminster boys long remembered what took place that day in the Abbey. Sprat, Bishop of Rochester, officiated there as Dean. As soon as he began to read the Declaration, murmurs and the noise of people crowding out of the choir drowned his voice. He trembled so violently that men saw the paper shake in his hand. Long before he had finished, the place was deserted by all but those whose situation made it necessary for them to remain.

Never had the Church been so dear to the nation as on the afternoon of that day. The spirit of dissent seemed to be extinct. Baxter from his pulpit pronounced an eulogium on the Bishops and parochial clergy. The Dutch minister, a few hours later, wrote to inform the States General that the Anglican priesthood had risen in the estimation of the public to an incredible degree. The universal cry of the Nonconformists, he said, was that they would rather continue to lie under the penal statutes than separate their cause from that of the prelates.

Another week of anxiety and agitation passed away. Sunday came again. Again the churches of the capital were thronged by hundreds of thousands. The Declaration was read nowhere except at the very few places where it had been read the week before. The minister who had officiated at the chapel in Saint James's Palace had been turned out of his situation: a more obsequious divine appeared with the paper in his hand: but his agitation was so great that he could not articulate. In truth the feeling of the whole nation had now become such as none but the very best and noblest, or the very worst and basest, of mankind could without much discomposure encounter.

Even the King stood aghast for a moment at the violence of the tempest which he had raised. What step was he next to take? * * * The prelates who had signed the petition might be cited before the Ecclesiastical Commission and deprived of their sees. But to this course strong objections were urged in Council. It had been announced that the Houses would be convoked before the end of the year. The Lords would assuredly treat the sentence of deprivation as a nullity, would insist that Sancroft and his fellow petitioners should be summoned to Parliament, and would refuse to acknowledge a new Archbishop of Canterbury or a new Bishop of Bath and Wells. * * * If therefore it were thought necessary to punish the Bishops, the punishment ought to be inflicted according to the known course of English law. * * * It was accordingly resolved that the Archbishop and the six other petitioners should be brought before the Court of King's Bench on a charge of seditious libel. That they would be convicted it was scarcely possible to doubt. The Judges and their officers were tools of the Court. Since the old charter of the City of London had been forfeited, scarcely one prisoner whom the government was bent on bringing to punishment had been absolved by a jury. The refractory prelates would probably be condemned to ruinous fines and to long imprisonment, and would be glad to ransom themselves by serving, both in and out of Parliament, the designs of the Sovereign.

On the evening of the eighth of June the seven prelates, furnished by the ablest lawyers in England with full advice, repaired to the palace, and were called into the Council chamber. Their petition was lying on the table. The Chancellor took the paper up, showed it to the Archbishop, and said, "Is this the paper which your Grace wrote, and which the six Bishops present delivered to His Majesty?" Sancroft looked at the paper, turned to the King, and spoke thus: "Sir, I stand here a culprit. I never was so before. * * * Since I am so unhappy as to be in this situation, Your Majesty will not be offended if I avail myself of my lawful right to decline saying anything which may criminate me." "This is mere chicanery," said the King. "I hope that Your Grace will not do so ill a thing as to deny your own hand." * * * "Sir," said the Archbishop, "I am not bound to accuse myself. Nevertheless, if Your Majesty positively commands me to answer, I will do so in the confidence that a just and generous prince will not suffer what I say in obedience to his orders to be brought in evidence against me." "You must not capitulate with your Sovereign," said the Chancellor. "No," said the King; "I will not give any such command. If you choose to deny your own hands, I have nothing more to say to you."

The Bishops were repeatedly sent out into the antechamber, and repeatedly called back into the Council room. At length James positively commanded them to answer the question. He did not expressly engage that their confession should not be used against them. But they, not unnaturally, supposed that, after what had passed, such an engagement was implied in his command. Sancroft acknowledged his handwriting; and his brethren followed his example. * * * The Chancellor then told them that a criminal information would be exhibited against them in the Court of King's Bench, and called upon them to enter into recognisances. They refused. They were peers of Parliament, they said. They were advised by the best lawyers in Westminster Hall that no peer could be required to enter into a recognisance in a case of libel; and they should not think themselves justified in relinquishing the privilege of their order. The King was so absurd as to think himself personally affronted because they chose, on a legal question, to be guided by legal advice. "You believe every body," he said, "rather than me." He was indeed mortified and alarmed. For he had gone so far that, if they persisted, he had no choice left but to send them to prison; and, though he by no means foresaw all the consequences of such a step, he foresaw probably enough to disturb him. They were resolute. A warrant was therefore made out directing the Lieutenant of the Tower to keep them in safe custody, and a barge was manned to convey them down the river. * * * When the Seven came forth under a guard, the emotions of the people broke through all restraint. Thousands fell on their knees and prayed aloud for the men who had, with the Christian courage of Ridley and Latimer, confronted a tyrant inflamed by all the bigotry of Mary. Many dashed into the stream, and, up to their waists in ooze and water, cried to the holy fathers to bless them. * * * The very sentinels who were posted at the Traitors' Gate reverently asked for a blessing from the martyrs whom they were to guard. Sir Edward Hales was Lieutenant of the Tower. He was little inclined to treat his prisoners with kindness. For he was an apostate from that Church for which they suffered; and he held several lucrative posts by virtue of that dispensing power against which they had protested. He learned with indignation that his soldiers were drinking the health of the Bishops. He ordered his officers to see that it was done no more. But the officers came back with a report that the thing could not be prevented, and that no other health was drunk in the garrison. * * * All day the coaches and liveries of the first nobles of England were seen round the prison gates. * * *

* * *

The Bishops edified all who approached them by the firmness and cheerfulness with which they endured confinement, by the modesty and meekness with which they received the applauses and blessings of the whole nation, and by the loyal attachment which they professed for the persecutor who sought their destruction. They remained only a week in custody. On Friday, the fifteenth of June, the first day of term, they were brought before the King's Bench. An immense throng awaited their coming. From the landing place to the Court of Requests they passed through a lane of spectators who blessed and applauded them. "Friends," said the prisoners as they passed, "honour the King; and remember us in your prayers." These humble and pious expressions moved the hearers even to tears. When at length the procession had made its way through the crowd into the presence of the Judges, the Attorney General exhibited the information which he had been commanded to prepare, and moved that the defendants might be ordered to plead. The counsel on the other side objected that the Bishops had been unlawfully committed, and were therefore not regularly before the Court. The question whether a peer could be required to enter into recognisances on a charge of libel was argued at great length, and decided by a majority of the Judges in favour of the crown. The prisoners then pleaded Not Guilty. That day fortnight, the twenty-ninth of June, was fixed for their trial. In the meantime they were allowed to be at large on their own recognisances. The crown lawyers acted prudently in not requiring sureties. For Halifax had arranged that twenty-one temporal peers of the highest consideration should be ready to put in bail, three for each defendant; and such a manifestation of the feeling of the nobility would have been no slight blow to the government. * * *

The Bishops were now permitted to depart to their own homes. The common people, who did not understand the nature of the legal proceedings which had taken place in the King's Bench, and who saw that their favourites had been brought to Westminster Hall in custody and were suffered to go away in freedom, imagined that the good cause was prospering. Loud acclamations were raised. The steeples of the churches sent forth joyous peals. * * *

Such was the concourse, and such the agitation, that the Dutch Ambassador was surprised to see the day close without an insurrection. The King had been anxious and irritable. In order that he might be ready to suppress any disturbance, he had passed the morning in reviewing several battalions of infantry in Hyde Park. It is, however, by no means certain that his troops would have stood by him if he had needed their services.   *   *   *   There were   *   *   * many bonfires that evening in the City. Two Roman Catholics, who were so indiscreet as to beat some boys for joining in these rejoicings, were seized by the mob, stripped naked, and ignominiously branded.

Sir Edward Hales now came to demand fees from those who had lately been his prisoners. They refused to pay anything for a detention which they regarded as illegal to an officer whose commission was, on their principles, a nullity. The Lieutenant hinted very intelligibly that, if they came into his hands again, they should be put into heavy irons and should lie on bare stones. "We are under our King's displeasure," was the answer; "and most deeply do we feel it: but a fellow subject who threatens us does but lose his breath."   *   *   *

Before the day of trial the agitation had spread to the farthest corners of the island. From Scotland the Bishops received letters assuring them of the sympathy of the Presbyterians of that country, so long and so bitterly hostile to prelacy. The people of Cornwall, a fierce, bold, and athletic race, among whom there was a stronger provincial feeling than in any other part of the realm, were greatly moved by the danger to Trelawney, whom they reverenced less as a ruler of the Church than as the head of an honourable house, and the heir through twenty descents of ancestors who had been of great note before the Normans had set foot on English ground. All over the country the peasants chanted a ballad * of which the burden is still remembered:

And shall Trelawney die, and shall Trelawney die?

Then thirty thousand Cornish boys will know the reason why.

The miners from their caverns reechoed the song with a variation:

Then twenty thousand under ground will know the reason why.

The rustics in many parts of the country loudly expressed a strange hope which had never ceased to live in their hearts. Their Protestant Duke, their beloved Monmouth, would suddenly appear, would lead them to victory, and would tread down the King and the Jesuits under his feet.

The ministers were appalled.   *   *   *   But the King's resolution was fixed. "I will go on," he said. "I have been only too indulgent. Indulgence ruined my father."

*   *   *

* There is some doubt about the authenticity of this ballad. Macaulay's source for this "was given to inventing Cornish traditions and fictitious historical documents." Sir Charles Firth, A Commentary on Macaulay's History of England 103–104 (1938).

[The Day of the Trial Arrived]

On the twenty-ninth of June, Westminster Hall, Old and New Palace Yard, and all the neighbouring streets to a great distance were thronged with people. Such an auditory had never before and has never since been assembled in the Court of King's Bench. Thirty-five temporal peers of the realm were counted in the crowd.

All the four Judges of the Court were on the bench. Wright, who presided, had been raised to his high place over the heads of many abler and more learned men solely on account of his unscrupulous servility. Allibone was a Papist, and owed his situation to that dispensing power, the legality of which was now in question. Holloway had hitherto been a serviceable tool of the government. Even Powell, whose character for honesty stood high, had borne a part in some proceedings which it is impossible to defend.   *   *   *

The counsel were by no means fairly matched. The government had required from its law officers services so odious and disgraceful that all the ablest jurists and advocates of the Tory party had, one after another, refused to comply, and had been dismissed from their employments. Sir Thomas Powis, the Attorney General, was scarcely of the third rank in his profession. Sir William Williams, the Solicitor General, had great abilities and dauntless courage: but he wanted discretion; he loved wrangling; he had no command over his temper; and he was hated and despised by all political parties.   *   *   *

On the other side were arrayed almost all the eminent forensic talents of the age. Sawyer and Finch, who, at the time of the accession of James, had been Attorney and Solicitor General, and who, during the persecution of the Whigs in the late reign, had served the crown with but too much vehemence and success, were of counsel for the defendants. With them were joined two persons   *   *   * reputed the two best lawyers that could be found in the Inns of Court; Pemberton, who had, in the time of Charles the Second, been Chief Justice of the King's Bench, who had been removed from his high place on account of his humanity and moderation, and who had resumed his practice at the bar; and Pollexfen, who had long been at the head of the Western circuit, and who   *   *   * was known to be at heart a Whig, if not a republican. Sir Creswell Levinz was also there, a man of great knowledge and experience, but of singularly timid nature. He had been removed from the bench some years before, because he was afraid to serve the purposes of the government. He was now afraid to appear as the advocate of the Bishops, and had at first refused to receive their retainer: but it had been intimidated to him by the whole body of attorneys who employed him that, if he declined this brief, he should never have another.

*   *   *

The junior counsel for the Bishops was a young barrister named John Somers. He had no advantages of birth or fortune; nor had he yet had any opportunity of distinguishing himself before the eyes of the public: but his genius, his industry, his great and various accomplishments, were well known to a small circle of friends; and in spite of his Whig opinions, his pertinent and lucid mode of arguing and the constant propriety of his demeanour had already secured to him the ear of the Court of King's Bench.   *   *   *

The jury was sworn. It consisted of persons of highly respectable station. The foreman was Sir Roger Langley, a baronet of old and honourable family. With him were joined a knight and ten esquires, several of whom are known to have been men of large possessions. There were some Nonconformists in the number: for the Bishops had wisely resolved not to show any distrust of the Protestant Dissenters. One name excited considerable alarm, that of Michael Arnold. He was brewer to the palace; and it was apprehended that the government counted on his voice. The story goes that he complained bitterly of the position in which he found himself. "Whatever I do," he said, "I am sure to be half ruined. If I say Not Guilty, I shall brew no more for the King; and if I say Guilty, I shall brew no more for anybody else."

*   *   *

The information charged the Bishops with having written or published, in the county of Middlesex, a false, malicious, and seditious libel. The Attorney and Solicitor first tried to prove the writing. For this purpose several persons were called to speak to the hands of the Bishops. But the witnesses were so unwilling that hardly a single plain answer could be extracted from any of them. Pemberton, Pollexfen, and Levinz contended that there was no evidence to go to the jury. Two of the Judges, Holloway and Powell, declared themselves of the same opinion; and the hopes of the spectators rose high. All at once the crown lawyers announced their intention to take another line. Powis, with shame and reluctance which he could not dissemble, put into the witness box Blathwayt, a Clerk of Privy Council, who had been present when the King interrogated the Bishops. Blathwayt swore that he had heard them own their signatures. His testimony was decisive. "Why," said Judge Holloway to the Attorney, "when you had such evidence, did you not produce it at first, without all this waste of time?" It soon appeared why the counsel for the crown had been unwilling, without absolute necessity, to resort to this mode of proof. Pemberton stopped Blathwayt, subjected him to a searching cross examination, and insisted upon having all that had passed between the King and the defendants fully related. "That is a pretty thing indeed," cried Williams. "Do you think," said Powis, "that you are at liberty to ask our witnesses any impertinent question that comes into your heads?" The advocates of the Bishops were not men to be so put down. "He is sworn," said Pollexfen, "to tell the truth and the whole truth; and an answer we must and will have." The witness shuffled, equivocated, pretended to misunderstand the questions, implored the protection of the Court. But he was in hands from which it was not easy to escape. At length the Attorney again interposed. "If," he said, "you persist in asking such a question, tell us, at least, what use you mean to make of it." Pemberton, who, through the whole trial, did his duty manfully and ably, replied without hesitation: "My Lords, I will answer Mr. Attorney. I will deal plainly with the Court. If the Bishops owned this paper under a promise from His Majesty that their confession should not be used against them, I hope that no unfair advantage will be taken of them." "You put on His Majesty what I dare hardly name," said Williams. "Since you will be so pressing, I demand, for the King, that the question may be recorded." "What do you mean, Mr. Solicitor?" said Sawyer, interposing. "I know what I mean," said the apostate: "I desire that the question may be recorded in court." "Record what you will. I am not afraid of you, Mr. Solicitor," said Pemberton. Then came a loud and fierce altercation, which Wright could with difficulty quiet. In other circumstances, he would probably have ordered the question to be recorded, and Pemberton to be committed. But on this great day the unjust judge was overawed. He often cast a side glance towards the thick rows of Earls and Barons by whom he was watched, and before whom, in the next Parliament, he might stand at the bar. He looked, a bystander said, as if all the peers present had halters in their pockets. At length Blathwayt was forced to give a full account of what had passed. It appeared that the King had entered into no express covenant with the Bishops. But it appeared also that the Bishops might not unreasonably think that there was an implied engagement. Indeed, from the unwillingness of the crown lawyers to put the Clerk of the Council into the witness box, and from the vehemence with which they objected to Pemberton's cross examination, it is plain that they were themselves of this opinion.

However, the handwriting was now proved.   *   *   *

The crown lawyers then   *   *   *   undertook to prove that the Bishops had published a libel in the county of Middlesex. The difficulties were great. The delivery of the petition to the King was undoubtedly, in the eye of the law, a publication. But how was this delivery to be proved? No person had been present at the audience in the royal closet except the King and the defendants. The King could not well be sworn. It was therefore only by the admissions of the defendants that the fact of publication could be established. Blathwayt was again examined, but in vain. He well remembered, he said, that the Bishops owned their hands; but he did not remember that they owned the paper which lay on the table of the Privy Council to be the same paper which they had delivered to the King, or that they were even interrogated on that point.   *   *   *   As witness after witness answered in the negative, roars of laughter and shouts of triumph, which the Judges did not even attempt to silence, shook the hall.

It seemed that at length this hard fight had been won. The case for the crown was closed. Had the counsel for the Bishops remained silent, an acquittal was certain; for nothing which the most corrupt and shameless Judge could venture to call legal evidence of publication had been given. The Chief Justice was beginning to charge the jury, and would undoubtedly have directed them to acquit the defendants; but Finch, too anxious to be perfectly discreet, interfered, and begged to be heard. "If you will be heard," said Wright, "you shall be heard; but you do not understand your own interests." The other counsel for the defence made Finch sit down, and begged the Chief Justice to proceed. He was about to do so, when a messenger came to the Solicitor General with news that Lord Sunderland could prove the publication, and would come down to the court immediately. Wright maliciously told the counsel for the defence that they had only themselves to thank for the turn which things had taken. The countenances of the great multitude fell. Finch was, during some hours, the most unpopular man in the country. Why could he not sit still as his betters, Sawyer, Pemberton, and Pollexfen, had done? His love of meddling, his ambition to make a fine speech, had ruined everything.

Meanwhile the Lord President was brought in a sedan chair through the hall. Not a hat moved as he passed; and many voices cried out "Popish dog." He came into court pale and trembling, with eyes fixed on the ground, and gave his evidence in a faltering voice. He swore that the Bishops had informed him of their intention to present a petition to the King, and that they had been admitted into the royal closet for that purpose. This circumstance, coupled with the circumstance that, after they left the closet, there was in the King's hands a petition signed by them, was such proof as might reasonably satisfy a jury of the fact of the publication.

Publication in Middlesex was then proved. But was the paper thus published a false, malicious, and seditious libel? Hitherto the matter in dispute had been whether a fact which everybody well knew to be true could be proved according to technical rules of evidence; but now the contest became one of deeper interest. It was necessary to enquire into the limits of prerogative and liberty, into the right of the King to dispense with statutes, into the right of the subject to petition for the redress of grievances. During three hours the counsel for the petitioners argued with great force in defence of the fundamental principles of the constitution, and proved from the Journals of the House of Commons that the Bishops had affirmed no more than the truth when they represented to the King that the dispensing power which he claimed had been repeatedly declared illegal by Parliament. Somers rose last. He spoke little more than five minutes: but every word was full of weighty matter; and when he sate down his reputation as an orator and a constitutional lawyer was established. He went through the expressions which were used in the information to describe the offence imputed to the Bishops, and showed that every word, whether adjective or substantive, was altogether inappropriate. The offence imputed was a false, a malicious, a seditious libel. False the paper was not; for every fact which it set forth had been shown from the journals of Parliament to be true. Malicious the paper was not; for the defendants had not sought an occasion of strife, but had been placed by the government in such a situation that they must either oppose themselves to the royal will, or violate the most sacred obligations of conscience and honour. Seditious the paper was not; for it had not been scattered by the writers among the rabble, but delivered privately into the hands of the King alone; and a libel it was not, but a decent petition such as, by the laws of England, nay by the laws of imperial Rome, by the laws of all civilised states, a subject who thinks himself aggrieved may with propriety present to the sovereign.

The Attorney replied shortly and feebly. The Solicitor spoke at great length and with great acrimony, and was often interrupted by the clamours and hisses of the audience. He went so far as to lay it down that no subject or body of subjects, except the Houses of Parliament, had a right to petition the King. The galleries were furious; and the Chief Justice himself stood aghast at the effrontery of this venal turncoat.

At length Wright proceeded to sum up the evidence. His language showed that the awe in which he stood of the government was tempered by the awe with which the audience, so numerous, so splendid, and so strongly excited, had impressed him. He said that he would give no opinion on the question of the dispensing power; that it was not necessary for him to do so; that he could not agree with much of the Solicitor's speech; that it was the right of the subject to petition; but that the particular petition before the Court was improperly worded, and was, in the contemplation of law, a libel. Allibone was of the same mind * * * Holloway evaded the question of the dispensing power, but said that the petition seemed to him to be such as subjects who think themselves aggrieved are entitled to present, and therefore no libel. Powell took a bolder course. He avowed that, in his judgment, the Declaration of Indulgence was a nullity, and that the dispensing power, as lately exercised, was utterly inconsistent with all law. If these encroachments of prerogative were allowed, there was an end of Parliaments. The whole legislative authority would be in the King. "That issue, gentlemen," he said, "I leave to God and to your consciences."

It was dark before the jury retired to consider of their verdict. The night was a night of intense anxiety. * * *

The solicitor for the Bishops sate up all night with a body of servants on the stairs leading to the room where the jury was consulting. It was absolutely necessary to watch the officers who watched the doors; for those officers were supposed to be in the interest of the crown, and might, if not carefully observed, have furnished a courtly juryman with food, which would have enabled him to starve out the other eleven. Strict guard was therefore kept. Not even a candle to light a pipe was permitted to enter. Some basins of water for washing were suffered to pass at about four in the morning. The jurymen, raging with thirst, soon lapped up the whole. * * * Voices, high in altercation, were repeatedly heard within the room: but nothing certain was known.

At first nine were for acquitting and three for convicting. Two of the minority soon gave way: but Arnold was obstinate. Thomas Austin, a country gentleman of great estate, who had paid close attention to the evidence and speeches, and had taken full notes, wished to argue the question. Arnold declined. He was not used, he doggedly said, to reasoning and debating. His conscience was not satisfied; and he should not acquit the Bishops. "If you come to that," said Austin, "look at me. I am the largest and strongest of the twelve; and before I find such a petition as this a libel, here I will stay till I am no bigger than a tobacco pipe." It was six in the morning before Arnold yielded. It was soon known that the jury were agreed: but what the verdict would be was still a secret.

At ten the Court again met. The crowd was greater than ever. The jury appeared in the box; and there was a breathless stillness.

Sir Samuel Astry spoke. "Do you find the defendants, or any of them, guilty of the misdemeanour whereof they are impeached, or not guilty?" Sir Roger Langley answered, "Not Guilty." As the words were uttered, Halifax sprang up and waved his hat. At that signal, benches and galleries raised a shout. In a moment ten thousand persons, who crowded the great hall, replied with a still louder shout, which made the old oaken roof crack; and in another moment the innumerable throng without set up a third huzza, which was heard at Temple Bar. The boats which covered the Thames gave an answering cheer. A peal of gunpowder was heard on the water, and another, and another; and so in a few moments, the glad tidings went flying past the Savoy and the Friars to London Bridge, and to the forest of masts below. As the news spread, streets and squares, market places and coffeehouses, broke forth into acclamations. Yet were the acclamations less strange than the weeping. For the feelings of men had been wound up to such a point that at length the stern English nature, so little used to outward signs of emotion, gave way, and thousands sobbed aloud for very joy. * * *

* * *

The prosecution of the Bishops is an event which stands by itself in our history. It was the first and the last occasion on which two feelings of tremendous potency, two feelings which have generally been opposed to each other, and either of which, when strongly ex-

cited, has sufficed to convulse the state, were united in perfect harmony. Those feelings were love of the Church and love of freedom.
* * * In 1688 the cause of the hierarchy was for a moment that of the popular party. More than nine thousand clergymen, with the Primate and his most respectable suffragans at their head, offered themselves to endure bonds and the spoiling of their goods for the great fundamental principle of our free constitution. The effect was a coalition which included the most zealous Cavaliers, the most zealous Republicans, and all the intermediate sections of the community.
* * * Those classes of society which are most deeply interested in the preservation of order, which in troubled times are generally most ready to strengthen the hands of government, and which have a natural antipathy to agitators, followed, without scruple, the guidance of a venerable man, the first peer of the Parliament, the first minister of the Church, a Tory in politics, a saint in manners, whom tyranny had in his own despite turned into a demagogue. Many, on the other hand, who had always abhorred episcopacy, as a relic of Popery, and as an instrument of arbitrary power, now asked on bended knees the blessing of a prelate who was ready to wear fetters and to lay his aged limbs on bare stones rather than betray the interests of the Protestant religion and set the prerogative above the laws. With love of the Church and with love of freedom was mingled, at this great crisis, a third feeling which is among the most honourable peculiarities of our national character. An individual oppressed by power, even when destitute of all claim to public respect and gratitude, generally finds strong sympathy among us. * * * It is probable, therefore, that, even if no great political or religious interest had been staked on the event of the proceeding against the Bishops, England would not have seen, without strong emotions of pity and anger, old men of stainless virtue pursued by the vengeance of a harsh and inexorable prince who owed to their fidelity the crown which he wore.

Actuated by these sentiments our ancestors arrayed themselves against the government in one huge and compact mass. All ranks, all parties, all Protestant sects, made up that vast phalanx. * * *
The Archbishop soon after his acquittal put forth a pastoral letter which is one of the most remarkable compositions of that age. He had, from his youth up, been at war with the Nonconformists, and had repeatedly assailed them with unjust and unchristian asperity.
* * * But now his heart was melted and opened. He solemnly enjoined the Bishops and clergy to have a very tender regard to their brethren the Protestant Dissenters, to visit them often, to entertain them hospitably, to discourse with them civilly, to persuade them, if it might be, to conform to the Church, but, if that were found impossible, to join them heartily and affectionately in exertions for the blessed cause of the Reformation.

Many pious persons in subsequent years remembered that time with bitter regret. They described it as a short glimpse of a golden age between two iron ages. Such lamentation, though natural, was not reasonable. The coalition of 1688 was produced, and could be produced, only by tyranny which approached to insanity, and by danger which threatened at once all the great institutions of the country. If there has never since been similar union, the reason is that there has never since been similar misgovernment. It must be remembered that, though concord is in itself better than discord, discord may indicate a better state of things than is indicated by concord. Calamity and peril often force men to combine. Prosperity and security often encourage them to separate.

NOTES AND QUESTIONS

1. James's Declarations of Indulgence, which appear to be based on the proposition that there ought to be religious liberty for English subjects should have been popular measures, shouldn't they? Why were they not? In answering this question ask yourself, "What is the connection between the trial of the Seven Bishops and the controversy between Sir Edward Coke and James I?"

2. James II seems honestly to have believed that he had the power and the right to suspend operation of statutes passed by Parliament (the "dispensing power"). Was this a novel idea? Would his grandfather, James I, have agreed? Why did the Seven Bishops disagree? When James II's brother, Charles II, had tried to exercise this power, as you read in the beginning of this excerpt, Charles II was persuaded to back down. Why did he forbear exercise of the dispensing power when James II did not? Does it help to know that James II regarded the word "republican" as an epithet? See J. P. Kenyon, The Stuarts 147 (1958). It is possible, of course, that James II did not perceive the issue as a political one at all, but acted simply as a result of his adherence to the Catholic faith. He was reported to have said, for example, that "his principle aim" was "the advancement of the Catholic religion." Kenyon, supra, at 155. Still, does it seem to you that the Catholic-Protestant controversy in England is a sufficient explanation for the affair of the Seven Bishops? Note that the author of this excerpt, Lord Macaulay, frequently stresses that the Bishops were members of one of the Houses of Parliament, the House of Lords. Note also that when the Bishops were incarcerated in the Tower of London "[a]ll day the coaches and liveries of the first nobles of England were seen round the prison gates," and that "twenty-one temporal peers of the highest consideration [were] ready to put in bail, three for each defendant." Why?

3. If Macaulay's account is accurate, the Trial of the Seven Bishops excited not only the nobles, but also the common people. Why do you suppose Macaulay finds it necessary to tell us that if King James II had put the Bishop of Cornwall, Trelawney, to death "Then thirty thousand Cornish boys" and "twenty thousand under ground" "will know the reason why?" Why would the "rustics in many parts of the country" expect at this time the resurrection of the Duke of Monmouth? For a somewhat dryer-eyed version of James II's struggles to preserve Stuart principles of Royal supremacy, see J. R. Jones, Country and Court: England 1658–1714 234–255 (1978).

4. The procedures before and during the actual trial are worth some comment. Why did the Seven Bishops believe that they should be set free without posting bond? Note that this demand was not acquiesced in. We learn from this excerpt that it was the usual practice for prisoners held at the tower to pay the costs of their detention, even where, as here, they were released pending trial. Does this practice make sense to you?

5. Why was it that only "third-rank" lawyers could be induced to prosecute the Bishops, and how was it that the Bishops were able to recruit the best legal talent in England for their defense? You have seen that one of the Bishops' lawyers, the experienced but timid Sir Creswell Levinz, was even blackmailed into serving as defense counsel "by the whole body of attorneys who employed him," who told him that, "if he declined this brief, he should never have another." Why was this threat by "attorneys" that Creswell would never have another "brief" an effective one?

6. For our purposes we can assume that the prosecution in a case of seditious libel must prove two elements—(1) publication, and (2) seditiousness. You will have seen that in the attempt to prove publication it was necessary for the Crown to prove that the document in question was actually written by the Bishops. The King had extracted this admission from them when he interrogated them in the Privy Council chambers. Why was the prosecution so hesitant to produce this particular bit of evidence? When the evidence was introduced, and it resulted in defense counsel Pemberton's accusing the King of breaking his promise to the Bishops, Macaulay suggests that Pemberton could have been immediately imprisoned by the Chief Judge, Wright. On what basis? Why did Wright decline to commit Pemberton after this affront to the King? How could Wright be "overawed" when he saw "the thick Rows of Earls and Barons by whom he was watched"?

7. On the basis of this excerpt, what do you take to be the test for "seditiousness?" Note that Macaulay says that to determine this question "It was necessary to enquire into the limits of prerogative and liberty, into the right of the King to dispense with statutes, into the right of the subject to petition for the redress of grievances." Did everyone involved agree that it was necessary to reach these "Constitutional" issues?

8. When one of the prosecutors argued that "no subject or body of subjects, except the Houses of Parliament, had a right to petition the King," writes Macaulay, "The galleries were furious * * * the Chief Justice himself stood aghast at the effrontery of this venal turncoat." Was the prosecutor's position really so ridiculous? Consider these comments from the actual charge to the jury of Allybone, J., commenting on whether the Bishop's petition "shall be in the construction of law a libel in itself, or a thing of great innocence.":

> * * * [N]o man can take upon him to write against the actual exercise of the government, unless he have leave from the government, but he makes a libel, be what he writes true or false; for if once we come to impeach the government by way of argument, it is the argument that makes it the government or not the government.

> * * * [N]o private man can take upon him to write concerning the government at all; for what has any private man to do

with the government if his interest be not stirred or shaken? It
is the business of the government to manage matters relating to
the government. It is the business of subjects to mind only their
own properties and interests. * * * If the government does
come to shake my particular interest, the law is open for me, and
I may redress myself by law. And when I intrude myself into
other men's business that does not concern my particular interest,
I am a libeller.

     * * * I do agree that every man may petition the govern-
ment or the king in a matter that relates to his own private interest, but to meddle with a matter that relates to the government,
I do not think my lords the bishops had any power more than any
others. When the Houses of Lords and Commons are in being
it is a proper way of applying to the king. * * * if every private man shall come and interpose his advice, I think there can
never be an end to advising the government. * * *

12 Howell's State Trials 183, 427–28 (1688). Powell, J., disagreed with the
interpretation of the law offered by Allybone. Powell maintained that
unless a petition to the King was accompanied by "threats of the people's
being discontented," it would not amount to seditious libel. Allybone replied that "every libel against the government carries in it sedition, and
all the other epithets that are in the information." Id., at 429. What is
Allybone's great concern about "popular petitions?" Can you relate this
to Macaulay's discussion about the relative *benefits* of discord?

    9. What does the outcome of this trial suggest as to the connection
between the crime of seditious libel and the rights and powers of King,
parliament, and people? The notion that there is such a connection was
clearly rejected by some of the Judges in the trial of the Seven Bishops,
but do you think the jury agreed with these judges? Does it surprise you
to learn that before the jury reached a verdict they were not permitted
to eat, drink, or use candles? In the next reading, the trial of John Peter
Zenger, we will further explore the early role of the jury, the nature of
the law of seditious libel, and the implications for executive power.

    10. Very soon after the trial of the Seven Bishops a coalition of
English nobles invited the Protestant William, King of the Netherlands,
to come to England. In the "Glorious Revolution" of 1688 William forced
James II to flee England for France, and in 1689 William and his wife
Mary (daughter of James II) became King and Queen of England. They
were granted their crowns by the House of Lords and the House of Commons, which should tell you what implications about Parliamentary supremacy can be drawn from the events of 1688–89. It is probably not
too much to say that James's excesses in the Trial of the Seven Bishops
went far toward provoking those who finally replaced him. See, e. g.
Kenyon, supra, at 158–159, Cf. L. Smith, This Realm of England 294 (3rd.
ed. 1976), W. Willcox, The Age of Aristocracy 9–12 (3rd. ed. 1976). In
American law, however, the importance of the trial of the Seven Bishops
has more to do with the jury's supposed defense of English liberties than
it does with the power politics of Crown and Nobles, as you will see not
only in the Zenger trial, but in the trial of Gideon Henfield, infra. The
terms of the settlement of the crown on William and Mary, which altered

the "constitution" of England, were written into the Bill of Rights of 1689, enacted in Parliament, and appeared in the Act of Settlement of 1701. So ended the battle between Coke and James at the beginning of the century, and between divine right of Kings and Parliamentary Sovereignty during the Civil War. Perhaps the greatest legacy of the seventeenth century to Americans, however, was not so much in the eventual outcome of the struggle—Parliamentary sovereignty—as in the means of its accomplishment: the "people" had taken into their own hands the right and power to set up a new form of government in accordance with a theory of the state.

11. Those interested in pursuing the historical and legal dimensions of sixteenth and seventeenth century England should find W. Notestein, The English People on the Eve of Colonization (Harper Torchbook ed. 1962) useful for its discussion of the English social structure; T. Plucknett, A Concise History of the Common Law (5th ed. 1956) and W. Holdsworth, I A History of English Law (7th ed. 1956) are invaluable mines of information on English law.

Chapter 1

THE EMERGENCE OF THE THEORY OF THE POPULAR WILL AS THE BASIS OF LAW IN THE AMERICAN COLONIES: LEGAL AND CONSTITUTIONAL PERSPECTIVES ON THE AMERICAN REVOLUTION

SECTION A. INTRODUCTION

The seventeenth century was not only an age of political revolution for the English, but also marked the beginnings of English imperialism. The English attempted to colonize America in accordance with the dominant international economic strategy of the day: Mercantilism. England, Spain, France, and the Netherlands each sought to increase national wealth to the point of self-sufficiency, in order to avoid debilitating and expensive diplomatic and military entanglements. Foreign colonies were thus to serve as a market for surplus home manufactures; and the colonies were to supply the mother country with raw materials to sustain the productivity and profit of home industries. The production, manufacturing and distribution of commodities wholly within the empire would further permit the mother country to enjoy a favourable balance of trade. By exporting more than was imported, she could accumulate gold to be used to finance large armies for national defense and to reinvest in colonization and manufacturing.

The settlement of Virginia in 1607, the first permanent English transplantation, was to be such a mercantilist operation. Even the settlement of Massachusetts Bay in 1629 resulted from commercial as well as religious motives; it was a product both of mercantilism and of Puritan discontent under the absolutist Stuarts. By 1700 England had ten colonies on the eastern seaboard of the North American continent, but they had not realized mercantilist expectations. Instead, these early settlements were a drain on English capital. Still, the unsettling political situation at home and the boom-and-bust cycles of the English economy produced a steady stream of migrants with some capital and a great deal of desire to make their way in a New World. Political uncertainty in seventeenth century England also detracted from imperial administration, leading to a sort of "benign neglect" of the colonies, and a concomitant slippage of the rigors of mercantilism. Accordingly, in less than a century, the North American colonies evolved from distant outposts into smaller-scaled replicas of English society, enjoying a high degree of political independence, each possessing a unique landed and commercial economy. By the middle of the eighteenth century, some of the colonies were beginning to rival the mother country in volume of trade and in population. In fact, after London, the largest urban concentrations of Englishmen were in the New World.

The colonies remained cognizant of their English commercial and political heritage. In places like New York, originally a Dutch settlement, the colonists themselves could be merciless cultural imperialists. As much as they could, they patterned their executive, legislative and judicial branches of government after the English; colonial lawyers purchased English law books and pleading manuals and cited English precedent in their courts. Colonials read English newspapers, followed London gossip and politics, and, when they could, journeyed to London itself to view the seat of learning and culture of their Empire. There was also considerable movement back and forth among top-level imperial personnel. Royal governors and their advisors generally resided in America for short periods of time, using colonial office as a stepping stone for some higher or more lucrative position in England. Deeper, more personal bonds between colony and mother country formed out of common language, culture, and kinship.

Ironically, their practical success in mimicking English society produced great stress for Americans. Colonials were acutely aware of the subtle differences that remained. They never quite replicated English government, nor were they permitted to. There were hedges, accretions of power peculiar to local circumstances, and legal peculiarities because of the particular necessities and customs of settlements. Together, these anomalies made colonial political life factious, unstable, and highly introspective. The royal governor of the colony was not quite a king, true to the English model, for his opponents could appeal over his head to the English Parliament or the administrative agency for the colonies, the "Board of Trade." The colonial assemblies were not quite like Parliament, since their enactments were subject to stringent review by the King and his ministers in London. The colonial councils, modeled on the English House of Lords, lacked real dignity and legitimacy in the absence of a titled American nobility. Finally, colonial law was not quite like the English, since everyone recognized the futility of applying *in toto* a common law, with its hoary medieval origins, to a society as diverse and derivative as America. As America lacked a traditional social structure and hierarchy of institutions based on legal privilege, the rulers were never far removed from the people. Self-rule became a way of life long before it became an article of belief. Nevertheless, the fiction of imperial societal identity persevered as long as colonials thought of themselves as Englishmen. And, as long as they thought of themselves primarily as participants in an English empire, they were bound to think of their political peculiarities in negative terms, as imperfect fragments needing repair or restructuring to bring them more in accord with the English originals.

The movement toward American independence could not begin until a new vision of American society recognized political validity in the historically determined colonial systems of government. When Americans began to view their "imperfections" as plusses, and when the eighteenth-century English polity, instead of being idealized, came to be perceived as a corruption of some ancient constitutional order, then the logic of distant rule began to recede. This realization that classic English liberty remained pristine *only* in America was slow in coming. The feeling was encouraged by American observation of the newly-acquired sovereignty of the eighteenth century English Parliament, and by the perception of arbitrary rule by key ministers that Parliamentary absolutism eventually encouraged. The ultimate stimulus leading to a break was Parliament's dogged resolve in the 1760's to reestablish its mercantilist hold over the colonial economy. The most notorious of Parliamentary measures was the 1765 Stamp Tax. It was repealed within the year, but was soon followed by other taxing measures. These led to a vigorous debate among colonials over the province of English Parliamentary sovereignty in the New World. This pamphlet literature spawned a self-examination that grew into a wondrous self-discovery. The eventual severance from England from this point on became nearly inevitable.

The American Revolution was unlike any other; some have wondered if it was a revolution at all. The patriotic tracts of the 1760's and 1770's often read like debates over fine points of supposedly ancient law. Some have become classics of constitutional thought in the West. Official colonial resistance to Parliamentary enactments frequently took the form of colonial legislative "resolves." The Declaration of Independence itself issued from a "Congress duly convened," presented grievances in brief-like fashion, and appealed to a higher "law" than the dictates of the English Parliament or King. The new American "states" immediately set about constructing new governments based on written constitutions, and these documents were promoted as embodiments of the fundamental law that gave rise to the Declaration of Independence and was thought to have been reflected in the Magna Carta, the opinions and treatises of Sir Edward Coke, and the English Bill of Rights of 1689. Everywhere, it would seem, the language of the lawyer was evident, and this language, quoting ancient precedent, was used to support revolutionary acts.

It was in the sulphurous mix of law and politics of the 1760's and 1770's in America that a new ideology was born. The materials in this chapter are offered as glimpses into the process at work. True to the evolution of a Revolutionary frame of mind, they are set against the shifting background of individual personalities and local politics. Both factors we believe, help explain the halting nature of development, the uncertain groping toward new modes of thought within an inherited framework of ideas.

Those interested in pursuing these themes might begin with the discussion of the evolution of American politics in Bernard Bailyn's The Origins of American Politics (1965) and follow developments through his The Ideological Origins of the American Revolution (1967) and The Ordeal of Thomas Hutchinson (1974). Provocative insights into the nexus between colonial politics and law are to be found in Stanley N. Katz, The Politics of Law in Colonial America: Controversies Over Chancery Courts and Equity Law in the Eighteenth Century, 5 Perspectives in American History 257 (1971) (reprinted in hardcover as D. Fleming and B. Bailyn, eds., Law in American History (1971)) and Professor Katz's introduction and annotation of the trial of John Peter Zenger, A Brief Narrative of the Case and Trial of John Peter Zenger, by James Alexander (S. N. Katz, ed., 1963). Also useful for colonial legal history are the essays and the bibliographical introduction in David H. Flaherty, ed., Essays in the History of Early American Law (1969). Constitutional issues in the early state and federal governments are explored in Gordon S. Wood, The Creation of the American Republic 1776–1787 (1969), and legal issues are treated in Lawrence Friedman, A History of American Law 27–90 (1973), Morton Horwitz, The Transformation of American Law 1780–1860 1–30 (1977) and William Nelson, The Americanization of the Common Law: The Impact of Legal Change on Massachusetts Society, 1760–1830 1–64 (1975). Finally, and of importance throughout the readings in this casebook, cameos of English and American legal history are offered in the definitions of many terms in a good Law Dictionary such as Black's Law Dictionary (5th ed. 1979) or Ballantine's Law Dictionary (3rd ed. 1969). No fledgling legal historian should be without one.

SECTION B.   THE TRIAL OF JOHN PETER ZENGER FOR SEDITIOUS LIBEL

JAMES ALEXANDER, A BRIEF NARRATIVE OF THE CASE AND TRIAL OF JOHN PETER ZENGER, PRINTER OF THE NEW YORK WEEKLY JOURNAL * (1735)

S. Katz, ed., A Brief Narrative of the Case and Trial of John Peter Zenger Printer of the New York Weekly Journal by James Alexander 58–70, 71–77, 78–79, 81–83, 84–85, 87–88, 91–92, 95–96, 99–101 (1963).

[John Peter Zenger was a printer in the colony of New York in the early Eighteenth Century. By 1735 he had printed many items in his New York Weekly Journal which were critical of the Royal Governor of New York, William Cosby. These pieces were not written by Zenger, but were produced by political opponents of Cosby, one of whom was a man named James Alexander, an important New York lawyer. Zenger was prosecuted for the publication of these articles, pursuant to the legal doctrine of seditious libel, the same doctrine that was involved in the Seven Bishops' case. What follows are excerpts from what purports to be a report of Zenger's trial. Though it is supposedly written in the first person by Zenger, the document was actually produced by James Alexander, the anti-Cosby lawyer. This trial involves a number of complex matters, not all of which will be readily intelligible to you. As you read through the excerpts from the trial you should be looking principally for three things. First, the debate over the legal definition of the crime of seditious libel; second, the differing conceptions of the appropriate roles for judge and jury; and third, the ideas expressed about the proper participation in governance of the colony by governor and people. "Mr. Attorney" is the Attorney General of the colony of New York, the prosecutor in the trial. "Mr. Hamilton" is one of Zenger's lawyers, an outside counsel brought in from Philadelphia following the disbarment of Zenger's original attorneys by "Mr. Chief Justice." The narrative begins with Mr. Attorney explaining and reading the "Information," the document which sets forth Zenger's offense, to the Judge and jury.]

[1. *Zenger's Alleged Crime*]

Mr. Attorney. May it please Your Honors, and you, gentlemen of the jury; the information now before the Court, and to which the Defendant Zenger has pleaded not guilty, is an information for printing and publishing a false, scandalous and seditious libel, in which His Excellency the Governor of this Province, who is the King's immediate representative here, is greatly and unjustly scandalized as a person that has no regard to law nor justice; with much more, as will appear upon reading the information. This of libeling is what has always been discouraged as a thing that tends to create differences among men, ill blood among the people, and oftentimes great bloodshed between the party libeling and the party libeled. There can be no doubt but you gentlemen of the jury will have the same ill opinion of such practices as the judges have always shown upon such occasions: But I shall say no more at this time until you hear the information, which is as follows:

* * *

* * * John Peter Zenger, late of the City of New York, printer (being a seditious person and a frequent printer and publisher of false news and seditious libels, and wickedly and maliciously devising the government of our said lord the King of this His Majesty's Province of New York under the administration of His Excellency William Cosby, Esq.; Captain General and Governor-in-Chief of the said Province, to traduce, scandalize and vilify, and His Excellency the said Governor and the ministers and officers of our said lord the King, of and for the said Province to bring into suspicion and the ill opinion of the subjects of our said lord the King residing within the said Province) the twenty-eighth day of January * * * at the City of New York, *did falsely, seditiously and scandalously* print and publish * * * a certain *false, malicious, seditious, scandalous* libel, entitled

The New York Weekly Journal, containing the Freshest Advices, Foreign and Domestic; in which libel (of and concerning His Excellency the said Governor, and the ministers and officers of our said lord the King, of and for the said Province) among other things therein contained are these words:

Your appearance in print at last gives a pleasure to many, though most wish you had come fairly into the open field, and not appeared behind *retrenchments* made of the supposed laws against libeling and of what other men have said and done before; these *retrenchments,* gentlemen, may soon be shown to you and all men to be weak, and to have neither law nor reason for their foundation, so cannot long stand you in stead: Therefore, you had much better as yet leave them, and come to what *the people of this City and Province* (the City and Province of New York meaning) think are the points in question (*to wit*) *They* (the people of the City and Province of New York meaning) *think as matters now stand that their* LIBERTIES *and* PROPERTIES *are precarious, and that* SLAVERY *is like to be entailed on them and their posterity if some past things be not amended, and this they collect from many past proceedings.* (Meaning many of the past proceedings of His Excellency the said Governor, and of the ministers and officers of our said lord the King, of and for the said Province.)

[The information then quoted a second article, also said to be a "false malicious seditious and scandalous" libel:]

One of our neighbors (one of the inhabitants of New Jersey meaning) *being in company, observing the strangers* (some of the inhabitants of New York meaning) *full of complaints, endeavored to persuade them to remove into Jersey; to which it was replied, that would be leaping out of the frying pan into the fire, for, says he, we both are under the same Governor* (His Excellency the said Governor meaning) *and your Assembly have shown with a witness what is to be expected from them; one that was then moving to Pennsylvania,* (meaning one that was then removing from New York with intent to reside at Pennsylvania) *to which place it is reported several considerable men are removing* (from New York meaning) *expressed, in terms very moving, much concern for the circumstances of New York* (the bad circumstances of the Province and people of New York meaning) *seemed to think them very much owing to the influence that some men* (whom he called tools) *had in the administration* (meaning the administration of government of the said Province of New York) *said he was now going from them, and was not to be hurt by any measures they should take, but could not help having some concern for the welfare of his countrymen, and should be glad to hear that the Assembly* (meaning the General Assembly of the Province of New York) *would exert themselves as became them, by showing that they have the interest of their country more at heart than the gratification of any private view of any of their members, or being at all affected by the smiles or frowns of a governor* (His Excellency the said Governor meaning), *both which ought equally to be despised when the interest of their country is at stake. You, says he, complain of the lawyers, but I think the law itself is at an end;* WE (the people of the Province of New York meaning) SEE MEN'S DEEDS DESTROYED, JUDGES ARBITRARILY DISPLACED, NEW COURTS ERECTED WITHOUT CONSENT OF THE LEGISLATURE (within the Province of New York meaning) BY WHICH, IT SEEMS TO ME, TRIALS BY JURIES ARE TAKEN AWAY WHEN A GOVERNOR PLEASES (His Excellency the said Governor meaning), MEN OF KNOWN ESTATES DENIED THEIR VOTES CONTRARY TO THE RECEIVED PRACTICE, THE BEST EXPOSITOR OF ANY LAW: *Who is then in that Province* (meaning the Province of New York) *that call* (can call meaning) *anything his own, or enjoy any liberty* (liberty meaning) *longer than those in the administration* (meaning the administration of government of the said Province of New York) *will condescend to let them do it, for which reason I have left it* (the Province of New York meaning), *as I believe more will.* [The information concluded by charging that the publication of these articles by Zenger was:]

To the great disturbance of the peace of the said Province of New York, to the great scandal of our said lord the King, of His Excellency the said Governor, and of all others concerned in the administration of the government of the said Province, and against the peace of our sovereign lord the King his crown and dignity, etc. * * *

R. Bradley, Attorney General

To this information the Defendant has pleaded *not guilty,* and we are ready to prove it.

[2. *The Legal Arguments Begin*]

Mr. Hamilton. May it please Your Honor; I am concerned in this cause on the part of Mr. Zenger the Defendant. The information against my client was sent me a few days before I left home, with some instructions to let me know how far I might rely upon the truth of those parts of the papers set forth in the information and which are said to be libelous. * * * I cannot think it proper for me (without doing violence to my own principles) to deny the publication of a complaint which I think is the right of every free-born subject to make when the matters so published can be supported with truth; and therefore I'll save Mr. Attorney the trouble of examining his witnesses to that point; and I do (for my client) confess that he both printed and published the two newspapers set forth in the information, and I hope in so doing he has committed no crime.

Mr. Attorney. Then if Your Honor pleases, since Mr. Hamilton has confessed the fact, I think our witnesses may be discharged; we have no further occasion for them.

Mr. Hamilton. If you brought them here only to prove the printing and publishing of these newspapers, we have acknowledged that, and shall abide by it.

[Here my journeyman and two sons (with several others subpoenaed by Mr. Attorney, to give evidence against me) were discharged, and there was silence in the Court for some time.]

Mr. Chief Justice. Well Mr. Attorney, will you proceed?

Mr. Attorney. Indeed sir, as Mr. Hamilton has confessed the printing and publishing these libels, I think the jury must find a verdict for the King; for supposing they were true, the law says that they are not the less libelous for that; nay indeed the law says their being true is an aggravation of the crime.

Mr. Hamilton. Not so neither, Mr. Attorney, there are two words to that bargain. I hope it is not our bare printing and publishing a paper that will make it a libel: You will have something more to do before you make my client a libeler; for the words themselves must be libelous, that is, *false, scandalous, and seditious* or else we are not guilty.

[As Mr. Attorney has not been pleased to favor us with his argument, which he read, or with the notes of it, we cannot take upon us to set down his words, but only to show the book cases he cited and the general scope of his argument which he drew from those authorities. He observed upon the excellency as well as the use of government, and the great regard and reverence which had been constantly paid to it, both under the law and the gospel. That by government we were protected in our lives, religion and properties; and that for these reasons great care had always been taken to prevent everything that might tend to scandalize magistrates and others concerned in the administration of the government, especially the supreme magistrate. And that there were many instances of very severe judgments, and of punishments inflicted upon such, as had attempted to bring the government into contempt; by publishing false and scurrilous libels against it, or by speaking evil and scandalous words of men in authority; to the great disturbance of the public peace. And to support this, he cited 5 Coke 121 (suppose it should be 125), Wood's Instit. 430, 2 Lilly 168, I Hawkins 73.11.6. From these books he insisted that a libel was a malicious defamation of any person, expressed either in printing or writing, signs or pictures, to asperse the reputation of one that is alive or the memory of one that is dead; if he is a private man, the libeler deserves a severe punishment, but if it is against a magistrate or other public person, it is a greater offense; for this concerns not only the breach of the peace, but the scandal of the government; for what greater scandal of government can there be than to have corrupt or wicked magistrates to be appointed by the King to govern his subjects under him? And a greater imputation to the state cannot be than to suffer such corrupt men to sit in the sacred seat of justice, or to have any meddling in or concerning the administration of justice; And from the same books Mr. Attorney insisted that whether the person defamed is a private man or a magistrate, whether living or dead, whether the libel is true or false, or if the party against whom it is made is of good or evil fame, it is nevertheless a libel: For in a settled state of government the party aggrieved ought to complain for every injury done him in the ordinary course of the law. He said it was likewise evident that libeling was an offense against the law of God. Act. XXIII. 5. Then said Paul, I wist not brethren, that he was the High Priest: For it is written, thou shalt not speak evil of the ruler of the People. 2 Pet. X. II. Despise government, presumptuous are they, self-willed, they are not afraid to speak evil of dignitaries, etc. He then insisted that it was clear, both by the law of God and man, that it was a very great offense to speak evil of or to revile those in authority over us; and that Mr. Zenger had offended in a most notorious and gross manner in scandalizing His Excellency our Governor, who is the King's immediate representative and the supreme magistrate of this Province: For can there be anything more scandalous said of a Governor than what is published in those papers?

* * * If this was not a libel, he said, he did not know what was one. Such persons as will take those liberties with governors and magistrates he thought ought to suffer for stirring up sedition and discontent among the people. And concluded by saying that the government had been very much traduced and exposed by Mr. Zenger before he was taken notice of; that at last it was the opinion of the Governor and Council that he ought not to be suffered to go on to dis-

turb the peace of the government by publishing such libels against the Governor and the chief persons in the government * * *.]

* * *

[3. *Hamilton on the Rights of Subjects and the Differences in Law in England and America*]

Mr. Hamilton. May it please Your Honor; I agree with Mr. Attorney, that government is a sacred thing, but I differ very widely from him when he would insinuate that the just complaints of a number of men who suffer under a bad administration is libeling that administration. * * *

* * *

I was in hopes, as that terrible Court, where those dreadful judgments were given and that law established which Mr. Attorney has produced for authorities to support this cause, was long ago laid aside as the most dangerous court to the liberties of the people of England that ever was known in that kingdom; that Mr. Attorney knowing this would not have attempted to set up a Star Chamber here, nor to make their judgments a precedent to us: For it is well known that what would have been judged treason in those days for a man to speak, I think, has since not only been practiced as lawful, but the contrary doctrine has been held to be law.

* * *

Is it not surprising to see a subject, upon his receiving a commission from the King to be a governor of a colony in America, immediately imagining himself to be vested with all the prerogatives belonging to the sacred person of his Prince? And which is yet more astonishing, to see that a people can be so wild as to allow of and acknowledge those prerogatives and exemptions, even to their own destruction? Is it so hard a matter to distinguish between the majesty of our Sovereign and the power of a governor of the plantations? Is not this making very free with our Prince, to apply that regard, obedience and allegiance to a subject which is due only to our Sovereign? And yet in all the cases which Mr. Attorney has cited to show the duty and obedience we owe to the supreme magistrate, it is the King that is there meant and understood, though Mr. Attorney is pleased to urge them as authorities to prove the heinousness of Mr. Zenger's offense against the Governor of New York. * * * Let us not (while we are pretending to pay a great regard to our Prince and his peace) make bold to transfer that allegiance to a subject which we owe to our King only. What strange doctrine is it to press everything for law here which is so in England? I believe we should not think it a favor, at present at least, to establish this practice. In England so great a regard and reverence is had to the judges, that if any man strikes another in Westminster Hall while the judges are sitting, he shall lose his right hand and forfeit his land and goods for so doing. And though the judges here claim all the powers and authorities within this government that a Court of King's Bench has in England, yet I believe Mr. Attorney will scarcely say that such a punishment could be legally inflicted on a man for committing such an offense in the presence of the judges sitting in any court within the Province of New York. The reason is obvious; a quarrel or riot in New York cannot possibly be attended with those dangerous consequences that it might in Westminster Hall; nor (I hope) will it be alleged that any misbehavior to a governor in the plantations will, or ought to be, judged of or punished as a like undutifulness would be to our Sovereign. From all which, I hope Mr. Attorney will not think it proper to apply his law cases (to support the cause of his Governor) which have only been judged where the King's safety or honor was concerned. It will not be denied but that a freeholder in the Province of New York has as good a right to the sole and separate use of his lands as a freeholder in England, who has a right to bring an action of trespass against his neighbor for suffering his horse or cow to come and feed upon his land, or eat his corn, whether enclosed or not enclosed; and yet I believe it would be looked upon as a strange attempt for one man here to bring an action against another, whose cattle and horses feed upon his grounds not enclosed, or indeed for eating and treading down his corn, if that were not enclosed. Numberless are the instances of this kind that might be given, to show that what is good law at one time and in one place is not so at another time and in another place; so that I think the law seems to expect that in these parts of the world men should take care, by a good fence, to preserve their property from the injury of unruly beasts. And perhaps there may be as good reason why men should take the same care to make an honest and upright conduct a fence and security against the injury of unruly tongues.

Mr. Attorney. I don't know what the gentleman means, by comparing cases of freeholders in England with freeholders here. What has this case to do with actions of trespass, or men's fencing their ground? The case before the Court is whether Mr. Zenger is guilty of libeling His Excellency the Governor of New York, and indeed the whole administration of the government? Mr. Hamilton has confessed the printing and publishing, and I think nothing is plainer than that the words in the information are *scandalous, and tend to sedition, and to disquiet the minds of the people of this Province.* And if such papers are not libels, I think it may be said there can be no such thing as a libel.

Mr. Hamilton. May it please Your Honor; I cannot agree with Mr. Attorney: For though I freely acknowledge that there are such things as libels, yet I must insist at the same time that what my client is charged with is not a libel; and I observed just now that Mr. Attorney in defining a libel made use of the words *scandalous, sedi-*

tious, and tend to disquiet the people; but (whether with design or not I will not say) he omitted the word *false.*

Mr. Attorney. I think I did not omit the word *false:* But it has been said already that it may be a libel notwithstanding it may be true.

Mr. Hamilton. In this I must still differ with Mr. Attorney; for I depend upon it, we are to be tried upon this information now before the Court and jury, and to which we have pleaded *not guilty,* and by it we are charged with printing and publishing *a certain false, malicious, seditious and scandalous libel.* This word *false* must have some meaning, or else how came it there? I hope Mr. Attorney will not say he put it there by chance, and I am of opinion his information would not be good without it. But to show that it is the principal thing which, in my opinion, makes a libel, I put the case, if the information had been for printing and publishing a certain *true* libel, would that be the same thing? Or could Mr. Attorney support such an information by any precedent in the English law? No, the falsehood makes the scandal, and both make the libel. And to show the Court that I am in good earnest and to save the Court's time and Mr. Attorney's trouble, I will agree that if he can prove the facts charged upon us to be *false,* I'll own them to be *scandalous, seditious* and *a libel.* So the work seems now to be pretty much shortened, and Mr. Attorney has now only to prove the words *false* in order to make us guilty.

Mr. Attorney. We have nothing to prove; you have confessed the printing and publishing; but if it was necessary (as I insist it is not) how can we prove a negative? But I hope some regard will be had to the authorities that have been produced, and that supposing all the words to be true, yet that will not help them, that Chief Justice Holt in his charge to the jury in the case of Tutchin made no distinction whether Tutchin's papers were *true* or *false;* and as Chief Justice Holt has made no distinction in that case, so none ought to be made here; nor can it be shown in all that case there was any question made about their being *false* or *true.*

* * *

[4. *Hamilton Argues to the Court that*
Truth is a Defense]

Mr. Chief Justice. You cannot be admitted, Mr. Hamilton, to give the truth of a libel in evidence. A libel is not to be justified; for it is nevertheless a libel that it is *true.*

Mr. Hamilton. I am sorry the Court has so soon resolved upon that piece of law; I expected first to have been heard to that point. I have not in all my reading met with an authority that says we cannot be admitted to give the truth in evidence upon an information for a libel.

* * *

Mr. Chief Justice. I pray show that you can give the truth of a libel in evidence.

Mr. Hamilton. I am ready, both from what I understand to be the authorities in the case, and from the reason of the thing, to show that we may lawfully do so. But here I beg leave to observe that informations for libels is a child if not born, yet nursed up and brought to full maturity, in the Court of Star Chamber.

Mr. Chief Justice. Mr. Hamilton you'll find yourself mistaken; for in *Coke's Institutes* you'll find informations for libels long before the Court of Star Chamber.

* * *

Mr. Hamilton. I know it is said *that truth makes a libel the more provoking, and therefore the offense is the greater, and consequently the judgment should be the heavier.* Well, suppose it were so, and let us agree for once *that truth is a greater sin than falsehood:* Yet as the offenses are not equal, and as the punishment is arbitrary, *that is,* according as the judges in their discretion shall direct to be inflicted; is it not absolutely necessary that they should know whether the libel is *true* or *false,* that they may by that means be able to proportion the punishment? For would it not be a sad case if the judges, for want of a due information, should chance to give as severe a judgment against a man for writing or publishing a lie as for writing or publishing a truth? And yet this (with submission), as monstrous and ridiculous as it may seem to be, is the natural consequence of Mr. Attorney's doctrine *that truth makes a worse libel than falsehood,* and must follow from his not proving our papers to be *false,* or not suffering us to prove them to be *true.* But this is only reasoning upon the case, and I will now proceed to show what in my opinion will be sufficient to induce the Court to allow us to prove the truth of the words which in the information are called libelous. * * * [A]greeable to this it was urged by Sir Robert Sawyer in the trial of the seven bishops, *that the falsity, the malice, and sedition of the writing were all facts to be proved.* But here it may be said Sir Robert was one of the bishops' counsel, and his argument is not to be allowed for law: But I offer it only to show that we are not the first who have insisted that to make a writing a libel, it must be *false.* And if the argument of a counsel must have no weight, I hope there will be more regard shown to the opinion of a judge, and therefore I mention the words of Justice Powell in the same trial, where he says (of the petition of the bishops, which was called a libel, and upon which they were prosecuted by information) that *to make it a libel, it must be false and malicious and tend to sedition;* and declared, *as he saw no falsehood or malice in it, he was of opinion that it was no libel.* Now I should think this opinion alone, in the case of the King, and in a case which that King had so much at heart and which to this day has never been contradicted, might be a sufficient authority to entitle us to the liberty of proving the *truth* of the papers which in the information are called *false, malicious, seditious* and *scandalous*. If it be objected *that the opinions of the other three judges were against him,* I answer that the censures the judgments of these men have undergone, and the approbation Justice Powell's opinion, his judgment and conduct upon that trial has met with, and the honor he gained to himself for daring to speak truth at such a time, upon such an occasion, and in the reign of such a King, is more than sufficient in my humble opinion, to warrant our insisting on his judgment as a full authority to our purpose * * *. And in the case of Tutchin, which seems to be Mr. Attorney's chief authority, that case is against him; for he was upon his trial put upon showing the truth of his papers, but did not; at least the prisoner was asked by the King's counsel whether he would say they were *true?* And as he never pretended that they were true, the Chief Justice was not to say so. But the point will still be clearer on our side from Fuller's case, *for falsely and wickedly causing to be printed a false and scandalous libel, in which (amongst other things) were contained these words,* "Mr. Jones has also made oath that he paid £5000 more by the late King's order to several persons in places of trust, that they might complete my ruin, and invalidate me forever. Nor is this all; for the same Mr. Jones will prove by undeniable witness and demonstration that he has distributed more than £180,000 in eight years last past by the French King's order to persons in public trust in this kingdom." Here you see is a scandalous and infamous charge against the late King; here is a charge no less than high treason against the *men in public trust* for receiving money of the French King, then in actual war with the Crown of Great Britain; and yet the Court were far from bearing him down with that Star Chamber doctrine, *to wit, that it was no matter whether what he said was true or false;* no, on the contrary, Lord Chief Justice Holt asks Fuller, "Can you make it appear they are true? Have you any witnesses? You might have had subpoenas for your witnesses against this day. If you take upon you to write such things as you are charged with, it lies upon you to prove them true, at your peril. If you have any witnesses, I will hear them. How came you to write those books which are not true? If you have any witnesses, produce them. If you can offer any matter to prove what you have wrote, let us hear it." Thus said and thus did that great man Lord Chief Justice Holt upon a trial of the like kind with ours, and the rule laid down by him in this case is *that he who will take upon him to write things, it lies upon him to prove them at his peril.* Now, sir, we have acknowledged the printing and publishing of those papers set forth in the information, and (with the leave of the Court) agreeable to the rule laid down by Chief Justice Holt, we are ready to prove them to be true, at our peril.

Mr. Chief Justice. Let me see the book.

[Here the Court had the case under consideration a considerable time, and everyone was silent.]

Mr. Chief Justice. Mr. Attorney, you have heard what Mr. Hamilton has said, and the cases he has cited, for having his witnesses examined to prove the truth of the several facts contained in the papers set forth in the information, what do you say to it?

Mr. Attorney. The law in my opinion is very clear; they cannot be admitted to justify a libel; for, by the authorities I have already read to the Court, it is not the less a libel because it is true. I think I need not trouble the Court with reading the cases over again; the thing seems to be very plain, and I submit it to the Court.

Mr. Chief Justice. Mr. Hamilton, the Court is of opinion, you ought not to be permitted to prove the facts in the papers: These are the words of the book, "It is far from being a justification of a libel, that the contents thereof are true, or that the person upon whom it is made had a bad reputation, since the greater appearance there is of truth in any malicious invective, so much the more provoking it is." *

Mr. Hamilton. These are Star Chamber cases, and I was in hopes that practice had been dead with the Court.

Mr. Chief Justice. Mr. Hamilton, the Court have delivered their opinion, and we expect you will use us with good manners; you are not to be permitted to argue against the opinion of the Court.

Mr. Hamilton. With submission, I have seen the practice in very great courts, and never heard it deemed unmannerly to—

Mr. Chief Justice. After the Court have declared their opinion, it is not good manners to insist upon a point in which you are overruled.

Mr. Hamilton. I will say no more at this time; the Court I see is against us in this point; and that I hope I may be allowed to say.

Mr. Chief Justice. Use the Court with good manners, and you shall be allowed all the liberty you can reasonably desire.

[5. *Hamilton turns to the Jury. What is a Libel?*]

Mr. Hamilton. I thank Your Honor. Then, gentlemen of the jury, it is to you we must now appeal for witnesses to the truth of the facts we have offered and are denied the liberty to prove * * * And were you to find a verdict against my client, you must take upon you to say the papers referred to in the information, and which we acknowledge we printed and published, are *false, scandalous and seditious;* but of this I can have no apprehension. You are citizens of New York; you are really what the law supposes you to be, *honest and lawful men;* and, according to my brief, the facts which we offer to prove were not committed in a corner; they are notoriously known to be true; and therefore in your justice lies our safety. And as we

* Mr. Chief Justice was here reading from I William Hawkins, A Treatise of the Pleas of the Crown 194 (1716–1721).

are denied the liberty of giving evidence to prove the truth of what we have published, I will beg leave to lay it down as a standing rule in such cases, *that the suppressing of evidence ought always to be taken for the strongest evidence;* and I hope it will have that weight with you. But since we are not admitted to examine our witnesses, I will endeavor to shorten the dispute with Mr. Attorney, and to that end I desire he would favor us with some standard definition of a libel, by which it may be certainly known whether a writing be a libel, yea or not.

Mr. Attorney. The books, I think, have given a very full definition of a libel; they say *it is in a strict sense taken for a malicious defamation, expressed either in printing or writing, and tending either to blacken the memory of one who is dead, or the reputation of one who is alive, and to expose him to public hatred, contempt, or ridicule. § 2. But it is said that in a larger sense the notion of a libel may be applied to any defamation whatsoever, expressed either by signs or pictures, as by fixing up a gallows against a man's door, or by painting him in a shameful and ignominious manner. § 3. And since the chief cause for which the law so severely punishes all offenses of this nature is the direct tendency of them to a breach of public peace by provoking the parties injured, their friends and families, to acts of revenge, which it would be impossible to restrain by the severest laws, were there no redress from public justice for injuries of this kind, which of all others are most sensibly felt; and since the plain meaning of such scandal as is expressed by signs or pictures is as obvious to common sense, and as easily understood by every common capacity, and altogether as provoking as that which is expressed by writing or printing, why should it not be equally criminal? § 4. And from the same ground it seemeth also clearly to follow that such scandal as is expressed in a scoffing and ironical manner makes a writing as properly a libel, as that which is expressed in direct terms; as where a writing * * * pretending to recommend to one the characters of several great men for his imitation, instead of taking notice of what they are generally esteemed famous for, pitched on such qualities only which their enemies charge them with the want of, as by proposing such a one to be imitated for his courage who is known to be a great statesman but no soldier, and another to be imitated for his learning who is known to be a great general but no scholar, etc., which kind of writing is as well understood to mean only to upbraid the parties with the want of these qualities as if it had directly and expressly done so.**

Mr. Hamilton. Ay, Mr. Attorney; but what certain standard rule have the books laid down, by which we can certainly know whether the words or the signs are malicious? Whether they are defamatory? Whether they tend to the breach of the peace, and are a sufficient

---

* Also taken from Hawkins, supra.

ground to provoke a man, his family, or friends to acts of revenge, especially those of the ironical sort of words? And what rule have you to know when I write ironically? I think it would be hard, when I say *such a man is a very worthy honest gentleman, and of fine understanding,* that therefore I meant *he was a knave or a fool.*

* * *

Mr. Chief Justice. Mr. Hamilton, do you think it so hard to know words are ironical, or spoke in a scoffing manner?

Mr. Hamilton. I own it may be known; but I insist, the only rule to know is, as I do or can *understand* them; I have no other rule to go by, but as I *understand* them.

Mr. Chief Justice. That is certain. All words are libelous or not, as they are *understood.* Those who are to judge of the words must judge whether they *are scandalous* or *ironical, tend to the breach of peace,* or are *seditious:* There can be no doubt of it.

Mr. Hamilton. I thank Your Honor; I am glad to find the Court of this opinion. Then it follows that those twelve men must *understand* the words in the information to be *scandalous,* that is to say *false;* for I think it is not pretended they are of the *ironical* sort; and when they understand the words to be so, they will say we are guilty of publishing a *false libel,* and not otherwise.

Mr. Chief Justice. No, Mr. Hamilton; the jury may find that Zenger printed and published those papers, and leave it to the Court to judge whether they are libelous; you know this is very common; it is in the nature of a special verdict, where the jury leave the matter of law to the Court.

Mr. Hamilton. I know, may it please Your Honor, the jury may do so; but I do likewise know they may do otherwise. I know they have the right beyond all dispute to determine both the law and the fact, and where they do not doubt of the law, they ought to do so. This of leaving it to the judgment of the Court *whether the words are libelous or not* in effect renders juries useless (to say no worse) in many cases; but this I shall have occasion to speak to by and by; and I will with the Court's leave proceed to examine the inconveniences that must inevitably arise from the doctrines Mr. Attorney has laid down; and I observe, in support of this prosecution, he has frequently repeated the words taken from the case of *Libel. Famosis* in 5. Co. This is indeed the leading case, and to which almost all the other cases upon the subject of libels do refer; and I must insist upon saying that according as this case seems to be understood by the Court and Mr. Attorney, it is not law at this day: For though I own it to be base and unworthy to scandalize any man, yet I think it is even villainous to scandalize a person of public character, and I will go so far into Mr. Attorney's doctrine as to agree that if the faults, mistakes, nay even the vices of such a person be private and personal, and don't affect the peace of the public, or the liberty or property of our neighbor, it is unmanly and unmannerly to expose them either by word or writing. But when a ruler of a people brings his personal failings, but much more his vices, into his administration, and the people find themselves affected by them, either in their liberties or properties, that will alter the case mightily, and all the high things that are said in favor of rulers, and of dignities, and upon the side of power, will not be able to stop people's mouths when they feel themselves oppressed, I mean in a free government. It is true in times past it was a crime to speak truth, and in that terrible Court of Star Chamber, many worthy and brave men suffered for so doing; and yet even in that Court and in those bad times, a great and good man durst say, what I hope will not be taken amiss of me to say in this place, *to wit, The practice of informations for libels is a sword in the hands of a wicked king and an arrant coward to cut down and destroy the innocent; the one cannot because of his high station, and the other dares not because of his want of courage, revenge himself in another manner.*

*   *   *

[6.   *Hamilton Returns to the Theme of the Political Rights of the Subject*]

Mr. Hamilton.   *   *   *   I pray, what redress is to be expected for an honest man who makes his complaint against a governor to an Assembly who may properly enough be said to be made by the same governor against whom the complaint is made? The thing answers itself. No, it is natural, it is a privilege, I will go farther, it is right which all freemen claim, and are entitled to complain when they are hurt; they have a right publicly to remonstrate the abuses of power in the strongest terms, to put their neighbors upon their guard against the craft or open violence of men in authority, and to assert with courage the sense they have of the blessings of liberty, the value they put upon it, and their resolution at all hazards to preserve it as one of the greatest blessings heaven can bestow.   *   *   *   We know His Majesty's gracious intentions to his subjects; he desires no more than that his people in the plantations should be kept up to their duty and allegiance to the Crown of Great Britain, that peace may be preserved amongst them, and justice impartially administered; that we may be governed so as to render us useful to our Mother Country, by encouraging us to make and raise such commodities as may be useful to Great Britain. But will any one say that all or any of these good ends are to be effected by a governor's setting his people together by the ears, and by the assistance of one part of the people to plague and plunder the other?   *   *   *   when a governor departs from the duty enjoined him by his Sovereign, and acts as if he was less accountable than the Royal Hand that gave him all that power and honor which he is possessed of; this sets people upon examining and enquiring into the power, authority and duty of such a magistrate, and to compare those with his conduct, and just as far as they find he exceeds the bounds of his authority, or falls short in doing impartial justice to the people under his administration, so far they very often, in return, come short in their duty to such a governor. * * * For men who are not endued with wisdom and virtue can only be kept in bounds by the law; and by how much the further they think themselves out of the reach of the law, by so much the more wicked and cruel men are. I wish there were no instances of the kind at this day. And wherever this happens to be the case of a governor, unhappy are the people under his administration, and in the end he will find himself so too; for the people will neither love him nor support him. I make no doubt but there are those here who are zealously concerned for the success of this prosecution, and yet I hope they are not many, and even some of those I am persuaded (when they consider what lengths such prosecutions may be carried, and how deeply the liberties of the people may be affected by such means) will not all abide by their present sentiments. * * * There are others that are under stronger obligations, and those are such as are in some sort engaged in support of a governor's cause by their own or their relations' dependence on his favor for some post or preferment; such men have what is commonly called duty and gratitude to influence their inclinations, and oblige them to go his lengths. I know men's interests are very near to them, and they will do much rather than forgo the favor of a governor and a livelihood at the same time; but I can with very just grounds hope, even from those men, whom I will suppose to be men of honor and conscience too, that when they see the liberty of their country is in danger, either by their concurrence, or even by their silence, they will like Englishmen, and like themselves, freely make a sacrifice of any preferment of favor rather than be accessory to destroying the liberties of their country and entailing slavery upon their posterity.

* * *

* * * I think it will be agreed that ever since the time of the Star Chamber, where the most arbitrary and destructive judgments and opinions were given that ever an Englishmen heard of, at least in his own country: I say prosecutions for libels since the time of that arbitrary Court, and until the Glorious Revolution, have generally been set on foot at the instance of the Crown or its ministers; and it is no small reproach to the law that these prosecutions were too often and too much countenanced by the judges, who held their places at pleasure (a disagreeable tenure to any officer, but a dangerous one in the case of a judge). To say more to this point may not be proper. And yet I cannot think it unwarrantable to show the unhappy influence that a sovereign has sometimes had, not only upon judges, but even upon Parliaments themselves.

It has already been shown how the judges differed in their opinions about the nature of a libel in the case of the seven bishops. There you see three judges of one opinion, that is, of a wrong opinion in the judgment of the best men in England, and one judge of a right opinion. How unhappy might it have been for all of us at this day if that jury had understood the words in that information as the Court did? Or if they had left it to the Court to judge whether the petition of the bishops was or was not a libel? No they took upon them, to their immortal honor! to determine both *law* and *fact,* and to *understand* the petition of the bishops *to be no libel, that is, to contain no falsehood nor sedition,* and therefore found them *not guilty.*

* * *

[7. *Hamilton Reiterates the Task of the Jury.*
Closing Statements]

Mr. Hamilton. * * * I must insist that where matter of law is complicated with matter of fact, the jury have a right to determine both. As for instance; upon indictment for murder, the jury may, and almost constantly do, take upon them to judge whether the evidence will amount to murder or manslaughter, and find accordingly; and I must say I cannot see why in our case the jury have not at least as good a right to say whether our newspapers are a libel or no libel as another jury has to say whether killing of a man is murder or manslaughter. The right of the jury to find such a verdict as they in their conscience do think is agreeable to their evidence is supported by the authority of Bushel's case, in Vaughan's Reports, pag. 135, beyond any doubt. * * * The reason given in the same book is *because the judge (as judge) cannot know what the evidence is which the jury have,* that is, *he can only know the evidence given in court; but the evidence which the jury have may be of their own knowledge, as they are returned of the neighborhood. They may also know from their own knowledge that what is sworn in court is not true; and they may know the witnesses to be stigmatized, to which the Court may be strangers.* But what is to my purpose is that suppose that the Court did really know all the evidence which the jury know, yet in that case it is agreed *that the judge and jury may differ in the result of their evidence as well as two judges may,* which often happens. And in pag. 148, the judge subjoins the reason why it is no crime for a jury to differ in opinion from the Court, where he says *that a man cannot see with another's eye, nor hear by another's ear; no more can a man conclude or infer the thing by another's understanding or reasoning.* From all which (I insist) it is very plain *that the jury are by law at liberty (without any affront to the judgment of the Court) to find both the law and the fact in our case* * * *.

* * *

* * * I sincerely believe that were some persons to go through the streets of New York nowadays, and read a part of the Bible, if it was not known to be such, Mr. Attorney, with the help of his *innuendoes,* would easily turn it into a libel. As for instance, *Is.* IX. 16, *The leaders of the people cause them to err, and they that are led by them are destroyed.* But should Mr. Attorney go about to make this libel, he would read it thus; *The leaders of the people* [*innuendo,* the Governor and Council of New York] *cause them* [*innuendo,* the people of this Province] *to err, and they* [the people of this Province meaning] *that are led by them* [the Governor and Council meaning] *are destroyed* [*innuendo,* are deceived into the loss of their liberty] which is the worst kind of destruction. * * * Then if Mr. Attorney is at liberty to come into court, and file an information in the King's name without leave, who is secure whom he is pleased to prosecute as a libeler? And as the Crown law is contended for in bad times, there is no remedy for the greatest oppression of this sort, even though the party prosecuted is acquitted with honor. And give me leave to say as great men as any in Britain have boldly asserted that the mode of prosecuting by information (when a Grand Jury will not find *billa vera*) is a national grievance, and greatly inconsistent with that freedom which the subjects of England enjoy in most other cases. * * *

Gentlemen; the danger is great in proportion to the mischief that may happen through our too great credulity. A proper confidence in a court is commendable; but as the verdict (whatever it is) will be yours, you ought to refer no part of your duty to the discretion of other persons. If you should be of opinion that there is no falsehood in Mr. Zenger's papers, you will, nay (pardon me for the expression) you ought to say so; because you don't know whether others (I mean the Court) may be of that opinion. It is your right to do so, and there is much depending upon your resolution as well as upon your integrity.

* * *

* * * [T]he question before the Court and you gentlemen of the jury is not of small nor private concern, it is not the cause of a poor printer, nor of New York alone, which you are now trying: No! It may in its consequence affect every freeman that lives under a British government on the main of America. It is the best cause. It is the cause of liberty; and I make no doubt but your upright conduct this day will not only entitle you to the love and esteem of your fellow citizens; but every man who prefers freedom to a life of slavery will bless and honor you as men who have baffled the attempt of tyranny; and by an impartial and uncorrupt verdict, have laid a noble foundation for securing to ourselves, our posterity, and our neighbors that to which nature and the laws of our country have given us a right— the liberty—both of exposing and opposing arbitrary power (in these parts of the world, at least) by speaking and writing truth.

[Here Mr. Attorney observed that Mr. Hamilton had gone very much out of the way, and had made himself and the people very merry: But that he had been citing cases not at all to the purpose; * * * All that the jury had to consider of was Mr. Zenger's printing and publishing two scandalous libels, which very highly reflected on His Excellency and the principal men concerned in the administration of this government, which is confessed. That is, the printing and publishing of the *Journals* set forth in the information is confessed. And concluded that as Mr. Hamilton had confessed the printing and there could be no doubt but they were scandalous papers, highly reflecting upon His Excellency, and the principal magistrates in the Province. And therefore he made no doubt but the jury would find the Defendant guilty, and would refer to the Court for their direction.]

Mr. Chief Justice. Gentlemen of the jury. The great pains Mr. Hamilton has taken to show how little regard juries are to pay to the opinion of the judges, and his insisting so much upon the conduct of some judges in trials of this kind, is done no doubt with a design that you should take but very little notice of what I might say upon this occasion. I shall therefore only observe to you that as the facts or words in the information are confessed: The only thing that can come in question before you is whether the words as set forth in the information make a libel. And that is a matter of law, no doubt, and which you may leave to the Court. But I shall trouble you no further with anything more of my own, but read to you the words of a learned and upright judge * in a case of the like nature.

> To say that corrupt officers are appointed to administer affairs is certainly a reflection on the government. If people should not be called to account for possessing the people with an ill opinion of the government, no government can subsist, for it is very necessary for all governments that the people should have a good opinion of it. And nothing can be worse to any government than to endeavor to procure animosities; as to the management of it, this has been always looked upon as a crime, and no government can be safe without it be punished.

> Now you are to consider whether these words I have read to you, do not tend to beget an ill opinion of the administration of the government? To tell us, that those that are employed know nothing of the matter, and those that do know are not employed. Men are not adapted to offices, but offices to men, out of a particular regard to their interest, and not to their fitness for the places; this is the purport of these papers.

Mr. Hamilton. I humbly beg Your Honor's pardon: I am very much misapprehended, if you suppose what I said was so designed.

Sir, you know; I made an apology for the freedom I found myself under a necessity of using upon this occasion. I said there was nothing personal designed; it arose from the nature of our defense.

---

* The Chief Judge reads from the opinion of Chief Judge Holt in Tutchin's   Case, Rex v. Tutchin, 14 Howell's State Trials 1095, 1128 (1704).

The jury withdrew and in a small time returned and being asked by the Clerk whether they were agreed of their verdict, and whether John Peter Zenger was guilty of printing and publishing the libels in the information mentioned? They answered by Thomas Hunt, their foreman, *Not Guilty,* upon which there were three huzzas in the hall which was crowded with people and the next day I was discharged from my imprisonment.

NOTES AND QUESTIONS

1. What exactly did Zenger publish? He seems to have suggested that Governor Cosby was taking steps that would plunge the colony into "slavery." How could that have been taken seriously? Why did Governor Cosby and his followers think that it was so terrible for Zenger to report gossip that people were leaving the colony? On the other hand, could the real irritation be caused by Zenger's charges that the "law" was at an end in the colony, that judges were unfairly dismissed, and that trials by jury had been infringed? In this connection, is it important that, as was the case in the trial of the Seven Bishops, the proceeding was started against Zenger by an "Information?" The alternative to proceeding by information in a criminal matter is the securing of an indictment from a grand jury. Cosby tried and failed to obtain indictments against Zenger from grand juries.

The trial of Zenger was primarily the result of a struggle between opposing wealthy and powerful factions in the colony of New York. When Governor William Cosby arrived in 1732 he began a course of action by which he failed to steer between these contending groups of prominant New Yorkers. He soon collided with Lewis Morris, a New York and New Jersey politician who was then chief justice of the New York supreme court. In 1734, Governor Cosby replaced Morris with James Delancey, "Mr. Chief Justice" at the trial. Morris and his supporters then launched a vigorous campaign to discredit Cosby. First, Morris ran successfully as an Assembly candidate from Westchester County, overcoming efforts by a pro-Cosby sheriff to fix the election against him. Second, the Morrisite faction, which included James Alexander, Zenger's original lawyer, gained control of the New York city council. Finally, the Morrisites established Zenger's New York Weekly Journal in order to print materials critical of Cosby. James Alexander wrote most of the articles, while Zenger, a German immigrant, handled the printing.

Before Zenger's trial Lewis Morris had gone to London himself to plead for Cosby's removal and for his own reinstatement as Chief Justice. Morris argued, among other things, that Cosby had accepted an illegal gift of one thousand pounds, that he had upset certain land titles, that he had wrongly taken part in legislative proceedings, and that he had failed to summon some members of the colony's upper house, the Council (the Morrisite members). The verdict in the Zenger trial was an important political victory for the Morrisites, who were able to use the trial in order to paint themselves as popular champions struggling against the arbitrary rule of Cosby and his supporters. Still, Cosby maintained a tight control over the New York Assembly, and Cosby managed to convince royal officials in London of his propriety and his competence. Cosby soon died, however, and was replaced by George Clarke, a respected member of the Council, and a more astute politician than Cosby. Clarke managed to appease the rival New York factions by distributing political and financial rewards in generous quantities to prominant members of both what had been the Cosbyite and Morrisite factions. Lewis Morris was soon made governor of New Jersey, where he eventually found himself in grave difficulties with a "popular" faction. The broad ideas expressed in the Zenger trial on freedom of speech critical of government as essential to liberty do not seem to have been as important to the Morrisites once they regained power, and, as we will soon see, the doctrine of seditious libel in America was very much alive even after American independence *and* the First Amendment to the Federal Constitution of 1787.

For a discussion of the lack of immediate practical impact of the Zenger case, and for a discussion of early American notions about freedom of the press in general, see Leonard Levy's brilliant Freedom of Speech and Press in Early American History: Legacy of Suppression (Torchbook ed. 1963).

For an excellent and full account of the background of the Zenger trial and the legal issues involved see S. Katz, ed. A Brief Narrative of the Case and Trial of John Peter Zenger, Printer of the New York Weekly Journal 1–35 (1963). Whatever the immediate impact on American politics and law of the Zenger trial, however, these issues are still well worth our examination, as they were never far from the surface of American affairs in the late eighteenth and early nineteenth centuries. We proceed, then, to an examination of the law and the political theory of the case.

2. You will have noticed that almost at the very beginning of the case Hamilton admits for the record that Zenger published the newspaper articles in question, and that consequently many witnesses were discharged. Following this admission by Hamilton there was "silence for some time" in the court. Why? Apparently "Mr. Attorney" thought that this admission by Hamilton was tantamount to a guilty plea. How could he think this? Is an explanation suggested by Mr. Attorney's position that it was worse to publish a "true libel" than a false one? Why would a "true libel" be worse? Can you relate this theory to the fears expressed by Judge Allybone about "discord" in the trial of the Seven Bishops? Does it help make sense of Mr. Attorney's argument to know that the Bible is quoted by him on the point that governments are sanctified because of their protection of life, religion, and property, and that the Bible actually states that it is wrong to criticize governors?

3. Contrast Hamilton's views on the sanctity of government with those of Mr. Attorney. In particular, note that Hamilton is at great pains to point out that a colonial governor is quite a different man from a King. Note, however, that Hamilton is not above criticizing Kings either. It seems important to his argument for him to criticize the "Star Chamber," the court which decided some of the English seditious libel cases. Hamilton attempts to disparage this case law by disparaging the court of Star Chamber. By the end of the sixteenth century the Star Chamber, whose origins as a court were somewhat obscure, had become "a separate court which exercises 'the high and pre-eminent power' reserved to the King's Council 'in causes that might in example or consequence concern the state of the commonwealth.'" See generally I. W. Holdsworth, A History of

English Law 495–508 (paperback ed., 1969). Star Chamber was one of the "prerogative courts." Particularly under the Tudors, it was "bound to look into matters which might concern the safety of the state [and] it was not strictly bound by the straight rules of the common law in dealing with such matters." In addition to its work in punishing criminal libels, the Star Chamber court heard cases of conspiracy, riots, and "above all" it was used by the Tudor Kings to suppress religious dissidents, or "recusants." Holdsworth, supra, at 504. The court was able to act more effectively and swiftly than the common law courts, it had the power to examine witnesses on its own, and "where occasion required, it habitually employed torture." Id., at 505. The court of Star Chamber was formally abolished in 1641, a period when the English Parliament had begun to flex its muscles, to restrict the Royal prerogatives, and to set in motion the events that would lead to Revolution and Regicide. See, e. g. L. Smith, This Realm of England 1399–1688, 224–227 (Third Ed., 1976). In light of this history, can you see some connection between the episode involving Coke and James I, the trial of the Seven Bishops, and Hamilton's argument at Zenger's trial? Note that Hamilton refers several times to the trial of the Seven Bishops and the public approbation of Judge Powell's opinion and the verdict in that case.

4. Even if Mr. Attorney's views on the English law of seditious libel were correct, Hamilton would not be willing to concede that the law was the same in America, would he? For example, he points out that in America the law would not order the cutting off of the right hand and the forfeiture of goods of a man who struck another in the presence of sitting judges, though English law might theoretically require it. Hamilton also argues that the law of trespass would be different in America, since in America no one would have the right to bring an action for trespass when his neighbor's animals fed on his unenclosed land or ate his unenclosed corn, although such an action would lie for damage to enclosed or unenclosed land in England. Mr. Attorney replies to all of this by saying "I don't know what the gentleman means, by comparing cases of freeholders in England with freeholders here." He suggests that this has nothing to do with the case at hand. Do you see the connection?

5. The comparison of English and American law comes before Hamilton launches into his argument to the court that evidence of the "truth" of a seditious libel should be admitted. Hamilton wants, in fact, to get the court to rule that truth is a defense to the crime of seditious libel. He demonstrates that the information was for publishing a "*false*, malicious, seditious, and scandalous" libel, and that in one case, that of John de Northampton, the falsity of what the defendant published was emphasized in his trial. Furthermore, Hamilton argues that one of the counsel in the Seven Bishops' trial, and one of the judges in that case, Powell, both maintained that falsity was an element of the crime. Hamilton stated that when one considered the approbation that Powell's opinion had met with since the trial "and the honor he gained to himself for daring to speak truth at such a time, upon such an occasion, and in the reign of such a King, [it] is more than sufficient * * * to warrant our insisting on his judgment as a full authority to our purpose * * *." Do you agree? Does approbation and honor make good law?

6. As well as citing authorities, Hamilton argues from "the reason of the thing." This is his argument that it is appropriate to admit evidence of the truth of the libel, even if true libels are *worse* than false ones, so that the appropriate punishment can be meted out. In other words, if the libels are in fact true, Hamilton is implicitly suggesting, this evidence should be admitted into court so Zenger can be more severely punished. Do you think that Hamilton intends this argument seriously? To whom in the courtroom is Hamilton speaking? After examining the arguments that Hamilton makes in this case, and knowing that he was imported especially for the case from Philadelphia, do you understand what is meant by the term "Philadelphia lawyer?"

7. Assume that Hamilton wanted evidence of truth to be admitted for other purposes than punishing Zenger more severely. Note that the court rules that truth is *not* a defense, and further, that no evidence of truth may be introduced. The court makes this ruling after reading a contemporary law book, Hawkins, *Pleas of the Crown.* It is quite clear that the English law at the time of the Zenger trial was as stated in Hawkins. In light of this, how do you account for the fact that Hamilton is permitted to argue to the jury, following this ruling, that they can *presume* the truth of what Zenger published? Could it be that Hamilton is actually better off *not* being permitted to offer evidence of the truth of what Zenger published?

8. The jury finds Zenger "not guilty." Is this verdict in accordance with the instructions of the judge? Do you discern any differences between the manner in which the Zenger jury operated and your understanding of the way juries function today?

9. Though Hamilton implicitly criticizes Tudor and Stuart absolutism, Hamilton is careful in his arguments not to cast aspersions on the current English monarch. This attitude did not prevail forever, as shown in the dispute in Virginia over what has come to be called the "Parsons' cause."

NOTE ON THE PARSONS' CAUSE

During the colonial period in Virginia the Church of England, as an established church, was publicly supported. Pursuant to legislation in colonial Virginia ministers were to be paid, principally in tobacco, on an annual basis. Because the price of tobacco varied, so did the real wages of the clergy. In 1755 the first colony-wide attempt was made to provide for payments to the clergy in *currency* instead of tobacco. This statute "superceded" a 1748 Act on the same subject and provided for payment in currency at a rate slightly below the market value of the formerly-required tobacco payments.

At this time the activities of the colonial legislatures were circumscribed by the "Instructions" to the "Royal Governors," the Chief Executives of the colonies. These Instructions were written directions given by the King to his appointed governors, and, because they set certain limits on what the Governors and Colonial Legislatures could do, they were primitive analogues of our modern State and Federal Constitutions. See Generally L. Labaree, Royal Instructions to British Colonial Governors (2 vols., 1935). The King also had the power of "Disallowance," the right to set aside any law passed by the assembly of one of the colonies. When the

King formally approved of an Act, it was said to be "confirmed." In deciding whether to confirm or to disallow an Act the King was advised by various officials, including the Privy Council and a special committee for the colonies, the "Board of Trade."

The 1755 Act probably violated two Royal Instructions. First, the Act was only to be in force for ten months, while the Instructions barred laws enacted for periods of less than two years. Second, the Instructions prohibited acts repealing former laws unless they were accompanied by clauses suspending them until the Crown's officers could decide whether or not they should be allowed. There was no suspending clause in the 1755 Act, and arguably it repealed the former act setting salaries, since the monetary equivalents were slightly below the market value of tobacco.

The Virginia clergy, since they correctly perceived that payments according to the 1755 statute would mean a reduction in their salaries, sought to avoid the effects of that law both by appeal to the King and by seeking redress in the colonial courts. Since the 1755 Act probably violated Royal instructions, the argument for royal disallowance was a very persuasive one. To allow the Act to stand would have been derogatory to the Royal prerogative, not only because of the Royal instructions, but also because the 1748 Act had been "confirmed" by the King. The Parsons argued to the King's ministers on the Board of Trade that to allow the 1755 act to "supercede" the 1748 Act which had received the King's approval would be to suggest that the colonial legislature was superior to the King. Agents for the colonial legislature in London argued that the failure of the tobacco crop had made the 1755 Act (and a 1758 Act in the same terms as the 1755 Act) necessary, and that since the duty to pay in tobacco would have been so onerous, the "clergy, as such, from Principles of Christianity ought to be first to acquiesce" in it. The Board of Trade, however, was convinced of the danger of allowing infringements on the Royal prerogative, and recommended that the King disallow the 1755 and 1758 Acts. In addition, the Board of Trade, on behalf of the King, strongly enjoined the Virginia governor from acquiescing in acts which were contrary to his instructions. Neither the King nor his agents, however, would go so far as to declare that the 1755 and 1758 Acts, having been disallowed, were void *ab initio*, and that the colonial courts should treat them as if they never existed. Had they so acquiesced in the wishes of the Parsons, the declaration of nullity *ab initio* would have allowed the Parsons to sue for the wages in tobacco they would otherwise have collected. Still, since there was also no declaration that the acts were valid until disallowed, it remained the task of the Virginia courts to declare whether the salaries could be paid in currency until the Acts were disallowed.

In one case, that of Clergyman Alexander White, the Virginia court ruled that the 1758 Act could be treated as valid until the disallowance, and while the governor might be subject to royal censure for violation of his instructions, this had no effect on the interim validity of colonial legislation. Through a technical error in the record the court also prevented an appeal to the Courts in London. One case, that of John Camm, did make it on appeal to the King in Council, sitting, in effect, as a Supreme Court for the colonies. The ruling of the King in Council affirmed the Virginia court's holding against Camm, and the notes taken by the council's clerk suggest that the King in Council supported the argument that the Acts were not void *ab initio,* but remained in force until disallowed.   For an account of these cases, and a discussion of the English constitutional implications, see Joseph Henry Smith, Appeals to the Privy Council from the American Plantations 607–626 (1950), on which the foregoing account has been based.   Smith's recital of the circumstances of these cases strongly suggests that more was going on than the neutral application of constitutional or legal principles.   Consider Smith's report on suits brought by parsons while Camm's appeal to the King in Council was pending:

*   *   *   The conduct of these suits was apparently handicapped by the reluctance of able counsel to plead the clerical cause and by the prejudicial conduct of [Virginia officials.]   Cleric Thomas Warrington brought suit in the Elizabeth City County Court, but upon a special verdict the court as a matter of law adjudged the 1758 act valid.   Plaintiff appealed to the General Court with some hopes of success, but the appellate court refused to hear any further causes until Camm's appeal was determined. The most publicized cause was that commenced by James Maury, preceptor of Thomas Jefferson and rector of Fredericksville parish, in the Hanover County Court in 1763.   In this cause the court adjudged the 1758 act to be "no law," sustaining a demurrer that the act, not having received the royal assent, did not have the force of law and that it had been declared null and void by the King in Council.   But a jury summoned on a writ of inquiry to settle the damages brought in only one penny for the plaintiff. Although the evidence was uncontradicted that the tobacco commuted at £–/16/8 per hundred pounds had a market value of 50 shillings per hundred, the jury was swayed to this determination by the irrelevant rhetoric of young Patrick Henry.   This budding demagogue sought to show that the act of 1758 had every characteristic of a good law, that it was a law of general utility, and that it could not, consistently with an alleged original compact between the King and people, be annulled by the King.   From this it was inferred that the King, by disallowing acts of a salutary nature, from being the father of his people, degenerated into a tyrant and forfeited all rights to the obedience of his subjects. Further strictures followed upon the unbecoming conduct of the clergy in the cause and their proper place in the societal structure. Counsel for Maury in vain urged that as the verdict was contrary to the weight of the evidence, the jury ought to be sent out again.   The verdict was accepted by the bench; motions to have recorded the evidence of the plaintiff as to the quantum of damages and for a new trial were denied.   *   *   *

Joseph H. Smith, Appeals to the Privy Council from the American Plantations 620–621 (1950).   Copyright © 1950, by Columbia University Press, reprinted with the permission of the publisher and the author.

QUESTIONS

1.   Do Patrick Henry's statements sound to you like the same deference toward the King that Hamilton professed in *Zenger*?   Indeed, when clergy-

man Camm's suit was in the Virginia General Court, the highest court in the colony, after a lot of skirmishing in the pleadings, the defendants argued that "unless acts passed by the governor and legislature, although unjust and contrary to gubernatorial instructions and former confirmed acts, might stand as law, the people in Virginia were not free." Does this have anything to do with Henry's arguments?

2. Why does Professor Smith call Patrick Henry's comments on behalf of the defendants in Maury's case "irrelevant"? Henry argued that the 1758 Act "could not, consistently with an alleged original compact between the King and the people, be annulled by the King." What about the eventual verdict in Maury's case, said by Smith to have been produced by Henry? Why was the verdict, for the *Plaintiffs,* the clergymen, a verdict of one penny, said to be "contrary to the weight of the evidence"? Why was Henry's argument that of a "budding demagogue"?

3. Why do you suppose the King in council were unwilling to declare the 1758 Act void *ab initio*? Camm's final appeal to the King in Council was not decided until 1766. Note that shortly before this episode, in 1763, the French and Indian War was concluded. Could this be relevant? We turn next to the events of the 1760's and 1770's that might have concerned the King in Council, and that laid the foundation for the American Revolution.

From the original painting by Chappel in the possession of the publishers

JAMES OTIS, Jr.

SECTION C. THE WRITS OF ASSISTANCE CASE

Paxton's case (1761), more popularly known as the "writs of assistance" case, may have been the most important legal event leading up to the American Revolution. John Adams said of the case, sixty years later, "Then and there the child Independence was born." While other events of this era may have had more immediate political impact (for example the Stamp Act crisis of 1765), it is difficult to overestimate the importance of the legal and ideological thought that grew out of Paxton's case.

The "writ of assistance" took its name from the powers vested in the bearer, who could command the assistance of any local public official in making entry and seizure. Contraband goods discovered in the search were then placed in the custody of the Vice-Admiralty court sitting in Boston, where proceedings for condemnation and forfeiture were begun. Since Vice-Admiralty court typically sat without a jury and relied mainly on the testimony of customs officials and their informants, it was fairly easy for the government to produce a result favorable to its interests. Attorney-General Trowbridge drafted a "general" writ of assistance for the colony of Massachusetts in 1755. Customs officials had to apply to court for the writ, but from 1755 until 1760 the Chief Justice of the province, cooperating with the Attorney-General, routinely issued the general writ to customs officials allowing them to search houses and vessels for illegally imported merchandise.

In January 1760 the London Magazine published an article highly critical of "general" writs of assistance. The practice in English law, according to the anonymous author, was to countenance only "special" writs; writs issued on a one-time basis. This may have caused Chief Justice Sewall of the Massachusetts Superior Court to doubt the legality of the colony's general writ. Sewall died in September of 1760. Shortly thereafter James Paxton and others applied for the writ, but the Massachusetts court postponed acting in light of Sewall's "late doubt" and because of the vacancy on the court. In November, Thomas Hutchinson, then Lieutenant Governor of Massachusetts, was appointed to the vacancy. The new Chief Justice was widely known to be a friend of the general writ of assistance; he may even have had a hand in drafting the 1755 version. Paxton's application for the writ was to be heard in February of 1761. Hutchinson probably expected the hearing to be simply a conference before the bench involving no more than two or three attorneys.

A considerable public interest began to build, however. Paxton was growing notorious in the colony for his alleged racketeering in the customs business. He was currently a defendant in another government case, accusing him of embezzlement. The Boston Gazette reflected the ugliness of popular opinion when it labelled Paxton a "rat gnawing at the innards" of the city's life. The Gazette also portrayed the current Governor and Chief Justice Hutchinson as Paxton's patrons. The newspaper also reprinted the London Magazine article which questioned the legal basis of general writs. A group of prominent merchants petitioned the court to be heard on the question. The Massachusetts Surveyor-General of the Customs then entered the case and requested "to be heard on the same subject: And that writs of Assistance may be granted to himself and his officers as usual." The brilliant and fiery James Otis, Jr., then resigned his post as Advocate-General, which position would have required him to represent the Customs Office, and agreed to argue against the writ on behalf of Boston and of the petitioning merchants. The government then invited Jeremiah Gridley to argue its position in support of the general writs. Gridley was eminent in the colonial bar, and a whig in temperament and sympathy. He was the good friend and law teacher of both James Otis, Jr. and of John Adams. What had begun as a routine investigation was thus escalating into a great confrontation between Boston's merchants and the Royal provincial government.

Like the Zenger case, the writs case must also be understood in terms of local politics. An economic and political confrontation had been brewing in the colony for some years. Because of lax enforcement of the British customs laws, Boston smuggling was a common and respectable business in the eighteenth century. The entire molasses trade, essential to the New England economy, was built upon massive customs evasions. Royal customs officials at dockside often participated in evasions by extracting token customs for the sake of appearances in London, and many of these officials grew rich as a result. In the late 1750's, however, England needed money to finance the Seven Years War and sought it through customs revenue, pursuant to good mercantilist strategy. With the 1755 writ at their disposal, Boston officials began serious smuggling prosecutions. The Vice-Admiralty court cooperated, issuing judgments with uncommon speed and regularity. Especially galling to Bostonians was the fact that the admiralty judges, the customs officers, and customs informants were permitted a large share in forfeited booty. Nor were Bostonians unaware of the stinging inequities of their situation. Few judges in other colonies would grant the general writ of assistance. Neighboring Rhode Island, Boston's chief mercantile competitor, flouted the law with impunity. Rhode Island's Vice-Admiralty court uncharacteristically sat *with* a jury. Judgments against merchants were rare. Boston's economic woes worsened as the result of a disastrous fire in 1759. By 1760 a depression seemed to be settling over the city. In terms of total tonnage of trade, Boston slipped behind New York and Philadelphia.

Aggravating matters further was the instability of the current Massachusetts government. The years under Governor Shirley's administration, 1741–1757, had been politically harmonious because of his skill in dispensing patronage. Shirley was replaced by Thomas Pownall in 1757, and then Francis Bernard replaced Pownall in 1760. This rapid turn-over upset fragile political alliances, and set off a wild run on patronage and position. This political in-fighting infiltrated virtually every level of government, including the administration of justice.

The Hutchinson-Otis controversy, an important sidelight of the writs case, illustrates these precarious politics. James Otis, *Sr.,* actively lobbied for the Chief Justiceship after Sewall's death. Otis, Sr. had apparently understood that Lieutenant Governor Hutchinson, whose political star was on the rise, would lend his support. Besides, former Governor Pownall had promised Otis, Sr. a seat on the bench when one became available. One can thus understand Otis's anger and sense of betrayal when Governor Bernard appointed Hutchinson. Supporters of Otis and opponents of Bernard noted that the writs case was pending, Hutchinson's support of royal policy was well known, and that the Governor received one-third of all contraband confiscated in Massachusetts. Hutchinson retained his seat on the Council, a body usually allied with the Governor against the lower house. Otis, Sr., meanwhile, was the Speaker of the House. Both Otis, Sr. and Hutchinson were capable of using their authority in personal and partisan ways. It should be noted, finally, that in October and November James Otis, Jr., had represented his father in negotiating for Hutchinson's support for Otis, Sr.'s judicial ambitions, but resigned his government job immediately after his father's defeat. In such ways could personal animosity flare up into local political conflagration.

As you read the case and materials below, search for points of comparison and contrast with *Zenger.* Why was this case, more so than *Zenger,* so important to colonial radicals? In what ways are the two cases similar? Review the earlier discussion of Sir Edward Coke and his conflict with the King, for he will figure prominently in the argument of Otis. Pay strict attention to the politicking in the arguments of counsel on both sides, and in particular to the elliptical movement from the political to the legal to the ideological in Otis's presentation.

1. THE FEBRUARY HEARING

Our chief source for what occurred in Hutchinson's courtroom at the first hearing of the case is John Adams. Adams sat in the gallery and took notes. Later, he expanded these notes into what he called an "Abstract." Portions of this Abstract appear below. Crucial to an understanding of the arguments at the hearing is a knowledge of the legislation involved (three English statutes and one Massachusetts statute). For this reason we have included a short explanation of the legislation.

II L. KINVIN WROTH AND HILLER B. ZOBEL, eds.,
LEGAL PAPERS OF JOHN ADAMS *

107–113 (1965).

* * * The term "writ of assistance" had originally been applied to process in favor of a particular litigant in the Exchequer or in Chancery, enabling him to obtain the sheriff's help in collecting a debt or gaining possession of property to which he was entitled. The writs sought by the Crown officials in Boston in 1761, however, were general standing warrants, good from the date of issue until six months after the death of the issuing sovereign, which permitted the holder to enter any house by day, with a constable or other officer, and there search for smuggled goods without special application to a court.

The earliest relevant statute, an Act of Parliament passed in 1660, authorized the issuance "to any person or persons" of a warrant to enter any house to search for specific goods, upon oath made of their illegal entry before "the lord treasurer, or any of the barons of the Exchequer, or chief magistrate of the port or place where the offense shall be committed, or the place next adjoining thereto." ** Both the language and the legislative history of this enactment make reasonably clear that its purpose was to authorize a special search warrant of limited extent, under control of a higher authority. The statute central to the controversy was the Act of 1662, which, in setting up a comprehensive scheme of customs administration for the British Isles, first used "writ of assistance" to describe a customs search warrant. The act provided that "any person or persons, authorized by writ of assistance under the seal of his majesty's court of exchequer," might enter any premises in the day time, with a constable or other officer, using force if necessary, and there seize any contraband goods found.*** It has been argued on the basis of the language and legislative history of this and other contemporary acts, that the Act of 1662 was intended to incorporate no more than the special warrant embodied in the Act of 1660. The language of the two statutes is open to the contrary construction, however, and, since the parliamentary debates contain no affirmative statement on the precise point in question, contrary inferences may also be drawn from the legislative history. The actual intent of Parliament in the Act of 1662 thus cannot be determined.

Whatever the legislative intent, a course of practice under the statute soon developed which was a surer guide to construction in the courts than ambiguous language and incomplete history. There are

** 12 Car. 2, c. 19 § I. (1660).

*** 13 & 14 Car. 2, c. 11 ¶ 5(2) (1662).

some indications that in the years after 1662 searches were carried out under special warrant, probably as a result of an attempt to follow the former practice under the Act of 1660. Apparently, however, the view prevailed that the Act of 1662 had created a new process, limited neither by the earlier statute nor by practice under the ancient equitable writ. There is no reported decision on the point prior to the argument at Boston in 1761, but before 1685 a form of the writ granting unlimited powers of general search seems to have been in use in the Exchequer. Other evidence indicates that from some time in the first half of the 18th century, the writ was established as a general standing warrant issued by the Exchequer on the application of the Commissioners of Customs, to be held by the principal customs officers for use by them or their subordinates as the occasion demanded. Abuses of the instrument were probably avoided by virtue of the fact that ordinarily the principal officers required the same showing of information and probable cause that a justice would have required for the issue of a special search warrant. Furthermore, even with probable cause, the officer who searched and found nothing was liable in damages for the trespass.

The use of the writ in the colonies depended upon a third statute, the Act of 1696, by which colonial customs control was generally strengthened and reorganized, and colonial customs officials were given the powers of their English counterparts, whatever those might be.* In Massachusetts, both before and after the passage of this act, the powers of search granted to customs officers by statute and inherent in their commissions were exercised, but there is little affirmative evidence that general warrants were issued in support of these powers. According to Thomas Hutchinson, however, Governor Shirley, in office from 1741 until 1757, issued what were apparently general warrants to the customs officers. When Hutchinson himself pointed out the illegality of this practice, the Governor directed "the officers to apply for warrants from the superior court; and from that time, writs issued, not exactly in the form, but of the nature of writs of assistance issued from the court of exchequer in England."

This development brought a fourth act into play—a Province law of 1699 which conveyed to the Superior Court the powers of the Exchequer.**

* 7 & 8 Will. 3, c. 22 § 6 (2) (1696).   ** 11 Will. 3, c. 3, 1 A & R 370 (1699).

JOHN ADAMS, "ABSTRACT" OF THE ARGUMENT IN THE WRITS OF ASSISTANCE CASE

The speeches of Mr. Gridley and Mr. Thacher appear in Quincy's Reports of Cases Argued and Adjudged in the Superior Court of Judicature of the Province of Massachusetts Bay, Between 1761 and 1772 479–82 (1865), Otis's remarks appear in the Massachusetts Spy for April 29, 1773, p. 3, cols. 1–3. Boston Superior Court February 1761.

* * *

Mr. Gridley. I appear on the behalf of Mr. Cockle * and others, who pray "that * * * they cannot fully exercise their Offices in such a manner as his Majesty's Service and their Laws in such cases require, unless your Honors who are vested with the power of a Court of Exchequer for this Province will please to grant them Writs of Assistance * * *."

May it please your Honors, it is certain it has been the practice of the Court of Exchequer in England, and of this Court in this Province, to grant Writs of Assistance to Custom House Officers. Such Writs are mentioned in several Acts of Parliament, in several Books of Reports; and in a Book called the Modern Practice of the Court of Exchequer, We have a Precedent, a form of a Writ, called a Writ of Assistance for Custom House Officers, [which was issued in 1755] * * * to Mr. Paxton under the Seal of this Court, and tested by the late Chief Justice Sewall * * *.

The first Question therefore for your Honors to determine is, whether this practice of the Court of Exchequer in England * * * is legal or illegal. And the second is, whether the practice of the Exchequer (admitting it to be legal) can warrant this Court in the same practice.

In answer to the first, I cannot indeed find the Original of this Writ of Assistance. It may be of very ancient, to which I am inclined, or it may be of modern date. This however is certain, that the Stat. of the 14th. Char. 2nd.** has established this Writ almost in the words of the Writ itself. "And it shall be lawful to and for any person or persons *authorised by Writ of Assistance under the seal of his Majesty's Court of Exchequer* to take a Constable, Headborough, or other public Officer, inhabiting near unto the place, and in the day time to enter and go into any house, Shop, Cellar, Warehouse, room, or any other place, and in case of Resistance, to break open doors, Chests, Trunks and other Package, and there to seize any kind of Goods or Merchandize whatever prohibited, and to put the same into his Majesty's Warehouse in the Port where Seisure is made."

---

* James Cockle was Collector of Customs at Salem from 1760 to 1764. Cockle had applied for the Writ at about the same time Paxton did, although Paxton may have been the first to apply.

** The 1662 Act, 13 & 14 Car. 2, c. 11 § 5(2).

By this act and that of 12 Char. 2nd.* all the powers in the Writ of Assistance mentioned are given * * *. Now the Books in which we should expect to find these Writs, and all that relates to them are Books of Precedents, and Reports in the Exchequer, which are extremely scarce in this Country; we have one, and but one that treats of Exchequer matters, and that is called the "Modern practice of the Court of Exchequer," and in this Book we find one Writ of Assistance * * *. Books of Reports have commonly the Sanction of all the Judges, but books of Precedents never have more than that of the Chief Justice. Now this Book has the Imprimatur of Wright, who was Chief Justice of the King's Bench, and it was wrote by Brown, whom I esteem the best Collector of Precedents; I have Two Volumes of them by him, which I esteem the best except Rastall and Coke. But we have a further proof of the legality of these Writs, and of the settled practice at home of allowing them; because by the Stat. 6th Anne which continues all Processes and Writs after the Demise of the Crown, *Writs of Assistance are continued among the Rest.***

It being clear therefore that the Court of Exchequer at home has a power by Law of granting these Writs, I think there can be but little doubt, whether this Court as a Court of Exchequer for this Province has this power. By the Statute of the 7th. & 8th. W. 3d.,*** it is enacted "that all the Officers for collecting and managing his Majesty's Revenue, and inspecting the Plantation Trade in any of the said Plantations, shall have the same powers &c. as are provided for the Officers of the Revenue in England; also to enter Houses, or Warehouses, to search for and seize any such Goods, and that the like Assistance shall be given to the said Officers as is the Custom in England."

Now what is the Assistance which the Officers of the Revenue are to have here, which is like that they have in England? Writs of Assistance under the Seal of his Majesty's Court of Exchequer at home will not run here. They must therefore be under the Seal of this Court. For by the law of this Province 2 W. 3d. Ch. 3 **** "there shall be a Superior Court &c. over the whole Province &c. who shall have cognizance of all pleas &c. and generally of all other matters, as fully and [amply] to all intents and purposes as the Courts of King's Bench, Common Pleas and Exchequer within his Majesty's Kingdom of England have or ought to have."

It is true the common privileges of Englishmen are taken away in this Case, but even their privileges are not so in cases of Crime and fine. 'Tis the necessity of the Case and the benefit of the Revenue

---

* The 1760 Act, 12 Car. 2, c. 19 § I.

** Since the courts were thought to derive their power of granting writs from the individual King, when the King died the new King had to continue, or reaffirm this power.

*** The 1696 Act, 7 & 8 Will. 3, c. 22 § 6.

**** The 1699 Act, 11 Will. 3, c. 3, 1 A & R 370.

that justifies this Writ. Is not the Revenue the sole support of Fleets and Armies abroad, and Ministers at home? without which the Nation could neither be preserved from the Invasions of her foes, nor the Tumults of her own Subjects. Is not this I say infinitely more important, than the imprisonment of Thieves, or even Murderers? yet in these Cases 'tis agreed Houses may be broke open.

In fine the power now under consideration is the same with that given by the Law of this Province to Treasurers towards Collectors, and to them towards the subject. A Collector may when he pleases distrain my goods and Chattels, and in want of them arrest my person, and throw me instantly into Gaol. What! shall my property be wrested from me!—shall my Liberty be destroyed by a Collector, for a debt, unadjudged, without the common Indulgence and Lenity of the Law? So it is established, and the necessity of having public taxes effectually and speedily collected is of infinitely greater moment to the whole, than the Liberty of any Individual.

*Thacher.** In obedience to the Order of this Court I have searched * * * but have not found any such Writ as this Petition prays. * * * I have found Two Writs which bear the Title of Brev. Assistentice, but these are only to give possession of Houses &c. in cases of Injunctions and Sequestration in Chancery. By the Act of Parliament any private Person as well as Custom House Officer may take a Sheriff or Constable and go into any Shop &c. and seize &c. (here Mr. Thacher quoted an Authority * * * which intended to shew that Writs of Assistance were only temporary things).

The most material question is whether the practice of the Exchequer is good ground for this Court. * * *

In England all Informations of uncustomed or prohibited Goods are in the Exchequer, so that the Custom House Officers are the Officers of that Court under the Eye and Direction of the Barons ** and so accountable for any wanton exercise of power.

The Writ now prayed for is not returnable. If the Seizures were so, before your Honors, and this Court should enquire into them you'd often find a wanton exercise of power. At home they seize at their peril, even with probable Cause.

[*Otis:*]

I * * * appear not only in obedience to your order, but also in behalf of the inhabitants of this town, * * * and out of regard to the liberties of the subject. And I take this opportunity to declare, that whether under a fee or not, (for in such a cause as this I despise a fee) I will to my dying day oppose, with all the powers and faculties God has given me, all such instruments of slavery on the one

---

* Oxenbridge Thacher was asked by the court to argue. He appears to be allied with Otis.

** The Exchequer judges were called "Barons."

hand, and villainy on the other, as this writ of assistance is. It appears to me (may it please your honours) the worst instrument of arbitrary power, the most destructive of English liberty, and the fundamental principles of the constitution, that ever was found in an English law-book. I must therefore beg your honours patience and attention to the whole range of an argument, that may perhaps appear uncommon in many things, as well as points of learning, that are more remote and unusual, that the whole tendency of my design may the more easily be perceived, the conclusions better [discerned] and the force of them better felt.

I shall not think much of my pains in this cause as I engaged in it from principle. I was sollicited to engage on the other side. I was sollicited to argue this cause as Advocate-General, and because I would not, I have been charged with a desertion of my office; to this charge I can give a very sufficient answer, I renounced that office, and I argue this cause from the same principle; and I argue it with the greater pleasure as it is in favour of British liberty, at a time, when we hear the greatest monarch upon earth declaring from his throne, that he glories in the name of Briton, and that the privileges of his people are dearer to him than the most valuable prerogatives of his crown.* And as it is in opposition to a kind of power, the exercise of which in former periods of English history, cost one King of England his head and another his throne. I have taken more pains in this cause, than I ever will take again: Although my engaging in this * * * has raised much resentment; but I think I can sincerely declare, that I cheerfully submit myself to every odious name for conscience sake; and from my soul I despise all those whose guilt, malice or folly has made my foes. * * * The only principles of public conduct that are worthy a gentleman, or a man are, to sacrifice estate, ease, health and applause, and even life itself to the sacred calls of his country. * * * I will proceed to the subject of the writ. * * * I will admit, that writs of one kind, may be legal, that is, special writs, directed to special officers, and to search certain houses, &c. especially set forth in the writ, may be granted by the Court of Exchequer at home, upon oath made before the Lord Treasurer by the person, who asks, that he suspects such goods to be concealed in THOSE VERY PLACES HE DESIRES TO SEARCH. The Act of 14th Car. II. [1662] which Mr. Gridley mentions proves this. And in this light the writ appears like a warrant from a justice of peace to search for stolen goods. Your Honours will find in the old book, concerning the office of a justice of peace, precedents of general war-

---

* George III in his accession speech on November 18, 1760, had stated that "The civil and religious rights of my loving subjects are equally dear to me with the most valuable prerogatives of my crown: and, as the surest foundation of the whole, and the best means to draw down the divine favour on my reign, it is my fixed purpose to countenance and encourage the practice of true religion and virtue." Boston News-Letter, January 15, 1761, at 1 cols. 2–4.

rants to search suspected houses. But in more modern books you will find only special warrants to search such and such houses specially named, in which the complainant has before sworn he suspects his goods are concealed; and you will find it adjudged that special warrants only are legal. In the same manner I rely on it, that the writ prayed for in this petition being general is illegal. It is a power that places the liberty of every man in the hands of every petty officer.

*   *   *

In the first place the writ [that is sought by the customs officials in this case] is UNIVERSAL, being directed "to all and singular justices, sheriffs, constables and all other officers and subjects, &c." So that in short it is directed to every subject in the king's dominions; every one with this writ may be a tyrant: If this commission is legal, a tyrant may, in a legal manner also, controul, imprison or murder any one within the realm.

In the next place, IT IS PERPETUAL; there's no return, a man is accountable to no person for his doings, every man may reign secure in his petty tyranny, and spread terror and desolation around him, until the trump of the arch angel shall excite different emotions in his soul.

In the third place, a person with this writ, IN THE DAY TIME may enter all houses, shops, &c. AT WILL, and command all to assist.

Fourth, by this not only deputies, &c. but even THEIR MENIAL SERVANTS ARE ALLOWED TO LORD IT OVER US—What is this but to have the curse of Canaan with a witness on us, to be the servant of servants, the most despicable of God's creation. Now one of the most essential branches of English liberty, is the freedom of one's house. A man's house is his castle; and while he is quiet, he is as well guarded as a prince in his castle. This writ, if it should be declared legal, would totally annihilate this privilege. *   *   * This wanton exercise of this power is no chimerical suggestion of a heated Brain—I will mention some facts. Mr. Pew had one of these writs, and when Mr. Ware succeeded him, he endorsed this writ over to Mr. Ware, so that THESE WRITS ARE NEGOTIABLE from one officer to another,* and so your Honours have no opportunity of judging the persons to whom this vast power is delegated. Another instance is this.—Mr. Justice Wally had called this same Mr. Ware before him by a constable, to answer for a breach of the Sabbath day acts, or that of profane swearing. As soon as he had done, Mr. Ware asked him if he had done, he replied, yes. Well then, says he, I will shew you a little of my power—I command you to permit me to search

---

* The Editors of Adams's legal papers could find no documentation to support these charges of Otis's. Jonathan Pew was Searcher and Surveyor of the Port of Boston from 1735 until *Paxton* succeeded him in 1752. Nathaniel Ware was Comptroller of Customs for the Port of Boston from 1750 to 1764. II Wroth and Zobel, supra, note 144.

your house for unaccustomed goods; and went on to search his house from the garret to the cellar, and then served the constable in the same manner. But to shew another absurdity in this writ, if it should be established, I insist upon it EVERY PERSON by 14th of Car. II. HAS THIS POWER as well as Custom-house officers; the words are, "it shall be lawful for any person or persons authorized, &c." What a scene does this open! Every man prompted by revenge, ill humour or wantonness to inspect the inside of his neighbour's house, may get a writ of assistance; others will ask it from self defence; one arbitrary exertion will provoke another, until society will be involved in tumult and in blood. Again these writs ARE NOT RETURNED. Writs in their nature are temporary things; when the purposes for which they are issued are answered, they exist no more; but these monsters in the law live forever, no one can be called to account. Thus reason and the constitution are both against this writ. Let us see what authority there is for it. No more than one instance can be found of it in all our law books, and that was in the zenith of arbitrary power, viz. In the reign of [Charles II] when Star-chamber powers were pushed in extremity by some ignorant clerk of the Exchequer. But had this writ been in any book whatever it would have been illegal. ALL PRECEDENTS ARE UNDER THE CON-TROUL OF THE PRINCIPLES OF THE LAW. Lord Talbot says, it is better to observe these than any precedents though in the House of Lords, the last resort of the subject. No Acts of Parliament can establish such a writ; Though it should be made in the very words of the petition it would be void, "AN ACT AGAINST THE CON-STITUTION IS VOID." * * * But these prove no more than what I before observed, that *special* writs may be granted *on oath* and *probable suspicion*. The Act of 7th and 8th of William III. that the officers of the plantations shall have the same powers, &c. is confined to this sense, that an officer should show probable grounds, should take his oath on it, should do this before a magistrate, and that such magistrate, if he thinks proper should issue a special warrant to a constable to search the places. * * *

It is the business of this court to demolish this monster of oppression, and to tear into rags this remnant of Star Chamber tyranny— * * *

* * *

NOTES AND QUESTIONS

1. You will remember that the Otis family and Thomas Hutchinson collided over the appointment to the Superior Court. Did this influence Otis's conduct in this hearing? What, exactly, were Otis Sr.'s feelings toward Hutchinson? The old conflict erupted again in 1765 with acri-

* This last sentence does not appear in the account in the Massachusetts Spy, but is to be found in the "Joseph Hawley Common Place Book," a manu-script copy of Adams's "Abstract." See generally II Wroth & Zobel, supra, at 134 n., 149 n.

monious charges and countercharges appearing in the Massachusetts Gazette. Otis Jr. charged that in 1760 Hutchinson had violated an "agreement" to support his father, which was contained in a letter. Here is Hutchinson's own recollection, written in 1765:

> The next day after the death of the late Chief Justice several gentlemen spake to me and told me they hoped the Governor would nominate me for his successor. It was some surprize to me, and I answered them in no other way than by thanking them for their favourable opinion of me, and expressing a diffidence of my own abilities. I was not determined in my own mind that it would be adviseable for me to undertake so great a trust; nor did I know the Governor's mind concerning it. Before the Chief Justice was buried Mr. OTIS came to [me] with a letter from his father desiring me, whom he had always looked upon as his friend, to use my interest with the Governor that he might be one of the Justices of the Superior Court. While I was reading the letter Mr. OTIS said to me, that he had heard one proposed for the place of Chief Justice, and if I had any thoughts of it, neither he nor his father had a word more to say, no person in the Province would be more agreeable to them; but if I had not, he thought his father had a better pretence to a place in the Court than anybody else, having been longer at the bar than any other gentlemen and having had the promise of the place in former administrations, to which facts I was knowing. I told Mr. OTIS the proposal to me was new and what I had not time to consider of, and expressed my doubts of my abilities to give the Country satisfaction. I said many civil things of his father, as I had done before and have since, and of the friendship there had been between us; but I must deny that I gave him any reason to suppose that I was determined to refuse the place; or that I promised to use my interests with the Governor that his father should be appointed.
>
> A few days after I received it I was informed by Gentlemen of undoubted veracity, that Mr. OTIS the Son had declared that neither he nor his father would give up their pretensions to the Lieutenant Governor nor any other person, that he uttered many revengeful threats; particularly, that he would do all the mischief he could to the Government, and would set the Province in a flame, &c. if his father should not be appointed (the town was full of the talk of it) and I soon after had reason to suspect that these threats were carrying into execution. * * *

Quoted in M. H. Smith, The Writs of Assistance Case 216–217 (1978). When Hutchinson says that Otis had carried into execution his threat to "set the province aflame," what do you suppose he meant? Were Otis's arguments directed exclusively at the court?

2. Since Jeremiah Gridley was thought to be a friend of colonial liberty and a champion of Massachusetts causes, his willingness to argue the government's case must have raised a few eyebrows. Yet there may be something more in Gridley's decision. M. H. Smith, in his recent The Writs of Assistance Case (1978), suggests that Gridley *and* Otis met privately with John Adams after the hearing to fill in Adams's Notes, thus giving

birth to the remarkably complete "Abstract" in April, 1761. Id., at 285–287. Smith also believes that Gridley may have intentionally weakened the government's case. Id. at 282–285. Consider Gridley's interpretation of the 1660 and 1662 legislation, and Otis's point-by-point rebuttal. What would have been the effect of Gridley's talk of "necessity," and of his citation of Wright, C. J.? Where have you encountered Wright, C. J. before? If Gridley intentionally sabotaged the Government's case, and if Gridley helped Adams and Otis complete the account of the February hearing, what meaning, then, would Adams's Abstract have had?

3. Do you believe, with Otis, that the writs of assistance were the "worst instrument of arbitrary power, the most destructive of English liberty, and the fundamental principles of the constitution, that ever was found in an English lawbook?" Why does he think this? Incidentally, Otis suggests that the reign of Charles II was the "zenith of arbitrary power." Does that make sense? See generally Antonia Fraser, Royal Charles (1979). Is Otis's essentially rambling argument any more or less "relevant" than Hamilton's in the *Zenger* case or Henry's in the *Parsons' cause*?

4. By now you should be able to grasp why Adams saw the "birth of the child Independence" at this dispute. Otis seems to have used Coke as a sort of midwife to give birth to the "child Independence." The question which then needs to be answered is whether Otis's use of Coke was motivated by something other than an objective reading and a neutral application of legal precedent.

Consider Bernard Bailyn's comments, in I Pamphlets of the American Revolution 411–13 (1965).* His discussion of Otis carries the analysis beyond Otis's speech which you have just read, and shows on what authority Otis relied:

> * * * The ultimate problem, Otis said, was not so much the writs as the laws of Parliament controlling the American economy that made such writs necessary. These navigation laws and the writs issued to enforce them invaded the invaluable "privilege of house" by which every subject of English laws was rendered "as secure in his house as a prince in his castle." Both navigation laws and writs of assistance, therefore, violate "the fundamental principles of law"; both, therefore, run against the constitution, and they are, consequently, void. For "an act against the constitution is void: an act against natural equity is void: and * * * the executive courts must pass such acts into disuse," the common law having the power to control an act of Parliament.
>
> It was a doctrine familiar to English law; and to substantiate it Otis cited Coke's celebrated judgment in *Bonham's Case* (1610) that "it appears in our books that in many cases the common law will control acts of Parliament, and sometimes adjudge them to be utterly void: for when an act of Parliament is against common

* I Pamphlets of the American Revolution 1750–1776 411–413, Edited by Bernard Bailyn, with the assistance of Jane N. Garrett, Copyright © 1965 by the President and Fellows of Harvard College, published by the Belknap Press of the Harvard University Press. Reprinted with the permission of the publisher and the author.

right or reason, or repugnant, or impossible to be performed, the common law will control it, and adjudge such act to be void"— to which Otis would add for further support the dicta of other seventeenth-century justices endorsing Coke's words * * * [But Otis may not have accurately presented Coke's views, because] Coke had not meant that positive, statute laws were restricted to areas defined by a higher law binding on Parliament and that they could be nullified—declared to be legally nonexistent—by the judges as custodians of the higher law when they exceeded these bounds. Nor had Coke conceived of his dictum as going beyond private law considerations into the realm of constitutional construction. Coke had meant only that the basis of statute law, like that of common law, was reason and justice, and that when laws created unreasonable or manifestly unjust or self-contradictory situations—situations wherein law violated the principles of law—it was the duty of the courts, not to annihilate the statutory provisions, but, as Coke's successor Hobart put it, "to mold them to the truest and best use." Coke's concern had been the traditional one of interpreting statutes strictly when reason and justice required it, adjusting, that is, in the lower courts inequities and impracticalities created by decrees of the highest court, Parliament.

It was upon the judicial nature of Parliament, and its presumed devotion to the same principles of justice and reason that animated all courts of law that Coke's doctrine ultimately rested. And it was, consequently, the great historic shift in the understanding of Parliament's role that took place in the mid and later seventeenth century that gave a new meaning to Coke's doctrine, and that created for James Otis, a century later, the central intellectual problem of his life. In the course of the searing controversies of the English Civil War—controversies that destroyed the foundations of public order and touched off a series of penetrating discussions of public authority—Coke's assumption that Parliament was animated by the same sense of justice and reason as other courts, and that its pronouncements were susceptible to equitable interpretation by judges, fell away before a conception of Parliament as the monopolist of absolute sovereign power, the creator, not the discover, of law, unbound by any rulings but its own. In the Glorious Revolution, which secured the absolute supremacy of Parliament over all other agencies of government, Coke's presumptions in *Bonham's Case* were, in effect, abandoned, and the location of an absolute and arbitrary legislative authority fixed firmly and indisputably in Parliament.—In effect abandoned: but not in law; for Coke's words, reinforced by later, more expansive pronouncements, remained on the books, to the bewilderment of those who would apply them to an absolute, unchallengable legislative sovereign distinct from courts of law. * * * By 1761, when Otis introduced the doctrine of *Bonham's Case* into the discussion of Anglo-American relations, the dominant understanding of English jurists and scholars—an understanding which colonial resistance would only confirm—was classically phrased by

Blackstone, who admitted that the rule was familiar in law that acts of Parliament contrary to reason are void; "but if the Parliament will positively enact a thing to be done which is unreasonable, I know of no power that can control it." So too Lord Camden, who would oppose the Stamp Act on the ground that "there are some things" a sovereign body cannot rightfully do, in the end concluded that once Parliament did declare its will against right "he did not think himself, nor any man else, at liberty to call it any more in question."

* * *

5. It is the "legalism" of colonial resistance, implicit in Otis's use of precedent and authority—indeed in the expression of discontent within the framework of a law case—which makes it difficult to label the Revolutionary movement as "radical" or "conservative." As Bailyn notes, the emergence of a sovereign Parliament in the eighteenth century is an incident of the modernization of the state with a strong executive authority. The supremacy of the English common law as originally articulated by Coke would appear to be medieval in character, relying as it does on static and immutable principles of "right reason" and "justice." Is Otis's politico-legal philosophy, then, "antique?"

6. Hutchinson suspended judgment following the arguments in February. It is likely that the court leaned in favor of Otis, and against the writs. It also appears that Hutchinson wanted to know more about the practice in England. He asked William Bollan, the colony's agent in London, to submit a memorandum on the English practice. Bollan's memorandum reached Hutchinson in August. Bollan stated that the Chief Justice had asked him whether writs of assistance were issued by the exchequer only in cases where there was "special information" and only where particular houses and particular goods sought were specified. What happened next, as Bollan later recalled it, appears below:

* * *

Mr. Bollan sent [the Chief Justice] a copy of the writ of assistance, taken out of the court of exchequer, which writ is directed to the officers of the admiralty, justices of peace, mayors, sheriffs, constables, & all other his Majestys officers, ministers, & subjects in England, requiring them to permit the comissrs. of the customs, & their officers by night or day to enter on board any vessel to search &c & in the daytime to enter the vaults, cellars, warehouses, shops, & other places where any goods &c lye conceal'd, or are suspected to lye conceal'd, for which the customs are not paid, to inspect & search for the said goods &c and to do all things which according to the laws in that behalf shou'd be done, and comanding them to be aiding & assisting to the said comissrs. & their officers in the execution of the premises. On the copy sent this endorsement was made, NB. These writs upon any application of the comissrs. of the customs to the proper officer of the court of exchequer are made out of course by him, without any affidavit, or order of the court.

* * *

Quoted in M. H. Smith, supra at 541. Some time after the receipt of this copy of the English writ, the hearing was reconvened.

2. THE NOVEMBER, 1761 HEARING

PAXTON'S CASE OF THE WRIT OF ASSISTANCE

Samuel M. Quincy, ed. Reports of Cases Argued and Adjudged in the Superior
Court of the Province of Massachusetts Bay Between 1761 and 1762
by Josiah Quincy, Junior 51–57 (1865).

[We begin with Thacher's speech against the legality of the writs.]

Mr. Thacher first read the Acts of 14 Car. 2 [(1662)] and 7 & 8 of Wm. & Mary [1696], upon which the Request for this Writ is founded.

Though this Act of Parliament has existed 60 Years, yet it was never applied for, nor ever granted, till 1756; which is a great Argument against granting it; not that an Act of Parliament can be antiquated, but Non-user is a great Presumption that the Law will not bear it; this is the Reasoning of Littleton and Coke. * * * * Moreover, when an Act of Parliament is not express, but even doubtfull, and then has been neglected and not executed, in such a Case the Presumption is more violent.

Ch. Justice. The Custom House Officers have frequently applied to the Governour for this Writ, and have had it granted them by him, and therefore, though he had no Power to grant it, yet that removes the Argument of Non-user.

Mr. Thacher. If this Court have a Right to grant this Writ, it must be either *ex debita Justitia* or discretionary. If *ex debita Justitia,* it cannot in any Case be refused; which from the Act itself and its Consequences, he argued, could not be intended. It can't be discretionary; for it can't be in the Power of any Judge at discretion to determine that I shall have my House broken open or not. As says Just. Holt, "There can be no discretionary Power whether a Man shall be hanged or no." [Amstrong v. Lisle, Comb. 410 (1697)].

He moved further that such a Writ is granted and must issue from the Exchequer Court, and no other can grant it; 4 Inst. 103; and that no other officers but such as constitute that Court can grant it. 2 Inst. 551. That this Court is not such a one, * * * This Court has in the most solemn Manner disclaimed the Authority of the Exchequer; this they did in the Case of McNeal of Ireland & McNeal of Boston. [McNeal v. Brideoak, Quincy's Reports, at 470.] This they cannot do in Part; if the Province Law gives them any, it gives them all the Power of the Exchequer Court; nor can they chuse and refuse to act at Pleasure. But supposing this Court has the Power of the Exchequer, yet there are many Circumstances which render that Court in this Case an improper Precedent; for there the Officers are

---

* Thacher was here referring to Co. Lit.
81a, 81b.

sworn in that Court, and are accountable to it, are obliged there to pass their Accounts weekly; which is not the Case here. In that Court, there Cases are tried, and there finally; which is another Diversity. Besides, the Officers of the Customs are their Officers, and under their Check, and that so much, that for Misbehaviour they may punish with corporal punishment. * * * 7 & 8 W. & M. does not give the authority.

(Mr. Otis was of the same Side, but I was absent, while he was speaking, most of the Time, and so have but few Notes.)

Mr. Otis. * * * Let a Warrant come from whence it will improperly, it is to be refused, and the higher the Power granting it, the more dangerous. The Exchequer itself was thought a Hardship in the first Constitution. [Otis here cited precedents from the time of Charles I, when the Privy Council authorized customs officers to break into houses, and he refers to practices in Massachusetts prior to 1755, when customs officers, simply by virtue of their commissions, engaged in similar breaking and entering. Is this relevant?]

It is worthy Consideration whether this Writ was constitutional even in England; and I think it plainly appears it was not; much less here, since it was not there invented till after our Constitution and Settlement. Such a Writ is generally illegal. Hawkins, B. 2, ch. 1, Of Crim.Jur., Viner, Tit. Commission, A., 1 Inst. 464 29M.*

Mr. Auchmuty. [arguing on behalf of the government.] * * * From the Words of the Law, this Court may have the Power of the Exchequer. Now the Exchequer always had that Power; the Court cannot regard Consequences, but must follow Law. * * *

Mr. Gridley. This is properly a Writ of Assist*ants*, not Assistance; not to give the Officers a greater Power, but as a Check upon them. For by this they cannot enter into any House, without the Presence of the Sheriff or civil Officer, who will always be supposed to have an Eye over and be a Check upon them. Quoting History is not speaking like a Lawyer. If it is Law in England, it is Law here; it is extended to this Country by Act of Parliament. * * * By Act of Parliament they are entitled to like Assistants, if the court cannot grant them it; and how can the Court grant them like Assistance, if they cannot grant this Writ. Pity it would be, they should have like Right, and not like Remedy; the Law abhors Right without Remedy. But the General Court has given this Court Authority to grant it, and so has every other Plantation Court given their Superior Court.

---

* The authorities here referred to include the statements that "If commission issues to take J.S. and his goods, without indictment, or suit of the party, or other process, this is not good; for it is against the law." and "The surest construction of a statute is by the rule and reason of the common law." Otis probably is also here referring to Chapter 29 of Magna Carta, which provided (freely translated) that "No free man shall be taken, imprisoned * * * except by the law of the land."

The Justices were unanimously of Opinion that the Writ might be granted   *   *   *.

3. BOSTON GAZETTE, 4 JAN. 1762

[Though appearing unsigned, this broadside was probably written by Otis.]

SINCE the advancement of so great a lawyer as the Hon. Mr. H-TCH-NS-N to the *first* J-st-s seat, it would be deem'd the highest impertinence for any one to express the least surprize, that the Superior Court of this province, should after *solemn hearing,* adjudge themselves authoriz'd to grant *such* a writ, as the WRIT OF ASSISTANCE; or even to doubt, whether *by law,* they have power so to do: I hope however, I may say without offence   *   *   *   that I heartily wish it never may [be used.]

*   *   *   I do therefore *from principle* declare against an illicit trade; I would have it *totally* suppress'd, with this proviso only, *that* it may have the same fate in the other governments; otherwise all the world will judge it unequitable: it is because we only are severely dealt with, that we complain of unreasonable treatment   *   *   *.

But it is not trade only that will be affected by this new severity: every householder in this province, will necessarily become *less secure* than he was before this writ had any existence among us; for by it, a *custom house officer* or ANY OTHER PERSON *has a power given him, with the assistance of a peace officer,* to ENTER FORCEABLY *into a* DWELLING HOUSE, *and rifle every part of it where he shall* PLEASE *to suspect uncustomed goods are lodgd!*   *   *   * Will any one then under *such* circumstance, ever again boast of *british* honor or *british* privilege?—I expect that some *little leering* tool of power will tell us, that the publick is now amus'd with *mere chimeras* of an overheated brain; but I desire that men of understanding, and morals, would only recollect an instance of this sort; when a late comptroller of this port, by virtue of his *writ of assistance,* FORCEABLY enter'd into and rummag'd the house of a *magistrate* of this town; and what render'd the insolence intollerable, was, that he did not pretend a suspicion of contraband goods as a reason for his conduct, but it was only because the honest magistrate had a day before taken the liberty to execute a good and wholesome law of this province against the comptroller.—

IT is granted that upon *some occasions,* even a *brittish* freeholder's house may be forceably opened; but   *   *   * it ought never to be done, and it never is done, but in cases of the most urgent necessity and importance; and this necessity and importance always is, and always ought to be determin'd by *adequate* and *proper* judges: Shall so tender a point as this is, be left to the discretion of ANY person, to whomsoever this writ may be given! shall the *jealousies* and *mere imaginations* of a custom house officer,   *   *   * be accounted a sufficient reason for his breaking into a freeman's house! * * * what, if it should appear, that there was no just grounds of suspicion; what reparation will he make? is it enough to say, that damages may be recover'd against him in the law? * * * Is not this vexation *itself* to a man of a well disposed mind? and besides, may we not be insolently treated by our *petty tyrants* in *some* ways, for which the law prescribes no redress? and if this should be the case, what man will hereafter think his rights and privileges worth contending for, or even worth *enjoying.*

* * *

BUT admitting *there is such* a practice at home, and that it is not disputed, even at this time, when there is so warm a sense of liberty there; it may nevertheless be an Infringement upon the constitution: and let it be observed, there may be at some times a necessity of conceeding to measures there, which bear hard upon liberty; which measures ought not to be drawn into precedent here, because there is not, nor can be such necessity for them here; and to take such measures, without any necessity at all, would be as violent an infraction on our liberties, as if there was no pretence at all to law or precedent. It is idle then, to tell us we ought to be content under the same restrictions which they are under at home * * * when it is tolerated then only *thro' necessity,* and there is no necessity for it here. In *England* something may be said for granting these writs, tho' I am far from saying that anything can justify it. In *England* the revenue and the support of government, in some measure, depend upon the customs; but is this the case here? are any remittances made from the officers here? has the king's revenue, or the revenue of the province ever received the addition of a farthing, from all the collections, and all the seizures that have been made and forfeited, excepting what has been remitted by the late worthy collector Mr. *B-r-ns?*—I assert nothing: but if no benefit accrues to the publick, either here or at home, from all the monies that are receiv'd *for the use of the publick.* Is not this PECULATION? and what reason can there be, that *a free people* should be expos'd to all the insult and abuse, to the risque and even the *fatal consequences,* which may arise from the execution of a writ of assistance, ONLY TO PUT FORTUNES INTO PRIVATE POCKETS.

I desire it may be further consider'd, that the custom house officers at home, are under certain *checks* and *restrictions,* which they cannot be under here; * * * In *England* the exchequer has the power of controuling them in *every respect;* * * * and they do in fact account to it for money receiv'd, and for their BEHAVIOR, once every week—so that the people there have a short and easy method of redress, in case of injury receiv'd from them: but is it so here? Do the officers of the customs here account with the Superior Court, or lodge monies received into the hands of that court; or are they as officers under any sort of check from it?—Will they *concede* to such powers in the Superior Court? or does this court, notwithstanding *these* are powers *belonging* to the exchequer—notwithstanding *it is said to be vested with* ALL THE POWERS *belonging to the exchequer*—and, further, notwithstanding *this very writ of assistance* is to be granted AS a power belonging to the exchequer, will the Superior Court itself, assume the power of calling these officers to account, and punish them for misbehavior? * * * Have we not seen already, ONE of those officers, and he an *inferior* one too, REFUSING to account to *any power* in the province, for monies receiv'd by him *by virtue of his office,* belonging to the province, and which we are assured by the JOINT DECLARATION of the three branches of the legislature is UNJUSTLY as well as *illegally* detain'd by him? Does not every one then see that a writ of assistance in the hands of a custom house officer here, is in reallity a *greater* power & more to be dreaded, than it is in England? *greater* because UNCONTROUL'D—and can a community be safe with an uncontroul'd power lodg'd in the hands of *such* officers, some of whom have given abundant proofs of the danger there is in trusting them with ANY?

NOTES AND QUESTIONS

1.   Thacher's February and November arguments are largely concerned with jurisdiction. Why is it such a matter of concern to Thacher that the Massachusetts Superior Court of Judicature be limited to common-law jurisdiction? Why are the writs of assistance potentially more dangerous in the colonies, assuming that England and the colonies use the same form of writ? When Gridley intones that "Law and not History" should be used to resolve the case, what accusation is he levelling? Are not "law and history" the same things?

2.   In the "anonymous" editorial, Otis contends that colonials should not be bound by legal practices in England which "bear hard upon liberty." He does admit, though, that sometimes it is necessary to limit liberty in pursuit of some higher policy. Why? According to Otis, is there a "higher policy" to recommend the general writ of assistance? How does he interpret the application of the writ in Massachusetts? Why might he still be inclined to view the writ as a provocation toward "bloody tumults?" What do you suppose Otis would believe a colony can do, if the English have mistaken the law? Does he imply that the *people* have a role?

3.   Who was correct on the legality of the writs? The confusion about the actual state of the law in the writs case was evident as well in the Zenger case, but here it seems more profound. Consider the course of conduct and the views on the law of Writs of Assistance after 1761, discussed in the following reading. See if you can understand how law cases in the colonies became a means of resistance to England.

4. ENFORCING THE WRITS AFTER 1761: THE MALCOM–SHEAFFE EPISODE

While the writ of assistance was declared legal by the Superior Court, enforcing the writ was another matter. A successful search required the cooperation of an "assistant" to the customs officer, and, in a sense, the cooperation of the suspected smuggler. Does the following description of an encounter between a customs officer and a Boston merchant indicate that the cooperation of "the people" was also necessary? By this date, 1767, "the people" of Boston were an important political force. They rioted in 1765 when royal stamp officials attempted to enforce the infamous "Stamp Act." * Hutchinson's house was then burned to the ground with "special savagery," in the words of Governor Bernard, probably in "payment" not only for perceived sympathies for the Stamp Act, but also for Hutchinson's position in the writs case. Though most colonial judges in the 1760s refused to grant the writ, Hutchinson did not take this "popular" course. Much pressure was thus brought to bear on the Massachusetts court by the people of Boston.

As resistance moved out of the courtroom and into the street, so did the habit of thinking in legal terms. It was after 1765 that the Writs case began to grow in importance—when Parliament's exercise of sovereign power to tax American colonists seemed to confirm Otis's prediction of "bloody tumults." Recall Otis's statement of America's dilemma: were the colonists bound to follow England's law, right or wrong? And if English law was wrong, what was the appropriate response? As you read the next excerpt, ask yourself if any of the participants in the episode acted "unlawfully."

M. H. SMITH, THE WRITS OF ASSISTANCE CASE **

443–453 (1978).

* * * [T]he sequence of events seems to have started with information given to the Boston custom house * * * that illegally imported wines and spirits had been taken to the house of Captain Daniel Malcom, a former seafarer and now a small-time merchant, in the early hours of 23 September 1766. They belonged to "one Simenton of Casco Bay," with whom Malcom and his partner William Mackay were known to have had dealing. Benjamin Hallowell, comptroller of customs, and William Sheaffe, deputy collector, laid plans to search Malcom's house the following morning, 24 September. They determined to use a writ of assistance in Hallowell's possession, and

---

* The Stamp Act, 26 Statutes at Large 179 (1765), was the first direct tax levied by Parliament upon America. It was designed to raise £60,000 annually, and the revenues were to help provide for British military forces in America. Special "stamps" showing prepayment of tax were to be affixed to virtually all papers. The Act required "stamps" on all legal documents, printed matter, and playing cards. Penalties for non-payment could be imposed by vice-admiralty courts as well as the common law courts. Resistance to the act was unprecedented, and it was repealed in 1766. See generally Edmund S. & Helen M. Morgan, The Stamp Act Crisis: Prologue to Revolution (Rev. ed. 1962).

presumably it was in relation to this that they wrote to Stephen Greenleaf, sheriff of Suffolk County, asking him to meet with them at 8 A.M. However, Greenleaf was out of town; and a deputy sheriff, Benjamin Cudworth, * * * was enlisted instead. Two custom house understrappers attended in addition.

The party arriving at Malcom's dwelling, he admitted them, and allowed Hallowell and Sheaffe to look round the outbuildings and kitchen, and into a cellar. But when they asked to inspect a partitioned-off area of the cellar Malcom told them that this was in the tenancy of Mackay, and that he himself did not have the key. Sheaffe thereupon went off and asked for the key from Mackay, who protested that "it was very extraordinary Proceedings to search private Dwelling Houses," and instead accompanied Sheaffe back to Malcom's house. Outside he saw Deputy Sheriff Cudworth and the supporting customs men who had been posted there. * * * Mackay commented on this scene to Malcom: it was, he said, "beset by the whole Possey of the Custom House Officers and Mr. Cudworth the Deputy Sheriff." Malcom, who seems to have been fairly amiable up to now, reacted with an appropriate display of spirit. Or perhaps it was because the possibility of a forcible break-in was beginning to emerge. Hallowell and Sheaffe having, * * * "insisted upon having the said Cellar Door opened * * * Malcom solemnly swore that it should not be & if any Man attempted it he would blow his Brains out." * * *

At this, Malcom put on a sword, took up a brace of pistols, and repeated his intention (as he himself put it) that "the first Man that would break upon my House without having Legal Authority for the same, I would kill him on the Spot." An attempt to persuade him of the customs officers' "Legal Authority" availed nothing. * * * It was a convincing show (although Malcom afterward claimed that the pistols were not loaded). * * * "Mr. Hallowell called me aside," William Mackay testified, "and begged I would advice Malcom to open the Doors and if there was anything there * * * he would endeavour to make it as easy as possible and that for Peace sake he would give up his Part [his share in the seizure] and Mr. Sheaffe would do the same * * *." * * *

After "near two Hours" expostulating with Malcom, and "the Deputy Sheriff Benjamin Cudworth not being willing to enter the said Cellar by Force," Hallowell and Sheaffe * * * went off to report the morning's frustrations * * *. [A]t the custom house they met up with Sheriff Stephen Greenleaf, now returned to Boston. The discomfited pair told Greenleaf of the Malcom fracas, and Hallowell showed him the writ of assistance "and desired him to go with him & the said Collector to aid and assist them in making proper Search * * *." * * *

It may be a sign that Greenleaf was still unconvinced about the writ of assistance that when he met with Hallowell and Sheaffe after lunch they presented him with not only the writ but with a warrant they had procured from Justice Foster Hutchinson (a brother of Lieutenant Governor and Chief Justice Thomas Hutchinson, and himself a reliable establishmentarian). This warrant, * * * had been issued upon Hallowell and Sheaffe swearing to having received information of an illegal importation concealed in Malcom's house; it ordered "the Civil Officers * * * to be aiding & assisting" Hallowell and Sheaffe "to Enter the House & Cellar of * * * Daniel Malcom." * * *

However, the warrant proved as useless as the writ * * *. This time Malcom had shuttered his windows and locked his doors; and not only were the search party thus barred from the house itself, a fastened gate kept them out of the curtilage as well. While Malcom sat indoors with Mackay and a few other cronies the invaders fretted in the street outside, where the demeanor of bystanders was not such as to encourage heroic assault on the invested dwelling.

The possibility of public commotion had not gone unanticipated. [At a meeting of the Governor's Council called about this matter, where Sheriff Greenleaf was asked to assist the Customs officers] there had been talk of the sheriff raising the *posse comitatus,* an ancient institution of the common law whereby the "force of the county," consisting of practically all able-bodied men in the neighborhood, might be called out to quell tumultuous disorder. It was talk that accorded with the position taken by most of the councilors: the sheriff had powers enough of his own, and "any Aid from his Excellency and the Board does not appear, at present, to be needful." This was not steadiness of nerve, exactly. Rather it was the hesitation of councilors, whose concern for the government interest stopped well short of foolhardiness, to associate themselves with so unpopular a cause as customs search: under the stimulus of the Stamp Act experience the previous year a powerful patriot spirit was both in the air and on the streets. * * *

According to Sheriff Greenleaf and the customs men, the total failure that befell their afternoon expedition was explained and excused by the ugly rhubarbing of a hostile street mob whose numbers would be augmented in the event of an actual forcing of Malcom's house, by a ringing of the bell of the Old North meeting house. * * * The attitude of the onlookers/mobsters toward a call to assist was true to the local tradition of colorable legality: not so much outright refusal as insistence * * * that the name of the informer on Malcom first be made known and sworn to. Raising the *posse comitatus,* reported Sheriff Greenleaf rather needlessly, would have been "not only in vain, but highly imprudent." Time passed, darkness came on, and Greenleaf and the customs men called it a day: "The Warrant would not justify a forcible Entrance into any Dwelling House after sun set." The invaders thus routed, Malcom sent out some buckets of wine to his well-wishers in the street.

The sheriff and the customs men went straight to Governor Bernard to tell of the failure of their mission to search Malcom's house. They had been "obliged to quit it," they said, "having been assured that an Attempt to force it would cost some of them their Lives." Bernard had them return the following morning, to repeat their story before the Council. What he purposed—to gather attested descriptions of the Malcom affair that would remind Westminster yet again of Boston's incorrigible turbulence—naturally met with resistance from councilors of patriot sympathy. He was allowed to have his way, but apparently at the price of postponing actual despatch of the incriminating depositions. In the time thus gained a town meeting was convened, which set up a committee whose first task was to obtain copies of the tale as told by Sheriff Greenleaf and the custom house. This done, a bath of counterdepositions—orchestrated, probably, by James Otis—was collected, also for transmission to England.

Malcom himself disputed much that Hallowell and Sheaffe had said, he protested innocence of anything smuggled being under his roof, denied having seen (presumably in the afternoon, when he was barricaded indoors) "any Writ of Assistance nor any other Power or Authority whatsoever to break open my House," and asserted an intention to thwart or pursue the invaders only "in Law as far as Justice would go." * * * Benjamin Goodwin spoke of the bystanders he saw outside [Malcom's house]: "People that was passing by about their Business seeing the Officers in the Street askt what the Matter was and stood and talk't five 5 or 6 or so, and I never saw People that was going to a Funeral behave more solemn and concern'd than they did. * * *" Other deponents testified to their being about fifty onlookers, all well-behaved. * * * As for a reported plan to ring the bell of the Old North, Paul Revere swore he had heard nothing of it * * *.

The burden of the Boston town meeting's material was that the Malcom incident had been exaggerated out of all proportion to its true significance. * * * Probably [the Bostonians] were concerned lest the Malcom affair intensify British pressure for compensation of persons—Comptroller Hallowell among them—whose property had been despoiled in the Stamp Act riots. * * *

Counterdepositions playing down the Malcom incident were still being collected when Governor Bernard dispatched the originals, together with his own story, to the Earl of Shelburne and the Board of Trade on 10 October. But John Temple, surveyor general of customs, got in still earlier. Temple's report to the customs commissioners in London, * * * was dated 1 October. His turn of speed may have had something to do with an implacable hatred [of] Governor Bernard. Though the foot-dragging decision to leave Sheriff Greenleaf to his own resources in the afternoon expedition was less the governor's fault than the Council's, it would have been Bernard whom the authorities in London identified [as lacking firmness.] * * * It was all rather hard on Bernard. Not only was he belabored in the Boston press for letting on about the Malcom incident to the government in England: the man who got in first with the story, and whose own fealty to the crown interest was to become more and more ambiguous, was blaming him for the incident ever having happened.

The customs commissioners' reaction to the Temple report was not specially galvanic. * * * [T]he writ of assistance element had been overtaken by the Opinion of Attorney General De Grey on the question * * *. Writing to the Treasury on 31 October 1766, the commissioners had simply accepted De Grey's view that writ of assistance search had no lawful place in America and made the obvious recommendation, that it was "expedient to have the interposition of Parliament for granting the proper power to the Officers of the Revenue in America * * *": in other words, the situation following from the De Grey Opinion needed to be put right by legislation. [The English customs commissioners forwarded a report on the incident to the English Treasury, and stated,] "In the Case now laid before Your Lordships, it is stated that the Officers had a Writ of Assistants legally granted. The Writ of Assistants directed by the Act of the 14th of King Charles 2nd is to be under the Seal of the Court of Exchequer, but the Court of Exchequer do not issue their Writs into the Plantations." * * *

The Treasury made no overt move until 14 January 1767. By this time Governor Bernard's collection of depositions had arrived in England; and the Board of Trade, no doubt aware that the Treasury already had papers on the same subject and glad enough of a reason to drop this hot potato * * * passed the entire batch over. Stimulated, perhaps, by Board of Trade agitation over the general law and order aspect, the Treasury took a bolder line than that recommended by the customs commissioners. * * * The crown's legal advisers must be asked to think again. Causing all the Malcom papers to be sent to the attorney general and solicitor general, the Treasury made no bones about "the violent resistance made by * * * [Malcom] * * * and others to the Execution of a legal Writ commanding Aid and Assistance to be given to the Officers of his Majesty's Customs * * *", and squarely demanded "what proceedings may be fit to be carried on against the sd. Daniel Malcom for his Offences mentioned in the said Affidavits."

But there was no budging De Grey and his colleague. On February 6 De Grey and the Solicitor general again stated that

no Civil Action or Criminal Prosecution can be brought against any of the Parties complained of, for obstructing the Officers of the Customs in the execution of their office, inasmuch as the Writ of Assistance by virtue of which they entered the House and Cellar was not in this case a legal Authority.

[the Treasury]   *   *   *   On 14 February tried again   *   *   *:

It has occurred to their Lordships that an Act of Assembly of the province of Massachsets Bay had passed & been confirmed by the King in the 11th year of Wm. the 3d. intitled an Act for establishing a Superior Court of Judicature within that province by which Act Jurisdiction and cognizance is given to that Superior Court of all matters as fully and amply to all Intents and purposes whatsoever as the Courts of King's Bench Common Pleas & Exchqr. within his Majestys Kingdom of England have or ought to have and it also appearing to my Lords upon a search made by their order amongst the papers and Documents of the Plantation Office that Writts of Assistance have been by constant usage since the period of passing that Act issued out of the Superior Court at Boston as a Court of Exchequer. My Lords direct me to desire you forthwith to lay this matter before Mr. Attorney and Mr. Sollr. Genl, together with the case and their opinion for their reconsideration whether as this Act of Assembly duly passed into a Law of the province is made supplementary to and in aid of the Act of the 7 & 8 of King William [the Act of Frauds, 1696], and as in fact & by constant usage the superior Court of the Province has exercised the Jurisdiction as a Court of Exchequer of Granting Writts of Assistance such Writt of Assistance do not give a legal Authority to the Officers of the Customs to search &c.   *   *   *

Standards of historical research and reporting were none too high here: the Superior Court of Massachusetts, far from having issued writs of assistance from when it was first set up, took to the practice only in 1755; besides, any records of issuances were likelier to be with the customs commissioners than in the Plantation Office.   *   *   *

*   *   *   [T]here is no record of the law officers having replied   *   *   *. Of course, for a working department, even the mighty Treasury, to bandy points of law with the law officers of the crown was to court a snub. All the same, it was not necessarily a case of the law officers merely standing on their dignity. A sense of the practical probabilities could have come into it. Aside altogether from the point of law, the factual evidence was by no means unanimous in the custom house's favor. The law officers could not ignore the sheaf of pro-Malcom testimony gathered by the Boston town meeting, and the strong likelihood that a local jury would prefer it and acquit Malcom in triumph.

*   *   *

And so in 1767 the British government decided to do what the customs commissioners had been recommending since the previous fall.   The chancellor of the exchequer, Charles Townshend, included in his legislation for a new American import duty revenue a clause designed to establish writ of assistance search in all the colonies * * *:

> And whereas by an Act of Parliament made in the thirteenth and fourteenth Year of the Reign of King Charles the Second, intituled, An Act for preventing Frauds, and regulating Abuses, in his Majesty's Customs, and several other Acts now in Force, it is lawful for any Officer of his Majesty's Customs authorised by Writ of Assistances under the Seal of his Majesty's Court of Exchequer, to take a Constable, Headborough, or other Publick Officer inhabiting near unto the place, and in the Day-time to enter and go into any House, Shop, Cellar, Warehouse, or Room or other place, and, in case of Resistance, to break open Doors, Chests, Trunks, and other Package there, to seize, and from thence to bring, any Kind of Goods or Merchandize whatsoever prohibited or uncustomed, and to put and secure the same in his Majesty's Storehouse next to the Place where such Seizure shall be made: And whereas by an Act made in the seventh and eighth Years of the Reign of King William the Third, intituled, An Act for preventing Frauds, and regulating Abuses, in the Plantation Trade, it is, amongst other Things, enacted, that the Officers for collecting and managing his Majesty's Revenue, and inspecting the Plantation Trade, in America, shall have the same Powers and Authorities to enter Houses or Warehouses, to search for and seize Goods prohibited to be imported or exported into or out of any of the said Plantations, or for which any Duties are payable, or ought to have been paid; and that the like Assistance shall be given to the said Officers in the Execution of their Office, as, by the said recited Act of the fourteenth Year of King Charles the Second, is provided for the Officers in England: But, no Authority being expressly given by the said Act, made in the seventh and eighth Year of the Reign of King William the Third, to any particular Court to grant such Writs of Assistants for the Officers of the Customs in the said Plantations, it is doubted whether such Officers can legally enter Houses and other Places on Land, to search for and seize Goods, in the Manner directed by the said recited Acts: To obviate which Doubts for the future, and in order to carry the Intention of the said recited Acts into effectual Execution, be it enacted, and it is hereby enacted by the Authority aforesaid, That from and after the said twentieth Day of November, one thousand seven hundred and sixty-seven, such Writs of Assistants, to authorise and impower the Officers of his Majesty's Customs to enter and go into any House, Warehouse, Shop, Cellar, or other Place, in the British Colonies or

Plantations in America, to search for and seize prohibited or uncustomed Goods, in the Manner directed by the said recited Acts, shall and may be granted by the said Superior, or Supreme Court of Justice having Jurisdiction within such Colony or Plantation respectively.

* * *

Prominent among the draftsman's problems was that his phraseology could not allow it to appear, much less say outright, that customs search in the colonies was illegal. The law officers of the crown were free to say so in private exchanges with the Treasury and the customs commissioners [but] * * * care had to be taken that those notoriously litigious colonials were not given ideas. In Massachusetts searches with writ of assistance had been known for years; if the new legislation were so worded as to imply that every one of them had been unlawful, and therefore actionable as a trespass, the customs officers responsible would face ruinous liability in damages. Thus it was that section 10's recital of the pre-existing law, while initially faithful to the Opinion of Attorney General De Grey—spelling out the 1662 enactment for writ of assistance search and bracketing the obscure 1696 text on to it—eased itself toward an altogether less hard-nosed position than De Grey's. In contrast to the law officers' unequivocal repudiation of colonial writs of assistance, section 10 did not close the door on all possibility of such writs having been valid. What appeared in intradepartmental files as a firm denial was presented to the public as a mere doubt. To the innocent reader section 10 would signify not a headlong rush to panic stations but rather a helpful, though not strictly necessary, clarification of the law as it already was. And to Bostonians and others who might otherwise have moved in on customs officers with writs for trespass it would mean nothing doing.

Legislation ostensibly "To obviate * * * Doubts" but in truth to head off certainty of trouble in the courts is an old trick of the lawsmith's trade. Section 10 of the Revenue Act of 1767 is a prize specimen.

NOTES AND QUESTIONS

1. Does this last excerpt suggest to you that English views on the legality of general writs of assistance were any clearer than American ones? The excerpt reveals that whatever may have been desired by the Lords of the Treasury and the Board of Trade, the English Attorney General believed in 1767 that general writs of assistance were illegal in the colonies, and that the English thought that a statute was necessary to "clarify" matters. Subsequent to the passage of this legislation, in 1768, the English Attorney General declared that such general warrants were legal, but, in 1771 a new Attorney General expressed the opinion that notwithstanding the legality of the writs, colonial courts which refused to grant them could not be ordered to do so by English courts. (The opinions of these attorney generals are reproduced as Appendices A and B of Smith, supra, at 520–523).

2. As if the legal uncertainty in England were not enough, the local political situation also led to moves to counter the effect of the court's decision reached at the November hearing. The practice of plural office-holding, which was common in the colonies, seems to have aggravated the situation.

James Otis, Jr., serving in the Massachusetts House of Representatives, was a strong supporter of a 1762 bill that would have, in effect, forbidden Hutchinson's court to issue general writs of assistance. While there may have been some sympathy for the bill in the Governor's council as well, it is likely that the eventual veto of the bill by Governor Bernard was a result of persuasion by three of the Council members *who were also members of Hutchinson's court*, including Hutchinson himself! James Otis, Jr., "togeathere with a Number of Other firebrands" in the Assembly also saw to it that William Bollan was fired from his position as agent for the colonies in London.

Finally, shortly after the writs of assistance case, the Massachusetts House of Representatives, which set judicial salaries, reduced the salaries of the five judges of Hutchinson's court, and refused to vote Hutchinson the traditional extra payment for the Chief Justice. Smith, supra, at 434–437.

Plural office-holding was an aspect of colonial life that became an important grievance at the time of the American revolution, and which was subject to criticism much earlier, as you may have been able to discern from the materials regarding the Zenger trial. Do you understand why it was perceived as an "evil?" Would this disapproval of plural office-holding have anything in common with the colonists' (and Coke's) insistence that jurisdictional lines be kept clear and consistent?

3. Hutchinson's court upheld the issuance of the general writ of assistance in 1761, a decision favorable to the collection of English duties. What would happen, however, when a case involving compliance with British duties was to be decided by an American jury? You have seen how the Zenger jury responded to pleas on behalf of the government. How would you expect juries to behave in customs cases? A recent student of this matter has declared that the civil traverse jury "especially in Massachusetts" was "perhaps the most unrenowned instrument the whigs possessed" in "their arsenal of legal warfare," and that "Naval officers who seized vessels for violating the trade or navigation statutes faced the prospect of being sued for large sums and having both their assets and their careers tied up for years in litigation." John Reid, In a Defiant Stance: The Conditions of Law in Massachusetts Bay, the Irish Comparison, and the Coming of the American Revolution 27–28 (1977). What was an American Governmental official who considered himself a loyal servant of the British Empire to make of this? In the next reading we find out.

SECTION D.   MOVING TOWARD REVOLUTION

1.   THE ATTITUDE OF THE LOYALISTS

BERNARD BAILYN, THE ORDEAL OF THOMAS HUTCHINSON *

70–107.

[We have already seen something of Thomas Hutchinson's activities as Chief Justice of Massachusetts, in the materials on the Writs of Assistance.   He also served as the last Royal Governor of the colony of Massachusetts.   He held this position at the time we read of him here.]

[a.   *The Situation in 1765*]

* * *

There was no doubt by the summer of 1765 that the passions of the people had been aroused—aroused beyond anything Hutchinson, in his long career in public life, had ever seen before.   Some great transformation had taken place. * * * "Patriots" who now would die rather than submit to the Stamp Act, he wrote in March 1766, had been angling for jobs with the stamp distributors just a few months earlier.   When the inflammatory Virginia resolves ** were received in Boston "a new spirit appeared at once.   An act of Parliament against our natural rights was *ipso facto* void and the people were bound to unite against the execution of it * * * it is the universal voice of all people, that if the Stamp Act must take place we are absolute slaves.   There is no reasoning with them, you are immediately pronounced an enemy to your country." * * * He knew a country gentleman * * * whose servant on a dark night said he was afraid to go out to the barn: "Afraid of what," asked the gentleman.   "Of the Stamp Act," replied the servant. * * *

What had set off this madness of the people?   Not, Hutchinson believed, an understanding of the intrinsic impolicy of the Stamp Act, which had troubled him and other experienced public people.   And not the existence of an actual threat to liberty.   No such threat existed.   Americans were the freest people on earth, and the acts that they said threatened them had been undertaken, however mistakenly, to strengthen the bond between them and the homeland, which was

** The "Virginia Resolutions" were introduced by Patrick Henry before the Virginia House of Burgesses with his famous "treason" speech on May 29, 1765.   The gist of the "Resolutions" or "Resolves" was that the colonists' legislatures had the sole legal and constitutional right to regulate internal affairs and that there could be no Parliamentary taxation of Americans without American representation in Parliament.

the ultimate guarantor of liberty. The ostensible motivations behind the wild opposition therefore could not possibly be the real ones. Another explanation must be sought.

* * * The common run of the people, lacking the necessary education, leisure, and economic independence to make an impartial assessment of public problems, were mercurial playthings of leaders who could profit by exciting their fears. Some of these leaders were pure demagogues, lovers of power adept at manipulating the mob, men who "have nothing to lose and * * * will hold out, for, from public mischief and confusion they may have a chance for private advantage." But some of the leaders had only too much to lose—by certain policies. These men were impelled by a close sense of their own selfish interests as against the public good: they were "the illicit traders" whose animosity * * * had been excited by the threat of efficient enforcement of the customs laws and the renewal of writs of assistance. * * *

Together, these demagogues and malcontents had deliberately raised the fears of a people bred to liberty and set them against the government. Together, they had released the latent forces of anarchy, always threatening from below, and unraveled the fabric of civic order.

* * * The ministry in England, blinded to the realities of life in America and unable or unwilling to see the need to redefine the terms of Anglo-American relations, had blundered badly and created conditions ideal for the purposes of selfish commercial operators and ruthless demagogues. As late as 1764, * * * no one would have dreamt of defying Parliament; everyone would have agreed that such defiance was high treason. But the Sugar Act, which had suddenly posed the question of "how far the Parliament of right might impose taxes upon them"; the threat, immediately following, of internal taxes; and the failure of Parliament to distinguish between petitions that acknowledged its right to tax and those that did not—all of this had given the hard-core demagogues and the selfish opportunists the occasion they sought, of rallying to them the respectable, well-meaning, public-spirited part of the population. With this liberal support they had succeeded in making defiance of law and order respectable. * * * "Authority is in the populace," Hutchinson wrote, "no law can be carried into execution against their mind." No custom house officer would now dare make a seizure, and no law was safe from challenge. * * *

What was to be done? * * *

[b. *The Issues at Stake*]

Hutchinson had no illusions about the limits of his own wisdom, but in the five years after the Stamp Act riots he undertook * * * a thorough-going study of the fundamental issues at stake in the Anglo-

American controversy and of the courses of action open to the administration.   *   *   *

*   *   *

One catches a glimpse of the theoretical presumptions that underlay his conclusions and recommendations in his enthusiastic praise of Allan Ramsay's Thoughts on the Origin and Nature of Government [(1769)]   *   *   *   a handbook of applied Hobbesianism, cold, harsh, and disillusioned.   Men are in actuality unequal, Ramsey had written. The idea of human equality is a dangerous fiction which, when taken up by the "very lowest class of men" at the urging of demagogues, has in the end always resulted in slaughter and the plunder of property.   And society, Ramsay wrote, far from being the voluntary compact conjured up in "the idle dreams of metaphysicians" was in real life an inescapable organism created by the flight for survival of weak and solitary men to the protection of the strong.   From this natural origin flowed the equally natural and inevitable division between rulers and ruled and the necessity for the ruler's ultimate power to be supreme and absolute, though never arbitrary.   Taxing?   It was a necessary power of any government that sought to serve society, and in fact it did not—could not—rest   *   *   *   on the explicit consent of the governed, expressed either directly or through representatives.   Taxing was simply an attribute of supreme authority, a mechanism necessary for its survival, and "sovereignly admits of no degrees, it is always supreme, and to level it is in effect to destroy it."   For Britain, Ramsay concluded, this "absolute and supreme," this "uncontrollable" authority lay in Parliament, the ultimate proof of whose authority would be found in the coercive forces it could exert, force alone being the final, uncontrollable source of all law: "those," Ramsay said, "who try to separate law from force attempt impiously to put asunder whom God has been pleased to join."

*   *   *   [Hutchinson agreed] with Ramsay's view of sovereignty, representation, and taxation.   But he was not, like Ramsay, committed to basic notions systematically at variance with the liberal thought of the time.   While he shared Ramsay's cold view of human nature   *   *   *   he shared too the common premise of eighteenth-century British thought: that mankind was endowed in its original, pre-social state with unlimited rights to actions of all kinds but that these rights had been restricted upon entrance into organized society. From that original abridgment of natural rights, he believed, derived the compelling authority of law and the rightful power of government.   *   *   *

*   *   *   Though Hutchinson spoke of the abridgment of natural rights that takes place upon entrance into society, he stressed not its voluntary and hence its reversible character (which would become the theoretical justification for the American Revolution) but its "necessity."   *   *   *   And he believed that if one understood the political nature of the British empire one would see how reasonable Parliament's actions really were, and that therefore, though orderly protests were proper, extralegal agitation against the government was criminal.

* * * Hutchinson felt that Parliament fused, expressed, and protected all the liberties of Britons, and, because in its essence it was benign and freedom-enhancing, it justified its use of unlimited power. * * * For Hutchinson as for Ramsay and the ruling Whig governments of England, the ultimate fact of all political life * * * was the logical necessity for an absolute and unitary authority to exist somewhere in every government; in its essential definition, that is what government was: a unit of absolute and indivisible authority. Absolute, supreme authority, for Hutchinson, was neither good nor bad, neither a desirable nor an undesirable thing: it simply was. * * * [I]n the case of Britain that power, marvelously restricted by the balances of "mixed" government, was entrusted to Parliament in its totality: that is, to King, Lords, and Commons operating together as sovereign.

* * * [T]here were certain times when the effective use of state power was peculiarly urgent. His own time, he believed, was one such moment in history. If one understood the delicate balance of power and liberty in free states and understood too the movement of history in the eighteenth century, one must conclude, Hutchinson believed, that the age he lived in was "an age of liberty." Since the time of the Glorious Revolution the thirst for liberty had become so intense as to threaten stability everywhere. If the threat of despotism had been deflected, the threat of anarchy was rising. * * * He never doubted that in certain circumstances—in governments under the arbitrary rule of despots, for example—the drive to reinforce and enlarge the sphere of liberty could have a most salutary effect; but in the British colonies, "where as much freedom is enjoyed as can consist with the ends of government"—where * * * the laxness of government was known to be so extreme as to be positively embarrassing to pro-Americans in Parliament—the heedless enthusiasm for liberty "must work anarchy and confusion unless there be some external power to restrain it." * * * If, therefore, the delicate balance of Britain's famed mixed constitution * * * was to be preserved, it was the power element, not, as was the case before 1688, the liberty element, that needed most carefully to be protected.

[c. *Solutions to the Crisis*]

* * * [Following the working-out of these theoretical presumptions, Hutchinson went on] first to work out a program of action to deal with the immediate crisis, and then, beyond that, to sketch the terms of a rational system of imperial relations. * * *

Hutchinson's program of reconstruction and reordering was conceived as a series of stages. There was no doubt in his mind of the proper way to handle the immediate crisis. The Stamp Act must be repealed, he said, promptly and resoundingly. A stupidly conceived act in the first place * * * it had proved unenforceable: if allowed to remain on the books and not enforced it would destroy confidence in government; if attempts were made to enforce it, "there is no determining what desperate men will not attempt."

* * * But nothing more, he felt, should be done immediately after the repeal. There would have to be a pause * * * "until the minds of the people are somewhat calmed and the effect of the repeal * * * shall appear." * * * Strenuous efforts would then have to be made by the government to reach the great majority of moderate, sensible people—the "many good men among us who abhor the present anarchy"—and to rally their support for the steps that would be necessary. They must be made to see the basic fact of life, that the colonies must be subject to some power; if their protector were not Great Britain it could only be some other European state "which would allow them less liberty than they are sure of always enjoying whilst they remain English subjects." * * * [T]hen efforts could be taken to strengthen the effective power of government. And this would have to be done by measures "which shall evidently appear to be intended to preserve to [the colonies] all the rights and liberties which can consist with their connection with their mother country" * * *. Finally, when the government was thus strengthened and free to use its power to support the authority it claimed—then and only then * * * a coherent, rational, and mutually beneficial political reconstruction of the English-speaking world could be created.

[In order to restabalize relations disturbed in the crisis, Hutchinson was even prepared to be coldly cynical] * * * [H]e believed that Lord Chatham's distinction in the powers of Parliament, between the power to tax and the power to legislate, was as specious as all the other fanciful distinctions in parliament's power that had been suggested. But it was nevertheless true * * * that most of the colonists in fact believed in that distinction, even though it made no sense: therefore Parliament should act on it as if it did make sense; it should pass legislation on the basis of this distinction as soon as possible, before Americans became impressed with the logic of claiming that among their rights as Britishers was freedom from all laws, not only tax laws, to which they had not consented. * * * Use anything reasonable that comes to hand to create the stability that is needed: exploit division within and among the colonies if doing so will help maintain authority, for though in some situations such duplicity would be criminal, when the aim is to prevent greater mischief, it may be laudable.

* * *

Parliament must act, he wrote again and again; it must not only enforce the rule of law but articulate the principles of colonial dependency. One could already see the outlines of the future if Parliament failed in this. One could see it in the popular misreading of Lord Coke's maxim that "an act of Parliament against Magna Carta or the peculiar rights of Englishmen is *ipso facto* void": the opposition, taught by Otis, now took that quite traditional doctrine of judicial discretion to mean that the people had the right to say what laws they would and would not obey. When people feel justified in taking the law into their own hands * * * society will revert to the rules of the jungle; the fear of brutality will sweep across the community and terror will make savages of civilized men. * * * The thin membrane of law and civil discourse that constrained the natural forces of anarchy would be worn away slowly, in successive outbreaks of disorder, and reach the breaking point before men generally realized what was happening. * * * Riots, for some reason, Hutchinson said, do not seem to "strike the mind with so much abhorrence as some other offenses do"; yet they are self-intensifying, feeding upon themselves, and no one can predict where they will end. * * * The more frequently disorders occurred, the less they would seem unnatural and unthinkable and the less the public at large would react with effective repulsion, though riotous disorders, he said again and again, necessarily "sap the foundation of all government."

* * * Of course, he said, there were reasons for protest; of course some laws were offensive to some groups, others to other groups, and no doubt some actions of the government were generally offensive. But somehow people must be made to see that if the government offends, if the law is felt to be oppressive, remedies must be sought in law and not in illegality. * * *

* * *

* * * [Hutchinson] disagreed with almost all of the long-term programs of reform suggested by his correspondents * * *.

[One of Hutchinson's correspondents with plans for reform and for dealing with the current crisis was Sir Francis Bernard, Hutchinson's predecessor as Governor of Massachusetts] * * * Bernard justified the absolute sovereignty of the King-in-Parliament and its right to tax all units of the empire whether or not they were represented, but recommended, as a possible expedient, the granting of Parliamentary representation as a special privilege to certain colonies, and suggested that Parliament consider turning over the levying of "internal" taxes to the colonial Assemblies, so long as they continued to provide sums sufficient to maintain a dependable financial basis for the executive branch of the government. But his chief ideas had to do with plans for a permanent recasting of colonial institutions and society. The present colonies in America, he argued, were too many in number, too small, and too weakly structured internally. They should be combined into a smaller number of larger units so that the financial bases of the governments might be strengthened and the forms of their constitutions brought closer to the pattern of Eng-

land's. These enlarged colonies should have not only financially au-
tonomous executive branches but also—what they had so far completely lacked—"a real and distinct third legislative power mediating
between the King and the people, which is the peculiar excellence of
the British constitution." This independent middle order of society
was to be created by the appointment of American life peers, and the
resulting colonial nobility would not only complete the classic triad
of "mixed" government but also eliminate the need for the anomalous
and obstructive Councils that then existed, some of which, like that
of Massachusetts, Bernard said, had thrown the whole weight of the
constitution to the popular side and had paralyzed the operation of
government. *   *   *

*   *   *

[Another of Hutchinson's correspondents who addressed these issues
was Thomas Pownall, who was also a former Governor of Massachusetts.] His main point was simply that Britain must reorganize
the structure of its empire into a "grand marine dominion" with efficient, forceful administrative direction at the center. A single
colonial office, combining the work of the Board of Trade and the
secretary of state's office, should be created. Trade, justice, law must
all center in Britain and be controlled by Britain. *   *   *   [T]he
existing administrative structure of the empire was intolerable;
sweeping changes must be made which would replace the present
hodgepodge of disparate offices and scattered responsibilities that had
evolved through the accidents of history with a streamlined, logical,
and efficiently centralized organization.

*   *   *

[A third correspondent was Richard Jackson,] formerly secretary
to the chancellor of the exchequer and then a Member of Parliament,
agent for Connecticut, Pennsylvania, and Massachusetts, and counsel
to the South Sea Company. [In November 1766, Jackson] sought
Hutchinson's opinion (which he said he valued more highly than his
own) of an intricate argument. *   *   *   Having opposed the Stamp
Act, Jackson, like many Americans, was seeking to define some kind
of limitation on Parliament's rightful power. Was it truly necessary,
he asked Hutchinson, for governments to exercise both legislative
and taxing powers? Neither, he said, was an inevitable attribute of
government. Sparta after the Lycurgan laws, he pointed out, had had
no legislative body at all, and innumerable perfectly stable and viable
if despotic governments had raised money by simple fiat or by
"plunder, rapine, or the spoils of a disgraced minister." Only free
states raise money by acts of representative legislatures, but they succeed in doing so only because of the confidence of the people in the
legislature. The American colonists, however, had clearly proved
that they had no confidence in Parliament as a legislature for them,
for the very good reason that they were not represented in it. Even
if Parliament rightly had the power to tax, therefore, it "was mani-

festly inconsistent with policy and the principles of our constitution to exercise it until the Parliament itself was improved to the perfection the principles of the constitution require." Someday perhaps the irregular constitution of England with respect to America would be improved to the point where the necessary confidence would exist, and at that point taxation might begin. At the moment its imperfections stood out—imperfections the more difficult to change, Jackson said, because of the total ignorance in England of the nature of government in the colonies.

In his lengthy reply Hutchinson sketched the parameters of his own thought. Legislation, he insisted, is a fundamental attribute of government, notwithstanding the example of Sparta * * *. And if by rectifying the inadequacies of the imperial constitution Jackson had meant introducing colonial representation into Parliament, he was—like both Bernard and Pownall—ignoring logical as well as political difficulties. Logically, colonial representation was irrelevant since the power to tax did not rest on representation; politically, it was clearly unacceptable to Americans since they quite correctly understood that it would only lend a specious approval to acts over which they would still have no control and of which they would still disapprove. Direct representation was one of the privileges enjoyed by some (and only some) Englishmen, and it simply could not be enjoyed by the colonists. This limitation was not a matter of will or desire or policy; it was certainly not something he personally advocated. It was, he wrote, simply a matter of evident logic and palpable fact.

For himself, he told Jackson * * * there was no mystery about the grounds for constructing a sensible colonial policy and a rational imperial constitution. Everything flowed from one simple but inescapable and undeniable fact: The American colonies were too weak to survive independently in a world of rival nation-states. * * * As a consequence of this necessary dependence, compounded by the colonists' remoteness, certain privileges enjoyed by Englishmen could not be held by them. It was simply a matter * * * of what was and what was not possible, not of what was theoretically good or bad. No amount of theorizing or wishful thinking could change the necessity for "an abridgment of what is called English liberty." * * *

The colonists' necessary and limiting dependence did not mean, however, that they need be victims of oppression. "I am as much against arbitrary government," he wrote to a correspondent in England in 1769, "as any person living. The more favor you show the colonies in freeing them from taxes of every sort and indulging them in such forms of constitution, civil and ecclesiastical, as they have been used to, the more agreeable it will be to me, provided you do not wholly relinquish us and take away the claim we have to your protection." Not only as a matter of sensible policy should the parent state allow the colonies every possible liberty * * * but * * * the parent state should compensate for the inescapable restrictions on liberty in overseas territories with extraordinary indulgences, so as to bring the condition of colonists and Englishmen into as close a general equality as possible. This * * * would merely formalize traditional practices. If partisans on both sides would put aside their passions, their delusions, and ambitions, they would see, he believed, that for over a century precisely such a balance had been struck and had proved workable and liberty-preserving. It had been this balance, established in many spheres, that had accounted for the prosperity, indeed the continuing existence, of the Anglo-American empire. For four generations there had been a major limitation on liberty in America in the restrictions on colonial trade, but Americans had not objected because there had been a compensating indulgence in freedom from Parliamentary taxation. * * *

What was needed to regain this long-successful set of balances between inescapable limitations and wise indulgences was not institutional restructuring, as Bernard, Pownall, and so many facile theoreticians claimed, but statesmanship. * * * He openly condemned the proposal of Chief Justice William Smith of New York that a single vice-regal government be created in America, including an American parliament, not only because he thought such an arrangement would be impracticable but because it would destroy the existing structure of authority * * *. Even the simpler and apparently more sensible idea, rapidly gaining popularity in America, that the colonies be associated with England through the King alone and not through Parliament—what later generations would call dominion status—he felt sacrificed reality to an attractive theory. For in such an arrangement, he pointed out, there would be a withdrawal of effective governmental power from communities already beset by civil disorder, and the result would simply be chaos. If order was to be restored and maintained, the ultimate power of the King-in-Parliament must remain as unitary and total over the colonies as it was over England. * * *

* * *

* * * [The proper course] was the most difficult and the most complicated: it was, simply, "to bear with their disorderly behavior until they have distressed themselves so as to bear their distresses no longer. Encourage the animosities already begun between the colonies, and distinguish one colony from another by favor for good behavior and frowns for the contrary. Lay aside taxation, not upon the principle that it is to be distinguished from legislation in general but because it is inexpedient. Keep up every other part of legislation and familiarize every colony to acts of Parliament. This may in time bring the colonies to their old state."

* * * Let the House of Commons appoint a permanent committee for America, and let that committee generate enactments

that are manifestly to the colonists' advantage. Show Americans the favorable aspects of Parliament's authority; provide them with instruments and powers that they need and would welcome, and that might also have political support in England. * * * Only in that way would the colonists learn to respect English authority—indeed, all authority; authority as such—and see the folly of resistance. If such steps had been taken five years ago, he wrote in 1770, all the trouble would have been nipped in the bud.

* * *

* * * The whole mess, he exploded uncharacteristically to an English friend and business associate of thirty years standing, was the result of gross errors in high places. "You have brought all this trouble upon yourselves and upon us by your own imprudence. You never ought to have made any concessions from your own power over the colonies, and you ought not to have attempted an exertion of power which caused such a general dissatisfaction through the colonies. God only knows when the ill effects of this mistake will cease."

* * * [In the summer of 1768] as the Massachusetts House defied the ministry's order to rescind its inflammatory circular letter; as mobs assaulted the customs officers who had seized John Hancock's sloop Liberty and drove them to the refuge of the harbor fort; as the nonimportation committees tightened their boycott of British goods; and as plans were almost publicly made to oppose the landing of the two regiments of troops known to be en route to Boston— Thomas Hutchinson retired to the peace of his house in Milton to write what he hoped would be a definitive refutation of all the mistaken notions that had been circulating since the Stamp Act resistance had begun. * * *

[d. *Hutchinson's Definitive Statement*]

[The Document Hutchinson produced during this summer] may be called "A Dialogue between Europe and America" and it is written entirely as a dramatic exchange * * *. The purpose of the piece was not to set out new terms of imperial relations but to demonstrate the irrationality of the arguments of the American opposition, the impossibility of constructing a workable imperial system on the principles that the opposition had suggested, and the inescapable necessity of settling the current controversy on terms dictated by the historical tradition that Britain and America had inherited.

* * *

[The most important matters addressed in the Dialogue were] the central and universal questions of the grounds of personal obedience to the state and the limits, if any, of this obligation. * * * What kind of a society, *Europe* asks, would there be if individuals were empowered to tell judges and executives when to enforce the law and when not?

Judges themselves, *America* replied, should decide not to enforce immoral laws or laws contrary to the purposes of the government. *Europe*: but if judges were to select which laws to enforce and which to ignore they would be making, not enforcing, the law, and that would violate a primary precept of free government. * * * For there is no agreed-on, absolute, and objective definition of morality and immorality that judges or anyone else can simply invoke. Justice and morality are relative to the circumstances and culture. * * *

Let us suppose, *Europe* says, that a person believes his government is engaged in an immoral war. * * * Is he thereby free to refuse to pay taxes in support of that war? Perhaps not, *America* replied, but the British constitution does not provide for "an umpire or judge" to determine when the government has exceeded its authority—the courts, which were in fact as well as in name "executive courts," had never been given that power—and since that is the case, "every man's own conscience must be the judge, and he must follow the evidence of truth in his own mind, and submit or not accordingly." This. Europe replies, would be a constitution that is no constitution at all but "a mere rope of sand." No government in the history of the world has ever survived for long on the principle that individuals may claim an exemption to the law when they decide their rights have been infringed. Nor, indeed, has the definition of fundamental rights been constant in any nation's history. The British constitution—every constitution ever known—has been in flux at all times, and it is in fact through successive alterations of the British constitution that, historically, adjustments have been made to accommodate personal or group grievances. Instead of individuals personally defying the government in order to right wrongs they claim have been committed, the supreme authority itself has modified its own actions, "and such alterations become to all intents and purposes parts of the constitution." For constitutions are not immutable blueprints of government inscribed on parchment at a particular point in time; they are living, growing, malleable arrangements of things, and it is a contradiction in terms to think that an agency of government could serve as umpire to rule the government itself out of order when it impinged on individual rights. Courts are part of the law enforcement procedure, not a check upon it. The only restraint on the action of the state is the state's *self*-restraint, and in a balanced, "mixed" constitution that is an effective limitation indeed on the abuse of power.

Well, *America* replies, you may use any argument you wish, but it is still true that the government is wrong to take my property without my consent, expressed either directly or through a personally chosen representative. * * * the same immutable principles are embedded in English history and immemorial English law.

How "obstinately tenacious" you are, *Europe* replies. Let us indeed turn to the history of the English constitution. Does it justify an individual's refusal to obey the law? No—and more important, it does not contain immutable principles that might serve as the basis for such resistance.   True, it is one of the glories of the English constitution that there are "certain fundamental principles, plain and intelligible," which can guide the courts in deciding difficult and uncertain cases, but these principles are far from being or having been immutable; they have always changed when circumstances changed. Magna Carta, surely, is a fundamental document in the English constitution.   Yet it provides for the continuing jurisdiction of the then-existing Church, from which it follows at the very least that there should be a bishop of the Church in America.   But is there one? And how have Americans in fact responded to the suggestion that there be one?   If the Church really occupied the role conceded to it in Magna Carta, consider what a deplorable state we Protestants would all be in.   Consider how many other provisions of that great charter of constitutional liberty have also been repealed by acts of Parliament. In fact there is only one absolutely immutable principle in the British constitution and certain to remain such: "that no act can be made or passed in any Parliament which it shall not be in the power of a subsequent Parliament to alter and repeal."   No government or constitution on earth is immutable: "the power which established it may dissolve it."   Yes, the British government has fundamental principles, "but if King, nobles, and people agree to make an alteration in what were before fundamentals, who is there to complain"?

The people, *America* replies, may complain, for they alone, as opposed to the other two elements of the constitution, do not personally participate in such decisions but act only through representatives.   If these representatives exercise a power they were never given, they may be repudiated.   Nor need this be only a majority's action: a *minor* part of the people may feel themselves free to repudiate such irresponsible actions by representatives.   *Europe:* but it is an historical fact that the government was formed by representatives; surely it can be altered by representatives.   *America*: I never gave my representative unlimited power; for him to give away my rights is to assume a power he never had, and any act of that sort "is void."   If it is void, *Europe* replies, then there is an end to all organized government.

*   *   *

What must be done in the present circumstances?   *Europe* asks. If America is exempt from any law, it is exempt from all laws.   The law as it stands must be enforced, though the supreme authority may ultimately wish to alter the law.   "I would not give up the least iota of our right, but I would exercise this right with discretion, with equity, and even with a degree of partiality, but when I had once determined how far I would exercise it * * * such determination should never be departed from."   If such a policy were now followed it would easily succeed, for the extremists among the colonial leaders are simply desperadoes who stand to gain by reducing everything to chaos and then starting things over again. But the generality of the people, "who are in easy circumstances," will not risk their property and security for the benefit of a few irresponsible agitators. The present popular frenzy will pass, for "you are Englishmen. * * * No people upon the globe have been oftener in a frenzy and none return sooner to their senses than Englishmen."

2. A MIDDLE VIEW

OXENBRIDGE THACHER, THE SENTIMENTS OF A BRITISH AMERICAN * (1764).

It well becomes the wisdom of a great nation, having been highly successful in their foreign wars and added a large extent of country to their dominions, to consider with a critical attention their internal state lest their prosperity should destroy them.

Great Britain at this day is arrived to an heighth of glory and wealth which no European nation hath ever reached since the decline of the Roman Empire. Everybody knows that it is not indebted to itself alone for this envied power: that its colonies, placed in a distant quarter of the earth, have had their share of efficiency in its late successes, as indeed they have also contributed to the advancing and increasing its grandeur from their very first beginnings.

In the forming and settling, therefore, the internal policy of the kingdom, these have reason to expect that *their* interest should be considered and attended to, that *their* rights, if they have any, should be preserved to them, and that *they* should have no reason to complain that they have been lavish of their blood and treasure in the late war only to bind the shackles of slavery on themselves and their children.

* * *

The writer of this, being a native of an English colony, will take it for granted that the colonies are not the mere property of the mother state; that they have the same rights as other British subjects. He will also suppose that no design is formed to enslave them, and that the justice of the British Parliament will finally do right to every part of their dominions.

These things presupposed, he intends to consider the late act made in the fourth year of his present Majesty entitled *An Act for Granting Certain Duties in the British Colonies and Plantations in America*, etc., to show the real subjects of grievance therein to the colonists, and that the interest of Great Britain itself may finally be greatly affected thereby. * * *

* Reprinted in I. B. Bailyn, ed. Pamphlets of the American Revolution 490–498 (1965).

[I.]   The first objection is that a tax is thereby laid on several commodities, to be raised and levied in the plantations, and to be remitted home to England.   This is esteemed a grievance inasmuch as the same are laid without the consent of the representatives of the colonists.   It is esteemed an essential British right that no person shall be subject to any tax but what in person or by his representative he hath a voice in laying.   The British Parliament have many times vindicated this right against the attempts of Kings to invade it.   And though perhaps it may be said that the House of Commons, in a large sense, are the representatives of the colonies as well as of the people of Great Britain, yet it is certain that these have no voice in their election.   Nor can it be any alleviation of their unhappiness that if this right is taken from them, it is taken by that body who have been the great patrons and defenders of it in the people of Great Britain.

Besides, the colonies have ever supported a subordinate government among themselves.

*   *   *   Now the colonies have always been taxed by their own representatives and in their respective legislatures, and have supported an entire domestic government among themselves.   Is it just, then, they should be doubly taxed?   *   *   *

The reason given for this extraordinary taxation, namely, that this war was undertaken for the security of the colonies, and that they ought therefore to be taxed to pay the charge thereby incurred, it is humbly apprehended is without foundation.   For—

(1) It was of no less consequence to Great Britain than it was to the colonies that these should not be overrun and conquered by the French.   *   *   *   Put the case that the town of Portsmouth or any other seaport had been besieged and the like sums expended in its defense, could any have thought that town ought to be charged with the expense?

(2) The colonies contributed their full proportion to those conquests which adorn and dignify the late and present reign.   One of them in particular raised in one year seven thousand men   *   *   *. All of them by their expenses and exertions in the late war have incurred heavy debts, which it will take them many years to pay.

(3) The colonies are no particular gainers by these acquisitions. None of the conquered territory is annexed to them.   All are acquisitions accruing to the crown.   *   *   *   It is true they have more security from having their throats cut by the French while the peace lasts; but so have also all His Majesty's subjects.

(4) Great Britain gaineth immensely by these acquisitions.   The command of the whole American fur trade and the increased demand for their woolen manufactures from their numerous new subjects in a country too cold to keep sheep: these are such immense gains as in a commercial light would refund the kingdom, if every farthing of the expense of reducing Canada were paid out of the exchequer.

But to say the truth, it is not only by the taxation itself that the colonists deem themselves aggrieved by the act we are considering. For—

II.   The power therein given to courts of admiralty alarms them greatly.   The common law is the birthright of every subject, and trial by jury a most darling privilege.   *   *   *   Many struggles had [our ancestors]   *   *   *   with courts of admiralty, which, like the element they take their name from, have divers times attempted to innundate the land.   Hence the statutes of *Richard* II, of *Henry* IV, and divers other public acts.   Hence the watchful eye the reverend sages of the common law have kept over these courts.   Now by the act we are considering, the colonists are deprived of these privileges: of the common law, for these judges are supposed to be connusant only of the civil law; of juries, for all here is put in the breast of one man.   He judges both law and fact, and his decree is final; at least it cannot be reversed on this side of the Atlantic.   In this particular the colonists are put under a quite different law from all the rest of the King's subjects: jurisdiction is nowhere else given to courts of admiralty of matters so foreign from their connusance.   In some things the colonists have been long subject to this cruel yoke, and have indeed fully experienced its galling nature.   Loud complaints have been long made by them of the oppressions of these courts, their exhorbitant fees, and the little justice the subject may expect from them in cases of seizures.   Let me mention one thing that is notorious: these courts have assumed (I know not by what law) a commission of five per cent to the judge on all seizures condemned.   What chance does the subject stand for his right upon the best claim when the judge, condemning, is to have an hundred or perhaps five hundred pounds, and acquitting, less than twenty shillings?   *   *   *

*   *   *

But in the act we are considering, the power of these courts is even much enlarged and made still more grievous.   For it is thereby enacted that the seizor may inform in any court of admiralty for the particular colony, or in any court of admiralty to be appointed over all America, at his pleasure.   Thus a malicious seizor may take the goods of any man, ever so lawfully and duly imported, and carry the trial of the cause to a thousand miles distance, where for mere want of ability to follow, the claimer shall be incapable of defending his right.   *   *   *

III.   The empowering commanders of the King's ships to seize and implead, as is done in this act and a former act and by special commission from the commissioners of the customs, is another great hardship on the colonies.   The knowledge of all the statutes relating to the customs, of the prohibitions on exports and imports, and of various intricate cases arising on them, requires a good lawyer.   How can this science ever be expected from men educated in a totally different way, brought up upon the boisterous element and knowing no law aboard their ships but their own will? * * * [While this power in the captains might work less damage in England because there] no jurisdiction is given to any other than the common law courts; there too the subjects are near the throne, where, when they are oppressed, their complaints may soon be heard and redressed; but with respect to the colonies, far different is the case! Here it is their own courts that try the cause! Here the subject is far distant from the throne! His complaints cannot soon be heard and redressed. The boisterous commander may take for his motto, *Procul a Jove, a fulmine procul.* [Far from Jove, far from his thunder.]

* * *

There is yet another very great objection the colonists make to this act, of no less weight than the other three. It is this:

IV. Whereas it is good law that all officers seizing goods seize at their peril, and if the goods they seize are not liable to forfeiture they must pay the claimant his cost, and are liable to his action besides, which two things have been looked upon as proper checks of exorbitant wanton power in the officer: both these checks are taken off. They, the officers, may charge the revenue with the cost, with the consent of four of the commissioners of the customs. And if the judge of admiralty will certify that there was probable cause of seizure, no action shall be maintained by the claimant though his goods on trial appear to be ever so duly imported and liable to no sort of forfeiture, and he hath been forced to expend ever so much in the defense of them. * * * .

Much more might be said on these subjects, but I aim at brevity. * * *

What we are now considering is how the mere present self-interest of Great Britain is affected by these new regulations.

Now everybody knows that the greatest part of the trade of Great Britain is with her colonies. This she enjoyeth, exclusive of any other European county, and hath entirely at her own command. Further, it may be made out that the greatest part of the profits of the trade of the colonies, at least on the continent, centers in Great Britain. The colonists, settled in a wide and sparse manner, are perpetually demanding the linen, woolen, and other manufacturers of Great Britain. * * * Great Britain, besides, is the mart which supplieth the colonies with all the produce of the other countries in Europe which the colonies use.

Considering the vast numbers supported by these manufactures vended in the colonies, and by the articles of foreign trade brought into the kingdom and thence exported and consumed in the plantations, doubtless even the luxury of the colonists is the gain of Great Britain. So thought wise ministers in the late reign: on which ground they repealed two or three sumptuary laws made in the colonies for restraining that luxury.

Now as the colonies have no gold or silver mines in them, it is certain that all their remittances they make must be from their trade. * * *

One grand source of these remittances is the fishery, which by the duty of three pence a gallon on molasses must entirely be at an end. That branch can never bear the high duties imposed, nor subsist without the molasses which the trade to the foreign islands furnisheth. Not only by their connection with this but by the mere effect of the new regulations, all the other trade of the colonists must be at an end. * * *

Hence, one or other of these consequences will follow: either (1) the colonies will universally go into such manufactures as they are capable of doing within themselves, or (2) they will do without them, and being reduced to mere necessaries, will be clothed like their predecessors the Indians with the skins of beasts, and sink into like barbarism. * * *

Now, either of these events taking place, how will it affect the island of Great Britain? The answer is obvious. The exports to the colonies wholly stopped or greatly diminished, the demands for those manufactures in Great Britain must be in proportion lessened. The substance of those manufacturers, merchants, and traders whom this demand supports is then gone. They who live from supplying these manufacturers, etc., must decay and die with them. Lastly, as trade may be compared to a grand chain made up of innumerable links, it is doubtful whether the British trade, great as it is, can bear the striking out so many without greatly endangering the whole.

What now is the equivalent for all this to the nation? A tenth part of one year's tax, at the extent two years' tax upon the colonies (for after that time all their money will be gone) to be lodged in the exchequer and thence issued as the Parliament shall direct. Doth not this resemble the conduct of the good wife in the fable who killed her hen that every day laid her a *golden egg?*

* * *

NOTES AND QUESTIONS

1. With these last two readings we open up the area of the causes of the American Revolution and the importance of law to the Whigs and the Loyalists. We cannot, of course, solve the problem of causation of the American Revolution here; it is still the subject of heated debate among American historians. There is no agreement about whether the primary causes were economic, social, or political. For a summary of nearly current historiography on the American Revolution see Jack P. Greene, ed., The Reinterpretation of the American Revolution, 1763–1789 (1968). For more recent efforts at coming to grips with the philosophical underpinnings of the American Revolution see Henry Steele Commager, The Empire of Reason (1977), Morton White, The Philosophy of the American Revolution (1978), and Garry Wills, Inventing America: Jefferson's Declaration of Independence (1978).

2.   One way of approaching the problem of American revolutionary ideology is to study what there was to rebel against. Governor Hutchinson was perhaps one of the most articulate theorists of the loyalist cause, even if his theoretical formulations were not generally known at the time. Why doesn't Hutchinson sympathize with the popular critics of the Royal administration? Is it simply that he *is* the King's officer in the colony of Massachusetts, or does his hostility to what was to become the patriot cause run deeper?

3.   Does Hutchinson believe that the majority of the American people are dissatisfied with royal rule? Who then is causing the disaffection that he is able to perceive on all sides? What does Hutchinson mean when he refers to "popular demagogues?"

4.   Hutchinson is greatly troubled by recent riots and popular disturbances in Massachusetts. As indicated earlier, in 1765 a savage mob wrecked and torched his house, destroying virtually all of his belongings. There has been something of a recent explosion in the scholarship on the American Revolutionary mob. See, e. g., Pauline Maier, "Popular Uprisings and Civil Authority in Eighteenth-Century America," 27 Will. & Mary Q. 3 (1970). It is clear that American mobs played a prominent role in the agitation against royal policy, and that some of them destroyed property and physically abused royal officials. Popular mobs had been fixtures in the colonial political process at least since the late 1600's. Mob activity extended over a wide range, including rioting, tarring and feathering, obstructing customs enforcement and service of process, and highly selective damaging of property, such as brothels, private dwellings, or ships.

Still, is it correct to describe most American mobs as "lawless?" Were they really undisciplined and anarchic? John Reid argues that while Whig mobs in the 1760's and 1770's may have been "unlawful," they were not "lawless." Does the following discussion from Reid's 1977 book In a Defiant Stance, supra, at 162–163, shed any light on the differences of opinion between Hutchinson, Otis, and Oxenbridge Thacher?*

We must not demand precise rules or definitive principles. In the fluid rivalry of two competing governments what is "legal" may be as often a subjective as an objective judgment. *   *   *

Consider the possibility that there are often two sides to lawlessness. A tory conscious of how the Massachusetts whigs departed from traditional principles of English common law by employing the civil traverse jury and the writ system to impose a criminal-law type sanction upon customs officials would have said that they abused the judicial process. Yet that same tory might not have thought it an abuse when the commissioners of the customs departed from similar principles of English common law and attempted to use the admiralty jurisdiction to impose a criminal-law

* From John Phillip Reid, In a Defiant Stance: The Conditions of Law in Massachusetts Bay, The Irish Comparison, and the Coming of the American Revolution 162–163, Copyright © 1977 The Pennsylvania State University, Published by the Pennsylvania State University Press, University Park and London, reprinted with the permission of the publisher and the author.

type sanction upon John Hancock.** The tory who saw a violation of the constitution when whig juries ignored admiralty judgments and rendered common-law verdicts despite being instructed that the admiralty decree had settled all legal questions, probably did not recognize a comparable violation of the constitution in that section of the Sugar Act freeing customs officers from common-law damage suits whenever an admiralty court in a nonjury *ex parte* hearing ruled that they had acted with "probable cause." * * * Should Hutchinson concede that Whigs acted within the law when their grand jurors refused to indict the rioters who destroyed his house, yet assert they acted without principle, the complaint could with equal fairness be made about him, for Hutchinson kept imperial officials informed about secret grand jury proceedings and when men such as Gage or Bernard were indicted he saw to it that the law did not take its normal course.

The judicial process was such in eighteenth-century British North America that it could be used by the political process, and each side of the controversy was willing to take whatever advantages fell its way. Most dropped on the whig side, but the whigs should not be accused of unlawful manipulations merely because the tories thought them unlawful. The whigs, for their part, believed that the British were altering an immutable constitution and Hutchinson's "manipulations" were part of their story.

A more serious charge, as it troubled Americans who accepted implicitly the whig tale of constitutional abuse yet retained a conservative's respect for the rule of law, was the assertion that much of whig violence was lawless. We have seen whigs reject this contention yet none has articulated a satisfactory argument for the legality of their use of force. Implicit in their legal theory—in John Adams's distinction between legitimate and illegitimate mobs and his praise of the Boston Tea Party—was the concept that what is "unlawful" under imperial law is not always "lawless." "Lawlessness" in the whig sense implied that the act complained of—such as a riot—was not only in violation of constituted law but was performed either for an irrational purpose or for personal gain or had a negative or antisocial aim. "Lawful" or "semilawful" in the whig sense was an act contrary to statutory or common law, but when tory or imperial law was broken and the purpose was to defend whig constitutional principles the act was not necessarily "lawless." * * *

It is fair to say that Governor Francis Bernard was one high tory who never understood what whigs were up to. That rebels might be governed by a legal theory was beyond his imagination. Yet even Bernard grasped the whig distinction between the lawless rioters who sacked Hutchinson's house and the semilawful rioters who forced Andrew Oliver to resign as stamp agent. It was this legal theory—a theory that apparently had no limits as it

** Hancock's sloop, The Liberty, was seized by royal customs officials in 1768, on charges of illegal trading.

led directly to mob rule—that persuaded other Americans to recoil from the whig program.   *   *   *

5.   Thacher was reacting against the "Sugar Act," of 1764, 4 George III, c. 15, VII Statutes at Large 457 (1764).   The principal substantive provision of the act was a three pence per gallon duty on molasses imported into the colonies.   This duty, which was of primary concern to rum distillers, was not thought to be excessively harsh by Parliament, and was approximately half of the former duty on molasses.   Still, since this duty was to be enforced, and the former duty had been all but ignored, because of the importance of the trade in rum, many in America believed that the duty would cripple American commerce.   See, e. g. Lawrence H. Gipson, The Coming of the Revolution 65–68 (1954).   For Thacher, however, the *governmental philosophy* that appeared to be behind some of the enforcement provisions of the Sugar Act may have suggested a greater threat than the immediate economic impact.   Here is how Professor Bernard Bailyn describes these provisions:

> To facilitate prosecution of violators of the navigation laws, the burden of proof was shifted to the defendant in cases brought by the customs officials; whatever the outcome of such cases, the defendant was obliged to pay costs; and the defendant was, in effect, prevented from entering retaliatory suits against customs officials.   Above all, the law allowed all suits involving alleged violations of the navigation laws to be tried, if the "informer or prosecutor" wished, in the juryless admiralty courts: either the vice-admiralty court in the colony concerned "or in any court of vice-admiralty which may   *   *   *   be appointed over all *America*"—an alternative that referred to a projected new tribunal with jurisdiction over all the colonies, concurrent with that of the provincial vice-admiralty courts, which was created in fact in June 1764 in the remote hamlet of Halifax, Nova Scotia.

B. Bailyn, ed., I Pamphlets of the American Revolution 487 (1965).*

6.   Thacher refers to some British statutes that restricted the jurisdiction of the English Admiralty courts.   Bailyn's notes on these state that the statutes were "[1.] 13 Richard II c. 5, which declared that "admirals and their deputies shall not meddle from henceforth of anything done within the realm, but only of a thing done upon the sea"; [2.] 15 Richard II c. 3, which added that over all matters "rising within the bodies of the counties, as well by land as by water, and also of wreck of the sea, the admiral's court shall have no jurisdiction" and [3.] 2 Henry IV c. 11, which confirmed 13 Richard II c. 5."   Bailyn, supra note 5, at 726–727. Can one reconcile Parliament's motives in passing and maintaining this legislation restricting admiralty jurisdiction in England and its passage of the Sugar Act expanding admiralty jurisdiction in the colonies?

7.   The formal break with Great Britain did not come until 1776, approximately ten years after the events discussed in these excerpts.   By that time, in the wake of the Boston Tea Party, Parliament had passed

* Bernard Bailyn, Editor, I Pamphlets   Harvard University Press, reprinted
   of the American Revolution (1965),   with the permission of the publisher.
   published by the Belknap Press of the

the infamous "Coercive Acts," closing Boston's Port and severely restricting popular participation in the governance of Massachusetts. See, e. g. Gipson, supra note 5, at 223–225. These measures led directly to the convening of the Continental Congress which, following the failure of attempts at reconciliation, issued the Declaration of Independence. Compare the final version of the Declaration, which follows, with Hutchinson's, Otis's, and Thacher's comments.

When in the Course of human events, it becomes necessary for one people to dissolve the political bands which have connected them with another, and to assume among the powers of the earth, the separate and equal station to which the Laws of Nature and of Nature's God entitle them, a decent respect to the opinions of mankind requires that they should declare the causes which impel them to the separation. We hold these truths to be self-evident, that all men are created equal, that they are endowed by their Creator with certain unalienable Rights, that among these are Life, Liberty and the pursuit of Happiness. That to secure these rights, Governments are instituted among Men, deriving their just powers from the consent of the governed, That whenever any Form of Government becomes destructive of these ends it is the Right of the People to alter or to abolish it, and to institute new Government, laying its foundation on such principles and organizing its powers in such form, as to them shall seem most likely to effect their Safety and Happiness. Prudence, indeed, will dictate that Governments long established should not be changed for light and transient causes; and accordingly all experience hath shewn, that mankind are more disposed to suffer, while evils are sufferable, than to right themselves by abolishing the forms to which they are accustomed. But when a long train of abuses and usurpations, pursuing invariably the same Object evinces a design to reduce them under absolute Despotism, it is their right, it is their duty, to throw off such Government, and to provide new Guards for their future security. Such has been the patient sufferance of these Colonies; and such is now the necessity which constrains them to alter their former Systems of Government. The history of the present King of Great Britain is a history of repeated injuries and usurpations, all having in direct object the establishment of an absolute Tyranny over these States. To prove this, let Facts be submitted to a candid world. He has refused his Assent to Laws, the most wholesome and necessary for the public good. He has forbidden his Governors to pass Laws of immediate and pressing importance, unless suspended in their operation till his Assent should be obtained; and when so suspended, he has utterly neglected to attend to them. He has refused to pass other Laws for the accommodation of large districts of people, unless those people would relinquish the right of Representation in the Legislature, a right inestimable to them and formidable to tyrants only. He has called together legislative bodies at places unusual, uncomfortable, and distant from the depository of their public Records, for the sole purpose of fatiguing them into compliance with his measures. He has dissolved Representative Houses repeatedly, for opposing with manly firmness his invasions on the rights of the people. He has refused for a long time, after such dissolutions, to cause others to be elected; whereby the Legislative powers, incapable of Annihilation, have returned to the People at large for their exercise; the State remaining in the mean time exposed to all the dangers of invasion from without, and convulsions within. He has endeavoured to prevent the population of these States; for that purpose obstructing the Laws for Naturalization of Foreigners; refusing to pass others to encourage their migrations hither, and raising the conditions of new Appropriations of Lands. He has obstructed the Administration of Justice, by refusing his Assent to Laws for establishing Judiciary powers. He has made Judges dependent on his Will alone, for the tenure of their offices, and the amount and payment of their salaries. He has erected a multitude of New Offices, and sent hither swarms of Officers to harass our people, and eat out their substance. He has kept among us, in times of peace, standing Armies without the Consent of our legislatures. He has affected to render the Military independent of and superior to the Civil power. He has combined with others to subject us to a jurisdiction foreign to our constitution, and unacknowledged by our laws; giving his Assent to their Acts of pretended Legislation: For Quartering large bodies of armed troops among us: For protecting them, by a mock Trial, from punishment for any Murders which they should commit on the Inhabitants of these States: For cutting off our Trade with all parts of the world: For imposing Taxes on us without our Consent: For depriving us in many cases of the benefits of Trial by Jury: For transporting us beyond Seas to be tried for pretended offences: For abolishing the free System of English Laws in a neighbouring Province, establishing therein an Arbitrary government, and enlarging its Boundaries so as to render it at once an example and fit instrument for introducing the same absolute rule into these Colonies: For taking away our Charters, abolishing our most valuable Laws, and altering fundamentally the Forms of our Governments: For suspending our own Legislatures, and declaring themselves invested with power to legislate for us in all cases whatsoever. He has abdicated Government here, by declaring us out of his Protection and waging War against us. He has plundered our seas, ravaged our Coasts, burnt our towns, and destroyed the Lives of our people. He is at this time transporting large Armies of foreign Mercenaries to compleat the works of death, desolation and tyranny, already begun with circumstances of Cruelty & perfidy scarcely paralleled in the most barbarous ages, and totally unworthy the Head of a civilized nation. He has constrained our fellow Citizens taken Captive on the high Seas to bear Arms against their Country, to become the executioners of their friends and Brethren, or to fall themselves by their Hands. He has excited domestic insurrections amongst us, and has endeavoured to bring on the inhabitants of our frontiers, the merciless Indian Savages, whose known rule of warfare, is an undistinguished destruction of all ages, sexes and conditions. In every stage of these Oppressions We have Petitioned for Redress in the most humble terms: Our repeated Petitions have been answered only by repeated injury. A Prince, whose character is thus marked by every act which may define a Tyrant, is unfit to be the ruler of a free people. Nor have We been wanting in attentions to our Brittish brethren. We have warned them from time to time of attempts by their legislature to extend an unwarrantable jurisdiction over us. We have reminded them of the circumstances of our emigration and settlement here. We have appealed to their native justice and magnanimity, and we have conjured them by the ties of our common kindred to disavow these usurpations, which, would inevitably interrupt our connections and correspondence. They too have been deaf to the voice of justice and of consanguinity. We must, therefore, acquiesce in the necessity, which denounces our Separation, and hold them, as we hold the rest of mankind, Enemies in War, in Peace Friends.

We, therefore, the Representatives of the United States of America, in General Congress, Assembled, appealing to the Supreme Judge of the world for the rectitude of our intentions, do, in the Name, and by Authority of the good People of these Colonies, solemnly publish and declare, That these United Colonies are, and of Right ought to be Free and Independent States; that they are Absolved from all Allegiance to the British Crown, and that all political connection between them and the State of Great Britain, is and ought to be totally dissolved; and that as Free and Independent States, they have full Power to levy War, conclude Peace, contract Alliances, establish Commerce, and to do all other Acts and Things which Independent States may of right do. And for the support of this Declaration, with a firm reliance on the protection of divine Providence, we mutually pledge to each other our Lives, our Fortunes and our sacred Honor.

8. Note, for example, that Thacher's pamphlet seems to be directed against parliament and the British government generally while Jefferson's Declaration singles out the King as the villain. Why? Note the reference in the beginning of the Declaration to the "Laws of Nature and of Nature's God" which are said to guarantee "separate and equal" stations to the peoples of the world. Note, as you probably have frequently, the ideas that "all men are created equal," that their "Creator" endows them with "certain unalienable Rights," that governments are instituted to secure these rights and that these governments derive "their just powers from the consent of the governed." Do these political premises have any bearing on the debate between Hutchinson and Thacher? Does Jefferson have anything to say about the security of property rights? What does this suggest to you about the ideals, if not the motives, of the Revolutionaries? Note also that while the King is accused of dissolving "Representative Houses repeatedly," the "Legislative Powers, incapable of Annihilation, have returned to the People at large for their exercise." How could this be? And why is it critical that Jefferson establish this point in the Declaration? See generally Carl Becker's little classic, The Declaration of Independence (1922), and see also the provocative recent treatment by the contemporary political commentator Garry Wills, Inventing America: Jefferson's Declaration of Independence (1978).

9. Part of what was ultimately at stake here, of course, was the idea of Constitutionalism, that there are certain fundamental principles or laws which are sacred, transcendent, and immutable, and which circumscribe the activities of the Government. How would Hutchinson have reacted to this idea? Does he suggest that there are any inherent limits on the powers of Parliament? Does Thacher? Does Jefferson? What about Hutchinson's ideas on the allegiance of the subject? Would Jefferson agree with these? Note that Hutchinson indicates toward the close of his dialogue that there could be no organ of government capable of declaring that the actions of the government are "unconstitutional." Why is that? Do you agree with Hutchinson?

10. In the next set of readings and in Chapter Two we will attempt to come to grips with some of the practical problems of Constitutionalism in the early American republic.

SECTION E. TOWARDS POPULAR SOVEREIGNTY AND CONSTITUTIONALISM

We begin our examination of the political, constitutional and legal philosophies in the early American republic with the Pennsylvania Constitution of 1776, usually thought to have been the most "democratic" or "radical" frame of government to emerge out of the American revolution. We will then compare and contrast the constitutional and legislative experience in Virginia, as described by Thomas Jefferson. Finally, in the beginning of the next Chapter, we will examine the thought of the "Federalists," the political group which dominated the national government for twelve years after the adoption of the United States Constitution in 1789. As you examine these materials, try to determine how the governments and the laws they describe are consisent or inconsistent with current American practice.

1. THE PENNSYLVANIA CONSTITUTION OF 1776

THE PROCEEDINGS RELATIVE TO THE CALLING OF THE CONVENTIONS OF 1776 AND 1790 * * *
54–65 (1825).

WHEREAS all government ought to be instituted and supported for the security and protection of the community as such, and to enable the individuals who compose it, to enjoy their natural rights, and the other blessings which the author of existence has bestowed upon man; and whenever these great ends of government are not obtained, the people have a right by common consent to change it, and take such measures as to them may appear necessary, to promote their safety and happiness. And whereas the inhabitants of this commonwealth, have, in consideration of protection only, heretofore acknowledged allegience to the king of Great Britain, and the said king has not only withdrawn that protection, but commenced and still continues to carry on with unabated vengeance, a most cruel and unjust war against them, employing therein not only the troops of Great Britain, but foreign mercenaries, savages and slaves, for the avowed purpose of reducing them to a total and abject submission to the despotic domination of the British parliament * * * whereby all allegiance and fealty to the said king and his successors are dissolved and at an end, and all power and authority derived from him ceased in these colonies. And whereas it is absolutely necessary for the welfare and safety of the inhabitants of said colonies, that they be henceforth free and independent states, and that just, permanent and proper forms of government exist in every part of them, derived from, and founded on the authority of the people only, agreeable to the directions of the honorable American congress. WE, the representatives of the freemen of Pennsylvania, in general convention met, for the express purpose of framing such a government, * * * and being fully convinced, that it is our indispensible duty to establish such original principles of government, as will best promote the general happiness of the people of this state and their posterity, and provide for future improvements, without partiality for, or prejudice against, any particular class, sect or denomination of men whatsoever, do, by virtue of the authority vested in us by our constituents, ordain, declare and establish the following declaration of rights, and frame of government, to be the constitution of this commonwealth, and to remain in force therein for ever unaltered, except in such articles as shall hereafter, on experience, be found to require improvement, and which shall by the same authority of the people, fairly delegated, as this frame of government directs, be amended or improved for the more effectual obtaining and securing the great end and design of all government, herein before mentioned.

Chapter I

A declaration of the rights of the inhabitants of the commonwealth or state of Pennsylvania

I.   That all men are born equally free and independent, and have certain natural, inherent and unalienable rights, amongst which are the enjoying and defending life and liberty, acquiring, possessing and protecting property, and pursuing and obtaining happiness and safety.

II.   That all men have a natural and unalienable right to worship Almighty God, according to the dictates of their own consciences and understanding, and that no man ought, or of right can be compelled to attend any religious worship, or erect or support any place of worship, or maintain any ministry, contrary to, or against his own free will and consent, nor can any man who acknowledges the being of a God, be justly deprived or abridged of any civil right as a citizen, on account of his religious sentiments, or peculiar mode of religious worship; and that no authority can, or ought to be vested in, or assumed by any power whatever, that shall in any case interfere with, or in any manner controul the right of conscience in the free exercise of religious worship.

III.   That the people of this state have the sole, exclusive and inherent right of governing and regulating the internal police of the same.

IV.   That all power being originally inherent in, and consequently derived from the people; therefore all officers of government, whether legislative or executive, are their trustees and servants, and at all times accountable to them.

V.   That government is, or ought to be, instituted for the common benefit, protection, and security of the people, nation or community; and not for the particular emolument or advantage of any single man, family, or set of men, who are a part only of that community; and that the community hath an indubitable, unalienable and indefeasible right to reform, alter or abolish government, in such manner as shall be by that community judged most conducive to the public weal.

VI.   That those who are employed in the legislative and executive business of the state, may be restrained from oppression, the people have a right, at such periods as they may think proper, to reduce their public officers to a private station, and supply the vacancies by certain and regular elections.

VII.   That all elections ought to be free, and that all free men, having a sufficient evident common interest with and attachment to the community, have a right to elect officers, or to be elected into office.

VIII.   That every member of society hath a right to be protected in the enjoyment of life, liberty and property, and therefore is bound to contribute his proportion towards the expense of that protection, and yield his personal service when necessary, or an equivalent thereto; but no part of a man's property can be justly taken from him or applied to public uses, without his own consent or that of his legal representatives; nor can any man who is conscientiously scrupulous of bearing arms be justly compelled thereto if he will pay such equivalent; nor are the people bound by any laws but such as they have in like manner assented to, for their common good.

IX.   That in all prosecutions for criminal offences, a man hath a right to be heard by himself and his council; to demand the cause and nature of his accusation; to be confronted with the witnesses, to call for evidence in his favor, and a speedy public trial by an impartial jury of the country, without the unanimous consent of which jury he cannot be found guilty; nor can he be compelled to give evidence against himself; nor can any man be justly deprived of his liberty, except by the laws of the land or the judgment of his peers.

X.   That the people have a right to hold themselves, their houses, papers and possessions free from search and seizure; and therefore warrants, without oaths or affirmations first made, affording a sufficient foundation for them, and whereby any officer or messenger may be commanded or required to search suspected places, or to seize any person or persons, his or their property not particularly described, are contrary to that right, and ought not to be granted.

XI.   That in controversies respecting property, and in suits between man and man, the parties have a right to trial by jury, which ought to be held sacred.

XII.   That the people have a right to freedom of speech, and of writing and publishing their sentiments; therefore the freedom of the press ought not to be restrained.

XIII.   That the people have a right to bear arms for the defence of themselves, and the state; and as standing armies in the time of peace, are dangerous to liberty, they ought not to be kept up; and that the military should be kept under strict subordination to, and governed by the civil power.

XIV.   That a frequent recurrence to fundamental principles and a firm adherence to justice, moderation, temperance, industry and frugality, are absolutely necessary to preserve the blessings of liberty, and, keep a government free. The people ought therefore to pay particular attention to these points in the choice of officers and representatives, and have a right to exact a due and constant regard to them from their legislatures and magistrates, in the making and executing such laws as are necessary for the good government of the state.

XV.   That all men have a natural inherent right to emigrate from one state to another that will receive them, or to form a new state in vacant countries, or in such countries as they can purchase, whenever they think that thereby they may promote their own happiness.

XVI.   That the people have a right to assemble together to consult for their common good, to instruct their representatives, and to apply to the legislature for redress of grievances by address, petition or remonstrance.

Chapter II

Plan or frame of government for the commonwealth or state of Pennsylvania

[A.   *General Provisions*]

Section 1.   The commonwealth or state of Pennsylvania shall be governed hereafter by an assembly of the representatives of the freemen of the same, and a president and council, in manner and form following:—

Sect. 2.   The supreme legislative power shall be vested in a house of representatives of the freemen of the commonwealth or state of Pennsylvania.

Sect. 3.   The supreme executive power shall be vested in a president and council.

Sect. 4.   Courts of justice shall be established in the city of Philadelphia, and in every county of this state.

Sect. 5.   The freemen of this commonwealth and their sons shall be trained and armed for its defence, under such regulations, restrictions and exceptions as the general assembly shall by law direct; preserving always to the people the right of choosing their colonels and all commissioned officers under that rank, in such manner, and as often as by the said laws shall be directed.

Sect. 6.   Every freeman of the full age of twenty-one years, having resided in this state for the space of one whole year next before the day of election for representatives, and paid public taxes during that time, shall enjoy the right of an elector: Provided always, That sons of freeholders of the age of twenty-one years shall be entitled to vote, although they have not paid taxes.

[B.   *The House of Representatives*]

Sect. 7.   The house of representatives of the freemen of this commonwealth shall consist of persons most noted for wisdom and virtue, to be chosen by the freemen of every city and county of this commonwealth respectively, and no person shall be elected unless he has resided in the city or county for which he shall be chosen two years immediately before the said election, nor shall any member, while he continues such, hold any other office except in the militia.

Sect. 8.   No person shall be capable of being elected a member to serve in the house of representatives of the freemen of this commonwealth more than four years in seven.

Sect. 9.   The members of the house of representatives shall be chosen annually by ballot, by the freemen of the commonwealth * * * and shall have power to choose their speaker, the treasurer of the state, and their other officers; sit on their own adjournments; prepare bills and enact them into laws; judge of the elections and qualifications of their own members; they may expel a member, but not a second time for the same cause; they may administer oaths or affirmations on examination of witnesses; redress grievances; impeach state criminals; grant charters of incorporation; constitute towns, boroughs, cities and counties; and shall have all other powers necessary for the legislature of a free state or commonwealth; but they shall have no power to add to, alter, abolish or infringe any part of this constitution.

Sect. 10.   A quorum of the house of representatives shall consist of two-thirds of the whole number of members elected, and having met and chosen their speaker, shall each of them, before they proceed to business, take and subscribe as well the oath or affirmation of fidelity and allegiance hereinafter directed, as the following oath or affirmation, viz.

I _____ _____ do swear (or affirm) that as a member of this assembly, I will not propose or assent to any bill, vote or resolution, which shall appear to me injurious to the people, nor do or consent to any act or thing whatever, that shall have a tendency to lessen or abridge their rights and privileges as declared in the constitution of this state, but will in all things conduct myself as a faithful honest representative and guardian of the people, according to the best of my judgment and abilities.

And each member, before he takes his seat, shall make and subscribe the following declaration, viz.

I do believe in one God, the creator and governor of the universe, the rewarder of the good and punisher of the wicked, and I do acknowledge the scriptures of the Old and New Testament to be given by Divine Inspiration.

And no further or other religious test shall ever hereafter be required of any civil officer or magistrate in this state.

Sect. 11.   Delegates to represent this state in congress shall be chosen by ballot by the future general assembly at their first meeting, and annually for ever afterwards as long as such representation shall be necessary.   Any delegate may be superseded at any time, by the general assembly appointing another in his stead.   No man shall sit in congress longer than two years successively, nor be capable of re-election for three years afterwards; and no person who holds any office in the gift of the congress shall hereafter be elected to represent this commonwealth in congress.

* * *

Sect. 13.   The doors of the house in which the representatives of the freemen of this state shall sit in general assembly, shall be and remain open for the admission of all persons, who behave decently, except only when the welfare of this state may require the doors to be shut.

Sect. 14.   The votes and proceedings of the general assembly shall be printed weekly, during their sitting, with the yeas and nays on any question, vote or resolution, where any two members require it, except when the vote is taken by ballot; and when the yeas and nays are so taken, every member shall have a right to insert the reasons of his vote upon the minutes, if he desires it.

Sect. 15.   To the end that laws before they are enacted, may be more maturely considered, and the inconvenience of hasty determinations as much as possible prevented, all bills of a public nature shall be printed for the consideration of the people, before they are read in general assembly the last time for debate and amendment; and except on occasions of sudden necessity, shall not be passed into laws until the next session of assembly; and for the more perfect satisfaction of the public, the reasons and motives for making such laws shall be fully and clearly expressed in the preambles.

* * *

Sect. 17. * * * as representation in proportion to the number of taxable inhabitants is the only principle which can at all times secure liberty and make the voice of a majority of the people the law of the land; therefore the general assembly shall cause complete lists of the taxable inhabitants in the city and each county in the commonwealth respectively, to be taken and returned to them on or before the last meeting of the assembly elected in the year one thousand seven hundred and seventy-eight, who shall appoint a representation to reach in proportion to the number of taxables in such returns, which representation shall continue for the next seven years afterwards, at the end of which, a new return of the taxable inhabitants shall be made, and a representation agreeable thereto appointed by the said assembly, and so on septennially for ever.

* * *

[C.   *The Executive*]

Sect. 19.   For the present the supreme executive council of this state shall consist of twelve persons chosen in the following manner: The freemen of the city of Philadelphia, and of the counties of Philadelphia, Chester and Bucks respectively, shall choose by ballot one person for the city and one for each county aforesaid, to serve for three years and no longer, at the time and place for electing representatives in general assembly. The freemen of the counties of Lancaster, York, Cumberland, and Berks, shall in like manner elect one person for each county respectively, to serve as councillors for two years and no longer. And the counties of Northampton, Bedford, Northumberland and Westmoreland respectively, shall in like manner elect one person for each county, to serve as councillors for one year and no longer: And at the expiration of the time for which each councillor was chosen to serve, the freemen of the city of Philadelphia and of the several counties in this state respectively, shall elect one person to serve as councillor for three years and no longer, and so on every third year for ever. By this mode of election and continual rotation more men will be trained to public business, there will in every subsequent year be found in the council a number of persons acquainted with the proceedings of the foregoing years, whereby the business will be more consistently conducted, and moreover the danger of establishing an inconvenient aristocracy will be effectually prevented. * * * No member of the general assembly or delegate in Congress, shall be chosen a member of the council. The president and vice-president shall be chosen annually by the joint ballot of the general assembly and council, of the members of the council. Any person having served as a councillor for three successive years, shall be incapable of holding that office for four years afterwards. Every member of the council shall be a justice of the peace for the whole commonwealth, by virtue of his office.

The council shall meet annually, at the same time and place with the general assembly.

The treasurer of the state, trustees of the loan-office, naval officers, collectors of customs or excise, judge of the admiralty, attornies-general, sheriffs and prothonotaries, shall not be capable of a seat in the general assembly, executive council or continental congress.

Sect. 20. The president, and in his absence the vice-president, with the council, five of whom shall be a quorum, shall have power to appoint and commissionate judges, naval officers, judge of the admiralty, attorney-general and all other officers, civil and military, except such as are chosen by the general assembly or the people * * *. They are to correspond with other states, and transact business with the officers of government, civil and military, and to prepare such business as may appear to them necessary, to lay before the general assembly. They shall sit as judges, to hear and determine on impeachments, taking to their assistance, for advice only, the justices of the supreme court. And shall have power to grant pardons and remit fines in all cases whatsoever, except in cases of impeachment; and in cases of treason and murder shall have power to grant reprieves, but not to pardon, until the end of the next session of assembly, but there shall be no remission or mitigation of punishment on impeachments, except by act of the legislature; they are also to take care that the laws be faithfully executed; they are to expedite the execution of such measures as may be resolved upon by the general assembly; and they may draw upon the treasury for such sums as shall be appropriated by the house. They may also lay embargoes, or prohibit the exportation of any commodity, for any time, not exceeding thirty days, in the recess of the house only. They may grant such licences as shall be directed by law, and shall have power to call together the general assembly when necessary, before the day to which they shall stand adjourned. The president shall be commander in chief of the forces of the state, but shall not command in person, except advised thereto by the council, and then only so long as they shall approve thereof. The president and council shall have a secretary, and keep fair books of their proceedings, wherein any councillor may enter his dissent, with his reasons in support of it.

* * *

Sect. 22. Every officer of state, whether judicial or executive, shall be liable to be impeached by the general assembly, either when in office or after his resignation or removal for mal-administration. All impeachments shall be before the president or vice-president and council, who shall hear and determine the same.

[D. *The Judiciary*]

Sect. 23. The judges of the supreme court of judicature shall have fixed salaries, be commissioned for seven years only, though capable of re-appointment at the end of that term, but removable for misbehaviour at any time by the general assembly; they shall not be allowed to sit as members in the continental congress, executive council or general assembly, nor to hold any other office, civil or military, nor take or receive fees or perquisites of any kind.

* * *

Sect. 25. Trials shall be by jury as heretofore, and it is recommended to the legislature of this state to provide by law against every corruption or partiality in the choice, return or appointment of juries.

Sect. 26. Courts of sessions, common pleas and orphans' courts shall be held quarterly in each city and county, and the legislature shall have power to establish all such other courts as they may judge for the good of the inhabitants of the state; all courts shall be open, and justice shall be impartially administered without corruption or unnecessary delay: All their officers shall be paid an adequate but moderate compensation for their services, and if any officer shall take greater or other fees than the laws allow him, either directly or indirectly, it shall ever after disqualify him from holding any office in this state.

* * *

[E. *Other*]

Sect. 28. The person of a debtor, where there is not a strong presumption of fraud, shall not be continued in prison after delivering up, *bona fide,* all his estate real and personal for the use of his creditors, in such manner as shall be hereafter regulated by law. All prisoners shall be bailable by sufficient suretie, unless for capital offences, when the proof is evident or presumption great.

Sect. 29. Excessive bail shall not be exacted for bailable offences: And all fines shall be moderate.

* * *

Sect. 32. All elections, whether by the people or in general assembly, shall be by ballot, free and voluntary: And any elector, who shall receive any gift or reward for his vote, in meat, drink, monies or otherwise, shall forfeit his right to elect for that time, and suffer such other penalty as future laws shall direct. And any person who shall directly or indirectly give, promise or bestow any such rewards to be elected, shall be thereby rendered incapable to serve for the ensuing year.

* * *

Sect. 35.   The printing presses shall be free to every person, who undertakes to examine the proceedings of the legislature, or any part of government.

Sect. 36.   As every freeman, to preserve his independence, (if without a sufficient estate,) ought to have some profession, calling, trade or farm, whereby he may honestly subsist, there can be no necessity for nor use in establishing offices of profit, the usual effects of which are dependence and servility, unbecoming freemen, in the possessors and expectants, faction, contention, corruption, and disorder among the people: but if any man is called into public service to the prejudice of his private affairs, he has a right to a reasonable compensation: And whenever an office, through increase of fees, or otherwise becomes so profitable as to occasion many to apply for it, the profits ought to be lessened by the legislature.

Sect. 37.   The future legislature of this state shall regulate entails in such manner as to prevent perpetuities.

Sect. 38.   The penal laws as heretofore used, shall be reformed by the future legislature of this state, as soon as may be, and punishments made in some cases less sanguinary, and in general more proportionate to the crimes.

Sect. 39.   To deter more effectually from the commission of crimes, by continued visible punishment of long duration, and to make sanguinary punishments less necessary, houses ought to be provided for punishing by hard labour, those who shall be convicted of crimes not capital; wherein the criminals shall be employed for the benefit of the public, or for reparation of injuries done to private persons. And all persons at proper times shall be admitted to see the prisoners at their labour.

*   *   *

Sect. 41.   No public tax, custom or contribution shall be imposed upon, or paid by the people of this state, except by a law for that purpose; and before any law be made for raising it, the purpose for which any tax is to be raised, ought to appear clearly to the legislature to be of more service to the community than the money would be, if not collected, which being well observed, taxes can never be burthens.

*   *   *

Sect. 43.   The inhabitants of this state shall have liberty to fowl and hunt in seasonable times on the lands they hold, and on all other lands therein not inclosed, and in like manner to fish in all boatable waters and others not private property.

Sect. 44.   A school or schools shall be established in each county by the legislature for the convenient instruction of youth, with such salaries to the masters paid by the public as may enable them to instruct youth at low prices: And all useful learning shall be duly encouraged and promoted in one or more universities.

Sect. 45.   Laws for the encouragement of virtue, and prevention of vice and immorality, shall be made and constantly kept in force, and provision shall be made for their due execution: And all religious societies or bodies of men heretofore united or incorporated for the advancement of religion and learning, or for other pious and charitable purposes, shall be encouraged and protected in the enjoyment of the privileges, immunities and estates which they were accustomed to enjoy or could of right have enjoyed under the laws and former constitution of this state.

*   *   *

[F.   *Council of Censors*]

Sect. 47.   In order that the freedom of this commonwealth may be preserved inviolate for ever, there shall be chosen, by ballot, by the freemen in each city and county respectively, on the second Tuesday in October, in the year one thousand seven hundred and eighty-three, and on the second Tuesday in October, in every seventh year thereafter, two persons in each city and county of this state, to be called THE COUNCIL OF CENSORS, who shall meet together on the second Monday of November next ensuing their election; the majority of whom shall be a quorum in every case, except as to calling a convention, in which two-thirds of the whole number elected shall agree, and whose duty it shall be to enquire whether the constitution has been preserved inviolate in every part; and whether the legislative and executive branches of government have performed their duty, as guardians of the people, or assumed to themselves or exercised other or greater powers than they are entitled to by the constitution; they are also to enquire whether the public taxes have been justly laid and collected in all parts of this commonwealth, in what manner the public monies have been disposed of, and whether the laws have been duly executed: For these purposes they shall have power to send for persons, papers and records; they shall have authority to pass public censures, to order impeachments, and to recommend to the legislature the repealing such laws as appear to them to have been enacted contrary to the principles of the constitution.   These powers they shall continue to have for and during the space of one year, from the day of their election, and no longer.   The said council of censors shall also have power to call a convention, to meet within two years after their sitting, if there appear to them an absolute necessity of amending any article of the constitution, which may be defective, explaining such as may be thought not clearly expressed, and of adding such as are necessary for the preservation of the rights and happiness of the people; but the articles to be amended, and the amendments proposed,   *   *   *   shall be promulgated at least six months before the day appointed for the election of such convention, for the previous consideration of the people, that they may have an opportunity of instructing their delegates on the subject.

NOTES AND QUESTIONS

1.   Of all the state constitutions, Pennsylvania's was the purest application of revolutionary political theory to government; it also reflects many of the experiences and concerns of the colonists in the 1760's and 1770's. Do you see, for example, any similarities in the preamble to the Pennsylvania Constitution and the Declaration of Independence? Can you explain any specific provisions of the Constitution by reference to other readings in the course?

2.   Note what rights the Pennsylvania Constitution-makers deemed to be fundamental. For example, in Section VIII of Chapter I (the Declaration of Rights) the right of Pennsylvanians to enjoy "life, liberty, and property" is acknowledged. Also in that section the Constitution suggests that none of these rights, especially property, are to be infringed except by consent of the individual involved or by that of his legal representatives. How effective a protection is this? Who would be his "legal representatives?"

3.   Why is this constitution thought to be so democratic? Examine, for example, the section of the Declaration of Rights which refers to the franchise (Section VII), but see the qualification to this principle in the Constitution itself (Chapter II, Section 6). Note that elections to the House of Representatives are to be held annually. Why is this? Note also the provision prohibiting any persons from serving in the House of Representatives for more than four years out of seven. Why?

4.   Examine the powers of the House Representatives, and compare these to the powers of the other branches of government (Executive Council, Judiciary, Council of Censors). Which do you regard as the most important? How are representatives to the Continental Congress to be chosen?

5.   Note that the Executive powers (Section 20 of Chapter II) are vested in a council, originally to consist of twelve persons elected to represent respectively the counties of the state and the city of Philadelphia. Why do you suppose the Pennsylvanians thought it wise to place executive powers in plural hands? Do the provisions for rotation in office of the members of the Executive Council (Section 19 of Chapter II) give you any clues?

6.   In connection with the philosophy behind the concept of a plural executive, consider several other bold provisions in Chapter II. Section 36 discourages "offices of profit". What are these? Section 37 discourages "entails." Why? Section 28 abolishes imprisonment for debt, providing the debtor takes certain steps to liquidate his assets. Is this a significant advance? What about the philosophy of crimes limned in Sections 38 and 39? Do you suppose that the resolution of criminal matters in Pennsylvania was to follow the same course as in England?

7.   Finally, consider this body to be called the "Council of Censors," created by Section 47. Why is there a need for such a body? What institution would today perform their function of scrutinizing the Constitutionality of the activities of the other branches of government?

8.   The Pennsylvania Constitution of 1776 lasted only fourteen years. Why do you suppose it had such a short lifespan? The Constitution of 1790, which replaced the document which you have just read

* * *   [W]as exceedingly reactionary and undid much of the work of the early framers. In the new Constitution the legislative, executive, and judicial powers were distinguished and defined according to the now classic American method. Provision was made for a governor, an assembly, and a senate. A judiciary serving during good behavior was also established—an ideal strongly opposed in the Convention of 1776 as entirely too aristocratic.

J. Paul Selsam, The Pennsylvania Constitution of 1776: A Study in Revolutionary Democracy 259 (1971). The United States Constitution of 1787 has been labelled by some historians as a "counter revolution" or "a revolution of conservatism." Can something similar be said of the revised Pennsylvania Constitution?

9. As you read the excerpts from Jefferson's Notes on Virginia which follow, see if you can determine to what extent he favors the political philosophy behind the Pennsylvania Constitution of 1776. You should also try to determine how closely the government of Virginia in 1776 corresponds to the Pennsylvania institutions.

2. THOMAS JEFFERSON, NOTES ON THE STATE OF VIRGINIA (1781)

[In the excerpt which follows Jefferson is describing the Government of Virginia formed under the Virginia Constitution of 1776.]

* * *

* * *   The executive powers are lodged in the hands of a governor, chosen annually, and incapable of acting more then three years in seven. He is assisted by a council of eight members. * * * Legislation is exercised by two houses of assembly, the one called the house of Delegates, composed of two members from each county, chosen annually by the citizens, possessing an estate for life in one hundred acres of uninhabited land, or twenty-five acres with a house on it, or in a house or lot in some town: the other called the Senate, consisting of twenty-four members, chosen quadrennially by the same electors, who for this purpose are distributed into twenty-four districts. The concurrence of both houses is necessary to the passage of a law. They have the appointment of the governor and council, the judges of the superior courts, auditors, attorney-general, treasurer, register of the land office, and delegates to Congress. * * *

This constitution was formed when we were new and unexperienced in the science of government. It was the first, too, which was formed in the whole United States. No wonder then that time and trial have discovered very capital defects in it.

1. The majority of the men in the State, who pay and fight for its support, are unrepresented in the legislature, * * *.

2. Among those who share the representation, the shares are very unequal. Thus the county of Warwick, with only one hundred fighting men, has an equal representation with the county of Loudon, which has one thousand seven hundred and forty-six. So that every

man in Warwick has as much influence in the government as seventeen men in Loudon.   *   *   *

*   *   *   [N]ineteen thousand men, living below the falls of the rivers, [occupying only 10% of the land] possess half the senate, and want four members only of possessing a majority of the house of delegates; a want more than supplied by the vicinity of their situation to the seat of government, and of course the greater degree of convenience and punctuality with which their members may and will attend in the legislature. These nineteen thousand, therefore, living in one part of the country, give law to upwards of thirty thousand living in another, and appoint all their chief officers, executive and judiciary.   *   *   *

3.   The senate is, by its constitution, too homogenous with the house of delegates. Being chosen by the same electors, at the same time, and out of the same subjects, the choice falls of course on men of the same description. The purpose of establishing different houses of legislation is to introduce the influence of different interests or different principles. Thus in Great Britain it is said their constitution relies on the house of commons for honesty, and the lords for wisdom; which would be a rational reliance, if honesty were to be bought with money, and if wisdom were hereditary. In some of the American States, the delegates and senators are so chosen, as that the first represent the persons, and the second the property of the State. But with us, wealth and wisdom have equal chance for admission into both houses. We do not, therefore, derive from the separation of our legislature into two houses, those benefits which a proper complication of principles are capable of producing, and those which alone can compensate the evils which may be produced by their dissensions.

4.   All the powers of government, legislative, executive, and judiciary, result to the legislative body. The concentrating these in the same hands is precisely the definition of despotic government. It will be no alleviation that these powers will be exercised by a plurality of hands, and not by a single one. One hundred and seventy-three despots would surely be as oppressive as one. Let those who doubt it turn their eyes on the republic of Venice.   *   *   *   An elective despotism was not the government we fought for, but one which should not only be founded on free principles, but in which the powers of government should be so divided and balanced among several bodies of magistracy, as that no one could transcend their legal limits, without being effectually checked and restrained by the others. For this reason that convention which passed the ordinance of government, laid its foundation on this basis, that the legislative, executive, and judiciary departments should be separate and distinct, so that no person should exercise the powers of more than one of them at the same time. But no barrier was provided between these several powers. The judiciary and executive members were left dependent on the

legislative, for their subsistence in office, and some of them for their continuance in it. If, therefore, the legislature assumes executive and judiciary powers, no opposition is likely to be made * * *. They have, accordingly, in many instances, decided rights which should have been left to judiciary controversy; and the direction of the executive, during the whole time of their session, is becoming habitual and fa- miliar. * * * The views of the present members are perfectly upright. When they are led out of their regular province, it is by art in others, and inadvertence in themselves. * * * The public money and public liberty, intended to have been deposited with three branch- es of magistracy, but found inadvertently to be in the hands of one only, will soon be discovered to be sources of wealth and dominion to those who hold them * * *. With money we will get men, said Caesar, and with men we will get money. Nor should our assembly be deluded by the integrity of their own purposes, and conclude that these unlimited powers will never be abused, because themselves are not disposed to abuse them. They should look forward to a time, and that not a distant one, when a corruption in this, as in the country from which we derive our origin, will have seized the heads of gov- ernment, and be spread by them through the body of the people * *. Human nature is the same on every side of the Atlantic, and will be alike influenced by the same causes. The time to guard against cor- ruption and tyranny, is before they shall have gotten hold of us. It is better to keep the wolf out of the fold, than to trust to drawing his teeth and talons after he shall have entered. * * *

5. That the ordinary legislature may alter the constitution it- self. [The 1776 "Constitution" was actually a statute passed by the Virginia "Convention" of 1776, a body of elected officials then serv- ing as the new state's legislature.] * * * [T]his very convention, meeting as a house of delegates in general assembly with the Senate in the autumn of that year, passed acts of assembly in contradiction to their ordinance of government; and every assembly from that time to this has done the same. * * * [Jefferson proceeds to indicate his belief that a special convention should be called to approve a new Constitution and to make clear that it is not amendable by ordinary legislatures.] True it is, this is no time for deliberating on forms of government. While an enemy is within our bowels, the first object is to expel him. But when this shall be done, when peace shall be es- tablished, and leisure given us for intrenching within good forms, the rights for which we have bled, let no man be found indolent enough to decline a little more trouble for placing them beyond the reach of question. * * *

6. That the assembly exercises a power of determining the quorum of their own body which may legislate for us. After the es- tablishment of the new form they adhered to the *Lex majoris partis,* founded in common law as well as common right. It is the natural law of every assembly of men, whose numbers are not fixed by any

other law. They continued for some time to require the presence of a majority of their whole number, to pass an act. But the British parliament fixes its own quorum; our former assemblies fixed their own quorum; and one precedent in favor of power is stronger than an hundred against it. The house of delegates, therefore, have lately voted that, during the present dangerous invasion, forty members shall be a house to proceed to business. * * * But this danger could not authorize them to call that a house which was none; and if they may fix it at one number, they may at another, till it loses its fundamental character of being a representative body. * * *

* * *

* * * In December 1776, our circumstances being much distressed, it was proposed in the house of delegates to create a dictator, invested with every power legislative, executive, and judiciary, civil and military, of life and of death, over our persons and over our properties; and in June 1781, again under calamity, the same proposition was repeated, and wanted a few votes only of being passed. One who entered into this contest from a pure love of liberty, and a sense of injured rights, who determined to make every sacrifice, and to meet every danger, for the re-establishment of those rights on a firm basis, who did not mean to expend his blood and substance for the wretched purpose of changing this matter for that, but to place the powers of governing him in a plurality of hands of his own choice, so that the corrupt will of no one man might in future oppress him, must stand confounded and dismayed when he is told, that a considerable portion of that plurality had mediated the surrender of them into a single hand, and, in lieu of a limited monarchy, to deliver him over to a despotic one! * * * In God's name, from whence have they derived this power? * * * Is it from any principle in our new constitution expressed or implied? Every lineament, expressed or implied, is in full opposition to it. Its fundamental principle is, that the State shall be governed as a commonwealth. It provides a republican organization, proscribes under the name of prerogative the exercise of all powers undefined by the laws; places on this basis the whole system of our laws * * *. Our ancient laws expressly declare, that those who are but delegates themselves shall not delegate to others powers which require judgment and integrity in their exercise. * * * They never admit the idea that [the people] like sheep or cattle, may be given from hand to hand without an appeal to their own will. Was it from the necessity of the case? Necessities which dissolve a government, do not convey its authority to an oligarchy or a monarchy. They throw back, into the hands of the people, the powers they had delegated, and leave them as individuals to shift for themselves. A leader may offer, but not impose himself, nor be imposed on them. * * * The necessity which should operate these tremendous effects should at least be palpable and irresistible. Yet in

both instances, where it was feared, or pretended with us, it was be-
lied by the event.   *   *   *

In this State alone did there exist so little virtue, that fear was
to be fixed in the hearts of the people, and to become the motive of
their exertions, and principle of their government? The very thought
alone was treason against the people; was treason against mankind
in general; as rivetting forever the chains which bow down their
necks, by giving to their oppressors a proof, which they would have
trumpeted through the universe, of the imbecility of republican government, in times of pressing danger, to shield them from harm.
*   *   *   What a cruel moment was this for creating such an embarrassment, for putting to the proof the attachment of our countrymen
to republican government! Those who meant well, of the advocates
of this measure, (and most of them meant well, for I know them personally   *   *   *) had been seduced in their judgment by the example of an ancient republic, whose constitution and circumstances
were fundamentally different. They had sought this precedent in the
history of Rome   *   *   *. They had taken it from a republic rent
by the most bitter factions and tumults where the government was
of a heavy-handed unfeeling aristocracy, over a people ferocious, and
rendered desperate by poverty and wretchedness; tumults which could
not be allayed under the most trying circumstances, but by the omnipotent hand of a single despot. Their constitution, therefore, allowed a temporary tyrant to be erected, under the name of a dictator;
and that temporary tyrant, after a few examples, became perpetual.
They misapplied this precedent to a people mild in their dispositions,
patient under their trial, united for the public liberty, and affectionate to their leaders.   *   *   *   Searching for the foundations of this
proposition, I can find none which may pretend a color of right or
reason, but the defect before developed, that there being no barrier
between the legislative, executive, and judiciary departments, the legislature may seize the whole; that having seized it, and possessing a
right to fix their own quorum, they may reduce that quorum to one,
whom they may call a chairman, speaker, dictator, or by any other
name they please.   *   *   *

NOTES AND QUESTIONS

1. Based on what you have just read, do you think Thomas Jefferson
would have voted for the adoption of the *Pennsylvania* constitution of 1776?
What does Jefferson see as the chief defect of the Virginia Constitution
of 1776? What does he mean when he suggests several times that the
Virginia Assembly has the potential to be despotic? Why does he believe
that there must be different houses in a legislature, and they must be differently chosen? Would the framers of the Pennsylvania Constitution of
1776 have agreed with him?

2. Why is Jefferson disturbed that the Virginia legislature possesses
the power to amend the Constitution? What might he prefer as an alter-

native means of amendment? Why do you suppose, in an explanation of the workings of the Virginia Constitution, Jefferson feels that it is necessary to discuss the two bizarre episodes when the Virginia Assembly considered the creation of a "Dictator?" What heuristic purpose is to be served by the allusion to the practice in ancient Rome? What does it reveal about Jefferson's attitude toward the American people?

3. Jefferson's thoughts on the nature of Americans are perhaps more clearly stated in the excerpt which follows, from the next section of the Notes on Virginia, dealing with the revision of the Virginia substantive laws undertaken in 1776. Jefferson was the leading figure in the revisal. See Generally "Editorial Note," II The Papers of Thomas Jefferson 305–324 (Julian P. Boyd, ed. 1950), and Edward Dumbauld, Thomas Jefferson and the Law (1979).

3. JEFFERSON'S NOTES ON THE STATE OF VIRGINIA (CONTINUED)

The plan of the revisal was this. The common law of England, by which is meant, that part of the English law which was anterior to the date of the oldest statutes extant, is made the basis of the work. It was thought dangerous to attempt to reduce it to a text; it was therefore left to be collected from the usual monuments of it. Necessary alterations in that, and so much of the whole body of the British statutes, and of acts of assembly, as were thought proper to be retained, were digested into one hundred and twenty-six new acts, in which simplicity of style was aimed at, as far as was safe. The following are the most remarkable alterations proposed:

To change the rules of descent, so as that the lands of any person dying intestate shall be divisible equally among all his children, or other representatives, in equal degree.

To make slaves distributable among the next of kin, as other movables.

* * *

To establish religious freedom on the broadest bottom.

To emancipate all slaves born after the passing the act. The bill reported by the revisers does not itself contain this proposition; but an amendment containing it was prepared, to be offered to the legislature whenever the bill should be taken up, and farther directing, that they should continue with their parents to a certain age, then to be brought up, at the public expense, to tillage, arts, or sciences, according to their geniuses, till the females should be eighteen, and the males twenty-one years of age, when they should be colonized to such place as the circumstances of the time should render most proper, sending them out with arms, implements of household and of the handicraft arts, seeds, pairs of the useful domestic animals, &c., to declare them a free and independent people, and extend to them our alliance and protection, till they have acquired strength; and to send vessels at the same time to other parts of the world for an equal number of white inhabitants; to induce them to migrate hither, proper encouragements were to be proposed. It will probably be asked, Why not retain and incorporate the blacks into the State, and thus save the expense of supplying by importation of white settlers, the vacancies they will leave? Deep-rooted prejudices entertained by the whites; ten thousand recollections, by the blacks, of the injuries they have sustained; new provocations; the real distinctions which nature has made; and many other circumstances, will divide us into parties, and produce convulsions, which will probably never end but in the extermination of the one or the other race. To these objections, which are political, may be added others, which are physical and moral. The first difference which strikes us is that of color. * * * And is this difference of no importance? Is it not the foundation of a greater or less share of beauty in the two races? Are not the fine mixtures of red and white, the expressions of every passion by greater or less suffusions of color in the one, preferable to that eternal monotony, which reigns in the countenances, that immovable veil of black which covers the emotions of the other race? Add to these, flowing hair, a more elegant symmetry of form, their own judgment in favor of the whites, declared by their preference of them * * *. The circumstance of superior beauty, is thought worthy attention in the propagation of our horses, dogs, and other domestic animals; why not in that of man? * * * They have less hair on the face and body. They secrete less by the kidneys, and more by the glands of the skin, which gives them a very strong and disagreeable odor. This greater degree of transpiration, renders them more tolerant of heat, and less so of cold than the whites. * * * They seem to require less sleep. A black after hard labor through the day, will be induced by the slightest amusements to sit up till midnight, or later, though knowing he must be out with the first dawn of the morning. They are at least as brave, and more adventuresome. But this may perhaps proceed from a want of forethought, which prevents their seeing a danger till it be present. When present, they do not go through it with more coolness or steadiness than the whites. They are more ardent after their female; but love seems with them to be more an eager desire, than a tender delicate mixture of sentiment and sensation. Their griefs are transient. * * * In general, their existence appears to participate more of sensation than reflection. To this must be ascribed their disposition to sleep when abstracted from their diversions, and unemployed in labor. * * * Comparing them by their faculties of memory, reason, and imagination, it appears to me that in memory they are equal to the whites: in reason much inferior, as I think one could scarcely be found capable of tracing and comprehending the investigations of Euclid; and that in imagination they are dull, tasteless, and anomalous. * * * It will be right to make great allowances for the difference of condition, of education, of conversation, of the sphere in which they move. Many millions of them have been brought to, and born in America. Most of them, indeed, have been confined to tillage, to their own homes, and their own society; yet many have been so situated, that they might have availed themselves of the conversation of their masters * * *. Some have been liberally educated, and all have lived in countries where the arts and sciences are cultivated to a considerable degree, and all have had before their eyes samples of the best works from abroad. The Indians, with no advantages of this kind, will often carve figures on their pipes not destitute of design and merit. They will crayon out an animal, a plant, or a country, so as to prove the existence of a germ in their minds which only wants cultivation. They astonish you with strokes of the most sublime oratory; such as prove their reason and sentiment strong, their imagination glowing and elevated. But never yet could I find that a black had uttered a thought above the level of plain narration; never saw even an elementary trait of painting or sculpture. In music they are more generally gifted than the whites with accurate ears for tune and time, and they have been found capable of imagining a small catch. Whether they will be equal to the composition of a more extensive run of melody, or of complicated harmony, is yet to be proved. Misery is often the parent of the most affecting touches in poetry. Among the blacks is misery enough, God knows, but no poetry. Love is the peculiar oestrum of the poet. Their love is ardent, but it kindles the senses only, not the imagination. * * * The improvement of the blacks in body and mind, in the first instance of their mixture with the whites, has been observed by everyone, and proves that their inferiority is not the effect merely of their condition of life. We know that among the Romans, about the Augustan age especially, the condition of their slaves was much more deplorable than that of the blacks on the continent of America. The two sexes were confined in separate apartments, because to raise a child cost the master more than to buy one. Cato, for a very restricted indulgence to his slaves in this particular, took from them a certain price. But in this country the slaves multiply as fast as the free inhabitants. Their situation and manners place the commerce between the two sexes almost without restraint. The same Cato, on a principle of economy, always sold his sick and superannuated slaves. * * * The American slaves cannot enumerate this among the injuries and insults they receive. It was the common practice to expose in the island Aesculapius, in the Tyber, diseased slaves whose cure was like to become tedious. The emperor Claudius, by an edict, gave freedom to such of them as should recover, and first declared that if any person chose to kill rather than to expose them, it should not be deemed homicide. The exposing them is a crime of which no instance has existed with us; and were it to be followed by death, it would be punished capitally. We are told of a certain Vedius Pollio, who, in the presence of Augustus, would have given a slave as food to his fish, for having broken a glass. With the Romans, the regular method of taking the evidence of their slaves was under torture. Here it has been thought better never to resort to their evidence. When a master was murdered, all his slaves, in the same house or within hearing, were condemned to death. Here punishment falls on the guilty only, and as precise proof is required against him as against a freeman. Yet notwithstanding these and other discouraging circumstances among the Romans, their slaves were often their rarest artists. They excelled too in science, insomuch as to be usually employed as tutors to their master's children. Epictetus, Terence, and Phaedrus, were slaves. But they were of the race of whites. It is not their condition then, but nature, which has produced the distinction. Whether further observation will or will not verify the conjecture, that nature has been less bountiful to them in the endowments of the head, I believe that in those of the heart she will be found to have done them justice. That disposition to theft with which they have been branded, must be ascribed to their situation, and not to any depravity of the moral sense. The man in whose favor no laws of property exist, probably feels himself less bound to respect those made in favor of others. When arguing for ourselves, we lay it down as a fundamental, that laws, to be just, must give a reciprocation of right; that, without this, they are mere arbitrary rules of conduct, founded in force, and not in conscience; and it is a problem which I give to the master to solve, whether the religious precepts against the violation of property were not framed for him as well as his slave? And whether the slave may not as justifiably take a little from one who has taken all from him, as he may slay one who would slay him? * * * Notwithstanding these considerations which must weaken their respect for the laws of property, we find among them numerous instances of the most rigid integrity, and as many as among their better instructed masters, of benevolence, gratitude, and unshaken fidelity. The opinion that they are inferior in the faculties of reason and imagination, must be hazarded with great diffidence. To justify a general conclusion, requires many observations, even where the subject may be submitted to the anatomical knife, to optical glasses, to analysis by fire or by solvents. How much more then where it is a faculty, not a substance, we are examining; where it eludes the research of all the senses * * * let me add too, as a circumstance of great tenderness, where our conclusion would degrade a whole race of men from the rank in the scale of beings which their Creator may perhaps have given them. To our reproach it must be said, that though for a century and a half we have had under our eyes the races of black and of red men, they have never yet been viewed by us as subjects of natural history. I advance it, therefore, as a suspicion only, that the blacks, whether originally a distinct race, or made distinct by time and circumstances, are inferior to the whites in the endowments both of body and mind. It is not against experience to suppose that different species of the same genus, or varieties of the same species, may possess different qualifications. * * * This unfortunate difference of color, and perhaps of faculty, is a powerful obstacle to the emancipation of these people. Many of their advocates, while they wish to vindicate the liberty of human nature, are anxious also to preserve its dignity and beauty. Some of these, embarrassed by the question, "What further is to be done with them?" join themselves in opposition with those who are actuated by sordid avarice only. Among the Romans emancipation required but one effort. The slave, when made free, might mix with, without staining the blood of his master. But with us a second is necessary, unknown to history. When freed, he is to be removed beyond the reach of mixture.

The revised code further proposes to proportion crimes and punishments.

This is attempted on the following scale:

I. Crimes whose punishment extends to LIFE.

    1. High treason. Death by hanging.
        Forfeiture of lands and goods to the commonwealth.

    2. Petty treason. Death by hanging. Dissection.
        Forfeiture of half the lands and goods to the representatives of the party slain.

    3. Murder. 1. By poison. Death by poison.
                 Forfeiture of one-half, as before.

           2. In duel. Death by hanging. Gibbeting, if the challenger.
              Forfeiture of one-half as before, unless it be the party challenged, then the forfeiture is to the commonwealth.

           3. In any other way. Death by hanging.
              Forfeiture of one-half as before.

    4. Manslaughter. The second offence is murder.

II. Crimes whose punishment goes to LIMB.

    1. Rape
    2. Sodomy   } Dismemberment.

    3. Maiming
    4. Disfiguring } Retaliation, and the forfeiture of half of the lands and goods to the sufferer.

III. Crimes punishable by LABOR.

    1. Manslaughter, 1st offence.   Labor VII. years for the public.   Forfeiture of half, as in murder.

    2. Counterfeiting money.   Labor VI. years   Forfeiture of lands and goods to the commonwealth.

    3. Arson.
    4. Asportation of vessels. } Labor V. years   Reparation threefold.

5. Robbery.	} Labor IV. years	Reparation double.
6. Burglary.		
7. House-breaking.	} Labor III. years	Reparation.
8. Horse-stealing.		
9. Grand larceny.	Labor II. years	Reparation. Pillory.
10. Petty larceny.	Labor I. year	Reparation. Pillory.
11. Pretensions to witch-craft, &c.	Ducking.	Stripes.
12. Excusable homicide.	} To be pitied, not punished.	
13. Suicide.		
14. Apostasy. Heresy.		

* * *

Another object of the revisal is, to diffuse knowledge more generally through the mass of the people. This bill proposes to lay off every county into small districts of five or six miles square, called hundreds, and in each of them to establish a school for teaching, reading, writing, and arithmetic. The tutor to be supported by the hundred, and every person in it entitled to send their children three years gratis, and as much longer as they please, paying for it. These schools to be under a visitor who is annually to choose the boy of best genius in the school, of those whose parents are too poor to give them further education, and to send him forward to one of the grammar schools, of which twenty are proposed to be erected in different parts of the country, for teaching Greek, Latin, Geography, and the higher branches of numerical arithmetic. Of the boys thus sent in one year, trial is to be made at the grammar schools one or two years, and the best genius of the whole selected, and continued six years, and the residue dismissed. By this means twenty of the best geniuses will be raked from the rubbish annually, and be instructed, at the public expense, so far as the grammar schools go. At the end of six years instruction, one half are to be discontinued (from among whom the grammar schools will probably be supplied with future masters); and the other half, who are to be chosen for the superiority of their parts and disposition, are to be sent and continued three years in the study of such sciences as they shall choose, at William and Mary college. * * * The ultimate result of the whole scheme of education would be the teaching all the children of the State reading, writing, and common arithmetic; turning out ten annually, of superior genius, well taught in Greek, Latin, Geography, and the higher branches of arithmetic; turning out ten others annually, of still superior parts, who, to those branches of learning, shall have added such of the sciences as their genius shall have led them to; the furnishing to the wealthier part of the people convenient schools at which their children may be educated at their own expense. The general objects of this law are to provide an education adapted to the years, to the capacity, and the con-

dition of everyone, and directed to their freedom and happiness. * * *
The first stage of this education being the schools of the hundreds,
wherein the great mass of the people will receive their instruction, the
principal foundations of future order will be laid here. Instead,
therefore, of putting the Bible and Testament into the hands of the
children at an age when their judgments are not sufficiently matured
for religious inquiries, their memories may here be stored with the
most useful facts from Grecian, Roman, European and American history. The first elements of morality too may be instilled into their
minds; such as, when further developed as their judgments advance
in strength, may teach them how to work out their own greatest happiness, by showing them that it does not depend on the condition of
life in which chance has placed them, but is always the result of a
good conscience, good health, occupation, and freedom in all just pursuits. Those whom either the wealth of their parents or the adoption
of the State shall destine to higher degrees of learning, will go on to
the grammar schools, which constitute the next stage, there to be
instructed in the languages. The learning Greek and Latin, I am told,
is going into disuse in Europe * * * it would be very ill judged
in us to follow their example in this instance. There is a certain period of life, say from eight to fifteen or sixteen years of age, when the
mind like the body is not yet firm enough for laborious and close
operations. * * * The memory is then most susceptible and tenacious of impressions; and the learning of languages being chiefly a
work of memory, it seems precisely fitted to the powers of this period, which is long enough too for acquiring the most useful languages,
ancient and modern. * * * that time is not lost which is employed
in providing tools for future operation; more especially as in this
case the books put into the hands of the youth for this purpose may
be such as will at the same time impress their minds with useful facts
and good principles. * * * As soon as they are of sufficient age,
it is supposed they will be sent on from the grammar schools to the
university, which constitutes our third and last stage, there to study
those sciences which may be adapted to their views. By that part
of our plan which prescribes the selection of the youths of genius from
among the classes of the poor, we hope to avail the State of those
talents which nature has sown as liberally among the poor as the
rich, but which perish without use, if not sought for and cultivated.
But of the views of this law none is more important, none more legitimate, than that of rendering the people the safe, as they are the ultimate, guardians of their own liberty. For this purpose the reading in
the first stage, where they will receive their whole education, is proposed, as has been said, to be chiefly historical. History, by apprizing
them of the past, will enable them to judge of the future; it will avail
them of the experience of other times and other nations; it will qualify them as judges of the actions and designs of men; it will enable
them to know ambition under every disguise it may assume; and

knowing it, to defeat its views. In every government on earth is some trace of human weakness, some germ of corruption and degeneracy, which cunning will discover, and wickedness insensibly open, cultivate and improve. Every government degenerates when trusted to the rulers of the people alone. The people themselves therefore are its only safe depositories. And to render even them safe, their minds must be improved to a certain degree. * * * An amendment of our constitution must here come in aid of the public education. The influence over government must be shared among all the people. If every individual which composes their mass participates of the ultimate authority, the government will be safe; because the corrupting the whole mass will exceed any private resources of wealth * * *. The government of Great Britain has been corrupted, because but one man in ten has a right to vote for members of parliament. The sellers of the government, therefore, get nine-tenths of their price clear. It has been thought that corruption is restrained by confining the right of suffrage to a few of the wealthier of the people; but it would be more effectually restrained by an extension of that right to such numbers as would bid defiance to the means of corruption.

Lastly, it is proposed, by a bill in this revisal, to begin a public library and gallery, by laying out a certain sum annually in books, paintings, and statues.

* * *

NOTES AND QUESTIONS

1. Why is it that the basis of Virginia law is still principally to be the English common law? Why is it that Jefferson wishes to change some parts and not others? Why, for example, change the common law rules of descent? Did the old common law rules reflect principles "inconsistent with republicanism?" What is meant by "republicanism?" Why was Jefferson opposed to the reducing of law "to a text;" an enterprise which he regarded as "dangerous?"

2. While Jefferson appears to have hoped for eventual emancipation of slaves, the Committee of Revisors reported a draft bill to the legislature which, in effect, perpetuated bondage. On the substance of the proposed law, see J. Noonan, Persons and Masks of the Law 51–54 (1976). Can you determine from this excerpt why Jefferson favored emancipation? What do you make of Jefferson's explanation of the necessity for "colonizing" emancipated Blacks? What conclusions does Jefferson reach regarding differences between the races? Do you find him consistent on this point throughout this passage? How, if at all, do you reconcile Jefferson's comments on Blacks with his assertion in the Declaration of Independence that "all men are created equal?"

3. Can it be said that Jefferson thinks little of the qualities of Blacks when he suggests that if "nature has been less bountiful to them in the endowments of the head, I believe that in those of the heart she will have been found to have done them justice?" What does Jefferson mean by "justice?"

4. Why do you suppose that in this section of the Notes on Virginia, a section that is supposed to be concerned with the substantive revisions in Virginia law, Jefferson spends most of his time discussing slaves? Of what relevance is the discussion contrasting American practice regarding slaves with that of Greece and Rome?

5. Do you find any philosophical similarities among Jefferson's comments on the nature of American slaves, his ideas on the appropriate punishments for crimes and his views on public education? What is the reasoning behind the plan to "proportion crimes and punishments?" Is there an ideological dimension to this plan as well; does it have any bearing on Jefferson's conception of humankind and the proper ends of government amplified in his draft of the Declaration of Independence? What does it mean that the plan of the proposed educational system "is to provide an education adapted to the years, to the capacity, and the condition of everyone?" What does "condition" mean? Does Jefferson's suggestion that by means of his scheme "twenty of the best geniuses will be raked from the rubbish annually" tell you anything about his social views? Yet can these views necessarily be described as "anti-republican?" What value, then, was education? Why, by the way, does Jefferson want Americans to learn Greek and Latin if Europeans have found it no longer necessary?

6. Jefferson is one of the most intriguing of America's historical figures. At one time or another he expressed an opinion on almost everything, and he has been cited to support innumerable causes, many of them in opposition to each other. Merrill Peterson's Jeffersonian Image in the American Mind (1960), Daniel Boorstin's The Lost World of Thomas Jefferson (1948), and Edmund Morgan's recent and provocative American Slavery—American Freedom (1975) are good starting places for understanding Jefferson as an eighteenth century enlightenment product. Fawn Brodie's popular analysis of Jefferson's supposed relationship with his slave, Sally Hemings, helps illuminate the complexities and contradictions in Jefferson's thinking about Blacks, Thomas Jefferson: An Intimate History (1974). Edward Dumbauld, Thomas Jefferson and the Law (1978), and John T. Noonan, Jr., Persons and Masks of the Law (1976), contain valuable materials on Jefferson's legal activities and social views during the Revolutionary era. Jefferson's rationalism in his proposals for reforming criminal law follows the thinking of the Italian, Cesare Beccaria, whose influence extended throughout Europe and influenced Blackstone, Bentham, and John Adams. See, e. g. Beccaria, On Crimes and Punishments (Paolucci, trans. 1963).

Chapter 2

FEDERALISM VERSUS REPUBLICANISM IN THE COURTS: CONCEPTIONS OF NATIONAL LAW

SECTION A.   THE FEDERALIST PERSUASION

If the conflict between colonial patriots and high-handed Parliamentarians taught the Americans anything, it was that absolute power corrupted absolutely.   At the root of the perceived oppression of the colonies was the "sovereign" Parliament, a body answerable only to itself.   The state and national governments erected during the War for Independence reflected this new political wisdom.   The Pennsylvania constitution, as we have seen, practically obliterated the executive authority in the name of liberty.   Still, most of the new state constitutions followed Virginia's example, allowing governors, but hedging executive power.   Many restricted their governors to one-year terms; some denied governors the veto power over legislation; and, in eight states, governors were selected by members of the legislature.   Real power in the new United States thus resided in the assemblies, the branches of government ostensibly closest to the people.   Unlike the English Parliament, it was believed, the American people themselves were able to maintain their sovereignty over their legislative bodies.

The Articles of Confederation formed the basis of the new national government, and were ratified by the states in 1781.   The Articles recognized that "Each state" was to "retain its sovereignty, freedom, and independence."   The new national government lacked coercive powers, could merely request funds from the states, had no control over interstate commerce or the money supply, and had no powerful chief executive or effective judiciary.   The national government implemented under the articles was to be more an advisory than a ruling body.   If effective national government under the Articles was difficult, however, it was so by design.   Few wished to see a strong central government while memories of the abuses that led to the Revolution were still fresh.

Events in the 1780's forced some to alter their opinions about the virtues of limited central power.   Post-war periods are usually times of economic turmoil and adjustment.   The war had disrupted agriculture, interrupted trade, and raised staggering public debts.   States attempted to finance the Revolutionary War by selling securities to their citizens.   But, after the war, the new states were reluctant to levy unpopular taxes to repay their obligations.   The Treaty of

Paris (1781), which ended the war, required the states to recognize the pre-war claims of British citizens and to compensate loyalists for their property which had been confiscated by patriot state governments. Following the treaty, an unfavorable balance of trade (as imports far overtook exports) aggravated the economic situation, as gold and silver flowed from the country. Under these circumstances few foreign governments or banks were willing to grant American state or national governments the loans needed to rekindle the economy. The states responded by issuing paper currency with each negative fluctuation of the business cycle, in such quantities that the currencies depreciated almost daily. "Rag money," it came to be called; in effect it allowed debtors to repay loans at a reduced rate, but the uncertain value of money badly hampered American trade.

Agrarian and backcountry elements removed from the market economy and from centers of commerce and transportation saw no great cause for alarm in these developments. A certain amount of economic disorganization may have been seen as the price of liberty. But when economic instability began to mix with the spectre of popular rebellion, the situation took on an alarming aspect. In 1786–87, one Daniel Shays, a former officer in Washington's Continental Army, gathered a force in excess of one thousand men (many former revolutionary soldiers) and proceeded to close down the courts in the western counties of Massachusetts. Law enforcement in that area ceased.

The "Shaysites" acted because they resented the high burden of taxes imposed on already distressed farmers and the zeal of courts in collecting private debts. Merchants in Boston raised money for a military expedition to restore order, but only after seven months were the insurgents routed. Similar, though less spectacular, incidents occurred in other states. Added to the disorder was a growing cacaphony of criticism directed at the young state assemblies. "We daily see laws repealed or suspended," went one charge, "before any trial can be made of their merits, and even before a knowledge of them can have reached the remoter districts within which they were to operate." A prominent New York politician exclaimed that "the people do not exhibit the virtue that is necessary to support a republican government." An observer of North Carolina politics was more blunt. He described that state's session laws as "the vilest collection of trash ever framed by a legislative body." Much of this criticism was prompted by state legislative attempts to suspend or obliterate contractual debts. In the turmoil, moderates and conservatives alike began to fear that the great republican experiment was on the verge of collapsing.

Historians now doubt that affairs in America were as precarious as they seemed. Most of the states appear to have experienced modest growth and comparative prosperity despite the economic difficulties, while social discontent may never have run as deeply as alarmists claimed. Nor did the young state legislatures compile only abysmal records. Virginia's revisal of her colonial laws, for example, was a model of circumspection. Nevertheless, contemporaries persisted in seeing these years as a "critical period," and a growing number of nationalists called for a new central government that could arrest the perceived decline. They sought a structure with the military might to preserve the social order; a government sufficiently strong to bring the economy under control, to negotiate favorable trade agreements with foreign nations, and to tap the collective resources of the states.

In Philadelphia, in May of 1787, with news of Shay abroad, a meeting of delegates from every state but Rhode Island took place. The conferees were charged with finding a way to amend the Articles of Confederation to make the government more effective. Instead, the convention reported out an entirely new plan of government, a Constitution which created a national republic. The proposed Constitution was the product of many compromises, especially between smaller and larger and between slave-holding and free states. Still, there was a central vision of government implicit in the document which has led some historians to refer to the Philadelphia Constitutional Convention as a "second American Revolution." The new Constitution provided for a bicameral national legislature and co-equal executive and judicial branches of government. It gave the national legislature, congress, the power to levy taxes, to coin and borrow money, to regulate interstate commerce, to raise an army, to create a federal court system, and to "make all Laws which shall be necessary and proper for carrying into execution" its enumerated powers. The document also circumscribed the workings of the state legislatures, forbidding them, *inter alia*, from abridging existing contractual rights.

The Constitution created a national chief executive with a veto power over legislation, command of the national armed forces, freedom to conduct foreign affairs, and vast appointive powers. The Constitution, then, rejected the assumptions of the political theory which had generated the "first" American Revolution, when it placed considerable power in the hands of a centralized government.

The struggle for ratification of the proposed national Constitution occupied national political life for the next several months. The so-called "Anti-Federalists" opposed ratification. They objected to the proposal for a strong central government, and railed against the absence of any Bill of Rights. Some Anti-Federalists also accused the Convention delegates of harboring monarchical and aristocratic sympathies. Nor were these opponents confident that an American national republic could survive free. The conventional political wisdom, supplied principally from ancient history, limited the successful operation of free republics to small geographical areas; to attempt a large-scale republic, they feared, would risk anarchy or despotism, and might thus spell the end of liberty.

The "Federalists," the proponents of ratification, at first claimed that a Bill of Rights was unnecessary, since the powers of the new national government were to be limited and enumerated. Nevertheless, they eventually pledged their support for Constitutional amendments to guarantee basic liberties. To the charge of secretly harboring anti-republican sympathies, the Federalists responded that by separating, checking and disbursing power, as their Constitution would, a balanced republican polity could be created. James Madison, in the Federalist, turned the conventional position of republican theory on its head when he argued that a national republic would actually better preserve liberty, because the clash of interests in as vast a land as America would prevent any faction from dominating the government. Finally, the Federalists reminded their critics that they were simply *proposing* a constitution. They were leaving to "the people," meeting in popularly constituted state conventions, the task of ratification of the document. The Federalists argued that the people ought to accept their proposal, because their Constitution would implement a government strong enough to meet the needs of the times, but limited enough to ensure the preservation of individual liberty and essential state sovereignty.

The Constitution was finally ratified by the requisite number of states in 1789. But the political divisions which were manifest in the debate over ratification persisted, although in somewhat altered forms. Thomas Jefferson and Alexander Hamilton both served in President Washington's first cabinet, but held divergent views on national priorities. The differences between these two men, and the factions that formed around them (the Jeffersonian "Republicans" and the Hamiltonian "Federalists") were more than political. Hamiltonian policies favored commerce and manufacturing as well as a vigorous central government. Jeffersonian desires were more in the direction of limited government in a prosperous but stable agrarian economy. These differences determined these groups' differing visions of the future, their attitudes toward popular authority, and their regard for the functions of a judicial system in a republic. For the 1790's the Federalists held the balance of power: they occupied the Presidency and appointed Federalists to the national bench. In the following documents we will study these divergent views in the context of the early operation of the national judiciary. We begin with an excerpt from the Federalist, authored by Alexander Hamilton, and directed at the voters of New York. This material concerns judicial tenure under the proposed federal constitution.

1. ALEXANDER HAMILTON ON THE FEDERAL JUDICIARY

"PUBLIUS" [ALEXANDER HAMILTON], THE FEDERALIST PAPERS *

464–491; 520–527 (Clinton Rossiter, ed. 1961).

No. 78

* * *

* * * [A]ll judges who may be appointed by the United States are to hold their offices during good behavior; which is conformable to the most approved of the State constitutions, and among the rest, to that of this State. Its propriety having been drawn into question by the adversaries of that plan is no light symptom of the rage for objection which disorders their imaginations and judgments. The standard of good behavior for the continuance in office of the judicial magistracy is certainly one of the most valuable of the modern improvements in the practice of government. In a monarchy it is an excellent barrier to the despotism of the prince; in a republic it is a no less excellent barrier to the encroachments and oppressions of the representative body. And it is the best expedient which can be devised in any government to secure a steady, upright, and impartial administration of the laws.

Whoever attentively considers the different departments of power must perceive that, in a government in which they are separated from each other, the judiciary, from the nature of its functions, will always be the least dangerous to the political rights of the Constitution; because it will be least in a capacity to annoy or injure them. The executive not only dispenses the honors but holds the sword of the community. The legislature not only commands the purse but prescribes the rules by which the duties and rights of every citizen are to be regulated. The judiciary, on the contrary, has no influence over either the sword or the purse; no direction either of the strength or of the wealth of the society, and can take no active resolution whatever. It may truly be said to have neither FORCE nor WILL but merely judgment; and must ultimately depend upon the aid of the executive arm even for the efficacy of its judgments.

* * * [T]he judiciary is beyond comparison the weakest of the three departments of power; * * * it can never attack with success either of the other two; and * * * all possible care is requisite to enable it to defend itself against their attacks. * * * [T]hough individual oppression may now and then proceed from the courts of justice, the general liberty of the people can never be endan-

---

gered from that quarter; I mean so long as the judiciary remains truly distinct from both the legislature and the executive. For I agree that "there is no liberty if the power of judging be not separated from the legislative and executive powers." * * * * [F]rom the natural feebleness of the judiciary, it is in continual jeopardy of being overpowered, awed, or influenced by its co-ordinate branches; and * * * as nothing can contribute so much to its firmness and independence as permanency in office, this quality may therefore be justly regarded as an indispensable ingredient in its constitution, and, in a great measure, as the citadel of the public justice and the public security.

The complete independence of the courts of justice is peculiarly essential in a limited Constitution. By a limited Constitution, I understand one which contains certain specified exceptions to the legislative authority; such, for instance, as that it shall pass no bills of attainder, no *ex post facto* laws, and the like. Limitations of this kind can be preserved in practice no other way than through the medium of courts of justice, whose duty it must be to declare all acts contrary to the manifest tenor of the Constitution void. Without this, all the reservations of particular rights or privileges would amount to nothing.

Some perplexity respecting the rights of the courts to pronounce legislative acts void, because contrary to the Constitution, has arisen from an imagination that the doctrine would imply a superiority of the judiciary to the legislative power. It is urged that the authority which can declare the acts of another void must necessarily be superior to the one whose acts may be declared void. As this doctrine is of great importance in all the American constitutions, a brief discussion of the grounds on which it rests cannot be unacceptable.

There is no position which depends on clearer principles than that every act of a delegated authority, contrary to the tenor of the commission under which it is exercised, is void. No legislative act, therefore, contrary to the Constitution, can be valid. To deny this would be to affirm that the deputy is greater than his principal; that the servant is above his master; that the representatives of the people are superior to the people themselves * * *.

If it be said that the legislative body are themselves the constitutional judges of their own powers and that the construction they put upon them is conclusive upon the other departments it may be answered that this cannot be the natural presumption where it is not to be collected from any particular provisions in the Constitution. It is not otherwise to be supposed that the Constitution could intend to enable the representatives of the people to substitute their *will* to that of their constituents. It is far more rational to suppose that the courts

* 1 Montesquieu, Spirit of the Laws 181.

were designed to be an intermediate body between the people and the legislature in order, among other things, to keep the latter within the limits assigned to their authority. The interpretation of the laws is the proper and peculiar province of the courts. A constitution is, in fact, and must be regarded by the judges as, a fundamental law. It therefore belongs to them to ascertain its meaning as well as the meaning of any particular act proceeding from the legislative body. If there should happen to be an irreconcilable variance between the two, that which has the superior obligation and validity ought, of course, to be preferred; or, in other words, the Constitution ought to be preferred to the statute, the intention of the people to the intention of their agents.

Nor does this conclusion by any means suppose a superiority of the judicial to the legislative power. It only supposes that the power of the people is superior to both, and that where the will of the legislature, declared in its statutes, stands in opposition to that of the people, declared in the Constitution, the judges ought to be governed by the latter rather than the former. They ought to regulate their decisions by the fundamental laws rather than by those which are not fundamental.

* * *

It can be of no weight to say that the courts, on the pretense of a repugnancy, may substitute their own pleasure to the constitutional intentions of the legislature. This * * * might as well happen in every adjudication upon any * * * statute. The courts must declare the sense of the law; and if they should be disposed to exercise WILL instead of JUDGMENT, the consequence would equally be the substitution of their pleasure to that of the legislative body. The observation, if it proved anything, would prove that there ought to be no judges distinct from that body.

* * *

This independence of the judges is equally requisite to guard the Constitution and the rights of individuals from the effects of those ill humors which the arts of designing men, or the influence of particular conjunctures, sometimes disseminate among the people themselves, and which, though they speedily give place to better information, and more deliberate reflection, have a tendency, in the meantime, to occasion dangerous innovations in the government, and serious oppressions of the minor party in the community. Though [we would never question] * * * that fundamental principle of republican government which admits the right of the people to alter or abolish the established Constitution whenever they find it inconsistent with their happiness; yet it is not to be inferred from this principle that the representatives of the people, whenever a momentary inclination happens to lay hold of a majority of their constituents incompatible with the provisions in the existing Constitution would, on that account, be justifiable in a violation of those provisions; or that the courts would be under a greater obligation to connive at infractions in this shape than when they had proceeded wholly from the cabals of the representative body. Until the people have, by some solemn and authoritative act, annulled or changed the established form, it is binding upon themselves collectively, as well as individually; and no presumption, or even knowledge of their sentiments, can warrant their representatives in a departure from it prior to such an act. But it is easy to see that it would require an uncommon portion of fortitude in the judges to do their duty as faithful guardians of the Constitution, where legislative invasions of it had been instigated by the major voice of the community.

* * * The benefits of the integrity and moderation of the judiciary have already been felt in more States than one; and though they may have displeased those whose sinister expectations they may have disappointed, they must have commanded the esteem and applause of all the virtuous and disinterested. Considerate men of every description ought to prize whatever will tend to beget or fortify that temper in the courts; as no man can be sure that he may not be tomorrow the victim of a spirit of injustice, by which he may be a gainer today. And every man must now feel that the inevitable tendency of such a spirit is to sap the foundations of public and private confidence and to introduce in its stead universal distrust and distress.

* * * Periodical appointments, however regulated, or by whomsoever made, would, in some way or other, be fatal to [the judges'] necessary independence. If the power of making them was committed either to the executive or legislature there would be danger of an improper complaisance to the branch which possessed it; if to both, there would be an unwillingness to hazard the displeasure of either; if to the people, or to persons chosen by them for the special purpose, there would be too great a disposition to consult popularity to justify a reliance that nothing would be consulted but the Constitution and the laws.

* * * It has been frequently remarked with great propriety that a voluminous code of laws is one of the inconveniences necessarily connected with the advantages of a free government. To avoid an arbitrary discretion in the courts, it is indispensable that they should be bound down by strict rules and precedents which serve to define and point out their duty in every particular case that comes before them; and it will readily be conceived from the variety of controversies which grow out of the folly and wickedness of mankind that the records of those precedents must unavoidably swell to a very considerable bulk and must demand long and laborious study to acquire a competent knowledge of them. Hence it is that there can be but few men in the society who will have sufficient skill in the laws to qualify them for the stations of judges. And making the proper deductions for the ordinary depravity of human nature, the number must be still smaller of those who unite the requisite integrity with the requisite knowledge.

These considerations apprise us that the government can have no great option between fit characters; and that a temporary duration in office which would naturally discourage such characters from quitting a lucrative line of practice to accept a seat on the bench would have a tendency to throw the administration of justice into hands less able and less well qualified to conduct it with utility and dignity. * * *

* * * The experience of Great Britain affords an illustrious comment on the excellence of the institution [of good behavior tenure.]

No. 79

Next to permanency in office, nothing can contribute more to the independence of the judges than a fixed provision for their support. The remark made in relation to the President is equally applicable here. In the general course of human nature, *a power over a man's subsistence amounts to a power over his will.* And we can never hope to see realized in practice the complete separation of the judicial from the legislative power, in any system which leaves the former dependent for pecuniary resources on the occasional grants of the latter. * * * The plan of the convention accordingly has provided that the judges of the United States "shall at *stated times* receive for their services a compensation which shall not be *diminished* during their continuance in office."

* * *

The precautions for their responsibility are comprised in the article respecting impeachments. They are liable to be impeached for malconduct by the House of Representatives and tried by the Senate; and, if convicted, may be dismissed from office and disqualified for holding any other. This is the only provision on the point which is consistent with the necessary independence of the judicial character, and is the only one which we find in our own Constitution in respect to our own judges.

* * *

The constitution of New York, to avoid investigations that must forever be vague and dangerous, has taken a particular age as the criterion of inability. No man can be a judge beyond sixty. I believe there are few at present who do not disapprove of this provision. There is no station in relation to which it is less proper than to that of a judge. The deliberating and comparing faculties generally preserve their strength much beyond that period in men who survive it; and when, in addition to this circumstance, we consider how few there are who outlive the season of intellectual vigor and how improbable it is that any considerable portion of the bench, whether more or less numerous, should be in such a situation at the same time, we shall be ready to conclude that limitations of this sort have little to recommend them. In a republic where fortunes are not affluent and pensions not expedient, the dismission of men from stations in which they have served their country long and usefully, on which they depend for subsistence, and from which it will be too late to resort to any other occupation for a livelihood, ought to have some better apology to humanity than is to be found in the imaginary danger of a superannuated bench.

No. 80

[Objects of the Federal Judiciary]

* * *

It seems scarcely to admit of controversy that the judiciary authority of the Union ought to extend to these several descriptions of cases: 1st, to all those which arise out of the laws of the United States * * * ; 2nd, to all those which concern the execution of the provisions expressly contained in the articles of Union; 3rd, to all those in which the United States are a party; 4th, to all those which involve the PEACE of the CONFEDERACY, whether they relate to the intercourse between the United States and foreign nations or to that between the States themselves; 5th, to all those which originate on the high seas, and are of admiralty or maritime jurisdiction; and lastly, to all those in which the State tribunals cannot be supposed to be impartial and unbiased.

* * * The States, * * * are prohibited from doing a variety of things, some of which are incompatible with the interests of the Union and others with the principles of good government. The imposition of duties on imported articles and the emission of paper money are specimens of each kind. No man of sense will believe that such prohibitions would be scrupulously regarded without some effectual power in the government to restrain or correct the infractions of them. This power must either be a direct negative on the State laws, or an authority in the federal courts to overrule such as might be in manifest contravention of the articles of Union. There is no third course that I can imagine. The latter apears to have been thought by the convention preferable to the former, and I presume will be most agreeable to the States.

* * * If there are such things as political axioms, the propriety of the judicial power of a government being coextensive with its legislative may be ranked among the number. The mere necessity of uniformity in the interpretation of the national laws decides the question. Thirteen independent courts of final jurisdiction over the same causes, arising upon the same laws, is a hydra in government from which nothing but contradiction and confusion can proceed.

* * * Controversies between the nation and its members or citizens can only be properly referred to the national tribunals. Any other plan would be contrary to reason, to precedent, and to decorum.

* * *

A method of terminating territorial disputes between the States, under the authority of the federal head, was not unattended to, even in the imperfect system by which they have been hitherto held together. But there are many other sources, besides interfering claims of boundary, from which bickerings and animosities may spring up among the members of the Union. * * * It will readily be conjectured that I allude to the fraudulent laws which have been passed in too many of the States. And though the proposed Constitution establishes particular guards against the repetition of those instances which have heretofore made their appearance, yet it is warrantable to apprehend that the spirit which produced them will assume new shapes that could not be foreseen nor specifically provided against. Whatever practices may have a tendency to disturb the harmony between the States are proper objects of federal superintendence and control.

* * * [I]f it be a just principle that every government ought to possess the means of executing its own provisions by its own authority it will follow that in order [for] * * * the inviolable maintenance of that equality of privileges and immunities to which the citizens of the Union will be entitled, the national judiciary ought to preside in all cases in which one State or its citizens are opposed to another State or its citizens. To secure the full effect of so fundamental a provision against all evasion and subterfuge, it is necessary that its construction should be committed to that tribunal which, having no local attachments, will be likely to be impartial between the different States and their citizens and which, owing its official existence to the Union, will never be likely to feel any bias inauspicious to the principles on which it is founded.

* * * The most bigoted idolizers of State authority have not thus far shown a disposition to deny the national judiciary the cognizance of maritime cases. These so generally depend on the laws of nations and so commonly affect the rights of foreigners that they fall within the considerations which are relative to the public peace. * * *

The reasonableness of the agency of the national courts in cases in which the State tribunals cannot be supposed to be impartial speaks for itself. No man ought certainly to be a judge in his own cause, or in any cause in respect to which he has the least interest or bias. * * * Claims to land under grants of different States, founded upon adverse pretensions of boundary, are of this description. The courts of neither of the granting States could be expected to be unbiased. The laws may have even prejudged the question and tied the courts down to decisions in favor of the grants of the State to which they belonged. And even where this had not been done, it would be natural that the judges, as men, should feel a strong predilection to the claims of their own government.

* * *

NOTES AND QUESTIONS

1. Why is it true that "there is no liberty if the power of judging be not separated from the legislative and executive powers?" What exactly is *good behavior* tenure? What was the role of judicial tenure in the colonies? Why would good behavior tenure be popular then, and perhaps less so later among groups such as the Anti-Federalists? Note the idea of the judiciary serving as a barrier to both the monarchy (in England) and the legislature (in America). In a republic why do you need a barrier between the people and the legislature? What view does Hamilton have of humankind, and what bearing does this have on his thinking about a national judiciary? Hamilton appears to believe that the judiciary is the weakest and the least dangerous branch of government. Why might he think this, and what does he offer as proof? Do you agree?

2. Why is the necessity for judicial review a self-evident truth in a society with a "limited Constitution?" Incidentally, can you understand what would be meant by a Constitution that would be "unlimited?" What, if anything, does judicial review have to do with popular sovereignty? According to Hamilton, what kind of men should staff the national judiciary? What rules and procedures ought to guide their decision-making? What objections might an Anti-Federalist or a radical republican theorist have to Hamilton's proposals? Is judicial review necessarily a conservative or a liberal doctrine?

3. Do you agree with Hamilton's argument in Federalist 78 that the process of impeachment is a sufficient guarantee of judicial "competence?" What else is it a guarantee of? Do you think that Hamilton would have it apply *only* to questions of competence? Why does Hamilton note in this connection that the United States is a republic "where fortunes are not affluent and pensions not expedient?" Do you think that Hamilton expects the United States to remain this kind of a republic for very long?

4. In Federalist 80, Hamilton argues, *inter alia*, the need for national tribunals to resolve controversies between the nation and its members or citizens, but his argument seems not very detailed, relying instead on first principles. Do you think that jurisdiction would be necessarily so limited as Hamilton implies? Why might this trouble an Anti-Federalist? Concerning the controversies between the nation and its members or citizens, why would it be contrary to "reason, to precedent, and to decorum" to have state courts resolve these matters? What does Hamilton mean by "decorum"? What do you take to be Hamilton's opinion of state courts? Why? Would Hamilton's arguments be weaker or stronger if it turned out that Federal district judges were usually citizens of the states in which their courts sat?

5. The Federalist papers which are excerpted here were originally published in New York newspapers and were designed to persuade the New Yorkers to approve the proposed Federal Constitution. Why do you think that Alexander Hamilton and his co-authors, Madison and Jay, instead of signing their own names, wrote as "Publius?" In this connection, note that much of these Federalist papers was devoted to stressing the need for quick action of approval of the proposed constitution, as it then existed, leaving the constitutional amendment process to correct remaining errors.

Why the rush? Consider these excerpts from the concluding paper, Federalist 85, and see if they sound familiar:

> The additional securities to republican government, to liberty, and to property, to be derived from the adoption of the plan under consideration, consist chiefly in the restraints which the preservation of the Union will impose on local factions and insurrections, and on the ambition of powerful individuals in single States who might acquire credit and influence enough from leaders and favorites to become the despots of the people; in the diminution of the opportunities to foreign intrigue, which the dissolution of the Confederacy would invite and facilitate; in the prevention of extensive military establishments, which could not fail to grow out of wars between the States in a disunited situation; in the express guaranty of a republican form of government to each; in the absolute and universal exclusion of titles of nobility; and in the precautions against the repetition of those practices on the part of the State governments which have undermined the foundations of property and credit, have planted mutual distrust in the breasts of all classes of citizens, and have occasioned an almost universal prostration of morals.

*   *   *

> I shall not dissemble that I feel an entire confidence in the arguments which recommend the proposed system [but,] *   *   * I am persuaded that it is the best which our political situation, habits, and opinions will admit, and superior to any the revolution has produced.

> Concessions on the part of the friends of the plan that it has not a claim to absolute perfection have afforded matter of no small triumph to its enemies. "Why," say they, "should we adopt an imperfect thing? Why not amend it and make it perfect before it is irrevocably established?" *   *   * This, as far as I have understood the meaning of those who make the concessions, is an entire perversion of their sense. No advocate of the measure can be found who will not declare as his sentiment that the system, though it may not be perfect in every part, is, upon the whole, a good one *   *   *; and is such a one as promises every species of security which a reasonable people can desire.

*   *   *

> The zeal for attempts to amend, prior to the establishment of the Constitution, must abate in every man who is ready to accede to the truth of the following observations *   *   * "To balance a large state or society *   *   * whether monarchical or republican, on general laws, is a work of so great difficulty that no human genius, however comprehensive, is able, by the mere dint of reason and reflection, to effect it. The judgments of many must unite in the work; EXPERIENCE must guide their labor; TIME must bring it to perfection, and the FEELING of inconveniences must correct the mistakes which they *inevitably* fall into in their first trials and experiments." * These judicious reflections *   *   *

* David Hume, I Essays 128, "The Rise of Arts and Sciences."

ought to put [us] upon [our] guard against hazarding anarchy, civil war, a perpetual alienation of the States from each other, and perhaps the military despotism of a victorious demagogue, in the pursuit of what [we] are not likely to obtain, but from TIME and EXPERIENCE. It may be in me a defect of political fortitude but I acknowledge that I cannot entertain an equal tranquility with those who affect to treat the dangers of a longer continuance in our present situation as imaginary. A NATION, without a NATIONAL GOVERNMENT, is, in my view, an awful spectacle. The establishment of a Constitution, in time of profound peace, by the voluntary consent of a whole people, is a PRODIGY, to the completion of which I look forward with trembling anxiety. * * * I dread the more the consequences of new attempts because I KNOW that POWERFUL INDIVIDUALS, in this and in other States, are enemies to a general national government in every possible shape.

7. With the next group of selections we begin to find out whether the national judiciary evolved along the lines Hamilton promised. As you read these materials, determine whether the Federal judges were performing according to the theory of popular sovereignty that seems to underlie the Federalist papers.

2. A SELECTION FROM THE UNITED STATES DISTRICT COURT FOR THE DISTRICT OF PENNSYLVANIA

(a) THE NATURE OF ADMIRALTY JURISPRUDENCE

RICE ET AL. v. THE POLLY & KITTY

20 Fed.Cas. 666 (1789).

BY THE COURT. The libellants had been cruelly beaten and abused both by the captain and one Shirtliff, the mate * * * insomuch that on account of extreme illusage and dangerous threats, they were obliged to leave the brig at Lisbon in the midst of her voyage, and return to Philadelphia in another vessel; and the principal question was, whether this desertion did not incur a forfeiture of wages under the articles.

* * *

When mariners enter into articles for a voyage, they do not thereby put themselves out of the protection of the laws, or subject their limbs and lives to the capricious passions of a master or his mate. On account of the great charge entrusted to the master, and for the benefit of commerce, the law holds his office in high estimation, and vests him with a great extent of discretionary power. It gives him absolute command over the seamen in all matters concerning their duty and the object of their service, but not an absolute command over their persons. The master has a right to correct a refractory, disobedient mariner; but wherever this right is recognized in the books, moderate chastisement is always express or intended. For the law always watches the exercise of discretionary power with a jealous eye. The relation between a master and his servant or apprentice is such, that of necessity a discretionary authority is allowed by law to the master, yet nothing is more frequent than the intervention of the civil power to dissolve this connection, when the master is found to abuse his authority by undue severity and cruelty. Under such circumstances, the servant is justified in leaving his master. Keeping a servant from meat and drink, or battery, are good causes for a departure from the service. Fitzh.Nat.Brev. 391; 1 Bl.Comm. 428. The shipping articles, indeed, declare that forty-eight hours absence from the vessel, during the voyage, without leave, shall be deemed a total desertion, and incur a forfeiture of wages. But * * * although the sole contract mentioned in these articles on the part of the master or owner, is the payment of wages, yet law and reason will imply other obligations—such as, that the vessel shall be sea-worthy and properly fitted for navigation—that the mariners shall be supplied with sufficient meat and drink, and that they shall be treated with, at least, decent humanity.

From a general review of the testimony, and indeed from the mate's own account, it is manifest that the libellants have been cruelly beaten and abused on board this brig at sundry times, and especially in the port of Lisbon, where the captain found it necessary to take one of them on shore and put him under the care of a surgeon to be cured of the wounds and bruises he had suffered under the chastisement given him by the captain and his mate. The only justifications alleged for this great severity, are a general charge against the mariners of disobedience and insufficiency in their duty, without specifying any particulars, and an appearance of a mutinous combination between them in the port of Lisbon. * * * But what I principally look to, is the general conduct of the mariners on this occasion. Finding themselves so cruelly treated by the mate, they first made their complaint to the captain; instead of obtaining the redress they expected, the captain joined the mate in punishing them still more severely for making this complaint. This extreme severity, together with the declaration of the mate, that he would make them glad to jump overboard before they got to America, seems to have taken away all hope of redress or even safety on board, and the whole crew left the vessel. When on shore, they did not secrete themselves, but frequently sought for and met the captain, and openly demanded their wages and clothes; and finally, they applied to the legal authority at Lisbon, and obtained a process against the captain. This conduct on the part of the mariners, seems to remove every appearance of an intended mutiny or a voluntary desertion. If the suspicion of either had been well founded, why did not the captain apply to the courts of law at Lisbon, to have them secured and tried for their offences. This he did not do, but on the contrary, promised to pay them their wages, and anxiously avoided the process they had taken out against him.

* * * The libellants have not voluntarily deserted, but have been forced from a service in which neither the rights of humanity nor personal safety could be depended upon or even expected.

I adjudge that the libellants have and receive their wages to the time of their leaving the vessel at Lisbon (for this is all the libellants ask for), and that the respondent pay the costs of suit.

(b) THE SOURCES OF ADMIRALTY JURISPRUDENCE

THOMPSON ET AL. v. THE CATHERINA

23 Fed.Cas. 1028 (1795).

[This case, by Judge Richard Peters, relates the American law of admiralty to that of other countries. Pay particular attention to the footnotes; do not memorize the detail, but note the scope of authorities cited.]

This was the case of a foreign ship, which came before the court on a claim for wages by her seamen * * * who by their contracts had engaged to return to the port from which they shipped. * * *

An objection is made * * * to my decision on a point, on which our own municipal laws are silent. This objection * * * obliges me to give my sentiments on the question, 'What laws or rules shall direct or govern the decisions of maritime courts here, in points on which we have no regulations established by our own national legislature?' There are, in most nations concerned in commerce, municipal and local laws relative to contracts with mariners, and other maritime covenants and agreements; though the great leading principles, or outlines, are in all nearly the same. On this account among others, I have avoided taking cognizance, as much as possible, of disputes in which foreign ships and seamen, are concerned. * * * But where the voyage of a foreign ship ended here, or was broken up, and no treaty or compact designated the mode of proceeding, I have permitted suits to be prosecuted. In such cases, I have determined according to the laws of the country to which the ship belonged, if there existed any peculiar variance of difference from those generally prevailing. I have seldom found any very material difference in principle. The laws and customs of Spain, relating to mariners, are more rigid than those of other nations, on similar points. Among other points of variance from other laws, those of Spain grant the master a lien on the ship, for his wages. In the present case, the contract was, in part, with mariners of the United States; and these seamen were to be discharged in an American port. I apply the authority of this court to the case of our own citizens. If by our own municipal laws, there are rules established, our courts are bound exclusively to follow them. But in cases where no such rules are instituted, we must resort to the regulations of other maritime countries, which have stood the test of time and experience, to direct our judgments, as rules of decision. We ought not to betray so much vanity, as to take it for granted, that we could establish more salutary and useful regulations than those which have, for ages, governed the most commercial and powerful nations, and led them to wealth and greatness.

The laws of the Rhodians were followed and adopted by the Romans, in their most prosperous state of commerce and power. Those in the celebrated Consolato del Mare,[3] prevailing in the Mediterranean, and established, in concert with other trading states and countries, by the Venetians and Genoese, in the periods of their naval power and commercial prosperity, are collections of, and improvements on, more ancient customs and laws. Of these, the Amalfitan Code * * * furnished the predominant and most generally received principles.[4] The laws of Oleron occupy now a portion of the famous Black Book of the British Admiralty, which is consulted by all their courts on subjects of maritime and commercial controversy. These laws of Oleron were not entirely of British growth. They were compiled at first * * * by Queen Eleonora, Duchess of Guienne, for her continental dominions, and afterwards improved and enlarged by her son Richard the First, of England, in no small degree from the maritime laws and customs, not only of his own country, but also from the laws and customs prevailing among the continental trading nations. Of these, the Saxons were, at an early period, the most conspicuous and practically intelligent in nautical affairs. They introduced into England their maritime knowledge, as they did some valuable principles of the common law. * * * The maritime ordinances of France (where also the laws of Oleron, or Roll d'Oleron, are in force, and claimed, as of French origin) are very much grounded on the sea laws of other nations, mixed with their own. * * * The laws of the Hanse Towns,[5] are nearly in substance the same with

3. Consolato del Mare. These are the most ancient, celebrated and authentic sea laws, after those of the Rhodians, Greeks, and Romans. * * * As a respectable part of the laws of nations, they have always been received in the English courts of admiralty, and those of this country. Their origin is enveloped in obscurity, though attributed to several nations * * *. Their influence, value and authority, have been appreciated by claims to their origin, set up by various people of maritime countries. Those laws have prevailed in the countries occupying the coasts of the Mediterranean, and in the neighbouring parts of Southern Europe, for centuries. * * * This body of maritime law is a compilation of the best maritime laws then existing, comprising judicial proceedings, principles and decisions, settled by men of great experience and consummate prudence; who, having reason and custom for their guides, established these excellent regulations * * *.

4. The city of Amalfi was situate in what is now called the province of Salerno, in the kingdom of Naples. Nothing great remains of it, but its celebrity for the most extensive commerce of its time, its immense wealth and magnificence, and its great weight in all questions of maritime concern. * * *

5. The laws of the Hanse Towns were published first in 1591, and reviewed in 1614, and posterior to those of Wisbuy or Oleron. The history of this commercial confederacy is well known. Although in itself and its de-

those called the laws of Wisbuy, and both are principally founded on those of Oleron. The sea laws of Spain are, in no small degree, collections from those of other nations. There is a striking similarity in the leading principles of all these laws. So far from sound principles becoming obsolete, or injured by time, that it will be found, on careful investigation, that the oldest sea laws we know, those of the Rhodians,[6] have furnished the outline and leading character of the whole. With such examples before us, we need not hesitate to be guided by the rules and principles, established in the maritime laws of other countries. * * *

I shall not contend with those who say, we ought to have a maritime code of our own, about the binding force of all these laws on us. By the general laws of nations we certainly are bound. These apply, most frequently, in the prize court; but there are many cases of salvage, wreck, &c. on the instance or civil side of the court, which necessarily must be determined under the general law. The wisdom and experience, evidenced in the particular maritime institutions of other commercial countries, ought at least to be greatly respected. If they serve only as faithful guides, and tried and long established rules of decision, in similar cases, they are of high and exemplary importance. It must be granted, that it is safer to follow them, than to trust entirely to the varying and crooked line of discretion.[7]

Where a reciprocity of decision, in certain cases, is necessary, the court of one country is often guided by the customs, laws, and decisions of the tribunals of another, in similar cases. But the change in the form of our government has not abrogated all the laws, customs and principles of jurisprudence we inherited from our ancestors and possessed at the period of our becoming an independent nation. The people of these states, both individually and collectively, have the common law,[8] in all cases, consistent with the change of our government,

pendencies, it consisted of 62 cities, originally, it is now reduced to six, consisting of Lubeck, Hamburgh, Dantzig, Brenten, Rostock, and Cologne. * * *

6. * * * The Rhodians applied themselves exclusively to commerce, and avoided every idea of extension of territory. Their fleet was so powerful, and their naval regulations so excellent, that they were courted by the most mighty nations of their time. They held the empire of the sea, and by confining their strength and resources to maritime objects, they not only protected and extended their own commerce, but scoured the ocean of pirates who annoyed the trade of all countries. Alexander the Great treated them with marked distinction. * * * Their superiority, in mercan-tile and naval talent and enterprise, gained them the admiration and respect of their contemporaries; when a spirt of monopoly, jealousy and plunder, would have handed them down to us, not to be imitated, but detested.

7. The foregoing enumeration of some of the maritime codes, is not intended to comprehend the whole, which would swell the account too extensively. It is given merely to show, that the most renowned maritime nations always adopted the principles, when long tried and tested, of their predecessors or contemporaries. * * *

8. The feudal parts of this law, and such as are inconsistent with the principles of our government are not, nor can they be, in force. Those who and the principles on which it is founded. They possess, in like manner, the maritime law, which is part of the common law, existing at the same period; and this is peculiarly within the cognizance of courts, invested with maritime jurisdiction; although it is referred to, in all our courts on maritime questions. It is, then, not to be disputed, on sound principles, that this court must be governed in its decisions, by the Maritime Code we possessed at the period before stated; as well as by the particular laws since established by our own government, or which may hereafter be enacted. * * * Whatever may, in strictness, be thought of their binding authority, I shall always be ready to hear the opinions of the learned and wise jurisprudents or judicial characters of any country on subjects agitated in this court * * *. I am not so confident in my own judgment, as not to wish for all the lights and information, it may be in my power to obtain, from any respectable sources. * * * [Peters proceeded, apparently on the basis of many maritime authorities discussed, to determine that the plaintiffs, American seamen, were entitled to the wages they sought from the foreign owner of their ship. According to admiralty practice, the ship was to be sold to pay the wages if the owner did not.]

(c) THE AIM OF ADMIRALTY JURISPRUDENCE

WILLINGS ET AL. v. BLIGHT

30 Fed.Cas. 50 (1800).

This was a petition to permit the majority of owners to proceed with the brig Amelia on a voyage, after giving stipulation for value of the recusant owner's share. In this case the proceedings will shew the course originally taken by the parties. The court was clearly of opinion that the cause was one of admiralty jurisdiction; and that it had power to authorize the majority of owners to fit out and expedite the vessel on a voyage to be designated in the stipulation, and it directed accordingly. The question of freight was accommodated; and the court gave no final judgment. An opinion was however intimated that no freight was legally demandable by a recusant owner,

are best acquainted with its wise and just principles, as they relate to contracts, and the property, as well as the personal rights of individuals, admire the common law as the venerable and solid bulwark of both liberty and property. Statute laws innovating upon it, have seldom been found, on experience, to be real improvements. Those who do not know the common law suppose it to be everything, that it is not. Its rules and principles are not arbitrary, but fixed and settled by the wisdom and decisions of the most respectable and intelligent sages, of both ancient and modern times. Many of the objections raised against it shew a want of acquaintance with its system and principles. Some of these objections are founded in innovation made by statutes altering or obscuring, the common law. Others have nothing in either common or statute law to support them.

who would neither sell at a reasonable appraisement, nor make advances for outfit; but his share of the vessel should be secured to him, that as he gains no profit, he may incur no loss. It appeared unreasonable, that those who were prepared, and desirous to put their property into a state of activity, should use their funds disproportionably for the benefit of a delinquent owner.

During the progress of the cause the following opinion was given by the court.

Whether the minority shall or shall not be compelled to sell, has not, in the opinion of the court, been here judicially determined. It is asserted (Beawes, Lex.Merc. 49) that if the majority of owners refuse to fit out, they are compellable to sell at a valuation; and so are part-owners, deficient and unable to fit out the vessel. This majority or minority, means those who hold the greater or less proportion of property. In the Sea Laws (3d Ed. 442), it is said, that "upon any probable design, the major part of the owners may, even against the consent, though not without the privity and knowledge of the rest, freight out their vessel to sea." "If it should so fall out that the major part, in number, protest against the voyage, and but one left that is for the voyage, yet the same may be effected by that party, if there be equality in partnership." "If it falls out that one is so obstinate, that his consent cannot be had, the law will enforce him either to hold or to sell his proportion; but if he will set no price, the rest may rig her out, at their own costs and charges, and whatsoever freight she earns, he is not to have any share or benefit in the same. But if such vessel happens to miscarry, or to be cast away, the rest must answer him his part, or proportion, in the vessel. But if it should fall out, that the major part of the owners in value, refuse to set out the vessel to sea; there by reason of the inequality, they may not be compelled; but then such vessel is to be valued and sold: the like, whether part of the owners become deficient, or unable to set her forth to sea." The sixth article of the twenty-third section of the ordinances of Louis XIV of France, enacts, that "no person may constrain his partner to proceed to the sale of a ship, except the opinions of the owners be equally divided about the undertaking of the voyage." Here "equally" means equality of property.

It is a principle discernable in all maritime codes, that every encouragement and assistance should be afforded to those, who are ready to give to their ships constant employment; and this, not only for the particular profit of owners, but for the general interests and prosperity of commerce. If agriculture be, according to the happy allusion of the great Sully,* "one of the breasts from which the state

---

* Maximilian de Béthune, duc de Sully (1560–1641), a brilliant administrator and visionary, was superintendent of finances for Henry IV of France. Sully helped make France prosperous in the late sixteenth and seventeenth centuries by his encouragement of agriculture, roads and canals.

must draw its nourishment," commerce is certainly the other. The earth, the parent of both, is the immediate foundation and support of the one, and ships are the moving powers, instruments and facilities of the other.—Both must be rendered productive by industry and ingenuity. The interests and comforts of the community will droop, and finally perish, if either be permitted to remain entirely at rest. The former will less ruinously bear neglect, and throw up spontaneous products; but the latter require unremitted employment, attention and enterprize, to ensure utility and profit. A privation of freight, the fruit and crop of shipping, seems therefore to be an appropriate mulct, on indolent, perverse, or negligent part-owners. The drones ought not to share in the stores, acquired and accumulated by the labour, activity, foresight and management of the bees. Although the hive may be common property, it is destructively useless to all, if not furnished with means of profit and support by industry and exertion; which should be jointly applied by all, before they participate in beneficial results. Nor should the idle and incompetent be permitted to hold it vacant and useless to the injury and ruin of the industrious and active.

NOTES AND QUESTIONS

1. The Constitution and the Judiciary Act of 1789 gave admiralty jurisdiction to the federal courts, but did not spell out what substantive maritime law the federal courts were to apply. Some of the cases you have just read are addressed to this problem. In the first one, Rice v. The Polly (p. 152), you will notice that there is very little citation of authority. The law of the case seems to be drawn from the "shipping articles" and also from "law and reason," or the "rights of humanity." Does this strike you as a wise approach? The federal admiralty courts, following the English practice, proceeded without a jury. In light of the American objections to the colonial English Vice-Admiralty courts on the grounds of their lack of juries, such as those made by Oxenbridge Thacher and Thomas Jefferson, was this a sensible manner of proceeding in America? In some states, immediately after the revolution, admiralty courts were created which functioned *with* juries. Why were the *federal* courts which replaced them juryless?

2. In Thompson v. The Catherina, Judge Peters displays his knowledge of the maritime laws of ancient and modern nations. Much of this knowledge he acquired from his own translations of ancient and modern authorities from many European nations. Peters indicates that these authorities will be used in his decisions. Does this seem correct? Why? Reread footnote 8 of the *Thompson* case, and its accompanying text. Does the attitude that one should reject the "feudal" parts of the common law, but keep its provisions with regard to contract, property, and individual rights make sense to you? How do you explain the attitude in the footnote that statutes, more often than not, miss the mark? Is this attitude dominant today? Should it be?

3. What does Willings v. Blight tell you about its author's (Judge Peters) ideas about the aims of admiralty jurisprudence? In another ad-

miralty case, Hollingsworth v. The Betsey, 12 Fed.Cas. 348 (D.C.D.Pa.1798), Judge Peters found his court asked to assess damages for the unlawful capture and detention of the brigantine *Betsey* and her cargo. Peters ordered the clerk of his court "to associate with him three intelligent and disinterested merchants of this district, who, or any two of them with the clerk, shall examine into all circumstances relative to the vessel and cargo and the losses and damages consequent thereon, and ascertain the amount thereof, according to justice and good conscience * * *." Why would Peters make such an order? Would you have approved of it? During most of American history most Americans were engaged in the practice of agriculture. Do *Willings* and *Hollingsworth* seem consistent with the spirit of American agrarianism? Is the Constitutional theory that seems implied by the Federalist consistent with this spirit?

4. In the two cases which follow, you will see a clash between rural agrarian Americans and the Federalist judges, growing out of two actual rebellions in Pennsylvania in the late eighteenth century. Does the attitude of the Federalist judges in these two cases seem different from that displayed in the three admiralty opinions?

SECTION B.   THE FIRST FEDERAL TREASON TRIALS

1.   THE TRIAL OF THE WESTERN INSURGENTS (1794–95)

In 1794 the United States Government sought to collect long overdue revenues under a 1791 excise tax on whiskey in several western Pennsylvania counties. The tax struck hard at the economy of this region, as the manufacture of whiskey was viewed as the best means of preserving the grain crop. The tax was figured on the basis of quantity, and since the selling price of whiskey was lowest in Western Pennsylvania, the tax burden was especially great. Many of the residents of that region engaged in attacks on federal excise officials in the summer of 1794, often resorting to the use of tar and feathers. For several months federal authority was suspended. Federal commissioners sent to observe the situation concluded that "nothing less than the physical strength of the nation could enforce the law." Several thousand men of Western Pennsylvania took up arms in opposition to the federal statute, and President Washington finally dispatched a contingent of 15,000 federal troops which restored the authority of the national government. Several of the ringleaders were brought to trial in Philadelphia before the United States Circuit Court.

THE UNITED STATES v. VIGOL

United States Circuit Court for the District of Pennsylvania, 1795.
28 Fed.Cas. 376.

Indictment for High Treason, in levying war against the United States. The prisoner was one of the most active insurgents in the Western counties of Pennsylvania, and had accompanied the armed party, who attacked the house of the excise officer (Reigan's) in Westmoreland with guns, drums, &c., insisted upon his surrendering his official papers, and extorted an oath from him, that he would never act again in the execution of the excise law. The same party then proceeded to the house of Wells, the excise officer, in Fayette county, swearing that the excise law should never be carried into effect, and that they would destroy Wells and his house. On their arrival, Wells had fled, and concealed himself; whereupon they ransacked the house, burned it, with all its contents, including the public books and papers, and afterwards discovering Wells, seized, imprisoned, and compelled him to swear that he would never act again as excise officer. Witnesses were likewise examined to establish that the general combination and scope of the insurrection, were to prevent the execution of the excise law by force   *   *   *.

Paterson, Justice: [charging the jury] The first point for consideration, is the evidence, which has been given to establish the case stated in the indictment; the second point turns upon the criminal intention of the party; and from these points (the evidence and intention) the law arises.

With respect to the evidence, the current runs one way. It harmonizes in all its parts. It proves that the prisoner was a member of the party, who went to Reigan's house, and afterwards to the house of Wells, in arms, marshalled and arrayed, and who, at each place, committed acts of violence and devastation.

With respect to the intention, likewise, there is not, unhappily, the slightest possibility of doubt. To suppress the office of excise, in the fourth survey of this State, and particularly in the present instance, to compel the resignation of Wells, the excise officer, so as to render null and void, in effect, an act of Congress, constituted the apparent, the avowed object of the inspection, and of the outrages which the prisoner assisted to commit.

Combining these facts, and this design, the crime of High Treason is consummate in the contemplation of the Constitution and law of the United States.

The counsel for the prisoner have endeavoured, in the course of a faithful discharge of their duty, to extract from the witnesses some testimony, which might justify a defence upon the ground of duress and terror, but in this they have failed, for the whole scene exhibits a disgraceful unanimity; and, with regard to the prisoner, he can only be distinguished for a guilty pre-eminence in zeal and activity. It may not, however, be useless on this occasion, to observe, that the fear, which the law recognizes as an excuse for the perpetration of an offence, must proceed from an immediate and actual danger, threatening the very life of the party. The apprehension of any loss of property, by waste or fire; or even an apprehension of a slighter remote injury to the person, furnish no excuse. If, indeed, such circumstances could avail, it would be in the power of every crafty leader of tumults and rebellions to indemnify his followers, by uttering previous menaces; an avenue would be forever open for the escape of unsuccessful guilt; and the whole fabric of society must inevitably be laid prostrate.

    *   *   *   Verdict guilty.

THE UNITED STATES v. MITCHELL

United States Circuit Court for the District of Pennsylvania, 1795.
26 Fed.Cas. 1277.

Indictment for High Treason for levying war against the United States. * * *

[Following the testimony of witnesses] The attorney of the district (Mr. Rawle) [began his argument on the law of the case:] * * * Kings, it is true, have endeavoured to augment the number, and to perplex the descriptions of treasons, as an instrument to enlarge their powers, and to oppress their subjects; but in republics, and particularly in the American Republic, the crime of treason is naturally reduced to a single head, which divides itself into these constitutional propositions. 1st. Levying war against the government; and 2d. Adhering to its enemies and giving them aid and comfort. In other words, exciting internal, or waging external war against the State. * * *

What constitutes a levying of war, however, must be the same in technical interpretation, whether committed under a republican or a regal form of government, since either institution may be assailed and subverted by the same means. Hence we are enabled * * * to acquire precise and satisfactory ideas upon the subject, from the matured experience of another government * * *. By the English authorities it is uniformly and clearly declared, that raising a body of men to obtain by intimidation or violence the repeal of a law, or to oppose and prevent by force or terror the execution of the law, is an act of levying war. Doug. 570. Again; an insurrection with an avowed design to suppress public offices, is an act of levying war, and, although a bare conspiracy to levy war may not amount to that species of treason; yet, if any of the conspirators actually levy war, it is treason in all the persons that conspired * * *. Those, likewise, who join afterwards, though not concerned at first in the plot, are as guilty as the original conspirators; for in treason all are principals * * *.

The evidence, unfortunately, leaves no room for excuse or extenuation, in the application of the law to the prisoners' cases. The general and avowed object of the conspiracy at Couche's Fort, was to suppress the offices of excise in the Fourth Survey. As an important measure for that purpose, it was agreed to go to Gen. Neville's house, and to compel him to surrender his office and official papers. Some of the persons who were at Couche's Fort went, accordingly, to General Neville's and terminated a course of lawless and outrageous proceedings, by burning his house. The prisoner is proved by four witnesses to have been at Couche's Fort; and so far from opposing the expedition to General Neville's, he offered himself to reconnoitre. Being thus originally combined with the conspirators, in a treasonable purpose, to levy war, it was unnecessary that the purpose should be afterwards executed, in order to convict them all of treason, and much less is it necessary to his conviction, that he should have been present at the burning of General Neville's house, which was the consummation of their plot, or that the burning should be proved by two witnesses. But he is, likewise, discovered, by one of the witnesses at least, within a few rods of the General's, at the moment of the conflagration, and he is seen marching in the cavalcade, which escorted the dead body of their leader, in melancholy triumph, from the scene of action to Barclay's house. * * *.

The counsel for the prisoner * * * premised, that they did not conceive it to be their duty to show, that the prisoner was guiltless of any description of crime against the United States, or the State of Pennsylvania. But they contended, that he had not committed the crime of high treason, and ought, therefore, to be acquitted upon the present indictment. The adjudications in England upon the various descriptions of treason, have been worked, incautiously, into a system, by the destruction of which, at this day, the government itself would be seriously affected; but even there, the best judges, and the ablest commentators, while they acquiesce in the decisions that have already taken place, furnish a strong caution against the too easy admission of future cases, which may seem to have a parity of reason. Constructive, or interpretative treasons, must be the dread and scourge of any nation that allows them. 1 Hale P.C. 132, 259; 4 Bl.Com. 85. Take then, the distinction of treason by levying war, as laid down by the attorney of the district, and it is a constructive or interpretative weapon, which is calculated to annul all distinctions heretofore wisely established in the grades and punishments of crimes; and by whose magic power a mob may easily be converted into a conspiracy; and a riot aggravated into high treason. Such, however, is not the sense which Congress has expressed upon this very subject; for, if a bare opposition to the execution of a law can be considered as constituting a traitorous offence, as levying war against the government, it must be equally so, in relation to every other law, as well as in relation to the excise law * * *. And yet, in the penal code of the United States, the offence of wilfully obstructing, resisting or opposing, any officer, in serving, or attempting so serve any process, is considered and punished merely as a misdemeanour. * * * Let it be granted, that to compel Congress to repeal a law, by violence, or intimidation, is treason, (and the English authorities rightly construed, claim no greater concession,) it does not follow, that resisting the execution of a law, or attempting to coerce an officer into the resignation of his commission, will amount to the same offence. Let it be granted, also that an insurrection for an avowed purpose of suppressing all the excise offices in the United States, may be construed into an act of levying war against the government * * it does not follow that an attempt to oblige one officer to resign, or to suppress all the offices in one district, will be a crime of the same denomination. 1 Hal.P.C. 135. * * * [A] bare conspiracy to levy war, does not amount to treason; but, it is contended, that if, at any time afterwards, a part of the conspirators should execute the plot, the whole of them will be involved in the guilt and punishment. Thus, no opportunity is left for repentance * * *. The state of the evidence, however, renders it unavoidable, that this ground should be taken; for, unless the proceedings at Couche's Fort, and at General Neville's house, can be so combined and interwoven, as to form one action, there are not two witnesses to prove that the prisoner was at the latter place; and the conduct at the former, could only amount, under the most rigid construction, to a conspiracy to levy war, not to an actual levying of war against the government. With the necessity for two witnesses to an overt act of treason, it is not in the power of the judge or juries to dispense; it is a shield from oppression, with which the constitution furnishes the prisoner * * *.

If this view of the law is correct, it will be easy to show, that its operation upon the facts, will entitle the prisoner to an acquittal. * * With respect to the criminal proceedings at General Neville's house, (which after all, amount to the crime of arson, not of treason,) it is agreed that only one positive witness proves the fact of his having been there; but, even that Witness states, that the prisoner was alone, at the distance of thirty or forty rods; and it is not recollected whether he had a gun. Then it only remains to consider of the prisoner's presence at Couche's Fort * * *. It does not, then, appear by the testimony of two witnesses, that the meeting at Couche's Fort was convened for the purpose of accomplishing a compulsory repeal of the excise laws, or a suppression of the excise offices. The meeting seems to have originated merely in a wish to consider what it was best to do in the actual state of the country. On this point a committee was chosen, or rather was self-created, and the members determined to send a flag to General Neville. It does not appear with what view the flag was to be sent; but it will not be presumed, when the evidence is silent, to be with a view to attack the General's house, to force a repeal of the excise law, or to compel the officer's resignation; and even the fact itself is only proved by one witness. Besides, the conduct of the Committee, however culpable, will not be sufficient to involve the whole assembly in the guilt of treason. It is true, that the prisoner expressed his willingness to reconnoitre General Neville's house; but this expression, likewise, is only proved by one witness; and even if it were proved by fifty witnesses, it does not amount to an overt act of treason by levying war; nor does it appear that he even did reconnoitre, or furnish intelligence to the Committee. * * *.

The Attorney General of the United States (Mr. Bradford) in reply. * * * If * * * the principles asserted in the course of the prisoner's defence should prevail, a flagrant attempt to obstruct the legitimate operations of the government, to prevent the execution of its laws, and to coerce its officers into a dereliction of their trusts, must no longer be regarded as high treason. * * *

[I]t has been argued, that Congress has provided a specific punishment, for the offence of resisting or obstructing the service of process, obviously distinguishing it from treason; and that it is as much treason to resist the execution of one law as another; to resist the marshal of a court, as much as the supervisor of a district. The analogy is, in a great measure, just; in either case, if the resistance is made by a few persons, in a particular instance, and under the impulse of a particular interest, the offence would not amount to high treason; but if, in either case, there is a general rising of a whole county, to prevent the officer from discharging his duty in relation to the public at large, the offence is unquestionably high treason. * * *

Again, it has been urged, that the criminal intention must point to the suppression of all the excise offices in the United States, or it cannot amount to high treason. * * * [I]f it was intended that, by their lawless career and example, Congress should be forced into a repeal of the obnoxious law, it necessarily followed, that from the same cause, the offices of excise would be suppressed throughout the Union. * * *

The truth is, however, that the insurgents did not entertain a personal dislike for General Neville, but in every stage of their proceedings * * * they were actuated by one single traitorous motive, a determination if practicable, to frustrate and prevent the execution of the excise law. The whole was one great insurrection, and it is immaterial at what point of time or place, from its commencement to its termination, any man became an agent in carrying it on. * * * To render any man criminal, he must not only have been present, but he must have taken part with the insurgents; yet, whether he was present at Couche's Fort, or the march to General Neville's, or at the burning of the General's house, if his intention was traitorous, his offence was treason. 3 Inst. 9. The overt act laid in the indictment (which is drawn from the most approved precedents) is levying war; and war may be levied, though not actually made. Fost. 218. It is agreed that this overt act must be proved by two witnesses; but there is a difference as to what constitutes the act itself. Now it is manifest from every authority, that to assemble in a body armed and arrayed for some treasonable purpose, is an act of levying war; this was the case at Couche's Fort, and the prisoner's active attendance there is proved by a number of witnesses. * * * The conspiracy to levy war being effected, all the conspirators are guilty, though they did not all attend at General Neville's house. 1 Hale P.C. 132. Fost. 213, 215. * * *

The charge of the Court was delivered to the jury * * *:

Paterson, Justice. The first question to be considered is, what was the general object of the insurrection? If its object was to suppress the excise offices and to prevent the execution of an act of Congress, by force and intimidation, the offence in legal estimation is high treason; it is an usurpation of the authority of government; it is high treason by levying of war. Taking the testimony in a rational and connected point of view, this was the object. It was of a general nature, and of national concern. * * * With what view was the attack made on General Neville's house? Was it to gratify a spirit of revenge against him as a private citizen, as an individual? No! as a private citizen he had been highly respected and beloved; it was only by becoming a public officer that he became obnoxious, and it was on account of his holding the excise office alone, that his house had been assailed, and his person endangered. On the first day of attack, the insurgents were repulsed, but they rallied, returned with greater force, and fatally succeeded in the second attempt. They were arrayed in a military manner; they affected the military forms of negotiation by a flag; they pretended no personal hostility to General Neville; but they insisted on the surrender of his commission. Can there be a doubt, then, that the object of the insurrection was of a general and public nature?

The second question to be considered is, how far was the prisoner traitorously connected with the insurgents? It was proved by four witnesses, that he was at Couche's Fort, at a great distance from his own home, and that he was armed. One witness proves, positively, that he was at the burning of General Neville's house; and another says, "it runs in his head, that he also saw the prisoner there." On this state of the facts, a difficulty has been suggested. It is said, that no act of treason was committed at Couche's Fort; and that however treasonable the proceedings at General Neville's may have been, there are not two witnesses who prove that the prisoner was there. Of the overt act of treason, there must, undoubtedly, be proof by two witnesses * * *. But let us consider the prisoner's conduct in a regular and connected course. He is proved, by a competent number of witnesses, to have been at Couche's Fort. At Couche's Fort the conspiracy was formed, for attacking General Neville's house; and the prisoner was actually passed on the march thither. Now, in Foster, 213, the very act of marching is considered as carrying the traitorous intention into effect; and the jury * * * will consider how far this aids the doubtful language of the second witness, even as to the fact of the prisoner's being at General Neville's house.

On the personal motives and conduct of the prisoner, it would be superfluous to make a particular commentary. He was armed, he was a volunteer, he was a party to the various consultations of the insurgents; and in every scene of the insurrection, from the assembly at Couche's Fort to the day prescribed for submission to the government, he makes a conspicuous appearance * * * Upon the whole, whether the conspiracy at Couche's Fort may of itself be deemed treason, or the conspiracy there, and the proceedings at General Neville's house, are considered as one act, (which is, perhaps, the true light to view the subject in,) the prisoner must be pronounced guilty. The consequences are not to weigh with the jury:—it is their province to do justice; the attribute of mercy is placed by our Constitution in other hands. *Verdict—Guilty*.

NOTES AND QUESTIONS

1. These were the first trials for treason in the federal courts, and established the precedent that widespread armed opposition to execution of a United States statute amounted to "levying war" against the United States, and thus came within the Constitutional definition of treason. Are you satisfied with this definition of treason? What of the distinction, made by counsel for the prisoner, between resisting or opposing any officer attempting to serve process, which was only a misdemeanor, and the treatment of Neville, which Paterson defines as "levying war?" Has the prosecutor satisfactorily met this argument? The prosecutor, William Rawle, argues that "What constitutes a levying of war * * * must be the same, in technical interpretation, whether committed under a republican, or a regal form of government; since either institution may be assailed and subverted by the same means." What force should the English common-law rule of conspiracy to commit treason have in a republic? Is Rawle sensitive enough to the differences between regal and republican governments? What might those differences be, and what bearing might they have on the concept of "treason"?

2. The prosecution of the insurgents was not particularly smooth. In the first trial, United States v. Porter, 28 Fed.Cas. 376 (C.C.D.Pa.1794) a verdict of not guilty was directed when court discovered that another man having the same name as the defendant was the culprit sought by the government. In some other early skirmishing, Judge Peters advanced his opinion that the federal judiciary should not be hamstrung by delicate niceties of state procedure. Counsel for some of the prisoners had argued that the prosecutions were not being carried on in conformity with the requirements of section 29 of the Judiciary Act, which ordered that certain matters of jury selection should be in accordance with state practice. Peters diplomatically accepted some of these objections, and accordingly post-

poned the trials until compliance with state law could be accomplished, but he rejected arguments based on other technical infractions of state law:

> Although, in ordinary cases, it would be well to accommodate our practice with that of the state, yet the judiciary of the United States should not be fettered and controlled in its operations, by a strict adherence to state regulations and practice * * *. The legislature of a state have in their consideration a variety of local arrangements, which cannot be adapted to the more expanded policy of the nation. It never could have been in the contemplation of congress, by any reference to state regulations, to defeat the operation of the national laws.

United States v. Insurgents, 26 Fed.Cas. 499, 511–12 (C.C.D.Pa.1795). Peters cited no authority in support of these propositions.

3. Consider Justice Paterson's jury charges in the two cases that resulted in treason convictions. In both these cases Paterson makes extensive comments on the credibility of the evidence, and, in *Mitchell*, the second case, he goes so far as to say, "Upon the whole, * * * the prisoner must be pronounced guilty." Is this what a judge is supposed to do?

4. To what degree was Justice Paterson's and Judge Peters's intolerance of social upheaval a reflection of changed attitudes toward mob behavior since the Revolution? In colonial America the mob, as we have seen, might have often functioned as an extra-legal arm of the community. In particular, where mob action was taken in resistance to imperial authority, mob actions might have been generally perceived by colonials as emanations of the popular will in support of liberty. Moreover, mob actions might have been resorted to generally only after the normal remedies for legal redress had been exhausted, when other means of preserving liberty did not exist, or when royal policies (and royal courts) were prepared to ignore colonial law. While the means adopted by colonials who took to the streets might be condemned as an "evil," in the language of Jefferson, mobs were "productive of good," since they held rulers "to the true principles of their institutions;" they provided a "medicine necessary for the sound health of the government." XII Boyd et. al, The Papers of Thomas Jefferson 356. Even Lt. Governor Thomas Hutchinson could state in 1768 that "mobs * * * are constitutional." Hutchinson to Grant, XXVI Massachusetts Archives, 317. Both Hutchinson and Jefferson are quoted in Pauline Maier's perceptive article on the post-revolutionary mobs, "Popular Uprisings and Civil Authority in Eighteenth-Century America," 27 Wm. & Mary Q. 3 (3rd Ser. 1970).

Professor Maier suggests that after 1776 "changing attitudes toward popular uprisings turned upon fundamental transformations in the political perspective of Americans," and that many Americans

> began to see domestic turbulence not as indictments but as insults to government that were likely to discredit American republicanism in the eyes of European observers. "Mobs are a reproach to Free Governments," where all grievances could be legally redressed through the courts or the ballot box, it was argued in 1783. They originated there "not in Oppression, but in Licentiousness," an "ungovernable spirit" among the people. Under republican gov-

ernments even that distrust of power colonists had found so necessary for liberty, and which uprisings seemed to manifest, could appear outmoded.

27 Wm. & Mary Q. (3rd Ser.) at 34. Yet, Ms. Maier urges that this change in attitude toward popular uprisings might not be a distinctly American phenomenon:

> a century earlier, when England passed beyond her revolutionary era and progressed toward political "stability," radical ideology with its talk of resistance and revolution was gradually left behind. A commitment to peace and permanence emerged from decades of fundamental change. In America as in England this stability demanded that operative sovereignty, including the right finally to decide what was and was not in the community's interest, and which laws were and were not constitutional, be entrusted to established governmental institutions. The result was to minimize the role of the people at large, who had been the ultimate arbiters of those questions in English and American revolutionary thought.*

Id., at 34–35. Do these observations make it any easier to understand why President Washington might have pardoned the convicted defendants? Would you have recommended such a pardon if you were one of Washington's advisors?

2.   THE FIRST TRIAL OF JOHN FRIES **

PRESSER, A TALE OF TWO JUDGES: RICHARD PETERS, SAMUEL CHASE, AND THE BROKEN PROMISE OF FEDERALIST JURISPRUDENCE

73 Nw.L.Rev. 83–88 (1978).

* * * Five years after the Whisky Rebellion, the "Fries Rebellion" took place in eastern Pennsylvania. The levy which was the object of the Fries Rebellion, a tax on houses, had become necessary because of the high cost of troops used to quell the Whisky Rebellion, and also because of the expenditures for anticipated hostilities against France. The yeomen of [three] counties in eastern Pennsylvania organized protests against the new federal taxes and succeeded in preventing their collection. While there was no real bloodshed, there was, during the months of 1799, much marching around by armed troops in uniform, and at least one overt act of rebellion—the liberation of prisoners from the custody of a federal marshal * * *.

The chief perpetrators of agitation, including John Fries, who led the freeing of the federal prisoners, were brought to trial for treason before Judge Peters and Justice Iredell in 1799. The case aroused in-

---

* Reprinted by permission of the author and the publisher.

**As the official report of this trial runs to hundreds of pages, this summary is provided instead.

terest in the Pennsylvania press, and the trial immediately took on dramatic political overtones. Acting as lawyers for the defense were William Lewis, a former federal judge, and Alexander James Dallas, fast becoming the kingpin of the emerging Pennsylvania Republican organization. Their arguments * * * were clearly designed to stir popular sympathies.

* * * On April 30, 1799, Lewis moved for the Fries trial to be removed from Philadelphia to Northampton County, the place where Fries's offense was alleged to have been committed. His motion was made pursuant to section 29 of the Judiciary Act, which mandated trial in the county where the offense had occurred. The motion was denied by Iredell and Peters. In his opinion Peters announced, considering fairness to the prosecution, that "a fair and impartial trial ought to be had, which he was certain could not be held in the county of Northampton." Similarly, Iredell questioned: "If nearly one whole county has been in state of insurrection, can it be said that a fair trial can be had there? " * * *

Most of the arguments of Fries's counsel at trial went to the law of the case. The thrust of their defense was to persuade the jury that armed resistance to a federal officer's execution of a federal statute was not the crime of treason. Lewis and Dallas, in short, were exhorting the jurors in Fries's case to arrive at the opposite conclusion from that laid down by Justice Paterson, Judge Peters, and by the jurors in the trials of the Whisky Rebels.

The technique of arguing the law to the jury was tacitly approved by Peters and Iredell. Peters was later to write that the latitude permitted counsel in this trial was "unbounded" or even "unjustifiable" as to "both Law & Fact." Indeed, Peters remembered five years later that defense counsel was permitted to charge that the law laid down in the [Whiskey Rebels Trials] * * * was as "unsound as the worst opinion, delivered in the worst of times in England."

Fries's counsel did not argue that their client was innocent of all crimes, but simply that he was not guilty of the heinous crime of treason. The strategy of Lewis and Dallas was to parade before the jury a series of "horribles" drawn from the English common law to show that a broad definition of "treason" led to gross tyranny. Judge Peters's reflection on this tactic was: "All the abominable and reprobated cases of constructive treason in England were sufferred to be read."
* * *.

Two such examples were cited with great enthusiasm. For one, defense counsel described how once, in the "dark ages of English jurisprudence" when the king killed a yeoman's stag, the yeoman, in a fit of anger "wished the horns of the stag in the king's belly." The yeoman was swiftly, and apparently successfully, prosecuted for treason. As an even more egregious travesty, for the second example, the case was given of an innkeeper who kept an inn called "the sign of the crown." He had bragged that he would make his son "heir to the crown," and so he was convicted of treason. * * *

Lewis and Dallas used these abuses from the English common law to distinguish the only English precedent holding that the "rescue" of prisoners from official hands could amount to treason. Since it came from the time of the absolute monarchy of Henry VIII, [they argued that] it should be ignored by the jury as reflective of despotic excess. * * *

In contrast to the abuses of the treason doctrine they cited from England, they argued that in a "free republic" like America, the application of the doctrine of treason should be so limited that the phrase "levying war" would only apply to cases where armed men sought "to put an end to the government," where a part of "the Union" sought to "throw off the authority of the United States," or where rebels actually marched on the legislature or the executive. It should not be treason, they argued, where insurgents simply opposed the implementation of the republic's laws. The latter activity, they urged, might constitute "sedition" or common law "rescue," but not the capital crime of treason. * * *

After more than a week of impassioned arguments by Lewis and Dallas, Iredell and Peters charged the jury. Peters stated his opinion first. He maintained that the *Vigol* and *Mitchell* cases (the Whisky Rebellion trials) governed: "It is treason to oppose or prevent by force, numbers or intimidation, a public and general law of the United States, with intent to prevent its operation or compel its repeal." By opposing a law, said Peters, "the rights of all are invaded by the force and violence of a few" and "a deadly blow is aimed at the government, when its fiscal arrangements are forcibly destroyed, distracted and impeded; for on its revenues its very existence depends." * * * Justice Iredell opened his charge by declaring, in sharp contrast to the attitude of Justice Paterson in the trials of the Whisky Rebels, * * * that he would not usurp the role of the jury * * * "[I]t is not for the court," he stated, "to say whether there was treasonable intention or act as charged in the indictment; that is for the jury to determine; we have only to state the law, we therefore should have no right to give out opinion on it." * * *

A verdict of "guilty" was rendered. Given the latitude that Lewis and Dallas were allowed by the judges in arguing the law to the jury, and given the force of their arguments that their client at most had committed sedition, but not treason, the verdict is somewhat surprising. It may be that public opinion in the city of Philadelphia, where the trial took place, was strongly against the rural insurgents and influenced the jury. It may be, however, that the federal marshal, who had some discretion in picking the jury, was careful to choose members sensitive to the need for peace and good order. * * *

The possibility of a biased jury is strongly suggested * * * by subsequent events. Five days after the verdict was announced, Mr.

Lewis moved for a new trial for Fries on the ground that a Mr. John Rhoad, one of the jurors, had "declared a prejudice against the prisoner after he was summoned as a juror on the trial. [Though Rhoad denied it under oath, five sworn witnesses stated that after Rhoad was summoned for jury duty but before the trial, he had said that Fries "ought to be hung" and that "it would not be safe at home unless they hung them all."] Justice Iredell, probably much relieved, issued an opinion that Fries was entitled to a new trial. [Justice Iredell had earlier written his wife that when the jury's verdict was announced, "I could not bear to look upon the poor man, but I am told he fainted away * * * I dread the task I have before me in pronouncing sentence on him."] Judge Peters gave his opinion that there was no reason to grant a new trial. * * * Peters implied that even if Rhoad had made the statement attributed to him, Rhoad only reflected "the facts" as they "appeared then to the public." In any event, Peters finally concluded that "as a division in the court might lessen the weight of the judgement if finally pronounced and the great end of the law in punishments being example," he reluctantly went along with Iredell's opinion, and the new trial was granted.

NOTES AND QUESTIONS

1. Do you have any difficulties with the conception of "fair trial" invoked by Judge Peters and Justice Iredell in rejecting Fries's motion for a trial in Northampton? On the other hand, why did Peters and Iredell allow Fries's counsel such latitude in arguing that the law set down in the Whiskey Rebels' case should be rejected? Do the trials of Zenger and the Seven Bishops shed any light here? Compare the attitude toward the prerogatives of the jury of Peters and Iredell to that of Justice Chase (in the case which follows). How do Iredell's comments on the roles of judge and jury compare to the comments by Justice Paterson in the trials of the Whiskey Rebels? Note that Peters seems to use interchangeably the notions of "opposing," "preventing" by force, and "compelling" repeal of a law. Are there differences in these acts? Is passive resistance treasonable?

2. Though the Fries trial lasted for nine or ten days, Justice Iredell seemed quite ready to subject the federal courts to repeating the process once it was discovered that a juror was prejudiced. Why didn't Peters reach the same initial conclusion? Peters commented:

I am in sentiment against granting the motion for a new trial, Because:

1. The juror said no more than all friends to the laws and the government were warranted in thinking and saying as the facts appeared then to the public. Fries being generally alleged to be the most prominent character, it was on this account, and not with special or particular malice, that Rhoad's declaration was made.

2. If a juror was rejected on account of such declarations, trials, where the community at large are intimately affected by

crimes of such general importance and public notoriety, must be had, in all probability, by those who only openly or secretly approved of the conduct of the criminals. This would be unjust and improper, as it affects the government in its public prosecutions. Little success could be expected from proceedings against the most atrocious offenders, if great multitudes were implicated in their delusions or guilt.

3. It is natural for all good citizens, when atrocious crimes, of a public nature, are known to have been committed, to express their abhorrence and disapprobation both of the offences and the perpetrators. It is their duty so to express themselves. This is not like the case of murder, or any offence against an individual; or where several are charged, and none remarkably prominent. In this latter case, selecting one out of the mass might evince particular malice.

4. I have no doubt that declarations of an opposite complexion could be proved; and yet the jurors were unanimous in their verdict. The defendant has had a fair, and I think an impartial trial.

9 Fed.Cas., at 923. Does this seem persuasive to you? How could Peters then turn around and vote with Iredell for a retrial?

3. As you read the next excerpts, dealing with the retrial, decide whether you would have found Fries guilty of treason.

SAMUEL CHASE

3. THE SECOND TRIAL OF JOHN FRIES * (1800)

Fries was tried again in April of 1800, when Justice Samuel Chase was sitting on Circuit with Judge Peters. Before the trial, Chase had indicated to Peters that the Judges needed to devise some way to "get through all the business which had accumulated on the civil side" as a result of the great amount of time spent in the last session with the criminal trials resulting from the Fries Rebellion. Chase had heard an account of the first Fries trial and believed that what then took 10 days should have taken no more than "one third" of the time. Chase was determined that *this* time there should not be so much leeway in citing "irrelevant authorities & unnecessary discussions." Chase therefore drafted an opinion, which he hoped to use as the opinion of the court on the law, and thus prevent counsel from straying. He showed the draft opinion to Peters, who approved of it, later indicating that "he had expressed what I had before delivered as my opinion better than I had done it myself." At this point Chase had not settled on the manner of delivering this opinion, and Peters had told him that it should be done with "Prudence." Peters was left with the impression that Chase would consult him about the "time & manner of delivery" of the opinion. Peters, who believed in circumspection, had begun to be uneasy, "lest a premature Declaration of the Opinion of the Court might be made."

The day assigned to the Fries trial arrived, and as the proceedings opened, a juror came up to Judge Peters on the bench "to make some excuses for non attendance." Peters then noticed some commotion and discovered that while his "attention had been thus engaged" Chase had distributed copies of his opinion, one to defense counsel, one for the District attorney, and one for the Jury. "I felt uneasy," Peters later wrote, "& silently waited to see the effect, which did not surprize me." Chase had apparently engaged in the very "premature" conduct that Peters had feared. At the time he passed out this opinion, which he said was the opinion of the court, Chase told defense counsel that the opinion contained the court's view of the law of treason, which view was that articulated by Justice Paterson in the "Whiskey Rebels" case and Judge Peters and Justice Iredell in the first *Fries* trial: that armed opposition to United States statutes was treason. Since this was the law, Chase went on, the court would not permit arguments that such conduct was not treason to be made to the jury. In particular, Chase was determined that the jury not be distracted with odious English treason cases like that of the yeoman who wished the stag's horns in the King's belly, or the boastful innkeeper.

When Mr. Lewis, one of Fries' two lawyers, realized that the tactics he and Dallas had used in the first Fries trial would be foreclosed,

---

* The quoted portions of the introductory account of the second Fries trial are from a letter from Richard Peters to Timothy Pickering (Jan. 24, 1804), 10 Peters Papers 91 (Historical Society of Pennsylvania).

he threw down Chase's opinion in anger.   Peters then whispered to Chase that he believed the two Fries counsel would "take the studs & abandon the Cause, or take advantage of [the delivery of this statement of Chase's view] to operate on public opinion, or on that of the jury at least."   Peters reprimanded Chase, and reminded him of "my having 'told him so' or 'predicted it'."   Chase replied that "[H]e did not think the counsel would quit the Cause," and that "it was only a *Threat*, or some such expression."   Peters was right.   Lewis and Dallas announced their intention of withdrawing from the case, since the court had prejudged what they wished to argue.

Chase and Peters then repaired to the office of Mr. Rawle, the prosecutor.   Rawle (who was present for this discussion) and Peters then persuaded Chase that his opinion "should be recalled."   Chase "readily consented, declaring his intention to be merely to save time & accelerate business."

The next morning Lewis and Dallas were again in court, and Peters told them that "they might proceed in the Cause."   He assured them expressly that "you may, & I *hope* will, proceed in your own way, as if nothing had happened."   Chase was not as conciliatory as Peters, and though he did not contradict Peters, Chase "administered no emolients."   Chase, said Peters later, appeared "animated—if not irritated.   He declared 'The council could not embarrass him.   He knew what it was about'."   Chase agreed that he was "*willing* and *desirous to hear*," counsel's opinion on the law, and that "it might be controverted either with the Jury or any other Way."   He cautioned Lewis and Dallas, however, that "he would not permit improper or irrelevant authorities," and he probably told them that if they stepped out of bounds in their citation of authority they would be proceeding "at the hazard of [their] reputation."   Dallas later said that "This had the contrary effect rather than to induce me to proceed," and he and Lewis remained firm in their determination to leave the case.

Chase and Peters then offered to appoint other counsel for Fries, and gave him a day to think it over.   Fries declined other counsel, however, having been persuaded by Lewis and Dallas that to proceed without counsel would generate sympathy for him that might result in a Presidential pardon.   Chase then informed the prisoner that since he refused to accept other counsel, but was instead relying on the court "to be his counsel," he, Chase, would take it upon himself to serve as attorney for the defense, as well as judge.

UNITED STATES v. JOHN FRIES

United States Circuit Court for the District of Pennsylvania, 1800.
9 Fed.Cas. 826.

* * *

Thursday, April 24.—Before the jurors were sworn in, they were individually asked (upon oath)   * * *   "Have you ever formed or delivered an opinion as to the guilt or innocence of the prisoner, or that he ought to be punished? * * * Some of the jurors said they had given their sentiments generally, disapprobatory of the transaction, but not as to the prisoner particularly. These were admitted.

One of the jurors (Mr. Taggert) after he was sworn, expressed himself to the court to be very uneasy under his oath; he then meant that he never had made up his mind that the prisoner should be hung, but very often had spoken his opinion that he was very culpable; he did not, when he took the oath, conceive it so strict, and therefore wished, if possible, to be excused. The court informed the juror it was impossible to excuse him, now he was sworn.

The court informed the prisoner, that he had a right to challenge thirty-five without showing cause, and as many more as he could show cause for. Thirty-four were challenged * * *.

* * *

Mr. Rawle then * * * observed that the jury must be aware of the very unpleasant duty he had to perform: he felt an extreme difficulty of situation—called forth by his duty to exhibit a charge against the prisoner at the bar of the highest magnitude, who now stood to answer, unattended by any legal advice * * *.

Mr. Rawle then proceeded to open the charge. He said, he should be able to prove, that John Fries, the prisoner at the bar, did oppose the execution of two laws of the United States, to effectuate which he was provided with men, who, as well as himself, were armed with guns, swords, and other warlike weapons [and that Fries and his accomplices also did] release from the custody of the Marshal of Pennsylvania a number of persons who were held in prison by the said marshal, and * * * prevent him executing process upon others * * *.

Mr. Rawle then proceeded, under the direction of the court, to state the law. The treason whereof the prisoner was charged was, "levying war against the United States." U.S.Const., Art. 3, Sec. 3.

He conceived himself authorized, upon good authority, to say, levying war did not only consist in open, manifest, and avowed rebellion against the government, with a design of overthrowing the Constitution; but it may consist in assembling together in numbers, and by actual force, or by terror, opposing any particular law or laws. * * The endeavour, by intimidation, to do the act, whether it be accomplished or not, amounts to treason, provided the object of those concerned in the transaction, is of a general nature, and not applied to a special or private purpose.

* * * If a particular friend of the party had been in the custody of the marshal; if even a number sufficient for the purpose should step forward and rescue such a person, if it was not with a view to rescue prisoners generally, it would amount to no more than a rescue; but, if general, it is treason. * * *

* * * [In the cases of Vigol and Mitchell, said Rawle,] the attack on Gen. Neville's house was of this general nature, because he was an officer appointed to execute the obnoxious law; and being to the officer and not to the man that they objected, it was thought to be treason * * *.

He observed, that the clause in our Constitution was founded on a statute which was passed in England, to prevent the ever-increasing and ever-varying number of treasons, upon the general and undefined opposition to royal prerogative: the situation of things was such, previous to that period, as to call forth from the statesman, from the philosopher, and from the divine, even in those dark ages, the most vehement complaints: in attendance to these reasonable and just murmurs, the statute was passed.

Mr. Rawle was then producing an authority, when Judge Chase said, the court would admit, as a general rule, of quotations which referred to what constituted actual or constructive levying war against the King of Great Britain, in his regal capacity; or, in other words, of levying war against his government, but not against his person * * —they may, any of them, be read to the jury, and the decisions thereupon—not as authorities whereby we are bound, but as the opinions and decisions of men of great legal learning and ability. But even then, the court would attend carefully to the time of the decisions, and in no case must it be binding upon our juries.

Mr. Rawle quoted Hawkins, b. 1, chap. 17, sec. 23, as an authority of authenticity to prove that * * * those who withstood [The King's] lawful authority, and who endeavoured to oppose his government; who withstood the king's forces, or attacked any of his fortresses * * * were guilty of high treason. He also read Sir John Friend's case from Holt, 681, and Damarree and Pinchases' case, 8 State Trials, 289.

Judge Chase begged the counsel to read only those parts of the cases which referred to what could be treason in the United States, and nothing which related to compassing the king's death. It would be found, he observed, by an attention to the last case, that because the intention was arising to demolish ALL meeting-houses, generally, it was considered to be an insurrection against the Toleration Act, by numbers and open force, setting the law at defiance. * * *

Mr. Rawle said, that he conceived that, even if the matter made a grievance of, was illegal, the demolition of it in this way was, nevertheless, high treason, because of the people so assembled taking the law into their own hands; thus, in *Foster*, it would be seen that demolishing all bawdy-houses, as such, was high treason * * *. He also read Douglas, 570, Lord George Gordon's case, when it was Lord Mansfield's opinion that any attempt, by violence, to force the repeal of a law, or to prevent its execution, is levying war, and treason.

* * *

Mr. Rawle then proceeded to state the most prominent facts * * in which it would fully appear, he presumed, that John Fries, the prisoner, * * * in every instance showed his aversion of, and opposition to, the assessors, and determination by threats and menaces to prevent them doing their duty, and that whenever any force was used, * * * he was the commander, * * * and that finally, by threats and intimidation, equally the same in the eyes of the law as force, he, the prisoner, did attain his object, to wit, the release of a number of prisoners who were confined for opposing the execution of the law, and were actually in custody of the marshal in a house at Bethlehem, which, by reason of his having prisoners there, and his having an armed posse to protect his lawful authority, was to all intents a fortress of the United States; and further, that he did, completely for a time, prevent the execution of the laws intended * * *.

Judge Chase then said to the prisoner:

John Fries, you will attend to all the evidence * * * and ask any questions you please of the several witnesses, or of the court; but be careful to ask no questions wherein you may possibly criminate yourself, for remember, whatever you say to your own crimination, is evidence with the jury; but if you say anything to your justification, it is not evidence. The court will be watchful of you; they will check anything that may injure yourself: they will be your counsel, and give you every assistance and indulgence in their power.

[The evidence adduced on this trial is of so similar a character to that reported on the former occasion, as to render a report of it unnecessary. The defendant produced no testimony.]

Mr. Rawle said he felt himself so very peculiarly situated in this case, that he would wish the opinion of the court. The unfortunate prisoner at the bar appeared to answer to a charge, the greatest that could be brought against him, without the assistance of counsel, or any friend to advise with. * * * I believe it will be found that in no *material* point have I failed to substantiate what I first gave notice that I could prove. I therefore conceive the charges are fully confirmed.

But although, if this trial was conducted in the usual way * * * it would now be proper, on my part, to sum up the evidence as produced to the jury, and apply it to the law, in order to see whether the crime was fixed or not. Under the present circumstances, I feel very great reluctance to fulfil what would, in other circumstances, be my bounden duty, lest it should appear to be going further than the rigid requisition of my office compels me to. I therefore shall rest the evidence and the law here, unless the court think that my office as public prosecutor, demands of me to do it * * *.

Judge Chase.—It is not unfrequent for a prisoner to appear in a court of justice without counsel, but it is uncommon for a prisoner not to accept of legal assistance. It is the peculiar lenity of our laws that makes it the duty of a court to assign counsel to the person accused. With respect to your situation, sir, it is a matter entirely discretionary with you whether you will state the evidence and apply it to the law or not. There is great justice due to a prisoner arraigned on a charge so important as the present: there is great justice also due to the government. * * * If you do not please to proceed, I shall consider it my duty to apply the law to the facts. The prisoner may therefore offer what he pleases to the jury.

Prisoner.—I submit to the court to do me that justice which is right.

Judge Chase.—That I will, by the blessing of God, do you every justice.

Judge Peters.—Mr. Attorney, while you are justifiable in considering this situation of the prisoner * * * there is another consideration deserving attention—there is justice due to the United States. * * * I wish it to be done for the due execution of public justice, and, God knows, I do it not with a desire to injure the prisoner, for I wish not the conviction of any man. It is a painful task, but we must do our duty. Still I think you are at liberty to fulfil your own pleasure.

Mr. Rawle [then stated that he would give a brief summary of the facts and the law of the case.]

As he stated before, Mr. Rawle said * * * in relation to the republican form of government existing among us, [levying war] could only consist in an opposition to the will of the society * * * declared and established by a majority; in short, an opposition to the acts of Congress, in whole or in part, so as to prevent their execution * * * to procure a repeal or a suspension of the law, by rendering it impracticable to carry such law or laws into effect * * *.

The question, then, is, how far the case of the prisoner and his conduct merit this definition? * * *

It will first be observed by the testimony of several respectable witnesses * * * that attempts were made and executed, by a combination, in which, unfortunately for him, the prisoner at the bar was very active, to prevent the assessors from doing the duty required of them when they accepted their office, and that this combination existed both in Northampton and Bucks counties, and to such a degree that it was impossible to carry the law into effect * * *. This spirit of opposition to the laws, as exhibited generally, is also related by Mr. Henry and Col. Nichols, the marshal, wherein it appears that process could not be served, and that witnesses could not be subpoenaed, being deterred from the threats made to them by this extensive combination; and that, in the serving of process, personal abuse was given, as well as to the assessors who attempted to execute the law. In short the law was *prostrate* at the feet of a powerful combination.

Mr. Rawle here called to view the occurrences in Bucks county, as deposed by Messrs. Foulke, Rodrick, Chapman, Thomas, Mitchell, and Wiedner, exhibiting a disposition to insurrection by a great number of persons, and who engaged in its acts; he referred to the meeting at Jacob Fries', where John Fries, the prisoner at the bar, expressed himself as determining to oppose and continue hostile to the laws; also to the circumstance afterwards near Singmaster's, where Mr. Rodrick made his escape, and where, as well as at other times, the prisoner forbade those officers to proceed, under threats of personal danger. * * * However, the assessors met the next day, but were stopped at Quaker town, where they were extremely abused. To be sure, while the prisoner at the bar was in the room, and whenever he was present, their abuse was suspended; when he absented himself, it was renewed. * * * Here it must be observed, in justice to the prisoner, that one more of his few good actions appeared, which Mr. Rawle wished in his heart had been more numerous. Fries assisted Mr. Foulke to get out of the house the back way, and advised him to keep out of the way of the men.

* * * The next morning they met and went on as far as Ritters, where it appeared they were stopped for a short period by young Marks, who had been sent forward, with information that the prisoners were gone on to Bethlehem: a doubt being stated whether they would not be too late, it was debated, and at last determined to go forward: of this latter opinion was the prisoner at the bar. It was in evidence that none of those people knew the prisoners whom they were going to release * * * this, Mitchel and others swore.

Here Mr. Rawle thought commenced the overt act in the indictment. * * * They proceeded to Bethlehem, and here the officer of militia, the man who derived his power from the people, the prisoner, Captain John Fries, whose duty it was to support the law and Constitution of the United States, made a most distinguished figure. At Bethlehem it appeared that the prisoner was to step forward to effect the surrender of the prisoners, and of course to lay prostrate the legal arm of the United States. * * * The prisoner with an armed force arrived at Bethlehem, and proceeded on his mission to the marshal * * * to wit, demanding the surrender of the prisoners; the marshal answered, that he could not deliver them up. John Fries then returned to his men; and * * * said, "They must be taken by force; the marshal says he cannot deliver them up; if you are willing, we will take them by force: I will go foremost; if I drop, then take your own command." Words were followed by actions; they went into the house, and the prisoners were given up.

This, Mr. Rawle thought, was an unquestionable, full and complete proof of the commission of the overt act; and that overt act is high treason * * *.

To him, Mr. Rawle said, there was no doubt but the act of levying war was completed in the county of Bucks, independently of all those actions at Bethlehem; for there the prisoner and others were armed, and arrayed with all the appearances of war—with drums and fifes, and at times firing their pieces; and this to oppose the laws and prevent their execution * * *.

Gentlemen, said Mr. Attorney, you will consider how far the individual witnesses are deserving your credit. If you consider them worthy of being believed, and if the facts related apply to the law which I submitted to your consideration * * * there can be but little doubt upon your minds, that the prisoner is guilty: if it be not so, in your opinion, you must find him otherwise.

* * *

Court.   John Fries, you are at liberty to say anything you please to the jury.

Prisoner.   It was mentioned, that I collected a parcel of people to follow up the assessors; but I did not collect them. They came and fetched me out from my house to go with them.

I have nothing to say, but leave it to the court.

Judge Chase then addressed the jury * * *.

Too much praise cannot be given to [the] constitutional definition of treason, and the requiring such full proof for conviction; and declaring, that no attainder of treason shall work corruption of blood or forfeiture, except during the life of the person attainted.

This constitutional definition of treason is a question of law. * * * What is the true meaning and true import of any statute, and whether the case stated comes within it, is a question of law, and not of fact. The question in an indictment for levying war against * * * the United States, is, whether the facts stated do, or do not amount to levying war, within the contemplation and construction of the Constitution.

It is the duty of the court in this case, and in all criminal cases, to state to the jury their opinion of the law arising on the facts; but the jury are to decide on the present, and in all criminal cases, both the law and the facts, on their consideration of the whole case.

It is the opinion of the court, that any insurrection or rising of any body of the people, within the United States, to attain or effect by force or violence any object of a great public nature, or of public and general (or national) concern, is a levying of war against the United States, within the contemplation and construction of the Constitution.

* * *

The true criterion to determine whether acts committed are treason, or a less offence (as a riot), is the *quo animo,* or the intention, with which the people did assemble. When the intention is universal or general, as to effect some object of a general public nature, it will be treason, and cannot be considered, construed, or reduced to a riot. * * *

The court are of opinion, that if a body of people conspire and meditate an insurrection to resist or oppose the execution of any statute of the United States by force, that they are only guilty of a high misdemeanour; but if they proceed to carry such intention into execution by force, that they are guilty of the treason of levying war, and the quantum of the force employed neither lessens nor increases the crime   *   *   *.

*   *   *   [I]t is altogether immaterial whether the force used is sufficient to effectuate the object—any force connected with the intention will constitute the crime of levying war.

This opinion of the court is founded on the same principles, and is, in substance, the same as the opinion of the Circuit Court for this district, on the trials (in April, 1795) of Vigol and Mitchell, who were both found guilty by the jury, and afterwards pardoned by the late President.

At the Circuit Court for the district (April term, 1799), on the trial of the prisoner at the bar, Judge Iredell delivered the same opinion, and Fries was convicted by the jury.

To support the present indictment against the prisoner at the bar, two facts must be proved to your satisfaction:

First. That some time *before* the finding of the indictment, there was an insurrection (or rising) of a body of people in the *County of Northampton,* in this State, *with intent* to oppose and prevent, by means of *intimidation* and *violence,* the execution of a law of the United States   *   *   *   and that *some acts of violence* were committed by *some* of the people so assembled, *with intent* to oppose and prevent, by means of intimidation and violence, the execution   *   *   *   of the said law of Congress.

*   *   *

If, from a careful examination of the evidence, you shall be convinced that the real object and intent of the people assembled at Bethlehem was of a *public nature* (which it certainly was, if they assembled with intent to prevent the execution of   *   *   *   the above-mentioned laws   *   *   *,   it must then be proved to your satisfaction, that the prisoner at the bar incited, encouraged, promoted, or *assisted* in the insurrection, or rising of the people, at Bethlehem   *   *   *   and that *some force* was used by *some* of the people assembled at Bethlehem.

In the consideration of this fact, the court think proper to assist your inquiry by giving you their opinion.

In treason, all the *participes criminis* are principals; there are no accessories to this crime.   *   *   *   All persons *present*, aiding, assisting, or abetting any *treasonable act,* are *principals.*   All persons, who are present and countenancing, and are ready to afford assistance, if necessary, to those who actually commit any *treasonable act,* are also *principals.* If a number of persons assemble and set out upon a *common design,* as to resist and prevent, by force, the execution of any law, and some of them commit acts of force and violence, *with intent* to oppose the execution of any law, and others are present to aid and assist, if necessary, they are all *principals.*   *   *   *   If persons collect together to act *for one and the same common end,* any act done by any one of them, with intent to effectuate such common end, is a fact that may be given in evidence against all of them; the act of each is evidence against ALL concerned.

*   *   *

If, upon consideration of the whole matter (law as well as fact), you are *not* fully satisfied, *without any doubt,* that the prisoner is guilty of the treason charged in the indictment, you will find him *not guilty;* but if, upon consideration of the *whole* matter (law as well as *fact*), you are convinced that the prisoner is guilty of the treason charged in the indictment, you will find him guilty.

The jury retired, for the space of two hours, and brought in their verdict, GUILTY.

After the verdict was given, Judge Chase with great feeling and sensibility, addressed the prisoner, observing that, as he had no counsel on the trial, if he, or any person for him, could point out any flaw in the indictment, or legal ground for arrest of judgment, ample time would be allowed for that purpose.

*   *   *

The prisoner being set at the bar, Judge CHASE   *   *   *   proceeded:—

John Fries—*   *   *   You have had a LEGAL, FAIR, and IMPARTIAL trial, with every indulgence that the law would permit. Of the whole panel, you PEREMPTORILY challenged thirty-four, and with truth I may say, that the jury who tried you were of your *own selection and choice.* Not one of them *before* had ever formed and delivered any opinion respecting your guilt or innocence. The verdict of the jury against you was founded on the testimony of many creditable and unexceptionable witnesses. It was apparent from the conduct of the jury   *   *   *   that they pronounced their verdict against you with great concern and reluctance, from a sense of duty to their country, and a *full conviction* of your guilt.

The crime of which you have been found guilty is *treason;* a crime considered, in the most civilized and the most free countries in the world, as the *greatest* that any man can commit.   *   *   *

You are a *native* of this country—you live under a constitution (or form of government) framed by the people themselves; and under laws made by *your* representatives, faithfully executed by independent and impartial judges. Your government secures to every member of the community *equal liberty* and *equal rights;*   *   *   *   every person, without any regard to wealth, rank, or station, may enjoy an *equal* share of *civil liberty,* and *equal* protection of *law,* and an *equal* security for his *person* and *property.* * * *

If experience should prove that the *Constitution* is defective, *it* provides a mode to *change* or *amend* it, without any danger to public order, or any injury to *social* rights.

If Congress * * * should pass any law in violation of the Constitution, or burdensome or oppressive to the people, a peaceable, safe and *ample* remedy is provided by the *Constitution.* * * * If Congress should pass a law contrary to the *Constitution,* such law would be *void,* and the courts of the United States possess complete authority, and are the only tribunal to decide, whether any law is contrary to the *Constitution.* If Congress should pass *burdensome* or *oppressive* laws, the remedy is with their constituents, from whom they derive their existence and authority. If any law is made repugnant to the voice of a *majority* of their constituents, it is in their power to make choice of persons to repeal it; but until it is repealed, it is the duty of every citizen to submit to it, and to give up his *private* sentiments to the *public will.* If a law which is burdensome, or even oppressive in its *nature* or *execution,* is to be opposed by *force;* and obedience cannot be compelled, there must soon be an end to all government in this country. * * * The most ignorant man must know, that Congress can make *no law* that will not affect them *equally, in every respect,* with their constituents. Every law that is detrimental to their constituents must prove hurtful to themselves. From these considerations, every one may see, that Congress can have *no interest in oppressing their fellow-citizens.*

It is almost incredible, that a people living under the best and mildest government in the whole world, should not only be dissatisfied and discontented, but should break out into open resistance and opposition to its laws.

The insurrection in 1794 * * * is still fresh in memory * * *. Either persons disaffected to our government, or wishing to aggrandize themselves, deceived and misled the ignorant and uninformed class of the people. The opposition commenced in meetings of the people, with threats against the officers, which ripened into acts of outrage against *them* * * * Committees were formed to systematize and inflame the spirit of opposition. Violence succeeded to violence, and the collector of Fayette county was compelled to surrender his commission and official books; the dwelling house of the inspector * * * was attacked and burnt; and the marshal was seized, and obtained his liberty on a promise to serve no other process on the *west side of the Alleghany mountain.* To compel submission to the laws, the government were obliged to march an army against the insurgents, and the expense was above one million one hundred thousand dollars. Of the whole number of insurgents (many hundreds) only a *few* were brought to trial; and of them only *two* were sentenced to die (Vigol and Mitchell,) and they were pardoned by the late President. Although the insurgents made no resistance to the army sent against them, yet not a few of our troops lost their lives, in consequence of their great fatigue, and exposure to the severity of the season.

This great and remarkable clemency of the government had no effect upon *you,* and the deluded people in your neighbourhood. The rise, progress, and termination of the *late* insurrection bear a strong and striking analogy to the former; and it may be remembered that it has cost the United States 80,000 dollars. It cannot escape observation, that the ignorant and uninformed are taught to complain of taxes, which are necessary for the support of government, and yet they permit themselves to be seduced into insurrections which have so enormously increased the public burthens   *   *   *.

*   *   *   The expense, and all the consequences, therefore, are not imputable to the government, but to the insurgents. The mildness and lenity of our government are as striking on the *late* as on the *former* insurrection. Of nearly one hundred and thirty persons who might have been put on their trial for *treason,* only five have been prosecuted and tried for that crime.

*   *   *   It was the height of folly in you to suppose that the great body of our citizens, blessed in the enjoyment of a free republican government of their own choice   *   *   *   and conscious that the laws are the only security for their preservation from violence, would not rise up as one man to oppose and crush so ill-founded, so unprovoked an attempt to disturb the public peace and tranquility. If you could see in a proper light your own *folly* and *wickedness,* you ought now to bless God that your insurrection was so happily and speedily quelled by the vigilance and energy of our government *   *   *.

The annual, necessary expenditures for the support of any extensive government like ours must be great; and the sum required can only be obtained by *taxes,* or loans. In all countries the levying taxes is unpopular, and a subject of complaint.   *   *   *   [I]t becomes you to reflect that the time you chose to rise up in arms to oppose the laws of your country, was when it stood in a very critical situation with regard to France, and on the eve of a rupture with that country.

*   *   *

The end of all *punishment* is *example*; and the enormity of your crime requires that a severe example should be made to deter others from the commission of *like* crimes in future. You have forfeited your life to justice. Let me, therefore, earnestly recommend to you most seriously to consider your situation—to take a review of your past life, and to employ the very little time you are to continue in this world in endeavors to make your peace with that God whose mercy is equal to his justice. I suppose that you are a Christian; and as *such* I address you. Be assured, my guilty and unhappy fellow-citizen, that without serious repentance of *all* your sins, you cannot expect happiness in the world to come * * *. Your *day* of *life* is almost spent; and the *night* of *death* fast approaches. Look up to the Father of mercies, and God of comfort. You have a great and immense work to perform, and but little time in which you must finish it. There is no repentance in the grave, for after death comes judgment; and as you die, so you must be judged. * * * If you will sincerely repent and believe, God has pronounced his forgiveness; and there is no crime too great for his mercy and pardon.

Although you must be strictly confined for the very short remainder of your life, yet the mild government and laws which you have endeavoured to destroy, permit you (if you please) to converse and commune with ministers of the gospel; to whose pious care and consolation, in fervent prayers and devotion, I most cordially recommend you.

What remains for me is a very painful but, a very necessary part of my duty. It is to pronounce that judgment, which the law has appointed for crimes of this magnitude. The judgment of the law is, and this Court doth award "that you be hanged by the neck *until dead*:" and I pray God Almighty to be merciful to your soul!

NOTES AND QUESTIONS

1. Judge Peters worried that Chase's hasty opinion-giving would have an adverse affect on public opinion. Why was he concerned with this? Should he have been?

2. Note that Chase cautioned the jury that English authority was not binding on them. This came right after the prosecutor, Rawle, praised the English treason statute, on which Article 3, Section 3, of the United States Constitution was modelled. Was Chase's comment favorable to the prosecution? How good a job overall did Chase do as both defense counsel *and* judge? The prosecutor, William Rawle, probably embarrassed by Fries's lack of counsel, indicated a willingness to go easy on Fries, and to decline from summing up the evidence against him. *Both* Peters *and* Chase then indicated that the interests of the United States called for a summing up of the facts against Fries. Which should be more jealously guarded—the rights of the defendant or the rights of the country? Would your answer have been different in 1800?

3. What is Chase's attitude toward the jury? Chase says to the jury that they are to decide on both "the law and the facts." Is this consistent with his attempted delivery of an opinion to them at the beginning of the trial and his refusal to let certain legal arguments be made to them? Is there any other conduct of Chase's that you found to be improper? Were you surprised that Fries was convicted again?

4. Is Chase some kind of ogre? He has been recently described as "A hanging judge," and has often been called an "American Jeffreys." See, e. g., J. Miller, The Federalist Era 248 (1960). Is his political and judicial philosophy the work of the devil? What did you make of his remarks to

John Fries after Fries's conviction? Compare Chase's thinking on American political principles and the importance of judicial review to that of John Marshall in Marbury v. Madison.

5. Shortly after the Second Fries trial, President Adams, against the advice of Alexander Hamilton, pardoned John Fries and all others who had taken part in the insurrection. This helped destroy the Federalist party from within. Instead of being hung, then, Fries walked away a free man. How could Adams do this? Even more remarkable than Adams pardon of Fries is Fries's attitude toward Chase. Shortly after his pardon, Fries journeyed to Chase's home in Maryland, and there thanked the justice "for his impartial, fair, and equitable conduct" during the trial. 9 J. Sanderson, Biography of the Signers to the Declaration of Independence 230 (1827). Was Fries completely unhinged, or did people behave differently at the turn of the eighteenth country? What might account for this behavior?

6. Recall Jefferson's proposals for reforming the law of crime and punishment (pp. 134–135, supra). Contrast these with Chase's statement at the end of the Fries trial that "the end of all punishment is example." Does this suggest anything about Chase's view of the purpose of government in general and criminal law in particular?

SECTION C. THE FEDERAL COMMON LAW OF CRIMES

By late 1798 the question of whether there were federal non-statutory crimes that could be punished in the federal courts was a hot political issue. The Federalists, with one significant exception (as you will soon see), unanimously maintained that the federal bench could punish "common law crimes" in the same manner as could the state courts. The Republicans, again almost without exception, felt equally strongly that to allow the federal courts to punish common law crimes would be an unconstitutional and unwarranted usurpation of power. These materials are to illustrate the divergent approaches to the problem of common law crimes. Your task is to determine which view or views you find convincing, and to determine whether the positions of the Federalist judges, and particularly Judge Peters and Justice Chase, seem consistent with what you have seen of them so far.

1. JAY'S AND WILSON'S JURY CHARGES

PRESSER, A TALE OF TWO JUDGES: RICHARD PETERS, SAMUEL CHASE, AND THE BROKEN PROMISE OF FEDERALIST JURISPRUDENCE

73 Nw.L.Rev. 48–52 (1978).

The Judiciary Act of 1789 gave the federal circuit courts jurisdiction over "crimes and offenses cognizable under the authority of the United States," but the statute did not specify what acts were "crimes and offenses," nor did it specify the extent of the "authority" of the United States. Much of the prevailing jurisprudence can be derived from contemporary jury charges. The first official interpretation of federal criminal jurisdiction, in 1790, signalled that it was to be broadly construed. Chief Justice John Jay charged the Grand Juries of the Eastern Circuit in the spring of that year as follows: * * * Your province and your duty extend * * * to the enquiry and presentment of all offenses of every kind, committed against the United States in this district, or on the high seas by persons in it." Jay did not define the term "offenses," * * * Nevertheless, Jay did provide some clues * * *.

First, he suggested that the jurors

would recollect that the laws of nations make part of the laws of this, and of every other civilized nation. They consist of those rules for regulating the conduct of nations towards each other, which, resulting from right reason, receive their obligation from that principle and from general assent and practice.

The jurors were thus to use their own common sense and their knowledge of world and national history to guide them in their search for criminal acts.

Second, Jay acknowledged that some federal statutes defined crimes, but he maintained that these statutes would not serve alone as indicators of what offenses the jurors should present:

The penal statutes of the United States are few and principally respect the revenue. The right ordering and management of this important business is very essential to the credit, character, and prosperity of our country. On the citizens at large is placed the burden of providing for the public exigencies. Whoever therefore fraudulently withdraws his shoulder from the common burthen necessarily leaves his portion of the weight to be born by the others, and thereby does injustice not only to the government, but to them.

Here Jay's focus would seem to be not on particular violations of the terms of revenue statutes but more broadly on "whoever fraudulently withdraws his shoulder from the common burthen."

Finally Jay told the grand jurors * * * to "direct your conduct also to the conduct of the national officers, and let not any corruptions, frauds, extortions or criminal negligence with which you may find any of them justly chargeable pass unnoticed." Jay thus seemed to be defining "offenses against the United States" [at least as committed by government officials] to include virtually any examples of [what the grand jurors might conceive as] wrongdoing against the government or the public. * * *

Three years later, in a charge to the Grand Jury for the Middle Circuit in the District of Virginia, Jay   *   *   *   seemed most concerned with violations of the "law of nations." This was a result of the outbreak of war between England and France in January 1793, which had violently split American public opinion and had just resulted in the "Neutrality Proclamation" issued by President Washington. Jay quoted extensively from the Proclamation and indicated that Washington's instructions to prosecute persons who committed, aided, or abetted hostilities against any of the belligerents, or who furnished them contraband, were "exactly consistent with and declaratory of the conduct enjoined by the law of nations." Jay closed his charge with comments indicating that the United States' treaties of "firm and perpetual peace" also enjoined American citizens from aiding the belligerent powers, and that such conduct, as a violation of a treaty, was punishable as a crime [but it appears clearly from Jay's charge that an offense against the "law of nations" would be criminal even without a treaty.]

Later, in July 1793, Justice James Wilson of the Supreme Court charged a Grand Jury for the Middle Circuit in Philadelphia. One of the matters which this grand jury was to investigate involved one Gideon Henfield, who was accused of engaging in acts hostile to nations at peace with the United States. Henfield had allegedly assisted in the capture of an English prize ship by a French privateer. [In Wilson's charge he stressed that]   *   *   *   the basis of the American judicial system, and indeed, the basis of any civilized system of jurisprudence was what he called the "common law."   *   *   *   Unlike the contemporary English common law   *   *   *   Wilson suggested, American common law was closer to the common law of the ancient Saxons than it was to that of the Normans. The Saxons, like the Americans, had a more expansive notion of individual liberty and popular sovereignty. Nevertheless, Wilson went on, the American common law, like every other, was "a social system of jurisprudence; and associates to herself those who can give her information, or advice, or assistance." Thus, when a court was faced with a problem involving the law of other countries, the law of merchants, or the law of nations, those bodies of doctrine would become assimilated into the common law and would be used in the disposition of particular cases.

In this manner Wilson arrived at the same point Jay started with in his jury charge two months earlier—the United States law incorporated the law of nations. Unlike Jay, however, Wilson carefully explained that he had arrived at this destination through the vehicle of what he called the "common law." For Wilson, the "Law of nations" (and by implication, "the common law") was not simply a set of arbitrary rules. The "law of nations" was "the law of nature," it was "of obligation indispensible" and "of origin divine." Moreover, the "law of nations" was not simply limited to regulating the affairs of one nation with another. By becoming a nation, citizens created certain duties which they owed to each other and to the nation itself, duties specified by the "law of nations." Among these duties which devolved on individuals (and on nations) was that of keeping "peace on earth," of living in amity with one's neighbors. * * * [G]iven the primary duty of citizens to be peaceful [, Wilson told the jurors,] "[A] citizen, who in our state of neutrality, and without the authority of the nation, takes an hostile part with either of the belligerent powers, violates thereby his duty, and the laws of his country * * *."

Five days later, on July 27, 1793, the grand jury returned an indictment against Henfield. The indictment said that his conduct was "to the evil example of all others in like cases offending, in violation of the laws of nations, against the laws of the United States in such case made and provided, and against the Constitution of the United States, and against the peace and dignity of the said United States." * * *

* * *

2. HENFIELD'S TRIAL

UNITED STATES v. HENFIELD

United States Circuit Court for the District of Pennsylvania, 1793.
11 Fed.Cas. 1099.

* * *

It appeared in evidence that Gideon Henfield was a citizen of the United States and that his family resided in Salem, Massachusetts. Being a sea-faring man he had been absent from them some time, and about the 1st of May, 1793, being then at Charleston, South Carolina, and desirous of coming to Philadelphia * * * he entered on board the Citizen Genet, a French privateer, commissioned by the French Republic and commanded by Pierre Johannen. Captain Johannen, it appeared, promised him the berth of prize-master on board the first prize they should capture, and the ship William belonging to British subjects, having been captured about the 5th of May, he was put on board her as prize-master, with another person, and arrived in that capacity at Philadelphia. It appeared that on his examination before the magistrate, he protested himself an American, that as such he would die, and therefore could not be supposed likely to intend anything to her prejudice. He declared if he had known it to be contrary to the President's proclamation, or even the wishes of the President, for whom he had the greatest respect, he would not have entered on board. About a month afterwards, being before the same magistrate, he declared he had espoused the cause of France, that he now considered himself as a Frenchman, and meant to move his family within their dominions.

Mr. Rawle, District Attorney [argued that:] * * *

1. *Every* member is accountable to society for those actions which may affect the *interest* of that society.

2. The United States being in perfect peace with *all* nations, and allied in friendly bonds with *some,* their national situation requires a *perfect neutrality* from *every* motive applicable to our *common interest.*

3. An aggression on the subjects of other nations done in an *hostile* manner and under *colour of war* is a violation of that neutrality.

4. If *not* under the colour of war it would be an act of *piracy.*

But by the laws of nations if one of the belligerent powers should capture a neutral subject fighting under a commission from the other belligerent powers he could not punish him as a pirate, but must *treat him as an enemy,* and it would be a good cause of declaring war against the nation to which he belonged; and if treated as an enemy without *just* cause it is the duty of the nation to which he belongs to interfere in his behalf; and thus arises another cause of war.

Hence the act of the individual is an *injury* to the nation, and the *right of punishment* follows the existence of the *injury.*

5. The right of peace and war is always vested in the government.

In the United States, but Congress alone possesses it.

By the formation of the society every individual has consented to its being thus exclusively deposited for the general benefit.

No individual, therefore, can assume the exercise of this right.

* * *

6. If *one* individual has a right to associate with the subjects of one of the belligerent powers, *another* individual has an equal right to do the same with the other belligerent power; thus the citizens of the neutral nation might be fighting *with each other.*

Under this unhappy prospect, the national *character* and *existence* of America are lost; and instead of being members of a *great nation,* we become a band of *miserable Algerines.*

* * *

France is at war with Austria, Spain, Portugal, and Sardinia, with whom we are at peace; with Great Britain, with whom a treaty of peace exists; and with the United Netherlands and Prussia, with whom there is peace, amity, and commerce.

* * *

With Great Britain is a treaty of peace, by Article 7 of which it is provided that there shall be a *firm* and *perpetual peace* between his Britannic Majesty and the United States, and the subjects of the one and the citizens of the other.

* * *

Thus, an infraction of *this kind,* unless punished, becomes a good cause of war on the part of the *offended* nation.—Vat. b. 4, § 52; Bynk, Jus.Pub. b. 1, c. 8, p. 178.

It is an offence against *our own* country, at common law, because the right of war is vested in the *government* only.—Puffendorf, b. 8, c. 6, sec. 8; Vat. b. 3, § 4; b. 4, § 223.

In a *state of nature* the right adhered to the individual.

It is lost by *joining* society.

* * *

Nor are these only the speculations of the closet. We see them carried into effect in England in affirmation of national common law, i. e., *the law of nations.*—4 Black.Com. 69.

The English statute is not in force here, because the specific remedy for which alone it was made cannot be had, but the *law* which it aided, not introduced, is in force.

The law of nations is part of the law of the land.—4 Black.Com. 66; 1 Dallas 111; C.L. 11 b.

This is an offence against the laws of nations. It is punishable by indictment on information as such.—1 Dallas, 114, &c.; 3 Burr. 1480.

* * *

* * * That the Executive should be inadequate to sudden and unusual exertions of power is our pride and happiness; and that our Courts should, with that impartial and unbiased dignity which characterizes their judicial investigations of truth, apply the law of nations to men, of which nations are composed, and substitute the scales of justice for the sword of war.

But it is said that there is a want of *precedent* for this prosecution.

The first answer is, that it is demonstrated that the law of nations is part of the law of the land.

The second answer is, that in numerous other instances, enumerated by Blackstone, the law of nations is enforced by the judiciary. * * *

It is urged, also, that the right of emigration is natural to freemen. It is no crime to become a French subject, and being a French subject, the defendant may lawfully enlist in this command.

The answer is, that when a man has fairly and deliberately emigrated * * * *previously* to the commission of the hostile act, and *without a view to it,* there is no offence in an act *of this kind.* * * *

But, at all events, if *at the time* the act was committed, the party was unquestionably a citizen, had *not renounced* his country, and was not domiciliated elsewhere, he cannot escape punishment by becoming a citizen *afterwards.* * * *

Is not the defendant's *family* still at Massachusetts?

Is he not *still* upon the *roll* of their citizens; were his family in want, would they not be entitled to public relief?

Did he not declare that, as an American he would die?

* * *

Let us suppose America engaged in war, and that one of her faithless children prefers the other party, joins an hostile detachment which has already invaded his own country, or enters on board a foreign privateer lying in our bay, and commits those acts, which in war are lawful, in peace, crimes. Does the right to emigrate, the right to choose his country, to renounce his former allegiance protect him here?

* * *

Let it not be said that this doctrine violates the rights of man. It is on the rights of man that it is established. The rights of man are the rights of all men in relation to each other, and when voluntarily assumed in society founded on principles of genuine freedom, they form a useful, benevolent and endearing system, in which as much is received as is given. Perfect equality is one of those rights. We render ourselves equal when we all submit to the laws. That equality is destroyed if one man can set himself above them. That equality is destroyed if one man with impunity may involve three millions in war.

* * *

Is it not fair to ask * * * by what authority have you or I delegated to an individual the right of subjecting us to the pressure of heavy taxes, to the desolation of property, to the destruction of agriculture and of commerce, to the dangers of military service, in short, to the havoc and miseries of war? * * * Our excellent constitution has wisely vested this solemn, awful step in the collected wisdom and patriotism of the whole country. There the necessity of the war and the means of defence will be compared by men selected by their country and responsible to it, but not by men who involve us in what they profess they will not share with us, and in the very act which draws on us the greatest political affliction renounce the very connexion which has alone rendered us liable for their conduct.
* * *

Mr. Duponceau, Mr. Ingersoll and Mr. Sergeant addressed the jury at great length; and insisted—

1.   That the indictment did not include an offence at common law.

2.   That if the President's proclamation created such an offence, the case before the Court was committed before the proclamation was made.

3.   That though the treaty with Morocco prohibited the enlisting of American citizens under such circumstances as the present, yet there was no such provision in the treaty with France, and hence the

inference from its express introduction into the former treaty is that it was intentionally omitted from the latter.

4.   That independently on these grounds, as there was no statute giving jurisdiction, the Court could take no cognizance of the offence.

*   *   *

Judge Wilson, (with whom were Judge Iredell and Judge Peters,) charged the jury as follows: *   *   *

It has not been contended, on the present occasion, that the defendant has any peculiar exclusive right to take a part in the present war between the European powers, in relation to all whom the United States are in a state of peace and tranquillity.

If he has no peculiar or exclusive right, it naturally follows, that what he may do every other citizen of the United States may also do *   *   *   and thus thousands of our fellow-citizens may associate themselves with different belligerent powers, destroying not only those with whom we have no hostility, but destroying each other.   In such a case, can we expect peace among their friends who stay behind?   And will not a civil war, with all its lamentable train of evil, be the natural effect?

*   *   *

Two principal questions of fact have arisen, and require your determination.   The first is, that the defendant, Gideon Henfield, has committed an act of hostility against the subjects of a power with whom the United States are at peace: this has been clearly established by the testimony.   The second object of inquiry is, whether Gideon Henfield was at that time a citizen of the United States.   This he explicitly acknowledged to Mr. Baker; and if he declared true, it was at that time the least of his thoughts to expatriate himself.

The questions of law coming into joint consideration with the facts, it is the duty of the Court to explain the law to the jury, and give it to them in direction.

It is the joint and unanimous opinion of the Court, that the United States, being in a state of neutrality relative to the present war, the acts of hostility committed by Gideon Henfield are an offence against this country, and punishable by its laws.

It has been asked by his counsel, in their address to you, against what law has he offended?   The answer is, against many and binding laws.   As a citizen of the United States, he was bound to act no part which could injure the nation; he was bound to keep the peace in regard to all nations with whom we are at peace.   This is the law of nations; not an *ex post facto* law, but a law that was in existence long before Gideon Henfield existed.   There are, also, positive laws, existing previous to the offence committed, and expressly declared to be part of the supreme law of the land.   The Constitution of the United States has declared that all treaties made, or to be made, under the authority of the United States, shall be part of the supreme law of the land. * * *

The seventh article of the definitive treaty of peace between the United States and Great Britain, declares that there shall be a firm and perpetual peace between His Britannic Majesty and the United States, and between the subjects of the one and the citizens of the other.

* * *

These treaties were in the most public, the most notorious existence, before the act for which the prisoner is indicted was committed.

* * *

* * * [T]he Judge concluded by remarking, that the jury, in a general verdict must decide both law and fact, but that this did not authorize them to decide it as they please;

They were as much bound to decide by law as the judges: the responsibility was equal upon both.

The jury retired about nine on Saturday evening, and came into court again about half-past eleven, when they informed the Court they had not agreed. They were desired to retire again which they did, and returned on Monday morning * * *.

One of the jurymen now expressed some doubts, which occasioned the judges separately to deliver their sentiments on the points of law adverted to in the charge on Saturday evening, each of them assenting to the same, particularly as to the change of political relation in the defendant, from his having been some time absent from home previous to his entering on board the privateer.

The jury again retired, and the Court adjourned. At half-past four the Court was convened, and the jury presented a written verdict, which the Court refused to receive, as being neither general nor special. Another adjournment took place, and about seven o'clock a verdict of "Not Guilty" was delivered.

NOTES AND QUESTIONS

1. As indicated in these materials, before Henfield's trial, but *after* Henfield's offense, President Washington issued a proclamation urging citizens *not* to get involved in the current war between European nations. The relevant text of this proclamation was:

Whereas, it appears that a state of war exists between Austria, Prussia, Sardinia, Great Britain, and the United Netherlands of the one part, and France of the other, and the duty and interest of the United States, require that they should with sincerity and good faith, adopt and pursue a conduct friendly and impartial towards the belligerent powers:

I have, therefore, thought fit by these presents, to declare the disposition of the United States to observe the conduct aforesaid towards these powers respectively, and to exhort and warn the citizens of the United States, carefully to avoid all acts and proceedings whatsoever, which may in any manner tend to contravene such disposition.

I do hereby make known, that whosoever of the citizens of the United States, shall render himself liable to punishment or forfeiture, under the law of nations, by committing, aiding, or abetting hostilities against any of the said powers, or by carrying to them those articles which are deemed contraband, by the modern usage of nations, will not receive the protection of the United States against such punishment or forfeiture; and further, that I have given instructions to those officers to whom it belongs, to cause prosecutions to be instituted against all persons who shall within the cognizance of the Courts of the United States, violate the law of nations, with respect to the powers at war, or any of them.

Was it true, as Henfield's counsel maintained and as the anti-Federalist, "Democratic," or "Republican" press urged, that the Proclamation created a new offense, which did not exist at the time Henfield committed the acts complained of?

2.   The prosecutor, William Rawle, and the judges, notably Justice Wilson, indicate that the law Henfield violated was in existence long before Henfield. Where exactly did this law come from?

3.   What is the difference between "the law of nations," as that term is used by the authors in this section, and the "common law"?

4.   How would you have voted if you were a juror in *Henfield's* case? The opposition press hailed the acquittal of Henfield. See, e. g. John Marshall, II Life of Washington 273–274 (1807). Indeed, these newspapers suggested that the Henfield victory was as great a triumph for liberty as the verdict in the *Seven Bishops'* case. What might the anti-Federalist press have meant by "liberty?" What is the connection between the two trials? Does it help to know that there was no doubt that Henfield had done the acts charged against him?

5.   Immediately below is the report of a case decided a year after Henfield's, United States v. Ravara, 27 Fed.Cas. 714 (C.C.D.Pa.1793). Note the verdict. What is the difference between the issue in the *Henfield* case and the issue in *Ravara's* case? Why the difference in the verdicts?

The defendant, a Consul from Genoa, was indicted for a misdemeanour, in sending anonymous and threatening letters to Mr. Hammond, the British Minister, to Mr. Holland, a citizen of Philadelphia, and to several other persons, with a view to extort money.
* * *

The defendant was tried in April Session, 1794, before Jay, Chief Justice, and Peters, Justice; and was defended * * * on the following points: 1st. That the matter charged in the indictment was not a crime by the Common Law, nor is it made such by any positive law of the United States. In England it was once treason; it is now felony; but in both instances it was the effect of positive law. It can only, therefore, be considered as a bare menace of bodily hurt; and, without a consequent inconvenience, it is no injury public or private. 4 Bl.C. 5; 8 Hen. VI. c. 6, 9;

Geo. I. c. 22; 4 Bl.C. 144; 3 Bl.C. 120. 2d. That considering the official character of the defendant, such a proceeding ought not to be sustained, nor such a punishment inflicted. The law of nations is a part of the law of the United States; and the law of nations seems to require, that a counsel should be independent of the ordinary criminal justice of the place where he resides. Vat. b. 2, c. 2, s. 34. 3d. But that, exclusive of the legal exceptions, the prosecution had not been maintained in point of evidence; for, it was all circumstantial and presumptive, and that too, in so slight a degree, as ought not to weigh with a jury on so important an issue. * * *

Mr. Rawle, in reply, insisted that the offence was indictable at common law; that the consular character of the defendant gave jurisdiction to the Circuit Court, and did not entitle him to an exemption from prosecution agreeably to the law of nations; and that the proof was as strong as the nature of the case allowed, or the rules of evidence required. * * *

The Court were of opinion in the charge, that the offence was indictable, and that the defendant was not privileged from prosecution, in virtue of his consular appointment.

The Jury, after a short consultation, pronounced the defendant guilty; but he was afterwards pardoned, on condition (*as stated by Mr. Dallas*) that he surrendered his commission * * *.

3. WORRALL'S CASE

UNITED STATES v. ROBERT WORRALL

United States Circuit Court for the District of Pennsylvania, 1798.
28 Fed.Cas. 774.

[The defendant had been indicted for attempting to bribe Tench Coxe, the United States Commissioner of Revenue. Pursuant to federal legislation Coxe had been authorized to let a contract for the building of a lighthouse on Cape Hatteras, in North Carolina. The relevant part of the indictment charged that Robert Worrall] * * * yeoman, being an ill-disposed person, and wickedly contriving and contending to bribe and seduce the * * * Commissioner of the Revenue, from the performance of the trust and duty so in him reposed, on the said 28th day of September, 1797 * * * wickedly, advisedly and corruptly, did compose, write, utter and publish, and cause to be delivered to the said Tench Coxe, a letter * * *:

DEAR SIR:

Having had the honour of waiting on you, at different times, on the light house business, and having delivered a fair, honest estimate, and I will be candid to declare, that with my diligent and industrious attendance, and sometimes taking an active part in the work, and receiving a reasonable wages for attending the same, I will be bold to say, that when the work is completed in the most masterly manner, the job will clear at the finishing, the sum of £1000. * * *

* * * [G]ood sir, as having always been brought up in a life of industry, [I] should, be happy in serving you in the executing this job, and always content with a reasonable profit; therefore, every reasonable person would say that £1400 was not unreasonable * * *. If I should be so happy in your recommendation of this work, I should think myself very ungrateful, if I did not offer you one-half of the profits as above stated, and would deposit in your hand at receiving the first payment £350, and the other £350 at the last payment, when the work is finished and completed. * * * In the mean time I shall subscribe myself to be, your obedient and very humble servant to command.

ROBERT WORRALL.

* * *

* * * On the receipt of the letter Mr. Coxe immediately consulted Mr. Ingersoll (the Attorney General of the State), communicated the circumstance that had occurred to the President, and invited the defendant to a conference at Burlington. In this conference, the defendant acknowledged having written and sent the letter; declared that no one else knew its contents, for "in business done in his chamber, he did not let his left hand know what his right hand did;" and repeated the offer of allowing Mr. Coxe a share in the profits of the contract. * * *

[The two counts of the indictment charged Mr. Worrall with (1) offering the bribe in the letter, and (2) repeating the offer orally.] On these facts, Mr. M. Levy, for the defendant, observed, that it was not sufficient for the purpose of conviction to prove that the defendant was guilty of an offence, but the offence must also appear to be legally defined * * *.

The attorney of the district (Mr. Rawle) * * * To show that the offer of a bribe is indictable, though the bribe is not accepted, * * * referred to 4 Burr. 2494, 1 Ld.Raym. 1377.

* * * Verdict—*guilty* on both counts of the indictment.

Mr. Dallas, (who had declined speaking on the facts before the jury) now moved in arrest of judgment, alleging that the Circuit Court could not take cognizance of the crime charged in the indictment. * * * It will be admited, [Dallas stated,] that all the judicial authority of the Federal Courts, must be derived, either from the Constitution of the United States, or from the Acts of Congress made in pursuance of that Constitution. It is, therefore, incumbent upon the prosecutor to show, that an offer to bribe the Commissioner of the Revenue, is a violation of some constitution, or legislative prohibition. The Constitution contains express provisions in certain cases, which are designated by a definition of the crimes; by a reference to the characters of the parties offending; or by the exclusive jurisdiction of the place where the offences were perpetrated: but the crime of attempting to bribe, the character of a Federal officer, and the place where the present offence was committed, do not form any part of the constitutional express provisions, for the exercise of judicial authority in the courts of the Union. The judicial power, however, extends, not only to all cases, in law and equity, arising under the Constitution; but, likewise, to all such as shall arise under the laws of the United States, (Art. 3, § 2,) and besides the authority, specially vested in Congress, to pass laws for enumerated purposes, there is a general authority given "to make all laws which shall be necessary and proper for carrying into execution all the powers vested by the Constitution in the government of the United States, or in any department or office thereof." Art. 1, Sect. 8. Whenever, then, Congress think any provision necessary to effectuate the constitutional power of the government, they may establish it by law; and whenever it is so established, a violation of its sanctions will come within the jurisdiction of this Court, under the 11th Section of the Judicial Act, which declares, that the Circuit Court "shall have exclusive cognizance of all crimes and offences cognizable under the authority of the United States," &c.   *   *   *   Thus, Congress have provided by law, for the punishment of treason, misprision of treason, piracy, counterfeiting any public certificate, stealing or falsifying records, &c.; for the punishment of various crimes, when committed within the limits of the exclusive jurisdiction of the United States; and for the punishment of bribery itself in the case of a judge, an officer of the customs, or an officer of the excise.   *   *   *   But in the case of the Commissioner of the Revenue, the act constituting the office does not create or declare the offence;   *   *   *   it is not recognized in the act, under which proposals for building the light house were invited;   *   *   *   and there is no other act that has the slightest relation to the subject.

    *   *   *   A case arising under a law, must mean a case depending on the exposition of a law, in respect to something which the law prohibits, or enjoins. There is no characteristic of that kind in the present instance. But, it may be suggested, that the office being established by a law of the United States, it is an incident naturally attached to the authority of the United States, to guard the officer against the approaches of corruption, in the execution of his public trust. It is true, that the person who accepts an office may be supposed to enter into a compact to be answerable to the government, which he serves, for any violation of his duty; and, having taken the oath of office, he would unquestionably be liable, in such case, to a prosecution for perjury in the Federal Courts. But because one man, by his own act, renders himself amenable to a particular jurisdiction, shall another man, who has not incurred a similar obligation, be implicated? If, in other words, it is sufficient to vest a jurisdiction in this court, that a Federal officer is concerned; if it is a sufficient proof of a case arising under a law of the United States to affect

other persons, that such officer is bound, by law, to discharge his duty with fidelity;—a source of jurisdiction is opened, which must inevitably overflow and destroy all the barriers between the judicial authorities of the state and the general government. Any thing which can prevent a Federal officer from the punctual, as well as from an impartial performance of his duty; an assault and battery; or the recovery of a debt, as well as the offer of a bribe, may be made a foundation of the jurisdiction of this court; and, considering the constant disposition of power to extend the sphere of its influence, fictions will be resorted to, when real cases cease to occur. A mere fiction, that the defendant is in the custody of the marshal, has rendered the jurisdiction of the King's Bench universal in all personal actions. Another fiction, which states the plaintiff to be a debtor of the crown, gives cognizance of all kinds of personal suits to the Exchequer * * *. If, therefore, the disposition to amplify the jurisdiction of the Circuit Court exists, precedents of the means to do so are not wanting; and it may hereafter be sufficient to suggest, that the party is a Federal officer, in order to enable this court to try every species of crime, and to sustain every description of action.

But another ground may, perhaps, be taken to vindicate the present claim of jurisdiction: it may be urged, that though the offence is not specified in the Constitution, nor defined in any act of Congress; yet, that it is an offence at common law; and that the common law is the law of the United States, in cases that arise under their authority. The nature of our Federal compact will not, however, tolerate this doctrine. The twelfth article of the amendment stipulates, that "the powers not delegated to the United States by the Constitution, nor prohibited by it to the States, are reserved to the States respectively, or to the people." In relation to crimes and punishments, the objects of the delegated power of the United States are enumerated and fixed. Congress may provide for the punishment of counterfeiting the securities and current coin of the United States; and may define and punish piracies and felonies committed on the high seas, and offences against the law of nations. Art. 1, § 8. And, so likewise Congress may make all laws which shall be necessary and proper for carrying into execution the powers of the general government. But here is no reference to a common law authority: Every power is matter of definite and positive grant; and the very powers that are granted cannot take effect until they are exercised through the medium of a law. Congress had undoubtedly a power to make a law, which should render it criminal to offer a bribe to the Commissioner of the Revenue; but not having made the law the crime is not recognized by the Federal code, constitutional or legislative; and, consequently, it is not a subject on which the judicial authority of the Union can operate.

The cases that have occurred, since the establishment of the Federal Constitution, confirm these general principles. The indictment against Henfield, an American citizen, for enlisting and serving on board a French privateer, while she captured a Dutch merchant ship, &c., expressly charged the defendant with a violation of the treaties existing between the United States and the United Netherlands, Great Britain, &c., which is a matter cognizable under the Federal authority by the very words of the Constitution. The jurisdiction in the indictment against Ravara, was sustained by reason of the defendant's official character as Consul.   *   *   *

Mr. Rawle (the attorney of the district) observed, that the exception, taken in support of the motion in arrest of judgment, struck at the root of the whole system of the national government; for, if opposition to the pure, regular and efficient administration of its affairs could thus be made by fraud, the experiment of force might next be applied; and doubtless with equal impunity and success. He concluded, however, that it was unnecessary to reason from the inconveniency and mischief of the exception; for, the offence was strictly within the very terms of the Constitution, arising under the laws of the United States. If no such office had been created by the laws of the United States, no attempt to corrupt such an officer could have been made; and it is unreasonable to insist, that merely because a law has not prescribed an express and appropriate punishment for the offence, therefore, the offence, when committed, shall not be punished by the Circuit Court, upon the principles of common law punishment. The effect, indeed, of the position is still more injurious; for, unless this offence is punishable in the Federal courts, it certainly is not cognizable before any State tribunal. The true point of view for considering the case, may be ascertained, by an inquiry whether, if Mr. Coxe had accepted the bribe, and betrayed his trust, he would not have been indictable in the courts of the United States? If he would be so indictable, upon the strongest principles of analogy, the offence of the person who tempted him, must be equally the subject of animadversion before the same judicial authority. The precedents cited by the defendant's counsel, are distinguishable from the present indictment. The prosecution against Henfield was not expressly on the treaty, but on the law of nations, which is a part of the common law of the United States; and the power of indicting for a breach of treaty, not expressly providing the means of enforcing performance in the particular instance, is itself a common law power. Unless the judicial system of the United States justified a recourse to common law against an individual guilty of a breach of treaty, the offence, where no specific penalty was to be found in the treaty, would therefore remain unpunished. So, likewise, with respect to Ravara, although he held the office of a Consul, he was indicted and punished at the common law.   *   *   *

Chase, Justice. Do you mean, Mr. Attorney, to support this indictment solely at common law? If you do, I have no difficulty upon the subject: The indictment cannot be maintained in this Court.

Mr. Rawle, answering in the affirmitive, Chase * * * delivered an opinion to the following effect.

Chase, Justice. This is an indictment for an offence highly injurious to morals, and deserving the severest punishment; but, as it is an indictment at common law, I dismiss, at once, everything that has been said about the Constitution and laws of the United States.

In this country, every man sustains a twofold political capacity; one in relation to the State, and another in relation to the United States. In relation to the State, he is subject to various municipal regulations, founded upon the State Constitution and policy, which do not affect him in his relation to the United States: For, the Constitution of the Union is the source of all the jurisdiction of the national government; so that the departments of the government can never assume any power, that is not expressly granted by that instrument, nor exercise a power in any other manner than is there prescribed. Besides the particular cases, which the 8th section of the 1st article designates, there is a power granted to Congress to create, define, and punish crimes and offences, whenever they shall deem it necessary and proper by law to do so, for effectuating the objects of the government; and although bribery is not among the crimes and offences specifically mentioned, it is certainly included in this general provision. The question, however, does not arise about the power; but about the exercise of the power:—Whether the courts of the United States can punish a man for any act, before it is declared by a law of the United States to be criminal? Now, it appears to my mind, to be as essential, that Congress should define the offences to be tried, and apportion the punishments to be inflicted, as that they should erect courts to try the criminal, or to pronounce a sentence on conviction.

It is attempted, however, to supply the silence of the Constitution and statutes of the Union by resorting to the common law for a definition and punishment of the offence which has been committed: but, in my opinion, the United States, as a Federal government, have no common law; and, consequently, no indictment can be maintained in their courts, for offences merely at the common law. If, indeed, the United States can be supposed, for a moment, to have a common law, it must, I presume, be that of England; and, yet, it is impossible to trace when, or how, the system was adopted, or introduced. With respect to the individual States, the difficulty does not occur. When the American colonies were first settled by our ancestors, it was held, as well by the settlers, as by the judges and lawyers of England, that they brought hither, as a birth-right and inheritance, so much of the common law as was applicable to their local situation and change of circumstances. But each colony judged for itself what parts of the common law were applicable to its new condition; and in various modes by legislative acts, by judicial decisions, or by constant usage, adopted some parts, and rejected others. Hence, he who shall travel through the different States, will soon discover, that the whole of the common law of England has been nowhere introduced; that some States have rejected what others have adopted; and that there is, in short, a great and essential diversity in the subjects to which the common law is applied, as well as in the extent of its application. The common law, therefore, of one State, is not the common law of another; but the common law of England, is the law of each State, so far as each State has adopted it; and it results from that position, connected with the judicial act, that the common law will always apply to suits between citizen and citizen, whether they are instituted in a Federal or State court.

But the question recurs, when and how have the courts of the United States acquired a common law jurisdiction in criminal cases? The United States must possess the common law themselves, before they can communicate it to their judicial agents: Now, the United States did not bring it with them from England; the Constitution does not create it; and no act of Congress has assumed it. Besides, what is the common law to which we are referred? Is it the common law entire, as it exists in England; or modified, as it exists in some of the States; and of the various modifications, which are we to select, the system of Georgia or New Hampshire, of Pennsylvania or Connecticut?

Upon the whole it may be a defect in our political institutions, it may be an inconvenience in the administration of justice, that the common law authority, relating to crimes and punishments, has not been conferred upon the government of the United States, which is a government in other respects also of a limited jurisdiction; but judges cannot remedy political imperfections, nor supply any legislative omission. * * * [C]ertainly, Congress might have provided by law for the present case, as they have provided for other cases, of a similar nature; and yet if Congress had ever declared and defined the offence, without prescribing a punishment, I should still have thought it improper to exercise a discretion upon that part of the subject.

Peters, Judge. Whenever a government has been established, I have always supposed, that a power to preserve itself, was a necessary and an inseparable concomitant. But the existence of the Federal government would be precarious, and it could no longer be called an independent government, if, for the punishment of offences of this nature, tending to obstruct and pervert the administration of its affairs, an appeal must be made to the State tribunals, or the offenders must escape with absolute impunity.

The power to punish misdemeanours is originally and strictly a common law power; of which I think the United States are constitutionally possessed. It might have been exercised by Congress in the form of a legislative act; but it may also, in my opinion, be enforced in a course of judicial proceeding. Whenever an offence aims at the subversion of any Federal institution, or at the corruption of its public officers, it is an offence against the well-being of the United States; from its very nature, it is cognizable under their authority; and, consequently, it is within the jurisdiction of this court, by virtue of the 11th section of the judicial act.

The court being divided in opinion, it became a doubt, whether sentence could be pronounced upon the defendant; and a wish was expressed by the judges and the attorney of the district, that the case might be put into such a form, as would admit of obtaining the ultimate decision of the Supreme Court, upon the important principle of the discussion: But the counsel for the prisoner did not think themselves authorized to enter into a compromise of that nature. The court, after a short consultation, and declaring that the sentence was mitigated in consideration of the defendant's circumstances, proceeded to adjudge,

That the defendant be imprisoned for three months; that he pay a fine of two hundred dollars; and that he stand committed until this sentence be complied with, and the costs of prosecution paid.

NOTES AND QUESTIONS

1. This case is probably our most important case on the federal common law of crimes because it involved *both* Peters and Chase, whom we are able to study in a variety of contexts. Does Peters's opinion in this case, that there *is* a federal common law of crimes, seem consistent with his opinions in the other cases which you have seen? What of Justice Chase? In *Worrall*, Chase states his opinion that there is *no* federal common law of crimes. Does this seem consistent with his conduct in the *Fries* trial? Chase's opinion in *Worrall*, according to a compiler of early federal criminal cases, Francis Wharton, "greatly surprised not only the bar but the community." Wharton suggests that Chase's opinion might have sprung from "the 'persuasions' of the 'metaphysical' Virginia lawyers, who led Judge Chase into the belief that the United States had no common law." "But the oddest part of the case," says Wharton, "is that though Judge Chase expressly denied that there was jurisdiction, and though there must have been at best a divided bench, the court, 'after a short consultation' imposed a sentence of unequivocally common law stamp." Wharton's theory is that "Judge Chase had used this 'short consultation' to acquaint himself with the views of his brethren on the supreme bench, about which after Henfield's case, there could then have been no doubt." Wharton, State Trials 199 n. (1849).

2. What is the nature of the dispute between those who believed in a federal common law of crimes and those who did not? Is the issue over the constitutional extent of Federal sovereignty? Could something more basic be involved? What is meant by Chase's suggestion that it is "as essential, that Congress should define the offences to be tried, and apportion the punishments to be inflicted, as that they should erect courts to try the criminal, or to pronounce a sentence on conviction?" Professor Morton Horwitz believes that something deeper *is* involved in the split between Chase and Peters. It is his opinion that the attack on common law crimes "emerged from a distinctively post-revolutionary conviction that the com-

mon law was both uncertain and unpredictable." Morton Horwitz, The Transformation of American Law 1780–1860 14 (1977). Horwitz suggests that the opposition to the Federal common law of crimes was part of a larger movement against common law crimes even at the state level. Here is Horwitz's analysis of the views of two anti-state common law men, Justices Chipman and Swift:

> * * * In his "Dissertation on the Act adopting the Common and Statute Laws of England" (1793), Vermont Chief Justice Nathaniel Chipman "lay[s] it down as an unalterable rule that no Court, in this State, ought ever to pronounce sentence of death upon the authority of a common law precedent, without the authority of a statute." And two years later, in his treatise on Connecticut law, Zepheniah Swift, soon to be that state's chief justice, indicated that he too was troubled by the doctrine "that every crime committed against the law of nature may be punished at the discretion of the judge, where the legislature has not appointed a particular punishment." Distinguishing between "crimes which are expressly defined by statute or common law" and those actions over which "courts of law have assumed a discretionary power of punishing," he warned that judges "ought to exercise [the latter] power with great circumspection and caution," since "the supreme excellency of a code of criminal laws consists in defining every act that is punishable with such certainty and accuracy, that no man shall be exposed to the danger of incurring a penalty without knowing it." It would be unjust, he continued, for "a man [to] do an act, which he knows has never been punished, and against which there is no law, yet upon a prosecution for it, the court may by a determination subsequent to the act, judge it to be a crime, and inflict on him a severe punishment." * * * Swift * * * was no longer prepared to assume that even the first judicial pronouncement of a legal rule was merely a declaration of some known and preexisting standard of natural law. Indeed, his entire discussion assumed the inability of individuals to know their legal duties without some express legislative or judicial pronouncement. * * * Swift's * * * preoccupation with the unfairness of administering a system of judge-made criminal law was a distinctly postrevolutionary phenomenon, reflecting a profound change in sensibility. For the inarticulate premise that lay behind Swift's warnings against the danger of judicial discretion was a growing perception that judges no longer merely discovered law; they also made it.*

Horwitz, supra, at 14–15 (footnotes omitted). Do you agree with Horwitz that this deeper philosophical view on the nature of the common law is what motivated Chase? How, then, do you explain Chase's ultimately agreeing to punish Worrall? Did Chase reverse himself on the issue of common law crimes? If so, why?

3. The last two excerpts in this section on the Federal common law of crimes are, respectively, the clearest articulation of the Republican position on the issue, and the Supreme Court's ultimate resolution of the problem. As you read them ask yourself again whether they seem to be concerned with the constitutional dimensions of the problem or whether they seem to be addressed to deeper questions about the nature of the American polity or the nature of law itself.

4. VIRGINIA "INSTRUCTION"

INSTRUCTION FROM THE GENERAL ASSEMBLY OF VIRGINIA TO THE SENATORS FROM THAT STATE IN CONGRESS, JANUARY 11, 1800

I St. George Tucker, ed., Blackstone's Commentaries 438 (1803).

The general assembly of Virginia would consider themselves unfaithful to the trust reposed in them, were they to remain silent, whilst a doctrine has been publicly advanced, novel in its principle, and tremendous in its consequences: That the common law of England is in force under the government of the United States. It is not at this time proposed to expose at large the monstrous pretentions resulting from the adoption of this principle. It ought never, however, to be forgotten, and can never be too often repeated, that it opens a new tribunal for the trial of crimes never contemplated by the federal compact. It opens a new code of sanguinary criminal law, both obsolete and unknown, and either wholly rejected or essentially modified in almost all its parts by state institutions. It arrests, or supercedes, state jurisdictions, and innovates upon state laws. It subjects the citizen to punishment, according to the judiciary will, when he is left in ignorance of what this law enjoins as a duty, or prohibits as a crime. It assumes a range of jurisdiction for the federal courts, which defies limitation or definition. In short it is believed, that the advocates for the principle would, themselves, be lost in an attempt to apply it to the existing institutions of federal and state courts, by separating with precision their judiciary rights, and thus preventing the constant and mischievous interference of rival jurisdictions.

Deeply impressed with these opinions, the general assembly of Virginia, instruct the senators, and request the representatives from this state, in congress, to use their best efforts * * *.

To oppose the passing of any law, founded on, or recognizing the principle lately advanced, "that the common law of England, is in force under the government of the United States;" excepting from such opposition, such particular parts of the common law, as may have a sanction from the constitution, so far as they are necessarily comprehended in the technical phrases which express the powers delegated to the government; * * * and excepting, also, such other parts thereof as may be adopted by congress as necessary and proper for carrying into execution the powers expressly delegated.

5. THE SUPREME COURT ON THE FEDERAL COMMON LAW

UNITED STATES v. HUDSON & GOODWIN

United States Supreme Court, 1812.
7 Cranch 32.

This was a case certified from the Circuit Court for the district of Connecticut, in which, upon argument of a general demurrer to an indictment for a libel on the president and congress of the United States, contained in the Connecticut Currant, of the 7th of May 1806, charging them with having in secret voted $2,000,000 as a present to Bonaparte, for leave to make a treaty with Spain, the judges of that court were divided in opinion upon the question, whether the circuit court of the United States had a common-law jurisdiction in cases of libel?

Pinkney, Attorney-General, in behalf of the United States, and *Dana,* for the defendants, declined arguing the case.

The Court, having taken time to consider, the following opinion was delivered (on the last day of the term, all the judges being present) by JOHNSON, J.—The only question which this case presents is, whether the circuit courts of the United States can exercise a common-law jurisdiction in criminal cases. We state it thus broadly, because a decision on a case of libel will apply to every case in which jurisdiction is not vested in those courts by statute.

Although this question is brought up now, for the first time, to be decided by this court, we consider it as having been long since settled in public opinion. In no other case, for many years, has this jurisdiction been asserted; and the general acquiescence of legal men shows the prevalence of opinion in favor of the negative of the proposition.

The course of reasoning which leads to this conclusion is simple, obvious, and admits of but little illustration. The powers of the general government are made up of concessions from the several states— whatever is not expressly given to the former, the latter expressly reserve. The judicial power of the United States is a constituent part of those concessions; that power is to be exercised by courts organized for the purpose; and brought into existence by an effort of the legislative power of the Union. Of all the courts which the United States may, under their general powers, constitute, one only, the supreme court, possesses jurisdiction derived immediately from the constitution, and of which the legislative power cannot deprive it. All other courts created by the general government possesses no jurisdiction but what is given them by the power that creates them, and can be vested with none but what the power ceded to the general government will authorize them to confer.

It is not necessary to inquire, whether the general government, in any and what extent, possesses the power of conferring on its courts a jurisdiction in cases similar to the present; it is enough, that such jurisdiction has not been conferred by any legislative act, if it does not result to those courts as a consequence of their creation. And such is the opinion of the majority of this court: for the power which congress possess to create courts of inferior jurisdiction, necessarily implies the power to limit the jurisdiction of those courts to particular objects; and when a court is created, and its operations confined to certain specific objects, with what propriety can it assume to itself a jurisdiction, much more extended, in its nature very indefinite, applicable to a great variety of subjects, varying in every state in the Union and with regard to which there exists no definite criterion of distribution between the district and circuit courts of the same district.

The only ground on which it has ever been contended that this jurisdiction could be maintained is, that, upon the formation of any political body, an implied power to preserve its own existence and promote the end and object of its creation, necessarily results to it. But, without examining how far this consideration is applicable to the peculiar character of our constitution, it may be remarked that it is a principle by no means peculiar to the common law. It is coeval, probably, with the first formation of a limited government; belongs to a system of universal law, and may as well support the assumption of many other powers as those more peculiarly acknowledged by the common law of England.

But if admitted as applicable to the state of things in this country, the consequence would not result from it, which is here contended for. If it may communicate certain implied powers to the general government, it would not follow, that the courts of that government are vested with jurisdiction over any particular act done by an individual, in supposed violation of the peace and dignity of the sovereign power. The legislative authority of the Union must first make an act a crime, affix a punishment to it, and declare the court that shall have jurisdiction of the offence.

Certain implied powers must necessarily result to our courts of justice, from the nature of their institution. But jurisdiction of crimes against the state is not among those powers. To fine for contempt, imprison for contumacy, enforce the observance of order, &c., are powers which cannot be dispensed within a court, because they are necessary to the exercise of all others: and so far our courts, no doubt, possess powers not immediately derived from statute; but all exercise of criminal jurisdiction in common-law cases, we are of opinion, is not within their implied powers.

QUESTIONS

1. Why did the lawyers decline to argue the case?

2. The Supreme Court in *Hudson* says that no "legislative act" has conferred common law jurisdiction on the lower Federal Courts. What about the 1789 Judiciary Act itself, which gave the Circuit Court jurisdiction, presumably over *all* "crimes and offenses congnizable under the authority of the United States."

3. What decided the question in "public opinion?" Could it have been the seditious libel cases which you will encounter in the next section?

SECTION D.   THE TRIALS FOR SEDITIOUS LIBEL

ACT FOR THE PUNISHMENT OF CERTAIN CRIMES,*
JULY 14, 1798

1 Stat. 596.

* * *

§ 2.   * * *   if any person shall write, print, utter, or publish; or shall cause or procure to be written, printed, uttered, or published, or shall knowingly and willingly assist or aid in writing, printing, uttering, or publishing, any false, scandalous, and malicious, writing or writings, against the government of the United States, or either house of the congress of the United States, or the president of the United States, with intent to defame the said government, or either house of the said congress, or the said president, or to bring them, or either of them, into contempt or disrepute; or to excite against them, or either or any of them, the hatred of the good people of the United States, or to stir up sedition within the United States; or to excite any unlawful combinations therein, for opposing or resisting any law of the United States, or any act of the president of the United States, done in pursuance of any such law, or of the powers in him vested by the constitution of the United States; or to resist, oppose, or defeat, any such law or act; or to aid, encourage, or abet any hostile designs or any foreign nation against the United States, their people, or government, then such person, being thereof convicted before any court of the United States having jurisdiction thereof, shall be punished, by a fine not exceeding two thousand dollars, and by imprisonment not exceeding two years.

§ 3.   * * *   if any person shall be prosecuted under this act, for the writing or publishing any libel aforesaid, it shall be lawfull for the defendant, upon the trial of the cause, to give in evidence in his defense, the truth of the matter contained in the publication charged as a libel.   And the Jury who shall try the cause, shall have

---

* The act, by its own terms, expired on
March 3, 1801.

a right to determine the law and the fact, under the direction of the court, as in other causes.

UNITED STATES v. MATTHEW LYON

United States Circuit Court for the District of Vermont, 1798.
15 Fed.Cas. 1183.

[Lyon was charged in an indictment with committing the offense specified in § 2 of the Act. The first count charged him with publishing the following allegedly criminal matter:]

As to the Executive, when I shall see the efforts of that power bent on the promotion of the comfort, the happiness, and accommodation of the people, that executive shall have my zealous and uniform support: but whenever I shall, on the part of the Executive, see every consideration of the public welfare swallowed up in a continual grasp for power, in an unbounded thirst for ridiculous pomp, foolish adulation, and selfish avarice; when I shall behold men of real merit daily turned out of office, for no other cause but independency of sentiment; when I shall see men of firmness, merit, years, abilities, and experience, discarded in their application for office, for fear they possess that independence, and men of meanness preferred for the ease with which they take up and advocate opinions, the consequence of which they know but little of—when I shall see the sacred name of religion employed as a state engine to make mankind hate and persecute one another, I shall not be their humble advocate.

The second count consisted of having * * * published a letter [said to be from a French diplomat, including these words:] * * *

The misunderstanding between the two governments (France and the United States), has become extremely alarming; confidence is completely destroyed, mistrusts, jealousy, and a disposition to a wrong attribution of motives, are so apparent, as to require the utmost caution in every word and action that are to come from your Executive. I mean, if your object is to avoid hostilities. Had this truth been understood with you before the recall of Monroe, before the coming and second coming of Pinckney; had it guided the pens that wrote the bullying speech of your President, and stupid answer of your Senate, at the opening of Congress in November last, I should probably had no occasion to address you this letter.

—But when we found him borrowing the language of Edmund Burke, and telling the world that although he should succeed in treating with the French, there was no dependence to be placed on any of their engagement, that their religion and morality were at an end, that they would turn pirates and plunderers, and it would be necessary to be perpetually armed against them, though you were at peace: We wondered that the answer of both Houses had not been an order to send him to a mad house. Instead of this the

Senate have echoed the speech with more servility than ever George III. experienced from either House of Parliament. * * *

Several witnesses were called to show that the defendant, both in public and in private, had extensively used the letter for political purposes, and in doing so had frequently made use of language highly disrespectful to the administration. * * *

The prosecution having closed its case, the defendant stated his defence to consist in three points: first, that the court had not jurisdiction of the offence, the act of Congress being unconstitutional and void, * * * second, that the publication was innocent; and third, that the contents were true.

On the first two points he offered no testimony, but on the third he proposed to call Judge Paterson, the presiding judge, and Judge Israel Smith.

Judge Paterson being then on the bench, was then asked by the defendant, whether he had not frequently "dined with the President, and observed his ridiculous pomp and parade?"

Judge Paterson replied, that he had sometimes, though rarely, dined with the President, but that he had never seen any pomp or parade; he had seen, on the contrary, a great deal of plainness and simplicity.

The defendant then asked whether he (the judge) had not seen at the President's more pomp and servants there, than at the tavern at Rutland? To this no answer was given.*

No other witness was * * * called.

* * * The defendant addressed the jury at great length, insisting on the unconstitutionality of the law, and the insufficiency of the evidence to show anything more than a legitimate opposition.

PATERSON, J., circuit judge, * * * charged the jury substantially as follows:

> You have nothing whatever to do with the constitutionality or unconstitutionality of the sedition law. Congress has said that the author and publisher of seditious libels is to be punished; and until this law is declared null and void by a tribunal competent for the purpose, its validity cannot be disputed. Great would be the abuses were the constitutionality of every statute to be submitted to a jury, in each case where the statute is to be applied. The only question you are to determine is * * * Did Mr. Lyon publish the writing given in the indictment? Did he do so seditiously?

On the first point * * * he himself concedes the fact of publication * * *. As to the second point, you will have to consider

---

* A report of this part of the trial in the Philadelphia *Aurora*, a Republican newspaper, states that "The judge, conscious that there was some difference between the table at Braintree, and the humble fare of a country tavern, with the privileges of half a bed, made no reply, but smoked a cigar."

whether language such as that here complained of could have been uttered with any other intent than that of making odious or contemptible the President and government, and bringing them both into disrepute. If you find such is the case, the offence is made out, and you must render a verdict of guilty. Nor should the political rank of the defendant,* his past services, or the dependent condition of his family, deter you from this duty. Such considerations are for the court alone in adjusting the penalty they will bestow. * * * In order to render a verdict of guilty, you must be satisfied beyond all reasonable substantial doubt that the hypothesis of innocence is unsustainable. * * *

At about eight o'clock in the evening of the same day, after about an hour's absence, the jury returned with a verdict of guilty.

The defendant being called up for sentence * * * Judge Paterson addressed him as follows:

> Matthew Lyon, as a member of the federal legislature, you must be well acquainted with the mischiefs which flow from an unlicensed abuse of government, and of the motives which led to the passage of the act under which this indictment is framed. * * * What, however, has tended to mitigate the sentence which would otherwise have been imposed, is, what I am sorry to hear of, the reduced condition of your estate. The judgement of the court is, that you stand imprisoned four months, pay the cost of prosecution, and a fine of one thousand dollars * * *.

UNITED STATES v. THOMAS COOPER

United States Circuit Court for the District of Pennsylvania, 1800.
25 Fed.Cas. 631.

* * *

Judge Chase * * * charged the jury as follows: * * * When men are found rash enough to commit an offence such as the traverser is charged with, it becomes the duty of the government to take care that they should not pass with impunity. * * *

Thomas Cooper * * * stands charged with having published a false, scandalous and malicious libel against the President of the United States, in his official character as President. There is no civilized country that I know of, that does not punish such offences; and it is necessary to the peace and welfare of this country, that these offences should meet with their proper punishment, since ours is a government founded on the opinions and confidence of the people. The Representatives and the President are chosen by the people. It is a government made by themselves; and their officers are chosen

---

* The defendant was a feisty Irish member of the United States Congress from Vermont. A stout Republican, the Federalists said of him, "a strange offensive brute, too wild to tame, too base to shoot." Quoted in Roger Butterfield, The American Past 28 (2nd. ed. 1966).

by themselves; and, therefore, if any improper law is enacted, the people have it in their power to obtain the repeal of such law, or even of the Constitution itself, if found defective, since provision is made for its amendment. Our government, therefore, is really republican; the people are truly represented, since all power is derived from them: it is a government of representation and responsibility: all officers of the government are liable to be displaced or removed, or their duration in office limited by elections at fixed periods * * *. All governments which I have ever read or heard of punish libels against themselves. If a man attempts to destroy the confidence of the people in their officers, their supreme magistrate, and their legislature, he effectually saps the government. A republican government can only be destroyed in two ways; the introduction of luxury, or the licentiousness of the press. This latter is the more slow, but most sure and certain, means of bringing about the destruction of the government. The legislature of this country, knowing this maxim, has thought proper to pass a law to check this licentiousness of the press * * *.

Thomas Cooper, then, stands indicted for having published a false, scandalous and malicious libel upon the President of the United States, with intent to defame the President, to bring him into contempt and disrepute, and to excite against him the hatred of the good people of the United States. * * * The traverser has pleaded not guilty, and that he has not published, &c., with these views: he has also pleaded in justification (which the law provides for), that the matters asserted by him are true, and that he will give the same in evidence.

It is incumbent on the part of the prosecution to prove * * * That he did publish with intent to defame, &c.

For the intent * * * must be proved in the same manner as other facts; and must be proved as stated in the law of Congress— the mere publication is no offence; and in making up your verdict, though you consider them separately, you must take the whole tenor and import of the publication * * *.

* * *

The fact of writing and publishing is clearly proved; nay, in fact, it is not denied * * *. It appears from the evidence that the traverser went to the house of a justice of the peace with this paper, whom, of all others, he ought to have avoided: for he must know that it was duty of the justice of the peace to deliver it immediately to those who administer the government. * * * It was indecent to deliver such a paper to a justice of the peace, and the manner in which it was delivered was yet more outrageous—if it was done in joke, as the traverser would wish to imply, it was still very improper —but there was the same solemnity in his expression, "this is my name, and I am the author of this handbill," as if the traverser was going to part with an estate. This conduct showed that he intended to dare and defy the government, and to provoke them, and his subsequent conduct satisfies my mind that such was his disposition. For he justifies the publication in all its parts, and declares it to be founded in truth: it is proved most clearly to be his publication. It is your business to consider the intent as coupled with that, and view the whole together. * * * If there are doubts as to the motives of the traverser, he has removed them; for, though he states in his defence that he does not arraign the motives of the President, yet he has boldly avowed that his own motives in this publication were to censure the conduct of the President * * *. Now, gentlemen, the motives of the President, in his official capacity, are not a subject of inquiry with you. Shall we say to the President, you are not fit for the government of this country? It is no apology for a man to say, that he believes the President to be honest, but that he has done acts which prove him unworthy the confidence of the people, incapable of executing the duties of his high station, and unfit for the important office to which the people have elected him * * *.

Now we will consider this libel as published by the defendant, and observe what were his motives. You will find the traverser speaking of the President in the following words: "Even those who doubted his capacity, thought well of his intentions." This the traverser might suppose would be considered as a compliment as to the intentions of the President; but I have no doubt that it was meant to carry a sting with it which should be felt; for it was in substance saying of the President, "you may have good intentions, but I doubt your capacity."

He then goes on to say, "Nor were we yet saddled with the expense of a permanent navy, nor threatened, under his (the President's) auspices, with the existence of a standing army. Our credit was not yet reduced so low as to borrow money at eight per cent, in *time of peace*." Now, gentlemen, if these things were true, can any one doubt what effect they would have on the public mind? * * * What! the President of the United States saddle us with a permanent navy, encourage a standing army, and borrow money at a large premium? * * * If you believe this to be true, what opinion can you, gentlemen, form of the President? * * * The President is further charged for that "the unnecessary violence of his official expressions might *justly* have provoked a war." * * * I say, gentlemen, again, if you believe this, what opinion can you form of the President? Certainly the worst you can form: you would certainly consider him totally unfit for the high station which he has so honourably filled, and with such benefit to his country.

The traverser states that, under the auspices of the President, "our credit is so low that we are obliged to borrow money at eight per cent. in time of peace." I cannot suppress my feelings at this gross attack upon the President. Can this be true? Can you believe it? Are we now in time of peace? Is there no war? No hostilities with France? Has she not captured our vessels and plundered us of our property to the amount of millions? Has not the intercourse been prohibited with her? Have we not armed our vessels to defend ourselves, and have we not captured several of her vessels of war? Although no formal declaration of war has been made, is it not notorious that actual hostilities have taken place? And is this, then, a time of peace? The very expense incurred, which rendered a loan necessary, was in consequence of the conduct of France. The traverser, therefore, has published an untruth, knowing it to be an untruth.

The other part of the publication is much more offensive * * *. The part to which I allude is that where the traverser charges the President with having influenced the judiciary department. * * * [T]he judicature of the country is of the greatest consequence to the liberties and existence of a nation. If your Constitution was destroyed, so long as the judiciary department remained free and uncontrolled, the liberties of the people would not be endangered. Suffer your courts of judicature to be destroyed: there is an end to your liberties. * * *

The traverser goes on thus—"This melancholy case of Jonathan Robbins, a native of America, forcibly impressed by the British, and delivered, with the advice of Mr. Adams, to the mock trial of a British court-martial, had not yet astonished the republican citizens of this free country. A case too little known, but of which the people ought to be fully apprised before the election, and they SHALL be." Now, gentlemen, there are circumstances in this publication which greatly aggravate the offence. The traverser [states that] the President interfered * * * in order to deliver up a native American citizen to be executed by a British court-martial under a mock trial, against law and against mercy. * * * I can scarcely conceive a charge can be made against the President of so much consequence, or of a more heinous nature. * * * It appears then that this is a charge on the President, not only false and scandalous, but evidently made with intent to injure his character, and the manner in which it is made is well calculated to operate on the passions of Americans, and I fear such has been the effect. If this charge were true, there is not a man amongst you but would hate the President; I am sure I should hate him myself if I had thought he had done this. Upon the purity and independence of the judges depend the existence of your government and the preservation of your liberties. They should be under no influence—they are only accountable to God and their own consciences * * *.

There is a little circumstance which the attorney-general, in his observations to you, omitted to state, but which I think it right to recall to your recollection, as it appears with what design the traverser made this publication. In this allusion to Jonathan Robbins he expressly tells you this is "a case too little known, but of which the people ought to be fully apprised before the election, and they shall be." Here, then, the evident design of the traverser was, to arouse the people against the President so as to influence their minds against him on the next election. I think it right to explain this to you, because it proves, that the traverser was actuated by improper motives to make this charge against the President. * * *

Now, gentlemen, with regard to this delivery of Jonathan Robbins, I am clearly of opinion that the President could not refuse to deliver him up. This same Jonathan Robbins, whose real name appears to have been Nash, was charged with murder committed on board the *Hermione* British ship of war. This Nash being discovered in America, the British Minister made a requisition to the President that he should be delivered up. * * * By the 27th article of the treaty with Great Britain, it is stipulated, "that either of the contracting parties will deliver up to justice all persons who, being charged with murder or forgery committed within the Jurisdiction of either, shall seek an asylum within any of the countries of the other, provided this shall be done only on such evidence of criminality as, according to the laws of the place where the fugitive or person so charged shall be found, would justify his apprehension and commitment for trial, if the offence had been there committed." If the President, therefore, by this treaty, was bound to give this Nash up to justice, he was so bound by law; for the treaty is the law of the land: if so, the charge of interference to influence the decisions of a court of justice, is without foundation. * * * Nash was charged with having committed murder on board a British ship of war: now a dispute has arisen whether murder committed on board such a ship of war, was committed within the jurisdiction of Great Britain: I have no doubt as to the point. All vessels, whether public or private, are part of the territory and within the jurisdiction of the nation to which they belong. This is according to the law of nations. * * * The President was the only person to take the proper steps, and to take cognizance of the business. He represents the United States in their concerns with foreign powers: this affair could not be tried before a court of law. No court of justice here has jurisdiction over the crime of murder committed on board a British ship of war. Now, as the requisition was made to the President on the part of the British government to deliver this man up, it became necessary to know whether there was sufficient evidence of his criminality pursuant to the treaty. The judge of the court of Carolina was therefore called upon to inquire into the evidence of his criminality: he was the instrument made use of by the President, which he was by the treaty and the law of the land, bound to perform; and had he not done so, we should have heard louder complaints from the party who are incessantly opposing and calumniating the government, that the President had grossly neglected his duty by not carrying a solemn treaty into effect. Was this, then, an interference on the part of the President with the judiciary without precedent, against law and against mercy; for doing an act which he was bound by the law of the land

to carry into effect, and over which a court of justice had no jurisdiction? Surely not; neither has it merited to be treated in the manner in which the traverser has done in his publication.   *   *   *

Take this publication in all its parts, and it is the boldest attempt
I have known to poison the minds of the people. He asserts that Mr.
Adams has countenanced a navy, that he has brought forward measures for raising a standing army in the country.   *   *   *   [T]o assert, as he has done, that we have a standing army in this country,
betrays the most egregious ignorance, or the most wilful intentions to
deceive the public. We have two descriptions of armies in this country—we have an army which is generally called the Western army,
enlisted for five years only—can this be a standing army? Who raises
them? Congress. Who pays them? The people. We have also another army, called the provisional army, which is enlisted during the
existence of the war with France—neither of these can, with any propriety, be called a standing army. In fact, we cannot have a standing
army in this country, the Constitution having expressly declared that
no appropriation shall be made for the support of any army longer
than two years.   *   *   *

There is no subject on which the people of America feel more
alarm, than the establishment of a standing army. Once persuade
them that the government is attempting to promote such a measure,
and you destroy their confidence in the government.   *   *   *

It is too much to press this point on the traverser. But he deserves it. This publication is evidently intended to mislead the ignorant, and inflame their minds against the President, and to influence their votes on the next election.

*   *   *

The traverser has, to prove these points, read to you many extracts from the addresses and answers to the President. He has selected a number of passages, which, he asserts, prove the approbation
of the President to the creation of a navy, and forming a standing
army. But we are to recollect gentlemen, that when in consequence
of the unjust proceedings of France, the great mass of the people
thought proper to address the President, expressing in those addresses, sentiments of attachment and confidence in the President, and
their determination to resist the oppression of the French government: the President replied to them, in answers which generally were
the echo of their sentiments, and in fact, his expressions were as general as the nature of the addresses would permit—therefore, the
traverser ought to have blamed the addressers, and not the President.
*   *   *

*   *   *

You will please to notice, gentlemen, that the traverser in his
defence must prove every charge he has made to be true; he must
prove it to the marrow.   *   *   *   If he were to prove, that the Presi-

dent had done everything charged against him in the first paragraph of the publication—though he should prove to your satisfaction, that the President had interfered to influence the decisions of a court of justice, that he had delivered up Jonathan Robbins without precedent, against law and against mercy, this would not be sufficient, unless he proved at the same time, that Jonathan Robbins was a native American, and had been forcibly impressed, and compelled to serve on board a British ship of war. If he fails, therefore, gentlemen, in this proof, you must then consider whether his intentions in making these charges against the President were malicious or not. It is not necessary for me to go more minutely into an investigation of the defence. You must judge for yourselves—you must find the publication, and judge of the intent with which that publication was made, whether it was malice or not? If you believe that he has published it without malice, or an intent to defame the President of the United States, you must acquit him; if he has proved the truth of the facts asserted by him, you must find him Not Guilty.

After the jury had returned with a verdict of Guilty:—

Judge Chase. Mr. Cooper, as the jury have found you guilty, we wish to hear any circumstances you have to offer in point of the mitigation of the fine the court may think proper to impose on you, and also in extenuation of your punishment. We should therefore wish to know your situation in life, in regard to your circumstances. * * *

Mr. Cooper. * * * I think it right to say, that my property in this country is moderate. That some resources I had in England, commercial failures there have lately cut off: that I depend principally on my practice: that practice, imprisonment will annihilate. Be it so. I have been accustomed to make sacrifices to opinion, and I can make this. As to circumstances in extenuation, not being conscious that I have set down aught in malice, I have nothing to extenuate.

Judge Chase. * * * I am sorry you did not think proper to make an affidavit in regard to your circumstances * * *. I do not know you personally—I know nothing of you, more than having lately heard your name mentioned in some publication. Every person knows the political disputes which have existed amongst us. It is notorious that there are two parties in the country; you have stated this yourself. You have taken one side—we do not pretend to say, that you have not a right to express your sentiments, only taking care not to injure the characters of those to whom you are opposed.

* * *

If we were to indulge our own ideas, there is room to suspect that in cases of this kind, where one party is against the government, gentlemen, who write for that party, would be indemnified against any pecuniary loss; and that the party would pay any fine which might be imposed on the person convicted. * * * If the fine were only to fall on yourself, I would consider circumstances; but, if I could believe you were supported by a party inimical to the government, and that they were to pay the fine, not you, I would go the utmost extent of the power of the court. I understand you have a family, but you have not thought proper to state that to the court. From what I can gather from you, it appears that you depend on your profession for support; we do not wish to impose so rigorous a fine as to be beyond a person's abilities to support, but the government must be secured against these malicious attacks. You say that you are not conscious of having acted from malicious motives. It may be so; saying so, we must believe you; but, the jury have found otherwise. You are a gentleman of the profession, of such capacity and knowledge, as to have it more in your power to mislead the ignorant. I do not want to oppress, but I will restrain, as far as I can, all such licentious attacks on the government   *   *   *.

Mr. Cooper.   *   *   *   Sir, I solemnly aver, that throughout my life, here and elsewhere, among all the political questions in which I have been concerned, I have never so far demeaned myself as to be a party writer.   *   *   *   The exertions of my talents, such as they are, have been unbought, and so they shall continue; they have indeed been paid for, but they have been paid for by myself, and by myself only, and sometimes dearly. The public is my debtor, and what I have paid or suffered for them, if my duty should again call upon me to write or to act, I shall again most readily submit to. I do not pretend to have no party opinions, to have no predilection for particular descriptions of men or of measures; but I do not act upon minor considerations; I belong here, as in my former country, to the great party of mankind. With regard to any offers which may have been made to me, to enable me to discharge the fine which may be imposed, I will state candidly to the court what has passed   *   *   *. [M]any of my friends have, in the expectation of a verdict against me, come forward with general offers of pecuniary assistance; these offers I have, hitherto, neither accepted nor rejected. If the court should impose a fine beyond my ability to pay, I shall accept them without hesitation; but if the fine be within my circumstances to discharge, I shall pay it myself. But the insinuations of the court are ill founded, and if you, sir, from misapprehension or misinformation have been tempted to make them, your mistake should be corrected.

Judge Peters. I think we have nothing to do with parties; we are only to consider the subject before us. I wish you had thought proper to make an affidavit of your property. I have nothing to do, sitting here, to inquire whether a party in whose favour you may be, or you, are to pay the fine. I shall only consider your circumstances, and impose a fine which I think adequate; we ought to avoid any oppression. It appears that you depend chiefly upon your profession for support. Imprisonment for any time would tend to increase the fine, as your family would be deprived of your professional abilities to maintain them.

Judge Chase. We will take time to consider this. [The following day the court sentenced Cooper to pay a fine of four hundred dollars and to be imprisoned for six months.]

* * *

UNITED STATES v. JAMES THOMPSON CALLENDER

United States Circuit Court for the District of Virginia, 1800.
25 Fed.Cas. 239.

The matter set out in the indictment as libellous was as follows:

The reign of Mr. Adams has been one continued tempest of malignant passion. As President, he has never opened his lips, or lifted his pen without threatening and scolding; the grand object of his administration has been to exasperate the rage of contending parties, to calumniate and destroy every man who differs from his opinions. Mr. Adams has laboured, and with melancholy success, to break up the bonds of social affection, and under the ruins of confidence and friendship, to extinguish the only gleam of happiness that glimmers through the dark and despicable farce of life. [The allegedly libelous publication proceeds in this vein, accusing Adams of "corruption," "malignant designs," and of being Pro-Aristocrat, Anti-French, Pro-British, "grossly prejudiced," and a "hoary headed incendiary."]

* * *

[We enter the trial at the conclusion of the presentation of the prosecutor, Mr. Nelson.]

* * * [I]t is the peculiar privilege of every citizen of this happy country to place confidence in whom he pleases, and at the constitutional periods of making new elections, to withdraw his confidence from a former representative, and place his trust in another; and even expatiate on the virtues of the new candidate; but this does not warrant him to vilify, revile, and defame another individual, who is a candidate. Cannot a good thing be said of one individual, without saying black and damnable things of another? * * *

The attorney for the United States having concluded, the counsel for the traverser introduced Colonel John Taylor (of Caroline county) as a witness, and he was sworn; but at the moment the oath was administered, the Judge called on them, and desired to know what they intended to prove by the witness.

They answered that they intended to examine Colonel Taylor to prove that he had avowed principles in his presence which justified Mr. Callender in saying that the President was an aristocrat; that he had voted against the sequestration law, and the resolutions concerning the suspension of commercial intercourse with Great Britain, by which he defeated every effort of those who were in favour of those beneficial measures which were well calculated to promote the happiness of their country.

The Judge demanded a statement in writing of the questions intended to be put to the witness.

Mr. Nicholas remarked, that * * * this requisition had not been made of the attorney, when he introduced witnesses on behalf of the United States, nor was it according to the practice of the State courts; that he wished the witness to state all he knew that would apply to the defence of his client; that he did not know what the witness would precisely prove, but that if the court insisted upon it, he would furnish a statement of the question which he should first propound, but requested that he might not be considered as confined, in the examination of the witness, to the question so stated.

Judge Chase.   It is right to state the questions intended to be propounded to witnesses, in all cases, and the reason is extremely plain.   Juries are only to hear legal evidence, and the court are the only judges of what is or is not legal evidence, to support the issue joined between the parties.   To say that you will correct improper evidence, after it shall have been given, is improper, because illegal evidence, once heard, may make an undue impression, and, therefore, ought not to be heard at all by the jury; and the attorney for the United States had, in opening the cause, stated the purpose for which he introduced the witnesses.

Judge Chase, having received a statement of the questions meant to be put,* and which were propounded by Mr. Nicholas, declared Colonel Taylor's evidence to be inadmissible.   No evidence, said the Judge, is admissible that does not go to justify the whole charge.   The charge you mean to justify by this witness, as I understand you, is, that the President is a professed aristocrat, and that he has proved serviceable to the British interest.   You must prove both these points, or you prove nothing.   Now as you do not attempt to prove the whole of one specific charge, but only a part of it, your evidence cannot be received. * * *   It may be said that this will preclude the party from the privilege of his testimony; but this will only be a misrepresentation, it precludes them from no legal benefit.   My country has made me a judge, and you must be governed now by my opinion, though I may be mistaken; but if I am not right, it is an error in judgment, and you can state the proceedings on the record so as to

---

* Ques. 1st.   Did you ever hear Mr. Adams express any opinion favourable to monarchy and aristocracy: and what were they?

Ques. 2d.   Did you ever hear Mr. Adams, whilst Vice President, express his disapprobation of the funding system?

Ques. 3d.   Do you know whether Mr. Adams did not, in the year 1794, vote against the sequestration law, and the bill for suspending commercial intercourse with Great Britain?

show any error, and I shall be the first man to grant you the benefit of a new trial by granting you a writ of error in the Supreme Court. * * * The very argument assigned by the young gentleman who spoke last, has convinced my mind that I am right. The offered testimony has no direct and proper application to the issue; it would deceive and mislead the jury; an argumentative justification of a trivial, unimportant part of a libel, would be urged before a jury as a substantial vindication of the whole. * * *

Mr. Nicholas suggested that it might be proper to prove one part of a specific charge by one witness, and another part by another, and thereby prove the charge.

Judge Chase, in answer, repeated some of his former arguments, and added, that the very argument suggested by the young gentleman who spoke last, convinced his mind that it would be improper to admit the testimony now offered to the court; that to admit evidence, which went to an argumentative establishment of the truth of a minute part of the charge by one witness, and another minute part by another witness, would be irregular, and subversive of every principle of law; that it had no relation to the issue; that it was a popular argument, calculated to deceive the people, but very incorrect. * *

* * * This is a new doctrine, inculcated in Virginia. You have all along mistaken the law, and press your mistakes on the court. The United States must prove the publication, and the fallacy of it. When these things are done, you must prove a justification, and this justification must be entire and complete, as to any one specific charge; a partial justification is inadmissible. * * *

Mr. Hay spoke thus. * * * One specific charge is twofold; that the President is an aristocrat; and that he proved serviceable to the British interest. The evidence, we suppose, will support this charge; we wish to prove the truth of the whole charge if we can, though I do not know that it is in our power. The evidence, we have reason to believe, goes first to prove that he is an aristocrat, and secondly, that he *did* prove serviceable to the British interest; if the testimony *will* in fact prove these two points, whatever may be the opinion of the court, I do not hesitate to say that, in my estimation, it will fully excuse and justify the traverser * * *. As to the first part, I can prove by the words of Mr. Adams, published by himself, in his book called A Defence of the American Constitution, that he thinks a government of three parts, a king, lords, and commons, the best in the world. Suppose, in addition to this it could be proved that a law passed the House of Representatives of the United States, to sequester British property; and suppose that one-half the Senate of the United States were in favour of it; and that the policy of passing the law was advocated by the best and wisest men in this country, who have the same pretensions to patriotism and virtue that Mr. Adams has, but that its passage was prevented by the casting vote of

Mr. Adams as speaker of the Senate, would not the traverser be justified as to this charge? Would it not demonstrate that he proved serviceable to the British interest? By the answers to the first and third questions we expect to prove both these points.

Here *Mr. Nelson* objected to the introduction of such testimony, as being altogether inadmissible * * *, that it would be a departure from the universal principle of law, which required the production of the best testimony which the nature of every case admitted, and that the journals and records of Congress were the best evidence of what votes had been given on any subject discussed before that body.

Judge Chase then addressed himself to Mr. Nelson thus:—Being very much pressed, by the young gentlemen who defend the traverser, to admit this testimony, I was going to recommend to you to permit those questions to be put to the witness, though they are certainly irregular. I wish you could consent that they should be propounded.

Mr. Nelson declared that he did not feel himself at liberty to consent to such a departure from legal principles.

Mr. Wirt then rose and addressed the jury.—He premised that the situation of the defendant and his counsel was extremely embarrassing; that as Mr. Callender had been presented, indicted, arrested and tried, during this term, he had not been able to procure the testimony essential to his defence, nor was his counsel prepared to defend him; and he insinuated that the conduct of the court was apparently precipitate, in not postponing the trial until the next term.

Judge Chase told him he must not reflect on the court.

* * *

Mr. Wirt.—Gentlemen of the jury, I am prevented from explaining to you the causes which have conspired to weaken our defence, and it is no doubt right that I should be prevented, as the court have so decided * * *. You will find that a material part of your inquiry will relate to the power of a jury over the subject committed to them, whether they have the right to determine the law, as well as the fact. In Virginia, an act of the assembly has adopted the common law of England; that common law, therefore, possesses in this state all the energy of a legislative act. By an act of Congress, the rules of proceedings in the federal courts, in the several states, are directed to conform to the rules of the states in which such court may be in session; by that act of Congress, it is therefore provided, that the practice of the courts of Virginia shall be observed in this court: to ascertain your power, therefore, as a jury, we have only to refer to the common law of England, which has been adopted in the laws of this state, and which defines the powers of juries in the state courts. By the common law of England, juries possess the power of considering and deciding the law as well as the fact in every case which may come before them.   *   *   *   If, then, a jury in a court of the state would have a right to decide the law and the fact, so have you.   The federal Constitution is the supreme law of the land; and a right to consider the law, is a right to consider the Constitution: if the law of Congress under which we are indicted, be an infraction of the Constitution, it has not the force of a law, and if you were to find the traverser guilty, under such an act, you would violate your oaths.

Here *Judge Chase*—Take your seat sir, if you please.   If I understand you rightly, you offer an argument to the petit jury, to convince them that the statute of Congress, entitled, "An act, &c., commonly called the Sedition Law," is contrary to the Constitution of the United States, and, therefore, void.   Now I tell you that this is irregular and inadmissible; it is not competent to the jury to decide on this point; but if you address yourself, gentlemen, to the court, they will with pleasure hear any reason you may offer, to show that the jury have the right contended for.   *   *   *

Here the Judge then read part of a long opinion, to show that the jury had not the right contended for   *   *   *.

*   *   *

Judge Chase.   *   *   *   [W]e all know that juries have the right to decide the law, as well as the fact—and the Constitution is the supreme law of the land, which controls all laws which are repugnant to it.

Mr. Wirt.—Since, then, the jury have a right to consider the law, and since the constitution is law, the conclusion is certainly syllogistic, that the jury have a right to consider the Constitution.

Judge Chase.—A *non sequitur,* sir.

Here Mr. Wirt sat down.

Mr. Nicholas then addressed the court.   *   *   *   I intend to defend Mr. Callender by the establishment of two points.

First, that a law contrary to the Constitution is void; and, secondly, that the jury have a right to consider the law and the fact.   First, it seems to be admitted on all hands, that, when the legislature exercise a power not given them by the Constitution, the judiciary will disregard their acts.   The second point, that the jury have a right to decide the law and the fact, appears to me equally clear.   In the exercise of the power of determining law and fact, a jury cannot be controlled by the court.   The court have a right to instruct the jury, but the jury have a right to act as they think right; and if they find contrary to the directions of the court, and to the law of the case, the court may set aside their verdict and grant a new trial.

Judge Chase.—Courts do not claim the right of setting aside the verdict in criminal cases.

Mr. Nicholas.—From this right of the jury to consider law and fact in a general verdict, it seems to follow, that counsel ought to be permitted to address a jury on the constitutionality of the law in question;—this leads me back to my first position, that if an act of Congress contravene the Constitution of the United States, a jury have a right to say that it is null * * *; if this jury believed that the Sedition Act is not a law of the land, they cannot find the defendant guilty. The Constitution secures to every man a fair and impartial trial by jury * * *. If ever a precedent is established, that the court can control the jury so as to prevent them from finding a general verdict, their important right, without which every other right is of no value, will be impaired, if not absolutely destroyed. Juries are to decide according to the dictates of conscience and the laws of the country * * *.

* * * I do not deny the right of the court to determine the law, but I deny the right of the court to control the jury; though I have not bestowed a very particular attention on this subject, I am perfectly convinced that the jury have the right I contend for; and, consequently that counsel have a right to address them on that subject.

The act of Congress to which I have alluded, appears to have given to the jury the power of deciding on the law and the fact * * *.

Mr. Hay * * * I entertained doubts at first; but a calm and dispassionate inquiry, and the most temperate investigation and reflection, have led me to believe and to say, that the jury have a right to determine every question which is necessary to determine, before sentence can be pronounced upon the traverser. I contend that the jury have a right to determine whether the writing charged in the indictment to be false, scandalous and malicious, be libel or not. If this question should be decided in the affirmative by the court, I shall endeavour to convince the jury that it is not a libel, because there is no law in force, under the government of the United States, which defines what a libel is, or prescribes its punishment. It is a universal principle of law, that questions of law belong to the court, and that the decision of facts belongs to the jury; but a jury have a right to determine both law and fact in all cases.

Judge Chase * * * interrupted Mr. Hay, and briefly expressed his opinion of the law. And then Mr. Hay folded up and put away his papers, seeming to decline any further argument.

Judge Chase observed, that though he thought it his duty to stop the counsel when mistaking the law, yet he did not wish to interrupt them improperly; that there was no occasion to be captious * * *.

Judge Chase then proceeded. * * *

* * *

To support this indictment on behalf of the government of the United States, it must be proved to the jury; first, that the traverser did write, print, utter or publish * * * a false and scandalous writing against the President of the United States; secondly, that the said writing is false, scandalous, and malicious; and thirdly, that it was published with intent to defame the President, &c., as stated in the statute and charged in the indictment.

If these three facts shall be established to the satisfaction of the jury they must find the traverser guilty, generally, unless he can prove to them the truth of the matter contained in the publication * * *. If all the twenty sets of words, stated in the indictment as charges against the traverser, shall not be proved against him * * *, the jury will acquit him of such of them as shall not be established against him, and also of such of them as he can prove to be true; and they will find him guilty of the residue.

* * * The issue joined, therefore, is, whether the traverser is guilty of the several offences charged in the indictment; and to this issue no evidence is admissible * * * but what is pertinent or applicable to it. The petit jury, to discharge their duty, must first inquire, whether the traverser committed all or any of the facts alleged in the indictment to have been done by him some time before the indictment. If they find that he did commit all or any of the said facts, their next inquiry is, whether the doing such facts have been made criminal and punishable by the statute of the United States, on which the traverser is indicted. * * *

* * * The statute, on which the traverser is indicted, enacts "that the jury who shall try the cause shall have a right to determine the law and the fact, under the direction of the court, as in other cases." By this provision, I understand that a right is given to the jury to determine what the law is in the case before them; and not to decide whether a statute of the United States produced to them, is a law or not, or whether it is void, under an opinion that it is unconstitutional, that is, contrary to the Constitution of the United States. I admit that the jury are to compare the statute with the facts proved, and then to decide whether the acts done are prohibited by the law * * *. This power the jury necessarily possesses, in order to enable them to decide on the guilt or innocence of the person accused. It is one thing to decide what the law is, on the facts proved, and another and a very different thing, to determine that the statute produced is no law. * * *

* * * To determine the validity of the statute, the Constitution of the United States must necessarily be resorted to and considered, and its provisions inquired into. It must be determined whether the statute alleged to be void, because contrary to the Constitution, is prohibited by it expressly or by necessary implication. Was it ever intended, by the framers of the Constitution, or by the people of America, that it should ever be submitted to examination of a jury, to decide what restrictions are expressly or impliedly imposed by it on the national legislature? I cannot possibly believe that

Congress intended, by the statute, to grant a right to a petit jury to declare a statute void.   *   *   *

  *   *   *   Congress had no authority to vest it in any body whatsoever; because, by the Constitution,   *   *   *   this right is expressly granted to the judicial power of the United States, and is recognized by Congress by a perpetual statute.   *   *   *

*   *   *

It never was pretended, as I ever heard, before this time, that a petit jury in England (from whence our common law is derived,) or in any part of the United States ever exercised such power. If a petit jury can rightfully exercise this power over one statute of Congress, they must have an equal right and power over any other statute, and indeed over all the statutes; for no line can be drawn, no restriction imposed on the exercise of such power; it must rest in discretion only.

If this power be once admitted, petit jurors will be superior to the national legislature, and its laws will be subject to their control. The power to abrogate or to make laws nugatory, is equal to the authority of making them. The evident consequences of this right in juries will be, that a law of Congress will be in operation in one state and not in another. A law to impose taxes will be obeyed in one state and not in another, unless force be employed to compel submission.

*   *   *

The effects of the exercise of this power by petit jurors may be readily conceived. It appears to me that the right now claimed has a direct tendency to dissolve the Union of the United States, on which, under Divine Providence, our political safety, happiness, and prosperity depend.

*   *   *

Every man must admit that the power of deciding the constitutionality of any law of the United States, or of any particular state, is one of the greatest and most important powers the people could grant.

Such power is   *   *   *   not absolute and unlimited, but confined to such cases only where the law in question shall clearly appear to have been prohibited by the Federal Constitution, and not in any doubtful case. On referring to the ninth section of the first article of the Constitution, there may be seen many restrictions imposed on the powers of the national legislature, and also on the powers of the several state legislatures. Among the special exceptions to their authority, is the power to make ex post facto laws, to lay any capitation, or other direct tax, unless in proportion to the census; to lay any tax or duty on articles exported from any state, &c. &c.

It should be remembered that the judicial power of the United States is co-existent, co-extensive, and co-ordinate with, and altogether independent of, the Federal legislature, or the executive. By the sixth article of the Constitution, among other things, it is declared that the Constitution shall be the supreme law of the land. By the third article, it is established "that the judicial power of the United States shall be vested in one supreme court, and in such other inferior courts as Congress may from time to time ordain and establish; and that the judicial power shall extend to all cases in law and equity, arising under the Constitution and laws of the United States."

Among the cases which may arise under the Constitution, are all the restrictions on the authority of Congress, and of the state legislatures.

It is very clear, that the present case arises under the Constitution, and also under a law of the United States, and therefore it is the very case to which the Constitution declares the judicial powers of the United States shall extend.

*   *   *

From these considerations I draw this conclusion, that the judicial power of the United States is the only proper and competent authority to decide whether any statute made by Congress (or any of the state legislatures) is contrary to, or in violation of, the Federal Constitution.

*   *   *   [A provision of the Federal Judiciary Act of 1789 states] "that the justices of the Supreme Courts, and the district judges, shall take an oath or affirmation in the following words, to wit:

"I, A.B., do solemnly swear or affirm, that I will administer justice without respect to persons, and do equal right to the poor and to the rich, and that I will faithfully and impartially discharge and perform all the duties incumbent on me as _____, according to the best of my abilities and understanding, agreeably to the Constitution and laws of the United States."

No position can be more clear than that all the federal judges are bound by the solemn obligation of religion, to regulate their decisions agreeably to the Constitution of the United States, and that it is the standard of their determination in all cases that come before them.

I believe that it has been the general and prevailing opinion in all the Union, that the power now wished to be exercised by a jury, properly belonged to the federal courts.

It was alleged that the tax on carriages was considered by the people of this commonwealth to be unconstitutional, and a case was made to submit the question to the Supreme Court of the United States, and they decided that the statute was not unconstitutional, and their decision was acquiesced in.

I have seen a report of a case (Kamper v. Hawkins) decided in 1793, in the general court of this commonwealth, respecting the constitutionality of a law which gave the district courts a power of granting injunctions in certain cases, in which case the judges of the general court [four to one] determined that the law was unconstitutional and void. * * *

* * * It is now contended, that the constitutionality of the laws of Congress should be submitted to the decision of a petit jury. May I ask, whence this change of opinion? I declare that the doctrine is entirely novel to me, and that I never heard of it before my arrival in this city. * * *

It must be evident, that decisions in the district or circuit courts of the United States will be uniform, or they will become so by the revision and correction of the Supreme Court; and thereby the same principles will pervade all the Union; but the opinions of petit juries will very probably be different in different states.

The decision of courts of justice will not be influenced by political and local principles, and prejudices. If inferior courts commit error, it may be rectified; but if juries make mistakes, there can be no revision or control over their verdicts, and therefore, there can be no mode to obtain uniformity in their decisions. Besides, petit juries are under no obligation by the terms of their oath, to decide the constitutionality of any law; their determination, therefore, will be extra judicial. I should also imagine, that no jury would wish to have a right to determine such great, important, and difficult questions; and I hope no jury can be found, who will exercise the power desired over the statutes of Congress, against the opinion of the federal courts.

I have consulted with my brother, Judge Griffin, and I now deliver the opinion of the court, "That the petit jury have no right to decide on the constitutionality of the statute on which the traverser is indicted; and that, if the jury should exercise that power, they would thereby usurp the authority entrusted by the Constitution of the United States to this court." * * *

The gentlemen of the profession know, that questions have sometimes occurred in state courts, whether acts of assembly had expired, or had been repealed; but no one will say that such questions were ever submitted to a jury.

* * *

Judge Chase concluded with observing, that, if he knew himself, the opinion he had delivered and the reasons offered in its support, flowed not from political motives, or reasons of state, with which he had no concern, and which he conceived never ought to enter courts of justice; but from a deliberate conviction of what the Constitution and the law of the land required. "I hold myself equally bound," said he, "to support the rights of the jury, as the rights of the court." I consider it of the greatest consequence to the administration of justice, that the powers of the court, and the powers of the petit jury, should be kept distinct and separate. I have uniformly delivered the opinion, "that the petit jury have a right to decide the law as well as the fact, in criminal cases;" but it never entered into my mind that they, therefore, had a right to determine the constitutionality of any statute of the United States. It is my duty to execute the laws of the United States with justice and impartiality, with firmness and decision, and I will endeavour to discharge this duty with the assistance of the Fountain of wisdom, and the Giver of all human reason and understanding.

After two hours, the jury returned with a verdict of guilty, upon which the court sentenced the traverser to a fine of two hundred dollars, and an imprisonment of nine months.

JAMES MORTON SMITH, FREEDOM'S FETTERS: THE ALIEN AND SEDITION LAWS AND AMERICAN CIVIL LIBERTIES *

270–274 (1956).

* * * After Congress adjourned in July, 1798, President John Adams made preparations for his usual retreat from the summer heat of Philadelphia for the cool shade of his home in Quincy, Massachusetts. On the twenty-seventh, he and Mrs. Adams passed through Newark, New Jersey, which celebrated the event as a festive occasion. * * * "The Association of Young Men" manned an artillery piece and paraded at the flagstaff while awaiting the president's arrival.

As the Chief magistrate entered Broad Street about eleven o'clock, he was greeted by the firing of the artillery piece, the ringing of church bells, and, as he passed the flagstaff, a chant by the young men who had fired the salute: "Behold the Chief who now commands." Three cheers followed, bells again pealed forth, and as the president's party withdrew into the distance the cannon boomed a sixteen-gun salute.

There was one inebriated Republican, however, who took no delight in the festival. Luther Baldwin happened to be coming toward John Burnet's dram shop when one of the tavern's plain-spoken customers, noting that the cannon was firing after the president had passed, observed to Baldwin: "There goes the President and they are firing at his a___." * * *

Luther, a little merry, replies, that he did not care if they fired thro' [sic] his a___: Then exclaims the dram seller, that is seditious—a considerable collection gathered—and the pretended federalists, being much disappointed that the president had not stopped that they might have had the honor of kissing his hand, bent their malice on poor Luther and the cry was, that he must be punished.

Not until two months after these unguarded remarks did Supreme Court Justice William Cushing arrive in New Jersey to instruct the grand jury of the Circuit Court on the intricacies of the new sedition statute. After hearing his charge, [and after being informed of the remarks of Baldwin and his cronies by the tavernkeeper] the grand jury not only accused Baldwin but also indicted two of his tavern cronies, Brown Clark and a person identified only as Lespenard. [All three eventually pleaded guilty.] * * * For speaking "seditious words tending to defame the President and Government of the United States," both were fined, assessed court costs and expenses, and committed to federal jail until fine and fees were paid.

Baldwin's trial afforded the Republican papers a field day. * * *

"Here's *Liberty* for you," jeered a Newark newspaper in reporting Baldwin's arrest. "When we heard that Luther Baldwin was indicted for sedition," the New York *Argus* agreed, "we supposed that he had been guilty of something criminal. * * * When cognizance is taken of such a ridiculous expression," it concluded, every Republican could see "the extraordinardy malignancy of the federal faction."

According to the Argus * * * Royalists in Europe would be pleased to read an account of this curious trial as evidence that their cause "might yet succeed in this country." * * * The editor bluntly charged that "the federalists are resolved that if they cannot force the republicans to admire John Adams, they shall not speak what they think of him." Happily, he concluded, the Democratic-Republicans at least could think their thoughts to themselves without being controlled.

Nothing about the case was overlooked; its every feature became grist for the Republican mill. The only power which the Federalists now lacked, the Newark Centinel asserted, was that of prosecuting and treading underfoot all those who refused "to be duped into their measures." Other opposition newspapers pointed to the rise of the "useful profession of informers" and recommended the tavernkeeper in Newark to any person needing such services. * * *

The Argus [called the tavernkeeper] * * * a "wretched tool, who, for the sake of a little patronage, we need not add, a little pelf, would sacrifice a neighbour, and at the same time know him to be a good citizen, an honest man and a friend to his country." A correspondent from Newark strengthened this hypothesis when he reported that "the *dram-seller*, the celebrated John Burnet," was being considered as the Federalist candidate for coroner. In an ironical letter, the writer, obviously a Republican, argued somewhat facetiously that since the tavernkeeper had risked so much for the president he ought to be rewarded with any office that the people of Newark could bestow on him. Not only had he turned informer; he had "nobly persevered in prosecuting the old fellow for daring to utter such a contemptuous expression of our beloved president, whom every one knows is one of the best of men, and thank God, we have shewn the cursed democrats that we will let none of them speak disrespectfully of any part of that dear man."

* * *

NOTES AND QUESTIONS

1. Historians have argued over whether the Federalist attempts to punish seditious libel represented a "reign of terror" (See, e. g., J. Miller, Crisis in Freedom: The Alien and Sedition Laws and American Civil Liberties (1956)) or whether, instead, these measures were a "natural reaction" to an "extremely indecent campaign of public mendacity" on the part of the Republicans. (See 2 W. W. Crosskey, Politics and the Constitution 767 (1953).) The term "reign of terror", of course, is taken from the nearly universal description of the contemporary acts during the French Revolution, where more than 20,000 people lost their lives. Are the efforts of the Federalists comparable?

2. You have studied seditious libel before, in the cases of the Seven Bishops and John Peter Zenger. The two key legal issues in those cases were 1) whether truth was to be a defense to a charge of seditious libel, and 2) whether the jury was to decide on anything other than the question of publication *vel non*. Does the 1798 Act work any change in the common law? Why, incidentally, was a statute needed? Why not simply proceed to prosecute seditious libel under the federal common law of crimes?

3. Compare the standard of proof of guilt used by Justices Paterson in (*Lyon*) and Chase (in *Cooper*). Paterson, whom we observed dictating conclusions to the jury in the Whiskey Rebels case, told the *Lyon* jury that to return a guilty verdict the jury must be satisfied "beyond all reasonable substantial doubt that the hypothesis of innocence is unsustainable." Chase told the *Cooper* jury that Cooper had the burden of proving his defense, truth, "beyond a marrow." Is this the same standard? Which is correct? How would the different standards affect the outcome of verdicts? Do the different standards suggest different conceptions of government or liberty? Which standard would be most compatible with the republican theory of the American revolution?

4. One thing on which both Paterson (in *Lyon*) and Chase (in *Callender*) agreed was that it was improper for arguments to be made to the jury on the alleged unconstitutionality of the Sedition Act. Given that the Sedition Act itself said that the jury "shall have a right to determine the law and the fact, under the direction of the court, as in other cases," were the Justices correct? Is Chase's view on this question consistent with his statement in *Cooper* that "If your Constitution was destroyed, so long as the judiciary department remained free * * * the liberties of the people would not be endangered?" What would be the consequences for "national law" if juries could rule on constitutionality? Why might *Virginians* advance such a theory? What sort of constitutional jurisprudence might you expect a Virginia jury to implement?

5. In each of the cases where we have observed Chase there has been some debate about the province of the jury. Can you determine Chase's attitude with regard to the competence and reliability of jurors? Does

his attitude suggest anything about his views regarding the role which he believes the citizenry generally should play in government? If the Republican printers whom Chase excoriates were making such notorious, scurrilous, and unfounded accusations; if, in short, they were so wide of the mark; how can Chase be concerned that they will have a negative effect on popular attitudes toward government? Who, or what, does Chase fear?

6. Consider the conduct of Justice Chase in the *Callender* trial. You are not given the full report of the case, but you have enough to give you the flavor of the proceedings. Do you agree with the legal rulings made by Chase? What about Chase's attitude during this trial? Do you notice anything unusual? Chase indicated that the opinions on the law which he delivered "flowed not from political motives, or reasons of state, with which he had no concern, and which he conceived never ought to enter courts of justice; but from a deliberate conviction of what the Constitution and the law of the land required." Do you agree? The court, after the guilty verdict in *Callender*, fined the defendant $200, and sentenced him to a term of nine months. Was this a severe penalty?

7. What does the material on the *Baldwin* case reveal about the good faith of the Federalists? Can you relate the attitude of the *Baldwin* court to the attitude of the courts in the treason trials? Do the facts surrounding the *Baldwin* prosecution differ from the facts of the other cases in this section? If you were a Republican, over which trials would you be the most upset?

8. Soon after the *Callender* case, the event which all God-fearing Federalists had been dreading, the election of the man they believed to be a shameless atheist and vivisectionist, Thomas Jefferson, as President of the United States, occurred. One of the most prominant targets of the new rulers of the Federal government was to be Samuel Chase. The following materials are drawn from his trial pursuant to an impeachment for "high crimes and misdemeanors." As you examine these materials, determine how you would have voted if you were a member of the Senate which tried Chase.

SECTION E.   THE IMPEACHMENT OF SAMUEL CHASE

---

1.   CHASE'S CHARGE TO THE BALTIMORE
GRAND JURY (1803)

SAMUEL H. SMITH AND THOMAS LLOYD, II TRIAL OF SAMUEL
CHASE, AN ASSOCIATE JUSTICE OF THE SUPREME
COURT OF THE UNITED STATES, IMPEACHED BY THE
HOUSE OF REPRESENTATIVES, FOR HIGH CRIMES AND
MISDEMEANORS, BEFORE THE SENATE OF THE UNITED
STATES *

Appendix, pp. v–viii (1805).

* * *

It is essentially necessary at all times, but more particularly at
the present, that the public mind should be truly informed; and that
our citizens should entertain correct principles of government, and
fixed ideas of their social rights. It is a very easy task to deceive or
mislead the great body of the people by propagating plausible, but
false doctrines; for the bulk of mankind are governed by their passions and not by reason.

Falsehood can be more readily disseminated than truth, and the
latter is heard with reluctance if repugnant to popular prejudice.
From the year 1776, I have been a decided and avowed advocate for
a representative or republican form of government, as since established by our state and national constitutions. It is my sincere wish
that freemen should be governed by their representatives, fairly and
freely elected by that class of citizens described in our bill of rights,
who have property in, a common interest with, and an attachment
to, the community.

* * *   [T]he history of mankind (in ancient and modern times)
informs us "that a monarchy may be free, and that a republic may be
a tyranny." The true test of liberty is in the practical enjoyment of
protection to the person and the property of the citizen, from all enquiry. Where the same laws govern the whole society without any
distinction, and there is no power to dispense with the execution of
the laws; where justice is impartially and speedily administered, and
the poorest man in the community may obtain redress against the
most wealthy and powerful, * * * in that country the people are
free. This is our present situation.—Where law is uncertain, partial
or arbitrary; where justice is not impartially administered to all;
where property is insecure, and the person is liable to insult and violence without redress by law, the people are not free, whatever may

* Hereafter cited as "CHASE TRIAL."

be their form of government. To this situation, I greatly fear we are fast approaching.

        *   *   *   [T]he late alteration of the federal judiciary by the abolition of the office of the sixteenth circuit judges, and the recent change in our state constitution by the establishing of universal suffrage,   *   *   *   will, in my judgment, take away all security for property and personal liberty. The independence of the national judiciary is already shaken to its foundation, and the virtue of the people alone can restore it. The independence of the judges of this state will be entirely destroyed, if the bill for the abolition of the two supreme courts [is enacted]. The change of the state constitution, by allowing universal suffrage, will, in my opinion, certainly and rapidly destroy all protection to property, and all security to personal liberty; and our republican constitution will sink into a mobocracy, the worst of all possible governments.

*   *   *

I cannot but remember the great and patriotic characters by whom your state constitution was framed. I cannot but recollect that attempts were then made in favor of universal suffrage; and to render the judges dependent upon the legislature. You may believe that the gentlemen who framed your constitution, possessed the full confidence of the people of Maryland, and that they were esteemed for their talents and patriotism, and for their public and private virtues. You must have heard that many of them held the highest civil and military stations, and that they, at every risk and danger, assisted to obtain and establish your independence.   *   *   *   With great concern I observe, that the sons of some of these characters have united to pull down the beautiful fabric of wisdom and republicanism that their fathers erected!

The declarations respecting the natural rights of man, which originated from the claim of the British parliament to make laws to bind America in all cases whatsoever; the publications since that period, of visionary and theoretical writers, asserting that men in a state of society, are entitled to exercise rights which they possessed in a state of nature; and the modern doctrines by our late reformers, that all men in a state of society, are entitled to enjoy equal liberty and equal rights, have brought this mighty mischief upon us; and I fear that it will rapidly progress, until peace and order, freedom and property shall be destroyed.   *   *   *

I have long since subscribed to the opinion, that there could be no rights of man in a state of nature, previous to the institution of society; and that liberty properly speaking, could not exist in a state of nature. I do not believe that any number of men ever existed together in a state of nature, without some head, leader or chief, whose advice they followed, and whose precepts they obeyed.   *   *   *   The great object for which men establish any form of government, is to obtain security to their persons and property from violence, destroy the security to either and you tear up society by the roots. It appears to me that the institution of government is really no sacrifice made, as some writers contend, to natural liberty, for I think that previous to the formation of some species of government, a state of liberty could not exist. It seems to me that personal liberty and rights can only be acquired by becoming a member of a community, which gives the protection of the whole to every individual. * * * From hence I conclude that liberty and rights, (and also property) must spring out of civil society, and must be forever subject to the modification of particular governments. * * * I cheerfully subscribe to the doctrine of equal liberty and equal rights, if properly explained. I understand by equality of liberty and rights, only this, that every citizen, without respect to property or station, should enjoy an equal share of civil liberty; an equal protection from the laws, and an equal security for his person and property. Any other interpretation of these terms, is in my judgment, destructive of all government and all laws. * * * Will justice be impartially administered by judges dependant on the legislature for their continuance in office, and also for their support? Will liberty or property be protected or secured, by laws made by representatives chosen by electors, who have no property in, a common interest with, or attachment to the community?

NOTES AND QUESTIONS

1. It was the delivery of this charge which inexorably led to Chase's impeachment by the Jeffersonian-controlled House of Representatives, and his trial in the Senate. What was so exceptionable about this charge? Is it Chase's statement that "the bulk of mankind are governed by their passions and not by reason?" Could it be his idea of "representative or republican" form of government? Do not forget that the party which opposed Chase often called themselves "Republican." How did their ideas on government differ from Chase's? Would they have shared Chase's notion that those who should vote to elect representatives should be those "who have property in, a common interest with, and an attachment to, the community?"

2. Chase seems to have been agitated by three recent developments. The first was at the national level, the repeal of the Judiciary Act of 1801 by the Jeffersonian Congress. This repeal resulted in the abolition of the sixteen Federal Circuit judgeships which the 1801 act had created, and which the Federalist President, John Adams, had filled in the closing days of his administration. Since that time, as you may know, the 1801 Act has been known as the "Midnight Judges' Act." See generally Turner, The Midnight Judges, 109 U.Pa.L.Rev. 494 (1961). Adams had filled the new judgeships with the party faithful, and the new administration was anxious to repeal the act (and get rid of the new judges) even though the act contained many provisions which made access to the federal courts speedier and more efficient. Was the repeal a wise measure?

3. The second and third new thorns in Chase's side were the attempts to circumscribe the judiciary in Maryland and the recent change in the

Maryland Constitution to provide for "universal sufferage." Why would Chase regard these changes as dangerous? Consider how Chase would define "liberty" and "equality," and his discussion of "civil society" and the "state of nature." Can you discern a set of attitudes about liberty, equality, and natural rights which Chase was attacking?

2. THE POLITICS OF THE IMPEACHMENT OF SAMUEL CHASE

RICHARD E. ELLIS, THE JEFFERSONIAN CRISIS: COURTS AND POLITICS IN THE YOUNG REPUBLIC *

76–82 (1971).

* * *

* * * A prominent and militant proponent of colonial rights in the Maryland legislature during the 1760's, [Chase] had signed the Declaration of Independence and served as an active member of the Continental Congress between 1775–78. His congressional career was suddenly cut short in 1778, when Alexander Hamilton denounced him for using privileged information to speculate in the flour market. Chase returned to Baltimore, where he continued to speculate in mercantile and land ventures, practiced law, rebuilt his political reputation, and became an influential Anti-Federalist leader.

After the ratification of the Constitution, for reasons that are obscure, Chase became an ardent Federalist. A hard worker, willing to fight uncompromisingly for his beliefs, his turbulent disposition made him an ally who often proved more of a liability than an asset. * * *

In the years immediately following Chase's promotion to the nation's highest tribunal, he conducted himself well and delivered several influential and learned decisions. But at the same time he was becoming increasingly aroused by vitriolic Republican attacks upon the Adams administration, until, finally, when he made his circuit ride in 1800, his partisan nature got the better of him. * * *

* * *

Yet, despite the popular groundswell against Chase and the desire of radical Republicans for impeachment proceedings, Jefferson, after becoming President, adopted a cautious attitude toward the Judge. This was part of his larger policy to establish a live-and-let-live arrangement with the judiciary, and it implied the administration's willingness to forget past excesses in return for good behavior in the future. * * *

Chase, however, increasingly bitter, adopted the hard line policy of the High Federalists and totally rejected any kind of accommodation with the administration. "There can be no union between the Heads of the two Parties," he wrote. "Confidence is destroyed; if attempted they will be branded as *Deserters,* and lose all Influence. Things must take their natural Course, from *bad* to *worse.*"

Less than two months later, on 2 May 1803, Chase delivered his charge to the federal grand jury in Baltimore, a charge that was soon to be famous. * * *

Chase's charge was published in a Baltimore newspaper, and an outraged Republican member of the Maryland legislature sent a copy to Jefferson. * * * Jefferson reacted immediately. He wrote to [Republican Congressman] Joseph Hooper Nicholson, asking "Ought the seditious and official attack on the principles of our Constitution and of a State to go unpunished? And to whom so pointedly as yourself will the public look for the necessary measures?" Because Republican conversations about Chase almost always turned to impeachment, and because Nicholson had definite Old Republican sympathies * * * there can be no doubt that the President was giving his consent to having Chase removed. It appears that Jefferson expected the impeachment of Chase to be hazardous politically, for he added, significantly, "for myself, it is better that I should not interfere."

* * * Nicholson * * * requested the opinion of the Speaker of the House, Nathaniel Macon. Macon indicated his own dislike for the Judge, but pointed out that since Nicholson would probably be appointed to the Supreme Court if Chase were convicted, it would be impolitic for him to prosecute. He then questioned the legitimacy of impeaching Chase for his political opinions. Thinking, undoubtedly, of the increasing number of Republicans using the state benches for partisan purposes, he warned, "it deserves the most serious consideration before a single step be taken. * * *

Throughout the spring and summer of 1803, the Republican press, led by the National Intelligencer, assailed Chase, but no official action was taken. * * * Then, suddenly, on 5 January 1804, John Randolph rose in the House and demanded an investigation of Chase's conduct. Only after three days of debate and the extension of the investigation of Chase to encompass the activities of Richard Peters, district judge of Pennsylvania, did the House pass the motion. The inclusion of Peters, made at the request of Pennsylvania's militant Republicans, was designed to discredit him, but no one seriously expected his impeachment. The committee, headed by Randolph, reported its findings on 6 March. It cleared Peters, but recommended impeachment proceedings against Chase. Five days later the report was approved by a vote of 73 to 32. * * *

Meanwhile, Chase, though publicly silent, was busy. He appointed Robert Goodloe Harper his chief counsel, and between them they began to solicit the aid of the most distinguished Federalist lawyers in the country. "Fees, of course," wrote Harper, "are out of the question."

If you concur with me in opinion, that this is a great public cause, in which the honour of the federal party, the independence of the judiciary, and even the personal safety of the judges are involved, you will require no further motives for uniting with those who place themselves in the breach, and endeavor to resist the terror which threatens us with ruin. * * *

Chase, never an easy opponent, was under these circumstances formidable. True, he had acted with partiality in the courtroom. Richard Peters, for example, admitted that he "never sat with him without pain, as he was forever getting into some intemperate and unnecessary squabble." But it was one thing to accuse a Supreme Court justice of excessive partisanship, and another to convict him of criminal behavior. * * *

3. THE TEXT OF THE IMPEACHMENT ARTICLES *

I CHASE TRIAL 5–8

Article I

That, unmindful of the solemn duties of his office, and contrary to the sacred obligation by which he stood bound to discharge them "faithfully and impartially, and without respect to persons," the said Samuel Chase, on the trial of John Fries, charged with treason * * * did, in his judicial capacity, conduct himself in a manner highly arbitrary, oppressive, and unjust, viz.

1. In delivering an opinion, in writing, on the question of law, on the construction of which the defense of the accused materially depended, tending to prejudice the minds of the jury against the case of the said John Fries, the prisoner, before counsel had been heard in his defense.

2. In restricting the counsel for the said Fries from recurring to such English authorities as they believed apposite, or from citing certain statutes of the United States, which they deemed illustrative of the positions upon which they intended to rest the defense of their client.

3. In debarring the prisoner from his constitutional privilege of addressing the jury (through his counsel) on the law, as well as on the fact, which was to determine his guilt, or innocence, and at the same time endeavoring to wrest from the jury their indisputable right to hear argument, and determine upon the question of law, as well as on the question of fact, involved in the verdict which they were required to give.

---

* In the materials which follow, references to Articles II, V, VI, and VII of the Impeachment Articles are omitted. These were principally concerned with arcane procedural matters, and the final vote on them in the Senate was decidedly in favor of Chase.

In consequence of which irregular conduct of the said Samuel Chase, as dangerous to our liberties, as it is novel to our laws and usages, the said John Fries was deprived of the right, secured to him by the eighth article amendatory of the constitution, and was condemned to death without having been heard by counsel, in his defense, to the disgrace of the character of the American bench, in manifest violation of law and justice, and in open contempt of the rights of juries, on which, ultimately, rest the liberty and safety of the American people.

Article III *

That, with intent to oppress and procure the conviction of the prisoner, the evidence of John Taylor * * * was not permitted by the said Samuel Chase to be given in, on pretence that the said witness could not prove the truth of the whole of one of the charges, contained in the indictment, although the said charge embraced more than one fact.

Article IV

That the conduct of the said Samuel Chase, was marked, during the whole course of the said trial, by manifest injustice, partiality, and intemperance; viz.

1. In compelling the prisoner's counsel to reduce to writing, and submit to the inspection of the court, for their admission, or rejection, all questions which the said counsel meant to propound to the above named John Taylor, the witness.

2. In refusing to postpone the trial, although an affidavit was regularly filed, stating the absence of material witnesses on behalf of the accused; and although it was manifest, that, with the utmost diligence, the attendance of such witnesses could not have been procured at that term.

3. In the use of unusual, rude, and contemptuous expressions towards the prisoner's counsel; and in falsely insinuating that they wished to excite the public fears and indignation, and to produce that insubordination to law, to which the conduct of the judge did, at the same time, manifestly tend:

4. In repeated and vexatious interruptions of the said counsel, on the part of the said judge, which, at length, induced them to abandon their cause and their client, who was thereupon convicted and condemned to fine and imprisonment:

5. In an indecent solicitude, manifested by the said Samuel Chase, for the conviction of the accused, unbecoming even a public prosecutor, but highly disgraceful to the character of a judge as it was subversive of justice.

* Articles III and IV dealt with Chase's
conduct in the Callender trial.

Article VIII

And whereas mutual respect and confidence between the government of the United States and those of the individual states, and between the people and those governments, respectively, are highly conducive to that public harmony, without which there can be no public happiness, yet the said Samuel Chase * * * did, at a circuit court, * * * held at Baltimore, * * * pervert his official right and duty to address the grand jury then and there assembled * * * for the purpose of delivering to the said grand jury an intemperate and inflammatory political harangue, with intent to excite the fears and resentment of the said grand jury, and of the good people of Maryland against their state government, and constitution, a conduct highly censurable in any, but peculiarly indecent and unbecoming in a judge of the supreme court of the United States: and moreover, that the said Samuel Chase * * * did, in a manner highly unwarrantable, endeavor to excite the odium of the said grand jury, and of the good people of Maryland, against the government of the United States, by delivering opinions, which, even if the judicial authority were competent to their expression, on a suitable occasion and in a proper manner, were at that time and as delivered by him, highly indecent, extra-judicial, and tending to prostitute the high judicial character with which he was invested, to the low purpose of an electioneering partizan.

And the House of Representatives * * * do demand that the said Samuel Chase may be put to answer the said crimes and misdemeanors, and that such proceedings, examinations, trials, and judgments may be thereupon had and given, as are agreeable to law and justice * * *.

4. CHASE'S ANSWER TO THE ARTICLES OF IMPEACHMENT

I CHASE TRIAL 25–103

[Chase begins with a defense of his delivery of his written opinion in the *Fries* case. Chase refers to himself in the third person.]

* * *

With respect to the opinion, which is alleged to have been delivered by this respondent, at the above-mentioned trial, he begs leave to lay before this honorable court, the true state of that transaction, and to call its attention to some facts and considerations, by which his conduct on that subject will, he presumes, be fully justified.

The constitution of the United States, in the third section of the third article, declares that "treason against the United States, shall consist only in levying war against them, or in adhering to their enemies, giving them aid and comfort."

* * *

[Chase proceeds to explain the action he took after considering "with great care and deliberation" the indictment against Fries;]

* * * [F]inding from the three overt facts of treason which it charged, that the question of law arising upon it, was the same question which had already been decided twice in the same court, on solemn argument and deliberation, and once in that very case, he considered the law as settled by those decisions, with the correctness of which on full consideration he was entirely satisfied; and by the authority of which he should have deemed himself bound, even had he regarded the question as doubtful in itself. They are moreover in perfect conformity with the uniform tenor of decisions in the courts of England and Great Britain, from the revolution, in 1688, to the present time, which, in his opinion, added greatly to their weight and authority.

And surely he need not urge to this honorable court, the correctness, the importance, and the absolute necessity of adhering to principles of law once established, and of considering the law as finally settled, after repeated and solemn decisions by courts of competent jurisdiction. A contrary principle would unsettle the basis of our whole system of jurisprudence, hitherto our safeguard and our boast; would reduce the law of the land, and subject the rights of the citizen, to the arbitrary will, the passions, or the caprice of the judge in each particular case; and would substitute the varying opinions of various men, instead of that fixed, permanent rule, in which the very essence of law consists. * * *

Under the influence of these considerations, this respondent drew up an opinion on the law arising from the overt acts stated in the * * * indictment * * * conformable to the decisions before given as above mentioned, and which he sent to his colleague the said Richard Peters, for his consideration. That gentleman returned it to this respondent, with some amendments * * *, but not in any manner touching the substance.

The opinion thus agreed to, this respondent thought it proper to communicate to the prisoner's counsel * * *.

In the first place, this respondent considered himself and the court, as bound by the authority of the former decisions; especially the last of them, which was on the same case. * * * It was not suggested or understood, that any new evidence was to be offered; and he knew that if any should be offered, which could vary the case, it would render wholly inapplicable both the opinion and the former decisions on which it was founded. And he could not and did not suppose, that the prisoner's counsel would be desirous of wasting very precious time, in addressing to the court an useless argument, on a point which that court held itself precluded from deciding in their favor. He therefore conceived that it would be rendering the counsel a service and a favor, to apprise them before hand of the view which the court had taken of the subject; so as to let them see in time, the necessity of endeavoring to produce new testimony, which might vary the case, and take it out of the authority of former decisions.

Secondly, There were more than one hundred civil causes then depending in the said court * * *. Many of those causes had already been subjected to great delay, and it was the peculiar duty of this respondent, as presiding judge, to take care, that as little time as possible should be unnecessarily consumed * * *. He did believe, that an early communication of the court's opinion, might tend to the saving of time * * *.

Thirdly, As the court held itself bound by the former decisions, and could not therefore alter its opinion in consequence of any argument; and as it was the duty of the court to charge the jury on the law, in all cases submitted to their consideration, he knew that this opinion must not only be made known at some period or other of the trial, but must at the end of the trial be expressly delivered to the jury by him * * * and he could not suppose and cannot yet imagine, that an opinion * * * could make any additional impression on their minds, from the circumstance of its being intimated to the counsel before the trial began, in the hearing of those who might be afterwards sworn on the jury.

And, lastly, it was then his opinion, and still is, that it is the duty of every court of this country * * * to guard the jury against erroneous impressions respecting the laws of the land. He well knows, that it is the right of juries in criminal cases, to give a general verdict of acquittal, which cannot be set aside on account of its being contrary to law, and that hence results the power of juries, to decide on the law as well as on the facts, in all criminal cases. This power he holds to be a sacred part of our legal privileges, which he never has attempted, and never will attempt to abridge or to obstruct. But he also knows, that in the exercise of this power, it is the duty of the jury to govern themselves by the laws of the land, over which they have no dispensing power; and their right to expect and receive from the court, all the assistance which it can give, for rightly understanding the law. To withhold this assistance, in any manner whatever; to forbear to give it in that way, which may be most effectual for preserving the jury from error and mistake; would be an abandonment or forgetfulness of duty * * *. In this case, therefore, where the question of law arising on the indictment, had been finally settled by authoritative decisions, it was the duty of the court * * * early to apprise the counsel and the jury of these decisions, and their effect, so as to save the former from the danger of making an improper attempt, to mislead the jury in a matter of law, and the jury from having their minds preoccupied by erroneous impressions.

* * *

[Chase's long argument explaining the legal accuracy of his opinion is omitted.]

If, however, this opinion were erroneous, this respondent would be far less censurable than his predecessors, by whose example he was led astray, and by whose authority he considered himself bound. Was it an error to consider himself bound * * *? If it were, he was led into the error by the uniform course of judicial proceedings, in this country and in England * * *. Can such an error be a crime or misdemeanor?

If, on the other hand, the opinion be in itself correct * * * could the expression of a correct opinion on the law, wherever and however made, mislead the jury, infringe their rights, or give an improper bias to their judgments? Could truth excite improper prejudice? * * * And is not that a new kind of offence, in this country at least, which consists in telling the truth, and giving a correct exposition of the law.

As to the second specific charge * * * "of restricting the counsel for the said Fries, from recurring to such English authorities as they believed apposite * * *" this respondent admits that he did * * * express it as his opinion to the * * * counsel * * * "that the decisions in England, in cases of indictments for treason at common law, against the person of the king, ought not to be read to the jury, on trials for treason under the constitution and statutes of the United States; because such decisions could not inform, but might mislead and deceive the jury: that any decisions on cases of treason, in the courts of England, before the revolution of 1688, ought to have very little influence in the courts of the United States * * *."

* * * The counsellors admitted to practice in any court of justice are, in his opinion, and according to universal practice, to be considered as officers of such courts, and ministers of justice therein, and as such subject to the direction and control of the court, as to their conduct in its presence, and in conducting the defence of criminals on trial before it.—As counsel, they owe to the person accused diligence, fidelity, and secrecy, and to the court and jury, due and correct information, according to the best of their knowledge and ability * * *. The court * * * is bound in duty, to decide and direct what evidence, whether by record or by precedents of decisions in courts of justice, is proper to be admitted for the establishment of any matter of law or fact. Consequently, should counsel attempt to read to a jury, as a law still in force, a statute which had been repealed, or a decision which had been reversed, or the judgments of courts in countries whose laws have no connection with ours, it would be the duty of the court to interpose, and prevent such an imposition from being practised on the jury. For these reasons, this respondent thinks that his conduct was correct, in expressing to the counsel for Fries, the opinions stated above. He is not bound to answer here for the correctness of those principles * * * but merely for the correct-

ness of his motives * * *. A contrary opinion would convert this honorable court, from a court of impeachment into a court of appeals; and would lead directly to the strange absurdity, that whenever the judgment of an inferior court should be reversed on appeal or writ of error, the judges of that court must be convicted of high crimes and misdemeanors, and turned out of office * * * and that crimes may be committed without any criminal intention. * * *

* * * [The correctness of motives in delivering opinions] ought to be presumed, unless the contrary appear by some direct proof, or by some violent presumption, arising from his general conduct on the trial, or from the glaring impropriety of the opinion itself. * * *

Do the opinions now under consideration bear any of these marks? * * * [T]here has existed in England, no such thing as treason at common law, since the year 1350, when the statute of the 25th Edward III, chap. 2 * * * was passed. Is it perfectly clear that decisions made before that statute, 450 years ago, when England, together with the rest of Europe, was still wrapped in the deepest gloom of ignorance and barbarism * * * when law, justice and reason, were perpetually trampled under foot by feudal oppression and feudal anarchy; when, under an able and vigorous monarch, every thing was adjudged to be treason which he thought fit to call so, and under a weak one, nothing was considered as treason which turbulent, powerful, and rebellious nobles thought fit to perpetrate: is it perfectly clear that decisions, made at such a time, and under such circumstances, ought to be received by the courts of this country as authorities to govern their decisions, or lights to guide the understanding of juries? * * *

* * * [A]fter the above mentioned proceedings had taken place in the said trial, it was postponed until the next day * * * when at the meeting of the court, this respondent told both the above mentioned counsel for the prisoner, "that to prevent any misunderstanding of any thing that had passed the day before, he would inform them, that although the court retained the same opinion of the law * * * yet the counsel would be permitted to offer arguments to the court, for the purpose of shewing them that they were mistaken in the law * * * and also that the counsel would be permitted to argue before the petit jury, that the court were mistaken in the law." * * *

After some observations by the said William Lewis and Alexander James Dallas, they both declared to the court, "that they did not any longer consider themselves as the counsel for John Fries the prisoner." This respondent then asked the said John Fries, whether he wished the court to appoint other counsel for his defense? He refused to have other counsel assigned; in which he acted, as this respondent believes and charges, by the advice of the said William Lewis and Alexander James Dallas" whereupon the court ordered the said trial to be had on the next day * * *.

And this respondent * * * saith, that * * * the * * * charge * * * "that the said Fries was thereby deprived of the benefit of counsel for his defence," is not true. He insists that the said Fries was deprived of the benefit of counsel, not by any misconduct of this respondent, but by the conduct and advice of the above mentioned William Lewis and Alexander James Dallas, who * * * withdrew from his defence, and advised him to refuse other counsel when offered to him by the court, under pretence that the law had been prejudged, and their liberty of conducting the defence, according to their own judgment, improperly restricted by this respondent; but in reality because they knew the law and the facts to be against them, and the case to be desperate, and supposed that their withdrawing themselves under this pretence, might excite odium against the court; might give rise to an opinion that the prisoner had not been fairly tried; and in the event of a conviction * * * might aid the prisoner in an application to the President for a pardon. * * *

As little can this respondent be justly charged with having by any conduct of his, endeavored to "wrest from the jury their indisputable right to hear argument, and determine upon the question of law as well as the question of fact involved in the verdict which they were required to give." * * * It was expressly stated in the copy of his opinion delivered as above set forth to William Lewis, that the jury had a right to determine the law as well as the fact * * *. This respondent believes that the said William Lewis did not read the opinion delivered to him as aforesaid, except a very small part at the beginning of it, and of course, acted upon it without knowing its contents: and that the said Alexander James Dallas read no part of the said opinion until about a year ago * * *.

* * *

[Chase then turns to the charge that he improperly refused to admit testimony by John Taylor in the Callender trial.]

The indictment against James Thompson Callender * * * consisted of two distinct and separate counts, each of which contained twenty distinct and independent charges * * *. Each of those sets of words was charged as a libel against John Adams, as President of the United States, and the twelfth charge embraced the following words, "He (meaning President Adams) was a professed aristocrat; he proved faithful and serviceable to the British interest." The defence set up was confined to this charge, and was rested upon the truth of the words. * * * It was to prove the truth of these words, that John Taylor, the person mentioned in the article of impeachment now under consideration, was offered as a witness. It can hardly be necessary to remind this honorable court, that when an indictment for a libel contains several distinct charges, founded on distinct sets of words, the party accused, who in such cases is called the "traverser," must be convicted, unless he makes a sufficient defence against every charge. His innocence on one, does not prove him innocent on the others. * * * This conviction on nineteen charges, would put the traverser as completely in the power of the court, by which the amount of the fine and the term of the imprisonment were to be fixed, as a conviction upon all the twenty charges. * * * If then this respondent were desirous of procuring the conviction of the traverser, he was sure of his object, without rejecting the testimony of John Taylor. * * *

That the court did not feel this vindictive spirit, is clearly evinced by the moderation of the punishment, which actually was inflicted on the traverser, after he was convicted of the whole twenty charges. Instead of two thousand dollars, he was fined only two hundred, and was sentenced to only nine months imprisonment, instead of two years. And this respondent avers * * * that in this decision, as well as in every other given in the course of the trial, he fully and freely concurred with his colleague, judge Griffin.

[Chase next defends the correctness of his ruling]

* * * It is clear that no words are indictable as libellous, except such as expressly, or by plain implication, charge the person against whom they are published, with some offence either legal or moral. To be an "aristocrat," is not in itself an offence, either legal or moral * * * neither was it an offence either legal or moral, for Mr. Adams to be "faithful and serviceable to the British interest," unless he thereby betrayed or endangered the interests of his own country; which does not necessarily follow, and is not directly alleged in the publication. These two phrases, therefore, taken separately, charge Mr. Adams with no offence of any kind; and, consequently, could not be indictable as libellous: but taken together, they convey the implication that Mr. Adams, being an "aristocrat," that is, an enemy to the republican government of his own country, had subserved the British interest, against the interest of his own country; which would, in his situation, have been an offence both moral and legal; to charge him with it was, therefore, libellous.

Admitting, therefore, these two phrases to constitute one distinct charge, and one entire offence, this respondent considers and states it to be law, that no justification which went to part only of the offence, could be received. The plea of justification must always answer the whole charge, or it is bad * * *; for this plain reason, that the object of the plea is to shew the party's innocence; and he cannot be innocent, if the accusation against him be supported in part. * * * Evidence, therefore, which goes only to justify the charge in part, cannot be received. It is not indeed necessary, that the whole of this evidence should be given by one witness. The justification may consist of several facts, some of which may be proved by one person, and some by another. But proof, in such cases, must be offered as to the whole, or it cannot be received.

In the case under consideration, no proof was offered as to the whole matter contained in the twelfth article. No witness except the above mentioned John Taylor, was produced or mentioned.

* * *

For these reasons this respondent did concur with his colleague, the said Cyrus Griffin, in rejecting the three above mentioned questions; but not any other testimony that the said John Taylor might have been able to give. * * *

If his error was an honest one, which as his colleague also fell into it, might in charity be supposed; and, as there is not a shadow of evidence to the contrary, must in law be presumed; he cannot, for committing it, be convicted of any offence, much less a high crime and misdemeanor, for which he must, on conviction, be deprived of his office.

* * *

The fourth article of impeachment alleges, that during the whole course of the trial of James Thompson Callender, above mentioned, the conduct of this respondent was marked by "manifest injustice, partiality, and intemperance;" and five particular instances of the "injustice, partiality, and intemperance," are adduced.

* * *

This respondent, in answer to this part of the article now under consideration, admits that the court, consisting of himself and the above mentioned Cyrus Griffin, did require the counsel for the traverser, on the trial of James Thompson Callender, above mentioned, to reduce to writing the questions which they intended to put to the said witness. But he denies that it is more his act than the act of his colleague, who fully concurred in this measure. The measure, as he apprehends and insists, was strictly legal and proper; * * * if he, in common with his colleague, committed an error, it was an error into which the best and wisest men might have honestly fallen.

* * * [A]ccording to our laws, evidence, whether oral or written, may be rejected and prevented from going before the jury, on various grounds.—1st, For incompetency: where the source from which the evidence is attempted to be drawn, is an improper source: as if a witness were to be called who was infamous, or interested in the event of the suit * * *. 2d, For irrelevancy: when the evidence offered is not such, as in law will warrant the jury to infer the fact intended to be proved; or where that fact, if proved, is immaterial to the issue. * * *

It being thus the right and duty of a court before which a trial takes place, to inform itself of the nature of the evidence offered, so as to be able to judge whether such evidence be proper, it results necessarily that they have a right to require, that any question intended to be put to a witness, should be reduced to writing, for that is the form in which their deliberation upon it may be most perfect, and their judgment will be most likely to be correct.   *   *   *   When the testimony of John Taylor was offered, the court enquired of the traverser's counsel, what that witness was to prove. The statement of his testimony given in answer, induced the court to suspect that it was irrelevant and inadmissible. They therefore, that they might have an opportunity for more careful and accurate consideration, called upon the counsel to state in writing, the questions intended to be put to the witness.   *   *   *

The next circumstance   *   *   *   is [the] refusal to postpone the trial of the said James Thompson Callender, "although an affidavit was regularly filed, stating the absence of material witnesses on behalf of the accused, and although it was manifest that with the utmost diligence, the attendance of such witnesses could not have been procured at that term."

This respondent   *   *   *   admits, that   *   *   *   the traverser's counsel did move the court   *   *   *   for a continuance of the case until the next term   *   *   *   and did file as the ground work of their motion, an affidavit of the traverser   *   *   *   but he denies that any sufficient ground for a continuance until the next term, was disclosed by this affidavit   *   *   *.

The affidavit   *   *   *   states, that the traverser wished to procure, as material to his defence, authentic copies of certain answers made by the President of the United States, Mr. Adams, to addresses from various persons; and also, a book entitled "an Essay on Canon and Feudal Law,"   *   *   *   which was ascribed to the President, and which the traverser believed to have been written by him; and also, evidence to prove that the President was in fact the author of that book.

[Chase goes on to explain that defendant did *not* allege that the evidence and witnesses in question *could* be produced if a continuance or a postponement had been granted.]

*   *   *

But in order to afford every accommodation to the traverser and his counsel, which it was in his power to give, this respondent did offer to postpone the trial for a month or more, in order to afford them full time for preparation, and for procuring such testimony as was within their reach. This indulgence they thought proper to refuse.   *   *   *

To the third charge adduced in support of the article now under consideration, the charge of using "unusual, rude, and contemptuous expressions, towards the prisoner's counsel,"   *   *   *   he cannot answer otherwise than by a general denial. A charge so vague, admits not of precise or particular refutation. He denies that there was any thing unusual or intentionally rude or contemptuous in his conduct   *   *   *.

On the contrary, it was his wish and intention, to treat the counsel with the respect due to their situation and functions, and with the decorum due to his own character. He thought it his duty to restrain such of their attempts as he considered improper, and to overrule motions made by them, which he considered as unfounded in law; but this it was his wish to accomplish in the manner least likely to offend * * *. He did indeed think * * * that the conduct of the traverser's counsel * * * was disrespectful, irritating, and highly incorrect. That conduct which he viewed in this light, might have produced some irritation in a temper naturally quick and warm, and that this irritation might, not withstanding his endeavors to suppress it, have appeared in his manner and in his expressions, he thinks not improbable; for he has had occasions of feeling and lamenting the want of sufficient caution and self-command, in things of this nature. But he confidently affirms, that his conduct in this particular was free from intentional impropriety; and this respondent denies, that any part of his conduct was such as ought to have induced the traverser's counsel to "abandon the cause of their client," nor does he believe that any such cause did induce them to take that step. On the contrary, he believes that it was taken by them under the influence of passion * * *. And this respondent admits, that the said traverser was convicted and condemned to fine and imprisonment, but not by reason of the abandonment of his defence by his counsel; but because the charges against him were clearly proved, and no defence was made or attempted against far the greater number of them.

The fourth charge in support of this article, attributes to this respondent, "repeated and vexatious interruptions of the said counsel, which at length induced them to abandon the cause of their client, who was therefore, convicted, and condemned to fine and imprisonment." To this charge also, it is impossible to give any other answer but a general denial. * * *

Lastly, this respondent is charged under this article, with an "indecent solicitude, manifested by him, for the conviction of the accused, unbecoming even a public prosecutor, but highly disgraceful to the character of a judge, as it was subversive of justice." * * * He denies that he felt any solicitude whatever for the conviction of the traverser; other than the general wish natural to every friend of truth, decorum, and virtue, that persons guilty of such offences * * * should be brought to punishment, for the sake of example. He has no hesitation to acknowledge, that his indignation was strongly excited, by the atrocious and profligate libel which the traverser was charged with having written and published. This indignation, he believes, was felt by every virtuous and honorable man in the community, of every party, who had read the book in question, or become acquainted with its contents * * *.

And this respondent thinks it his duty, on this occasion, to enter his solemn protest against the introduction in this country, of those arbitrary principles, at once the offspring and the instruments of despotism, which would make "high crimes and misdemeanors" to consist in "rude and contemptuous expressions," in "vexatious interruptions of counsel," and in the manifestation of "indecent solicitude" for the conviction of a most notorious offender. Such conduct is no doubt, improper and unbecoming in any person, and much more so in a judge: but, it is too vague, too uncertain, and too susceptible of forced interpretations, according to the impulse of passion or the views of policy, to be admitted into the class of punishable offences, under a system of law whose certainty and precision in the definition of crimes, is its greatest glory, and the greatest privilege of those who live under its sway.

* * *

[What follows is Chase's response to the eighth article, regarding his charge to the Baltimore Grand jury in 1803.]

In answer to this charge this respondent admits, that he did * * deliver a charge to the grand jury, and express in the conclusion of it some opinions as to certain public measures, both of the government of Maryland and of that of the United States. But he denies that in thus acting, he disregarded the duties and dignity of his judicial character, perverted his official right and duty to address the grand jury, or had any intention to excite the fears or resentment of any person whatever, against the government and constitution of the United States or of Maryland. * * * He denies that he did any thing that was unusual, improper or unbecoming in a judge, or expressed any opinions, but such as a friend to his country, and a firm supporter of the governments both of the state of Maryland and of the United States, might entertain. For the truth of what he here says, he appeals confidently to the charge itself * * *.

* * *

Admitting these opinions to have been incorrect and unfounded, this respondent denies that there was any law which forbid him to express them * * *. The very essence of despotism consists, in punishing acts which, at the time when they were done, were forbidden by no law. Admitting the expression of political opinions by a judge, in his charge to a jury, to be improper and dangerous; there are many improper and very dangerous acts, which not being forbidden by law cannot be punished. Hence the necessity of new penal laws; which are from time to time enacted for the prevention of acts not before forbidden, but found by experience to be of dangerous tendency. It has been the practice in this country, ever since the beginning of the revolution, which separated us from Great Britain, for the judges to express from the bench, by way of charge to the grand jury, and to enforce to the utmost of their ability, such political opinions as they thought correct and useful. There have been instances in which the legislative bodies of this country, have recommended this practice to the judges; and it was adopted by the judges of the supreme court of the United States, as soon as the present judicial system was established. If the legislature of the United States considered this practice as mischievous, dangerous, or liable to abuse, they might have forbidden it by law * * *. By not forbidding it, the legislature has given to it an implied sanction; and for that legislature to punish it now by way of impeachment, would be to convert into a crime, by an ex post facto proceeding * * *. Such conduct would be utterly subversive of the fundamental principles on which free government rests; and would form a precedent for the most sanguinary and arbitrary persecutions, under the forms of law.

Nor can the incorrectness of the political opinions thus expressed, have any influence in deciding on the guilt or innocence of a judge's conduct in expressing them. For if he should be considered as guilty or innocent, according to the supposed correctness or incorrectness of the opinion, thus expressed by him, it would follow, that error in political opinion however honestly entertained, might be a crime; and that a party in power might, under this pretext, destroy any judge, who might happen in a charge to a grand jury, to say something capable of being construed by them, into a political opinion adverse to their own system. * * *

* * * Confiding in the impartiality, independence and integrity of his judges, and that they will patiently hear, and conscientiously determine this case, without being influenced by the spirit of party, by popular prejudice, or political motives, he cheerfully submits himself to their decision. * * *

This respondent now stands not merely before an earthly tribunal, but also before that awful Being whose presence fills all space, and whose all-seeing eye more especially surveys the temples of justice and religion. In a little time, his accusers, his judges, and himself, must appear at the bar of Omnipotence, where * * * every human being shall answer for his deeds done in the body, and shall be compelled to give evidence against himself, in the presence of an assembled universe. To his Omniscient Judge, at that awful hour, he now appeals for the rectitude and purity of his conduct, as to all the matters of which he is this day accused.

He hath now only to adjure each member of this honorable court, by the living GOD, and in his holy name, to render impartial justice to him, according to the constitution and laws of the United States. He makes this solemn demand of each member, by all his hopes of happiness in the world to come, which he will have voluntarily renounced by the oath he has taken; if he shall wilfully do this respondent injustice, or disregard the constitution or laws of the United States, which he has solemnly sworn to make the rule and standard of his judgment and decision.

5. CONGRESSMAN RANDOLPH'S OPENING ARGUMENT FOR THE CONVICTION OF JUSTICE CHASE

I CHASE TRIAL 108–127

It is a painful but indispensible task which we are called upon to perform:—to establish the guilt of a great officer of government, of a man, who, if he had made a just use of those faculties which God and Nature bestowed upon him, would have been the ornament and benefactor of his country, would have rendered her services as eminent and useful as he has inflicted upon her outrages and wrongs deep and deadly. * * * Base is that heart which could triumph over him.

* * * [Chase's] answer to the first of these charges is by evasive insinuation and misrepresentation, by an attempt to wrest the accusation from its true bearing, the manner and time of delivering the opinion, and the intent with which it was delivered, to the correctness of the opinion itself, which is not the point in issue. * * * It is not for the opinion itself, that the respondent is impeached; it is for a daring inroad upon the criminal jurisprudence of his country, by delivering that opinion at a time and in a manner (in writing) before unknown and unheard of. The criminal intent is to be inferred from the boldness of the innovation itself * * *. The admission of the respondent ought to secure his conviction on this charge. * * *

* * * For the truth of this opinion, and, as it would seem, for the propriety of this proceeding, the respondent takes shelter under precedent. He tells you, sir, this doctrine had been repeatedly decided on solemn argument and deliberation, twice in the same court, and once in that very case.—What is this, but a confession, that he himself hath been the first man to venture on so daring an innovation on the forms of our criminal jurisprudence? To justify himself for having given a written opinion *before* counsel had been heard for the prisoner, he resorts to the example set by his predecessors, who had delivered the customary verbal opinion, after solemn argument and deliberation. And what do these repeated arguments and solemn deliberations prove, but that none of his predecessors ever arrogated to themselves the monstrous privilege of breaking in upon those sacred institutions, which guard the life and liberty of the citizen from the rude inroads of powerful injustice? * * *

* * * I beg this honorable court never to lose sight of the circumstance, that this was a *criminal* trial, for a *capital* offence, and that the offence charged was *treason*. The respondent also admits, that the counsel for Fries, not meaning to contest the truth of the facts charged in the indictment, rested their defence altogether upon the law, which he declared to have been settled in the cases of Vigol and Mitchel: a decision which, although it might be binding on the court, the jury were not obliged to respect, and which the counsel had a right to controvert before them, the sole judges, in a case of that

nature, both of the *law* and the *fact*. * * * If they verily believed that the overt acts charged in the indictment, did not amount to treason, they could not without a surrender of their consciences into the hands of the court, without a flagrant violation of all that is dear and sacred to man, bring in a verdict of Guilty. * * * In civil cases, indeed, the verdict may be set aside and a new trial granted—but in a criminal prosecution, the verdict, if not guilty, is final and conclusive. * * * When I concede the right of the court to explain the law to the jury in a criminal, and especially in a capital case, I am penetrated with a conviction that it ought to be done, if at all, with great caution and delicacy. * * * There is, in my mind, a material difference between a naked definition of law, the application of which is left to the jury, and the application by the court, of such definition to the particular case * * *. But it is alleged, on behalf of the respondent, that the law in this case was settled, and upon this he rests his defence. Will it be pretended by any man that the law of treason is better established than the law of murder? * * * And because what constitutes murder has been established and settled through a long succession of ages and adjudications, has any judge for that reason, been ever daring enough to assert that counsel should be precluded from endeavoring to convince the jury that the overt acts, charged in the indictment, did not amount to murder? * * *

* * *

* * * [Chase] confesses that he would not permit the prisoner's counsel to cite certain cases, "because they could not inform but might deceive and mislead the jury." Mr. President, * * * in criminal prosecutions * * * the jury are the sole judges, and where they acquit the prisoner, the judges, without appeal, both of law and fact. And what is the declaration of the respondent but an admission that he wished to take from the jury their indisputable privilege to hear argument and determine upon the law, and to usurp to himself that power, which belonged to them, and to them only? It is one of the most glorious attributes of jury trial, that in criminal cases (particularly such as are capital) the prisoner's counsel may (and they often do) attempt "to deceive and mislead the jury." It is essential to the fairness of the trial, that it should be conducted with perfect freedom. * * * Hence, a greater latitude is allowed to the accused, than is permitted to the prosecutor. The jury, upon whose verdict the event is staked, are presumed to be men capable of understanding what they are called upon to decide, and the attorney for the state, a gentleman learned in his profession, capable of detecting and exposing the attempts of the opposite counsel to mislead and deceive. * * * [T]o what purpose has treason been defined by the constitution itself, if overbearing arbitrary judges are permitted to establish among us the odious and dangerous doctrine of constructive treason? The acts of Congress which had been referred to on the former trial, but which the respondent said he would not suffer to be cited again, tended to

shew that the offence committed by Fries did not amount to treason. That it was a misdemeanor, only, already provided for by law and punishable with fine and imprisonment. * * * And are the laws of our own country (as well as foreign authorities) not to be suffered to be read in our courts, in justification of a man whose life is put in jeopardy!

* * *

The 3d article relates to the rejection of John Taylor's testimony. * * * [A]n attempt is made to justify it, on the ground of its *"irrelevancy,"* on the pretext that the witness could not prove the whole of a particular charge [which] * * * consists of two distinct sentences. Taken separately the respondent asserts that they mean nothing; taken together, a great deal. And because the respondent undertook to determine (without any authority as far as I can learn) that col. Taylor could not prove the whole, that is both sentences, he rejected his evidence entirely, for *"irrelevancy."* Might not his testimony have been relevant to that of some other witness, on the same, or on another charge? I appeal to the learning and good sense of this honorable court, whether it is not an unheard of practice (until the present instance) in a criminal prosecution, to declare testimony inadmissible because it is not expected to go to the entire exculpation of the prisoner? * * * Suppose for instance that the testimony of two witnesses would establish all the facts, but that each of those facts are not known by either of them. According to this doctrine the evidence of both might be declared inadmissible, and a man whose innocence, if the testimony in his favor were not rejected, might be clearly proved to the satisfaction of the jury, may thus be subjected by the verdict of that very jury to an ignominious death. Shall principles so palpably cruel and unjust be tolerated in this free country? I am free to declare that the decision of Mr. Chase, in rejecting col. Taylor's testimony, was contrary to the known and established rules of evidence * * *. There is one ground of defence taken by the respondent, which I did suppose, a gentleman of his discernment would have sedulously avoided. That although the traverser had justified nineteen out of twenty of the charges, contained in the indictment, if he could not prove the truth of the twentieth, it was of little moment, as he was, "thereby, put into the power of the court." Gracious God! Sir, what inference is to be drawn from this horrible insinuation?

* * * Sir, in the famous case of Logwood, whereat the chief justice of the United States presided, I was present, being one of the grand jury who found a true bill against him. It must be conceded that the government was as deeply interested in arresting the career of this dangerous and atrocious criminal, who had aimed his blow against the property of every man in society, as it could be in bringing to punishment a weak and worthless scribbler. And yet, although much testimony was offered by the prisoner, which did, by no means, go to his entire exculpation, although much of that testimony was of a

very questionable nature, none of it was declared *inadmissible*; it was suffered to go to the jury, who were left to judge of its weight and credibility, nor were any interrogatories to the witnesses required to be reduced to writing. And I will go farther, and say that it never has been done before, or since Callender's trial, in any court of Virginia, (and I believe I might add in the United States) whether state or federal. * * *

The respondent also acknowledges his refusal to postpone the trial of Callender, although an affidavit was regularly filed stating the absence of material witnesses on his behalf * * *. The dispersed situation of the witnesses, which he alleges to have been the motive of his refusal, is, to my mind, one of the most unanswerable reasons for granting a postponement. * * *

The 8th and last article remains to be considered. [article read.] I ask this honorable court whether the prostitution of the bench of justice to the purposes of an hustings is to be tolerated? We have nothing to do with the politics of the man. * * * If he must electioneer and abuse the government under which he lives, I know no law to prevent or punish him, provided he seeks the wonted theatres for his exhibition. * * * Shall he not put off the political partizan when he ascends the tribune; or shall we have the pure stream of public justice polluted with the venom of party virulence? In short, does it follow that a judge carries all the rights of a private citizen with him upon the bench * * *?

But, Sir, we are told that this high court is not a court of errors and appeals, but a court of impeachment, and that however incorrectly the respondent may have conducted himself, proof must be adduced of criminal intent, of wilful error, to constitute guilt. * * * It is not an indictable offence under the laws of the United States for a judge to go on the bench in a state of intoxication—it may not be in all the state courts. But it is indictable no where, for him to omit to do his duty, to refuse to hold a court. And who can doubt that both are impeachable offences, and ought to subject the offender to removal from office? But in this long and disgusting catalogue of crimes and misdemeanors (which he has in a great measure confessed) the respondent tells you he had accomplices and that what was guilt in him could not be innocence in them. I must beg the court to consider the facts alleged against the respondent in all their accumulated atrocity;—not to take them, each in an insulated point of view, but as a chain of evidence indissolubly linked together, and establishing the indisputable proof of his guilt. Call to mind his high standing and character, and his superior age and rank, and then ask yourselves whether he stands justified in a long course of oppression and injustice, because men of weak intellect, and yet feebler temper—men of far inferior standing to the respondent, have tamely acquiesced in such acts of violence and outrage? * * * But, sir, would the establishment of their guilt prove his innocence?   At most it would only prove that they too ought to be punished.   *   *   *

I have endeavored, Mr. President, in a manner, I am sensible, very lame and inadequate, to discharge the duty incumbent on me   *   *   *. We shall bring forward in proof, such a specimen of judicial tyranny, as, I trust in God, will never be again exhibited in our country.

The respondent hath closed his defence by an appeal to the great Searcher of hearts for the purity of his motives.   For his sake, I rejoice, that, by the timely exercise of that mercy, which, for wise purposes, has been reposed in the executive, this appeal is not drowned by the blood of an innocent man crying aloud for vengeance;   that the mute agony of widowed despair and the wailing voice of the orphan do not plead to heaven for justice on the oppressor's head.   *   *   * On that awful day the blood of a poor, ignorant, friendless, unlettered German, murdered under the semblance and color of law, sent without pity to the scaffold, would have risen in judgment at the Throne of Grace, against the unhappy man arraigned at your bar.   But the President of the United States by a well timed act, at once of justice and of mercy, (and mercy like charity covereth a multitude of sins,) wrested the victim from his grasp, and saved him from the countless horrors of remorse, by not suffering the pure ermine of justice to be dyed in the innocent blood of John Fries.

*   *   *

NOTES AND QUESTIONS

1.   You have now been given enough materials (the reports in *Fries*, *Cooper* and *Callender*;   the charge to the Baltimore Grand Jury;   the Articles of Impeachment;   Chase's Answer;   and Randolph's argument) to permit you to understand how law in the early republic might be freighted with ideological baggage, and how otherwise reasonable men might so vehemently disagree over the merits of particular laws.   By now you should also be able to arrive at some conclusion whether or not Chase should have been found Guilty of high crimes and misdemeanors at his Senate Trial.   Let's take the charge relating to Chase's hasty opinion-giving in the Fries's case.   Why was this regarded as criminal by Randolph? Consider Chase's defense to this charge.   He believed that the law on the matter was settled, he wanted to save time so that the court could get on to its overcrowded civil docket, and he believed that it was his duty to prevent the jury from straying from what had been previously found to be the law.   Are these reasons persuasive?   Do they meet Randolph's criticisms?

2.   What about the charges relating to Chase's conduct of the Callender trial?   Some of these are very technical, but the thrust of all of the charges is that Chase's bias against the defendant led him to deprive the defendant of a chance to defend himself in court.   Do you agree with this charge? How effective is Chase's defense that the other Judge, Griffin, acquiesced in Chase's rulings?   Note that Chase makes the same defense (substituting Judge Peters for Judge Griffin) with regard to the *Fries* trial.   Why do you suppose there were no impeachments of Peters and Griffin?

3. Note, especially in the case of the eighth count, the Baltimore Grand Jury charge, Chase comes down hard on the notion that while what he did may have been improper or inappropriate it was *not* a crime. Is this a good defense? What is the meaning of the Constitutional provision (Article II, Section 4) which states that "The President, Vice President and all Civil Officers of the United States, shall be removed from Office on Impeachment for, and Conviction of, Treason, Bribery, or other high Crimes and Misdemeanors." Former President Gerald Ford, when a Congressman seeking the impeachment of Justice Douglas, stated that an impeachable offense was "whatever a majority of the House of Representatives considers it to be   .   ." 116 Cong.Rec. H 3113–3114 (daily ed., April 15, 1970). Imagine, if you can, with what joy Mr. Ford's definition was cited to former President Nixon's lawyers who attempted to argue to the House of Representatives, in 1974, that Nixon could only be impeached for a criminal offense. One scholar has concluded that while Mr. Ford may not have been entirely correct, the phrase "high crimes and misdemeanors" at least when it refers to the conduct of a judge, *is* much broader than criminal acts, and probably extends to anything that could be construed as *not* good behavior. See R. Berger, Impeachment: The Constitutional Problems 53–102 (1973). Raoul Berger believes that Chase's "rabid partisanship" and his "implacable intention to convict" Callender should have resulted in his conviction by the Senate. Berger, supra, at 229, 250–251.

4. In order for Chase to have been convicted by the Senate, twenty-three Senators would have to have voted against him on any one charge. On the first count of the impeachment (improper conduct in delivering his opinion in the *Fries* case) sixteen senators voted *guilty* and eighteen *not guilty*. On the third and fourth counts (events at Callender's trial) eighteen voted *guilty* and sixteen *not guilty*. On the eighth count (the Baltimore Grand Jury charge) nineteen voted *guilty* and fifteen voted *not guilty*. On the other four charges there were never more than ten votes of guilty, and on one charge there were no guilty votes at all. Accordingly, Chase was acquitted and continued in office, though he was reported to be somewhat subdued by the experience. Wharton, State Trials, at 46. Most commentators have believed that Chase's acquittal was the proper result, and have suggested that since the time of the Chase impeachment, never again has the impeachment remedy been used as a means of punishing merely errant politics on the part of judges. See, e. g. 1 C. Warren, The Supreme Court in United States History 292–95 (rev. ed. 1947). Do you agree with Warren or Berger? Should impeachment be a means of keeping judges' politics in line? What, if anything, was resolved by the trial of Chase?

5. How do you explain the closing references to God and an afterlife made by *both* Chase and Randolph? Which is more effective? Why?

Chapter 3

SECURING THE REVOLUTION OF 1800
THROUGH THE COMMON LAW

Jefferson styled his victory over the Federalists in the election of 1800 a "Revolution." This was a play on the spirit of '76, and the Federalists expected Jefferson's election, like the recent French Revolution, to result in bloody purges, anarchy, and rampaging hordes ravishing Federalist women and private property. This never occurred, but in retrospect Jefferson's election *was* like a revolution. It marked the first peaceful transfer of power between opposing factions under the new Constitution. Still, Jefferson attempted to steer a middle course between radical and Federalist interests. "We are all Federalists, we are all Republicans," he had said in his inaugural. Eventually he broke with the radical agrarian wing of his party; he tolerated the first National Bank, a Hamiltonian creation; he grudgingly accepted the Federalist Supreme Court, and he came to acknowledge the importance of commercial and manufacturing interests to the life of the nation. He even unwittingly supported the Federalist principles of centralization and promotion of American industry, when he went beyond express Constitutional executive powers to purchase the Louisiana Territory in 1803. While some political divisiveness persisted for much of his Presidency, there was a pronounced movement in the direction of American consensus. Administrations after the War of 1812 flourished in an atmosphere of "Good Feeling." Lasting until the mid-1820s, this period is characterized by a relative absence of political rancor, a decline of agrarian and Federalist stridency and the emergence of widespread agreement on basic values of democracy, economic progress, and social mobility.

The generation coming of age in the 1820s could look back in wistful wonder at the achievements of the Founding Fathers. Some grand old men of that time still lingered. After years of political enmity, Adams the Federalist and Jefferson the Republican once again engaged in a lively correspondence on all manner of things, but in particular on their mutual sense of alienation from the bustling society of the early nineteenth century. Their eerily-timed deaths (both on the fourth of July in 1826) soon symbolized for the rising generation the irrevocable passage of the old order.

The new generation of Americans found new heroes: Daniel Webster, Henry Clay, and especially Andrew Jackson, who captured the Presidency in 1828 on a tidal wave of popular support. These men and others like them had temporarily resolved many of their political differences and were embarked on the common enterprise of national expansion.

The rate of demographic, territorial and economic growth during these years was astounding. United States population grew from almost 4 million in 1790 to more than 31 million in 1860. This growth sprang not only from a prolific birth rate, but also from an influx of European immigrants who sought to farm western land and to fill the demand for labor in the expanding cities. The percentage of urban population climbed from a meagre 3.3 percent in 1790 to 16.1 percent in 1860. The construction of turnpikes, canals and, after 1830, the railroads, facilitated internal migration and the westward movement. In 1790 most Americans were clustered east of the Alleghenies. By the Civil War, settlements had spread from the Atlantic to the Pacific. The new transportation network aided in the development of an internal economy by linking the regions of the country and by creating vast new markets for goods and services. Americans learned to look less and less to Europe for commercial progress. The Northeastern states supplied the rest of the country with manufactured commodities; the Western regions concentrated on agricultural production for both national and international trade; the Southern states grew cotton for the New England finishing mills and for export. State and local governments promoted growth by encouraging immigration, by liberalizing land policy, and by subsidizing transportation, manufacturing and education. The national government constructed tariff barriers, removed impediments to interstate commerce, and opened up new reserves of land.

A new national ideology of the antebellum era equated material progress with the fulfillment of the principles of the Revolution of 1776. Mining America's vast human and physical resources, spreading out across the face of the continent was seen as a patriotic mission, the realization of a providentially ordained "manifest destiny."

Often, of course, such chauvinism barely concealed crass materialism. Still, national growth revealed an important intellectual change, at the root of which was a new conception of man. The Americans of the Founding Fathers' generation feared authority and the inherent tendency toward corruption in mankind, and thus built checks, balances and separations of power into government. Most clung to the Calvinist belief that man was born in sin; his capacity for doing evil, his lust for power, could be thwarted only by the erection of earthly restraints. In antebellum America, however, man was more often seen as innately good, even perfectible. Traditional institutions which had been used to restrain men and thus preserve what freedom remained, gave way before a new regard for liberty that sought instead to enlarge the opportunities for action. The national policy was not only to voice platitudes of popular sovereignty, but actually to place power in the hands of the people. This new spirit was most clearly revealed in the "ferment of reform." The removal of property qualifications for voting, the improvements in the status of women and children, the establishment of free public schools, abolitionism, temperance, and religious revivalism were but another side of expansionism: both expansionism and reform were born of an optimistic faith in mankind, and both ostensibly sought to expand the boundaries of opportunity for all.

The transformation of American values was carried through in the changing social structure of society. The Jacksonian Era has been called the Age of the Common Man, and has been supposed to have been characterized by boundless opportunity. Quantitative studies seem to bear out the existence of substantial fluidity between classes, and of great economic potential, at least compared to the contemporary situation in other countries. Millions of acres of cheap, fertile farmland in the West operated as a steady lure for restless Easterners and for immigrants. Developments in transportation, the expansion of capital, and the growth of consumer demand also insured that farmers would profit as never before. Businessmen benefitted as the proliferation of banks, the relaxation of debtor laws, liberal lending policies, and the willingness of Western Europeans to invest here spurred risk-taking, entrepreneurial ventures.

The new manufacturing industries made the city a center of economic activity, a new "urban frontier." There was a continual demand for skilled and for semi-skilled labor. The diligent workingman might eventually save enough to buy a farm in the West, or at least to provide his children with hopes for the future. Manufacturing also gave rise to a new class of white-collar employees—salesmen, accountants, clerks, draftsmen, engineers, and managers. New public schools and relatively inexpensive colleges became available to many seeking the skills to advance in the urban world.

Not all Americans shared in these new opportunities. Most women, nearly all Blacks, and many unskilled laborers remained poor and powerless. But the rest could hope, and often expect, to rise or fall according to their individual initiative and abilities.

The materials of this chapter are designed to suggest how the spirit of expansion permeated American law and produced new rules to govern private economic behavior. There was a broad consensus that material progress would benefit all of American society. In practice, however, clear formulations of these legal rules were not easily drawn. It gradually became apparent that there *were* divisions in the economy and advocates for differing approaches to legal problems. There were disagreements between industrial developers and agrarian users of property, between groups of developers or industries, between competitors for some scarce resources, and between some advocates of change and some forces of conservatism. How American courts perceived these divisions, the legal conclusions they reached, and the manner in which private judicial decision-making became clothed in the language of public policy is the subject of this chapter.

NOTES

Overviews of American politics and social values for this period appear in John R. Howe, From the Revolution Through the Age of Jackson (1973); Marvin Meyers, The Jacksonian Persuasion: Politics and Belief (1960); and David M. Potter and Don E. Fehrenbacher, The Impending Crisis, 1848–61 (1976). A good introduction to the antebellum economy is George R. Taylor, The Transportation Revolution, 1815–1860 (1951). Quantitative growth is detailed in Douglass C. North, The Economic Growth of the United States, 1790–1860 (1961) and Peter Temin, The Jacksonian Economy (1965). The social, cultural and political context of growth is provocatively presented in Richard D. Brown, Modernization: The Transformation of American Life, 1600–1865 (1976) and Stuart Bruchey, The Roots of American Economic Growth, 1607–1861 (1965). The role of local government in the economy is well portrayed in Carter Goodrich, ed., The Government and the Economy, 1783–1861 (1967). A comprehensive approach to the efforts of a single state appears in the monograph by Oscar and Mary Handlin, Commonwealth: A Study of the Role of Government in the American Economy, Massachusetts, 1774–1861 (Rev. ed. 1969).

The growth of the American city during this period is described in Richard Wade, The Urban Frontier (1959). Good local studies developing antebellum themes include Sam Bass Warner, The Private City (1968), examining Philadelphia; Robert G. Albion, The Rise of New York Port, 1815–60 (1939), and Stuart Blumin, The Urban Threshold (1976), dealing with Poughkeepsie, New York. The finest introduction to the literature of mobility is Stephen Thernstrom, Poverty and Progress (1964), focusing on Newburyport, Massachusetts. Alice Felt Tyler's Freedom's Ferment (1944) and Russell B. Nye's Society and Culture in America, 1830–60 (1974) are good starting places for examining American reform.

Some of the most valuable recent work on Nineteenth Century American Law is Maxwell Bloomfield, American Lawyers in a Changing Society 1776–1876 (1976); Lawrence M. Friedman, A History of American Law (1973); Morton J. Horwitz, The Transformation of American Law 1780–1860 (1977); J. Willard Hurst, Law and the Conditions of Freedom in the Nineteenth Century United States (1956); Leonard W. Levy, The Law of the Commonwealth and Chief Justice Shaw (1957); Perry Miller, The Life of the Mind in America (1965); William E. Nelson, The Americanization of the Common Law (1975); and G. Edward White, The American Judicial Tradition (1976). Roscoe Pound's The Formative Era of American Law (1938) is something of a classic, although Pound's sanguine views about the nature and motives of nineteenth century legal change have been subjected to heavy criticism. Treatments of individual topics may be found in Wythe Holt, editor, Essays in Nineteenth Century American Legal History (1976). Finally, some historiographical perspective can be gained by consulting three valuable essays, Gordon, J. Willard Hurst and the Common Law Tradition in American Legal Historiography, 10 Law & Society Review 9 (1975); Horwitz, The Conservative Tradition in the Writing of American Legal History, 17 American Journal of Legal History 275 (1973), and Katz, Looking Backward: The Early History of American Law, 33 University of Chicago Law Review 867 (1966).

A. THE LAW AND AMERICAN DEMOCRACY

HONESTUS [Benjamin Austin, Jr.], OBSERVATIONS ON THE PERNICIOUS PRACTICE OF THE LAW, AS PUBLISHED OCCASIONALLY IN THE INDEPENDENT CHRONICLE, IN THE YEAR 1786

7–10 (1819).

The following observations are meant, in general, to apply to the practitioners of the law in their malpractice, and not intended to reflect on them in their particular character, as many individuals among them are gentlemen of high esteem and confidence. But as it has lately been asserted * * * that they are a "necessary order in a republic," it is presumed the subject is open to inquiry, and consequently there can be no objection in applying the general practice to support a contrary hypothesis.

Among the multiplicity of evils which we at present suffer, there are none more justly complained of, than those we labor under by the many pernicious practices in the profession of the law. It has therefore, become a subject of serious inquiry, whether this body of men, in a young republic, ought not to be controuled in their pleas.

Laws are necessary for the safety and good order of society, and consequently the execution of them is of great importance to be attended to. When therefore, *finesse* and gross impositions are practised, and under sanction of the law, every principle of equity and justice is destroyed, the persons concerned in such pernicious measures ought to be brought forward, and their conduct arraigned before the impartial tribunal of the people.

The study and practice of the law are doubtless an honourable employment; and when a man acts becoming the dignity of the profession, he ought to be esteemed by every member in the community. But when any number of men under sanction of this character are endeavouring to perplex and embarrass every judicial proceeding; who are rendering intricate even the most simple principles of law; who are involving individuals, applying for advice, in the most distressing difficulties; who are practising the greatest art in order to delay every process; who are taking the advantage of every accidental circumstance which an unprincipled person might have, by the lenity and indulgence of an honest creditor; who stand ready to strike up a bargain, (after rendering the property in a precarious state) to throw an honest man out of three quarters of his property. When such men pretend to cloak themselves under the sacredness of law, it is full time the people should inquire, "by what authority they do these things."

* * *

The distresses of the people are now great, but if we examine particularly, we shall find them owing, in a great measure, to the conduct of some practitioners of the law. Seven-eighths of the causes which are now in their hands might have been settled by impartial referees. Why cannot the disputes of the merchant, &c. be adjusted by reference, rather than by a long tedious Court process? Or why should we engage lawyers who are wholly unacquainted with all mercantile concerns? Is it to swell the cost and then by a rule of Court have them finally determined by referees, which is generally the case? * * * [I]f we look through the different counties throughout the Commonwealth, we shall find that the troubles of the people arise principally from debts enormously swelled by tedious law-suits.

The many pernicious modes of judiciary process which have taken place within a few years, are too notorious to mention; scarcely a petty office but has become a little distinct tribunal. What flagrant impositions are daily practised under sanction of law! The distressed individual is often reduced to the humiliating state of submitting to the extortion of official fees without any remedy. Is it not a disgrace to a free republic that the citizens should dread appealing to the laws of their country? To what purpose have we laws? * * *

It has, therefore, become necessary for the welfare and security of the Commonwealth, that some mode be adopted in order to render the laws a blessing, instead of an evil. For this purpose, it is requested that some acts should be passed, declaring that in all cases left to reference in future, the decision of the referees should be binding on the parties. In all judiciary processes, the Jury, to receive the evidence from the parties, and the Judges to give their opinion on any controverted points of law. The Jury in this manner would be possessed of all that was necessary to determine on the cause, viz. Law and Evidence, without the false glosses and subterfuges too often practised by lawyers.

If such regulations were made in our Courts, the Judges could determine with more precision; the Jury by taking the evidence, and points of law from the Judges, could, with more clearness, determine the cause; as in many instances, a Jury becomes puzzled in their judgment by the variety of sentiments advanced by lawyers. By this method the laws would be more justly executed, as the judges are under no influence from either party, their salaries being independent. But by our present mode, the lawyers become parties by their fees, and are too apt to delay the business while there is any prospect of further profit.

I would ask, whether there are many cases, that absolutely require the assistance of this "order?" Or if they were not admitted, whether any great inconvenience could arise? The law and evidence are all the essentials required, and are not the Judges with the Jury competent for these purposes? Why then this intervening "order?" The important study of law, should be followed solely with a view of doing justice; and gentlemen of talents, who meant to serve their country as Judges, should make the public good their chief object. They would not take up the profession as a set of needy persons, who meant by chicanery and finesse, to get a living by their practice; but they would make it a point of duty, so to understand the laws, as to distribute equal justice to the rich and poor; each individual would receive the benefit of the laws, and by a speedy and impartial determination, every man would have his cause decided without the imposition of enormous Court charges, and lawyers' fees. There would be no great danger of the Judges converting their authority to any destructive purposes, "as the municipal institutions are so fixed and determined, in this Commonwealth, that it must be difficult for the Judicial Authority to trample upon them with impunity." The perplexity of our laws, therefore, are chiefly owing to the embarrassments thrown in the way by many in the profession.

* * *

NOTES AND QUESTIONS

1. What is the meaning of this piece? Note that this was first published in 1786, the year of Shay's rebellion, which sought to put an end to debt collection in Massachusetts, and the year before the convention that drafted the Federal Constitution. Honestus takes issue with those who have "lately * * * asserted" that "lawyers are a necessary order in a republic." With whom might he be disagreeing? Why might lawyers be referred to as an "order?" Why might anyone think them "necessary?" Why should it make a difference that America is a "republic?"

2. Honestus advocates that lawyers be "controlled in their pleas." Does he mean by this that page limits on court documents should be established? Concerning lawyers, he rails against "finesse," "the greatest art," and, in general, against the lawyers' ability to make the simple complex. These have been perennial complaints about common lawyers, but is Honestus's complaint just with the "lawyers," or does his disaffection cut much deeper? Where would you place him in the political spectrum we observed in the last Chapter? Note that he comments on the high judicial fees, and suggests that most matters ought to be handled by referees instead of courts. Could Honestus be correct when he argues that at present the courts and lawyers are "wholly unacquainted with all mercantile concerns?" If Honestus was correct on this matter, how could such a situation have come about?

3. Note Honestus's observation that it would be desirable if, for the most part, we did without lawyers, and "In all judiciary processes, the Jury to receive the evidence from the parties, and the Judges to give their opinion on any controverted points of law." Is this a radical proposal? Do you share Honestus's confidence that judges and juries, functioning without lawyers, would consistently arrive at equitable results? What evidence within these materials can you cite to support your answer?

ROBERT RANTOUL, JR., ORATION AT SCITUATE, DELIVERED ON THE FOURTH OF JULY, 1836

The Common Law sprung from the dark ages; the fountain of justice is the throne of the Deity. The Common Law is but the glimmering taper by which men groped their way through the palpable midnight in which learning, wit, and reason were almost extinguished; justice shines with the splendor of that fulness of light which beams from the Ineffable Presence. The Common Law had its beginning in time, and in the time of ignorance; justice is eternal, even with the eternity of the allwise and just Lawgiver and Judge. The Common Law had its origin in folly, barbarism, and feudality; justice is the irradiance of divine wisdom, divine truth, and the government of infinite benevolence. * * * Older, nobler, clearer, and more glorious, then, is everlasting justice, than ambiguous, baseborn, purblind, perishable Common Law. That which is older than the creation may indeed be extolled for its venerable age; but among created things, the argument from antiquity is a false criterion of worth. Sin and death are older than the Common Law; are they, therefore, to be preferred to it? * * *

Judge-made law is *ex post facto* law, and therefore unjust. An act is not forbidden by the statute law, but it becomes void by judicial construction. The legislature could not effect this, for the Constitution forbids it. * * *

Judge-made law is special legislation. The judge is human, and feels the bias which the coloring of the particular case gives. If he wishes to decide the next case differently, he has only to distinguish, and thereby make a new law. The legislature must act on general views, and prescribe at once for a whole class of cases.

No man can tell what the Common Law is; therefore it is not law: for a law is a rule of action; but a rule which is unknown can govern no man's conduct. Notwithstanding this, it has been called the perfection of human reason.

The Common Law is the perfection of human reason,—just as alcohol is the perfection of sugar. The subtle spirit of the Common Law is reason double distilled, till what was wholesome and nutritive becomes rank poison. * * *

The judge makes law, by extorting from precedents something which they do not contain. He extends his precedents, which were themselves the extension of others, till, by this accommodating principle, a whole system of law is built up without the authority or interference of the legislator.

The judge labors to reconcile conflicting analogies, and to derive from them a rule to decide future cases. No one knows what the law is, before he lays it down; for it does not exist even in the breast of the judge. * * *

No man knows what the law is after the judge has decided it. Because, as the judge is careful not to decide any point which is not brought before him, he restricts his decision within the narrowest possible limits; and though the very next case that may arise may seem, to a superficial observer, and even upon a close inspection by an ordinary mind, to be precisely similar to the last, yet the ingenuity of a thorough-bred lawyer may detect some unsuspected shade of difference upon which an opposite decision may be founded.   *   *   *

Statutes, enacted by the legislature, speak the public voice. Legislators, with us, are not only chosen because they possess the public confidence, but after their election, they are strongly influenced by public feeling. They must sympathize with the public, and express its will: should they fail to do so, the next year witnesses their removal from office, and others are selected to be the organs of the popular sentiment. The older portions of the Common Law are the work of judges, who held their places during the good pleasure of the king, and of course decided the law so as to suit the pleasure of the king. In feudal times it was made up of feudal principles, warped, to be sure, according to the king's necessities. Judges now are appointed by the executive, and hold their offices during good behavior,—that is, for life, and are consequently out of the reach of popular influence. They are sworn to administer Common Law as it came down from the dark ages, excepting what has been repealed by the Constitution and the statutes, which exception they are always careful to reduce to the narrowest possible limits. With them, wrong is right, if wrong has existed from time immemorial: precedents are every thing: the spirit of the age is nothing. And suppose the judge prefers the Common Law to the Constitutions of the State and of the Union; or decides in defiance of the statute; what is the remedy?   *   *   *   Impeachment is a bugbear, which has lost its terrors. We must have democratic governors, who will appoint democratic judges, and the whole body of the law must be codified.

It is said, that where a chain of precedents is found running back to a remote antiquity, it may be presumed that they originated in a statute which, through lapse of time, has perished. Unparalleled presumption this! To suppose the legislation of a barbarous age richer and more comprehensive than our own. It was without doubt a thousand times more barren. But what if there were such statutes? The specimens which have survived do not impress us with a favorable opinion of those that may have been lost. Crudely conceived, savage in their spirit, vague, indeterminate, and unlimited in their terms, and incoherent when regarded as parts of a system, the remains of ancient legislation are of little use at present, and what is lost was probably still more worthless. If such laws were now to be found in our statute book, they would be repealed at once; the innumerable judicial constructions which they might have received would not save them.   *   *   *

These objections to the Common Law have a peculiar force in America, because the rapidly advancing state of our country is continually presenting new cases for the decision of the judges; and by determining these as they arise, the bench takes for its share more than half of our legislation, notwithstanding the express provisions of the Constitution, that the judiciary shall not usurp the functions of the legislature. If a Common Law system could be tolerable anywhere, it is only where every thing is stationary. With us, it is subversive of the fundamental principles of a free government, because it deposits in the same hands the power of first making the general laws, and then applying them to individual cases; powers distinct in their nature, and which ought to be jealously separated.

* * * All American Law must be statute law.

NOTES AND QUESTIONS

1. Compare Robert Rantoul's attitude toward the common law with that of Alexander Hamilton expressed in the Federalist. Would Hamilton have agreed with the position that the common law is reason "double distilled" and that judge-made law is *"ex post facto law?"* Would Hamilton have agreed that impeachment is a "bugbear, which has lost its terrors?" The Oxford English Dictionary defines "bugbear" as "A sort of hobgoblin, presumably in the shape of a bear, supposed to devour naughty children; hence, generally, any imaginary being invoked by nurses to frighten children. *Obs.*" When and how did impeachment lose its terrors?

2. Rantoul especially objects to the common law because it is unsuited to "the rapidly advancing state of our country." He then says that if it "could be tolerable anywhere, it is only where every thing is stationary." What does this mean? Could you advance a counter argument?

3. Do you see any common thread which runs through Honestus's criticism of American lawyers as non-commercially oriented and Rantoul's criticism of the common law based on its affinity with "folly, barbarism, and feudality?" Which man's statements seem to you to be the most tightly reasoned, serious of purpose, and ideologically consistent? Do you agree with Rantoul that the only sensible law is statute law? Why might he say this? Would Richard Peters have agreed? Robert Rantoul, incidentally, was a Jacksonian Democrat from Massachusetts, a spokesman for reformist causes, and an advocate of the urban workingman. Is this evident from this excerpt?

4. Rantoul advocates the "codification" of the law, and seems to be suggesting that it would be possible for comprehensive legislation enacted on the basis of reasoned principles to replace what he perceives to be the outmoded common law. Did Rantoul's views win wide acceptance? Of what does "law" primarily consist today, statutes or court decisions?

5. Was the lawyer "order" abolished? Why not? Consider the argument in the next few excerpts, the famous analysis of American law and lawyers by Alexis de Tocqueville.

I ALEXIS DE TOQUEVILLE, DEMOCRACY IN AMERICA *

48–56, 102–107, 247–250, 256–258, 282–290 (1840).

[(a) *The Social and Political Conditions of America*]

* * *

* * * The social condition of the Americans is eminently democratic; this was its character at the foundation of the colonies, and it is still more strongly marked at the present day.

* * * [G]reat equality existed among the immigrants who settled on the shores of New England. Even the germs of aristocracy were never planted in that part of the Union. The only influence which obtained there was that of intellect * * *. Some of their fellow citizens acquired a power over the others that might truly have been called aristocratic if it had been capable of transmission from father to son.

* * * In most of the states situated to the southwest of the Hudson some great English proprietors had settled who had imported with them aristocratic principles and the English law of inheritance. * * * In the South one man, aided by slaves, could cultivate a great extent of country; it was therefore common to see rich landed proprietors. But their influence was not altogether aristocratic, as that term is understood in Europe, since they possessed no privileges; and the cultivation of their estates being carried on by slaves, they had no tenants depending on them, and consequently no patronage. Still, the great proprietors south of the Hudson constituted a superior class, having ideas and tastes of its own and forming the center of political action. This kind of aristocracy sympathized with the body of the people, whose passions and interests it easily embraced; but it was too weak and too shortlived to excite either love or hatred. This was the class which headed the insurrection in the South and furnished the best leaders of the American Revolution.

At this period society was shaken to its center. The people, in whose name the struggle had taken place, conceived the desire of exercising the authority that it had acquired; its democratic tendencies were awakened; and having thrown off the yoke of the mother country, it aspired to independence of every kind. * * *

But the law of inheritance was the last step to equality. * * * It is true that these laws belong to civil affairs; but they ought, nevertheless, to be placed at the head of all political institutions; for they exercise an incredible influence upon the social state of a people, while political laws show only what this state already is. * * * Through their means man acquires a kind of preternatural power over the future lot of his fellow creatures. When the legislator has once reg-

---

ulated the law of inheritance, he may rest from his labor. The machine once put in motion will go on for ages * * *. When framed in a particular manner, this law unites, draws together, and vests property and power in a few hands; it causes an aristocracy, so to speak, to spring out of the ground. If formed on opposite principles, its action is still more rapid; it divides, distributes, and disperses both property and power. * * * When the law of inheritance permits, still more when it decrees, the equal division of a father's property among all his children, its effects are of two kinds: it is important to distinguish them from each other, although they tend to the same end.

As a result of the law of inheritance, the death of each owner brings about a revolution in property; not only do his possessions change hands, but their very nature is altered, since they are parceled into shares, which become smaller and smaller at each division. This is the direct and as it were the physical effect of the law. In the countries where legislation establishes the equality of division, property, and particularly landed fortunes, have a permanent tendency to diminish. * * *

* * *

Among nations whose law of descent is founded upon the right of primogeniture, landed estates often pass from generation to generation without undergoing division; the consequence of this is that family feeling is to a certain degree incorporated with the estate. The family represents the estate, the estate the family, whose name, together with its origin, its glory, its power, and its virtues, is thus perpetuated in an imperishable memorial of the past and as a sure pledge of the future.

When the equal partition of property is established by law, the intimate connection is destroyed between family feeling and the preservation of the paternal estate; the property ceases to represent the family * * *. The sons of the great landed proprietor, if they are few in number, or if fortune befriends them, may indeed entertain the hope of being as wealthy as their father, but not of possessing the same property that he did; their riches must be composed of other elements than his. Now, as soon as you divest the landowner of that interest in the preservation of his estate which he derives from association, from tradition, and from family pride, you may be certain that, sooner or later, he will dispose of it; for there is a strong pecuniary interest in favor of selling, as floating capital produces higher interest than real property and is more readily available to gratify the passions of the moment.

* * *

And now, after a lapse of a little more than sixty years, the aspect of society is totally altered; the families of the great landed proprietors are almost all commingled with the general mass. * * *

I do not mean that there is any lack of wealthy individuals in the United States; I know of no country, indeed, where the love of money has taken stronger hold on the affections of men and where a profounder contempt is expressed for the theory of the permanent equality of property. But wealth circulates with inconceivable rapidity, and experience shows that it is rare to find two succeeding generations in the full enjoyment of it.

*　*　*

It is not only the fortunes of men that are equal in America; even their acquirements partake in some degree of the same uniformity. I do not believe that there is a country in the world where, in proportion to the population, there are so few ignorant and at the same time so few learned individuals. Primary instruction is within the reach of everybody; superior instruction is scarcely to be obtained by any. This is not surprising; it is, in fact, the necessary consequence of what I have advanced above. Almost all the Americans are in easy circumstances and can therefore obtain the first elements of human knowledge.

In America there are but few wealthy persons; nearly all Americans have to take a profession. Now, every profession requires an apprenticeship. The Americans can devote to general education only the early years of life. At fifteen they enter upon their calling, and thus their education generally ends at the age when ours begins. If it is continued beyond that point, it aims only towards a particular specialized and profitable purpose * * *.

In America most of the rich men were formerly poor; most of those who now enjoy leisure were absorbed in business during their youth; the consequence of this is that when they might have had a taste for study, they had no time for it, and when the time is at their disposal, they have no longer the inclination.

There is no class, then, in America, in which the taste for intellectual pleasures is transmitted with hereditary fortune and leisure and by which the labors of the intellect are held in honor. Accordingly, there is an equal want of the desire and the power of application to these objects.

*　*　*

It is impossible to believe that equality will not eventually find its way into the political world, as it does everywhere else. To conceive of men remaining forever unequal upon a single point, yet equal on all others, is impossible; they must come in the end to be equal upon all.

Now, I know of only two methods of establishing equality in the political world; rights must be given to every citizen, or none at all to anyone. For nations which are arrived at the same stage of social existence as the Anglo-Americans, it is, therefore, very difficult to discover a medium between the sovereignty of all and the absolute power of one man * * *.

There is, in fact, a manly and lawful passion for equality that incites men to wish all to be powerful and honored. This passion tends to elevate the humble to the rank of the great; but there exists also in the human heart a depraved taste for equality, which impels the weak to attempt to lower the powerful to their own level and reduces men to prefer equality in slavery to inequality with freedom. Not that those nations whose social condition is democratic naturally despise liberty; on the contrary, they have an instinctive love of it. But liberty is not the chief and constant object of their desires; equality is their idol: they make rapid and sudden efforts to obtain liberty and, if they miss their aim, resign themselves to their disappointment; but nothing can satisfy them without equality, and they would rather perish than lose it.

On the other hand, in a state where the citizens are all practically equal, it becomes difficult for them to preserve their independence against the aggressions of power. No one among them being strong enough to engage in the struggle alone with advantage, nothing but a general combination can protect their liberty. Now, such a union is not always possible.

* * *

The Anglo-Americans are the first nation who, having been exposed to this formidable alternative, have been happy enough to escape the dominion of absolute power. They have been allowed by their circumstances, their origin, their intelligence, and especially by their morals to establish and maintain the sovereignty of the people.

* * *

[At the time before the American Revolution, the principle of popular sovereignty was not yet established.] * * * Intelligence in New England and wealth in the country to the south of the Hudson * * * long exercised a sort of aristocratic influence, which tended to keep the exercise of social power in the hands of a few. Not all the public functionaries were chosen by popular vote, nor were all the citizens voters. The electoral franchise was everywhere somewhat restricted and made dependent on a certain qualification, which was very low in the North and more considerable in the South.

The American Revolution broke out, and the doctrine of the sovereignty of the people came out of the townships and took possession of the state. Every class was enlisted in its cause; battles were fought and victories obtained for it; it became the law of laws.

A change almost as rapid was effected in the interior of society, where the law of inheritance completed the abolition of local influences.

As soon as this effect of the laws and of the Revolution became apparent to every eye, victory was irrevocably pronounced in favor of the democratic cause. All power was, in fact, in its hands, and resistance was no longer possible. The higher orders submitted without

a murmur and without a struggle to an evil that was thenceforth inevitable. The ordinary fate of falling powers awaited them; each
of their members followed his own interest; and as it was impossible
to wring the power from the hands of a people whom they did not
detest sufficiently to brave, their only aim was to secure its goodwill
at any price. The most democratic laws were consequently voted by
the very men whose interests they impaired: and thus, although
the higher classes did not excite the passions of the people against
their order, they themselves accelerated the triumph of the new state
of things; so that, by a singular change, the democratic impulse was
found to be most irresistible in the very states where the aristocracy
had the firmest hold. The state of Maryland, which had been founded
by men of rank, was the first to proclaim universal suffrage and to
introduce the most democratic forms into the whole of its government.

When a nation begins to modify the elective qualification, it may
easily be foreseen that, sooner or later, that qualification will be entirely abolished. There is no more invariable rule in the history of society
* * * for after each concession the strength of the democracy increases, and its demands increase with its strength. The ambition
of those who are below the appointed rate is irritated in exact proportion to the great number of those who are above it. The exception
at last becomes the rule, concession follows concession, and no stop
can be made short of universal suffrage.

* * *

[(b) *Judicial Power in the United States, and Its Influence on Political Society*]

* * * Confederations have existed in other countries besides
America; I have seen republics elsewhere * * *; the representative
system of government has been adopted in several states of Europe;
but I am not aware that any nation of the globe has hitherto organized
a judicial power in the same manner as the Americans. The judicial
organization of the United States is the institution which a stranger
has the greatest difficulty in understanding. He hears the authority
of a judge invoked in the political occurrences of every day, and he
naturally concludes that in the United States the judges are important
political functionaries; nevertheless, when he examines the nature of
the tribunals, they offer at the first glance nothing that is contrary
to the usual habits and privileges of those bodies * * *.

* * *

The first characteristic of judicial power in all nations is the
duty of arbitration. But rights must be contested in order to warrant
the interference of a tribunal; and an action must be brought before
the decision of a judge can be had. * * * When a judge in a given
case attacks a law relating to that case, he extends the circle of his
customary duties, without, however, stepping beyond it, since he is
in some measure obliged to decide upon the law in order to decide the

case. But if he pronounces upon a law without proceeding from a case, he clearly steps beyond his sphere and invades that of the legislative authority.

The second characteristic of judicial power is that it pronounces on special cases, and not upon general principles. If a judge, in deciding a particular point, destroys a general principle by passing a judgment which tends to reject all the inferences from that principle, and consequently to annul it, he remains within the ordinary limits of his functions. But if he directly attacks a general principle without having a particular case in view, he leaves the circle in which all nations have agreed to confine his authority * * *.

The third characteristic of the judicial power is that it can act only when it is called upon, or when, in legal phrase, it has taken cognizance of an affair. * * *

[Americans have adopted these three judicial principles. Why, then are their judiciaries regarded as more powerful than those of other nations?] * * * The cause of this difference lies in the simple fact that the Americans have acknowledged the right of judges to found their decisions on the Constitution rather than on the laws. In other words, they have permitted them not to apply such laws as may appear to them to be unconstitutional.

I am aware that a similar right has been sometimes claimed, but claimed in vain, by courts of justice in other countries; but in America it is recognized by all the authorities; and not a party, not so much as an individual, is found to contest it. This fact can be explained only by the principles of the American constitutions. In France the constitution is, or at least is supposed to be, immutable; and the received theory is that no power has the right of changing any part of it. In England the constitution may change continually, or rather it does not in reality exist; the Parliament is at once a legislative and a constituent assembly. * * * An American constitution is not supposed to be immutable, as in France; nor is it susceptible of modification by the ordinary powers of society, as in England. It constitutes a detached whole, which, as it represents the will of the whole people, is no less binding on the legislator than on the private citizen, but which may be altered by the will of the people in predetermined cases, according to established rules. In America the Constitution may therefore vary; but as long as it exists, it is the origin of all authority, and the sole vehicle of the predominating force.

* * *

Whenever a law that the judge holds to be unconstitutional is invoked in a tribunal of the United States, he may refuse to admit it as a rule; this power is the only one peculiar to the American magistrate, but it gives rise to immense political influence. In truth, few laws can escape the searching analysis of the judicial power for any length of time, for there are few that are not prejudicial to some private interest or other, and none that may not be brought before a court of justice * * *. But as soon as a judge has refused to apply any given law in a case, that law immediately loses a portion of its moral force. Those to whom it is prejudicial learn that means exist of overcoming its authority, and similar suits are multiplied until it becomes powerless. The alternative, then, is, that the people must alter the Constitution or the legislature must repeal the law. The political power which the Americans have entrusted to their courts of justice is therefore immense, but the evils of this power are considerably diminished by the impossibility of attacking the laws except through the courts of justice. * * * It will be seen, also, that by leaving it to private interest to censure the law, and by intimately uniting the trial of the law with the trial of an individual, legislation is protected from wanton assaults and from the daily aggressions of party spirit * * *.

I am inclined to believe this practice of the American courts to be at once most favorable to liberty and to public order. If the judge could attack the legislator only openly and directly, he would sometimes be afraid to oppose him; and at other times party spirit might encourage him to brave it at every turn. The laws would consequently be attacked when the power from which they emanated was weak, and obeyed when it was strong * * *. But the American judge is brought into the political arena independently of his own will. He judges the law only because he is obliged to judge a case. The political question that he is called upon to resolve is connected with the interests of the parties, and he cannot refuse to decide it without a denial of justice. * * * It is true that, upon this system, the judicial censorship of the courts of justice over the legislature cannot extend to all laws indiscriminately, inasmuch as some of them can never give rise to that precise species of contest which is termed a lawsuit; and even when such a contest is possible, it may happen that no one cares to bring it before a court of justice. The Americans have often felt this inconvenience; but they have left the remedy incomplete, lest they should give it an efficacy that might in some cases prove dangerous. Within these limits the power vested in the American courts of justice of pronouncing a statute to be unconstitutional forms one of the most powerful barriers that have ever been devised against the tyranny of political assemblies.

[(c) *American Laws*]

[De Toqueville proceeds from a discussion of the judiciary to a discussion of American Laws.] * * * The laws of the American democracy are frequently defective or incomplete; they sometimes attack vested rights, or sanction others which are dangerous to the community; and even if they were good, their frequency would still be a great evil. How comes it, then, that the American republics prosper and continue? * * *

Democratic laws generally tend to promote the welfare of the greatest possible number * * *. The laws of an aristocracy tend, on the contrary, to concentrate wealth and power in the hands of the minority * * *. It may therefore be asserted, as a general proposition, that the purpose of a democracy in its legislation is more useful to humanity than that of an aristocracy. This, however, is the sum total of its advantages.

Aristocracies are infinitely more expert in the science of legislation than democracies ever can be. They are possessed of a self-control that protects them from the errors of temporary excitement; and they form far-reaching designs, which they know how to mature till a favorable opportunity arrives. Aristocratic government proceeds with the dexterity of art; it understands how to make the collective force of all its laws converge at the same time to a given point. Such is not the case with democracies, whose laws are almost always ineffective or inopportune. The means of democracy are therefore more imperfect than those of aristocracy, and the measures that it unwittingly adopts are frequently opposed to its own cause; but the object it has in view is more useful.

Let us now imagine a community so organized by nature or by its constitution that it can support the transitory action of bad laws, and that it can await, without destruction, the general tendency of its legislation: we shall then conceive how a democratic government, notwithstanding its faults may be best fitted to produce the prosperity of this community. This is precisely what has occurred in the United States * * *.

* * *

No political form has hitherto been discovered that is equally favorable to the prosperity of the development of all the classes into which society is divided. These classes continue to form, as it were, so many distinct communities in the same nation; and experience has shown that it is no less dangerous to place the fate of these classes exclusively in the hands of any one of them than it is to make one people the arbiter of the destiny of another. * * * The advantage of democracy does not consist, therefore, as has sometimes been asserted, in favoring the prosperity of all, but simply in contributing to the well-being of the greatest number.

The men who are entrusted with the direction of public affairs in the United States are frequently inferior, in both capacity and morality, to those whom an aristocracy would raise to power. But their interest is identified and mingled with that of the majority of their fellow citizens. They may frequently be faithless and frequently mistaken, but they will never systematically adopt a line of conduct hostile to the majority; and they cannot give a dangerous or exclusive tendency to the government.

* * *

The common purpose which in aristocracies connects the interest of the magistrates with that of a portion of their contemporaries identifies it also with that of future generations; they labor for the future as well as for the present. The aristocratic magistrate is urged at the same time towards the same point by the passions of the community, by his own, and, I may almost add, by those of his posterity. Is it, then, wonderful that he does not resist such repeated impulses? And, indeed, aristocracies are often carried away by their class spirit without being corrupted by it; and they unconsciously fashion society to their own ends and prepare it for their own descendants.

The English aristocracy is perhaps the most liberal that has ever existed, and no body of men has ever, uninterruptedly, furnished so many honorable and enlightened individuals to the government of a country. It cannot escape observation, however, that in the legislation of England the interests of the poor have often been sacrificed to the advantages of the rich, and the rights of the majority to the privileges of a few. * * *

In the United States, where public officers have no class interests to promote, the general and constant influence of the government is beneficial, although the individuals who conduct it are frequently unskillful and sometimes contemptible. There is, indeed, a secret tendency in democratic institutions that makes the exertions of the citizens subservient to the prosperity of the community in spite of their vices and mistakes; while in aristocratic institutions there is a secret bias which, notwithstanding the talents and virtues of those who conduct the government, leads them to contribute to the evils that oppress their fellow creatures. * * *

* * *

[(d) *Respect for Law in the United States*]

* * *

In the United States, except slaves, servants, and paupers supported by the township, there is no class of persons who do not exercise the elective franchise and who do not indirectly contribute to make the laws. Those who wish to attack the laws must consequently either change the opinion of the nation or trample upon its decision.

* * * [I]n the United States everyone is personally interested in enforcing the obedience of the whole community to the law; for as the minority may shortly rally the majority to its principles, it is interested in professing that respect for the decrees of the legislator which it may soon have occasion to claim for its own. However irksome an enactment may be, the citizen of the United States complies with it, not only because it is the work of the majority, but because it is his own, and he regards it as a contract to which he is himself a party.

In the United States, then, that numerous and turbulent multitude does not exist who, regarding the law as their natural enemy, look upon it with fear and distrust. It is impossible, on the contrary, not to perceive that all classes display the utmost reliance upon the legislation of their country and are attached to it by a kind of parental affection.

I am wrong, however, in saying all classes; for as in America the European scale of authority is inverted, there the wealthy are placed in a position analogous to that of the poor in the Old World, and it is the opulent classes who frequently look upon law with suspicion. * * * In the United States, where the poor rule, the rich have always something to fear from the abuse of their power. This natural anxiety of the rich may produce a secret dissatisfaction; but society is not disturbed by it, for the same reason that withholds the confidence of the rich from the legislative authority makes them obey its mandates: their wealth, which prevents them from making the law, prevents them from withstanding it. Among civilized nations, only those who have nothing to lose ever revolt; and if the laws of a democracy are not always worthy of respect, they are always respected; for those who usually infringe the laws cannot fail to obey those which they have themselves made and by which they are benefited; while the citizens who might be interested in their infraction are induced, by their character and station, to submit to the decisions of the legislature, whatever they may be. * * *

[(e) *The Temper of the Legal Profession in the United States, and How It Serves as a Counterpoise to Democracy*]

* * *

* * * Men who have made a special study of the laws derive from occupation certain habits of order, a taste for formalities, and a kind of instinctive regard for the regular connection of ideas, which naturally render them very hostile to the revolutionary spirit and the unreflecting passions of the multitude.

The special information that lawyers derive from their studies ensures them a separate rank in society, and they constitute a sort of privileged body in the scale of intellect. This notion of their superiority perpetually recurs to them in the practice of their profession: they are the masters of a science which is necessary, but which is not very generally known; they serve as arbiters between the citizens; and the habit of directing to their purpose the blind passions of parties in litigation inspires them with a certain contempt for the judgment of the multitude. * * *

Some of the tastes and the habits of the aristocracy may consequently be discovered in the characters of lawyers. They participate in the same instinctive love of order and formalities; and they entertain the same repugnance to the actions of the multitude, and the same secret contempt of the government of the people. I do not mean to say that the natural propensities of lawyers are sufficiently strong to sway them irresistibly; for they, like most other men, are governed by their private interests, and especially by the interests of the moment.

* * * When an aristocracy excludes the leaders of that profession from its ranks, it excites enemies who are the more formidable as they are independent of the nobility by their labors and feel themselves to be their equals in intelligence though inferior in opulence and power. But whenever an aristocracy consents to impart some of its privileges to these same individuals, the two classes coalesce very readily and assume, as it were, family interests.

I am in like manner inclined to believe that a monarch will always be able to convert legal practitioners into the most serviceable instruments of his authority. * * *

Lawyers are attached to public order beyond every other consideration, and the best security of public order is authority. It must not be forgotten, also, that if they prize freedom much, they generally value legality still more: they are less afraid of tyranny than of arbitrary power; and, provided the legislature undertakes of itself to deprive men of their independence, they are not dissatisfied.

I am therefore convinced that the prince who, in presence of an encroaching democracy, should endeavor to impair the judicial authority in his dominions, and to diminish the political influence of lawyers, would commit a great mistake: he would let slip the substance of authority to grasp the shadow. He would act more wisely in introducing lawyers into the government; and if he entrusted despotism to them under the form of violence, perhaps he would find it again in their hands under the external features of justice and law.

The government of democracy is favorable to the political power of lawyers; for when the wealthy, the noble, and the prince are excluded from the government, the lawyers take possession of it, in their own right, as it were, since they are the only men of information and sagacity, beyond the sphere of the people, who can be the object of the popular choice. If, then, they are led by their tastes towards the aristocracy and the prince, they are brought in contact with the people by their interests. They like the government of democracy without participating in its propensities and without imitating its weaknesses; whence they derive a twofold authority from it and over it. The people in democratic states do not mistrust the members of the legal profession, because it is known that they are interested to serve the popular cause; and the people listen to them without irritation, because they do not attribute to them any sinister designs. The lawyers do not, indeed, wish to overthrow the institutions of democracy, but they constantly endeavor to turn it away from its real direction by means that are foreign to its nature. Lawyers belong to the people by birth and interest, and to the aristocracy by habit and taste; they may be looked upon as the connecting link between the two great classes of society.

The profession of the law is the only aristocratic element that can be amalgamated without violence with the natural elements of democracy and be advantageously and permanently combined with them. I am not ignorant of the defects inherent in the character of this body of men; but without this admixture of lawyer-like sobriety with the democratic principle, I question whether democratic institutions could long be maintained; and I cannot believe that a republic could hope to exist at the present time if the influence of lawyers in public business did not increase in proportion to the power of the people.

*   *   *

The French codes are often difficult to comprehend, but they can be read by everyone; nothing, on the other hand, can be more obscure and strange to the uninitiated than a legislation founded upon precedents. The absolute need of legal aid that is felt in England and the United States, and the high opinion that is entertained of the ability of the legal profession, tend to separate it more and more from the people and to erect it into a distinct class. The French lawyer is simply a man extensively acquainted with the statutes of his country; but the English or American lawyer resembles the hierophants of Egypt, for like them he is the sole interpreter of an occult science *   *   * [since most of American law is based on judicial precedent.]

*   *   *

In America there are no nobles or literary men, and the people are apt to mistrust the wealthy; lawyers consequently form the highest political class and the most cultivated portion of society. They have therefore nothing to gain by innovation, which adds a conservative interest to their natural taste for public order. *   *   *

The more we reflect upon all that occurs in the United States, the more we shall be persuaded that the lawyers, as a body, form the most powerful, if not the only, counterpoise to the democratic element. In that country we easily perceive how the legal profession is qualified by its attributes, and even by its faults, to neutralize the vices inherent in popular government. When the American people are intoxicated by passion or carried away by the impetuosity of their ideas, they are checked and stopped by the almost invisible influence of their legal counselors. These secretly oppose their aristocratic propensities to the nation's democratic instincts, their superstitious attachment to what is old to its love of novelty, their narrow views to its immense designs and their habitual procrastination to its ardent impatience.

The courts of justice are the visible organs by which the legal profession is enabled to control the democracy. *   *   *

*   *   * I am aware that a secret tendency to diminish the judicial power exists in the United States; and by most of the constitutions of the several states the government can, upon the demand of the two houses of the legislature, remove judges from their station. Some other state constitutions make the members of the judiciary elective, and they are even subjected to frequent re-elections. I venture to predict that these innovations will sooner or later be attended with fatal consequences; and that it will be found out at some future period that by thus lessening the independence of the judiciary they have attacked not only the judicial power, but the democratic republic itself.

It must not be supposed, moreover, that the legal spirit is confined in the United States to the courts of justice; it extends far beyond them. As the lawyers form the only enlightened class whom the people do not mistrust, they are naturally called upon to occupy most of the public stations. They fill the legislative assemblies and are at the head of the administration; they consequently exercise a powerful influence upon the formation of the law and upon its execution. The lawyers are obliged, however, to yield to the current public opinion, which is too strong for them to resist; but it is easy to find indications of what they would do if they were free to act. The Americans, who have made so many innovations in their political laws, have introduced very sparing alterations in their civil laws, and that with great difficulty, although many of these laws are repugnant to their social condition. The reason for this is that in matters of civil law the majority are obliged to defer to the authority of the legal profession, and the American lawyers are disinclined to innovate when they are left to their own choice.

The influence of legal habits extends beyond the precise limits I have pointed out. Scarcely any political question arises in the United States that is not resolved, sooner or later, into a judicial question. Hence all parties are obliged to borrow, in their daily controversies, the ideas, and even the language, peculiar to judicial proceedings. As most public men are or have been legal practitioners, they introduce the customs and technicalities of their profession into the management of public affairs. The jury extends this habit to all classes. The language of the law thus becomes, in some measure, a vulgar tongue; the spirit of the law, which is produced in the schools and courts of justice, gradually penetrates beyond their walls into the bosom of society, where it descends to the lowest classes, so that at last the whole people contract the habits and the tastes of the judicial magistrate. The lawyers of the United States form a party which * * * acts upon the country imperceptibly, but finally fashions it to suit its own purposes.

NOTES AND QUESTIONS

1. As you are probably aware, Tocqueville understood America better than most Americans before or since. He was a French aristocrat, lawyer, and legislator who was sent to America to study penal reform. He proceeded to write a wide-ranging survey of American social and political life. For a short and penetrating analysis of his work, see Richard Hofstadter, Alexis de Tocqueville, in L. Kronenberger, ed., Atlantic Brief

Lives 795 (1971). Tocqueville believed that the world was moving in the direction of democracy, and that America was in the vanguard. He was not overwhelmingly pleased with what the future offered, and believed that modern pressures for equality would extinguish some excellence that the *ancien regime* had encouraged. Can you discern, from these excerpts, Tocqueville's personal attitude toward American law and lawyers?

2. Your excerpts begin with Tocqueville's views on the general social and political conditions in America. His major premise is that America seems to have moved furthest towards a classless society. What part did American law play in this movement? Would Tocqueville have approved of Thomas Jefferson's efforts to do away with entail and primogeniture? Was Tocqueville correct when he predicted that either all Americans would come to have all rights or all but one man would have rights? Why or why not?

3. What about the established American political institutions Tocqueville describes? He suggests that the overriding principle in American politics is the "sovereignty of the people?" Can you discern what is meant by this phrase? Would you agree with Tocqueville that it was the aristocrats in Maryland who led the way toward universal suffrage? What relevance does Samuel Chase's attitude toward universal suffrage have here?

4. What relevance does American judicial power have to the principle of popular sovereignty? Why doesn't an American "turbulent multitude" regard law as its enemy? Why is it, as Tocqueville observes, that in America the judiciary has more power than in other countries? How does it come about that in America nearly every political dispute sooner or later winds up in the courts? You are probably familiar with this phenomenon, but note that Tocqueville was describing it almost one and one half centuries ago.

5. What relationship is there between the prominence of judicial power in America and the prominence of American lawyers? Why is it that Tocqueville believes that the only true American aristocracy is the lawyers? How does one reconcile the idea that the American lawyers are aristocrats, the spirit of equality of Americans, and Tocqueville's notion that Americans have a special veneration and respect for the law? Are Tocqueville's observations on lawyers consistent with those of Honestus? Does he explain the anti-lawyer sentiment in America? Note that although Tocqueville suggests that while it is the special province of lawyers to be well-informed and sagacious, they also have a tendency to gravitate toward the centers of power, and can just as easily serve a monarchy as a democracy. Towards what center of power would Tocqueville suggest that American lawyers would eventually gravitate? Consider his comments on the inevitability of another American aristocracy:

> As the conditions of men constituting the nation become more and more equal, the demand for manufactured commodities becomes more general and extensive, and the cheapness that places these objects within the reach of slender fortunes becomes a great element of success. Hence there are every day more men of great opulence and education who devote their wealth and knowledge to manufactures and who seek, by opening large establishments and

by a strict division of labor, to meet the fresh demands which are made on all sides. Thus, in proportion as the mass of the nation turns to democracy, that particular class which is engaged in manufactures becomes more aristocratic.   *   *   *

But this kind of aristocracy by no means resembles those kinds which preceded it.   *   *   *   To tell the truth, though there are rich men, the class of rich men does not exist; for these rich individuals have no feelings or purposes, no traditions or hopes, in common; there are individuals, therefore, but no definite class.

Not only are the rich not compactly united among themselves, but there is no real bond between them and the poor. Their relative position is not a permanent one; they are constantly drawn together or separated by their interests. The workman is generally dependent on the master, but not on any particular master; these two men meet in the factory, but do not know each other elsewhere; and while they come into contact on one point, they stand very far apart on all others. The manufacturer asks nothing of the workman but his labor; the workman expects nothing from him but his wages. The one contracts no obligation to protect nor the other to defend, and they are not permanently connected either by habit or by duty.   *   *   *

The territorial aristocracy of former ages was either bound by law, or thought itself bound by usage, to come to the relief of its serving-men and to relieve their distresses. But the manufacturing aristocracy of our age first impoverishes and debases the men who serve it and then abandons them to be supported by the charity of the public.   *   *   *

I am of the opinion, on the whole, that the manufacturing aristocracy which is growing up under our eyes is one of the harshest that ever existed in the world; but at the same time it is one of the most confined and least dangerous. Nevertheless, the friends of democracy should keep their eyes anxiously fixed in this direction; for if ever a permanent inequality of conditions and aristocracy again penetrates into the world, it may be predicted that this is the gate by which they will enter.

II Democracy in America 169–171 (Vintage Books ed. 1945).

6. Tocqueville, and, for that matter, Robert Rantoul, suggest that the American common law is essentially conservative. Is this correct? How do these two men divide over the value placed on conservatism? "Honestus" was a Boston merchant, Tocqueville a French Aristocrat. Do their different backgrounds lead to a different evaluation of American lawyers? As you read the cases on contracts, property, torts, and corporations which follow, and which are ostensibly American common-law decisions, see if you find "essentially conservative" results in the cases. In making this determination, consider what the terms "conservative" and "liberal" might mean to a nineteenth-century American.

SECTION B. THE RISE OF THE "CLASSICAL THEORY" OF CONTRACTS

SEARIGHT v. CALBRAITH

United States Circuit Court for the District of Pennsylvania, 1796.
21 Fed.Cas. 927.

[In February 1792, Mr. Searight sold Calbraith & Co. a bill of exchange (a negotiable piece of paper, like a check, which entitles the bearer to receive from a person or bank a certain sum of money) for 150,000 *livres tournois* (French units of currency). The bill of exchange was payable in Paris, six months from the date of sale. Calbraith & Co. promised to pay £10,625 in Pennsylvania currency for the Bill of Exchange, on or after July 1, 1792. The agent of Calbraith & Co. presented the bill of exchange for payment at the appointed time in Paris. The bank which was to pay on the bill of exchange offered payment in "assignats" (French paper currency) "which, by the then existing laws of France, were made a lawful tender, in payment of debts." Calbraith & Co.'s agent refused to accept the offered assignats, "declaring at the same time, that he would receive no other money than French crowns" (specie). Following these events Calbraith & Co., which had not yet paid Searight for the Bill of Exchange, refused to do so. Searight then sued Calbraith & Co. for their failure to pay the £10,625. Calbraith & Co., in turn, sued Searight for damages because of the French bank's failure to pay in specie. There was apparently no *explicit* agreement regarding whether the French bank would pay in paper money or in specie.]

* * *

On the trial of the cause, evidence was produced, on both sides, to ascertain and fix the precise terms of the original contract, for the sale and purchase of the bill of exchange * * * as to the knowledge and view of the parties, relative to the existence of assignats, or the law of France, making them a legal tender in payment of debts. And the great question of fact for decision, was, whether the parties contracted for a payment in gold and silver; or tacitly left the medium of payment, to the laws of France, where the bill was payable? The law arising from the fact, was discussed at large, according to the different positions of the parties in interest.

For Searight, it was shown, by the decrees of the French government, that assignats were established as a circulating medium for the payment of debts, before, and at the time of, the contract for the bill of exchange. * * * And this fact being known, it was contended, that the purchase of a bill payable in France, must in itself import an agreement to receive in satisfaction, the lawful current medium of that country, unless the contract expressly provides against it, which, on the present occasion, was controverted and denied. * * *

For Calbraith and Co. it was contended, that an express contract had been proved to pay the bill in specie; that the very terms of the bill import the same understanding of the parties; that however binding the law of France may be on cases between French citizens, or between American and French citizens, it did not affect contracts between Americans; that, in legal contemplation, there has been neither a payment, nor a tender of payment; and that Searight has sustained no damage, nor shown any right to recover.   *   *   *

Before IREDELL, Circuit Justice, and PETERS, District Judge.

IREDELL, Circuit Justice.   *   *   *   The sole question   *   *   * is, whether the tender of assignats in payment of the bill, was a compliance with that contract?   *   *   *

*   *   *

*   *   * Every man is bound to know the laws of his own country; but no man is bound to know the laws of foreign countries.

In two cases, indeed, (and, I believe, only in two cases) can foreign laws affect the contracts of American citizens: 1st. Where they reside, or trade, in a foreign country; and 2d. Where the contracts, plainly referring to a foreign country for their execution, adopt and recognize the lex loci. The present controversy, therefore, turns upon the fact, whether the parties meant to abide by the law of France? And this fact the jury must decide.

As to the damages, if the verdict should be for Searight, though it is true that in actions for a breach of contract, a jury should, in general, give the whole money contracted for and interest; yet, in a case like the present, they may modify the demand, and find such damages, as they think adequate to the injury actually sustained. *   *   *

Peters, District Judge. The decision depends entirely on the intention of the parties, of which the jury must judge. If a specie payment was meant, a tender in assignats was unavailing. But if the current money of France was in view, the tender in assignats was lawfully made, and is sufficiently proved.

When the jury were at the bar, ready to deliver verdicts, the plaintiff in each action voluntarily suffered a nonsuit. It was afterwards declared, however, that in Searight v. Calbraith and Co. the verdict would have been, generally, for the defendants; and that in Calbraith and Co. v. Searight, the verdict would have been for the plaintiffs, but with only six pence damages.

NOTES AND QUESTIONS

1. "Livres Tournois" were French coins in use before the French Revolution of 1789. What effect would you have given the use of that term in the contract if you were a member of this jury, and you knew that the coins were no longer in use? By the way, what do you take to be the reason for the transaction in the case? Does the fact that at this time the political situations in both France (the creation in 1792 of the French Republic and the outbreak of the French Revolutionary Wars in Europe) and America (the experiment with the new national government) were somewhat uncertain help in interpreting the deal?

2. How much discretion does the jury have to find the law and the facts in this case? Does this discretion seem to be more or less than that which you saw the jury exercise in criminal cases? In which type of case, criminal or civil, is it more important that the jury be given great discretion? Why? Why do you suppose that *after* the judges' instructions to the jury, but *before* "a verdict was rendered," the plaintiff in each action voluntarily suffered a nonsuit?" What is the meaning of the verdict that the jury would have delivered?

3. In the beginning of the nineteenth century, in many states, efforts were undertaken to modernize legal procedure, and to improve the overall efficiency of courts. In Massachusetts, Theodore Sedgwick, a prominent Federalist, advanced many proposals for judicial reform. What follows is the description in Richard E. Ellis, The Jeffersonian Crisis: Courts and Politics in the Young Republic 190–191, 198 (1971) of Sedgwick's opinions on the jury, and the political reaction to his ideas. Do these excerpts help to understand what the jury was up to in Searight v. Calbraith?

Sedgwick * * * counseled that under no circumstances should juries be permitted to interpret the law. Allowing juries, as was sometimes done in post-revolutionary Massachusetts, to mingle law with fact in arriving at their decisions, he believed, had contributed greatly to the disastrous inefficiency of the state's legal system. "In all instances where trial by jury has been practiced, and a separation of the law from the fact has taken place, there have been expedition, certainty, system and their consequences, general approbation. Where this has not been the case, neither expedition, certainty nor system have prevailed."

He also argued that the quality of juries had to be improved. Under an existing act justices of the peace, "men of the first consideration and weight of character in their counties," were exempted from jury duty. He advised that the act be repealed, otherwise the community would be denied the services of educated men upon whose "intelligence, integrity and independence," a successful administration of justice was so dependent.

* * *

Republican writers, on the other hand, defended the jury's right to interpret the law and to bring in a decision contrary to that ordered by the court. * * * [One wrote] that on points of law the greatest attention should be given the opinion of the court, but went on to argue that the question still remained: "suppose a difference in sentiment between the judges and the jury with regard to the law . . . What is to be done?—The jury must do their duty, and their whole duty; they must decide upon the law as well as upon the fact." To do otherwise would be to ask a man "to judge against his own judgment; in other words to sacrifice his honor and conscience—who would willingly be a juror upon these degrading terms?"

Reprinted from Richard E. Ellis, The Jeffersonian Crisis: Courts and Politics in the Young Republic, Copyright © 1971 by Oxford University Press, with the permission of the publisher.

4. Consider the implications for national or international trade of the behavior of the judges and jury in this case and the implications of Sedgwick's comments. If you were involved in such trade would you have confidence about the decision American courts might render if you were forced to litigate? Is it relevant that the American economy was capital-scarce until about the middle of the nineteenth century? Technological development, internal improvements, and manufacturing enterprise in America depended upon the availability of vast sums of venture capital, and much of it had to come in the form of investment by Europeans. See generally Stuart Bruchey, The Roots of American Economic Growth 1607–1861 (1965). Would you expect the scarcity of capital to effect American law?

WHITE v. FLORA AND CHERRY

Supreme Court of Tennessee, 1815.
2 Tenn. (2 Overt.) 426.

In Equity—COOKE, J., delivered the following opinion of the Court:—The bill charges that a grant issued to Lazarus Flora by the State of North Carolina for 274 acres of land, by whom previous to his death the same was devised to the defendant, Jesse Flora; that Jesse Flora, not knowing where the land was situated, applied to the complainant [White], and proposed to give him the one-half of the tract if he would find it and be at the expense of investigating the title, and to sell him the other half at a price to be fixed by valuers chosen for that purpose, payable in horses, and that a contract was made and reduced to writing in pursuance of such proposition; that the complainant made search in the land office and other places, and found the situation of the land; that afterwards Jesse Flora, with a view to cheat the complainant, sold and conveyed the whole tract to the defendant, Daniel Cherry, who at the same time had full knowledge of the equity on the part of the complainant. It is also charged that the complainant let Flora have a horse, bridle, and saddle at the price of one hundred dollars, and that it was agreed that, should the land be found, it was to stand as so much paid towards the purchase of half of the tract according to the agreement.

The bill prays that the land may be conveyed to the complainant.

Flora answers, in substance, that the agreement was made as set forth in the bill, but that White was guilty of great fraud and concealment in the transaction; that the land did not lie more than three miles from White's house, and that the situation of it was well known to White at the time the contract was made, although he represented himself to be entirely ignorant upon the subject; and indeed caused Flora to believe it would require great labor and influence to ascertain where the land lay. Flora admits that he sold and conveyed the land to Cherry, believing that White could not compel a performance of the contract, in consequence of the fraud and misrepresentation which he used; that he is willing to pay White the hundred dollars mentioned in the bill upon application, but denies that the horse, bridle, and saddle were received in part payment of the land.

Cherry's answer contains the same allegations as to the fraud practised by White, of which transaction he admits he was well informed when he took the deed from Flora. * * *

The proof in the cause shows that young Flora and a man by the name of Biggs had been hunting for the land, and, being unsuccessful, came to White's and inquired of him if he knew any thing of the land; he replied that he did not. Flora then pressed him to take a part of the land for finding it and paying the expense of investigating the title, which White at first refused to do; but finally, after much persuasion, the contract was closed as set forth in the bill. The parties than went to an attorney to have writings drawn; and the attorney is particular in stating that he was careful in making Flora understand the nature of the agreement. Flora said he was illiterate, and a stranger in the country, and was willing to make a liberal allowance for finding and securing the land. * * * The agreement was signed on the 18th day of August, 1807, and both parties went on to Nashville, which was only a few miles, to search the register's office. White got a copy of the grant, and the next day, on application to one Thomas Bradley, White found where the land was, and that it lay within two or three miles of his own house. * * *

There is no satisfactory proof going to show that White knew where the land was situated, before he made the contract with Flora.

The purchase of the horse, bridle, and saddle was proved to be in the manner set forth in the bill; and that the day after Bradley told White where the land lay, White and Flora went together on the land, and verbally agreed that the half to be purchased by White should be valued by Bradley. Flora seemed then well pleased with the contract he had made. Some short time after this, Cherry made propositions to Flora, to get a deed for the land, which were at first rejected, but finally agreed to, and the deed made as set forth by Cherry in his answer. Cherry at the same time gave Flora a bond of indemnity against the claim of White.

To the specific execution of the contract sought by the complainant, the defendant's counsel in the argument objected * * *:

1st. The fraud alleged to have been practised by the complainant upon Flora.

2d. The inadequacy of the consideration given by the complainant.

* * *

1st. There is no proof of fraud on the part of White. It is true, when he was first applied to by the defendant Flora, he represented himself as wholly ignorant of the situation of the land, but it is equally true that no proof has been shown to us that this representation was false. If the fact had been with the defendant upon that point, we should have no hesitation in saying the complainant ought not to have a decree. When the complainant was applied to, with a view to ascertain his knowledge upon the subject of this land, if he then knew where it was, a representation on his part that he did not know, would have been a fraud, inasmuch as by means of it Flora would, in all probability, have been induced to give a greater price for the trouble and labor of searching, and the expenses incident to an investigation of the title. In all cases of contract, any representation of a falsehood or concealment of a truth, which, if correctly known, would probably be a reason for making the terms of the contract different, will be a good ground for rescinding the agreement in a court of equity. Equity delights in doing justice, it delights in compelling men, by means of an appeal to the conscience, to do those things which ought to be done. To effect so desirable an object, strict regard must be had that no one is permitted to enjoy property which has been procured through means of an unreal appearance of things, more particularly if that appearance is the result of the fraudulent machinations of the person who seeks to be availed of it.

* * *

Had White known where to find the land, and apprised Flora of such knowledge, it is more than probable that Flora would not have given so much for the information as if he imagined that White was as ignorant of its situation as himself, and would most likely be put to some considerable trouble and expense in finding it. Therefore the representation on the part of White, that he knew not where the land was, if he did know, was a fraud; but there is no proof that he concealed any fact within his knowledge, or made any suggestion inconsistent with truth.

2d. It is also urged that there is in this case great inadequacy of consideration; and that therefore the Court ought not to decree a specific performance of the contract with Flora. * * *

When a complainant comes into a court of equity for the purpose of having a contract rescinded on the ground of mere inadequacy of consideration, all the books agree that relief cannot be afforded. The mere circumstance of the sum paid being greatly inferior in value to the thing contracted to be purchased, will not, of itself, be sufficient to set aside an agreement; but it is in many instances strong evidence of fraud and imposition, and, coupled with other matters, such as the embarrassment of one of the parties, or the like, may frequently occasion the interference of a court of equity. But the situation of a complainant seeking to enforce the execution of an unreasonable and unconscientious bargain is placed on a ground very different. In such cases, the Court has a discretionary power; it will either cause the agreement to be executed or not, depending upon the equity of the whole case. * * *

What cases of mere inadequacy of consideration will authorize the Court to refuse lending its aid to enforce an agreement, is not now necessary to be specified, as we are of opinion this is not one of them.

The sum it really cost White to find this land is, as we conceive, not the proper question; the bargain was clearly a risking one; it might cost only a few dollars to find the land, or it might cost the worth of the land itself.   At the time the contract was made, it was utterly unknown to the parties, and impossible to tell which had the advantage; for any thing then known, the result might prove equally valuable, or much more advantageous to one than to the other.   Every fact, tending to remove uncertainty, was wholly unknown.   If White had in the end been put to an expense more than sufficient to absorb the whole value of the land, an event which no man can say was impossible, could a court of equity have relieved him?   Could Flora be compelled to pay him for his trouble and expense, and rescind the contract as to land?   Clearly not.   Why not, then, make the situation of the parties reciprocal?   Here, White found this land at a cost much beneath what probably would have been given, had the trouble and expense been previously known.   But is that any reason why the contract ought not to be specifically executed?   When we are asked not to enforce an agreement merely upon the ground of the consideration being inadequate, in a case where that consideration was to be performed in services of an uncertain and dubious value, it is impossible for us not to look at what might have been the amount.   When we look at that, we believe there is nothing in it to prevent the interference of this court.

*   *   *

The complainant is therefore entitled to a decree * * * [that will compel Cherry to deed him the land] upon his paying up to the defendant, Daniel Cherry, the value of the one-half * * * in horses, agreeably to the contract made with Flora.

NOTES AND QUESTIONS

1.   As you have learned if you have had a course in contracts, courts of equity are ancient institutions borrowed from England and used for relaxing the rigors of the common law.   For example, as suggested by the first defense in this case, if Mr. White had defrauded Mr. Flora by representing that he (White) knew nothing about the location of the land in question, this fraud would have been "a good ground for rescinding the agreement [to sell the land to White] in a court of equity."   As this court remarks, this is because the equity court "delights in doing justice," and "in compelling men * * * to do those things which ought to be done."   Of more importance to us at this point, however, is the discretion to refuse specific enforcement of land sale contracts possessed by equity court judges.   By this time, the beginning of the nineteenth century, it had been clear for many years that inadequacy of consideration was *not* a *legal* defense to a contract; what do you understand from this case to be the *equity* judge's discretion to refuse enforcement of a land sale contract on the grounds of inadequacy of consideration?   Why was the contract enforced in this case?

2.   An important case on this issue arose in New York, Seymour v. Delancey, 6 Johns Ch. 222 (1822), and was first heard by that state's great

Chancellor, James Kent. The case involved a contract for an exchange of two country farms for a one-third interest in two city lots. The action for specific performance of the exchange was brought by a descendant of the party who was to receive the two farms. According to Chancellor Kent's interpretation of the "weight of the testimony" the two farms were worth $14,000 at the date of the agreement, and the one-third interest in the lots was worth $5,000. There was great disagreement among the witnesses called for valuation, however, with some putting the disparity within about $2,000 or less. Still Kent stated that "I am satisfied, that * * * the village lots were not worth half the value of the country farms * * * ".

Kent proceeded to announce that "It is a settled principle, that a specific performance of a contract of sale is not a matter of course, but rests entirely in the discretion of the Court, upon a view of all the circumstances." "A Court of Equity," Kent went on "must be satisfied that the claim for a deed is fair and just, and reasonable, and the contract equal in all its parts, and founded on an adequate consideration, before it will interpose with this extraordinary assistance." After examining a nearly interminable series of English and Roman decisions, Kent confessed that in the most recent cases "there is a doubt thrown over the question, whether inadequacy of price alone, though not so great as to be evidence of fraud, will be sufficient * * * to withhold the decree for specific performance." Apparently, however, Kent was more struck with the preponderance of earlier cases in which no such doubts were raised. Said he:

> There is a very great weight of authority against enforcing a contract, where the consideration is so inadequate as to render it a hard bargain, and an unequal and an unreasonable bargain; the argument is exceedingly strong against it in such cases, when it is considered that if equity acts at all, it must act *ex vigore,* and carry the contract into execution, with unmitigated severity: Whereas, if the party be sent to law, to submit his case to a jury, relief can be afforded in damages, with a moderation agreeable to equity and good conscience, and when the claims and pretensions of each party can be duly attended to, and be admitted to govern the assessment.

What did Kent mean when he suggested that if an equity court declined specific enforcement, the party seeking such enforcement could then "be sent to law" where the jury could offer "relief * * * agreeable to equity and good conscience"? Does the proposed jury verdict in Searight v. Calbraith & Co. help in understanding this? Suppose Sedgwick's views on jury discretion were to predominate. Would this undercut Kent's reasoning?

3. After observing that under the civil law contracts for sale of land were rescinded by judicial authority if the price was below half the value of the land, and that even under the Code Napoleon rescission could be granted if the price was 7/12ths below the "real value", Kent refused specific performance. Kent's refusal was reversed by a vote of 14–10 of the New York Court for the Trial of Impeachment and the Correction of Errors, a unique New York judicial institution, now extinct, which consisted of the Members of the New York Senate, the Chief Judge of

the New York Supreme Court, and the Equity Chancellor. Seymour v. Delancey, 3 Cow. 445 (1824).

Senator Sudam, who wrote the opinion for the majority, stated that Kent was wrong because his holding amounted to an assertion that *mere inequality* in value, which is not so gross as to strike the moral feeling of an indifferent man, would be sufficient to warrant the Chancellor in withholding a decree for specific performance. Sudam acknowledged the "sound discretion" of the equity court in its decision on granting the decree, but stated that "sound legal discretion" was not to be used as "an arbitrary power, interfering with the contracts of individuals, and sporting with their vested rights." Sudam brought out some facts that Kent had failed to mention, in particular that the owner of the two farms against whom the action was brought had previously purchased the two-thirds interest in the city lots, and that he might have suspected that the city lots would dramatically rise in value if a proposed Navy Yard were built in town.

Sudam went on to suggest that where there was inadequacy of consideration which was "so flagrant and palpable as to convince a man at the first blush that one of the contracting parties had been imposed on by some false pretense" no equity court should enforce a contract. For Sudam, however, this was not such a case. Sudam observed that "There is no question so well calculated to generate a variety of opinion, as that which regards the value of a village lot, or a farm in the country," and that the wide variance in witness valuations illustrated this. Sudam concluded that people will always disagree on the value of land and on the wisdom of particular speculative purchases. Here, said Sudam, the parties were entering into a transaction which none was really capable of evaluating, and there was no evidence to suggest "fraud, surprise, misrepresentation, or deceit." "What right have we," asked Sudam, "to sport with the contracts of parties fairly and deliberately entered into and prevent them from being carried into effect?"

4. With whom do you agree, Kent or Sudam? You have already seen, from Tocqueville, that fortunes in America tended to rise and fall with astonishing rapidity. It should come as no surprise to learn that land values could similarly fluctuate. Indeed, the entire nineteenth century economy in America could be viewed as careening up and down, from boom to bust, as wildly as a roller-coaster. See e. g., Charles Warren, Bankruptcy in United States History (1935), Douglass C. North, The Economic Growth of the United States 1790–1860, 66–71 (Norton library ed. 1966). What should have been the effect of this fluctuation in economic value on contract law? Can you imagine what contract law would have been like in a society where economic values were stable? Once you conclude that economic values will always be in a state of fluctuation, however, to whom is it wisest for the law to turn for determinations of value?

5. By now you have probably suspected that the rules of American contract law reflected *social* as well as economic values. Whose interests would be promoted by the rule of equity discretion to refuse to enforce specific performance of unfair contracts? Is there anything in the reading from Tocqueville which sheds light on why this rule was weakened in the nineteenth century?

GOULDING v. SKINNER

Supreme Judicial Court of Massachusetts, 1822.
18 Mass. (1 Pick.) 162.

In an action of *assumpsit* to recover damages for the breach of a warranty made on the sale of certain machine cards, the declaration alleged, that the defendants warranted them to be good and merchantable, and that in truth they were not so, but were of little or no value. At the trial * * * before Wilde, J., the plaintiffs, to prove the warranty, read to the jury an advertisement stating that machine cards were manufactured by the defendants, warranted equal to any in America. The judge instructed the jury, that a warranty in these terms was equivalent to the warranty set forth in the declaration. The jury having returned a verdict for the plaintiffs, the defendants moved for a new trial, partly on the ground of the misdirection of the judge in this particular.

Phinney, for the defendants. A warranty should be proved as it is set forth in the declaration. * * * A warranty that the cards should be equal to any in America cannot be considered the same with a warranty that they should be good and merchantable, although an article agreeing with the former warranty might be superior to one agreeing with the latter. Proof which would support one of these warranties might not support the other. The best cards in America might not be merchantable.

Webster, for the plaintiffs. * * * The object of the plaintiffs was to purchase good cards; they did not want the very best. Neither did the defendants want to sell any but such as were of the ordinary quality. The expression in the advertisement is equivalent to the word *warranted* simply; which means that the article should be of the ordinary quality. What would have been the result, if the defendants had proved that the cards sold were as good as other cards usually are, and the plaintiffs had proved, that, in some particular place in America, cards of an extraordinary good quality were manufactured? Would this show that the warranty had been broken? A common advertisement is not to be viewed with as much strictness as a deed * * * . It was a question for the jury to determine, whether the cards were not warranted to be of the ordinary quality, and they have found for the plaintiffs. The warranty, indeed, set out in the declaration is not so strong as that in the advertisement, but it is not for the defendants to make this an objection. The plaintiffs have taken the substantial part, and a recovery here will be a bar to any future action on the warranty.

The cause was continued *nisi* for advisement, and at the following March term, at Concord, the Court granted a new trial, on account of variance between the warranty alleged in the declaration and the contract proved.

NOTES AND QUESTIONS

1.   Who won in this decision? What sort of an attitude toward business-men does the ruling of the court reveal? How might you explain that attitude?   Would Honestus have been pleased with the result? The jury, in the first trial, found for the plaintiff. Note that a new trial is granted. What does this tell us about the jury's role in decisions on the law in contract cases? Would Sedgwick have been pleased?

2.   Goulding v. Skinner arrives at a result that is not inconsistent with one of the great maxims in the nineteenth century American law of con-tract, *caveat emptor*. The legal principle behind this maxim gained wide-spread acceptance in the course of the first half of the century. Why? What does the rise of *caveat emptor* have to do with the ultimate result in White v. Flora & Cherry and Seymour v. Delancey?   Consider these comments on the doctrine taken from Horwitz, *Historical Foundations of Modern Contract Law*, 87 Harv.L.Rev. 945–946 (1974):

> The nineteenth century departure from the equitable concep-tion of contract is particularly obvious in the rapid adoption of the doctrine of *caveat emptor*. * * * despite the supposed ancient lineage of *caveat emptor*, eighteenth century English and American courts embraced the doctrine that "a sound price war-rants a sound commodity." It was only after Lord Mansfield declared in 1778, in one of those casual asides that seem to have been so influential in forging the history of the common law, that the only basis for an action for breach of warranty was an express contract, that the foundation was laid for reconsidering whether an action for breach of an implied warranty would lie. In 1802 the English courts finally considered the policies behind such an action deciding that no suit on an implied warranty would be allowed. Two years later, in the leading American case of Seixas v. Woods, the New York Supreme Court, relying on a doubtfully reported seventeenth century English case, also held that there could be no recovery against a merchant who could not be proved knowingly to have sold defective goods. Other American jurisdic-tions quickly fell into line.

> While the rule of caveat emptor established in Seixas v. Woods seems to be the result of one of those frequent accidents of his-torical misunderstanding, this is hardly sufficient to account for the widespread acceptance of the doctrine of caveat emptor else-where in America. Nor are the demands of a market economy a sufficient cause. Although the sound price doctrine was at-tacked on the ground that there "is no standard to determine whether the vendee has paid a sound price," the most consistent legal theorist of the market economy, Gulian Verplanck, devoted his impressive analytical talents to an elaborate critique of the doc-trine of caveat emptor. The sudden and complete substitution of caveat emptor in place of the sound price doctrine must therefore be understood as a dramatic overthrow of an important element of the eighteenth century's equitable conception of contract.

* * *

I have not meant to assert that *caveat emptor* is more conducive to a market economy than the contrary doctrine of *caveat venditor*, though this might be independently demonstrated. Rather, I have argued that the importance of caveat emptor lies in its overthrow of both the sound price doctrine and the latter's underlying conception of objective value.

We can best see the nature of the attack on the "sound price" doctrine in South Carolina, the only state in which it persisted well into the nineteenth century. Urging reversal of the sound price doctrine and adoption in its place of a rule of *caveat emptor*, the Attorney General of South Carolina argued in 1802 that "[s]uch a doctrine * * * if once admitted in the formation of contracts, would leave no room for the exercise of judgment or discretion, but would destroy all free agency; every transaction between man and man must be weighed in the balance like the precious metals, and if found wanting in * * * adequacy, must be made good to the uttermost farthing * * *." Whitefield v. McLeod, 2 Bay 380, 382, (S.C.1802) (argument of counsel). If a court should refuse to enforce a contract made by a man who has had "an equal knowledge of all the circumstances" as well as "an opportunity of informing himself, and the means of procuring information * * *," he maintained, "good faith and mutual confidence would be at an end * * *." * * * According to South Carolina lawyer Hugh Legare, the rule of caveat emptor was desirable because it rejected the "refined equity" of the civil law in favor of "the policy of society." Though there was "something captivating in the equity of the principle, that a sound price implies a warranty of the soundness of the commodity," he was "certain that this rule is productive of great practical inconveniences * * *." 2 Writings of Hugh Swinton Legare 110 (M. Legare ed. 1845). * * *

Copyright © 1974 by the Harvard Law Review Association, reprinted with the permission of that Association and of the author. Perhaps the most important aspect of this excerpt from Horwitz's work to us is his assertion that nineteenth century contract law rejected the dominant notion of eighteenth century contract law, that there were "objective" values in contracting that might be implemented by judges or juries in deciding which contracts ought to be enforced. Suppose Horwitz is right. Would this change in the law be approved of by Honestus, Rantoul, or Tocqueville? If you are interested in pursuing this question further, see, in addition to Horwitz's article, the criticism in Simpson, The Horwitz Thesis and the History of Contracts, 46 U.Chi.L.Rev. 533 (1979).

SECTION C. PROPERTY: FROM ASCRIPTION TO UTILIZATION

III WILLIAM BLACKSTONE, COMMENTARIES ON THE LAWS OF ENGLAND

216–221 (1768).

* * * Nuisance, *nocumentum,* or annoyance, signifies any thing that worketh hurt, inconvenience, or damage. And nuisances are of two kinds; *public* or *common* nuisances, which affect the public, and are an annoyance to all the king's subjects; for which reason we must refer them to the class of public wrongs, or crimes and misdemeanors: and *private* nuisances, which are the objects of our present consideration, and may be defined, any thing done to the hurt or annoyance of the lands, tenements, or hereditaments of another. * * *

I. In discussing the several kinds of nuisances, we will consider, first, such nuisances as may affect a man's corporeal hereditaments, and then those that may damage such as are incorporeal.

1. FIRST, as to *corporeal* inheritances. If a man builds a house so close to mine that his roof overhangs my roof, and throws the water off his roof upon mine, this is a nuisance, for which an action will lie. Likewise to erect a house or other building so near to mine, that it obstructs my ancient lights and windows, is a nuisance of a similar nature. But in this latter case it is necessary that the windows be *ancient*; that is, have subsisted there time out of mind; otherwise there is no injury done. For he hath as much right to build a new edifice upon his ground, as I have upon mine: since every man may erect what he pleases upon the upright or perpendicular of his own soil, so as not to prejudice what has long been enjoyed by another; and it was my folly to build so near another's ground. Also, if a person keeps his hogs, or other noisome animals, so near the house of another, that the stench of them incommodes him and makes the air unwholesome, this is an injurious nuisance, as it tends to deprive him of the use and benefit of his house. A like injury is, if one's neighbour sets up and exercises any offensive trade; as a tanner's, a tallow-chandler's or the like; for though these are lawful and necessary trades, yet they should be exercised in remote places; for the rule is, "*sic utere tuo, ut alienum non laedas:*" this therefore is an actionable nuisance. So that the nuisances which affect a man's dwelling may be reduced to these three: 1. Overhanging it: which is also a species of trespass, for *cujus est solum ejus est usque ad coelum:* 2. Stopping ancient lights: and, 3. Corrupting the air with noisome smells: for light and air are two indispensable requisites to every dwelling. But depriving one of a mere matter of pleasure, as of a fine prospect, by building a wall, or the like; this, as it abridges nothing really con-

SIR WILLIAM BLACKSTONE

venient or necessary, is no injury to the sufferer, and is therefore not an actionable nuisance.

As to nuisance to one's *lands*: if one erects a smelting house for lead so near the land of another, that the vapor and smoke kills his corn and grass, and damages his cattle therein, this is held to be a nuisance. And by consequence it follows, that if one does any other act, in itself lawful, which yet being done in that place necessarily tends to the damage of another's property, it is a nuisance: for it is incumbent on him to find some other place to do that act, where it will be less offensive. * * *

With regard to *other* corporeal hereditaments: it is a nuisance to stop or divert water that used to run to another's meadow or mill; to corrupt or poison a water-course, by erecting a dye-house or a lime-pit for the use of trade, in the upper part of the stream; or in short to do any act therein, that in its consequences must necessarily tend to the prejudice of one's neighbour. So closely does the law of England enforce that excellent rule of gospel-morality, of "doing to others, as we would they should do unto ourselves."

2. As to *incorporeal* hereditaments, the law carries itself with the same equity. If I have a way, annexed to my estate, across another's land, and he obstructs me in the use of it, either by totally stopping it, or putting logs across it, or ploughing over it, it is a nuisance: for in the first case I cannot enjoy my right at all, and in the latter I cannot enjoy it so commodiously as I ought. Also, if I am entitled to hold a fair or market, and another person sets up a fair or market so near mine that he does me a prejudice, it is a nuisance to the freehold which I have in my market or fair. But in order to make this out to be a nuisance, it is necessary, 1. That my market or fair be the elder, otherwise the nuisance lies at my own door. 2. That the market be erected within the third part of twenty miles from mine. For sir Matthew Hale construes the *dieta,* or reasonable day's journey mentioned by Bracton, to be twenty miles * * *. So that if the new market be not within seven miles of the old one, it is no nuisance: for it is held reasonable that every man should have a market within one-third of a day's journey from his own home; that the day being divided into three parts, he may spend one part in going, another in returning, and the third in transacting his necessary business there. If such market or fair be on the same day with mine, it is *prima facie* a nuisance to mine, and there needs no proof of it, but the law will intend it to be so; but if it be on any other day, it *may be* a nuisance; though whether it *is* so or not, cannot be intended or presumed, but I must make proof of it to the jury. If a ferry is erected on a river, so near another ancient ferry as to draw away its custom, it is a nuisance to the owner of the old one. For where there is a ferry by prescription, the owner is bound to keep it always in repair and readiness, for the ease of all the king's subjects; otherwise he may be grievously amerced: it would be therefore ex-

tremely hard, if a new ferry were suffered to share his profits, which does not also share his burden.   But where the reason ceases, the law also ceases with it: therefore it is no nuisance to erect a mill so near mine, as to draw away the custom unless the miller also intercepts the water.   Neither is it a nuisance to set up any trade, or a school, in neighbourhood or rivalship with another: for by such emulation the public are like to be gainers; and, if the new mill or school occasion a damage to the old one, it is *damnum absque injuria.*

II.   Let us next attend to the remedies, which the law has given for this injury of nuisance.   *   *   *

The remedies by suit are, 1.   By action *on the case* for damages; in which the party injured shall only recover a satisfaction for the injury sustained; but cannot thereby remove the nuisance.   Indeed every continuance of a nuisance is held to be a fresh one; and therefore a fresh action will lie, and very exemplary damages will probably be given, if, after one verdict against him, the defendant has the hardiness to continue it.   Yet the founders of the law of England did not rely upon probabilities merely, in order to give relief to the injured. They have therefore provided two other actions; the *assize of nuisance,* and the writ of *quod permittat prosternere:* which not only give the plaintiff satisfaction for his injury past, but also strike at the root and remove the cause itself, the nuisance that occasioned the injury.   *   *   *

*   *   *

Both these actions, of *assize of nuisance,* and of *quod permittat prosternere,* are now out of use, and have given way to the action on the case   *   *   *.   [T]he effect will be much the same, unless a man has a very obstinate as well as an ill-natured neighbour: who had rather continue to pay damages, than remove his nuisance.   For in such a case, recourse must at last be had to the old and sure remedies, which will effectually conquer the defendant's perverseness, by sending the sheriff with his *posse comitatus,* or power of the county, to level it.

NOTES AND QUESTIONS

1.   "In the history of American institutions, no other book—except the Bible—has played so great a role as Blackstone's Commentaries on the Laws of England."   D. Boorstin, The Mysterious Science of the Law iii (Peter Smith, ed. 1973).   When he was training as a lawyer, Lincoln is said to have read his *Blackstone* (and his Coke) by candlelight.   While Blackstone's books, composed of his Oxford lectures, and originally published from 1765 to 1769, were to be a major source of American private law for roughly fifty years after the American Revolution, and were continually updated by American editors, there were some Americans, for example, Thomas Jefferson, who opposed the influence of Blackstone.   Jefferson felt that Blackstone and those nurtured on him were "Tories," and that Blackstone's influence was harmful in America, where more attention

needed to be paid to the needs of "whiggism" or "republicanism." See generally Waterman, Thomas Jefferson and Blackstone's Commentaries, 27 Illinois Law Review (now the "Northwestern University Law Review") 629 (1933), reprinted in Flaherty, ed. Essays in the History of Early American Law, at 451 (1969), and see also Edward Dumbauld, Thomas Jefferson and the Law (1979). What did Jefferson mean by this criticism of Blackstone? Can you make out anything in this excerpt that causes you to agree or disagree with Jefferson? Ask yourself again whether you agree or disagree with Jefferson after you have considered the following questions.

2. Blackstone begins his discussion of nuisance by a discussion of the doctrine of "ancient lights." Why must the lights be "ancient" for them to be preserved? What impact would this doctrine have on societal "progress?"

3. Two Latin maxims are of primary importance to Blackstone in this excerpt:

(1) *sic utere tuo, ut alienum non laedas* ("Use your own property in such a manner as not to injure that of another") and

(2) *cujus est solem ejus est usque ad coelum* ("The owner of the soil owns to the sky.").

These maxims are said to be the central principles of Blackstonian property law. Do you see any conflict between them? Consider, for example, how you reconcile the doctrine of "ancient lights" with these two maxims.

4. Why, if blocking off "ancient lights" is a nuisance, is it not a nuisance to block off a "fine prospect?" What, exactly, is a "nuisance?"

5. Note that Blackstone says that it may be a nuisance for one person to erect a "market" in a manner that draws off the trade of another's market. Similarly, it may be a nuisance to operate a ferry that competes with another's ferry. When is it such a nuisance, and why? Why is it never a nuisance merely to compete with an already existing mill or school?

6. Why, in the "action on the case" for nuisance, was there no injunctive relief? What about Blackstone's idea that the action will be effective simply because of the availability of "exemplary damages" for repeat offenders—do you agree? "Exemplary damages," or "punitive damages" as they are sometimes called, are not unknown in modern American private actions, although they are nearly unknown in breach of contract cases. Why not allow them in contract cases if we allow them in property and tort actions?

VAN NESS v. PACARD

United States Supreme Court, 1829.
27 U.S. (2 Pet.) 137, 7 L.Ed. 842.

Mr. Justice *Story* delivered the opinion of the Court.

* * *

The original was an action on the case brought by the plaintiffs in error against the defendant for waste committed by him, while tenant of the plaintiffs, to their reversionary interest, by pulling down and removing from the demised premises a messuage or dwelling-house erected thereon and attached to the freehold. [The tenant won below, the landlords have brought the case to the Supreme Court for review.]   *   *   *

By the bill of exceptions, filed at the trial, it appeared that the plaintiffs in 1820 demised to the defendant, for seven years, a vacant lot in the city of Washington, at the yearly rent of one hundred and twelve dollars and fifty cents, with a clause in the lease that the defendant should have a right to purchase the same at any time during the term for one thousand eight hundred and seventy-five dollars. After the defendant had taken possession of the lot, he erected thereon a wooden dwelling-house, two stories high in front, with a shed of one story, a cellar of stone or brick foundation and a brick chimney. The defendant and his family dwelt in the house from its erection until near the expiration of the lease, when he took the same down and removed all the materials from the lot. The defendant was a carpenter by trade; and he gave evidence, that upon obtaining the lease he erected the building above mentioned, with a view to carry on the business of a dairyman, and for the residence of his family and servants engaged in his said business; and that the cellar, in which there was a spring, was made and exclusively used for a milk cellar, in which the utensils of his said business were kept and scalded, and washed and used; and that feed was kept in the upper part of the house, which was also occupied as a dwelling for his family. That the defendant had his tools as a carpenter, and two apprentices in the house, and a work-bench out of doors; and carpenter's work was done in the house, which was in a rough unfinished state, and made partly of old materials. That he also erected on the lot a stable for his cows of plank and timber fixed upon posts fastened into the ground, which stable he removed with the house before the expiration of his lease.

*   *   *

The first exception raises the important question, what fixtures erected by a tenant during his term are removable by him?

The general rule of the common law certainly is, that whatever is once annexed to the freehold becomes part of it, and cannot afterwards be removed, except by him who is entitled to the inheritance. The rule, however, never was, at least as far back as we can trace it in the books, inflexible, and without exceptions. It was construed most strictly between executor and heir in favour of the latter; more liberally between tenant for life or in tail, and remainderman or reversioner, in favour of the former; and with much greater latitude between landlord and tenant, in favour of the tenant. But an exception of a much broader cast, and whose origin may be traced almost as high as the rule itself, is of fixtures erected for the purposes of trade. Upon principles of public policy, and to encourage trade and manufactures, fixtures which were erected to carry on such business were allowed to be removed by the tenant during his term, and were deemed personalty for many other purposes. [In a leading English case,] * * * Elwes v. Maw, 3 East's R. 38, [it was] * * * decided, that in the case of landlord and tenant, there had been no relaxation of the general rule in cases of erections, solely for agricultural purposes, however beneficial or important they might be as improvements of the estate. Being once annexed to the freehold by the tenant, they became a part of the realty, and could never afterwards be severed by the tenant. The distinction is certainly a nice one between fixtures for the purposes of trade, and fixtures for agricultural purposes; at least in those cases where the sale of the produce constitutes the principal object of the tenant, and the erections are for the purpose of such a beneficial enjoyment of the estate. But that point is not now before us; and it is unnecessary to consider what the true doctrine is or ought to be on this subject. How ever well settled it may now be in England, it cannot escape remark that learned judges at different periods in that country have entertained different opinions upon it * * *.

The common law of England is not to be taken in all respects to be that of America. Our ancestors brought with them its general principles, and claimed it as their birthright; but they brought with them and adopted only that portion which was applicable to their situation. There could be little or no reason for doubting, that the general doctrine as to things annexed to the freehold, so far as it respects heirs and executors, was adopted by them. The question could arise only between different claimants under the same ancestor, and no general policy could be subserved, by withdrawing from the heir those things, which his ancestor had chosen to leave annexed to the inheritance. But, between landlord and tenant, it is not so clear that the rigid rule of the common law, at least as it is expounded in 3 East, 38, was so applicable to their situation, as to give rise to necessary presumption in its favour. The country was a wilderness, and the universal policy was to procure its cultivation and improvement. The owner of the soil, as well as the public, had every motive to encourage the tenant to devote himself to agriculture and to favour any erections which should aid this result; yet, in the comparative poverty of the country, what tenant could afford to erect fixtures of much expense or value, if he was to lose his whole interest therein by the very act of erection? His cabin or log-hut, however necessary for any improvement of the soil would cease to be his the moment it was finished. It might, therefore, deserve consideration, whether, in case the doctrine were not previously adopted in a state by some authoritative practice or adjudication, it ought to be assumed by this Court as a part of the jurisprudence of such state, upon the mere footing of its existence in the common law. At present, it is unnecessary to say more, than that we give no opinion on this question. The case, which has been argued at the bar may well be disposed of without any discussion of it.

It has been already stated, that the exception of buildings and other fixtures, for the purpose of carrying on a trade or manufacture, is of very ancient date, and was recognised almost as early as the rule itself. The very point was decided in 20 Henry VII. 13, a. and b., where it was laid down, that if a lessee for years made a furnace for his advantage, or a dyer made his vats or vessels to occupy his occupation, during the term, he may afterwards remove them. That doctrine was recognised by Lord Holt, in Poole's case, 1 Salk. 368, in favour of a soap-boiler, who was tenant for years. He held that the party might well remove the vats he set up in relation to trade; and that he might do it by the common law (and not by virtue of any custom) in favour of trade, and to encourage industry. In Lawton v. Lawton, 2 Atk.R. 13, the same doctrine was held in the case of a fire engine, set up to work a colliery by a tenant for life. Lord Hardwicke, there said, that since the time of Henry the Seventh, the general ground the Courts have gone upon of relaxing the strict construction of law is, that it is for the benefit of the public to encourage tenants for life to do what is advantageous to the estate during the term. * * * The case too of a cider mill, between the executor and heir, &c., is extremely strong, for though cider is a part of the profits of the real estate, yet, it was held by Lord Chief Baron Comyns, a very able common lawyer, that the cider mill was personal estate, notwithstanding, and that it should go to the executor. * * *.

It has been suggested at the bar, that this exception in favour of trade has never been applied to cases like that before the Court, where a large house has been built and used in part as a family residence. But the question, whether removable or not, does not depend upon the form or size of the building, whether it has a brick foundation or not, or is one or two stories high, or has a brick or other chimney. The sole question is, whether it is designed for purposes of trade or not. *. * *

Then, as to the residence of the family in the house, this resolves itself into the same consideration. If the house were built principally for a dwelling-house for the family, independently of carrying on the trade, then it would doubtless be deemed a fixture, falling under the general rule, and immovable. But if the residence of the family were merely an accessory for the more beneficial exercise of the trade, and with a view to superior accommodation in this particular, then it is within the exception. There are many trades, which cannot be carried on well, without the presence of many persons by night as well as by day. It is so in some valuable manufactories. It is not unusual for persons employed in a bakery to sleep in the same building. Now, what was the evidence in the present case? It was, "that the defendant erected the building before mentioned, with a view to carry on the business of a dairyman, and for the residence of his family and servants engaged in that business." The residence of the family was then auxiliary to the dairy; it was for the accommodation and beneficial operations of his trade.

Surely it cannot be doubted, that in a business of this nature, the immediate presence of the family and servants was, or might be, of very great utility and importance. The defendant was also a carpenter, and carried on his business, as such, in the same building. It is no objection that he carried on two trades instead of one. There is not the slightest evidence of this one being a mere cover or evasion to conceal another, which was the principal design; and, unless we were prepared to say (which we are not) that the mere fact, that the house was used for a dwelling-house, as well as for a trade, superseded the exception in favour of the latter, there is no ground to declare that the tenant was not entitled to remove it. * * * In our opinion, the Circuit Court was right in refusing the first instruction.

The second exception proceeds upon the ground, that it was not competent to establish a usage and custom in the city of Washington for tenants to make such removals of buildings during their term. We can perceive no objection to such proof. Every demise between landlord and tenant in respect to matters, in which the parties are silent, may be fairly open to explanation by the general usage and custom of the country or of the district where the land lies. Every person under such circumstances is supposed to be cognizant of the custom, and to contract with a tacit reference to it. Cases of this sort are familiar in the books; as, for instance, to prove the right of a tenant to an away-going crop. In the very class of cases now before the Court the custom of the country has been admitted to decide the right of the tenant to remove fixtures. * * *

The third exception turns upon the consideration, whether the parol testimony was competent to establish such a usage and custom. Competent it certainly was, if by competent is meant that it was admissible to go to the jury. Whether it was such as ought to have satisfied their minds on the matter of fact was solely for their consideration, open indeed to such commentary and observation, as the Court might think proper in its discretion to lay before them for their aid and guidance. We cannot say, that they were not at liberty, by the principles of law, to infer from the evidence the existence of the usage. The evidence might be somewhat loose and indeterminate, and so be urged with more or less effect upon their judgment; but in a legal sense it was within their own province to weigh it as proof or as usage.

The last exception professes to call upon the Court to institute a comparison between the testimony introduced by the plaintiff and that introduced by the defendant against and for the usage. It requires from the Court a decision upon its relative weight and credibility, which the Court were not justified in giving to the jury in the shape of a positive instruction.

Upon the whole, in our judgment there is no error in the judgment of the Circuit Court; and it is affirmed with costs.

* * *

NOTES AND QUESTIONS

1. Mr. Justice Story, who wrote the opinion of the Court in Van Ness v. Pacard, has often been described as the "American Blackstone." He, and the other towering figure of early nineteenth century law, James Kent, are usually thought to have been orthodox, or conservative legal thinkers, and to have been concerned with serving "the interests of the wealthy, and the powerful." See, e. g. Morton Horwitz, The Transformation of American Law 1780–1860, 257–259 (1977), and John Horton, James Kent, A Study in Conservatism, 1763–1847 (1939). Does Story's opinion in this case fit this description?

2. Why was it a "general rule of the common law" (of England) that "whatever is once annexed to the freehold becomes part of it, and cannot afterwards be removed, except by him who is entitled to the inheritance?" What does the rule mean? Does Story believe that the rule is in effect in America? Why or why not?

3. What, exactly, is the holding in Van Ness v. Pacard? Does it necessarily involve the question of whether or not the English common law rule regarding "waste," that is, the removal of fixtures, is in force in America? If not, why does Story discuss it at all? Does it turn on more narrow concerns relating to the "trade fixtures" exception to the "waste" doctrine? What is this "trade fixtures" exemption? Is a building which houses the defendant's family (and also his dairy operations) necessarily a "trade fixture?" Does Story say it is? Are you persuaded?

4. What is the importance of the "custom" in the District of Columbia to the holding in this case? Should these matters turn on local custom? What would you expect to be the economic effect of Story's decision? Do you approve or disapprove of the consequences?

PARKER v. FOOTE

Supreme Court of New York, 1838.
19 Wend. 309.

This was an action on the case for stopping lights in a dwelling house. * * *

In 1808 the defendant being the owner of two village lots situate in the Village of Clinton, adjoining each other, sold one of them to Joseph Stebbins, who in the same year erected a dwelling house thereon on the line adjoining the other lot with windows in it overlooking the other lot. The defendant also, in the same year, built an addition to a house which stood on the lot which he retained, leaving a space of about 16 feet between the house erected by Stebbins and the addition put up by himself. This space was subsequently occupied by the defendant as an alley leading to buildings situate on the rear of his lot, and was so used by him until the year 1832, when (24 years after the erection of the house by Stebbins) he erected a store on the alley, filling up the whole space between the two houses, and consequently stopping the lights in the house erected by Stebbins. At the time of the erection of the store, the plaintiffs were the owners of the lot originally conveyed to Stebbins, by title derived from him, and were in the actual possession thereof, and brought this action for the stopping of the lights. Stebbins, the original purchaser, from the defendants, was a witness for the plaintiffs, and on his cross examination, testified that he never had any written agreement, deed or writing granting permission to have windows overlook the defendant's lot, and that nothing was ever said upon the subject. * * * On motion for a nonsuit, the defendant's counsel insisted that there was no evidence of a user authorizing the presumption of a grant as to the windows; that the user in this case was merely permissive, which explained and rebutted all presumption of a grant. That if the user, in the absence of other evidence, authorized the presumption of a grant, still that here the presumption was rebutted by the proof that, in fact, there never had been a grant. The circuit judge expressed a doubt whether the modern English doctrine in regard to stopping lights, was applicable to the growing villages of this country, but said he would rule in favor of the plaintiffs, and leave the question to the determination of this court. He also decided that the fact, whether there was or was not a grant in writing as to the windows, was not for the jury to determine; that the law presumed it from the user, and it could not be rebutted by proving that none had in truth been executed. After the evidence was closed, the judge declined leaving to the jury the question of presumption of right, and instructed them that the plaintiffs were entitled to their verdict. The jury accordingly found a verdict for the plaintiffs, with $225 damages. The defendant having excepted to the decisions of the judge, now moved for a new trial.

* * *

By the Court, BRONSON, J. The modern doctrine of presuming a right, by grant or otherwise, to easements and incorporeal hereditaments after 20 years of uninterrupted adverse enjoyment, exerts a much wider influence in quieting possession, than the old doctrine of title by prescription, which depended on immemorial usage. The period of 20 years has been adopted by the courts in analogy to the statute limiting an entry into lands; but as the statute does not apply to incorporeal rights, the adverse user is not regarded as a legal bar, but only as a ground for presuming a right, either by grant or in some other form. * * *

To authorize the presumption, the enjoyment of the easement must not only be uninterrupted for the period of 20 years, but it must be adverse, not by leave or favor, but under a claim or assertion of right; and it must be with the knowledge and acquiescence of the owner. * * * It is said that there may be cases relating to the use of water, which form exceptions to the rule that the enjoyment must be adverse to authorize the presumption of a grant. See Bealey v. Shaw, 6 East, 208; Ingraham v. Hutchinson, 2 Conn. 584. To this doctrine I cannot subscribe. * * * I think it sufficient at this time to say, that in whatever manner the water may be appropriated or enjoyed, it must, of necessity, be either rightful or wrongful. The use of the stream must be such as is authorized by the title of the occupant to the soil over which the water flows, or it must be a usurpation on the rights of another. If the enjoyment is rightful, there can be no occasion for presuming a grant. The title of the occupant is as perfect at the outset, as it can be after the lapse of a century. If the user be wrongful, a usurpation to any extent upon the rights of another, it is then adverse; and if acquiesced in for 20 years, a reasonable foundation is laid for presuming a grant. If the enjoyment is not according to the title of the occupant, the injured party may have redress by action. His remedy does not depend on the question whether he has built on his mill site or otherwise appropriated the stream to his own use. It is enough that his right has been invaded; and although in a particular case he may be entitled to recover only nominal damages, that will be a sufficient vindication of his title, and will put an end to all ground for presuming a grant. * * *

The presumption we are considering is a mixed one of law and fact. The inference that the right is in him who has the enjoyment, so long as nothing appears to the contrary, is a natural one—it is a presumption of fact. But adverse enjoyment, when left to exert only its natural force as mere presumptive evidence, can never conclude the true owner. No length of possession could work such a consequence. Hence the necessity of fixing on some definite period of enjoyment, and making that operate as a presumptive bar to the rightful owner. This part of the rule is wholly artificial; it is a presumption of mere law. In general, questions depending upon mixed presumptions of this description must be submitted to the jury, under proper instructions from the court. The difference between length of time which operates as a bar to a claim and that which is only used by way of evidence was very clearly stated by Ld. Mansfield, in the Mayor, etc., v. Horner, Cowp., 102. "A jury is concluded," he says, "by length of time that operates as a bar, as where the Statute of Limitations is pleaded in bar to a debt; although the jury is satisfied that the debt is due and unpaid, it is still a bar. So in the case of prescription, if it be time out of mind, a jury is bound to conclude the right from that prescription, if there could be a legal commencement of the right. But length of time used merely by way of evidence may be left to the consideration of a jury to be credited or not, and to draw their inference one way or the other, according to circumstances." In Darwin v. Upton, 2 Saund. 175, n. 2, the question related to lights, and it was said by the same learned judge that "Acquiescence for 20 years is such decisive presumption of a right by grant or otherwise, that unless contradicted or explained, the jury ought to believe it; but it is impossible that length of time can be said to be an absolute bar, like a Statute of Limitations; it is certainly a presumptive bar which ought to go to the jury." * * *

Some of the cases speak of the presumption as conclusive. Bealey v. Shaw, 6 East 208; Tyler v. Wilkinson, 4 Mas., 397. This can only mean that the presumption is conclusive where there is no dispute about the facts upon which it depends. It has never been doubted that the inference arising from 20 years' enjoyment of incorporeal rights might be explained and repelled; nor, so far as I have observed, has it ever been denied that questions of this description belong to the jury. The presumption we are considering has often been likened to the inference which is indulged that a bond or mortgage has been paid, when no interest has been demanded within 20 years. Such questions must be submitted to the jury to draw the proper conclusion from all the circumstances of each particular case. * * *

In a plain case, where there is no evidence to repeal the presumption arising from 20 years' uninterrupted adverse user of an incorporeal right, the judge may very properly instruct the jury that it is their duty to find in favor of the party who has had the enjoyment; but still it is a question for the jury. The judge erred in this case in wholly withdrawing that question from the consideration of the jury. On this ground, if no other, the verdict must be set aside.

The bill of exceptions presents another question which may probably arise on a second trial, and it seems proper, therefore, to give it some examination.

As neither light, air nor prospect can be the subject of a grant, the proper presumption, if any, to be made in this case, is that there was some covenant or agreement not to obstruct the lights. * * *

Most of the cases on the subject we have been considering relate to ways, commons, markets, water-courses, and the like, where the user or enjoyment, if not rightful, has been an immediate and continuing injury to the person against whom the presumption is made. His property has either been invaded, or his beneficial interest in it has been rendered less valuable. The injury has been of such a character that he might have immediate redress by action. But in the case of windows overlooking the land of another, the injury, if any, is merely ideal or imaginary. The light and air which they admit are not the subjects of property beyond the moment of actual occupancy; and for overlooking one's privacy no action can be maintained. The party has no remedy but to build on the adjoining land, opposite the offensive window. * * * Upon what principle the courts in England have applied the same rule of presumption to two classes of cases so essentially different in character, I have been unable to discover. If one commit a daily trespass on the land of another, under a claim of right to pass over, or feed his cattle upon it; or divert the water from his mill, or throw it back upon his land or machinery; in these and the like cases long continued acquiescence affords strong presumptive evidence of right. But in the case of lights there is no adverse user, nor, indeed, any use whatever of another's property; and no foundation is laid for indulging any presumption against the rightful owner.

Although I am not prepared to adopt the suggestion of Gould, J., in Ingraham v. Hutchinson, 2 Conn., 597, that the lights which are protected may be such as project over the land of the adjoining proprietor, yet it is not impossible that there are some considerations connected with the subject which do not distinctly appear in the reported cases.   *   *   *

The learned judges who have laid down this doctrine have not told us upon what principle or analogy in the law it can be maintained. They tell us that a man may build at the extremity of his own land, and that he may lawfully have windows looking out upon the lands of his neighbor.   *   *   *   The reason why he may lawfully have such windows must be because he does his neighbor no wrong; and, indeed, so it is adjudged, as we have already seen; and yet, somehow or other, by the exercise of a lawful right in his own land for 20 years, he acquires a beneficial interest in the land of his neighbor. The original proprietor is still seised of the fee, with the privilege of paying taxes and assessments; but the right to build on the land, without which city and village lots are of little or no value, has been destroyed by a lawful window. How much land can thus be rendered useless to the owner remains yet to be settled.   *   *   *   Now what is the acquiescence which concludes the owner?   *   *   *   How, then, has he forfeited the beneficial interest in his property? He has neglected to incur the expense of building a wall 20 or 50 feet high, as the case may be—not for his own benefit, but for the sole purpose of annoying his neighbor. That was his only remedy. A wanton act of this kind, although done in one's own land, is calculated to render a man odious. Indeed, an attempt has been made to sustain an action for erecting such a wall. Mahan v. Brown, 13 Wend., 261.

There is, I think, no principle upon which the modern English doctrine on the subject of lights can be supported. It is an anomaly in the law. It may do well enough in England; and I see that it has recently been sanctioned with some qualification, by an Act of Parliament. Stat. 2 & 3 Wm. IV., ch. 71, sec. 3. But it cannot be applied in the growing cities and villages of this country, without working the most mischievous consequences. It has never, I think, been deemed a part of our law. 3 Kent, Com., 446, n. a. Nor do I find that it has been adopted in any of the States.   *   *   *   It cannot be necessary to cite cases to prove that those portions of the common law of England which are hostile to the spirit of our institutions, or which are not adapted to the existing state of things in this country, form no part of our law. And besides, it would be difficult to prove that the rule in question was known to the common law previous to Apr. 19, 1775. Const.N.Y., art. 7, sec. 13.   *   *   *

There is one peculiar feature in the case at bar. It appears affirmatively that there never was any grant, writing or agreement about the use of the lights. A grant may under certain circumstances be presumed, although, as Ld. Mansfield once said, the court does not really think a grant has been made. Eldridge v. Knott, Cowp., 214. But it remains to be decided that a right by grant or otherwise can be presumed when it plainly appears that it never existed. If this had been the case of a way, common, or the like, and there had actually been an uninterrupted adverse user for 20 years under a claim of right, to which the defendant had submitted, I do not intend to say that proof that no grant was, in fact, made would have overturned the action. It will be time enough to decide that question when it shall be presented. But in this case the evidence of Stebbins, who built the house, in connection with the other facts which appeared on the trial, proved most satisfactorily that the windows were never enjoyed under a claim of right, but only as a matter of favor. If there was anything to leave to the jury, they could not have hesitated a moment about their verdict. But I think the plaintiffs should have been nonsuited.

The CHIEF JUSTICE concurred on both points.

COWEN, J., only concurred in the opinion that the question of presumption of a grant should have been submitted to the jury.

New trial granted.

NOTES AND QUESTIONS

1.   It has become a cliché in American legal history to say that the English common law or at least the English common law method of deciding cases won wide acceptance in the United States during the early nineteenth century. While some, like Robert Rantoul, whom we have already met, advocated the creation of statutes to encompass all of American law, nineteenth century American private law was primarily the work of courts. Rantoul, as you saw, resisted this trend, Why? Do the decisions in the last two cases suggest that Rantoul was correct or incorrect in his objections to the "common law?"

2.   Parker v. Foote, and particularly the majority opinion that there should be no conclusive presumption of a grant to the plaintiff, present problems of understanding. How would Blackstone have decided the case? Defense counsel had argued that since there was no "adversity" in plaintiff's possession, he should lose. Much of the difficulty here comes from the fact that by this time (1838), there had been many cases involving prescription in the area of water rights. In those cases it had been held that there was no requirement of "adversity" for one seeking to establish prescriptive rights to an undiminished flow of water. See, e. g. Ingraham v. Hutchinson, 2 Conn. 584 (1818), and Professor Horwitz's discussion of that case, Horwitz, Transformation of American Law, at 44–45. We most commonly think of the doctrine of "prescription" as adverse possession; one who adversely possesses a piece of land for a certain number of years (often twenty) thereby gains legal title. The water-rights prescription cases granted legal rights after twenty years possession with no requirement of *adverse* possession. Can you understand why? How would you adversely possess a naturally flowing body of water? Why should adversity be an element of prescription? What, if anything does this have to do with the idea that title by "prescription" is said to involve a "lost grant?"

3. Does Judge Bronson decide Parker v. Foote on the law regarding presumptions of grants, or on the unsuitability of the doctrine of "ancient lights" to America? Why do you suppose that Cowen J. "only concurred in the opinion that the question of presumption of a grant should have been submitted to the jury?" Does it strike you as strange that a question of "legal" presumptions should go to the jury? Is this case atavistic?

SECTION D. THE FALL OF NUISANCE AND RISE OF NEGLIGENCE

III WILLIAM BLACKSTONE, COMMENTARIES ON THE LAWS OF ENGLAND

165–166 (1768).

* * *

The last class of contracts, implied by reason and construction of law, arises upon this supposition, that every one who undertakes any office, employment, trust, or duty, contracts with those who employ or intrust him, to perform it with integrity, diligence, and skill. And, if by his want of either of those qualities any injury accrues to individuals, they have therefore their remedy in damages by a special action on the case. A few instances will fully illustrate this matter. If an officer of the public is guilty of neglect of duty, or a palpable breach of it, of non-feasance or of mis-feasance, as, if the sheriff does not execute a writ sent to him, or if he wilfully makes a false return thereof; in both these cases the party aggrieved shall have an action on the case, for damages to be assessed by a jury. If a sheriff or gaoler suffers a prisoner * * * during the pendency of a suit * * * to escape, he is liable to an action on the case. But if, after judgment, a gaoler or a sheriff permits a debtor to escape, who is charged in execution for a certain sum; the debt immediately becomes his own, and he is compellable by action of debt, being for a sum liquidated and ascertained, to satisfy the creditor his whole demand * * *. An advocate or attorney that betray the cause of their client, or, being retained, neglect to appear at the trial, by which the cause miscarries, are liable to an action on the case for a reparation to their injured client. There is also in law always an implied contract with a common inn-keeper, to secure his guest's goods in his inn; with a common carrier, or bargemaster, to be answerable for the goods he carries; with a common farrier, that he shoes a horse well, without laming him; with a common tailor, or other workman, that he performs his business in a workmanlike manner: in which if they fail, an action on the case lies to recover damages for such breach of their general undertaking. But if I employ a person to transact any of these concerns, whose common profession and business it is not, the law implies no such general undertaking; but, in order to charge him with damages, a special agreement is required. Also, if an inn-keeper, or other victualler, hangs out a sign

and opens his house for travellers, it is an implied engagement to entertain all persons who travel that way; and upon this universal *assumpsit* an action on the case will lie against him for damages, if he without good reason refuses to admit a traveller. If any one cheats me
with false cards or dice, or by false weights and measures, or by selling
me one commodity for another, an action on the case also lies against
him for damages upon the contract which the law always implies, that
every transaction is fair and honest. In contracts likewise for sales, it
is constantly understood that the seller undertakes that the commodity
he sells is his own; and if it proves otherwise, an action on the case
lies against him, to exact damages for this deceit. In contracts for
provisions it is always implied that they are wholesome; and, if they
be not, the same remedy may be had. * * *

Besides the special action on the case, there is also a peculiar remedy, entitled an action of deceit, to give damages in some particular
cases of fraud; and principally where one man does any thing in the
name of another, by which he is deceived or injured; as if one brings
an action in another's name, and then suffers a nonsuit, whereby the
plaintiff becomes liable to costs: or where one obtains or suffers a
fraudulent recovery of lands, tenements, or chattels, to the prejudice
of him that hath right. As when by collusion the attorney of the
tenant makes default in a real action, or where the sheriff returns that
the tenant was summoned when he was not so, and in either case he
loses the land, the writ of deceit lies against the demandant, and also
the attorney or the sheriff and his officers; to annul the former proceedings, and recover back the land. * * *

* * *

PATTEN v. HALSTED

Supreme Court of New Jersey, 1795.
1 N.J.Law 277.

This was an action on the case against defendant as sheriff, for
the escape of one Freeman. The declaration charged that the plaintiff in November Term, 1790, had sued out a writ of *capias ad respon-
dendum* against Clarkson, Freeman and others, by virtue of which
Halsted, the sheriff, on the 10th of March, 1791, arrested Freeman
only, and in April Term succeeding returned him in custody * * *;
that in November Term, there was a *nol. pros.* as to the other defendants, and plaintiff recovered against Freeman the sum of £1526 19s. 6d.
for his damages, costs and charges; and that afterwards the defendant
suffered Freeman to escape.

There were two counts in the declaration, one for a voluntary,
and the other for a negligent escape.

The cause was tried at bar.

After having proved the writ, the arrest, the judgment roll, and
the escape, plaintiff rested his cause.

Aaron Ogden, for defendant, moved for a non-suit, on the following grounds:

1.   That special bail could not be required in the action against Freeman; and the sheriff, therefore, had a right to discharge him from custody on the entering of an appearance, which had been done. The writ in this case was to answer a plea of trespass on the case, and agreeably to the practice in the English courts, which has ever been adopted as the rule for our government, unless expressly altered or repealed, special bail is not required except in actions of debt.   3 Bl. Com. 292.   In the present case the entering an appearance was sufficient.   3 Bl. Com. 290.   *   *   *

If, therefore, the writ was erroneous, and Freeman himself might have been relieved from the arrest, the sheriff was entitled to assume the risk himself, to release the prisoner, and to avail himself in his defence of every defect which the person arrested would have been permitted to urge against its sufficiency.   The statute of Charles is directory to the sheriff, and from it he was to learn the course to be pursued, and to judge of the legality of the arrest.

*   *   *

R. Stockton, contra   *   *   *   contended that the sheriff was obliged to look only to the writ placed in his hands, and to comply with its directions; if defendant had been improperly arrested, let him make his application to the court in a regular manner for his discharge.   It was not to be endured, that the sheriff was to assume upon himself an authority to decide in what cases bail was required, and when it might be dispensed with.   His own interests were in no degree jeopardized by executing the arrest, and it was a business in which he had no concern, and no right to interfere.   Nor was it a matter of which the sheriff could avail himself, that an appearance had been entered.   That was a proceeding in the court under his own eye, and the legal operation of it could not be inquired into and determined by the sheriff.   He contended, that if Freeman was arrested without sufficient authority, or upon defective process, an application should have been made to the court to have him discharged on a common appearance.   *   *   *

The court overruled the motion   *   *   *.   On the question as to the right of taking bail, Kinsey, C. J., observed, that the writ was directory to the sheriff   *   *   *.   That when the writ was put in his hands, he was not to determine whether it was a case in which special bail was required; he was bound to imprison the defendant, unless sufficient bail was found.

The ground of defence adopted by the defendant, was to prove that there was no want of attention on his part; that every precaution consistent with humanity, and sometimes even bordering on rigor, had been adopted with regard to Freeman.   This was made out by several witnesses, and it was proved that the escape was occasioned by circumstances not to be foreseen, and which could not be prevented by even more than ordinary exertions and caution.

On the trial, John Gifford was offered as a witness on the part of the defendant, and objected to by Stockton, on the ground of his being the gaoler and sheriff's deputy, and consequently interested to exonerate himself, as well as Halsted, from responsibility. * * * A release, however, from the sheriff being produced, he was admitted by the court.

The court, in their charge to the jury, said that there appeared to be no evidence warranting a suspicion that the escape was collusive or voluntary, so far as it was within their authority to express an opinion on the subject. This, however, was a subject exclusively for the decision of the jury, who were to consider and weigh all the circumstances that had been proved. If they should be of opinion that the escape was connived at by the sheriff, it was their duty to find the whole amount of the judgment against Freeman as the damages.

On the count for a negligent escape, the court said that every escape not happening by the act of God, or the public enemies, was, in the eye of the law, considered a negligent escape. The law admits no other excuse, and if the prisoner is rescued by a mob, whose power the sheriff is unable to withstand, even with the aid of his *posse comitatus,* yet he is answerable for an escape; he must keep him, at all events. The reasons are obvious. If it were otherwise, the creditor would be exposed to imposition and hardship. He must be constantly watching the conduct of the sheriff, and guarding against any collusion between him and the debtor; always liable to deceptions, which it would be impossible to thwart in their progress, or to unravel after their accomplishment. It does not, therefore, lie in the mouth of the sheriff to say that the gaol was insufficient, or that he took all possible care; that the prisoner escaped by means of a false key, or that he was rescued by a mob. He knows at the time of his election, before he enters upon the execution of his office, upon what terms and conditions he is to hold it, and how far the law makes him answerable for any accidents that may occur. He can examine the gaol, but if, after having done what it behooves a prudent man to do, he takes the office and enjoys its benefits, he must submit to the inconveniences, and be answerable for escapes, however innocent he may be of any connivance. O'Niel v. Marson, 5 Burr. 2812.

In cases, however, where the action is for a negligent escape, the jury are not bound to make the original debt the measure of damages against the sheriff. They may take into consideration the circumstances of the case, and find such a measure of damages as the more or less favorable view of the facts which appear in evidence will warrant. On the point, therefore, of the *quantum* of damages in this case, it is a matter upon which the jury are to exercise their own discretion and judgment, and the court ought not, nor will they, direct you.

The jury found a verdict in favor of the plaintiff for £1545 6d. 6s.

* * *

A rule to show cause why a new trial should not be awarded had been obtained in May, and came on for argument in September Term, 1795.

In support of the motion, it was argued * * * * * * That the court misdirected the jury in stating that the insufficiency of the gaol was not a bar to the action. In England there can be no doubt that the law is as stated by the court; but there the sheriff provides the gaol as well as keeps it, and in case of its weakness, the original and real cause of the escape is his own negligence and inattention. In this country, the county is bound to build the gaol and keep it in repair, and the sheriff should not be made answerable for their remissness in preparing a suitable place for the reception and safe custody of prisoners.

It was further stated that in this case it appeared on the trial that Halsted had made a regular protest against the sufficiency of the gaol. * * *

Stockton, contra * * *. * * * The distinction attempted to be drawn between the different extent to which the sheriff's responsibility ought to be carried in this country and in England, from the circumstance that with us the county is obliged to build and repair the gaol, is without foundation; and this is the first time that it has been thought of. The sheriff was bound to keep his prisoners safely, and if he suffered any injury from the insufficiency of the prison, it was his own loss, and a question between him and the county; but it cannot affect the interests of the plaintiff, who has a right to look immediately to him in case of a loss by an escape.

PER CURIAM * * * Until our own legislature change the common law in this particular, we must adopt it as the rule for our government; and by that the sheriff is answerable for an escape under circumstances like the present.

* * *

Rule discharged.

NOTES AND QUESTIONS

1.   The excerpt from Blackstone is from his discussion of the law of "contract." Does it seem to you that he is talking about "contracts?" When Blackstone uses the word "neglect," for example, as in the case he describes of a lawyer guilty of "neglect to appear at the trial," what does he mean, and how would you describe the cause of action?

2.   Does the law that is applied in Patten v. Halsted (a case which occurs approximately a generation after Blackstone) follow Blackstone? Note that Blackstone is cited by defendant's attorney in his unsuccessful attempt to have the action dismissed because of procedural irregularities. In particular, the defendant's claim is that "special bail" should not have been required, and thus there was no original right to imprison the defendant for his failure to make bail. It is argued that since this case

called for no "special bail," the sheriff should have dismissed the defendant on personal recognizance. The court holds that the writ given to the sheriff made no express mention that it was not a case requiring special bail, and merely directed the sheriff to imprison the defendant. The court held that the sheriff was not at liberty "to determine whether it was a case in which special bail was required," and that thus unless the defendant himself posted sufficient bail (which he apparently did not) it was the sheriff's duty to imprison him without asking questions. Does this sound right to you? Once the procedural objections are defeated, what becomes the defendant's defense?

3. Note that the judge takes it upon himself to tell the jury that "there appeared to be no evidence warranting a suspicion that the escape was collusive or voluntary * * *." Was it appropriate for the judge so to comment on the evidence? What about the liability on the count for "negligent escape?" According to the judge, what would be the resultant liability of the sheriff if the escape is caused by mob action "whose power the sheriff is unable to withstand, even with the aid of his *posse comitatus?*" Why is the reason for this result so "obvious" to the judge?

4. Is the operation of this rule, liability for "negligent escape," necessarily unjust? What about the operation of the rule in this particular case? What was the measure of damages used here? Note that there was a motion for a new trial. Do you agree with the court's position on disposition of this motion, that "Until our own legislature change the common law in this particular, we must adopt it as the rule for our government * * *." Does this square with the cases you have read before? Would you expect this attitude of not changing the English common law of torts to continue for very long? What does the next case suggest about American willingness to examine English precedent?

BROWN COUNTY v. BUTT

Supreme Court of Ohio, 1826.
2 Ohio R. 348.

* * *

Opinion of the court by Judge HITCHCOCK:

The first and most important question presented to the court for decision in the present case is, whether a county can be made responsible for the escape of a prisoner, confined for debts where the escape happens in consequence of the want of a jail, or where the jail furnished by the county commissioners is insufficient. It is necessary to dispose of this question in the first place, because if the county is not liable, the judgment of the court of common pleas was erroneous, and must be reversed.

The law has been long settled in England, the country from which we derive most of our laws, as well as our ideas of jurisprudence, that the sheriff is liable for escapes. It is to him, and him alone, in such cases, that the judgment creditor can look for redress. The same principle prevails in some, although not in all, our sister states.

Whenever a question of law has been settled in England, the courts in this country are in the habit of adhering to such decision. It is undoubtedly correct that such should, as a general rule, be the case. But to adhere blindly to English decisions when no good reason can be assigned for them, or when no other reason can be assigned than that it has been thus decided, to do this without inquiring what influenced the courts to make such decisions, to do it without inquiring whether the same reasons exist in this country as in that, would be foolish in the extreme. It is a useful maxim that when the reason of a law ceases, the law itself should cease. A particular law, or rule of law, might be very beneficial in England, or one of our sister states, which, if enforced in Ohio, would be attended with injurious consequences. Influenced by these circumstances, this court has ever been in the habit of looking to the effects which would follow the adoption of any particular rule of decision. Why is the sheriff in England made liable for an escape? The reason is obvious. The sheriff in that country, as well as in this, is the keeper of the jail. But he is not bound to confine the debtor in the public jail of the county, if there be one, but he may confine him in a house or prison furnished by himself. If the public prison is insufficient he can make all necessary repairs or alterations, and for the expense will be indemnified. In short, he may adopt any course which is essentially necessary to secure his prisoner, provided he confines him within the proper bailiwick. Such being his situation, it is perfectly proper that if the prisoner escapes, he should be liable. The escape will not happen without a violation or neglect of duty on his part, and whenever an individual sustains an injury in consequence of the violation or neglect of duty on the part of a public officer, justice requires that the officer should make reparation for that injury. But to make the officer liable where no such circumstance intervenes, when he has in fact complied with the requisitions of law and with his own duty, would be manifestly unjust. What, then, is the situation of the sheriff in Ohio? Can he confine the debtor in such place as he thinks proper? Can he confine him in a prison of his own choice? It will not be pretended. On the contrary, the law requires that the debtor shall be confined in the jail of the county. And should he be confined in any other place, the sheriff would be liable to the creditor for an escape, or to the debtor for false imprisonment. * * * Is the sheriff authorized to fix upon the place for, or to erect a jail for the county? In the "act providing for the erection of public buildings," passed January 22, 1810, the law in force when the escape now complained of happened, but which does not materially vary from the present law on the subject, these duties are assigned to the county commissioners.

The sheriff has no power to provide a prison, nor can he repair one unless at his own expense. Under these circumstances, to make the sheriff ultimately liable for the escape of a prisoner, when the

escape happens for the want of a jail, the law giving him no power
to furnish such jail, or to make him liable when the escape happens through the insufficiency of the jail, the law conferring no right
upon him to make necessary repairs, would be manifestly unjust. It
would be to inflict a penalty on an officer who had violated no law,
who had been guilty of no violation or neglect of duty. It would, in
fact, be to punish him for a neglect of duty on the part of others.

When the escape is voluntary, or where it happens in consequence
of the negligence of the sheriff, he ought to be liable. But where it
happens in consequence of circumstances not within his control, the
principles of justice require that he should be exonerated.

It may, perhaps, be thought by some that if the sheriff is to be
exonerated on the grounds before specified, it would be proper to make
the county commissioners liable in their individual capacity. But
we must consider the capacity in which the county commissioners act.
They are the representatives of the county. The money which they
expend is the money of the county. The funds with which public
buildings are erected, are the funds of the county. In fact, the acts
of the commissioners are the acts of the county, and it is only through
them that the business of the county can be transacted. And when
it is said that it is the duty of the commissioners to furnish public
buildings, nothing more is intended than that this should be done by
the county. It is true the commissioners may, in some cases, be punished criminally for a neglect of duty, but this is a civil action, the
object of which is to recover remuneration for a civil injury. The injury has been sustained in consequence of a neglect of duty on the
part of the commissioners, not as individuals, but in their corporate
capacity as the representatives of the county of Brown. If liable at
all, therefore, they must be liable in this capacity.

Inasmuch, then, as it is duty of the commissioners of a county,
or, in other words, of the county itself, acting by its commissioners,
to furnish a good and sufficient jail; and, inasmuch, as the sheriff
has no voice nor control in this business, it is the opinion of a majority of the court that where an escape happens in consequence of
the want of, or insufficiency of a jail, the county must be eventually
liable for such escape.   *   *   *

*   *   *   It being the duty of the county to furnish a prison,
and the escape having happened in consequence of a neglect of this
duty, it would seem to be proper that the county should be directly
liable to the party injured. By adopting such course, circuity of action would be avoided. The party in fault would suffer for his negligence, while an innocent individual would not be put to the trouble of
defending or prosecuting a suit. But I do not consider this question
as open for discussion. It has been repeatedly decided that the judgment creditor must look to the sheriff for his remedy, and in this
case we settle the principle that the sheriff shall be indemnified by
the county.   *   *   *

Judge BURNET'S Dissenting Opinion:

The ground on which I dissent from the opinion of the court in this case is, that I can not consider a county, in its corporate capacity, as liable for the illegal conduct of its officers; and if it is not so liable, I do not perceive any ground on which this action can be sustained. There is no statute in this state, by which it is made responsible, and if there be any principle of common law that can sustain the suit, it has escaped my observation. There is not any contract, either express or implied, subsisting between the plaintiff and the county of Brown, on which the claim can be founded, nor has the county, in its corporate capacity, been guilty of a tort to his prejudice. If the commissioners, by a willful omission of duty, have caused him an injury, they may be answerable for the consequences, in an action properly framed for that purpose. The statute made it the duty of the commissioners to provide a sufficient jail, and gave them the means of doing so. They voluntarily accepted the trust, and if they have neglected to execute it, and by that negligence the plaintiff has been injured, the injury has not proceeded from the county, but has been occasioned by the illegal conduct of the commissioners for which they are personally responsible.

Reference has been had to considerations of policy. If there be any weight in these arguments, they are better calculated for the legislative hall than for a court of justice. They might influence the legislature to provide a remedy, but they do not show that it already exists. It may, however, be fairly questioned whether good policy requires such a recourse. A county can not provide public buildings, in any other way than by the agency of its officers. If those officers may neglect their duty with impunity, as will be the case if they can transfer the consequences of their negligence to the county, a strong inducement to the faithful and punctual discharge of duty is lost. It will be a matter of but little moment, as it regards them personally, whether they provide a sufficient jail or not, if the consequence of their negligence is to operate on the public treasury, instead of their own purses. If considerations of policy can be properly used in a case like this, I incline to the opinion that it is better to let the officers bear the consequences of their omissions of duty than invite them to such omissions, by providing an indemnity, or by suffering them to offend with impunity. It can not be good policy to remove incentives to duty. If it be said that cases of hardship may arise, in which the commissioners are not chargeable with inexcusable neglect, so as to be personally liable, it may be replied, that in such cases the sheriff, or other person injured by an escape, may petition for relief, with a fair prospect of success, if his claim be a meritorious one. But it does not follow that a legal right of recovery must exist for every loss attended with hardship. There are cases without number in which such losses are sustained, and the sufferers are destitute of a remedy, because there is no person legally bound to indemnify.

It can not be overlooked, however, that in the case before us, all the parties acted voluntarily and advisedly. The sheriff knew the situation of the public buildings when he accepted his office, and the defendant had the same knowledge when he caused his debtor to be imprisoned. The hardship, therefore, is not as good as it would seem at first view.

If the liability contended for really existed, it is a natural inference that some adjudged cases might be found to support it, but the research of counsel has not enabled them to produce a solitary case, in which the funds of the county, or corporation, have been rendered liable for injuries sustained by the unauthorized, illegal, and tortious actions of its officers.   *   *   *

The books abound in cases, both English and American, in which recoveries have been had against sheriffs for escapes, but not an instance can be found in which they have recovered an indemnity against the county. If it be replied that this is because the sheriffs in England are not bound to confine debtors in the public jail, but may, at their election, provide a private jail, or may repair the old one, if necessary, for which they are to be remunerated; the same reply may be given, with equal force, in the present case. In Ohio, the county commissioners are authorized and directed to provide sufficient jails, and it is their duty to levy and collect money, or to contract debts for that purpose if necessary. Consequently, they stand in the situation of sheriffs in England, in relation to escapes, and ought to be answerable for the insufficiency of the jail, in the same manner, and to the same extent. They, as well as the sheriff, are county officers, and in providing public buildings, they all act as agents of the county.

If an escape happens in England, through the insufficiency of the jail, the sheriff must answer for it, and he has no recourse on the county. For the same reason, the commissioners in Ohio should be answerable without recourse. It is a just maxim, that "the reason of the law is the life of the law." The sheriff, in the case put, is liable without recourse on the county. Why? Because he has been guilty of a misfeasance, in not providing a *sufficient* jail. Therefore, and for the same reason, the commissioners should be liable without recourse, they having been guilty of a nonfeasance, in not *providing* a jail.

In every instance, within my knowledge, in which a county has been held liable for an escape, it has been made so by statute. It is by statute, the hundred in England is made liable for robberies, in certain cases, and under our territorial government, a statute was adopted by the governor and judges, in August, 1792, declaring the counties liable for escapes that should happen through the insufficiency of the jail. The act pointed out the manner in which the money should be assessed and paid; and also the mode of commencing and conducting suits for the recovery thereof, in case the courts should not order it assessed and paid. The frauds that were practiced on the counties, under that law, by collusions between plaintiffs and defendants, when no debts were really due, and when defendants were utterly insolvent, became so apparent and oppressive, that the first territorial legislature, in 1799, repealed the act, and no subsequent legislature has seen proper to revive it.

Prior to the adoption of that law, I believe no attempt was made to charge a county in such a case, and this is the first suit that has been brought for that purpose, within my knowledge, since the repeal of the law, although escapes have been numerous, for which the sheriffs have been held answerable to the persons injured. The natural inference is, that it has been the prevailing opinion that such actions could not be sustained at common law.

From the most careful view I have been able to take of this case, it appears to me that the county of Brown is not liable, either by statute, or by contract, to pay the money demanded, nor do I discern that she has committed any tort to the injury of the plaintiffs, and I do not know of any ground, distinct from these, on which the action can be sustained.

The duty and the power of the commissioners is created by statute. While they act within the scope of their powers, the county must be bound, but if they should make a contract, to remove the seat of justice, or should seize on private property, for county purposes, contrary to law, the county would not be bound by the contract, or liable for the trespass; they would be responsible in their private capacities. The proposition, therefore, that "the act of the commissioners is the act of the county," must be taken in a restricted sense. It would be mischievous, as well as unprecedented, to hold the county answerable for their tortious and illegal proceedings.

NOTES AND QUESTIONS

1. Do you perceive any change in the liability of the sheriff for negligent escape? What does the word "negligent" mean as it is used by the judge who writes the majority opinion in this case? Is the dissent consistent in its usage of the concept of negligence? With which opinion do you agree?

2. Seven years after the *Brown County* case, the Ohio Supreme Court held again in Richardson v. Spencer, 6 Ohio R. 13 (1833) that a sheriff could not escape from liability for negligent escape by showing that the jail was insufficient, even if his county would be liable to indemnify him if the escape resulted from such insufficiency. Nevertheless, the Supreme Court did suggest that where "the escape was not voluntary on the part of the officer," the sheriff might present evidence that the escaped debtor was insolvent, and thus limit his initial liability. The court held that the evidence of the involuntary or voluntary nature of the escape *and* the insolvency of the debtor were all facts which should go to the jury, which should receive instructions on the law from the trial judge

and then reach a damage figure on its own. Would the Patten v. Halsted court sympathize with the notion of differentiating between voluntary and involuntary escapes? In the cases which you have read thus far, note that the term "negligent" might refer to either a "voluntary" or an "involuntary" escape.

GREGORY, TRESPASS TO NEGLIGENCE TO ABSOLUTE LIABILITY *

37 Virginia Law Review 359, 360–370 (1951).

In this essay I am concerned * * * with liability for harm which defendants caused to others under circumstances where they did not intend to indulge in behavior directed in any way at the interests of such others. On the contrary, these defendants are minding their own business and get involved with the interests of others either because things get out of hand or because they are negligent. Nevertheless, those others sustain damage in some way because of the defendants' behavior; and the task of the courts is to decide whether or not there shall be compensation for such damage. * * *

Civil liability in the common law was originally based on a fairly simple concept—trespass. The King's Court in early England issued the writ of trespass to any litigant who could show that he had sustained a physical contact on his person or property, due to the activity of another. If this litigant-plaintiff could then convince the court that the defendant had intentionally brought about this contact, he had judgment for damages because of the trespass—unless the defendant could justify his act. But if the plaintiff could not establish intent, then in order to recover he had to go ahead and show that he had sustained some actual damage * * *. [T]his ancient concept of trespass had reference to any contact achieved as the consequence of one's conduct against the interest of another, no matter under what circumstances it occurred, as long as the defendant's causative conduct was his voluntary act.

In the early days of the King's Court, the only available writ was that of trespass. Plaintiffs who sustained harm under non-trespassory circumstances were not able to bring suit in the King's Court. Thus, suppose the defendant in a particular instance was building a house adjacent to the highway. As he was carrying a beam along a scaffold, he stumbled and unintentionally dropped the beam on the sidewalk, so that it hit a passerby named White on the head, causing him severe harm. White could easily procure a writ of trespass and recover damages. It was immaterial that the defendant dropped the beam unintentionally; and it made no difference whether or not the defendant was negligent or otherwise at fault. This was a trespass under the early law; and this primitive conception of trespass implied all the fault that was necessary for liability.

Shortly thereafter, let us assume, Black came walking along and stumbled over the beam, falling so that his head hit the beam, with the result that he sustained identically the same harm as that suffered by White. Suppose that the defendant had not had time to remove the beam from the sidewalk nor to post warnings; and also assume that Black neither saw the beam as he walked along nor was careless in having failed to see it. When Black sought a writ entitling him to sue the defendant, there was none available which was appropriate for his case; and he was unable to recover damages. That was because there was no trespass by the defendant against him, since the force initiated by the defendant had come to rest before Black was hurt. Indeed, the only force involved in Black's case was that supplied by Black himself when he came walking along and stumbled.

Poor Black never could understand why White was allowed recovery and he was denied it. Each had sustained the same hurt from the same unintended conduct of the same defendant—the dropping of the beam. The only difference Black could perceive was that White was "lucky" enough to get hit by the beam, so that he was allowed to recover with no questions asked. In the meantime, there were people who were accidentally hit by arrows shot at targets and by limbs cut off trees—all of whom were allowed to recover; while others who were hurt "consequentially"—that is, on whose person there had been no direct contact resulting from unexpended forces initiated by others—were denied recovery. This apparent unbalance of justice was no doubt responsible for the creation of a new writ, to be issued in situations where harm had occurred otherwise than by a "direct" or trespassory contact. The new writ was called "trespass in a similar case"—a misnomer, because it was intended to function in the absence of trespassory contact. Lawyers, however, soon came to refer to this new writ as the action on the case and nicknamed it "case", in contradistinction to trespass.

This development occurred in the thirteenth and fourteenth centuries. Thereafter, people in Black's position were enabled to bring their suits before the King's Court. But that did not mean that they were necessarily entitled to recover. Since they could not show a trespassory contact, they had to supply some other element justifying the imposition of liability on the people who had been instrumental in causing their harm. For by this time even an unintended trespassory contact was regarded as tantamount to *a trespass*; and a trespass of any kind was accepted as a wrong in itself, without inquiry into the circumstances leading up to it. Those who sued in case, therefore, because they could not show a trespassory contact, had to submit some item of illegality or fault to take the place of the missing element of trespass in order to establish liability. In actions on the case for inadvertently caused harm to person or property, this new item of illegality or fault ultimately became what we now speak of as negligence. For negligence, as it has operated during the past century or so to afford a basis of liability, is a fairly modern concept. Certainly its modern significance was completely unknown at the time when the action on the case was developing. But something of the sort no doubt operated to furnish the basis for liability during these early times in the absence of the trespassory contact.

At any rate, as the centuries rolled around, it became apparent that Black's descendants in the law were not much better off than they had been when only the writ of trespass was available—certainly in comparison with litigants who fell into White's category. For plaintiffs like White found trespassory contacts so easy to prove; and legal fault or the early counterpart of negligence was not at all easy to establish. To illustrate, let us return to the instance of the defendant who dropped the beam which hit White and over which Black stumbled. Whatever the circumstances were which governed the defendant's dropping of the beam, they were by hypothesis identically the same as far as the two hurt litigants were concerned. Yet all White has to do under this new development is still merely to show contact and damages, while Black has to undertake the burden of proving fault, at the risk of losing his suit if he cannot do so. If we assume that there was some explanation of the incident showing that defendant's conduct was reasonable and not due to his fault, then if Black cannot offer convincing evidence to the contrary, defendant will get the judgment in his case. But White, on the other hand, will still recover damages.

The frequent recurrence of this state of affairs was bound to irritate litigants in Black's position—not so much because they failed to recover as that White did recover without any real showing of fault. And they were not satisfied with the explanation that the unintended contact was trespassory and that such trespass implied fault in itself. To them the courts seemed to be maintaining a double standard for determining liability to govern unintentionally caused harm—that of fault or social inadequacy in cases like Black's and absolute liability without fault in cases like White's.

Moreover, defendants themselves began to notice this double standard and to complain bitterly about it. Builders whose non-negligently dropped beams hit plaintiffs before they came to rest on the ground felt themselves unfairly treated under a system of alleged justice which excused other builders from liability for harm caused after their beams had reached the ground. Such a capricious and one-sided administration of civil liability might even become a factor tending to discourage them from enterprise and investment!

This very consideration began to worry American judges during the first half of the nineteenth century. They disliked the imposition of liability without fault and reacted against any manifestation of this notion. * * * [M]any of our judges believed that the development of this young country under a system of private enterprise would be hindered and delayed as long as the element of chance exposed enterprisers to liability for the consequences of pure accident, without fault of some sort. * * *

Chief Justice Lemuel Shaw, of the Massachusetts Supreme Court, gets most of the credit for the establishment of a consistent theory of liability for unintentionally caused harm. The case in which he marked the departure from the past was Brown v. Kendall, decided in 1850. There it appeared that two dogs, belonging respectively to the plaintiff and defendant, were engaged in mortal combat. Defendant undertook to separate the dogs by beating them with a stick. Of course, the dogs moved about a good deal as they fought; and both plaintiff and defendant anxiously followed them around. At a certain point defendant raised his stick over his shoulder to strike the dogs, and the end of the stick then happened to hit the plaintiff in the eye while he was standing behind the defendant, causing him serious damage. * * * It does not appear from the report that either the defendant or the plaintiff was in any way negligent * * *.

The plaintiff sued the defendant in trespass for damages. After all, he had been hit in the eye by a stick set in motion by the defendant—a clear case of direct contact. He thought that this contact or, as he called it, this trespass entitled him to recover damages for the resulting harm, without showing anything else. Such a theory of liability, he claimed, was historically traditional * * *.

But the Massachusetts Supreme Court turned the plaintiff down cold. Shaw denied that the contact between defendant's stick and plaintiff's eye had any substantive significance at all. Certainly he did not believe that this unintended contact amounted to the tort of trespass, on which liability could be established. He admitted that the contact had procedural significance, enabling the plaintiff to bring his suit under the action of trespass rather than in case. And he declared that all of the old precedents cited by the plaintiff, in which it appeared that unintentionally caused direct physical contacts amounted to trespass, meant no more than that. They did not imply that any such contact was a trespass in the sense that it was a tort, in itself. Apparently that would be true only if the contact were intentionally inflicted. He then stated as a general principle that when harm occurs as the consequence of an unintended contact, it is actionable only on the basis of negligence, just as if there had been no contact at all in the causing of the harm. Thus, according to Shaw's principle, White and Black in the hypothetical case discussed above, would henceforth be treated exactly the same and White would have no advantage over Black merely because he sustained his harm by a direct hit while Black suffered consequentially.

Now Shaw, of course, had indicated in his opinion that White and Black had always been treated the same—that one who had been hurt by an unintended contact had never enjoyed any advantage over others whose unintentionally caused harm had not resulted from a direct hit. The available evidence, however, indicates that this was not so. * * *

As an alternative basis of liability in the absence of available evidence of negligence, the plaintiff in this dog fight case sought a ruling to the effect that one who sustained harm as the consequence of an unintended direct hit resulting from another's conduct, was entitled to a sort of presumption that such other was negligent and that the burden of disproving negligence was on such other. Thus, he wanted to have the jury instructed that, in view of the direct contact resulting from the defendant's act, even though it was not intended, the defendant must offer convincing evidence that he was not negligent in order to escape liability and that otherwise he would be liable. But Shaw and his court refused to compromise their new principle in this way. They said that the burden of proving negligence in a case of this type always lay on the plaintiff and that it never shifted, leaving the defendant free to sit tight and wait for the plaintiff to show that he had been negligent. For if the burden of disproving negligence were placed on the defendant, simply because of the chance that plaintiff's harm had occurred as the result of a direct hit, then the courts would be lending the element of contact or "trespass" a substantive significance similar to that which they had already denied. Whenever the defendant in such a case was unable to convince the jury of his due care or lack of negligence, liability would be imposed on him in the absence of any proof of fault. He would thus have lost the benefit of the doubt which was still accorded to the defendant whose conduct allegedly harms another, but not under the circumstances of a direct hit. Such a result would go far to cancel out the consistency in theory of liability which the Massachusetts court was endeavoring to establish.

BROWN v. KENDALL, the dog-fight case, quickly became a landmark in the law of torts. * * * If he wanted to win thereafter, a plaintiff hurt by an unintended contact would have to prove the commission of a tort based on negligence, just as if there had been no trespassory contact at all. And with this consistency of theory came another basic notion: no longer was there any theory of absolute liability without fault in our common law to govern the disposition of cases where one sustained harm unintentionally inflicted as the result of another's conduct.

* Harvey v. Dunlop, Hill & Denio 193 (N.Y.1843). Morton Horwitz has argued that this case "merely represented the culmination of a uniform course of New York decisions which since 1820 had assumed that carelessness had to be shown in both trespass and case." Transformation of American Law 1780–1860 91 (1977).

While it is pure speculation, one of Chief Justice Shaw's motives underlying his opinion appears to have been a desire to make risk-creating enterprise less hazardous to investors and entrepreneurs than it had been previously at common law. Certainly that interpretation is consistent with his having furthered the establishment of the fellow servant doctrine and expansion of the assumption-of-risk defense in actions arising out of industrial injuries. Judicial subsidies of this sort to youthful enterprise removed pressure from the pocket-books of investors and gave incipient industry a chance to experiment on low-cost operations without the risk of losing its reserve in actions by injured employees. Such a policy no doubt seems ruthless; but in a small way it probably helped to establish industry, which in turn was essential to the good society as Shaw envisaged it. And, of course, he also had in mind the obvious advantages of consistency in legal theory.

Seven years earlier, in 1843, the highest New York court had enunciated a principle similar to that promulgated in Massachusetts.* There it appeared that a six-year old defendant had thrown a stone at random and it had struck the plaintiff's five-year old daughter in the eye, causing serious damage. The evidence indicated, however, that the young defendant was not at fault, which presumably meant that he did not intend to hit the little girl and was not to be held negligent in having done so. In any event, the jury seems to have found it to be a case of inevitable accident; and following the instructions of the trial court, it gave the verdict to the defendant. In his appeal the plaintiff assigned error in these instructions. After all, he contended, the defendant had thrown the stone, which had hit his daughter's eye. And while a child of six could hardly be held for negligence, at least he could be made liable at common law for his trespasses.

But the highest New York court affirmed the judgment for defendant, the Chief Judge declaring: "No case or principle can be found, or if found can be maintained, subjecting an individual to liability for an act done without fault on his part." He then went on to say, however, that where harm is inflicted by the defendant, "it should be presumed to have been done wrongfully or carelessly," the burden of proving the contrary to be placed on him.   *   *   *

A somewhat similar instance, illustrating the difficulty with which a few of our state courts made the break from the past, occurred in 1835. The Vermont Supreme Court then declared the law to be that a plaintiff who was run down by a horse and buggy driven by the defendant, could not recover damages if this occurrence was the "result of unavoidable accident" and if "there was no want of prudence or care on the part of the defendant." But then the court went on to say something inconsistent with this statement. "Therefore," its Chief Justice observed, "where a person is doing a voluntary act, which he is under no obligation to do, he is held answerable for any injury which may happen to another, either by carelessness or accident." Now much the same idea was later expressed, in a slightly different way, in the trial court's instructions to the jury in Brown v. Kendall, the Massachusetts dog-fight case. There the trial court said that if what the defendant did "was not a necessary act, and [he] was not in duty bound to part the dogs, but might with propriety interfere or not as he chose, [he] was responsible for the consequences of the blow, unless it appeared that he was in the exercise of extraordinary care, so that the accident was inevitable, using the word not in a strict but a popular sense."

The meaning of this kind of language is hard to grasp. But whatever it means, it runs counter to the main principle that Shaw ultimately stated in the dog-fight case. Certainly Shaw recognized it as drivel, since its validity depended upon drawing a distinction between human conduct which was "necessary," or performed pursuant to some duty, on the one hand, and that which the defendant merely had a right to engage in, on the other hand. Naturally the defendant in Brown v. Kendall didn't have to separate the fighting dogs. It was not a necessary act, in the sense that there was any compulsion on him to perform it. Shaw said, rather, that it "was a lawful and proper act, which he might do by proper and safe means." And he then made it clear that his new principle applied to all human conduct lawfully embarked upon, whether it was driving a horse for pleasure or profit, shooting at targets, building houses or anything else. The only test was to be whether or not such lawful conduct was carefully or negligently performed. Otherwise his new principle would not mean very much, since most human conduct is not compulsory or necessary but is undertaken either for economic gain, for personal value ends, including recreation, or just for something to do.

Perhaps judges using the kind of language which Shaw disapproved were somewhat uncertain about the relatively new concept of negligence. After all, that concept did not then have a very long tradition; and its career in the modern sense was entirely in the future. It is fairly apparent from the examples cited by these judges in their opinions that they were confusing so-called unnecessary conduct with what clearer-headed judges like Shaw would have called conduct from which a jury might be permitted to infer negligence. Again, it is barely possible that they were in this fashion attempting to explain away some of the older precedents which Shaw had preferred simply to ignore—that is, the earlier English decisions in which liability for unintentionally caused harm resulting from direct contacts was based on trespass regardless of the absence of negligence.

* * *

NOTES AND QUESTIONS

1. Gregory gives Shaw much of the credit (albeit unclaimed by Shaw) for changing the rule which imposed a different standard for liability in actions of trespass and case. Before Brown v. Kendall, according to Gregory, one seeking to recover on a writ in trespass need only prove that he was *directly injured* by the conduct of the defendant (e. g. by being hit by defendant's baseball bat wielded at the time by defendant). One seeking to recover in an action on the case (the action brought for indirect injuries—one hurt for example by stumbling over defendant's baseball bat left on the floor by defendant), however, needed to prove some "fault," e. g. a lack of "due care" on the part of defendant. Shaw is said to have swept all this away, and to have applied the same "fault" standard in trespass and case. If Shaw's opinion was such a novel development, why did he claim it wasn't? Consider Professor Horwitz's statements in The Transformation of American Law 1780–1860 (1977) where he comments on the importance of the trespass/case distinction. Do they accord with those of Gregory? What follows is the footnote (number 146, on pages 297–298) which Horwitz uses to support his statement (p. 90) that " * * * there is no indication that American judges, unlike their English brethren, * * * ever regarded the substantive law governing the two writs as turning on a distinction between strict liability and negligence.":

In Taylor v. Rainbow, 2 H&M (12 Va.) 423 (1808) we find the court reporter observing of the difference between trespass and case that "the law says there is a nice distinction, but the reason * * * is often difficult to discover." Id. at 423. And the defendant's counsel, in arguing that the plaintiff brought the wrong action, declared: "It is unnecessary to reason on the propriety of keeping up the boundaries of action: it is a settled rule of law that they must be preserved." Id. at 430. Of the three judges who wrote opinions in the case, none puts the distinction on substantive law. Judge Fleming, for example, emphasized that he saw no substantive difference between the two writs, since the ends of justice would be served by either, yet he felt "tied down, and bound by precedents" establishing the direct-indirect distinction. Id. at 444.

* * * In Gates v. Miles, 3 Conn. 64, 67 (1819), the Connecticut Supreme Court also spelled out only procedural reasons for preserving the difference between the actions: "As no suit can be maintained for trespass *vi et armis* after three years, and as in trespass on the case there is no limitation, it becomes highly important to preserve the established boundaries between these actions."

An 1817 case in New York, Foot v. Wiswall, 14 Johns. 304, marks a significant turning point because it emphasizes how late it was before lawyers came to regard even the allegation of negligence in an action on the case as limiting liability. In a ship collision case, the plaintiff's counsel still argued the strict liability doctrine that the defendant had "acted at his peril." The action was brought in case, he pointed out, only because that form of action was required when a servant brought about an injury. "If the defendant had been at the helm of his boat at the time," he concluded, "there is no doubt that the plaintiffs could have recovered in an action of trespass; and there is no reason why they should not be equally entitled to recover in an action of trespass on the case, or for negligence; the distinction between the two actions being purely technical." Id. at 306. Nevertheless, the New York Supreme Court upheld the verdict for the defendant, clearly indicating for the first time it was for the plaintiff to prove and for the jury to determine whether the defendant had violated some standard of care. Three years later the court also upheld a trespass action for a collision only after minutely examining the evidence for proof of carelessness. Percival v. Hickey, 18 Johns. 257, 289–90 (1820). Thus, it is not surprising that by 1826, when the New York court elaborately explained why "it is still important to preserve the distinction between the actions" it failed to discuss any differences in substantive law, mentioning only technical differences in costs and pleadings. M'Allister v. Hammond, 6 Cow. 342, 344 (N.Y.1826). For within a few short years, actions in both trespass and case had been simultaneously put to the test of negligence.

Outside New York, Benjamin L. Oliver, Jr., of Massachusetts was the first clearly to state that "without any negligence or fault whatever, it seems no action can be maintained" in either trespass or case. B. Oliver, Forms of Practice; or American Precedents 619 (1828).

2. Still, Horwitz believes that the substantive law of both trespass and case did change from the application of a *strict liability* standard in both to the application of a "fault" or "due care" (modern "negligence") standard in both. Horwitz might well agree with Gregory on the reasons for such a change. What do you suppose that those reasons would be? Could they be the same ones that led, for example, to a change in the American common law regarding ancient lights?

3. In Callender v. Marsh, 18 Mass. (1 Pick.) 418 (1823), a homeowner whose foundation walls were seriously weakened by the lowering of a street adjacent to his property brought an action of trespass on the case against Boston's surveyor of highways, who had ordered the "improvement" in the road. The plaintiff had owned his property for more than twenty years, and the original road had been in existence some time before that. Massachusetts statutes gave the surveyor of highways the "power and duty" to make the public ways "safe and convenient." The court stated that "If the public safety and convenience require a levelling of the road, [the surveyor] must do it with as much care in relation to property bordering on the road, as it is possible for him to use; and if he should abuse his authority by digging down or raising up, where it might not be neces-

sary for the reasonable repair and amendment of the road, he would be amenable to any suffering party for his damages." In *Callender*, however, there was no allegation that the surveyor had failed to use "as much care * * * as it is possible for him to use." The plaintiff seems rather to have relied on his argument that the statute giving the surveyor the power to lower the roads in a manner that injured his foundations was unconstitutional, and thus could not be relied on by the surveyor. The Massachusetts Declaration of Rights provided in pertinent part that "whenever the public exigencies require that the property of any individual should be appropriated to public uses, he shall receive a reasonable compensation therefor," and there was no provision made by the surveyor for compensating homeowners whose foundations were weakened. *Held*, by the Supreme Court, *per* Parker, C. J., the plaintiff must be nonsuited. There was no problem with the constitutionality of the statute, since the provision of the Declaration of Rights could not be construed "to extend the benefit of it to one who suffers an indirect or consequential damage or expense, by means of the right use of property already belonging to the public." "Those who purchase house lots bordering upon streets," said the court, "are supposed to calculate the chances of such elevations and reductions as the increasing population of a city may require * * * [and] may indemnify themselves in the price of the lot which they buy, or take the chance of future improvements, as they shall see fit."

The surveyor, was, of course, a public official, and the plaintiff a citizen damaged by the conduct of such an official. How is it that in Patten v. Halsted there is relief for such damage, but not in Callender v. Marsh? Does Gregory's article on trespass suggest any explanations?

HENTZ v. THE LONG ISLAND RAILROAD CO.

Supreme Court of New York, 1852.
13 Barb. 646.

S. B. STRONG, J. The plaintiff alleges in his complaint that he has been for the last five years, and is, lawfully possessed of a lot in the village of Hempstead, in the county of Queens * * * comprising half an acre; on which there are a dwelling house and shop fronting on Main-street, and a barn and other out buildings on Fulton-street. That while he has been so possessed of the said premises, the defendants having previously, and in or about the year 1837, laid down and along Main-street, and upon such premises, certain timbers and iron rails, constituting their railroad track, continued them thereon, running over the same with passenger and freight cars drawn by horses, greatly to his injury * * *. That about the 5th of last August, the defendants took up the old timbers and rails and tore up the soil of his land, and laid down in their place other timbers and iron rails, and have at various times since * * * run upon the said rails * * * with their locomotives, propelled by steam; that "by the coming of the said locomotives upon and running the same over his said close, the health and lives of his family, tenants and inmates, are prejudiced and endangered, and the value of his property lessened; that an offensive smoke has filled his dwelling house; that the same is a nuisance of the most flagrant character," and that the continuance thereof would be an irreparable injury to his said property and the enjoyment thereof; and that his tenants are likely to abandon the same. That the defendants have since such 5th of August last, run upon and over the said premises certain freight cars loaded with manure and merchandise, propelling the same by means of their steam engine and horses, often without agents to watch and conduct them, and to the danger, nuisance and inconvenience of himself and family; and that from the contiguity of his land to the depot, the locomotives frequently stop opposite to his premises, and he is thus injured more than the rest of mankind.

He therefore claims two thousand dollars damages, and prays for an order of injunction restraining the defendants during the pendency of this suit from running their locomotives or cars of any description upon or over his said premises, and that a judgment may be given him for his damages, and for a perpetual injunction.

*   *   *

The only remaining question is whether the road where it passes the plaintiff's premises is a nuisance. * * * The legislature has expressly authorized various companies to lay and use their track through many of our cities and villages, and cars are now drawn by locomotives propelled by steam through Albany, Schenectady, Utica, Syracuse, Rochester, Buffalo, Poughkeepsie, Brooklyn, Jamaica, and many other cities and villages. It was held in the case of Drake v. The Hudson River Railroad Company, (7 Barb. 509,) that a road passing through the streets in the city of New York, and when the cars are drawn by steam-power into a crowded part of the city (although not to the terminus of the road) was not a nuisance. Similar decisions were made in the cases of Hamilton v. The New York and Harlem Railroad Company, (9 Paige, 171); The Lexington and Ohio Railroad Co. v. Applegate, (8 Dana, 289); and Chapman v. The Albany and Schenectady Railroad Company, (10 Barb. 360). Is there then any thing peculiar to Main-street, or in the management of the defendants, which makes the railroad where it passes the plaintiff's house a nuisance? It is not averred in the complaint that the railroad constitutes any serious impediment to the travel, along the highway. It no where appears that the rails are badly laid down, so as to create any obstruction on the surface, and it is apparent that the street is of sufficient width for carriages to pass each other without danger or difficulty, on either side of the railway. Besides, a number of respectable inhabitants of the place deposed that the condition of the street as a passway has been considerably improved by the defendants' works upon it.

Is there any thing in the management of the road and its appendages which renders it offensive to the plaintiff, to such an extent as to justify the interposition of this court by way of restraint upon the action of the defendants? One of the causes of complaint is that the steam locomotive passes as far south as Fulton-street, and occasionally below it. It is apparent that many of those who have favored the introduction of the road into the village have acted on the supposition that the locomotive was not to proceed below Fulton-street, but there is no evidence of any definite agreement with the defendants to that effect; and as their charter does not restrict them as to the means of transportation on any part of their route, I am not authorized to interfere, but must leave the matter to the good sense of those who may be intrusted with the management of the affairs of the company. It is manifestly for their interest to conduct its operations in such a manner as to gratify the reasonable wishes of that part of the community which gives to the company an efficient support. The plaintiff complains that about two years ago, and for about a year, the track was disused and suffered "to go to ruin," its shattered state embarrassing the travel upon the highway, causing the breaking of vehicles, and hindering their passage to and from his premises. There were no doubt serious grievances at the time, but they resulted from the then impaired condition of the track. The cause has since been removed, and the papers furnish us no reasons to apprehend a recurrence of the same or similar evils. None of the papers mention any serious accidents since the track has been relaid and the locomotive has passed over it, and if there had been any, they would no doubt have been discovered by the plaintiff, or the learned member of the bar who has resided during the past summer with him, who acts as one of his counsel in this action, and has shown a laudable zeal, and made strenuous exertions in behalf of his client. The plaintiff complains also of the smoke from the locomotive, on the ground that it is prejudicial to the health and comfort of himself and his family, and he alleges that the establishment as now conducted is a "nuisance of the most flagrant character," and the lives of his family, tenants and inmates are endangered. The general charge that it is a flagrant nuisance, cannot be taken into consideration, any further than as it may be supported by the facts. In this case there are none except those which I have mentioned. The smoke must undoubtedly be annoying to some extent, but not more disagreeable or prejudicial than what may proceed from many lawful establishments in the village, nor is the inconvenience so constant or continuous. There may be some danger to human life from the rapid passage of a railroad train, but in the opinion of many, not more than what results from the passage of ordinary carriages. Accidents to children, or to adults who are not grossly careless, from the locomotives when passing through our most populous cities, are very rare. The times of their passage are generally known, and the noise made by the movement over the rails, and the engineer's whistle, give timely notice of the approach of the train. When the usual precautions are practiced the

danger is very slight, and when there is any carelessness or mismanagement the company and its officers are very properly held to a rigid
accountability.   It is true that there can be no satisfaction for the
loss of life, nor any adequate remuneration for the deprivation of a
limb, but the strong probability that the company will encounter a
serious loss of property, and that a careless or notoriously incompetent conductor, or engineer, will undergo a disgraceful punishment
where serious injuries are inflicted, must necessarily lead to great
caution and to consequent security.   The evils of which the plaintiff
complains are by no means peculiar to himself.   They are the necessary concomitants of this species of locomotion, whether in the city
or in the country.   They cannot be prevented without an entire suspension of one of the greatest improvements of modern times.

Private rights should undoubtedly be effectually guarded, but
the courts cannot extend the protection of the interest of any one so
far as to restrict the lawful pursuits of another.   The maxim *sic uteri
tuo ut non alienum laedas* is true when correctly construed.   It extends to all damages for which the law gives redress, but no further.
If it should be applied literally, it would deprive us to a great extent
of the legitimate use of our property, and impair, if not destroy its
value.   A man who sets up a new store or hotel in the vicinity of an
old one, or who discovers and makes a new machine which wholly
supersedes a prior invention, or who erects a new dwelling house so
near that of his neighbor as to endanger it from the cinders which
may escape from the chimney, or as to interrupt some fine prospect,
or who plants a grove so near the boundary line of another as to shade
a valuable garden, or prevent the free circulation of air around a
dwelling house, inflicts an injury for which the law gives no redress,
and which cannot be averted by the tribunals intrusted with its administration.   So too there are some useful employments which endanger the lives of human beings which cannot and ought not to be
prohibited.   Lives are sometimes destroyed by an omnibus, a carman's
cart, a stage or a steamboat, but so long as they are not imminently
dangerous they cannot be prohibited.   We cannot enjoy our private
rights, nor can we avail ourselves of the many advantages resulting
from modern discoveries, without encountering some risk to our lives,
or our property, or to some extent endangering the lives or injuring
the property of others.   The questions in all such cases are, is the
business a lawful one, and is the injury or danger to others by or from
its legitimate pursuit inevitable?   If they are, the law furnishes no
remedy either by way of indemnity or prevention.

* * *

Upon the whole I am satisfied that the case presented in behalf
of the plaintiff does not call for, or warrant, the interposition of this
court by way of restriction upon the future action of the defendants.

The motion for an injunction must therefore be denied, and the
order temporarily restraining the defendants must be vacated.

NOTES AND QUESTIONS

1. How would Blackstone have decided this case, and why?

2. As noted by this court, its opinion, that a railroad was *not* a nuisance *per se*, followed earlier cases. In one of the first of these, Lexington & Ohio Railroad Co. v. Applegate, 38 Ky. (8 Dana.) 289 (1839), there are some poignant comments about the implications of declaring steam locomotives *not* nuisances:

> * * * [E]ven though some persons owning property on the railroad street may be subjected to some inconvenience, and even loss, by the construction and use of the road, yet, if the use made of the road be consistent with the purpose for which the street was established, and also consistent with the just rights of all, such persons have no right either to damages or to an injunction; because they purchased their property, and must hold it—as all others purchase and must hold town lots—subject to any consequences that may result, whether advantageously or disadvantageously, from any public and authorized use of the streets, in any mode promotive of, and consistent with, the purposes of establishing them as common highways in town, and compatible with the reasonable enjoyment by all others entitled thereto.

> * * *

> Main street, in Louisville, was established as a common highway for the universal public; and, as said in Rex v. Russel, "the right of the public is not confined to the purposes of passage; trade and commerce are the chief objects, and the right of passage is chiefly subservient to those ends."

> * * *

> The onward spirit of the age must, to a reasonable extent, have its way. The law is made for the times, and will be made or modified by them. The expanded and still expanding genius of the common-law should adapt it here, as elsewhere, to the improved and improving condition of our country and our countrymen. And, therefore, railroads and locomotive steam-cars—the offsprings, as they will also be the parents, of progressive improvement—should not, in themselves, be considered as nuisances, although, in ages that are gone, they might have been so held, because they would have been comparatively useless, and, therefore, more mischievous.

> We know that a zealous and inconsiderate spirit of innovation and improvement requires the vigilance and restraint of both reason and law. We are fully aware, also, of the fact that, when such a spirit is abroad, private rights are in peculiar danger, unless sternly guarded by the judiciary; and we are not sure that such guardianship is not most needed in a government where whatever is popular is apt to prevail at first, and often at last, only because it is the *vox populi*.

> * * *

Note the comments of this court that when a spirit of "innovation and improvement" is abroad in a situation where the *vox populi* tends to prevail, the court's task is the vigilent protection of private rights. Based on what you have seen of the law of torts in the early nineteenth century, how well did nineteenth century American courts perform this task? Would you say that tort liability increased or decreased? What implications would this have for the bearing of the costs of industrial and commercial development? Do you think this is a "democratic," or "anti-democratic" result?

SECTION E. THE EVOLUTION OF THE AMERICAN BUSINESS CORPORATION

1. THE STATE AND THE CORPORATION

CURRIE'S ADMINISTRATORS v. THE MUTUAL ASSURANCE SOCIETY

Supreme Court of Virginia, 1809.
4 Hen. & M. (14 Va.) 315.

[This case concerns an attempt by an early insurance ("assurance") company to rationalize its risk/reward calculations by allocating premiums from owners of town dwellings to pay only for damage to town dwellings, and "country" premiums for "country" damages. Formerly there had been only one pool. The change, made pursuant to an 1805 statute, had the effect of raising the plaintiff town dweller's premium. He sued to have the 1805 Act declared void. The plaintiff lost in the Virginia District Court, and appealed to the Virginia Supreme Court.]

Judge ROANE. In the year 1794, the legislature passed an act, at the suggestion of an individual, "for establishing a Mutual Assurance Society against fire, upon buildings in this state." It provided for a subscription to the scheme, by individuals, and declared that the principle of the assurance should be, "that the citizens of this state may insure their buildings against losses and damages occasioned accidentally by fire, and that the insured pay the losses and expenses, each his share, according to the sum insured." * * * The act further provided, that as soon as three millions of dollars should be subscribed, the subscribers should meet together, examine the system submitted to the legislature, and conclude on such rules and regulations, as to a majority of the subscribers might seem best; and that the said society should be at liberty, from time to time, to alter and amend the said rules and regulations, as they may judge necessary; and in particular, that they should agree upon the premiums to be paid. The act also provided, that as soon as the society should have acted in the premises, and elected their agents and officers, it should be considered as incorporated by virtue of the act.

It is evident, that every thing touching the question before us, is left to the pleasure of the society itself by this act * * * and that some of the powers expressly recognised by the act, as appertaining to the society itself, (that of fixing and altering the premiums for example,) are equally as important and as liable to be abused as the principle in question; which, it is urged, has been infringed by the act of 1805, effecting a separation between the interests of the towns and those of the country. * * * The true question, therefore, before us is, whether any fundamental principle exists in the case at bar, interdicting the separation of the interests in question—and if there be, whether the subsequent legislature had power to invade it?

* * *

In order to shew that the act in question is no law, and therefore, it is further urged, is a compact, and as such is beyond the power of a succeeding legislature, Blackstone's definition of municipal law has been relied on. Municipal law is defined by him to be "a rule of civil conduct prescribed by the supreme power of the state, commanding what is right, and prohibiting what is wrong;" and it is argued, that the act in question is no law, under this definition, for want of the generality implied by the term "rule," and because it is said to be not so much in the nature of a command by the legislature, as of a promise or contract proceeding from it. When we consider, that mere private statutes and acts of parliament, are (even by this writer himself) universally classed among the municipal laws of England; nay, even that the particular customs of that kingdom, are admitted to form a part of the municipal code, it is evident, that this definition of municipal law, is by far too limited and narrow. I would rather adopt the definition of Justinian, that civil (or municipal) law, is, *"quoad quisque sibi populus constituit;"* bounded only in this country in relation to legislative acts, by the constitutions of the general and state governments; and limited also by considerations of justice. It was argued by a respectable member of the bar, that the legislature had a right to pass any law, however just, or unjust, reasonable, or unreasonable. This is a position which even the courtly Judge Blackstone was scarcely hardy enough to contend for, under the doctrine of the boasted omnipotence of parliament. What is this, but to lay prostrate, at the footstool of the legislature, all our rights of person and of property, and abandon those great objects, for the protection of which, alone, all free governments have been instituted?

For my part, I will not outrage the character of any civilized people, by supposing them to have met in legislature, upon any other ground, than that of morality and justice. In this country, in particular, I will never forget, "that no free government, or the blessing of liberty, can be preserved to any people, but by a firm adherence to justice, moderation, temperance, frugality, and virtue, and by frequent recurrence to fundamental principles." [a] I must add, however, that

(a) Virginia Bill of Rights, art. 15.

when any legislative act is to be questioned, on the ground of conflicting with the superior acts of the people, or of invading the vested
rights of individuals, the case ought to be palpable and clear: in an
equivocal or equiponderant case, it ought not easily to be admitted,
that the immediate representatives of the people, representing as well
the justice as the wisdom of the nation, have forgotten the great injunctions under which they are called to act. In such case, it ought
rather to be believed, that the judging power is mistaken.

With respect to acts of incorporation, they ought never to be
passed, but in consideration of services to be rendered to the public.
This is the principle on which such charters are granted even in England; (1 Bl.Com. 467,) and it holds *a fortiori* in this country, as our
bill of rights interdicts all "exclusive and separate emoluments or
privileges from the community, but in consideration of public services." (Art. 4.) It may be often convenient for a set of associated individuals, to have the privileges of a corporation bestowed upon them;
but if their object is merely private or selfish; if it is detrimental to,
or not promotive of, the public good, they have no adequate claim
upon the legislature for the privilege. But as it is possible that the
legislature may be imposed upon in the first instance; and as the public good and the interests of the associated body, may, in the progress
of time, by the gradual and natural working of events, be thrown entirely asunder, the question presents itself, whether, under such and
similar circumstances, the hands of a succeeding legislature are tied
up from revoking the privilege. My answer is, that they are not. In
the first case, no consideration of public service ever existed, and in
the last, none continues to justify the privilege. It is the character of
a legislative act to be repealable by a succeeding legislature; nor can
a preceding legislature limit the power of its successor, on the mere
ground of volition only. That effect can only arise from a state of
things involving public utility, which includes the observance of justice and good faith towards all men.

These ideas are not new; they are entirely sanctioned by the sublime act of our legislature, "for establishing religious freedom." That
act, after having declared and asserted certain self-evident principles,
touching the rights of religious freedom, concludes in this manner:
"And though we well know that this assembly, elected by the people
for the ordinary purposes of legislation only, have no power to restrain
the acts of succeeding assemblies, constituted with powers equal to
our own, and that, therefore, to declare this act irrevocable, would be
of no effect in law, yet we are free to declare, that the rights hereby
asserted, are of the natural rights of mankind, and that if any act shall
be hereafter passed, to repeal the present, or to narrow its operation,
such act will be an infringement of natural right." Conforming to the
principles declared in this luminous exposition, I infer, irresistibly,
that the power of a succeeding legislature is bounded only, (and that
in cases of no equivocal complexion,) by the principles and provisions

of the constitution and bill of rights, and by those great rights and principles, for the preservation of which all just governments are founded. *   *   *

Under the actual case before us, I might, perhaps have spared myself the necessity of this discussion. The principle stated in the act of 1794, which is supposed to have interdicted the separation in question, is couched in terms extremely abstract and general. While other principles declared by this act, have clearly and expressly confined the benefits of the institution to citizens of this state, and limited insurances to losses occasioned accidentally by fire; while it is clearly provided that retribution is to be made by the insured, and that according to the sum insured, the principle now immediately in question does not seem to prohibit a division or distribution of the members, or their interests into classes, or districts. *   *   *

From these considerations, it would, perhaps, result, that the regulation in question did not require legislative aid to carry it into operation, but might have been effected by the society itself. That, however, is taking a broader ground than is necessary to be maintained on the present occasion. That aid having been afforded by the legislature, it is enough for our purpose that the act of 1805, if it has produced any injustice at all to any class of subscribers, has fallen short of the crying grade of injustice, which alone can disarm the act of its operation. The society itself, at least, considered this, on the contrary, as a measure essential to the equalization of the risks; and, in this respect, I see no cause to differ from them in opinion.

By referring to the principle of our law respecting corporations, the foregoing results will be fully justified. Those artificial persons are rendered necessary in the law from the inconvenience, if not impracticability of keeping alive the rights of associated bodies, by devolving them on one series of individuals after another. The effect of them is, to consolidate the will of the whole, which is collected from the sense of the majority of those who constitute them. This decision by a majority is a fundamental law of corporations in this country and in England *   *   *. It is also a fundamental principle of corporations, that this majority may establish rules and regulations for the corporation, (which are considered as a sort of municipal law for the body corporate,) subject only to a superior and fundamental law which may have been prescribed by the founder thereof, or by the legislature which grants the privilege perhaps, also, these petty legislatures ought further to be limited by all those considerations, (including the due observance of justice,) which I have endeavoured to shew, ought to bound the proceedings of all legislatures whatsoever. If, however, there be no such paramount law, or overruling principle, the mere will of the majority is competent to any regulation. *   *   * But further, a corporation may be extinguished by the surrender of its rights and franchises; as to which the unanimous assent of every individual is not requisite. The will of the majority must prevail in this, as in other cases. It is not to be expected that this kind of suicide will be committed for light causes; and where cases of greater exigency require it, the corporation should not hesitate to make the surrender.

*   *   *

As it is not expected, that corporations shall exist for ever, when the reasons for granting them shall have passed away, and no public utility can ensue from their continuance, this right of surrender must incontrovertibly exist, even in derogation of the fundamental laws and principles. In the case before us, the resolution of the society, on which the act of 1805 was bottomed, may be considered as such surrender, and that act as the acceptance thereof. The interest of the institution commenced thereafter, as it were, *de novo;* and provision was made for a revision, and revaluation of the houses in the towns and in the country, as thus separated. Whether, therefore, the measure adopted by the society in 1805, and sanctioned by the legislature, be considered as a legitimate change, by the society itself, of an ordinary regulation, or as a surrender which destroyed a fundamental one, the effect as to the question before us, is precisely the same.

*   *   *

In every view of this case, therefore, I am of opinion, that the judgment of the District Court is correct, and ought to be affirmed.

NOTES AND QUESTIONS

1. Why do you suppose Judge Roane finds it necessary to suggest that "morality and justice" are the only grounds on which a legislature would ever choose to act? Is there something suspect in what the legislature did here? Do you believe that there is anything inherently wrong with the idea that the legislature has the power to alter an insurance company's charter in order to alter the rates it charges?

2. Surely one of the core ideas in Judge Roane's opinion is the notion that incorporation is only to be allowed when the corporation will operate in the public interest. Corporations are still chartered by the fifty states today, and the rationale for granting charters is that corporations serve the public interest. Do you see how the notion that corporations are to operate in the public interest leads to the conclusions that legislatures may alter corporate charters?

3. When Judge Roane is speaking of the power that legislatures have to undo the work of their predecessors, he suggests that the only "bounds" on the action of a successor legislature are set "by the principles and provisions of the constitution and bill of rights, and by those great rights and principles, for the preservation of which all just governments are founded." What are "those great rights and principles, for the preservation of which all just governments are founded?" Do they have anything at all to do with corporations? Was any of this discussion of the power of legislatures necessary to the resolution of this case?

4. What purposes of corporations does Judge Roane recognize as legitimate? Does he make incorporation sound very attractive to you?

What about Judge Roane's suggestion that corporate charters are like "fundamental law." With what is Judge Roane thereby comparing corporate charters? Does that suggest that legislatures should feel free about changing charters? Compare Roane's attitude toward corporations and corporate charters with that of Justices Marshall and Story in the case which follows.

DARTMOUTH COLLEGE v. WOODWARD

United States Supreme Court, 1819.
17 U.S. (4 Wheat.) 518.

[Acts of the New Hampshire Legislature sought to change the terms of the corporate charter of Dartmouth College. The Dartmouth Trustees argued that a corporate charter was a "contract," and that a legislative act unilaterally changing that "contract" violated the United States Constitution. We begin with an edited version of the opinion of the Court, delivered by Chief Justice Marshall.]

* * *

* * * [T]his Court has * * * declared, that, in no doubtful case, would it pronounce a legislative act to be contrary to the constitution. But the American people have said, in the constitution of the United States, that "no State shall pass any bill of attainder, *ex post facto* law, or law impairing the obligation of contracts." In the same instrument they have also said, "that the judicial power shall extend to all cases in law and equity arising under the constitution." On the judges of this Court, then, is imposed the high and solemn duty of protecting, from even legislative violation, those contracts which the constitution of our country has placed beyond legislative control; and, however irksome the task may be, this is a duty from which we dare not shrink.

* * *

It can require no argument to prove, that the circumstances of this case constitute a contract. An application is made to the crown for a charter to incorporate a religious and literary institution. In the application, it is stated that large contributions have been made for the object, which will be conferred on the corporation, as soon as it shall be created. The charter is granted, and on its faith the property is conveyed. Surely in this transaction every ingredient of a complete and legitimate contract is to be found.

The points for consideration are,

1. Is this contract protected by the constitution of the United States?

* * *

1. On the first point it has been argued, that the word "contract," in its broadest sense, would comprehend the political relations between the government and its citizens, would extend to offices held within a

State for State purposes, and to many of those laws concerning civil institutions, which must change with circumstances, and be modified by ordinary legislation; which deeply concern the public, and which, to preserve good government, the public judgment must control. That even marriage is a contract, and its obligations are affected by the laws respecting divorces. That the clause in the constitution, if construed in its greatest latitude, would prohibit these laws. * * * That as the framers of the constitution could never have intended to insert in that instrument a provision so unnecessary, so mischievous, and so repugnant to its general spirit, the term "contract" must be understood in a more limited sense. That it must be understood as intended to guard against a power of at least doubtful utility, the abuse of which had been extensively felt; and to restrain the legislature in future from violating the right to property. That anterior to the formation of the constitution, a course of legislation had prevailed in many, if not in all, of the States, which weakened the confidence of man in man, and embarrassed all transactions between individuals, by dispensing with a faithful performance of engagements. To correct this mischief, by restraining the power which produced it, the State legislatures were forbidden "to pass any law impairing the obligation of contracts," that is, of contracts respecting property, under which some individual could claim a right to something beneficial to himself; and that since the clause in the constitution must in construction receive some limitation, it may be confined, and ought to be confined, to cases of this description * * *.

The general correctness of these observations cannot be controverted. That the framers of the constitution did not intend to restrain the States in the regulation of their civil institutions, adopted for internal government, and that the instrument they have given us, is not to be so construed, may be admitted. The provision of the constitution never has been understood to embrace other contracts, than those which respect property, or some object of value, and confer rights which may be asserted in a court of justice. * * *

The parties in this case differ less on general principles, less on the true construction of the constitution in the abstract, than on the application of those principles to this case, and on the true construction of the charter of 1769. This is the point on which the cause essentially depends. If the act of incorporation be a grant of political power, if it create a civil institution to be employed in the administration of the government, or if the funds of the college be public property, or if the State of New Hampshire, as a government, be alone interested in its transactions, the subject is one in which the legislature of the State may act according to its own judgment, unrestrained by any limitation of its power imposed by the constitution of the United States.

But if this be a private eleemosynary institution, endowed with a capacity to take property for objects unconnected with government, whose funds are bestowed by individuals on the faith of the charter;

if the donors have stipulated for the future disposition and management of those funds in the manner prescribed by themselves; there
may be more difficulty in the case * * *. Those who are no longer
interested in the property, may yet retain such an interest in the
preservation of their own arrangements, as to have a right to insist,
that those arrangements shall be held sacred. Or, if they have themselves disappeared, it becomes a subject of serious and anxious inquiry, whether those whom they have legally empowered to represent
them forever, may not assert all the rights which they possessed, while
in being * * *.

* * *

From the [original charter] itself, it appears, that about the year
1754, the Rev. Eleazer Wheelock established at his own expense, and
on his own estate, a charity school for the instruction of Indians in the
christian religion. The success of this institution inspired him with
the design of soliciting contributions in England for carrying on, and
extending, his undertaking. In this pious work he employed the Rev.
Nathaniel Whitacker, who, by virtue of a power of attorney from Dr.
Wheelock, appointed the Earl of Dartmouth and others, trustees of the
money, which had been, and should be, contributed; which appointment Dr. Wheelock confirmed by a deed of trust authorizing the trustees to fix on a site for the college. They determined to establish the
school on Connecticut river, in the western part of New Hampshire
* * * and the proprietors in the neighborhood * * * made large
offers of land, on condition, that the college should there be placed.
Dr. Wheelock then applied to the crown for an act of incorporation;
and represented the expediency of appointing those whom he had, by
his last will, named as trustees in America, to be members of the proposed corporation. "In consideration of the premises," "for the education and instruction of the youth of the Indian tribes," &c. "and also of
English youth, and any others," the charter was granted, and the trustees of Dartmouth College were by that name created a body corporate,
with power, for the use of the said college, to acquire real and personal
property, and to pay the president, tutors, and other officers of the
college, such salaries as they shall allow.

The charter proceeds to appoint Eleazer Wheelock, "the founder
of said college," president thereof, with power by his last will to appoint
a successor, who is to continue in office until disapproved by the trustees. In case of vacancy, the trustees may appoint a president, and in
case of the ceasing of a president, the senior professor or tutor, being
one of the trustees, shall exercise the office, until an appointment shall
be made. The trustees have power to appoint and displace professors,
tutors, and other officers, and to supply any vacancies which may be
created in their own body, by death, resignation, removal, or disability;
and also to make orders, ordinances, and laws, for the government of
the college, the same not being repugnant to the laws of Great Britain,
or of New Hampshire, and not excluding any person on account of his

speculative sentiments in religion, or his being of a religious profession different from that of the trustees.

This charter was accepted, and the property both real and personal, which had been contributed for the benefit of the college, was conveyed to, and vested in, the corporate body.

* * * [I]t is apparent, that the funds of the college consisted entirely of private donations. * * *

The origin of the institution was, undoubtedly, the Indian charity school, established by Dr. Wheelock, at his own expense. It was at his instance, and to enlarge this school, that contributions were solicited in England. The person soliciting these contributions was his agent; and the trustees, who received the money, were appointed by, and act under, his authority. It is not too much to say, that the funds were obtained by him, in trust, to be applied by him to the purposes of his enlarged school. The charter of incorporation was granted at his instance. The persons named by him in his last will, as the trustees of his charity school, compose a part of the corporation, and he is declared to be the founder of the college, and its president for life. Were the inquiry material, we should feel some hesitation in saying, that Dr. Wheelock was not, in law, to be considered as the founder of this institution, and as possessing all the rights appertaining to that character. But be this as it may, Dartmouth College is really endowed by private individuals, who have bestowed their funds for the propagation of the christian religion among the Indians, and for the promotion of piety and learning generally. * * * It is then an eleemosynary, and, as far as respects its funds, a private corporation.

Do its objects stamp on it a different character? * * *

That education is an object of national concern, and a proper subject of legislation, all admit. That there may be an institution founded by government, and placed entirely under its immediate control, the officers of which would be public officers, amenable exclusively to government, none will deny. But is Dartmouth College such an institution? Is education altogether in the hands of government? Does every teacher of youth become a public officer, and do donations for the purpose of education necessarily become public property, so far that the will of the legislature, not the will of the donor, becomes the law of the donation? * * *

Doctor Wheelock, as the keeper of his charity school, instructing the Indians in the art of reading, and in our holy religion; sustaining them at his own expense, and on the voluntary contributions of the charitable, could scarcely be considered as a public officer, exercising any portion of those duties which belong to government; nor could the legislature have supposed, that his private funds, or those given by others, were subject to legislative management, because they were applied to the purposes of education. * * *

A corporation is an artificial being, invisible, intangible, and existing only in contemplation of law. Being the mere creature of law, it possesses only those properties which the charter of its creation confers upon it, either expressly, or as incidental to its very existence. These are such as are supposed best calculated to effect the object for which it was created. Among the most important are immortality, and, if the expression may be allowed, individuality; properties, by which a perpetual succession of many persons are considered as the same, and may act as a single individual. They enable a corporation to manage its own affairs, and to hold property without the perplexing intricacies, the hazardous and endless necessity, of perpetual conveyances for the purpose of transmitting it from hand to hand. It is chiefly for the purpose of clothing bodies of men, in succession, with these qualities and capacities, that corporations were invented, and are in use. By these means, a perpetual succession of individuals are capable of acting for the promotion of the particular object, like one immortal being. But this being does not share in the civil government of the country, unless that be the purpose for which it was created. Its immortality no more confers on it political power, or a political character, than immortality would confer such power or character on a natural person. It is no more a State instrument, than a natural person exercising the same powers would be. If, then, a natural person, employed by individuals in the education of youth * * * would not become a public officer, or be considered as a member of the civil government, how is it, that this artificial being, created by law, for the purpose of being employed by the same individuals for the same purposes, should become a part of the civil government of the country? Is it because its existence, its capacities, its powers, are given by law? Because the government has given it the power to take and to hold property in a particular form, and for particular purposes, has the government a consequent right substantially to change that form, or to vary the purposes to which the property is to be applied? This principle has never been asserted or recognized, and is supported by no authority. Can it derive aid from reason?

The objects for which a corporation is created are universally such as the government wishes to promote. They are deemed beneficial to the country; and this benefit constitutes the consideration, and, in most cases, the sole consideration of the grant. In most eleemosynary institutions, the object would be difficult, perhaps unattainable, without the aid of a charter of incorporation. Charitable, or public spirited individuals, desirous of making permanent appropriations for charitable or other useful purposes, find it impossible to effect their design securely, and certainly, without an incorporating act. They apply to the government, state their beneficent object, and offer to advance the money necessary for its accomplishment * * *. The proposition is considered and approved. The benefit to the public is considered as an ample compensation for the faculty it confers, and the corporation is created. If the advantages to the public constitute a full compensation for the faculty it gives, there can be no reason for exacting a further compensation, by claiming a right to exercise over this artificial being a power which changes its nature, and touches the fund, for the security and application of which it was created. There can be no reason for implying in a charter, given for a valuable consideration, a power which is not only not expressed, but is in direct contradiction to its express stipulations.

* * *

* * * It requires no very critical examination of the human mind to enable us to determine, that one great inducement to these gifts is the conviction felt by the giver, that the disposition he makes of them is immutable. It is probable, that no man ever was, and that no man ever will be, the founder of a college, believing at the time, that an act of incorporation constitutes no security for the institution; believing, that it is immediately to be deemed a public institution, whose funds are to be governed and applied, not by the will of the donor, but by the will of the legislature. * * * If every man finds in his own bosom strong evidence of the universality of this sentiment, there can be but little reason to imagine, that the framers of our constitution were strangers to it, and that, feeling the necessity and policy of giving permanence and security to contracts, of withdrawing them from the influence of legislative bodies, whose fluctuating policy, and repeated interferences, produced the most perplexing and injurious embarrassments, they still deemed it necessary to leave these contracts subject to those interferences. The motives for such an exception must be very powerful, to justify the construction which makes it.

The motives suggested at the bar grow out of the original appointment of the trustees, which is supposed to have been in a spirit hostile to the genius of our government, and the presumption, that, if allowed to continue themselves, they now are, and must remain forever, what they originally were. Hence is inferred the necessity of applying to this corporation, and to other similar corporations, the correcting and improving hand of the legislature.

It has been urged repeatedly * * * that the trustees deriving their power from a regal source, must, necessarily, partake of the spirit of their origin; and that their first principles, unimproved by that resplendent light which has been shed around them, must continue to govern the college, and to guide the students. * * * The first trustees were undoubtedly named in the charter by the crown; but at whose suggestion were they named? * * * The charter informs us. Dr. Wheelock had represented, "that, for many weighty reasons, it would be expedient, that the gentlemen whom he had already nominated, in his last will, to be trustees in America, should be of the corporation now proposed." * * * Some were probably added by the crown, with the approbation of Dr. Wheelock. Among these is the Doctor himself. If any others were appointed at the instance of the crown, they are the governor, three members of the council, and the speaker of the house of representatives, of the colony of New Hampshire. The stations filled by these persons ought to rescue them from any other imputation than too great a dependence on the crown. If in the revolution that followed, they acted under the influence of this sentiment, they must have ceased to be trustees; if they took part with their countrymen, the imputation, which suspicion might excite, would no longer attach to them. * * *

The only evidence which we possess of the character of Dr. Wheelock is furnished by this charter. The judicious means employed for the accomplishment of his object, and the success which attended his endeavours, would lead to the opinion, that he united a sound understanding to that humanity and benevolence which suggested his undertaking. It surely cannot be assumed, that his trustees were selected without judgment. With as little probability can it be assumed, that, while the light of science, and of liberal principles, pervades the whole community, these originally benighted trustees remain in utter darkness, incapable of participating in the general improvement; that, while the human race is rapidly advancing, they are stationary. Reasoning *a priori*, we should believe, that learned and intelligent men, selected by its patrons for the government of a literary institution, would select learned and intelligent men for their successors; men as well fitted for the government of a college as those who might be chosen by other means. Should this reasoning ever prove erroneous in a particular case, public opinion, as has been stated at the bar, would correct the institution. The mere possibility of the contrary would not justify a construction of the constitution, which should exclude these contracts from the protection of a provision whose terms comprehend them.

The opinion of the Court, after mature deliberation, is, that this is a contract, the obligation of which cannot be impaired, without violating the constitution of the United States. * * *

* * *

NOTES AND QUESTIONS

1. Pursuant to the legislative acts mentioned in Justice Marshall's opinion, the New Hampshire legislature sought to change the method of appointment of trustees of Dartmouth College, in order to have appointments made by the state government. Since the trustees had the power to hire and fire Dartmouth instructors and officers, the acts of the legislature were an attempt to change Dartmouth from what we would consider to be a "private" college to a "public" one. This case is one of the great old "chestnuts" of American constitutional law.

"It is a small college," Daniel Webster is supposed to have said in his argument on behalf of the trustees, "but there are those who love it."

There was, however, much more to the case than love of *alma mater*. Consider some of the closing remarks which Webster made to the Supreme Court:

> The case before the court is not of ordinary importance, nor of everyday occurrence. It affects not this college only, but every college, and all the literary institutions of the country. They have flourished, hitherto, and have become in a high degree respectable and useful to the community. They have all a common principle of existence, the inviolability of their charters. It will be a dangerous, a most dangerous experiment, to hold these institutions subject to the rise and fall of popular parties, and the fluctuations of political opinions. If the franchise may be at any time taken away, or impaired, the property also may be taken away, or its use perverted. Benefactors will have no certainty of effecting the object of their bounty; and learned men will be deterred from devoting themselves to the service of such institutions, from the precarious title of their offices. Colleges and halls will be deserted by all better spirits, and become a theatre for the contention of politics. Party and faction will be cherished in the places consecrated to piety and learning. These consequences are neither remote nor possible only. They are certain and immediate.

Webster's argument is from Timothy Farrar, Report of the Case of the Trustees of Dartmouth College against William H. Woodward 282–283 (1819). Do you discern any similarities between Webster's argument here and Justice Chase's charge to the Baltimore grand jury in 1803, the charge which led to his impeachment?

2. Justice Marshall holds that the Dartmouth College charter is a contract. Can you follow his reasoning? Are you impressed with the number and scope of authorities which Justice Marshall cites in support of his arguments? Do you agree with the following assessment of Justice Marshall by Professor G. Edward White:

> The ability to "master the most complicated subjects with facility" was joined in Marshall with a certain disinclination toward academic learning and "some little propensity for indolence." His legal education consisted of a six-week lecture course given by George Wythe at William & Mary College in 1780, during which, if Marshall's notebook may be trusted, he devoted at least as much thought to the pursuit of his future wife, Polly Ambler (whose name was scrawled at prominent places throughout his law notes), as to the offerings of Mr. Wythe. As a lawyer in Virginia, and later as a judge, he was not prone to the use of legal authorities, and on several occasions his arguments in Virginia rested on no precedents at all. On the Supreme Court his "original bias," according to his colleague Story, "was to general principles and comprehensive views, rather than to technical or recondite learning."

White, The American Judicial Tradition 11 (1976) (footnotes omitted) copyright © 1976 by Oxford University Press, Inc. Reprinted by permission. If this is correct, why is Justice Marshall nearly universally regarded as the greatest Supreme Court justice?

3. After reading Marshall's opinion in this case can you explain why he decided it in the manner he did? Do you detect any sympathy for Webster's arguments?

DARTMOUTH COLLEGE v. WOODWARD (continued)

[We next consider the opinion of Mr. Justice Story. As the excerpt from his opinion begins, he is discussing the different types of corporations. Many citations are here omitted.]

*   *   *

* * * Eleemosynary corporations are such as are constituted for the perpetual distribution of the free alms and bounty of the founder, in such manner as he has directed; and in this class are ranked hospitals for the relief of poor and impotent persons, and colleges for the promotion of learning and piety, and the support of persons engaged in literary pursuits.

Another division of corporations is into public and private. Public corporations are generally esteemed such as exist for public political purposes only, such as towns, cities, parishes, and counties; and in many respects they are so, although they involve some private interests; but strictly speaking, public corporations are such only as are founded by the government for public purposes, where the whole interests belong also to the government. If, therefore, the foundation be private, though under the charter of the government, the corporation is private * * *. For instance, a bank created by the government for its own uses, whose stock is exclusively owned by the government, is, in the strictest sense, a public corporation. * * * But a bank, whose stock is owned by private persons, is a private corporation, although it is erected by the government, and its objects and operations partake of a public nature. The same doctrine may be affirmed of insurance, canal, bridge, and turnpike companies. In all these cases, the uses may, in a certain sense, be called public, but the corporations are private * * *.

This reasoning applies in its full force to eleemosynary corporations. A hospital founded by a private benefactor is, in point of law, a private corporation, although dedicated by its charter to general charity. So a college, founded and endowed in the same manner, although, being for the promotion of learning and piety, it may extend its charity to scholars from every class in the community, and thus acquire the character of a public institution. * * *

It was indeed supposed at the argument, that if the uses of an eleemosynary corporation be for general charity, this alone would constitute it a public corporation. But the law is certainly not so. * * * That the mere act of incorporation will not change the charity from a private to a public one, is most distinctly asserted in the authorities. Lord Hardwicke * * * says, "the charter of the crown cannot make a charity more or less public, but only more permanent than it would otherwise be; but it is the extensiveness, which will constitute it a public one. A devise to the poor of the parish is a public charity. Where testators leave it to the discretion of a trustee to choose out the objects, though each particular object may be said to be private, yet in the extensiveness of the benefit accruing from them, they may properly be called public charities. A sum to be disposed of by A.B. and his executors, at their discretion, among poor house-keepers, is of this kind." The charity, then, may, in this sense, be public, although it may be administered by private trustees; and, for the same reason, it may thus be public, though administered by a private corporation. The fact, then, that the charity is public, affords no proof that the corporation is also public; and, consequently, the argument, so far as it is built on this foundation, falls to the ground. If, indeed, the argument were correct, it would follow, that almost every hospital and college would be a public corporation * * *.

When, then, the argument assumes, that because the charity is public, the corporation is public, it manifestly confounds the popular, with the strictly legal sense of the terms. * * * But it is on this foundation, that a superstructure is erected, which is to compel a surrender of the cause. When the corporation is said at the bar to be public, it is merely meant, that the whole community may be the proper objects of the bounty, but that the government have the sole right, as trustees of the public interests, to regulate, control, and direct the corporation, and its funds and its franchises, at its own good will and pleasure. Now, such an authority does not exist in the government, except where the corporation is in the strictest sense public; that is, where its whole interests and franchises are the exclusive property and domain of the government itself. If it had been otherwise, Courts of law would have been spared many laborious adjudications in respect to eleemosynary corporations * * *. Nay, more, private trustees for charitable purposes would have been liable to have the property confided to their care taken away from them without any assent or default on their part, and the administration submitted, not to the control of law and equity, but to the arbitrary discretion of the government. Yet, who ever thought before, that the munificent gifts of private donors for general charity became instantaneously the property of the government; and that the trustees appointed by the donors, whether corporate or unincorporated, might be compelled to yield up their rights to whomsoever the government might appoint to administer them? If we were to establish such a principle, it would extinguish all future eleemosynary endowments * * *.

* * *

When a private eleemosynary corporation is * * * created by the charter of the crown, it is subject to no other control on the part of the crown, than what is expressly or implicitly reserved by the charter itself. Unless a power be reserved for this purpose, the crown cannot, in virtue of its prerogative, without the consent of the corporation, alter or amend the charter, or divest the corporation of any of its franchises, or add to them, or add to, or diminish, the number of the trustees, or remove any of the members, or change, or control the administration of the charity, or compel the corporation to receive a new charter. This is the uniform language of the authorities, and forms one of the most stubborn, and well settled doctrines of the common law.

* * *

We are now led to the consideration of the first question in the cause, whether this charter is a contract, within the clause of the constitution prohibiting the States from passing any law impairing the obligation of contracts. In the case of Fletcher v. Peck, [6 Cranch 87 (1810)] this Court [stated] * * * "A contract is a compact between two or more persons, and is either executory or executed. An executory contract is one, in which a party binds himself to do or not to do a particular thing. A contract executed is one in which the object of the contract is performed; and this, says Blackstone, differs in nothing from a grant. A contract executed, as well as one that is executory, contains obligations binding on the parties. A grant in its own nature amounts to an extinguishment of the right of the grantor, and implies a contract not to reassert that right. A party is always estopped by his own grant." This language is perfectly unambiguous, and was used in reference to a grant of land by the Governor of a State under a legislative act. It determines, in the most unequivocal manner, that the grant of a State is a contract within the clause of the constitution now in question, and that it implies a contract not to reassume the rights granted. *A fortiori*, the doctrine applies to a charter or grant from the king.

But it is objected, that the charter of Dartmouth College is not a contract contemplated by the constitution, because no valuable consideration passed to the king as an equivalent for the grant * * * and further, that no contracts merely voluntary are within the prohibitory clause. It must be admitted, that mere executory contracts cannot be enforced at law, unless there be a valuable consideration to sustain them; and the constitution certainly did not mean to create any new obligations, or give any new efficacy to nude pacts. But it must, on the other hand, be also admitted, that the constitution did intend to preserve all the obligatory force of contracts, which they have by the general principles of law. Now, when a contract has once passed, *bona fide,* into grant, neither the king nor any private person, who may be the grantor, can recall the grant of the property, although the conveyance may have been purely voluntary. A gift, completely executed, is irrevocable. * * * And a gift by the crown of incorporeal hereditaments, such as corporate franchises, when executed, comes completely within the principle, and is, in the strictest sense of the terms, a grant. Was it ever imagined that land, voluntarily granted to any person by a State, was liable to be resumed at its own good pleasure? Such a pretension would, under any circumstances, be truly alarming; but in a country like ours, where thousands of land titles had their origin in gratuitous grants of the States, it would go far to shake the foundations of the best settled estates. And a grant of franchises is not, in point of principle, distinguishable from a grant of any other property. If, therefore, this charter were a pure donation   *   *   *   it involved a contract, that the grantees should hold, and the grantor should not reassume the grant, as much as if it had been founded on the most valuable consideration.

But it is not admitted that this charter was not granted for what the law deems a valuable consideration. For this purpose it matters not how trifling the consideration may be; a pepper corn is as good as a thousand dollars. Nor is it necessary that the consideration should be a benefit to the grantor. It is sufficient if it import damage or loss, or forbearance of benefit, or any act done, or to be done, on the part of the grantee.   *   *   *

With these principles in view, let us now examine the terms of this charter.   *   *   *   [The charter] on its face, purports to be granted in consideration of the premises in the introductory recitals. Now, among these recitals it appears, that Dr. Wheelock had founded a charity school at his own expense, on his own estate; that divers contributions had been made in the colonies, by others, for its support; that new contributions had been made, and were making, in England for this purpose   *   *   *   that Dr. Wheelock had consented to have the school established at such other place as the trustees should select; that offers had been made by several of the governments in America, inviting the establishment of the school among them; that offers of land had also been made by divers proprietors of lands in the western parts of New Hampshire, if the school should be established there; that the trustees had finally consented to establish it in New Hampshire; and that Dr. Wheelock represented that, to effectuate the purposes of all parties, an incorporation was necessary. Can it be truly said that these recitals contain no legal consideration of benefit to the crown, or of forbearance of benefit on the other side? Is there not an implied contract by Dr. Wheelock, if a charter is granted, that the school shall be removed from his estate to New Hampshire? and that he will relinquish all his control over the funds collected, and to be collected, in England, under his auspices, and subject to his authority? that he will yield up the management of his charity school to the trustees of the college? that he will relinquish all the offers made by other American governments, and devote his patronage to this institution?   *   *   *

*   *   *

This is not all. A charter may be granted upon an executory, as well as an executed or present consideration.   *   *   *   Upon the acceptance there is an implied contract on the part of the grantees, in consideration of the charter, that they will perform the duties; and exercise the authorities conferred by it. This was the doctrine asserted by the late learned Mr. Justice Buller, in a modern case. He there said, "I do not know how to reason on this point better than in the manner urged by one of the relator's counsel, who considered the grant of incorporation to be a compact between the crown, and a certain number of the subjects, the latter of whom undertake, in consideration of the privileges which are bestowed, to exert themselves for the good government of the place," (i. e. the place incorporated.) It will not be pretended, that if a charter be granted for a bank, and the stockholders pay in their own funds, the charter is to be deemed a grant without consideration, and, therefore, revocable at the pleasure of the grantor. Yet here, the funds are to be managed, and the services performed exclusively for the use and benefit of the stockholders themselves. And where the grantees are mere trustees to perform services without reward, exclusively for the benefit of others, for public charity, can it be reasonably argued, that these services are less valuable to the government, than, if performed for the private emolument of the trustees themselves? * * *

There is yet another view of this part of the case, which deserves the most weighty consideration. The corporation was expressly created for the purpose of distributing in perpetuity the charitable donations of private benefactors. * * * The crown, then, upon the face of the charter, pledged its faith that the donations of private benefactors should be perpetually devoted to their original purposes, without any interference on its own part, and should be forever administered by the trustees of the corporation, unless its corporate franchises should be taken away by due process of law. From the very nature of the case, therefore, there was an implied contract on the part of the crown with every benefactor, that if he would give his money, it should be deemed a charity protected by the charter * * *. As soon, then, as a donation was made to the corporation, there was an implied contract springing up, and founded on a valuable consideration, that the crown would not revoke, or alter the charter, or change its administration, without the consent of the corporation. There was also an implied contract between the corporation itself, and every benefactor upon a like consideration, that it would administer his bounty according to the terms, and for the objects stipulated in the charter.

* * *

The principal objections having been thus answered satisfactorily, at least to my own mind, it remains only to declare, that my opinion, after the most mature deliberation is, that the charter of Dartmouth College, granted in 1769, is a contract within the purview of the constitutional prohibition.

* * *

The remaining inquiry is, whether the acts of the legislature of New Hampshire now in question, or any of them, impair the obligations of the charter of Dartmouth College   *   *   *.

[As you might have suspected, Justice Story finds that the Acts, in changing the methods of choosing trustees and administering the corporation, impair the obligations of the original charter.]

*   *   *

If these are not essential changes, impairing the rights and authorities of the trustees, and vitally affecting the interests and organization of Dartmouth College under its old charter, it is difficult to conceive what acts, short of an unconditional repeal of the charter, could have that effect. If a grant of land or franchises be made to A., in trust for special purposes, can the grant be revoked, and a new grant thereof be made to A., B., and C., in trust for the same purposes, without violating the obligation of the first grant? If property be vested by grant in A. and B., for the use of a college, or a hospital, of private foundation, is not the obligation of that grant impaired when the estate is taken from their exclusive management, and vested in them in common with ten other persons?   *   *   * If a bank, or insurance company, by the terms of its charter, be under the management of directors, elected by the stockholders, would not the rights acquired by the charter be impaired if the legislature should take the right of election from the stockholders, and appoint directors unconnected with the corporation? These questions carry their own answers along with them. The common sense of mankind will teach us, that all these cases would be direct infringements of the legal obligations of the grants to which they refer; and yet they are, with no essential distinction, the same as the case now at the bar.

In my judgment it is perfectly clear, that any act of a legislature which takes away any powers or franchises vested by its charter in a private corporation or its corporate officers, or which restrains or controls the legitimate exercise of them, or transfers them to other persons, without its assent, is a violation of the obligations of that charter. If the legislature mean to claim such an authority, it must be reserved in the grant. The charter of Dartmouth College contains no such reservation; and I am, therefore, bound to declare, that the acts of the legislature of New Hampshire, now in question, do impair the obligations of that charter, and are, consequently, unconstitutional and void.

In pronouncing this judgment, it has not for one moment escaped me how delicate, difficult, and ungracious is the task devolved upon us. The predicament in which this Court stands in relation to the nation at large, is full of perplexities and embarrassments. It is called to decide on causes between citizens of different States, between a State and its citizens, and between different States. It stands, therefore, in the midst of jealousies and rivalries of conflicting parties, with the most momentous interests confided to its care. Under such circumstances, it never can have a motive to do more than its duty; and, I trust, it will always be found to possess firmness enough to do that.

Under these impressions I have pondered on the case before us with the most anxious deliberation. I entertain great respect for the legislature, whose acts are in question. I entertain no less respect for the enlightened tribunal whose decision we are called upon to review. In the examination, I have endeavoured to keep my steps *super antiquas vias* of the law, under the guidance of authority and principle. It is not for judges to listen to the voice of persuasive eloquence or popular appeal. We have nothing to do but to pronounce the law as we find it; and having done this, our justification must be left to the impartial judgment of our country.

NOTES AND QUESTIONS

1. Which opinion strikes you as the more lawyer-like, that of Marshall or that of Story? Which opinion would you rather have written? Are Story's reasons for deciding the case the same as Marshall's? What is the importance of Story's distinction between public and private corporations? Why is a bank a public or a private corporation? Why does Story make so many references to banks and other types of business corporations in this opinion?

2. Once Story and Marshall's opinions pass into law, is there no way that a state legislature can alter corporate charters? Do these opinions really affect the ability of state legislatures to amend corporate charters of corporations not yet in existence? If, as Story suggests, future corporate charters may contain a clause reserving to the state legislature the right to amend or alter the charter, isn't the *Dartmouth College* case much ado about nothing? What is the meaning of the last two paragraphs of Story's opinion, where he suggests that the task of the Supreme Court is "difficult" and "ungracious?"

3. Justice Joseph Story began his political career as a Jeffersonian Republican, and was appointed to the Supreme Court by Jefferson's political heir, James Madison, in 1811. Once on the court, however, Story's views were perceived to be of a similar nationalist character to those of John Marshall, and Story's view on the common law of crimes was probably not different from those of the hard-line Federalist judges we saw in Chapter Two. See United States v. Coolidge, 25 Fed.Cas. 619 (C.C.D.Mass. 1813), reversed 14 U.S. (1 Wheat.) 415, 4 L.Ed. 124 (1816). What political views, if any, are reflected in Story's *Dartmouth College* opinion? A recent biographer of Story states that this opinion was "displayed [by him] with pride to confidents both on and off the bench." Gerald Dunne, Justice Joseph Story and the Rise of the Supreme Court 180 (1970). Mr. Dunne appears to hint that this might have had something to do with the fact that Story was, at the time he wrote this opinion, not only a Justice on the Supreme Court, but the President of the *Merchants' Bank* of Salem, Massachusetts. Id., at 181. Can you see the connection? "[B]y the stan-

dards of the day," writes Dunne of Story's presidency of the bank, "it involved no conflict with his judicial duties." Id., at 268. Would this be true today? Why the change?

2. THE CORPORATION AND ITS SHAREHOLDERS

ELLIS v. MARSHALL

Supreme Judicial Court of Massachusetts, 1807.
2 Mass. 269.

[By an 1804 Statute the Massachusetts legislature chartered a "corporation" for the purpose of making a street. The defendant, Mr. Marshall, was named as one of the "members" of the corporation, but he apparently had never consented to join. He was, however, one of the landowners adjoining the road that the corporation was to build, and a majority of such landowners *had* agreed to become members of the corporation. The Act of the legislature authorized the corporation to assess its members for the costs of building the road, and to sell the lands of members who refused to pay their assessments. Marshall refused to pay his assessments, and the corporation sold his land to the plaintiff, Ellis. Ellis brought an action in Ejectment to get possession of the property from Marshall. The court's opinion follows. Is the "corporation" involved in this case anything like what you understand by the term "corporation?" You will soon see that the court decides that Mr. Marshall could not be compelled to be a member of the corporation, and thus doesn't have to give up his land; but the interesting question is why did the plaintiff and the other members of the corporation think that he *could* be compelled to be a member?]

PARKER, J. * * * [Addressing himself to the plaintiff's two arguments: (1) that the legislature had the power to compel Marshall to become a member of the corporation, and (2) that the facts show Marshall's consent.]

* * *

The determination of the first point requires that we should ascertain the true nature and character of this legislative proceeding. If it were a public act, predicated upon a view to the general good, the question would be more difficult. If it be a private act, obtained at the solicitation of individuals, for their private emolument, or for the improvement of their estates, it must be construed, as to its effect and operation, like a grant. We are all of opinion that this was a grant or charter to the individuals who prayed for it, and those who should associate with them; and all incorporations to make turnpikes, canals, and bridges, must be so considered.

Can then one, whose name is, by mistake or misrepresentation, inserted in such an act, refuse the privileges it confers, and avoid the burdens it imposes? If he cannot, then the legislature may, at all times, press into the service of such corporations those whose lands may be wanted for such objects, whenever they may be prevailed on to insert the names of such persons by the intrigue or mistake of those more interested in the success of the object. No apprehension exists in the community that the legislature has such power. That the land of any person, over or through which a turnpike or canal may pass, may be taken for that purpose, if the legislature deem it proper, is not doubted. The constitution gives power to do this, provided compensation is made. But it was never before known that they have power over the person, to make him a member of a corporation, and subject him to taxation, *nolens volens*, for the promotion of a private enterprise.

That a man may refuse a grant, whether from the government or an individual, seems to be a principle too clear to require the support of authorities. That he may decline to improve his land, no one will doubt. Although the legislature may wisely determine that a certain use of his property will be highly beneficial to him, he has a right to judge for himself on points of this nature. The fact therefore in the case, that *Marshall* is benefited equally with the other owners by the making of this street, is of no importance. In *Bagg's* case [3] it seems to be agreed by the Court, that a patent procured by some persons of a corporation shall not bind the rest, unless they assent. And in *Brownlow's* Reports, 100, there is this passage: "It was said that inhabitants of a town cannot be incorporated without the consent of the major part of them, and an incorporation without their consent is void."

In *Comberbach,* 316, *Holt,* speaking of a new charter made to the city of *Norwich* by *Henry* 4, and confirmed by *Charles* 2, says the new charter had been void if the corporation had refused it; but when they accept it, and put it in execution, it is good.

If these principles were correct in *England* in times when prerogative ran high,—and the crown or the Parliament could not force charters or patents upon the subject without his assent,—surely in this free country, where the legislature derives its power from the people, such authority cannot be contended for.

It being, then, the opinion of the Court that this act is of a nature to require the assent of *Marshall,* either express or implied, before it can operate upon him, it is necessary to inquire into the second point, *viz.,* whether the facts agreed on in this case furnish evidence of such assent.

It is contended that the act itself, as it contains *Marshall's* name, furnishes such evidence, since it must be presumed that the legislature were satisfied on this point before they passed the act.

* * * It appearing that Marshall did not sign the petition; that he did not, in word or writing, assent to it, or to the act founded upon it; that he did not attend before the committee; and that, in the only transaction in which he noticed the corporation, he protested against its authority over him,—the presumption arising from his name being in the act is weakened, if not destroyed.

(3) Roll's Rep. 224.

It is then said that, public notice having been given of the hearing intended by the committee, his silence is evidence of his tacit assent to the passage of the act. As we are bound to presume every thing in favor of the doings of the legislature, we should think this a strong, if not a conclusive argument, if the notice given had been such as necessarily to signify to *Marshall* that he was to be included in the act prayed for. But on perusing the petition, which probably was published in the papers, we find nothing in it from which he could infer that his property or rights were to be affected, in the manner contemplated by this act. He may be considered as notified that a street was intended to be built over his ground; and all that he could infer from this was, that so much of his land as the street would pass over would be taken for this purpose, and that he would receive indemnity for it in the usual way; and that any opposition to it would be unavailing. He certainly could never have understood that it was intended to make him a member of the corporation without his consent. * * *

Upon the whole, therefore, we are of opinion that the act under which the plaintiff sets up his title could not bind Marshall without his assent; that he, having uniformly, whenever opportunity occurred, signified his dissent, is not a member of the corporation it created, was not liable to their assessments, and therefore that the sale of his land was without authority of law, and is void. According to the agreement of the parties, therefore, the plaintiff must become nonsuit, and judgment be given for costs to the defendant.

It having been said in argument that the acts relative to fencing common fields, and the act providing for the appointment of commissioners of common sewers, are within the principle of this act, it is proper to observe that we do not consider this decision as involving principles which militate with the provisions of those acts.

Those are public acts, promotive of general convenience, and operating equally upon all citizens whose property is intended to be secured or improved by them.

This is a private act, obtained at the solicitation of individuals, for their emolument or advantage.

The act relative to common fields, also, is predicated upon the assent of all who are to be affected by it; and that which provides for the appointment of commissioners of sewers gives an eventual trial by jury of all questions arising under it. These circumstances so materially vary those laws from the act under consideration, that our decisions upon the latter can by no means be considered as questioning the validity of the former.

* * *

Plaintiff nonsuit.

ANDOVER AND MEDFORD TURNPIKE CORP.
v. ABRAHAM GOULD

Supreme Judicial Court, 1809.
6 Mass. 40.

This was an action of *assumpsit*, to recover the amount of certain assessments upon the share in the said turnpike owned by the defendant, who was one of the original associates for making the same.

The cause was tried upon the general issue, before *Parker,* J., at the sitting after the last October term in this county, and a verdict found for the defendant, which was to be set aside, and a new trial granted, if the Court should be of opinion, that upon the evidence, as reported by the judge, the defendant was liable in this action.

The report states that there was regular evidence of the several assessments, and of a demand made on the defendant for payment. The only evidence produced by the plaintiffs of any promise or engagement on the part of the defendant to pay such sums as should be assessed on his share, was the subscription paper, which was in the following form, *viz.:—*

"Whereas the legislature has, at the last session, granted leave for making a turnpike road from," &c., [describing the course.] *"We, the subscribers, desirous of having the same completed as soon as possible, agree to take in said road the number of shares set against our names, and be proprietors therein.*

"*Medford*, Sept. 9, 1805."

To this paper the defendant, among others, had set his name, and against it had set *"one share."*

This being considered by the judge as insufficient to maintain the action, he directed the jury that no promise was proved in the case, either express or implied; and that the sale of the shares, as provided for by the act of incorporation, was the only remedy the corporation had for the delinquency of the defendant.

* * *

PARSONS, C. J. The question submitted to us in this case is, whether the direction of the judge to the jury was, or was not, legal.

This corporation was created by the statute of 1805, c. 14, by which six persons named, with such others as might afterwards associate with them, and their successors and assigns, are made a body corporate for the purpose of making the turnpike road. * * *

The expenses of making a turnpike road are certain, and frequently very great; and the money to defray them must be advanced, before any profit can be derived from the road; while the future toll to be received depends on the travel of passengers, and must be uncertain. The value of the shares will always depend on the expenses of making the road, compared with the expected profits from the toll. Although, when the incorporation is procured, the presumption is, that the toll will be an indemnity,—otherwise the undertakers would act a very unwise part,—yet, as this presumption may fail, it may be very reasonable for the corporation not to trust to the sale of the shares for a reimbursement of the expense, but, before any expense be incurred, to require an express undertaking from the corporators, that they will pay the several assessments on their shares. Where this express agreement has been made, we have decided that it may be enforced by action, there being a legal consideration for the contract.

Where no express agreement has been made by the corporators to pay their assessments, it has not been determined that the corporation can maintain an action to recover them, upon an implied *assumpsit* arising from their being voluntarily members of the corporation. That point is now before us, and if this should be decided against the plaintiffs, another point is made, that the subscription signed by the defendant, upon a fair construction of it, is evidence of an express agreement with the plaintiffs to pay the assessments.

If the plaintiffs can maintain this action, as upon an implied promise, it must be on the principle that the defendant is obliged by law to pay his assessment. * * *

Let us now consider whether the defendant is in law bound to pay his assessments. If he is, this obligation must result from the powers of the corporation, and the due execution of those powers. The statute creating it refers, for its powers and duties, to the statute of 1804, c. 125. All the powers and duties of the plaintiffs result from this statute, or are incident to it at common law. But very clearly a corporation has not power, as incident to it at common law, to assess for its own use a sum of money on the corporators, and compel them, by action at law, to the payment of it. To authorize this assessment, the power must be derived from the general statute. In the twelfth section, power is expressly given to choose the necessary officers, and to establish rules and regulations for the well-ordering of the affairs of the corporation.

The power to make assessments on the shares of the corporators for the use of the corporation is not in that act expressly given; but it impliedly results from the construction of the tenth section. It is there enacted that, whenever any proprietor shall neglect or refuse to pay a tax or assessment agreed on by the corporation to their treasurer in sixty days after the time set for payment, the treasurer may sell the share of the delinquent proprietor at public auction for the payment of the tax and the charges for sale. From this section we must conclude that the corporation have power to agree on a tax on the shares of the proprietors.

But it is a rule founded in sound reason, that when a statute gives a new power, and at the same time provides the means of executing it, those who claim the power can execute it in no other way. When we

find a power in the plaintiffs to make the assessments, they can enforce the payment in the method directed by the statute, and not
otherwise; and that method is by the sale of the delinquent's shares.
This rule applies to all taxes, public and private. No action can be
maintained to compel the payment of state, county, or town taxes,
except in the particular cases in which an action is expressly given by
the statute of 1789, c. 4. The same rule applies to taxes assessed by
parishes, and also, by statute of 1785, c. 53, § 3, by the proprietors of
general fields.

* * *

This rule of law is, in cases like the present, reasonable. Persons not interested in having the turnpike, either from their situation
or private property, may be requested to associate and become corporators. They may not be able to judge of the probable expenses or
profits. But if they know, that if the assessments become grievous,
they may abandon the enterprise by suffering their shares to be sold,
they may on this principle join the association. And it may be observed that it must be presumed that the legislature considered the
sale of the shares as an adequate remedy to recover the assessments;
for it is not to be supposed that corporate powers were applied for,
to subject the adventurers to a probable loss.

As we are of opinion that the plaintiffs cannot maintain this action on an implied promise, we shall now consider whether the subscription paper, upon a fair construction, is evidence of an express
promise.

The agreement there expressed is, that the subscribers will take
in the said road the number of shares set against their names,
and will be proprietors therein. These words certainly cannot
amount, upon any reasonable construction, to a promise to pay the
assessments that shall be made on their shares.

But the plaintiffs rely on the motives, expressed by the subscribers, of their taking shares and becoming proprietors. The
words are, "We the subscribers, desirous of having the said turnpike road completed as soon as possible, agree," &c. Now, perhaps
no man ever associated in a turnpike corporation without some hope
of profit; and if so, he must be desirous of having the road completed
as soon as possible, that he may be in the reception of the supposed
profits. Whether this motive to make the agreement is, or is not, expressed, it can have no effect in the construction of the contract.

We are therefore satisfied that the terms of the association do
not in law amount to an agreement to pay the assessments that may
be made on the shares.

* * *

Judgment on the verdict.

NOTES AND QUESTIONS

1. In the course of its opinion holding that Mr. Marshall could not be compelled to be a member of the road corporation the court in Ellis v. Marshall quotes a passage from Brownlow's Reports: "It was said that inhabitants of a town cannot be incorporated without the consent of the major part of them, and an incorporation without their consent is void." What relevance does a case involving a "town" have to a road corporation? Does this statement from Brownlow's Reports suggest that it was correct or incorrect to decide that Mr. Marshall could not be compelled to become a member of the road corporation?

2. Do you agree with the *Ellis* court that the situation of the corporation for construction of a road by private property holders is different in kind from the acts for fencing common fields and for commissioners of common sewers, or other corporations formed for purposes "promotive of general convenience?" Do you agree that the road corporation in *Ellis* is no different in kind from "all incorporations to make turnpikes, canals, and bridges?" Why the distinctions? Does the Ellis court classify corporations in the same manner Story did?

3. In the *Andover* case, the court indicates that it will strictly construe the powers of the corporation, and will not find a power to sue members for unpaid assessments, but will limit the corporation's remedy for unpaid assessments to sale of the delinquent member's shares. What policy does the court believe that it is encouraging by this holding? Incidentally, does the method of raising funds by assessment of members strike you as a reasonable way for a corporation to raise funds? Was it correct to rely on the analogy provided by Massachusetts statutes regarding state, county, or town taxes and general fields?

4. Is the Massachusetts court correct about the limitation on the powers of corporations at common law? In Culcullu v. Union Ins. Co., 2 Rob. 573 (La.1842), plaintiff was a judgment creditor of the Union Insurance Co., the defendant, and sought to compel one of the company's shareholders to pay money previously subscribed on shares, so that the money could be used to satisfy the judgment. The shareholder was itself a corporation, the Atchafalya Rail Road and Banking Company. When Atchafalya and the other shareholders of Union Insurance Co. originally received their shares, pursuant to the legislative charter, they each paid five dollars for each share, and gave notes for additional sums to be paid in installments until a total of $50.00 per share had been paid by each shareholder. Another provision of the charter, an act passed by the Louisiana legislature, stated that "any subscriber or stockholder who shall neglect to pay any installment * * * shall forfeit to the Company all previous payments, and shall cease to be a stockholder in said corporation, unless the Board of Directors, in their discretion, should determine to compel the payment of said subscription by suit." Atchafalya had never paid anything other than the initial $5, and argued that since the Board of Directors had never sued for additional payments, it could simply forfeit its shares and have its liability to the corporation end. The court held for the plaintiff, explaining its decision in the following language:

> A person who, with others, signs an agreement or promise to take stock in an incorporated company, thereby promises to pay

the corporation the sum necessary to cover every share set opposite to his name, and an action will lie to recover it. This point has been repeatedly decided, both in England and the United States, and rests upon the plainest principles of law and justice. 6 Barn. & Cress. 341. 1 Maule & Selwyn, 569. 9 Johns.Rep. 217. 14 Ibid. 238. 16 Mass. 94. Angel on Corporations, 293. This action may be maintained for the purpose of getting in the stock to carry on the business, or to execute the purposes for which the corporation was created, and also to pay the debts it may contract.

We are, further, of opinion, that whenever the stockholders in an incorporated company neglect or refuse to elect Directors to manage its affairs, and keep it in operation, or elect persons who will not call in the stock to pay the debts which may have been contracted, the creditors will have an action to compel them to pay, and that each will be responsible for the amount subscribed, if so much be necessary to pay the debts. It is not to be permitted to any number of individuals to get up incorporated companies for insurance, banking, or other operations, and, after enabling them to get in debt, to throw the loss upon the creditors, by refusing to pay their stock, or forfeiting it, or dissolving the corporation and releasing themselves by non-user. 2 Rob., at 202.

Is this decision consistent with Andover and Medford Turnpike Corp. v. Gould?

5. Selma and Tennessee Rail Road Co. v. Tipton, 5 Ala. 787, 39 Am. Dec. 344 (1843), involved another corporation's charter which provided a remedy for failure to pay amounts subscribed. The charter provision in question was:

"if any stockholder shall fail, or neglect to pay any instalment required to be paid, for the period of ninety days next after the same shall be due and payable, the stock on which it is demanded, shall be forfeited to the company, together with the instalments which may have been paid thereon, and a new subscription may be opened to make up such deficiency as may be caused by the non-payment aforesaid: *Provided*, that nothing in this section shall be so construed as to prevent the President and Directors of [the company] from offering for sale the stock of any defaulting stockholder, or so much thereof as may be necessary to pay such defalcation, after giving twenty days notice of the time and place of said sale, in some newspaper, and out of the proceeds of said sale, after paying the amount of such defalcation, * * * the residue, if any, shall be paid over to the said defaulting stockholder."

The defendant paid an initial $5.00 for his shares, but refused to pay additional amounts when the Board of Directors, pursuant to the plan eventually to collect an additional $95.00 on each share, made a call for a second installment. The defendant, who had originally been a director in the corporation, argued that the corporation's only remedy was to declare his shares forfeited, and sell them pursuant to the charter provision. The remaining directors disagreed, and sued him for the unpaid assessments. At the time of becoming a shareholder, the defendant had signed a "book of subscription" which indicated that he undertook to pay the full $100.00 per share, as required by the Board of Directors in installments. The exact language of the book, however, was: "We the undersigned agree to pay the sums annexed to our respective names, towards the capital stock of the Selma and Tennessee rail road company, in conformity with the provisions of the act incorporating said company." For whom would you have decided this case?

Quoting language from previous decisions, the *Selma* court declared that "it is a maxim of the common law, that an affirmative statute does not take away the common law," and that thus "the provision of the act giving to the company the right to sell the shares of a delinquent subscriber does not amount to a negative of their right to any other remedy * * *." This meant, said the court, that the company was still perfectly free to sue the subscriber, in a contract action, upon his original promise to pay the full subscription price. "A subscriber," said the court "cannot speculate upon the chances of a rise in stocks, and if the enterprise promises to be unprofitable, elect at his pleasure, to avoid a direct promise to pay by failing to meet calls made under the authority of the charter." 5 Ala., at 798–799. Does this attitude toward risk-taking by shareholders seem consistent or inconsistent with that of the court in *Andover*?

6. Suppose that you owned 100 shares of American Telephone & Telegraph Co., and that the company owed the Bank of America several million dollars on an outstanding loan. If A, T & T defaulted, could the Bank of America come after you? Why or why not?

JOSEPH STORY

Chapter 4

CONSOLIDATING THE GAINS AND EXTENDING THE BENEFITS: LAW IN THE MID–NINETEENTH CENTURY

SECTION A. THE NATURE OF NINETEENTH CENTURY LAW

SWIFT v. TYSON

United States Supreme Court, 1842.
41 U.S. (16 Pet.) 1, 10 L.Ed. 865.

Mr. Justice STORY delivered the opinion of the Court.

* * *

There is no doubt, that a bonâ fide holder of a negotiable instrument for a valuable consideration, without any notice of facts which impeach its validity as between the antecedent parties, if he takes it under an endorsement made before the same becomes due, holds the title unaffected by these facts, and may recover thereon, although as between the antecedent parties the transaction may be without any legal validity. * * *

In the present case, the plaintiff is a bonâ fide holder without notice for what the law deems a good and valid consideration, that is, for a pre-existing debt; and the only real question in the cause is, whether, under the circumstances of the present case, such a pre-existing debt constitutes a valuable consideration in the sense of the general rule applicable to negotiable instruments. We say, under the circumstances of the present case, for the acceptance having been made in New York, the argument on behalf of the defendant is, that the contract is to be treated as a New York contract, and therefore to be governed by the laws of New York, as expounded by its Courts, as well upon general principles, as by the express provisions of the thirty-fourth section of the judiciary act of 1789, ch. 20. And then it is further contended, that by the law of New York, as thus expounded by its Courts, a pre-existing debt does not constitute, in the sense of the general rule, a valuable consideration applicable to negotiable instruments. * * *

[Justice Story's discussion of individual New York cases is omitted.]

But, admitting the doctrine to be fully settled in New York, it remains to be considered, whether it is obligatory upon this Court, if it differs from the principles established in the general commercial law. It is observable that the Courts of New York do not found

367

their decisions upon this point upon any local statute, or positive, fixed, or ancient local usage: but they deduce the doctrine from the general principles of commercial law. It is, however, contended, that the thirty-fourth section of the judiciary act of 1789, ch. 20, furnishes a rule obligatory upon this Court to follow the decisions of the state tribunals in all cases to which they apply. That section provides "that the laws of the several states, except where the Constitution, treaties, or statutes of the United States shall otherwise require or provide, shall be regarded as rules of decision in trials at common law in the Courts of the United States, in cases where they apply." In order to maintain the argument, it is essential, therefore, to hold, that the word "laws," in this section, includes within the scope of its meaning the decisions of the local tribunals. In the ordinary use of language it will hardly be contended that the decisions of Courts constitute laws. They are, at most, only evidence of what the laws are; and are not of themselves laws. They are often reexamined, reversed, and qualified by the Courts themselves, whenever they are found to be either defective, or ill-founded, or otherwise incorrect. The laws of a state are more usually understood to mean the rules and enactments promulgated by the legislative authority thereof, or long established local customs having the force of laws. In all the various cases which have hitherto come before us for decision, this Court have uniformly supposed, that the true interpretation of the thirty-fourth section limited its application to state laws strictly local, that is to say, to the positive statutes of the state, and the construction thereof adopted by the local tribunals, and to rights and titles to things having a permanent locality, such as the rights and titles to real estate, and other matters immovable and intraterritorial in their nature and character. It never has been supposed by us, that the section did apply, or was designed to apply, to questions of a more general nature, not at all dependent upon local statutes or local usages of a fixed and permanent operation, as, for example, to the construction of ordinary contracts or other written instruments, and especially to questions of general commercial law, where the state tribunals are called upon to perform the like functions as ourselves, that is, to ascertain upon general reasoning and legal analogies, what is the true exposition of the contract or instrument, or what is the just rule furnished by the principles of commercial law to govern the case. And we have not now the slightest difficulty in holding, that this section, upon its true intendment and construction, is strictly limited to local statutes and local usages of the character before stated, and does not extend to contracts and other instruments of a commercial nature, the true interpretation and effect whereof are to be sought, not in the decisions of the local tribunals, but in the general principles and doctrines of commercial jurisprudence. Undoubtedly, the decisions of the local tribunals upon such subjects are entitled to, and will receive, the most deliberate attention and respect of this Court; but they cannot furnish positive rules, or conclusive authority, by which our own judgments are to be bound up and governed. The law respecting negotiable instruments may be truly declared in the language of Cicero, adopted by Lord Mansfield in Luke v. Lyde, 2 Burr.R. 883, 887, to be in a great measure, not the law of a single country only, but of the commercial world. * * *

It becomes necessary for us, therefore, upon the present occasion to express our own opinion of the true result of the commercial law upon the question now before us. And we have no hesitation in saying, that a pre-existing debt does constitute a valuable consideration in the sense of the general rule already stated, as applicable to negotiable instruments. Assuming it to be true * * * that the holder of a negotiable instrument is unaffected with the equities between the antecedent parties, of which he has no notice, only where he receives it in the usual course of trade and business for a valuable consideration, before it becomes due; we are prepared to say, that receiving it in payment of, or as security for a pre-existing debt, is according to the known usual course of trade and business. And why upon principle should not a pre-existing debt be deemed such a valuable consideration? It is for the benefit and convenience of the commercial world to give as wide an extent as practicable to the credit and circulation of negotiable paper, that it may pass not only as security for new purchases and advances, made upon the transfer thereof, but also in payment of and as security for pre-existing debts. The creditor is thereby enabled to realize or to secure his debt, and thus may safely give a prolonged credit, or forbear from taking any legal steps to enforce his rights. The debtor also has the advantage of making his negotiable securities of equivalent value to cash. But establish the opposite conclusion, that negotiable paper cannot be applied in payment of or as security for pre-existing debts, without letting in all the equities between the original and antecedent parties, and the value and circulation of such securities must be essentially diminished, and the debtor driven to the embarrassment of making a sale thereof, often at a ruinous discount, to some third person, and then by circuity to apply the proceeds to the payment of his debts. What, indeed, upon such a doctrine would become of that large class of cases, where new notes are given by the same or by other parties, by way of renewal or security to banks, in lieu of old securities discounted by them, which have arrived at maturity? Probably more than one-half of all bank transactions in our country, as well as those of other countries, are of this nature. The doctrine would strike a fatal blow at all discounts of negotiable securities for pre-existing debts.

This question has been several times before this Court, and it has been uniformly held, that it makes no difference whatsoever as to the rights of the holder, whether the debt for which the negotiable instrument is transferred to him is a pre-existing debt, or is contracted at the time of the transfer. In each case he equally gives credit to the instrument. The cases of Coolidge v. Payson, 2 Wheaton, R. 66, 70, 73, and Townsley v. Sumrall, 2 Peters, R. 170, 182, are directly in point.

In England the same doctrine has been uniformly acted upon. * * *

*   *   *

In the American Courts, so far as we have been able to trace the decisions, the same doctrine seems generally but not universally to prevail. In Brush v. Scribner, 11 Conn.R. 388, the Supreme Court of Connecticut, after an elaborate review of the English and New York adjudications, held, upon general principles of commercial law, that a pre-existing debt was a valuable consideration, sufficient to convey a valid title to a bonâ fide holder against all the antecedent parties to a negotiable note. There is no reason to doubt, that the same rule has been adopted and constantly adhered to in Massachusetts; and certainly there is no trace to be found to the contrary. In truth, in the silence of any adjudications upon the subject, in a case of such frequent and almost daily occurrence in the commercial states, it may fairly be presumed, that whatever constitutes a valid and valuable consideration in other cases of contract to support titles of the most solemn nature, is held à fortiori to be sufficient in cases of negotiable instruments, as indispensable to the security of holders, and the facility and safety of their circulation. Be this as it may, we entertain no doubt, that a bonâ fide holder, for a pre-existing debt, of a negotiable instrument, is not affected by any equities between the antecedent parties, where he has received the same before it became due, without notice of any such equities. We are all, therefore, of opinion, that the question on this point, propounded by the Circuit Court for our consideration, ought to be answered in the negative; and we shall accordingly direct it so to be certified to the Circuit Court.

NOTES AND QUESTIONS

1. A complete understanding of the particular legal point involved in this case is not crucial to an appreciation of the importance of Swift v. Tyson, but some remarks on the legal issue might help to clarify this apparently esoteric matter of commercial exchange. The case arose because the plaintiff, Mr. Swift, had been refused payment when he attempted to cash a bill of exchange, a negotiable instrument something like a check. The bill of exchange had not originally been made out to Swift, but Swift acquired rights in it because it had been "endorsed" (signed over to him) by the man to whom it originally belonged, one Norton. The bill of exchange was, in effect, an order to Mr. Tyson (on whom it was "drawn") to pay a certain amount of money to Norton, or to anyone to whom Norton might legally endorse the bill. For our purposes, we can assume that Tyson refused to pay Swift because he claimed that Swift had not given Norton sufficient consideration to support the transfer to Swift, since Swift had given Norton nothing new for the bill, although Norton *had* received something from Swift some time prior to the endorsement of the

bill. It was conceded by Swift that by the law of negotiable instruments, in order for an endorsee to have the legal rights to sue on a bill of exchange, free from any legal disabilities of the previous holders of the bill, the endorsee had to furnish valuable consideration. The question in the case then became, simply, whether the pre-existing debt which Norton owed Swift constituted such valuable consideration. The court decisions on this point differed. There had been some decisions of New York courts which had held that a pre-existing debt could *not* constitute the requisite consideration. Our real interest is in answering the question, "Why wasn't Story inclined to follow the New York decisions?"

2. Most law students know the case of Swift v. Tyson chiefly as a decision that was "correctly" overruled by the United States Supreme Court in Erie Railroad Co. v. Tompkins, 304 U.S. 64, 58 S.Ct. 817, 82 L.Ed. 1188 (1938). Many of them learn that Erie v. Tompkins not only overruled a case, but also overruled a particular way of looking at the common law. In *Swift,* it has been said, Justice Story was reflecting the position that "there is one august corpus" of law; "a transcendental body of law outside of any particular state but obligatory within it unless and until changed by statute * * *." Black & White Taxicab & Transfer Co. v. Brown & Yellow Taxicab and Transfer Co., 276 U.S. 518, 532–34, 48 S.Ct. 404, 408, 409, 72 L.Ed. 681 (1928) (Holmes, J. dissenting). In other words, so the critics of Swift v. Tyson were once given to arguing, Story believed in a "brooding omnipresence" of the law, a common law that existed like some Platonic form, of which certain state courts could see only dim shadows, like the men in Plato's cave. Is this characterization of Story's opinion accurate? Would Story apply the conceptions in his *Swift* opinion in any other contexts?

3. You have already read Story's opinion in *Dartmouth College.* Are there similar jurisprudential principles being applied by Story in that case? Would Story consider most of the private law developments reviewed in Chapter Three to be "local law," or emanations of "general principles and doctrines?" What, by the way, do you suppose would be the sources of "general principles and doctrines," and who might determine their content?

NOTE, SWIFT v. TYSON EXHUMED *

79 Yale L.J. 284 (1969).

* * *

* * * From 1818 to 1823, three decisions suggested that the deference given to state court decisions by the Supreme Court was a matter of gracious acquiescence not compelled by statute or Constitution. But in Jackson v. Chew in 1827, the Court held, in a well-reasoned opinion by Justice Thompson, that the federal courts must follow settled principles of state law with regard to construction of transfers of land by will. Justice Thompson relied somewhat disingenuously on

* Reprinted by permission of the Yale Law Journal Company and Fred B.   Rothman & Company from the Yale Law Journal.

> the rule which has uniformly governed this court, that where any principle of law, establishing a rule of real property, has been settled in the state courts, the same rule will be applied by this court, that would be applied by the state tribunals. This is a principle so obviously just, and so indispensably necessary, under our system of government, that it cannot be lost sight of.

The Supreme Court had always followed state courts' constructions of their own statutes; Justice Thompson saw no reason why the Court should not honor state constructions of transfers of land as well "when [a federal court] is applying settled rules of real property."

What emerges from Jackson v. Chew is a policy in favor of the stability of land titles rather than against federal interference with state law in general. Certainly there is no suggestion that deference to state court decisions is compelled by the theory of federalism. Even in the area of land title the Court characterized its actions as "acquiescence," and cautioned that it would acquiesce readily if state decisions could be reconciled with English law, reluctantly if not. By the 1830's, however, all reservations about applying the state law of land titles had disappeared, and the Supreme Court followed settled local rules about wills and statutes of limitations, of uses, and of frauds, even when it believed the state rule unreasonable. Nevertheless, the case law before 1842 did not justify Justice McLean's dictum that "it is clear, there can be no common law of the United States." Strictly read, the cases established a rule about property in land which was justified on independent grounds concerning the policy of stability in land title, without reference to a theory of federalism.

Swift v. Tyson presented a simple question of contract law involving the validity of past consideration. New York law was almost certainly against plaintiff, though the rule elsewhere, which his counsel contended was the general commercial law, favored him. Plaintiff argued that the Supreme Court should construe Section 34 to cover only statutes, not simply because the language of the section supported such a construction, but for broader reasons as well:

> How can this court preserve its control over the reason and the people of the United States; that control in which its usefulness consists, and which its own untrammeled learning and judgment would enable it naturally to maintain; if its records show that it has decided * * * the same identical question, arising on a bill of exchange, first one way, and then another, with vacillating inconsistency? In what light will the judicial character of the United States appear abroad, under such circumstances?

* * *

Despite some uncertainty in the New York law, Justice Story assumed that the state law was against plaintiff, presumably out of respect for the lower court's decision. He then construed Section 34 as referring to statutes and constructions thereof, and "to rights and titles to things having a permanent locality, such as rights and titles to real estate, and other matters immovable and intraterritorial in their nature and character." Most critics of *Swift* contend that Story's jurisprudence was unsound, that he believed there existed, outside and independent of the decisions of courts, some entity called The Common Law. But this misconceives Story's approach to the case. The core of the opinion makes it clear that he was concerned with the functions inherent in a court, and not with the existence of a transcendent body of law.

* * *

To Story it would demean the Supreme Court to preclude it from "general reasoning and legal analogies": as a court it *must* reason and analogize. Federal jurisdiction over civil cases under the common law existed neither to promote uniformity nor to enforce a nationalist theory of federalism. *Swift* meant that federal courts could draw on cases arising in all jurisdictions, English, state, and federal, and need not consider themselves limited to cases arising in the state where the action was brought. It had little to do with the existence of an entity called The Law; it dealt with the materials available for a federal court to use when it acted as courts must act.

To read *Swift* as an unlimited victory for national supremacy is misleading. As historians since Charles Warren have found, the major concern of the Taney Court was to develop doctrines which, while maintaining the power of the federal government, would leave the states some scope for regulation and innovation. The development of commerce-clause doctrine provides the clearest example of this. When the Marshall Court was confronted with what it saw as challenges to federal power, it had attempted to find a conflict between state regulation and some federal statute, and had rejected the extreme position that the dormant commerce power precluded any state regulation of interstate commerce. The Taney Court made the notion of the police power of the states more explicit, and finally adopted Justice Curtis' formulation, that states could regulate subjects not "in their nature national, [nor which] admit only of one uniform system." State and nation could regulate commerce jointly unless there was either a conflict inherent in the subject matter, where congressional inaction had to be taken as a specific policy of non-regulation, or an actual conflict. Such a recognition of the dual sovereignties in the commercial field strongly suggests a similar interpretation of *Swift*.

Though on its face *Swift* appears to be an expansion of federal power *tout court*, it need not be so treated. In 1842, it could not be predicted with certainty that the federal common law which was to be developed in the future would conflict with the common law of any state. This uncertainty is precisely what gives *Swift* its importance in the intellectual development of American law. * * * *Swift* gave federal courts the power to develop the common law in isolation from the confusion and ideological partisanship of the state judicial systems. But it also left the future substance of federal law unclear * * *.

NOTES AND QUESTIONS

1. The author of this note, Professor Mark Tushnet, argues that the conventional ideas about Swift v. Tyson—(1) that it was based on an "erroneous" construction of Section 34 of the Judiciary Act of 1789, (2) that its jurisprudential basis is inconsistent with "modern ideas about the nature of law derived from Austin and Holmes," and (3) that its view of federal-state relations is unacceptable—"miss the point." What do you suppose Tushnet believes is the "point" of Swift v. Tyson?

2. Tushnet stresses Story's desire to maintain the ability for the Supreme Court to act "as courts *must* act." Why would that desire be so strong for Story? How should courts "act?"

3. What is the virtue of a common law which could "develop * * * in isolation from the confusion and ideological partisanship of state judicial systems?" Does the fact that *Swift* concerns commercial law seem especially important? Is it troubling to you that *Swift* might also leave the future substance of federal law unclear? On the basis of what you have read so far, why or why not? Compare the views of Professor Morton Horwitz, described in the next two excerpts, with that of Professor Randall Bridwell, given in the third.

MORTON HORWITZ, THE RISE OF LEGAL FORMALISM *

19 Am.J.Leg.Hist. 251–253 (1975).

For seventy or eighty years after the American Revolution the major direction of common law policy reflected the overthrow of eighteenth century pre-commercial and anti-developmental common law values. As political and economic power shifted to merchant and entrepreneurial groups in the post-revolutionary period, they began to forge an alliance with the legal profession to advance their own interests through a transformation of the legal system.

By around 1850, that transformation was largely complete. Legal rules providing for the subsidization of enterprise and permitting the legal destruction of old forms of property for the benefit of more recent entrants had triumphed. Anti-commercial legal doctrines had been destroyed or undermined and the legal system had almost completely shed its eighteenth century commitment to regulating the substantive fairness of economic exchange. Legal relations that had once been conceived of as deriving from natural law or custom were

* Published in the American Journal of Legal History, Copyright © 1975 by Temple University. Reprinted with the permission of the publisher and the author. Reprinted as Chapter VIII of Morton Horwitz, The Transformation of American Law 1780–1860 (1977).

increasingly subordinated to the disproportionate economic power of individuals or corporations that were allowed the right to "contract out" of many existing legal obligations. Law, once conceived of as protective, regulative, paternalistic and, above all, a paramount expression of the moral sense of the community, had come to be thought of as facilitative of individual desires and as simply reflective of the existing organization of economic and political power.

This transformation in American law both aided and ratified a major shift in power in an increasingly market-oriented society. By the middle of the nineteenth century the legal system had been reshaped to the advantage of men of commerce and industry at the expense of farmers, workers, consumers and other less powerful groups within the society. Not only had the law come to establish legal doctrines that maintained the new distribution of economic and political power, but, wherever it could, it actively promoted a legal redistribution of wealth against the weakest groups in the society.

The rise of legal formalism can be fully correlated with the attainment of these substantive legal changes. If a flexible, instrumental conception of law was necessary to promote the transformation of the post-revolutionary American legal system, it was no longer needed once the major beneficiaries of that transformation had obtained the bulk of their objectives. Indeed, once successful, those groups could only benefit if both the recent origins and the foundations in policy and group self-interest of all newly established legal doctrines could be disguised. There were, in short, major advantages in creating an intellectual system which gave common law rules the appearance of being self-contained, apolitical, and inexorable, and which, by making "legal reasoning seem like mathematics," conveyed "an air * * * of * * * inevitability" about legal decisions.

* * *

The sources of legal formalism as it developed after 1850 can be traced to a much earlier bifurcation of American legal thought, for in reality two competing ideological tendencies operated on American law after the Revolution. The first, which dominated the law until around 1850, was largely shaped by the efforts of mercantile and industrial groups to capture and transform the system of private law that existed in 1776.

In commercial law, entrepreneurial groups from the beginning sought to change the law inherited from the colonial period and to restrict the power of the state to enforce substantive standards of fair dealing. They also regularly sought the state's aid in creating a more efficient system of debt collection, and, after the Panic of 1819, they strongly increased their enthusiasm for bankruptcy legislation, seeking, however, to limit its benefits to "merchants and traders." In general, the course of commercial law during the nineteenth century was to perfect the remedial system while circumscribing the power of courts—and, far more importantly, legislatures—to intervene substantively.

In property and tort law, the interventionist state was inseparably linked to the earliest goals of low cost development. In this area, it was the constant aspiration of the developers first to seek as much support for change as they could from the courts, while only involving the more politically volatile legislatures when they could not. It is remarkable how well they succeeded. The basic system of tort and property law (other than rules of inheritance and systems of title recordation) was judicially created. And, by and large, it was strongly geared to the aspirations of those that benefited most from low cost economic development.

These efforts to overthrow pre-commercial and anti-developmental legal doctrines and institutions powerfully supported the instrumentalist character of private law before the Civil War. A second, seemingly contradictory, tendency, however, was also established quite early in post-revolutionary constitutional law. By forging constitutional doctrines under the Contracts Clause barring retroactive laws and giving constitutional status to "vested rights," this line of intellectual development sought basically to limit the ability of the legal system—more specifically of the legislature—to bring about redistributions of wealth.   *   *   *

While commercial and entrepreneurial interests thus saw the private law shaped to their own needs and interests, they managed also to derive the benefits of an anti-distributive ideology developed in public law. One cannot but be struck by the sharp contrast between the utilitarian and instrumentalist character of early nineteenth century private law and the equally emphatic anti-utilitarian, formalistic cast of public law. If public law during this period was dominated by a conservative fear that legislatures might invade "vested property rights"—that is, that it might be used to redistribute wealth for equalitarian ends— the reality of the private law system was that it invariably tolerated and occasionally encouraged disguised forms of judicially sanctioned economic redistribution that actually increased inequality.

More than any other jurist of the nineteenth century, Joseph Story brought each of these two contradictory tendencies to their highest fulfillment. His private law opinions are, by and large, highly utilitarian and self-consciously attuned to the goals of promoting pro-commercial and developmental legal doctrines. By contrast, his public law opinions are usually starkly formalistic, often antiquarian, and therefore have frequently puzzled historians by running contrary to the supposed "prevailing economic needs" of his day.

These differences between the character of public and private law, however, can be traced directly to an underlying conviction held by all orthodox nineteenth century legal thinkers that the course of

American legal change should, if possible, be developed by courts and not by legislatures. The persistent formalism of public law, in short, was related to the infinitely greater threat of redistribution that statutory interferences with the economy represented.

* * *

STEPHEN PRESSER, REVISING THE CONSERVATIVE TRADITION: TOWARDS A NEW AMERICAN LEGAL HISTORY *

52 N.Y.U.L.Rev. 700 (1977).

Dark and Doestoyevskyan is the world of Morton Horwitz. In The Transformation of American Law, Professor Horwitz portrays nineteenth-century private law as a battleground where God and the Devil fight over the soul of man. Legal principles are subverted (p. 99), "class bias" prevails (p. 188), and "gross disparities of bargaining power" are brushed behind a facade of "neutral and formal rules" (p. 201). In sum, legal power is ruthlessly exercised to bring about economic redistributions, by powerful groups who carefully "disguise" their activities from the majority of Americans (p. 266). When all of this is over, the forces of goodness and morality in private law have been completely thrashed by emergent entrepreneurial and commercial groups, who manage "to win a disproportionate share of wealth and power in American society" (p. xvi).

* * *

Obvious questions are raised by this description of the American common law's fashioning and dismantling of legal rights in the service of economic growth. How was it that judges could be so obviously inconsistent in their adherence to legal doctrines? How could rational men so cavalierly condone the creation and destruction of important legal rights? Horwitz answers these questions with his theory of the lawyer-merchant alliance.

In colonial times, Horwitz explains, lawyers chiefly served the interests of landed wealth. The common law rules enforced in the courts were suited to this service, and were not particularly hospitable to other areas of economic exchange, such as trade, finance, and manufacturing (pp. 140–41). As a consequence, merchants employed their own mechanisms for dispute settlement, like arbitration and penal bonds. The common law even encouraged this self-regulation by permitting the practice of "struck" juries—juries composed solely of members of the merchant class.

After about 1790, however, the merchant and entrepreneurial classes began to seek advice from lawyers in such matters as marine insurance and speculation in state securities (pp. 140–41, 174). This shift in their clientele encouraged lawyers (and thus courts) to focus more closely on commercial interests. * * * The effect of specialization in the commercial community was to diminish the role of self-regulation, since the increasing fragmentation of interest made consensus difficult to achieve. This drove merchants to litigation, and thus gave lawyers and courts a more prominent role in the settlement of commercial disputes.

* * * Jury discretion became strictly limited to matters of fact; all questions of law were reserved for the court. Cutting back the role of the jury, Horwitz argues, enhanced the prospects for certainty and predictability of judicial decisions, thus promoting merchant resort to the courts. At the same time, the courts' consolidation of their law-declaring function explains the increasing hostility to extra-judicial dispute settlement, manifested by refusals to enforce arbitration awards or to permit struck juries.

The increasing judicial hostility to merchants' settling their own disputes did not, however, reflect a more general hostility to merchants. In his most provocative stroke, Horwitz argues that the exact opposite inference should be made. Perhaps seeing where the future of lucrative legal practice lay, the courts embarked on a program of writing a procommercial common law. * * * This procommercial transformation of the common law was most striking in the area with the most immediate impact on trade—the law of contracts. Horwitz forcefully maintains that, despite ostensible justification in the needs of the whole society, the procommercial transformation in contracts disproportionately benefitted the newly blessed merchant and entrepreneurial interests.

* * *

For these commercial doctrines to triumph, Horwitz believes, their political implications had to be disguised to an extent that has completely escaped contemporary historians. The chief instrument of deception was the fiction that in implementing commercial doctrines, judges were merely applying "scientific" general principles of law. This attitude, Horwitz argues (pp. 245–50), occurs as early as 1842 in Chief Justice Story's opinion in Swift v. Tyson. In *Swift*, Story overruled New York decisions on the basis of a "general" commercial law that, Story said, the federal courts were qualified to expound authoritatively. In Horwitz's view, *Swift* was designed to impose procommercial doctrines on reluctant state courts (p. 250), but in light of the prevailing anticommercial attitudes in the states, it was premature.

Horwitz's final chapter details the eventual victory of the attitudes reflected in Swift v. Tyson. In the first half of the nineteenth century, the ease with which early nineteenth-century private law decisions dispensed with contrary precedent had bothered some of the more conservative and "scientifically minded" treatise writers. These commentators felt that, for law to call itself a science, it was at least necessary for rules and doctrines to be consistently applied (p. 258).

In the beginning of the nineteenth century, this conservative attitude was reflected in the law as well as the treatises, although its ambit was restricted to a strain of constitutional law doctrines that protected vested rights from public appropriation (p. 255). The *Dartmouth College* case is a fine example of this trend. Private law, however, had played fast and loose with vested rights, and seemed to set them aside with impunity. By about 1850, according to Horwitz, the lawyer-merchant alliance, having secured most of the things it wanted out of private law, made the tactical decision to freeze legal doctrines where they were. The adherence to precedent required by this strategy dovetailed nicely with the treatise writers' "scientific" attitudes, and with the lawyers' aspirations to the mantle of non-political professionals. So it was that the conservative doctrines of public law began to merge with private law. By the middle of the century, the same notion of protection of vested rights prevailed in both private law and constitutional cases, and the inventiveness of early nineteenth-century private law was no more. No longer would judges rewrite the rules of property, torts, and contracts to conform with their notions of social policy. Now, with the advent of "formalism," *stare decisis* would be the rule, the inherent redistributive dangers of an expansive private law would be diminished, and the lawyer-merchant alliance would be able to consolidate its gains.

* * *

R. RANDALL BRIDWELL, THEME v. REALITY IN AMERICAN LEGAL HISTORY *

53 Ind.L.J. 450, 473–487 (1978).

* * *

As Professor Horwitz correctly observes, "One of the most interesting and puzzling developments in all of American legal history is the appearance of the Supreme Court's decision in Swift v. Tyson in 1842." As a case brought under the diversity of citizenship jurisdiction, *Swift* raised questions about the effect of local or state common law rules and, should state law be inapplicable, the content of potentially alternative rules of decision. Horwitz attempts to analyse both the independence of the federal judiciary from peculiar "localized" rules of commercial law, which would have in the absence of diversity jurisdiction been applied by state courts, and the *appar-*

ent variations in the opinions of the Supreme Court about the status and content of the general commercial law. However, he does so within the "transformation" dialectic applied to state cases. Further, this shift from purely state cases to the federal opinions involves a set of totally new relationships between the federal and state governments and, in the context of the diversity jurisdiction, among the states themselves—a point either generally unknown to or ignored by Professor Horwitz.

* * *

In the context of Horwitz's thesis, the basic issue is this: was there a growing body of transcendent legal rules known as the "general commercial law" which was acknowledged by the federal courts and which would literally supercede otherwise applicable state rules of law, and if this is so, is this evidence of a willingness of the federal courts, like their state bretheren, to engage in self conscious, interest-oriented judicial legislation?

* * *

In order to deal with this dual question it is necessary to first consider the true scope of the federal power in regard to diversity jurisdiction. In Swift v. Tyson, Mr. Justice Story construed § 34 of the Judiciary Act of 1789 to make certain local laws obligatory in the federal courts, but to exclude certain kinds of laws from its operation. Justice Story regarded as obligatory "the positive statutes of the state * * *" and state cases construing them, and laws pertaining "to things having a permanent locality," such as real estate, *and* other "matters * * * intraterritorial in their nature." Contrariwise, nothing required the federal courts to follow state laws applicable "to questions of a more general nature." Furthermore, Story clearly did not make the distinction between statutes and case law determinative of what was obligatory, but rather included both within the scope of the obligation to follow local law. The obligation was determined by the nature of the question and not by the nature of the legal pronouncement.

In the first place, Story referred not only to statutes as obligatory but also [to] "established local customs having the force of laws." Further it was clear that there was a distinct interplay between extraterritorial matters and local customs, which could become sufficiently developed and certain to counteract the general principles, in which case they would control. Additionally, commercial cases arising under the diversity jurisdiction were by definition extraterritorial to the sovereignty of any single state. Clearly Justice Story recognized that this implicated a pool of case law including but not limited to that of any given states, and called for an independent judgment on the part of the federal courts. In such cases "the state tribunals are called upon to perform the like function as ourselves, that is, to ascertain upon general reasoning and legal analogies, what is the true exposition of the contract or instrument, or what is the just rule furnished by the principles of commercial law to govern the case." To have done otherwise would have been to abdicate their primary function in diversity cases—to insure impartial justice between citizens of different states.

Equally important, however, was the recognition of a variety of subject matters which were or could be "localized" by a state, so that the local rule could be obligatory on the federal courts. Most importantly, "localization" required a *particular form* of local pronouncement about the legal issue in question *and* a congruity between the commercial and private international law conflict principles. A body of interstate common law rules dictated when and under what circumstances one state could localize a transaction *vis a vis* another. The case law taken as a whole reveals that federal courts would defer to localization, by statute or judicial decision, only in accordance with general conflict of laws principles. * * * Under these conceptions, sufficiently clear local laws—either statutes or decisions—would be obligatory when they pertained to matters local per se, such as real property within the state, and where they pertained to certain features of commercial transactions as well. The federal case law makes it clear that the judges were concerned with determining which set of potentially relevant rules the private parties may legitimately have assumed were relevant to their transaction. In cases where an articulate localization had taken place, even if the rule thereby promulgated differed from the general rules of the law merchant, and the shared extraterritorial rules of sovereignty—the conflict of laws rules—pointed to the state where the localization had occurred, the rule would be followed, but not otherwise. Thus, rather than the "either-or" conflict between the transcendent and instrumental general law and applicable local law, the pattern that *actually* emerged was one in which parties to commercial transactions were obligated under the conflict of laws principles which controlled commercial cases to look to the appropriate state, in order to determine whether there had been a localization by statute or custom, of the relevant controlling law. If none was found, it could be presumed that the general custom prevailing in the commercial world would be applied, at least in the federal courts in cases within the diversity jurisdiction. This did not, of course, eliminate all uncertainty from interstate commercial dealings; but it did provide a regularized, relatively coherent system within which the expectations of the parties to various commercial transactions could be generally preserved intact. Moreover, it provided ample space for local variations from general commercial jurisprudence, enforceable in both state and federal courts, thus securing the only important state and party interests in the application of local rules.

* * *

Critical to the understanding of the actual significance of the general commercial law and conflict of laws principles as employed by the federal judiciary and their relationship to the source of legal obligation is an understanding of the relationship between these subjects and the law of nations generally. Just as the law of nations must deal with multinational transactions, the creation of a federal government in the United States required a means of dealing with multistate transactions. The means employed were not novel in that they followed the pattern set by international law, and followed a pattern of judicial decision-making which repeated the earlier incorporation of multinational principles in the English common law. In understanding the role of commercial law as a part of the law of nations, it is important to recognize that there was originally no sharp distinction drawn between civil admiralty and maritime jurisprudence and commercial law. They were one and the same jurisprudence, and only after the passage of time did they become thought of as separate parts of international law. Consequently, because commercial law was originally customary law, and because it was also a branch of private international law, it was dealt with in the same fashion by the courts as cases within the general customary system of common law adjudication.

Similarly there was eventually a clear identity of function between substantive commercial law rules and conflict of laws rules which governed their application. It was thus quite appropriate for eminent writers on these subjects to describe conflict of laws doctrine as but a "branch of commercial law." The conflict of laws rules designed to serve legitimate party expectations and intentions by making it universally obvious which of the potentially involved substantive rules applied to any given case. The commercial law rules interacted with the conflict of laws rules to serve this end. This was possible because of the increasingly regular, stereotyped forms which the commercial law had in many of its aspects assumed. It had become, as it were, a sort of international or interstate language, which enabled the parties to engage in "reciprocal orientation of their actions" across state lines.

For example, it was clear to parties in commerce from the facts of a transaction, particularly the forms by which it was conducted, whether or not it pertained to an extraterritorial as opposed to a purely municipal or local set of governing rules. Various sets of rules, including customary ones both recorded and unrecorded in precedent, were present to govern or control [al]most any transaction, and the conflict of laws principles when logically applied to a given transaction revealed whether it was confined to a particular sovereign or not. Thus, in creating a negotiable bill of exchange, certain commonly recognized features were necessary before the instrument became negotiable, a quality considered to be the very essence of such an instrument, and to constitute "its true character." Such terms as "or order" and "or bearer" were, according to the general or extraterritorial methods of commerce, essential to negotiability. The form which the transaction assumed according to the common multistate language of commerce determined whether its consequences were to be measured by one set of rules or another, that is by particular, or local, as opposed to general, or multistate rules.

* * * Indeed, the employment of common rules either implicitly or explicitly observed by all concerned sovereigns to mitigate the inevitable differences in the substantive rules and their application among different nations and states, was essential to the successful settlement of multistate problems. The form in which a particular multistate transaction was conducted would in the contemplation of *both* the state and federal courts implicate a body of law which no state alone was constitutionally competent to supply because of the limiting conception of sovereign authority embodied in private international law rules.

This will, if properly understood, explain why the various state cases were not thought to be in direct conflict with some obligatory pronouncement about the correct rule of general commercial law by a federal diversity court and why most state decisions were not in any case obligatory on the federal diversity courts. Professor Horwitz's "Federal Court v. Local Rule" metaphor is, it will be observed, entirely inaccurate. To fully understand the litigation in the early federal cases, it must be understood that the ability to discern in advance which body of rules and usages would be deemed relevant to a transaction was the key to understanding the early commercial decisions. * * *

The value of a judicial decision as precedent in extraterritorial cases was determined with reference to a wider field of data and by different standards than was the case with purely municipal rules, and this was so without affecting any considerations of federalism whatsoever. It is enough for our present purpose to note the implication of prevailing extraterritorial custom through the use of well understood transactional forms and the role this played in judicial settlement of private disputes. Quite naturally the federal court sitting in a diversity case which *per se* involved *some* multistate elements (and usually in the commercial law cases actually involved in interstate or multistate transaction) would have to determine what the appropriate source of the governing rule was, and by adverting to the presumptively applicable multistate rules of a customary origin in such cases should not be confused with a pretension to "make" the governing law by blatantly ignoring a local state rule. Further, in deciding controversies within the context of this multistate customary system, state judges would thus resort to extraterritorial considerations, and in so doing they did not manifest the act of a sovereign "freezing" a rule within its geographical power to do so, but rather acted in a cooperative fashion in an area over which they could not pretend absolute authority. The originally non-sovereign origin of commercial rules in the common law process, of course, accounts for the fact that judicial opinions were not referred to as laws but only as evidence of the law, and this aphorism was even more apt in the state cases admittedly dealing with transactions over which the state involved could not pretend any absolute authority, that is in cases involving extraterritorial or multistate rules. Thus, if a large portion of the common law rules involved "interstate common law," then federal judicial exegesis of the principles contained in these rules posed no direct conflict with state sovereignty at all. And more to the point, such cases cannot be construed as examples of judicial creativity in conflict with presumptively applicable state rules, because under such an interpretation the conflict is absent. At least no more of a conflict or deviation from state case law would be represented than is present in the *ordinary* common law process of construing precedent which takes place *within* the state. * * *

Under this view of the commercial law as originally customary law, and as subject to the common law process, the nature of diversity jurisdiction in commercial cases should be apparent. In a customary law system in which the purpose of a grant of subject matter jurisdiction is to protect nonresidents from local bias, it would be essential that the intentions and expectations of the parties to every dispute be determined by a tribunal independent of the apprehended local prejudice. The law applied would be determined by the exercise of independent judgment by the impartial tribunal, just as factual disputes between the parties would be resolved by a presumptively unbiased trier of fact. * * *

* * *

NOTES AND QUESTIONS

1. Professor Horwitz sees two potentially conflicting tendencies in antebellum legal development. The one concerns the "utilitarian and instrumentalist character" of private law, such as torts and contracts, and the other the "anti-utilitarian, formalistic cast of public law." In what ways are these tendencies contradictory? What explanation does Horwitz offer for their existence? How does Story bring them to their "highest fulfillment?"

2. Who benefits most from Story's resolution of these legal issues? What does Horwitz's analysis add to that of Professor Tushnet? Are you persuaded by Horwitz in light of the development of private law reviewed in Chapter 3? Incidentally, as you have seen, Horwitz suggests that the "policy and group self-interest of all newly established legal doctrines" were "disguised" through "judicial forms." Do you understand how this could be? Why do you suppose it would be necessary to disguise them?

3. Would Professor Bridwell agree that the world of mid-century law was a "Dark and Doestoyevskyan" one? What, precisely, does Bridwell

see as dictating the decision in Swift v. Tyson? What does Bridwell mean when he speaks of "private international law?"

4. Consider the title of Bridwell's piece from which these excerpts are taken, "Theme v. Reality in American Legal History." What do you suppose that this means with regard to Bridwell's analysis of Horwitz's work? For the elaboration of Bridwell's differences with Horwitz see generally R. Bridwell and R. Whitten, The Constitution and the Common Law (1977).

5. In light of all you have read up to this point, what meaning would *you* give to antebellum legal change?

SECTION B.   THE CODIFICATION MOVEMENT

---

1. WILLIAM SAMPSON

MAXWELL BLOOMFIELD, AMERICAN LAWYERS IN A CHANGING SOCIETY *

60–80 (1976).

* * *

* * * Promoted by liberal practitioners with no political axes to grind, the codification movement of the 1820s sought to close the gap between legal dogmatism and the changing needs of a democratic society. In a wide-ranging debate that spilled over from law journals to newspapers and literary magazines, reformers raised fundamental questions about the nature of the judicial process, the relative merits of courts and legislatures as policymaking agencies, and the feasibility of legislative planning for the general welfare. As in any large movement, a complex interaction of circumstances and personalities contributed to the final outcome of the codification effort, but in its impact upon popular opinion it owed a unique debt to the tireless public relations work of one man—the flamboyant Irish émigré lawyer William Sampson (1764–1836). * * *

To an English statesman of the mid-eighteenth century plagued by reports of increasing militancy among American colonists, the latest dispatches from Ireland must have come as a welcome relief. In that neighboring island dependency a close-knit Anglo-Irish oligarchy of landlords and bureaucrats ruled with an iron hand, ruthlessly repressing all efforts by the native population to secure civil or political rights. Although numerically an insignificant minority, the so-called Anglican "ascendancy" owned five-sixths of all Irish lands, controlled the Irish Parliament at Dublin, and monopo-

---

lized key administrative positions within the government and the established Church of Ireland. Through a battery of harsh penal laws—a by-product of England's climactic battlefield victories of the previous century—the Roman Catholic "natives," who made up three-fourths of the Irish population, were reduced to the status of a permanently depressed tenantry. Forbidden to vote or to hold public office, to attend a university or to enter a profession, to purchase land or to practice their religion, the Irish Catholics were more viciously exploited on the whole than any comparable social group in Western Europe prior to the French Revolution. * * * Besides the tiny Anglican aristocracy at the top of the social pyramid, a middle strata of some one million Presbyterians—merchants, tradesmen, linen weavers, artisans, and farmers—shared the ruling-class mystique, even as they chafed under lesser political and religious disabilities that were still imposed upon Dissenters throughout the British Isles. With each class insulated from the others by law, custom, and religion, Ireland thus formed a model caste system * * *.

Into this closed and seemingly unshakable society William Sampson was born on January 17, 1764. The son of an Anglican clergyman, he had every reason to court favor with the Establishment * * *. But the times were anything but normal, and the rising generation, caught up in a vortex of revolutionary political upheaval, had no choice but to confront endemic social ills that earlier elites had managed to ignore.

* * * Growing up at Londonderry in northern Ireland, where the Presbyterians formed a compact majority, he was early exposed to the Dissenters' hostile view of bishops and landed aristocrats * * *. The outbreak of the American Revolution three months after his eleventh birthday provided an object lesson in democratic nation-building and fired him with enthusiasm for the cause of "liberty" and electoral reform at home. As he later noted approvingly, the transatlantic rebels "had reduced the theories of the great philosophers of England, France, and other countries into practice * * *.

Middle-class Irishmen responded to the American example by organizing in 1778 an armed militia, the Irish Volunteers, to wrest major concessions from the hard-pressed English government. Commanded by liberal aristocrats such as Henry Grattan, the Protestant Volunteers enjoyed for a time unparalleled popular support, even among the Catholic masses. As British troops suffered one setback after another on the battlefields of North America, Irishmen of every description rejoiced at the prospect of their own impending national liberation. By 1782, when Sampson at eighteen joined the Volunteers as a commissioned officer, the organization numbered 80,000 potential fighting men, and the war-weary English, unwilling to engage in a new police action, acceded to Irish demands for legislative autonomy without a struggle. * * *

Once the victory celebrations died down in Dublin, however, the old divisions within Irish society speedily reasserted themselves. Political reformers secured a few piecemeal civil rights for Catholics and Dissenters, but all moves toward Catholic emancipation or agrarian relief encountered a solid wall of conservative resistance. While the franchise was broadened somewhat to include a slightly larger proportion of middle-class property owners, the entrenched Anglo-Irish aristocracy stubbornly pursued its traditional shortsighted policies with even greater irresponsibility than before. * * *

In these troubled transition years Sampson completed his education and settled down into family life and a professional career. After * * * "keeping his terms" at Lincoln's Inn, [o]n his return to Ireland in 1791 he was promptly admitted to the Irish bar and began a promising practice in Belfast, then a bustling seaport as well as the intellectual capital of the country.

* * * [H]e found himself drawn almost at once into the ranks of anti-government activists * * *. [N]ow, with the great changes wrought in France by the Revolution of 1789 before their eyes, Irish liberals found further procrastination intolerable and began to reorganize for a new assault upon their caretaker regime. Again leadership was provided by the alienated sons of the Anglican elite, strongly supported by the middle classes, but this time the reformers sought from the outset to create a mass base by appealing directly to the Catholic natives. So was born the Society of United Irishmen, founded in Belfast late in 1791 by Sampson's friend Theobold Wolfe Tone to work toward the twin objectives of complete religious toleration and universal manhood suffrage in Ireland.

At first an open and orderly pressure group, the United Irishmen spread reform ideas to the remotest parts of the country through the pages of their official organ, the Belfast Northern Star, one of the most significant democratic newspapers of the English-speaking world at the time. * * * Sampson was an important contributor, as well as the paper's legal counsel, from its beginnings down to its final suppression by the government in 1797. His barbed satires ranged widely over the abuses of the existing political system, but he scored his greatest success with a series of articles attacking legal obscurantism as a major obstacle to the emergence of popular government among his countrymen.

* * * While Sampson zestfully demolished the pretentious formalities of courtroom procedure, he struck his most telling blows at the partisanship of Irish judges, in whose hands an ambiguous law could be transformed into a powerful bulwark of the ruling classes. Whenever the law was oracular, he maintained, judges usurped the functions of both jurors and legislators. Trials then became mere puppet shows, with jurors forbidden even to reason about the facts, "but on the contrary they are to hear with the law's ear, see with the

law's eye, speak wtih the law's voice, of which law the courts are alone to judge."

    *   *   *   Sampson practiced on the Northeast Circuit, which included the most militant counties of Ireland, and as the associate and protégé of the brilliant defense counsel John Philpot Curran he early became involved in some of the most famous political trials of the decade.   *   *   *   But the chances of winning an acquittal almost disappeared with the passage of increasingly repressive legislation and the vesting of broad discretionary power in the bench over the conduct of causes and the fixing of punishments.   The United Irish Societies were outlawed and driven underground after England went to war with France, and by 1797 mere membership in the organization was punishable by death.   Sampson, who regarded himself as a moderate and had for tactical reasons refused to join the Irish underground, now felt compelled to side openly with the cause of his clients [, and actually took the oath of the United Irishmen in open court during a trial of one of his clients for being a member of that organization.]   *   *   *   Thereafter he was a marked man in the eyes of the authorities   *   *   *.   Actually he was a most reluctant rebel, never comfortable in the presence of violence, and convinced that the government was deliberately prodding the nation toward revolution, in a calculated bid for stronger military support from England.   The events that sparked the abortive "rebellion of '98" seemed to demonstrate the truth of this proposition   *   *   *.

    "Nothing but terror will keep them in order," wrote the commander of the Irish garrison to his British superiors late in 1797. For months fresh troops had been arriving from England to help keep the peace against the dual threat of Irish insurrection and a combined naval invasion from France   *   *   *.   An Insurrection Act passed by the Dublin Parliament the previous year placed all Ireland under virtual military rule and sanctioned the most extreme measures of repression under the plea of necessity.   *   *   *   Agents provocateurs infiltrated the United Irish Societies and reported their plans to the authorities; suspected militants were arrested without warrant and imprisoned without trial; illegal searches and seizures became commonplace, as did looting, arson, and various forms of physical torture. *   *   *

    Early in 1798 the government began a systematic roundup of all remaining radical leaders, as rumors circulated that a vast expeditionary force—Napoleon's shadowy *Armée d' Angleterre*—was being assembled on the channel coast of France.   Mass arrests took place in Dublin on March 12, with Sampson's name on the list of the accused.   Forewarned, he went into hiding, after notifying the authorities that he would give himself up as soon as he was officially assured of a speedy trial.   The charges of high treason against him were, so far as he could tell, wild fabrications: a militiaman who had searched his rooms claimed to have turned up a commission appointing him a lieutenant general in the French army, as well as a list of individuals marked for assassination in Ireland! Sampson could not believe that the government seriously proposed to prosecute him on such trumped-up grounds; the real design, he reasoned, was to imprison him indefinitely without bail, thereby depriving his clients of legal counsel and cutting short his work on a projected history of the times, for which he had begun to collect documentary evidence of military atrocities committed against the peasants in the southern counties. After waiting in vain for some official response to his offer of conditional surrender, he managed to take ship for England disguised as a female passenger, but midway in the crossing someone spotted him shaving, and he was arrested as soon as he set foot on English soil at Whitehaven.

* * *

* * * [By the time Sampson was returned to Ireland the Irish Rebellion had grown to massive proportions, many had died, and it took 140,000 troops to restore peace.] To a matter-of-fact Englishman like Charles Cornwallis, who had been thrust somewhat reluctantly upon the scene as commander of all British forces, the perfervid emotionalism of the Irish crisis dwarfed anything in his previous experience, including the American Revolution. * * *

Resolved to set an example of clemency for others to follow, Cornwallis gave his support to a compromise arrangement involving Sampson (whom he considered one of the "principal criminals") and the other prisoners who were still awaiting trial. They were guaranteed their freedom if they testified fully concerning the United Irish organization and agreed to exile in some European country not then at war with England. To save the life of a condemned fellow prisoner, all accepted these terms. Sampson, whose health had begun to break during his months of confinement, chose Portugal as his place of asylum and, after many frustrating delays, reached Oporto in March 1799.

* * * He had scarcely settled down at the country home of a hospitable English merchant when he was arrested by the Portuguese government on vague charges, the exact nature of which he could never discover. Since his papers were repeatedly ransacked, however, he guessed that the English minister was somehow responsible for this "persecution," which must have been expected to turn up fresh subversive writings. Shuttled from one jail to another for the next two months, he experienced at first hand the uncertainty and helplessness that made daily life a Kafkaesque nightmare for those enmeshed in an arbitrary criminal process * * *.

After an absurd hearing before a Portuguese judge who could not speak English, Sampson was left largely to his own devices. He spent long hours reading or playing the flute, drawing charcoal designs on his prison walls or composing romantic notes to a dark-eyed young girl whose balcony he could see from his window. (These billets-doux he then lowered, with commendable Irish resourcefulness, in a hollowed-out orange fastened to the end of a stocking thread.) Just as these random activities were settling down into a fixed routine he was abruptly released and transported to a miserable fishing boat about to weigh anchor in Lisbon harbor. Only when well out to sea did he learn for the first time that he was being officially deported to France as an undesirable alien.

During the next six years (June 1799–May 1805) he remained in France as a prisoner of war—first at Bordeaux, then in Paris, where his wife and two children (whom he had not seen since he left Ireland) joined him early in 1802. Despite the almost continuous state of hostilities with England, he was permitted to move about freely (for who could doubt his ardent Anglo-phobia?) and even to criticize, from the high ground of revolutionary principle, the growing authoritarianism of Napoleon's rule. Spending his summers at the fashionable spas of Montmorency and his winters in the capital, he hobnobbed with the great and near-great of French society, including Josephine and her redoubtable mother-in-law, Letizia Bonaparte. * * *

An interested foreign observer could scarcely have chosen a better time to study the mechanics of societal evolution at close range. Under Napoleon all France was transformed into a vast social laboratory, in which government planners labored to provide the postrevolutionary public with a set of stabilizing institutions. Rationalization achieved its most impressive results in the area of jurisprudence, where the comprehensive Code Napoleon supplanted the divergent usages of local *parlements* after March 1804. Sampson watched the progress of the codification experiment with growing admiration, and a personal acquaintance with several French statesmen and jurists made him even more appreciative of the merits of a code system, as opposed to the uncertainties of judicial precedent. * * *

* * *

[In 1806 Sampson managed to get permission to bring his family to England, to wind up his affairs, in order to emigrate to America.] Their subsequent appearance in London created as much joy in official circles as a visitation of the plague. After trading insults for more than an hour with His Majesty's first lord of the admiralty, Sampson was placed under house arrest, to be shipped off to America at the earliest possible opportunity. * * * But seven weeks at sea revived his spirits, until he felt almost a new man by the time his ship arrived in New York harbor on July 4, 1806. An auspicious date to begin life in the New World, he thought. By the time he got ashore it was late, but scattered bonfires were still blazing and the mayor and other dignitaries were out celebrating in the streets with their constituents. Best of all, there were no troops around to repress popular enthusiasm. Here at last, it seemed, was a "land of peace and liberty" where reason prevailed over force and the institutional forms of Old World corruption had not taken root.

Sampson was forty-two years old when he arrived in America—a somewhat advanced age to begin afresh the practice of a profession he had been forced to abandon eight years earlier. Besides the usual difficulties of adjustment, he encountered much personal ill will from a legal community that still remained largely Federalist and anti-revolutionary in character. Only a short time earlier James Kent and other bar leaders had voiced strong objections to the very idea of permitting a "fugitive jacobin" like Sampson's friend Thomas Addis Emmet to practice in the New York courts. While Emmet did manage to obtain a counselor's license in February 1805 under a ruling of the New York Supreme Court that his alien status did not bar him from pursuing a legal career in the state, a strong conservative faction of lawyers continued to oppose the admission of any other Irishmen. When Sampson applied for his license in August 1806 the controversy reached a climax. It was finally decided that he should be admitted under the Emmet precedent, but at the same time the supreme court renounced any further flirtation with European radicalism by ruling "that hereafter no person, not being a natural born or naturalized citizen of the United States, shall be admitted as an attorney or counsellor of this court."

* * * [E]ven after he achieved full acceptance in legal circles he never managed to build up a very large or lucrative American practice. One reason—perhaps the chief reason—for his qualified professional success lay in his own quixotic personality. To his contemporaries he seemed, above all, a figure of fun—a warmhearted, gregarious Irishman whose infectious good humor few could resist. Even those like Chancellor Kent, who thought "his notions of law & Government were utopian, & wild, & radical," came in time to relish his wit and polished manners and to seek out his company on social occasions. * * * A portrait of 1807 shows * * * dark wavy hair brushed negligently over a high forehead; shrewd, piercing eyes, suggestive alike of boldness and suppressed mirth; prominent nose and ears; and a wide, sensuous mouth. * * * an appropriate treatment of one who could describe American woman as "fair-haired Dryads of the woods" while criticizing their haughty European rivals for having "cheeks of brass and eye-balls of stone." * * *

In his penchant for the picturesque phrase he was, of course, by no means unique. Most lawyers and judges of the time, however they declaimed in favor of "chaste" and restrained eloquence, liked nothing better than to wallow in sentimentality when occasion offered. (Did not even Webster and Marshall reportedly shed tears over the proprietary claims of little Dartmouth College?) Yet in an age of long-winded oratory, when many other practitioners thought that "getting back to first principles" meant starting with Genesis and working their way up, Sampson was in a class by himself. For one thing, he was not limited to classical, biblical, or Shakespearean allusions; he could (and did) drag the manifold wrongs of oppressed Ireland into his cases, whether the issue was rape, fraud, or the proper interpretation of a contract. * * *

But Sampson's courtroom flamboyance, however unprofessional, fitted into a larger pattern of divided loyalties, since he remained at heart a publicist as well as a lawyer. In America, to be sure, he rarely engaged in the kind of partisan polemics that had made him notorious in Ireland. He saw little need for such broadsides, since he adhered to a consensus theory of American politics that minimized party differences on most issues. Only in 1812 did his admiration for Jefferson (with whom he carried on an intermittent correspondence for some ten years) lead him to publish anonymously two small pamphlets in which he defended Republican policy and lashed out at England's violations of international law * * *.

He had first taken up shorthand as a fledgling Irish lawyer, to preserve for posterity the moving speeches of John Philpot Curran in defense of the United Irishmen, and in the United States he became a pioneer court reporter whose stenographic skills enabled him to produce for the public authentic accounts of celebrated cases, in several of which he had taken part as counsel. * * * He went to the trouble of publishing his cases partly for ideological reasons and partly to supplement the inadequate income he obtained from his practice.

* * * The reports * * * demonstrate that besides being primarily a trial lawyer Sampson tended to specialize to a great extent in civil rights litigation, and that a substantial proportion of his clients came from foreign-born or low-income groups. * * * The ideological components discernible in many individual cases were linked to broader questions of legal reform in his stenographic publications. One reported trial in particular pointed up the need for a massive restructuring of American law along more democratic lines. The Case of the Journeymen Cordwainers of the City of New York (1809) marked one of the earliest attempts to establish the legality of collective bargaining in America. A group of workers had formed an association to improve their lot and sought to enforce a demand for higher wages through strike activity. While no American statute prohibited such conduct, it stood condemned as an illegal conspiracy at common law. Should English doctrine on this point control the decision of a New York judge? Sampson argued that it should not.

The common law, he observed, had never been adopted in full by the American colonies. Even Blackstone acknowledged that the colonists took with them only those legal precepts and institutions that were suited to conditions in the New World. And now that independence had been achieved it was more important than ever to guard against any foreign doctrines that might impair the growth of a democratic society. English conspiracy statutes, directed against working-class organizations, had no place in a free America. * * * He attacked the class bias of English legislators and judges, whose reactionary pronouncements, he claimed, were held in superstitious awe by American jurists. Such blind adherence to common-law precedents could undermine the very ideals for which the Revolution had been fought * * *.

Sampson's oratory failed, however, to convince the court to reconsider the reasonableness of common-law doctrines adopted as the basis of New York jurisprudence by the framers of the state constitution of 1777. For all the local interest aroused by his cases, he remained a minor critic of the law—indistinguishable from other shadowy agitators in Ohio, Kentucky, and Pennsylvania—until a chance invitation to address the New York Historical Society in December 1823 brought him and his ideas at last to the attention of a nation-wide audience.

[The speech that he gave] contained the most devastating critique of common-law idealism ever written in America, [and] relied less upon erudition than upon wit and irony to achieve its effects. By tracing legal history back to the customs of barbaric German tribes, Sampson sought to dispel forever the myth that a golden age of English jurisprudence had existed prior to the Norman Conquest. This was no exercise in pedantry, for the "Saxon idols" still held a firm place in American legal folklore. Even such a staunch opponent of Blackstone and Mansfield as Thomas Jefferson professed a sentimental loyalty to the "pure" institutions and practices of the Saxon era.

But what relevance had the Saxon experience for nineteenth century America? Sampson queried. * * * Of modern commercial transactions they had no inkling; their criminal laws did not progress beyond the brutalities of the *lex talionis*; and there was little evidence to suggest that they originated the jury system, which they seldom employed in comparison with the trial by water or red-hot ploughshares. Yet their primitive codes, with all their deficiencies, proved more humane than the legal system subsequently imposed upon them by their Norman conquerors. It took centuries after the Battle of Hastings for judges to reestablish the rights of the individual citizen, by resorting to a series of awkward fictions that made the law unintelligible to the average man.

Was it not high time to discard such mummery and pretense and place the law upon a rational and scientific footing? "The well-being of society requires that a subject of such vital importance should be brought to the test of reason in the open light of day," Sampson urged. "Having adopted the common law of England, so far as it is not repugnant to our constitutions, we have a mighty interest to know clearly what it is, and from what stock it comes. * * *

Since history demonstrated that no part of the common-law tradition deserved special veneration, it was all the more imperative that every doctrine be tested by the principles of "natural reason, universal justice, and present convenience." In championing the cause of innovation, however, Sampson was by no means simply following a course already mapped out by earlier reformers; in fact a wide gap separated him from even the politically oriented Jeffersonian agitators of the pre-1812 years. Those men, as loyal party cadre, had typically attacked the law as an instrument of class domination in America. They had tried to stir up the feelings of backwoods "republicans" against a privileged establishment of urban lawyers and judges whose mastery of abstruse legal doctrines enabled them to promote the ends of a wealthy elite at the expense of the democratic masses. * * *

But it was precisely this element of class antagonism that Sampson and his adherents rejected in the 1820s. They worked for reform *within* the legal profession, looking to the scholar rather than the demagogue to carry through their program. Sampson thought of himself as a latter-day Luther, called to purge the law of its superstitious and irrational features so that it might be reestablished on a basis of sound principles intelligible to the average man. Far from desiring to uproot accepted doctrines recklessly, he conceded that "the English reports contain, amidst a world of rubbish, rich treasures of experience, and that those of our own courts contain materials of inestimable worth, and require little more than regulation and systematic order." The task of culling useful precepts from a mass of conflicting court decisions could only be entrusted to the legislature, however, because judges were disinclined by temperament and training to challenge past authorities. Indeed, as Sampson pictured them, judges were little more than slaves to precedent. Whenever a case arose, he argued, the doctrine of stare decisis required that a judge suspend his own views and seek instead to fit the facts into some line of previously reported opinions. Since these opinions were both voluminous and at variance with one another, a litigant had no way to predict the outcome of his case. Even where the circumstances proved unique, and a judge found himself compelled to render a verdict on the basis of his own beliefs, one of the parties necessarily fell victim to the announcement of the new rule.

By its very nature, then, judicial policymaking could lead only to arbitrary and highly personal results; yet Sampson was careful to avoid imputing any sinister or undemocratic motives to the judges themselves. It was the system that was at fault, he insisted, a system adapted to the needs of a society in which the masses could neither read nor write and had therefore to rely upon haphazard decisions from the bench to determine their lawful rights. But in America, where popular education was the rule, each citizen had an obligation to study and comprehend the law for himself. A legislative code modeled upon the Code Napoleon would provide comprehensive guidelines for both lawyers and laymen and would insure popular control over any future changes of policy.

To reduce the amorphous bulk of the law to a system of scientific axioms would prove an immense task, of course, but the first steps in the process had already been taken. Most states periodically revised and digested their written statutes; why not complete the picture by systematizing court decisions as well? Present conditions appeared peculiarly ripe for such an experiment. While European nations still suffered from wars and domestic tyranny, the United States had entered upon an era of unprecedented peace and prosperity, in which the fierce party feuds of the Jeffersonian years seemed buried forever. Citizens of all political faiths could now unite behind the labors of enlightened jurists who would reform the law with a "tender, patient, kindly, and experienced hand."

*   *   *

Encouraged by the public's response to his general propositions, Sampson now launched a promotional campaign designed to point up in greater detail the practical advantages of codification. For two years (1824–1826) he maintained an active correspondence with politicians and jurists throughout the Union, spreading his ideas through local newspapers and national magazines. The cream of this correspondence reappeared in book form in 1826, by which time legal reform had become a commonplace topic of discussion in literary periodicals and a source of increasing comment among foreign observers.

Sampson and his supporters were ardent Francophiles who looked to the Code Napoleon as a model for American legislators. In their eyes the French experience demonstrated the limits of improvement possible under a code system. While they agreed that no set of general principles could answer all human problems, they believed that the wisest precedents of the past might be summarized in definitive fashion as a guide to the future. *   *   * Instead of acting as a deterrent to further social change, every code would necessarily have to be revised from time to time to incorporate new rights and remedies. "But is it nothing," [one] argued, "that we have, or can have if we please, a new starting place every half century, leaving behind us the accumulated rubbish of years' proceedings?"

*   *   * [T]he general public would reap the greatest benefits under a code system, according to its proponents, since law would cease to be a mysterious science beyond the ken of the masses. Once reduced to fixed moral principles, its methods and objectives could be appreciated by the average layman, who would find the printed code an indispensable textbook of social ethics. A wiser and more responsible citizenry had reportedly emerged in France since the enactment of the Code Napoleon, while in Louisiana, where a civil code had recently gone into effect, the transplanted New York attorney Charles Watts observed: "The planters and well informed men have the code in their hand, and discuss it as a branch of politics; while, on the contrary, the community here [in New York] are involved in Egyptian darkness."

If laymen, were to play a more meaningful role in legal deliberations, however, that did not imply the destruction of a professional bar. The codifiers compared the law to a skilled trade whose practitioners required specialized talents and training. Could every man be his own cobbler? they asked. Obviously not. Yet the principles of shoemaking were known to all, and a customer could readily detect the difference between a good pair of shoes and those of inferior quality. So it would be with the law; a thorough grounding in basic principles would enable the average man to exercise a healthy check upon legal fraud and mysticism, as the Reformation had established popular control of religion without lessening the need for trained ministers. Codes could never produce a lawyerless utopia, for litigation was rooted in the selfish nature of man. But the caliber of the bar would be immensely improved under a code system that would eliminate the uncertain precedents and archaic technicalities that played into the hands of the shyster class of common-law pleaders.

* * *

NOTES AND QUESTIONS

1. Note that in Sampson's early days he was an associate of the United Irishmen, the "democratic" organization that worked for "complete religious toleration and universal manhood suffrage" in Ireland. At about this time, Pennsylvania was described by one American Federalist as a state given over to "United Irishmen, Free Masons, and the most God-provoking Democrats on this side of Hell." J. Miller, The Federalist Era 255 (1960). What was meant by this description, and why include the United Irishmen in this parade of horribles?

2. The William Sampson of this excerpt flees the authorities disguised as a woman, and is exposed when he is caught shaving. He plays the flute in Portuguese prisons, and sends a dark-eyed young girl notes in a hollowed-out orange. Would you expect people to take his legal reform proposals seriously? Why, exactly, was Sampson called the "Flaming Irishman?" Can you believe in his commitment to "revolutionary principle" once you have realized that in France he spent "his summers at the fashionable spas of Montmorency and * * * hob-nobbed with the great and near-great of French society * * *"? On the other hand, to what extent do his experiences in Ireland influence his attitudes toward the judiciary and the law in America?

3. Why didn't the judge in the New York Cordwainer's case buy Sampson's idea that the English common law of conspiracy should *not* be applied when workmen try to raise their wages?

4. Is it true, as Sampson thought, that a "code" is necessary "to place the law upon a rational and scientific footing?" Why is a code more

rational or scientific than a judicial opinion? Was Sampson's primary interest in rationality? Why did Sampson not push his position to an ideological extreme (as, for example, did Rantoul)? Does the author of this excerpt, Professor Bloomfield of Catholic University, believe that Sampson was a "radical"? Why or why not? Who do you suppose Sampson wanted to write codes? In order to put this issue into further perspective, consider this summary of the codification movement, from the Note, Swift v. Tyson Exhumed, 79 Yale L.J. 284, text accompanying notes 61–73 (1969).

In 1811, Jeremy Bentham wrote James Madison, offering his services to codify American law. He proposed a code which would cover all matters of importance with rules justified by the principle of utility, using prior cases only as general guides. Madison received this offer coolly, deferring his reply until 1816, when he wrote to suggest that the United States did not need Bentham's aid in developing a better system of laws. Over the next ten years, however, a movement did begin among [American] lawyers to "codify" the common law.   *   *   *

These codifiers based their position on a sharp distinction between the forms and organization of the inherited common law on the one hand and its substance and intellectual method on the other. The principles of the common law were admirable, and the techniques represented the perfection of Reason. Principles and techniques were therefore to be preserved, not because they had been handed down from the feudal past but because they were independently valid. However, the codifiers regarded the forms and organization of the law as encumbrances, inefficient in practice and dangerous because they drew the law into disrepute among the people.

Though codification was the goal, European codes and civil law were not regarded as models; they relied too much on "untried speculations" of civilian jurists, and were looked to only as examples of legal systems which did not rely on acquiescence in the unexamined inheritance of an existing body of law. American codification as a method of applying reason to law would isolate maxims whose validity had been tested by experience, and these maxims would serve as general guides to judges in the process of analogistic reasoning by which the common law constantly adjusted itself to new situations.

*   *   *

But during the 1830's the movement was transformed into one closer to Bentham's reformist vision. The later codifiers would simplify the law, and in the process reform its substance, stripping it of its mysteries and giving it popular sanction. One leading reformer, Thomas Walker of Ohio, wrote: "My creed is that the law should be made as simple, as intelligible, and as certain as possible. To this end, written or statute law should, as far as practicable, supply the place of unwritten or common law * * *." He echoed Bentham's distrust of lawyers:

If legal reform be called for, the people must bring it about. If opposition come from any quarter, we anticipate it from lawyers. And the reason is natural. They are the most directly interested in keeping things as they are. The more abstruse and recondite you make the law, the more indispensable will be their professional services.

* * *

* * * Walker thought that his codification would change the fundamental nature of the common law by removing the judge's discretion to overrule or ignore prior cases and evolve new rules. Under the new system the judges would still apply the general principles of the code to new situations, but they would not be "changing" the law, as common-law judges had, since in every case they would be bound by the clear expression of legislative will.

* * *

5. Sampson refers favorably to the Code Napoleon, as did other proponents of codification. But the detractors of codification argued that European codes were models of despotic ideology, rigid and authoritarian. Do you agree with this criticism? What in the common law tradition of adjudication would you suppose such critics of codification wanted to preserve?

6. Can you discern from this excerpt the position of the "old guard," the conservative bar, on the question of the applicability of the English common law to America and the desirability of an American code? Is this why they resisted Sampson, or was his rejection more for reasons of character and style of courtroom advocacy? One of the classic statements on English common law and American codification, not surprisingly, is that of Justice Story, which follows. See if you can determine the extent of Story's agreement or disagreement with both William Sampson and the more "popular" advocates of codification. With whom do you agree?

2. JOSEPH STORY, REPORT OF THE COMMISSION ON CODIFICATION OF THE LAW TO THE GOVERNOR OF MASSACHUSETTS (1837)

W. STORY, ED. THE MISCELLANEOUS WRITINGS OF JOSEPH STORY

698–703, 706–716 (1852).

When our ancestors first emigrated to this country * * *, they brought with them the common law of the mother country (England) so far, as from its nature and objects, it then was or might be applicable to their situation, as colonists, distant from and possessing institutions and political arrangements varying from those of the parent country. * * * Thus, for example, many of the feudal tenures, then in force in England, were never known here, all tenures of land here being from the beginning in free and common socage. * * *

Nor was this an artificial principle assumed for the occasion to govern the colonies. It was a part of the general law of the land, at the time of the emigration of our ancestors, that all new settlements made by Englishmen, in desert and uncultivated regions, were to be governed by the law of England, subject to the qualifications already stated. It was also a principle, fully recognized in the charters granted to the colonies, either in direct terms, or by necessary implication. * * * There is also to be found in all the charters, except that of Pennsylvania, (where it was probably omitted by mistake or accident,) an express clause, declaring, that all English subjects and their children, inhabiting in the colonies, shall be deemed natural born subjects, and shall enjoy all the privileges and immunities thereof. * * *

* * * The revolutionary Congress of 1774, accordingly, unanimously resolved, "that the respective colonies are entitled to the common law of England, and more especially to the great and inestimable privilege of being tried by their peers, in the vicinage, according to the course of that law;" and "that they were entitled to the benefit of such of the English statutes as existed at the time of their colonization, and which they have by experience respectively found to be applicable to their several local circumstances."

But notwithstanding this general adoption of the common law of England, it is obvious, that the qualifications annexed to it must have given rise to many very perplexing doubts and difficulties. What portions of the common law were applicable to the situation of the colonies, was an inquiry perpetually presented in the course of forensic discussions in former times. And though by the gradual operation of judicial decisions, and the positive enactments of the colonial, provincial, and state legislatures, the field of controversy has been greatly narrowed; yet there still remain some topics of debate upon which it would not be easy to affirm, whether the common law of England had been adopted here or not. * * *

Besides the common law of England, there are to be found in Massachusetts some few local usages, and principles, which properly constitute a part of our common law, though unknown to that of England. * * *

* * *

The next inquiry is, what is the true nature or character of the common law, so recognized and established, and where are its doctrines and principles to be found. In relation to the former part of the inquiry, it may be generally stated, that the common law consists of positive rules and remedies, of general usages and customs, and of elementary principles, and the developments or applications of them, which cannot now be distinctly traced back to any statutory enactments, but which rest for their authority upon the common recognition, consent and use of the State itself. Some of these rules, usages and principles are of such high antiquity, that the time cannot be assigned, when they had not an existence and use. Others of them are of a comparatively modern growth, having been developed with the gradual progress of society; and others, again, can hardly be said to have had a visible and known existence until our own day. Thus, for example, many of the rights and remedies, which ascertain and govern the titles to real estate, are of immemorial antiquity. On the other hand, the law of commercial contracts, and especially the law of insurance, of shipping, of bills of exchange, and of promissory notes, has almost entirely grown up since the time (1756) when Lord Mansfield was elevated to the bench. And again, the law of aquatic rights and water courses, and the law of corporations can scarcely be said to have assumed a scientific form until our day.

In truth, the common law is not in its nature and character an absolutely fixed, inflexible system, like the statute law, providing only for cases of a determinate form, which fall within the letter of the language, in which a particular doctrine or legal proposition is expressed. It is rather a system of elementary principles and of general juridical truths, which are continually expanding with the progress of society, and adapting themselves to the gradual changes of trade, and commerce, and the mechanic arts, and the exigencies and usages of the country. There are certain fundamental maxims in it, which are never departed from; there are others again, which, though true in a general sense, are at the same time susceptible of modifications and exceptions, to prevent them from doing manifest wrong and injury.

When a case, not affected by any statute, arises in any of our courts of justice, and the facts are established, the first question is, whether there is any clear and unequivocal principle of the common law, which directly and immediately governs it, and fixes the rights of the parties. If there be no such principle, the next question is, whether there is any principle of the common law, which, by analogy, or parity of reasoning, ought to govern it. If neither of these sources furnishes a positive solution of the controversy, resort is next had (as in a case confessedly new) to the principles of natural justice which constitute the basis of much of the common law; and if these principles can be ascertained to apply in a full and determinate manner to all the circumstances, they are adopted, and decide the rights of the parties. If all these sources fail, the case is treated as remediless at the common law, and the only relief, which remains, is by some new legislation, by statute, to operate upon future cases of the like nature.

* * *

[Story then proceeds to address the] * * * practicability of reducing to a written and systematic Code the Common Law of Massachusetts, or of any part thereof.

* * * If by those terms is to be intended not only all the general principles of that law, but all the diversities, ramifications, expansions, exceptions and qualifications of those principles, as they ought to be applied, not only to the past and present, but, to all future combinations of circumstances in the business of human life, it may require one answer. If, on the other hand, those terms are to be understood in a more restricted sense, as importing only the reduction to a positive code of those general principles, and of the expansions, exceptions, qualifications and minor deductions, which have already, by judicial decisions or otherwise, been engrafted on them, and are now capable of a distinct enunciation, then a very different answer might be given. In the former sense, the Commissioners have no doubt, that it is not practicable to reduce the common law of Massachusetts to a written code; in the latter sense, they have no doubt, that it is so practicable * * *.

* * * It is not an uncommon opinion, that all law is capable of being reduced to a specific form, which shall apply with equal clearness and certainty to the solution of all cases, past, present and future. In short, it is frequently supposed and frequently asserted, that a code may be compiled of all the law, which is to regulate the rights and titles, the property, the business and the contracts of a nation, so definite, full and exact, that it shall furnish a complete guide, not only for the decisions of courts of justice, but for intelligent citizens throughout the country, in all cases, and shall supersede, if not the necessity of new legislation, at least the necessity of new rules, and the modification of old rules by courts of justice, to reach the exigencies of every variety of controversy. * * * It is very certain, that no nation, whose legal institutions are known to us, ever had a code of the nature above supposed, namely, one, which was comprehensive enough to embrace all the doctrines and details required for the private concerns and business of its whole population. That it never has been done, however, furnishes no absolute proof, that it cannot be done. But at the same time, since it is well known, that many partial codes or collections of laws have been made, the fair presumption is, that it has been deemed impracticable or unwise to attempt more.

In proportion as nations advance in civilization and commerce, the business of the people and the rights and modifications of property, become necessarily more complicated and difficult, and various in their relations and circumstances. * * * Of the innumerable questions which arise in any one age, and admit of forensic controversy and doubt, probably not one in a hundred, perhaps it would be more correct to say, not one in a thousand, ever comes before a court of justice to be there finally settled by adjudication. Many are settled by compromise; many by arbitration, or the intervention of friends: many are neglected or abandoned, from their comparatively slight importance, or the poverty of the claimants, or their ignorance of, or indifference to, their rights, or from other causes tending to suppress litigation. Hence it is, that the basis of the actual administration of justice in every country must comprehend principles of far more extensive reach than those which become the subjects of direct adjudication in courts of justice, and be capable of a progressive adaptation to new cases as they arise, or the most manifold public and private mischiefs must pervade the whole community.

It may be asked, why may not a nation require all the laws, which are to govern it, to be clearly made known and promulgated before they are acted upon? Certainly it is competent for a nation so to act. It may declare, that the administration of justice shall be applied only to rights and titles and claims which have been previously ascertained by the terms of express laws, leaving nothing to the judgment of courts of justice, beyond the direct application of the text to the very cases thus ascertained. But what would be the consequence of such a course of legislation? It would be, that every case of wrong and injustice and oppression, not thus foreseen and provided for, would be wholly remediless. And the mass of such cases would be perpetually accumulating, since positive legislation, however, rapid and constant, can never keep up in any just proportion with the actual permutations and combinations of the business of an active, enterprising, and industrious people. * * *

It is obviously impossible to make a positive code, which shall be adequate to the business and rights and modifications of property in any one single age, unless the Legislature can foresee every possible as well as every probable combination of circumstances applicable to every subject-matter in that age. Such a degree of wisdom and foresight belongs not to any human beings. If it were possible to foresee and provide for all such exigencies of a single age, having a determinate course of business, and institutions, no one would be rash enough to assert, that it was possible to foresee and provide for the exigencies, rights, duties, and business of the same nation throughout all time. A code, therefore, however full, would be perpetually growing more and more defective, unless resort was had to new legislation; and such legislation to be either wise or effective, must allow a great number of cases of the same sort to arise under various aspects, before the proper remedy or principle, which ought to be generally applied, could be clearly perceived, or safely adopted. * * *

* * * Of the reported cases, which were decided in England before the middle of the last century, consisting principally of cases at the common law, an abridgment has been published in twenty-four folio volumes * * *. An abridgment of the reported cases at the common law, from that time down to the present, has also been published in fifteen volumes * * *. These voluminous works are but specimens of what a code must be, which should attempt to enumerate in detail the doctrines of the common law, which have been in dispute in courts of justice, and have been established by decisions. If the enumeration of these is so voluminous, we may readily see, what space would be required for those which are known and not disputed, and for those which are unknown, or uncertain in their application,

and whose circumstances have never been discussed in tribunals of justice. A code, which should embrace the doctrines of all the reported cases of the common law, from the most important to the most minute, with accuracy and clearness, would of itself be exceedingly voluminous, and require many years, if not an age, for its preparation, and then would be mastered only by those, who could afford to devote a large portion of their lives to the study and exposition of it. For the purposes of common life, it would be like a sealed book, which would neither enlighten nor aid practical inquirers, and perhaps by a partial examination might mislead them. * * *

The civil code and the commercial code of France are probably as perfect specimens of legislation as ever have been, or ever can be produced, having been prepared with great care and diligence, by the most learned jurists of France, after repeated revisions, and with the assistance of the ablest and the most experienced judges of the tribunals of all the departments of that extensive kingdom. Yet it is well known, that a great variety of questions, as to the true construction of the text, and a still greater variety of questions, arising from new and unforeseen cases, have been discussed in their judicial tribunals, which already occupy many volumes of reports, and must constitute a continually augmenting mass of materials, alternately for litigation and for legislation. * * *

Considerations of this sort, which cannot fail to force themselves upon the mind upon a close survey of the subject, have led the Commissioners to the conclusion, that it is not possible to establish in any written code all the positive laws, and applications of laws * * *. If it were possible to provide such a written code, the Commissioners are of opinion, that the present state of the common law does not furnish sufficient materials for the purpose. An infinite number of new rules and doctrines, and modifications, limitations and enlargements of old rules and doctrines, would be required even for an approximation to such a code. * * * It seems to them, that private convenience as well as public policy requires, that the common law should be left in its prospective operations in future (as it has been in the past) to be improved, and expanded, and modified to meet the exigencies of society, by the gradual application of its principles in courts of justice to new cases, assisted from time to time, as the occasion may demand, by the enactments of the legislature.

* * *

In respect to the general principles of the common law of Massachusetts, it may be affirmed, that they are not positively incapable of being generally collected into a code. We say generally, because there may still be some question, whether particular principles of the common law of England constitute a part of the common law of Massachusetts. But in relation to a very large mass, there is no difficulty whatsoever of this nature. These general principles are to be found, for the most part, collected in elementary treatises now extant, upon the whole or particular branches of the common law. They are capable of being stated in the very form and language, in which they are there enunciated, as they have, from long examinations and critical trials, acquired a precision and exactness, which approach very near to scientific accuracy; and for all the ordinary uses of life, they are sufficiently clear in their interpretations and qualifications. * * *

In respect to the details of these general principles in their actual application to particular cases, where they have necessarily undergone modifications, exceptions and qualifications, as they are chiefly, if not exclusively, to be gathered from actual adjudications in courts of justice, it may also be affirmed, that they are not positively incapable, so far at least as reported cases go, of being generally reduced to a written code. We say generally * * * because there are to be found conflicting decisions upon some points, so that it may not be easy to affirm, upon the weight of authority, what the true doctrine is; and because some branches of the common law of England have become so nearly obsolete * * * that, if they constitute a part of our common law, it would be very difficult to collect all the true doctrines, and to express them in an unexceptionable form. Time here, as everywhere else, has wrought such great changes in rights, remedies, institutions, and usages, that it would be almost a hopeless task to suit the ancient forms and the ancient language of particular doctrines to the present state of things. * * *

These considerations naturally conduct us to the second and very important inquiry, as to the expediency of reducing the common law of Massachusetts, or any part thereof, (in the narrower sense already stated) to a written and systematic code, so far as the same is practicable. * * *

* * *

I.   The Commissioners are, in the first place, of opinion, that it is not expedient to attempt the reduction to a code of the entire body of the common law of Massachusetts, either in its general principles or in the deduction from, or the applications, of those principles, so far as they have been ascertained by judicial decisions, or are incontrovertibly established.

II.   The Commissioners, are, in the next place, of opinion, that it is expedient to reduce to a code those principles, and details of the common law of Massachusetts in civil cases, which are of daily use and familiar application to the common business of life, and the present state of property and personal rights and contracts, and which are now so far ascertained and established, as to admit of a scientific form and arrangement, and are capable of being announced in distinct and determinate propositions. * * * [The Commissioners also recommended that criminal law and the law of evidence could be "reduced" to codes. What does this leave not codified?]

* * * [T]he Commissioners propose to insert in such a code the following fundamental rules for its interpretation and application.

I.   The code is to be interpreted and applied to future cases, as a code of the common law of Massachusetts, and not as a code of mere positive or statute law. It is to be deemed an affirmance of what the common law now is, and not as containing provisions in derogation of that law, and therefore subject to a strict construction.

II.   Consequently, it is to furnish the rules for decisions in courts of justice, not only in cases directly (*ex directo*) within its terms, but indirectly, and by analogy in cases, where as a part of the common law, it would and ought to be applied by courts of justice, in like manner.

III.   In all cases not provided for by the code, or governed by the analogies therein contained, the common law of Massachusetts, as now existing, is to furnish the rules for decision, unless so far as it is repugnant to the common law affirmed in the code, or to the statute law of the state.

Such is the basis of the code proposed by the Commissioners, and such the principles, by which they propose, that those who shall be called upon to perform the duty of codification, should be guided.

NOTES AND QUESTIONS

1.   According to Story, how does a common law judge go about ascertaining the law of a case? Has Story left anything out?

2.   Story comes out in favor of codification of Massachusetts common law, but only in a "restricted sense." What are the "restrictions?" Story suggests that as "nations advance in civilization and commerce," legal rights and social relations become more "complicated and difficult." What do you suppose Story means here? In light of this supposedly increasingly complexity in society, why would a "systematic Codification" of the law soon be rendered "defective?" Incidentally, what do you suppose "defective" would mean for Story?

3.   Pay close attention to the rules of interpretation that would be inserted into the proposed code. If we begin with the proposition that Story is a defender of the common law and the methods of adjudication associated with that system, what concessions has he made toward codification? What are the implications of Story's statement in "I." that a code of common law in Massachusetts would not be interpreted as a "code of mere positive * * * law?" Incidentally, is it not a contradiction to speak of "common law affirmed in the code?"

4.   Although Swift v. Tyson is still five years away, do you believe Story's opinion in that case and his "Report * * * on Codification" are cut from the same cloth? How would you compare Story to Sampson? To Rantoul?

DAVID DUDLEY FIELD

3. DAVID DUDLEY FIELD

DAVID DUDLEY FIELD, WHAT SHALL BE DONE WITH
THE PRACTICE OF THE COURTS? (1847)

I. A. P. SPRAGUE, ED. SPEECHES, ARGUMENTS, AND MISCELLANEOUS
PAPERS OF DAVID DUDLEY FIELD 226 (1884)

* * *

The profession stands at this time in a position in which it has not
before been placed. Shall it set itself in opposition to the demands of
a radical reform? shall it be indifferent to it? or shall it unite heartily
in its prosecution? None can reform so well as we, as none would be
benefited so much. We can not remain motionless. We must either
take part in the changes or set ourselves in opposition to them, and
then, as I think, be overwhelmed by them. * * *

* * *

If it had depended upon the bar alone, I believe that many important amendments would have been made, which we are now without. Various causes have contributed to prevent their doing as much
as they would otherwise have done, the principle of which is, the
jealousy with which concert of action on their part was regarded by
others. It is a mistake to suppose that our present legal machinery
has been regarded by them with much favor. On the contrary, I think
they have disliked it generally. They would choose something better
to drive over our modern ways, than this cumbrous thing—three hundred years old and more—ill-adapted to our present circumstances,
unequal to our present wants, and so altered and mended that scarce
any two parts seem of a piece. * * *

Every consideration, as it seems to me, makes it expedient for
us all now to enter heartily upon the work of amendment. Those of
us who have long been laboring for a radical reformation of the law,
and those who have felt less inclination for it, should find this an
occasion to act together in the common pursuit of thorough and wise
reforms. We feel the inconvenience of the present state of things.
We know that the technicality and the drudgery of legal proceedings are discreditable to our profession. Justice is entangled in the
net of forms.

* * *

For all reasons, therefore, it appears to me the wiser and safer
plan, when we are about it, to make a radical reform; in short, to
go back to first principles, break up the present system, and recon-
struct a simple and natural scheme of legal procedure. * * *

* * *

Such a reform, I am persuaded, should have in view nothing less
than a uniform course of proceeding, in all cases, legal and equitable.

A legal proceeding has three principal stages: the allegations of the parties, the proofs, and the decision upon the law and the facts. * * *

What is meant by a uniform course of proceeding? Not that precisely the same shall take place, for all demands, and all kinds of relief. That is not possible, so long as the cases themselves differ from each other. * * *

* * * [I]s it practicable to abolish all the forms of action now in use in common law cases, and to substitute in their place a complaint and answer, according to the fact * * * ? By practicable, I mean not possible only, but capable of being done, without failing of any of the purposes subserved by the present forms of pleading. Are these forms necessary? Are they useful? * * *

In the earliest periods of our law, every cause was commenced by an original writ, issuing out of the Court of Chancery, describing briefly the cause of action, and returnable before some of the courts of law. It was this writ which gave jurisdiction of the cause to those Courts, the writ combining the two qualities of a summons to the defendant and a commission to the Judges to hear and determine the controversy. * * * They were conceived in certain fixed forms, and, unless an original writ could be found or devised for the case, the suitor was without remedy in the courts of law.

The writs, being thus confined within certain established forms, were soon classified, and all actions at common law were accordingly divided into a certain number of classes, fifty-nine in all, according to some enumerations; the more common of which were the writ of right, dower, ejectment, debt, covenant, detinue, trespass, trespass on the case, and replevin.

These actions were all known in the time of Edward I, and, though some of them have been modified and made more comprehensive, no new action has been devised within the last three hundred years, although property has taken many new shapes, and the business of mankind has undergone a complete revolution. * * *

On the return of the original writ into the Court of Common Law, the pleadings there commenced. The plaintiff repeated the original writ, the defendant answered it. The answers also soon fell into set forms. At first the allegations were made orally, and taken down by the clerk. About the middle of the fourteenth century oral pleadings were discontinued, but the same forms were used as before, and to this day the record is framed as though the parties or their attorneys actually made their allegations in open court. * * *

Originally the pleadings were short and simple, as may be seen on looking into Glanville or the Year-Books. * * * In process of time they became extremely technical. * * * When the pleadings came to be written in English, they were in a great degree mere translations of the Norman and Latin forms. * * *

The narrow spirit in which the Courts construed the language, and required the proof to correspond with the allegation, in the strictest literal sense, led to repetitions, pleonasms, and to the introduction of different counts as different ways of stating the same case. For these reasons the pleadings came in process of time to be long, overloaded with verbiage, uncouth phrases, and endless repetitions. Many rules have been established by the Courts and pleaders together, prescribing the manner of pleading and the forms of the allegations. These rules, and the commentaries upon them, form, as every lawyer knows, one of the most technical and abstruse branches of the law. They are ingenious, everybody will admit; the principal ones are founded on sound logic; others are founded on distinctions purely verbal; and many of them tend to shut out the truth, and embarrass the party in a labyrinth of forms. * * *

It was early found that a form of plea could be devised which in many actions would virtually deny every material allegation of the declaration, without disclosing any particular defense. The Courts have been constantly admitting new defenses under these general issues. The Legislature has also provided by law that the defendant may plead the general issue, and give notice with it of any defense which he could not regularly introduce under such issue. It has even gone further, and provided that any public officers, when prosecuted for acts done by virtue of their offices, may plead the general issue, and give any defense in evidence without notice. There could scarcely be a more glaring inconsistency; for, either special pleading is a help to justice, and should therefore be adhered to in all cases, or it is a hindrance and a burden, from which all parties should be free.

Besides the general pleas, which we call general issues, we have general declarations, or common counts, as they are called. These have been so contrived as to give no information of the particular demand. This form has been encouraged by the Courts, so as to allow a vast number of demands to be given in evidence under it. * * It appears, therefore, that there has been a constant struggle of the lawyers and the Courts to evade the rules which [they] themselves have framed. * * *

* * *

After the declaration the defendant may demur, or he may put in a dilatory plea in bar. * * *

The defendant may indeed plead as many pleas in bar as he likes, but each plea must either deny some allegation of the declaration, or aver new facts, which, without denying the declaration, do away with their effect; that is, he must plead by way of traverse, or by way of confession and avoidance. And the plaintiff, if he replies to the pleas, must conform to the same rules; and so on with each party, through all the successive stages of allegation and counter-allegation, till some proposition, either real or verbal, is evolved, which one party avers and the other traverses, or to which one demurs and the other joins in demurrer. * * *

Of what real utility is this system? * * * [T]here can not be any good reason why the story should not be told in the ordinary language of life, in the only language intelligible to the juries who are to decide the causes; and if that were done, the distinction of actions would cease, of course.

* * * Doubtless the change from Norman-French into Latin was thought a most dangerous innovation in its day, and that from Latin to English ridiculed as unnecessary, unworthy of the law, and quite beneath the learned special pleaders of 1730. * * *

* * *

What I propose, then, in respect to cases of legal cognizance, is this: that the present forms of action be abolished, and in their stead a complaint and answer required, each setting forth the real claim and defense of the parties. * * *

Let the plaintiff set forth his cause of action in his complaint briefly, in ordinary language, and without repetition; and let the defendant make his answer in the same way. * * * The disputed facts will be sifted from the undisputed, and the parties will go to trial knowing what they have to answer. The plaintiff will state his case as he believes it, and as he expects to prove it. The defendant, on his part, will set forth what he believes and expects to establish, and he need set forth no more. He will not be likely to aver what he does not believe. His answer will disclose the whole of his defense, because he will not be allowed to prove anything which the answer does not contain. * * *

* * *

* * * But suppose the answer to set up new facts, which the plaintiff can not deny, but which he can answer by new matter, explaining away the effect of the new facts of the answer, how, it may be asked, is the plaintiff to bring the new matter out? I answer, he may bring it out in his proof in answer to the proof on the defendant's part * * *. How will the question appear upon the pleadings? So far as the record is concerned, it will appear thus: The allegations of the complaint are admitted; a new fact is alleged on the part of the defendant; this new fact the plaintiff is considered as opposing, either by a positive denial or as capable of being explained away by other facts, and therefore not having the effect claimed for it.

Either this may be done, or the course now pursued in equity cases may be followed, of amending the complaint when new facts are brought forward by the answer. Or still another mode may be adopted—that of requiring the parties respectively to give notice to each other of their points before the trial. Something of the sort now prevails in the Court of Admiralty of this district, and in the common-law Courts of Massachusetts.

The most ample power of amendment should likewise be given to the Courts. They should be enabled to amend the pleadings, in furtherance of justice, either when they are not sufficiently precise, or when they vary from the proofs; taking care to guard the parties against injury from surprise. * * *

Will it be said that the mode of pleading by complaint and answer, in the way I propose, will not put the case in a position to be tried by a jury? Let us see.

In the first place, is not the experience of Louisiana * * * decisive? * * * There, as I have already observed, the only pleadings are petition and answer. These are laid before the jury, who endorse their verdict upon the petition. All civil causes are tried by jury when either party desires it. Has any complaint been heard that the issues are not well defined, or that the juries can not perform their appropriate functions?

But if there were no experience in its favor, might we not reasonably expect that it would succeed? Any system would be better than the present. What with the common counts, and the general issues, we have now in most cases really no pleadings, no statement of the claim or defense, till the cause is called on for trial. * * *

You might just as well require the parties to copy and file each a verse of the "Iliad," and call that coming to an issue. * * *

The legitimate end of every administration of law is to do justice, with the least possible delay and expense. Every system of pleading is useful only as it tends to this end. This it can do but in one of two ways: either by enabling the parties the better to prepare for trial, or by assisting the jury and the Court in judging the cause. Let us consider it, then, in these two aspects:

First, as it enables the parties to prepare for trial. This it can only do by informing them of each other's case. To make them settle beforehand wherein they disagree, so as to enable them to dispense with unnecessary proofs, and to be prepared with those which are necessary, is the legitimate end of pleadings, so far as the parties are concerned. Now, no system could accomplish this more effectually than the one proposed. * * *

Is not this a certain way of apprising the parties of what they have to try? And is it not a simpler and easier way of doing it, than by the long labyrinth of replications, rejoinders, and the like? All this excessive subtlety and refinement on the one hand, and this monstrous jargon and prolixity on the other, can not be necessary to inform the parties of the points in dispute between them. * * *

Second, as it assists the jury and the Court in performing their functions. An opinion prevails that nothing but common-law issues are fit for a jury. Many lawyers are wedded to the system of pleading according to the ancient rules, though they admit and deplore the imperfections of our present practice. It is said that the production of the issue disentangles the case, lessens the number of questions of fact, and separates them from the questions of law.

Now, I deny, in the first place, that the production of an issue, according to the course of the common law, does really lessen the number of questions of fact. The declaration may contain any number of counts, each setting forth different causes of action, or the same cause of action in different forms. If the same plea is put into all the counts, there will be as many issues as there are counts. But the defendant may plead as many pleas to each count as he likes; and the plaintiff, with leave of the Court, may put in as many replications to each plea as he may happen to have answers to it.   *   *   *

But, apart from this, is it possible for any system of pleading to lessen the number of real questions without doing injustice? The jury must pass upon all the disputed questions of fact in a cause, or it must be imperfectly understood. No pleading can lessen the number of questions really disputed; it may lessen the number apparently disputed but the apparent dispute disappears the moment the trial is opened.   *   *   *

As to disentangling the questions, and separating those of fact and of law, it may be answered that it does it very imperfectly. It is impossible it should be otherwise.   *   *   * Take, for example, the issue of tender, payment, fraud, release, marriage, devise, property in trover, or replevin or title in trespass or ejectment. These are all complex questions, and to decide some of them may require the decision of many subordinate ones.

The attempt to reduce questions to all their elements before trial, must commonly fail. What subordinate ones may arise can scarcely be known till the evidence is all disclosed. The greatest diligence and skill will lead only to an approximation, greater or less according to the nature of the original questions. The first one is always this: Has the plaintiff the right, or the defendant? This depends upon others.   *   *   *

So apparent is it that our issues generally do not present simple questions, but complex ones, both of law and fact, that the law allows the jury, in all cases upon every issue, to find a special verdict, setting forth in detail all the facts tending to prove or disprove the affirmative of the issue, and referring the conclusion, from these facts, to the Court.

But suppose that the pleading did develop the questions, and quite separate those of fact from those of law, of how much advantage would it be to the jury, or the Court, in the exercise of their functions? The jury do not look into the record.   *   *   * They hear the testimony and arguments of counsel, and take the points in dispute from the Judge. He tells them that they are to pass upon certain questions of fact. That is all they know of them.

The most accurate analysis of a cause takes place at the trial, and then there really is something analogous to the ancient oral pleading. Indeed, we must not forget that our system of pleading had its origin in a practice which no longer exists. Being carried on orally by the parties, in the presence of the Court, it rested always under its supervision. It was, in fact, nothing more than the forming of an issue, by the Court, from the respective allegations of the parties.

When the presence of the Judge was withdrawn it lost an essential part of its original character. The substitute for that now is the trial. First, the plaintiff opens his case, and calls his witnesses; the defendant then does the same. After the testimony is finished, the defendant goes over his case again, and makes his analysis of the points and of the evidence. The plaintiff follows with his analysis and arguments, and upon this the Judge charges the jury. Then comes the true analysis of the case—the fullest development of all the points in the controversy, which no system of special pleading can dispense with.

* * *

So far we have considered the question without reference to the expense and delay of the old system of pleading. These are, however, important elements in the question. To do justice with the least expense and delay is, I repeat, the object of every administration of law. It has been said that it is better to have a Judge decide wrong, than not to decide soon. Without going so far as this, I must think time one of the most important elements in the proper administration of justice. Suppose it were certain that a cause would be better decided if the parties were allowed five years to get their proofs, and the Court five years to decide: Who would think of allowing any such thing? The expensiveness of lawsuits is also a consideration of immense consequence. Dear justice is no justice to the largest class of litigants.

* * *

Two objections have been made to the abolition of the present modes of pleading, of so singular a nature that I can not pass them over. I have been told, I know not how many times, that it would lessen the learning of the profession, and reduce the Courts to the level of justices' courts.

And is, indeed, the learning of the profession bound up with the system of common-law pleading? Is the noble science of jurisprudence—the fruit of the experience of ages, at once the monument and the record of civilization—inseparable from such paltry learning as that, "after the declaration, the parties must at each stage demur, or plead by way of traverse, or by way of confession and avoidance," or that "upon a traverse issue must be tendered," or anything of that sort? Lawyers have enough to learn if their studies are confined to useful knowledge. To assert that the great body of the law, civil and criminal—the law which defines rights and punishes crimes; the law which regulates the proprietorship, the enjoyment, and the transmission of property in all its forms; which explains the nature and the obligations of contracts through all their changes; the law that prevails equally on the sea and the land; the law that is enforced in courts of chancery and courts of admiralty, as well as in the courts of common law—to assert that this vast body of law requires the aid of that small portion which regulates the written statement of the parties in the courts of common law, is to assert a monstrous paradox, fitter for ridicule than for argument.

* * *

Many of the rules of pleading, I am ready to admit, are logical; but a logical exercise, however proper for young men in a college, is not a very proper exercise to be had at the expense of litigating parties. Logic can be taught in other ways, and at a less expense.

* * *

As to the other objection, that our superior courts would fall to the level of justices' courts by changing the forms of written pleadings, it proceeds upon the extraordinary assumption that the dignity and decorum of a court depend upon what passes in writing between the parties beforehand. If there be any connection between the two things, I am unable to see it. The dignity of a court depends not upon such matters, but upon him who sits upon its seat of judgment— upon his learning, his character, and his manners. * * *

The change which I recommend can not affect, in the slightest degree, the substantial rights of any party. No rule of law by which rights and injuries are judged will be touched, the object and effect of the change being simply the removal of old obstructions in the way of asserting the rights and redressing the injuries. * * *

* * *

Six sections like the following, incorporated into the new code of procedure, with a few forms annexed, would contain all the provisions necessary to establish the course of pleading, which I propose in all civil cases:

§ 1. The first proceeding shall be a complaint filed with the Clerk of the Court, setting forth briefly, in ordinary language, and without repetition, the nature and particulars of the cause of suit, and praying for the relief to which the complainant thinks himself entitled. * * *

§ 2. Within ten days after the day of appearance, the defendant shall file with the Clerk of the Court his answer to the complaint, setting forth briefly, in ordinary language, and without repetition, the nature and particulars of his defense. But further time to answer may be granted by a Judge of the Court, for good cause shown. * *

§ 3. No other pleading shall be allowed than the complaint and answer aforesaid, and, upon the filing of the answer, the cause shall be deemed at issue.   If the defendant shall neglect to file his answer within the time aforesaid, the allegations of the complaint shall, for the purposes of that suit, be taken to be true.   And when an answer is filed containing new matter, not responsive to the complaint, the Court may require from either party notice of any other facts, intended to be proved on the trial, relating to such new matter.

§ 4.   The defendant shall not be required to make any discovery by answer, nor shall the answer, in any cases, be deemed evidence against the complainant.   But any party to the suit may be examined as a witness at the instance of the opposite party, and for that purpose he shall be subject, like any other witness, to subpoena, to examination conditionally, or upon commission.

§ 5.   The Court shall have power at any time, in its discretion, to amend any process, pleading, or proceeding in furtherance of justice, taking care to guard the parties against injury from surprise, by correcting any mistake in the name of any complainant or defendant, or by adding or striking out the name of any complainant or defendant, or by conforming any pleading or proceeding to the facts proved, whenever the variance between the allegation and the proof is not material to the right of the case.   And the Court may also compel the parties respectively to amend the complaint or answer for want of sufficient precision therein;   and the defendant may be allowed, in the discretion of the Court, and after notice to the complainant, to file a supplemental answer containing any new defense occurring after the former answer.   And the Court may, also, upon the trial, disregard any variance between the allegation and the proof not material in substance.

§ 6.   All suits shall be brought in the name of the real party in interest, and against the party as to whom relief is prayed.

* * *

I lay out of view the advantage that this change would be to the profession itself.   This is altogether too narrow a view of the question, although I think it quite apparent that the real usefulness and dignity of the profession would be increased by it.   The practice is now too technical.   It requires a vast amount of drudgery to be performed; too many and too long papers; too many steps to be taken; too many motions to be made.   In short, instead of a straight path to an object in sight, we have to grope our way through a labyrinth of old passages, some of them in decay, some of them dark, many of them blocked up, and quite uncertain when we shall emerge to the light.   Most fervently do I hope that the year 1847 will see this labyrinth uncovered and demolished.

NOTES AND QUESTIONS

1.   In this excerpt Field indicates that he is responding to "demands for radical reform," and in a part that is omitted he notes "manifesta-

tions of public sentiment out of doors." Do his proposals strike you as "radical" ones? Do you believe that he is responding principally to the people "out of doors?" Who *are* the people "out of doors?" Whom would you expect Field's proposed codes to benefit, and why? In this connection, what does Field say is the attitude of the bar (or segments of the bar) toward the changes he proposes?

2. Can you detect any difference in the *espirit* of Field's proposals, and the pronouncements of Sampson? Rantoul? Story? Can you learn anything from this excerpt about Field's *concrete* political beliefs: whether he is a liberal or conservative, a Republican or Democrat or Whig, an ideologue or pragmatist? Field does use the word "justice" to recommend his reforms. What sort of "justice" is he talking about? Is it the same kind of justice that the radical Jeffersonians had wished to advance?

3. Field seems to make a distinction between law as writs-and-procedure, and law-as-substance. William Nelson has argued that this attitudinal change ranks as a major intellectual development in the history of American law. Do you understand why? Can you see how this intellectual distinction between writs (procedure) and substance would emerge naturally out of the kinds of legal changes studied in Chapter 3?

4. Field's paramount goal expressed here is to reform civil procedure, especially the common law actions. Do his proposals for the reform of common law pleading make sense to you? How could anyone oppose them? Indeed, how could anyone, even lawyers, ever live with the archaic common law writ system? Consider the following reading, and see if it explains why the old system lasted as long as it did.

WILLIAM E. NELSON, AMERICANIZATION OF THE COMMON LAW *

21–26 (1975).

Under the common law writ system, which was given wide application in prerevolutionary Massachusetts, pleading can serve the function of not only giving parties notice of each others' claims but also framing a single, simple factual question for the jury, to which the jury can return an answer of yes or no that will completely dispose of the case. The key to such a system is widespread use of special pleading and adherence to the rule that in giving evidence of the facts of their case parties "must abide by their Allegations." When this is done, no legal issues can come before the jury, for all questions of law are removed from the case by the court's prior determination of the legal sufficiency of proffered pleas. Moreover, the jury is not confused by extraneous facts, since the court excludes from evidence all facts that do not tend to prove or disprove the single issue of fact raised by the pleadings. * * *

* Reprinted from **William E. Nelson,** **Americanization of the Common Law:** The Impact of Legal Change on Massachusetts Society, 1760–1830, copyright © 1975 by the President and Fellows of Harvard University, published by the Harvard University Press, Cambridge, **Massachusetts** and London, England, in association with the American Society for Legal History, with the permission of the publisher and the author.

The effect of special pleading can be seen in a typical action of debt on a penal bond with a conditional defeasance. When the defendant pleaded his performance of the condition, the plaintiff could interpose a demurrer to his plea—a demurrer that would require the court to decide whether performance was a good defense. On the other hand, the plaintiff could deny the defendant's performance; then only the factual issue of the defendant's performance or nonperformance would remain in the case. Evidence on such matters as the execution of the bond, fraud, or usury could not come before the jury, since such evidence could not assist the jury in rendering a yes or no answer to the question whether the defendant had performed the act constituting the condition. Moreover, the jury might not even know the legal consequences of its answer; if, for example, it answered affirmatively the question whether John Doe had completed construction of a house for Richard Roe in 1763, it might not know whether its answer rendered Roe liable to Doe for the price of the house or Doe liable to Roe for failure to complete the house on time. Special pleading thus had the capacity of limiting the jury only to find facts and depriving it of all discretion in applying law to the facts.

If a defendant wished merely to deny the allegations advanced in the plaintiff's writ, he would plead what was known as the general issue in lieu of a special plea. The general issue was so called because it imported an absolute and general denial of each and every allegation in the plaintiff's declaration; all those allegations were put in issue before the jury. A plea of the general issue did not frame a single, precise factual question for the jury. There were two reasons for this. The first was that a typical plaintiff's declaration alleged several facts, all of which were put in issue by a general denial. The second was that the courts did not, as they did in the case of a special plea, restrict parties to proof only of facts tending to establish their allegations. The test of admissibility of facts under the general issue was not relevancy thereto but whether, as a matter of law, the proposed evidence ought to constitute a good defense to the plaintiff's action. * * * The consequence of permitting proof of special facts under the general issue [was that] * * * instead of being confronted with a single issue on which they heard only directly relevant evidence, juries heard evidence on several issues, among which legal relationships were unclear and subject to determination during the course of the jury's deliberations. Jurors thus had to find not only facts but also the legal consequences of facts; that is, in the absence of other restrictions they possessed power to decide the law as well as the facts.

Juries were frequently put in a position to exercise such power, for parties usually preferred to try cases under the general issue rather than under a special plea. Special pleading beyond the initial plea by the defendant and replication by the plaintiff was rare. * * * [Perhaps] judges and lawyers preferred to have juries rather than judges decide the law as well as the facts of their cases; whatever the cause may have been, this was the consequence of their infrequent use of special pleading. * * *

In addition to the rules of evidence discussed above, which excluded proof of facts deemed irrelevant to the issues, Massachusetts common law during this period had several other rules that excluded evidence deemed unreliable. * * *

The exclusionary rule most frequently invoked was that which rendered "Persons interested in the Matter in Question" incompetent as witnesses. The theory for exclusion was that "from the nature of human Passions and Actions, there * * * [was] more Reason to distrust such a biased Testimony than to believe it." * * * Much technical law became encrusted on that basic rule. Members of a corporation, for example, even if they themselves were not parties, were not permitted to testify in a suit involving the corporation since they would be liable for costs if the suit were lost. * * * The rule was extended further to exclude testimony of witnesses who had no such direct interest. Thus in Rex v. Jackson, a criminal prosecution for assault, it was doubted whether either the complainant or the defendant's wife could testify, even though neither had a direct pecuniary interest in the prosecution's outcome. And in Bartlett v. White the Superior Court extended the rule even further, holding that Baptists other than the plaintiff, a Baptist who had sued to recover damages for an allegedly unlawful collection of a religious tax, could not testify. * * *

A rule analogous to the one rendering interested witnesses incompetent was one that excluded the testimony of people convicted of serious crimes. The theory was that "when the Crime is so great and of such a Nature * * * it is to be supposed that the Person guilty has lost all Sense of Truth, and would not hesitate at violating his Oath * * *."

The final rule seeking to keep unreliable evidence away from the jury was the hearsay rule. * * * Two reasons were given for excluding hearsay. First, such testimony was not based on the witness's first-hand knowledge but on his mere "credulity"; second, it was not a statement made under oath. * * * The oath—and the moral and religious sanction that it implied—was seen as the best way of insuring that witnesses would tell the truth. The immense weight that colonials attached to oaths can also be seen from the instructions given to jurors to direct their evaluation of testimony. Prerevolutionary jurors were not told, as jurors are today, to weigh the credibility of witnesses and to consider the inherent probability or improbability of their testimony. Instead they were directed, in effect, to presume that all witnesses who had sworn an oath had told the truth. * * *

The colonial approach to evidentiary questions rested in large part, then, on a conception of truth that we do not share. The conception—that truth would emerge not from a weighing of credibilities and probabilities but from the sanctity of an oath—looked backward to earlier times, in which God-fearing men had attached enormous importance to a solemn oath. To the extent that such notions persisted, they reduced somewhat the power of juries to determine facts both by keeping evidence from them and by reducing their freedom in weighing the evidence that they heard.

NOTES AND QUESTIONS

1. In light of the workings of the system as Nelson explains them, are you persuaded that the common law procedures needed the fundamental alterations that Field proposed? Does Field himself give any evidence that the common law is capable of changing by itself? Could one take (1) the changes from Norman French to Latin and from Latin to English in the courts, (2) the introduction of the general issue, and (3) the development of the common counts, as such evidence? Is radical change necessarily better than this type of change?

2. Do you agree with Field that the enforced erudition of the bar was not a good reason for maintaining a regime of special pleading? Could that argument pass the red-face test? Do you agree that "a logical exercise, however proper for young men in a college, is not a very proper exercise to be had at the expense of litigating parties?"

3. What was the ultimate result of Field's championing the cause of Law Reform? The first installment of Field's proposed code of court procedure, which you have read about, *was* passed in 1848. See generally Reppy, "The Field Codification Concept," in Reppy, ed. Field Centenary Essays 17, 33–34 (1949) Field eventually threw his energies into efforts to have the New York legislature pass codifications of New York's substantive law. For an appraisal of Field's latter codification efforts, we have the comments of his biographer, Henry M. Field.

HENRY M. FIELD, THE LIFE OF DAVID DUDLEY FIELD

73–75, 76–77, 86–88 (1898).

* * * [Field's aim] was not to be a breaker of the precious traditions of the past. He had no purpose or desire to destroy the Common Law, but to preserve it and exalt it by cutting off its excrescences, and by translating it into the language of the people, so as to make it worthy, not only of the free States of America, but of all English-speaking peoples on the habitable globe.

But the stronger the argument for the Code, the more violent was the opposition. * * * The chief opposition came from the older members of the bar, who seemed to have a power in the Legislature to obstruct and defeat any action to which they were opposed. * * * [Still, in] 1857, on the 6th of April * * * an Act which he had himself drawn up with the greatest care, was passed by the Legislature, that a new Commission be appointed "to reduce into a written and systematic Code the whole body of the law of this State, or so much and such parts thereof as shall seem to them practicable and expedient * * *."

Very simple words are these to "lay readers," who do not take in all their meaning. But to the legal mind that one sentence, "to reduce into a written and systematic Code the whole body of the law," was the foretokening of a Revolution. With this came to Mr. Field the opportunity of his life. From the time that he entered on the practice of law, he had been possessed with the idea of Reform: it had been his one thought by day and his dream by night. A part of his scheme had been realized in the Code of Procedure, but the greater task of reconstructing and codifying the substance of the Law itself, yet remained. * * *

* * *

With such natural repugnance to change, it was not surprising that the adoption of the Codes was slow. Even the Codes of Procedure, though they concerned but the outward forms of administration of justice, instead of the substance of the law, met with opposition both within and without the Legislature. Although they had been submitted complete on the first of January, 1850, they had to wait long for recognition, and even as yet are only adopted in part. * * * The Code of Criminal Procedure was not adopted until 1882.

Thus the progress of reform was slow: it was only the outer walls of Conservatism that had been carried, the fortress itself was still to be stormed and taken. The revision of the Codes had taken the Commissioners, with all their assistants, eight years of the hardest labor. Not only had they been outlined with the utmost care, but every chapter and article had been revised and re-revised, till some portions were changed no less than eighteen times. * * * There was not a meeting of the Legislature that Mr. Field had not to make a pilgrimage to Albany, to appear before the Committee of the Senate or of the Assembly, where he was always sure to meet the determined opposition of some of the ablest members of the Bar in the State, in which they were supported by a large number of the legislators, who, from professional instinct, were opposed to innovations which would oblige them to re-learn, at least to some extent, both the substance and the practice of the law.

These were heavy odds, against which the Reformer had to stand almost alone, using all his power of argument and of persuasion, with only partial success. The Penal Code was indeed enacted in 1881, and has been the law of the great State of New York for fifteen years; but the Civil and the Political Codes have not been adopted to this day! The Civil Code, which he looked upon as the most important of all, has passed one of the houses, the Senate or the Assembly, again and again; twice it has passed both by large majorities; but failed in either case of receiving the signature of the Governor, who shrank from the responsibility of putting his name to a Reform which reconstructed the very substance of the Law.

* * *

FIELD, REASONS FOR THE ADOPTION OF THE CODES

(1873) Sprague, supra, at 361.

[Field wrote this twenty-five years before his brother's biography. These are *his* thoughts on the success or failure of his endeavors.]

Gentlemen of the Committee: Twenty-three years ago the Commissioners on Practice and Pleadings reported to the Legislature complete Codes of Civil and Criminal Procedure. These still await your action. Thirteen years ago the Commissioners of the Code reported the Political Code complete, and five years later they reported complete the Civil and Penal Codes, thus completing the system of codification which the Constitution had prescribed. These last three Codes, like their complements and predecessors, the completed Codes of Procedure, remain to be acted upon. * * *

* * *

These works, five of them in all, making, with the Book of Forms, six volumes, are, or, rather I should say, profess to be, a collection, in a compact and easily accessible form, of the general rules of our law, civil and criminal, substantive and remedial, or, in other words, "a complete digest of our existing law, common and statute, dissected and analyzed, avoiding repetitions and rejecting contradictions, molded into distinct propositions, and arranged in scientific order, with proper amendments." They were prepared not as a matter of speculation, but in obedience to two separate provisions of the Constitution, and pursuant to repeated acts of the Legislature, for the purpose of being enacted, so far as they were found worthy, and made part of the law of the State.

Why have they not been considered by the Legislature? The chief reason is that it has had too much to do, or, rather, it has done too much else. * * * Now, if the Legislature will occupy itself with special legislation at the rate of eight or nine statutes a day, it is easy to see that it will have neither time nor inclination for the consideration of a code. "How, then, is a code to be passed at all?" you will ask. I answer, it can be only in one of two ways; either by holding an extra session for the purpose, as was done when the Revised Statutes were enacted, or by taking the codes from the hands of a select body, either a commission of lawyers or a committee of the Legislature. This was substantially the method adopted in Massachusetts for passing the Revised Statutes of that Commonwealth, and it was also the method by which the French Codes were adopted. There is nothing in this course inconsistent with the duty of any legislator. A personal acquaintance with the details of every bill for which he votes is not expected or required of him. He contents himself with knowing its general scope, and relies upon the good sense and fidelity of the committees by which it has been examined and reported, and also, perhaps, upon the judgment of other members more competent or more conversant with the subject than himself. Then the Governor approves a bill because, on the whole, he prefers that it should, rather than it should not, become a law. Every section may not be such as he would himself have framed if he had been draughtsman of the bill, yet he does not, for that reason, withhold his approval. So a member of the Legislature, called on to vote upon the enactment of a code, may say to himself: "I have not thoroughly examined every section of this bill, but I understand its theory and design, and the general scope of its provisions; they have been framed under the authority of law; they have been a sufficient time before the public to enable any one desirous of studying them carefully to do so; they have been examined by persons competent to decide upon their merits, and I think that upon the whole it is safe to put them upon trial. They must, at all events, be better than the chaos that we have now. Great and glaring imperfections they are not likely to have after the ordeal they have undergone. * * * Such may be the wise conclusion of the most conscientious legislator. For my own part, I do not think it would be an advantage to have a code considered in a legislative body section by section, and amended or changed by a word or phrase inserted here or omitted there. A code is or should be an homogeneous work. It should have the impress of one mind, or at most of a few minds. Unity of design and uniformity of expression are important to it.

* * * I do not think our Revised Statutes were made better by the minute criticism to which they were subjected in the Legislature at an extra session; on the contrary, I think they were injured by it. If they had been accepted as they came from the hands of the revisers, it would have been better for us all. It should be remembered that the draughts of the Codes prepared by the Code Commission were first distributed among lawyers and judges for examination and suggestion, prior to a final revision; that, after they had been thus widely circulated, they were subjected to most careful reëxamination, and that no pains were spared to make them as perfect as possible. I think it safe to say that a greater amount of examination by lawyers or by the public at large could hardly be obtained previous to enactment, and I do not believe that a more painstaking commission could ever be organized. * * *

Another reason, perhaps, why all the Codes have not been adopted, is the opposition which the Code of Civil Procedure, or that part of it which has passed into law, encountered from the beginning. And yet this opposition was but natural. The new system was a complete overthrow of the old. Nothing of the kind had ever before been attempted. It shocked the theories and prejudices of the profession, hardened by the incrustation of centuries. No wonder that it was received with amazement at the audacity of proposing it, with scorn for the reasoning with which it was supported, and with hate for its destruction of the learning of so many lifetimes. No wonder that lawyers scoffed at it, and judges rebuked it. We had then—we have now a little improved, perhaps—one of the worst judicial systems which an enlightened community ever established: thirty-two Judges of the Supreme Court elected in eight districts, each Judge chosen by one constituency to serve for seven others which had no part in electing him, and all with coördinate powers reaching through the State. Given these conditions, and adding this other, that three fourths of the Judges were amazed, indignant, and disgusted at this sudden, daring, and, as they thought, visionary innovation; and it must needs follow that, what with dislike, misconception, unwillingness to assist and willingness to embarrass, a series of discordant decisions in the different districts would crowd the reports, great and small, to the annoyance equally of the lawyer and the suitor. Then add to the other sources of trouble, that so much of the Code as was enacted was a part—confessedly a part only—of a larger work which was promised at the time the first was received, and which was necessary to make a harmonious whole, and you have a condition of things which would have created embarrassment at first even with the most favorably disposed bench, and bar, but which, when both were, as a body, hostile, made an easy working of the system impossible. It is not, therefore, matter of surprise, though it be of reproach, that, in one State at least which has adopted the New York Code, the New York interpretation of it has been rejected, and the citation of New York decisions forbidden. Thus it has happened that the enactment of the remaining portions of the Code of Civil Procedure—three fourths of the whole, for the portion enacted was but about one fourth—has been resisted and defeated from 1850 to the present day; and we are now working the new but imperfect machinery in connection with the old. * * *

*   *   *

* * * There is another class of objections, however, which I ought to discuss * * *. It has been said * * * that an unwritten is, after all, preferable to a written law. You, of course, understand very well what is meant by these expressions "written and unwritten" law. In point of fact there is no such thing in this country at the present day as law known only through usage or tradition, and never committed to writing * * *. All law, deserving of the name, is written, and the distinction lies between that which is scattered up and down in enormous piles of cases, reports, treatises, and digests, without having had the sanction of the legislator, and that which has been enacted by the law-making department of the government. * * * The objectors whom I am now answering reject the latter and prefer the former.

The reasons advanced by them, or the principal reasons, are three—the impossibility of foreseeing and providing for all future cases, the supposed uncertainty and the supposed inflexibility of a code. That all future cases can not be foreseen is certain; and, therefore, that the code can not provide for them specifically and expressly is equally certain, but no more can an unwritten law provide for them; if there be any difference in this respect, it is in favor of the Code, because that is framed with an endeavor to provide for the future so far as it is possible to do so; whereas the unwritten law has no such aim and makes no such endeavor. It is the product of particular cases as they arise, is made for them, and limited to them. * * * An edict of the lawgiver reaches further and takes in more cases than a decree of the Judge.

Here let me correct a misapprehension into which some are apt to fall. The province of a code is not to give all the rules of law, general and particular, but only such as are general and fundamental. Some one has estimated the whole number of rules laid down in the reports at two million. No man would dream of collecting and arranging all these in a code. Most of them are mere deductions from other rules more general; the latter are those only which it would be useful or possible to bring together in a convenient form. * * * So it is with that rule of the common law, that a contract against public policy is void. This is a rule of general application to all cases. But public policy changes from time to time, and a contract which is valid today may not be valid half a century hence. A covenant to bring slaves from Africa, for example, might have been considered in accordance with public policy two hundred years ago. It certainly is against public policy now. * * *

And here I may mention an advantage of written over unwritten law; of statute law over case law; of legislator-made law over judge-made law—namely, that the latter is always made at the expense and risk of the suitor. Two citizens differ about the validity or performance of a contract, and go into court. If the law is already established, it should have been written and made known to the citizen before the lawsuit began; if it is not established, then the defeated party, an innocent person, innocent so far as knowledge of the law goes, must suffer the loss of property, the expense of litigation, in order that it may be established: a great hardship, as it seems to me, and one which society should have relieved him from, if it were possible to do so, by making and promulgating a rule beforehand. * * *

* * *

The last objection to a code, which I am here to consider, is its supposed inflexibility. If by this is meant that a statute once enacted will stand without the risk of appeal by the Courts so long as the Legislature leaves it alone, while, on the contrary, a decision, though pronounced and pronounced again, may be overruled the next day or the next year, then I must insist that the former condition is preferable to the latter. In this sense, flexibility is uncertainty, and, of course, inflexibility is certainty, which, so far from being a fault, is, to my thinking, a merit of the highest value.

If, however, by flexibility, as applied to the common law, it be meant that this law accommodates itself to the ever-changing circumstances and necessities of men, while a code could not thus adapt itself, I answer that, not only is the statement untrue in fact, but it would never have found believers except through a confusion of ideas. The common law, as I have said, is recorded somewhere, and wherever that may be its rules can be extracted and inserted in a code. The same words are as flexible in the one place as in the other. Therefore, the objection means, if it means anything, that it is better to have no record and no law than to have a code; better to have judges to make the rule at the same time that they apply it than to have the Legislature make it beforehand. The proposition thus stated will commend itself to no one in this country of popular institutions where it is a fundamental idea that the functions of government should be devolved upon distinct departments, where the Legislature can not encroach upon the Executive, and the Judiciary can not encroach upon either.

* * *

A code will lessen the labor of Judges and lawyers in the investigation of legal questions. Instead of searching, as now, through large libraries filled with the judicial records, not only of all the American States, but of England, Scotland, and Ireland, it will be sufficient to examine the articles of the Code relating to the subject.

* * *

Not only will there be a saving of labor but a saving of capital. The outlay required for the furnishing of law libraries will be greatly reduced. We forget how great is this outlay at present. Supposing the number of lawyers in the State of New York to be, as computed, ten thousand, and the average expense of their libraries to be three hundred dollars—too low, I think—the whole capital invested in lawyers' libraries will reach in this State alone three million dollars. This makes no account of the public libraries. I believe it is safe to estimate the whole capital invested in law libraries in this State to be not less than four millions. Three fourths of this, at least, may be saved, and a burden, grievous to be borne, taken from the shoulders of young men starting in professional life.

Besides the saving of labor and capital, there will ensue this additional advantage from a code, which is, that an opportunity will thus be afforded for settling vexed questions of law. We lawyers know that these vexed questions are many. We know better than all others into what a chaos our law has fallen. * * *

* * * And not only may doubtful questions be freed from doubt, but needed reforms may be effected through a code with greater facility than is possible without it. * * * How, with the greatest ease and certainty, can the law of real and personal property be assimilated? In what way can these modifications, in the relations

of husband and wife which modern society demands, be wrought with safety so readily as in the form of a general code of all the law? And, when a code is once formed, those necessary changes, which time and experience may show to be desirable, can be made without the confusion and uncertainty which are inseparable concomitants of our present annual legislation.   *   *   *

And last, but not least, of all the benefits of a code, is the diffusion among the people of a knowledge of the laws under which they live, and to which they must conform their conduct. Here, more than anywhere else in the world, is it needful that the people should know the law. They are supposed to make it. They, at least, are responsible for it. They by their agents administer it and execute it. *   *   *

It may interest you to know the working of codification in India, and I will give you the following extracts from the opening address at the session of 1872, of the English Law Amendment Society, delivered by Mr. Fitzjames Stephen, lately legal adviser of council in India   *   *   *.

> I once had occasion to consult a military officer upon certain matters connected with habitual criminals. He was a man whose life was passed in the saddle, and who hunted down Thugs and Dacoits as if they were game. Upon some remark which I made, he pulled out of his pocket a little Code of Criminal Procedure, bound like a memorandum-book, turned up to the precise section which related to the matter in hand, and pointed out the way in which it worked with perfect precision. It is one of the many odd sights of Calcutta to see native policemen learning by heart the parts of the police act which concern them. The sergeant shouts it out phrase by phrase, and his squad obediently repeat it after him till they know it by heart. The only thing which prevents English people from seeing that law is really one of the most interesting and instructive studies in the world is, that English lawyers have thrown it into a shape which can only be described as studiously repulsive.   *   *   *

*   *   *

NOTES AND QUESTIONS

1. This speech was made to the joint Judiciary Committee of the two houses of the New York legislature. Does it seem likely to you that a legislator seriously committed to serving his constituents would be persuaded to take the advice of Field's Code Commission and pass the Field codes without debate or close scrutiny? Does it make the passage of Field's codes in New York any more likely when Field labels the New York judiciary "one of the worst judicial systems which an enlightened community ever established?" Why would he say such a thing?

2. Note that by the time of this speech, 1873, Field's work had expanded from revisions in the writ system to, as his commission put it,

"reduce into a written and systematic Code the whole body of the law. * * *" How well did Field succeed? He never got all his codes passed in New York, but what about his success elsewhere? By 1898 both California and Montana, for example, had enacted *all five* of the Field codes, so that his dream of a Code to cover *all the law* of a state was realized. Why did the codes find more acceptance in the West than the East?

3. Field suggests that his codes were in keeping with the "popular institutions" of America. What did he mean by that? He also said, in response to critics, that his plan of codification would not intrude upon the functions of separate government departments (legislature, executive, judiciary). Whom would he need to convince of this, and why?

4. Field was said to have been influenced at an early age by the work of William Sampson (Henry M. Field, The Life of David Dudley Field 44 (1898)). Do you see any evidence of this influence? Do you see any evidence, on the other hand, of the influence of more traditional theorists, like Joseph Story? And how is he unlike Story?

5. James Coolidge Carter (1827–1905), a prominent member of the New York bar, successfully led the opposition to the enactment of Field's substantive codes in New York. Much of his argument against the codes is contained in the following passages from The Proposed Codification of Our Common Law 86ff (1894), a paper Carter prepared at the request of a Committee of the Bar Association of the city of New York:

> * * * It cannot too often be repeated that the Practical business of administering private law consists in the application by the courts of the national standard of justice to the business and dealings of men. This national standard of justice is something which cannot be embodied in written rules, or set down in any form of words. It is the product of the combined operation of the thought, the morality, the intellectual and moral culture of the time. Under our present unwritten system of law it is ascertained and made effective by the judges, who know it and feel it because they are a part of the community. They cannot but recognize it and yield to it, because their judgements are subject to the instant and close scrutiny of keen professional observers, not to mention the oversight of the press and the general public. This national standard or ideal of justice grows and develops with the moral and intellectual growth of the community, and through the operation of judicial decision is transferred to the province of the law. Hence a gradual change, unperceived and unfelt in its progress, is continually going on in the jurisprudence of every progressive State. The natural agency through which this healthy progress is effected is that of the devoted students and authoritative interpreters of the law. * * * The question is, shall this growth, development and improvement of the law remain under the guidance of men selected by the people on account of their special qualifications for the work, or be transferred to a numerous legislative body, disqualified by the nature of their duties for the discharge of this supreme function. * * *

* * *

(1) It is agreed on all hands that private jurisprudence is a science; whence it follows that it can be cultivated, developed and advanced only by the masters of that science.

(2) It is also agreed that a legislative body consisting principally of laymen, possesses no single qualification which enables it to prosecute the cultivation and improvement of this science, and its adaptation to human affairs.

How, if at all, does Field deal with the arguments propounded by Carter? Are Field and Carter in disagreement on all points? With which one do you agree? How do you account for the fact that in New York, at least, Carter's views were the immediate victors? On the other hand, whose views do you suppose prevail today, and why?

6. Who really stood to benefit from the Field codes? Was it the common man, or perhaps the cop on the beat, as is suggested by the little anecdote from India? Could something far subtler have been going on? Of what importance are the facts that Field was also the lawyer for "Boss" Tweed, the counsel to two of the great "robber barons," Jay Gould and James Fiske, and that Field helped found one of New York's largest and most influential law firms?

SECTION C. THE MOVEMENT FOR AN ELECTIVE JUDICIARY

ROBERT M. IRELAND, "AN INDEPENDENT JUDICIARY" THE POPULAR ELECTION OF JUDGES IN AMERICAN HISTORY *

[At approximately the same time as the passage of Field's Code of Civil Procedure, there was a nationwide movement for State Constitutional Reform and for the popular election of State Judges. According to Professor Ireland:]

States which converted wholly to an elective judiciary [were] * * * Illinois (1848), Indiana (1851), Kentucky (1850), Louisiana (1852), Maryland (1851), Michigan (1850), Missouri (1851), Ohio (1851), Pennsylvania (1850), Tennessee (1853), and Virginia (1851). Two newly admitted states, California (1849) and Wisconsin (1848) adopted elective judiciaries. Five others, Alabama (1850), Arkansas (1848), Connecticut (1850), Iowa (1846), and Vermont (1850) began electing inferior court judges. In 1852, Georgia's general assembly provided for popularly elected superior court judges leaving only the newly created Supreme Court subject to legislative appointment. Voters in New Hampshire (1851) and Massachusetts (1853) bucked the American mainstream and rejected proposed constitutions with reformed judiciaries. * * *

* * *

---

* Unpublished paper by Professor Ireland, of the University of Kentucky Department of History, reprinted with the permission of the author.

[The following excerpt from the preface to Professor Ireland's study gives some of the background for the movement towards an elective judiciary. Do you discern any common causes or tactics between the movement for an elective judiciary and the movement for codification of the common law?]

Almost from their beginning Americans have brooded about the problem of how to select their judges and for what period of time. During the colonial era the principal question was that of tenure; the Crown insisted that colonial judges be chosen for a period at the pleasure of the King, while certain colonists, most often speaking from assemblies, demanded that jurists be appointed for life on the condition of good behavior. Before 1701 most English judges were appointed for a tenure at the pleasure of the King. After more than a century of turmoil which saw some of the Stuart kings, especially James II, implement a type of judicial tyranny, English reformers in the Act of Settlement of 1701 secured the appointment of judges for the life of the monarch on the condition of good behavior. In 1760, Parliament specified that the death of the monarch would not terminate judicial tenure. But the mother country refused to extend these reforms to her colonies * * *.

Colonists argued that it was unfair for the royal government (most often acting through the governors) both to appoint judges and be able to remove them at pleasure. * * * Only life tenure could protect the judiciary and the people from a dependent judiciary acting under the influence of the Crown and its agents, the governors. The royal government disputed this argument, noting that the legislatures maintained leverage over the judiciary by controlling its salaries * * *. [The Governors also argued that] lack of legal talent in the colonies necessitated tenure at the pleasure of the King * * * to remove incompetent jurists.

* * *

The Revolution may have rendered most judiciaries independent of the executive, but in most cases it did not completely remove their dependence upon the legislature. The new state constitutions generally codified the colonial conception of the ideal judiciary; legislatures most often had the right to appoint judges, usually for life and seldom had to provide them with permanent and sufficient salaries. Furthermore they often won a right rarely recognized during the colonial period, to remove judges by impeachment or by joint address. * * * [In] the first decade of independence legislatures added to their newly gained authority by trespassing on territory traditionally occupied by the courts, overturning judicial decisions by special statutes and the like.

But the judiciary did not sit by idly * * *. The period 1776–1800 also witnessed the emergence of the judiciary as a powerful constitutional institution regarded by increasing numbers of influential * * * thinkers as an essential check on legislative power.

With this transformation of the judiciary came new appreciation for judicial independence and power. State appellate courts even before the Constitution of 1787 began to claim the right to declare unconstitutional legislative statutes. By 1790 trial judges also commenced claiming more authority at the expense of juries. And finally, judges, however gradually, began to regard the common law as an instrument of social and economic change rather than simply fixed doctrine. * * * [A]ll three states entering the Union between 1780 and 1800 provided for good behavior judicial tenure, and by the latter date eleven of sixteen states had lifetime judges. Delegates to the [Federal] Constitutional Convention of 1787 generally endorsed the newly found significance of the judiciary and without much debate provided for good behavior judicial tenure and salaries that could not be diminished.

Alexander Hamilton * * * in his Federalist Paper Number Seventy-Eight * * * submitted that an independent judiciary was essential to a republican government and was best achieved by good behavior tenure. Hamilton's devotion to judicial independence resulted in large part from his fear of the legislature which he believed would exceed its powers under the constitution should the courts not have the power to declare its statutes unconstitutional. Furthermore, unless checked by an independent judiciary, a legislature might do "injury" to the "private rights of particular classes of citizens, by unjust and partial laws." Thus by 1787 many political leaders applauded the newly asserted power of judges, but most discussed this power and its foundation, judicial independence, only in the narrow terms of preventing legislative tyranny. * * * Hamilton and others believed that the people [should involve] themselves only by their selection of delegates to constitutional conventions and their indirect ratification of constitutions. Constitutions represented the supreme embodiment of the will of the people and the courts upheld this will against legislative usurpation. But the people could not claim the power to elect those charged with interpreting constitutions.

Even critics of the new Constitution did not [seriously] question the newly [derived notions about the need for an] independent judiciary. During the debate over the constitution in 1787 and 1788, antifederalists rarely attacked the proposed provisions regarding judicial tenure and selection and when they did so, most often suggested that federal judges would not be independent enough. Pennsylvania's John Smilie contended that the mere existence of an impeachment power would seriously compromise the judicial will, whereas Patrick Henry and Luther Martin implied that state judges were more secure from undue pressure. * * *

If antifederalists were generally silent regarding the new nation's general allegiance to non-popular life-tenured judges, so-called "radical republicans" of the early national period were not. Eager to reform the bar and bench in drastic ways, a few radicals wrote detailed pamphlets calling for an elective judiciary for limited terms. Typical was the effort in 1805 of John Leland, Protestant minister of western Massachusetts, who called for an elective judiciary both federal and state, issuing an elaborate denial that the people were incompetent to choose their judges and that popular selection would impair the independence of the judiciary. Yet Leland, not confident of success, ended his tract with the standard radical plea for the masses to ignore judges and lawyers and to settle their own disputes. More withdrawn and philosophical was Thomas Jefferson whose antipathy toward the judiciary, especially that of the federal government, deepened in retirement at Monticello. In letters to friends and in his autobiography, he castigated federal judges as "miners and sappers" and seemed to call for an elective judiciary for a term of years.

Leland's pessimism was well-placed, for his and Jefferson's diatribes did not spark national debate on judicial selection and tenure, and few states seriously entertained the notion of an elective judiciary before 1830. * * *

SAMUEL M. SMUCKER, POPULAR ARGUMENTS IN FAVOR OF AN ELECTIVE JUDICIARY*

(1850).

The Statesmen of this Commonwealth [Pennsylvania] have at length arrived at the assertion of a very important and fundamental principle, which belongs to the great system of rational and republican freedom under which we live; we mean the Election of the Judiciary at the polls. The minds of thinking men and patriots are, however, divided, as to the desirableness of anything in the structure of our Constitution with reference to this point. This difference of opinion among men of equal sagacity, experience and patriotism, shows that the question must be involved in serious difficulty. * * *

We invite the attention, therefore, of both the approvers and opposers of this measure, to the consideration of the following brief and popular arguments, which, as we think, powerfully commend its unqualified adoption.

§ I. The selection of the Judges, when chosen by the people will be accomplished with less mercenary motive and influence *on the part of the electors themselves,* then is the case under the present system of appointment by the Governor.

* * *

How then, have most of the Judges in this Commonwealth been chosen, for the last thirty years? Have not the majority of them been

---

* This, and the following two readings, are taken from some of the debates in the states which arose as a result of Constitutional Conventions and reforms.

the relations,—the brothers, the cousins, or the sons-in-law of the acting executive? Or else, if the Cornucopia of official abundance has not poured out its riches upon these, probably because none such were in existence; have not many of the vacant Judgeships been conferred upon those faithful, but obscure friends of the Executive, who, for many long years, had groped with him, shoulder to shoulder, amid the obscure drudgery of some country law-office, or worked up with him the petty county politics of some remote section of the state? *Such has been the fact.* Faithful to the often bitter memories of the past, the successful aspirant after the supreme seat in the Commonwealth, casts his eye, from his lofty eminence, upon his ancient, less fortunate allies, who still grope among the subterranean shades below; he dips the Executive arm far down the declivity, and heaves up his expectant friends to the elevation of the Judiciary.

Now, we maintain that this is not the way to elect suitable wise and able Judges; that this is the very way to fill the bench with the most incompetent incumbents. And we maintain that the election of the Judges, by the people, would entirely remove this evil. In the election of their legislators, the people are not under the influence of any selfish or improper motive. They uniformly choose men who, if they are not always able and enlightened, are at the least the object of no personal or family partiality; and they are generally men well adapted to the part which they are called upon to perform. If they are under any obligations whatever, it is not one of individual favors, but only those which they owe their party, whose principles they have publicly espoused, and are supposed, in common honor and honesty, faithfully to maintain.

But this partial kind of obligation for party preferences, however it may operate in inducing legislators to vote for party measures in the halls of legislation, cannot possibly operate upon the Bench, where the whole sphere of the incumbent is one altogether professional, scientific, and extra-popular. No Judge can rule a cause in favor of a *party*. Corruption, in such cases, is utterly impossible. And therefore, when the people assemble at the polls, to choose the men who are to hold offices, which afford so little opportunity to reward those to whose votes they owe their election, they will vote under the influence of no selfish bias whatever. * * * The people would at once be thrown upon the necessity of voting for men whose only recommendation was their legal distinction and their personal worth.

§ II. From this first position necessarily follows our second one; that by the election of the Judges by the people, there will be less subserviency, less timeserving, and less mercenary place-hunting *on the part of the applicants.*

The reason for this will be, because it will be impossible for the candidates, from the nature of the case, to display the same degree of unprincipled subserviency to the countless members of a vast community, which they can and will display toward one single and all-potent individual. That the applicants for the Judgeship under the proposed change, will make all possible efforts to secure their aims, is of course to be expected. But what means can they employ to attain those ends? None which savor of bribery or corruption. None which can result in benefits unjustly and unfairly bestowed by the successful applicant, upon those who lift him up to power; because they are too numerous. The only way by which the popular favor could be courted, with reference to election to the Judiciary, is by the attainment of general popularity; by the display of those qualities which will commend men, as Judges, to the people. For will the people elect to that high responsible office, men who are notoriously corrupt or mercenary; or men who are notoriously irascible or selfish or incompetent? * * *

* * *

AN ELECTIVE JUDICIARY

Baltimore Sun, June 4, 1851, page 1, col. 4.

A writer in the Georgetown Reporter has the following excellent remarks on the great principle of an elective Judiciary. He is a native of Maryland and speaks with reference to the new Constitution:

" * * * That which is most novel to us, and most calculated to strike our attention, is in the organization of the Judiciary department. The change here proposed, I suppose, may safely be regarded as one of the most material points upon which its opponents will turn the thunder of their batteries. The bare idea of allowing the people to elect the Judges of their courts, has filled with a sort of magical apprehension the minds of some * * *.

"The masses of the people must be a singular and rather strange intellectual and moral compound, to be held universally to be capable of self-government, and yet have that capability limited, so as to exempt from the exercise of the elective franchise the Judges of our courts. * * * The people are either capable of self-government, or they are not. To admit that they are, is to be consistent, not only with the idea of liberty, but also with the theory which runs throughout the framework of that stupendous government which unites into one republic the thirty States of which it is composed. To deny it, is but a bold declaration that the whole is but one magnificent falsehood.

"What, then, is the effect of this limitation of the right of the people to govern in the judiciary department? It is that the people are qualified to govern in the legislative and executive departments of the government, but not there; as if qualifications of a high order, and purity of character were not as necessary in the two, as in the other grand department of government. We are told, that in order to keep the ermine pure, and to secure the efficient administration of justice, the Judge must be independent of, and not accountable to the people. This is a doctrine which belongs to the ages that have past and gone—certainly not to this in which we live.

"It is this doctrine alone, of 'irresponsibility to the people' which has spotted the annals of our race with so many instances of wanton and odious cruelty. It is the prolific parent of all kinds and modes of tyranny. Place your fellow man in a position wholly independent of you, invest him with the attribute of irresponsibility, and that *human sympathy* which stimulates to virtuous actions, and guides one on to the accomplishment of a noble and praiseworthy destiny, will certainly be extinguished. In its stead, selfishness, with all its little, bigoted, and concomitant auxiliaries, will enthrone itself * * *.

"Why, then, shall the people of Maryland retain such an antagonistical doctrine in the organization of their Judiciary department? Now that they have an opportunity to do so peacefully, I hope that on the 4th of June next they will vote to strike down into the dust this modern Moloch of unreasonable power, which has been so long enthroned in the very Temples of Justice."

* * *

J. M. LOVE, THE ELECTION OF JUDGES BY THE PEOPLE FOR SHORT TERMS OF OFFICE

3 So.L.Rev. (New Series) 18 (1877).

The inevitable tendency of all free institutions is to radicalism. Free thought and free discussion bring two great forces into perpetual conflict—the one radical, the other conservative. The former is positive and aggressive; the latter, negative and defensive. The first assails, the last resists. It is a conflict of ideas, in which there can be no doubtful result. The active, positive, moving force ever prevails against the negative, quiescent, resisting force. This active force in a free country is democratic sentiment, the constant tendency of which is to carry all established institutions irresistibly forward in the direction of radicalism. * * *

There is nothing more natural to the human mind than to accept abstract propositions and follow them to their logical consequences, without regard to the existing conditions to which they are to be applied. * * * The shallow thinker imagines that he sees in this logical process profound philosophy. The lazy investigator finds in it a ready solution of all difficult problems, without the painstaking labor required by the process of induction from innumerable facts. * * * But to determine truly with what modifications abstract truths are to be applied to existing conditions, so as to avert possible evils and promote the well-being of society, demands the profoundest insight into men and things, as well as careful investigation and thorough knowledge. A great scholar and legist has said with sententious wisdom that "many things which are true in the abstract are not true in the concrete." The founders of our institutions understood the full truth of this apothegm, and they acted upon it in laying the foundations of the system which they established. They were not mere theorists, nor *doctrinaires*, nor utopian legislators. They were great lawyers, practical philosophers, and wise statesmen, experienced in affairs. They recognized the principle of popular sovereignty. They were too wise not to know that the will of the people must needs be a great factor—nay, the greatest factor in any system of government to be established in a state of society where neither military power nor traditional rights exists. Hence, they skilfully wrought into the framework of our institutions the principle that the consent of the governed is the only legitimate source of human authority over the people. But in framing our early constitutions the fathers did by no means blindly follow the doctrine of popular sovereignty to its logical consequences. On the contrary * * * they carefully and studiously erected powerful barriers to arrest, control, and sometimes defeat, the popular will. * * * The fathers evidently believed that between the tyranny of one man and the tyranny of an unrestrained popular majority, the balance of evil would be largely with the latter. Did they recognize the absurd dogma that all men, all women, and all children, at the age of discretion, have an inalienable right, without experience or training, to participate in the government of the country? Did they for a moment assent to the proposition that to fight and to vote are correlative rights, and that the bullet and the ballot must be wielded by the same hand? On the contrary, they postponed universal suffrage for many years after the close of the Revolution, and until the people who had been living under monarchical form, without the training required to vote intelligently in a republic, became, to a certain extent, politically educated. * * * Little did they dream of perpetuating the monstrous and criminal folly of introducing, without the least preparation, into the body politic vast hordes of ignorant, illiterate, and semi-barbarous men, to vote away the property of their fellow-men, and subvert all civil order! If the fathers had been called upon to consider the question of negro suffrage under the same circumstances in which this generation of statesmen had to deal with that problem, they would probably have reasoned thus: "Let us by no means establish a constitution excluding these four millions of freedmen absolutely from the suffrage, lest we make the whole race enemies of the government under which they are to live. It is not consistent with the true idea of a republican commonwealth to exclude by arbitrary designation large numbers of people from all participation in the government. The deprivation of essential rights tends inevitably to make those who are thus excluded, enemies of the government. Let us, therefore, take measures to prepare these people, by education and political training, for the great duties of citizenship; and let us introduce them slowly and gradually as members of the political community. Thus may we at once satisfy the just and natural aspirations of the colored race, and prevent them from becoming the victims of demagogues and designing politicians, who will otherwise mislead them to their own injury, and to the irreparable detriment of society."

Many were the barriers which the wise fathers erected * * *. Consider the Senate of the United States. The people are not represented in that body at all. Its members are not elected by the people.* * * * Two senators, speaking for that little commonwealth [Delaware] of one hundred thousand people, may negative the voice of the great state of New York, with its five millions of inhabitants. * * * The Senate was intended to be, and is, an obstruction to the popular will; yet what American citizen would consent to abolish the Senate? * * *

Again, in the organization of the executive department our ancestors sought to raise restraining obstacles to the will of popular majorities. It is well known that it was not their purpose that the president should be elected directly by the people. On the contrary, they intended so to organize the electoral colleges as to place the election of president in the hands of the small number of independent men elected, indeed, by the people, but free to exercise their own judgment and discretion in the choice of the chief magistrate of the nation. * * * Thus they made it quite possible that a president should be chosen by a popular minority, and it is a familiar fact of our history that several of our presidents were elected in opposition to a majority of the popular vote. * * *

* * *

The fathers were too wise and too honest to give assent to the false and blasphemous dogma, that "the voice of the people is the voice of God." They had read history, and from its "pictured page" they had learned that the voice of the people is not unfrequently the voice of the devil! They had heard the voice of the people in the enlightened, polite, and art-loving Athenian democracy, condemning to death without cause their wisest citizen, and banishing another equally illustrious, because they were "vexed" to hear him everywhere called "the just." They had heard that potential voice in the Roman forum— now applauding one usurper, now another; today following with shouts of approbation the tyrant Sylla, tomorrow the tyrant Marius! They had heard it uttered in the streets of the great city at the death of the usurper in wild cries for vengeance against their own deliverers! They had heard the voice of the people in the mother country, de-

* Article I, Section 3 of the Constitution originally provided that Senators were to be chosen by the state legislatures. By the Seventeenth Amendment to the United States Constitution, ratified in 1913, the mechanism for election of Senators was changed from selection by the legislatures to direct election by the people of each state. Does the passage of this amendment strengthen or weaken Love's argument?

manding the burning of witches and heretics, sustaining the accursed slave trade, and approving of the judicial murder of many illustrious men. * * * The fathers well knew what history, ancient and modern, but too clearly reveals that faction and party spirit not frequently prevail in republics over truth, reason, and justice * * *.

* * * It was evidently their purpose to make the judiciary perfectly independent of the people, as well as the government. This they sought to accomplish by the manner of their appointment, the tenure of office, and the mode of compensation.

* * * They would not consent even to allow the House, in which the people are directly represented, to participate in the appointment of the judges. * * * They withheld from the whole government the power to remove a judge except by impeachment. They forbade any reduction of the salary of a judge during the time of his continuance in office. But in a large number of the states of the Federal Union this wise policy respecting the judiciary has been swept away by the drift of public sentiment toward radicalism. The judges in many states are now elected by universal suffrage for a short term of office, and the manifest tendency in all the states is strongly in the same direction. This is a momentous change! Is it a wise one? Or, on the contrary, is it but another proof, of which history furnishes so many, that all change is not progress—all innovation not improvement.

The fathers had read the history of the mother country * * *. They had noted the corruption, the craft, the self-abasement of English judges when it became their interest to conciliate that power in the state upon which they depended for their continuance in office and their salaries. They had seen exhibited in English history the amazing and humiliating spectacle of illustrious magistrates, judges of the highest dignity, crawling to the footstool of kingly power, like prostrate slaves before some eastern despot! * * *

Then, again, the founders of the government had seen a great change in the history of English jurisprudence. At the Revolution of 1688 the judges were made partially independent. * * * [By the time of the American Revolution, Parliament had] provided that the commissions of the judges should continue during good behavior, notwithstanding any demise of the crown, and that their full salaries should be absolutely secured to them during the continuance of their commissions. The great and salutary change which resulted from these facts in the administration of English law is well known to every student of the judicial history of England. * * *

* * * We have in our day and generation taken a vast stride in the opposite direction. We have in a great number of states made the judges dependent, not upon the executive government, but upon the popular will. Is the change a wise one? The American bar certainly does not approve of it; and the members of the bar are not

only the best judges of such a matter, but they have had the best possible opportunities of observing the results of the change, and of forming a correct judgment concerning it. What is the difference in the principle and practice between making the judges dependent upon the people and dependent upon the executive head of the government? In my judgment it would be far better to make them dependent, if dependent at all, upon the executive than upon the people. It is only in political questions sometimes, though rarely involved in private litigation, that the executive government takes any special interest in the administration of justice by the courts. Even the kings of England desired to see the laws impartially administered between private litigants. * * * They rarely interfered with the courts, except in cases involving the interests and prerogatives of the crown. But how is it with King Public Opinion? Does he not interest himself in a vast variety of cases, involving mere individual right and private litigation? Does he not often, as well in the remote corners of the land as at the seat of government, assume to influence, revise, and sometimes overrule, judges as well as juries? Is he not often arbitrary, one-sided, prejudiced, ill-informed, yet violent and dominating? * * * [I]t is equally well known that public opinion is not seldom influenced and controlled by party spirit, religious bigotry, and personal prejudices. Now, a judge sitting to administer justice in the midst of an excited populace, upon whose will his future judicial existence depends, must be elevated above ordinary human nature not to be removed or affected by such influence. * * *

Nothing surely could be more shocking to our sense of justice and propriety than that a court of justice should be influenced in its judgments between man and man by outside popular opinion. * * * Yet, with strange inconsistency, our people have in many states * * exposed their judges to such temptations that nothing but that lofty virtue and independence of personal character, which cannot be expected in the ordinary incumbent of judicial office, can give assurance that the courts will not be influenced by the prevailing popular opinion. * * *

The fundamental objection to an elective judiciary is that the people have no right to be represented in a judicial proceeding. * * On the contrary, if all the people in all America should demand judgment against the humblest individual, yet, if right and justice were with him, a court of justice should, in disregard of universal opinion, give judgment in his favor. * * * The people ought of right to be represented in the making of the laws, but not in their administration by the courts. The legislator enacts a general law, the burdens and obligations of which fall alike upon his friends and foes, and in this we have a sufficient guaranty that the legislator will not pass oppressive laws. But the judge pronounces sentence in a particular case between individuals, or between the government and individuals, and he may therefore, if so disposed, without wounding his own friends and supporters, give judgment in favor of the party who controls the greater power or commands the greater number of votes. * * *

Since all men reject without the least hesitation the idea that the popular voice should be heard in a court of justice * * * what are the reasons which have induced the change in our state constitutions by which the judges are made elective by the people? It is surely not that judges should be responsible to the people for decisions made by them in the administration of justice; for how are the great mass of the people to know whether the decisions of the judge are right or wrong—in accordance with law or otherwise? Perhaps the idea underlying the great change of policy respecting the mode of appointing judges may be found in the belief that the people are capable of making a wiser choice of judges than the executive head of the state would be. There are many demagogues who affect to believe, and some honest people who, by dint of repetition, have brought themselves to believe, that the popular judgment of men and things is well nigh infallible. * * *

But without questioning the infallibility of the popular mind, let us for a moment enquire what are the inevitable consequences of making the judiciary subject to popular election. Is it not notorious that it brings the judicial office into direct connection with party politics and all the bad methods and influences of faction? Who will deny the somewhat startling assertion that, under the elective system, the party caucus does, in fact, appoint the judges of the land? Wherever either party is dominant, it makes the election of judges strictly partisan, and uses the judicial office as a part of its patronage. * * * And who is the man most likely to get a caucus nomination? Is the thoughtful, studious, and upright lawyer, the man of ideas and books and nice scruples, or the man of inflexible love of right, truth, and justice, likely to prove acceptable to a party caucus? Is such a candidate likely to succeed in getting a nomination in opposition to the adroit wire-puller, the man of popular ways and manners, voluble tongue, and little law? * * *

* * * Now, what would be said of a law or constitution enacted in these terms: Be it ordained, or enacted, that the party caucus of the majority faction shall choose the judges of the state! Such a statute or constitution, made in direct terms, would startle everybody, and meet probably with universal reprobation; yet such is the undoubted practical result of making the judges elective.

And here I may remark that it is one of the singular and, it seems to me, anomalous workings of our free institutions that the country is practically deprived by party usage of the services of nearly one-half its citizens. All the offices and honors of the state are engrossed by the majority. The minority, without respect to their own merits and qualifications, and often in utter disregard of the interests of the public service, are excluded by a rigid and inflexible party usage. * *

Now, it would seem to be to the highest degree unjust and impolitic in a free republican commonwealth that the community should not be perfectly free to choose from the entire body of its citizens the individual best qualified for the public service in a given capacity; and, theoretically, our American republics enjoy this liberty, but practically it is not so. Could a democrat in Iowa or republican in Missouri, by any conceivable means, be chosen as a supreme judge of the state in the face of existing party usages and organizations, which rule elections with a rod of iron? * * *

* * * With respect to executive and legislative offices, the majority have at least the entire body of their own partisans and followers from whom to make their selection. But judges have to be chosen from the very small number of citizens who form the body of a learned profession * * *.

* * * To say nothing of the evil influence that such a relation to party must exert upon the mind of the judge himself, it is obvious that he is, more or less, an object of distrust to his political opponents, and that he takes his seat without that full and unreserved confidence which would attend him if freely chosen by the whole people instead of a faction. There is, perhaps, no mode of election in this country by which the evil in question could be entirely cured. By whomsoever appointed, party views would, perhaps, have undue influence in the choice of judges, but the incumbent himself, if the old plan of appointment by the executive and senate prevailed, would be, to a considerable extent, removed from popular and partisan influences, and the candidate for judge would certainly, under that mode of selection, be less exposed to the temptation of plying the arts of popularity in obtaining and administering his high office.

Again, it is evident that the sense of responsibility is lessened as you divide and diffuse it. * * * Now, the appointment of a judge imposes upon the appointing power a heavy responsibility, and if this responsibility could be concentrated upon the executive head of the state, that officer would, I think, very rarely provoke the censure of the legal profession, and the indignation of the whole community, by the appointment of a bad or incompetent judge.

But what sense of responsibility can be brought home to an entire people for the election of a bad judge? * * *

I do not myself believe that the law for the popular election of judges can be changed. Popular privileges, once granted, are not likely to be surrendered, especially where the people are taught to believe themselves an unfailing source of all political wisdom. The only practicable remedy consists, in my judgment, in greatly enlarging the terms of judicial office, and in making the incumbent ineligible to a second election. To this, I think, the people would consent, and it would place the judge in a position of *quasi* independence. * * *

Finally, let me say, that although the election of judges for short terms by the people is not, in my judgment, a wise institution, and although we have certainly taken a wrong step in that direction, yet the system does not seem to work as badly as one would be led to suppose, reasoning from cause to effect. There is, I think, far less ground of complaint than might be expected, since private justice is, in the main, administered in the states which have adopted the elective system with at least tolerable ability and impartiality. The reason is obvious. The offence of judicial corruption or partiality is so heinous a crime in the eyes of all men, and especially of the legal profession, that few judges would have the hardihood to face the community and the bar under a sense of judicial delinquency. There is very little intemperance among women, because the public sentiment will not tolerate drunkenness in a woman. A female inebriate is a spectacle shocking to behold. The same stern and inexorable sentiment of condemnation against judicial delinquencies stares every judge in the face, and deters him in general, even if so inclined, from the commission of any serious offences against the rights of litigants, and the usages, traditions, and proprieties of his station.

NOTES AND QUESTIONS

There were efforts in many jurisdictions, especially in states where there were effective political machines, to end judicial selection by popular election. Until approximately the middle of the twentieth century, however, there were virtually no changes, and elected judiciaries were to be found in a clear majority of the states. In the beginning of the twentieth century, debate on judicial reform began to focus on the "merit plan" as an alternative to popular election. A merit plan was first adopted in Missouri, in 1949, following some particularly egregious conduct on the part of the Pendergast machine in Kansas City. The way that such a merit plan worked was that a commission, normally consisting of jurists, lawyers, and laymen, would recommend several names to governors, who would then appoint judges from the recommended list. The judges so appointed would serve for a term of years, and their terms would be subject to renewal in periodic non-competitive elections. According to Professor Ireland's unpublished study, as of late 1976, 13 states used some variant of the merit plan, 28 elected judges (14 by partisan nominations, 14 by non-partisan), five had their judges appointed by governors, and four had the legislature appoint judges. Which plan of judicial selection do you favor, and why? Does the merit plan solve the difficulties that are inherent in the other schemes? How do you explain the pervasiveness and tenacity of popular election for the judiciary? On the other hand, why do you suppose that the United States Constitution was never amended to provide for election of judges?

SECTION D. SLAVERY

1. SLAVERY LEGISLATION

KENNETH STAMPP, THE PECULIAR INSTITUTION *

206–216 (1956).

Every slave state had a slave code. Besides establishing the property rights of those who owned human chattels, these codes supported masters in maintaining discipline and provided safeguards for the white community against slave rebellions. In addition, they held slaves, as thinking beings, morally responsible and punishable for misdemeanors and felonies.

Fundamentally the slave codes were much alike. Those of the Deep South were somewhat more severe than those of the Upper South, but most of the variations were in minor details. * * *,

After a generation of liberalization following the American Revolution, the codes underwent a reverse trend toward increasing restrictions. This trend was clearly evident by the 1820's, when rising slave prices and expansion into the Southwest caused more and more Southerners to accept slavery as a permanent institution. * * *

In practice the slave codes went through alternating periods of rigid and lax enforcement. Sometimes slaveholders demanded even more rigorous codes, and sometimes they were remiss in enforcing parts of existing ones. When the danger of attack from without or of rebellion from within seemed most acute, they looked anxiously to the state governments for additional protection. * * *

At the heart of every code was the requirement that slaves submit to their masters and respect all white men. The Louisiana code of 1806 proclaimed this most lucidly: "The condition of the slave being merely a passive one, his subordination to his master and to all who represent him is not susceptible of modification or restriction * * * he owes to his master, and to all his family, a respect without bounds, and an absolute obedience, and he is consequently to execute all the orders which he receives from him, his said master, or from them." A slave was neither to raise his hand against a white man nor to use insulting or abusive language. Any number of acts, said a North Carolina judge, may constitute "insolence"—it may be merely "a look, the pointing of a finger, a refusal or neglect to step out of the way when a white person is seen to approach. But each of such acts violates the rules of propriety, and if tolerated, would destroy that subordination, upon which our social system rests."

The codes rigidly controlled the slave's movements and his communication with others. A slave was not to be "at large" without a pass which he must show to any white man who asked to see it; if he forged a pass or free papers he was guilty of a felony. Except in a few localities, he was prohibited from hiring his own time, finding his own employment, or living by himself. A slave was not to preach, except to his master's own slaves on his master's premises in the presence of whites. A gathering of more than a few slaves (usually five) away from home, unattended by a white, was an "unlawful assembly" regardless of its purpose or orderly decorum.

No person, not even the master, was to teach a slave to read or write, employ him in setting type in a printing office, or give him books or pamphlets. A religious publication asked rhetorically: "Is there any great moral reason why we should incur the tremendous risk of having our wives slaughtered in consequence of our slaves being taught to read incendiary publications?" * * *

Farms and plantations employing slaves were to be under the supervision of resident white men, and not left to the sole direction of slave foremen. Slaves were not to beat drums, blow horns, or possess guns; periodically their cabins were to be searched for weapons. They were not to administer drugs to whites or practice medicine. "A slave under pretence of practicing medicine," warned a Tennessee judge, "might convey intelligence from one plantation to another, of a contemplated insurrectionary movement; and thus enable the slaves to act in concert."

A slave was not to possess liquor, or purchase it without a written order from his owner. He was not to trade without a permit, or gamble with whites or with other slaves. He was not to raise cotton, swine, horses, mules, or cattle. Allowing a slave to own animals, explained the North Carolina Supreme Court, tended "to make other slaves dissatisfied * * * and thereby excite * * * a spirit of insubordination."

* * * Richmond required Negroes and mulattoes to step aside when whites passed by, and barred them from riding in carriages except in the capacity of menials. Charleston slaves could not swear, smoke, walk with a cane, assemble at military parades, or make joyful demonstrations. In Washington, North Carolina, the town Commissioners prohibited "all disorderly shouting and dancing, and all disorderly * * * assemblies * * * of slaves and free Negroes in the streets, market and other public places." In Natchez, all "strange slaves" had to leave the city by four o'clock on Sunday afternoon.

Violations of the state and local codes were misdemeanors or felonies subject to punishment by justices, sheriffs, police, and constabulary. Whipping was the most common form of public punishment for less than capital offenses. Except in Louisiana, imprisonment was rare. By mid-nineteenth century branding and mutilation had declined, though they had not been abolished everywhere. South Carolina did not prohibit branding until 1833, and occasionally thereafter slave felons still had their ears cropped. Mississippi and Alabama continued to enforce the penalty of "burning in the hand" for felonies not capitally punished.

But most slave offenders were simply tied up in the jail or at a whipping post and flogged. Some states in the Upper South limited to thirty-nine the number of stripes that could be administered at any one time, though more could be given in a series of whippings over a period of days or weeks. In the Deep South floggings could legally be more severe. Alabama permitted up to one hundred stripes on the bare back of a slave who forged a pass or engaged in "riots, routs, unlawful assemblies, trespasses, and seditious speeches."

State criminal codes dealt more severely with slaves and free Negroes than with whites. In the first place, they made certain acts felonies when committed by Negroes but not when committed by whites; and in the second place, they assigned heavier penalties to Negroes than whites convicted of the same offense. Every southern state defined a substantial number of felonies carrying capital punishment for slaves and lesser punishments for whites. In addition to murder of any degree, slaves received the death penalty for attempted murder, manslaughter, rape and attempted rape upon a white woman, rebellion and attempted rebellion, poisoning, robbery, and arson. A battery upon a white person might also carry a sentence of death under certain circumstances. In Louisiana, a slave who struck his master, a member of the master's family, or the overseer, "so as to cause a contusion, or effusion or shedding of blood," was to suffer death—as was a slave on a third conviction for striking a white.

The codes were quite unmerciful toward whites who interfered with slave discipline. Heavy fines were levied upon persons who unlawfully traded with slaves, sold them liquor without the master's permission, gave them passes, gambled with them, or taught them to read or write. North Carolina made death the penalty for concealing a slave "with the intent and for the purpose of enabling such slave to escape." Aiding or encouraging a bondsman to rebel was the most heinous crime of all. "If a free person," said the Alabama code, "advise or conspire with a slave to * * * make insurrection, * * * he shall be punished with death, whether such rebellion or insurrection be made or not."

Every slave state made it a felony to say or write anything that might lead, directly or indirectly, to discontent or rebellion. In 1837, the Missouri legislature passed an act "to prohibit the publication, circulation, and promulgation of the abolition doctrines." The Virginia code of 1849 provided a fine and imprisonment for any person who maintained "that owners have not right of property in their slaves." Louisiana made it a capital offense to use "language in any public discourse, from the bar, the bench, the stage, the pulpit, or in any place whatsoever" that might produce "insubordination among the slaves." Most southern states used their police power to prohibit the circulation of "incendiary" material through the United States mail; on numerous occasions local postmasters, public officials, or mobs seized and destroyed antislavery publications.

* * *

* * * If a white man fraternized with another man's slave, he became an object of suspicion; sometimes he found himself in trouble with the law. "On Sunday evening last," ran an item in a Richmond newspaper, "while Officer Reed, of the Police, was passing down Broad Street, he met a white man, walking arm-in-arm with a black man. Officer Reed stopped them and demanded to know the why and the wherefore of such a cheek by jowl business. * * * They were both arrested and taken to the cage." Happily for the white man, he could produce witnesses who testified that he was a person "of general good character, who happened to be 'on a spree' at the time he was found in the company with the negro." He was therefore discharged "with an admonition."

Southern slave codes protected the owners of bondsmen who attempted to abscond by requiring officers to assist in their recapture and by giving all white men power to arrest them. Every state required the owner of a fugitive to compensate the captor for his trouble. Because of the magnitude of the problem, Kentucky obligated masters to pay a reward of one hundred dollars for runaways taken "in a State where slavery is not tolerated by law." In an effort to induce the return of fugitives escaping to Mexico, Texas promised a reward of one-third the value of a slave who fled "beyond the limits of the slave territories of the United States." * * *

North Carolina authorized the outlawing of a "vicious" runaway. For example, two justices of New Hanover County gave notice that the slave London was "lurking about" and "committing acts of felony and other misdeeds." London was therefore outlawed; unless he surrendered immediately, "any person may KILL and DESTROY the said slave by such means as he or they may think fit, without accusation or impeachment of any crime or offense for so doing." At the same time, London's master offered a reward of fifty dollars for his confinement in jail, or one hundred dollars for his head. Louisiana permitted a person to shoot a runaway who would not stop when ordered to do so. * * *

Occasionally a band of runaways was too formidable to be dispersed by volunteers, and the governor called upon the militia to capture or destroy it. Ordinarily, however, this and other organized police activity was delegated to the slave patrols. A system of patrols, often more or less loosely connected with the militia, existed in every slave state. Virginia empowered each county or corporation court to "appoint, for a term not exceeding three months, one or more patrols" to visit "all negro quarters and other places suspected of having therein unlawful assemblies," and to arrest "such slaves as may stroll from one plantation to another without permission." Alabama compelled every slaveowner under sixty and every nonslaveholder under forty-five to perform patrol duty. The justices of each precinct divided the eligible males into detachments which had to patrol at least one night a week during their terms of service. Everywhere the patrols played a major role in the system of control.

*   *   *

*   *   * The nonslaveholding whites, to whom most patrol service was relegated, frequently disliked the masters almost as intensely as the Negroes, and as patrollers they were in a position to vent their feelings toward both. Slaveholders repeatedly went to the courts with charges that patrollers had invaded their premises and whipped their slaves excessively or illegally. The slaves in turn both hated and feared the "paterollers" and retaliated against them when they could. Yet masters looked upon the patrol as an essential police system, and none ever seriously suggested abolishing it.

The final clauses in the southern legal codes relating directly to the control of slaves were those governing free Negroes. The laws reflected the general opinion that these people were an anomaly, a living denial "that nature's God intended the African for the status of slavery." They "embitter by their presence the happiness of those who remain slaves. They entice them and furnish them with facilities to elope." They were potential allies of the slaves in the event of a rebellion. In 1830, David Walker, a free Negro who moved from North Carolina to Boston, wrote and attempted to circulate in the South a pamphlet which urged the slaves to fight for their freedom. He thus aroused southern legislatures to the menace of the free Negro.

The trend of ante-bellum legislation was toward ever more stringent controls. Free Negroes could not move from one state to another, and those who left their own state for any purpose could not return. In South Carolina and the Gulf states Negro seamen were arrested and kept in custody while their vessels were in port. Though free Negroes could make contracts and own property, in most other respects their civil rights were as circumscribed as those of slaves. They were the victims of the white man's fears, of racial prejudice, and of the desire to convince slaves that winning freedom was scarcely worth the effort.

Many Southerners desired the complete expulsion of the free Negroes, or the re-enslavement of those who would not leave. Petitions poured in to the state legislatures demanding laws that would implement one or the other of these policies. In 1849, a petition from Augusta County, Virginia, asked the legislature to make an appropriation for a program of gradual removal; all free Negroes who refused to go to Liberia should be expelled from the state within five years. In 1859, the Arkansas legislature required sheriffs to order the state's handful of free Negroes to leave. Those who remained were to be hired out as slaves for a year, after which those who still remained were to be sold into permanent bondage.

* * *

NOTES AND QUESTIONS

1. This first excerpt is to give you an overview of conditions under the American slavery laws. For a detailed and absorbing description of Southern slave society see Eugene D. Genovese, Roll, Jordan, Roll: The World the Slaves Made (Vintage paperbacks, 1976).

2. Note that the author of this excerpt comments on the reversal of a "generation of liberalization" in slavery legislation which followed the American Revolution. What would have caused this liberalization, and what does Professor Stampp suggest brought about the reversal?

3. You may have noticed that as the nineteenth century progressed some aspects of the slave laws seem to reflect humanitarian concerns, for example, there is less toleration for mutilation of slaves. Still, the harshness of the laws which aimed to prevent runaways or slave rebellions tended to increase until the Civil War. Why? Note, in particular, that much of the enforcement of these laws may have been in the hands of the "slave patrols," many members of which were not themselves slave-owners. Does this strike you as an intelligent system? How do you explain the pre-eminence of the slave patrols?

4. In 1837 Senator John C. Calhoun of South Carolina responded to abolitionist critics of slavery by claiming that slavery, instead of being an "evil", had proved to be a "good." Calhoun observed that "there never has yet existed a wealthy and civilized society in which one portion of the community did not, in point of fact, live on the labor of the other." Calhoun explained that each society had concocted its own devices for ensuring the inevitable and necessary unequal division of wealth between the laboring and consuming classes, and that they ranged "from the brute force and gross superstition of ancient times, to the subtle and artful fiscal contrivances of modern." Turning to the South's own solution, Calhoun claimed that "the more direct, simple and patriarchal mode by which the labor of the African race is * * * commanded by the European" compared favorably with the means of maldistribution in other societies. Calhoun concluded by stating that "I fearlessly assert that the existing relation between the two races in the South, against which these blind fanatics [the abolitionists] are waging war, forms the most solid and durable foundation on which to rear free and stable political institutions." I Calhoun, Works 630–632 (R. K. Cralle, ed. 1853–1855, repr. 1968), quoted in H. W. Farnam, Chapters in the History of Social Legislation in the United States to 1860 173–174 (1938). How could Calhoun believe such things? Would you have subscribed to these views in 1837? For a discussion of Calhoun's acumen as a political theorist see "John C. Calhoun: The Marx of the Master Class," Chapter IV of Richard Hofstadter, The

American Political Tradition & The Men Who Made It (Vintage Books ed., 1974). How inhuman was the overall system of slavery? Consider the following continuation of Stampp's discussion.

KENNETH STAMPP, THE PECULIAR INSTITUTION

217–222 (1956).

"A slave," said a Tennessee judge, "is not in the condition of a horse. * * * He has mental capacities, and an immortal principle in his nature." The laws did not "extinguish his high-born nature nor deprive him of many rights which are inherent in man." * * * Many state constitutions required the legislature "to pass such laws as may be necessary to oblige the owners of slaves to treat them with humanity; to provide for them necessary clothing and provisions; [and] to abstain from all injuries to them, extending to life or limb."

The legislatures responded with laws extending some protection to the persons of slaves. Masters who refused to feed and clothe slaves properly might be fined; in several states the court might order them to be sold, the proceeds going to the dispossessed owners. Those who abandoned or neglected insane, aged, or infirm slaves were also liable to fines. In Virginia the overseers of the poor were required to care for such slaves and to charge their masters.

Now and then a master was tried and convicted for the violation of one of these laws. In 1849, the South Carolina Supreme Court upheld the conviction of a slaveholder who "did not give his negroes enough even of [corn] meal, the only provision he did give." In such a case, said the court, the law had to be enforced for the sake of "public sentiment, * * * and to protect property from the depredation of famishing slaves." But prosecutions were infrequent. * * *

Some of the codes regulated the hours of labor. As early as 1740, South Carolina limited the working day to fifteen hours from March to September and fourteen hours from September to March. All the codes forbade field labor on Sunday. * * * It was permissible, however, to let slaves labor on the Sabbath for wages * * *. With rare exceptions, masters who were so inclined violated these laws with impunity.

The early colonial codes had assessed only light penalties, or none at all, for killing a slave. * * *

After the American Revolution there was a drastic change of policy. Virginia, in 1788, and North Carolina, in 1791, defined the malicious killing of a slave as murder subject to the same penalty imposed upon the murderer of a freeman. In 1817, North Carolina applied this principle to persons convicted of manslaughter. Georgia's Constitution of 1798 contained a clause that was copied, in substance, into the constitutions of several states in the Southwest: "Any person who shall maliciously dismember or deprive a slave of life shall suffer such punishment as would be inflicted in case the like offence had been committed on a free white person."

Eventually all the southern states adopted laws of this kind. * * * In Alabama a person who, "with malice aforethought," caused the death of a slave "by cruel whipping or beating, or by any inhuman treatment, or by the use of any weapon in its nature calculated to produce death," was guilty of murder in the first degree. A master or overseer causing death by cruel whipping or by other cruel punishment, "though without any intention to kill," was guilty of murder in the second degree.

By the 1850's, most of the codes had made cruelty a public offense even when not resulting in Death. * * * Louisiana prohibited the owner from punishing a slave with "unusual rigor" or "so as to maim or mutilate him." Georgia more explicitly prohibited "cutting, or wounding, or * * * cruelly and unnecessarily biting or tearing with dogs." In Kentucky, a slave who was treated cruelly might be taken from his master and sold.

But these laws invariably had significant qualifications. For example the accidental death of a slave while receiving "moderate correction" was not homicide. Killing a slave in the act of rebellion or when resisting legal arrest was always "justifiable homicide." South Carolina permitted a white person to "apprehend and moderately correct" a slave who was at large without a pass and refused to submit to examination; "and, if any such slave shall assault and strike such white person, such slave may be lawfully killed." * * *

Under most circumstances a slave was powerless to defend himself from an assault by a white man. According to the Tennessee Supreme Court, severe chastisement by the master did not justify resistance. If a master exercised his right to punish, "with or without cause, [and] the slave resist and slay him, it is murder * * * because the law cannot recognize the violence of the master as a legitimate cause of provocation." According to the Georgia Supreme Court, even if the owner should "exceed the bounds of reason * * * in his chastisement, the slave must submit * * * unless the attack * * * be calculated to produce death."

* * *

In a few notable cases the courts enforced the laws against the killing of slaves. A North Carolinian was sentenced to death for the murder of his own female chattel. * * * The Virginia Court of Appeals, in approving a similar conviction, explained precisely how far a master could go before the law would intervene. For the sake of securing "proper subordination and obedience" the master would not be disturbed even though his punishment were "malicious, cruel and excessive." But he "acts at his peril; and if death ensues in consequence of such punishment, the relation of master and slave affords no ground of excuse or palliation." In Mississippi, too, a white man was hanged for killing another man's slave. "In vain," argued the state Supreme Court, "shall we look for any law passed by the * * * philanthropic legislature of this state, giving even to the master, much less to a stranger, power over the life of a slave."

Decisions such as these were exceptional. Only a handful of whites suffered capital punishment for murdering slaves, and they were usually persons who had committed the offense upon slaves not their own. * * *

* * *

NOTES AND QUESTIONS

1. Does this second excerpt from Stampp make you feel any more sanguine about the laws of slavery? Stampp seems to suggest that the laws offered relatively little protection, and that convictions were rare. Does this necessarily mean that the laws were ineffective? Do you note any trend in this legislation that seems to run counter to the trends discussed in the first excerpt from Professor Stampp?

2. Is the existence of slavery inconsistent with the existence of principles of political freedom? This problem is addressed in David Brion Davis, The Problem of Slavery in Western Culture (1966). Turning to the ancient past, Davis observes:

> Though actual slaves never formed a significant percentage of the populations of China or ancient Egypt, in Greece, where they were treated as commodities and put to industrial and commercial employments, the number kept increasing from the Persian Wars to the time of Alexander. Historians disagree on the exact percentage of slaves in the total population of fourth-century Athens, but Moses Finley states that the proportion was as great as in the combined slave states of America in 1860, and that the ownership of slaves in Greece was even more widely distributed among the free population than in America. * * * Finley argues persuasively that the institution was an integral element in Hellenic society. Moreover, "the cities in which individual freedom reached its highest expression—most obviously Athens—were cities in which chattel slavery flourished." Thus the history of ancient Greece presents the same paradox that has perplexed Americans since the eighteenth century: freedom and slavery seemed to advance together.*

Id., at 35–36. How might we go about expressing and solving the American paradox? Virginia, for example, had been the source of much of the Revolutionary ideology and doctrines of political equality, and yet Virginia had one of the largest slave populations. Were slaveholding Virginians mere hypocrites? Was Jefferson? Does the following excerpt suggest a means of reconciling the ideal of political liberty and the realities of slavery?

* Reprinted from David Brion Davis: The Problem of Slavery in Western Culture. Copyright © 1966 by Cornell University. Used by permission of the publisher, Cornell University Press.

STANLEY M. ELKINS, SLAVERY *

81–87 (3rd ed., 1976).

An examination of American slavery, checked at certain critical points against a very different slave system, that of Latin America, reveals that a major key to many of the contrasts between them was an institutional key: The presence or absence of other powerful institutions in society made an immense difference in the character of slavery itself. In Latin America, the very tension and balance among three kinds of organizational concerns—church, crown, and plantation agriculture—prevented slavery from being carried by the planting class to its ultimate logic. For the slave, in terms of the space thus allowed for the development of men and women as moral beings, the result was an "open system": a system of contacts with free society through which ultimate absorption into that society could and did occur with great frequency. The rights of personality implicit in the ancient traditions of slavery and in the church's most venerable assumptions on the nature of the human soul were thus in a vital sense conserved, whereas to a staggering extent the very opposite was true in North American slavery. The latter system had developed virtually unchecked by institutions having anything like the power of their Latin counterparts; the legal structure which supported it, shaped only by the demands of a staple-raising capitalism, had defined with such nicety the slave's character as chattel that his character as a moral individual was left in the vaguest of legal obscurity. In this sense American slavery operated as a "closed" system—one in which, for the generality of slaves in their nature as men and women, *sub specie aeternitatis,* contacts with free society could occur only on the most narrowly circumscribed of terms. The next question is whether living within such a "closed system" might not have produced noticeable effects upon the slave's very personality.

The name "Sambo" has come to be synonymous with "race stereotype." Here is an automatic danger signal, warning that the analytical difficulties of asking questions about slave personality may not be nearly so great as the moral difficulties. The one inhibits the other; the morality of the matter has had a clogging effect on its theoretical development that may not be to the best interest of either.
*   *   *

Is it possible to deal with "Sambo" as a type? The characteristics that have been claimed for the type come principally from Southern lore. Sambo, the typical plantation slave, was docile but irrespon-

---

* Reprinted from Stanley M. Elkins, Slavery: A Problem in American Institutional and Intellectual Life (3rd ed., rev.) Copyright © 1959, 1968, 1976 by the University of Chicago, published by the University of Chicago Press, by permission of the author and of the University of Chicago Press.

sible, loyal but lazy, humble but chronically given to lying and steal-ing; his behavior was full of infantile silliness and his talk inflated with childish exaggeration. His relationship with his master was one of utter dependence and childlike attachment: it was indeed this childlike quality that was the very key to his being. Although the merest hint of Sambo's "manhood" might fill the Southern breast with scorn, the child, "in his place," could be both exasperating and lovable.

* * * Is there a "scientific" way to talk about this problem? For most Southerners in 1860 it went without saying not only that Sambo was real—that he was a dominant plantation type—but also that his characteristics were the clear product of racial inheritance. * * * But in recent times, the discrediting, as unscientific, of racial explanations for any feature of plantation slavery has tended in the case of Sambo to discredit not simply the explanation itself but also the thing it was supposed to explain. * * * This modern approach to Sambo had a strong counterpart in the way Northern reformers thought about slavery in ante-bellum times: they thought that nothing could actually be said about the Negro's "true" nature because that nature was veiled by the institution of slavery. * * *

There ought, however, to be still a third way of dealing with the Sambo picture, some formula for taking it seriously. The picture has far too many different brushes, for it to be denounced as counter-feit. Too much folk-knowledge, too much plantation literature, too much of the Negro's own lore, have gone into its making to entitle one in good conscience to condemn it as "conspiracy." One searches in vain through the literature of the Latin-American slave systems for the "Sambo" of our tradition—the perpetual child incapable of ma-turity. How is this to be explained? If Sambo is not a product of race (that "explanation" can be consigned to oblivion) and not simply a product of "slavery" in the abstract (other societies have had slav-ery), then he must be related to our own peculiar variety of it. And if Sambo is uniquely an American product, then his existence, and the reasons for his character, must be recognized in order to appre-ciate the very scope of our slave problem and its aftermath. The abso-luteness with which such a personality ("real" or "unreal") had been stamped upon the plantation slave does much to make plausible the ante-bellum Southerner's difficulty in imagining that blacks anywhere could be anything but a degraded race—and it goes far to explain his failure to see any sense at all in abolitionism. * * *

If it were taken for granted that a special type existed in sig-nificant numbers on American plantations, closer connections might be made with a growing literature on personality and character types, the investigation of which has become a widespread, respectable, and productive enterprise among our psychologists and social scientists. Realizing that, it might then seem not quite so dangerous to add that the type corresponded in its major outlines to "Sambo."

* * *

It should be understood that to identify a social type in this sense is still to generalize on a fairly crude level—and to insist for a limited purpose on the legitimacy of such generalizing is by no means to deny that, on more refined levels, a great profusion of individual types might have been observed in slave society. Nor need it be claimed that the "Sambo" type, even in the relatively crude sense employed here, was a universal type. It was, however, a plantation type, and a plantation existence embraced well over half the slave population.

* * *

* * *

NOTES AND QUESTIONS

1. The "Elkins thesis" about the nature of plantation slavery (which will be developed further in the next reading) has been one of the most controversial topics in American historiography. See, e. g. Ann J. Lane, ed., Debate Over Slavery: Stanley Elkins and His Critics (1971). What is the nature of Elkins' explanation for the behavior of plantation slaves that the "Sambo" stereotype is said to describe? Is it a racial explanation? Why, then, has Elkins been accused of denigrating Blacks?

2. The key to Elkins's explanation for the personality type of plantation slaves lies within his conception of a "closed system" that was present on the plantations of the Southern United States, but not in Latin America. How would you explain why Latin America was an "open system," and how might this lessen the chance of the "Sambo" stereotype?

3. Elkins proceeds to discuss the process of assimilation of slaves into Southern society, and stresses the aspects of brutalization and shock involved in the capture in Africa, the horrible conditions of the sea passage to America, and the degradations of final sale in the South. Elkins then proceeds to the most controversial and disturbing aspect of his analysis of the personality types of Southern slaves, his analogy to German concentration camps.

STANLEY M. ELKINS, SLAVERY

104–113 (3rd ed., 1976).

The system of the concentration camps was expressly devised in the 1930's by high officials of the German government to function as an instrument of terror. The first groups detained in the camps consisted of prominent enemies of the Nazi regime; later, when these had mostly been eliminated, it was still felt necessary that the system be institutionalized and made into a standing weapon of intimidation —which required a continuing flow of incoming prisoners. The categories of eligible persons were greatly widened to include all real, fancied, or "potential" opposition to the state. They were often selected on capricious and random grounds, and together they formed a cross-section of society which was virtually complete: criminals, workers, businessmen, professional people, middle-class Jews, even members of the aristocracy. The teeming camps thus held all kinds

—not only the scum of the underworld but also countless men and women of culture and refinement. During the war a specialized objective was added, that of exterminating the Jewish populations of subject countries *   *   *. Yet the basic technique was everywhere and at all times the same: the deliberate infliction of various forms of torture upon the incoming prisoners in such a way as to break their resistance and make way for their degradation as individuals. These brutalities were not merely "permitted" or "encouraged"; they were prescribed. *   *   *

*   *   * The undenied existence of the camps cast a shadow of nameless dread over the entire population; on the other hand the individual who actually became a prisoner in one of them was in most cases devasted with fright and utterly demoralized to discover that what was happening to him was not less, but rather far more terrible than anything he had imagined. *   *   *

The arrest was typically made at night, preferably late; this was standing Gestapo policy, designed to heighten the element of shock, terror, and unreality surrounding the arrest. After a day or so in the police jail came the next major shock, that of being transported to the camp itself. *   *   * It involved a planned series of brutalities inflicted by guards making repeated rounds through the train over a twelve- to thirty-six-hour period during which the prisoner was prevented from resting. If transported in cattle cars instead of passenger cars, the prisoners were sealed in, under conditions not dissimilar to those of the Middle Passage* [Upon arrival at the camps,] the newcomers would file past an SS doctor who indicated, with a motion of the forefinger, whether they were to go to the left or to the right. To one side went those considered capable of heavy labor; to the other would go wide categories of "undesirables"; those in the latter group were being condemned to the gas chambers. Those who remained would undergo the formalities of "registration," full of indignities, which culminated in the marking of each prisoner with a number.

There were certain physical and psychological strains of camp life, especially debilitating in the early stages, which should be classed with the introductory shock sequence. There was a state of chronic hunger whose pressures were unusually effective in detaching prior scruples of all kinds; even the sexual instincts no longer functioned in the face of the drive for food. The man who at his pleasure could bestow or withhold food thus wielded, for that reason alone, abnormal power. Another strain at first was the demand for absolute obedience, the slightest deviation from which brought savage punishments. *   * The power of the SS guard, as the prisoner was hourly reminded, was that of life and death over his body. A more exquisite form of pressure

---

* The passage of Black slaves across the Atlantic in conditions of utter degradation and inhuman discomfort.

lay in the fact that the prisoner had never a moment of solitude: he no longer had a private existence; it was no longer possible, in any imaginable sense, for him to be an "individual."

Another factor having deep disintegrative effects upon the prisoner was the prospect of a limitless future in the camp. In the immediate sense this meant that he could no longer make plans for the future. But there would eventually be a subtler meaning: it made the break with the outside world a real break; in time the "real" life would become the life of the camp, the outside world an abstraction. * * * It was this that underlay the "egalitarianism" of the camps; old statuses had lost their meaning. A final strain, which must have been particularly acute for the newcomer, was the omnipresent threat of death and the very unpredictable suddenness with which death might strike. Quite aside from the periodic gaschamber selections, the guards in their sports and caprices were at liberty to kill any prisoner any time.

In the face of all this, one might suppose that the very notion of an "adjustment" would be grotesque. The majority of those who entered the camps never came out again, but our concern here has to be with those who survived—an estimated 700,000 out of nearly eight million. For them, the regime must be considered not as a system of death but as a way of life. * * * After the initial shocks, what was the nature of the "normality" that emerged?

* * * The very extremity of the initial tortures produced in the prisoner what actually amounted to a sense of detachment; these brutalities went so beyond his own experience that they became somehow incredible—they seemed to be happening no longer to him but almost to someone else. "[The author] has no doubt," writes Bruno Bettelheim, "that he was able to endure the transportation, and all that followed, because right from the beginning he became convinced that these horrible and degrading experiences somehow did not happen to 'him' as a subject, but only to 'him' as an object." * * * This splitting-off of a special "self"—a self which endured the tortures but which was not the "real" self—also provided the first glimpse of a new personality which, being not "real", would not need to feel bound by the values which guided the individual in his former life. * * *

* * *

"If you survive the first three months you will survive the next three years." Such was the formula transmitted from the old prisoners to the new ones, and its meaning lay in the fact that the first three months would generally determine a prisoner's capacity for survival and adaptation. "Be inconspicuous": this was the golden rule. The prisoner who called attention to himself, even in such trivial matters as the wearing of glasses, risked doom. Any show of bravado, any heroics, any kind of resistance condemned a man instantly. There were no rewards for martyrdom: not only did the martyr himself suffer, but mass punishments were wreaked upon his fellow inmates. To "be inconspicuous" required a special kind of alertness—almost an animal instinct [58]—against the apathy which tended to follow the initial shocks. To give up the struggle for survival was to commit "passive suicide"; a careless mistake meant death. There were those, however, who did come through this phase and who managed an adjustment to the life of the camp. * * *

The most immediate aspect of the old inmates' behavior * * * was its childlike quality. "The prisoners developed types of behavior which are characteristic of infancy or early youth. * * * They lost many of the customary inhibitions as to soiling their beds and their persons. Their humor was shot with silliness and they giggled like children when one of them would expel wind. Their relationships were highly unstable. "Prisoners would, like early adolescents, fight one another tooth and nail * * * only to become close friends within a few minutes." Dishonesty became chronic. * * * "In hundreds of ways," writes Colasco Belmonte, "the soldier, and to an even greater extent the prisoner of war, is given to understand that he is a child. * * * Then dishonesty, mendacity, egotistic actions in order to obtain more food or to get out of scrapes reach full development, and theft becomes a veritable affliction of camp life." * * * Benedikt Kautsky observed such things in his own behavior: "I myself can declare that often I saw myself as I used to be in my school days, when by sly dodges and clever pretexts we avoided being found out, or could 'organize' something." Bruno Bettelheim remarks on the extravagance of the stories told by the prisoners to one another. "They were boastful, telling tales about what they had accomplished in their former lives, or how they succeeded in cheating foremen or guards, and how they sabotaged the work. Like children they felt not at all set back or ashamed when it became known that they had lied about their prowess."

This development of childlike behavior in the old inmates was the counterpart of something even more striking that was happening to them: "Only very few of the prisoners escaped a more or less intensive identification with the SS." As Mr. Bettelheim puts it: "A prisoner had reached the final stage of adjustment to the camp situation when he had changed his personality so as to accept as his own the values of the Gestapo." * * * The old prisoners came to share the attitude of the SS toward the "unfit" prisoners; newcomers who behaved badly in the labor groups or who could not withstand the strain became a liability for the others, who were often instrumental in get-

[58.] This should in no sense be considered as a calculating, "rational" alertness, but rather as something quite primitive. "Of myself," writes Dr. Cohen, "I know that I was not continuously occupied by the reflection: I am going to win through. The actions which contributed to my survival were performed instinctively rather than consciously. * * * Like animals warned by their instinct that danger is imminent, we would act instinctively at critical moments. These instinctive acts must, I think, be considered as manifestations of the life instinct. * * *"

ting rid of them.   Many old prisoners actually imitated the SS; they would sew and mend their uniforms in such a way as to make them look more like those of the SS—even though they risked punishment for it.   * * *   Some took great enjoyment in the fact that during roll call "they really had stood well at attention."   There were cases of nonsensical rules, made by the guards, which the older prisoners would continue to observe and try to force on the others long after the SS had forgotten them.   Even the most abstract ideals of the SS, such as their intense German nationalism and anti-Semitism, were often absorbed by the old inmates—a phenomenon observed among the politically well-educated and even among the Jews themselves. The final quintessence of all this was seen in the "Kapo"—the prisoner who had been placed in a supervisory position over his fellow inmates.   These creatures, many of them professional criminals, not only behaved with slavish servility to the SS, but the way in which they often outdid the SS in sheer brutality became one of the most durable features of the concentration camp legend.

To all these men, reduced to complete and childish dependence upon their masters, the SS had actually become a father symbol. * * *   The closed system, in short, had become a kind of grotesque patriarchy.

NOTES AND QUESTIONS

1.   Much of Elkins's psychological theoretical apparatus for his analogy to slavery has been omitted, but enough description has been given here to enable you to judge for yourself whether the comparison with American slavery is instructive.   Does Elkins's analysis of German prison camps persuade you that American slaves behaved in a child-like manner?   What are the weaknesses in the analogy?   What are its strengths?   For a summary of the reception of this aspect of Elkins's thesis, see Richard E. Beringer, Historical Analysis: Contemporary Approaches to Clio's Craft 109–114 (1978).

2.   One of the most vocal of Elkins's critics, and perhaps the one with the greatest familiarity with the conditions of plantation slavery, is Eugene D. Genovese.   What follows is an excerpt from his article, "Rebelliousness and Docility in the Negro Slave: A Critique of the Elkins Thesis," 13 Civil War History 293, 307–309.   Does Genovese persuade you that Elkins is wrong about the prominence of the "Sambo" personality type?

The fundamental differences between the concentration camp and plantation experience may be gleaned from a brief consideration of some of the points made in Bruno Bettelheim's study, on which Elkins relies heavily.   Prisoners received inadequate clothing and food in order to test their reaction to extremities of inclement weather and their ability to work while acutely hungry. Slaves received clothing and food designed to provide at least minimum comfort.   Slaves suffered from dietary deficiencies and hidden hungers, but rarely from outright malnutrition.   In direct contrast to prisoners, slaves normally did not work outdoors in the rain or extreme cold; usually, they were deliberately ordered to stay indoors. Pneumonia and other diseases killed too many slaves every winter for planters not to take every precaution to guard their health. Therein lay the crucial differences: prisoners might be kept alive for experimental purposes, but slaves received treatment designed to grant them long life. Prisoners often did useless work as part of a deliberate program to destroy their personality; slaves did, and knew they did, the productive work necessary for their own sustenance. Prisoners were forbidden to talk to each other much of the day and had virtually no privacy and no social life. Slaves maintained a many-sided social life, which received considerable encouragement from their masters. The Gestapo deliberately set out to deny the individuality of prisoners or to distinguish among them. Planters and overseers made every effort to take full account of slave individuality and even to encourage it up to a point. Prisoners were deliberately subjected to torture and arbitrary punishment; those who followed orders endured the same indignities and blows as those who did not. Slaves, despite considerable arbitrariness in the system, generally had the option of currying favor and avoiding punishment. * * * Concentration camp prisoners changed work groups and barracks regularly and could not develop attachments. Slaves had families and friends, often for a lifetime. The Gestapo had no interest in indoctrinating prisoners. They demanded obedience, not loyalty. Masters wanted and took great pains to secure the loyalty and ideological adherence of their slaves. In general, the slave plantation was a social system, full of joys and sorrows and a fair degree of security, notwithstanding great harshness and even brutality, whereas the concentration camp was a particularly vicious death-cell. They shared a strong degree of authoritarianism, but so does the army or a revolutionary party, or even a family unit.

Reprinted from Civil War History, Vol. 13 copyright © 1967 by the University of Iowa, with the permission of the Kent State University Press.

3. But even if the "closed system" which Elkins posits is not present in Southern plantation slavery, would this necessarily mean that Elkins is wrong when he implies that the slaveowners thought of their slaves as being like children? What do you infer about this from Genovese's own description of the way masters behaved following the Civil War and the emancipation of their slaves, which is the next reading?

EUGENE D. GENOVESE, ROLL, JORDON, ROLL: THE WORLD THE SLAVES MADE *

97–99, 102–103, 105–112 (Vintage Books, ed. 1976).

The slaveholders' understanding of themselves and their world suffered a severe shock during and immediately after the war, when "their black family" appeared in a new light. * * * Their behavior presented their masters with a terrible moment of truth. Could it be that they had never known "their people" at all? that they had been deceiving themselves? * * *

The masters had expected more than obedience from their slaves; they had expected faithfulness—obedience internalized as duty, respect, and love. They had had little choice, for anything less would have meant a self-image as exploitative brutes. This insistence on the slaves' constituting part of the family and these expressions of belief in their loyalty lay at the heart of the masters' world-view and, abolitionist criticism notwithstanding, embraced little insincerity. Thus the leading southern ideologues, who wrote the pro-slavery polemics of the late antebellum period, were deceiving none so much as themselves. In 1837, Chancellor Harper blithely wrote of docile and faithful slaves' adding greatly to southern military strength. * * * In 1850, a young aristocratic South Carolinian gloomily told Fredrika Bremer, "The world is against us, and we shall be overpowered by voices and condemned without justice, for what we are, and for what we are doing on behalf of our servants." And as late as 1864, with the cause lost, a lawyer in Memphis lamented, "I believe too that a very large number of the negroes will not accept their freedom and that, by one name or another, pretty much of the old relations will be re-established." * * *

The wartime and immediate postwar trauma derived less from the sudden confrontation with the true attitudes of their slaves than from the enforced confrontation with themselves. The experience proved all the more bitter since that organic relationship of master and slave which the slaveholders always celebrated had so clearly rebounded against them: any change in their perception of the slaves intrinsically meant a change in their perception of themselves. The freedmen often had a better sense of this relationship and of the nature of the slaveholders' reaction than did the slaveholders. They spoke of masters and mistresses who died of broken hearts both for the loss of their property and for their sense of having been betrayed. * * *

The great shock to the planters came with the defection of their most trusted and pampered slaves—the drivers and especially the more intimate of the house servants. That many of these remained loyal did not offset the shock at the behavior of those who did not. The slaveholders might reconcile themselves to the defection of their field hands, for it struck at their pocketbooks but not necessarily at their self-esteem. They could explain the exodus from the fields by reasoning that these were inexperienced, simple people whom the Yankees could mislead. No such reasoning would serve to explain the behavior of the house slaves or the drivers. Their desertion, in the minds of the slaveholders, constituted the essence of ingratitude, of unfaithfulness, of disloyalty, of treason.

* * *

Eliza Frances Andrews noted in her diary for January 16, 1865, that the most well-behaved and docile blacks became increasingly unruly as Yankee troops got close. On May 27, she celebrated the loyalty of her own servants, whom she called "treasures": "I really love them for the way they have stood by us." A month later she told of the adventures of a neighbor's favorite pampered, loyal, religiously devout, superannuated slave. One day, as usual without the slightest provocation so far as the slaveholders were concerned, he slandered his white family, which had sheltered and befriended him, and—of all things—had the temerity to claim the plantation as his own. Years later, when Miss Andrews had grown into a woman of considerable intellectual sophistication, she reflected on these pages of her diary and recalled how her aunt, who had had no children of her own, had compensated by spoiling a "pet" servant. The boy had been orphaned by the death of his mother, the aunt's favorite maid. As soon as the war ended he "deserted." "The kind-hearted old lady never ceased to mourn over his ingratitude." Miss Andrews recalled this story along with another. Arch, her father's favorite dining-room servant, was the first black to leave the plantation. Yet he had not sneaked off. He had asked his old master's permission, which could hardly have been refused, and had expressed all possible respect. But the time had come. For many years afterwards he visited the white family, which continued to employ his sister.

This ambivalence in the Big House often broke into its antagonistic components, with some white families experiencing only the slaves' "loyalty" and others only their "desertion." And for many whites the fact of freedom itself constituted a desertion. One planter in Georgia burned his slave cabins to the ground and expelled his people. He had no use for them any longer, he said, nor they for him. In 1871 a hysterical old white man "denounced, with bitter curses, his negroes, saying that they had abandoned him when set free and left him to starve in his old age, knowing as they did what he had intended to do for them [that is, to care for them] if he could have had his own way."

* * *

Several entries in the journal of Mrs. Mary Jones during January, 1865, taken together, reveal the deepening despair and sense of abandonment and betrayal:

[Jan. 6, 1865.] The people are all idle on the plantations, most of them seeking their own pleasure. Many servants have proven faithful, others false and rebellious against all authority and restraint. Susan, a Virginia Negro and nurse to my little Mary Ruth, went off with Mac, her husband, to Arcadia the night after the first day the Yankees appeared, with whom she took every opportunity of conversing, informing them that the baby's father was Colonel Jones. She has acted a faithless part as soon as she could. Porter left three weeks since. * * * Gilbert, Flora, Lucy, Tenah, Sue, Rosetta, Fanny, Little Gilbert, Charles, Milton, and Elsie and Kate have been faithful to us. Milton has been a model of fidelity. He will not even converse with the Yankees. * * * His brother, Little Pulaski * * * took himself off a week since.

[Jan. 21, 1865.] Kate daughter's servant who has been cooking for us, took herself off today, influenced, as we believe, by her father. Sent for cook Kate to Arcadia. She refuses to come.

Their condition is one of perfect anarchy and rebellion. They have placed themselves in perfect antagonism to their owners and to all government and control.

[Jan. 24, 1865.] Nearly all the house servants have left their homes, and from most of the plantations they have gone in a body.

* * * After receiving more reports of the awful behavior of trusted servants, Mrs. Mary Jones pronounced herself "thoroughly disgusted with the whole race." By November, 1865, despite continued affectionate references to some of the old servants, she burst out:

My life long (I mean since I had a home) I have been laboring and caring for them, and since the war have labored with all my might to supply their wants, and expended everything I had upon their support, directly or indirectly; and this is their return.

* * *

It is impossible to get at any of their intentions, and it is useless to ask them. I see only a dark future for the whole race.

A month later, with cotton stolen, Mrs. Mary Jones's "heart is pained and sickened with their vileness and falsehood in every way. I long to be delivered from the race." * * *

The struggle of the members of the Jones family to keep faith with their past in the face of what they regarded as the most severe provocations emerges from two letters with which we may close our account of them. Charles C. Jones wrote to his mother from New York in May, 1866:

I regret deeply to hear that you have been subjected to "severe trials" at Montevideo, and heartily unite with you in the hope that they are now overpassed. The transition in the status of the Negro has been such a marked and violent one that we cannot wonder that he does not at once adapt himself rationally and intelligently to the change. He has always been a child in intellect—improvident, incapable of appreciating the obligations of a contract, ignorant of the operation of any law other than the will of his master, careless of the future, and without the most distant conception of the duties of life and labor now devolved upon him. Time alone can impart the necessary intelligence; and the fear of the law, as well as kindness and instruction, must unite in compelling an appreciation and discharge of the novel duties and responsibilities resting upon him.

But his mother had remained on the plantation and could not manage to be quite so philosophical. On May 28, she replied with news about a strike over contract terms that had been put down by Federal troops:

> I have told the people that in doubting my word they have offered me the greatest insult I ever received in my life; that I had considered them friends and treated them as such, giving them gallons of clabber every day and syrup once a week with rice and extra dinners; but that now they were only laborers under contract, and only the law would rule between us, and I would require every one of them to come up to the mark in their duty on the plantation. The effect has been decided, and I am not sorry for the position we hold mutually. They have relieved me of the constant desire and effort to do something to promote their comfort.
> * * *

Everything lies bare in these letters and in numerous others like them. The "ingratitude" of the blacks. But then, we must try to understand that their condition opens them to temptation and error. Still, how could they do this to us? What about Cato—a favorite, wonderful at ingratiating himself? Why was he the one to stir up trouble among the slaves so much earlier than the bad characters among them? They are hateful. But we cannot hate them, for we are good Christians. And, they really still do love us. Of course they do—some of them. They must. They are confused. They will come to their senses. Some of the old affection remains. How are we supposed to live without it? They do love us, in their own irritating childish, perverse way. The ungrateful wretches. What can they be thinking of? What is in their enigmatic heads? * * *

* * *

* * * Three ex-slaves from Texas said their own piece, in terms essentially the same as those used everywhere else. Anderson Edwards had been a slave on a small unit of three black families. His master had treated them with kindness and as part of his own family but could not cope with their emancipation. "Gawd," he exploded, "never did 'tend to free niggers." Isaac Martin described how his master grieved himself to death, although his own slaves had remained loyal and had cried when freedom came. And Anne Miller watched her master go mad when emancipation came. He left the area, screaming that he would not live in a country in which blacks were free. A year later he committed suicide.

The blacks knew what they saw. They saw the trauma and often felt compassion despite their determination to assert themselves. Jane Simpson of Kentucky was stern: "I never heard of white folks giving niggers nothing. * * * Dey was so mad 'cause dey had to set 'em free, dey just stayed mean as dey would allow 'em to be anyhow, and is yet, most of 'em." Willis of Georgia, who had been foreman of a plow gang, recalled that he had wanted to stay with his former master but that his wife had insisted on leaving. Naturally, he chose his wife. But his master had trouble understanding the decision. He burst out crying: "I didn't thought I could raise up a darkey dat would talk dat-a-way." Robert Falls of Tennessee told of his good master's announcement that his slaves had been freed:

> "Sit down there all of you and listen to what I got to tell you. I hates to do it but I must. You-all ain't my niggers no more. You is free. Just as free as I am. Here I have raised you all to work for me, and now you are going to leave me. I am an old man, and I can't get along without you. I don't know what I am going to do." Well, sir, it killed him. He was dead in less than ten months.

The Memphis Argus, a conservative southern newspaper, summed up part of the story in 1865:

> The events of the last five years have produced an entire revolution in the social system of the entire Southern country. The old arrangement of things is broken up. The relation of master and servant is severed. Doubt and uncertainty pervade the mind of both. * * * The transition state of the African from the condition of slaves to that of freemen has placed him in a condition where he cannot avoid being suspicious of his newly acquired privilege of freedom. He looks with a jealous eye upon anything like an encroachment on what he esteems his rights. * * * We fear that too many of the former masters of the negro, forced by the events of a mighty revolution to relinquish their rights in the persons of slaves as property, do it with a bitter reluctance, amounting to absolute hatred.

* * *

For many, the old paternalism died hard. * * *

But for many, especially those whose spirit had shaped the old ruling class, the defection of so many blacks had spelled the end. No matter that 80 percent or more had stood fast. More would have gone if they had had the chance or the courage. Many others wisely waited for the end of the war to go their own way. They were faithless. The "loyalty" of the many could never, in any case, have compensated for the "betrayal" of so many trusted others. Betrayal! For that was the point. The slaveholders had been deserted in their time of need. Abandoned. * * *

The old paternalistic sensibility, in its best and basest manifestations, withered. In some cases it died quickly, with screams of most foul and bloody murder; in others, it declined slowly, with brave attempts to forget and forgive or with pathetic groans. To a decreasing extent it lingered on well into the twentieth century * * *.

The temper of the times may be discerned in a deposition filed by a Louisiana planter with the Union army: "When I owned niggers, I used to pay medical bills. I do not think I shall trouble myself." * *

And above all, it may be discerned in a letter to the New York Tribune, written in 1865 by Augustin L. Taveau of Charleston, South Carolina * * *:

> Apart from religious considerations, by the loss of the cause and the institution I have suffered like the rest, yet am I content, for the conduct of the Negro in the late crisis of our affairs has convinced me that we were all laboring under a delusion. Good masters and bad masters all alike, shared the same fate—the sea of the Revolution confounded good and evil; and, in the chaotic turbulence, all suffer in degree. Born and raised amid the institution, like a great many others, I believed it was necessary, to our welfare, if not to our very existence. I believed that these people were content, happy, and attached to their masters. But events and reflection have caused me to change these opinions; for if they were necessary to our welfare, why were four-fifths of the plantations of the Southern States dilapidated caricatures of that elegance and neatness which adorn the Country-seats of other people? If as a matter of profit they were so valuable, why was it that nine-tenths of our planters were always in debt and at the mercy of their factors? If they were content, happy and attached to their masters, why did they desert him in the moment of his need and flock to an enemy, whom they did not know; and thus left their perhaps really good masters whom they did know from infancy?

2. SLAVERY IN THE STATE COURTS

ROBERT M. COVER, JUSTICE ACCUSED *

67–75 (1975).

Prior to 1782, manumission of slaves within Virginia, without special act of the legislature, was forbidden. The Quakers, led by Robert Pleasants, mounted a campaign of correspondence to major liberal Virginians to change that law. In 1782 these efforts were successful. The Act of 1782 provided:

That it shall hereafter be lawful for any person by his or her last will and testament, or by any other instrument in writing, under his or her hand and seal attested and proved in the county court by two witnesses, or acknowledged by the party in the court of the county where he or she resides, to emancipate and set free his or her slaves, or any of them.
* * *

* * *

* * * Undoubtedly, for many of the moving forces behind the original statute, this act was meant to be only the first step in the gradual vitiation of slavery in Virginia. They hoped that the combined force of private manumission, prohibitions against importation, and public distaste for slavery would lead to withering away of the institution. The cotton gin was still eleven years away, and almost everybody seemed agreed that prohibitions against importation ought to be strictly enforced. The hope for a relatively painless end to slavery was not quixotic. Quakers and others knew that the key to public acceptance of emancipation was public tolerance of the free black. In a real sense, therefore, the private manumission law was a trial balloon. The free black population would increase and with it the opportunity to test public reaction to such a class.

Not all of the support for the Act of 1782 came from those who imperfectly programmed an ultimate emancipation. There were many who simply felt that the property rights of a master ought to extend to the power of liberating his property if he so chose. * * *

In construing this apparently simple statute, courts could choose from a variety of interpretive principles. Clearly, they ought to effectuate legislative intent. However, * * * the larger purposes of the act were not clear. Was this simply tolerance for whim or an invitation to the end of slavery? The courts could also choose to appeal to the normal principles of construction for the instruments of gratuitous transfers: wills and trusts. * * * Appeal to such principles carried

* Reprinted from Justice Accused: Antislavery and the Judicial Process, Copyright © 1975 by Yale University, published by the Yale University Press, New Haven and London, with the permission of the publisher and the author.

with it the question of whether and how the normal limits on the capacity of a testator or settlor would be effectuated. Were there public policy limitations? Did the Rule against Perpetuities apply? How should formalities be treated? * * *

At the outset, in the first cases under the act decided at the turn of the century, the Virginia court made eclectic use of equitable, common law and statutory devices all informed by and infused with a favorable attitude toward manumission. * * * Later judges came to implicitly and explicitly reject the earlier cases and—most important—the interpretive principles on which they rested.

The first of the Virginia cases was Pleasants v. Pleasants, decided in 1799. * * * It was a significant case for three reasons. It involved the leading Quaker family in the state; it construed an instrument affecting the freedom of literally hundreds of Negroes; and it afforded an opportunity to explore the foundations and purposes of the Manumission Act.

John Pleasants died before passage of the Act of 1782. He provided in his will that his slaves "shall be free if they chose it when they arrive at the age of thirty years, and the laws of the land will admit them to be set free. * * * " He provided further that should the laws not so permit, the slaves were to be bequeathed to various members of the family subject to the condition that they allow the slaves to be set free "if the laws of the land would admit of it." The *Pleasants* litigation was instituted by John's son, Robert, as executor under his father's will. Robert sought to enforce the slaves' rights to freedom as against various legatees and their successors in interest who had refused to free the Negroes after the Act of 1782.

From a legal standpoint, Pleasants's will presented a number of difficulties. Most important, when executed and when probated, the will could not legally operate to free these slaves, for manumission was prohibited. Thus, if it were to have effect at all, the will would have to be construed as creating a trust with the legatees as trustees who would be under a duty to effectuate the freedom of the slaves "if the laws allow." Such an appointment, however, presented two problems. First, if construed to affect unborn generations of blacks, it would violate the rule against perpetuities. The "Rule," as stated in the roughly contemporaneous Dane's *Abridgment*, provided:

> that all * * * executory interests whatever, including executory devises, must * * * cease to become contingent, and become vested within a life or lives in being, * * * with a mother's pregnancy and the child's minority added; this rule applies not only to inheritances in lands, * * * but to personal estate and chattels real.

The contingency contemplated in the Pleasants will was the passage of a statute or some other change in Virginia law that would permit

manumission. There was no certainty, then, that the interest in freedom provided for in the will would vest within lives in being plus
twenty-one years nine months, at least as to the interest in freedom of
remote generations. Second, perpetuities aside, the question remained
whether the 1782 Act would operate to posthumously ratify a settlor's
act for which no capacity existed at the time of his death. * * *

The *Pleasants* case was first heard by Chancellor George Wythe.
Wythe, not surprisingly, ruled in favor of the slaves, requiring the
legatees and their successors to do their duty under the instrument.
He went still farther and ordered an accounting of the Negroes'
profits for the period of their wrongful enslavement. On appeal, the
Supreme Court of Appeals upheld Wythe on most major points, but
reversed as to the accountings. Each of the judges wrote a separate
opinion.

Judge Spencer Roane thought that if an analogy to ordinary property and trust principles would arguably suffice to validate the
Negroes' interests, then the result "will hold with increased force,
when the case is considered in its true point of view, as one which
involves human liberty." Thus, the preference for liberty is an explicit principle of construction, a necessary part of the reasoning
a minori ad majus. This preference goes hand-in-hand with a reading
of the animus of the statute as not simple toleration, but a "policy of
authorizing or *encouraging* emancipation." Pendleton and Carrington, the other two judges, agreed that the major goal ought to be effectuating the object of the testator and of the Negroes. They, too,
read the act to be applied to retroactively ratify Pleasants's will.

The judges were equally expansive in dealing with the Rule
against Perpetuities. Roane stated his respect for the public policy
behind the Rule—the refusal to let the disposition of property be
governed too long by the dead—however, he doubted "whether the
doctrine of perpetuities is applicable to cases in which human liberty
is challenged." The policy of freedom is of greater weight. Carrington agreed that devises respecting liberty are not subject to the limitations on those respecting chattel interests. And Pendleton thought,
"That it would be too rigid to apply that rule, with all its consequences, to the present case."

* * *

The *Pleasants* case was extended four years later in Charles v.
Hunnicutt. * * * The Quaker testator, Gloister Hunnicutt, died in
1781 leaving a will that provided

> that the following negroes should be manumitted on or be-
> fore the first month next 1782. * * * I give the above
> named Negroes to the monthly meeting, of which I am a
> member, to be manumitted by such members of the said
> meeting, as the meeting shall appoint.

This provision differed significantly from *Pleasants* in that it purported not to direct a manumission when the laws should allow, but to direct a manumission on a date certain; which date, unfortunately, was prior to the effective date of the Act of 1782.

The *Pleasants* case was relied on by the plaintiff, one of the named Negroes, in suing for his freedom. His counsel, the reporter Call, and Taylor asserted that *Pleasants* stood for application of the broad proposition that "subsequent statutes will embrace anterior dispositions made with a view to the existence of future laws." The opposition claimed that *Pleasants*, by its own terms, explicitly distinguished the case of a bequest that purported to make a manumission when it was not permitted by law.

St. George Tucker read the language of the will as not being an immediate act of manumission, but rather the settling of a trust. Accordingly, the trust instrument should be read to effectuate the settlor's intent "and that such intention be construed, if it be possible, not to be repugnant to the law, or the policy of the law." He construed the will as if it had been written like that of Pleasants, supplying the phrase "if the laws allow." Roane embraced a similar reading. The president of the court, Peter Lyons, brought the preference for liberty to the fore:

> Devises in favor of charities, and particularly those in favor
> of liberty, ought to be liberally expounded: and upon the
> present occasion, it is fair to infer, that the testator meant
> that the deed of manumission should not take place, until an
> act of assembly, to authorize it, should pass * * *.

As in the case of *Pleasants*, the court also deemed it advisable to take a very flexible view of procedure. The plaintiff had sued for his freedom in an action at law. There was some doubt as to whether the common law court ought to apply rules and standards involving the obligations of the "Quakers meeting" as trustee as against the claim of an executor of the estate, or whether such relief would be available only in a Court of Equity. Roane argued strongly that "The courts of law will rather stand in the place of courts of equity in relation to the principles of their decision." Roane thought that even the more rigid of common law judges "would have approved that system in relation to the case before us: a case involving human liberty."

*   *   *

By 1821 decisions in the area of conflict of laws already foretold a decisive shift in the attitude and technique of the Virginia court. In 1824, in Maria v. Surbaugh that shift manifested itself in a private manumission case with the disclaimer that principles of interpretation favoring liberty have any place in decisions on private emancipation.
* * *

In *Maria* the court held that an instrument providing for the manumission of a slave upon her reaching a specific age would not have the effect of rendering free children born to her between the effective date of the instrument and her attainment of the given age. Spencer Roane had reached the opposite conclusion in *Pleasants* and on natural rights grounds, though the rest of that court had chosen other inconclusive reasoning. Even more significant than the result, for purposes of this analysis, is Judge Green's perception of the interpretive process:

> in deciding upon questions of liberty and slavery, * * * it is the duty of the Court, uninfluenced by considerations of humanity on the one hand, or of policy (except so far as the policy of the law appears to extend) on the other, to ascertain and pronounce what the law is: leaving it to the legislature, * * * to deal * * * with a subject involving * * * such important moral and political considerations.

If any doubt might have remained about an explicit rejection of earlier standards, they were certainly dispelled by the court in Gregory v. Baugh in 1831:

> But all who have examined the earlier cases in our books, must admit, that our judges (from the purest motives, I am sure) did, *in favorem libertatis*, sometimes relax, rather too much, the rules of law. * * * Of this, the court in later times, has been so sensible, that it has felt the propriety of gradually returning to the legal standard, and of treating these precisely like any other questions of property.

*   *   *

NOTES AND QUESTIONS

1. Why was there no legislation permitting "private manumission" in Virginia until 1782? How do you explain the fact that the pressure for manumission came from a "quaker-dominated" anti-slavery upper class? Wouldn't that class have benefitted the most from slavery? How do you explain the increasing trend toward libertarian slavery decisions in Virginia, and then the shift away from that attitude after 1821? Did you notice anything similar in the development of slavery legislation generally?

2. In the Virginia case of Maria v. Surbaugh, 2 Rand (23 Va.) 228 (1824), as you have seen, the judge stated that the court must remain "uninfluenced by considerations of humanity on the one hand, or of policy (except so far as the policy of the law appears to extend) on the other * * *." Rather the court was supposed to leave "such important moral and political considerations" to the legislature. Why? Why did this attitude not appear earlier? Does this attitude seem consistent with the opinions you read in Chapter Three involving contracts, property, torts and corporations?

3. How free were judges to decide slavery cases according to their consciences? We can perhaps derive some perspective on this problem by comparing the decisions of Judges Ruffin and Shaw, which follow.

STATE v. MANN

Supreme Court of North Carolina, 1829.
13 N.C. (2 Dev.) 263.

The Defendant was indicted for an assault and battery upon *Lydia*, the slave of one *Elizabeth Jones*.

On the trial it appeared that the Defendant had hired the slave for a year—that during the term, the slave had committed some small offence, for which the Defendant undertook to chastise her—that while in the act of so doing, the slave ran off, whereupon the Defendant called upon her to stop, which being refused, he shot at and wounded her.

His honor Judge DANIEL charged the Jury, that if they believed the punishment inflicted by the Defendant was cruel and unwarrantable, and disproportionate to the offence committed by the slave, that in law the Defendant was guilty, as he had only a special property in the slave.

A verdict was returned for the State, and the Defendant appealed.

No Counsel appeared for the Defendant.

The Attorney General contended, that no difference existed between this case and that of the State v. Hall, (2 Hawks, 582.) In this case the weapon used was one calculated to produce death. He assimilated the relation between a master and a slave, to those existing between parents and children, masters and apprentices, and tutors and scholars, and upon the limitations to the right of the Superiors in these relations, he cited Russell on Crimes, 866.

RUFFIN, Judge. A Judge cannot but lament when such cases as the present are brought into judgment. It is impossible that the reasons on which they go can be appreciated, but where institutions similar to our own, exist and are thoroughly understood. The struggle, too, in the Judge's own breast between the feelings of the man, and the duty of the magistrate is a severe one, presenting strong temptation to put aside such questions, if it be possible. It is useless however, to complain of things inherent in our political state. And it is criminal in a Court to avoid any responsibility which the laws impose. With whatever reluctance therefore it is done the Court is compelled to express an opinion upon the extent of the dominion of the master over the slave in North Carolina.

The indictment charges a battery on *Lydia*, a slave of Elizabeth Jones. Upon the face of the indictment, the case is the same as the State v. Hall, (2 Hawks, 582.) No fault is found with the rule then adopted; nor would be, if it were now open. But it is not open; for the question, as it relates to a battery on a slave by a stranger, is considered as settled by that case. But the evidence makes this a different case. Here the slave had been hired by the Defendant, and was in his possession and the battery was committed during the period of hiring. * * * The enquiry here is, whether a cruel and unreasonable battery on a slave, by the hirer, is indictable. The Judge below instructed the Jury, that it is. He seems to have put it on the ground, that the Defendant had but a special property. Our laws uniformly treat the master or other person having the possession and command of the slave, as entitled to the same extent of authority. The object is the same—the services of the slave; and the same powers must be confided. In a criminal proceeding, and indeed in reference to all other persons but the general owner, the hirer and possessor of a slave, in relation to both rights and duties, is, for the time being, the owner. * * *

[U]pon the general question, whether the owner is answerable *criminaliter*, for a battery upon his own slave, or other exercise of authority or force, not forbidden by statute, the Court entertains but little doubt.—That he is so liable, has never yet been decided; nor, as far as is known, been hitherto contended. There have been no prosecutions of the sort. The established habits and uniform practice of the country in this respect, is the best evidence of the portion of power, deemed by the whole community, requisite to the preservation of the master's dominion. If we thought differently, we could not set our notions in array against the judgment of every body else, and say that this, or that authority, may be safely lopped off. This has indeed been assimilated at the bar to the other domestic relations; and arguments drawn from the well established principles, which confer and restrain the authority of the parent over the child, the tutor over the pupil, the master over the apprentice, have been pressed on us. The Court does not recognize their application. There is no likeness between the cases. They are in opposition to each other, and there is an impassable gulf between them. The difference is that which exists between freedom and slavery—and a greater cannot be imagined. In the one, the end in view is the happiness of the youth, born to equal rights with that governor, on whom the duty devolves of training the young to usefulness, in a station which he is afterwards to assume among freemen. To such an end, and with such a subject, moral and intellectual instruction seem the natural means; and for the most part, they are found to suffice. Moderate force is superadded, only to make the others effectual. If that fails, it is better to leave the party to his own headstrong passions, and the ultimate correction of the law, than to allow it to be immoderately inflicted by a private person. With slavery it is far otherwise. The end is the profit of the master, his security and the public safety; the subject, one doomed in his own person, and his posterity, to live without knowledge, and without the capacity to make any thing his own, and to toil that another may reap the fruits. What moral considerations shall be addressed to such a being, to convince him what, it is impossible but that the most stupid must feel and know can never be true—that he is thus to labor upon a principle of natural duty, or for the sake of his own personal happiness, such services can only be expected from one who has no will of his own; who surrenders his will in implicit obedience to that of another. Such obedience is the consequence only of uncontrolled authority over the body. There is nothing else which can operate to produce the effect. The power of the master must be absolute, to render the submission of the slave perfect. I most freely confess my sense of the harshness of this proposition, I feel it as deeply as any man can. And as a principle of moral right, every person in his retirement must repudiate it. But in the actual condition of things, it must be so.—There is no remedy. This discipline belongs to the state of slavery. They cannot be disunited, without abrogating at once the rights of the master, and absolving the slave from his subjection. It constitutes the curse of slavery to both the bond and free portions of our population. But it is inherent in the relation of master and slave.

That there may be particular instances of cruelty and deliberate barbarity, where, in conscience the law might properly interfere, is most probable. The difficulty is to determine, where *a Court* may properly begin. Merely in the abstract it may well be asked, which power of the master accords with right. The answer will probably sweep away all of them. But we cannot look at the matter in that light. The truth is, that we are forbidden to enter upon a train of general reasoning on the subject. We cannot allow the right of the master to be brought into discussion in the Courts of Justice. The slave, to remain a slave, must be made sensible, that there is no appeal from his master; that his power is in no instance, usurped; but is conferred by the laws of man at least, if not by the law of God. The danger would be great indeed, if the tribunals of justice should be called on to graduate the punishment appropriate to every temper, and every dereliction of menial duty. No man can anticipate the many and aggravated provocations of the master, which the slave would be constantly stimulated by his own passions, or the instigation of others to give; or the consequent wrath of the master, prompting him to bloody vengeance, upon the turbulent traitor—a vengeance generally practised with impunity, by reason of its privacy. The Court therefore disclaims the power of changing the relation, in which these parts of our people stand to each other.

We are happy to see, that there is daily less and less occasion for the interposition of the Courts. The protection already afforded by several statutes, that all powerful motive, the private interest of the owner, the benevolences towards each other, seated in the hearts of those who have been born and bred together, the frowns and deep execrations of the community upon the barbarian, who is guilty of excessive and brutal cruelty to his unprotected slave, all combined, have produced a mildness of treatment, and attention to the comforts of the unfortunate class of slaves, greatly mitigating the rigors of servitude, and ameliorating the condition of the slaves. The same causes are operating, and will continue to operate with increased action, until the disparity in numbers between the whites and blacks, shall have rendered the latter in no degree dangerous to the former, when the police now existing may be further relaxed. This result, greatly to be desired, may be much more rationally expected from the events above alluded to, and now in progress, than from any rash expositions of abstract truths, by a Judiciary tainted with a false and fanatical philanthropy, seeking to redress an acknowledged evil, by means still more wicked and appalling than even that evil.

I repeat, that I would gladly have avoided this ungrateful question. But being brought to it, the Court is compelled to declare, that while slavery exists amongst us in its present state, or until it shall seem fit to the Legislature to interpose express enactments to the contrary, it will be the imperative duty of the Judges to recognize the full dominion of the owner over the slave, except where the exercise of it is forbidden by statute. And this we do upon the ground, that this dominion is essential to the value of slaves as property, to the security of the master, and the public tranquility, greatly dependent upon their subordination; and in fine, as most effectually securing the general protection and comfort of the slaves themselves.

PER CURIAM. Let the judgment below be reversed and judgment entered for the Defendant.

NOTES AND QUESTIONS

1. This opinion "has both attracted and repulsed commentators for over a century." Robert Cover, Justice Accused: Anti-Slavery and the Judicial Process 77n (1975). Were you attracted or repulsed? Cover quotes Harriet Beecher Stowe's comments:

No one can read this decision, so fine and clear in expression, so dignified and solemn in its earnestness, and so dreadful in its results, without feeling at once deep respect for the man and horror for the system. The man, judging him from this short specimen, * * * has one of that high order of minds, which looks straight through all verbiage and sophistry to the heart of every subject which it encounters. He has, too, that noble scorn of dissimulation, that straight forward determination not to call a bad thing by a good name, even when most popular and reputable and legal, which it is to be wished could be more frequently seen, both in our Northern and Southern States. There is but one sole regret; and that is that such a man, with such a mind, should have been merely an *expositor*, and not a *reformer* of law."

Id., at 77–78n, *quoting* Harriet Beecher Stowe, The Key to Uncle Tom's Cabin 78–79 (1853). Do you agree with her analysis?

2. Does it seem to you that Ruffin's attitude toward slavery, or his legal analysis, support Elkins's and/or Genovese's descriptions of the relationship between slaves and masters? How do you explain the note of optimism that creeps into Ruffin's opinion at the end? Was it justified?

COMMONWEALTH v. AVES

Supreme Judicial Court of Massachusetts, 1836.
35 Mass. (18 Pick.) 193.

SHAW, C. J., delivered the opinion of the Court. The question now before the Court arises upon a return to a habeas corpus * * * for the purpose of bringing up the person of a colored child named Med, and instituting a legal inquiry into the fact of her detention, and the causes for which she was detained. * * *

* * *

The precise question presented by the claim of the respondent is, whether a citizen of any one of the United States, where negro slavery is established by law, coming into this State, for any temporary purpose of business or pleasure, staying some time, but not acquiring a domicil here, who brings a slave with him as a personal attendant, may restrain such slave of his liberty during his continuance here, and convey him out of this State on his return, against his consent. * * *

* * *

It is now to be considered as an established rule, that by the constitution and laws of this Commonwealth, before the adoption of the constitution of the United States, in 1789, slavery was abolished, as being contrary to the principles of justice, and of nature, and repugnant to the provisions of the declaration of rights, which is a component part of the constitution of the State.

* * *

How, or by what act particularly, slavery was abolished in Massachusetts, whether by the adoption of the opinion in Sommersett's case, as a declaration and modification of the common law, or by the Declaration of Independence, or by the constitution of 1780, it is not now very easy to determine, and it is rather a matter of curiosity than of utility; it being agreed on all hands, that if not abolished before, it was so by the declaration of rights. In the case of Winchendon v. Hatfield, 4 Mass.R. 123, which was a case between two towns respecting the support of a pauper, Chief Justice Parsons, in giving the opinion of the Court, states, that in the first action which came before the Court after the establishment of the constitution, the judges declared, that by virtue of the declaration of rights, slavery in this State was no more. * * *

It has recently been stated as a fact, that there were judicial decisions in this State prior to the adoption of the present constitution, holding that negroes born here of slave parents were free. A fact is stated in the above opinion of Chief Justice Parsons, which may account for this suggestion. He states that several negroes, born in this country, of imported slaves, had demanded their freedom of their masters by suits at law, and obtained it by a judgment of court. The defence of the master, he says, was faintly made, for such was the temper of the times, that a restless, discontented slave was worth little, and when his freedom was obtained in a course of legal proceedings, his master was not holden for his support, if he became poor. It is very probable, therefore, that this surmise is correct, and that records of judgments to this effect may be found; but they would throw very little light on the subject.

Without pursuing this inquiry farther, it is sufficient for the purposes of the case before us, that by the constitution adopted in 1780, slavery was abolished in Massachusetts, upon the ground that it is contrary to natural right and the plain principles of justice. The terms of the first article of the declaration of rights are plain and explicit. "All men are born free and equal, and have certain natural, essential, and unalienable rights, which are, the right of enjoying and defending their lives and liberties, that of acquiring, possessing, and protecting property." It would be difficult to select words more precisely adapted to the abolition of negro slavery. According to the laws prevailing in all the States, where slavery is upheld, the child of a slave is not deemed to be born free, a slave has no right to enjoy and defend his own liberty, or to acquire, possess, or protect property. That the description was broad enough in its terms to embrace negroes, and that it was intended by the framers of the constitution to embrace them, is proved by the earliest contemporaneous construction, by an unbroken series of judicial decisions, and by a uniform practice from the adoption of the constitution to the present time. The whole tenor of our policy, of our legislation and jurisprudence, from that time to the present, has been consistent with this construction, and with no other.

Such being the general rule of law, it becomes necessary to inquire how far it is modified or controlled in its operation; either,

1. By the law of other nations and states, as admitted by the comity of nations to have a limited operation within a particular state; or

2. By the constitution and laws of the United States.

In considering the first, we may assume that the law of this State is analogous to the law of England, in this respect; that while slavery is considered as unlawful and inadmissible in both, and this because contrary to natural right and to laws designed for the security of personal liberty, yet in both, the existence of slavery in other countries is recognized, and the claims of foreigners, growing out of that condition, are, to a certain extent, respected. Almost the only reason assigned by Lord *Mansfield* in Sommersett's case was, that slavery is of such a nature, that it is incapable of being introduced on any reasons moral or political, but only by positive law; and, it is so odious, that nothing can be suffered to support it but positive law.

The same doctrine is clearly stated in the full and able opinion of Marshall C. J., in the case of the *Antelope*, 10 Wheat. 120. He is speaking of the slave trade, but the remark itself shows that it applies to the state of slavery. "That it is contrary to the law of nature will scarcely be denied. That every man has a natural right to the fruits of his own labor, is generally admitted, and that no other person can rightfully deprive him of those fruits, and appropriate them against his will, seems to be the necessary result of the admission."

But although slavery and the slave trade are deemed contrary to natural right, yet it is settled by the judicial decisions of this country and of England, that it is not contrary to the law of nations. * * * The consequence is, that each independent community, in its intercourse with every other, is bound to act on the principle, that such other country has a full and perfect authority to make such laws for the government of its own subjects, as its own judgment shall dictate and its own conscience approve, provided the same are consistent with the law of nations; and no independent community has any right to interfere with the acts or conduct of another state, within the territories of such state, or on the high seas, which each has an equal right to use and occupy; and that each sovereign state, governed by its own laws, although competent and well authorized to make such laws as it may think most expedient to the extent of its own territorial limits, and for the government of its own subjects, yet beyond those limits, and over those who are not her own subjects, has no authority to enforce her own laws, or to treat the laws of other states as void, although contrary to its own views of morality.

This view seems consistent with most of the leading cases on the subject.

Sommersett's case, 20 Howell's State Trials, 1, as already cited, decides that slavery, being odious and against natural right, cannot exist, except by force of positive law. But it clearly admits, that it may exist by force of positive law. And it may be remarked, that by positive law, in this connection, may be as well understood customary law as the enactment of a statute; and the word is used to designate rules established by tacit acquiescence or by the legislative act of any state, and which derive their force and authority from such acquiescence or enactment, and not because they are the dictates of natural justice, and as such of universal obligation.

Le Louis, 2 Dodson, 236. This was an elaborate opinion of Sir William Scott. It was the case of a French vessel seized by an English vessel in time of peace, whilst engaged in the slave trade. It proceeded upon the ground, that a right of visitation, by the vessels of one nation, of the vessels of another, could only be exercised in time of war, or against pirates, and that the slave trade was not piracy by the laws of nations, except against those by whose government it has been so declared by law or by treaty. And the vessel was delivered up.

* * *

Two cases are cited from the decisions of courts of common law, which throw much light upon the subject.

Madrazo v. Willes, 3 Barn. & Ald. 353. It was an action brought by a Spaniard against a British subject, who had unlawfully, and without justifiable cause, captured a ship with three hundred slaves on board. The only question was the amount of damages. Abbott C. J., who tried the cause, in reference to the very strong language of the acts of Parliament, declaring the traffic in slaves a violation of right and contrary to the first principles of justice and humanity, doubted whether the owner could recover damages, in an English court of justice, for the value of the slaves as property, and directed the ships and the slaves to be separately valued. On further consideration, he and the whole court were of opinion, that the plaintiff was entitled to recover for the value of the slaves. That opinion went upon the ground, that the traffic in slaves, however wrong in itself, if prosecuted by a Spaniard between Spain and the coast of Africa, and if permitted by the laws of Spain, and not restrained by treaty, could not be lawfully interrupted by a British subject, on the high seas, the common highway of nations. And Mr. Justice Bayley, in his opinion, after stating the general rule, that a foreigner is entitled, in a British court of justice, to compensation for a wrongful act, added, that although the language used by the statutes was very strong, yet it could only apply to British subjects. * * *

Forbes v. Cochrane, 2 Barn. & Cressw. 448; S.C. 3 Dowl. & Ryl. 679. * * * The plaintiff, a British subject, domiciled in East Florida, where slavery was established by law, was the owner of a plantation, and of certain slaves, who escaped thence and got on board a British ship of war on the high seas. It was held, that he could not maintain an action against the master of the ship for harbouring the slaves after notice and demand of them. * * * Best, J. declared * * * "Slavery is a local law, and therefore if a man wishes to preserve his slaves, let him attach them to him by affection, or make fast the bars of their prison, or rivet well their chains, for the instant they get beyond the limits where slavery is recognized by the local law, they have broken their chains, they have escaped from their prison, and are free."

* * *

This view of the law applicable to slavery, marks strongly the distinction between the relation of master and slave, as established by the local law of particular states, and in virtue of that sovereign power and independent authority which each independent state concedes to every other, and those natural and social relations, which are everywhere and by all people recognized, and which, though they may be modified and regulated by municipal law, are not founded upon it, such as the relation of parent and child, and husband and wife. Such also is the principle upon which the general right of property is founded, being in some form universally recognized as a natural right, independently of municipal law.

This affords an answer to the argument drawn from the maxim, that the right of personal property follows the person, and therefore, where by the law of a place a person there domiciled acquires personal property, by the comity of nations the same must be deemed his property everywhere. It is obvious, that if this were true, in the extent in which the argument employs it, if slavery exists anywhere, and if by the laws of any place a property can be acquired in slaves, the law of slavery must extend to every place where such slaves may be carried. The maxim, therefore, and the argument can apply only to those commodities which are everywhere, and by all nations, treated and deemed subjects of property. But it is not speaking with strict accuracy to say, that a property can be acquired in human beings, by local laws. Each state may, for its own convenience, declare that slaves shall be deemed property, and that the relations and laws of personal chattels shall be deemed to apply to them. * * * But it would be a perversion of terms to say, that such local laws do in fact make them personal property generally; they can only determine, that the same rules of law shall apply to them as are applicable to property, and this effect will follow only so far as such laws *proprio vigore* can operate.

* * *

The conclusion to which we come from this view of the law is this:

That by the general and now well established law of this Commonwealth, bond slavery cannot exist, because it is contrary to natural right, and repugnant to numerous provisions of the constitution and laws, designed to secure the liberty and personal rights of all persons within its limits and entitled to the protection of the laws.

* * *

That, as a general rule, all persons coming within the limits of a state, become subject to all its municipal laws, civil and criminal, and entitled to the privileges which those laws confer; that this rule applies as well to blacks as whites, except in the case of fugitives, to be afterwards considered; that if such persons have been slaves, they become free, not so much because any alteration is made in their *status*, or condition, as because there is no law which will warrant, but there are laws, if they choose to avail themselves of them, which prohibit, their forcible detention or forcible removal.

That the law arising from the comity of nations cannot apply; because if it did, it would follow as a necessary consequence, that all those persons, who, by force of local laws, and within all foreign places where slavery is permitted, have acquired slaves as property, might bring their slaves here, and exercise over them the rights and power which an owner of property might exercise, and for any length of time short of acquiring a domicil; that such an application of the law would be wholly repugnant to our laws, entirely inconsistent with our policy and our fundamental principles, and is therefore inadmissible.

* * *

The question has thus far been considered as a general one, and applicable to cases of slaves brought from any foreign state or country; and it now becomes necessary to consider how far this result differs, where the person is claimed as a slave by a citizen of another State of this Union. * * *

In art. 4, § 2, the constitution declares that no person held to service or labor in one State, under the laws thereof, escaping into another, shall in consequence of any law or regulation therein, be discharged from such service or labor, but shall be delivered up on claim of the party to whom such service or labor may be due.

The law of congress made in pursuance of this article provides, that when any person held to labor in any of the United States, &c. shall escape into any other of the said States or Territories, the person entitled, &c. is empowered to arrest the fugitive, and upon proof made that the person so seized, under the law of the State from which he or she fled, owes service, &c. Act of February 12, 1793, c. 7, § 3.

In regard to these provisions, the Court are of opinion, that as by the general law of this Commonwealth, slavery cannot exist, and the rights and powers of slave owners cannot be exercised therein; the effect of this provision in the constitution and laws of the United States, is to limit and restrain the operation of this general rule, so far as it is done by the plain meaning and obvious intent and import of the language used, and no further. The constitution and law manifestly refer to the case of a slave escaping from a State where he owes service or labor, into another State or Territory. He is termed a fugitive from labor; the proof to be made is, that he owed service or labor, under the laws of the State or Territory *from which he fled,* and the authority is given to remove such fugitive to the State *from which he fled.* This language can, by no reasonable construction, be applied to the case of a slave who has not fled from the State, but who has been brought into the State by his master.

The same conclusion will result from a consideration of the well known circumstances under which this constitution was formed. Before the adoption of the constitution, the States were to a certain extent, sovereign and independent, and were in a condition to settle the terms upon which they would form a more perfect union. It has been contended by some overzealous philanthropists, that such an article in the constitution could be of no binding force or validity, because it was a stipulation contrary to natural right. But it is difficult to perceive the force of this objection. It has already been shown, that slavery is not contrary to the laws of nations. It would then be the proper subject of treaties among sovereign and independent powers. * * * Now the constitution of the United States partakes both of the nature of a treaty and of a form of government. It regards the States, to a certain extent, as sovereign and independent communities, with full power to make their own laws and regulate their own domestic policy, and fixes the terms upon which their intercourse with each other shall be conducted. * * * It is well known that when this constitution was formed, some of the States permitted slavery and the slave-trade, and considered them highly essential to their interest, and that some other States had abolished slavery within their own limits, and from the principles deduced and policy avowed by them, might be presumed to desire to extend such abolition further. * * * Under these circumstances the clause in question was agreed on and introduced into the constitution; and as it was well considered, as it was intended to secure future peace and harmony, and to fix as precisely as language could do it, the limit to which the rights of one party should be exercised within the territory of the other, it is to be presumed that they selected terms intended to express their exact and their whole meaning; and it would be a departure from the purpose and spirit of the compact to put any other construction upon it, than that to be derived from the plain and natural import of the language used. Besides, this construction of the provision in the constitution, gives to it a latitude sufficient to afford effectual security to the owners of slaves. The States have a plenary power to make all laws necessary for the regulation of slavery and the rights of the slave owners, whilst the slaves remain within their territorial limits; and it is only when they escape, without the consent of their owners, into other States, that they require the aid of other States, to enable them to regain their dominion over the fugitives.

But this point is supported by most respectable and unexceptionable authorities.

In the case of Butler v. Hopper, 1 Wash.C.C.Rep. 499, it was held by Mr. Justice Washington, in terms, that the provision in the constitution which we are now considering, does not "extend to the case of a slave voluntarily carried by his master into another State, and there leaving him under the protection of some law declaring him free." In this case, however, the master claimed to hold the slave in virtue of a law of Pennsylvania, which permitted members of congress and sojourners, to retain their domestic slaves, and it was held that he did not bring himself within either branch of the exception, because he had, for two years of the period, ceased to be a member of congress, and so lost the privilege; and by having become a resident could not claim as a sojourner. The case is an authority to this point, that the claimant of a slave, to avail himself of the provisions of the constitution and laws of the United States, must bring himself within their plain and obvious meaning, and they will not be extended by construction; and that the clause in the constitution is confined to the case of a slave escaping from one State, and fleeing to another.

But in a more recent case, the point was decided by the same eminent judge. Ex parte Simmons, 4 Wash.C.C.R. 396. It was an application for a certificate under § 3, of the act of February 12, 1793. He held that both the constitution and laws of the United States apply only to fugitives, escaping from one State and fleeing to another, and not to the case of a slave voluntarily brought by his master.

Another question was made in that case, whether the slave was free by the laws of Pennsylvania, which, like our own in effect, liberate slaves voluntarily brought within the State, but there is an exception in favor of members of congress, foreign ministers and consuls, and *sojourners*: but this provision is qualified as to sojourners and persons passing through the State, in such manner as to exclude them from the benefit of the exception, if the slave was retained in the State longer than six months. The slave in that case having been detained in the State more than six months, was therefore held free.

This case is an authority to this point;—the general rule being, that if a slave is brought into a State where the laws do not admit slavery, he will be held free, the person who claims him as a slave under any exception or limitation of the general rule, must show clearly that the case is within such exception.

*   *   *

In Louisiana, it has been held, that if a person with a slave, goes into a State to reside, where it is declared that slavery shall not exist, for ever so short a time, the slave *ipso facto* becomes free, and will be so adjudged and considered afterwards in all other States; and a person moving from Kentucky to Ohio to reside, his slaves thereby became free, and were so held in Louisiana. This case also fully recognizes the authority of States to make laws dissolving the relation of master and slave; and considers the special limitation of the general power, by the federal constitution, as a forcible implication in proof of the existence of such general power. Lunsford v. Coquillon, 14 Martin's Rep. 403.

*   *   *

The same rule of construction is adopted in analogous cases in other countries, that is, where an institution is forbidden, but where for special reasons and to a limited extent such prohibition is relaxed, the exemption is to be construed strictly, and whoever claims the exemption, must show himself clearly within it, and where the facts do not bring the case within the exemption, the general rule has its effect.

*   *   *

The constitution and laws of the United States, then, are confined to cases of slaves escaping from other States and coming within the limits of this State without the consent and against the will of their masters, and cannot by any sound construction extend to a case where the slave does not escape and does not come within the limits of this State against the will of the master, but by his own act and permission. The provision is to be construed according to its plain terms and import, and cannot be extended beyond this, and where the case is not that of an escape, the general rule shall have its effect. It is upon these grounds we are of opinion, that an owner of a slave in another State where slavery is warranted by law, voluntarily bringing such slave into this State, has no authority to detain him against his will, or to carry him out of the State against his consent, for the purpose of being held in slavery.

* * *

NOTES AND QUESTIONS

1. Shaw's biographer, Leonard W. Levy, has written that Northern Abolitionists greeted the opinion in Commonwealth v. Aves with great joy, and that Boston's Columbian Centinel "called the decision 'THE MOST IMPORTANT' ever made in any one of the free states." The opinion in the South, however, was considerably less sanguine:

> The Baltimore *Chronicle* fumed over judicial confiscation of property and declared that whereas the Constitution had provided for the restoration of slaves fleeing from one state to another, "the decision of Chief Justice Shaw virtually annuls this security * * *." * * * The *Augusta Sentinel* * * * exclaimed that the Union was worthless if its members were able to destroy the right of private property and to deprive the people of the South "of what is justly theirs." "This is the strongest and boldest step ever yet taken against the rights of the South, and leaves the puny efforts of the abolitionists at an immeasureable distance in the rear," the paper trumpeted, as it demanded of Southerners whether they would submit to the outrage.

Levy, The Law of the Commonwealth and Chief Justice Shaw 67–68 (1957).* (Levy's book is one of the best-written and most provocative works in American legal history, and should be read by everyone seriously interested in the field.) Were the Southerners over-reacting? Can you think of a legal basis for deciding the case differently? How do you suppose Thomas Ruffin would have resolved the issue?

2. Consider Shaw's explanation for the lack of positive law to support slavery in Massachusetts. Shaw concedes that slavery once existed in the state, but that it has since become illegal. What led to the changed legal status for slavery? Shaw offers three possibilities: (1) *Sommersett's* case, a British opinion written in 1772; (2) the Declaration of Independence, adopted by the Continental Congress in 1776; and (3) The Massachusetts

Constitution of 1780 (Article One of the Declaration of Rights). Do you have any problems with using the first two as authorities for the abolition of slavery in Massachusetts? What about the third? The Massachusetts Declaration of Rights provided in article one that "All men are born free and equal, and have certain natural, essential, and unalienable rights; which are, the right of enjoying and defending their lives and liberties, that of acquiring, possessing, and protecting property." Shaw says that "It would be difficult to select words more properly adjudged to the abolition of negro slavery." Can you come up with words "more properly adjudged" for that purpose?

3. Are the cases construing Pennsylvania's statute authorizing the temporary transit of slaves through the state, Butler v. Hopper and Ex Parte Simms, good authority for Shaw to cite in support of his opinion that Med was freed by bringing her to Massachusetts? Consider Shaw's construction of the fugitive slave clause of the Constitution. Shaw says that the clause's "plain meaning" is the only acceptable construction. Why should this be so? Could it be argued that its "plain meaning" could be extended to include the case of a slave who comes willingly with his or her master to Massachusetts and then refuses to go home?

4. How can Shaw suggest that one of the bases for his decision is that slavery is contrary to "natural right and to laws designed for the security of personal liberty," and yet dismiss as "overzealous philanthropists" abolitionists like William Lloyd Garrison who argued that the fugitive slave provisions of federal law were void because they were "contrary to natural right?" Garrison, incidentally, was apparently "thrilled" by this decision of Shaw's, but a few years later, when Shaw participated in a Massachusetts decision which upheld the federal law regarding fugitive slaves, Garrison denounced Shaw as willing " * * * to act the part of Pilate in the Crucifixion of the Son of God" or " * * * the slave pirate on the African coast," and complained that Shaw "had betrayed the honor of Massachusetts 'when Liberty lay bleeding.'" Levy, supra, at 67, 82. Would you have predicted, on the basis of the *Aves* opinion, that Shaw would be willing to suffer the vilest personal abuse to support the apprehension of fugitive slaves? Compare the sophistication and subtlety of Shaw's analysis of the state and federal laws regarding slavery with those of Justices Story and Taney which you will read next.

3. THE UNITED STATES SUPREME COURT ON SLAVERY

PRIGG v. PENNSYLVANIA

Supreme Court of the United States, 1842.
41 U.S. (16 Pet.) 539, 608, 10 L.Ed. 1060.

* * *

Mr. Justice STORY delivered the opinion of the Court.

* * *

The facts are briefly these: The plaintiff in error was indicted in the Court of Oyer and Terminer for York county, for having, with force and violence, taken and carried away from that county to the state of Maryland, a certain negro woman, named Margaret Morgan, with a design and intention of selling and disposing of, and keeping her as a slave or servant for life, contrary to a statute of Pennsylvania, passed on the 26th of March, 1826. That statute in the first section, in substance, provides, that if any person or persons shall from and after the passing of the act, by force and violence take and carry away * * * [or] shall by fraud or false pretence, seduce, or cause to be seduced * * * any negro or mulatto from any part of that commonwealth, with a design and intention of selling and disposing of * * * or of keeping and detaining * * * such negro or mulatto as a slave or servant for life * * * every such person or persons, his or their aiders or abettors, shall, on conviction thereof, be deemed guilty of a felony, and shall forfeit and pay a sum not less than five hundred, nor more than one thousand dollars; and moreover, shall be sentenced to undergo a servitude for any term or terms of years, not less than seven years nor exceeding twenty-one years; and shall be confined and kept to hard labour, &c. * * *

The plaintiff in error pleaded not guilty to the indictment; and at the trial the jury found a special verdict * * * that the negro woman, Margaret Morgan, was a slave for life, and held to labour and service under and according to the laws of Maryland, to a certain Margaret Ashmore, a citizen of Maryland; that the slave escaped and fled from Maryland into Pennsylvania in 1832; that the plaintiff in error, being legally constituted the agent and attorney of the said Margaret Ashmore, in 1837, caused the said negro woman to be taken and apprehended as a fugitive from labour by a state constable, under a warrant from a Pennsylvania magistrate; that the said negro woman was thereupon brought before the said magistrate, who refused to take further cognisance of the case; and thereupon the plaintiff in error did remove, take, and carry away the said negro woman and her children out of Pennsylvania into Maryland, and did deliver the said negro woman and her children into the custody and possession of the said Margaret Ashmore. * * *

Upon this special verdict, the Court of Oyer and Terminer of York county adjudged that the plaintiff in error was guilty of the offence charged in the indictment. * * *

Before proceeding to discuss the very important and interesting questions involved in this record, it is fit to say, that the cause has been conducted in the Court below, and has been brought here by the co-operation and sanction, both of the state of Maryland, and the state of Pennsylvania, in the most friendly and courteous spirit, with a view to have those questions finally disposed of by the adjudication of this Court; so that the agitations on this subject in both states, which have had a tendency to interrupt the harmony between them, may subside, and the conflict of opinion be put at rest. * * *

* * *

There are two clauses in the Constitution upon the subject of fugitives, * * * They are both contained in the second section of the fourth article, and are in the following words: "A person charged in any state with treason, felony, or other crime, who shall flee from justice, and be found in another state, shall, on demand of the executive authority of the state from which he fled, be delivered up, to be removed to the state having jurisdiction of the crime."

"No person held to service or labour in one state under the laws thereof, escaping into another, shall in consequence of any law or regulation therein, be discharged from such service or labour; but shall be delivered up, on claim of the party to whom such service or labour may be due."

The last clause is that, the true interpretation whereof is directly in judgment before us. Historically, it is well known, that the object of this clause was to secure to the citizens of the slaveholding states the complete right and title of ownership in their slaves, as property, in every state in the Union into which they might escape from the state where they were held in servitude. The full recognition of this right and title was indispensable to the security of this species of property in all the slaveholding states; and, indeed, was so vital to the preservation of their domestic interests and institutions, that it cannot be doubted that it constituted a fundamental article, without the adoption of which the Union could not have been formed. Its true design was to guard against the doctrines and principles prevalent in the non-slaveholding states, by preventing them from intermeddling with, or obstructing, or abolishing the rights of the owners of slaves.

By the general law of nations, no nation is bound to recognise the state of slavery, as to foreign slaves found within its territorial dominions, when it is in opposition to its own policy and institutions, in favour of the subjects of other nations where slavery is recognised. If it does it, it is a matter of comity, and not as a matter of international right. The state of slavery is deemed to be a mere municipal regulation, founded upon and limited to the range of the territorial laws. * * *

It is manifest from this consideration, that if the Constitution had not contained this clause, every non-slaveholding state in the Union would have been at liberty to have declared free all runaway slaves coming within its limits, and to have given them entire immunity and protection against the claims of their masters; a course which would have created the most bitter animosities, and engendered perpetual strife between the different states. * * *

The clause manifestly contemplates the existence of a positive, unqualified right on the part of the owner of the slave, which no state law or regulation can in any way qualify, regulate, control, or restrain. The slave is not to be discharged from service or labour, in consequence of any state law or regulation. Now, certainly, without indulging in any nicety of criticism upon words, it may fairly and reasonably be said, that any state law or state regulation, which interrupts, limits, delays, or postpones the right of the owner to the immediate possession of the slave, and the immediate command of his service and labour, operates, pro tanto, a discharge of the slave therefrom. The question can never be, how much the slave is discharged from; but whether he is discharged from any, by the natural or necessary operation of state laws or state regulations. * * *

We have said, that the clause contains a positive and unqualified recognition of the right of the owner in the slave, unaffected by any state law or regulation whatsoever, because there is no qualification or restriction of it to be found therein; and we have no right to insert any which is not expressed, and cannot be fairly implied. * * * If this be so, then all the incidents to that right attach also. The owner must, therefore, have the right to seize and repossess the slave, which the local laws of his own state confer upon him as property; and we all know that this right of seizure and recaption is universally acknowledged in all the slaveholding states. * * * Upon this ground we have not the slightest hesitation in holding, that, under and in virtue of the Constitution, the owner of a slave is clothed with entire authority, in every state in the Union, to seize and recapture his slave, whenever he can do it without any breach of the peace, or any illegal violence. In this sense, and to this extent this clause of the Constitution may properly be said to execute itself, and to require no aid from legislation, state or national.

But the clause of the Constitution does not stop here * * *. Many cases must arise in which, if the remedy of the owner were confined to the mere right of seizure and recaption, he would be utterly without any adequate redress. He may not be able to lay his hands upon the slave. * * * He may be restricted by local legislation as to the mode of proofs of his ownership; as to the Courts in which he shall sue, and as to the actions which he may bring; or the process he may use to compel the delivery of the slave. Nay, the local legislation may be utterly inadequate to furnish the appropriate redress, by authorizing no process in rem, or no specific mode of repossessing the slave, but a mere remedy in damages; and that perhaps against persons utterly insolvent or worthless. * * *

And this leads us to the consideration of the other part of the clause, which implies at once a guaranty and duty. It says, "But he (the slave) shall be delivered up on claim of the party to whom such service or labour may be due." Now, we think it exceedingly difficult, if not impracticable, to read this language and not to feel, that it contemplated some farther remedial redress than that, which might be administered at the hands of the owner himself. A claim is to be made. What is a claim? It is, in a just juridical sense, a

demand of some matter as of right made by one person upon another, to do or to forbear to do some act or thing as a matter of
duty. [This means, said Story, that there must be] * * * legislation to protect the right, to enforce the delivery, and to secure the
subsequent possession of the slave. If, indeed, the Constitution guarantees the right * * * the natural inference certainly is, that the
national government is clothed with the appropriate authority and
functions to enforce it. * * * The clause is found in the national
Constitution, and not in that of any state. It does not point out any
state functionaries, or any state action to carry its provisions into
effect. The states cannot, therefore, be compelled to enforce them;
and it might well be deemed an unconstitutional exercise of the power
of interpretation, to insist that the states are bound to provide means
to carry into effect the duties of the national government, nowhere
delegated or intrusted to them by the Constitution. * * *

Congress has taken this very view of the power and duty of the
national government. As early as the year 1791, the attention of
Congress was drawn to it * * *. The result of their deliberations,
was the passage of the act of the 12th of February, 1793, ch. 51, (7,)
which * * * proceeds, in the third section, to provide, that when
a person held to labour or service in any of the United States, shall
escape into any other of the states or territories, the person to whom
such labour or service may be due, his agent or attorney, is hereby
empowered to seize or arrest such fugitive from labour, and take him
or her before any judge of the Circuit or District Courts of the United States * * * or before any magistrate of a county, city, or
town corporate, wherein such seizure or arrest shall be made; and
upon proof to the satisfaction of such judge or magistrate, either by
oral evidence or affidavit, &c., that the person so seized or arrested,
doth, under the laws of the state or territory from which he or she
fled, owe service or labour to the person claiming him or her, it shall
be the duty of such judge or magistrate, to give a certificate thereof
to such claimant, his agent or attorney, which shall be sufficient warrant for removing the said fugitive from labour, to the state or territory from which he or she fled. The fourth section provides a penalty against any person, who shall knowingly and willingly obstruct
or hinder such claimant, his agent, or attorney, in so seizing or arresting such fugitive from labour, or rescue such fugitive from the
claimant, or his agent, or attorney when so arrested * * *.

In a general sense, this act may be truly said to cover the whole
ground of the Constitution * * *; not because it exhausts the
remedies which may be applied by Congress to enforce the rights, if
the provisions of the act shall in practice be found not to attain the
object of the Constitution; but because it points out fully all the
modes of attaining those objects, which Congress, in their discretion,
have as yet deemed expedient or proper to meet the exigencies of
the Constitution. If this be so, then it would seem, upon just princi-

ples of construction, that the legislation of Congress, if constitutional, must supersede all state legislation upon the same subject; and by necessary implication prohibit it. For, if Congress have a constitutional power to regulate a particular subject, and they do actually regulate it in a given manner, and in a certain form, it cannot be that the state legislatures have a right to interfere, and, as it were, by way of complement to the legislation of Congress, to prescribe additional regulations, and what they may deem auxiliary provisions for the same purpose. In such a case, the legislation of Congress, in what it does prescribe, manifestly indicates, that it does not intend that there shall be any further legislation to act upon the subject-matter. Its silence as to what it does not do, is as expressive of what its intention is as the direct provisions made by it.

*　　*　　*

But it has been argued, that the act of Congress is unconstitutional, because it does not fall within the scope of any of the enumerated powers of legislation confided to that body; and therefore it is void. Stripped of its artificial and technical structure, the argument comes to this, that although rights are exclusively secured by, or duties are exclusively imposed upon, the national government, yet, unless the power to enforce these rights, or to execute these duties can be found among the express powers of legislation enumerated in the Constitution, they remain without any means of giving them effect by any act of Congress;　*　*　*　even although, in a practical sense, they may become a nullity from the want of a proper remedy to enforce them, or to provide against their violation.　*　*　*　Such a limited construction of the Constitution has never yet been adopted as correct, either in theory or practice. No one has ever supposed that Congress could, constitutionally, by its legislation, exercise powers, or enact laws beyond the powers delegated to it by the Constitution. But it has, on various occasions, exercised powers which were necessary and proper as means to carry into effect rights expressly given, and duties expressly enjoined thereby. The end being required, it has been deemed a just and necessary implication, that the means to accomplish it are given also　*　*　*.

*　　*　　*

[Story then proceeds to give two instances where Congress exercised implied powers in order to accomplish express constitutional ends: apportionment of Congressional representatives among the states and preventing the suspension of the writ of habeas corpus.]

*　　*　　*

The very act of 1793, now under consideration, affords the most conclusive proof, that Congress has acted upon a very different rule of interpretation, and has supposed that the right as well as the duty of legislation on the subject of fugitives from justice, and fugitive slaves, was within the scope of the constitutional authority conferred on the national legislature. In respect to fugitives from justice, the Constitution, although it expressly provides, that the demand shall be made by the executive authority of the state from which the fugitive has fled, is silent as to the party upon whom the demand is to be made, and as to the mode in which it shall be made. This very silence occasioned embarrassments in enforcing the right and duty at an early period after the adoption of the Constitution; and produced a hesitation on the part of the executive authority of Virginia to deliver up a fugitive from justice, upon the demand of the executive of Pennsylvania, in the year 1791; and as we historically know from the message of President Washington and the public documents of that period, it was the immediate cause of the passing of the act of 1793, which designated the person (the state executive) upon whom the demand should be made, and the mode and proofs upon and in which it should be made. From that time down to the present hour not a doubt has been breathed upon the constitutionality of this part of the act; and every executive in the Union has constantly acted upon and admitted its validity. * * * This very acquiescence, under such circumstances, of the highest state functionaries, is a most decisive proof of the universality of the opinion that the act is founded in a just construction of the Constitution, independent of the vast influence, which it ought to have as a contemporaneous exposition of the provisions by those, who were its immediate framers, or intimately connected with its adoption.

The same uniformity of acquiescence in the validity of the act of 1793, upon the other part of the subject-matter, that of fugitive slaves, has prevailed throughout the whole Union until a comparatively recent period. * * * So far as the judges of the Courts of the United States have been called upon to enforce it, and to grant the certificate required by it, it is believed that it has been uniformly recognised as a binding and valid law, and as imposing a constitutional duty. Under such circumstances, if the question were one of doubtful construction, such long acquiescence in it, such contemporaneous expositions of it, and such extensive and uniform recognition of its validity, would in our judgment entitle the question to be considered at rest * * *.

But we do not wish to rest our present opinion upon the ground either of contemporaneous exposition, or long acquiescence * * *. On the contrary, our judgment would be the same, if the question were entirely new, and the act of Congress were of recent enactment. We hold the act to be clearly constitutional in all its leading provisions, and, indeed, with the exception of that part, which confers authority upon state magistrates, to be free from reasonable doubt and difficulty upon the grounds already stated. As to the authority so conferred upon state magistrates, while a difference of opinion has existed, and may exist still on the point, in different states, whether state magistrates are bound to act under it, none is entertained by this Court, that state magistrates may, if they choose, exercise that authority, unless prohibited by state legislation.

The remaining question is, whether the power of legislation upon this subject is exclusive in the national government, or concurrent in the states, until it is exercised by Congress. In our opinion it is exclusive * * *. "Wherever," said Mr. Chief Justice Marshall, in delivering the opinion of the Court [in Sturgis v. Crowninshield, 4 Wheat.Rep. 122, 193,] "the terms in which a power is granted to Congress, or the nature of the power require, that it should be exercised exclusively by Congress, the subject is as completely taken from the state legislatures, as if they had been forbidden to act." * * *

In the first place, it is material to state * * * that the right to seize and retake fugitive slaves, and the duty to deliver them up, * * * and of course the corresponding power in Congress to use the appropriate means to enforce the right and duty, derive their whole validity and obligation exclusively from the Constitution of the United States * * *. Before the adoption of the Constitution, no state had any power whatsoever over the subject, except within its own territorial limits, and could not bind the sovereignty or the legislation of other states. * * * Under the Constitution it is recognized as an absolute, positive, right and duty, pervading the whole Union with an equal and supreme force, uncontrolled and uncontrollable by state sovereignty or state legislation. * * * The natural inference deducible from this consideration certainly is, in the absence of any positive delegation of power to the state legislatures, that it belongs to the legislative department of the national government, to which it owes its origin and establishment. It would be a strange anomaly, and forced construction, to suppose, that the national government meant to rely for the due fulfillment of its own proper duties and the rights, which it intended to secure, upon state legislation, and not upon that of the Union. * *

In the next place, the nature of the provision and the objects to be attained by it, require that it should be controlled by one and the same will, and act uniformly by the same system of regulations throughout the Union. If, then, the states have a right, in the absence of legislation by Congress, to act upon the subject, each state is at liberty to prescribe just such regulations as suit its own policy, local convenience, and local feelings. * * * One state may require the owner to sue in one mode, another in a different mode. One state may make a statute of limitations as to the remedy, in its own tribunals, short and summary; another may prolong the period, and yet restrict the proofs. * * * The duty might be enforced in some states; retarded, or limited in others; and denied, as compulsory in many, if not in all. Consequences like these must have been foreseen as very likely to occur in the non-slaveholding states, where legislation, if not silent on the subject, and purely voluntary, could scarcely be presumed to be favorable to the exercise of the rights of the owner.

It is scarcely conceivable, that the slaveholding states would have been satisfied with leaving to the legislation of the non-slaveholding states, a power of regulation, in the absence of that of Congress, which would or might practically amount to a power to destroy the rights of the owner. * * * Surely such a state of things never could have been intended, under such a solemn guarantee of right and duty. On the other hand, construe the right of legislation as exclusive in Congress, and every evil, and every danger vanishes. The right and the duty are then co-extensive and uniform in remedy and operation throughout the whole Union. The owner has the same security, and the same remedial justice, and the same exemption from state regulation and control, through however many states he may pass with his fugitive slave in his possession, in transitu, to his own domicile. * *

These are some of the reasons, but by no means all, upon which we hold the power of legislation on this subject to be exclusive in Congress. To guard, however, against any possible misconstruction of our views, it is proper to state, that we are by no means to be understood in any manner whatsoever to doubt or to interfere with the police power belonging to the states in virtue of their general sovereignty. * * * We entertain no doubt whatsoever, that the states, in virtue of their general police power, possess full jurisdiction to arrest and restrain runaway slaves, and remove them from their borders, and otherwise to secure themselves against their depredations and evil example, as they certainly may do in cases of idlers, vagabonds, and paupers. * * * But such regulations can never be permitted to interfere with or to obstruct the just rights of the owner to reclaim his slave, derived from the Constitution of the United States, or with the remedies prescribed by Congress to aid and enforce the same.

Upon these grounds, we are of opinion that the act of Pennsylvania upon which this indictment is founded, is unconstitutional and void. It purports to punish as a public offence against that state, the very act of seizing and removing a slave by his master, which the Constitution of the United States was designed to justify and uphold. * *

NOTES AND QUESTIONS

1. What do you understand to have been the purpose of the Pennsylvania Act of March 26, 1826, described in the second paragraph of Story's opinion? Many of these "personal liberty laws," passed at about this time, did not expressly reject the Constitution's fugitive slave clause, but did require certain safeguards, such as jury trials or a certificate from a state officer before a fugitive could be taken. Is such legislation consistent with the text of the clause of Article IV, Section 2 of the U.S. Constitution which provides that "No person held to service or labour in one state under the laws thereof, escaping into another, shall in consequence of any law or regulation therein, be discharged from such service or labour * * *." Would you have voted for such a "personal liberty law" if you were a Pennsylvania state legislator?

2.   How do you explain that it is not until 1842 that the United States Supreme Court passes on the Constitutionality of the Fugitive Slave Act of 1793?   According to your edited version of the opinion, what was the argument that the Act was unconstitutional and did you find it persuasive? Can you imagine how this argument could be advanced by anyone who took seriously the idea that the United States Constitution was to be the "supreme law" of the land?   Do you see any similarities in this argument and the debate over the federal common law of crimes which we studied in Chapter Two?   Are the problems of conceptions of the allocation of powers between the state and federal governments similar?   How would you have dealt with the argument, also made, that the federal fugitive slave act was unconstitutional because it deprived alleged fugitives of their freedom without a jury trial?

3.   Is the problem of the constitutionality of the 1793 Act confined to fugitive *slaves*?   Suppose Story had decided that the federal legislation on fugitive slaves was unconstitutional.   What would have been the effect on other fleeing felons?

4.   Is Story necessarily correct that the power to legislate regarding fugitive slaves is exclusively vested in congress?   Is this necessarily a pro-slavery holding?   Chief Justice Taney dissented from this part of Story's opinion:

> The language used in the Constitution does not, in my judgment, justify the construction given to it by the Court.   It contains no words prohibiting the several states from passing laws to enforce this right.   They are in express terms forbidden to make any regulation that shall impair it.   But, there the prohibition stops.   And according to the settled rules of construction for all written instruments, the prohibition being confined to laws injurious to the right, the power to pass laws to support and enforce it, is necessarily implied.   And the words of the article which direct that the fugitive "shall be delivered up," seem evidently designed to impose it as a duty upon the people of the several states to pass laws to carry into execution, in good faith, the compact into which they thus solemnly entered with each other.   The Constitution of the United States, and every article and clause in it, is a part of the law of every state in the Union; and is the paramount law.   *   *   *   And why may not a state protect a right of property, acknowledged by its own paramount law?   Besides, the laws of the different states, in all other cases, constantly protect the citizens of other states in their rights of property, when it is found within their respective territories; and no one doubts their power to do so.   And in the absence of any express prohibition, I perceive no reason for establishing, by implication, a different rule in this instance; where, by the national compact, this right of property is recognised as an existing right in every state of the Union.   41 U.S., at 627–633.

Who is correct, Justice Story or Justice Taney?   Was it necessary for Story to decide the question of whether a state could pass legislation to aid in the enforcement of the fugitive slave act?   What are we to make of Story's offhand suggestions that state magistrates may have the right to "choose" whether to act pursuant to the 1793 Act, and that states might "prohibit" them from doing so? How could Story's son claim that this opinion was a "charter of freedom?" II William W. Story, Life and Letters of Joseph Story 381–98 (1851).

5. The leading abolitionist newspaper greeted Story's decision in the following manner: "*It is not law * * * It is to be spit upon,* hooted at, trampled in the dust resolutely and openly." The Liberator, March 11, 1842. This prompted Story to rail "from his Harvard classroom at the 'madmen' who would pull down the house of Union to exorcise its defects." Gerald T. Dunne, Justice Joseph Story and the Rise of the Supreme Court 401 (1970). Imagine the effect of the next case on these "madmen."

SCOTT v. SANDFORD

Supreme Court of the United States, 1856.
60 U.S. (19 How.) 393, 400, 15 L.Ed. 691.

[In this suit Dred Scott sought to assert "the title of himself and his family to freedom." Chief Justice Taney's opinion begins with a discussion of whether or not the United States Circuit Court had diversity jurisdiction over this case. The first point to be addressed is whether the plaintiff, who then lived in Missouri, and who had once been held by the defendant as a slave in Missouri, could be considered to be a "citizen" of Missouri. If so, then the requisite diversity was present, since the defendant was a citizen of New York.]

[(a) *Is a Negro a "Citizen?"*]

* * *

The words "people of the United States" and "citizens" are synonymous terms, and mean the same thing. They both describe the political body who, according to our republican institutions, form the sovereignty, and who hold the power and conduct the Government through their representatives. They are what we familiarly call the "sovereign people," and every citizen is one of this people, and a constituent member of this sovereignty. The question before us is, whether the class of persons described in the plea in abatement compose a portion of this people, and are constituent members of this sovereignty? We think they are not, and that they are not included, and were not intended to be included, under the word "citizens" in the Constitution, and can therefore claim none of the rights and privileges which that instrument provides for and secures to citizens of the United States. On the contrary, they were at that time considered as a subordinate and inferior class of beings, who had been subjugated by the dominant race, and, whether emancipated or not, yet remained subject to their authority, and had no rights or privileges but such as those who held the power and the Government might choose to grant them.

It is not the province of the court to decide upon the justice or injustice, the policy or impolicy, of these laws. The decision of that question belonged to the political or law-making power; to those who formed the sovereignty and framed the Constitution. The duty of the court is, to interpret the instrument they have framed, with the best lights we can obtain on the subject, and to administer it as we find it, according to its true intent and meaning when it was adopted.

* * *

* * * The Constitution has conferred on Congress the right to establish an uniform rule of naturalization, and this right is evidently exclusive, and has always been held by this court to be so. Consequently, no State, since the adoption of the Constitution, can by naturalizing an alien invest him with the rights and privileges secured to a citizen of a State under the Federal Government, although, so far as the State alone was concerned, he would undoubtedly be entitled to the rights of a citizen, and clothed with all the rights and immunities which the Constitution and laws of the State attached to that character.

It is very clear, therefore, that no State can, by any act or law of its own, passed since the adoption of the Constitution, introduce a new member into the political community created by the Constitution of the United States. * * *

The question then arises, whether the provisions of the Constitution, in relation to the personal rights and privileges to which the citizen of a State should be entitled, embraced the negro African race, at that time in this country, or who might afterwards be imported, who had then or should afterwards be made free in any State; and to put it in the power of a single State to make him a citizen of the United States, and endue him with the full rights of citizenship in every other State without their consent? * * *

The court think the affirmative of these propositions cannot be maintained. * * *

* * * In the opinion of the court, the legislation and histories of the times, and the language used in the Declaration of Independence, show, that neither the class of persons who had been imported as slaves, nor their descendants, whether they had become free or not, were then acknowledged as a part of the people, nor intended to be included in the general words used in that memorable instrument.

It is difficult at this day to realize the state of public opinion in relation to that unfortunate race, which prevailed in the civilized and enlightened portions of the world at the time of the Declaration of Independence, and when the Constitution of the United States was framed and adopted. But the public history of every European nation displays it in a manner too plain to be mistaken.

They had for more than a century before been regarded as beings of an inferior order, and altogether unfit to associate with the white race, either in social or political relations; and so far inferior, that they had no rights which the white man was bound to respect; and that the negro might justly and lawfully be reduced to slavery for his benefit. * * * This opinion was at that time fixed and universal in the civilized portion of the white race. It was regarded as an axiom in morals as well as in politics, which no one thought of disputing, or supposed to be open to dispute * * *.

And in no nation was this opinion more firmly fixed or more uniformly acted upon than by the English Government and English people. They not only seized them on the coast of Africa, and sold them or held them in slavery for their own use; but they took them as ordinary articles of merchandise to every country where they could make a profit on them, and were far more extensively engaged in this commerce than any other nation in the world.

The opinion thus entertained and acted upon in England was naturally impressed upon the colonies they founded on this side of the Atlantic. And, accordingly, a negro of the African race was regarded by them as an article of property, and held, and bought and sold as such, in every one of the thirteen colonies which united in the Declaration of Independence, and afterwards formed the Constitution of the United States. * * *

The legislation of the different colonies furnishes positive and indisputable proof of this fact. * * * They show that a perpetual and impassable barrier was intended to be erected between the white race and the one which they had reduced to slavery, and governed as subjects with absolute and despotic power, and which they then looked upon as so far below them in the scale of created beings, that intermarriages between white persons and negroes or mulattoes were regarded as unnatural and immoral, and punished as crimes, not only in the parties, but in the person who joined them in marriage. * * *

We refer to these historical facts for the purpose of showing the fixed opinions concerning that race, upon which the statesmen of that day spoke and acted. It is necessary to do this, in order to determine whether the general terms used in the Constitution of the United States, as to the rights of man and the rights of the people, was intended to include them, or to give to them or their posterity the benefit of any of its provisions.

The language of the Declaration of Independence is equally conclusive. * * *

The general words [of the Declaration] would seem to embrace the whole human family, and if they were used in a similar instrument at this day would be so understood. But it is too clear for dispute, that the enslaved African race were not intended to be included, and formed no part of the people who framed and adopted this declaration; for if the language, as understood in that day, would embrace them, the conduct of the distinguished men who framed the Declaration of Independence would have been utterly and flagrantly inconsistent with the principles they asserted * * *.

Yet the men who framed this declaration were great men—high in literary acquirements—high in their sense of honor, and incapable

of asserting principles inconsistent with those on which they were acting. They perfectly understood the meaning of the language they
used, and how it would be understood by others; and they knew that
it would not in any part of the civilized world be supposed to embrace
the negro race, which, by common consent, had been excluded from
civilized Governments and the family of nations, and doomed to
slavery. * * *

This state of public opinion had undergone no change when the
Constitution was adopted, as is equally evident from its provisions and
language.

   * * * It speaks in general terms of the people of the United
States, and of citizens of the several States, when it is providing for
the exercise of the powers granted or the privileges secured to the
citizen. It does not define what description of persons are intended
to be included under these terms, or who shall be regarded as a citizen
and one of the people. * * *

But there are two clauses in the Constitution which point directly
and specifically to the negro race as a separate class of persons, and
show clearly that they were not regarded as a portion of the people
or citizens of the Government then formed.

One of these clauses reserves to each of the thirteen States the
right to import slaves until the year 1808, if it thinks proper. * * *
And by the other provision the States pledge themselves to each other
to maintain the right of property of the master, by delivering up to
him any slave who may have escaped from his service, and be found
within their respective territories. * * * And these two provisions
show, conclusively, that neither the description of persons therein referred to, nor their descendants, were embraced in any of the other
provisions of the Constitution; for certainly these two clauses were
not intended to confer on them or their posterity the blessings of liberty, or any of the personal rights so carefully provided for the citizen.

No one of that race had ever migrated to the United States voluntarily; all of them had been brought here as articles of merchandise.
The number that had been emancipated at that time were but few in
comparison with those held in slavery; and they were identified in the
public mind with the race to which they belonged, and regarded as a
part of the slave population rather than the free. * * *

Indeed, when we look to the condition of this race in the several
States at the time, it is impossible to believe that these rights and
privileges were intended to be extended to them.

It is very true, that in [some states] * * * few slaves were
held at the time of the Declaration of Independence; and when the
Constitution was adopted, it had entirely worn out in one of them, and
measures had been taken for its gradual abolition in several others.
But this change had not been produced by any change of opinion in
relation to this race; but because it was discovered, from experience,

that slave labor was unsuited to the climate and productions of these States: for some of the States, where it had ceased or nearly ceased to exist, were actively engaged in the slave trade * * *. And it can hardly be supposed that, in the States where it was then countenanced in its worst form—that is, in the seizure and transportation— the people could have regarded those who were emancipated as entitled to equal rights with themselves.

[Even in Massachusetts, said Taney,] The law of 1786, like the law of 1705, forbids the marriage of any white person with any negro, Indian, or Mulatto * * *. And this mark of degradation was renewed, and again impressed upon the race, in the careful and deliberate preparation of their revised code published in 1836. [And the same law can be found in Connecticut and Rhode Island at the time of framing the Federal Constitution.]

* * *

By the laws of New Hampshire, collected and finally passed in 1815, no one was permitted to be enrolled in the militia of the State, but free white citizens * * *. Nothing could more strongly mark the entire repudiation of the African race. The alien is excluded, because, being born in a foreign country, he cannot be a member of the community until he is naturalized. But why are the African race, born in the State, not permitted to share in one of the highest duties of the citizen? The answer is obvious; he is not, by the institutions and laws of the State, numbered among its people. He forms no part of the sovereignty of the State, and is not therefore called on to uphold and defend it.

* * *

* * * Chancellor Kent, whose accuracy and research no one will question, states in the sixth edition of his Commentaries, (published in 1848, 2 vol., 258, note b.) that in no part of the country except Maine, did the African race, in point of fact, participate equally with the whites in thee exercise of civil and political rights.

The legislation of the States therefore shows, in a manner not to be mistaken, the inferior and subject condition of that race at the time the Constitution was adopted * * *. [It] is hardly consistent with the respect due to these States, to suppose that they regarded at that time, as fellow-citizens and members of the sovereignty, a class of beings whom they had thus stigmatized * * *, or, that when they met in convention to form the Constitution, they looked upon them as a portion of their constituents, or designed to include them in the provisions so carefully inserted for the security and protection of the liberties and rights of their citizens.

* * *

[Furthermore,] no State was willing to permit another State to determine who should or should not be admitted as one of its citizens, and entitled to demand equal rights and privileges with their own people, within their own territories. The right of naturalization was therefore, with one accord, surrendered by the States, and confided to the Federal Government. And this power granted to Congress to establish an uniform rule of *naturalization* is, by the well-understood meaning of the word, confined to persons born in a foreign country, under a foreign Government. It is not a power to raise to the rank of a citizen any one born in the United States, who, from birth or parentage, by the laws of the country, belongs to an inferior and subordinate class. And when we find the States guarding themselves from the indiscreet or improper admission by other States of emigrants from other countries, by giving the power exclusively to Congress, we cannot fail to see that they could never have left with the States a much more important power—that is, the power of transforming into citizens a numerous class of persons, who in that character would be much more dangerous to the peace and safety of a large portion of the Union, than the few foreigners one of the States might improperly naturalize. * * *

* * *

To all this mass of proof we have still to add, that Congress has repeatedly legislated upon the same construction of the Constitution that we have given. Three laws, two of which were passed almost immediately after the Government went into operation, will be abundantly sufficient to show this. * * *

The first of these acts is the naturalization law, which was passed at the second session of the first Congress, March 26, 1790, and confines the right of becoming citizens "to aliens being free white persons."

Now, the Constitution does not limit the power of Congress in this respect to white persons. And they may, if they think proper, authorize the naturalization of any one, of any color, who was born under allegiance to another Government. But the language of the law above quoted, shows that citizenship at that time was perfectly understood to be confined to the white race; and that they alone constituted the sovereignty in the Government.

Another of the early laws of which we have spoken, is the first militia law, which was passed in 1792, at the first session of the second Congress. The language of this law is equally plain and significant with the one just mentioned. It directs that every "free able-bodied white male citizen" shall be enrolled in the militia. The word white is evidently used to exclude the African race, and the word "citizen" to exclude unnaturalized foreigners; the latter forming no part of the sovereignty, owing it no allegiance, and therefore under no obligation to defend it. The African race, however, born in the country, did owe allegiance to the Government, whether they were slave or free; but it is repudiated, and rejected from the duties and obligations of citizenship in marked language.

The third act to which we have alluded is even still more decisive; it was passed as late as 1813, (2 Stat., 809,) and it provides: "That from and after the termination of the war in which the United States are now engaged with Great Britain, it shall not be lawful to employ, on board of any public or private vessels of the United States, any person or persons except citizens of the United States, or persons of color, natives of the United States.

* * *

And even as late as 1820, (chap. 104, sec. 8,) in the charter to the city of Washington, the corporation is authorized "to restrain and prohibit the nightly and other disorderly meetings of slaves, free negroes, and mulattoes," thus associating them together in it legislation * * *. And in a subsequent part of the same section, the act authorizes the corporation "to prescribe the terms and conditions upon which free negroes and mulattoes may reside in the city."

This law, like the laws of the States, shows that this class of persons were governed by special legislation directed expressly to them, and always connected with provisions for the government of slaves, and not with those for the government of free white citizens. * * *

The conduct of the Executive Department of the Government has been in perfect harmony upon this subject with this course of legislation. The question was brought officially before the late William Wirt, when he was the Attorney General of the United States, in 1821, and he decided that the words "citizens of the United States" were used in the acts of Congress in the same sense as in the Constitution; and that free persons of color were not citizens, within the meaning of the Constitution and laws; and this opinion has been confirmed by that of the late Attorney General, Caleb Cushing, in a recent case, and acted upon by the Secretary of State, who refused to grant passports to them as "citizens of the United States."

* * *

No one, we presume, supposes that any change in public opinion or feeling, in relation to this unfortunate race, in the civilized nations of Europe or in this country, should induce the court to give to the words of the Constitution a more liberal construction in their favor than they were intended to bear when the instrument was framed and adopted. Such an argument would be altogether inadmissible in any tribunal called on to interpret it. If any of its provisions are deemed unjust, there is a mode prescribed in the instrument itself by which it may be amended; but while it remains unaltered, it must be construed now as it was understood at the time of its adoption. * * Any other rule of construction would abrogate the judicial character of this court, and make it the mere reflex of the popular opinion or passion of the day. This court was not created by the Constitution for such purposes. Higher and graver trusts have been confided to it, and it must not falter in the path of duty.

* * *

And upon a full and careful consideration of the subject, the court is of opinion, that, upon the facts stated in the plea in abatement, Dred Scott was not a citizen of Missouri within the meaning of the Constitution of the United States, and not entitled as such to sue in its courts; and, consequently, that the Circuit Court had no jurisdiction of the case * * *.

[(b) *Was Scott Free?*]

[Taney proceeds to note that if Scott *was* a slave he certainly could not have been a citizen, and since he (Taney) has just proven that even free Blacks are not citizens, there is no jurisdiction, and the case must be dismissed. Still, because the lower court's holding that Scott was no longer a slave might be treated as precedent, Taney goes on to evaluate Scott's assertion of his right to freedom.]

* * *

The plaintiff was a negro slave, belonging to Dr. Emerson, who was a surgeon in the army of the United States. In the year 1834, he took the plaintiff from the State of Missouri to the military post at Rock Island, in the State of Illinois, and held him there as a slave until the month of April or May, 1836. At the time last mentioned, said Dr. Emerson removed the plaintiff from said military post at Rock Island to the military post at Fort Snelling * * * in the Territory known as Upper Louisiana * * * north of the State of Missouri. Said Dr. Emerson held the plaintiff in slavery at said Fort Snelling, from said last-mentioned date until the year 1838. [Scott argued that he had become free, *inter alia*, because Congress had forbidden slavery in the part of the Louisiana territory where Fort Snelling was located.]

The act of Congress, upon which the plaintiff relies, declares that slavery and involuntary servitude, except as a punishment for crime, shall be forever prohibited in all that part of the territory ceded by France, under the name of Louisiana, which lies north of thirty-six degrees thirty minutes north latitude, and not included within the limits of Missouri. And the difficulty which meets us at the threshold of this part of the inquiry is, whether Congress was authorized to pass this law under any of the powers granted to it by the Constitution * * *.

The counsel for the plaintiff has laid much stress upon that article in the Constitution which confers on Congress the power "to dispose of and make all needful rules and regulations respecting the territory or other property belonging to the United States;" but, in the judgment of the court, that provision has no bearing on the present controversy, and the power there given, whatever it may be, is confined, and was intended to be confined, to the territory which at that time belonged to, or was claimed by, the United States, and was within their boundaries as settled by the treaty with Great Britain * * *.

It will be remembered that, from the commencement of the Revolutionary war, serious difficulties existed between the States, in relation to the disposition of large and unsettled territories which were included in the chartered limits of some of the States. And some of the other States, and more especially Maryland, which had no unsettled lands, insisted that as the unoccupied lands, if wrested from Great Britain, would owe their preservation to the common purse and the common sword, the money arising from them ought to be applied in just proportion among the several States to pay the expenses of the war * * *.

* * *

These fears and dangers were, however, at once removed, when the State of Virginia, in 1784, voluntarily ceded to the United States the immense tract of country lying northwest of the river Ohio, and which was within the acknowledged limits of the State. * * *

The example of Virginia was soon afterwards followed by other States * * *. The main object for which these cessions were desired and made, was on account of their money value, and to put an end to a dangerous controversy, as to who was justly entitled to the proceeds when the lands should be sold. * * *

Undoubtedly the powers of sovereignty and the eminent domain were ceded with the land. * * * But it must be remembered that, at that time, there was no Government of the United States in existence with enumerated and limited powers; what was then called the United States, were thirteen separate, sovereign, independent States, which had entered into a league or confederation for their mutual protection and advantage, and the Congress of the United States was composed of the representatives of these separate sovereignties, meeting together, as equals * * *. But this Confederation had none of the attributes of sovereignty in legislative, executive, or judicial power. It was little more than a congress of ambassadors, authorized to represent separate nations, in matters in which they had a common concern.

It was this Congress that accepted the cession from Virginia. They had no power to accept it under the Articles of Confederation. But they had an undoubted right, as independent sovereignties, to accept any cession of territory for their common benefit, which all of them assented to; and it is equally clear, that as their common property, and having no superior to control them, they had the right to exercise absolute dominion over it * * *. It was by a Congress, representing the authority of these several and separate sovereignties, and acting under their authority and command, (but not from any authority derived from the Articles of Confederation,) that the instrument usually called the ordinance of 1787 was adopted; regulating in much detail the principles and the laws by which this territory should be governed; and among other provisions, slavery is prohibited in it. We do not question the power of the States, by agreement among themselves, to pass this ordinance, nor its obligatory force in the territory, while the confederation or league of the States in their separate sovereign character continued to exist.

This was the state of things when the Constitution of the United States was formed. The territory ceded by Virginia belonged to the several confederated States * * *. They were about to dissolve this federative Union, and to surrender a portion of their independent sovereignty to a new Government, * * * but this Government was to be carefully limited in its powers, and to exercise no authority beyond those expressly granted by the Constitution, or necessarily to be implied from the language of the instrument, and the objects it was intended to accomplish; and as this league of States would, upon the adoption of the new Government, cease to have any power over the territory, and the ordinance they had agreed upon be incapable of execution, and a mere nullity, it was obvious that some provision was necessary to give the new Government sufficient power to enable it to carry into effect the objects for which it was ceded * * *. It was necessary that the lands should be sold to pay the war debt; that a Government and system of Jurisprudence should be maintained in it, to protect the citizens of the United States who should migrate to the territory, in their rights of person and of property. * * * [For these reasons,] the clause was inserted in the Constitution which gives Congress the power "to dispose of and make all needful rules and regulations respecting the territory or other property belonging to the United States." * * *. It applied only to the property which the States held in common at that time, and has no reference whatever to any territory or other property which the new sovereignty might afterwards itself acquire.

* * * It does not speak of *any territory,* nor of *Territories,* but uses language which, according to its legitimate meaning, points to a particular thing. The power is given in relation only to the territory of the United States—that is, to a territory then in existence, and then known or claimed as the territory of the United States. It begins its enumeration of powers by that of disposing, in other words, making sale of the lands, or raising money from them, which, as we have already said, was the main object of the cession, and which is accordingly the first thing provided for in the article. It then gives the power which was necessarily associated with the disposition and sale of the lands—that is, the power of making needful rules and regulations respecting the territory. And whatever construction may now be given to these words, every one, we think, must admit that they are not the words usually employed by statesmen in giving supreme power of legislation. * * *

* * *

* * * The concluding words of the clause appear to render this construction irresistible; for, after the provisions we have mentioned, it proceeds to say, "that nothing in the Constitution shall be so construed as to prejudice any claims of the United States, or of any particular State."

Now, * * * all of the States, except North Carolina and Georgia, had made the cession before the Constitution was adopted * * *. The claims of other States, that the unappropriated lands in these two States should be applied to the common benefit, in like manner, was still insisted on, but refused by the States. And this member of the clause in question evidently applies to them, and can apply to nothing else. It was to exclude the conclusion that either party, by adopting the Constitution, would surrender what they deemed their rights. And when the latter provision relates so obviously to the unappropriated lands not yet ceded by the States, and the first clause makes provision for those then actually ceded, it is impossible, by any just rule of construction, to make the first provision general, and extend to all territories, which the Federal Government might in any way afterwards acquire, when the latter is plainly and unequivocally confined to a particular territory; which was a part of the same controversy, and involved in the same dispute, and depended upon the same principles. * * *

The Constitution has always been remarkable for the felicity of its arrangement of different subjects, and the perspicuity and appropriateness of the language it uses. But if this clause is construed to extend to territory acquired by the present Government from a foreign nation, outside of the limits of any charter from the British Government to a colony, it would be difficult to say, why it was deemed necessary to give the Government the power to sell any vacant lands belonging to the sovereignty which might be found within it; and if this was necessary, why the grant of this power should precede the power to legislate over it and establish a Government there; and still more difficult to say, why it was deemed necessary so specially and particularly to grant the power to make needful rules and regulations in relation to any personal or movable property it might acquire there. * * *

The words "needful rules and regulations" would seem, also, to have been cautiously used for some definite object. They are not the words usually employed by statesmen, when they mean to give the powers of sovereignty, or to establish a Government, or to authorize its establishment. Thus, in the law to renew and keep alive the ordinance of 1787, and to re-establish the Government, the title of the law is: "An act to provide for the government of the territory northwest of the river Ohio." And in the Constitution, when granting the power to legislate over the territory that may be selected for the seat of Government independently of a State, it does not say Congress shall have power "to make all needful rules and regulations respecting the territory;" but it declares that "Congress shall have power to exercise exclusive legislation in all cases whatsoever over such District * * *".

The words "rules and regulations" are usually employed in the Constitution in speaking of some particular specified power which it means to confer on the Government, and not, as we have seen, when granting general powers of legislation. * * * But if confined to a particular Territory, in which a Government and laws had already been established, but which would require some alterations to adapt it to the new Government, the words are peculiarly applicable and appropriate for that purpose.

* * * Consequently, the power which Congress may have lawfully exercised in this Territory, while it remained under a Territorial Government, and which may have been sanctioned by judicial decision, can furnish no justification and no argument to support a similar exercise of power over territory afterwards acquired by the Federal Government. We put aside, therefore, any argument, drawn from precedents, showing the extent of the power which the General Government exercised over slavery in this Territory, as altogether inapplicable to the case before us.

* * *

This brings us to examine by what provision of the Constitution the present Federal Government, under its delegated and restricted powers, is authorized to acquire territory outside of the original limits of the United States, and what powers it may exercise therein over the person or property of a citizen of the United States * * *.

There is certainly no power given by the Constitution to the Federal Government to establish or maintain colonies bordering on the United States or at a distance, to be ruled and governed at its own pleasure; nor to enlarge its territorial limits in any way, except by the admission of new States. That power is plainly given; and if a new State is admitted, it needs no further legislation by Congress, because the Constitution itself defines the relative rights and powers, and duties of the State, and the citizens of the State, and the Federal Government. But no power is given to acquire a Territory to be held and governed permanently in that character.

* * *

We do not mean, however, to question the power of Congress in this respect. The power to expand the territory of the United States by the admission of new States is plainly given; and in the construction of this power by all the departments of the Government, it has been held to authorize the acquisition of territory, not fit for admission at the time, but to be admitted as soon as its population and situation would entitle it to admission. * * * All we mean to say on this point is, that, as there is no express regulation in the Constitution defining the power which the General Government may exercise over the person or property of a citizen in a Territory thus acquired, the court must necessarily look to the provision and principles of the Constitution, and its distribution of powers, for the rules and principles by which its decision must be governed.

Taking this rule to guide us, it may be safely assumed that citizens of the United States who migrate to a Territory belonging to the people of the United States, cannot be ruled as mere colonists, dependent upon the will of the General Government, and to be governed by any laws it may think proper to impose. The principle upon which our Governments rest, and upon which alone they continue to exist, is the union of States, sovereign and independent within their own limits in their internal and domestic concerns, and bound together as one people by a General Government, possessing certain enumerated and restricted powers * * *. Whatever it acquires, it acquires for the benefit of the people of the several States who created it. It is their trustee acting for them, and charged with the duty of promoting the interests of the whole people of the Union in the exercise of the powers specifically granted.

At the time when the Territory in question was obtained by cession from France, it contained no population fit to be associated together and admitted as a State; and it therefore was absolutely necessary to hold possession of it, as a Territory belonging to the United States, until it was settled and inhabited by a civilized community capable of self-government * * *.

* * * The form of government to be established necessarily rested in the discretion of Congress. It was their duty to establish the one that would be best suited for the protection and security of the citizens of the United States * * *.

[Taney proceeds to suggest the scope of permissible
legislation for territories.]

* * *

For example, no one, we presume, will contend that Congress can make any law in a Territory respecting the establishment of religion, or the free exercise thereof, or abridging the freedom of speech or of the press, or the right of the people of the Territory peaceably to assemble, and to petition the Government for the redress of grievances.

Nor can Congress deny to the people the right to keep and bear arms, nor the right to trial by jury, nor compel any one to be a witness against himself in a criminal proceeding.

These powers, and others, in relation to rights of person, which it is not necessary here to enumerate, are, in express and positive terms, denied to the General Government; and the rights of private property have been guarded with equal care. Thus the rights of property are united with the rights of person, and placed on the same ground by the fifth amendment to the Constitution, which provides that no person shall be deprived of life, liberty, and property, without due process of law. And an act of Congress which deprives a citizen of the United States of his liberty or property, merely because he came himself or brought his property into a particular Territory of the United States, and who had committed no offence against the laws, could hardly be dignified with the name of due process of law.

*   *   *

The powers over person and property of which we speak are not only not granted to Congress, but are in express terms denied, and they are forbidden to exercise them. And this prohibition is not confined to the States, but the words are general, and extend to the whole territory over which the Constitution gives it power to legislate, including those portions of it remaining under Territorial Government, as well as that covered by States. *   *   * And if Congress itself cannot do this—if it is beyond the powers conferred on the Federal Government—it will be admitted, we presume, that it could not authorize a Territorial Government to exercise them. It could confer no power on any local Government, established by its authority, to violate the provisions of the Constitution.

It seems, however, to be supposed, that there is a difference between property in a slave and other property, and that different rules may be applied to it in expounding the Constitution of the United States. And the laws and usages of nations, and the writings of eminent jurists upon the relation of master and slave and their mutual rights and duties, and the powers which Governments may exercise over it, have been dwelt upon in the argument.

But in considering the question before us, it must be borne in mind that there is no law of nations standing between the people of the United States and their Government, and interfering with their relation to each other. The powers of the Government, and the rights of the citizen under it, are positive and practical regulations plainly written down. *   *   * It has no power over the person or property of a citizen but what the citizens of the United States have granted. And no laws or usages of other nations, or reasoning of statesmen or jurists upon the relations of master and slave, can enlarge the powers of the Government, or take from the citizens the rights they have reserved. And if the Constitution recognises the right of property of the master in a slave, and makes no distinction between that description of property and other property owned by a citizen, no tribunal, acting under the authority of the United States, whether it be legislative, executive, or judicial, has a right to draw such a distinction, or deny to it the benefit of the provisions and guarantees which have been provided for the protection of private property against the encroachments of the Government.

Now * * * the right of property in a slave is distinctly and expressly affirmed in the Constitution. The right to traffic in it, like an ordinary article of merchandise and property, was guaranteed to the citizens of the United States, in every State that might desire it, for twenty years. And the Government in express terms is pledged to protect it in all future time, if the slave escapes from his owner. * * * And no word can be found in the Constitution which gives Congress a greater power over slave property, or which entitles property of that kind to less protection than property of any other description. The only power conferred is the power coupled with the duty of guarding and protecting the owner in his rights.

Upon these considerations, it is the opinion of the court that the act of Congress which prohibited a citizen from holding and owning property of this kind in the territory of the United States north of the line therein mentioned, is not warranted by the Constitution, and is therefore void; and that neither Dred Scott himself, nor any of his family, were made free by being carried into this territory; even if they had been carried there by the owner, with the intention of becoming a permanent resident.

* * *

[Taney concluded his opinion by holding that even though Scott temporarily resided in a free State, Illinois, this had no effect on his status in Missouri, since, as an independent State, Missouri was not required to give effect to Illinois law regarding slavery. By the relevant laws of Missouri, then, Scott was still a slave.]

NOTES AND QUESTIONS

1. Scott v. Sandford is one of the most important decisions ever rendered by the United States Supreme Court. It has been the subject of controversy and study since it was first decided. For a recent, thorough treatment of the case, see Don E. Fehrenbacher, The Dred Scott Case: Its Significance in American Law and Politics (1978).

The crucial decision in the case, as you may have guessed, was not the determination of the personal status of Dred Scott, but was the ruling on Congress's ability to forbid slavery in the federal territories acquired after the Constitution of 1789, such as those of Louisiana. After the "era of good feelings" passed, during the years before the Civil War (1830–1860), the dominant national issues were those of allocation of power and wealth between the states of the North and South. To simplify matters, Southerners feared that the uncouth masses of the North were conspiring to end Southern Civilization, while Northerners were worried that the mandarins of the Southern "slavocracy" were conspiring to impose slavery on the entire nation. Some sort of balance was struck by Congress in the "Missouri Compromise" of 1820, when legislation was passed admitting Missouri as a slave state, admitting Maine as a free state, and forbidding slavery in the territories North of the line 36 degrees and 30 minutes in latitude.

What do you suppose the Court's opinion in Dred Scott did to the delicate balance struck in 1820? The decision was the Supreme Court's first declaration since Marbury v. Madison (1803) that an Act of Congress was unconstitutional. President Buchanan had predicted in his inaugural address two days before the *Dred Scott* opinion was issued that the current controversy over the status of slavery in the territories would be "speedily and finally settled" by the Supreme Court. Immediately prior to his inaugural speech Buchanan was seen huddled with Chief Justice Taney, and from that time to this the Dred Scott decision has been seen as evidence of the Southern Conspiracy, which allegedly included Taney and Buchanan among the principals, and which amounted to the President's playing politics with the members of the Court. Whether or not Taney's whispering to Buchanan on the day of the Inaugural revealed what the Supreme Court was to do two days later, it now seems clear that Buchanan *was* in correspondence with at least two of the judges of the Supreme Court, and that he did know exactly what the court was up to. Fehrenbacher, supra, at 305–314.

The abolitionist newspapers attacked the Dred Scott opinion in a manner that almost makes their comments about Prigg v. Pennsylvania seem like paeans. Horace Greeley's New York Tribune described the decision as "atrocious," "wicked," "abominable," and "no better than what might be obtained in any 'Washington bar-room.'" He excoriated Taney, the "'cunning chief' whose 'collation of false statements and shallow sophistries' revealed a 'destestable hypocrisy' and a 'mean and skulking cowardice.'" Fehrenbacher, supra, at 417. As late as 1865 Senator Charles Sumner declared that "the name of Taney is to be hooted down the page of history. Judgement is beginning now; and an emancipated country will fasten upon him the stigma which he deserves * * *. He administered justice at least wickedly, and degraded the age." Cong.Globe, 38th Cong. 2d Sess. 1012 (1865). More recently Taney has been rehabilitated, and he has been recognized, his opinion in Dred Scott notwithstanding, as one of the greatest of American Chief Justices. See generally Carl Brent Swisher, Roger B. Taney (1935) and Walker Lewis, Without Fear or Favor, A Biography of Chief Justice Roger Brook Taney (1965). Were the critics right about the quality of the decision in *Dred Scott*?

2. If Missouri had the power, as Taney acknowledges, to make Dred Scott a "citizen" of Missouri, why exactly does Taney maintain that he was not to be considered a "citizen" of Missouri for the purposes of diversity jurisdiction? What bearing does Article 4, Section 2, of the United States Constitution, "The citizens of each state shall be entitled to all privileges and immunities of citizens in the several states," have on this problem?

3. Are you impressed with Taney's abilities as an historian? How accurately does he present English attitudes on Negroes and on slavery which were contemporary with the Constitution? How important is the intention of the Constitutional framers to Taney? Do you find his attitude towards effectuating the intentions of the framers consistent throughout his opinion? Are you persuaded by Taney's proof that the authors of the Declaration of Independence could not have meant to have referred to the "African race" when it was written that "all men are created equal?" What about Taney's argument that even in the states where, at the time

of the Constitution, no slaves or few slaves were held, Blacks were still regarded as an inferior race and *not* accorded the privileges of citizenship? Does it necessarily follow that if a race is regarded by many as "inferior" it cannot contribute "citizens?"

4. What are the essential qualifications for United States Citizenship under the Constitution? There is one Constitutional provision which refers to Blacks that Taney never discusses. Article One, Section Two of the Constitution provides that " * * * Representatives and direct Taxes shall be apportioned among the several States which may be included within this Union, according to their respective Numbers, which shall be determined by adding to the whole Number of free Persons, * * * three fifths of all other Persons." Does the provision affect Taney's argument?

5. Is Taney correct when he presumes that no one would suppose "that any change in public opinion or feeling in relation to this unfortunate race * * * should induce the court to give the words of the Constitution a more liberal construction in their favor than they were intended to bear when the instrument was framed and adopted?" Is this a proper view of the task of Constitutional exposition? Is this consistent with the Supreme Court's ultimate resolution of the issue of common law crimes in *Hudson & Goodwin*, supra page 208? If not, why the change?

6. What is the ground upon which Taney decides the second issue in this case, whether Scott was entitled to freedom? How is it that Taney believes it was permissible for the Continental Congress under the Articles of Confederation to forbid slavery in the Northwest Territory in 1787, but the United States Congress *after* the Constitution lacked Constitutional authority to prohibit slavery in the territories of the Louisiana Purchase? Why do you suppose it has been suggested that *Dred Scott* helped cause the Civil War? What do you suppose Taney would have had to say about the Constitutionality of President Lincoln's Emancipation Proclamation?

7. If Taney concedes the Constitutional power in Congress to acquire territories later to be admitted as states, and if, as Taney says, "[t]he power to acquire necessarily carries with it the power to preserve and apply to the purposes for which [territories are] acquired," then why, where Congress has decided that the preservation of the national union requires the prohibition of slavery in part of newly-acquired territories, does Taney say it is unconstitutional? Would Taney's analysis crumble if he is wrong in his assertion that "there is no law of nations standing between the people of the United States and their Government"? Is he wrong? What does it mean to suggest that a "law of nations" might "stand between" Americans and the government? Would you agree with this anthropomorphic notion?

Chapter 5

COMPETITION AND LABOR LAW IN ANTE–
BELLUM AND LATE NINETEENTH
CENTURY AMERICA

SECTION A. DIFFERING MODELS FOR ECONOMIC
DEVELOPMENT (1808–1837)

In his *Commentaries*, as you may remember, Blackstone wrote that it was an actionable nuisance to set up a fair or a market "so near" to an already-existing one that it "does * * * a prejudice." Blackstone also indicated, however, that it was no nuisance simply to erect a new mill near an old one, or to set up "any trade, or a school, in neighborhood or rivalship with another * * *." (Pp. 299–300, supra.) Why do you suppose the English common law, as Blackstone described it, maintained what amounts to two differing models for enterprise—monopoly in the case of fairs or ferries and competition in the case of mills, schools, or trades? As you read the following materials on the early law of competition in America try to determine which of these models is favored, and why.

DONELLY v. VANDENBERGH

Supreme Court of New York, 1808.
3 Johns 27.

[An 1803 Act of the New York legislature authorized seven named persons to operate stage-wagons over a particular route between Albany and the New Jersey border, and provided that any person operating a competing stage-wagon on that route would be liable to pay a penalty of $500.00. The seven divided up responsibility for operation along the route, and one part of the service was allocated to the plaintiff, Mr. Donelly, one of the original seven. Apparently Donelly failed to keep up operation along the route, and two of the other six (Tremble and Vanderhoff) authorized the defendant, Mr. Vandenbergh, to run a stage-wagon along Donelly's part of the route. Vandenbergh was not one of the original seven beneficiaries of the New York legislation, but Vandenbergh had been running a stage-wagon along Tremble and Vanderhoff's sections of the route, because they had assigned their right to run stage-wagons along their sections to him. Donelly brought suit against Vandenbergh to recover the statutory penalty, $500.00. He won in the trial court, and what follows are excerpts from the opinions of the judges who reviewed the case on appeal.]

THOMPSON, J. * * * This penalty was given by the act to secure the grantees in the privilege thereby vested in them, against any encroachment by strangers, and not as a security against the acts of each other. As long as they remain tenants in common, they must be subject to the same rules, and like remedies, as other tenants in common. The statute vested a joint interest in them. There is no limitation as to the number of stages to be run, and if each of the grantees had undertaken to run a line the whole extent of the road, the penalty would not have been incurred.

It is said, however, that previous to the license under which the defendant acted, the proprietors had divided the road among themselves, by which division those who undertook to license the defendant had parted with their interest in that portion of the road for which they gave the license. I should much doubt whether the privilege or franchise granted by this act is, according to the spirit and intention of the act, susceptible of partition, so as to give exclusive and independent rights in distinct parcels of the road. Public accommodation and convenience were the objects the Legislature had in view, and a common interest to each proprietor in the whole extent of the road, would seem necessary, to prevent confusion with respect to the continuation of the line of stages. If the franchise may be so divided as to vest separate right, in distinct parts, what would be the consequence of a neglect by anyone to perform the duties enjoined by the act? Would his portion of the road only be forfeited, or the whole extent? I apprehend the latter; and this would subject the other individuals to a forfeiture, without a default. 　* 　* 　*

> [Judge Thompson concluded that, in any event, there was not sufficient evidence that the route had been divided, and thus Tremble and Vanderhoff were authorized to assign Donelly's part of the route to Vandenbergh, as any "tenant in common" might do.]

KENT, Ch. J., declared himself to be of the same opinion.

SPENCER, J. [dissenting], 　* 　* 　*

This act, like others, and like the contracts of individuals, must have a reasonable construction so as to effectuate, not defeat, the intention of parties. The inhibition to establish a stage on the route must be intended as an inhibition to establish one on any part of the route, otherwise the act grants nothing. From the nature of the thing, the right granted by the Legislature to Donelly and the six others is partible; and it appears that it was partitioned among the grantees. The act contemplated the interest conveyed as capable of being so assigned, and I know of no principle which forbids it. 　* 　* 　* If so, then the assignment to the defendant of a precise portion of the route can give him no more right than a total stranger, to erect stages on a different part.

　* 　* 　*

NOTES AND QUESTIONS

1. Judges Thompson and Spencer differed on the question of whether a legal distribution had taken place, but our concern is more with their differences over the partible nature of the grant of the route. Can you discern the public policies that Judge Thompson seeks to implement? Would you have expected the then Chief Justice Kent (later Chancellor Kent) to agree? Kent, you may remember, was the New York Chancellor who sought to maintain an equitable discretion in courts asked to grant specific performance of contracts involving unequal values, in Seymour v. Delancey, supra at 291. What might be Spencer's policy preferences?

2. Does the per curiam opinion in the next case seem more in accordance with Thompson's or Spencer's views?

ALMY v. HARRIS

Supreme Court of New York, 1809.
5 Johns 175.

Harris sued Almy in the court below, in an action on the case, for disturbing him in the enjoyment of a ferry across the Cayuga Lake, at the village of Cayuga, granted to Harris, by the Courts of Common Pleas, for the Counties of Cayuga and Seneca. A judgment for damages was given in favor of Harris * * *.

PER CURIAM. There is one error which we consider fatal, and for that we think there must be a judgment of reversal. The Act to Regulate Ferries within this State (20 sess. ch. 64, sec. 1) prohibits any person * * * from keeping or using a ferry, for transporting across any river, stream, or lake, any person or persons, or any goods or merchandise, for profit or hire, unless licensed in the manner directed by that [act] under a penalty of five dollars.

If Harris had possessed a right at the common law, to the exclusive enjoyment of this ferry, then the statute giving a remedy in the affirmative, without a negative expressed or implied, for a matter authorized by the common law, he might, notwithstanding the statute, have his remedy by action at the common law. * * * But Harris had no exclusive right at the common law, nor any right but what he derived from the statute. Consequently, he can have no right, since the statute, but those it gives; and his remedy, therefore, must be under the statute, and the penalty only can be recovered.

Judgment reversed.

NOTES AND QUESTIONS

The *Almy* court seems to be suggesting that there is no "common law" right "to the exclusive enjoyment" of a ferry. Do you agree? And yet, recall Blackstone's reason for permitting ferry owners to sue competitors in an action of nuisance: "For where there is a ferry by prescription, the owner is bound to keep it always in repair and readiness, for the ease of all the king's subjects; otherwise he may be grievously amerced: it would be therefore extremely hard, if a new ferry were suffered to share his profits, which does not also share his burden." Would this argument necessarily compel an action of nuisance in American common law?

LIVINGSTON v. VAN INGEN

New York Court for the Trial of Impeachments and The Correction of Errors, 1812.
9 Johns 507.

THE CHANCELLOR. An application was made by the complainants * * * for an injunction to restrain the defendants from using a steamboat * * * in the navigation of Hudson's River * * *.

* * * [O]n the part of the defendants, it was objected that the complainants' claim to an exclusive navigation of steamboats was:

1.   Contrary to the Constitution of the United States.

2.   That the statutes under which the complainants claim having prescribed a remedy for violations of the exclusive right, chancery must leave them to pursue it, without its interference.

The complainants applied for an injunction, on the ground of a clear exclusive right granted to them by an Act of the Legislature of this State, secured and extended by several successive acts.

* * *

When Justinian, the Emperor of the East, devised his code of civil law, he acknowledged the source of the right to the common enjoyment of air and water to be paramount to his authority, and bestowed, as a common boon, by the hand of nature, or, as we would express the same sentiment, by Nature's God * * *.

The civil code was, in its origin, merely municipal; but * * * from the amelioration which the experience, wisdom, and science of successive ages had infused, from the sound maxims of justice and jurisprudence it contained * * * as well as its intrinsic worth, it has been deservedly held in reverence by all the civilized world * * *.

In the Institutes, lib. 3., tit. 1., De aere, aqua profluente, &c., it is laid down, that those things which are given to mankind, in common, by the law of nature, are the air, running water, the sea, &c.

The general principles applied to the sea have as uniformly been extended to rivers in which the tide ebbs and flows, as arms of the sea. * * *

The common law doctrine is conformable to those principles; and is conceived in such terms, and to be traced to so early a day, as to warrant a presumption that it is derived from the civil law.

* * *

* * * In the case from 6 Mod., 73, Holt held that the king's grant could not bar a common right of fishing in a navigable river.

But Hale, in his treatise, shows a number of cases in which a grant of that kind was held available, and that a subject might possess a franchise in a port; as customs arising from its use, or even the soil; and so is now the acknowledged doctrine; but though all these rights might exist in subjects, the jus publicum of passage and repassage was not thereby destroyed, and no annoyance or obstacle was to be tolerated to interrupt or incommode the navigation.

* * *

Navigable rivers, in which the tide ebbs and flows, are within the same reason, and subject to the same distinctions. They admit of private interests in them; but they must all be subservient to the public interest, to promote and protect which, in England, the king has a general conservancy: but whenever he makes a grant of the soil or franchise of a port, or of a navigable river, the legal construction is, that it must be in subserviency to the public rights, and the common use of all the subjects of the realm, and even the foreigners.

None of the books I have consulted on the subject, and none of those cited in argument, have shown a case in which a grant of a navigable river or port vested in the grantor a right to the exclusive enjoyment of its use. * * * [I]t would seem that it was considered contrary to the *jus publicum* that such a grant should be made.

* * *

If by the common law of England, navigable rivers, in which the tide ebbs and flows, were deemed consecrated to the common use of all, as of common right, if no impediment or obstruction was to be admitted to impede the navigation; if a grant, which, by its terms, in all other cases, would have passed a fee, *usque ad coelum* was, by the established construction of law, to glance from the surface of a navigable river, or attach to its bottom, and give only an exclusive right to the grantee, to catch the swimming fish, while within the bounds of his grant; if the common law was the law of all the states in the Union, at the time the Constitution was adopted, as it certainly was in this, it may be a question of very serious import, how far a particular state may detract from privileges and immunities, at common law incapable of anihilation or restraint, common to all, at the time the Constitution was adopted, and regulated by principles which shielded them from every species of private appropriation.

The claim of the complainants is not founded on original invention. The mode of generating steam and its properties was known as early as the seventeenth century * * *. Projects for propelling boats by steam have been under the public eye for near twenty-five years * * *. It is a matter of public notoriety that they are now in a train of successful operation; and whenever the exertion of the ingenuity and perseverance, which perfected them to the point at which they have now arrived, can become the legitimate object of judicial cognizance, the incalculable utility and convenience which the public experience from the invention merit every consideration in favor of the inventors which a court can possibly yield to, consistent with the correct administration of justice; but here they were not brought into view, and could have no weight.

The laws of the State alluded to have granted the exclusive right of using vessels impelled by steam, in the navigable waters of this State, to the complainants. Suppose this grant valid; if the Legislature of this State could make an exclusive grant of that nature, could they not have extended it to vessels impelled by the winds or by oars, and to vessels of every other description capable of floating * * *. If carried to this extent, would it not be an abridgment of common rights? Could it comport with the constitutional provision that the citizens of all the states are to have like privileges and immunities with the citizens of the several states? With whom are they to be ranked? With the class who hold exclusive rights in the State, or with the excluded class of citizens? If the most favored citizens are not to give the test, what proportion of the collective number of the citizens of this State are to constitute it? * * * And should the grant in this case partake of the nature of a contract, could its consideration be legally carved out of the *jus publicum* of the citizens of the United States?

These are questions which, at the first blush, must appear of much moment; certainly too much so to admit of being determined without the fullest investigation. Without meaning to decide upon any, the mere propounding them must carry conviction to every mind that the subject is involved in much doubt and difficulty, and that, from its novelty, its importance and perplexity, it constitutes a case incapable of being considered so clear and plain as not to admit of doubt, which is the only ground upon which an injunction could have been then granted on the bill of the complainants.

* * *

[Accordingly, Chancellor Lansing refused to issue an injunction. We next read the decision by Chief Justice Kent rendered on appeal of Lansing's refusal.]

KENT, Ch. J. The great point in this cause is, whether the several acts of the Legislature which have been passed in favor of the appellants, are to be regarded as constitutional and binding.

* * *

In the first place, the presumption must be admitted to be extremely strong in favor of their validity. There is no very obvious constitutional objection, or it would not so repeatedly have escaped the notice of the several branches of the government, when these acts were under consideration. There are, in the whole, five different statutes, passed in the years 1798, 1803, 1807, 1808 and 1811, all relating to one subject, and all granting or confirming to the appellants, or one of them, the exclusive privilege of using steamboats upon the navigable waters of this State. The last Act was passed after the right of the appellants was drawn into question, and made known to the Legislature, and that Act was, therefore, equivalent to a declaratory opinion of high authority, that the former laws were valid and constitutional. The Act in the year 1798 was peculiarly calculated to awaken attention, as it was the first Act that was passed upon the subject, after the adoption of the federal Constitution, and it would naturally lead to a consideration of the power of the State to make such a grant. That Act was, therefore, a legislative exposition given to the powers of the state governments, and there were circumstances existing at the time, which gave that exposition singular weight and importance. It was a new and original grant to one of the appellants, encouraging him, by the pledge of an exclusive privilege for twenty years, to engage, according to the language of the preamble to the statute, in the "uncertainty and hazard of a very expensive experiment." The Legislature must have been clearly satisfied of their competency to make this pledge, or they acted with deception and injustice towards the individual on whose account it was made. There were members in that Legislature, as well as in all the other departments of the government, who had been deeply concerned in the study of the Constitution of the United States, and who were masters of all the critical discussions which had attended the interesting progress of its adoption.   *   *   *

*   *   *   Unless the court should be able to vindicate itself by the soundest and most demonstrable argument, a decree prostrating all these laws would weaken, as I should apprehend, the authority and sanction of law in general, and impair, in some degree, the public confidence, either in the intelligence or integrity of the government.

*   *   *

*   *   *   No one can entertain a doubt of a competent power existing in the Legislature, prior to the adoption of the federal Constitution. The capacity to grant separate and exclusive privileges appertains to every sovereign authority. It is a necessary attribute of every independent government. All our bank charters, turnpike, canal and bridge companies; ferries, markets, &c., are grants of exclusive privileges for beneficial public purposes.   *   *   *   The legislative power, in a single, independent government, extends to every proper object of power, and is limited only by its own constitutional provisions, or by the fundamental principles of all government, and the unalienable rights of mankind. In the present case, the grant to the appellants took away no vested right. It interfered with no man's property. It left every citizen to enjoy all the rights of navigation, and all the use of the waters of this State which he before enjoyed. There was, then, no injustice, no violation of first principles, in a grant to the appellants, for a limited time, of the exclusive benefit of their own hazardous and expensive experiments. The first impression upon every unprejudiced mind would be, that there was justice and policy

in the grant. Clearly then, it is valid, unless the power to make it be taken away by the Constitution of the United States.

* * * It does not follow, that because a given power is granted to Congress, the states cannot exercise a similar power. We ought to bear in mind certain great rules or principles of construction peculiar to the case of a confederated government, and by attending to them in the examination of the subject, all our seeming difficulties will vanish.

When the people create a single, entire government, they grant at once all the rights of sovereignty. * * * But when a federal government is erected with only a portion of the sovereign power, the rule of construction is directly the reverse, and every power is reserved to the member that is not, either in express terms, or by necessary implication, taken away from them, and vested exclusively in the federal head. * * *

This principle might be illustrated by other instances of grants of power to Congress with a prohibition to the states from exercising the like powers; but it becomes unnecessary to enlarge upon so plain a proposition, as it is removed beyond all doubt by the tenth article of the amendments to the Constitution. That article declares that "the powers not delegated to the United States by the Constitution, nor prohibited by it to the states, are reserved to the states respectively, or to the people." * * *

Our safe rule of construction and of action is this, that if any given power was originally vested in this State, if it has not been exclusively ceded to Congress, or if the exercise of it has not been prohibited to the states, we may then go on in the exercise of the power until it becomes practically in collision with the actual exercise of some congressional power. * * *

* * *

I now proceed to apply these general rules to those parts of the Constitution which are supposed to have an influence on the present question.

The provision that the citizens of each state shall be entitled to all privileges and immunities of citizens in the several states, has nothing to do with this case. It means only that citizens of other states shall have equal rights with our own citizens, and not that they shall have different or greater rights. * * * The two paragraphs of the Constitution by which it is contended that the original power in the state governments to make the grant has been withdrawn, and vested exclusively in the Union, are, 1. The power to regulate commerce with foreign nations, and among the several states; and, 2. The power to secure to authors and inventors the exclusive right to their writings and discoveries.

1. As to the power to regulate commerce. This power is not, in express terms, exclusive, and the only prohibition upon the states

is, that they shall not enter into any treaty or compact with each other, or with a foreign power, nor lay any duty on tonnage, or on imports or exports, except what may be necessary for executing their inspection laws. Upon the principles above laid down, the states are under no other constitutional restriction, and are, consequently, left in possession of a vast field of commercial regulation * * *. The congressional power relates to external not to internal commerce, and it is confined to the regulation of that commerce. * * * The states are under no other restrictions than those expressly specified in the Constitution, and such regulations as the national government may, by treaty, and by laws, from time to time, prescribe. * * * This does away [with] all color for the suggestion that the steamboat grant is illegal and void under this clause in the Constitution. It comes not within any prohibition upon the states, and it interferes with no existing regulation. * * * [W]hen there is no existing regulation which interferes with the grant, nor any pretense of a constitutional interdict, it would be most extraordinary for us to adjudge it void, on the mere contingency of a collision with some future exercise of congressional power. Such a doctrine is a monstrous heresy. It would go, in a great degree, to annihilate the legislative power of the states. * * *

* * * Hudson River is the property of the people of this State, and the Legislature have the same jurisdiction over it that they have over the land, or over any of our public highways, or over the waters of any of our rivers or lakes. They may, in their sound discretion, regulate and control, enlarge or abridge the use of its waters, and they are in the habitual exercise of that sovereign right. If the Constitution had given to Congress exclusive jurisdiction over our navigable waters, then the argument of the respondents would have applied; but the people never did, nor ever intended, to grant such a power; and Congress has concurrent jurisdiction over the navigable waters no further than may be incidental and requisite to the due regulation of commerce between the states and with foreign nations.

What has been the uniform, practical construction of this power? Let us examine the code of our statute laws. Our turnpike roads, our toll-bridges, the exclusive grant to run stage wagons, our laws relating to paupers from other states, our Sunday laws, our rights of ferriage over navigable rivers and lakes, our auction licenses, our licenses to retail spirituous liquors, the laws to restrain hawkers and peddlers; what are all these provisions but regulations of internal commerce, affecting as well the intercourse between the citizens of this and other states, as between our own citizens? * * *

Are we prepared to say, in the face of all these regulations, which form such a mass of evidence of the uniform construction of our powers, that a special privilege for the exclusive navigation by a steamboat upon our waters is void, because it may, by possibility, and in the course of events, interfere with the power granted to Congress to regulate commerce? Nothing, in my opinion, would be more preposterous and extravagant.   *   *   *

*   *   *

[Kent then turns to the Constitutional provision regarding exclusive rights of inventors. He notes that the federal Constitution is concerned with providing federal control over rights of exclusivity for *novel* forms of technology. He then turns to English practice.]

The creation of monopolies was anciently claimed and exercised as a branch of the royal prerogative. Lord Coke, 3 Inst., 181, defines a monopoly to be "an institution or allowance by the king's grant, for the sole using of anything;" and he considers such royal grants to have been against the ancient and fundamental laws of the realm. Parliament at last interposed to check the abuse of these grants, which had been issued, under Elizabeth, with inconsiderate profusion; and by the statute of 21 Jac. I., ch. 3, commonly called the statute of monopolies, there were due limitations placed upon the exercise of this branch of the prerogative. That statute, by a general sweeping clause, demolished all the existing monopolies that were not specially excepted; and some of those exceptions are worthy of our particular notice. In the first place, all grants of privileges by act of Parliament were saved; for no one ever doubted (unless it be since the origin of this controversy) of the power of the Legislature to create an exclusive privilege. The statute also allowed grants to be made for a limited time, by the authority of the crown, for the sole working or making of any new manufacture not before used in the realm. Upon this clause it has been held by such distinguished judges as Holt and Pollexfen (2 Salk. 447), that if the invention be new in England, a patent may be granted, though the thing was practiced beyond sea before; for the statute, as they observed, intended to encourage new devices useful to the kingdom, and whether learned by travel or by study, it is the same thing.   *   *   *

*   *   *   And can we for a moment suppose that such a power does not exist in the several states? We have seen that it does not belong to Congress, and if it does not reside in the states, it resides nowhere, and is wholly extinguished. This would be leaving the states in a condition of singular and contemptible imbecility. The power is important in itself, and may be most beneficially exercised for the encouragement of the arts; and if well and judiciously exerted, it may ameliorate the condition of society, by enriching and adorning the country with useful and elegant improvements.   *   *   *   And permit me here to add, that I think the power has been wisely applied, in the instance before us, to the creation of the privilege now in controversy. Under its auspices the experiment of navigating boats by steam has been made, and crowned with triumphant success. Every lover of the arts, every patron of useful improvement, every friend to his country's honor, has beheld this success with pleasure and admiration. From this single source the improvement is progressively ex-

tending to all the navigable waters of the United States, and it promises to become a great public blessing, by giving astonishing facility, dispatch and safety, not only to traveling, but to the internal commerce of this country. It is difficult to consider even the known results of the undertaking, without feeling a sentiment of good will and gratitude towards the individuals by whom they have been procured, and who have carried on their experiment with patient industry, at great expense, under repeated disappointments, and while constantly exposed to be held up, as dreaming projectors, to the whips and scorns of time. So far from charging the authors of the grant with being rash and inconsiderate, or from wishing to curtail the appellants of their liberal recompense, I think the prize has been dearly earned and fairly won, and that the statutes bear the stamp of an enlightened and munificent spirit.

If the legal right be in favor of the appellants, the remedy prayed for by their bill is a matter of course. * * *

Injunctions are always granted to secure the enjoyment of statute privileges of which the party is in the actual possession * * *. I believe there is no case to the contrary * * *. It appears, by the facts stated in the bill * * * that the appellants had been, for three years, in the actual and exclusive enjoyment of their statute privilege, when the respondents interfered to disturb that right and that enjoyment.

* * * The Act which the Legislature passed at the last session, making it expressly the duty of the Chancellor to grant an injunction as to all other boats except the two then built, proves very clearly the sense of the Legislature that this was a fit and proper remedy in the case. Those two boats were excepted out of the law, merely because it was improper to interfere with a pending suit, and the statute did not impair the pre-existing remedy by injunction; it only made it more clear and peremptory thereafter; and there is no reason why the injunction should issue against one set of boats, and not against another.

* * *

I am sensible that the case is calculated to excite sympathy. I feel it with others, and I sincerely wish that the respondents had brought the laws to a test, at less risk and expense; for every one who had eyes to read, or ears to hear the contents of our statute book, must have been astonished at the boldness and rashness of the experiment. But in proportion to the respectability and strength of the combination, should be the vigor of our purpose to maintain the law. If we were to suffer the plighted faith of this State to be broken, upon a mere pretext, we should become a reproach and a by-word throughout the Union. It was a saying of Euripides, and often repeated by Caesar, that if right was ever to be violated, it was for the sake of power. We follow a purer and nobler system of morals, and one which teaches us that right is never to be violated. This principle ought to be kept steadfast in every man's breast; and above all, it ought to find an asylum in the sanctuary of justice.

I am, accordingly, of opinion that the order of the Court of Chancery be reversed, and that an injunction be awarded.

* * *

Judgment of reversal.

NOTES AND QUESTIONS

1.   Chancellor Lansing was a firm adherent of Jeffersonian principles. Do you see this reflected in his opinion denying the injunction? Robert Fulton and Robert Livingston, to whom the New York legislature had granted a steamboat monopoly on the Hudson were also supposed to be Jeffersonians. Do you see anything inconsistent with being a "good Jeffersonian" and accepting an exclusive franchise? Can you understand why Fulton and Livingston sought to argue that what they had was not a "monopoly," but rather a "legislative franchise." What's the difference? Jefferson himself, although he supervised the United States Patent Office when he was secretary of state, and although he was an inventor of considerable creativity, refused to take out any patents. Floyd L. Vaughan, The United States Patent System 6, 18 (1956). Why might Jefferson adopt this posture?

2.   Consider Lansing's opinion. Can you discern Lansing's attitude toward steam power and commercial progress generally? Lansing seems to feel that the state must not be permitted to parcel out exclusive franchises for operation on navigable waterways. Why not? Do you detect any similarities between Lansing's mode of analysis and the opinions in *Almy* and *Donelly*? Kent went along with the majority in the *Donelly* case, where the court apparently refused to allow private partition of a state franchise, and in the *Almy* case, where the court held there was no common-law right to provide an action for nuisance to stop a competing ferry. Is Kent's position in *Livingston* consistent with these opinions?

3.   Does Kent actually come to grips with the problems Chancellor Lansing has with the issuance of the injunction? Kent, by the way, was not a Jeffersonian, but note the line he attempts to draw between grants of monopolies by the King and grants of privileges by Parliament. Does he persuade you that though Royal monopolies were despicable, legislative grants were not? Three years later, when Kent had become Chancellor of New York, he issued an injunction sought by a turnpike company in order to prevent competition from a recently-built public (free) road which threatened severely to diminish the tolls collectable by the turnpike company. Kent called the right to collect tolls an "exclusive right," and cited as precedent Livingston v. Van Ingen. Croton Turnpike Road Co. v. Ryder, 1 Johns.Ch. 611 (N.Y.1815). Similarly, in Newburgh Turnpike Co. v. Miller, 5 Johns.Ch. 101 (N.Y.1821), Chancellor Kent held that where the legislature had granted a franchise to the plaintiff to take a toll from persons passing over its bridge, the construction of a nearby bridge which created "a competition injurious to such franchise" was an actionable nuisance, calling for a perpetual injunction. Do these latter holdings go beyond *Livingston*?

4.   Kent's opinion in *Livingston* was, after twelve years, reversed by the United State Supreme Court, in the great Constitutional case of Gib-

bons v. Ogden, 22 U.S. (9 Wheat.) 1, 6 L.Ed. 23 (1824). In that case, which turned on the construction of the interstate commerce clause, Chief Justice Marshall concluded that the regulation of steam traffic on the Hudson was exclusively in the jurisdiction of Congress. This opinion thus did not squarely address the more interesting question raised in the Lansing-Kent debate, the appropriateness of monopolies or franchises generally. This question was one of the central issues in the next case we consider.

PROPRIETORS OF CHARLES RIVER BRIDGE v. PROPRIETORS OF WARREN BRIDGE

Supreme Court of the United States, 1837.
36 U.S. (11 Pet.) 420, 9 L.Ed. 773.

Mr. Chief Justice TANEY delivered the opinion of the court.

* * *

It appears, from the record, that in the year 1650, the legislature of Massachusetts granted to the president of Harvard College "the liberty and power," to dispose of the ferry from Charlestown to Boston, by lease or otherwise, in the behalf, and for the behoof of the college: that, under that grant, the college continued to hold and keep the ferry by its lessees or agents, and to receive the profits of it until 1785. In the last mentioned year, a petition was presented to the legislature, by Thomas Russell and others, stating the inconvenience of the transportation by ferries, over Charles river, and the public advantages that would result from a bridge; and praying to be incorporated for the purpose of erecting a bridge in the place where the ferry between Boston and Charlestown was then kept. Pursuant to this petition, the legislature, on the 9th of March, 1785, passed an act incorporating a company, by the name of "The Proprietors of the Charles River Bridge," for the purposes mentioned in the petition. Under this charter the company were empowered to erect a bridge, in "the place where the ferry was then kept;" certain tolls were granted, and the charter was limited to forty years, from the first opening of the bridge for passengers; and from the time the toll commenced, until the expiration of this term, the company were to pay, two hundred pounds, annually to Harvard College; and, at the expiration of the forty years, the bridge was to be the property of the commonwealth; "saving (as the law expresses it) to the said college or university, a reasonable annual compensation, for the annual income of the ferry, which they might have received had not the said bridge been erected."

The bridge was accordingly built, and was opened for passengers on the 17th of June, 1786. In 1792, the charter was extended to seventy years, from the opening of the bridge; and at the expiration of that time it was to belong to the commonwealth. * * *

In 1828, the legislature of Massachusetts incorporated a company by the name of "The Proprietors of the Warren Bridge," for the purpose of erecting another bridge over Charles river. This bridge is only sixteen rods, at its commencement, on the Charlestown side, from the commencement of the bridge of the plaintiffs; and they are about fifty rods apart at their termination on the Boston side. * * *

The Warren bridge, by the terms of its charter, was to be surrendered to the state, as soon as the expenses of the proprietors in building and supporting it should be reimbursed; but this period was not, in any event, to exceed six years from the time the company commenced receiving toll.

* * * The bill, among other things, charged as a ground for relief, that the act for the erection of the Warren bridge impaired the obligation of the contract between the commonwealth and the proprietors of the Charles river bridge; and was therefore repugnant to the constitution of the United States. * * *

In the argument here, it was admitted, that since the filing of the supplemental bill, a sufficient amount of toll had been received by the proprietors of the Warren bridge to reimburse all their expenses, and that the bridge is now the property of the state, and has been made a free bridge and that the value of the franchise granted to the proprietors of the Charles river bridge, has by this means been entirely destroyed.

* * *

The plaintiffs in error insist * * * [t]hat the acts of the legislature of Massachusetts of 1785, and 1792, by their true construction, necessarily implied that the legislature would not authorize another bridge, and especially a free one, by the side of this, and placed in the same line of travel, whereby the franchise granted to the "proprietors of the Charles river bridge" should be rendered of no value * * *.

* * *

* * * It does not, by any means, follow, that because the legislative power in Massachusetts, in 1650, may have granted to a justly favoured seminary of learning, the exclusive right of ferry between Boston and Charlestown, they would, in 1785, give the same extensive privilege to another corporation, who were about to erect a bridge in the same place. * * * Increased population longer experienced in legislation, the different character of the corporations which owned the ferry from that which owned the bridge, might well have induced a change in the policy of the state in this respect; and as the franchise of the ferry, and that of the bridge, are different in their nature, and were each established by separate grants, which have no words to connect the privileges of the one with the privileges of the other; there is no rule of legal interpretation, which would authorize the court to associate these grants together * * *. The charter to the bridge

is a written instrument which must speak for itself, and be interpreted by its own terms.

This brings us to the act of the legislature of Massachusetts, of 1785, by which the plaintiffs were incorporated * * *.

* * * It is the grant of certain franchises by the public to a private corporation, and in a matter where the public interest is concerned.   The rule of construction in such cases is well settled, both in England, and by the decisions of our own tribunals.   In 2 Barn. & Adol. 793, in the case of the Proprietors of the Stourbridge Canal against Wheely and others, the court say, "the canal having been made under an act of parliament, the rights of the plaintiffs are derived entirely from that act.   This, like many other cases, is a bargain between a company of adventurers and the public, the terms of which are expressed in the statute; and the rule of construction in all such cases, is now fully established to be this; that any ambiguity in the terms of the contract, must operate against the adventurers, and in favour of the public, and the plaintiffs can claim nothing that is not clearly given them by the act." * * *

Borrowing, as we have done, our system of jurisprudence from the English law; and having adopted, in every other case, civil and criminal, its rules for the construction of statutes; is there any thing in our local situation, or in the nature of our political institutions, which should lead us to depart from the principle where corporations are concerned? * * * We think not; and it would present a singular spectacle, if, while the courts in England are restraining, within the strictest limits, the spirit of monopoly, and exclusive privileges in nature of monopolies, and confining corporations to the privileges plainly given to them in their charter; the courts of this country should be found enlarging these privileges by implication; and construing a statute more unfavourably to the public, and to the rights of the community, than would be done in a like case in an English court of justice.

* * *

* * * [T]he case most analogous to this, and in which the question came more directly before the court, is the case of the Providence Bank v. Billings & Pittmann, 4 Pet. 514; and which was decided in 1830.   In that case, it appeared that the legislature of Rhode Island had chartered the bank; in the usual form of such acts of incorporation.   The charter contained no stipulation on the part of the state, that it would not impose a tax on the bank, nor any reservation of the right to do so.   It was silent on this point.   Afterwards, a law was passed, imposing a tax on all banks in the state; and the right to impose this tax was resisted by the Providence Bank, upon the ground, that if the state could impose a tax, it might tax so heavily as to render the franchise of no value, and destroy the institution; that the charter was a contract, and that a power which may in effect destroy

the charter is inconsistent with it, and is impliedly renounced by granting it. But the court said that the taxing power was of vital importance, and essential to the existence of government; and that the relinquishment of such a power is never to be assumed. And in delivering the opinion of the court, the late chief justice states the principle, in the following clear and emphatic language. Speaking of the taxing power, he says, "as the whole community is interested in retaining it undiminished, that community has a right to insist that its abandonment ought not to be presumed, in a case in which the deliberate purpose of the state to abandon it does not appear." The case now before the court is, in principle, precisely the same. It is a charter from a state. The act of incorporation is silent in relation to the contested power. The argument in favour of the proprietors of the Charles river bridge, is the same, almost in words, with that used by the Providence Bank; that is, that the power claimed by the state, if it exists, may be so used as to destroy the value of the franchise they have granted to the corporation. The argument must receive the same answer; and the fact that the power has been already exercised so as to destroy the value of the franchise, cannot in any degree affect the principle. The existence of the power does not, and cannot depend upon the circumstance of its having been exercised or not.

It may, perhaps, be said, that in the case of the Providence Bank, this court were speaking of the taxing power; which is of vital importance to the very existence of every government. But the object and end of all government is to promote the happiness and prosperity of the community by which it is established; and it can never be assumed, that the government intended to diminish its power of accomplishing the end for which it was created. And in a country like ours, free, active, and enterprising, continually advancing in numbers and wealth; new channels of communication are daily found necessary, both for travel and trade; and are essential to the comfort, convenience, and prosperity of the people. A state ought never to be presumed to surrender this power, because, like the taxing power, the whole community have an interest in preserving it undiminished. And when a corporation alleges, that a state has surrendered for seventy years, its power of improvement and public accommodation, in a great and important line of travel, along which a vast number of its citizens must daily pass; the community have a right to insist, in the language of this court above quoted, "that its abandonment ought not to be presumed, in a case, in which the deliberate purpose of the state to abandon it does not appear." * * *

Adopting the rule of construction above stated as the settled one, we proceed to apply it to the charter of 1785, to the proprietors of the Charles river bridge. This act of incorporation is in the usual form, and the privileges such as are commonly given to corporations of that kind. It confers on them the ordinary faculties of a corporation, for the purpose of building the bridge; and establishes certain rates of toll, which the company are authorized to take. This is the whole grant. There is no exclusive privilege given to them over the waters of Charles river, above or below their bridge. No right to erect another bridge themselves, nor to prevent other persons from erecting one. No engagement from the state, that another shall not be erected; and no undertaking not to sanction competition, nor to make improvements that may diminish the amount of its income. Upon all these subjects the charter is silent; and nothing is said in it about a line of travel, so much insisted on in the argument, in which they are to have exclusive privileges. * * *

* * *

* * * Can such an agreement be implied? The rule of construction before stated is an answer to the question. In charters of this description, no rights are taken from the public or given to the corporation, beyond those which the words of the charter, by their natural and proper construction, purport to convey. * * *

But the case before the court is even still stronger against any such implied contract, as the plaintiffs in error contend for. * * *

The act of 1792, which extends the charter of this bridge, incorporates another company to build a bridge over Charles river; furnishing another communication with Boston, and distant only between one and two miles from the old bridge.

The first six sections of this act incorporate the proprietors of the West Boston bridge * * *. In the seventh section there is the following recital: "And whereas the erection of Charles river bridge was a work of hazard and public utility, and another bridge in the place of West Boston bridge may diminish the emoluments of Charles river bridge; therefore, for the encouragement of enterprise," they proceed to extend the charter of the Charles river bridge, and to continue it for the term of seventy years from the day the bridge was completed * * *. It appears, then, that by the same act that extended this charter, the legislature established another bridge, which they knew would lessen its profits * * *; thereby showing, that the state did not suppose that, by the terms it had used in the first law, it had deprived itself of the power of making such public improvements as might impair the profits of the Charles river bridge * * *.

* * * The extension [of the term to seventy years] was given because the company had undertaken and executed a work of doubtful success; and the improvements which the legislature then contemplated, might diminish the emoluments they had expected to receive from it. It results from this statement, that the legislature in the very law extending the charter, asserts its rights to authorize improvements over Charles river which would take off a portion of the travel from this bridge and diminish its profits; and the bridge company accept the renewal thus given, and thus carefully connected with this assertion of the right on the part of the state. * * *

Indeed, the practice and usage of almost every state in the Union, old enough to have commenced the work of internal improvement, is opposed to the doctrine contended for on the part of the plaintiffs in error. Turnpike roads have been made in succession, on the same line of travel; the later ones interfering materially with the profits of the first. These corporations have, in some instances, been utterly ruined by the introduction of newer and better modes of transportation, and travelling. In some cases, rail roads have rendered the turnpike roads on the same line of travel so entirely useless, that the franchise of the turnpike corporation is not worth preserving.

Yet in none of these cases have the corporation supposed that their privileges were invaded, or any contract violated on the part of the state. * * * The absence of any such controversy, when there must have been so many occasions to give rise to it, proves that neither states, nor individuals, nor corporations, ever imagined that such a contract could be implied from such charters. * * *

And what would be the fruits of this doctrine of implied contracts on the part of the states, and of property in a line of travel by a corporation, if it should now be sanctioned by this court? To what results would it lead us? If it is to be found in the charter to this bridge, the same process of reasoning must discover it, in the various acts which have been passed, within the last forty years, for turnpike companies. * * * If this court should establish the principles now contended for, what is to become of the numerous rail roads established on the same line of travel with turnpike companies; and which have rendered the franchises of the turnpike corporations of no value? Let it once be understood that such charters carry with them these implied contracts, and give this unknown and undefined property in a line of travelling; and you will soon find the old turnpike corporations awakening from their sleep, and calling upon this court to put down the improvements which have taken their place. The millions of property which have been invested in rail roads and canals, upon lines of travel which had been before occupied by turnpike corporations, will be put in jeopardy. We shall be thrown back to the improvements of the last century, and obliged to stand still, until the claims of the old turnpike corporations shall be satisfied; and they shall consent to permit these states to avail themselves of the lights of modern science, and to partake of the benefit of those improvements which are now adding to the wealth and prosperity, and the convenience and comfort, of every other part of the civilized world. * * *

*   *   *

The judgment of the supreme judicial court of the commonwealth of Massachusetts, dismissing the plaintiffs' bill, must, therefore, be affirmed, with costs.

Mr. Justice STORY, dissenting.

*   *   *

* * * [W]ith a view to induce the Court to withdraw from all the common rules of reasonable and liberal interpretation in favour of grants, we have been told at the argument, that this very charter is a restriction upon the legislative power; that it is in derogation of the rights and interests of the state, and the people; that it tends to promote monopolies, and exclusive privileges; and that it will interpose an insuperable barrier to the progress of improvement. Now, upon every one of these propositions, which are assumed, and not proved, I entertain a directly opposite opinion; and, if I did not, I am not prepared to admit the conclusion for which they are adduced. If the legislature has made a grant, which involves any or all of these consequences, it is not for courts of justice to overturn the plain sense of the grant, because it has been, improvidently or injuriously made.

But I deny the very ground work of the argument. This charter is not * * * any restriction upon the legislative power; unless it be true, that because the legislature cannot grant again, what it has already granted, the legislative power is restricted. If so, then every grant of the public land is a restriction upon that power; a doctrine, that has never yet been established, nor (as far as I know) ever contended for. Every grant of a franchise is, so far as that grant extends, necessarily exclusive; and cannot be resumed, or interfered with. * *

Then again, how is it established that this is a grant in derogation of the rights and interests of the people? No individual citizen has any right to build a bridge over navigable waters; and consequently he is deprived of no right, when a grant is made to any other persons for that purpose. * * * But that is not the sense in which the argument is pressed; for, by derogation, is here meant an injurious or mischievous detraction from the sovereign rights of the state. * * * If it had been said that the grant of this bridge was in derogation of the common right of navigating the Charles river, by reason of its obstructing, pro tanto, a free and open passage, the ground would have been intelligible. * * * But, if at the same time, equivalent public rights of a different nature, but of greater public accommodation and use, had been obtained; it could hardly have been said, in a correct sense, that there was any derogation from the rights of the people, or the rights of the state. * * *

* * * The erection of a bridge may be of the highest utility to the people. It may essentially promote the public convenience, and aid the public interests, and protect the public property. And if no persons can be found willing to undertake such a work, unless they receive in return the exclusive privilege of erecting it, and taking toll; surely it cannot be said, as of course, that such a grant, under such circumstances, is, per se, against the interest of the people. * * *

* * *

Again, it is argued that the present grant is a grant of a monopoly, and of exclusive privileges; and therefore to be construed by the most narrow mode of interpretation. * * *

There is great virtue in particular phrases; and when it is once suggested, that a grant is of the nature or tendency of a monopoly, the mind almost instantaneously prepares itself to reject every construction which does not pare it down to the narrowest limits. It is an honest prejudice, which grew up in former times from the gross abuses of the royal prerogatives; to which, in America, there are no analogous authorities. But, what is a monopoly, as understood in law? It is an exclusive right granted to a few, of something which was before of common right. Thus, a privilege granted by the king for the sole buying, selling, making, working, or using a thing, whereby the subject, in general, is restrained from the liberty of manufacturing or trading, which before he had, is a monopoly * * *.

No sound lawyer will, I presume, assert that the grant of a right to erect a bridge over a navigable stream, is a grant of a common right. * * * It was neither a monopoly; nor, in a legal sense, had it any tendency to a monopoly. It took from no citizen what he possessed before; and had no tendency to take it from him. It took, indeed, from the legislature the power of granting the same identical privilege or franchise to any other persons. But this made it no more a monopoly, than the grant of the public stock or funds of a state for a valuable consideration. * * *

But it has been argued, and the argument has been pressed in every form which ingenuity could suggest, that if grants of this nature are to be construed liberally, as conferring any exclusive rights on the grantees, it will interpose an effectual barrier against all general improvements of the country. * * * This is a subject upon which different minds may well arrive at different conclusions, both as to policy and principle. * * * For my own part, I can conceive of no surer plan to arrest all public improvements, founded on private capital and enterprise, than to make the outlay of that capital uncertain, and questionable both as to security, and as to productiveness. No man will hazard his capital in any enterprise, in which, if there be a loss, it must be borne exclusively by himself; and if there be success, he has not the slightest security of enjoying the rewards of that success for a single moment. If the government means to invite its citizens to enlarge the public comforts and conveniences, to establish bridges, or turnpikes, or canals, or railroads, there must be some pledge, that the property will be safe; that the enjoyment will be co-extensive with the grant: and that success will not be the signal of a general combination to overthrow its rights, and to take away its profits. * * * And yet, we are told, that all such exclusive grants are to the detriment of the public.

But if there were any foundation for the argument itself in a general view, it would totally fail in its application to the present case. Here, the grant, however exclusive, is but for a short and limited period, more than two-thirds of which have already elapsed; and, when it is gone, the whole property and franchise are to revert to the state.

The legislature exercised a wholesome foresight on the subject; and within a reasonable period it will have an unrestricted authority to do whatever it may choose, in the appropriation of the bridge and its tolls. There is not, then, under any fair aspect of the case, the slightest reason to presume that public improvements either can, or will, be injuriously retarded by a liberal construction of the present grant.

* * * In order to entertain a just view of this subject, we must go back to that period of general bankruptcy, and distress and difficulty. The constitution of the United States was not only not then in existence, but it was not then even dreamed of. The union of the states was crumbling into ruins, under the old confederation. Agriculture, manufactures and commerce, were at their lowest ebb. There was infinite danger to all the states from local interests and jealousies, and from the apparent impossibility of a much longer adherence to that shadow of a government, the continental congress. * * *

This is not all. It is well known, historically, that this was the very first bridge ever constructed in New England, over navigable tide waters so near the sea. The rigours of our climate, the dangers from sudden thaws and freezing, and the obstructions from ice in a rapid current, were deemed by many persons to be insuperable obstacles to the success of such a project. It was believed, that the bridge would scarcely stand a single severe winter. * * * If Charles river bridge had been carried away during the first or second season after its erection, it is far from being certain, that up to this moment another bridge, upon such an arm of the sea, would ever have been erected in Massachusetts. I state these things which are of public notoriety, to repeal the notion that the legislature was surprised into an incautious grant, or that the reward was more than adequate to the perils. * *

But I do not insist upon any extraordinary liberality in interpreting this charter. All I contend for is, that it shall receive a fair and reasonable interpretation; so as to carry into effect the legislative intention, and secure to the grantees a just security for their privileges. * * *

* * *

* * * Taking this to be a grant of a right to build a bridge over Charles river, in the place where the old ferry between Charlestown and Boston was then kept, (as is contended for by the defendants;) still it has, as all such grants must have, a fixed locality, and the same question meets us: is the grant confined to the mere right to erect a bridge on the proper spot, and to take toll of the passengers, who may pass over it, without any exclusive franchise on each side to an extent, which shall shut out any injurious competition? * * * The defendants contend, that the exclusive right of the plaintiffs extends no further than the planks and timbers of the bridge; and that the legislature is at full liberty to grant any new bridge, however near * * *.

The argument of the defendants is, that the plaintiffs are to take nothing by implication. Either (say they) the exclusive grant extends only to the local limits of the bridge; or it extends the whole length of the river, or at least up to old Cambridge bridge. The latter construction would be absurd and monstrous; and therefore the former must be the true one. Now, I utterly deny the alternative involved in the dilemma. The right to build a bridge over a river, and to take toll, may well include an exclusive franchise beyond the local limits of the bridge; and yet not extend through the whole course of the river, or even to any considerable distance on the river. There is no difficulty in common sense, or in law, in maintaining such a doctrine. But then, it is asked, what limits can be assigned to such a franchise? The answer is obvious; the grant carries with it an exclusive franchise to a reasonable distance on the river; so that the ordinary travel to the bridge shall not be diverted by any new bridge to the injury or ruin of the franchise. A new bridge, which would be a nuisance to the old bridge, would be within the reach of its exclusive right. The question would not be so much as to the fact of distance, as it would be as to the fact of nuisance. There is nothing new in such expositions of incorporeal rights; and nothing new in thus administering, upon this foundation, remedies in regard thereto. The doctrine is coeval with the common law itself. Suppose an action is brought for shutting up the ancient lights belonging to a messuage; or for diverting a water-course; or for flowing back a stream; or for erecting a nuisance near a dwelling house; the question in cases is not a question of mere distance; of mere feet and inches, but of injury; permanent, real, and substantial injury, to be decided upon all the circumstances of the case. * * *

Now, I put it to the common sense of every man, whether if at the moment of granting the charter the legislature had said to the proprietors; you shall build the bridge; you shall bear the burthens; you shall be bound by the charges; and your sole reimbursement shall be from the tolls of forty years: and yet we will not even guaranty you any certainty of receiving any tolls. On the contrary we reserve to ourselves the full power and authority to erect other bridges, toll, or free bridges, according to our own free will and pleasure, contiguous to yours, and having the same termini with yours; and if you are successful we may thus supplant you, divide, destroy your profits, and annihilate your tolls, without annihilating your burthens: if, I say, such had been the language of the legislature, is there a man living of ordinary discretion or prudence, who would have accepted such a charter upon such terms? * * *

* * *

But it is said that there is no prohibitory covenant in the charter, and no implications are to be made of any such prohibition. The proprietors are to stand upon the letter of their contract * * *. And yet it is conceded, that the legislature cannot revoke or resume this grant. Why not, I pray to know? There is no negative covenant in the charter; there is no express prohibition to be found there. The reason is plain. The prohibition arises by natural, if not by necessary implication. It would be against the first principles of justice to presume that the legislature reserved a right to destroy its own grant. * * * If it cannot take away, or resume the franchise itself, can it take away its whole substance and value? If the law will create an implication that the legislature shall not resume its own grant, is it not equally as natural and as necessary an implication, that the legislature shall not do any act directly to prejudice its own grant, or to destroy its value? * * *

But it is said, if this is the law, what then is to become of turnpikes and canals? Is the legislature precluded from authorizing new turnpikes or new canals, simply because they cross the path of the old ones, and incidentally diminish their receipt of tolls? The answer is plain. Every turnpike has its local limits and local termini; its points of beginning and of end. No one ever imagined that the legislature might grant a new turnpike, with exactly the same location and termini. That would be to rescind its first grant. * * * And the opinion of Mr. Chancellor Kent, and all the old authorities on the subject of ferries, support me in the doctrine.

* * *

But then again, it is said, that all this rests upon implication, and not upon the words of the charter. * * * What objection can there be to implications, if they arise from the very nature and objects of the grant? If it be indispensable to the full enjoyment of the right to take toll, that it should be exclusive within certain limits, is it not just and reasonable, that it should be so construed? * * *

* * *

The truth is, that the whole argument of the defendants turns upon an implied reservation of power in the legislature to defeat and destroy its own grant. The grant, construed upon its own terms, upon the plain principles of construction of the common law, by which alone it ought to be judged, is an exclusive grant. It is the grant of a franchise, *publici juris*, with a right of tolls; and in all such cases the common law asserts the grant to be exclusive, so as to prevent injurious competition. The argument seeks to exclude the common law from touching the grant, by implying an exception in favour of the legislative authority to make any new grant. * * *

To the answer already given to the objection, that, unless such a reservation of power exists, there will be a stop put to the progress of all public improvements; I wish, in this connexion, to add, that never can any such consequence follow upon the opposite doctrine. If the public exigencies and interests require that the franchise of Charles river bridge should be taken away, or impaired; it may be lawfully done upon making due compensation to the proprietors. * * *

* * *

* * * I maintain, that under the principles of the common law, there exists no more right in the legislature of Massachusetts, to erect the Warren bridge, to the ruin of the franchise of the Charles river bridge, than exists to transfer the latter to the former, or to authorize the former to demolish the latter. If the legislature does not mean in its grant to give any exclusive rights, let it say so, expressly; directly; and in terms admitting of no misconstruction. The grantees will then take at their peril, and must abide the results of their overweening confidence, indiscretion, and zeal.

My judgment is formed upon the terms of the grant, its nature and objects, its design and duties; and, in its interpretation, I seek for no new principles, but I apply such as are as old as the very rudiments of the common law.

* * *

Before I close, it is proper to notice, and I shall do it briefly, another argument strongly pressed at the bar against the plaintiffs; and that is, that the extension of the term of the franchise of the plaintiffs for thirty years, by the act of 1792, (erecting the West Boston bridge, between Boston and Cambridge,) and the acceptance thereof by the plaintiffs, amounted to a surrender or extinguishment of their exclusive franchise, if they ever had any, to build bridges over Charles river; so that they are barred from now setting it up against the Warren bridge. * * * But there is no warrant for the objection in any part of the language of the act. The extension of the term is not granted upon any condition whatsoever. No surrender of any right is asked, or required. The clause extending the term, purports, in its face, to be a mere donation or bounty of the legislature, founded on motives of public liberality and policy. It is granted expressly, as an encouragement to enterprise, and as a compensation for the supposed diminution of tolls, which West Boston bridge would occasion to Charles river bridge; and in no manner suggests any sacrifice or surrender of right whatsoever, to be made by the plaintiffs. In the next place, the erection of West Boston bridge was no invasion, whatsoever, of the franchise of the plaintiffs. Their right, as I have endeavoured to show, was limited to a bridge, and the travel between Charlestown and Boston; and did not extend beyond those towns. West Boston bridge was between Boston and Cambridge, at the distance of more than a mile by water, and by land of nearly three miles; and as the roads then ran, the line of travel for West Boston bridge would scarcely ever, perhaps never, approach nearer than that distance to Charles river bridge. The grant, therefore, could not have been founded in any notion of any surrender or extinguishment of the exclusive franchise of the plaintiffs; for it did not reach to such an extent. It did not reach Cambridge, and never had reached it.

* * *

Upon the whole, my judgment is, that the act of the legislature of Massachusetts granting the charter of Warren bridge, is an act impairing the obligation of the prior contract and grant to the proprietors of Charles river bridge; and, by the constitution of the United States, it is, therefore utterly void. I am for reversing the decree of the state court, (dismissing the bill;) and for remanding the cause to the state court for further proceedings, as to law and justice shall appertain.

NOTES AND QUESTIONS

1. Stanley I. Kutler's excellent study of this decision was entitled Privilege and Creative Destruction: The Charles River Bridge Case (1971). Why the choice of title? In his biography of Joseph Story, Gerald T. Dunne thus describes the Whig "wrath" upon the rendering of the decision for the Warren bridge:

> Webster assured Story that his dissent * * * left the Chief Justice "not an inch of ground to stand on," and young Charles Sumner adopted a British simile to write that reading Taney after Story was "hog wash after champagne." He reported a similar reaction from Chancellor Kent: "The Chancellor abused Taney & yr. associates to my heart's content. He thought Taney's opinion in the Warren Bridge case was miserable and yours gigantic." In fact, Kent had difficulty in reading Taney's views through; he dropped the pamphlet [containing the opinion] in shuddering disgust on the first effort and managed to finish it later by an effort of will, but with increased repugnance.

Justice Joseph Story and the Rise of the Supreme Court 365–366 (1970.) Copyright © 1970 by Gerald T. Dunne, reprinted with the permission of the publisher, Simon and Schuster. Would you have expected this reaction from Chancellor Kent? You will remember that Story cites Kent's opinions regarding ferries as authority in his dissent. Do Kent's opinions in Livingston v. Van Ingen, Croton Turnpike, and Newburgh Turnpike support Story?

Whatever Kent's support of Story's opinion in *Charles River Bridge*, however, there is some evidence that even Kent was concerned about threats to society posed by the growth of corporations. In 1831 he wrote that "Considering that corporations and privileges are multiplying upon us in every direction, and upon all possible subjects with astonishing fertility, the reservation of a power to *alter and modify* [by the legislature when it grants a charter] becomes most important to the safety and prosperity of the state. The reservation ought to be liberally construed. Grants are rapidly and heedlessly made." *quoted in* Morton Horwitz, The Transformation of American Law 1780–1860 138 (1977).

If even a conservative, like Kent, could discern the need for some restraint on the part of legislatures dealing with corporations, imagine the reaction of the Democrats to Taney's decision. The Charles River Bridge company, whatever the riskiness of its initial venture, had multiplied its capital 500%, and, although this appreciation may not have been more than that of most private property in Massachusetts, "customers came to regard the company as an objectionable monopoly extorting tolls which it had no right to collect. The company refused to make concessions either in the way of improved services or reduced tolls." Carl B. Swisher, V History of the Supreme Court of the United States: The Taney Period 1836–64 76 (1974). Professor Swisher thus describes the attitude of the Democrats:

> With the announcement of the decision in the *Bridge Case,* some Democratic spokesmen leaped to the conclusion that the millennium had arrived. The editor of the Boston Advocate joyously proclaimed that the victory was due to the democratic principles of the Administration and to democratic judges on the Supreme Bench. * * * Had the majority of the Court been composed of Whig judges, had vacancies been filled by guardians of vested rights such as Clay and Webster, the Warren Bridge would never have been free. Judge Story had "read a book, occupying over three hours in its delivery,* in which he undertook to show that the bigoted blockheads who lived in the time of the old year books and my Lord Coke, were incomparably wiser than the present race, and that we had no business to do anything which they had not sanctioned! * * * There was not one liberal principle in it."

Id., at 90. Copyright © 1974 by Macmillan Publishing Co., Inc., reprinted by permission of the publisher.

2. Story seems to have recognized that after what happened in the *Charles River Bridge* case, a new era had been entered. "I am sick at heart," he wrote Kent "and now go to the discharge of my judicial duties in the Supreme Court with a firm belief that the future cannot be as the past." Id., at 93, quoting Joseph Story to James Kent, June 26, 1837. What had changed? Is Taney's opinion in *Charles River Bridge* consistent with Story's and Marshall's opinions in the *Dartmouth College* case?

The *Charles River Bridge* case was originally argued before the Supreme Court in 1831, at which time the then Chief Justice Marshall and Justice Story were persuaded that the Charles River Bridge proprietors were right. An opinion by Story was drafted, but Marshall ordered it withheld until a majority of the court could concur with it. This took six years, and when a majority coalesced it was after Justice Marshall had been replaced by Justice Taney and it was in favour of the Warren Bridge. Accordingly, Story dissented. See Walker Lewis, Without Fear or Favor 281–294 (1965). Lewis calls this case "a crucial test between the views of the old-line Federalists and the newer theories of the Jacksonians." Id. at 283. Morton Horwitz says that "The *Charles River Bridge* case represented the last great contest in America between two different models of economic development." Horwitz, Transformation of American Law 134 (1977). What does he mean? Do you discern any similarities in the changes of the nineteenth century American law of competition and the changes in the law of property which we examined in Chapter III?

---

* Story's opinion, which includes dozens of references to English and American authorities, has been edited considerably from its original length of sixty-five pages.

SECTION B. THE CASE OF THE PHILADELPHIA CORDWAINERS (1806) AND THE DEVELOPMENT OF EARLY AMERICAN LABOR LAW

Boston's "Company of Shoemakers," chartered by the Colony of the Massachusetts Bay in 1648, was probably the first craft guild in America. The purpose of the guild was the suppression of "bad ware." The guild officers examined local workmen, and could secure from the county court an order prohibiting incompetent workmen from practicing the trade. The charter also empowered the association to regulate the labor of shoemakers, to "change and reform" the trade as appropriate, and to impose penalties on their members and "levy the same by distresse." The colonial authorities, however, reserved the right of "inhancinge the prices of shoes, bootes, or wages." III J. Commons et al., A Documentary History of American Industrial Society 20–22 (1910). Each member of this early guild performed the functions of "merchant" and "journeyman." Each shoemaker possessed his own tools, owned or rented his own shop, procured his own leather, and personally cut, stitched, and sold his shoes. The "bespoke" system was in effect: customers placed individual orders in advance. The style of the shoe and the quality and speed of the work usually determined price.

The appearance of the *retail* shoe shop, in Philadelphia by 1789, marks the beginning of a distinction between labor and capital, "employee" and "employer." At this time some of the more enterprising "cordwainers" (taking their name from the "cordevan" leather they worked), instead of receiving orders in advance from customers, began building an inventory of shoes standardized by shape and size for random sale in the local market. Such an undertaking required a considerable capital investment and a reorganization of the manner of doing business. In order to take advantage of economies of scale, money had to be found for acquiring more raw materials and for paying wages to an increased number of employees. The extension of credit, and the opening of accounts with customers became commonplace. Soon, a few retail merchant-employers saw the opportunity to expand their businesses by producing shoes wholesale for a new export market. As the nature of the shoe business changed, a competitive edge at the retail and wholesale levels was often maintained by mass producing shoes of minimum quality at low cost. By the 1790s, then, three grades of work existed in the Philadelphia shoe industry, and different persons were engaged in the shoe trade as "merchant-employers" and "journeymen-workers." "Bespoke" work still commanded the highest price and wages, and included the most talented journeymen. The retail and wholesale businesses offered low-priced shoes, and paid the lowest wages. The conflict between journeymen and their employers grew from this differentiation in pay scale, as many workers found themselves "locked" into the retail and wholesale business, toiling for what was perceived as a "knocked down" wage. In 1794 many of the Philadelphia shoemakers organized the "Federal Society of Journeymen Cordwainers," and by a succession of strikes and lockouts, attempted to peg all wages at the "bespoke" level.

The success of the Society of Cordwainers, the first "union" of its kind in America, was mixed. From 1794 to 1804 they secured several moderate wage increases, but these apparently did not extend to workers in the wholesale trade. In the spring of 1805, the Society demanded a flat, across-the-board wage increase for all city workers, but after several weeks the workers were compelled to return to work at the "knocked down" wage. By this time the merchants had formed their own organization to resist the union. In the Summer of 1805 the workmen voluntarily agreed to a slight reduction in wage, because of slack in the market, but when they later demanded a return to the earlier scale, the merchants refused. The Cordwainers struck in November, 1805. The vote to strike was split, 50 to 60, a measure of the relative complacency of bespoke and retail workers, and the strike collapsed following the indictment and arrest of the strike leaders for the common-law crime of "conspiracy."

The arrest and trial in January of 1806 occurred during a particularly turbulent period in Pennsylvania political history. The radical wing of the Republican party, strengthened by Jefferson's reelection, was calling for a complete reconstruction of government and society, in accordance with democratic principles. These men sought particularly to disband the legal profession, to permit anyone to argue his own case, to abolish the common law, replacing it with a written "code" drafted by "the people," to simplify legal procedure, and to replace the adversarial process with a simple system of arbitration before a panel of laymen. The moderate wing of the Republican party differed with the radicals on the extent of needed reform. In September of 1805 the moderates united with the Federalists, (who were bitterly opposed to any changes), in electing Thomas McKean governor of Pennsylvania. McKean, a Republican, had earlier expressed some sympathy for the radicals' goals, and they placed severe pressure on him to undertake some reform of the law and the legal system. The arrest of the Cordwainers exacerbated radical grievances, and the trial became a forum to assail unjust law. The report of the trial from which you will read excerpts was taken in short-hand by Thomas Lloyd, a radical Republican printer. Lloyd dedicated his report to McKean and the Pennsylvania legislature. He called the Cordwainer's trial "the most interesting law case, which has occurred in this state since our revolution," and he stated that his dedication was "with the hope of attracting * * * particular attention, at the next meeting of the Legislature."

The prosecutors, Attorney General Joseph Reed, Joseph Hopkinson, and Jared Ingersoll were all ardent Federalists. Ceasar A. Rodney, for the Cordwainers, as a congressman from Delaware, managed the impeachment trial of Samuel Chase. Walter Franklin, Rodney's co-counsel, was also a radical Republican, and a partisan of the workingman's cause in Philadelphia.

COMMONWEALTH v. PULLIS

Mayor's Court of Philadelphia, 1806.

III J. COMMONS ET AL., A DOCUMENTARY HISTORY OF AMERICAN INDUSTRIAL SOCIETY 60 (1910)

* * *

Mr. HOPKINSON: This prosecution has been commenced, not from any private pique, or personal resentment, but solely, with a view, to promote the common good of the community: and to prevent in future the pernicious combinations, of misguided men, to effect purposes not only injurious to themselves, but mischievous to society. Yet infinite pains have been taken to represent this prosecution, as founded in very improper motives. * * *

The newspaper called the Aurora, has teemed with false representations and statements of this transaction; and the most insolent abuse of the parties, who have brought it before this tribunal, with a view * * * to poison the public mind, and obstruct the pure streams of justice flowing from the established courts of law. * * * When the true nature of the case shall be explained, and the plain narrative of the facts, shall be laid before you gentlemen of the jury, we feel confident that you will not be biased by newspaper attempts, to delude and mislead you. * * *

Let it be well understood that the present action, is not intended to introduce the doctrine, that a man is not at liberty to fix any price whatsoever upon his own labour; we disclaim the idea, in the most unqualified terms * * *. We have no design to prevent him. * * *

* * * [W]e shall shew you that some journeymen, with families, have been forbid to work at prices with which they were perfectly satisfied, and thereby been brought into deep distress.

* * * [W]e shall also shew the mode by which they compel men to join their society * * *. A journeyman arriving from Europe, or any part of the United States, an apprentice who has served * * * his time, must join the association, or be shut out from every shop in the city, if he presumes to work at his own price. Nay, every master shoemaker must decline to employ such journeyman or his shop will be abandoned, by all the other workmen. * * * [T]his compulsion from its nature seldom fails. If the master discharges the non conformist, and he gets employed at another shop, the body pursue him, and order the new master to drive him away, and threaten in case of refusal that they will draw off all the members of the society, and so on, until the persecuted man either joins their body or is driven from the city. * * *

This is the chief charge in the indictment; and you now see that the action is instituted to maintain the cause of liberty and repress that of licentiousness. It is to secure the rights of each individual to obtain and enjoy the price he fixes upon his own labour.

* * * I have thought it necessary to say thus much that you might not suppose we are attempting to deprive any man of his constitutional rights and privileges, as has been represented. * * *

* * *

Our position is, that no man is at liberty to combine, conspire, confederate, and unlawfully agree to regulate the whole body of workmen in the city. * * *

It must be known to you, that every society of people are affected by such private confederacies: that they are injurious to the public good and against the public interest. The law therefore forbids conspiracies of every kind which puts in jeopardy the interest and well being of the community; what may be lawful in an individual, may be criminal in a number of individuals combined, with a view to carry it into effect. * * *

You will also please to observe that this body of journeymen are not an incorporated society * * * neither are they a society instituted for benevolent purposes. But merely a society for compelling by the most arbitrary and malignant means, the whole body of the journeymen to submit to their rules and regulations; it is not confined even to the members of the society, it reaches every individual of the trade, whether journeymen or master. * * * You will find that they not only determine the price of labour for themselves, but compel every one to demand that price and receive no other, they refuse to hold communion with any person who shall disobey their mandates, in fine, they regulate the whole trade under the most dreadful pains and penalties, such I believe as never was heard of in this or any other civilized country.

[There followed two days of testimony, which did show that the Journeymen behaved in the manner Hopkinson described: that they attempted to enforce uniformity in their demands for raised wages, and ostracized scabs. We continue with Hopkinson's comments on the law as applied to the evidence.]

* * *

Why a combination in such case is criminal, will not be difficult to explain: we live under a government composed of a constitution and laws * * * and every man is obliged to obey the constitution, and the laws made under it. When I say he is bound to obey these, I mean to state the whole extent of his obedience. Do you feel yourselves bound to obey any other laws, enacted by any other legislature, than that of your own choice? Shall these, or any other body of men, associate for the purpose of making new laws, laws not made under the constitutional authority, and compel their fellow citizens to obey them, under the penalty of their existence? This prosecution contravenes no man's right, it is to prevent an infringement of right; it is in favour of the equal liberty of all men, this is the policy of our laws; but if private associations and clubs, can make constitutions and laws for us * * * if they can associate and make bye-laws paramount, or inconsistent with the state laws; What, I ask, becomes of the liberty of the people * * *?

There is evidence before you that shews this secret association, this private club, composed of men who have been only a little time in your country, (not that they are the worse for that,) but they ought to submit to the laws of the country, and not attempt to alter them according to their own whim or caprice.

* * *

* * * I now am to speak to the policy of permitting such associations. This is a large, increasing, manufacturing city. Those best acquainted with our situation, believe that manufactures will, by and by, become one of its chief means of support. * * * [W]e rival the supplies from England in many things, and great sums are annually received in returns. It is then proper to support this manufacture. Will you permit men to destroy it, who have no permanent stake in the city; men who can pack up their all in a knapsack, or carry them in their pockets to New-York or Baltimore? * * * Other articles, to a great amount, are manufactured here, and exported; such as coaches and other pleasurable carriages; windsor chairs, and particular manufactures of iron. * * *

* * * [W]hen orders arrive for considerable quantities of any article, the association may determine to raise the wages, and reduce the contractors to diminish their profit; to sustain a loss, or to abandon the execution of the orders, as was done in Bedford's case * * *. When they found he had a contract, they took advantage of his necessity. What was done by the journeymen shoemakers, may be done by those of every other trade, or manufacturer in the city * * *. A few more things of this sort, and you will break up the manufactories; the master will be afraid to make a contract, therefore he must relinquish the export trade, and depend altogether upon the profits of the work of Philadelphia, and confine his supplies altogether to the city. The last turn-out had liked to have produced that effect: Mr. Ryan told you he had intended to confine himself to bespoke work.

It must be plain to you, that the master employers have no particular interest in the thing * * * if they pay higher wages, you must pay higher for the articles. They, in truth, are protecting the community. * * *

* * *

If this conspiracy was to be confined to the persons themselves, it would not be an offence against the law; but they go further. There are two counts in the indictment; you are to consider each, and to give your verdict on each. The first is for contriving, and intending, unjustly, and oppressively, to encrease and augment the wages usually allowed them. The other for endeavouring to prevent, by threats, menaces, and other unlawful means, other journeymen from working at the usual prices, and that they compelled others to join them.

* * *

It may be answered, that when men enter into a society, they are bound to conform to its rules; they may say, the majority ought to govern the minority * * * granted * * * but they ought to leave a man free to join, or not to join the society. * * * The man who seeks an asylum in this country, from the arbitrary laws of other nations, is coerced into this society, though he does not work in the article intended to be raised; he must leave his seat and join the turn-out. This was Harrison's case * * * he worked exclusively in shoes, they in boots; he was a stranger, he was a married man, with a large family; he represented his distressed condition; they entangle him, but shew no mercy. The dogs of vigilance find, by their scent, the emigrant in his cellar or garret: they drag him forth, they tell him he must join them; he replies, I am well satisfied as I am * * *. No * * * they chase him from shop to shop; they allow him no resting place, till he consents to be one of their body; he is expelled [from] society, driven from his lodgings, proscribed from working; he is left no alternative, but to perish in the streets, or seek some other asylum on a more hospitable shore. * * *

* * * It will be seen that the mere combination to raise wages is considered an offence at common law: the reason is founded in common sense. Suppose the bakers were to combine, and agree not to sell a loaf of bread, only for one week, under a dollar, would not this be an injury to the community? * * * Extend the case to butchers, and all others who deal in articles of prime necessity, and the good policy of the law is then apparent.

Hawkins, c. 72, § 2, in note, was cited. Speaking of combinations, he says * * * "Where divers persons confederate together, in order to prejudice a third person, it is indictable as highly criminal at common law." "Journeymen confederating and refusing to work, unless at encreased prices, is indictable!" * * *

Mr. Hopkinson next cited 8 Mod. p. 11. Wise against the journeymen taylors at Cambridge. "A conspiracy is unlawful, even though the matter might have been lawful, if done by them individually. * * * "

He trusted the jury would see the present cause in this double point of view; the general policy, as it relates to the good of the community, and the flourishing state of our manufactures: the liberty of individuals, and the enjoyment of common and equal rights, secured by the constitution and laws. * * * [W]as our state legislature to dare to pass such laws as these men have passed, it would be a just cause of rebellion. I will go further, and say, it would produce rebellion if the legislature should say, that a man should not work under a certain sum * * * it would lead to beggary, and no man would submit to it. Then, shall a secret body exercise a power over our fellow-citizens, which the legislature itself is not invested with? * * *

* * *

One word more; we are told the prices asked by these men, are those given at New-York and Baltimore: if so, why do not these men go there? They know if their wages are higher there, their expences also are higher: they do not stay here out of patriotism; they know their own interests, and can calculate them with accuracy * * *.

[*Mr. Franklin*:] Has the master then the sole right of determining the wages which are to be given for the labour of his journeymen? This would be too arbitrary a power for any man to contend for; it would be an insult to your understandings, to insist upon it. * * * As to the price which any particular employer may pay his workmen, that must be regulated by the contract between them. If they can mutually agree upon a price to be given, the master is bound to give, and the journeymen must abide by the sum stipulated. A different price will be given to different workmen; some deserve more than others, either on account of their greater industry and application, or their greater skill and ingenuity.

But if the employer and journeyman cannot agree upon the work to be done, or the price to be paid, neither is bound to recede from his determination.

If then, any one man has this right, has not every other man the same privilege? If one journeyman has a right to adopt measures to prevent the effects of the obstinacy or combination of the master shoemakers, may not a number unite for the same object? A purpose innocent or lawful in one man, cannot be otherwise in a society or body of men. Supposing, therefore, that the facts charged in the first count were true; that the men refused to work but at certain prices, it is no crime, and they cannot be punished for it.

* * *

Now, if any journeyman who chose to work at the rates or prices offered by the employers, contrary to the wish of other journeymen, were threatened by them, or any of them, with injury to his person or property, he has a complete and ample remedy provided for him by law without resorting to the measures which have been adopted.

He might have them bound over to their good behaviour, and if they afterwards were guilty of any threats, their recognizance would be forfeited, and they would be obliged to pay the penalty. * * *

If any employer suffer inconvenience or mischief, in consequence of his journeymen being seduced or driven from his employment, he has his remedy by a civil action, in which he may recover from the offender, damages equal to the injury sustained. * * *

* * * What proof is there of the association having made any unlawful or arbitrary bye laws? * * * None * * *. But supposing that such laws had been enacted by the society, are the defendants to answer for them in this way? Should it not appear clearly, that they assented to them? When the question was taken, the defendants might have been in the minority; and shall they be punished for an act of the society of which they have shewn their disapprobation? * * *

* * *

[Franklin then turns to the charges of ostracizing scabs and preventing masters from hiring them.]

* * * Is there the slightest evidence, that the defendants ever compelled a single journeyman to leave his employers? How did they compel? Did they use any violence? If they had they were subject to the laws and might have been individually punished for it. But neither violence, threats, nor menaces, were used * * *. No man was the object of force or compulsion. * * * "The very head and front of their offending was:" their refusing to work for any master who employed such journeymen as infringed the rules of the society to which they belonged.

This I deny to be an offence. * * * The motive for my refusal may be illiberal, but it furnishes no legal foundation for a prosecution: I cannot be indicted for it. Every man may chuse his company, or refuse to associate with any one whose company may be disagreeable to him, without being obliged to give a reason for it: and without violating the laws of the land. * * *

I will conclude this part of my argument, with the remarks of a very sensible and judicious writer * * * 1. Smith's Wealth of Nations, page 89. "Workmen desire to get as much, masters to give as little, as possible. * * * It is not, however, difficult to foresee which of the two parties must, upon all ordinary occasions, have the advantage in the dispute * * *. The masters being fewer in number, can combine much more easily; and the law, besides, authorises, or at least does not prohibit their combinations, while it prohibits those of the workmen. We have no acts of parliament against combining to lower the price of work; but many against combining to raise it. In all such disputes the masters can hold out much longer. A landlord, a farmer, a master manufacturer, or merchant, though they did not employ a single workman, could generally live a year or two upon the stocks which they have already acquired. Many work-men could not subsist a week * * *. We rarely hear, it has been said, of the combinations of masters; though frequently of those of workmen. But whoever imagines, upon this account, that masters rarely combine, is as ignorant of the world as the subject. Masters are always and every where in a sort of tacit, but constant and uni-form combination, not to raise the wages of labour above their actual rate. To violate this combination is everywhere a most unpopular action, and a sort of reproach to a master among his neighbours and equals. * * * "

* * *

[Franklin moved then into the law of conspiracy.] 1 Hawk. b. 1, c. 72, § 2, note 2, is cited. This point rests on 8 Mod. p. 11. Rex. vs. the journeymen taylors * * *. "It is not for the denial, &c. but for the conspiracy they were indicted; and a conspiracy of any kind is illegal, though the matter about which they conspired might have been lawful for them, or any of them to do, if they had not con-spired to do it."

And is it contended that the doctrine contained in this case is law in Pennsylvania? It may be adapted to the meridian of Lon-don, Paris, Madrid, or Constantinople, but can never suit the free state of Pennsylvania. * * * By this authority, whatever is in-nocent or laudable in one, becomes criminal if he unite with others in doing it.

It is lawful for an individual to use his best endeavours to ex-tinguish the fire which burns his neighbour's house, but he must not unite with others in doing it. What then becomes of your fire com-panies, your hose companies, and other institutions of a similar nature * * * none of which are incorporated by law?

It is lawful for a man to improve himself in any art or science, but he must not join with others for the purpose. What then be-comes of the numerous literary associations which do so much honour to Philadelphia?

* * *

* * * [The English] Parliament [has passed laws] to limit the prices of work in various branches of business, and under those acts it is made criminal to combine for the purpose of raising the wages, otherwise than as the acts direct. I believe the journeymen shoemakers would be punishable in England for an attempt to raise their wages, not by the common law, but under the provisions of acts of parliament, made expressly for the purpose.

Admitting, for argument sake, however, that they would be amenable to the common law in England, independent of the statute, they should shew us that this part of the common law has been ex-tended to Pennsylvania * * *. Of the applicability of the [Eng-lish] law to the circumstances of the country, the colonists even when in a state of dependence on the mother country, undertook to decide, and were allowed the privilege of determining for themselves. * * *

How is it to be ascertained what parts of the common law are, or are not, applicable to the condition and circumstances of the country, and therefore to be adopted or rejected? The only modes in which this can be done are by legislative acts, judicial decisions, or constant usage or practice. * * *

I need not, I am sure, go into an argument to shew, that laws of the kind contended for, are neither necessary for us, applicable to our situation, nor suitable to our circumstances. You might as well introduce that part of the common law relative to cutting off a man's right hand for striking in court, &c. mentioned in 4 Black. p. 124. * * *

* * *

It is acknowledged, that there is no express statute on the subject in this country. It therefore must be by the common law or it cannot be punished at all. Where is the evidence of this common law? Is it founded on practice or usage? None can be proved! Is it founded on any legal decision? None can be produced!

* * *

It is true that precedents innumerable may be imported from Great Britain. But very different are the genius and feelings of the two countries, on the subject of criminal law * * *. The theory and practice of the criminal law of England, form an object of horror to every feeling and reflecting mind. [Franklin then quotes former Supreme Court Justice James Wilson:] * * * "Instead of being, as it ought to be, an emanation from the law of nature and morality, it has too often been avowedly and systematically the reverse. It has been a combination of the strong against the weak, of the rich against the poor, of pride and interest against justice and humanity. Unfortunate, indeed, it is, that this has been the case; for we may truly say, that on the excellence of the criminal law, the liberty and the happiness of the people chiefly depend."

In Great Britain * * * the prices of every kind of work and labour are fixed by law; and very high penalties are imposed upon those who transgress them. * * *

You will readily perceive the spirit of partiality, which breathes through their statutes * * * and the strong inclinations which they evince to favor the rich at the expence of the poor * * * the master at the expence of the servant.

If you are desirous of introducing a similar spirit of inequality into our government and laws * * * such disposition and opinions will lead you to convict the defendants. If * * * you are contented with the blessings enjoyed under our free constitution, which secures to the citizens an equality of rights, and recognizes no distinction of classes * * * I shall look for the result of these feelings and these sentiments in a verdict of acquittal.

* * *

Mr. Rodney: [He begins his argument with an evaluation of Mr. Hopkinson's claim that the merchants who sought to keep down wages were disinterested public servants.] He has attempted to excite your feelings and sympathy, in behalf of those, who can scarce refrain from smiling in your face; he has set forth their merits, their disinterestedness, and their magnanimity, in stepping between you and the impositions of their workmen * * *. Is this a true picture of the case before you? * * * It is nothing more or less than this, whether the wealthy master shoemakers of this populous and flourishing city, shall charge you and me what price they please for our boots and shoes, and at the same time have the privilege of fixing the wages of the poor journeymen they happen to employ. * * *

* * *

Much has been said of the importance of manufactures to this city, and the injury manufacturing interest would sustain, if journeymen were permitted to regulate the price of their own labour. The gentleman has shewn you one side of the picture; I wish to call your attention to the other. The great advantage possessed by Philadelphia over New York and Baltimore, is the extent of her monied capital. Those cities give more wages, and we have proved them to be given at this very time: and we wish to receive merely the same prices, and no more.

The gentleman calls out, why do they not go there? Suppose they should at his bidding take wing and fly away, how would Mr. Bedford and Mr. Ryan make their boots, and what is to become of their export trade? Do you wish to banish them? The verdict called for by the prosecutors, will effectually answer the purpose. * * * New York and Baltimore wisely hold out good prices to attract them; and good policy ought to dictate to the employers here, to allow them as liberal a compensation. Leather is said to be cheaper here, and I do not believe, living costs more than at either New York or Baltimore. * * * New York and Baltimore will gladly receive them, as they take care to profit by every other advantage which our inattention or narrow policy throws into their way. * * *

Philadelphia is a great commercial and manufacturing city; that the legislature of the state by its fostering care, in opening new roads and cutting canals, may render it still more prosperous * * * must be the sincere wish of us all. * * * Do not then, I beg of you bring on a premature old age, by establishing the principle, that labourers or journeymen, in every trade, are to submit to the prices which their employers, in the plenitude of their power, choose to give them. * * * The moment you destroy the free agency of this meritorious part of the community (for remember the principle is undeniable, that labour constitutes the real wealth of a country) the verdict which you will pronounce, will proclaim the decline and the fall of Philadelphia. * * * Let them ask as freely as they breathe the air, wages for their services. No person is compelled to give them more than their work is worth, the market will sufficiently and correctly regulate these matters. If you adhere to our doctrines * * * I venture to predict * * * that scarcely a breeze will blow, but what will waft to our shores, experienced workmen from those realms, where labour is regulated by statutable provisions * * *. Give me leave however, frankly to declare, that I would not barter away our dear bought rights and American liberty, for all the warehouses of London and Liverpool, and the manufactures of Birmingham and Manchester: no; not if were to be added to them, the gold of Mexico, the silver of Peru, and the diamonds of Brazil.

* * *

One word in reply to the observations on the subject of aliens. From the moment we declared independence, we stood with open arms to receive the oppressed of all nations and countries. * * * We want workmen of every kind. Let us preserve this asylum. * * * It is the last retreat of freedom and liberty.

* * * [T]he law should be no respecter of persons * * * like the light of the sun, it should shine on all. Whether they are as rich as Croesus, or as poor as Belisarius * * * whether their complexion be as black as jet, or as white as the driven snow!

* * *

[*Mr. Ingersoll*:] The defendants formed a society, the object of which was * * *. What? That they should not be obliged to work for wages which they did not think a reasonable compensation? No: If that was the sole object of the society, I approve it * * *. No man is to work without a reasonable compensation: they may legally and properly associate for that purpose. * * * If they go beyond this, and say we will not work, but we will compel the employers to give more, not according to contract, but such as they separately think themselves entitled to receive [then there is a violation of law.] * * *

[Ingersoll turns to a defense of the common law.] Whence comes this enmity to the common law? It is of mushroom growth. Look through the journals of congress during the revolutionary war, you will find it claimed as the great charter of liberty; as the best birthright and noblest of inheritance. Caesar A. Rodney, the revolutionary patriot, hazarded his life to secure and perpetuate the blessing. * * *

But the common law is in some respects faulty, as in the case cited from 4 Black. p. 124, and 4 Inst. p. 143. The sun too has its spots, but will you extinguish that luminary from the firmament?

But the common law, as adopted and practised in Pennsylvania, is the least exceptionable criminal code in the world. In England, it is said to be sanguinary and cruel. In England there are 176 offences punishable by death, of which there are only 16 so punished by the common law.

Why do I love the common law, especially the criminal part? * * * Because, to the common law we are indebted for trial by jury, grand and petit, without the unanimous consent of which latter, I cannot be convicted. * * * Because, it secures me a fair trial by challenges, the laws of evidence, confronting me with my accuser, and exempting me from accusing myself, or being twice liable to trial for the same offence. * * *

* * *

Abolish the common law, judging not by instances, but by principle, where are you? Shew me an indictment of any kind, even for assault and battery, it is bottomed on common law; with us we have no cause of proceeding in criminal cases, but by the modes of the common law * * *.

Recorder Levy [Instructing the Jury]:

* * *

The moment courts of justice lose their respectability from that moment the security of persons and of property is gone. The moment courts of justice have their characters contaminated by a well founded suspicion, that they are governed by caprice, fear or favour; from that moment they will cease to be able to administer justice with effect, and redress wrongs of either a public or a private nature. Every consideration, therefore, calls upon us to maintain the character of courts and juries; and that can only be maintained by undeviating integrity, by an adhesion to the rules of law, and by deciding impartially in conformity to them.

* * * As far as the arguments of counsel apply to your understanding and judgment, they should have weight: but, if the appeal has been made to your passions, it ought not to be indulged. * * * An attempt has been made to shew that the spirit of the revolution and the principle of the common law, are opposite in this case. That the common law, if applied in this case, would operate an attack upon the rights of man. The enquiry on that point, was unnecessary and improper. Nothing more was required than to ascertain what the law is. The law is the permanent rule, it is the will of the whole community. After that is discovered, whatever may be its spirit or tendency, it must be executed, and the most imperious duty demands our submission to it.

* * *

* * * The prosecutors are not on their trial, if they have proved the offence, alleged in the indictment against the defendants;

and if the defendants are guilty, will any man say, that they ought not to be convicted: because the prosecution was not founded in motives of patriotism? Certainly the only question is, whether they are guilty or innocent. * * *

* * *

It is proper to consider, is such a combination consistent with the principles of our law, and injurious to the public welfare? The usual means by which the prices of work are regulated, are the demand for the article and the excellence of its fabric. * * * To make an artificial regulation, is not to regard the excellence of the work or quality of the material, but to fix a positive and arbitrary price, governed by no standard, controlled by no impartial person, but dependent on the will of the few who are interested * * *. It is an unnatural, artificial means of raising the price of work beyond its standard, and taking an undue advantage of the public. Is the rule of law bottomed upon such principles, as to permit or protect such conduct? * * * Is there any man who can calculate (if this is tolerated) at what price he may safely contract to deliver articles, for which he may receive orders, if he is to be regulated by the journeymen in an arbitrary jump from one price to another? * * * What then is the operation of this kind of conduct upon the commerce of the city? It exposes it to inconveniences, if not to ruin; therefore, it is against the public welfare. How does it operate upon the defendants? We see that those who are in indigent circumstances, and who have families to maintain, and who get their bread by their daily labour, have declared here upon oath, that it was impossible for them to hold out * * * and it has been admitted by the witnesses for the defendants, that such persons, however sharp and pressing their necessities, were obliged to stand to the turn-out, or never afterwards to be employed. * * * Can such a regulation be just and proper? Does it not tend to involve necessitous men in the commission of crimes? If they are prevented from working for six weeks, it might induce those who are thus idle, and have not the means of maintenance, to take other courses for the support of their wives and children. It might lead them to procure it by crimes—by burglary, larceny, or highway robbery! A father cannot stand by and see, without agony, his children suffer; if he does, he is an inhuman monster; he will be driven to seek bread for them, either by crime, by beggary, or a removal from the city. * * * Does this measure tend to make good workmen? No: it puts the botch incapable of doing justice to his work, on a level with the best tradesman. The master must give the same wages to each. Such a practice would take away all the excitement to excel in workmanship or industry. * * * In every point of view, this measure is pregnant with public mischief and private injury * * *.

What has been the conduct of the defendants in this instance? They belong to an association, the object of which is, that every person who follows the trade of a journeyman shoemaker, must be a member of their body. * * * If they do not join the body, a term of reproach is fixed upon them. The members of the body will not work with them, and they refuse to board or lodge with them. * * * If the purpose of the association is well understood, it will be found they leave no individual at liberty to join the society or reject it. * * * Is there any reason to suppose that the laws are not competent to redress an evil of this magnitude? * * *

* * *

It is in the volumes of the common law we are to seek for information in the far greater number, as well as the most important causes that come before our tribunals. That invaluable code has ascertained and defined, with a critical precision, and with a consistency that no fluctuating political body could or can attain, not only the civil rights of property, but the nature of all crimes from treason to trespass, has pointed out the rules of evidence and the mode of proof, and has introduced and perpetuated, for their investigation, that admirable institution, the freeman's-boast, the trial by jury. * * * Much abuse has of late teemed upon its valuable institutions. Its enemies do not attack it as a system: but they single out some detached branch of it, declare it absurd or intelligible, without understanding it. * * * As well might a circle of a thousand miles diameter be described by the man, whose eye could only see a single inch * * *. Its rules are the result of the wisdom of ages. It says there may be cases in which what one man may do without offence, many combined may not do with impunity. * * *

* * * A combination of workmen to raise their wages may be considered in a two fold point of view: one is to benefit themselves * * * the other is to injure those who do not join their society. The rule of law condemns both. If the rule be clear, we are bound to conform to it even though we do not comprehend the principle upon which it is founded. * * * It is enough, that it is the will of the majority. * * * But the rule in this case is pregnant with sound sense and all the authorities are clear upon the subject. * * *

* * * In the turn-out of last fall, if each member of the body had stood alone, fettered by no promises to the rest, many of them might have changed their opinion as to the price of wages and gone to work * * *. The continuance in improper conduct may therefore well be attributed to the combination. The good sense of those individuals was prevented by this agreement, from having its free exercise. * * * Is this like the formation of a society for the promotion of the general welfare of the community, such as to advance the interests of religion, or to accomplish acts of charity and benevolence? * * * These are for the benefit of third persons, the society in question to promote the selfish purposes of the mem-

bers. * * * How can these cases be considered on an equal footing? The journeymen shoemakers * * * could not go farther than saying, no one should work unless they all got the wages demanded by the majority; is this freedom? * * * Was it the spirit of '76 that either masters or journeymen, in regulating the prices of their commodities should set up a rule contrary to the law of their country? General and individual liberty was the spirit of '76. It is our first blessing. It has been obtained and will be maintained * * *. It is not a question, whether we shall have an imperium in imperio, whether we shall have, besides our state legislature a new legislature consisting of journeymen shoemakers. * * * [T]hough we acknowledge it is the hard hand of labour that promises the wealth of a nation, though we acknowledge the usefulness of such a large body of tradesmen and agree they should have every thing to which they are legally entitled; yet we conceive they ought to ask nothing more. They should neither be the slaves nor the governors of the community.

* * *

* * * [The court has] given you the rule as they have found it in the book, and it is now for you to say, whether the defendants are guilty or not. The rule they consider as fixed, they cannot change it. * * * If you can reconcile it to your consciences, to find the defendants not guilty, you will do so; if not, the alternative that remains, is a verdict of guilty. [The jury returned a verdict of guilty, and the court fined the defendants eight dollars each, with costs of suit.]

* * *

NOTES AND QUESTIONS

1. Like the trial of Zenger, the Writs of Assistance Case, and the proceedings against Samuel Chase, the questions of "law" in the trial of the Cordwainers are entertwined with questions of political and economic ideology. These problems have been studied in some of the most exciting recent historiography.

On the outcome of legal reform in Pennsylvania, see R. Ellis, The Jeffersonian Crisis: Courts and Politics in the Young Republic (1971). On the conditions of work and unionization in Philadelphia, see E. Foner, Tom Paine (1976), and David Montgomery, "The Working Class of the Preindustrial American City, 1780–1830," 9 Labor History 1–22 (1968). On the link between radical Republicanism and urban workingmen, see A. Young, "The Mechanics and the Jeffersonians: New York, 1789–1801," 5 Labor History 247 (1964). The best recent general study of nineteenth century labor and unionization is probably H. Gutman, Work, Culture and Society in Industrializing America (1977).

2. According to the prosecution and Recorder Levy, what is the legal definition of conspiracy? What sort of "conspiracy law" would the defense counsel propose? What is the relevance of Franklin's and Rodney's digressions about the English common law of crimes? Can you perceive a link

between the Franklin-Rodney fulminations against the common law, the Hopkinson-Ingersoll defense, and the politics of Pennsylvania at the time of the trial?

3. Both prosecution and defense claim that "liberty" and the "rights of man" are on their side. Would they agree on the definitions of these terms? The prosecutor casts aspersions on the "alien" workingmen of the city who can pack all their belongings on their backs, and invites them to leave the city if they are unsatisfied with their work. While Rodney agrees on the social origins of the shoemakers, he doesn't share many of the attitudes of the prosecution. What power should the shoemakers exercise in society, according to Rodney?

4. The prosecutor objects to the Society of Cordwainers because they are like a "government unto themselves." What does this mean? What evidence can he offer for their "unconstitutionality?" Franklin and Rodney respond that it is in the nature of private associations to exercise some degree of compulsion and coercion on their members. Why this concern on both sides about possible abuses of power?

5. In 1776 Adam Smith published Wealth of Nations, still considered to be one of the most important statements on the virtues of a free market. Why did defense counsel quote favorably from it? Recorder Levy also has an opinion on the virtues of a free market. Does this opinion "interfere" with his judgment of the case? Do you think he correctly understands the motives of the Society of Cordwainers? What is the economic policy behind Levy's instructions? Should economic policy have a place in a criminal proceeding?

6. In his instructions to the jury, Levy waxes eloquent on the virtues of the common law. Does Levy's common law differ from that of the prosecution and the defense? What is Levy's attitude toward the jury? Levy instructs the jury to rely not on their "passions" but on their "judgment." What is the distinction? In the same vein, Levy reminds the jury that they must distinguish between "selfish purposes" and the "general welfare" in arriving at a verdict. What does Levy have in mind? Do you find his opinion more or less logical than those of counsel?

7. Jared Ingersoll, for the prosecution, chastizes Rodney, and accuses him of inconsistency, for being on the one hand a famous Revolutionary patriot, and on the other an opponent of the common law. Why would Ingersoll make such a charge? Could you answer for Rodney? Can you explain why a labor conspiracy case would be the battleground for interpreting the meaning of the Revolution?

8. One of the arguments of defense counsel, not included here, is that the merchants formed their own "combination" in 1789—five years before the Society—and that the Society of Cordwainers was actually an attempt to restore the balance of power in dealings between labor and management. The court believed the evidence insufficient to support this argument of the cordwainers. Yet both the prosecution and Recorder Levy seem to stress that the law, when conspiracy is involved, must be "blind," favoring neither merchant nor workingman.

9. An opportunity to determine the even-handedness of the Pennsylvania common law of conspiracy arose in 1821, in COMMONWEALTH v.

CARLISLE, Bright. 36. The defendants were master ladies' shoemakers who were accused of conspiring to lower the wages of their journeymen. Their principal defense was that they were merely seeking to reduce wages artificially inflated by a combination of the journeymen. Referring to the trial of the cordwainers, Chief Justice Gibson of the Pennsylvania Supreme Court stated that "there was no general principle distinctly asserted, but the case was considered only in reference to its particular circumstances, and in these it materially differed from that now under consideration." Id., at 37. Do you agree?

Turning to the English conspiracy cases against journeymen for combining to raise their wages, Gibson remarked that "we ought to pause before we adopt their law of conspiracy, as respects artisans, which may be said to have in some measure, indirectly received its form from the pressure of positive enactment, and which therefore may be entirely unfitted to the condition and habits of the same class here." Id., at 38. Gibson noted the confused state of the English law of conspiracy, and stressed that it would be a mistake to "impart criminality to the most laudable associations" merely because they were "combinations." Id., at 39. Gibson then concluded that the most important inquiries were those regarding "motive" and the "nature of the object to be attained." "Where the act is lawful for an individual," he stated, "it can be the subject of a conspiracy when done in concert, only where there is a direct intention that injury shall result from it, or where the object is to benefit the conspirators to the prejudice of the public or the oppression of individuals, and where such prejudice or oppression is the natural and necessary consequence." Id., at 39–40. Proceeding to give examples, Gibson said that if "persons should combine to establish a ferry, not from motives of public or private utility, but to ruin or injure the owner of a neighboring ferry," or "if the bakers of a town were to combine to hold up the article of bread, and by means of a scarcity thus produced, extort an exorbitant price for it," these would be indictable conspiracies under the Pennsylvania common law. The result would be otherwise, however, if the motives of those establishing a ferry, for example, were "fair competition" and not "oppression." Id., at 40.

Moving finally to the facts at hand, Gibson decided that "a combination of employers to depress the wages of journeymen below what they would be, if there was no recurrence to artificial means by either side, is criminal." Id. at 41. Gibson proceeded to give his thoughts on the necessity for such a rule:

> There is between the different parts of the body politic a reciprocity of action on each other, which, like the action of antagonizing muscles in the natural body, not only prescribes to each its appropriate state and condition, but regulates the motion of the whole. The effort of an individual to disturb this equilibrium can never be perceptible, nor carry the operation of his interest on that of any other individual beyond the limits of fair competition; but the increase of power by combination of means, being in geometrical proportion to the number concerned, an association may be able to give an impulse, not only oppressive to individuals, but mischievous to the public at large; and it is the employment of an engine so powerful and dangerous, that gives criminality to an act

that would be perfectly innocent, at least in a legal view, when done by an individual. The combination of capital for purposes of commerce, or to carry on any other branch of industry, although it may in its consequences indirectly operate on third persons, is unaffected by this consideration, because it is a common means in the ordinary course of human affairs, which stimulates to competition and enables men to engage in undertakings too weighty for an individual.

Id., at 41. Gibson then announced that a combination artificially to depress the price of labor would be just as criminal as a combination to raise the price of bread, since the "labouring classes purchase their bread with their labour." Id., at 42. Still, the essence of the crime was motive, and where the intention of masters was "not to give an undue value to labour, but to foil their antagonists [the journeymen] in an attempt to assign to it, by surreptitious means, a value which it would not otherwise have, they will make out a good defense." Id., at 42. While it was true that the masters might proceed against journeymen who combined artificially to raise their wages through the law of conspiracy, "the legal remedy is cumulative, and does not take away the preventive remedy by the act of the parties," so that the masters could lawfully combine to reduce artificially-raised wages. Id., at 43. Gibson then referred the matter to a jury, for a factual determination of the motives of the masters in combining to reduce the journeymen's wages. The report of the case contains no information on the jury's disposition of the matter, but it appears that "the prosecution was probably dropped." Nelles, "Commonwealth v. Hunt" 32 Col.L.Rev. 1167n. (1932).

Do you find Gibson's treatment of the law of conspiracy to be more or less satisfactory than those of counsel and Recorder Levy in the case of the cordwainers? Which treatment seems most in accord with what you take to be the American political values of freedom and liberty? How clear are the principles which Gibson lays down? Gibson seems to be relying on the same free-market model of the economy that Recorder Levy alluded to, and it is likely that both men subscribed to the wage-fund theory of labor (only a fixed part of the national income was available for wages). How easy do you think it would be for Gibson or for a jury to determine when a given combination was designed to produce "artificially" high or low wages? Gibson explains that combinations of capital are permissible where the object is not "oppression," but "fair competition." Is the distinction an easy one to make? If these would be difficult determinations, in whose favor would you assume they would be likely to be resolved?

10. How far was early American common law prepared to go in sanctioning competition among employers for labor? In Gibson's opinion in *Carlisle* he stated his belief that if merchants in one industry artificially lowered wages, workers would eventually leave that industry to enter others, and that the offending merchants would eventually (even without the help of the law of conspiracy) be forced to raise wages back to their natural level. Id., at 41. The willingness of the American common law to maintain a free market in labor was put to a test in BOSTON GLASS MANUFACTORY v. BINNEY, 21 Mass. (4 Pick.) 425 (1827). This was an action sounding in tort, in which the plaintiffs argued that the defendants,

their competitors, had unlawfully enticed skilled workmen from their employ. Lemuel Shaw, whose two opinions in labor cases we will soon read, appeared as counsel for the defendants. Relying on an English case cited by Shaw, the court held that " 'to induce a servant to leave his master's service at the expiration of the time for which the servant had hired himself, although the servant had no intention at the time, of quitting his master's service, was not the subject of an action.' *It is damnum absque injuria.*"   Id., at 428, citing Lord Kenyon in Nicol et al. v. Martyn, 2 Esp. R. 732. "If the law were otherwise," said Justice Wilde, "it would lead to the most mischievous consequences, and would operate injuriously both to laborers and their employers." In the course of its opinion in *Binney* the Supreme Judicial Court in effect rejected a jury instruction of the trial judge to the contrary, and held that it was not a tort for new employers to bargain with employees before their contracts with competitors had expired. Does the language from Nicol v. Martyn support this?

In the course of the trial in Binney, the plaintiffs sought to demonstrate that the defendants were liable not only for the common-law tort of enticement, but also because they had earlier signed an agreement among Boston glass-making merchants not to lure away each other's skilled workers. The trial judge rejected the evidence of the contract, on the grounds that it could not form the basis for an action in tort. (*Binney* was an "action on the case," a tort proceeding, and at this time one could not submit in the same proceeding claims in tort *and* contract.) Suppose that the contract had been properly sued upon. Was it enforceable? Would you consider such an agreement to be an "unlawful combination" under the doctrines of the *Cordwainer's case* or Commonwealth v. Carlisle? How do you suppose Justice Wilde would have disposed of a prosecution for a common-law conspiracy under the laws of Massachusetts? Can you discern the economic policies that might be behind Justice Wilde's ruling in *Binney*? Would they be in accordance with those of Recorder Levy and Judge Gibson? Does the Binney case favor the interests of the skilled worker? The employer? Both?

As you read the next two cases decided by Justice Shaw fifteen years later, see if you can discern his agreement or disagreement with the reasoning in these cases with regard to the importance of the free market and the proper solicitude to be shown to labor.

LEMUEL SHAW

SECTION C.   CHIEF JUSTICE SHAW ON LABOR LAW

FARWELL v. BOSTON AND WORCESTER RAIL ROAD CORP.

Supreme Judicial Court of Massachusetts, 1842.
45 Mass. (4 Metc.) 49.

* * *

The case was submitted to the court on the following facts agreed by the parties: "The plaintiff was employed by the defendants, in 1835, as an engineer, and went at first with the merchandize cars, and afterwards with the passenger cars, and so continued till October 30th 1837, at the wages of two dollars per day; that being the usual wages paid to engine-men, which are higher than the wages paid to a machinist, in which capacity the plaintiff formerly was employed.

"On the 30th of October 1837, the plaintiff * * * ran his engine off at a switch on the road, which had been left in a wrong condition * * * by one Whitcomb, another servant of the defendants, who had been long in their employment, as a switch-man or tender, and had the care of switches on the road, and was a careful and trustworthy servant, in his general character, and as such servant was well known to the plaintiff. By which running off, the plaintiff sustained the injury complained of in his declaration. [Loss of his right hand.]

* * *

C. G. Loring, for the plaintiff. The defendants, having employed the plaintiff to do a specified duty on the road, were bound to keep the road in such a condition that he might do that duty with safety. If the plaintiff had been a stranger, the defendants would have been liable; and he contends that the case is not varied by the fact that both the plaintiff and Whitcomb were the servants of the defendants; because the plaintiff was not the servant of the defendants in the duty or service, the neglect of which occasioned the injury sustained by him. He was employed for a distinct and separate service, and had no joint agency or power with the other servants whose duty it was to keep the road in order; and could not be made responsible to the defendants for its not being kept in order. He could not, by any vigilance or any power that he could exercise, have prevented the accident. His duties and those of Whitcomb were as distinct and independent of each other, as if they had been servants of different masters.

The plaintiff does not put his case on the ground of the defendants' liability to passengers, nor upon the general principle which renders principals liable for the acts of their agents; but on the ground, that a master, by the nature of his contract with a servant, stipulates for the safety of the servant's employment, so far as the master can regulate the matter.

The defence rests upon an alleged general rule, that a master is not liable to his servant for damage caused by the negligence of a fellow servant. But if that be sound, as a general rule, it does not apply here; for Whitcomb and the plaintiff, as has already been stated, were not fellow servants—that is, were not jointly employed for a common purpose.

* * *

No general rule can be laid down, which will apply to all cases of a master's liability to a servant. But it is submitted that a master is liable to one servant for the negligence of another, when they are engaged in distinct employments, though he is not so liable, where two servants are engaged jointly in the same service; because, in the latter case, each servant has some supervision and control of every other.

* * *

In case of servants jointly employed in the same business, it may reasonably be inferred that they take the hazard of injuries from each other's negligence; because such hazard is naturally and necessarily incident to such employment; because they have, to a great extent, the means of guarding against such injuries, by the exercise of mutual caution and prudence, while the master has no such means; and because, between persons employed in a joint service, there is a privity of contract, that renders them liable to each other for their carelessness or neglect in the discharge of such service.

It is a well settled general rule, that a servant is not liable to third persons for his neglect of duty. Story on Agency, §§ 308, 309. If that principle applies to this case, so that the plaintiff has no remedy against Whitcomb, it would seem to be a sufficient reason for holding the defendants liable.

It is also a well established rule, that if an agent, without his own default, has incurred loss or damage in transacting the business of the principal, he is entitled to full compensation. Story on Agency, § 339.

Fletcher & Morey, for the defendants. * * * [N]o rule of policy requires that masters shall be liable to one servant for injuries received by him from a fellow servant. On the contrary, policy requires an entirely different rule, especially in the present case. The aim of all the statutes concerning rail roads is to protect passengers; and if this action is maintained, it will establish a principle which will tend to diminish the caution of rail road servants, and thus increase the risk of passengers.

The defendants have been in no fault, in this case, either in the construction of their road, the use of defective engines, or the employment of careless or untrusty servants. So that the question is, whether they are liable to the plaintiff, on an implied contract of indemnity. The contract between the parties to this suit excludes the notion that the defendants are liable for the injury received by the plaintiff. He agreed to run an engine on their road, knowing the state of the road, and also knowing Whitcomb, his character, and the specific duty intrusted to him. The plaintiff therefore assumed the risks of the service which he undertook to perform; and one of those risks was his liability to injury from the carelessness of others who were employed by the defendants in the same service. As a consideration for the increased risk of this service, he received higher wages than when he was employed in a less hazardous business.

* * *

The only cases in which a servant has attempted to recover of a master for another servant's misconduct, are Priestley v. Fowler, 3 Mees. & Welsb. 1, and Murray v. South Carolina Rail Road Company, 1 McMullan, 385; and in both those cases, it was held that the action could not be maintained. In those cases, it is true that both servants were on the same carriage when the accident happened by which one of them was injured. And the counsel for the present plaintiff has invented a rule of law, in order to escape from the pressure of those decisions. But admitting the distinction, and the rule which he advances, to be sound, the case at bar is not thereby affected. The plaintiff and Whitcomb were not engaged in distinct and separate employments, but in the same service. They both were acting to the same end, although they had different parts to perform.

* * *

SHAW, C. J. This is an action of new impression in our courts, and involves a principle of great importance. It presents a case, where two persons are in the service and employment of one company, whose business it is to construct and maintain a rail road, and to employ their trains of cars to carry persons and merchandize for hire. They are appointed and employed by the same company to perform separate duties and services, all tending to the accomplishment of one and the same purpose—that of the safe and rapid transmission of the trains; and they are paid for their respective services according to the nature of their respective duties, and the labor and skill required for their proper performance. The question is, whether, for damages sustained by one of the persons so employed, by means of the carelessness and negligence of another, the party injured has a remedy against the common employer. It is an argument against such an action, though certainly not a decisive one, that no such action has before been maintained.

It is laid down by Blackstone, that if a servant, by his negligence, does any damage to a stranger, the master shall be answerable for his neglect. * * * 1 Bl.Com. 431. * * * This rule is obviously founded on the great principle of social duty, that every man, in the management of his own affairs, whether by himself or by his agents or servants, shall so conduct them as not to injure another; and if he does not, and another thereby sustains damage, he shall answer for it. * * * But this presupposes that the parties stand to each other in the relation of strangers, between whom there is no privity; and the action, in such case, is an action sounding in tort. * * *

But this does not apply to the case of a servant bringing his action against his own employer to recover damages for an injury arising in the course of that employment, where all such risks and perils as the employer and the servant respectively intend to assume and bear may be regulated by the express or implied contract between them, and which, in contemplation of law, must be presumed to be thus regulated.

The same view seems to have been taken by the learned counsel for the plaintiff in the argument * * *. The claim, therefore, is placed, and must be maintained, if maintained at all, on the ground of contract. As there is no express contract between the parties, applicable to this point, it is placed on the footing of an implied contract of indemnity, arising out of the relation of master and servant. It would be an implied promise, arising from the duty of the master to be responsible to each person employed by him * * * to pay for all damage occasioned by the negligence of every other person employed in the same service. If such a duty were established by law * * * it would be a rule of frequent and familiar occurrence, and its existence and application, with all its qualifications and restrictions, would be settled by judicial precedents. But we are of opinion that no such rule has been established, and the authorities, as far as they go, are opposed to the principle. Priestley v. Fowler, 3 Mees. & Welsb. 1.
* * *

The general rule, resulting from considerations as well of justice as of policy, is, that he who engages in the employment of another for the performance of specified duties and services, for compensation, takes upon himself the natural and ordinary risks and perils incident to the performance of such services, and in legal presumption, the compensation is adjusted accordingly. And we are not aware of any principle which should except the perils arising from the carelessness and negligence of those who are in the same employment. These are perils which the servant is as likely to know, and against which he can as effectually guard, as the master. They are perils incident to the service, and which can be as distinctly foreseen and provided for in the rate of compensation as any others. * * *

* * * In considering the rights and obligations arising out of particular relations, it is competent for courts of justice to regard considerations of policy and general convenience, and to draw from them such rules as will, in their practical application, best promote the safety and security of all parties concerned. This is, in truth, the basis on which implied promises are raised, being duties legally inferred from a consideration of what is best adapted to promote the benefit of all persons concerned, under given circumstances. To take the well known and familiar cases, * * * a common carrier, without

regard to actual fault or neglect in himself or his servants, is made liable for all losses of goods confided to him for carriage, except those caused by the act of God or of a public enemy, because he can best guard them against all minor dangers, and because, in case of actual loss, it would be extremely difficult for the owner to adduce proof of embezzlement, or other actual fault or neglect on the part of the carrier * * *. The risk is therefore thrown upon the carrier, and he receives, in the form of payment for the carriage, a premium for the risk which he thus assumes. So of an innkeeper; he can best secure the attendance of honest and faithful servants, and guard his house against thieves. Whereas, if he were responsible only upon proof of actual negligence, he might connive * * * and even participate in the embezzlement of the property of the guests, during the hours of their necessary sleep, and yet it would be difficult, and often impossible, to prove these facts.

The liability of passenger carriers is founded on similar considerations. They are held to the strictest responsibility for care, vigilance and skill, on the part of themselves and all persons employed by them, and they are paid accordingly. The rule is founded on the expediency of throwing the risk upon those who can best guard against it. Story on Bailments, § 590, & seq.

We are of opinion that these considerations apply strongly to the case in question. Where several persons are employed in the conduct of one common enterprise or undertaking, and the safety of each depends much on the care and skill with which each other shall perform his appropriate duty, each is an observer of the conduct of the others, can give notice of any misconduct, incapacity or neglect of duty, and leave the service, if the common employer will not take such precautions, and employ such agents as the safety of the whole party may require. By these means, the safety of each will be much more effectually secured, than could be done by a resort to the common employer for indemnity in case of loss by the negligence of each other. * * *

In applying these principles to the present case, it appears that the plaintiff was employed by the defendants as an engineer, at the rate of wages usually paid in that employment, being a higher rate than the plaintiff had before received as a machinist. It was a voluntary undertaking on his part, with a full knowledge of the risks incident to the employment; and the loss was sustained by means of an ordinary casualty, caused by the negligence of another servant of the company. Under these circumstances, the loss must be deemed to be the result of a pure accident, * * * and * * * it must rest where it first fell, unless the plaintiff has a remedy against the person actually in default; of which we give no opinion.

It was strongly pressed in the argument, that [this rule] could not apply where two or more are employed in different departments of duty, at a distance from each other, and where one can in no degree control or influence the conduct of another. But we think this is founded upon a supposed distinction, on which it would be extremely difficult to establish a practical rule. When the object to be accomplished is one and the same, when the employers are the same, and the several persons employed derive their authority and their compensation from the same source, it would be extremely difficult to distinguish, what constitutes one department and what a distinct department of duty. * * * If it were made to depend upon the nearness or distance of the persons from each other, the question would immediately arise, how near or how distant must they be, to be in the same or different departments. * * *

Besides, it appears to us, that the argument rests upon an assumed principle of responsibility which does not exist. The master, in the case supposed, is not exempt from liability, because the servant has better means of providing for his safety, when he is employed in immediate connexion with those from whose negligence he might suffer; but because the *implied contract* of the master does not extend to indemnify the servant against the negligence of any one but himself; and he is not liable in tort, as for the negligence of his servant, because the person suffering does not stand towards him in the relation of a stranger, but is one whose rights are regulated by contract express or implied. * * *

* * *

In coming to the conclusion that the plaintiff, in the present case, is not entitled to recover, considering it as in some measure a nice question, we would add a caution against any hasty conclusion as to the application of this rule to a case not fully within the same principle. * * * We are far from intending to say that there are no implied warranties and undertakings arising out of the relation of master and servant. Whether, for instance, the employer would be responsible to an engineer for a loss arising from a defective or ill-constructed steam engine: Whether this would depend upon an implied warranty of its goodness and sufficiency, or upon the fact of wilful misconduct, or gross negligence on the part of the employer * * * are questions on which we give no opinion. In the present case, the claim of the plaintiff is not put on the ground that the defendants did not furnish a sufficient engine, a proper rail road track, a well constructed switch, and a person of suitable skill and experience to attend it; the gravamen of the complaint is, that that person was chargeable with negligence in not changing the switch * * *. Upon this question, supposing the accident to have occurred, and the loss to have been caused, by the negligence of the person employed to attend to and change the switch, in his not doing so in the particular case, the court are of opinion that it is a loss for which the defendants are not liable, and that the action cannot be maintained.

Plaintiff nonsuit.

NOTES AND QUESTIONS

1. Note that as the plaintiff's attorney begins his argument he concedes that where two servants are in the *same* line of work for a common employer the employer is *not* liable for the damage caused one servant by the other. Why this concession? Why doesn't the plaintiff's attorney argue that the general rule of *respondeat superior* should apply in this situation?

2. Does Judge Shaw view this as a case of torts? What kind of a case is it, according to him? Is Shaw's view of the situation unprecedented? Can you make any comparisons between Shaw's analysis of this case and the case of the Sheriff who let his prisoner escape, Patten v. Halsted, supra page 313?

3. Judge Shaw says that considerations of "justice" lead him to conclude that fellow-servants such as Farwell and Whitcomb should not recover from their employers for each other's negligence. Why does Shaw believe that such a result is "just"? What does he understand the concept "justice" to mean? Shaw is not content to let his holding stand on considerations of "justice", however, but suggests also that the "policy" of protecting servants and passengers will best be served by his decision. How is that? And how does Judge Shaw deal with the plaintiff's argument that whatever the policy of cases like Priestly v. Fowler (the English case that established the fellow-servant rule), it is difficult to apply that policy to a situation where the servants are "in different departments of duty". Are you satisfied with Shaw's reasons for refusing to make this distinction?

4. Would you say that the opinion in *Farwell* is hostile to workers? Does Shaw suggest any circumstances under which the employer might be liable for the negligence of a fellow-servant? Roscoe Pound discusses Justice Shaw and the Farwell case in The Formative Era of American Law 86–87 (1938). Part of the purpose of Pound's book seems to be to refute a Marxist interpretation of the law. While he concedes that the *Farwell* decision might have sprung from the "pressure of new demands, problems created by the development of transportation, the effects of inventions, and the rise of industry * * * and * * * trade", this was *not* a reflection of the "Marxian class struggle" in the law. Id., at 86. The Marxists, suggested Pound, saw *Farwell's* reception of the English fellow-servant rule as "an arbitrary exception to a rule of law which expressed a fundamental and universal idea of justice". Here Pound was referring to the general doctrine of *respondeat superior*, from which *Farwell* was said by the Marxists to have departed. According to Pound, however, *Farwell* did not represent an "arbitrary departure", as the doctrine of *respondeat superior* was itself "an exception to a then generally received doctrine that liability must flow from fault." Shaw in *Farwell*, said Pound, merely "refused to extend further" this exception to the "no liability without fault" doctrine. Do you see the proposal for fellow-servant liability as a proposal to impose liability where there is no "fault"? What is meant by "fault" here? Furthermore, is Pound correct about the existence of a general doctrine of "no liability without fault?" Do the early trespass and nuisance cases we studied in Chapter III suggest the existence of such a doctrine?

5. The *Farwell* case outcome (implementation of the fellow-servant rule) obviously favored the defendant, the railroad. We have seen similar

protection of America's infant industries in Chapter III, in the materials on nuisance and negligence. For still another instance of the *respondeat superior* doctrine's failure to result in relief for negligence see Carey v. Berkshire Railroad Co., 55 Mass. (1 Cush.) 475 (1848). Employees of the railroad had negligently caused the deaths of the husband of one of the plaintiffs and the eleven-year-old son of another. Following a line of reasoning in English cases, the court appears to have held that the right to sue for tortious injury dies with the person injured, and neither plaintiff was allowed to recover. Two years prior to the case, "Lord Campbell's Act," 9 and 10 Vict. ch. 93, had provided such a cause of action in England, allowing the executor or administrator of persons killed by torts to bring actions for wrongful death for the benefit of the deceased's family. Eight years before the case, the Massachusetts legislature itself had provided for such an action in the case of *passengers* who lost their lives through the negligence of railroads, steamboats, or stagecoach proprietors or their agents, although such relief was limited to five thousand dollars. Massachusetts Statutes of 1840, ch. 80. The *Carey* court held that if an action for wrongful death in the circumstances of the case "would be expedient for us, it is for the legislature to make it." Is this a convincing argument? Why not extend the policy of the 1840 Massachusetts statute through the common law? Carey v. Berkshire R. R. was the "first distinct pronouncement by an American court that no cause of action for wrongful death exists at common law." Malone, The Genesis of Wrongful Death, 17 Stan. L.Rev. 1043, 1067 (1965). The prestige of the Massachusetts court led to its doctrine being widely accepted, but in the rest of the nineteenth century the states passed legislation permitting wrongful death claims of the type asserted in *Carey*. By 1883, in fact, Massachusetts appears to have weakened the rule in the *Farwell* case by passing a statute that gave relief to the families of railroad workers killed in their employment.

6. Does the doctrine of the *Carey* case, and the fellow-servant doctrine, which gained widespread American acceptance in the nineteenth century, reflect a general hostility on the part of the American common law to workers? In another line of cases, American unskilled laborers who had contracted to work for a certain contractual term (e. g. one year), were not allowed to recover for the value of work done (in *quantum meruit*) if they quit at any time before their terms expired. See, e. g. Stark v. Parker, 19 Mass. (2 Pick.) 267, but see Britton v. Turner, 6 N.H.Rep. (1st ser.) 481 (1834). In cases where contractors had failed to build houses "strictly according to contract, but still valuable and capable of being advantageously used or profitably rented," however, they were generally permitted to recover for the value of their performance, with the contract price as a ceiling, and with a deduction for any damages suffered by virtue of their failure to complete their contracts. See, e. g. Haywood v. Leonard, 24 Mass. (7 Pick.) 181 (1828). Why the difference in treatment? Morton Horwitz suggests that this is "an important example of class bias," and that nineteenth century common law doctrines "allowed judges to pick and choose among those groups in the population that would be its beneficiaries." The Transformation of American Law 1780–1860 188 (1977). Does Shaw's behavior as a judge support Horwitz's comments? Consider Shaw's opinion in the next case.

COMMONWEALTH v. HUNT

Supreme Judicial Court of Massachusetts, 1842.
45 Mass. (4 Metc.) 111.

This was an indictment against the defendants, (seven in number,) for a conspiracy. The first count alleged that the defendants * * * "on the first Monday of September 1840, at Boston, being workmen and journeymen in the art and manual occupation of bootmakers, unlawfully, perniciously and deceitfully designing and intending to continue, keep up, form, and unite themselves into an unlawful club, society and combination * * * and thereby govern themselves and other workmen in said art, and unlawfully and unjustly to extort great sums of money by means thereof, did * * * unjustly and corruptly combine, confederate and agree together, * * * that none of them would work for any master or person * * * who should employ any workman or journeyman * * * who was not a member of said club, society or combination, after notice given him to discharge such workman from the employ of such master; to the great damage and oppression, not only of their said masters employing them in said art and occupation, but also of divers other workmen and journeymen * * * to the evil example of all others in like case offending, and against the peace and dignity of the Commonwealth."

The second count charged that the defendants * * * did compel one Isaac B. Wait, a master cordwainer in said Boston, to turn out of his employ one Jeremiah Horne, a journeyman boot-maker, because said Horne would not pay a sum of money to said society for an alleged penalty of some of [its] unjust rules, orders and by-laws."

The third count averred that the defendants * * * [did] unlawfully and indirectly prevent him, the said Horne, from following his said art, occupation, trade and business, and did greatly impoverish him."

* * *

The defendants were found guilty, at the October term, 1840, of the municipal court, and thereupon several exceptions were alleged by them to the ruling of the judge at the trial. * * * "The defendants' counsel contended that the indictment did not set forth any agreement to do a criminal act, or to do any lawful act by criminal means; and that the agreements, therein set forth, did not constitute a conspiracy indictable by any law of this Commonwealth; and they moved the court so to instruct the jury: But the judge refused so to do, and instructed the jury that the indictment against the defendants did, in his opinion, describe a confederacy among the defendants to do an unlawful act, and to effect the same by unlawful means * * *.

* * *

Rantoul, for the defendants. As we have no statute concerning conspiracy, the facts alleged in the indictment constitute an offence, if any, at common law. But the English common law of conspiracy is not in force in this State. * * * So much only of the common law has been adopted, as is applicable to our situation, excluding "the artificial refinements and distinctions incident to the property of a great commercial people; the laws of revenue and police; such especially as are enforced by penalties." 1 Bl.Com. 107, & seq. 1 Tucker's Black. Appx. 406. * * * The English law, as to acts in restraint of trade, is generally local in its nature, and not suited to our condition. It has never been adopted here, and the colonies are not named in the statutes on that subject which have been passed in England since they were settled. Van Ness v. Pacard, 2 Pet. 144. * * * [T]he innumerable statutes of laborers, and the statutes against seducing artisans, &c. illustrate this point. All the law we ever had on these subjects was domestic, and is now obsolete. * * *

The original of the law of conspiracy is in St. Edw. I., (A.D. 1304) and includes in its definition only false and malicious indictments. 2 Inst. 561, 562. * * *

The next stage of the law of conspiracy appears in the early editions of 1 Hawk. c. 72, § 2: "That all confederacies wrongfully to prejudice a third person are criminal at common law; as a confederacy by indirect means to impoverish a third person, or falsely and maliciously to charge a man with being the reputed father of a bastard child * * *. By "indirect means," unlawful means are meant.

The case of The King v. Journeymen Tailors, 8 Mod. 10 [K.B. 1721], was decided after Hawkins's work was published, and is not a part of the law laid down by him, in his first editions. In that case, it was held that a conspiracy among workmen, to refuse to work under certain wages, is an indictable offence. This case, if correctly reported, introduced new law, unless it was decided on the statutes of laborers. * * * The doctrine of that case, therefore, is not a part of the law adopted in this State. It was not the doctrine of the common law, when our ancestors came hither, and is not suited to our condition.

* * *

Probably the indictment, in that case, was sustained on the statutes of laborers. Though the old precedents of indictments are *contra pacem* only, yet that is because a conspiracy to do acts contrary to those statutes is punishable at common law, in England. * * *

The statutes of laborers were blind struggles of the feudal nobles to avert from themselves the effects of great national calamities. * * * In the famine of 1315, and the plague of 1316, parliament vainly strove to alleviate the universal distress, by fixing a legal price for provisions. Yet the scarcity increased, so that the king, going to St. Albans, "had much ado to get victuals to sustain his family." 1

Parl. Hist. 152. And some months later, mothers ate their children. Monk of Malmsb. 166. * * * From the same motives, and with no better success, the plague of 1349 was followed by that remarkable statute *de servientibus*, from which have been derived all subsequent statutes of laborers. * * * The deaths in London were mostly of the laboring classes * * *. King Edward had just been debasing his coin. * * * From these causes, the wages of labor rose rapidly, and the law undertook to fix them. * * *

The case in 8 Mod. 10, was about the time of the bursting of the south sea bubble, when laborers sought to withstand the operation of the state of affairs then existing.

* * *

In most of the United States, conspiracies, that have been held indictable at common law, are all for acts that are indictable, immoral, or forbidden by statute. * * *

In New York and Massachusetts, the cases have gone further; and in Commonwealth v. Judd, 2 Mass. 337, Parsons, C.J. says a conspiracy is "the unlawful act for unlawful purposes." And all the Massachusetts cases come within this definition. * * *

A conspiracy to commit a mere civil injury to an individual is not indictable. * * * Yet nothing more is properly alleged against the present defendants.

A conspiracy to raise wages would not be indictable in England, if it were not unlawful for an individual to attempt to raise his wages. And the indictment, in the case at bar, is bad, because each of the defendants had a right to do that which is charged against them jointly.

* * *

Austin, (Attorney General,) for the Commonwealth. The common law doctrine of conspiracy is part of the law of this Commonwealth. It has been recognized by the legislature, in Rev.Sts. c. 82, § 28, and c. 86, § 10; and was long since enforced by this court. * *

The charge against the defendants is, in effect, an attempt to monopolize by them certain labor, on their own terms, and to prevent others from obtaining or giving employment. This is an indictable offence. Rex v. Bykerdike, 1 M. & Rob. 179. 3 Chit.Crim.Law, 1138, & seq. * * *

The case in 8 Mod. 10 * * * shows the fact, that defendants were convicted of an offence like that with which the present defendants are charged * * *.

The old statutes of laborers, which have been referred to, do not at all affect the common law doctrine. No reference is made to them in the English books of criminal law, or in the reports of the cases of conspiracy by workmen.

A conspiracy to raise wages is indictable in England, not because it is unlawful for an individual to attempt to raise his wages—as the defendants' counsel suggests—but because a combination for that purpose is criminal and punishable. * * *

                              * * *

It is not necessary, in order to render a conspiracy indictable, that the means, devised to carry it into effect, should be acts that are indictable. It is sufficient if they are unlawful. * * *

The People v. Fisher, 14 Wend. 1, is a strong authority in support of the present indictment. It is true that it was under the revised statutes of New York, and proceeded on the ground that the conspiracy was "injurious to trade or commerce." But the question, what is injurious to trade or commerce, is to be determined by the common law.

SHAW, C. J. * * *

We have no doubt, that by the operation of the constitution of this Commonwealth, the general rules of the common law, making conspiracy an indictable offence, are in force here * * *. It was so held in Commonwealth v. Boynton, and Commonwealth v. Pierpont, cases decided before reports of cases were regularly published, and in many cases since. * * * Still, it is proper in this connexion to remark, that although the common law in regard to conspiracy in this Commonwealth is in force, yet it will not necessarily follow that every indictment at common law for this offence is a precedent for a similar indictment in this State. The general rule of the common law is, that it is a criminal and indictable offence, for two or more to confederate and combine together, by concerted means, to do that which is unlawful or criminal, to the injury of the public, or portions or classes of the community, or even to the rights of an individual. This rule of law may be equally in force as a rule of the common law, in England, and in this Commonwealth; and yet it must depend upon the local laws of each country to determine, whether the purpose to be accomplished by the combination, or the concerted means of accomplishing it, be unlawful or criminal in the respective countries. All those laws of the parent country, whether rules of the common law, or early English statutes, which were made for the purpose of regulating the wages of laborers, the settlement of paupers, and making it penal for any one to use a trade or handicraft to which he had not served a full apprenticeship—not being adapted to the circumstances of our colonial condition—were not adopted, used or approved, and therefore [are not in force here.] * * * The King v. Journeymen Tailors of Cambridge, 8 Mod. 10, for instance, is commonly cited as an authority for an indictment at common law, and a conviction of journeymen mechanics of a conspiracy to raise their wages. It was there held, that the indictment need not conclude *contra forman statuti*, because the gist of the offence was the conspiracy, which was an offence at common law. At the same time it was conceded, that the unlawful object to be accomplished was the raising of wages above the rate fixed by a general act of parliament. It was therefore a conspiracy to violate a general statute law * * * and thus the object to be accomplished by the conspiracy was unlawful, if not criminal.

* * *

Let us, then, first consider how the subject of criminal conspiracy is treated by elementary writers. The position cited by Chitty from Hawkins, by way of summing up the result of the cases, is this: "In a word, all confederacies wrongfully to prejudice another are misdemeanors at common law, whether the intention is to injure his property, his person, or his character." And Chitty adds, that "the object of conspiracy is not confined to an immediate wrong to individuals; it may be to injure public trade, to affect public health, to violate public policy, to insult public justice, or to do any act in itself illegal." 3 Chit.Crim.Law, 1139.

* * *

From these views * * * it appears to us to follow, as a necessary legal conclusion, that when the criminality of a conspiracy consists in an unlawful agreement of two or more persons to compass or promote some criminal or illegal purpose, that purpose must be fully and clearly stated in the indictment; and if the criminality of the offence, which is intended to be charged, consists in the agreement to compass or promote some purpose, not of itself criminal or unlawful, by the use of fraud, force, falsehood, or other criminal or unlawful means, such intended use of fraud, force, falsehood, or other criminal or unlawful means, must be set out in the indictment. * * *

In the case of a conspiracy to induce a person to marry a pauper, in order to change the burden of her support from one parish to another, it was held by Buller, J. that, as the marriage itself was not unlawful, some violence, fraud or falsehood, or some artful or sinister contrivance must be averred, as the means intended to be employed to effect the marriage, in order to make the agreement indictable as a conspiracy. Rex v. Fowler, 2 Russell on Crimes, (1st ed.) 1812. S.C. 1 East P.C. 461.

* * *

With these general views of the law, it becomes necessary to consider the circumstances of the present case, as they appear from the indictment itself, and from the bill of exceptions filed and allowed.

One of the exceptions, though not the first in the order of time, yet by far the most important, was this:

The counsel for the defendants contended, and requested the court to instruct the jury, that the indictment did not set forth any agreement to do a criminal act, or to do any lawful act by any specified criminal means, and that the agreements therein set forth did not constitute a conspiracy indictable by any law of this Commonwealth. But the judge refused so to do * * *.

We are here carefully to distinguish between the confederacy set forth in the indictment, and the confederacy or association contained in the constitution of the Boston Journeymen Bootmakers' Society, as stated in the little printed book, which was admitted as evidence on the trial. Because, though it was thus admitted as evidence, it would not warrant a conviction for any thing not stated in the indictment. It was proof, as far as it went to support the averments in the indictment. If it contained any criminal matter not set forth in the indictment, it is of no avail. * * *

* * *

Now it is to be considered, that the preamble and introductory matter in the indictment—such as unlawfully and deceitfully designing and intending unjustly to extort great sums, &c.—is mere recital, and not traversable, and therefore cannot aid an imperfect averment of the facts constituting the description of the offence. The same may be said of the concluding matter, which follows the averment, as to the great damage and oppression not only of their said masters, employing them in said art and occupation, but also of divers other workmen in the same art, mystery and occupation, to the evil example, &c. If the facts averred constitute the crime, these are properly stated as the legal inferences to be drawn from them. If they do not constitute the charge of such an offence, they cannot be aided by these alleged consequences.

Stripped then of these introductory recitals and alleged injurious consequences, and of the qualifying epithets attached to the facts, the averment is this; that the defendants and others formed themselves into a society, and agreed not to work for any person, who should employ any journeyman or other person, not a member of such society, after notice given him to discharge such workman.

The manifest intent of the association is, to induce all those engaged in the same occupation to become members of it. Such a purpose is not unlawful. It would give them a power which might be exerted for useful and honorable purposes, or for dangerous and pernicious ones. If the latter were the real and actual object, and susceptible of proof, it should have been specially charged. Such an association might be used to afford each other assistance in times of poverty, sickness and distress; or to raise their intellectual, moral and social condition; or to make improvement in their art; or for other proper purposes. Or the association might be designed for purposes of oppression and injustice. But in order to charge all those, who become members of an association, with the guilt of a criminal conspiracy, it must be averred and proved that the actual, if not the avowed object of the association, was criminal. * * *

Nor can we perceive that the objects of this association whatever they may have been, were to be attained by criminal means. The means which they proposed to employ * * * were, that they would not work for a person, who, after due notice, should employ a journeyman not a member of their society. Supposing the object of the association to be laudable and lawful, or at least not unlawful, are these means criminal? The case supposes that these persons are not bound by contract, but free to work for whom they please, or not to work, if they so prefer. In this state of things, we cannot perceive, that it is criminal for men to agree together to exercise their own acknowledged rights, in such a manner as best to subserve their own interests. One way to test this is, to consider the effect of such an agreement, where the object of the association is acknowledged on all hands to be a laudable one. Suppose a class of workmen, impressed with the manifold evils of intemperance, should agree with each other not to work in a shop in which ardent spirit was furnished, or not to work in a shop with any one who used it, or not to work for an employer, who should, after notice, employ a journeyman who habitually used it. The consequences might be the same. A workman, who, should still persist in the use of ardent spirit, would find it more difficult to get employment; a master employing such an one might, at times, experience inconvenience in his work, in losing the services of a skilful but intemperate workman. Still it seems to us, that as the object would be lawful, and the means not unlawful, such an agreement could not be pronounced a criminal conspiracy.

* * * If a large number of men, engaged for a certain time, should combine together to violate their contract, and quit their employment together, it would present a very different question. Suppose a farmer, employing a large number of men, engaged for the year, at fair monthly wages, and suppose that just at the moment that his crops were ready to harvest, they should all combine to quit his service, unless he would advance their wages, at a time when other laborers could not be obtained. It would surely be a conspiracy to do an unlawful act, though of such a character, that if done by an individual, it would lay the foundation of a civil action only, and not of a criminal prosecution. * * *

The second count * * * alleges that the defendants * * * did assemble, conspire, confederate and agree together, not to work for any master or person who should employ any workman not being a member of a certain club, society or combination, called the Boston Journeymen Bootmaker's Society, or who should break any of their by-laws [and to] compel one Isaac B. Wait, a master cordwainer, to turn out of his employ one Jeremiah Horne * * *. So far as the averment of a conspiracy is concerned, all the remarks made in reference to the first count are equally applicable to this. * * * It was an agreement, as to the manner in which they would exercise an acknowledged right to contract with others for their labor. It does not aver a conspiracy or even an intention to raise their wages; and it appears by the bill of exceptions, that the case was not put upon the footing of a conspiracy to raise their wages. Such an agreement, as set forth in this count, would be perfectly justifiable under the recent English statute, by which this subject is regulated. * * *

As to the latter part of this count, which avers that by means of said conspiracy, the defendants did compel one Wait to turn out of his employ one Jeremiah Horne * * *; if this is to be considered as a substantive charge, it would depend altogether upon the force of the word "compel," which may be used in the sense of coercion, or duress, by force or fraud. * * * If, for instance, the indictment had averred a conspiracy, by the defendants, to compel Wait to turn Horne out of his employment, and to accomplish that object by the use of force or fraud, it would have been a very different case; especially if it might be fairly construed, as perhaps in that case it might have been, that Wait was under obligation, by contract, for an unexpired term of time, to employ and pay Horne. * * * To mark the difference between the case of a journeyman or a servant and master, mutually bound by contract, and the same parties when free to engage anew, I should have before cited the case of the Boston Glass Co. v. Binney, 4 Pick. 425. In that case, it was held actionable to entice another person's hired servant to quit his employment, during the time for which he was engaged; but not actionable to treat with such hired servant, whilst actually hired and employed by another, to leave his service, and engage in the employment of the person making the proposal, when the term for which he is engaged shall expire. It acknowledges the established principle, that every free man, whether skilled laborer, mechanic, farmer or domestic servant, may work or not work, or work or refuse to work with any company or individual, at his own option, except so far as he is bound by contract. But whatever might be the force of the word "compel," unexplained by its connexion, it is disarmed and rendered harmless by the precise statement of the means, by which such compulsion was to be effected. It was the agreement not to work for him, by which they compelled Wait to decline employing Horne longer. * * *

* * *

If the fact of depriving Jeremiah Horne of the profits of his business, by whatever means it might be done, would be unlawful and criminal, a combination to compass that object would be an unlawful conspiracy, and it would be unnecessary to state the means. * * *

Suppose a baker in a small village had the exclusive custom of his neighborhood, and was making large profits by the sale of his bread. Supposing a number of those neighbors, believing the price of his bread too high, should propose to him to reduce his prices, or if he did not, that they would introduce another baker; and on his refusal, such other baker should, under their encouragement, set up a rival establishment, and sell his bread at lower prices; the effect would be to diminish the profit of the former baker, and to the same extent to impoverish him. And it might be said and proved, that the purpose of the associates was to diminish his profits, and thus impoverish him, though the ultimate and laudable object of the combination was to reduce the cost of bread to themselves and their neighbors. The same thing may be said of all competition in every branch of trade and industry; and yet it is through that competition, that the best interests of trade and industry are promoted. It is scarcely necessary to allude to the familiar instances of opposition lines of conveyance, rival hotels, and the thousand other instances, where each strives to gain custom to himself, by ingenious improvements, by increased industry, and by all the means by which he may lessen the price of commodities, and thereby diminish the profits of others.

We think, therefore, that associations may be entered into, the object of which is to adopt measures that may have a tendency to impoverish another, that is, to diminish his gains and profits, and yet so far from being criminal or unlawful, the object may be highly meritorious and public spirited. The legality of such an association will therefore depend upon the means to be used for its accomplishment. If it is to be carried into effect by fair or honorable and lawful means, it is, to say the least, innocent; if by falsehood or force, it may be stamped with the character of conspiracy. It follows as a necessary consequence, that if criminal and indictable, it is so by reason of the criminal means intended to be employed for its accomplishment; and as a further legal consequence, that as the criminality will depend on the means, those means must be stated in the indictment.   *   *   *

*   *   *

One case was cited, which was supposed to be much in point, and which is certainly deserving of great respect. The People v. Fisher, 14 Wend. 1. But it is obvious, that this decision was founded on the construction of the revised statutes of New York, by which this matter of conspiracy is now regulated. It was a conspiracy by journeymen to raise their wages, and it was decided to be a violation of the statutes, making it criminal to commit any act injurious to trade or commerce. It has, therefore, an indirect application only to the present case.

*   *   *

*   *   *   [L]ooking solely at the indictment, disregarding the qualifying epithets, recitals and immaterial allegations, and confining ourselves to facts so averred as to be capable of being traversed and put in issue, we cannot perceive that it charges a criminal conspiracy punishable by law. The exceptions must, therefore, be sustained, and the judgment arrested.

*   *   *

NOTES AND QUESTIONS

1. Does Shaw's opinion in this case seem consistent with his opinion in Farwell? Roscoe Pound suggests that the "Marxist economic determinists" have a difficult time reconciling the decision in *Farwell* with the

decision in Commonwealth v. Hunt, and that they are forced to conclude that the latter decision was "dictated" by "fear of a radical movement in politics." They reached such a conclusion, said Pound, because "It seems to be impossible for a Marxian economic determinist to comprehend an honest man." Formative Era of American Law, at 88. What do you suppose Pound meant by that? Pound's attack seems aimed principally at Yale's Professor Walter Nelles. See Nelles, "Commonwealth v. Hunt," 32 Col.L.Rev. 1128 (1932), and, for Nelles's views on the economic determinants of the *Philadelphia Cordwainers'* case, see The First American Labor Case 41 Yale L.J. 165 (1931).

2. Note that Robert Rantoul is the counsel for the defendants. Given the excerpt from his oration, supra page 266, would you have expected to see him appearing as defense counsel here? Is the argument he advances consistent with his oration? Note that among the cases Rantoul cites in support of his argument that the English common law of conspiracy is not in force in Massachusetts in Story's opinion in Van Ness v. Pacard, supra page 301. What's the connection? Why does Rantoul find it necessary to tell the court that during the plague of 1316, following the famine of 1315, "mothers ate their children?" What kind of an authority is "Monk of Malmsb.?"

3. Does the attorney general, in his argument in support of the indictment, suggest that it would have been unlawful for the defendants, acting individually, to seek to raise their wages? If not, how does he explain why it becomes unlawful when organized groups seek to raise their wages? Would Recorder Levy and Justice Gibson have agreed? Did Shaw agree with the assertion that the doing of a lawful act, attempting to raise wages, automatically becomes a conspiracy when wage raises are sought, in concert, by groups?

4. Shaw holds that the "manifest intent" of the Journeymen bootmakers' association "is to induce all those engaged in the same occupation to become members of it. Such a purpose is not unlawful." Why not? Does Shaw cite any authority to support this proposition? Is Shaw's holding consistent with the case of the Philadelphia Cordwainers? Shaw says that the association might be used for "useful and honorable purposes, or for dangerous and pernicious ones," but that unless there was proof offered that the association was formed for bad purposes, or that illegal acts were taken to accomplish legal aims, there could be no finding of conspiracy. Commonwealth v. Hunt is Shaw's "best known and most widely praised opinion," and is "the Magna Charta of American trade unionism, for it removed the stigma of criminality from labor organizations." Leonard W. Levy, The Law of the Commonwealth and Chief Justice Shaw 183 (1957). Does Shaw's holding cover the case of employees *under contract* who go out on strike? Why or why not? When would employees be regarded by Shaw as under contract? Does the *Farwell* case give you any guidance here?

5. Whether or not the "Marxist economic determinists" were right about Shaw, the *Farwell* case does seem to be anti-labor, and the *Hunt* case seems pro-labor. Pound and the Marxists both found it necessary to "explain" this seeming inconsistency, and they have not been alone. In his biography of Chief Justice Shaw, The Law of the Commonwealth

and Chief Justice Shaw (1957), Leonard Levy advances several reasons for the decision in Commonwealth v. Hunt. First, says Levy, Shaw might have been seeking to respond to the movement for codification of the common law. Id., at 196. Second, notes Levy, quoting Pound, Shaw may have been simply following "received professional ideals of the social order in America." Id., at 202. And third, as the most "plausible if not a watertight explanation of Commonwealth v. Hunt", Levy suggests that Shaw may simply have believed that "combinations, whether by entrepeneurs or workers," were "inherent in a free, competitive society," and would contribute toward "social gain." Id., at 203. How would you argue in support of or against each of these three propositions? Do you see any links between *Charles River Bridge* and Commonwealth v. Hunt?

6. We will soon see whether Shaw's sanguine views on labor unions prevailed in the late nineteenth century, but before we are able to do that, we must explore the late-nineteenth century consequences of the view that "combinations * * * of entrepreneurs" were "inherent in a free competitive society," and determine whether such combinations were thought to have contributed to "social gain."

SECTION D.   THE TRUSTS AND THE SHERMAN ACT (1890)

---

1.   INTRODUCTION

The rhythm of American life changed profoundly after the Civil War. The American economy continued to grow; it was during these years that new national wealth transformed America into a significant political and economic world power. Yet American society between 1865 and 1915 exhibited stark contrasts. A few men, like John D. Rockefeller, grew almost unspeakably rich, and only after the civil war can we identify a "class" of millionaires. Many more men and women experienced economic uncertainty and powerlessness as part of a vast new industrial work force. At the same time, a growing minority were entering the ranks of white-collar respectability. This new middle class, comprised of legions of clerks, business managers, technicians, scientific experts, educators, doctors, and lawyers were the product of an urban industrial society, and upon them that society eventually came to depend.

The American Civil War may well have been the most cataclysmic event in American history, and it fundamentally altered the shape and direction of society. Years of waging war steeled the American spirit, and conditioned many to believe that immense sacrifice was a normal and necessary feature of life. This dark world view was congenial to the growth of scientific Darwinism in America after the war, and acceptance of its principles of "evolution" and "survival of the fittest." At the same time, many influential business and political figures subscribed to "social Darwinism," and its similar tenets, among which was the virtual relegation of government to bystander status in the economy. This perspective is also seen in the new pragmatism of American thought, where the result often justified the means, and in the naturalism and realism of American literature and art. The war left in its wake, then, a coldness to humanistic idealism that posed the most serious challenge yet to American principles of freedom, justice and equality.

The Civil War also left a legacy of economic organization and efficiency. Waging "total war" placed novel demands on government, in both the North and South. Managing resources, disciplining the military and civilian populations, coordinating industry, and harnessing the new technology and the transportation network to the war effort were achievements on an unparalled scale, requiring new sophistication in administration and consolidation. Ulysses S. Grant had led the North to victory not because of his skills as a tactician (he lost most of his battles), but because of his superior organizational ability and his brutal efficiency. The success of the North's military and civilian effort also resulted in the clear supremacy of the Federal Government. The Era of Reconstruction which followed marked the emergence of a truly *national* government capable of promulgating a unified *national* policy. The completed shift of the political centers of gravity, from the local to the state and national, mirrored the growing consolidation of many sectors of society after the war. The new modes of organization and operation appeared in areas as diverse as philanthropy and business. Doing-good, for example, increasingly became the domain of large-scale social and governmental organizations. The corporate philanthropic foundation, the modern hospital, the state and federal departments and bureaus of health and welfare were post-war creations. The trend toward vertical integration in industry, most notable in oil and beef processing, was applauded by many businessmen and social Darwinists as an advance over the chaos and unregulated competition of the free market. Stressing control, rationalization, consolidation and planning, these new large-scale industries, like government, exercised a truly national influence.

By about 1890, these massive changes were attended by a kind of crisis of national will. While power continued to gravitate away from town and county, there existed an uncertainty within the central government as to how to exercise national or state power. This malaise was in part the result of the awesomeness of problems that now were perceived as interconnected and national in scope, problems thought not to be susceptible to traditional solutions. The difficulties were also the result of deeper causes. Indeed, Americans seemed unsure about which of two models of civic culture should be embraced: that of the pre-war years, predominantly preindustrial and emphasizing limited government and personal liberty, or that of the Civil War and Reconstruction Eras which saw the expansion of central power and the emphasis on the rights of groups. There was no clear popular consensus that could guide government. Legislators and judges were whipsawed between conflicting demands produced as a result of growing class divisions. Huge corporations with almost limitless capital were expanding and gobbling up competition in quest of greater profits, and corporate minions applied legal and illegal pressures to government officials. At the same time, a growing proletariat, swelling the cities, working the factories, and chafing under the often harsh restraints of the new industrialism seemed to pose a potential threat to order, stability and prosperity. Squeezed between capital and labor was the voluble middle class, intent on preserving its prosperity and mobility, and eager to accentuate its power and influence. Also expressing heightened concern were American farmers, whose ranks still included 42% of the gainfully employed, and who found themselves suffering from lower prices offered by newly consolidated large-scale processors of raw materials, like the "cattle trust," the "linseed oil" and the "cotton oil trusts," and the higher costs of consumer goods and farming needs charged by such organizations as the "Jute Bag Trust," "the Standard Oil Trust", and the "Sugar Trust." Many of these farmers formed themselves into "Granges," local cooperatives and organizations. They, too, agitated for governmental reforms, not only to control the trusts, but also to reform the tax and transportation systems.

The so-called "Populist Revolt," coming out of the agrarian West and South, was directed at railroads, large corporate middlemen, and a government that failed to act. The growth of the Knights of Labor in 1878, the first attempt at establishing a national trade union, demonstrated the desire of workers to gain more control over their lives. The growth of the new professional organizations, such as the American Bar Association and the National Education Association, signaled the stirrings of the new "middle" class of experts who, like the laborers and the farmers, were in the process of organizing for national action. Even Businessmen moved to promote their interests, when, in 1895, they founded the National Association of Manufacturers.

Intellectually, Americans during this decade were breaking the grip of a post-war psychology. In the words of Eric Goldman, they were bursting the "steel chain of ideas" where laissez-faire thinking, buttressed by social Darwinism, tended to resist the expansion of regulatory government. Robert Wiebe has described these turn-of-the-century years as a "search for order." In this atmosphere, in 1889 and 1890, the United States Congress debated proposals for some national regulation of the economy, which debates we consider next. Still unclear was the role which the state and federal courts would play in this new national government.

Those wishing to pursue studies of the post-war era should consult Robert H. Wiebe, The Search for Order (1968). Morton Keller's recent study, Affairs of State (1978) examines the tensions between a preindustrial and industrial ethic as they related to the growth of the public sector. The clash between laissez-faire conservatism and liberal progressive reform is treated in Sidney Fine, Laissez-Faire and the General Welfare (1956) and Robert McCloskey, Conservatism in the Age of Enterprise (1951). The best single study of social Darwinism and its hold on American academic, intellectual and political life is Richard Hofstadter, Social Darwinism in American Thought (1945). The early chapters of Alfred D. Chandler, Jr., Strategy and Structure: Chapters in the History of American Industrial Enterprise (1966) describe the evolution of the internal structure of the giant business corporation in the Gilded Age. On the plight of labor in the new industrial society, see the relevant chapters in John A. Garraty, The New Commonwealth, 1877–90 (1968) and Samuel P. Hays, The Response to Industrialism (1957). The influence of the Civil War on a generation of American literature and values is brilliantly portrayed by George Frederickson, The Inner Civil War (1965) and Edmund Wilson, Patriotic Gore (1962). The growth of American nationalism after the Civil War can be found in Hans Kohn's American Nationalism (1957). A good overview of the agrarian Populist movement, and its discontents, is still John D. Hicks, Populist Revolt (1931).

2. THE PASSAGE OF THE SHERMAN ACT (1890)

ALBERT H. WALKER, HISTORY OF THE SHERMAN LAW OF THE UNITED STATES OF AMERICA

1–46 (1910).

[1. *The Sherman Bill*]

John Sherman during his life passed through a career of public service, which in continuous length and great value has never been equalled by any other American. That career began when he took the oath of office as a member of Congress in December, 1855, and it continued without any interruption until he resigned the office of Secretary of State forty-three years later * * *. During thirty-two of the intervening years he was a United States Senator from Ohio * * *. [H]e was generally and, indeed, uniformly reputed to be the ablest and most influential financial statesman in this country. * *

It was this influential statesman who, * * * on December 4, 1889, introduced Senate Bill No. 1 of that Congress, which bill he entitled, "A bill to declare unlawful, trusts and combinations in restraint of trade and production."

* * *

That Sherman bill of 1889, though never enacted into law, deserves to be read, analyzed and understood because its provisions, when considered in connection with the four months of consideration which it received in the Senate, furnish several valuable guides to the Congressional intention which was finally expressed in the Sherman law of July 2, 1890.

The Sherman bill of December 4, 1889, was as follows:

"Be it enacted by the Senate and House of Representatives of the United States of America in Congress assembled:

Sec. 1.   That all arrangements, contracts, agreements, trusts, or combinations between persons or corporations made with a view or which tend to prevent full and free competition in the importation, transportation or sale of articles imported into the United States, or in the production, manufacture, or sale of articles of domestic growth or production, or domestic raw material that competes with any similar article upon which a duty is levied by the United States, or which shall be transported from one State or Territory to another, and all arrangements, contracts, agreements, trusts or combinations between persons or corporations, designed or which tend to advance the cost to the consumer of any such articles, are hereby declared to be against public policy, unlawful and void.

Sec. 2.   That any person or corporation, injured or damnified by such arrangement, contract, agreement, trust or combination, may sue for and recover in any court of the United States of competent jurisdiction, of any person or corporation a party to a combination described in the first section of this act, the full consideration or sum paid by him for any goods, wares and merchandise included in or advanced in price by said combination.

Sec. 3.   That all persons entering into any such arrangement, contract, agreement, trust or combination, described in section 1 of this act, either on his own account or as an agent or attorney for another, or as an officer, agent or stockholder of any corporation, or as a trustee, committee or in any capacity whatever, shall be guilty of a high misdemeanor, and on conviction thereof in any district or circuit court of the United States, shall be subject to a fine of not more than $10,000, or to imprisonment in the penitentiary for a term of not more than five years, or both such fine and imprisonment, in the discretion of the court.   And it shall be the duty of the District Attorney of the United States of the district in which such persons reside, to institute the proper proceedings to enforce the provisions of this act."

*   *   *

It was Senator Sherman's opinion that the commerce clause of the Constitution justified all parts of Section 1 of the Sherman bill. *   *   *

*   *   *   [I]t is apparent that he wished to prohibit all decreases of competition and all increases of prices in respect of the transportation and also the sale of as many classes or articles as possible, so far as such decrease of competition or increase of prices might result from combinations between a plurality of persons   *   *   *.

* * *

[We turn next to consideration of the bill on the floor of the Senate, beginning with the remarks of Senator George, of Mississippi, February 27, 1890.]

Senator George began his speech by saying that he regarded legislation on the subject of this bill as probably the most important to be considered by the Fifty-first Congress, for which reason he had prepared with particular care the remarks which he proposed to submit to the Senate in opposition to the bill as it then stood * * *.

* * * Senator George took the ground that the bill was unconstitutional for several reasons, including the fact that it proposed to regulate not only interstate and foreign commerce, but also to regulate, under some circumstances, manufacture or other production within individual states, of some classes of commodities. * * * [He also] took the ground that the bill was inefficient, because while it proposed to prohibit "arrangements, contracts, agreements, trusts or combinations" that prohibition was confined, as Senator George thought, to plans to decrease competition or increase prices, and did not include any overt acts done in pursuance of those plans. In accordance with this view, Senator George argued that representatives of corporations or other persons might go to Canada or to any other foreign country, and there [plan to] * * * decrease competition or increase prices without violating the bill, because the bill if enacted into law would not be in force in Canada; and that having thus made their plans, they might return to the United States and execute those plans here without violating that bill * * *.

* * *

[On March 21, 1890, Sherman addressed the Senate generally on antitrust, and in particular on his bill.]

Speaking of Section 1 of the original Sherman bill, Senator Sherman said: "This section will enable the courts of the United States to restrain, limit and control such combinations as interfere injuriously with our foreign and interstate commerce to the same extent that the state courts habitually control such combinations as interfere with the commerce of the state;" and that "The first section being a remedial statute, would be construed liberally with a view to promote its object. It defines a civil remedy and the courts will construe it liberally; they will prescribe the precise limits of the constitutional power of the Government. They will distinguish between lawful combinations in aid of production, and unlawful combinations to prevent competition and in restraint of trade; they can operate on corporations by restraining orders and rules. They can declare the particular combination null and void, and deal with it according to the nature and extent of the injuries," and that "This bill does not seek to cripple combinations of capital and labor; the formation of partnerships or corporations; but only to prevent and control combinations made with a view to prevent competition or for the restraint of trade, or to increase the profits of the producer at the cost of the consumer."

Speaking of the wrongs which the Sherman bill proposed to remedy, Senator Sherman said: "Associated enterprise and capital are not satisfied with partnerships and corporations competing with each other, and have invented a new form of combination commonly called 'trusts,' that seeks to avoid competition by combining the controlling corporations, partnerships and individuals engaged in the same business, and placing the power and property of the combination under the government of a few individuals, and often under the control of a single man called a trustee, a chairman or a president. The sole object of such a combination is to make competition impossible. It can control the market, raise or lower prices as will best promote its selfish interests, reduce prices in a particular locality and break down competition, and advance prices at will where competition does not exist. Its governing motive is to increase the profits of the parties composing it. The law of selfishness uncontrolled by competition, compels it to disregard the interest of the consumer. It dictates terms to transportation companies. It commands the price of labor without fear of strikes, for in its field it allows no competitors. * * * It is a substantial monopoly injurious to the public, and by the rule of both the common law and the civil law is null and void and the just subject of restraint by the courts * * *.

"If the concentrated powers of this combination are entrusted to a single man, it is a kingly prerogative, inconsistent with our form of government, and should be subject to the strong resistance of the state and national authorities. * * * If the combination is confined to a state, the state should apply the remedy; if it is interstate and controls any production in many states, Congress must apply the remedy. If the combination affects interstate transportation or is aided in any way by a transportation company, it falls clearly within the power of Congress * * *.

"Now, Mr. President, what is this bill? A remedial statute to enforce, by civil process in the courts of the United States, the common law against monopolies. How is such a law to be construed? Liberally, with a view to promote its object. * * *

* * *

"What is the extent of [the Congressional power to regulate commerce]? What is the meaning of the word commerce? It means the exchange of all commodities between different places or communities. It includes all trade and traffic, all modes of transportation by land or by sea * * *. The power of Congress extends to all this commerce, except only that limited within the bounds of a state."

* * * "In no respect does the work of our fathers in framing the Constitution of the United States appear more like the work of the Almighty Ruler of the Universe, rather than the conception of human

minds, than by the powers conferred by it upon the branches of the Federal Government. Many of these powers have remained dormant, unused, but plainly there, awaiting the growth and progress of our country * * *.

"While we should not stretch the powers granted to Congress by strained construction, we cannot surrender any of them; they are not ours to surrender; but whenever occasion calls, we should exercise them for the benefit and protection of the people of the United States. And, sir, while I have no doubt that every word of this bill is within the powers granted to Congress, I feel that its defects are in its moderation, and that its best effect will be a warning that all trade and commerce, all agreements and arrangements, all struggles for money or property, must be governed by the universal law that the public good must be the test for all."

* * *

Senator Teller of Colorado next took the floor. He said: "There is not a civilized country anywhere in the world that is not more or less cursed with trusts. A trust may not always be an evil. A trust for certain purposes which may simply mean a combination of capital may be a valuable thing to the community and to the country. There have been trusts in this country that have not been injurious. But the general complaint against trusts is that they prevent competition." Having thus stated his view of the wrongs to be remedied, Senator Teller stated that he was inclined to vote for the Sherman bill, though he did not think it strong enough to accomplish the result at which it was aimed, and which appeared to be desired by the Senate.

The debate on the Sherman bill was resumed on March 24, 1890, beginning with a speech by Senator Turpie of Indiana [advocating criminal, as well as civil, penalties for those participating in trusts] who said: * * *

"There may be some difficulty in defining this offense; to describe it is impossible. It is like the penal offense of fraud. The courts have never attempted to define that. There may be no description, there can be none altogether applicable to fraudulent commercial trusts; they vary so much and are so multiform in their character * * *. The moment we denounce these trusts penally, the moment we declare these fraudulent trust combinations to be conspiracies, to be felonies or misdemeanors, that moment the courts are bound to carry out the intention and purpose of the legislation, and even to favor that purpose and intention, that the will of the people may prevail and not perish. I have no doubt that when this law comes into practical operation it will receive a construction and definition very useful to us. * * * It will be aided by advocates on both sides, in stating different views of construction; and, above all, it will be supported and upheld by public opinion, expressed in a denunciation of those evils which this kind of legislation would avert and avoid."

* * *

Senator Stewart of Nevada then delivered the only remarks which were made in either house of Congress in opposition to the proposed anti-trust legislation. Without making any comprehensive argument upon the point, he said: "I do not find any warrant in the Constitution for this particular class of legislation." His speech consisted mainly in contending that the true remedy against "trusts" organized among capitalists, manufacturers and railroad companies, would be found in counter combinations among the people. Senator Stewart did not explain in what way such counter combinations among the people could be made effective; but he must have meant to recommend boycotting for that purpose, because it must have been plain to him, as it is to us, that boycotting is the only means by which the people could resist combinations of railroad companies or manufacturing companies to charge excessive prices for commodities. The Senate did not appear to take Senator Stewart's argument on this subject seriously, for no other Senator mentioned it in his own speech, or took any time to controvert any such view.

Senator Hoar of Massachusetts made the last argument of the day relevant to the proposed anti-trust legislation. In that argument he criticised the Sherman bill in several respects. His first criticism was that in his opinion that bill was aimed at less than all of the offenders who ought to be subject to its penalties. And his second criticism was that the bill failed to provide any effective remedy for its violation, except so far as it gave power to private citizens to bring suits for private damagers.

[2.   *The Reagan Amendment*]

In the next day of debate the Senate decided by a vote of nearly three to one to add [certain amendments and additions drafted by Senator] Reagan to the Sherman bill   *   *   *.

*   *   *

Section 1 of the Reagan amendment was a penal provision, aimed at all persons engaged in the creation or in the management of any "trust," where that trust was employed in any international or interstate "business;" and that section provided that all such persons should be deemed guilty of high misdemeanor, and on conviction thereof should be fined not exceeding $10,000, or imprisoned at hard labor not exceeding five years, or should be punished by both of said penalties, at the discretion of the court.

To make section 1 of this amendment effective, it was necessary to define the pivotal word "trust," which that section contained; and section 2 of the Reagan amendment was devoted to that purpose. That section declared that a "trust" is a combination of capital, skill or acts by two or more persons, firms, corporations or associations of persons made for any or all of many specified purposes, namely: 1, to produce any restriction in trade; 2, to limit or reduce production of any commodity; 3, to increase or reduce the price of any commodity; 4, to prevent competition in the manufacture, transportation, purchase or sale of any commodity; 5, to fix a standard whereby the price of any commodity would be established or controlled; 6, to create a monopoly in the manufacture, purchase, sale or transportation of any commodity; 7, to enter into or to execute any contract, not to manufacture, sell or transport any commodity below a standard figure or to keep the price of any commodity at a fixed or graduated figure, or to establish the price of any commodity, or the price of transporting any commodity, so as to preclude unrestrained competition in the sale or transportation of any commodity, or to pool, combine or unite in any interest, relevant to the sale or transportation of any commodity, whereby its price might in any manner be affected.

* * *

[On March 27, 1890, debate continued, and Senator Edmunds of Vermont stated:]

"I am in favor of the scheme in its fundamental desire and motive —most heartily in favor of it—directed to the breaking up of great monopolies, which get hold of the whole or some parts of particular business in the country, and are enabled therefore to command everybody, laborer, consumer, producer and everybody else, as the Sugar Trust and the Oil Trust. I am in favor, most earnestly in favor, of doing anything that the Constitution of the United States has given Congress power to do, to repress and break up and destroy forever the monopolies of that character; because in the long run, however seductive they may appear in lowering prices to the consumer, for the time being, all human experience and all human philosophy has proved that they are destructive of the public welfare and come to be tyrannies, grinding tyrannies."

Having thus emphatically stated his opinion of the propriety and necessity of the object of the Sherman bill, Senator Edmunds stated that he thought that bill to be broader than the constitutional foundation therefor, in that it proposed to do more than to regulate foreign and interstate commerce, and that therefore it was impossible for him to vote for that bill.

* * *

[3. *The Hoar Substitute*]

[Because of the criticism made of the bill in debate, the Senate voted to send it to the Committee on the Judiciary, for revision.] On April 2, 1890, Senator Edmunds reported back the original Sherman bill and all its amendments, accompanied by a new substitute for all of them. * * *

* * * Inasmuch as the new substitute had the same general purpose as that of the original Sherman bill of December 4, 1889, and inasmuch as Senator Sherman was the author and had always been the leading advocate of the proposed anti-trust legislation, the substitute for his bill which was reported from the Judiciary Committee, continued to be known as the Sherman bill. Indeed, the name of the man who wrote the Judiciary Committee substitute was never mentioned [in debate]. [Thirteen years after the passage of this substitute bill as the "Sherman Act," however, in his autobiography] Senator [George F.] Hoar expressly stated that he was the author of the Judiciary Committee substitute for the Sherman bill, and that that substitute was finally passed, without any change, by both houses of Congress, as indeed it also appears in the Congressional Record to have been.

The history of Congressional legislation from its beginning in 1789 until now, probably presents no other instance of a statute so important, and relevant to a subject of such scope and complexity, being written by one man, exactly as it was passed by both houses of Congress, and approved by the President. But when Senator Hoar wrote the Sherman law he was sixty-four years old, and through a career of more than twenty years at the Massachusetts Bar, followed by a career of more than twenty years in the two houses of Congress, he had developed his remarkable original ability for clear statement, into an intellectual power on that point, which was not equalled by that of any other man in Congress. * * *

[The text of the Hoar substitute read in pertinent parts:]

Section 1. Every contract, combination in the form of trust or otherwise, or conspiracy, in restraint of trade or commerce among the several States, or with foreign nations, is hereby declared to be illegal. Every person who shall make any such contract, or engage in any such combination or conspiracy, shall be deemed guilty of a misdemeanor, and, on conviction thereof, shall be punished by a fine not exceeding five thousand dollars, or by imprisonment not exceeding one year, or by both said punishments, in the discretion of the court.

Sec. 2. Every person who shall monopolize, or attempt to monopolize, or combine or conspire with any other person or persons to monopolize any part of the trade or commerce among the several States, or with foreign nations, shall be deemed guilty of a misdemeanor, and, on conviction thereof, shall be punished by fine not exceeding five thousand dollars, or by imprisonment not exceeding one year, or by both said punishments, in the discretion of the court.

* * *

Sec. 4. The several circuit courts of the United States are hereby invested with jurisdiction to prevent and restrain violations of this act; and it shall be the duty of the several district attorneys of the United States, in their respective districts, under the direction of the Attorney-General, to institute proceedings in equity to prevent and restrain such violations. * * *

* * *

Sec. 7.   Any person who shall be injured in his business or property by any other person or corporation by reason of anything forbidden or declared to be unlawful by this act may sue therefor in any Circuit Court of the United States in the district in which the defendant resides or is found, without respect to the amount in controversy, and shall recover threefold the damages by him sustained, and the costs of suit, including a reasonable attorney's fee.

Sec. 8.   That the word "person" or "persons" wherever used in this act shall be deemed to include corporations and associations * * *.

The Senate began on April 8, 1890, its consideration of the Hoar substitute for the Sherman bill.   That consideration was begun on the motion of Senator Hoar, who thereupon said that he would not undertake to explain the bill, because it was already well understood.

Senator Sherman thereupon said that, after having fairly and fully considered the substitute prepared by the Committee on Judiciary for his own bill, he would vote for it.

* * *

Senator Reagan of Texas thereupon moved to amend Section 7 of the Judiciary Committee substitute by inserting therein after the word "found" the words "or any state court of competent jurisdiction," so as to give to state courts concurrent jurisdiction with United States courts, of actions brought by private persons for damages inflicted upon them by violators of the proposed law.   But the impracticability of that Reagan amendment was so clearly pointed out by Senator Edmunds and other Senators, that it was defeated by a vote of thirty-six nays to thirteen yeas. * * *

* * *

Senator Reagan of Texas thereupon moved to amend Section 3 of the Judiciary Committee substitute by adding thereto the proviso, "That each day's violation of any of the provisions of the act should be held to be a separate offense."   But that amendment was rejected without debate and without calling for the yeas and nays.

Senator Kenna, of West Virginia, thereupon asked Senator Edmunds to explain the meaning of the word "monopolize" in Section 2 of the Judiciary Committee substitute.   In explanation of this request, Senator Kenna asked whether that word would cover the conduct of a citizen who might secure the entire demand for some particular commodity by virtue of his superior skill or facilities for producing that article, and without any attempt to interfere with anybody else in trying to produce similar articles.   Senator Edmunds answered to this question in the negative, and supported that answer by stating that the word "monopolize" has a meaning in the dictionaries and in the law which confines its scope to conduct which includes some attempt made by the monopolist to impede competitors and to prevent them from having an equal opportunity with himself to engage in the particular business sought to be monopolized.

Senator Hoar expressed his agreement with the opinion of Senator Edmunds on this point, and stated that all the members of the Judiciary Committee agreed that the word "monopoly" is a technical term known to the common law and that in that law it signifies "the sole engrossing to a man's self, by means which prevent other men from engaging in fair competition with him."

Senator Kenna thereupon inquired of Senator Hoar whether such a monopoly as he had defined is prohibited at common law, and Senator Hoar replied that he so understood. Senator Kenna thereupon asked why the bill should denounce a monopoly already illegal at common law; to which Senator Hoar replied that there is not any common law of the United States, and that the common law prevailing in the separate states of the Union cannot, as such, be enforced by the Federal courts by means of any penalty or punishment.

* * *

* * * [T]he Hoar substitute was thereupon passed by fifty-two ayes to one nay. The only negative vote was given by the undistinguished Senator Blodgett, of New Jersey, who had taken no part whatever in any of the debates on the subject and who did not state any reason for his vote. * * *

* * *

[4. *The Debate in the House*]

[In the course of the debate over the bill in the House, Mr. Culberson, of Texas, explained the working of its provisions.]

Though Mr. Culberson did not attempt to foresee or foretell all of the transactions which the courts would find to be within the prohibitions of the bill he did mention some which he thought would be violative thereof. * * * [H]e stated, that he understood that the Standard Oil Company habitually made contracts with merchants which obliged them not to sell oil below a certain price, except where it might become necessary to do so, to drive some competitor out of business by underselling that competitor; in which case the Standard Oil Company would shoulder the temporary loss caused by such underselling. Mr. Culberson stated that such a contract as that would violate the proposed law.

* * *

Mr. Henderson, of Iowa * * * interrupted Mr. Culberson's speech * * *:

" * * * I think it has been well settled by the investigation of a Congressional committee within the last year that a trust or combination of a few men in Chicago, Illinois, has been able to reduce the price of western cattle from one-third to one-half, controlling as they do the stock yards, the cattle yards and the transportation in Chicago; and it seems at the same time they have been enabled to keep up the price of every beefsteak that is used in this country. Now I want to ask * * * whether this bill * * * reaches that difficulty or not." To this question Mr. Culberson replied by saying: "I believe it will if it is construed as we think it ought to be construed by the courts."

Mr. Henderson thereupon asked, "Does the bill go as far as Congress has the power to go to strike at that damnable system?" To which Mr. Culberson replied: "That is the opinion of the Committee."

* * *

Mr. Cannon, of Illinois [replying to some critics of the bill:] * * "Gentlemen say they do not know how the courts will construe the act. It is for us to enact the law, and for courts to construe and enforce it. If we do our duty, it is reasonable to believe that the co-ordinate branch of the Government will do its duty. I believe this is a valuable bill, and I shall vote for it with pleasure."

* * *

Many other speeches having been made in favor of the bill and none against it, Mr. Culberson called for the previous question on its passage. But pending that motion, Mr. Bland, of Missouri, was permitted to offer, and did offer, the following amendment thereto:

"Every contract or agreement entered into for the purpose of preventing competition in the sale or purchase of a commodity transported from one state or territory to be sold in another, or so contracted to be sold, or to prevent competition in transportation of persons or property from one state or territory into another, shall be deemed unlawful within the meaning of this act; provided that the contracts here enumerated shall not be construed to exclude any other contract or agreement declared unlawful in this act."

* * *

[5.   *Final Action by the Senate and House*]

On May 12, 1890, Senator Hoar reported back Senate Bill No. 1 with an amendment to the House amendment, which amendment consisted in so changing the House amendment as to make it read as follows:

"Every contract or agreement entered into for the purpose of preventing competition in transportation of persons or property from one state or territory to another shall be deemed unlawful within the meaning of this act."

Thereupon Senator Hoar explained that the Bland amendment proposed by the House contained two points. First, it provided that any contract or agreement entered into for the purpose of preventing competition in the sale or purchase of a commodity transported from one state or territory to another shall be prohibited; and second, that contracts to prevent competition in the transportation of persons or property from one state to another should be prohibited. Senator Hoar stated that the Committee on Judiciary objected to the first of these provisions, but approved the second one, though they supposed the second provision was already covered by the bill, because transportation is commerce as truly as sales are commerce.

The bill was then recommitted to the Senate Judiciary Committee, and reported back with the House amendment amended so as to read as follows:

"That every contract or agreement entered into for the purpose of preventing competition in transportation of persons or property from one state * * * into another, so that the rates of such transportation may be raised above what is just and reasonable, shall be deemed unlawful within the meaning of this act."

* * *

In the House on May 17, 1890, Mr. Taylor, of Ohio, chairman of the Judiciary Committee, moved that the House non-concur in the Senate amendment to the House amendment and agree to the conference asked by the Senate, which motion was agreed to by the House. * * *

On June 11, 1890, the Conference Committee agreed to amend the Bland amendment so as to read as follows:

"Every contract or agreement entered into for the purpose of preventing competition in the transportation of persons or property from one state or territory into another, so that the rates of said transportation may be raised above what is just and reasonable, shall be deemed unlawful within the meaning of this act, and nothing in this act shall be deemed or held to impair the powers of the several states in any of the matters in this act mentioned."

Thereupon a long debate ensued upon the question of agreeing to the conference report.

* * *

[Following another meeting of a conference committee,] on June 18, 1890, Senator Edmunds presented to the Senate the report of the Conference Committee, which was to the effect that both Houses should recede from their respective amendments to the Senate bill, and that report was immediately agreed to without debate and without opposition.

On June 20, 1890, Mr. Stewart, of Vermont, submitted to the House the same conference report which Senator Edmunds had submitted to the Senate. * * *

* * *

* * * [T]he conference report was adopted and the bill was passed by the House by a vote of two hundred and forty-two ayes to no nays on June 20, 1890.

* * *

President Harrison, on July 2, 1890, approved and signed Senate Bill No. 1, namely: "An Act to protect trade and commerce against unlawful restraints and monopolies."

NOTES AND QUESTIONS

1. "That so broad-gauged a law attacking such powerful interests could pass in a predominantly conservative Congress by such an overwhelming vote seems on the surface difficult to explain." John Garraty, The New Commonwealth 124 (1968). Do you have an explanation? Of what importance is the national crisis described in the Introduction to this section? "Some historians," says Garraty, "have concluded that a massive explosion of public wrath compelled Congress to act." Id., at 124. One senator remarked that his "colleagues were interested in only one thing, to get some bill headed, 'A Bill to Punish Trusts' with which to go to the country." Coolidge, An Old-Fashioned Senator: Orville H. Platt 444 (1910), quoted in Letwin, Congress and the Sherman Antitrust Law, 1887–1890, 23 U.Chi.L.Rev. 221 (1956). But how significant was this Congressional action?

2. Consider the bill first introduced by Senator Sherman on December 4, 1889. Does it strike you as an important piece of legislation? What would such a bill accomplish? Are its terms clear? Are you persuaded by Senator Sherman's argument for the Constitutionality of the Bill? Under Senator Sherman's original scheme, who was to be depended on to effectuate the purposes of the Bill? Under the original Sherman Bill, how would the courts go about determining when they had a case of "lawful combination in aid of production," and when they had a case of "unlawful combination to prevent competition and in restraint of trade"? Are the two categories of combinations mutually exclusive?

3. Senator Sherman was a Republican who had recently lost the battle for the Republican nomination as President to William Henry Harrison, who was elected in 1888. Did Senator Sherman think that his bill would work any fundamental change in business law? Do you? Do you detect differences in antitrust policy between the Congressmen? For example, how would you compare the views of Sherman with those of Senator Reagan, a Texas Democrat; or Senator George of Mississippi, also a Democrat and a former confederate general? Consider the point raised in support of the Sherman Act by Senator Turpie of Indiana. That Senator believed that the Federal Legislature should pass antitrust laws, but should not clearly define the offense of "fraudulent combinations," because to do so would invite avoidance of the spirit of the law. Is this a persuasive argument? Is it consistent with the theory of criminal legislation articulated almost a hundred years earlier by Justice Chase and Justice Johnson in the common law crimes cases?

4. Only one Congressman, Senator Stewart of Nevada, spoke against the advisability of Antitrust legislation. Is this surprising? Can you discern anything here of the conflict between civic ideologies referred

to in the Introduction? Do you find his reasoning, that the proper remedy for "trusts" is combination among the people, to be as ludicrous as the author of this excerpt suggests? Do the materials on labor law which we have just considered make his argument more or less persuasive? How was it, by the way, that Senator Edmunds of Vermont, the Chairman of the Senate Judiciary Committee, could suggest that the "Sugar Trust and the Oil Trust" should be repressed because, being monopolies, "all human experience and all human philosophy has proved that they are destructive of the public welfare and come to be tyrannies, grinding tyrannies." Do you wish that you could have been a member of the Senate and able to make a speech like that?

5.   After you have read about the debate and amendments to the original Sherman Bill and the Reagan Amendments, which were much subject to criticism and alteration, how do you account for the fact that the Hoar substitute was "identical in every section and in every word with the Sherman law as it was afterward passed by both houses?" Do you think the explanation was simply Senator Hoar's "remarkable original ability for clear statement" which Hoar had developed "into an intellectual power * * * which was not equalled by that of any other man in Congress"? Why do you suppose that Hoar didn't immediately reveal his authorship of the substitute Bill? It appears from the Judiciary Committee's "Minute Book" that Sections 1, 2, 5 and 6 and perhaps 3 and 8 of the "Hoar Substitute" were actually drafted by Senator Edmunds, that Senator George drafted Section 4 and that Senator Hoar drafted only Section 7. Letwin, Congress and the Sherman Antitrust Law 1887–1890, 23 U.Chi.L.Rev. 221, 254n. (1956). Would you agree with the author of this excerpt that the Sherman Act, as it was finally passed (the "Hoar Substitute") was an "admirable specimen of statute writing?"

6.   What changes did the final bill make in the original Sherman bill and Reagan amendments? Would you have favored such changes? Note that in explanation of his bill Senator Hoar stated that a federal law regarding monopolies was made necessary because "the common law prevailing in the separate states of the Union cannot, as such, be enforced by the Federal courts by means of any penalty or punishment." Was he right about that? What inferences might be drawn from the Senate's refusal to add to the substitute bill Senator Reagan's amendment "That each day's violation of any of the provisions of the act should be held to be a separate offense"? How do you explain that that amendment was "rejected without debate and without calling for the yeas and nays?"

7.   There seems to have been an understanding on the part of many of the men who joined to pass the Sherman Antitrust Act that they were merely enacting the common law regarding trusts, monopolies, and restraint of trade on a national scale. What did this mean? We have already observed the tendency of the American common law to favor competition, but was the common law any more precise, and did it offer any concrete hopes for control of the trusts? According to one recent student of the common law regarding competition, William Letwin, there were four separate areas of the common law that bore on this problem: (1) the common law concerning royally chartered monopolies, which had been used to "destroy or weaken" those monopolies, while maintaining the power of the

English legislature, Parliament, to charter corporations.   (2) The body of English cases and statutes which forbid "engrossing," that is, cornering the supply of a necessity of life and charging extortionate prices for it. (3) English and American doctrines on contracts in restraint of trade generally, which prohibited "unreasonable" restrictions by employers on whom their employees might work for in the future, or which forbade buyers of businesses from exacting "unreasonable" agreements not to compete from sellers.   (4) English and American precedents on conspiracies or combinations in restraint of trade, such as those we have studied regarding labor unions, merchants associations, or manufacturing associations.   See generally Letwin, Congress and the Sherman Antitrust Law: 1887–1890, 23 U.Chi.L.Rev. 221, 241–243 (1956), see also Letwin, The English Common Law Concerning Monopolies, 21 U.Chi.L.Rev. 355 (1954).   Letwin concludes that none of these four branches offered much hope of controlling the trusts.   Do you agree?

8.   Mr. Heard, of Missouri, said in debate on the Hoar substitute that "It is for us to enact the law, and for courts to construe and enforce it. If we do our duty, it is reasonable to believe that the co-ordinate branch of the Government will do its duty."   In the next few cases we find out whether or not he was right.

9.   In the House Mr. Bland offered an amendment to make clear that the antitrust law would apply to purveyors of interstate transportation.   A Senate amendment offered by Senator Hoar would have accomplished the same thing, although Hoar's amendment removed Bland's provision affecting "competition in the sale or purchase of a commodity transported from one state * * * to another."   Senator Edmunds's Judiciary committee amended the proposed amendment to indicate that such competition was only to be illegal where "the rates of such transportation may be raised above what is just and reasonable."   Following this proposed amendment to the amendment *both* the Senate and the House backed off from Bland's, Hoar's, and Edmunds's proposals, and the House passed the "Hoar substitute" as originally drafted.   This was done more or less "without debate and without opposition."   Why?

3.   THE SHERMAN ACT IN THE SUPREME COURT

UNITED STATES v. E. C. KNIGHT CO.

Supreme Court of the United States, 1895.
156 U.S. 1, 15 S.Ct. 249, 39 L.Ed. 325.

Mr. Chief Justice FULLER   *   *   *.

By the purchase of the stock of the four Philadelphia refineries with shares of its own stock the American Sugar Refining Company acquired nearly complete control of the manufacture of refined sugar within the United States.   The bill charged that the contracts under which these purchases were made constituted combinations in restraint of trade   *   *   *   contrary to the act of congress of July 2, 1890.

* * * [T]he primary equity, or ground of suit * * * was the existence of contracts to monopolize interstate or international trade or commerce, and to restrain such trade or commerce * * *.

In commenting upon the statute (21 Jac. I. c. 3), at the commencement of chapter 85 of the third institute, entitled "Against Monopolists, Propounders, and Projectors," Lord Coke, in language often quoted, said:

> It appeareth by the preamble of this act (as a judgment in parliament) that all grants of monopolies are against the ancient and fundamental laws of this kingdome. And therefore it is necessary to define what a monopoly is.
>
> A monopoly is an institution, or allowance by the king by his grant, commission, or otherwise to any person or persons, bodies politique, or corporate, of or for the sole buying, selling, making, working, or using of anything, whereby any person or persons, bodies politique, or corporate, are sought to be restrained of any freedome or liberty that they had before, or hindred in their lawfull trade.

* * *

Counsel contend that this definition, as explained by the derivation of the word, may be applied to all cases in which "one person sells alone the whole of any kind of marketable thing, so that only he can continue to sell it, fixing the price at his own pleasure," whether by virtue of legislative grant or agreement; that the monopolization referred to in the act of congress is not confined to the common-law sense of the term as implying an exclusive control, by authority, of one branch of industry without legal right of any other person to interfere therewith by competition or otherwise, but that it includes engrossing as well, and covers controlling the market by contracts securing the advantage of selling alone or exclusively all, or some considerable portion, of a particular kind of merchandise or commodity to the detriment of the public; and that such contracts amount to that restraint of trade or commerce declared to be illegal. But the monopoly and restraint denounced by the act are the monopoly and restraint of interstate and international trade or commerce, while the conclusion to be assumed on this record is that the result of the transaction complained of was the creation of a monopoly in the manufacture of a necessary of life.

* * *

The fundamental question is whether, conceding that the existence of a monopoly in manufacture is established by the evidence, that monopoly can be directly suppressed under the act of congress in the mode attempted by this bill.

* * *

The argument is that the power to control the manufacture of refined sugar is a monopoly over a necessary of life, to the enjoyment of which by a large part of the population of the United States inter-

state commerce is indispensable, and that, therefore, the general government, in the exercise of the power to regulate commerce, may repress such monopoly directly, and set aside the instruments which have created it.   But this argument cannot be confined to necessaries of life merely and must include all articles of general consumption. Doubtless the power to control the manufacture of a given thing involves, in a certain sense, the control of its disposition, but this is a secondary, and not the primary, sense; and, although the exercise of that power may result in bringing the operation of commerce into play, it does not control it, and affects it only incidentally and indirectly.   Commerce succeeds to manufacture, and is not a part of it.
* * *

It is vital that the independence of the commercial power and of the police power, and the delimitation between them, however sometimes perplexing, should always be recognized and observed, for, while the one furnishes the strongest bond of union, the other is essential to the preservation of the autonomy of the states as required by our dual form of government; and acknowledged evils, however grave and urgent they may appear to be, had better be borne, than the risk be run, in the effort to suppress them, of more serious consequences by resort to expedients of even doubtful constitutionality.

* * *   The regulation of commerce applies to the subjects of commerce, and not to matters of internal police.   Contracts to buy, sell, or exchange goods to be transported among the several states, the transportation and its instrumentalities, and articles bought, sold, or exchanged for the purposes of such transit among the states, or put in the way of transit, may be regulated.   * * *   The fact that an article is manufactured for export to another state does not of itself make it an article of interstate commerce, and the intent of the manufacturer does not determine the time when the article or product passes from the control of the state and belongs to commerce.   * * *

* * *   [I]n Kidd v. Pearson, 128 U.S. 1, 20, 24, 9 Sup.Ct. 6, where the question was discussed whether the right of a state to enact a statute prohibiting within its limits the manufacture of intoxicating liquors, except for certain purposes, could be overthrown by the fact that the manufacturer intended to export the liquors when made, it was held that the intent of the manufacturer did not determine the time when the article or product passed from the control of the state and belonged to commerce, and that, therefore, the statute, in omitting to except from its operation the manufacture of intoxicating liquors within the limits of the state for export, did not constitute an unauthorized interference with the right of congress to regulate commerce.   And Mr. Justice Lamar remarked

> * * *   Manufacture is transformation,—the fashioning of raw materials into a change of form for use.   The functions of commerce are different.   The buying and selling, and the transporta-

tion incidental thereto, constitute commerce; and the regulation of commerce in the constitutional sense embraces the regulation at least of such transportation. * * * If it be held that the term includes the regulation of all such manufactures as are intended to be the subject of commercial transactions in the future, it is impossible to deny that it would also include all productive industries that contemplate the same thing. The result would be that congress would be invested, to the exclusion of the states, with the power to regulate, not only manufactures, but also agriculture, horticulture, stock-raising, domestic fisheries, mining; in short, every branch of human industry. * * *

* * *

* * * [T]he contracts and acts of the defendants related exclusively to the acquisition of the Philadelphia refineries and the business of sugar refining in Pennsylvania, and bore no direct relation to commerce between the states or with foreign nations. The object was manifestly private gain in the manufacture of the commodity, but not through the control of interstate or foreign commerce. It is true that the bill alleged that the products of these refineries were sold and distributed among the several states, and that all the companies were engaged in trade or commerce with the several states and with foreign nations; but this was no more than to say that trade and commerce served manufacture to fulfill its function. Sugar was refined for sale, and sales were probably made at Philadelphia for consumption, and undoubtedly for resale by the first purchasers throughout Pennsylvania and other states, and refined sugar was also forwarded by the companies to other states for sale. Nevertheless it does not follow that an attempt to monopolize, or the actual monopoly of, the manufacture was an attempt, whether executory or consummated, to monopolize commerce, even though, in order to dispose of the product, the instrumentality of commerce was necessarily invoked. There was nothing in the proofs to indicate any intention to put a restraint upon trade or commerce, and the fact, as we have seen, that trade or commerce might be indirectly affected, was not enough to entitle complainants to a decree.

Mr. Justice HARLAN dissenting * * *

* * *

"The object," the court below said, "in purchasing the Philadelphia refineries was to obtain a greater influence or more perfect control over the business of refining and selling sugar in this country." * * * In its consideration of the important constitutional question presented this court assumes on the record before us that the result of the transactions disclosed by the pleadings and proof was the creation of a monopoly in the manufacture of a necessary of life. If this combination, so far as its operations necessarily or directly affect interstate commerce, cannot be restrained or suppressed under some power granted to congress, it will be cause for regret that the patriotic statesmen who framed the constitution did not foresee the necessity of investing the national government with power to deal with gigantic monopolies holding in their grasp, and injuriously controlling in their own interest, the entire trade among the states in food products that are essential to the comfort of every household in the land.

The court holds it to be vital in our system of government to recognize and give effect to both the commercial power of the nation and the police powers of the states, to the end that the Union be strengthened, and the autonomy of the states preserved. In this view I entirely concur.

* * * But it is equally true that the preservation of the just authority of the general government is essential as well to the safety of the states * * *. The constitution, which enumerates the powers committed to the nation for objects of interest to the people of all the states, should not, therefore, be subjected to an interpretation so rigid, technical, and narrow that those objects cannot be accomplished. Learned counsel in Gibbons v. Ogden, 9 Wheat. 1, 187, having suggested that the constitution should be strictly construed, this court, speaking by Chief Justice Marshall * * * [asked]: "What do gentlemen mean * * * by a strict construction? * * * If they contend for that narrow construction which, in support of some theory to be found in the constitution, would deny to the government those powers which the words of the grant, as usually understood, import, and which are consistent with the general views and objects of the instrument; for that narrow construction, which would cripple the government, and render it unequal to the objects for which it is declared to be instituted, and to which the powers given, as fairly understood, render it competent,—then we cannot perceive the propriety of this strict construction, nor adopt it as the rule by which the constitution is to be expounded." Id. 188. * * *

Congress is invested with power to regulate commerce with foreign nations and among the several states. * * *

* * *

What is commerce among the states? The decisions of this court fully answer the question. "Commerce, undoubtedly, is traffic, but it is something more; it is intercourse." It does not embrace the completely interior traffic of the respective states,—that which is "carried on between man and man in a state, or between different parts of the same state, and which does not extend to or affect other states,"—but it does embrace * * * such traffic or trade, buying, selling, and interchange of commodities, as directly affects or necessarily involves the interests of the people of the United States. "Commerce, as the word is used in the constitution, is a unit," and "cannot stop at the external boundary line of each state, but may be introduced into the interior." "The genius and character of the whole government seem to be that its action is to be applied to all the external concerns of the nation, and to those internal concerns which affect the states generally." * * *

In the light of these principles, determining as well the scope of the power to regulate commerce among the states as the nature of such commerce, we are to inquire whether the act of congress of July 2, 1890, entitled "An act to protect trade and commerce against unlawful restraints and monopolies" (26 Stat. 209, c. 647), is repugnant to the constitution.

* * *

It would seem to be indisputable that no combination of corporations or individuals can, of right, impose unlawful restraints upon interstate trade, whether upon transportation or upon such interstate intercourse and traffic as precede transportation, any more than it can, of right, impose unreasonable restraints upon the completely internal traffic of a state. * * * If it be true that a combination of corporations or individuals may, so far as the power of congress is concerned, subject interstate trade, in any of its stages, to unlawful restraints, the conclusion is inevitable that the constitution has failed to accomplish one primary object of the Union, which was to place commerce among the states under the control of the common government of all the people, and thereby relieve or protect it against burdens or restrictions imposed, by whatever authority, for the benefit of particular localities or special interests.

The fundamental inquiry in this case is, what, in a legal sense, is an unlawful restraint of trade?

Sir William Erle, formerly chief justice of the common pleas, in his essay on the Law Relating to Trade Unions, well said that "restraint of trade, according to a general principle of the common law, is unlawful"; that "at common law every person has individually, and the public also have collectively, a right, to require that the course of trade should be kept free from unreasonable obstruction"; and that "the right to a free course for trade is of great importance to commerce and productive industry, and has been carefully maintained by those who have administered the common law." Pages 5–7.

There is a partial restraint of trade which, in certain circumstances, is tolerated by the law. The rule upon that subject is stated in Navigation Co. v. Winsor, 20 Wall. 64, 66, where it was said that: "An agreement in general restraint of trade is illegal and void; but an agreement which operates merely in partial restraint of trade is good, provided it be not unreasonable, and there be a consideration to support it. In order that it may not be unreasonable, the restraint imposed must not be larger than is required for the necessary protection of the party with whom the contract is made. * * *"

But a general restraint of trade has often resulted from combinations formed for the purpose of controlling prices by destroying the opportunity of buyers and sellers to deal with each other upon the basis of fair, open free competition. Combinations of this character have frequently been the subject of Judicial scrutiny, and have always been condemned as illegal because of their necessary tendency to restrain trade. Such combinations are against common right, and are crimes against the public. *   *   *

In Morris Run Coal Co. v. Barclay Coal Co., 68 Pa. 173, 183–187, the principal question was as to the validity of a contract made between five coal corporations of Pennsylvania, by which they divided between themselves two coal regions of which they had the control. The referee in the case found that those companies acquired under their arrangement the power to control the entire market for bituminous coal in the northern part of the state, and their combination was, therefore, a restraint upon trade, and against public policy. In response to the suggestion that the real purpose of the combination was to lessen expenses, to advance the quality of coal, and to deliver it in the markets intended to be supplied in the best order to the consumer, the supreme court of Pennsylvania said:

> This is denied by the defendants, but it seems to us it is immaterial whether these positions are sustained or not. Admitting their correctness, it does not follow that these advantages redeem the contract from the obnoxious effects so strikingly presented by the referee. The important fact is that these companies control this immense coal field *   *   *; that by this contract they control the price of coal in this extensive market, and make it bring sums it would not command if left to the natural laws of trade; [and] that it concerns an article of prime necessity for many uses *   *   *. These being its features, the contract is against public policy, illegal, and therefore void. *   *   * Singly each might have suspended deliveries and sales of coal to suit its own interests, and might have raised the price, even though this might have been detrimental to the public interest. *   *   * When competition is left free, individual error or folly will generally find a corrective in the conduct of others. But here is a combination of all the companies operating in the Blossburg and Barclay regions, and controlling their entire productions. *   *   * This combination has a power in its confederated form which no individual action can confer. The public interest must succumb to it, for it has left no competition free to correct its baleful influence. When the supply of coal is suspended, the demand for it becomes importunate, and prices must rise; or, if the supply goes forward, the price fixed by the confederates must accompany it. The domestic hearth, the furnaces of the iron master, and the fires of the manufacturer all feel the ~~straint, while many dependent hands are paralyzed, and hungry mouths are stinted. The influence of a lack of supply or a rise in the price of an article of such prime necessity cannot be measured. *   *   * Such a combination is more than a contract; it is an offense. "I take it," said Gibson, J., "a combination is criminal whenever the act to be done has a necessary tendency to prejudice the public or to oppress individuals, by unjustly

subjecting them to the power of the confederates, and giving effect to the purpose of the latter, whether of extortion or of mischief." Com. v. Carlisle, Brightly, N.P. 40. * * * Men can often do by the combination of many what severally no one could accomplish, and even what, when done by one, would be innocent. * * * There is a potency in numbers when combined, which the law cannot overlook, where injury is the consequence.

* * *

In Salt Co. v. Guthrie, 35 Ohio St. 666, 672, the principal question was as to the legality of an association of substantially all the manufacturers of salt in a large salt-producing territory. * * * [T]he court said:

> Public policy unquestionably favors competition in trade to the end that its commodities may be afforded to the consumer as cheaply as possible, and is opposed to monopolies which tend to advance market prices, to the injury of the general public. * * * The clear tendency of such an agreement is to establish a monopoly, and to destroy competition in trade, and for that reason, on grounds of public policy, the courts will not aid in its enforcement. It is no answer to say that competition in the salt trade was not in fact destroyed, or that the price of the commodity was not unreasonably advanced. Courts will not stop to inquire as to the degree of injury inflicted upon the public; it is enough to know that the inevitable tendency of such contracts is injurious to the public.

* * *

A leading case on the question as to what combinations are illegal as being in general restraint of trade is Richardson v. Buhl, 77 Mich. 632, 635, 657, 660, 43 N.W. 1102, which related to certain agreements connected with the business and operations of the Diamond Match Company. From the report of the case it appears that that company was organized, under the laws of Connecticut, for the purpose of uniting in one corporation all the match manufactories in the United States, and to monopolize and control the business of making all the friction matches in the country, and establish the price thereof. * * * Chief Justice Sherwood of the supreme court of Michigan said:

> The sole object of the corporation is to make money by having it in its power to raise the price of the article, or diminish the quantity to be made and used, at its pleasure. Thus both the supply of the article and the price thereof are made to depend upon the action of a half dozen individuals, more or less, to satisfy their cupidity and avarice * * * an artificial person, governed by a single motive or purpose, which is to accumulate money regardless of the wants or necessities of over 60,000,000 people. The article thus completely under their control for the last fifty years has come to be regarded as one of necessity * * * in every household in the land * * *. It is difficult to conceive of a

monopoly which can effect a greater number of people, or one more extensive in its effect on the country than that of the Diamond Match Company. It was to aid that company in its purposes and in carrying out its object that the contract in this case was made between those parties, and which we are now asked to aid in enforcing. Monopoly in trade, or in any kind of business in this country, is odious to our form of government. It is sometimes permitted to aid the government in carrying on a great public enterprise or public work under government control in the interest of the public. Its tendency is, however, destructive of free institutions, and repugnant to the instincts of a free people, and contrary to the whole scope and spirit of the federal constitution, and is not allowed to exist under express provisions in several of our state constitutions. * * * All combinations among persons or corporations for the purpose of raising or controlling the prices of merchandise, or any of the necessaries of life, are monopolies, and intolerable; and ought to receive the condemnation of all courts.

In the same case, Mr. Justice Champlin, with whom Mr. Justice Campbell concurred, said: " * * * Such a vast combination as has been entered into under the above name is a menace to the public. Its object and direct tendency is to prevent free and fair competition, and control prices throughout the national domain. It is no answer to say that this monopoly has in fact reduced the price of friction matches. That policy may have been necessary to crush competition. The fact exists that it rests in the discretion of this company at any time to raise the price to an exorbitant degree. * * * "

This extended reference to adjudged cases relating to unlawful restraints upon the interior traffic of a state has been made for the purpose of showing that a combination such as that organized under the name of the American Sugar Refining Company has been uniformly held by the courts of the states to be against public policy, and illegal, because of its necessary tendency to impose improper restraints upon trade. * * * The judgments of the state courts rest upon general principles of law, and not necessarily upon statutory provisions expressly condemning restraints of trade imposed by or resulting from combinations. Of course, in view of the authorities, it will not be doubted that it would be competent for a state, under the power to regulate its domestic commerce, and for the purpose of protecting its people against fraud and injustice, to make it a public offense, punishable by fine and imprisonment, for individuals or corporations to make contracts, form combinations, or engage in conspiracies, which unduly restrain trade or commerce carried on within its limits, and also to authorize the institution of proceedings for the purpose of annulling contracts of that character, as well as of preventing or restraining such combinations and conspiracies.

But there is a trade among the several states which is distinct from that carried on within the territorial limits of a state. The regulation and control of the former are committed by the national constitution to congress. * * * Under the power with which it is invested, congress may remove unlawful obstructions, of whatever kind, to the free course of trade among the states. * * * Any combination * * * that disturbs or unreasonably obstructs freedom in buying and selling articles manufactured to be sold to persons in other states, or to be carried to other states, * * * affects, not incidentally, but directly, the people of all the states; and the remedy for such an evil is found only in the exercise of powers confided to a government which, this court has said, was the government of all, exercising powers delegated by all, representing all, acting for all. M'Culloch v. Maryland, 4 Wheat. 405. * * *

* * *

In Kidd v. Pearson we recognized, as had been done in previous cases, the distinction between the mere transportation of articles of interstate commerce and the purchasing and selling that precede transportation. It is said that manufacture precedes commerce, and is not a part of it. But it is equally true that when manufacture ends, that which has been manufactured becomes a subject of commerce; that buying and selling succeed manufacture, come into existence after the process of manufacture is completed, precede transportation, and are as much commercial intercourse, where articles are bought to be carried from one state to another, as is the manual transportation of such articles after they have been so purchased. The distinction was recognized by this court in Gibbons v. Ogden, where the principal question was whether commerce included navigation. Both the court and counsel recognized buying and selling or barter as included in commerce. Chief Justice Marshall said that the mind can scarcely conceive a system for regulating commerce, which was "confined to prescribing rules for the conduct of individuals in the actual employment of buying and selling, or of barter." Pages 189, 190, 9 Wheat.

The power of congress covers and protects the absolute freedom of such intercourse and trade among the states as may or must succeed manufacturer and precede transportation from the place of purchase. This would seem to be conceded, for the court in the present case expressly declare that "contracts to buy, sell, or exchange goods to be transported among the several states, the transportation and its instrumentalities, and articles bought, sold, or exchanged for the purpose of such transit among the states, or put in the way of transit, may be regulated, but this is because they form part of interstate trade or commerce." Here is a direct admission—one which the settled doctrines of this court justify—that contracts to buy, and the purchasing of goods to be transported from one state to another, and transportation, with its instrumentalities, are all parts of interstate trade or commerce. * * * And yet by the opinion and judgment in this case, if I do not misapprehend them, congress is without power to protect the commercial intercourse that such purchasing necessarily involves against the restraints and burdens arising from the existence of combinations that meet purchasers, from whatever state they come, with the threat—for it is nothing more nor less than a threat—that they shall not purchase what they desire to purchase, except at the prices fixed by such combinations.   *   *   *

In my judgment, the citizens of the several states composing the Union are entitled of right to buy goods in the state where they are manufactured, or in any other state, without being confronted by an illegal combination whose business extends throughout the whole country, which, by the law everywhere, is an enemy to the public interests, and which prevents such buying, except at prices arbitrarily fixed by it.   *   *   *

*   *   *   [The Constitution] gives to congress, in express words, authority to enact all laws necessary and proper for carrying into execution the power to regulate commerce; and whether an act of congress, passed to accomplish an object to which the general government is competent, is within the power granted, must be determined by the rule announced through Chief Justice Marshall *   *   * : "The sound construction of the constitution must allow to the national legislature the discretion with respect to the means by which the powers it confers are to be carried into execution, which will enable that body to perform the high duties assigned to it in the manner most beneficial to the people. Let the end be legitimate, let it be within the scope of the constitution; and all means which are appropriate, which are plainly adapted to that end, which are not prohibited, but consistent with the letter and spirit of the constitution, are constitutional." M'Culloch v. Maryland, 4 Wheat. 316, 421. The end proposed to be accomplished by the act of 1890 is the protection of trade and commerce among the states against unlawful restraints. Who can say that that end is not legitimate, or is not within the scope of the constitution? The means employed are the suppression, by legal proceedings, of combinations, conspiracies, and monopolies which, by their inevitable and admitted tendency, improperly restrain trade and commerce among the states. Who can say that such means are not appropriate *   *   * ?

*   *   *

It is said that there are no proofs in the record which indicate an intention upon the part of the American Sugar Refining Company and its associates to put a restraint upon trade or commerce. Was it necessary that formal proof be made that the persons engaged in this combination admitted in words that they intended to restrain trade or commerce? Did any one expect to find in the written agreements which resulted in the formation of this combination a distinct expression of a purpose to restrain interstate trade or commerce? Men who form and control these combinations are too cautious and wary to make such admissions orally or in writing. Why, it is conceded that the object of this combination was to obtain control of the business of making and selling refined sugar throughout the entire country. Those interested in its operations will be satisfied with nothing less than to have the whole population of America pay tribute to them. That object is disclosed upon the very face of the transactions described in the bill. And it is proved—indeed, is conceded—that that object has been accomplished to the extent that the American Sugar Refining Company now controls 98 per cent. of all the sugar refining business in the country, and therefore controls the price of that article everywhere. Now, the mere existence of a combination having such an object and possessing such extraordinary power is itself, under settled principles of law,—there being no adjudged case to the contrary in this country,—a direct restraint of trade in the article for the control of the sales of which in this country that combination was organized. * * *

A decree recognizing the freedom of commercial intercourse as embracing the right to buy goods to be transported from one state to another without buyers being burdened by unlawful restraints imposed by combinations of corporations or individuals, so far from disturbing or endangering would tend to preserve the autonomy of the states, and protect the people of all the states against dangers so portentous as to excite apprehension for the safety of our liberties. If this be not a sound interpretation of the constitution, it is easy to perceive that interstate traffic, so far as it involves the price to be paid for articles necessary to the comfort and well-being of the people in all the states, may pass under the absolute control of overshadowing combinations having financial resources without limit, and an audacity in the accomplishment of their objects that recognizes none of the restraints of moral obligations controlling the action of individuals; combinations governed entirely by the law of greed and selfishness, so powerful that no single state is able to overthrow them, and give the required protection to the whole country, and so all-pervading that they threaten the integrity of our institutions.

* * *

To the general government has been committed the control of commercial intercourse among the states, to the end that it may be free at all times from any restraints except such as congress may impose or permit for the benefit of the whole country. * * * Its authority should not be so weakened by construction that it cannot reach and eradicate evils that, beyond all question, tend to defeat an object which that government is entitled, by the constitution, to accomplish. "Powerful and ingenious minds," this court has said, "taking, as postulates, that the powers expressly granted to the government of the Union are to be contracted by construction into the narrowest possible compass, and that the original powers of the states are retained, if any possible construction will retain them, may, by a course of well digested but refined and metaphysical reasoning, founded on these premises, explain away the constitution of our country, and leave it, a magnificent structure, indeed, to look at, but totally unfit for use. * * * " Gibbons v. Ogden, 9 Wheat. 1, 222.

While a decree annulling the contracts under which the combination in question was formed may not, in view of the facts disclosed, be effectual to accomplish the object of the act of 1890, I perceive no difficulty in the way of the court passing a decree declaring that that combination imposes an unlawful restraint upon trade and commerce among the states, and perpetually enjoining it from further prosecuting any business pursuant to the unlawful agreements under which it was formed, or by which it was created. * * *

For the reasons stated, I dissent from the opinion and judgment of the court.

NOTES AND QUESTIONS

1. In light of the legislative history of the Sherman Act, how persuasive did you find the United States' argument that "the monopolization referred to in the act of congress is not confined to the common-law sense of the term as implying an exclusive control, by authority, of one branch of industry without legal right of any other person to interfere therewith * * * but that it includes engrossing as well, and covers controlling the market by contracts securing the advantage of selling alone or exclusively all, or some considerable portion, of a particular kind of merchandise or commodity to the detriment of the public; and that such contracts amount to that restraint of trade or commerce declared to be illegal."

2. Also in light of the legislative history of the Sherman Act, do you find support for Judge Fuller's distinction between "monopolies" of trade, and "monopolies" of manufacturing? Does the rationale for the distinction lie in his observation that "The regulation of commerce applies to the subjects of commerce, and not to matters of internal police"? What are matters of "internal police?"

3. Consider Justice Harlan's dissent. Why does Harlan find it necessary to state such a self-evident proposition as "It would seem to be indisputable that no combination of corporations or individuals can, of right, impose unlawful restraints upon interstate trade * * *." Would anyone challenge such a statement? On what problem is Harlan really seeking to focus attention?

4. Harlan spends some time with state cases which had found monopolistically-inclined organizations to be acting in restraint of trade. Are these cases distinguishable from a federal antitrust prosecution? What, exactly, is the common-law rationale of these cases? Must there be a finding that the culprits in question are *actually* injuring the public? What if the combination in question has actually *not* diminished competition and has *not* resulted in higher prices for consumers?

5. Consider the language quoted from the "Diamond Match" monopoly case, Richardson v. Buhl, to the effect that "Monopoly in trade, or in any kind of business in this country, is odious to our form of government." Do you agree? Why is the "tendency" of a monopoly "destructive of free

institutions, and repugnant to the instincts of a free people?" Are "all combinations * * * for the purpose * * * of controlling prices" necessarily "intolerable?" How much of this is law, and how much is political and social philosophy? Is there a difference? Should there be?

6. Does all of this necessarily mean, however, that the power of the federal government must be invoked in matters involving monopolization of the manufacture of sugar? Would Justice Harlan believe that the power of the federal government would reach a case, where, as was presumably alleged in this case, the sugar companies themselves delivered no sugar to out-of-state buyers, but sold to anyone who came to them?

7. Do Justice Harlan's views on the power of the federal government remind you of any that you have studied before? Is he employing these views in the service of the same or different social philosophies? For example, in terms of the idea of centralized supervision of the American economy, how would you compare Harlan's views with those of the Federalists we studied in Chapter II, and with those of Chief Justice Taney? Do Harlan's fears about arbitrary uses of economic power and in particular large concentrations of private power sound familiar? How, for example, are they similar to or different from those expressed by the bench and the prosecution in the *Cordwainer's* case? On Harlan, his times, and his social and judicial philosophy see White, The American Judicial Tradition 127–149 (1976), and sources there cited.

UNITED STATES v. TRANS–MISSOURI FREIGHT ASS'N

Supreme Court of the United States, 1897.
166 U.S. 290, 17 S.Ct. 540, 41 L.Ed. 1007.

[The great question in this case was whether the Sherman Act applied to railroads. Do you remember anything in the legislative history of the act that is relevant? This case involved an association of 18 railroads (the Trans-Missouri Freight Association), at least some of which competed directly with each other, to fix rates.

The association argued that such rate-fixing was necessary to set "reasonable" rates, and that such "reasonable" rates were necessary to prevent some of the competitors from falling into financial ruin. Such ruin, said the companies, would injure the public when rail service consequently diminished. The rate-fixing in question was done pursuant to a written agreement, entered into before the passage of the Sherman Act. While the actual association which had been originally prosecuted was dissolved before the case was ruled on by the Supreme Court, the court decided to go ahead and address the merits of the question, in light of the fact that similar associations had since been formed. It should be borne in mind, as you read this opinion, that Congress had begun to deal with the Railroads *before* the Sherman Act, by the creation of the Interstate Commerce Commission (ICC) in 1887. The Interstate Commerce Act provided that rates must be "reasonable and just," and also forbade some types of agreements among railroads, called "pooling agreements." The ICC was charged with the responsibility for conducting investigations and enforcing the law, where necessary by prosecuting violators in the federal courts. It had become apparent by 1889, however, that the ICC did not interpret the provision forbidding "pooling" to include "rate agreements between competing companies," as long as "freight and territories were not parcelled out among them." See, e. g. J. Garraty, The New Commonwealth 112–119 (1968). Accordingly, the Trans-Missouri Freight Association argued that since it had filed its rates *and* its rate agreement with the ICC, and had gained ICC approval, it should be immune from prosecution under the Sherman Act. In short, asked the railroad, if the government agency charged with such determinations had decided that its rates were "reasonable," and "just" how could its actions be illegal restraints of trade? Does the argument of the railroad have anything in common with Harlan's dissent?]

Mr. Justice PECKHAM for the court   *   *   *

The language of the act includes every contract, combination in the form of trust or otherwise, or conspiracy, in restraint of trade or commerce among the several States or with foreign nations.   *   * It cannot be denied that those who are engaged in the transportation of persons or property from one State to another are engaged in interstate commerce, and it would seem to follow that if such persons enter into agreements between themselves in regard to the compensation to be secured from the owners of the articles transported, such agreement would at least relate to the business of commerce, and might more or less restrain it. The point urged on the defendants' part is that the statute was not really intended to reach that kind of an agreement relating only to traffic rates entered into by competing common carriers by railroad; that it was intended to reach only those who were engaged in the manufacture or sale of articles of commerce, and who by means of trusts, combinations and conspiracies were engaged in affecting the supply or the price or the place of manufacture of such articles. The terms of the act do not bear out such construction.   *   *   *

We have held that the Trust Act did not apply to a company engaged in one State in the refining of sugar under the circumstances detailed in the case of United States v. E. C. Knight Company, 156 U.S. 1, because the refining of sugar under those circumstances bore no distinct relation to commerce between the States or with foreign nations. To exclude agreements as to rates by competing railroads for the transportation of articles of commerce between the States would leave little for the act to take effect upon.   *   *   *

But it is maintained that an agreement like the one in question on the part of the railroad companies is authorized by the Commerce Act, which is a special statute applicable only to railroads, and that a construction of the Trust Act (which is a general act) so as to include within its provisions the case of railroads, carries with it the repeal by implication of so much of the Commerce Act as authorized the agreement. It is added that there is no language in the Trust Act which is sufficiently plain to indicate a purpose to repeal those provisions of the Commerce Act which permit the agreement * * *. On a line with this reasoning it is said that if Congress had intended to in any manner affect the railroad carrier as governed by the Commerce Act, it would have amended that act directly and in terms, and not have left it as a question of construction to be determined whether so important a change in the commerce statute had been accomplished by the passage of the statute relating to trusts.

The first answer to this argument is that, in our opinion, the Commerce Act does not authorize an agreement of this nature. It may not in terms prohibit, but it is far from conferring either directly or by implication any authority to make it. * * * The fifth section prohibits what is termed "pooling," but there is no express provision in the act prohibiting the maintenance of traffic rates among competing roads by making such an agreement as this, nor is there any provision which permits it. * * *

The existence of agreements similar to this one may have been known to Congress at the time it passed the Commerce Act, although we are not aware, from the record, that an agreement of this kind had ever been made and publicly known prior to the passage of the Commerce Act. Yet if it had been known to Congress, its omission to prohibit it at that time, while prohibiting the pooling arrangements, is no reason for assuming that when passing the Trust Act it meant to except all contracts of railroad companies in regard to traffic rates from the operation of such act. * * *

It is also urged that the debates in Congress show beyond a doubt that the act as passed does not include railroads. Counsel for the defendants refer in considerable detail to its history from the time of its introduction in the Senate to its final passage. As the act originally passed the Senate the first section was in substance as it stands at present in the statute. On its receipt by the House that body proposed an amendment, by which it was in terms made unlawful to enter into any contract for the purpose of preventing competition in the transportation of persons or property. As thus amended the bill went back to the Senate, which itself amended the amendment by making the act apply to any such contract as tended to raise prices for transportation above what was just and reasonable. * * * The amendments were then considered by conference committees, and the first conference committee reported to each house in favor of the amendment of the Senate. This report was disagreed to and another committee appointed, which agreed to strike out both amendments and leave the bill as it stood when it first passed the Senate * * *.

Looking at the debates during the various times when the bill was before the Senate and the House, both on its original passage by the Senate and upon the report from the conference committees, it is seen that various views were declared in regard to the legal import of the act. Some of the members of the House wanted it placed beyond doubt or cavil that contracts in relation to the transportation of persons and property were included in the bill. Some thought the amendment unnecessary as the language of the act already covered it, and some refused to vote for the amendment or for the bill if the amendments were adopted on the ground that it would then interfere with the Interstate Commerce Act, and tend to create confusion as to the meaning of each act.

* * *

Looking simply at the history of the bill from the time it was introduced in the Senate until it was finally passed, it would be impossible to say what were the views of a majority of the members of each house in relation to the meaning of the act. It cannot be said that a majority of both houses did not agree with Senator Hoar in his views as to the construction to be given to the act as it passed the Senate. All that can be determined from the debates and reports is that various members had various views, and we are left to determine the meaning of this act, as we determine the meaning of other acts, from the language used therein.

There is, too, a general acquiescence in the doctrine that debates in Congress are not appropriate sources of information from which to discover the meaning of the language of a statute passed by that body. United States v. Union Pacific Railroad Company, 91 U.S. 72, 79; Aldridge v. Williams, 3 How. 9, 24, Taney, Chief Justice; Mitchell v. Great Works Milling & Manufacturing Company, 2 Story, 648, 653; Queen v. Hertford College, 3 Q.B.D. 693, 707.

The reason is that it is impossible to determine with certainty what construction was put upon an act by the members of a legislative body that passed it by resorting to the speeches of individual members thereof. Those who did not speak may not have agreed with those who did; and those who spoke might differ from each other; the result being that the only proper way to construe a legislative act is from the language used in the act, and, upon occasion, by a resort to the history of the times when it was passed. (Cases cited, supra.) If such resort be had, we are still unable to see that the railroads were not intended to be included in this legislation.

It is said that Congress had very different matters in view and very different objects to accomplish in the passage of the act in question; that a number of combinations in the form of trusts and conspiracies in restraint of trade were to be found throughout the country, and that it was impossible for the state governments to successfully cope with them because of their commercial character and of their business extension through the different States of the Union. Among these trusts it was said in Congress were the Beef Trust, the Standard Oil Trust, the Steel Trust, the Barbed Fence Wire Trust, the Sugar Trust, the Cordage Trust, the Cotton Seed Oil Trust, the

Whiskey Trust and many others * * *. To combinations and conspiracies of this kind it is contended that the act in question was directed, and not to the combinations of competing railroads to keep up their prices to a reasonable sum for the transportation of persons and property. It is true that many and various trusts were in existence at the time of the passage of the act, and it was probably sought to cover them by the provisions of the act. * * * But a further investigation of "the history of the times" shows also that those trusts were not the only associations controlling a great combination of capital which had caused complaint at the manner in which their business was conducted. There were many and loud complaints from some portions of the public regarding the railroads and the prices they were charging * * * and it was alleged that the prices * * * were unduly and improperly enhanced by combinations among the different roads. * * *

Our attention is also called to one of the rules for the construction of statutes which has been approved by this court; that while it is the duty of courts to ascertain the meaning of the legislature from the words used in the statute and the subject-matter to which it relates, there is an equal duty to restrict the meaning of general words, whenever it is found necessary to do so in order to carry out the legislative intent. * * * It is therefore urged that if, by a strict construction of the language of this statute it may be made to include railroads, yet it is evident from other considerations now to be mentioned that the real meaning of the legislature would not include them, and they must for that reason be excluded. It is said that this meaning is plainly to be inferred, because of fundamental differences both in an economic way and before the law between trade and manufacture on the one hand, and railroad transportation on the other. Among these differences are the public character of railroad business, and as a result the peculiar power of control and regulation possessed by the State over railroad companies. The trader or manufacturer, on the other hand, carries on an entirely private business, and can sell to whom he pleases; he may charge different prices for the same article to different individuals; he may charge as much as he can get for the article in which he deals, whether the price be reasonable or unreasonable; he may make such discrimination in his business as he chooses, and he may cease to do any business whenever his choice lies in that direction; while, on the contrary, a railroad company must transport all persons and property that come to it, and it must do so at the same price for the same service, and the price must be reasonable, and it cannot at its will discontinue its business. It is also urged that there are evils arising from unrestricted competition in regard to railroads which do not exist in regard to any other kind of property, that it is so admitted by the latest and best writers on the subject, and that practical experience of the results of unrestricted competition among railroads tends directly to the same view * * *. It is also said that the contemporaneous industrial history of the country, the legal situation in regard to railroad properties at the time of the enactment of this statute, its legislative history, the ancient and constantly maintained different legal effect and policy regarding railway transportation and ordinary trade and manufacture, together with a just regard for interests of such enormous magnitude as are represented by the railroads of the country, all tend to show that Congress in passing the Anti-Trust Act never could have contemplated the inclusion of railroads within its provisions. * * *

* * * While the points of difference just mentioned and others do exist between the two classes of corporations, it must be remembered they have also some points of resemblance. Trading, manufacturing and railroad corporations are all engaged in the transaction of business with regard to articles of trade and commerce * * *. A contract among those engaged in the latter business by which the prices for the transportation of commodities traded in or manufactured by the others is greatly enhanced from what it otherwise would be if free competition were the rule, affects and to a certain extent restricts trade and commerce, and affects the price of the commodity. * * * Why should not a railroad company be included in general legislation aimed at the prevention of that kind of agreement made in restraint of trade * * *? It is true the results of trusts, or combinations of that nature, may be different in different kinds of corporations, and yet they all have an essential similarity, and have been induced by motives of individual or corporate aggrandizement as against the public interest. In business or trading combinations they may even temporarily, or perhaps permanently, reduce the price of the article traded in or manufactured, by reducing the expense inseparable from the running of many different companies for the same purpose. Trade or commerce under those circumstances may nevertheless be badly and unfortunately restrained by driving out of business the small dealers and worthy men whose lives have been spent therein, and who might be unable to readjust themselves to their altered surroundings. Mere reduction in the price of the commodity dealt in might be dearly paid for by the ruin of such a class * * *. In any great and extended change in the manner or method of doing business it seems to be an inevitable necessity that distress and, perhaps, ruin shall be its accompaniment in regard to some of those who were engaged in the old methods.

It is wholly different, however, when such changes are effected by combinations of capital * * *. In this light it is not material that the price of an article may be lowered. It is in the power of the combination to raise it, and the result in any event is unfortunate for the country by depriving it of the services of a large number of small but independent dealers * * * who supported themselves and their families from the small profits realized therein. Whether they be able to find other avenues to earn their livelihood is not so material, because it is not for the real prosperity of any country that such changes should occur which result in transferring an independent business man, the head of his establishment, small though it might be, into a mere servant or agent of a corporation for selling the commodities which he once manufactured or dealt in, having no voice in shaping the business policy of the company and bound to obey orders issued by others.   Nor is it for the substantial interests of the country that any one commodity should be within the sole power and subject to the sole will of one powerful combination of capital. * * * It is entirely appropriate generally to subject corporations or persons engaged in trading or manufacturing to different rules from those applicable to railroads in their transportation business; but when the evil to be remedied is similar in both kinds of corporations * * * we see no reason why similar rules should not be promulgated in regard to both, and both be covered in the same statute by general language sufficiently broad to include them both. * * * We think, after a careful examination, that the statute covers, and was intended to cover, common carriers by railroad.

* * * The next question to be discussed is as to what is the true construction of the statute, assuming that it applies to common carriers by railroad. What is the meaning of the language as used in the statute, that "every contract, combination in the form of trust or otherwise, or conspiracy in restraint of trade or commerce among the several States or with foreign nations, is hereby declared to be illegal"? Is it confined to a contract or combination which is only in unreasonable restraint of trade or commerce, or does it include what the language of the act plainly and in terms covers, all contracts of that nature?

We are asked to regard the title of this act as indicative of its purpose to include only those contracts which were unlawful at common law, but which require the sanction of a Federal statute in order to be dealt with in a Federal court. It is said that when terms which are known to the common law are used in a Federal statute those terms are to be given the same meaning that they received at common law, and that when the language of the title is "to protect trade and commerce against unlawful restraints and monopolies," it means those restraints and monopolies which the common law regarded as unlawful, and which were to be prohibited by the Federal statute. We are of opinion that the language used in the title refers to and includes and was intended to include those restraints and monopolies which are made unlawful in the body of the statute. * * *

It is now with much amplification of argument urged that the statute, in declaring illegal every combination in the form of trust or otherwise, or conspiracy in restraint of trade or commerce, does not mean what the language used therein plainly imports, but that it only means to declare illegal any such contract which is in unreasonable restraint of trade * * *.

The term ["restraint of trade", as used in the statute] is not of such limited signification. Contracts in restraint of trade have been known and spoken of for hundreds of years both in England and in this country, and the term includes all kinds of those contracts which in fact restrain or may restrain trade. * * * A contract may be in restraint of trade and still be valid at common law. Although valid, it is nevertheless a contract in restraint of trade, and would be so described either at common law or elsewhere. By the simple use of the term "contract in restraint of trade," all contracts of that nature, whether valid or otherwise, would be included, and not alone that kind of contract which was invalid and unenforceable as being in unreasonable restraint of trade. * * *

It must also be remembered that railways are public corporations organized for public purposes, granted valuable franchises and privileges, among which the right to take the private property of the citizen *in invitum* is not the least, Cherokee Nation v. Southern Kansas Railway Co., 135 U.S. 641, 657; that many of them are the donees of large tracts of public lands and of gifts of money by municipal corporations, and that they all primarily owe duties to the public of a higher nature even than that of earning large dividends for their shareholders. The business which the railroads do is of a public nature, closely affecting almost all classes in the community—the farmer, the artisan, the manufacturer and the trader. It is of such a public nature that it may well be doubted, to say the least, whether any contract which imposes any restraint upon its business would not be prejudicial to the public interest.

We recognize the argument upon the part of the defendants that restraint upon the business of railroads will not be prejudicial to the public interest so long as such restraint provides for reasonable rates for transportation and prevents the deadly competition so liable to result in the ruin of the roads and to thereby impair their usefulness to the public, and in that way to prejudice the public interest. But it must be remembered that these results are by no means admitted with unanimity; on the contrary, they are earnestly and warmly denied on the part of the public and by those who assume to defend its interests both in and out of Congress. Competition, they urge, is a necessity for the purpose of securing in the end just and proper rates.
* * *
* * *

[Justice Peckham then quoted from the dissenting opinion below, on the railroads' argument that they should be permitted to fix rates to avoid ruinous competition.]

It may be entirely true that as we proceed in the development of the policy of public control over railway traffic, methods will

be devised and put in operation by legislative enactment whereby
railway companies and the public may be protected against the
evils arising from unrestricted competition and from rate wars
which unsettle the business of the community, but I fail to perceive the force of the argument that because railway companies
through their own action cause evils to themselves and the public
by sudden changes or reductions in tariff rates they must be permitted to deprive the community of the benefit of competition in
securing reasonable rates for the transportation of the products
of the country. Competition, free and unrestricted, is the general
rule which governs all the ordinary business pursuits and transactions of life. Evils, as well as benefits, result therefrom. In
the fierce heat of competition the stronger competitor may crush
out the weaker; fluctuations in prices may be caused that result
in wreck and disaster; yet, balancing the benefits as against the
evils, the law of competition remains as a controlling element in
the business world. * * * The time may come when the companies will be relieved from the operation of this law, but they cannot,
by combination and agreements among themselves, bring about
this change. The fact that the provisions of the Interstate Commerce Act may have changed in many respects the conduct of
the companies in the carrying on of the public business they are
engaged in does not show that it was the intent of Congress, in
the enactment of that statute, to clothe railway companies with the
right to combine together for the purpose of avoiding the effects
of competition on the subject of rates.

* * *

As a result of this review of the situation, we find two very widely divergent views of the effects which might be expected to result
from declaring illegal all contracts in restraint of trade, etc.; one
side predicting financial disaster and ruin to competing railroads,
including thereby the ruin of shareholders, the destruction of immensely valuable properties, and the consequent prejudice to the public interest; while on the other side predictions equally earnest are
made that no such mournful results will follow, and it is urged that
there is a necessity, in order that the public interest may be fairly
and justly protected, to allow free and open competition among railroads upon the subject of the rates for the transportation of persons
and property.

The arguments which have been addressed to us against the inclusion of all contracts in restraint of trade, as provided for by the
language of the act, have been based upon the alleged presumption
that Congress, notwithstanding the language of the act, could not have
intended to embrace all contracts, but only such contracts as were in
unreasonable restraint of trade. Under these circumstances we are,
therefore, asked to hold that the act of Congress excepts contracts
which are not in unreasonable restraint of trade, and which only
keep rates up to a reasonable price, notwithstanding the language of
the act makes no such exception. In other words, we are asked to

read into the act by way of judicial legislation an exception that is not placed there by the law-making branch of the Government, and this is to be done upon the theory that the impolicy of such legislation is so clear that it cannot be supposed Congress intended the natural import of the language it used.   This we cannot and ought not to do.   *   *   *   It may be that the policy evidenced by the passage of the act itself will, if carried out, result in disaster to the roads and in a failure to secure the advantages sought from such legislation. *   *   *   These considerations are, however, not for us.   If the act ought to read as contended for by defendants, Congress is the body to amend it and not this court, by a process of judicial legislation wholly unjustifiable.   *   *   *

The conclusion which we have drawn from the examination above made into the question before us is that the Anti-Trust Act applies to railroads, and that it renders illegal all agreements which are in restraint of trade or commerce as we have above defined that expression, and the question then arises whether the agreement before us is of that nature.

*   *   *   The question is one of law in regard to the meaning and effect of the agreement itself, namely: Does the agreement restrain trade or commerce in any way so as to be a violation of the act?   We have no doubt that it does.   The agreement on its face recites that it is entered into "for the purpose of mutual protection by establishing and maintaining reasonable rates, rules and regulations on all freight traffic, both through and local."   To that end the association is formed and a body created which is to adopt rates, which, when agreed to, are to be the governing rates for all the companies, and a violation of which subjects the defaulting company to the payment of a penalty, and although the parties have a right to withdraw from the agreement on giving thirty days' notice of a desire so to do, yet while in force and assuming it to be lived up to, there can be no doubt that its direct, immediate and necessary effect is to put a restraint upon trade or commerce as described in the act.

*   *   *

NOTES AND QUESTIONS

1.   Do you agree with Justice Peckham's conclusion that the existence of the ICC and the ICC Act has no bearing on the applicability of the Sherman Act to railroads?   How would you argue to reach the opposite conclusion?   What about Peckham's view of the importance of legislative history?   Would you participate in the "general acquiescence in the doctrine that debates in Congress are not appropriate sources of information from which to discover the meaning of the language of a statute passed by that body?"   What does such a doctrine suggest about the allocation of responsibility between courts and legislatures?

2.   In light of the *E. C. Knight Co.* case, which held that the antitrust law did not reach monopolization of manufacturing, do you think that

Justice Peckham concludes too quickly that the Antitrust Act does apply to common carriers, like railroads? Do you suppose that Peckham's ideology might have some influence on his judicial thinking? Do you find anything, for example, that suggests that Peckham might share Justice Harlan's social assumptions?

3. In light of what you have learned about the legislative history of the Sherman Act, and without regard to Justice Peckham's opinion about legislative history, do you agree with Peckham that one should interpret the Antitrust Act as forbidding all contracts and combinations in "restraint of trade," and that one should not read in the so-called "rule of reason" from the common law? In other words, is it correct that the Antitrust Act was *not* intended merely to Federalize the common law?

4. Even if Justice Peckham is correct that the Sherman Act was meant to prohibit all contracts in restraint of trade in interstate commerce, does it necessarily follow that the contract in this case is in "restraint of trade?" How does Peckham justify his finding to that effect?

5. If Justice Peckham was closer in judicial temperament to Justice Harlan than to Justice Fuller, would you expect Peckham to agree with the idea that the Antitrust Act was not designed to reach manufacturing? Peckham wrote an opinion on this question in Addyston Pipe and Steel Co. v. United States, 175 U.S. 211, 20 S.Ct. 96, 44 L.Ed. 136 (1899). The conventional wisdom on this opinion is that *Addyston Pipe* "for all practical purposes" reversed *E. C. Knight*. See, e. g. A. D. Neale, The Antitrust Laws of the United States of America 16n (2nd ed. 1970). *Addyston* involved an arrangement among six manufacturers of cast-iron pipe whereby the six agreed not to underbid each other in public bidding for contracts for the manufacture of pipe in certain territories. Each carried on business by submitting bids for the manufacture of pipe required in particular construction projects and then, if their bids were successful, by manufacturing and shipping pipe to the construction site. While this did involve interstate shipment of pipe, the defendants argued that since they were "manufacturers" of pipe, the *E. C. Knight* case covered their situation. What follows are the parts of Peckham's opinion in *Addyston* where he distinguishes the *E. C. Knight* case. See if you accept his arguments.

ADDYSTON PIPE AND STEEL CO. v. UNITED STATES

Supreme Court of the United States, 1899.
175 U.S. 211, 20 S.Ct. 96, 44 L.Ed. 136.

The direct purpose of the combination in the *Knight case* was the control of the manufacture of sugar. There was no combination or agreement, in terms, regarding the future disposition of the manufactured article; nothing looking to a transaction in the nature of interstate commerce * * * The various cases which had been decided in this court relating to the subject of interstate commerce, and to the difference between that and the manufacture of commodities, and also the police power of the States as affected by the commerce clause of the Constitution, were adverted to, and the case was decided upon the principle that a combination simply to control manufacture was not a violation of the act of Congress, because such a contract or combination did not directly control or affect interstate commerce, but that contracts for the sale and transportation to other States of specific articles were proper subjects for regulation because they did form part of such commerce.

We think the case now before us involves contracts of the nature last above mentioned, not incidentally or collaterally, but as a direct and immediate result of the combination engaged in by the defendants.

While no particular contract regarding the furnishing of pipe and the price for which it should be furnished was in the contemplation of the parties to the combination at the time of its formation, yet it was their intention, as it was the purpose of the combination, to directly and by means of such combination increase the price for which all contracts for the delivery of pipe within the territory above described should be made, and the latter result was to be achieved by abolishing all competition between the parties to the combination. The direct and immediate result of the combination was therefore necessarily a restraint upon interstate commerce in respect of articles manufactured by any of the parties to it to be transported beyond the State in which they were made. * * *

If dealers in any commodity agreed among themselves that any particular territory bounded by state lines should be furnished with such commodity by certain members only of the combination, and the others would abstain from business in that territory, would not such agreement be regarded as one in restraint of interstate trade? If the price of the commodity were thereby enhanced, (as it naturally would be,) the character of the agreement would be still more clearly one in restraint of trade. Is there any substantial difference where, by agreement among themselves, the parties choose one of their number to make a bid for the supply of the pipe for delivery in another State, and agree that all the other bids shall be for a larger sum, thus practically restricting all but the member agreed upon from any attempt to supply the demand for the pipe or to enter into competition for the business? * * *

* * *

The defendants allege, and it is true, that their business is not like a factory manufacturing an article of a certain kind for which there is at all times a demand, and which is manufactured without any regard to a particular sale or for a particular customer. In this respect as in many others the business differs radically from the sugar refiners. The business of defendants is carried on by obtaining particular contracts for the sale, transportation and delivery of iron pipe of a certain description, quality and strength, differing in different contracts as the intended use may differ. These contracts are, generally speaking, obtained at a public letting, at which there are many competitors, and the contract bid for includes, in its terms, the sale of the pipe and its delivery at the place desired, the cost of transportation being included in the purchase price of the pipe. The contract is one for the sale and delivery of a certain kind of pipe, and it is not generally essential to its performance that it should be manufactured for that particular contract, although sometimes it may be.

If the successful bidder had on hand iron pipe of the kind specified, or if he could procure it by purchase, he could in most cases deliver such pipe in fulfilment of his contract just the same as if he manufactured the pipe subsequently to the making of the contract and for the specific purpose of its performance. It is the sale and delivery, of a certain kind and quality of pipe, and not the manufacture, which is the material portion of the contract, and a sale for delivery beyond the State makes the transaction a part of interstate commerce. Municipal corporations and gas, railroad and water companies are among the chief customers for the pipe, and when they desire the article they give notice of the kind and quality, size, strength and purpose for which the pipe is desired, and announce that they will receive proposals for furnishing the same at the place indicated by them. * * * In certain sections of the country the defendants would have, by reason of their situation, such an advantage over all other competitors that there would practically be no chance for any other than one of their number to obtain the contract, unless the price bid was so exorbitant as to give others not so favorably situated an opportunity to snatch it from their hands. * * *

The combination thus had a direct, immediate and intended relation to and effect upon the subsequent contract to sell and deliver the pipe. It was to obtain that particular and specific result that the combination was formed, and but for the restriction the resulting high prices for the pipe would not have been obtained. It is useless for the defendants to say they did not intend to regulate or affect interstate commerce. They intended to make the very combination and agreement which they in fact did make, and they must be held to have intended (if in such case intention is of the least importance) the necessary and direct result of their agreement.

* * *

It is said that a particular business must be distinguished from its mere subjects, and from the instruments by which the business is carried on; that in most cases of a large manufacturing company it could only be carried on by shipping products from one State to another, and that the business of such an establishment would be related to interstate commerce only incidentally and indirectly. This proposition we are not called upon to deny. It is not, however, relevant. Where the contract is for the sale of the article and for its delivery in another State, the transaction is one of interstate commerce, although the vendor may have also agreed to manufacture it in order to fulfil his contract of sale. In such case a combination of this character would be properly called a combination in restraint of interstate commerce, and not one relating only to manufacture.

It is almost needless to add that we do not hold that every private enterprise which may be carried on chiefly or in part by means of interstate shipments is therefore to be regarded as so related to interstate commerce as to come within the regulating power of Congress. Such enterprises may be of the same nature as the manufacturing of refined sugar in the *Knight case*—that is, the parties may be engaged as manufacturers of a commodity which they thereafter intend at some time to sell, and possibly to sell in another State; but such sale we have already held is an incident to and not the direct result of the manufacture, and so is not a regulation of or an illegal interference with interstate commerce. That principle is not affected by anything herein decided.

* * *

SECTION E. INDUSTRIAL STRIFE: THE PULLMAN STRIKE, EUGENE V. DEBS, AND WORKMEN'S COMPENSATION

1. INTRODUCTION

As we have seen, one of the effects of commercial development in early nineteenth century America was the increasing diversity of interests between capital and labor. In the early years, however, conflict between the two was not often serious. The small-scale organization of business still maintained a personal employer-employee relationship, and the "master" still at least paid lip service to the tradition that he was guardian of his "servant's" welfare. Working conditions, though not luxurious, were often respectable, and occasionally satisfying. The importance of handicraft skills in early industry meant that workers could continue to think of themselves as craftsmen, and take pride in their work. The common ideology of expansion held out the hope that workers could share in the generally rising fortunes of business. As we have seen, some judges, like Shaw, even attempted to create tenets of jurisprudence to balance the competing interests of labor and capital.

After 1850, however, whatever balance had been struck began to tilt in favor of capital, as the trend toward large-scale industrialization continued. As this tilt continued, the conflict between owners and workers grew greater, until finally, in the late years of the century, a state very near to industrial warfare existed.

Labor grievances ordinarily concerned hours and wages. As late as 1910, only 8 percent of American laborers worked only an 8-hour day. In the steel industry, for example, 12-hour days and 6-day weeks were commonplace until 1923. In the textile industry, dependent primarily on women and young children, the work week ranged from 60 to 84 hours. Nor did munificent wages offset the burdensome hours. The unskilled laborer from 1880–1910 could expect to take home a little under $10 per week. Skilled workers rarely made more than $20. The average annual family income of industrial workers was never higher than $650, an amount which was often not enough for subsistence. Moreover, the closing decades of the nineteenth century included several recessions which brought on severe unemployment. The depression of 1894, the worst, left one in five workers jobless. City dwellers found it difficult if not impossible to procure food by gardening or raising livestock, and life was thus fragile for the American working class—it is not difficult to understand how frustration could lead to violence.

The first such significant instance was in 1877. In reaction to a business slump, the Baltimore & Ohio railroad had cut wages. The B & O workers struck, and were soon joined by a sympathy strike of employees on other lines. Soon, more than two-thirds of all American railway mileage was closed. Violence then flared in the face of company intransigence. Rail yards were burned, strikers were fired upon, and before the dispute was over, private armies were hired by businessmen to patrol the streets of Chicago and other cities. Business picked up in the 1880's, but strikes still came more often. More than 80,000 workers in Chicago went on strike in the spring of '86. A small group of vocal anarchists then took advantage of the situation to draw attention to their cause. These men called for a rally at Chicago's Haymarket Square in connection with a strike against the McCormick Harvesting Machine Company. Chicago police attempted to break up the meeting, and in the midst of the ensuing melee a bomb was thrown at the police. Seven officers were killed, and dozens injured. The identity of the person who actually threw the bomb was never discovered, but local prosecutors still placed many on trial and obtained a conviction on flimsy evidence. Meanwhile, a skittish press saw in the Chicago "massacre" part of a carefully orchestrated attempt by foreign radicals, with clear ties to labor organizers, to foment a working-class rebellion. No evidence was ever produced to substantiate this charge, but suspicions grew with the increasing number of "aliens" in the city's work force.

The pattern of violence and paranoia continued into the 1890s. In 1892, a violent strike in the silver mines of Coeur d'Alene, Idaho, left many dead and ended with a declaration of martial law and the dispatching of federal troops. More ominous events occurred that same year in Pennsylvania. Andrew Carnegie's Homestead Steel Company, near Pittsburgh, had been accusing workers of resisting technological innovations, while workers argued that they were being denied the financial benefits of the company's newly efficient operations. A sharp national business downturn threatened a loss of profits. Henry Clay Frick, left in charge of the Homestead plant while Carnegie was out of the country, decided to "teach our employees a lesson." Wages were summarily cut. A strike followed. Frick imported a force of strikebreakers, and protected them with 300 Pinkerton detectives. The Homestead strikers fired on the Pinkertons, as they were travelling by barge up the Monongahela. The Pinkertons fired back, killing seven workers, and forcing a humiliating "surrender." In the meantime, Alexander Berkman, a self-confessed anarchistic Communist, burst into Frick's office and attempted to kill him. Frick survived, and used the assassination attempt to turn national opinion against the strikers. The state militia was eventually summoned, and the strike collapsed.

By 1894, when the events we next consider occurred, the public had been aroused by almost two decades of violence between labor and capital. The pitched battles between strikers and militiamen, the attacks on the police, the assassination attempts, the rantings of a few radicals, and the massive economic dislocations all mingled to create public fears of bloody class revolt, of armed insurrection.

2. VIEWS OF THE PULLMAN STRIKE

LEON STEIN AND PHILIP TAFT, "INTRODUCTION," TO STEIN, ED., THE PULLMAN STRIKE *

v–vii (1969).

George M. Pullman developed a railroad car in which long-distance travelers could sleep in comfort * * *. To build and service his cars, Pullman created a model town, named "Pullman," just outside of Chicago, and he provided his workers with homes, water, gas, libraries—each at a fixed price and rent.

* * * It was an efficient plan to preserve intact a labor force of 5,800 men and to protect them from troublesome outside elements. Pullman saw no need to negotiate. He provided for their needs at his prices and rents.

But business is business, and when business took a bad turn early in 1893, Pullman laid off 3,000 workers and cut wages drastically for those not laid off—but rents and prices retained their usual high levels. For a time the men endured. Then they sent a grievance committee to see Mr. Pullman, with the assurance that none of the committee would be discharged. When three committee members were summarily fired, the men in the shops * * * walked out on May 11, 1894.

The world outside Pullman began to learn about the exorbitant rents in that "model town," the meager health facilities, the monopolistic service charges, the spy-ridden, dictatorial town rule. "Go and live in Pullman and find out how much Pullman gets sellin' city water and gas ten per cent higher to those poor fools," political boss Mark Hanna gibed. Nine years earlier, Richard T. Ely had concluded that "the idea of Pullman is un-American."

The Pullman strikers turned to the fledgling American Railway Union for aid. The ARU had come into existence with the help of Eugene V. Debs in June, 1893, and in its first year had won a major victory in an eighteen-day strike on the Great Northern Railroad. At the ARU convention, pent-up resentments swept the delegates. Despite Debs' reluctance to gamble with a general railroad strike in an unfavorable period, on June 21, the convention gave Pullman a five-day deadline—deal with the men's grievances or face a boycott. The five days passed, the boycott was declared in effect, and Debs, responding to the voice of the people, directed railroad workers to cut out Pullman cars, but to proceed with caution and to avoid violence.

A network of twenty-four railroads was centered in Chicago, where long strings of freight, mail, coach and Pullman cars were joined in vast yards. Chicago had a General Managers Association of top railroad executives whose purpose was not only to break the strike, but to destroy the union.

Toward this goal the GMA had, first of all, the aid of virtually the entire press. Newspapers across the country spread the cry that Debs was an anarchist's bloodthirsty dictator of a revolutionary strike whose purpose was the destruction of property.

Second, the GMA had the aid of the widespread unemployment of masses of hungry, roving men and women. Their violence was what the managers wanted as a prelude to stringent restraints. It is not surprising, therefore, that those men and women were frequently and easily able to enter the freight yards and set fire only to old, *discarded* equipment.

Third, the managers had a staunch ally in U.S. Attorney General Richard Olney, formerly a dedicated corporation lawyer with a passion for collecting railroad directorships. Olney devised a strategy that brought United States troops on the scene, despite the protest of liberal Illinois Governor John P. Altgeld, who was maintaining law and order with police and militia.

Strikebreakers were imported. The managers refused to uncouple the Pullman cars so that not even the mail cars could be moved. On July 2, Olney obtained a blanket injunction charging the strikers with obstructing the mails and interfering with interstate commerce, both of which were forbidden by the Sherman Antitrust Act of 1890, which, ironically, was supposed to be a weapon not against labor, but against powerful corporations. Debs was arrested for conspiracy to obstruct the mails. He was released on bail, rearrested, and found in contempt of court.

*   *   *

WILLIAM H. CARWARDINE, THE PULLMAN STRIKE *

118–125 (1894).

[Carwardine was pastor of the First M. E. Church, Pullman, Ill.]

*   *   * My position was peculiar. I did not endorse the strike, and never have. I did not endorse the boycott. *   *   * But I stood for justice. *   *   *

*   *   *

Holding this position, I was surprised to find how the fear of anarchy and mob rule blinded the eyes of true men and women to the injustice that had wrought all these things. *   *   *

The inequalities of life as indicated in the social fabric of modern society are simply fearful. In many respects we are living in the grandest age this old world has ever seen. And yet, with our boasted progress and advancement; I realize that something is radically wrong in a condition of society that permits some to be so poor and others to be so rich. *   *   *

No person who has ever read Sir Walter Scott's wonderful story of "Ivanhoe" can forget the picture of Gurth, the Swineherd. Describing him, Scott says: "One part of his dress only remains, but it is too remarkable to be suppressed. It was a brass ring, resembling a dog's collar, but without any opening, and soldered fast round his neck, so loose as to form no impediment to his breathing, yet so tight as to be incapable of being removed excepting by the use of the file. On this singular gorget was engraven in Saxon characters an inscription of the following purport: 'Gurth, the son of Beowulph, is the born thrall of Cedric of Rotherwood.' "

*   *   * Gurth, the son of Beowulph, is with us yet.

While he wears not the collar of Cedric of Rotherwood, yet he is to all intents and purposes the chattel or "White Slave," of the "corporation," "trust" or "millionaire lords," *   *   *.

We as a nation are dividing ourselves, like ancient Rome, into two classes, the rich and the poor, the oppressor and the oppressed. And on the side of the oppressor there is power and protection, class legislation and military support. Should this policy continue for a generation or two, there can be no doubt at all that working men who in times of war and invasion are the protectors of our liberties and homes, would refuse to take up arms in their defense. We are fol-

---

* Reprinted in Stein, ed., The Pullman Strike (1969).

lowing in the tracks of ancient Rome, instead of learning useful lessons from her failures and defeats. No country can prosper, no government long perpetuate itself and its institutions, which does not administer judgment and justice alike to all of its people. * * *

The oppressed of to-day are white laborers and mechanics who, evidently, though without a Supreme Court decision, have no rights which millionaires and moneyed corporations are bound to respect. * * * Men and nations sometimes oppress to their own hurt. An estimate of the money losses in the present strike up to July 9, '94, puts them at $6,560,500, of which the laborers have lost in wages $1,500,000. * * * And all this grows out of the oppression of one man who was once a poor mechanic. He has gained wealth, and risen into power on it so that he can now take advantage of the necessities and poverty of his fellowmen to crush and oppress them.

Whatever the fathers who organized this government intended it to be, we, their successors, have evidently drifted very far away from the original intention of the founders. It is no longer a government of equal rights for all. The present strike may be overcome by federal bayonets and bullets, but the trouble will not end here. There is deep unrest in the lowest strata of society, the real burden-bearers of our country, which augurs ill for capitalistic oppression in the future. * * * I therefore deprecate, though necessary, the use of federal troops in this strike as a precedent, pregnant with evil in years to come. Capital seems to be organized to destroy the independence of labor and defeat its efforts at elevation, and labor is organized not only to protect itself, but to retaliate on capital. * * *

I appeal to the great body of the laboring classes, in view of the developments of the past few weeks, hereafter and forever to use your ballot aright. It is the God-given privilege of every American citizen, purchased at the sacrifice of blood, tears and property, and which is the birthright of 4,000 years of slow and painful evolution from degradation, slavery, and tyranny to the liberty of this latter nineteenth century. A ballot unknown in ancient days, in the Mosaic economy, and Roman history; a ballot that first began to make its appearance when the Barons at Runnymede demanded the rights of Magna Charta from King John of England, when Oliver Cromwell rose against the despotism of Charles I, with his Star Chamber, and when Martin Luther blew a blast that awoke all Europe to the dawn of the Reformation; a ballot that was not born until the urgent demands of a home government once more created a rebellion and the American Colonies were established, and that masterpiece of human composition, the Declaration of Independence, given to the world; a ballot, forsooth, that did not reach its majority until Abraham Lincoln broke the manacles that enslaved 3,000,000 black men, and signed that Magna Charta of human liberty, the Act of Emancipation; a ballot that represents * * * free homes, free schools, free press, a united people, the right of every man unmolested to worship God according to the dictates of his own conscience; the greatest gift given by God to man outside of his Blessed Son, our Lord and Savior Jesus Christ, and one that can give us, if we use it right, the grandest type of government under the sun!

* * *

IN RE DEBS

Supreme Court of the United States, 1895.
158 U.S. 564, 15 S.Ct. 900, 39 L.Ed. 1092.

[Eugene V. Debs, through his attorney Clarence Darrow, argued that he was entitled to writ of habeas corpus, since there was insufficient legal basis to support his jailing for contempt.]

Mr. Justice BREWER * * *

The case presented by the bill is this: The United States, finding that the interstate transportation of persons and property, as well as the carriage of the mails, is forcibly obstructed, and that a combination and conspiracy exists to subject the control of such transportation to the will of the conspirators, applied to one of their courts, sitting as a court of equity, for an injunction to restrain such obstruction and prevent carrying into effect such conspiracy. * * *

* * * What are the relations of the general government to interstate commerce and the transportation of the mails? They are those of direct supervision, control, and management. While, under the dual system which prevails with us, the powers of government are distributed between the state and the nation, and while the latter is properly styled a government of enumerated powers, yet within the limits of such enumeration it has all the attributes of sovereignty, and, in the exercise of those enumerated powers, acts directly upon the citizen, and not through the intermediate agency of the state.

[In order to support his argument Brewer then quoted from earlier court opinions.]

"No trace is to be found in the constitution of an intention to create a dependence of the government of the Union on those of the states, for the execution of the great powers assigned to it. Its means are adequate to its ends, and on those means alone was it expected to rely for the accomplishment of its ends. To impose on it the necessity of resorting to means which it cannot control, which another government may furnish or withhold, would render its course precarious, the result of its measures uncertain, and create a dependence on other governments, which might disappoint its most important designs, and is incompatible with the language of the constitution." Chief Justice Marshall in McCulloch v. State of Maryland, 4 Wheat. 316, 405, 424.

* * *

"This power to enforce its laws and to execute its functions in all places does not derogate from the power of the state to execute its laws at the same time and in the same places. The one does not exclude the other, except where both cannot be executed at the same time. In that case the words of the constitution itself show which is to yield. 'This constitution, and all laws which shall be made in pursuance thereof, * * * shall be the supreme law of the land.'" Mr. Justice Bradley in Ex parte Siebold, 100 U.S. 371, 395.

* * *

Among the powers expressly given to the national government are the control of interstate commerce and the creation and management of a postoffice system for the nation. * * *

* * *

As, under the constitution, power over interstate commerce and the transportation of the mails is vested in the national government, and congress, by virtue of such grant, has assumed actual and direct control, it follows that the national government may prevent any unlawful and forcible interference therewith. But how shall this be accomplished? Doubtless, it is within the competency of congress to prescribe by legislation that any interferences with these matters shall be offenses against the United States, and prosecuted and punished by indictment in the proper courts. But is that the only remedy? Have the vast interests of the nation in interstate commerce, and in the transportation of the mails, no other protection than lies in the possible punishment of those who interfere with it? To ask the question is to answer it. By article 3, § 2, cl. 3, of the federal constitution, it is provided: "The trial of all crimes except in cases of impeachment shall be by jury; and such trial shall be held in the state where the said crime shall have been committed." If all the inhabitants of a state, or even a great body of them, should combine to obstruct interstate commerce or the transportation of the mails, prosecutions for such offenses had in such a community would be doomed in advance to failure. And if the certainty of such failure was known, and the national government had no other way to enforce the freedom of interstate commerce and the transportation of the mails than by prosecution and punishment for interference therewith, the whole interests of the nation in these respects would be at the absolute mercy of a portion of the inhabitants of that single state.

But there is no such impotency in the national government. The entire strength of the nation may be used to enforce in any part of the land the full and free exercise of all national powers and the security of all rights intrusted by the constitution to its care. * * * If the emergency arises, the army of the nation, and all its militia, are at the service of the nation, to compel obedience to its laws.

But * * * is there no other alternative than the use of force on the part of the executive authorities whenever obstructions arise to the freedom of interstate commerce or the transportation of the mails? * * * The existence of this right of forcible abatement is not inconsistent with, nor does it destroy, the right of appeal, in an orderly way, to the courts for a judicial determination, and an exercise of their powers, by writ of injunction and otherwise, to accomplish the same result. In Borough of Stamford v. Stamford Horse R. Co., 56 Conn. 381, 15 Atl. 749, an injunction was asked by the borough to restrain the company from laying down its track in a street of the borough. The right of the borough to forcibly remove the track was insisted upon as a ground for questioning the jurisdiction of a court of equity, but the court sustained the injunction, adding: "And none the less so because of its right to remove the track by force. As a rule, injunctions are denied to those who have adequate remedy at law. * * * In some cases of nuisance, and in some cases of trespass * * *. [But w]hen the choice is between redress or prevention of injury by force and by peaceful process, the law is well pleased if the individual will consent to waive his right to the use of force, and await its action. Therefore, as between force and the extraordinary writ of injunction, the rule will permit the latter."

So, in the case before us, * * * it is more to the praise than to the blame of the government that, instead of determining for itself questions of right and wrong on the part of these petitioners and their associates, and enforcing that determination by the club of the policeman and the bayonet of the soldier, it submitted all those questions to the peaceful determination of judicial tribunals * * *.

* * * It is said that equity only interferes for the protection of property, and that the government has no property, and that the government has no property interest. A sufficient reply is that the United States have a property in the mails, the protection of which was one of the purposes of this bill. [In] Searight v. Stokes, 3 How. 151 * * * Chief Justice Taney [said]: "The United States have unquestionably a property in the mails. They are not mere common carriers, but a government, performing a high official duty in holding and guarding its own property as well as that of its citizens committed to its care; for a very large portion of the letters and packages conveyed on this road, especially during the session of congress, consists of communications to or from the officers of the executive departments, or members of the legislature, on public service, or in relation to matters of public concern. * * * We think that a carriage, whenever it is carrying the mail, is laden with the property of the United States, within the true meaning of the compact."

* * *

It is obvious from these decisions that while it is not the province of the government to interfere in any mere matter of private controversy betwen individuals, or to use its great powers to enforce the rights of one against another, yet, whenever the wrongs complained of are such as affect the public at large, and are in respect of matters which by the constitution are intrusted to the care of the nation * * * then the mere fact that the government has no pecuniary interest in the controversy is not sufficient to exclude it from the courts * * *.

The national government, given by the constitution power to regulate interstate commerce, has by express statute assumed jurisdiction over such commerce when carried upon railroads. It is charged, therefore, with the duty of keeping those highways of interstate commerce free from obstruction, for it has always been recognized as one of the powers and duties of a government to remove obstructions from the highways under its control.

* * *

Indeed, the obstruction of a highway is a public nuisance (4 Bl. Comm. 167), and a public nuisance has always been held subject to abatement at the instance of the government * * *.

* * *

It is said that the jurisdiction heretofore exercised by the national government over highways has been in respect to waterways,—the natural highways of the country,—and not over artificial highways, such as railroads * * *, but the basis upon which [Congress] rests its jurisdiction over artificial highways is the same as that which supports it over the natural highways. Both spring from the power to regulate commerce. * * * The great case of Gibbons v. Ogden, 9 Wheat. 1, in which the control of congress over inland waters was asserted, rested that control on the grant of the power to regulate commerce. The argument of the chief justice was that commerce includes navigation, "and a power to regulate navigation is as expressly granted as if that term had been added to the word 'commerce.'" * * *

* * *

Constitutional provisions do not change, but their operation extends to new matters, as the modes of business and the habits of life of the people vary with each succeeding generation. The law of the common carrier is the same to-day as when transportation on land was by coach and wagon, and on water by canal boat and sailing vessel; yet in its actual operation it touches and regulates transportation by modes then unknown,—the railroad train and the steamship. Just so is it with the grant to the national government of power over interstate commerce. * * *

It is said that seldom have the courts assumed jurisdiction to restrain by injunction in suits brought by the government, either state or national, obstructions to highways either artificial or natural. This is undoubtedly true, but the reason is that the necessity for such interference has only been occasional. Ordinarily, the local authorities have taken full control over the matter, and by indictment for misdemeanor, or in some kindred way, have secured the removal of the obstruction and the cessation of the nuisance. * * * And, because the remedy by indictment is so efficacious, courts of equity entertain jurisdiction in such cases with great reluctance, * * * and they will only do so where there appears to be a necessity for their interference. Rowe v. Granite Bridge, 21 Pick. 347 * * *.

That the bill filed in this case alleged special facts calling for the exercise of all the powers of the court is not open to question. The picture drawn in it of the vast interests involved, not merely of the city of Chicago and the state of Illinois, but of all the states, and the general confusion into which the interstate commerce of the country was thrown; the forcible interference with that commerce; the attempted exercise by individuals of powers belonging only to government, and the threatened continuance of such invasions of public right, presented a condition of affairs which called for the fullest exercise of all the powers of the courts. * * *

* * *

Again, it is objected that it is outside of the jurisdiction of a court of equity to enjoin the commission of crimes. This, as a general proposition, is unquestioned. A chancellor has no criminal jurisdiction.

Something more than the threatened commission of an offense against the laws of the land is necessary to call into exercise the injunctive powers of the court. There must be some interferences, actual or threatened, with property or rights of a pecuniary nature; but when such interferences appear, the jurisdiction of a court of equity arises, and is not destroyed by the fact that they are accompanied by or are themselves violations of the criminal law. * * *

The law is full of instances in which the same act may give rise to a civil action and a criminal prosecution. An assault with intent to kill may be punished criminally, under an indictment therefor, or will support a civil action for damages; and the same is true of all other offenses which cause injury to person or property. In such cases the jurisdiction of the civil court is invoked, not to enforce the criminal law and punish the wrongdoer, but to compensate the injured party for the damages which he or his property has suffered; and it is no defense to the civil action that the same act by the defendant exposes him also to indictment and punishment in a court of criminal jurisdiction. * * *

Nor is there in this any invasion of the constitutional right of trial by jury. We fully agree with counsel that "it matters not what form the attempt to deny constitutional right may take; it is vain and ineffectual, and must be so declared by the courts." And we reaffirm the declaration made for the court by Mr. Justice Bradley in Boyd v. U. S., 116 U. S. 616, 635, 6 Sup.Ct. 524, that "it is the duty of courts to be watchful for the constitutional rights of the citizen, and against any stealthy encroachments thereon. Their motto should be obsta principiis." But the power of a court to make an order carries with it the equal power to punish for a disobedience of that order, and the inquiry as to the question of disobedience has been, from time immemorial, the special function of the court. * * * In Watson v. Williams, 36 Miss. 331, 341, it was said: "The power to fine and imprison for contempt, from the earliest history of jurisprudence, has been regarded as a necessary incident and attribute of a court, without which it could no more exist than without a judge. * * * A court without the power effectually to protect itself against the assaults of the lawless, or to enforce its orders, judgments, or decrees against the recusant parties before it, would be a disgrace to the legislation, and a stigma upon the age which invented it." In Cartwright's Case, 114 Mass. 230, 238, we find this language: "The summary power to commit and punish for contempts tending to obstruct or degrade the administration of justice is inherent in courts of chancery and other superior courts, as essential to the execution of their powers and to the maintenance of their authority, and is part of the law of the land, within the meaning of Magna Charta and of the twelfth article of our Declaration of Rights." [In] Commission v. Brimson, 154 U.S. 447–488, 14 Sup.Ct.1125, * * * it was said: "Surely it cannot be supposed that the question of contempt of the authority of a court of the United States, committed by a disobedience of its orders, is triable, of right, by a jury."

* * *

Further, it is said by counsel in their brief:

"No case can be cited where such a bill in behalf of the sovereign has been entertained against riot and mob violence, though occurring on the highway. It is not such fitful and temporary obstruction that constitutes a nuisance. The strong hand of executive power is required to deal with such lawless demonstrations.

"The courts should stand aloof from them and not invade executive prerogative, nor, even at the behest or request of the executive, travel out of the beaten path of well-settled judicial authority. A mob cannot be suppressed by injunction; nor can its leaders be tried, convicted, and sentenced in equity.

"It is too great a strain upon the judicial branch of the government to impose this essentially executive and military power upon courts of chancery."

We do not perceive that this argument questions the jurisdiction of the court, but only the expediency of the action of the government in applying for its process. It surely cannot be seriously contended that the court has jurisdiction to enjoin the obstruction of a highway by one person, but that its jurisdiction ceases when the obstruction is by a hundred persons. It may be true, as suggested, that in the excitement of passion a mob will pay little heed to processes issued from the courts, and it may be, as said by counsel in argument, that it would savor somewhat of the puerile and ridiculous to have read a writ of injunction to Lee's army during the late Civil War.   *   *   * But does not counsel's argument imply too much?   Is it to be assumed that these defendants were conducting a rebellion or inaugurating a revolution, and that they and their associates were thus placing themselves beyond the reach of the civil process of the courts? We find in the opinion of the circuit court a quotation from the testimony given by one of the defendants before the United States strike commission, which is sufficient answer to this suggestion:

"As soon as the employees found that we were arrested, and taken from the scene of action, they became demoralized, and that ended the strike.   It was not the soldiers that ended the strike.   It was not the old brotherhoods that ended the strike.   It was simply the United States courts that ended the strike.   Our men were in a position that never would have been shaken, under any circumstances, if we had been permitted to remain upon the field, among them.   Once we were taken from the scene of action, and restrained from sending telegrams or issuing orders or answering questions, then the minions of the corporations would be put to work.   *   *   *   Our headquarters were temporarily demoralized and abandoned, and we could not answer any messages.   The men went back to work, and the ranks were broken, and the strike was broken up.   *   *   *   not by the army, and not by any other power, but simply and solely by the action of the United States courts in restraining us from discharging our duties as officers and representatives of our employees."

*   *   *

It must be borne in mind that this bill was not simply to enjoin a mob and mob violence.   It was not a bill to command a keeping of the peace;   much less was its purport to restrain the defendants from abandoning whatever employment they were engaged in.   The right of any laborer, or any number of laborers, to quit work was not challenged.   The scope and purpose of the bill was only to restrain forcible obstructions of the highways along which interstate commerce travels and the mails are carried.   *   *   *

A most earnest and eloquent appeal was made to us in eulogy of the heroic spirit of those who threw up their employment, and gave up their means of earning a livelihood, not in defense of their own rights, but in sympathy for and to assist others whom they believed to be wronged.   We yield to none in our admiration of any act of heroism or self-sacrifice, but we may be permitted to add that it is a lesson which cannot be learned too soon or too thoroughly that under this government of and by the people the means of redress of all wrongs are through the courts and at the ballot box, and that no wrong, real or fancied, carries with it legal warrant to invite as a means of redress the co-operation of a mob, with its accompanying acts of violence.

* * *

We enter into no examination of the act of July 2, 1890 (26 Stat. 209), upon which the circuit court relied mainly to sustain its jurisdiction. It must not be understood from this that we dissent from the conclusions of that court in reference to the scope of the act, but simply that we prefer to rest our judgment on the broader ground which has been discussed in this opinion, believing it of importance that the principles underlying it should be fully stated and affirmed.

The petition for a writ of habeas corpus is denied.

NOTES AND QUESTIONS

1. As the introduction to this section suggests, in 1894 there was an intense mood of public apprehension. In many ways the feelings of those in the national government were similar to those of the Federalists one hundred years before. Many believed that the increasing patterns of radical agitation and labor unrest presaged open rebellion, and that strong measures from the central authorities were required. In this light, do the actions of President Cleveland and Attorney General Olney in sending federal troops to Chicago seem to result from national necessity or political expediency?

As you have seen from some of these materials, the workers of the American Railroad Union (ARU) of which Debs was President, *had* agreed to "support the Pullman strike by a boycott of Pullman cars on all railroads." The ARU, however, offered to uncouple the sleeping (Pullman) cars, so that the rest of the trains could go on, including the mail cars. The General Managers Association (GMA), the organization of the high officers of the railroads, refused to allow uncoupling of the Pullman cars, however, allegedly believing that if they capitulated, any one of them might later be injured by similar strikes. When the ARU then refused to let the trains pass, interstate commerce on the rails came to a halt. See, e. g. Iris Nobel, Labor's Advocate: Eugene V. Debs 99–101 (1966).

But whether or not the railroads took their actions because of fears that they might individually suffer in the future from strikes, it also seems clear that the GMA members believed that if they allowed the uncoupling of Pullman cars they would be violating contracts with Pullman, thus leaving themselves open to civil suits for breach of contract. It appears that such uncoupling could also have been viewed as illegal discrimination against Pullman under the Interstate Commerce Act. See, e. g., A. Paul, Conservative Crisis and the Rule of Law: Attitudes of Bench and Bar 1887–1895 143 (Torchbook ed. 1969). Still, there may have been opportunities to resolve some of the points in issue among the workers, Pullman, and the Railroads by mediation or arbitration, but Pullman and the Railroads refused to consider this option. Id. at 153. Who, then, was ultimately responsible for the disruption of interstate commerce?

The Governor of Illinois, John Peter Altgeld, was the state's first Democratic governor, and quite sympathetic to labor. Two years earlier he had risked denunciation as an anarchist because of his pardoning of three men convicted of starting the Haymarket riot of 1886. Altgeld believed that "the jury which had convicted them was packed, the judge prejudiced, and the defendants not proved guilty." Altgeld eventually tried in vain to persuade Cleveland that the situation in Chicago was perfectly capable of being controlled by state militia, that the press had overstated the dimensions of the problem, and that there was no need for federal troops. Cleveland and his advisors disagreed. Without a request from state authorities, and without consultation of Altgeld, on July 4, 1894, 2,000 federal troops arrived in Chicago:

> From then on * * * the American Railway Union lost all control of the situation. Mobs, which the Strike Commission [the federal body which later investigated events] described as "composed generally of hoodlums, women, a low class of foreigners, and recruits of the criminal classes," took possession of railroad yards, upsetting, burning, and destroying cars and stealing whatever property they could lay their hands on. Nevertheless, it was difficult to accept the President's opinion that terror reigned in Chicago. Few strikers were seen in the mobs or arrested, and none were killed by troops or deputies. The American Railway Union had no part in instigating mob violence. On the other hand, no one could deny that a great deal of property was destroyed. Twelve people were killed.

Harold U. Faulkner, Politics, Reform and Expansion 1890–1900 177–178, 179 (1959). The activity thus described took place *after* the injunction forbidding interference with the mails, but *before* the arrest and indictment of Debs and three other ARU officials. The four were indicted for conspiracy, and, a week later, Debs and the others were charged with contempt of court for having disobeyed the injunction. The conspiracy proceedings, as you will soon learn from Debs himself, were never completed. The same court which issued the injunction tried Debs and his colleagues for the contempt. Debs received a six month sentence, the others three months.

2. The introductory readings give you something of the ideological flavor of the dispute, and the conditions of the workers. Stein and Taft quote a contemporary's suggestion that the system at Pullman was "unAmerican." What was meant by that? Is Reverend Carwardine correct when he suggests that for "all intents and purposes" there is no difference between modern industrial workers at Pullman, and Gurth, the Swineherd? Consider whether the lot of the laborer at Pullman was what was envisioned by Shaw when he wrote his opinion in Commonwealth v. Hunt. Would Shaw have approved of Pullman? What about Recorder Levy?

3. Would you have concurred with the Supreme Court's opinion in the *Debs* case? Your version has been condensed, but you may still be able to sense that Justice Brewer spends much time stressing the nature of the United States' power to supervise interstate commerce. Is that really the issue in the *Debs* case? Do you find any similarities or differences between the approach in the *Debs* case and that of the *E. C. Knight* case? Are you convinced that the holding in contempt for disobedience to an injunction is *not* a matter of criminal law requiring a trial by jury? Does Brewer's conception of the permissible scope of federal court activity remind

you at all of that of the Federalist Peters, expressed in United States v. Worrall, supra p. 204?

4. Towards the close of his opinion, Justice Brewer states that in the course of the United States Government's actions in the Pullman strike, "The right of any laborer, or any number of laborers to quit work was not challenged." Given the effect of the labor injunction as a tool to control unions, do you think that the laborers' right to "quit work" may have been altered? Do you find any clues to the court's feelings on the appropriateness of strikes and boycotts as a bargaining tool when it declares almost immediately afterwards that "under this government of and by the people the means of redress of all wrongs are through the courts and at the ballot box * * *." Would lowering of wages be such a "wrong?" In any event, it appears that the Reverend Carwardine would be sympathetic to Justice Brewer's offering of the "ballot box" as a means of vindication of the workers' rights. Do you think that you would have found that satisfactory if you were a worker? Would Debs? Consider what he has to say about the ballot in the following excerpt.

5. Brewer ends his opinion with the assertion that "we enter into no examination of the act of July 2, 1890 (26 Stat. 209), upon which the circuit court relied mainly to sustain its jurisdiction." Is it not curious that the Supreme Court feels it necessary to adopt a different basis for jurisdiction from that of the circuit court? What was the act to which Brewer referred, and why did he "prefer to rest our judgment on the broader ground * * *?" Consider Stein & Taft's statement that Olney rested his request for injunction against the strikers on the charge that they were "obstructing the mails and interfering with interstate commerce, both of which were forbidden by the Sherman Antitrust Act of 1890 * * *." Would you have advised Olney thus to proceed?

EUGENE V. DEBS

EUGENE V. DEBS, "LIBERTY" *

3–27 (1895).

[This was a speech delivered by Debs following his release from jail.]

* * * I greet you to-night as lovers of liberty and despisers of despotism. * * * The vindication and glorification of American principles of government, as proclaimed to the world in the Declaration of Independence, is the high purpose of this convocation.

Speaking for myself personally, I am not certain whether this is an occasion for rejoicing or lamentation. I confess to a serious doubt as to whether this day marks my deliverance from bondage to freedom or my doom from freedom to bondage. Certain it is, in the light of recent judicial proceedings, that I stand in your presence stripped of my constitutional rights as a free-man and shorn of the most sacred prerogatives of American citizenship, and what is true of myself is true of every other citizen who has the temerity to protest against corporation rule or question the absolute sway of the money power. It is not law nor the administration of law of which I complain. It is the flagrant violation of the Constitution, the total abrogation of law and the usurpation of judicial and despotic power, by virtue of which my colleagues and myself were committed to jail * * *."

In a letter recently written by the venerable Judge Trumbull that eminent jurist says: "The doctrine announced by the Supreme Court in the Debs case, carried to its logical conclusion, places every citizen at the mercy of any prejudiced or malicious federal judge who may think proper to imprison him." * * * The authority of Judge Trumbull upon this question will not be impeached by anyone whose opinions are not deformed or debauched.

At this juncture I deem it proper to voice my demand for a trial by a jury of my peers. At the instigation of the railroad corporations centering here in Chicago I was indicted for conspiracy and I insist upon being tried as to my innocence or guilt. It will be remembered that the trial last winter terminated very abruptly on account of a sick juror. It was currently reported at the time that this was merely a pretext to abandon the trial and thus defeat the vindication of a favorable verdict * * *. Whether this be true or not, I do not know. * * * I am charged with conspiracy to commit a crime, and if guilty I should go to the penitentiary. All I ask is a fair trial and no favor. If the counsel for the government, alias the railroads, have been correctly quoted in the press, the case against me is "not to be pressed," as they "do not wish to appear in the light of persecuting the defendants." I repel with scorn their professed mercy. Simple justice is the demand. * * *

* Reprinted in Stein, ed., The Pullman
Strike (1969).

* * *

For the first time in the records of all the ages, the inalienable rights of man, "life, liberty and the pursuit of happiness," were proclaimed July 4th, 1776.

It was then that crowns, sceptres, thrones and the divine right of kings to rule sunk together and man expanded to glorious liberty and sovereignty. It was then that the genius of Liberty, speaking to all men in the commanding voice of Eternal Truth, bade them assert their heaven-decreed prerogatives and emancipate themselves from bondage. It was a proclamation countersigned by the Infinite—and man stood forth the coronated sovereign of the world, free as the tides that flow, free as the winds that blow, and on that primal morning when creation was complete, the morning stars and the sons of God, in anthem chorus, sang the song of Liberty. * * *

It does not matter that the Creator has sown with stars the fields of ether and decked the earth with countless beauties for man's enjoyment. It does not matter that air and ocean teem with the wonders of innumerable forms of life to challenge man's admiration and investigation. * * * If liberty is ostracised and exiled, man is a slave, and the world rolls in space and whirls around the sun a gilded prison, a domed dungeon, and though painted in all the enchanting hues that infinite art could command, it must stand forth a blotch amidst the singing spheres of the sidereal heavens * * *.

* * *

* * * As Americans, we have boasted of our liberties and continue to boast of them. They were once the nation's glory, and, if some have vanished, it may be well to remember that a remnant still remains. Out of prison, beyond the limits of Russian injunctions, out of reach of a deputy marshal's club, above the throttling clutch of corporations and the enslaving power of plutocracy, out of range of the government's machine guns and knowing the location of judicial traps and deadfalls, Americans may still indulge in the exaltation of liberty, though pursued through every lane and avenue of life by the baying hounds of usurped and unconstitutional power, glad if when night lets down her sable curtains, they are out of prison, though still the wage-slaves of a plutocracy which, were it in the celestial city, would wreck every avenue leading up to the throne of the Infinite by stealing the gold with which they are paved, and debauch Heaven's supreme court to obtain a decision that the command "thou shalt not steal" is unconstitutional.

Liberty, be it known, is for those only who dare strike the blow to secure and retain the priceless boon. * * * [E]ternal vigilance is the price of liberty."

Is it worthwhile to iterate that all men are created free and that slavery and bondage are in contravention of the Creator's decree and have their origin in man's depravity?

If liberty is a birthright which has been wrested from the weak by the strong, or has been placed in peril by those who were commissioned to guard it * * * what is to be done? Above all, what is the duty of American workingmen whose liberties have been placed in peril? They are not hereditary bondsmen. Their fathers were free born—their sovereignty none denied and their children yet have the ballot. It has been called "a weapon that executes a free man's will as lightning does the will of God." * * * There is nothing in our government it can not remove or amend. It can make and unmake Presidents and Congresses and Courts. It can abolish unjust laws and consign to eternal odium and oblivion unjust judges, strip from them their robes and gowns and send them forth unclean as lepers to bear the burden of merited obloquy as Cain with the mark of a murderer. It can sweep away trusts, syndicates, corporations, monopolies, and every other abnormal development of the money power designed to abridge the liberties of workingmen and enslave them by the degradation incident to poverty and enforced idleness * * *. It can give our civilization its crowning glory—the co-operative commonwealth.

* * *

* * * My theme expands to proportions which obscure the victims of judicial tyranny, and yet, regardless of reluctance, it so happens by the decree of circumstances, that personal references are unavoidable. To wish it otherwise would be to deplore the organization of the American Railway Union and every effort that great organization has made to extend a helping hand to oppressed, robbed, suffering and starving men, women and children, the victims of corporate greed and rapacity. * * *

* * *

I hold it to have been inconceivable that an organization of workingmen, animated by such inspirations and aspirations, should have become the target for the shafts of judicial and governmental malice.

But the fact that such was the case brings into haggard prominence a condition of affairs that appeals to all thoughtful men in the ranks of organized labor and all patriotic citizens, regardless of vocation, who note the subtle invasions of the liberties of the American people by the courts, sustained by an administration that is equally dead to the guarantees of the constitution.

* * *

In the great Pullman strike the American Railway Union challenged the power of corporations in a way that had not previously been done, and the analyzation of this fact serves to expand it to proportions that the most conservative men of the nation regard with alarm.

It must be borne in mind that the American Railway Union did not challenge the government. It threw down no gauntlet to courts or armies—it simply resisted the invasion of the rights of working-men by corporations. * * *

The corporations left to their own resources of money, mendacity and malice, of thugs and ex-convicts, leeches and lawyers, would have been overwhelmed with defeat and the banners of organized labor would have floated triumphant in the breeze.

This the corporations saw and believed—hence the crowning act of infamy in which the federal courts and the federal armies partici-pated, and which culminated in the defeat of labor.

* * * [T]he defeat of the American Railway Union involved questions of law, constitution and government which, all things con-sidered, are without a parallel in court and governmental proceedings under the constitution of the Republic. And it is this judicial and ad-ministrative usurpation of power to override the rights of states and strike down the liberties of the people that has conferred upon the incidents connected with the Pullman strike such commanding im-portance as to attract the attention of men of the highest attainments in constitutional law and of statesmen who, like Jefferson, view with alarm the processes by which the Republic is being wrecked and a despotism reared upon its ruins.

* * * [T]he country stood amazed as the corporations put forth their latent powers to debauch such departments of the govern-ment as were required to defeat labor in the greatest struggle for the right that was ever chronicled in the United States.

Defeated at every point, their plans all frustrated, out-generaled in tactics and strategy, while the hopes of labor were brightening and victory was in sight, the corporations, goaded to desperation, played their last card in the game of oppression by an appeal to the federal judiciary and to the federal administration. To this appeal the re-sponse came quick as lightning from a storm cloud. * * *

The corporations first attack the judicial department of the gov-ernment, a department which, according to Thomas Jefferson, has menaced the integrity of the Republic from the beginning.

* * *

I am aware that innuendoes, dark intimations of venality are not regarded as courageous forms of arraignment, and yet the judicial despotism which marked every step of the proceedings by which my official associates and myself were doomed to imprisonment, was marked by infamies, supported by falsehoods and perjuries as destitute of truth as are the Arctic regions of orange blossoms.

* * *

There is an adage which says, "fight the devil with fire." In this connection why may it not be intimated that a judge who pollutes his high office at the behest of the money power has the hinges of his knees lubricated with oil from the tank of the corporation that thrift may follow humiliating obedience to its commands?

If not this, I challenge the world to assign a reason why a judge * * * should in a temple dedicated to justice, stab the Magna Charta of American liberty to death in the interest of corporations * * * ?

* * *

Once upon a time a corporation dog of good reputation was charged with killing sheep, though he had never been caught in the act. The corporation had always found him to be an obedient dog, willing to lick the hand of his master, and they declared he was a peaceable and law-abiding dog; but one day upon investigation the dog was found to have wool in his teeth and thenceforward, though the corporation stood manfully by him, he was believed to be a sheep-killing dog. The world has no means of knowing what methods corporations employ to obtain despotic decrees in their interest, but it is generally believed that if an examination could be made, there would be found wool in the teeth of the judge.

* * *

No afflatus, however divine, no genius, though saturated with the inspiring waters of Hippocrene, could now write in a spirit of patriotic fire of the old constitution, nor ever again until the people by the all pervading power of the ballot have repaired the old chart, closed the rents and obscured the judicial dagger holes made for the accomodation of millionaires and corporations, through which they drive their four-in-hands as if they were Cumberland gaps.

* * *

It might be a question in the minds of some if this occasion warrants the indulgence of the fancy. It will be remembered that Aesop taught the world by fables and Christ by parables but my recollection is that the old "stone preachers" * were as epigrammatic as an unabridged dictionary.

I remember one old divine who, one night, selected for his text George M. Pullman, and said: "George is a bad egg—handle him with care. Should you crack his shell the odor would depopulate Chicago in an hour." * * * Another old sermonizer who said he had been preaching since man was a molecule, declared he had of late years studied corporations, and that they were warts on the nose of our national industries * * *. Another old Stone said he knew more about strikes than Carroll D. Wright,** and that he was present when the slaves built the pyramids; that God Himself had taught His light-

---

* Debs is here building on Shakespeare's observation that: "This is our life, exempt from public haunt, finds tongues in trees, books in running brooks, *sermons in stones*, and good in everything."

** A Commissioner of the United States Strike Commission.

ning, thunderbolts, winds, waves and earthquakes to strike, and that strikes would proceed, with bullets or ballots, until workingmen, no longer deceived and cajoled by their enemies, would unify, proclaim their sovereignty and walk the earth free men.

O, yes; Shakespeare was right when he said there were sermons in stones. I recall one rugged-visaged old Stone preacher who claimed to have been a pavement bowlder in a street of heaven before the gold standard was adopted, and who discussed courts. He said they had been antagonizing the decrees of heaven since the day when Lucifer was cast into the bottomless pit. Referring to our Supreme Court he said it was a nest of rodents forever gnawing at the stately pillars supporting the temple of our liberties. I recall how his eyes, as he lifted their stony lids, flashed indignation like orbs of fire, and how his stony lips quivered as he uttered his maledictions of judicial treason to constitutional liberty.

* * * One old divine, having read some of the plutocratic papers on the Pullman strike and their anathemas of sympathy, when one workingman's heart, throbbing responsive to the divine law of love, prompted him to aid his brother in distress, discussed sympathy. He said sympathy was one of the perennial flowers of the Celestial City * * *.

Referring to the men and women of other labor organizations who had sympathized with the American Railway Union in its efforts to rescue Pullman's slaves from death by starvation, the old preacher placed a crown of jewelled eulogies upon their heads and said that in all the mutations of life * * *, there would never come a time to them when * * * they would not cherish as a valued souvenir of all their weary years that one act of sympathy for the victims of the Pullman piracy, and that when presented at the pearly gate of paradise, it would swing wide open and let them in amidst the joyous acclaims of angels.

NOTES AND QUESTIONS

1. Debs's speech, delivered the evening of his release from jail, was not, of course, intended to be a model legal brief. It was given in the Chicago Armory on Michigan Avenue, immediately after Debs's arrival in Chicago, where he was greeted by a cheering, tearful crowd possibly one hundred thousand strong, wearing the white ribbons of the ARU, and singing union songs. Noble, Labor's Advocate: Eugene V. Debs 131–133 (1966). Still, there is some analysis in the speech that should seem familiar to you. For example, how would you compare Debs's statements regarding "liberty" and "slavery" with those of the American Revolutionaries like James Otis, John Adams, or Thomas Jefferson? Debs invokes Jefferson with some frequency. Do you suppose Jefferson and Debs would have agreed on the ultimate meaning of "liberty?" What, if anything, can the views of Jefferson tell Debs about appropriate ways of dealing with capital and labor in the industrial age?

2. Like Carwardine, and like Justice Brewer, Debs offers the "ballot" as a means of solving America's industrial problems. What social system does Debs believe is appropriate once reformers have been elected, however? What do you suppose Debs means when he proposes, as a "crowning glory" to our civilization, "the co-operative commonwealth?" Consider Debs's views about corporations, and the people who run them. Is this hostility philosophically close to Harlan's or Peckham's ideas on trusts? Do you believe that Debs would share their conceptions of the appropriate economic order? How about Debs's views on law, lawyers, and judges? Is he a latter-day Honestus? Does the legal profession have a place in Debs's "co-operative commonwealth?"

3. Some lawyers appear to have understood that the law would have to find means of reconciling emerging class conflicts. In a speech delivered in 1888, entitled "Impending Perils," Charles C. Bonney, a former president of the Illinois Bar Association, told his listeners that it was the duty of government "to protect the weak against the strong, and to prevent, by stringent laws and their vigorous enforcement, the oppression of the poor and friendless by the rich and powerful." Bonney proceeded to propose that the American bar take the side of the angels "in the great conflict now impending between the people and the giant forces that are striving for the practical control of the republic." Bonney suggested that the bar support "a comprehensive plan for the settlement of all labor disputes, beginning with collective bargaining, then mediation, and finally compulsory arbitration," and that the government involve itself more in the regulation of labor, production and trade. Quoted in A. Paul, Conservative Crisis and the Rule of Law 32–33 (Torchbook ed., 1969).

In 1895, however, Debs probably had few friends within the American legal profession. The Senior editor of the American Law Review, Seymour D. Thompson, whom Arnold Paul states "could generally be counted on the progressive side of public issues," called Debs an "adventurer," an "irresponsible vagabond," and a "fiend" who produced widespread calamities which he observed with "insane hilarity." Thompson saw the Pullman strike as an attempt "to wrest from intelligent and capable men the property which they have acquired, and to put it into the hands of the unintelligent and ignorant." 28 American Law Review 630–634, 637 (1894) *quoted* in Paul, supra, at 145–146. Accordingly, Thompson believed that the conduct of Pullman and the railroads was blameless, as "they represented the right of every man to manage his own business and to keep his own contracts without dictation from third persons. * * * They entered upon a struggle with an unknown and appalling force, which threatened to revolutionize the very foundations of society and to reverse all the processes by which our splendid industrial system has been built up." Id. Does Debs's speech suggest that Thompson was right or wrong?

4. How accurately did Debs characterize late nineteenth century American law? Reread Professor Morton Horwitz's conclusions regarding the style of judicial reasoning during this period, reproduced in Chapter Four, at 374, supra. Do you find support for Horwitz's view in the court decisions you have recently read?

5. Other scholars have found that, at least by the end of the nineteenth century, the judicial philosophy was not as uniform as Horwitz's analysis

suggests. For example, Professor Morton Keller, after commenting on some opinions that seemed to go against the workingmen, particularly on the ground that state laws regulating working conditions were unconstitutional tamperings with freedom of contract, nevertheless concluded that

> * * * the extent of this antilabor decisionmaking often has been exaggerated. An 1897 review of 1,639 state labor laws enacted during the preceding twenty years found that only 114 of them—7 percent—had been held unconstitutional. * * * The police power of the states to regulate working conditions continued to be a powerful and widely accepted legal doctrine. Critics of labor injunctions had a strong array of arguments. They held that when the courts ordered workers to return to their jobs this was in effect enforcing a form of slavery; and that when judges issued injunctions in their equity capacity, they were imposing criminal sanctions without a jury trial or other common law safeguards. Equity was being transformed, charged one critic, from the protection of private rights to "the perversion of public rights, or the punishment of private wrongs."
>
> The activism of the courts in labor matters was blamed on "the dry rot which has attacked our state executives and our state legislatures, which renders them unable to perform in anything like an efficient manner their proper functions." But precisely because so much was expected of the courts, they could not act indefinitely in a sensitive area like labor relations without taking account of public opinion or economic and social realities. By the late 1890s, the influential New York and Massachusetts courts were increasingly inclined to uphold state laws affecting the conditions of labor. In Holden v. Hardy (1898) the United States Supreme Court sustained a Utah eight-hour law for miners. The courts, in sum, were no more single-minded in their response to a new, industrial America than were the other sectors of the polity.

Morton Keller, Affairs of State 407–408 (1977). Copyright © 1977 by Morton Keller, published by the Belknap Press of the Harvard University Press, Cambridge Massachusetts, and London, England. Reprinted with the permission of the publisher and the author.

LAWRENCE M. FRIEDMAN AND JACK LADINSKY, SOCIAL CHANGE AND THE LAW OF INDUSTRIAL ACCIDENTS *

67 Col.L.Rev. 50, 59–79 (1967).

A general pattern may be discerned which is common to the judicial history of many rules of law. The courts enunciate a rule, intending to "solve" a social problem * * *. If the rule comports with some kind of social consensus, it will in fact work a solution— that is, it will go unchallenged, or, if challenged, will prevail. Challenges will not usually continue, since the small chance of overturning the rule is not worth the cost of litigation. If, however, the rule is weakened—if courts engraft exceptions to it, for example—then fresh challenges probing new weaknesses will be encouraged. Even if the rule retains some support, it will no longer be efficient and clear-cut. Ultimately, the rule may no longer serve anybody's purposes. At this point, a fresh (perhaps wholly new) "solution" will be attempted.

The history of the fellow-servant rule rather neatly fits this scheme. Shaw wrote his *Farwell* opinion in 1842. During the latter part of the century, judges began to reject his reasoning. The "tendency in nearly all jurisdictions," said a Connecticut court in 1885, was to "limit rather than enlarge" the range of the fellow-servant rule. * * *

The rule was strong medicine, and it depended for its efficacy upon continued, relatively certain, and unswerving legal loyalty. Ideally, if the rule were strong and commanded nearly total respect from the various agencies of law, it would eliminate much of the mass of litigation that might otherwise arise. Undoubtedly, it did prevent countless thousands of law suits; but it did not succeed in choking off industrial accident litigation. For example, industrial accident litigation dominated the docket of the Wisconsin Supreme Court at the beginning of the age of workmen's compensation; far more cases arose under that heading than under any other single field of law. Undoubtedly, this appellate case-load was merely the visible portion of a vast iceberg of litigation. Thus, the rule did not command the respect required for efficient operation and hence, in the long run, survival.

One reason for the continued litigation may have been simply the great number of accidents that occurred. At the dawn of the industrial revolution, when Shaw wrote, the human consequences of that technological change were unforeseeable. In particular, the toll it would take of human life was unknown. But by the last quarter of the nineteenth century, the number of industrial accidents had grown enormously. After 1900, it is estimated, 35,000 deaths and 2,000,000 injuries occurred every year in the United States. * * *

In addition to the sheer number of accidents, other reasons for the increasing number of challenges to the rule in the later nineteenth century are apparent. If the injury resulted in death or permanent disability, it broke off the employment relationship; the plaintiff or his family thereafter had nothing to lose except the costs of suit. The development of the contingent fee system provided the poor man with the means to hire a lawyer. * * *

The contingent fee system was no more than a mechanism, however. A losing plaintiff's lawyer receives no fee; that is the essence of the system. The fact is that plaintiffs won many of their lawsuits;

in so doing, they not only weakened the fellow-servant rule, but they encouraged still more plaintiffs to try their hand, still more attorneys to make a living from personal injury work. In trial courts, the pressure of particular cases—the "hard" cases in which the plight of the plaintiff was pitiful or dramatic—tempted judges and juries to find for the little man and against the corporate defendant. In Shaw's generation, many leading appellate judges shared his view of the role of the judge; they took it as their duty to lay down grand legal principles to govern whole segments of the economic order. Thus, individual hardship cases had to be ignored for the sake of higher duty. But this was not the exclusive judicial style, even in the appellate courts. And in personal injury cases, lower court judges and juries were especially prone to tailor justice to the case at hand. For example, in Wisconsin, of 307 personal injury cases involving workers that appeared before the state supreme court up to 1907, nearly two-thirds had been decided in favor of the worker in the lower courts. * * *

* * * [S]ympathy for injured workers manifested itself also in changes in doctrine. On the appellate court level, a number of mitigations of the fellow-servant rule developed near the end of the nineteenth century. For example, it had always been conceded that the employer was liable if he was personally responsible (through his own negligence) for his worker's injury. * * * Out of this simple proposition grew the so-called vice-principal rule, which allowed an employee to sue his employer where the negligent employee occupied a supervisory position such that he could more properly be said to be an alter ego of the principal than a mere fellow-servant. * * *

There were scores of other "exceptions" to the fellow-servant rule, enunciated in one or more states. * * * Among these was the duty to furnish a safe place to work, safe tools, and safe appliances. Litigation on these points was enormous, and here too the cases cannot readily be summed up or even explained. In Wedgwood v. Chicago & Northwestern Railway Co. [41 Wisc. 478 (1877)] the plaintiff, a brakeman, was injured by a "large and long bolt, out of place, and which unnecessarily, carelessly and unskillfully projected beyond the frame, beam or brakehead, in the way of the brakeman going to couple the cars." The trial court threw the case out, but the Wisconsin Supreme Court reversed:

> It is true, the defendant * * * is a railroad corporation, and can only act through officers or agents. But this does not relieve it from responsibility for the negligence of its officers and agents whose duty it is to provide safe and suitable machinery for its road which its employees are to operate.

So phrased, of course, the exception comes close to swallowing the rule. * * *

[There were many qualifications and exceptions to these rules, and this d]octrinal complexity and vacillation in the upper courts, coupled with jury freedom in the lower courts, meant that by the end of the century the fellow-servant rule had lost much of its reason for existence: it was no longer an efficient cost-allocating doctrine. * * *

The numerous judge-made exceptions reflected a good deal of uncertainty about underlying social policy. The same uncertainty was reflected in another sphere of legal activity—the legislature. Though the rule was not formally abrogated, it was weakened by statute in a number of jurisdictions. * * * The early nineteenth century cannot be uncritically described as a period that accepted without question business values and practices. Rather, it accepted the ideal of economic growth, which certain kinds of enterprise seemed to hinder. Thus in the age of Jackson, as is well known, popular feeling ran high against financial institutions, chiefly the chartered banks. Banks were believed to have far too much economic power; they corrupted both the currency and the government. They were a "clog upon the industry of this country." But many a good judge, who decried the soulless corporation (meaning chiefly the moneyed kind) in the best Jacksonian tradition, may at the same time have upheld the fellow-servant rule. * * *

* * * Great masses of people had come to accept the notion that the power of the railroads was a threat to farmers and a threat to the independence and stability of democratic institutions. Out of the ashes of ineffective and impermanent state regulation of railroads arose what ultimately became a stronger and more systematic program of regulation, grounded in federal power over the national economy.

The Interstate Commerce Commission was created in 1887, chiefly to outlaw discrimination in freight rates and other practices deemed harmful to railroad users. The original legislation had nothing to say about railroad accidents and safety. But this did not long remain the case. The railroads had become unpopular defendants relatively early in American legal history. By 1911, twenty-five states had laws modifying or abrogating the fellow-servant doctrine for railroads. * * * In 1893, Congress required interstate railroads to equip themselves with safety appliances, and provided that any employee injured "by any locomotive, car, or train in use" without such appliances would not "be deemed * * * to have assumed the risk thereby occasioned."

The Federal Employers' Liability Act of 1908 [FELA] went much further; it abolished the fellow-servant rule for railroads and greatly reduced the strength of contributory negligence and assumption of risk as defenses. * * *

FELA shows one of many possible outcomes of the decline in efficacy of the fellow-servant rule. Under it, the rule was eliminated, and the law turned to a "pure" tort system—pure in the sense that the proclivities of juries were not interfered with by doctrines designed to limit the chances of a worker's recovery. But the railroads were a special case. Aside from the special history of regulation, the interstate character of the major railroads made them subject to national safety standards and control by a single national authority. For other industrial employers, the FELA route was not taken; instead, workmen's compensation acts were passed. In either case, however, the fellow-servant rule was abolished, or virtually so. Either course reflects, we can assume, some kind of general agreement that the costs of the rule outweighed its benefits.

The common law doctrines were designed to preserve a certain economic balance in the community. When the courts and legislatures created numerous exceptions, the rules lost much of their efficiency as a limitation on the liability of businessmen. * * * There were costs of settlements, costs of liability insurance, costs of administration, legal fees and the salaries of staff lawyers. These costs rose steadily, at the very time when American business, especially big business, was striving to rationalize and bureaucratize its operations. * * * The costs of industrial accident liability were not easily predictable, partly because legal consequences of accidents were not predictable. * * *

In addition, industry faced a serious problem of labor unrest. Workers and their unions were dissatisfied with many aspects of factory life. The lack of compensation for industrial accidents was one obvious weakness. Relatively few injured workers received compensation. Under primitive state employers' liability statutes, the issue of liability and the amount awarded still depended upon court rulings and jury verdicts. Furthermore, the employer and the insurance carrier might contest a claim or otherwise delay settlement in hopes of bringing the employee to terms. * * *

When an employee did recover, the amount was usually small. The New York Commission found that of forty-eight fatal cases studied in Manhattan * * * most received less than $500. The deceased workers had averaged $15.22 a week in wages; only eight families recovered as much as three times their average yearly earnings. * * *

Litigation costs consumed much of whatever was recovered. It was estimated that, in 1907, "of every $100 paid out by [employers in New York] on account of work accidents but $56 reached the injured workmen and their dependents." * * *

These figures on the inadequacy of recoveries are usually cited to show how little the workers received for their pains. But what did these figures mean to employers? Assuming that employers, as

rational men, were anxious to pay as little compensation as was necessary to preserve industrial peace and maintain a healthy workforce,
the better course might be to pay a higher net amount direct to employees. Employers had little or nothing to gain from their big payments to insurance companies, lawyers, and court officials. Perhaps at some unmeasurable point of time, the existing tort system
crossed an invisible line and thereafter, purely in economic terms,
represented on balance a net loss to the industrial establishment.
From that point on, the success of a movement for change in the
system was certain, provided that businessmen could be convinced
that indeed their self-interest lay in the direction of reform and that
a change in compensation systems did not drag with it other unknow-
able and harmful consequences.

As on many issues of reform, the legal profession did not speak
with one voice. Certainly, many lawyers and judges were dissatisfied with the status quo. Judges complained about the burdens imposed on the court system by masses of personal injury suits; many
felt frustrated by the chaotic state of the law, and others were bothered by their felt inability to do justice to injured workmen. * * *
Some influential judges despaired of piecemeal improvements and
played an active role in working for a compensation system. In a
1911 opinion, Chief Justice J. B. Winslow of Wisconsin wrote:

> No part of my labor on this bench has brought such heart-
> weariness to me as that ever increasing part devoted to
> the consideration of personal injury actions brought by em-
> ployees against their employers. The appeal to the emotions
> is so strong in these cases, the results to life and limb and
> human happiness so distressing, that the attempt to honestly
> administer cold, hard rules of law * * * make[s] drafts
> upon the heart and nerves which no man can appreciate who
> has not been obliged to meet the situation himself * * *.
> These rules are archaic and unfitted to modern industrial
> conditions * * *.

> When [the faithful laborer] * * * has yielded up
> life, or limb, or health in the service of that marvelous in-
> dustrialism which is our boast, shall not the great public
> * * * be charged with the duty of securing from want the
> laborer himself, if he survive, as well as his helpless and
> dependent ones? Shall these latter alone pay the fearful
> price of the luxuries and comforts which modern machinery
> brings within the reach of all?

> These are burning and difficult questions with which
> the courts cannot deal, because their duty is to administer
> the law as it is, not to change it; but they are well within
> the province of the legislative arm of the government.

* * * Legal writers and law teachers also spoke out against the common law and in favor of a compensation system. Roscoe Pound voiced a common opinion in 1907:

> [I]t is coming to be well understood by all who have studied the circumstances of modern industrial employment that the supposed contributory negligence of employees is in effect a result of the mechanical conditions imposed on them by the nature of their employment, and that by reason of these conditions the individual vigilance and responsibility contemplated by the common law are impossible in practice.

* * *

When considerations of politics were added to those of business economics and industrial peace, it was not surprising to find that businessmen gradually withdrew their veto against workmen's compensation statutes. * * * In 1910, the president of the National Association of Manufacturers (NAM) appointed a committee to study the possibility of compensating injured workmen without time-consuming and expensive litigation, and the convention that year heard a speaker tell them that no one was satisfied with the present state of the law—that the employers' liability system was "antagonistic to harmonious relations between employers and wage workers." By 1911 the NAM appeared convinced that a compensation system was inevitable and that prudence dictated that business play a positive role in shaping the design of the law—otherwise the law would be "settled for us by the demagogue, and agitator and the socialist with a vengeance." Business would benefit economically and politically from a compensation system, but only if certain conditions were present. Business, therefore, had an interest in pressing for a specific kind of program * * *. For example, it was imperative that the new system be in fact as actuarially predictable as business demanded; it was important that the costs of the program be fair and equal in their impact upon particular industries, so that no competitive advantage or disadvantage flowed from the scheme. Consequently the old tort actions had to be eliminated, along with the old defenses of the company. In exchange for certainty of recovery by the worker, the companies were prepared to demand certainty and predictability of loss—that is, limitation of recovery. The jury's caprice had to be dispensed with. In short, when workmen's compensation became law, as a solution to the industrial accident problem, it did so on terms acceptable to industry. * * *

* * *

Between 1910 and 1920 the method of compensating employees injured on the job was fundamentally altered in the United States. In brief, workmen's compensation statutes eliminated (or tried to eliminate) the process of fixing civil liability for industrial accidents through litigation in common law courts. Under the statutes, compensation was based on statutory schedules, and the responsibility for initial determination of employee claims was taken from the courts and given to an administrative agency. Finally, the statutes abolished the fellow-servant rule and the defenses of assumption of risk and contributory negligence. Wisconsin's law, passed in 1911, was the first general compensation act to survive a court test. Mississippi, the last state in the Union to adopt a compensation law, did so in 1948.

Compensation systems varied from state to state, but they had many features in common. The original Wisconsin law was representative of the earlier group of statutes. It set up a voluntary system—a response to the fact that New York's courts had held a compulsory scheme unconstitutional on due process grounds. Wisconsin abolished the fellow-servant rule and the defense of assumption of risk for employers of four or more employees. In turn, the compensation scheme, for employers who elected to come under it, was made the "exclusive remedy" for an employee injured accidentally on the job. The element of "fault" or "negligence" was eliminated, and the mere fact of injury at work "proximately caused by accident," and not the result of "wilful misconduct," made the employer liable to pay compensation but exempt from ordinary tort liability. The state aimed to make it expensive for employers to stay out of the system. Any employer who did so was liable to suit by injured employees and the employer was denied the common law defenses.

The compensation plans strictly limited the employee's amount of recovery. In Wisconsin, for example, if an accident caused "partial disability," the worker was to receive 65% of his weekly loss in wages during the period of disability, not to exceed four times his average annual earnings. The statutes, therefore, were compensatory, not punitive, and the measure of compensation was, subject to strict limitations, the loss of earning power of the worker. In the original Wisconsin act, death benefits were also payable to dependents of the worker. If the worker who died left "no person dependent upon him for support," the death benefit was limited to "the reasonable expense of his burial, not exceeding $100." Neither death nor injury as such gave rise to a right to compensation—only the fact of economic loss to someone, either the worker himself or his family. * * *

* * *

NOTES AND QUESTIONS

1. Of what significance is it that "industrial accident litigation dominated the docket of the Wisconsin Supreme Court [in the early twentieth century] * * * far more cases arose under that heading than under any single field of law." Specifically, if one solves the industrial accident "problem," does this remove or increase pressure to solve other social problems? If the "contingency fee arrangement" was a significant factor in enabling injured workers to bring suit, and thus put pressure on the

"fellow-servant" rule—pressure that ultimately led to its demise—and if this represented a democratization of the furnishing of legal services, what is the effect on democracy of the abolition of the "fellow-servant" rule through workmen's compensation schemes? By the way, does the "safe-tool" exception to the fellow-servant rule remind you of the "trade fixtures" exemption to the "waste" doctrine? See Van Ness v. Pacard, supra page 301.

2. How do you evaluate the anguish suffered by some of the early twentieth century judges as they applied the legal doctrines regarding employer's liability? Note that in 1911 Chief Justice J. B. Winslow of Wisconsin called his task "distressing", and said that "These rules are archaic and unfitted to modern industrial conditions * * *." And yet, the Judge said that "These are burning and difficult questions with which the courts cannot deal, because their duty is to administer the law as it is, not to change it * * *." Is there a slip in reasoning there? Is Winslow's attitude consistent with that evidenced by Chief Justice Shaw in the labor cases? How about the perspective of the early nineteenth century judges we studied in Chapter III?

3. Why do you suppose that in 1911 the New York Court of Appeals unanimously declared the nation's first workmen's compensation statute unconstitutional in Ives v. South Buffalo R. Co., 201 N.Y. 271, 94 N.E. 431 (1911)? Why then, did the Wisconsin scheme, and later Workmen's Compensation Acts survive constitutional scrutiny? Indeed, two years later the New York State Constitution was amended to allow involuntary workmen's compensation legislation. Finally, four years after that, in New York Cent. R. R. Co. v. White, 243 U.S. 188, 37 S.Ct. 247, 61 L.Ed. 667 (1917) and Hawkins v. Bleakly, 243 U.S. 210, 37 S.Ct. 255, 61 L.Ed. 678 (1917) the United States Supreme Court held compulsory *and* elective workmen's compensation schemes to be constitutional.

4. Is the passage of workmen's compensation legislation a "victory of employees over employers?" Whom does it benefit to replace a "fault-oriented" compensation system with one unconcerned with fault? What does the history of workmen's compensation efforts, and the fall of the fellow-servant doctrine tell you about the workings of the late nineteenth century and early twentieth century judiciary and legislatures? Does the evidence support Horwitz's view of the judiciary, and its preoccupation with "formalism?" Does the evidence support Professor Keller's assessment of judicial uncertainty in the face of massive societal and economic change? Consider the free-market, contractarian model that Justice Shaw and Recorder Levy advanced. Given the social unrest and the judicial and legislative efforts which you have just read about, including the Sherman Act, *and* the workmen's compensation statutes, do you find that American law was still following Shaw's and Levy's model in the late nineteenth and early twentieth century? We will have further evidence with which to examine the nature of American law in the next Chapter.

Chapter 6

LAW AND JURISPRUDENCE FOR THE MODERN INDUSTRIAL AGE

SECTION A. THE SCIENCE OF LAW

DAVID DUDLEY FIELD, MAGNITUDE AND IMPORTANCE OF LEGAL SCIENCE *

(1859).

Address at the opening of the Law School of the University of Chicago, September 21, 1859.

* * *

* * * There are undoubtedly several topics, which might properly be considered, in connection with the establishment of this school—as, for example, its relations to the public, to the university and to its own pupils, or the most advisable course of study; but I shall only ask you to consider with me now the magnitude and importance of legal science. And though all knowledge has value, and all the arts their uses, yet, as there are differences in value as in use, I hope to show you that, of all the sciences and all the arts, not one can be named greater in magnitude or importance than * * * the science of the law.

Law is a rule of property and of conduct prescribed by the sovereign power of a state. The science of the law embraces, therefore, all the rules recognized and enforced by the state, of all the property and of all the conduct of men in all their relations, public and private. * * * No engagement can be entered into, no work undertaken, no journey made, but with the law in view. * * * This science, therefore, is equal in duration with histcry, in extent with all the affairs of men.

We can measure it best by tracing its progress. When men dwelt in tents and led a pastoral life, their laws might have been compressed in a few pages. They had, of course, some part of our law of personal rights, the law of succession, and of boundaries between the occupiers of adjoining pastures. This was the condition of the race in the primitive ages, and is even yet the condition of some parts of it. * * *

The next stage in the civilization of the race was the fixed habitation and the cultivation of the soil; and this brought with it

---

* Reprinted in I Sprague, ed., Speeches,
Arguments, and Miscellaneous Papers
of David Dudley Field 517–533 (1884).

the next stage in the development of the legal system—the law of land and of permanent structures—a department which, though it teaches of the most permanent of earthly things, has not partaken of their permanence, but has fluctuated with political condition. The distribution of the land has determined the policy and the fate of governments, and these in their turn have encouraged the aggregation or subdivision of estates, as they inclined to aristocratic or democratic institutions.

 * * * To possess land, to own an estate, to found a family, and to make for it an ancestral home, are objects of ambition almost universal. We seem to ourselves to be more firmly fixed when we are anchored in the soil. * * * And, notwithstanding the enormous increase of personal property in our modern society, the larger portion of man's wealth is still in the land. * * *

For these reasons, the law, which regulates the possession, enjoyment, and transfer of real property, has always been the subject of special attention. It has oscillated, as governments have swayed back and forth; at one time allodial, at another fuedal, sometimes comparatively simple; then excessively complex; in one country natural, in another artificial. But in all countries * * * the law of real property has ever been and must be large and difficult. The acquisition and use of land, the different kinds of ownership, the exclusive and perpetual, or the joint or temporary title, the conflicting interests of adjoining owners, the relative rights of landlord and tenant, and a thousand other conditions and incidents, can only be regulated upon a careful and minute analysis, by a series of rules adjusted with nice discrimination * * *..

In the next stage of civilization, the products of the soil were wrought into new forms, and manufactured fabrics added to the wealth and comfort of man. Manufactures required the purchase and collection of materials, the employment of workmen, and the sale of the fabric. Commerce led to navigation. Each of these operations added a new chapter to the law.

Of these three stages in civilization and in law, the ancient world was witness, but not in their highest development, though in forms of which the records will last for ever. The accumulation of lawbooks became so burdensome that, thirteen hundred years ago, it was found necessary to reduce them by substituting digests and codes. * * * Since then, however, materials have accumulated, greater by far than those out of which the Roman Codes were constructed.

 * * * The present law of real property in this country and in England was brought from the North or Northeast, by those conquering tribes, whose scheme of civil polity was a gradation of ranks, bound together by feudal ties. This feudal system, after having flourished through several centuries, has been gradually softening and disintegrating under the double influence of commerce and peace.

Our maritime law is also in great part of modern origin   *   *   *;
rules by which modern commerce is governed began with the activity
of the middle ages, and grew to maturity with the enterprise of our
own times.   The best part of our law of personal rights we owe to
the spirit of Christianity and the influence of chivalry.   A man's person is now sacred.   *   *   *   He may go or stay wheresoever he will;
he may engage in any pursuit which pleases him; he may embrace
any faith which appears right in his own eyes.   Associations being
more powerful than individuals, corporations scarcely known to the
ancients have become the most frequent and the most powerful agencies of modern society.   During all the while the machinery of government has been increasing and expanding, till volumes are filled
with the rules which relate to that alone.   And, last of all, there have
just appeared the three most marvelous inventions of all time—the
steamer, the railway, and the telegraph—which, while they have been
making a revolution in the social life of man, have, at the same time,
been adding three chapters to the books of his laws.   *   *   *

The more perfect is the civilization, the more complete is the
law.   The latter is, in many respects, both the cause and the consequence of the former.   *   *   *

*   *   *

*   *   *   Who that has studied the government of a country,
though occupying but a single department in its laws, but wonders
at the magnitude of the subject?   A lifetime seems scarcely sufficient
for its mastery.   Political philosophy and history are its adjuncts.
Take our political code, survey it generally, enter into its details,
study its history, consider how many good and wise men have participated in its framing, how cautiously it has been contrived, amended,
added to, debated, at every step in its progress, and then stand reverently before it as the grandest monument of human genius.   Time
would fail me if I were to attempt recounting even the principal
epochs in its history; the long and hardy training of our forefathers
beyond the sea, where their institutions were purified by blood and
fire, the transplanting of those institutions hither, their curtailment
of the monarchical portions, the amelioration which time and experience have wrought, the principle of federation, its origin and development, and the final completion of the vast structure of our Government, Federal and State, through all its parts.   *   *   *   Large
must be the book which shall even describe adequately this double
Government of ours—larger still that which shall contain all the laws
by which it moves and all the functions which it performs; its various departments, legislative, executive, and judicial, the powers and
duties of all its public officers, its revenues, and the different branches of the public service.

*   *   *

*   *   *   Let us select for example a single department and follow
out its subdivisions.   Take if you will the contract of sale, and see

into how many branches it divides itself. Whether the contract be written or unwritten, whether there be an actual transfer, or only an agreement to transfer, whether the thing agreed upon be already made or only to be made, whether it be sound or defective or deficient in quantity, whether there be fair dealing, concealment, or misrepresentation as to quality, existence, or value, whether the thing has been delivered or paid for in whole or in part, whether the seller or the purchaser ever, and if so when and upon what terms, may rescind the contract and be reinstated—all these, and many more, are considerations affecting the transaction, which the law has carefully provided for, by an appropriate rule.

The law may be compared to a majestic tree that is ever growing. It has a trunk heavy with centuries, great branches equal themselves to other trees, with their roots in the parent trunk; lesser branches, and from those lesser branches still, till you arrive at the delicate bud, which in a few years will be itself a branch, with a multitude of leaves and buds. * * * [T]he law appears infinite in its manifestations; the shelves of law libraries groan under the accumulation of their volumes. The curious in such matters have computed that the number of cases in the English Courts relating to practice alone equals twenty-five thousand, and that the common law has two million rules!

Compare this science with any of the other sciences; with those which are esteemed the greatest in extent, and the most exalted in subject. Take even astronomy, that noble science which * * * weighs the sun and the planets, measures their distances, traces their orbits, and penetrates the secrets of that great law which governs their motions. Sublime as this science is, it is but the science of inanimate matter, and a few natural laws; while the science which is the subject of our discourse governs the actions of human beings, intelligent and immortal, penetrates into the secrets of their souls, subdues their wills, and adapts itself to the endless variety of their wants, motives, and conditions.

Will you compare it with one of the exact sciences—as, for example, with mathematics? * * * Clear, precise, simple in its elements, far-reaching and sublime in its results, it has disciplined and exalted some of the greatest minds of our race, and been the nursery of other sciences, and of the mechanic arts. * * * But the science of calculation is occupied with a single principle. This it may go on to develop more and more, till the mind is almost lost in its immensity; yet the development of that one principle can never reach in extent, comprehensiveness, and variety the development of all the principles by which the actions of men toward each other are governed in all their relations. The law, it will be remembered, is the rule of all property and all conduct. * * *

* * *

This rapid survey may serve to give us some idea, imperfect, indeed, of the magnitude of legal science. Though it may be the most familiar of all things, it is also the most profound and immense. It surrounds us everywhere like the light of this autumnal day, or the breath of this all-comprehending air. It sits with us, sleeps beside us, walks with us abroad, studies with the inventor, writes with the scholar, and marches by the side of every new branch of industry and every new mode of travel. The infant of an hour old, the old man of threescore and ten, the feeble woman, the strong and hardy youth, are all under its equal care, and by it alike protected and restrained.

* * *

We have considered thus far the magnitude of legal science. Its importance is more than commensurate with its magnitude. Without it there could be no civilization and no order. Where there is no law, there can be no order, since order is but another name for regularity, or conformity to rule. Without order, society would relapse into barbarism. The very magnitude of the law is a proof of its necessity. It is great, because it is essential. There is a necessity, not only for law, but for a system, with arrangement and a due relation of parts; for, without this system, the administration of government, both in its judicial and its administrative departments, would fall into irretrievable confusion. * * *

The science of the law is our great security against the maladministration of justice. If the decision of litigated questions were to depend upon the will of the Judge or upon his notions of what was just, our property and our lives would be at the mercy of a fluctuating judgment, or of caprice. The existence of a system of rules and conformity to them are the essential conditions of all free government, and of republican government above all others. The law is our only sovereign. We have enthroned it. In other governments, loyalty to a personal sovereign is a bond for the State. * * * We have substituted loyalty to the State and the law for what with others is loyalty to the person. In place of a government of opposing interests, we have a double government of written Constitutions. The just interpretation of these Constitutions and the working of the double machinery, so that there may be no break and no jar, are committed in a great degree, how great few ever reflect, to the legal profession, and are dependent upon their knowledge of the science of law in all its departments, political, civil, penal, and remedial. Precisely, therefore, as free government and republican institutions are valuable, in the same proportion is the science of the law valuable as a means of preserving them.

* * *

I might add that, if there be any science and any culture tending to invigorate and sharpen the intellect, they are legal science and discipline. Every science rewards those who study it, by enlarging their minds to a comprehension of its learning; and the greater the science, the greater the reward. But there is something in the conduct of litigation which makes the judgment severe and keen, beyond any other discipline to which it is subjected. While, therefore, the study of the law has the effect of enlarging the vision of its practicers, it has also the effect of sharpening the intellect, leading to precision of thought and language, and acuteness in discovering the truth of facts. Who can unravel intrigues, lift the veil from hypocrisy, dissect evidence, and lay falsehood bare, like the practiced lawyer? Better men have never existed, more exalted in intellect, or purer in motive, or more useful in action, than our profession can show.

* * *

But I must return from this digression to the science which is the subject of this discourse. * * *

How shall this science best be learned? There are three methods: the private study of books; the advice and aid of practitioners, amid the bustle and interruptions of practice; and the teaching of public schools. The inadequacy of the first is obvious; the disadvantages of the second are too painfully known to all of us who studied in that way; the third is beyond question the most efficient and complete. There is as much need of public schools for the law as for any other science. There is more, for, the greater the science, the greater the need. Above all others, this science, so vast, so comprehensive, so complicated and various in its details, needs to be studied with all the aids which universities, professors, and libraries can furnish.

Where else so readily as here will the student obtain a view of the law as a whole, and of all its parts in their several relations and dependencies—here, where are collected the records of the science, where there are professors devoted to its teaching, where there are scholars emulous of distinction, and stimulating each other? * * *

* * *

NOTES AND QUESTIONS

1. What is the point of Field's speech? He calls it the "Magnitude and Importance" of legal science. What is the magnitude of legal science? Is the chief clue Field's proposition that the more perfect is the civilization, the more complete is the law?" Do you agree? In his controversial little book, The Ages of American Law (1977), Yale's Professor Grant Gilmore, a grand figure in the law of contract, admiralty, *and* legal history wrote:

Law reflects but in no sense determines the moral worth of a society. The values of a reasonably just society will reflect themselves in a reasonably just law. The better the society, the less law there will be. In Heaven there will be no law, and the lion will lie down with the lamb. The values of an unjust society will reflect themselves in an unjust law. The worse the society, the more law there will be. In Hell there will be nothing but law, and due process will be meticulously observed.*

The Ages of American Law, at 110–111. How do you account for the disagreement between Field and Gilmore? Do you suppose that Gilmore and Field share similar views of the course of history? What is Field's view? How would you compare Field's view of "the law" to that of Robert Rantoul or William Sampson?

2. What does Field mean when he suggests that "The law is our only sovereign. We have enthroned it?" Does this view explain his assertion that "legal science" is the most important science? Do you suppose that Chief Justice Shaw would have agreed with this assertion? Is Field merely making the point that ours is a government of laws, not men, or is he after something subtler? What does Field mean by "legal science?"

3. Field was speaking at the dedication of the institution that eventually became the Northwestern University School of Law. See Generally Rahl and Schwerin, Northwestern University School of Law: A Short History 5–6 (1960). What does Field see as the importance of law schools to legal science? Why was it, if legal science is so important, that the American law school as we know it did not appear as an institution until about the middle of the nineteenth century? Harvard and Yale both had law schools by the 1820's, but for the next thirty years these were moribund institutions, little better than "trade schools", with admissions requirements probably laxer than the colleges'. See Stevens, "Two Cheers for 1870: The American Law School," 5 Perspectives in American History 405, 415–424 (1971). Professor Stevens suggests that the real transformation in American legal education was accomplished during the tenure of Christopher Columbus Langdell at Harvard, Id., at 430–441, and it is to him that we now turn.

CHRISTOPHER COLUMBUS LANGDELL, SELECTION OF CASES ON THE LAW OF CONTRACTS

v–vii (1871).

* * *

I entered upon the duties of my present position, a year and a half ago, with a settled conviction that law could only be taught or learned effectively by means of cases in some form. I had entertained such an opinion ever since I knew any thing of the nature of law or of legal study; but it was chiefly through my experience as a learner that it was first formed, as well as subsequently strengthened and confirmed.

* * *

Now, however, I was called upon to consider directly the subject of teaching, not theoretically but practically. * * * I was expected to take a large class of pupils, meet them regularly from day to day, and give them systematic instruction in such branches of law as had been assigned to me. To accomplish this successfully, it was necessary, first, that the efforts of the pupils should go hand in hand with mine, that is, that they should study with direct reference to my instruction; secondly, that the study thus required of them should be of the kind from which they might reap the greatest and most lasting benefit; thirdly, that the instruction should be of such a character that the pupils might at least derive a greater advantage from attending it than from devoting the same time to private study. How could this threefold object be accomplished? Only one mode occurred to me which seemed to hold out any reasonable prospect of success; and that was, to make a series of cases, carefully selected from the books of reports, the subject alike of study and instruction. But here I was met by what seemed at first to be an insuperable practical difficulty, namely, the want of books; for though it might be practicable, in case of private pupils having free access to a complete library, to refer them directly to the books of reports, such a course was quite out of the question with a large class, all of whom would want the same books at the same time. Nor would such a course be without great drawbacks and inconveniences, even in the case of a single pupil. As he would always have to go where the books were, and could only have access to them there during certain prescribed hours, it would be impossible for him to economize his time or work to the best advantage; and he would be liable to be constantly haunted by the apprehension that he was spending time, labor, and money in studying cases which would be inaccessible to him in after life.

It was with a view to removing these obstacles, that I was first led to inquire into the feasibility of preparing and publishing such a selection of cases as would be adapted to my purpose as a teacher. The most important element in that inquiry was the great and rapidly increasing number of reported cases in every department of law. In view of this fact, was there any satisfactory principle upon which such a selection could be made? It seemed to me that there was. Law, considered as a science, consists of certain principles or doctrines. To have such a mastery of these as to be able to apply them with constant facility and certainty to the ever-tangled skein of human affairs, is what constitutes a true lawyer; and hence to acquire that mastery should be the business of every earnest student of law. Each of these doctrines has arrived at its present state by slow degrees; in other words, it is a growth, extending in many cases through centuries. This growth is to be traced in the main through a series of cases * * *. But the cases which are useful and necessary for this purpose at the present day bear an exceedingly small proportion to all that have been reported. The vast majority are useless and worse than useless for any purpose of systematic study. Moreover, the number of fundamental legal doctrines is much less than is commonly supposed; the many different guises in which the same doctrine is constantly making its appearance, and the great extent to which legal treatises are a repetition of each other, being the cause of much misapprehension. * * * It seemed to me, therefore, to be possible to take such a branch of the law as Contracts, for example, and, without exceeding comparatively moderate limits, to select, classify, and arrange all the cases which had contributed in any important degree to the growth, development, or establishment of any of its essential doctrines; and that such a work could not fail to be of material service to all who desire to study that branch of law systematically and in its original sources.

It is upon this principle that the present volume has been prepared. It begins the subject of Contracts, and embraces the important topics of Mutual Consent, Consideration, and Conditional Contracts. Though complete in itself, it is my expectation that it will be followed by other volumes upon the same plan * * *.

BOOK REVIEW [OF THE SECOND EDITION OF LANGDELL'S CASEBOOK]

14 Am.Law Rev. 233–235 (1880).

* * *

It is hard to know where to begin in dealing with this extraordinary production,—equally extraordinary in its merits and its limitations. No man competent to judge can read a page of it without at once recognizing the hand of a great master. Every line is compact of ingenious and original thought. Decisions are reconciled which those who gave them meant to be opposed, and drawn together by subtle lines which never were dreamed of before Mr. Langdell wrote. It may be said without exaggeration that there cannot be found in the legal literature of this country, such a *tour de force* of patient and profound intellect working out original theory through a mass of detail, and evolving consistency out of what seemed a chaos of conflicting atoms. But in this word "consistency" we touch what some of us at least must deem the weak point in Mr. Langdell's habit of mind. Mr. Langdell's ideal in the law, the end of all his striving, is the *elegantia juris,* or *logical* integrity of the system as a system. He is, perhaps, the greatest living legal theologian. But as a theologian he is less concerned with his postulates than to show that the conclusions from them hang together. A single phrase will illustrate what is meant. "It has been claimed that the purposes of substantial justice and the interests of contracting parties as understood by themselves will be best served by holding &c., * * * and cases have been put to show that the contrary view would produce not only unjust but absurd results. *The true answer to this argument is that it is irrelevant;* but" &c. (pp. 995, 996, pl. 15). The reader will perceive that the language is only incidental, but it reveals a mode of thought which becomes conspicuous to a careful student.

If Mr. Langdell could be suspected of ever having troubled himself about Hegel, we might call him a Hegelian in disguise, so entirely is he interested in the formal connection of things, or logic, as distinguished from the feelings which make the content of logic, and which have actually shaped the substance of the law. The life of the law has not been logic: it has been experience. The seed of every new growth within its sphere has been a felt necessity. The form of continuity has been kept up by reasonings purporting to reduce every thing to a logical sequence; but that form is nothing but the evening dress which the new-comer puts on to make itself presentable according to conventional requirements. The important phenomenon is the man underneath it, not the coat; the justice and reasonableness of a decision, not its consistency with previously held views. No one will ever have a truly philosophic mastery over the law who does not habitually consider the forces outside of it which have made it what it is. More than that, he must remember that as it embodies the story of a nation's development through many centuries, the law finds its philosophy not in self-consistency, which it must always fail in so long as it continues to grow, but in history and the nature of human needs. As a branch of anthropology, law is an object of science; the theory of legislation is a scientific study; but the effort to reduce the concrete details of an existing system to the merely logical consequence of simple postulates is always in danger of becoming unscientific, and of leading to a misapprehension of the nature of the problem and the data.

* * * But it is to be remembered that the book is published for use at a law school, and that for that purpose dogmatic teaching is a necessity, if any thing is to be taught within the limited time of a student's course. A professor must start with a system as an arbitrary fact, and the most which can be hoped for is to make the student see how it hangs together, and thus to send him into practice with something more than a rag-bag of details. For this purpose it is believed that Mr. Langdell's teachings, published and unpublished, have been of unequalled value.

* * *

NOTES AND QUESTIONS

1. The pedagogical philosophy that made Langdell's Harvard law school the greatest America had yet seen was fully embodied in the casebook on contracts. Langdell's aim was to train law students to derive "the few, ever-present, and ever-evolving and fructifying principles, which constituted the genius of the common law." Professor Lawrence Friedman, in his A History of American Law (1973) appears to criticize Langdell's notion that law was a science with independent logical principles. Friedman writes:

If law is at all the product of society, Langdell's science of law was a geology without rocks, an astronomy without stars. Lawyers and judges raised on the method, if they took their training at all seriously, came to speak of law mainly in terms of a dry, arid logic, divorced from society and life.*

Id., at 535. What do you think that Friedman believes is missing from Langdell's view of the law? If Friedman is right about the emptiness of Langdell's science of law, why did it almost immediately win acceptance at virtually all law schools, and why does it still form the basis of legal education? Friedman explains this by indulging in retrospective psycho-analysis. He states that the flourishing of Langdellian legal science in the law schools occurred because it exalted the prestige of law and legal learning in a period when lawyers needed to justify their monopoly of practice. Id., at 536. Is this a satisfactory explanation? Is there a danger in exposing law students to the "rag-bag of details," to the ex-perience of law, rather than to its "logic?"

2. Perhaps the most significant assumption of Langdellian theory is the assertion that the "vast majority" of reported decisions are "useless and worse than useless for any purpose of systematic study." Would you agree with this? Was Langdell right that "the number of fundamental legal doctrines is much less than is commonly supposed"? What is a "fundamental legal doctrine?" Do you see any similarities between Field's view of law, as reflected not only in his speech in this section but also in his codification efforts, and that of Langdell? Would Field and Langdell agree upon the nature of legal history?

3. Why does the author of this review of the second edition of Lang-dell's casebook suggest that it is "extraordinary" in its limitations? How is this assertion related to the characterization of Langdell as "perhaps * * * the greatest living legal theologian?" And yet, does the author of this review believe that Langdell's casebook is appropriate for law schools? The author of the review was Oliver Wendell Holmes, Jr., and the next excerpt develops his philosophical differences with Langdell.

* Lawrence M. Friedman, A History of American Law, copyright © 1973 by Lawrence M. Friedman, published by Simon and Schuster, reprinted with the permission of the publisher.

OLIVER WENDELL HOLMES, JR.

OLIVER WENDELL HOLMES, JR., THE COMMON LAW

1–18, 24–30, 34–38 (1881).

The object of this book is to present a general view of the Common Law. To accomplish the task, other tools are needed besides logic. * * * The life of the law has not been logic: it has been experience. The felt necessities of the time, the prevalent moral and political theories, intuitions of public policy, avowed or unconscious, even the prejudices which judges share with their fellow-men, have had a good deal more to do than the syllogism in determining the rules by which men should be governed. The law embodies the story of a nation's development through many centuries, and it cannot be dealt with as if it contained only the axioms and corollaries of a book of mathematics. In order to know what it is, we must know what it has been, and what it tends to become. We must alternately consult history and existing theories of legislation. But the most difficult labor will be to understand the combination of the two into new products at every stage. The substance of the law at any given time pretty nearly corresponds, so far as it goes, with what is then understood to be convenient; but its form and machinery, and the degree to which it is able to work out desired results, depend very much upon its past.

In Massachusetts to-day, while, on the one hand, there are a great many rules which are quite sufficiently accounted for by their manifest good sense, on the other, there are some which can only be understood by reference to the infancy of procedure among the German tribes, or to the social condition of Rome under the Decemvirs.

* * *

The first subject to be discussed is the general theory of liability civil and criminal. * * *

It is commonly known that the early forms of legal procedure were grounded in vengeance. Modern writers have thought that the Roman law started from the blood feud, and all the authorities agree that the German law began in that way. The feud led to the composition, at first optional, then compulsory, by which the feud was bought off. * * * The killings and house-burnings of an earlier day became the appeals of mayhem and arson. The appeals *de pace et plagis* and of mayhem became, or rather were in substance, the action of trespass which is still familiar to lawyers. But as the compensation recovered in the appeal was the alternative of vengeance, we might expect to find its scope limited to the scope of vengeance. Vengeance imports a feeling of blame, and an opinion, however distorted by passion, that a wrong has been done. It can hardly go very far beyond the case of a harm intentionally inflicted: even a dog distinguishes between being stumbled over and being kicked.

Whether for this cause or another, the early English appeals for personal violence seem to have been confined to intentional wrongs. * * * The cause of action in the cases of trespass reported in the earlier Year Books and in the Abbreviatio Placitorum is always an intentional wrong. It was only at a later day, and after argument, that trespass was extended so as to embrace harms which were foreseen, but which were not the intended consequence of the defendant's act.   Thence again it extended to unforeseen injuries.

* * *

The original principles of liability for harm inflicted by another person or thing have been less carefully considered hitherto than those which governed trespass, and I shall therefore devote the rest of this Lecture to discussing them.   I shall try to show that this liability also had its root in the passion of revenge, and to point out the changes by which it reached its present form.   * * *

A very common phenomenon, and one very familiar to the student of history, is this.   The customs, beliefs, or needs of a primitive time establish a rule or a formula.   In the course of centuries the custom, belief, or necessity disappears, but the rule remains.   The reason which gave rise to the rule has been forgotten, and ingenious minds set themselves to inquire how it is to be accounted for.   Some ground of policy is thought of, which seems to explain it and to reconcile it with the present state of things; and then the rule adapts itself to the new reasons which have been found for it, and enters on a new career. * * *   The subject under consideration illustrates this course of events very clearly.

I will begin by taking a medley of examples embodying as many distinct rules, each with its plausible and seemingly sufficient ground of policy to explain it.

* * *

A baker's man, while driving his master's cart to deliver hot rolls of a morning, runs another man down.   The master has to pay for it.   And when he has asked why he should have to pay for the wrongful act of an independent and responsible being, he has been answered from the time of Ulpian to that of Austin, that it is because he was to blame for employing an improper person.   If he answers, that he used the greatest possible care in choosing his driver, he is told that that is no excuse; and then perhaps the reason is shifted, and it is said that there ought to be a remedy against some one who can pay the damages, or that such wrongful acts as by ordinary human laws are likely to happen in the course of the service are imputable to the service.

* * *   In 1851, Congress passed a law, which is still in force, and by which the owners of ships in all the more common cases of maritime loss can surrender the vessel and her freight then pending to the losers; and it is provided that, thereupon, further proceedings against the owners shall cease.   The legislators to whom we owe this act argued that, if a merchant embark a portion of his property upon a hazardous venture, it is reasonable that his stake should be confined to what he puts at risk,—a principle similar to that on which corporations have been so largely created in America during the last fifty years.

It has been a rule of criminal pleading in England down into the present century, that an indictment for homicide must set forth the value of the instrument causing the death, in order that the king or his grantee might claim forfeiture of the deodand, "as an accursed thing," in the language of Blackstone.

I might go on multiplying examples; but these are enough to show the remoteness of the points to be brought together. * * *

* * * Plutarch, in his Solon, tells us that a dog that had bitten a man was to be delivered up bound to a log four cubits long. Plato made elaborate provisions in his Laws for many such cases. If a slave killed a man, he was to be given up to the relatives of the deceased. If he wounded a man, he was to be given up to the injured party to use him as he pleased. * * * If a beast killed a man, it was to be slain and cast beyond the borders. If an inanimate thing caused death, it was to be cast beyond the borders in like manner, and expiation was to be made. * * *

In the Roman law we find the similar principles of the *noxae deditio* * gradually leading to further results. The Twelve Tables (451 B.C.) provided that, if an animal had done damage, either the animal was to be surrendered or the damage paid for. We learn from Gaius that the same rule was applied to the torts of children or slaves * * *.

The Roman lawyers, not looking beyond their own system or their own time, drew on their wits for an explanation which would show that the law as they found it was reasonable. Gaius said that it was unjust that the fault of children or slaves should be a source of loss to their parents or owners beyond their own bodies * * *.

This way of approaching the question seems to deal with the right of surrender as if it were a limitation of a liability incurred by a parent or owner, which would naturally and in the first instance be unlimited. But if that is what was meant, it puts the cart before the horse. The right of surrender was not introduced as a limitation of liability, but, in Rome and Greece alike, payment was introduced as the alternative of a failure to surrender.

The action was not based, as it would be nowadays, on the fault of the parent or owner. If it had been, it would always have been brought against the person who had control of the slave or animal at the time it did the harm complained of, and who, if any one, was to blame for not preventing the injury. So far from this being the course, the person to be sued was the owner at the time of suing. * * * And in curious contrast with the principle as inverted to meet still more modern views of public policy, if the animal was of

---

* The Roman legal action resulting in the surrender of an "offending" animal, child, slave, or inanimate object to the injured victim or his or her family.

a wild nature, that is, in the very case of the most ferocious animals, the owner ceased to be liable the moment it escaped, because at that moment he ceased to be owner. There seems to have been no other or more extensive liability by the old law, even where a slave was guilty with his master's knowledge, unless perhaps he was a mere tool in his master's hands. * * *

All this shows very clearly that the liability of the owner was merely a way of getting at the slave or animal which was the immediate cause of offence. In other words, vengeance on the immediate offender was the object of the Greek and early Roman process, not indemnity from the master or owner. * * *

But it may be asked how inanimate objects came to be pursued in this way, if the object of the procedure was to gratify the passion of revenge. [Perhaps the reason is] * * * the personification of inanimate nature common to savages and children * * *.

In the Athenian process there is also, no doubt, to be traced a different thought. Expiation is one of the ends most insisted on by Plato, and appears to have been the purpose of the procedure mentioned by Eschines. * * *

Another peculiarity to be noticed is, that the liability seems to have been regarded as attached to the body doing the damage, in an almost physical sense. An untrained intelligence only imperfectly performs the analysis by which jurists carry responsibility back to the beginning of a chain of causation. The hatred for anything giving us pain, which wreaks itself on the manifest cause, and which leads even civilized man to kick a door when it pinches his finger, is embodied in the *noxae deditio* and other kindred doctrines of early Roman law. * * *

[Holmes proceeds to discuss some examples from Roman law, where, even in cases of breach of treaty or contract, a legal action might terminate in the body of the defendant being surrendered to the plaintiff.]

It might be asked what analogy could have been found between a breach of contract and those wrongs which excite the desire for vengeance. But it must be remembered that the distinction between tort and breaches of contract, and especially between the remedies for the two, is not found ready made. It is conceivable that a procedure adapted to redress for violence was extended to other cases as they arose. Slaves were surrendered for theft as well as for assault; and it is said that a debtor who did not pay his debts, or a seller who failed to deliver an article for which he had been paid, was dealt with on the same footing as a thief. This line of thought, together with the quasi material conception of legal obligations as binding the offending body, which has been noticed, would perhaps explain the well-known law of the Twelve Tables as to insolvent debtors. According to that law, if a man was indebted to several creditors and insolvent, after certain formalities they might cut up his body and divide it among them. If there was a single creditor, he might put his debtor to death or sell him as a slave.

If no other right were given but to reduce a debtor to slavery, the law might be taken to look only to compensation, and to be modelled on the natural working of self-redress. * * * But the right to put to death looks like vengeance, and the division of the body shows that the debt was conceived very literally to inhere in or bind the body * * *.

* * *

It will readily be imagined that such a system as has been described could not last when civilization had advanced to any considerable height. What had been the privilege of buying off vengeance by agreement, of paying the damage instead of surrendering the body of the offender, no doubt became a general custom. The Aquilian law, passed about a couple of centuries later than the date of the Twelve Tables, enlarged the sphere of compensation for bodily injuries. Interpretation enlarged the Aquilian law. Masters became personally liable for certain wrongs committed by their slaves with their knowledge, where previously they were only bound to surrender the slave. If a pack-mule threw off his burden upon a passer-by because he had been improperly overloaded, or a dog which might have been restrained escaped from his master and bit any one, the old noxal action, as it was called, gave way to an action under the new law to enforce a general personal liability.

Still later, ship-owners and innkeepers were made liable *as if* they were wrong-doers for wrongs committed by those in their employ on board ship or in the tavern, although of course committed without their knowledge. The true reason for this exceptional responsibility was the exceptional confidence which was necessarily reposed in carriers and innkeepers. But some of the jurists, who regarded the surrender of children and slaves as a privilege intended to limit liability, explained this new liability on the ground that the innkeeper or ship-owner was to a certain degree guilty of negligence in having employed the services of bad men. * * *

The law as to ship-owners and innkeepers introduced another and more startling innovation. It made them responsible when those whom they employed were free, as well as when they were slaves. For the first time one man was made answerable for the wrongs of another who was also answerable himself, and who had a standing before the law. This was a great change from the bare permission to ransom one's slave as a privilege. But here we have the history of the whole modern doctrine of master and servant, and principal and agent. All servants are now as free and as liable to a suit as their masters. Yet the principle introduced on special grounds in a special case, when servants were slaves, is now the general law of this country and England, and under it men daily have to pay large sums for other people's acts, in which they had no part and for which they are in no sense to blame. * * *

* * *

The reader may begin to ask for the proof that all this has any bearing on our law of to-day. So far as concerns the influence of the Roman law upon our own, especially the Roman law of master and servant, the evidence of it is to be found in every book which has been written for the last five hundred years. It has been stated already that we still repeat the reasoning of the Roman lawyers, empty as it is, to the present day. * * *

* * *

We will now follow the history of that branch of the primitive notion which was least likely to survive,—the liability of inanimate things.

It will be remembered that King Alfred ordained the surrender of a tree, but that the later Scotch law refused it because a dead thing could not have guilt. It will be remembered, also, that the animals which the Scotch law forfeited were escheat to the king. The same thing has remained true in England until well into this century, with regard even to inanimate objects. As long ago as Bracton, in case a man was slain, the coroner was to value the object causing the death, and that was to be forfeited as deodand *"pro rege."* It was to be given to God, that is to say to the Church, for the King, to be expended for the good of his soul. A man's death had ceased to be the private affair of his friends as in the time of the barbarian folk-laws. The king, who furnished the court, now sued for the penalty. He supplanted the family in the claim on the guilty thing, and the Church supplanted him.

In Edward the First's time some of the cases remind us of the barbarian laws at their rudest stage. If a man fell from a tree, the tree was deodand. If he drowned in a well, the well was to be filled up. It did not matter that the forfeited instrument belonged to an innocent person. * * * And it has been repeated from Queen Elizabeth's time to within one hundred years, that if my horse strikes a man, and afterwards I sell my horse, and after that the man dies, the horse shall be forfeited. Hence it is, that, in all indictments for homicide, until very lately it has been necessary to state the instrument causing the death and its value, as that the stroke was given by a certain penknife, value sixpence, so as to secure the forfeiture. It is said that a steam-engine has been forfeited in this way.

I now come to what I regard as the most remarkable transformation of this principle, and one which is a most important factor in our law as it is to-day. * * *

The most striking example of this sort is a ship. And accordingly the old books say that, if a man falls from a ship and is drowned, the motion of the ship must be taken to cause the death, and the ship is forfeited * * *.

A ship is the most living of inanimate things. Servants sometimes say "she" of a clock, but every one gives a gender to vessels. And we need not be surprised, therefore, to find a mode of dealing which has shown such extraordinary vitality in the criminal law applied with even more striking thoroughness in the Admiralty. It is only by supposing the ship to have been treated as if endowed with personality, that the arbitrary seeming peculiarities of the maritime law can be made intelligible, and on that supposition they at once become consistent and logical.

By way of seeing what those peculiarities are, take first a case of collision at sea. A collision takes place between two vessels * * *. [The ship which is responsible for the collision] is under a lease at the time, the lessee has his own master in charge, and the owner of the vessel has no manner of control over it. The owner, therefore, is not to blame, and he cannot even be charged on the ground that the damage was done by his servants. He is free from personal liability on elementary principles. Yet it is perfectly settled that there is a lien on his vessel for the amount of the damage done, and this means that that vessel may be arrested and sold to pay the loss in any admiralty court whose process will reach her. * * *

But, again, suppose that the vessel, instead of being under lease, is in charge of a pilot whose employment is made compulsory by the laws of the port which she is just entering. The Supreme Court of the United States holds the ship liable in this instance also. * * * [Our] Supreme Court has long recognized that a person may bind a ship, when he could not bind the owners personally, because he was not their agent.

It may be admitted that, if this doctrine were not supported by an appearance of good sense, it would not have survived. The ship is the only security available in dealing with foreigners, and rather than send one's own citizens to search for a remedy abroad in strange courts, it is easy to seize the vessel and satisfy the claim at home, leaving the foreign owners to get their indemnity as they may be able. I dare say some such thought has helped to keep the practice alive, but I believe the true historic foundation is elsewhere. The ship no doubt, like a sword, would have been forfeited for causing death, in whosesoever hands it might have been. * * * It seems most likely that the principle by which the ship was forfeited to the king for causing death, or for piracy, was the same as that by which it was bound to private sufferers for other damage, in whose hands soever it might have been when it did the harm.

* * *

* * * The following is a passage from a judgment by Chief Justice Marshall, which is quoted with approval by Judge Story in

giving the opinion of the Supreme Court of the United States.* "This is not a proceeding against the owner; it is a proceeding against the vessel for an offence committed by the vessel; which is not the less an offence, and does not the less subject her to forfeiture, because it was committed without the authority and against the will of the owner. It is true that inanimate matter can commit no offence. But this body is animated and put in action by the crew, who are guided by the master. The vessel acts and speaks by the master. She reports herself by the master. It is, therefore, not unreasonable that the vessel should be affected by this report." * * *

In other words, those great judges, although of course aware that a ship is no more alive than a mill-wheel, thought that not only the law did in fact deal with it as if it were alive, but that it was reasonable that the law should do so. The reader will observe that they do not say simply that it is reasonable on grounds of policy to sacrifice justice to the owner to security for somebody else, but that it is reasonable to deal with the vessel as an offending thing. Whatever the hidden ground of policy may be, their thought still clothes itself in personifying language.

*   *   *

We have now followed the development of the chief forms of liability in modern law for anything other than the immediate and manifest consequences of a man's own acts. * * * We have seen a single germ multiplying and branching into products as different from each others as the flower from the root. It hardly remains to ask what that germ was. We have seen that it was the desire of retaliation against the offending thing itself. * * * A consideration of the earliest instances will show, as might have been expected, that vengeance, not compensation, and vengeance on the offending things, was the original object. The ox in Exodus was to be stoned. The axe in the Athenian law was to be banished. * * * The slave under all the systems was to be surrendered to the relatives of the slain man, that they might do with him what they liked. The deodand was an accursed thing. The original limitation of liability to surrender, when the owner was before the court, could not be accounted for if it was his liability, and not that of his property, which was in question. * * *

The foregoing history, apart from the purposes for which it has been given, well illustrates the paradox of form and substance in the development of law. In form its growth is logical. The official theory is that each new decision follows syllogistically from existing precedents. But just as the clavicle in the cat only tells of the existence of some earlier creature to which a collar-bone was useful, precedents survive in the law long after the use they once served is at an end and the reason for them has been forgotten. The result

*The Malek Adhel, 43 U.S. (2 How.)
210, 233, 11 L.Ed. 239 (1844).

of following them must often be failure and confusion from the merely logical point of view.

On the other hand, in substance the growth of the law is legislative. And this in a deeper sense than that what the courts declare to have always been the law is in fact new. It is legislative in its grounds. The very considerations which judges most rarely mention, and always with an apology, are the secret root from which the law draws all the juices of life. I mean, of course, considerations of what is expedient for the community concerned. Every important principle which is developed by litigation is in fact and at bottom the result of more or less definitely understood views of public policy; most generally, to be sure, under our practice and traditions, the unconscious result of instinctive preferences and inarticulate convictions, but none the less traceable to views of public policy in the last analysis. And as the law is administered by able and experienced men, who know too much to sacrifice good sense to a syllogism, it will be found that, when ancient rules maintain themselves in the way that has been and will be shown in this book, new reasons more fitted to the time have been found for them, and that they gradually receive a new content, and at last a new form, from the grounds to which they have been transplanted.

But hitherto this process has been largely unconscious. It is important, on that account, to bring to mind what the actual course of events has been. If it were only to insist on a more conscious recognition of the legislative function of the courts, as just explained, it would be useful * * *.

What has been said will explain the failure of all theories which consider the law only from its formal side, whether they attempt to deduce the *corpus* from *a priori* postulates, or fall into the humbler error of supposing the science of the law to reside in the *elegantia juris*, or logical cohesion of part with part. The truth is, that the law is always approaching, and never reaching, consistency. It is forever adopting new principles from life at one end, and it always retains old ones from history at the other, which have not yet been absorbed or sloughed off. It will become entirely consistent only when it ceases to grow.

* * *

However much we may codify the law into a series of seemingly self-sufficient propositions, those propositions will be but a phase in a continuous growth. To understand their scope fully, to know how they will be dealt with by judges trained in the past which the law embodies, we must ourselves know something of that past. The history of what the law has been is necessary to the knowledge of what the law is.

Again, the process which I have described has involved the attempt to follow precedents, as well as to give a good reason for them.

When we find that in large and important branches of the law the various grounds of policy on which the various rules have been justified are later inventions to account for what are in fact survivals from more primitive times, we have a right to reconsider the popular reasons, and, taking a broader view of the field, to decide anew whether those reasons are satisfactory. * * *

But none of the foregoing considerations, nor the purpose of showing the materials for anthropology contained in the history of the law, are the immediate object here. My aim and purpose have been to show that the various forms of liability known to modern law spring from the common ground of revenge. * * * [This] shows that they have started from a moral basis, from the thought that some one was to blame.

It remains to be proved that, while the terminology of morals is still retained, and while the law does still and always, in a certain sense, measure legal liability by moral standards, it nevertheless, by the very necessity of its nature, is continually transmuting those moral standards into external or objective ones, from which the actual guilt of the party concerned is wholly eliminated.

NOTES AND QUESTIONS

1. In an omitted passage, Holmes asserts that there is a "mode in which the law has grown, without a break, from barbarism to civilization." Based on what you have read, are his views of the nature of the law's growth the same as those of Field and Langdell? What are their differences?

2. What is Holmes's excursion into the law of Greece and Rome designed to prove? The aim of the Greek law regarding masters and servants, says Holmes, was vengeance. Is this plausible to you? How does Holmes explain the ancient law that required the surrender or destruction of inanimate objects causing harm as an instrument of "vengeance?" Holmes makes a reference to Plato's *Laws* in this connection. Is there any significance in the fact that in another section of Plato's Laws, Book X, Plato provides extremely harsh penalties for religious heresy, even where the heresy stems only from personal agnosticism:

> For the morally inoffensive heretic the penalty, on conviction will in every case include at least five years of imprisonment in the "House of Correction," where he will see no one but members of the "nocturnal council," who are to visit him from time to time and to reason with him on the error of his ways. A second conviction is to be followed by death.

A. E. Taylor, Plato: The Man and His Work 494 (7th ed., 1960).

3. Holmes argues that civilization outgrew the old vengeance motive for law, and replaced it with a new one, while maintaining the old law's "principle" of master's liability for acts of servants. What is the new motive that Holmes ascribes to the law? Is this a motive that really reflects an advance in civilization? There is a similar discussion of admiralty law. What are the old and new rationales there?

4. How does Holmes use the analysis you have just read to arrive at the conclusion that "The very considerations which judges most rarely mention, and always with an apology, are the secret root from which the law draws all the juices of life?" How does this lead him to the observation that " * * * the law is always approaching, and never reaching, consistency?" What does this lead Holmes to conclude about the feasibility of attempts to systematize the law, like those of Field or Langdell? What do you suppose is the importance of his closing observation of this part of The Common Law, that the law's "moral standards" are "continually" being transmuted "into external or objective ones, from which the actual guilt of the party concerned is wholly eliminated." Do you suppose, for example, that Holmes's thoughts could be applied to Shaw's decision in Farwell v. Boston & Worcester R. R.? Was that a case about "moral" standards? Was that a case which had grown out of a response to some deeply "felt need" in the community? Returning to Holmes's view of the forward march of civilization, what makes him different from a Field or a Langdell? What makes him like them? Holmes refers to his brand of history as "anthropology." What does he mean by that? Does it surprise you, in light of all that you have read in this casebook, that Holmes should need to go back to Greece and Rome to prove his points?

5. What does all of this tell you about Holmes's view of mankind? Did you find anything in this excerpt that might cause you to agree with the assessment of Professor G. Edward White:

> * * * one finds a disturbing dissonance between Holmes's very conspicuous social and professional success—it is hard to imagine a life less marred by physical, social or economical deprivations or one marked by a greater length and breadth of achievement—and his gloomy musings that "the crowd has substantially all there is," that "we are all very near despair," that men are like "flies", and that "man has no more cosmic significance than a baboon or a grain of sand." * * * Holmes's skepticism appears to have been less a striving for a positive goal than a facile means of avoiding commitment, whether to beliefs, institutions, or mankind itself. One is struck by the comments of Holmes that he had remained childless because he could not bear bringing children into the world. * * *

White, Patterns of American Legal Thought 225 (1978). Copyright 1978 by the Bobbs-Merrill Company, Inc., reprinted with the permission of the publisher. Holmes was also given to tossing off splendid ascerbic epigrams, for example, "the notion that with socialized property we should have women free and a piano for everybody seems to me an empty humbug." Holmes, "Ideals and Doubts," 10 Ill.L.Rev. 1 (1915).

Still, Holmes's ultimate musings on the future of man may not have been negative:

> * * * [A]s I grow older I grow calm. If I feel what are perhaps an old man's apprehensions, that competition from new races will cut deeper than working men's disputes and will test whether we can hang together and can fight; if I fear that we are running through the world's resources at a pace that we cannot keep; I do

not lose my hopes. I do not pin my dreams for the future to my country or even to my race. I think it probable that civilization somehow will last as long as I care to look ahead—perhaps with smaller numbers, but perhaps also bred to greatness and splendor by science.

Holmes, "Law and the Court," (1913), in The Occasional Speeches of Justice Oliver Wendell Holmes 168, 173–174 (Howe ed., 1962).

By 1931, as Holmes's ninetieth birthday approached, and as he had completed twenty years on the Supreme Judicial Court of Massachusetts, and thirty years on the United States Supreme Court, Felix Frankfurter wrote that "no figure in the history of the Supreme Court, except Holmes, may fittingly be compared with the great Chief Justice [Marshall]." Frankfurter, ed., Mr. Justice Holmes vii (1931). As you will soon see, virtually every modern legal reformer or student of jurisprudence sooner or later invokes Holmes's name or his blessing. You have not seen much of Holmes's writing, of course, but as you read the materials which follow, see if you can guess why Holmes has been deified more than any judge since Marshall.

SECTION B. THE NEW DEAL AND THE NINE OLD MEN

In the late years of the nineteenth century and the early years of the twentieth century, at the height of what has been called the "Progressive Movement," there was much state legislation regarding working conditions. We have already alluded to legislation regarding compensation for injured workmen, which was commonplace. Other reforms included laws regarding wages and hours, the employment of women and children, and health and safety conditions of the workingplace. Advocates of freedom of contract fought some of this social legislation, arguing that it was unconstitutional under the prohibition against any state's passing a law "impairing the obligation of contracts." U. S. Constitution, Article I, Section 10. Nevertheless, in Holden v. Hardy, 169 U.S. 366, 18 S.Ct. 383, 42 L.Ed. 780 (1896), the United States Supreme Court upheld a Utah law limiting work hours in the mines, basing its decision on the state's "police power," and suggesting that considering the conditions of Utah's mines, the inequality of bargaining power between the miners and their employers required some modification of a strict "freedom-of-contract" approach. Still, in the infamous decision in Lochner v. New York, 198 U.S. 45, 25 S.Ct. 539, 49 L.Ed. 937 (1905), a majority of five justices held unconstitutional a New York maximum-hours law for bakers, as an unreasonable interference with "the right of the individual to his personal liberty or to enter into contracts in relation to labor which may seem to him appropriate or necessary for the support of himself and his family." This personal liberty and this right to contract, said the court, were secured by Section 1 of the Fourteenth Amendment, which provided that no state was to "deprive any person of life, liberty, or property, without due process of law." A blistering dissent was filed by Justice Harlan, with whom Justices White and Day concurred, but the most famous statements against the *Lochner* decision were made in the dissent of Justice Holmes.

Holmes suggested that the majority based its decision on its own ideological preferences for freedom of contract, and not on the law, which, under Holden v. Hardy and several other decisions, would seem to permit such state legislation. The Fourteenth Amendment, declared Holmes, "does not enact Mr. Herbert Spencer's Social Statics," referring to a work by an English Social Darwinist. A constitution, Holmes concluded, "is not intended to embody a particular economic theory, whether of paternalism and the organic relation of the citizen to the State or of *laissez faire*." From *Lochner* until the 1930's, the Supreme Court behaved erratically in the area of social legislation by the states, frequently invalidating state and federal legislation on grounds like those of *Lochner*, but occasionally upholding measures, as in Muller v. Oregon, 208 U.S. 412, 28 S.Ct. 324, 52 L.Ed. 551 (1908). (Oregon law limiting maximum hours of women), or Wilson v. New, 243 U.S. 332, 37 S.Ct. 298, 61 L.Ed. 755 (1917) (federal law limiting interstate railroad workers to eight-hour day).

In the twenties, as the Republican party in particular, and American business in general, flourished, the trend in Supreme Court decisions seemed to be decidedly against state or federal supervision of commerce or industry, on the theory that government should not be allowed to tinker with the obvious success of the free market. Before the Fall of 1929, indeed, America, or at least American corporations, appeared to be enjoying unparalled prosperity, although striking inequalities in the distribution of income existed, and the values of many shares of stock in industrial and commercial concerns were wildly inflated. Most businessmen and politicians appeared to have believed, however, that American business was quite sound, and that economic euphoria would, and ought to, continue indefinitely. Some thought that the current speculative fever ought to be contained, however, and the American Federal Reserve Board and the Bank of England took some modest steps in late summer and early fall of 1929 to reduce the availability of the "easy money" investors had been borrowing. Some speculators then sold out, and panic ensued. From September 1, 1929 to July 1, 1932, the market value of stocks listed on the New York Exchange fell from $89.6 billion to $15.6 billion, and similar, and in many cases, much greater, declines were experienced by other issues. Investors thus saw paper profits evaporate; many who had bought on margin were practically instantaneously ruined, and millions of other American investors were hit by the greatest financial distress they had ever known. See Generally John D. Hicks, Republican Ascendency 1921–33, 224–233 (1960).

Though business leaders and politicians minimized the impact of the Crash in the Fall of 1929, the American economy rapidly deteriorated:

> Prices dropped sharply, foreign trade fell off, factories closed, business failures multiplied, banks went under, unemployment began to mount * * *. Savings disappeared; purchases made on installments had to be returned; substantial citizens lost their homes on mortgages; * * * stores closed for lack of customers; * * * soup kitchens opened; bread lines began to form; local relief systems broke down; panhandlers roamed the streets; * * * the jobless slept on park benches, in the doorways of public buildings or on the ground * * *.

Hicks, supra, at 229.

The Republican Herbert Hoover tried to take measures that would improve the situation, but they were ineffectual. In 1932, disenchanted, the American electorate turned to the Democrat, Franklin D. Roosevelt. Once inaugurated, during the historic "Hundred Days," Roosevelt was able to get the now democratically-controlled congress to pass the most ambitious program of social legislation America had yet seen. These programs, known usually as the "First New Deal," were designed to produce relief for the unemployed, and to smooth the path to economic recovery for American business. Among other actions, the Emergency Banking Relief Act (March 9, 1932) gave the President broad discretion to regulate transactions in Gold and Silver, and validated the actions the President had already taken, including his enforced "Bank Holiday," whereby he closed the nation's banks on March 5, in order to prevent further financial deterioration. The act, drafted principally by members of the banking industry, also reorganized the nation's banking system, and attempted to prevent further deterioration of the country's gold reserves by limiting specie payments. Shortly thereafter the country went off the Gold Standard, and, pursuant to the Gold Reserve Act of 1934 (January 31, 1934), the dollar's value was halved. The Beer-Wine Revenue Act (March 22) legalized those beverages of 3.2% maximum alcoholic content by weight, and taxed them at $5.00 per barrel. The Civilian Conservation Corps Reforestation Relief Act (March 31) authorized jobs for 250,000, and the Federal Emergency Relief Act created an agency to distribute national revenues to states and municipalities (May 12). The Tennessee Valley Authority (TVA), an independent public corporation, was created to construct dams and power plants and generally to develop the economies of Tennessee, North Carolina, Kentucky, Virginia, Mississippi, Georgia, and Alabama. On June 13, the Home Owners Refinancing Act created a corporation to refinance home mortgage debts for nonfarm owners, and on June 16 the Farm Credit Act eased the way toward refinancing of farm mortgages. The

Federal Securities Act (May 27) required full disclosure of the facts regarding new securities, and provided for the registration of information on new issues with the Federal Government. The Banking Act of 1933 (June 16) created the Federal Bank Deposit Insurance Corporation which was to guarantee individual bank deposits under $5,000, and enacted several other banking reforms.

The two most important New Deal measures, however, were the Agricultural Adjustment Act (May 12) which set up the Agricultural Adjustment Administration (AAA) and the National Industrial Recovery Act (NIRA) (June 16). The task of the AAA was to improve the condition of farmers by curtailing the production of certain crops, and to set prices for them. Farmers were to be paid subsidies for reducing their production, and the money to pay the subsidies was to come from taxes on the food processors. The NIRA created the National Recovery Administration (NRA), which was charged with the responsibility for establishing (with the cooperation of the businesses themselves) codes for fair competition for American business. Such codes, which would set wages, hours, and working conditions, were to be drafted by members of the industries, and were to be exempt from federal Antitrust Law.

As you might well imagine, these bold measures were greeted with enthusiasm by most, but some were cautious. The New Deal meant a change in the nature of the Federal government, as it extended its influence over the national economy in previously unimagined ways. Many were concerned about the increased bureaucracy, and the possibility of losses of individual freedoms. Some were also disturbed by the manipulation of the dollar and the money markets. Bernard Baruch, a wall street financier, viewed the nation's going off the Gold standard as a move that "can't be defended except as mob rule." Lewis Douglas, the Director of the Budget, considering the acts to raise prices by "remonitizing silver, printing greenbacks, or altering the gold content of the dollar," observed that, "Well, this is the end of Western Civilization." See generally William E. Leuchtenburg, Franklin D. Roosevelt and the New Deal 41–62 (1963).

Others waited to see how the Supreme Court, which had recently been so hostile to social legislation, would view the New Deal measures. It was several years before any of these laws were constitutionally tested by the court. In the first few tests of New Deal measures, most of which were not crucial to Roosevelt's program, the Supreme Court displayed no consistent pattern, upholding some actions, e. g. many of the currency and gold measures, but rejecting others, as it did to a railroad pension program. The first clear indication of the court's attitude came in its review of the constitutionality of the important National Industrial Recovery Act, to which we now turn.

Historians have differed over the goals and the sources of Progressive Reform. G. Mowry, The California Progressives (1951), and R.

Hofstadter, The Age of Reform (1955) trace the origins of the movement to an "old" middle class, whose leaders sought to control the destabilizing forces of industrialism. Robert Wiebe, Businessmen And Reform (1962) and G. Kolko, The Triumph Of Conservatism (1963) suggest that the direction of reform followed the interests of the industrialists themselves. In his later work, The Search For Order, 1877–1920 (1967), Professor Wiebe emphasizes the leadership of a "new" middle class (composed of professionals and administrative and business experts), and the primacy of the social and economic order to Progressive thought. S. Hay's Response To Industrialism, 1885–1914 (1957) examines the problems of unregulated economic growth, and the ways in which industrialism altered the nation's social structure. Other standard works are: H. Faulkner, The Quest For Social Justice, 1898–1914 (1931); G. Mowry, The Era Of Theodore Roosevelt, 1900–1912 (1958); and A. Link, Woodrow Wilson And The Progressive Era, 1910–1917 (1954). The Relationship between the new academic disciplines and the progressive reliance on expertise, efficiency, and rationality is brilliantly recounted in M. White, Social Thought In America: The Revolt Against Formalism (1949).

Good reviews of some major cultural, social, and economic themes of the Twenties are W. Leuchtenburg, The Perils Of Prosperity, 1914–1932 (1958); P. Carter, The Twenties In America (1968); G. Soule, Prosperity Decade (1947); and L. Galambos, Competition & Cooperation: Emergence Of A National Trade Association (1966).

The history of the 1930's is the subject of several towering volumes. The collapse of the economy in 1929 is well told in J. Galbraith, The Great Crash (1959). A full single-volume reference for the period is W. Leuchtenburg's Franklin D. Roosevelt And The New Deal, 1932–1940 (1963). P. Conkin's slim volume, The New Deal (1968) is pathbreaking and provocative, and reviews the historiography of the decade. A very favorable view of Roosevelt and the New Deal, from the perspective of the New Dealers, is given by A. Schlesinger, Jr. in his The Coming Of The New Deal (1959) and his The Politics Of Upheaval (1960). The New Dealers' contributions to the rise of a national welfare state are examined in J. Huthmacher, Senator Robert F. Wagner And The Rise Of Urban Liberalism (1969), and Frances Perkins, The Roosevelt I Knew (1946).

Perhaps the best available way of approaching the legal issues of the early Twentieth century is through the reading of several scholarly biographies of lawyers. See, for example, W. Harbaugh, Lawyer's Lawyer: The Life Of John W. Davis (1973); M. Urofsky, A Mind Of One Piece: Brandeis And American Reform (1971); D. Wigdor, Roscoe Pound: Philosopher Of The Law (1974); D. Hollinger, Morris Cohen And The Scientific Ideal (1975); A. Sutherland, The Law At Harvard: A History Of Ideas And Men, 1817–1967 (1967); G. White, The American Judicial Tradition (1976); G. Dunne, Hugo

Black And The Judicial Revolution (1977); A. Mason, Harlan Fiske Stone: Pillar Of The Law (1956); and J. Howard, Mr. Justice Murphy: A Political Biography (1968). References to the literature on the developments of public and private law in these years appear in the notes and comments in this and the following Chapter.

SCHECHTER POULTRY CORP. v. UNITED STATES

Supreme Court of the United States, 1935.
295 U.S. 495, 55 S.Ct. 837, 79 L.Ed. 1570.

* * *

Mr. Chief Justice HUGHES delivered the opinion of the Court.

Petitioners * * * were convicted in the District Court of the United States for the Eastern District of New York on eighteen counts of an indictment charging violations of what is known as the "Live Poultry Code," [1] and on an additional count for conspiracy to commit such violations. * * * [T]he defendants contended (1) that the Code had been adopted pursuant to an unconstitutional delegation by Congress of legislative power [and] (2) that it attempted to regulate intrastate transactions which lay outside the authority of Congress * * *.

* * *

New York City is the largest live-poultry market in the United States. Ninety-six per cent of the live poultry there marketed comes from other States. Three-fourths of this amount arrives by rail and is consigned to commission men or receivers. * * * They sell to slaughterhouse operators who are also called market-men.

The defendants are slaughterhouse operators * * * in Brooklyn, New York City. Defendants ordinarily purchase their live poultry from commission men at the West Washington Market in New York City or at the railroad terminals serving the City, but occasionally they purchase from commission men in Philadelphia. They buy the poultry for slaughter and resale. After the poultry is trucked to their slaughterhouse markets in Brooklyn, it is there sold, usually within twenty-four hours, to retail poultry dealers and butchers who sell directly to consumers. * * * Defendants do not sell poultry in interstate commerce.

The "Live Poultry Code" was promulgated under § 3 of the National Industrial Recovery Act. That section * * * authorizes the President to approve "codes of fair competition." Such a code may be approved for a trade or industry, upon application by one or more trade or industrial associations or groups, if the President finds (1) that such associations or groups "impose no inequitable restrictions on admission to membership therein and are truly representative,"

---

1. The full title of the Code is "Code of Fair Competition for the Live Poul-   try Industry of the Metropolitan Area in and about the City of New York."

and (2) that such codes are not designed "to promote monopolies or to eliminate or oppress small enterprises and will not operate to discriminate against them, and will tend to effectuate the policy" of Title I of the Act. Such codes "shall not permit monopolies or monopolistic practices." As a condition of his approval, the President may "impose such conditions (including requirements for the making of reports and the keeping of accounts) for the protection of consumers, competitors, employees, and others, and in furtherance of the public interest, and may provide such exceptions to and exemptions from the provisions of such code as the President in his discretion deems necessary to effectuate the policy herein declared." Where such a code has not been approved, the President may prescribe one, either on his own motion or on complaint. Violation of any provision of a code (so approved or prescribed) "in any transaction in or affecting interstate or foreign commerce" is made a misdemeanor punishable by a fine of not more than $500 for each offense, and each day the violation continues is to be deemed a separate offense.

The "Live Poultry Code" was approved by the President on April 13, 1934. * * *

* * * The Code is established as "a code of fair competition for the live poultry industry of the metropolitan area in and about the City of New York." * * *

The "industry" is defined as including "every person engaged in the business of selling, purchasing for resale, transporting, or handling and/or slaughtering live poultry, from the time such poultry comes into the New York metropolitan area to the time it is first sold in slaughtered form," * * *.

The Code * * * provides that no employee, with certain exceptions, shall be permitted to work in excess of forty (40) hours in any one week, and that no employee, save as stated, "shall be paid in any pay period less than at the rate of fifty (50) cents per hour." The article containing "general labor provisions" prohibits the employment of any person under sixteen years of age, and declares that employees shall have the right of "collective bargaining," and freedom of choice with respect to labor organizations * * *. The minimum number of employees, who shall be employed by slaughterhouse operators, is fixed, the number being graduated according to the average volume of weekly sales.

Provision is made for administration through an "industry advisory committee," to be selected by trade associations and members of the industry, and a "code supervisor" to be appointed, with the approval of the committee, by agreement between the Secretary of Agriculture and the Administrator for Industrial Recovery. The expenses of administration are to be borne by the members of the industry proportionately upon the basis of volume of business, or such other factors as the advisory committee may deem equitable, "subject to the disapproval of the Secretary and/or Administrator."

The seventh article, containing "trade practice provisions," prohibits various practices which are said to constitute "unfair methods of competition." * * * The members of the industry are also required to keep books and records which "will clearly reflect all financial transactions of their respective businesses and the financial condition thereof," and to submit weekly reports showing the range of daily prices and volume of sales" for each kind of produce.

The President approved the Code by an executive order * * *.

* * *

First. Two preliminary points are stressed by the Government * * *. We are told that the provision of the statute authorizing the adoption of codes must be viewed in the light of the grave national crisis with which Congress was confronted. Undoubtedly, the conditions to which power is addressed are always to be considered when the exercise of power is challenged. Extraordinary conditions may call for extraordinary remedies. But the argument necessarily stops short of an attempt to justify action which lies outside the sphere of constitutional authority. Extraordinary conditions do not create or enlarge constitutional power. * * * Such assertions of extra-constitutional authority were anticipated and precluded by the explicit terms of the Tenth Amendment,—"The powers not delegated to the United States by the Constitution, nor prohibited by it to the States, are reserved to the States respectively, or to the people."

The further point is urged that the national crisis demanded a broad and intensive cooperative effort by those engaged in trade and industry, and that this necessary cooperation was sought to be fostered by permitting them to initiate the adoption of codes. But the statutory plan is not simply one for voluntary effort. * * * Violations of the provisions of the codes are punishable as crimes.

Second. The question of the delegation of legislative power. * * * The Constitution provides that "All legislative powers herein granted shall be vested in a Congress of the United States, which shall consist of a Senate and House of Representatives." Art. I, § 1. And the Congress is authorized "To make all laws which shall be necessary and proper for carrying into execution its general powers." Art. I, § 8, par. 18. The Congress is not permitted to abdicate or to transfer to others the essential legislative functions with which it is thus vested. We have repeatedly recognized the necessity of adapting legislation to complex conditions involving a host of details with which the national legislature cannot deal directly. * * * [T]he Constitution has never been regarded as denying to Congress the necessary resources of flexibility and practicality, which will enable it to perform its function in laying down policies and establishing standards, while leaving to selected instrumentalities the making of subordinate rules within prescribed limits and the determinations of facts to which the policy as declared by the legislature is to apply. But * * * the constant recognition of the necessity and validity of such provisions, and the wide range of administrative authority which has been developed by means of them, cannot be allowed to obscure the limitations of the authority to delegate, if our constitutional system is to be maintained. * * *

Accordingly, we look to the statute to see whether Congress has overstepped these limitations,—whether Congress in authorizing "codes of fair competition" has itself established the standards of legal obligation, thus performing its essential legislative function, or, by the failure to enact such standards, has attempted to transfer that function to others.

What is meant by "fair competition" as the term is used in the Act? Does it refer to a category established in the law, and is the authority to make codes limited accordingly? Or is it used as a convenient designation for whatever set of laws the formulators of a code for a particular trade or industry may propose * * *, or the President may himself prescribe, as being wise and beneficent provisions for the government of the trade or industry in order to accomplish the broad purposes of rehabilitation, correction and expansion which are stated in the first section of Title I? [9]

The Act does not define "fair competition." * * *

The Government urges that the codes will "consist of rules of competition deemed fair for each industry by representative members of that industry—by the persons most vitally concerned and most familiar with its problems." Instances are cited in which Congress has availed itself of such assistance; as e. g., in the exercise of its authority over the public domain, with respect to the recognition of local customs or rules of miners as to mining claims, or, in matters of a more or less technical nature, as in designating the standard height of drawbars. But would it be seriously contended that Con-

---

9. That section, under the heading "Declaration of Policy," is as follows: "Section 1. A national emergency productive of widespread unemployment and disorganization of industry, which burdens interstate and foreign commerce, affects the public welfare, and undermines the standards of living of the American people, is hereby declared to exist. It is hereby declared to be the policy of Congress to remove obstructions to the free flow of interstate and foreign commerce which tend to diminish the amount thereof; and to provide for the general welfare by promoting the organization of industry for the purpose of coöperative action among trade groups, to induce and maintain united action of labor and management under adequate governmental sanctions and supervision, to eliminate unfair competitive practices, to promote the fullest possible utilization of the present productive capacity of industries, to avoid undue restriction of production (except as may be temporarily required), to increase the consumption of industrial and agricultural products by increasing purchasing power, to reduce and relieve unemployment, to improve standards of labor, and otherwise to rehabilitate industry and to conserve natural resources."

gress could delegate its legislative authority to trade or industrial associations or groups so as to empower them to enact the laws they deem to be wise and beneficent for the rehabilitation and expansion of their trade or industries? Could trade or industrial associations or groups be constituted legislative bodies for that purpose because such associations or groups are familiar with the problems of their enterprises? * * * The answer is obvious. Such a delegation of legislative power is unknown to our law and is utterly inconsistent with the constitutional prerogatives and duties of Congress.

The question, then, turns upon the authority which § 3 of the Recovery Act vests in the President to approve or prescribe. * * * But Congress cannot delegate legislative power to the President to exercise an unfettered discretion to make whatever laws he thinks may be needed or advisable for the rehabilitation and expansion of trade or industry. * * *

Accordingly we turn to the Recovery Act to ascertain what limits have been set to the exercise of the President's discretion. *First,* the President, as a condition of approval, is required to find that the trade or industrial associations or groups which propose a code, "impose no inequitable restrictions on admission to membership" and are "truly representative." That condition, however, relates only to the status of the initiators of the new laws and not to the permissible scope of such laws. *Second,* the President is required to find that the code is not "designed to promote monopolies or to eliminate or oppress small enterprises and will not operate to discriminate against them." * * * But these restrictions leave virtually untouched the field of policy envisaged by section one, and, in that wide field of legislative possibilities, the proponents of a code, refraining from monopolistic designs, may roam at will and the President may approve or disapprove their proposals as he may see fit. That is the precise effect of the further finding that the President is to make—that the code "will tend to effectuate the policy of this title." * * *

* * *

Such a sweeping delegation of legislative power finds no support in the decisions upon which the Government especially relies. By the Interstate Commerce Act, Congress has itself provided a code of laws regulating the activities of the common carriers subject to the Act, in order to assure the performance of their services upon just and reasonable terms, with adequate facilities and without unjust discrimination. Congress from time to time has elaborated its requirements, as needs have been disclosed. To facilitate the application of the standards prescribed by the Act, Congress has provided an expert body. That administrative agency, in dealing with particular cases, is required to act upon notice and hearing, and its orders must be supported by findings of fact which in turn are sustained by evidence. * *
When the Commission is authorized to issue, for the construction, extension or abandonment of lines, a certificate of "public convenience

and necessity," or to permit the acquisition by one carrier of the control of another, if that is found to be "in the public interest," we have pointed out that these provisions are not left without standards to guide determination. The authority conferred has direct relation to the standards prescribed for the service of common carriers and can be exercised only upon findings, based upon evidence, with respect to particular conditions of transportation. * * *

Similarly, we have held that the Radio Act of 1927 established standards to govern radio communications and, in view of the limited number of available broadcasting frequencies, Congress authorized allocation and licenses. The Federal Radio Commission was created as the licensing authority, in order to secure a reasonable equality of opportunity in radio transmission and reception. The authority of the Commission to grant licenses "as public convenience, interest or necessity requires" was limited by the nature of radio communications, and by the scope, character and quality of the services to be rendered and the relative advantages to be derived through distribution of facilities. These standards established by Congress were to be enforced upon hearing, and evidence, by an administrative body acting under statutory restrictions adapted to the particular activity. * * *

To summarize and conclude upon this point: Section 3 of the Recovery Act is without precedent. It supplies no standards for any trade, industry or activity. It does not undertake to prescribe rules of conduct to be applied to particular states of fact determined by appropriate administrative procedure. Instead of prescribing rules of conduct, it authorizes the making of codes to prescribe them. For that legislative undertaking, § 3 sets up no standards, aside from the statement of the general aims of rehabilitation, correction and expansion described in section one. In view of the scope of that broad declaration, and of the nature of the few restrictions that are imposed, the discretion of the President in approving or prescribing codes, and thus enacting laws for the government of trade and industry throughout the country, is virtually unfettered. We think that the code-making authority thus conferred is an unconstitutional delegation of legislative power.

Third. The question of the application of the provisions of the Live Poultry Code to intrastate transactions. * * *

* * *

These provisions relate to the hours and wages of those employed by defendants in their slaughterhouses in Brooklyn and to the sales there made to retail dealers and butchers.

(1) Were these transactions "in" interstate commerce? Much is made of the fact that almost all the poultry coming to New York is sent there from other States. But the code provisions, as here applied, do not concern the transportation of the poultry from other

States to New York * * *. When defendants had made their purchases, whether at the West Washington Market in New York City or at the railroad terminals serving the City, or elsewhere, the poultry was trucked to their slaughterhouses in Brooklyn for local disposition. * * * Defendants held the poultry at their slaughterhouse markets for slaughter and local sale to retail dealers and butchers who in turn sold directly to consumers. Neither the slaughtering nor the sales by defendants were transactions in interstate commerce. * * *

The undisputed facts thus afford no warrant for the argument that the poultry handled by defendants at their slaughterhouse markets was in a "current" or "flow" of interstate commerce and was thus subject to congressional regulation. The mere fact that there may be a constant flow of commodities into a State does not mean that the flow continues after the property has arrived and has become commingled with the mass of property within the State and is there held solely for local disposition and use. * * * Hence, decisions which deal with a stream of interstate commerce—where goods come to rest within a State temporarily and are later to go forward in interstate commerce—and with the regulations of transactions involved in that practical continuity of movement, are not applicable here. * * *

(2) Did the defendants' transactions directly "affect" interstate commerce so as to be subject to federal regulation? The power of Congress extends not only to the regulation of transactions which are part of interstate commerce, but to the protection of that commerce from injury. It matters not that the injury may be due to the conduct of those engaged in intrastate operations. * * * We have held that, in dealing with common carriers engaged in both interstate and intrastate commerce, the dominant authority of Congress necessarily embraces the right to control their intrastate operations in all matters having such a close and substantial relation to interstate traffic that the control is essential or appropriate to secure the freedom of that traffic from interference or unjust discrimination and to promote the efficiency of the interstate service. * * * And combinations and conspiracies to restrain interstate commerce, or to monopolize any part of it, are none the less within the reach of the Anti-Trust Act because the conspirators seek to attain their end by means of intrastate activities. * * *

* * *

* * * This is not a prosecution for a conspiracy to restrain or monopolize interstate commerce in violation of the Anti-Trust Act. Defendants have been convicted, not upon direct charges of injury to interstate commerce or of interference with persons engaged in that commerce, but of violations of certain provisions of the Live Poultry Code and of conspiracy to commit these violations. Interstate commerce is brought in only upon the charge that violations of these pro-

visions—as to hours and wages of employees and local sales—"affected" interstate commerce.

In determining how far the federal government may go in controlling intrastate transactions upon the ground that they "affect" interstate commerce, there is a necessary and well-established distinction between direct and indirect effects. The precise line can be drawn
only as individual cases arise, but the distinction is clear in principle.
Direct effects are illustrated by the railroad cases we have cited, as
e. g., the effect of failure to use prescribed safety appliances on railroads which are the highways of both interstate and intrastate commerce, injury to an employee engaged in interstate transportation by
the negligence of an employee engaged in an intrastate movement, the
fixing of rates for intrastate transportation which unjustly discriminate against interstate commerce. But where the effect of intrastate
transactions upon interstate commerce is merely indirect, such transactions remain within the domain of state power. If the commerce
clause were construed to reach all enterprises and transactions which
could be said to have an indirect effect upon interstate commerce,
the federal authority would embrace practically all the activities of
the people and the authority of the State over its domestic concerns
would exist only by sufferance of the federal government.   *   *   *

The distinction between direct and indirect effects has been clearly recognized in the application of the Anti-Trust Act. Where a combination or conspiracy is formed, with the intent to restrain interstate commerce or to monopolize any part of it, the violation of the
statute is clear.   *   *   *   But where that intent is absent, and the
objectives are limited to intrastate activities, the fact that there may
be an indirect effect upon interstate commerce does not subject the
parties to the federal statute, notwithstanding its broad provisions.
*   *   *

                              *   *   *

The question of chief importance [here] relates to the provisions
of the Code as to the hours and wages of those employed in defendants' slaughterhouse markets. It is plain that these requirements are
imposed in order to govern the details of defendants' management of
their local business. The persons employed in slaughtering and selling
in local trade are not employed in interstate commerce.   *   *   *

The Government   *   *   *   makes the point that efforts to enact state legislation establishing high labor standards have been impeded by the belief that unless similar action is taken generally, commerce will be diverted from the States adopting such standards, and
that this fear of diversion has led to demands for federal legislation
on the subject of wages and hours. The apparent implication is that
the federal authority under the commerce clause should be deemed to
extend to the establishment of rules to govern wages and hours in
intrastate trade and industry generally throughout the country, thus

overriding the authority of the States to deal with domestic problems arising from labor conditions in their internal commerce.

It is not the province of the Court to consider the economic advantages or disadvantages of such a centralized system. It is sufficient to say that the Federal Constitution does not provide for it. * * * [T]he authority of the federal government may not be pushed to such an extreme as to destroy the distinction, which the commerce clause itself establishes, between commerce "among the several States" and the internal concerns of a State. The same answer must be made to the contention that is based upon the serious economic situation which led to the passage of the Recovery Act,—the fall in prices, the decline in wages and employment, and the curtailment of the market for commodities. Stress is laid upon the great importance of maintaining wage distributions which would provide the necessary stimulus in starting "the cumulative forces making for expanding commercial activity." Without in any way disparaging this motive, it is enough to say that the recuperative efforts of the federal government must be made in a manner consistent with the authority granted by the Constitution.

* * *

On both the grounds we have discussed, the attempted delegation of legislative power, and the attempted regulation of intrastate transactions which affect interstate commerce only indirectly, we hold the code provisions here in question to be invalid and that the judgment of conviction must be reversed.

NOTES AND QUESTIONS

1. The "delegation" ground of *Schechter* had been anticipated in Panama Refining Co. v. Ryan, 293 U.S. 388, 55 S.Ct. 241, 79 L.Ed. 446 (1935), when the court had held that certain procedural provisions pertaining to the "hot oil" industry under the NIRA involved excessive delegation of legislative power to the executive. The "interstate commerce clause" ground had also been anticipated, in Railroad Retirement Bd. v. Alton R. Co., 295 U.S. 330, 55 S.Ct. 758, 79 L.Ed. 1468 (1935), when the court held that the provisions of the Railroad Retirement Act of 1934 were unconstitutional, because they provided for pensions for workers in exclusively intrastate traffic. Still, *Schechter* had more impact than earlier decisions, because of the unanimous court's clear declaration that the industry code system (the heart of the NIRA) could not be based on the commerce clause. Most of the economic work of the New Deal may already have been accomplished by May 27, 1935, when *Schechter* was announced, but Roosevelt was genuinely concerned about what the Supreme Court's obdurate attitude might mean for future reform efforts. He stated at a press conference held a few days later that "We have been relegated to the horse-and-buggy definition of interstate commerce." See generally Leuchtenburg, The Origins of Franklin D. Roosevelt's "Court-Packing" Plan, 1966 Supreme Court Review 347, 356–357.

2. Given the seriousness of the problems confronting the nation, given the appeal to many of the country's most advanced thinkers of centralized

management of the economy, and given the cooperation of government and business mandated by the NIRA, how would *you* have construed the interstate commerce clause in *Schechter*? Also, would you have found any support for holding the NIRA to be constitutional in the Constitution's preamble that the national government was "ordained and established" to "promote the general welfare" or "secure domestic tranquility?" What about the clause in Article I, Section 8, that provides that the Congress shall have the power "to pay the Debts and provide for the common Defence and general Welfare of the United States?" Finally, would the last clause of Section 8, which gives Congress power "To make all Laws which shall be necessary and proper for carrying into Execution the foregoing Powers, and all other Powers vested by this Constitution in the Government of the United States, or in any Department or Officer thereof" have any bearing?

3. Why do you suppose there was unanimous concurrence in throwing out the NIRA? What is the fundamental difficulty with the system of codes, the exemption from the antitrust acts, and the enforced cooperation of government and industry? Would the result under the NIRA have been acceptable to most of the nineteenth century judges whose opinions we studied? Why or why not? Consider the "delegation" rationale of the Supreme Court. Where in the Constitution do you find support for such a rationale? Do you believe that the Supreme Court successfully distinguishes the ICC Act and the Radio Act, which passed constitutional muster? Why isn't the meaning of "fair competition" made clear by the reference to the purposes of the NIRA, set out in Section 1, the Act's "Declaration of Policy?"

4. For the next two years several other decisions of the United States Supreme Court invalidated New Deal measures. On January 6, 1936, for example, the Supreme Court declared that the scheme of the AAA processing tax, insofar as it took money from the processors to be given to the farmers in subsidy payments, was unconstitutional. United States v. Butler, 297 U.S. 1, 56 S.Ct. 312, 80 L.Ed. 477 (1936) Justice Roberts, speaking for a six to three majority (Stone, Cardozo, and Brandeis dissented), stated that the subsidy payments were, in effect "the expropriation of money from one group for the benefit of another." Id., at 61.

5. Franklin Roosevelt was re-elected in 1936, in a landslide victory that included the greatest majority of electoral votes yet seen, including those of all but two states. For months popular sentiment had been running strongly against the "Nine old men" who were frustrating his legislative efforts. In early February of 1937, President Roosevelt proposed that Congress enact the following legislation:

> When any judge of a court of the United States, appointed to hold his office during good behavior, has heretofore or hereafter attained the age of seventy years and has held a commission or commissions as a judge of any such court or courts at least ten years, continuously or otherwise, and within six months thereafter has neither resigned nor retired, the President, for each such judge who has not so resigned or retired, shall nominate, and by and with the advice and consent of the Senate, shall appoint one additional judge to the court to which the former is commissioned. * * * No more than fifty judges shall be appointed thereunder,

nor shall any judge be so appointed if such appointment would result in * * * more than fifteen members of the Supreme Court of the United States. * * *.

Quoted in G. Gunther, Constitutional Law: Cases and Materials 168 (9th ed. 1975). At the time of the proposed bill six justices were over seventy: Butler (71), Hughes (75), Sutherland (75), McReynolds (75), Van Devanter (78), and Brandeis (81). There was a certain delicious irony in the plan, since Mr. Justice McReynolds, when he was Woodrow Wilson's Attorney General, in 1913, noting that federal court judges had tended to remain "upon the bench long beyond the time that they are able to adequately discharge their duties," had proposed legislation requiring the President to appoint additional judges to the lower federal courts when older judges failed to take the retirement at full pay which federal law permitted them. Roosevelt's Attorney General, Homer Cummings, one of the chief architects of FDR's court-packing plan, was able to argue that their proposal merely extended McReynolds's to the Supreme Court, a logical extension. Leuchtenburg, supra, at 391–392.

6. On March 9, 1937, President Roosevelt addressed the nation by radio, commenting on the *Butler* and *Schechter* decisions:

*   *   *

When the Congress has sought to stabilize national agriculture, to improve the conditions of labor, to safeguard business against unfair competition, to protect our national resources, and in many other ways to serve our clearly national needs, the majority of the Court has been assuming the power to pass on the wisdom of these acts of the Congress—and to approve or disapprove the public policy written into these laws.

*   *   *

We have, therefore, reached the point as a Nation where we must take action to save the Constitution from the Court and the Court from itself. We must find a way to take an appeal from the Supreme Court to the Constitution itself. We want a Supreme Court which will do justice under the Constitution—not over it. In our courts we want a government of laws and not of men.

*   *   *

quoted in Gunther, supra at 169–170. The President proceeded to argue for the necessity of his plan to pass legislation authorizing him to appoint additional judges to the court. Do you think that the President, in the portions quoted from his speech, accurately presents the issues? How would you have reacted if you were a Justice of the Supreme Court?

7. On March 29, 1937, the Supreme Court decided West Coast Hotel Co. v. Parrish, 300 U.S. 379, 57 S.Ct. 578, 81 L.Ed. 703 (1937). That case, by a five to four majority, upheld the constitutionality of a Washington State law which set a minimum wage for women. The court expressly overruled Adkins v. Children's Hospital, 261 U.S. 525, 43 S.Ct. 394, 67 L.Ed. 785 (1923), which had rejected the District of Columbia's Women's Minimum Wage Act, as a violation of the due process clause of the Fifth Amendment. Chief Justice Hughes, writing for the majority in *Parrish*,

seemed to reject much of the Constitutional philosophy of the early twentieth century court:

> The Constitution does not speak of freedom of contract. It speaks of liberty and prohibits the deprivation of liberty without due process of law. In prohibiting that deprivation the Constitution does not recognize an absolute and uncontrollable liberty. Liberty in each of its phases has its history and connotation. But the liberty safeguarded is liberty in a social organization which requires the protection of law against the evils which menace the health, safety, morals and welfare of the people. Liberty under the Constitution is thus necessarily subject to the restraints of due process, and regulation which is reasonable in relation to its subject and is adopted in the interests of the community is due process.

300 U.S., at 391. Justice Hughes went on to suggest that because the health of women was peculiarly related to the vigor of the race, and because women were especially liable to be overreached and exploited by unscrupulous employers, the Washington Act was a "reasonable" exercise of the state's police power. The court buttressed its arguments with economic considerations:

> The exploitation of a class of workers who are in an unequal position with respect to bargaining power and are thus relatively defenceless against the denial of a living wage is not only detrimental to their health and well being but casts a direct burden for their support upon the community. What these workers lose in wages the taxpayers are called upon to pay. The bare cost of living must be met. We may take judicial notice of the unparalleled demands for relief which arose during the recent period of depression and still continue to an alarming extent despite the degree of economic recovery which has been achieved. It is unnecessary to cite official statistics to establish what is of common knowledge through the length and breadth of the land. While in the instant case no factual brief has been presented, there is no reason to doubt that the State of Washington has encountered the same social problem that is present elsewhere. The community is not bound to provide what is in effect a subsidy for unconscionable employers.

Id., at 399.

Mr. Justice Sutherland wrote a dissenting opinion in *Parrish*, and was joined by Mr. Justice Van Devanter, Mr. Justice McReynolds, and Mr. Justice Butler. These four, by the way, were often referred to as the "Four Horsemen." Why do you suppose that was? Justice Sutherland, casting doubt on the propriety of overruling the fourteen-year-old *Adkins* case, stated "It is urged that the question involved should now receive fresh consideration, among other reasons, because of 'the economic conditions which have supervened' but the meaning of the Constitution does not change with the ebb and flow of economic events." Id., at 402. Was he right? Would Taney have agreed?

Restating the Court's former thinking on the necessary liberty of contracting under the due process clauses of the Fifth or Fourteenth amendments, Justice Sutherland first observed that the Washington state legislation in question, which had originally been passed in 1913, and was general in its terms:

> does not deal with any business charged with a public interest, or with public work, or with a temporary emergency, or with the character, methods or periods of wage payments, or with hours of labor, or with the protection of persons under legal disability, or with the prevention of fraud. It is, simply and exclusively, a law fixing wages for adult women who are legally as capable of contracting for themselves as men, and cannot be sustained unless upon principles apart from those involved in cases already decided by the court.

Id., at 407. Stressing that the statute was arbitrary not only in its application to women and not men, but also in its application to *all* employers, Sutherland continued:

> It takes no account of periods of stress and business depression, or crippling losses, which may leave the employer himself without adequate means of livelihood. To the extent that the sum fixed exceeds the fair value of the services rendered, it amounts to a compulsory exaction from the employer for the support of a partially indigent person, for whose condition there rests upon him no peculiar responsibility, and therefore, in effect, arbitrarily shifts to his shoulders a burden which, if it belongs to anybody, belongs to society as a whole.

Id., at 409. Winding up with a flourish, Sutherland concluded:

> Difference of sex affords no reasonable ground for making a restriction applicable to the wage contracts of all working women from which like contracts of all working men are left free. Certainly a suggestion that the bargaining ability of the average woman is not equal to that of the average man would lack substance. The ability to make a fair bargain, as everyone knows, does not depend upon sex.

Id., at 413. From the point of view of feminism, which opinion is preferable, that of the majority, or the dissent? How about from the point of view of Constitutional law? Is there a difference?

Less than a year earlier, on June 1, 1936, when the Supreme Court decided Morehead v. People of State of New York ex rel. Tipaldo, 298 U.S. 587, 56 S.Ct. 918, 80 L.Ed. 1347 (1936), Justice Roberts had voted with the Four Horsemen in a decision which, by a bare majority, found unconstitutional a New York minimum wage law for women, and which had expressly declined to overrule *Adkins*. Roberts "change" of position, to vote with what became the majority in *Parrish*, has been called the "switch in time, which saved nine." Felix Frankfurter, having been given a "memorandum" on the relevant facts by Justice Roberts, has argued that since the court actually voted in *Parrish* weeks before the decision was announced, and since Roberts voted with the majority *before* Roosevelt's court-packing plan announcement took place in early February, his "switch" could *not* have been motivated by purely political considerations. This was expressly indicated by Roberts himself, who wrote Frankfurter that "no action taken by the President in the interim had any causal relation to my action in the *Parrish* case." Roberts also indicated that he might well have been prepared to overrule *Adkins* in the *Tipaldo* case, but since the New York state attorneys did not expressly ask for such an overruling, but preferred to have their statute upheld on other grounds, he went along with the majority in *Tipaldo*. Roberts (and Frankfurter) were thus claiming that Roberts indulged in *no switch at all*. Frankfurter, Mr. Justice Roberts, 104 U.Pa.L.Rev. 311, 314–315 (1955). See also Charles A. Leonard, A Search For a Judicial Philosophy: Mr. Justice Roberts and the Constitutional Revolution of 1937 (1971).

Whether or not Justice Roberts "switched" in *Parrish* from his opinion a year earlier in *Tipaldo*, what do you make of the fact that Roberts *and* Justice Hughes were in the majority in the *Schechter* case, decided on May 27, 1935, and in the majority in the *Jones & Laughlin* case, decided on April 12, 1937, which follows?

NATIONAL LABOR RELATIONS BD. v. JONES & LAUGHLIN STEEL CORP.

Supreme Court of the United States, 1937.
301 U.S. 1, 57 S.Ct. 615, 81 L.Ed. 893.

Mr. Chief Justice HUGHES delivered the opinion of the Court.

In a proceeding under the National Labor Relations Act of 1935, the National Labor Relations Board found that the respondent, Jones & Laughlin Steel Corporation, had violated the Act by engaging in unfair labor practices affecting commerce. The proceeding was instituted by the Beaver Valley Lodge No. 200 * * *, a labor organization. The unfair labor practices charged were that the corporation was discriminating against members of the union with regard to hire and tenure of employment, and was coercing and intimidating its employees in order to interfere with their self-organization. The discriminatory and coercive action alleged was the discharge of certain employees.

The National Labor Relations Board, sustaining the charge, ordered the corporation to cease and desist from such discrimination and coercion, to offer reinstatement to ten of the employees named, to make good their losses in pay, and to post for thirty days notices that the corporation would not discharge or discriminate against members, or those desiring to become members, of the labor union. As the corporation failed to comply, the Board petitioned the Circuit Court of Appeals to enforce the order. The court denied the petition, holding that the order lay beyond the range of federal power, 83 F. (2d) 998. We granted certiorari.

The scheme of the National Labor Relations Act—which is too long to be quoted in full—may be briefly stated. The first section sets forth findings with respect to the injury to commerce resulting from the denial by employers of the right of employees to organize and from the refusal of employers to accept the procedure of collective bargaining.* There follows a declaration that it is the policy of the United States to eliminate these causes of obstruction to the free flow of commerce. The Act * * * creates the National Labor Relations Board and prescribes its organization. * * * It sets forth the right of employees to self-organization and to bargain collectively through representatives of their own choosing. * * * It defines "unfair labor practices." * * * The Board is empowered to prevent the described unfair labor practices affecting commerce and the Act prescribes the procedure to that end. There is a separability clause to the effect that if any provision of the Act or its application to any person or circumstances shall be held invalid, the remainder of the Act or its application to other persons or circumstances shall not be affected. * * *

The procedure in the instant case followed the statute. The labor union filed with the Board its verified charge. The Board thereupon issued its complaint against the respondent alleging that its action in discharging the employees in question constituted unfair labor practices affecting commerce * * *. Respondent admitted the discharges, but alleged that they were made because of inefficiency or violation of rules or for other good reasons and were not ascribable to union membership or activities. As an affirmative defense, respondent challenged the constitutional validity of the statute and its applicability in the instant case. Notice of hearing was given and respondent appeared by counsel. * * * The Board received evidence upon the merits and at its close made its findings and order.

Contesting the ruling of the Board, the respondent argues (1) that the Act is in reality a regulation of labor relations and not of interstate commerce; (2) that the Act can have no application to the respondent's relations with its production employees because they

---

* This section is as follows:

"Section 1. The denial by employers of the right of employees to organize and the refusal by employers to accept the procedure of collective bargaining lead to strikes and other forms of industrial strife or unrest, which have the intent or the necessary effect of burdening or obstructing commerce by (a) impairing the efficiency, safety, or operation of the instrumentalities of commerce; (b) occurring in the current of commerce; (c) materially affecting, restraining, or controlling the flow of raw materials or manufactured or processed goods from or into the channels of commerce, or the prices of such materials or goods in commerce; or (d) causing diminution of employment and wages in such volume as substantially to impair or disrupt the market for goods flowing from or into the channels of commerce.

"The inequality of bargaining power between employees who do not possess full freedom of association or actual liberty of contract, and employers who are organized in the corporate or other forms of ownership association substantially burdens and affects the flow of commerce, and tends to aggravate recurrent business depressions, by depressing wage rates and the purchasing power of wage earners in industry and by preventing the stabilization of competitive wage rates and working conditions within and between industries.

* * *

are not subject to regulation by the federal government; and (3) that the provisions of the Act violate § 2 of Article III and the Fifth and Seventh Amendments of the Constitution of the United States.

* * * The Labor Board has found: The corporation is organized under the laws of Pennsylvania and has its principal office at Pittsburgh. It is engaged in the business of manufacturing iron and steel in plants situated in Pittsburgh and nearby Aliquippa, Pennsylvania. It manufactures and distributes a widely diversified line of steel and pig iron, being the fourth largest producer of steel in the United States. With its subsidiaries—nineteen in number—it is a completely integrated enterprise * * *. It owns or controls mines in Michigan and Minnesota. It operates four ore steamships on the Great Lakes * * *. It owns coal mines in Pennsylvania. It operates towboats and steam barges used in carrying coal to its factories. It owns limestone properties in various places in Pennsylvania and West Virginia. It owns the Monongahela connecting railroad which connects the plants of the Pittsburgh works and forms an interconnection with the Pennsylvania, New York Central and Baltimore and Ohio Railroad systems. * * * Much of its product is shipped to its warehouses in Chicago, Detroit, Cincinnati and Memphis * * *. In Long Island City, New York, and in New Orleans it operates structural steel fabricating shops in connection with the warehousing of semi-finished materials sent from its works. * * * It has sales offices in twenty cities in the United States and a wholly-owned subsidiary which is devoted exclusively to distributing its product in Canada. Approximately 75 per cent. of its product is shipped out of Pennsylvania.

* * *

Respondent points to evidence that the Aliquippa plant, in which the discharged men were employed, contains complete facilities for the production of finished and semi-finished iron and steel products from raw materials * * *.

Practically all the factual evidence in the case, except that which dealt with the nature of respondent's business, concerned its relations with the employees in the Aliquippa plant whose discharge was the subject of the complaint. These employees were active leaders in the labor union. * * *

While respondent criticises the evidence and the attitude of the Board, which is described as being hostile toward employers and particularly toward those who insisted upon their constitutional rights, respondent aid not take advantage of its opportunity to present evidence to refute that which was offered to show discrimination and coercion. In this situation, the record presents no ground for setting aside the order of the Board so far as the facts pertaining to the circumstances and purpose of the discharge of the employees are concerned. * * * We turn to the questions of law * * *.

First. The scope of the Act.—The Act is challenged in its entirety as an attempt to regulate all industry, thus invading the reserved powers of the States over their local concerns. It is asserted that the references in the Act to interstate and foreign commerce are colorable at best; that the Act * * * has the fundamental object of placing under the compulsory supervision of the federal government all industrial labor relations within the nation. The argument seeks support in the broad words of the preamble (section one) and in the sweep of the provisions of the Act, and it is further insisted that its legislative history shows an essential universal purpose in the light of which its scope cannot be limited by either consruction or by the application of the separability clause.

If this conception of terms, intent and consequent inseparability were sound, the Act would necessarily fall by reason of the limitation upon the federal power which inheres in the constitutional grant, as well as because of the explicit reservation of the Tenth Amendment. Schechter Corp. v. United States, 295 U.S. 495, 549, 550, 554. * * * That distinction between what is national and what is local in the activities of commerce is vital to the maintenance of our federal system. Id.

But we are not at liberty to deny effect to specific provisions, which Congress has constitutional power to enact, by superimposing upon them inferences from general legislative declarations of an ambiguous character, even if found in the same statute. The cardinal principle of statutory construction is to save and not to destroy. We have repeatedly held that as between two possible interpretations of a statute, by one of which it would be unconstitutional and by the other valid, our plain duty is to adopt that which will save the act. * * *

We think it clear that the National Labor Relations Act may be construed so as to operate within the sphere of constitutional authority. The jurisdiction conferred upon the Board, and invoked in this instance, is found in § 10(a), which provides:

"*SEC.* 10(a). The Board is empowered, as hereinafter provided, to prevent any person from engaging in any unfair labor practice (listed in section 8) affecting commerce." * * * The Act specifically defines the "Commerce" to which it refers (§ 2(6)):

> The term "commerce" means trade, traffic, commerce, transportation, or communication among the several States, or between the District of Columbia or any Territory of the United States and any State or other Territory, or between any foreign country and any State, Territory, or the District of Columbia, or within the District of Columbia or any Territory, or between points in the same State but through any other State or any Territory or the District of Columbia or any foreign country.

There can be no question that the commerce thus contemplated by the Act (aside from that within a Territory or the District of Columbia) is interstate and foreign commerce in the constitutional sense. The Act also defines the term "affecting commerce" (§ 2(7)):

The term "affecting commerce" means in commerce, or burdening or obstructing commerce or the free flow of commerce, or having led or tending to lead to a labor dispute burdening or obstructing commerce or the free flow of commerce.

*   *   *   The grant of authority to the Board does not purport to extend to the relationship between all industrial employees and employers. Its terms do not impose collective bargaining upon all industry regardless of effects upon interstate or foreign commerce. It purports to reach only what may be deemed to burden or obstruct that commerce and, thus qualified, it must be construed as contemplating the exercise of control within constitutional bounds. *   *   *   It is the effect upon commerce, not the source of the injury, which is the criterion. *Second Employers' Liability Cases*, 223 U.S. 1, 51. Whether or not particular action does affect commerce in such a close and intimate fashion as to be subject to federal control, and hence to lie within the authority conferred upon the Board, is left by the statute to be determined as individual cases arise. *   *   *

Second. The unfair labor practices in question.—*   *   *

*   *   *

*   *   *   [I]n its present application, the statute goes no further than to safeguard the right of employees to self-organization and to select representatives of their own choosing for collective bargaining or other mutual protection without restraint or coercion by their employers.

That is a fundamental right. Employees have as clear a right to organize and select their representatives for lawful purposes as the respondent has to organize its business and select its own officers and agents. Discrimination and coercion to prevent the free exercise of the right of employees to self-organization and representation is a proper subject for condemnation by competent legislative authority. Long ago we stated the reason for labor organizations. We said that they were organized out of the necessities of the situation; that a single employee was helpless in dealing with an employer; that he was dependent ordinarily on his daily wage for the maintenance of himself and family; that if the employer refused to pay him the wages that he thought fair, he was nevertheless unable to leave the employ and resist arbitrary and unfair treatment; that union was essential to give laborers opportunity to deal on an equality with their employers. *   *   *   Fully recognizing the legality of collective action on the part of employees in order to safeguard their proper interests, we said that Congress was not required to ignore this right but could safeguard it. * * * Hence the prohibition by Congress of interference with the selection of representatives for the purpose of negotiation and conference between employers and employees, "instead of being an invasion of the constitutional right of either, was based on the recognition of the rights of both." Texas & N.O.O. Co. v. Railway Clerks, [281 U.S. 548]. We have reasserted the same principle in sustaining the application of the Railway Labor Act as amended in 1934. Virginian Railway Co. v. System Federation, No. 40, [300 U.S. 515].

Third. The application of the Act to employees engaged in production.—The principle involved.—Respondent says that whatever may be said of employees engaged in interstate commerce, the industrial relations and activities in the manufacturing department of respondent's enterprise are not subject to federal regulation. The argument rests upon the proposition that manufacturing in itself is not commerce. * * * Schechter Corp. v. United States, supra, p. 547 * * *.

The Government distinguishes these cases [which hold that manufacturing is not commerce.] The various parts of respondent's enterprise are described as interdependent * * *. It is urged that these activities constitute a "stream" or "flow" of commerce, of which the Aliquippa manufacturing plant is the focal point, and that industrial strife at that point would cripple the entire movement. Reference is made to our decision sustaining the Packers and Stockyards Act. Stafford v. Wallace, 258 U.S. 495. The Court found that the stockyards were but a "throat" through which the current of commerce flowed and the transactions which there occurred could not be separated from that movement. * * * Applying the doctrine of Stafford v. Wallace, supra, the Court sustained the Grain Futures Act of 1922 with respect to transactions on the Chicago Board of Trade, although these transactions were "not in and of themselves interstate commerce." Congress had found that they had become "a constantly recurring burden and obstruction to that commerce." Chicago Board of Trade v. Olsen, 262 U.S. 1, 32 * * *.

Respondent contends that the instant case presents material distinctions. Respondent says that the Aliquippa plant is extensive in size and represents a large investment in buildings, machinery and equipment. The raw materials which are brought to the plant are delayed for long periods and, after being subjected to manufacturing processes, "are changed substantially as to character, utility and value." The finished products which emerge "are to a large extent manufactured without reference to pre-existing orders and contracts and are entirely different from the raw materials which enter at the other end." * * *

We do not find it necessary to determine whether these features of defendant's business dispose of the asserted analogy to the "stream of commerce" cases. The instances in which that metaphor has been used are but particular, and not exclusive, illustrations of the protective power which the Government invokes in support of the present Act. The congressional authority to protect interstate commerce from burdens and obstructions is not limited to transactions which can be deemed to be an essential part of a "flow" of interstate or foreign commerce. Burdens and obstructions may be due to injurious action springing from other sources. The fundamental principle is that the power to regulate commerce is the power to enact "all appropriate legislation" for "its protection and advancement" (*The Daniel Ball*, 10 Wall. 557, 564) ; to adopt measures "to promote its growth and insure its safety" (Mobile County v. Kimball, 102 U.S. 691, 696, 697) ; "to foster, protect, control and restrain." *Second Employers' Liability Cases*, supra, p. 47. See *Texas & N. O. R. Co.* v. *Railway Clerks*, supra. That power is plenary and may be exerted to protect interstate commerce "no matter what the source of the dangers which threaten it." *Second Employers' Liability Cases*, p. 51; Schechter Corp. v. United States, supra. * * * Undoubtedly the scope of this power must be considered in the light of our dual system of government and may not be extended so as to embrace effects upon interstate commerce so indirect and remote that to embrace them, in view of our complex society, would effectually obliterate the distinction between what is national and what is local and create a completely centralized government. Id. The question is necessarily one of degree. * * *

That intrastate activities, by reason of close and intimate relation to interstate commerce, may fall within federal control is demonstrated in the case of carriers who are engaged in both interstate and intrastate transportation. There federal control has been found essential to secure the freedom of interstate traffic from interference or unjust discrimination and to promote the efficiency of the interstate service. Shreveport Case, 234 U.S. 342, 351, 352; Wisconsin Railroad Comm'n v. Chicago, B. & Q. R. Co., 257 U.S. 563, 588. It is manifest that intrastate rates deal *primarily* with a local activity. But in rate-making they bear such a close relation to interstate rates that effective control of the one must embrace some control over the other. Id. * * *

The close and intimate effect which brings the subject within the reach of federal power may be due to activities in relation to productive industry although the industry when separately viewed is local. This has been abundantly illustrated in the application of the federal Anti-Trust Act. In the *Standard Oil* and *American Tobacco* cases, 221 U.S. 1, 106, that statute was applied to combinations of employers engaged in productive industry. Counsel for the offending corporations strongly urged that the Sherman Act had no application because the acts complained of were not acts of interstate or foreign commerce, nor direct and immediate in their effect on interstate or foreign commerce, but primarily affected manufacturing and not commerce. 221 U.S. pp. 5, 125. Counsel relied upon the decision in United States v. Knight Co., 156 U.S. 1. The Court stated their contention as follows: "That the act, even if the averments of the bill be true, cannot be constitutionally applied, because to do so would extend the power of Congress to subjects *dehors* the reach of its authority to regulate commerce, by enabling that body to deal with mere questions of production of commodities within the States." And the Court summarily dismissed the contention in these words: "But all the structure upon which this argument proceeds is based upon the decision in United States v. E. C. Knight Co., 156 U.S. 1. The view, however, which the argument takes of that case and the arguments based upon that view have been so repeatedly pressed upon this court in connection with the interpretation and enforcement of the Anti-Trust Act, and have been so necessarily and expressly decided to be unsound as to cause the contentions to be plainly foreclosed and to require no express notice" (citing cases). 221 U.S. pp. 68, 69.

* * *

It is thus apparent that the fact that the employees here concerned were engaged in production is not determinative. The question remains as to the effect upon interstate commerce of the labor practice involved. In the *Schechter* case, supra, we found that the effect there was so remote as to be beyond the federal power. To find "immediacy or directness" there was to find it "almost everywhere," a result inconsistent with the maintenance of our federal system. * * *

Fourth. Effects of the unfair labor practice in respondent's enterprise.—Giving full weight to respondent's contention with respect to a break in the complete continuity of the "stream of commerce" by reason of respondent's manufacturing operations, the fact remains that the stoppage of those operations by industrial strife would have a most serious effect upon interstate commerce. In view of respondent's far-flung activities, it is idle to say that the effect would be indirect or remote. It is obvious that it would be immediate and might be catastrophic. We are asked to shut our eyes to the plainest facts of our national life and to deal with the question of direct and indirect effects in an intellectual vacuum. * * * When industries organize themselves on a national scale, making their relation to interstate commerce the dominant factor in their activities, how can it be maintained that their industrial labor relations constitute a forbidden field into which Congress may not enter when it is necessary to protect interstate commerce from the paralyzing consequences of industrial war? We have often said that interstate commerce itself is a practical conception. It is equally true that interferences with that commerce must be appraised by a judgment that does not ignore actual experience.

Experience has abundantly demonstrated that the recognition of the right of employees to self-organization and to have representatives of their own choosing for the purpose of collective bargaining is often an essential condition of industrial peace. Refusal to confer and negotiate has been one of the most prolific causes of strife. This is such an outstanding fact in the history of labor disturbances that it is a proper subject of judicial notice and requires no citation of instances. * * *

* * * The steel industry is one of the great basic industries of the United States, with ramifying activities affecting interstate commerce at every point. * * * The fact that there appears to have been no major disturbance in that industry in the more recent period did not dispose of the possibilities of future and like dangers to interstate commerce which Congress was entitled to foresee and to exercise its protective power to forestall. It is not necessary again to detail the facts as to respondent's enterprise. Instead of being beyond the pale, we think that it presents in a most striking way the close and intimate relation which a manufacturing industry may have to interstate commerce and we have no doubt that Congress had constitutional authority to safeguard the right of respondent's employees to self-organization and freedom in the choice of representatives for collective bargaining.

Fifth. The means which the Act employs.—Questions under the due process clause and other constitutional restrictions.—Respondent asserts its right to conduct its business in an orderly manner without being subjected to arbitrary restraints. What we have said points to the fallacy in the argument. Employees have their correlative right to organize for the purpose of securing the redress of grievances and to promote agreements with employers relating to rates of pay and conditions of work. * * * Restraint for the purpose of preventing an unjust interference with that right cannot be considered arbitrary or capricious. * * *

The [National Labor Relations] Act does not compel agreements between employers and employees. It does not compel any agreement whatever. It does not prevent the employer "from refusing to make a collective contract and hiring individuals on whatever terms" the employer "may by unilateral action determine." The Act expressly provides in § 9(a) that any individual employee or a group of employees shall have the right at any time to present grievances to their employer. The theory of the Act is that free opportunity for negotiation with accredited representatives of employees is likely to promote industrial peace and may bring about the adjustments and agreements which the Act in itself does not attempt to compel. * * * The Act does not interfere with the normal exercise of the right of the employer to select its employees or to discharge them. The employer may not, under cover of that right, intimidate or coerce its employees with respect to their self-organization and representation, and, on the other hand, the Board is not entitled to make its authority a pretext for interference with the right of discharge when that right is exercised for other reasons than such intimidation and coercion. * * *

The procedural provisions of the Act are assailed. But these provisions, as we construe them, do not offend against the constitutional requirements governing the creation and action of administrative bodies. * * * The Act establishes standards to which the Board must conform. There must be complaint, notice and hearing. The Board must receive evidence and make findings. The findings as to the facts are to be conclusive, but only if supported by evidence. The order of the Board is subject to review by the designated court, and only when sustained by the court may the order be enforced. Upon that review all questions of the jurisdiction of the Board and the regularity of its proceedings, all questions of constitutional right or statutory authority, are open to examination by the court. We construe the procedural provisions as affording adequate opportunity to secure judicial protection against arbitrary action in accordance with the well-settled rules applicable to administrative agencies set up by Congress to aid in the enforcement of valid legislation. * * *

The order of the Board required the reinstatement of the employees who were found to have been discharged because of their "union activity" and for the purpose of "discouraging membership in the union." That requirement was authorized by the Act. § 10(c). * * *

Respondent complains that the Board not only ordered reinstatement but directed the payment of wages for the time lost by the discharge; less amounts earned by the employee during that period. This part of the order was also authorized by the Act. § 10(c). It is argued that the requirement is equivalent to a money judgment and hence contravenes the Seventh Amendment which provides that "In suits at common law, where the value in controversy shall exceed twenty dollars, the right of trial by jury shall be preserved." The Amendment thus preserves the right which existed under the common law when the Amendment was adopted. * * * It does not apply where the proceeding is not in the nature of a suit at common law. Guthrie National Bank v. Guthrie, 173 U.S. 528, 537.

The instant case is not a suit at common law or in the nature of such a suit. The proceeding is one unknown to the common law. It is a statutory proceeding. Reinstatement of the employee and payment for time lost are requirements imposed for violation of the statute and are remedies appropriate to its enforcement. The contention under the Seventh Amendment is without merit.

Our conclusion is that the order of the Board was within its competency and that the Act is valid as here applied.

* * *

NOTES AND QUESTIONS

1. Justice McReynolds wrote the dissent in *Jones & Laughlin*, which also served as a dissenting opinion in several other labor board cases disposed of by the Supreme Court at the same time. He was joined by Justices Van Devanter, Sutherland, and Butler. 301 U.S., at 76. McReynolds thus summed up the dissent:

> The Court, as we think, departs from well-established principles followed in Schechter Corp. v. United States, 295 U.S. 495 (May, 1935) and Carter v. Carter Coal Co., 298 U.S. 238 (May, 1936). Upon the authority of those decisions, the Circuit Court of Appeals of the Fifth, Sixth and Second Circuits in the causes now before us have held the power of Congress under the commerce clause does not extend to relations between employers and their employees engaged in manufacture, and therefore the Act conferred upon the National Labor Relations Board no authority in respect of matters covered by the questioned orders. * * *

301 U.S., at 76.

McReynolds ridiculed the majority's conception of the involvement of interstate commerce, even in the case of *Jones & Laughlin*, which involved the dismissals of ten men.

> In No. 419 [*Jones*] ten men out of ten thousand were discharged; in the other cases only a few. The immediate effect in the factory may be to create discontent among all those employed and a strike may follow, which, in turn may result in reducing production, which ultimately may reduce the volume of goods moving in interstate commerce. By this chain of indirect and progressively remote events we finally reach the evil with which it is said the legislation under consideration undertakes to deal. A more remote and indirect interference with interstate commerce or a more definite invasion of the powers reserved to the states is difficult, if not impossible, to imagine.

Id., at 97. In reply to contentions about the steel company's goods being in the "stream of commerce," McReynolds wrote:

> There is no ground on which reasonably to hold that refusal by a manufacturer, whose raw materials come from states other than that of his factory, and whose products are regularly carried to other states, to bargain collectively with employees in his manufacturing plant, directly affects interstate commerce. In such business, there is not one but two distinct movements or streams in interstate transportation. The first brings in raw material and there ends. Then follows manufacture, a separate and local activity. Upon completion of this, and not before, the second distinct movement or stream in interstate commerce begins and the products go to other states.

Id., at 98. Does this analysis, that there are two separate streams of commerce, neither of which flows through manufacturing, convince you? How about McReynolds's assertion that the majority went overboard because

"Almost anything—marriage, birth, death—may in some fashion affect commerce?" Id., at 99.

2. Justice McReynolds, as well as questioning the majority's views on interstate commerce, appears to have had some due process problems with the NLRB act's authorizing legislation, insofar as it rejected the dismissal of men or women for their union activities:

> The right to contract is fundamental and includes the privilege of selecting those with whom one is willing to assume contractual relations. This right is unduly abridged by the Act now upheld. A private owner is deprived of power to manage his own property by freely selecting those to whom his manufacturing operations are to be entrusted. We think this cannot lawfully be done in circumstances like those here disclosed.

Id., at 103.

It appears, does it not, that the majority had no such due process problems. Why not? Do you find anything in the majority's rationale on this point—labor's need for collective bargaining, self-organization, and representation—that resembles theories of labor law articulated by the judges we studied in Chapter Five? Still, is it appropriate to raise these theories to the level of federal policy? It has often been asserted that the line of Supreme Court cases beginning in 1937, which seemed to signal a new willingness to uphold Congressional acts addressing national economic concerns, signalled a "Constitutional Revolution." Would you agree with this term, as it might be applied to the *Jones* case?

3. Perhaps another aspect of a "Constitutional Revolution" which might be inherent in *Jones* has to do with administrative law, and with the remedies available to government agencies such as the labor board. The majority alludes to the argument that there is a problem with the Seventh Amendment insofar as the labor board is able to impose money judgments on employers, without a jury trial. Note the court simply brushes this aside, with the notion that since labor board actions are a statutory creation, there is no "common law" right to trial by jury that has been infringed. Given what you learned about the early American controversies over trial by jury in the Prologue and Chapters One and Two of the casebook, is this brusque dismissal of the argument appropriate? Is it correct to read the Seventh Amendment's prohibition regarding trials by jury at "common law" as leaving a wide area open for the shifting of assets without such a barrier of laymen between administrative agencies and the public? Do you find the majority exhibiting the same willingness to enter into the purposes and "spirit" of Constitutional provisions regarding trial by jury as it seems to be displaying with regard to the interpretation of the constitutional term "interstate commerce"?

4. Roughly two months after the *Jones* decision was announced, on June 14, 1937, the Senate's Judiciary Committee reported on the President's proposed bill to increase the number of Supreme Court Justices:

> We recommend the rejection of this bill as a needless, futile, and utterly dangerous abandonment of constitutional principle. * * *

> It would subjugate the courts to the will of Congress and the President and thereby destroy the independence of the judiciary,

the only certain shield of individual rights. * * * It stands now before the country, acknowledged by its proponents as a plan to force judicial interpretation of the Constitution, a proposal that violates every sacred tradition of American democracy.

* * * It is a measure which should be so emphatically rejected that its parallel will never again be presented to the free representatives of the free people of America.

Senate Report No. 711, 75th Cong., 1st Sess. (1937), quoted in Gunther, supra, at 170. As you might have guessed, the Judiciary Committee's views prevailed, and the "court-packing" bill was never passed. Still, given the decisions in *Jones, Parrish,* and a line of cases which followed, and given FDR's appointments of seven new Justices from 1937 through 1941 (Black, Reed, Frankfurter, Douglas, Murphy, Byrnes, and Jackson), even if FDR lost this "battle," who "won the war?"

5. After the rejection of the NIRA by the Supreme Court in *Schechter* in 1935, there appears to have been a shift in legislative philosophy on the part of Roosevelt's advisors, and perhaps on the part of the President himself. The measures which resulted from the shift have been frequently described as a "Second New Deal," in which the emphasis, instead of being on collective planning and cooperation between business and government, as was the case with the NIRA and the other measures of the "First New Deal," was on reform and strengthening of the bargaining power of workers and farmers. The NLRB Act, involved in *Jones,* of course, was one such measure. Arthur M. Schlesinger, Jr., in The Politics of Upheaval (1960) thus describes the differences:

> The early New Deal had accepted the concentration of economic power as the central and irreversible trend of the American economy, and had proposed the concentration of political power as the answer. The effort of 1933 had been to reshape American institutions according to the philosophy of an organic economy and a coordinated society. The new effort was to restore a competitive society within a framework of strict social ground rules and on the foundation of basic economic standards—accompanied, as time went on, by a readiness to use the fiscal pulmotor to keep the economy lively and expansive. * * *

Id., at 385. Copyright © 1960 by Arthur M. Schlesinger, Jr., reprinted by permission of the publisher, Houghton Mifflin Co.

The shift from the first to the second New Deal was probably prompted by much more than the Supreme Court's activities. Not only could intelligent Americans perceive what economic distress could do to foreign countries like Weimar Germany and Mussolini's Italy, but some thought that the anti-semitic demagoguery of the American "Radio Priest," Father Coughlin, or the machinations of the popular Louisiana dictator, Huey Long, were indications that Fascism could well come to America. See, e. g. William E. Leuchtenburg, Franklin D. Roosevelt and the New Deal, pp. 275–288 (1963), and sources there cited. Perhaps reflecting on similar considerations, Arthur M. Schlesinger, Jr., wrote that, "As children of light, the First New Dealers had believed in the capacity for justice which, in Niebur's phrase, makes democracy possible. As children of darkness, the Second New Dealers believed in the inclination to injustice which makes democracy necessary." Schlesinger, supra, at 397–8.

What effect would you have expected the legal and social events we have just considered to have had on American jurisprudence, and particularly the notion that American law exhibited the noble tenets of the "legal science" envisioned by Field and Langdell? In the next few readings, with our examination of "legal realism," we study the emergence of jurisprudential notions which seem to bear a far stronger resemblance to the ideas of Holmes than to those of Field or Langdell.

SECTION C. LEGAL REALISM

JEROME FRANK, LAW AND THE MODERN MIND *

3–11, 14–19, 253–260 (1930).

The lay attitude towards lawyers is a compound of contradictions, a mingling of respect and derision. Although lawyers occupy leading positions in government and industry, although the public looks to them for guidance in meeting its most vital problems, yet concurrently it sneers at them as tricksters and quibblers.

*   *   *

What is the source of these doubts of the lawyer's honesty and sincerity?

A false tradition "invented by twelfth-century priests and monks," replies Dean Roscoe Pound. "For the most part clerical jealousy of the rising profession of non-clerical lawyers was the determining element. * * * Naturally, the clergy did not relinquish the practice of law without a protest." What those priests began, says Pound, Luther developed, and since Luther's day the other learned professions have taken over. "Unless one perceives that a struggle of professions for leadership is involved," one cannot understand the distrust of the legal profession. The lawyer is today, as he was in the twelfth century, in a marked position of advantage. This irks the other learned men. * * *

An ingenious explanation, but patently superficial. * * * Modern dispraise of the Bar is not to be explained as merely an outcropping of angry rivalry; obviously it is not confined to members of competing professions. That lawyers are scheming hair-splitters is a popular commonplace.

* Reprinted from Jerome Frank, *Law and the Modern Mind,* originally published by Brentano's, Inc. in 1930. These excerpts are taken from the Anchor Books edition, published in 1963 by arrangement with Barbara Frank Kristein, and are here reprinted with the kind permission of Marvin Kristein, Esq., acting for the Estate of Barbara Frank Kristein. Copyright 1930, 1933, 1949 by Coward-McCann, Inc. Copyright 1930 by Brentano's, Inc. Copyright renewed in 1958 by Florence K. Frank. All Rights Reserved.

What lies back of this popular criticism? It appears to be founded on a belief that the lawyers complicate the law, and complicate it wantonly and unnecessarily, that, if the legal profession did not interpose its craftiness and guile, the law could be clear, exact and certain. * * * Public opinion agrees with Napoleon who was sure that "it would be possible to reduce laws to simple geometrical demonstrations, so that whoever could read and tie two ideas together would be capable of pronouncing on them."

* * *

Now it must be conceded that, if the law can be made certain and invariable, the lawyers are grievously at fault. For the layman is justified in his opinion that the coefficient of legal uncertainty is unquestionably large, that to predict the decisions of the courts on many a point is impossible. * * *

Yet the layman errs in his belief that this lack of precision and finality is to be ascribed to the lawyers. The truth of the matter is that the popular notion of the possibilities of legal exactness is based upon a misconception. The law always has been, is now, and will ever continue to be, largely vague and variable. And how could this well be otherwise? The law deals with human relations in their most complicated aspects. * * *

Even in a relatively static society, men have never been able to construct a comprehensive, eternized set of rules anticipating all possible legal disputes and settling them in advance. * * * How much less is such a frozen legal system possible in modern times. * * * When human relationships are transforming daily, legal relationships cannot be expressed in enduring form. * * * Our society would be strait-jacketed were not the courts, with the able assistance of the lawyers, constantly overhauling the law and adapting it to the realities of ever-changing social, industrial and political conditions; although changes cannot be made lightly, yet law must be more or less impermanent, experimental and therefore not nicely calculable. *Much of the uncertainty of law is not an unfortunate accident: it is of immense social value.*

In fields other than the law there is today a willingness to accept probabilities and to forego the hope of finding the absolutely certain. Even in physics and chemistry, where a high degree of quantitative exactness is possible, modern leaders of thought are recognizing that finality and ultimate precision are not to be attained. The physicists, indeed, have just announced the Principle of Uncertainty or Indeterminacy. If there can be nothing like complete definiteness in the natural sciences, it is surely absurd to expect to realize even approximate certainty and predictability in law, dealing as it does with the vagaries of complicated human adjustments.

Since legal tentativeness is inevitable and often socially desirable, it should not be considered an avoidable evil. But the public learns little or nothing of this desirability of legal tentativeness from the learned gentlemen of the law. Why this concealment? * * * If lawyers are not responsible for legal indefiniteness, are they not guilty, at any rate, of duping the public as to the essential character of law? Are they not a profession of clever hypocrites?

There is no denying that the bar appears to employ elaborate pretenses to foster the misguided notions of the populace. Lawyers do not merely sustain the vulgar notion that law is capable of being made entirely stable and unvarying; they seem bent on creating the impression that, on the whole, it is already established and certain. When a client indignantly exclaims, "A pretty state of affairs when I can't learn exactly what my rights are!" how does the lawyer usually respond? With assurances that the situation is exceptional, that generally speaking the law is clear enough, but that in this particular instance, for some reason or other the applicable rules cannot be definitely ascertained. * * *

Of course, such assurances are unwarranted. Each week the courts decide hundreds of cases which purport to turn not on disputed "questions of fact" but solely on "points of law." If the law is unambiguous and predictable, what excuses can be made by the lawyers who lose these cases? They should know in advance of the decisions that the rules of law are adverse to their contentions. Why, then, are these suits brought or defended? * * * [I]n many cases, honest and intelligent counsel on both sides of such controversies can conscientiously advise their respective clients to engage in the contest; they can do so because, prior to the decision, the law is sufficiently in doubt to justify such advice.

It would seem, then, that the legal practitioners must be aware of the unsettled condition of the law. Yet observe the arguments of counsel in addressing the courts, or the very opinions of the courts themselves: they are worded as if correct decisions were arrived at by logical deduction from a precise and pre-existing body of legal rules. Seldom do judges disclose any contingent elements in their reasoning, any doubts or lack of whole-hearted conviction * * *.

Why these pretenses, why this professional hypocrisy? The answer is an arresting one: There is no hypocrisy. The lawyers' pretenses are not consciously deceptive. The lawyers, themselves, like the laymen, fail to recognize fully the essentially plastic and mutable character of law. * * *

* * *

* * * Why do the generality of lawyers insist that law should and can be clearly knowable and precisely predictable although, by doing so, they justify a popular belief in an absurd standard of legal exactness? Why do lawyers, indeed, themselves recognize such an absurd standard, which makes their admirable and socially valuable

achievement—keeping the law supple and flexible—seem bungling
and harmful?   *   *   *

*   *   *

We are on the trail of a stubborn illusion.   Where better, then,
to look for clues than in the direction of childhood?   For in children's
problems, and in children's modes of meeting their problems, are to
be found the sources of most of the confirmed illusions of later years.

*   *   *   [O]nly today are psychologists noting that the behavior patterns of early childhood are the basis of many subsequent
adaptions.   At long last, they are using a genetic approach;   the emotional handicaps of adult life, they now tell us, "represent almost invariably, if not always, the unsolved problems or the partially solved
or badly solved problems of childhood."

*   *   *

The child at birth is literally forced from a small world of almost
complete and effortless security into a new environment which at
once sets up a series of demands.   Strange sensations of light, sound,
touch and smell attack him.   The nearly perfect pre-birth harmony
and serenity are over.   The infant now must breathe and eat.   His
struggle for existence has begun.   But his wants, at first, are few and
are satisfied with a minimum of strain on his own part.   The parents
do their best to meet, almost instantly, the infant's desires.   In this
sense, he approximates omnipotence, because, relative to his askings,
he achieves nearly complete obedience.   *   *   *

As infancy recedes his direct omnipotence diminishes.   But that
there is omnipotence somewhere the child does not doubt.   *   *   *
There is, he believes, no happening without a knowable reason.   *   *
There must always be whys and wherefores.   Chaos is beyond belief.
Order and rule govern all.

As early childhood passes and consciousness grows keener, now
and again the child becomes sharply aware of his incapacity for controlling the crushing, heedless, reluctant and uncertain facts of the
outer world.   *   *   *   Fears beset him—fear of the vague things
that stalk the darkness, fear of the unruly, the unseen, the horrible
bogies of the unknown.

Then he rushes to his parents for help.   They stand between him
and the multitudinous cruelties and vagaries of life.   They are all-
powerful, all-knowing.   *   *   *

The child still possesses omnipotence—but now, vicariously.
Through his dependence upon his parents' omnipotence he finds relief from unbearable uncertainty.   His overestimation of the parental
powers is an essential of his development.

It must not be overlooked that a significant division of parental
functions takes place early in the life of the child.   In all communities
where the father is head of the family, the mother comes to "repre-

sent the nearer and more familiar influence, domestic tenderness, the help, the rest and the solace to which the child can always turn," writes Malinowski in a recent anthropological study. But "the father has to adopt the position of the final arbiter in force and authority. He has gradually to cast off the roll of tender and protective friend, and to adopt the position of strict judge, and hard executor of law." * * * The child, in his struggle for existence, makes vital use of his belief in an omniscient and omnipotent father, a father who lays down infallible and precise rules of conduct.

Then, slowly, repeated experiences erode this fictional overestimate. * * * There are many things father doesn't know, things he can't do. Other humans successfully oppose him. And there are forces loose in the world beyond his control. One's own father is at times helpless, deficient; he is all-too-human. * * *

But the average child cannot completely accept this disillusionment. He has formed an irresistible need for an omniscient and omnipotent father who shall stand between him and life's uncertainties. * * * His attitudes and adaptations had been built upon his relations to his idealized, his incomparable father. The child is disoriented. Again panic fear attacks him. He is unwilling and largely unable to accept as realities the ungovernable, the unorderable aspects of life. Surely, he feels, somewhere there must be Someone who can control events, make the dark spots light, make the uncertain clear. * * *

Many are the persons who become substitutes for the deposed father: the priest or pastor, the rulers and leaders of the group. They, too, turn out to be disappointing. But the demand for fatherly authority does not die. To be sure, as the child grows into manhood, this demand grows less and less vocal, more and more unconscious. The father-substitutes become less definite in form, more vague and impersonal. * * * Concealed and submerged, there persists a longing to reproduce the father-child pattern, to escape uncertainty and confusion through the rediscovery of a father.

* * *

That religion shows the effects of the childish desire to recapture a father-controlled world has been often observed. But the effect on the law of this childish desire has escaped attention. And yet it is obvious enough: To the child the father is the Infallible Judge, the Maker of definite rules of conduct. * * * The Law—a body of rules apparently devised for infallibly determining what is right and what is wrong and for deciding who should be punished for misdeeds—inevitably becomes a partial substitute for the Father-as-Infallible-Judge.

* * *

[Much later in his analysis, Frank asks whether any American lawyers have surmounted the "childish" tendency to regard the law as certain and infallible. His answer follows.]

One wise leader pointing the way we have had with us many years. The judicial opinions and other writings of Mr. Justice Holmes —practitioner, teacher, historian, philosopher, judge—are a treasury of adult counsels, of balanced judgments as to the relation of the law to other social relations. There you will find a vast knowledge of legal history divorced from slavish veneration for the past, a keen sensitiveness to the needs of today with no irrational revolt against the conceptions of yesterday, a profound respect for the utility of syllogistic reasoning linked with an insistence upon recurrent revisions of premises based on patient studies of new facts and new desires. He has himself abandoned, once and for all, the phantasy of a perfect, consistent, legal uniformity, and has never tried to perpetuate the pretense that there is or can be one. * * *

Almost fifty years ago Holmes made the famous statement (the implications of which have not yet been thoroughly appreciated) that "The life of the law has not been logic; it has been experience." [He added] that the law "cannot be dealt with as if it contained only the axioms and corollaries of a book of mathematics."

* * *

As one of our foremost legal historians, he does not underestimate the value of the history of law. * * * Yet he calls attention to history's "almost deceptive charm" and bids us beware of "the pitfall of antiquarianism." His chief interest in the past is for the light it throws upon the present. * * *

He has often weighed and considered the value of rules of law which are survivals of ancient traditions, when the ancient meaning has been forgotten. In such cases the judges strive to give modern reasons for the old rules. Such reasons, Holmes finds, are, for the most part, artificial and unsatisfactory. * * *

But he concedes that sometimes the old rules have an actual present use. * * *

Ever and again he has reverted to his early position that "in substance the growth of the law is legislative," that "the secret root from which the law draws all the juices of life" are considerations of what is expedient for the community concerned, more or less definitely understood views of public policy. These are considerations "which judges most rarely mention and always with an apology." * * * The process of judicial law-making "has been largely unconscious." It is important to insist on a "more conscious recognition of the legislative function of courts." * * *

What has made lawyers overstress logic he has sensed accurately: "The logical method and form flatter that longing for certainty and for repose which is in every human mind. But certainty generally is illusion, and repose is not the destiny of man." * * *

He has been sound, too, about the function of doubt: "To have doubted one's own first principles is the mark of a civilized man." Accordingly he can afford to doubt even his own dogmas: "While one's experience thus makes certain preferences dogmatic for one's self, recognition of how they came to be so leaves one able to see that others, poor souls, may be equally dogmatic about something else." And, accordingly, he has developed that remarkable tolerance which is the mark of high maturity. Skeptical about the inevitable validity of existing rules merely because they exist, he is yet no fiery reformer eager to abandon all tradition merely because of its lack of novelty.

* * * [T]hirty years ago he said:

> I do not expect or think it desirable that the judges should undertake to renovate the law. That is not their province. Indeed precisely because I believe that the world would be just as well off if it lived under laws that differed from ours in many ways, and because I believe that the claim of our especial code to respect is simply that it exists, that it is the one to which we have become accustomed, and not that it represents an eternal principle, I am slow to consent to over-ruling a precedent * * *. But I think it is most important to remember whenever a doubtful case arises, with certain analogies on one side and other analogies on the other, that what really is before us is a conflict between two social desires, each of which cannot both have their way. The social question is which desire is stronger at the point of conflict. The judicial one may be narrower, because one or the other desire may have been expressed in previous decisions to such an extent that logic requires us to assume it to preponderate in the one before us. But if that be clearly so, the case is not a doubtful one. Where there is doubt the simple tool of logic does not suffice, and even if it is disguised and unconscious, the judges are called on to exercise the sovereign prerogative of choice.

In his constitutional opinions he has been in favor of allowing a wide latitude of freedom in experimentation and has accordingly sustained statutes involving "social experiments" even though, as he has said, they "may seem futile or even noxious to me and those whose judgment I most respect." Now over eighty years of age, just the other day he said from the bench that our Constitution

> "is an experiment, as all life is an experiment. Every year, if not every day, we have to wager our salvation upon some prophecy based upon imperfect knowledge. While that experiment is part of our system, I think that we should be eternally vigilant against attempts to check the expressions of opinions that we loathe and believe to be fraught with death unless they so imminently threaten immediate inter-

ference with the lawful and pressing purposes of the law
that an immediate check is required to save the country."

And most significant for our purposes is his recognition that
one's dogmas, the things in which one believes and for which one
will fight and die, one's essential attitudes towards the universe, are
"determined largely by early associations and temperament, coupled
with the desire to have an absolute guide."

*The great value of Holmes as a leader is that his leadership im-
plicates no effort to enslave his followers.* It would be grossly mis-
using his example to accept his judicial opinions or views on any
question of law as infallible. It may well be assumed that he would
be the readiest to urge a critical reconsideration of any doctrines
he has announced. He has attained an adult emotional status, a self-
reliant, fearless approach to life * * *. We might say that, being
rid of the need of a strict father, he can afford not to use his authority as if he, himself, were a strict father.

His legal skepticism is clear, sane, vital, progressive—not an
easy achievement, as one can see in the example [of] * * * Pound
* * *. One is reminded of Vaihinger's comments on the pessimistic
character of Greek skepticism: When the Greek skeptics realized
the deep chasm between thought and reality, there resulted a marked
depression. They despaired of thought. * * * This was inevitable,
says Vaihinger, because "mere subjective thinking" had not "yet
achieved these tremendous scientific feats which are distinctive of
modern times."

And so in law today, most men still recoil from the admission of
the "subjectivity" of law. * * * Holmes, almost alone among
lawyers, adopts that skeptical attitude upon which modern science
has builded, that modern skepticism which looks upon thought as
instrumental and acknowledges the transient and relative nature of
all human thought-contrivances. Holmes has been telling us for fifty
years that, in effect, the Golden Rule is that there is no Golden Rule.
But the old fascinations lure men away from the essential meaning
of his teaching.

For Holmes's thoroughly "scientific" view of law requires courage,
more courage than is required in the natural sciences. In those sciences, as Vaihinger points out, skepticism has proved its worth. Not
so, as yet, in the law. And it is courageous indeed to face the fact,
once and for all, that men have made the law and must take the responsibility for its good or bad workings.

If, like Holmes, we win free of the myth of fixed authoritarian
law, having neither to accept law because it comes from an authority
resembling the father's, nor to reject it for like reason, we shall, for
the first time, begin to face legal problems squarely. Without abating
our insistence that the lawyers do the best they can, we can then
manfully endure inevitable short-comings, errors and inconsistencies

in the administration of justice because we can realize that perfection is not possible. The legal profession will then for the first time be in a position to do its work well.

If that view of the law brings to the lawyer a large sense of the burdens of his responsibility, it may also bring its pleasures—the pleasures of self-confidence, self-authority, of the conscious use of one's abilities in one of the most important areas of human activity.

* * *

NOTES AND QUESTIONS

1. As you may have discerned, Frank's *Law and the Modern Mind* had as one of its principal purposes a questioning of the jurisprudential assumptions of Roscoe Pound, then the Dean of the Harvard Law School and, at that time, probably the most renowned legal scholar in America. What is hinted at in the excerpt is made explicit in other parts of the work. See, e. g., pp. 151–152, 221–231, and 312–326. In particular Frank criticizes Pound for what Frank finds to be Pound's unwillingness to concede the inevitability of and the necessity for discretion on the part of judges. While Frank concedes that Pound excoriates "mechanical jurisprudence" in matters of "human conduct," or those involving "the conduct of enterprise, or fraud, good faith, negligence, or fiduciary duties" he attacks Pound's apparent insistence that certainty is possible in matters of "property and commercial transactions." Pound's insistence on keeping up this distinction, says Frank, means that Pound has not yet reached the completely adult status of Holmes. At one point, Frank even asks, regarding one of Pound's theories, "are we not * * * listening to something like a small boy with a grown-up vocabulary talking of an ideal father?" Id., at 306. How might you expect Pound to respond to this sort of criticism? The next reading seems to be his reaction.

2. As did Stanley Elkins, whose treatment of slavery we read in Chapter IV, Frank leans heavily on the work of psychologists to aid in understanding legal developments. Do you think that laymen and lawyers' failure to see the inevitability of uncertainty in the law flows from a failure to "work through" childhood fixations on an omnipotent father? Frank seems to assume a differentiation in familial roles between mother (as nourishing and comforting) and father (as stern and all-knowing). Suppose, as seems to be happening in modern America, the traditional role-stereotypes are breaking down, and "parenting" is seen as a joint venture, with neither parent as stern authoritarian. What would someone like Frank argue that this change in familial roles might mean for the law? Do you see any evidence of legal change that might flow from such developments? Ask yourself that question again after reading the materials in the last Chapter.

3. Consider Frank's use of Holmes. Would you say that his characterization of Holmes is accurate? Is Holmes's "anthropology" the same thing as Frank's Freudian psychology? From what you have seen of Holmes, would he accept Frank's notion of the inevitable and necessary uncertainty of the law? Is this a notion that you find acceptable? Could one expect a republic to be governed by laws that are inherently uncertain?

Is it too much to expect a populace, or even most lawyers, to accept a legal world in which there is no one, no thing, or no being permanently at the helm?

4. When all is said and done, is it still true that Frank is still like Field and Langdell in that he thinks "like a lawyer?" Is Frank's preoccupation with uncertainty the most important issue in law making by judges? Does this "uncertainty" preoccupation conceal other issues only hinted at by Frank, but made more explicit in the work of nineteenth century "legal realists" like Honestus or Rantoul?

ROSCOE POUND, THE CALL FOR A REALIST JURISPRUDENCE *

44 Harv.L.Rev. 697 (1931).

A critic of nineteenth-century historical jurisprudence used to deplore that Savigny had not studied under Savigny in his youth. He had been trained in the eighteenth-century natural law and was unable to get away from certain presuppositions and modes of thought which his training had made part of his juristic make-up. Those of us who were brought up in the analytical and historical jurisprudence of the last century may well bear this in mind as we read and seek to appraise the work of the on-coming generation of American law teachers. * * *

Hence I approach the subject of the call for a realist jurisprudence, insistent on the part of our younger teachers of law, with some humility. But here is an important movement in the science of law, and it behooves us to understand it and be thinking about it.

I

First, then, what is meant by realism in this connection? As I read them, the new juristic realists hardly use realism in a technical philosophical sense. They use it rather in the sense which it bears in art. By realism they mean fidelity to nature, accurate recording of things as they are, as contrasted with things as they are imagined to be, or wished to be, or as one feels they ought to be. They mean by realism faithful adherence to the actualities of the legal order as the basis of a science of law. But a science of law must be something more than a descriptive inventory. There must be selection and ordering of the materials so as to make them intelligible and useful. * * * What does realism propose to do with them which we had not been doing in the past? * * *

* * * [T]here is nothing new in the assumption of those who are striking out new paths of juristic thought that those who have

gone before them have been dealing with illusions, while they alone
and for the first time are dealing with realities. The rationalists put
forward the same claim. They claimed to stand upon a solid and un-
challengeable ground of reason in contrast to an illusion of authority
and the broken down academic fiction of continuity of the empire on
which the medieval conception of the binding force of the *corpus
juris* had been built. When Kant's critical philosophy undermined
this supposed solid foundation, the historical jurists came forward
with a claim of substituting for the illusion of reason the reality of
experience. Historical study of experience of adjusting human relations was to show us the course of unfolding of the idea, which alone
had significance, as contrasted with the eighteenth-century illusion of
a natural law discoverable by sheer reason. Next the analytical
jurists made a like claim. They made no pretense of considering
what had been or what would be or what ought to be. It was their
boast that they treated of what was. They proceeded on the basis
of "the pure fact of law." * * * And then came the positivists.
They too stood and stood alone on a solid ground of reality. To them
reality was in laws of social and legal development discoverable by
observation of social and legal institutions among all peoples. Our
new realist rejects all these conceptions of juristic reality. Reason is
an illusion. Experience is not the unfolding of an idea. No "pure
fact of Law" is to be found in rules since the existence of rules of
law, as anything outside of the books, is an illusion. * * *

If recent philosophy teaches aright, there is no absolute reality.
What test of reality may a modern relativist assert in jurisprudence
other than significance? But there is no absolute significance. Significance is significance for or in relation to something. Is not a valuing in terms of significance for the ends of the legal order (as the
social utilitarians see it) or a valuing and defining of ends with
reference to significance for civilization (as the Neo-Hegelians see it)
as real as a looking at single phenomena as significant in their unique-
ness or at the alogical element in judicial or legislative or juristic
behavior as more significant than the logical? As in the disputes of
diverse schools of jurists in the past, the difference today is one of
emphasis. Received ideals, conceptions, the quest for certainty and
uniformity, an authoritative technique of using authoritative legal
materials, settled legal doctrines and modes of thought, and a traditional mode of legal reasoning are actual and everyday phenomena
of the legal order. The question at bottom is whether a faithful representation of realities shall paint them in the foreground or instead
shall put in the foreground the subjective features in the behavior
of particular judges, the elements in judicial action which stand in
the way of certainty and uniformity, the deficiencies of the received
technique, the undefined edges and overlappings of doctrines and the
deficiencies of legal reasoning. Emphasis on the fallings short of
these instruments is useful * * *. The new realists have been

doing good work at this point. But such critical activity, important as it is, is not the whole of jurisprudence, nor can we build a science of law which shall faithfully describe the actualities of the legal order and organize our knowledge of these actualities, merely on the basis of such criticism. * * *

There is nothing upon which the new realist is so insistent as on giving over all preconceptions and beginning with an objectively scientific gathering of facts. * * * But facts occur in a multifarious mass of single instances. To be made intelligible and useful, significant facts have to be selected, and what is significant will be determined by some picture or ideal of the science and of the subject of which it treats. * * * The new realists have their own preconceptions of what is significant, and hence of what juristically must be. Most of them merely substitute a psychological must for an ethical or political or historical must.

II

* * * [F]ive items are to be found so generally in the writings of the new school, that one may be justified in pronouncing them, or most of them, the ideas of current juristic realism:

(a) One of the most common is faith in masses of figures as having significance in and of themselves. * * * Very little experience of using current official statistics is required to convince that statistics gathered for no purpose beyond filling a report with impressive tabulations are seldom valuable for anything else. I would not for a moment belittle the importance of bringing together information as to exactly how legal precepts and doctrines and institutions are functioning. But statistics on these subjects are not the only objectively ascertainable data available to the jurist. In the reported decisions of the past we have a record of experience in the administration of justice, of how precepts or doctrines or institutions have worked or have failed to work, and of how and why they came to be formulated or shaped as we find them, which is as solid a basis for objectively scientific study as any mass of figures can be. * * * Chiefly we shall have to understand the doctrinal and institutional and legislative materials which have come down to us, both in their workings and in their possibilities, using such statistics as we find or may gather as helps toward that understanding.

(b) No less common is belief in the exclusive significance or reality of some one method or line of approach. One of these, much insisted on, is exact terminology. * * * But I venture to think that the utility of precise terminology and exact meanings is more in connection with differentiating problems from pseudo-problems and with formulation of results than in providing solutions. None of the fundamental problems of jurisprudence is solved by terminology, while there have been signs that rigid terminology has been used to create an appearance of solution of questions which have been left untouched at the core.

* * *

Still another [group] * * * seeks a science of law analogous to mathematical physics, and would refuse the name of science to a body of knowledge, or the epithet scientific to a method which does not conform to that type. It is conceived that observation of the phenomena of administration of justice, carried on objectively and scientifically, may give us formulas as rigidly exact and free from any personal or subjective element, either in formulation or application, as for example, those employed by the engineer. It is argued that the only objectively valid phenomena are those discoverable by statistical investigation of the operations of judicial institutions * * *.

* * * [W]e must consider how judges do decide, how they ought to decide to give effect to the ends of the legal order, and how to insure as far as may be the decisions that ought to be. Undoubtedly the gathering of statistics can show us much as to how justice is administered, and how and how far legal precepts are observed and enforced. But they are expected also to show how justice must (in a psychological sense) be administered, and so to dispense with the question how it ought to be administered. This question of ought, turning ultimately on a theory of values, is the hardest one in jurisprudence. Those who long for an exact science analogous to mathematics or physics or astronomy have been inclined to seek exactness by excluding this hard problem from jurisprudence altogether. But such a jurisprudence has only an illusion of reality. For the significant question is the one excluded.

* * *

Another mode of approach to jurisprudence, often asserted to be the one path to reality, is psychological. Psychological exposure of the role of reason in human behavior, of the extent to which so-called reasons come after action as explanations instead of before action as determining factors, has made a profound impression upon the rising generation of jurists. It has led many of them to insist on the non-rational element in judicial action as reality and the rational as illusion. In contrast to the nineteenth-century emphasis on certainty and uniformity and ignoring of the continual fallings short of those ideals, they emphasize the uncertainties, the lack of uniformity, and the influence of personal and subjective factors in particular cases. This leads us to a related characteristic of the new juristic realism.

(c) Along with the assertion that the sole valid approach is by way of psychology goes usually a presupposition that some one psychological starting point is the *unum necessarium*, and that a science of law which makes use of any other type or theory of psychology is unscientific and illusory. * * *

* * *

* * * On the contrary, I submit that jurisprudence can't wait for psychologists to agree (if they are likely to), and that there is no need of waiting. We can reach a sufficient psychological basis for juristic purposes from any of the important current psychologies. Here again real means significant. The things which are significant for jurisprudence are in all of them. We have problems enough of our own in the science of law without wasting our ammunition in broadsides at each other over our wrong choices of psychological parties.

Nor is the psychological neo-realism of the moment wholly emancipated from the *a prior* dogmatism with which it reproaches older types of juristic thought. Much of it consists in setting forth what it seems the course of judicial action or juristic thinking must be, in the light of some current psychological dogma, rather than investigation of recorded judicial experience and juristic development thereof in order to see what they reveal.

* * * [T]here is a distinct advance in [the new realists'] frank recognition of the alogical or non-rational element in judicial action which the legal science of the nineteenth century sought to ignore. But many of these realists seek to ignore the logical and rational element and the traditional technique of application, or art of the common-law lawyer's craft, which tends to stability and uniformity of judicial action in spite of the disturbing factors. * * * It is just as unreal to refuse to see the extent to which legal technique, with all its faults, applied to authoritative legal materials, with all their defects, keeps down the alogical or unrational element or holds it to tolerable limits in practice. In the field of the economic life (in the stricter sense) there is incomparably more significance on the one side than on the other. It is exactly this significance which makes legal and economic development go hand in hand.

(d) Another characteristic is insistence on the unique single case rather than on the approximation to a uniform course of judicial behavior * * *. The unique aspects of cases, the common aspects of them, and generalizations from the common aspects, may or may not be useful instruments according to the connection in which we look at them and the tasks to which we apply them. None of the three is an absolute and universal solvent.

Radical neo-realism seems to deny that there are rules or principles or conceptions or doctrines at all, because all judicial action, or at times much judicial action, can not be referred to them; because there is no definite determination whereby we may be absolutely assured that judicial action will proceed on the basis of one rather than another of two competing principles; because there is a no-man's land about most conceptions so that concrete cases have been known to fall down between them; because much takes place in the course of adjudication which does not fit precisely into the doctrinal plan. * * * But nothing would be more unreal—in the sense of at variance with what is significant for a highly specialized form of social control through politically organized society—than to conceive of the administration of justice, or the legal adjustment of relations, or, for that matter, the working out of devices for the more efficient functioning of business in a legally ordered society, as a mere aggregate of single determinations.

(e) Finally, many of the new juristic realists conceive of law as a body of devices for the purposes of business instead of as a body of means toward general social ends. They put the whole emphasis on the exigencies of one phase of the economic order. To them the significant feature of law is as a body of devices for enabling business and industry to achieve certain purposes. * * * Like the schools which have gone before them, the new realists take one aspect of the apparatus of the legal order and conceive it to be of paramount significance.

Looking at law as an aggregate of devices whereby business projects may be effected in a politically organized industrial society, there are two ways in which these devices are availed of. First, they are employed toward a better and more economical achievement of what the legal precepts in the books permit or do not forbid. Second, they are employed, or sought to be employed, to evade legal prohibitions and to enable things to be done which politically organized society has authoritatively pronounced anti-social. Thus, for example, statutes as to coöperative marketing may be used to permit mergers in contravention of the laws or policy of the laws as to restraint of trade. * * * Certainly, here is a feature of the legal order which deserves the attention of jurists from many standpoints, and the new realists do a service in bringing it out. But if their way of looking at law is modern in its recognition of actualities ignored in the last century, it is thoroughly tied to the past in its limitations. * * * As in the past, one item is made to stand out at the expense of a picture of the whole. As in the past, reality is taken to be exclusively at one point or in one item. Law is more than a body of devices for business purposes, just as it is more than a body of rules for the guidance of courts. * *

III

It is much more important to understand than to criticize. Too much criticism in jurisprudence has started from an assumption that critic and criticized were looking at the same things, or seeking to answer the same questions, and achieved an easy victory over straw men set up on that assumption. * * * It takes time for a new school to develop. One may point out work to be done in the progress of a school without implying that those engaged in the task are ignorant thereof, or that they do not intend to direct their energies thereto in due time.

With this caveat, let me essay a program of relativist-realist jurisprudence as I conceive it might be * * *:

1.   A functional attitude, i. e., study not only of what legal precepts and doctrines and institutions are, and how they have come to be, but of how they work. [* * * I] urge particularly study of concrete instances of rules or doctrines or institutions in action, in such number and by such methods as to be able to reach valid general conclusions.

2.   Recognition of the existence of an alogical, unrational, subjective element in judicial action, and attempt by study of concrete instances of its operation to reach valid general conclusions as to the kinds of cases in which it operates most frequently, and where it operates most effectively or most unhappily for the ends of the legal order.

3.   Recognition of the significance of the individual case, as contrasted with the absolute universalism of the last century, without losing sight of the significance of generalizations and conceptions as instruments toward the ends of the legal order. * * *

4.   Giving up of the idea of a necessary sequence from a single cause in a straight line to a single effect, and hence of the one sovereign legal remedy for every difficulty and one necessary solution of every problem. There will be recognition of a plurality of elements in all situations and of the possibility of dealing with human relations in more than one way. There will be recognition that the test of a legal precept or doctrine or institution is how and how far it helps to achieve the ends of the legal order. * * * Hence in the end I am confident there will be no abandonment of belief that the administration of justice may be improved by intelligent effort. I suspect also that study of single instances wisely directed and in sufficient number will show what study of the legal materials of all systems seems to reveal, namely, that the old straight line thinking is a useful instrument in parts of the administration of justice where the economic order demands the maximum of attainable certainty.

5.   A theory of interests and of the ends of the legal order based on or consistent with modern psychology, without being tied absolutely to any particular dogmatic brand of psychology of the moment.

6.   A theory of values, for the valuing of interests, consistent with modern psychology and philosophy, without being tied fast to any particular body of psychological or philosophical dogma of the moment.

7.   A recognition that there are many approaches to juristic truth and that each is significant with respect to particular problems of the legal order; hence a valuing of these approaches, not absolutely or with reference to some one assumed necessary psychological or philosophical basis of jurisprudence, but with reference to how far they aid law maker, or judge, or jurist in making law and the science of law effective, the one toward the maintaining, furthering, and transmit-

ting of civilization, the other toward organizing the materials and laying out the course of the legal order.

Perhaps it is asking too much of any school of jurists to call upon them for so broad an outlook. But in the house of jurisprudence there are many mansions. There is more than enough room for all of us and more than enough work. If the time and energy expended on polemics were devoted to that work, jurisprudence would be more nearly abreast of its tasks.

NOTES AND QUESTIONS

1. Would you say that Pound is able successfully to deflect any of the punches launched by Frank? This is, of course, one brief excerpt from a large corpus of Pound's legal thought, but do you find Pound offering here any creditable alternatives to the views of the legal realists (at least as we have them from the excerpt from Frank or from Pound's descriptions of their thinking)? At one point Pound seems almost to suggest that the thought of the realists shows a danger of "abandonment of belief that the administration of justice may be improved by intelligent effort." Is this a fair criticism of Frank? Why did Frank write his book?

2. You will have noted that Pound still maintains the necessity for considering discrete parts of the "legal order," and perhaps of prescribing different reforms for different sectors. In particular he insists that there are parts of the "economic order" which demand the "maximum of attainable certainty." Has he really been affected by Frank's criticism? Perhaps it should be noted, as Pound himself acknowledged, that this essay was "written in haste at a time when he was burdened with administrative duties, not least his work as a member of the National Commission on Law Observance and Enforcement." William Twining, Karl Llewellyn and The Realist Movement 72 (1973). If this is true, what does it suggest about Pound's evaluation of the legal realists? Pound's critique of the Realists led to the following article in their defense. See whether you agree with Llewellyn's characterization of Pound, and whether Pound's criticisms are successfully rebutted.

KARL N. LLEWELLYN, SOME REALISM ABOUT REALISM— RESPONDING TO DEAN POUND *

44 Harv.L.Rev. 1222 (1931).**

Ferment is abroad in the law. The sphere of interest widens; men become interested again in the life that swirls around things legal.
* * *

* Jerome Frank refused me permission to sign his name as joint author to this paper, on the ground that it was my fist which pushed the pen. But his generosity does not alter the fact that the paper could not have been written without his help. I therefore write the first sections, in partial recognition, as "We," meaning thereby Frank and myself. In the description of the realists, I turn to the first person singular, partly because any alignment of such diverse work is individually colored; partly because any phrasing which would seem to suggest a non-existent school would be unfortunate.

The ferment is proper to the time. The law of schools threatened at the close of the century to turn into words—placid, clear-seeming, lifeless, like some old canal. Practice rolled on, muddy, turbulent, vigorous. It is now spilling, flooding, into the canal of stagnant words. It brings ferment and trouble. So other fields of thought have spilled their waters in: the stress on behavior in the social sciences; their drive toward integration; the physicists' reexamination of final-seeming premises; the challenge of war and revolution. These stir. They stir the law. * * * And always there is this restless questing: what difference does statute, or rule, or court-decision, make?

* * *

And those involved are folk of modest ideals. * * * They want to check ideas, and rules, and formulas by facts, to keep them close to facts. They view rules, they view law, as means to ends * * *. They suspect, with law moving slowly and the life around them moving fast, that some law may have gotten out of joint with life. This is a question in first instance of fact: what does law *do*, to people, or for people? In the second instance, it is a question of ends: what *ought* law to do to people, or for them? But there is no reaching a judgment as to whether any specific part of present law does what it ought, until you can first answer what it is doing now. * * *

All this is, we say, a simple-hearted point of view, and often philosophically naive—though it has in it elements enough of intellectual sophistication. It denies very little, except the completeness of the teachings handed down. It knows too little to care about denying much. It affirms ignorance, pitched within and without. It affirms the need to know. Its call is for intelligent effort to dispel the ignorance. Intelligent effort to cut beneath old rules, old words, to get sight of current things. It is not a new point of view; it is as old as man. But its rediscovery in any age, by any man, in any discipline, is joyous.

* * *

Dean Pound has discussed the call and the ferment. * * * We rejoiced that a scholar of Dean Pound's standing and perspective found much * * * to appreciate. We agreed with him that it was important for the older thinking and the newer to make contact.

But the Dean's description did not stop with the points mentioned. It continued. On bones we knew was built a flesh we knew not of. An ugly flesh. The new realists, or "most of them," had, as the Dean read them, been guilty of a goodly number of things that careful thinkers would in the main not be proud to be caught doing. These intellectual offenses Dean Pound criticized. He criticized them tellingly. The question is one of fact: whether the offenses have been committed. For if they have, the Dean's rebukes are needed. Spare the rod and spoil the realist.

The question is one of fact. By fact it must be tried. And tried it must be. When Dean Pound speaks on jurisprudence, men listen. The profession has too long relied on him to discover, read, digest, classify and report on jurists foreign and ancient not to rely again when he speaks of would-be jurists modern and at home. * * *

I

The trial of Dean Pound's indictment is not easy. It is a blanket indictment. It is blanket as to time and place and person of each offense. It specifies no one offender by his name.

We have the general indications above-mentioned: "new realists" and the like. We have the more specific indications also mentioned. Taken together, they narrow the class that may come in question.[17] We can, therefore, check the items against a reasonable sampling of the men whom the rest of the description fits.[18] We have chosen twenty men and ninety-odd titles; representative men and pertinent titles. These we have canvassed in order to ascertain the extent to which the evidence supports the Dean's allegations. * * *

THE RESULTS OF THE TEST

* * *

[As a result of his survey of the writings of the twenty "realists," Llewellyn declares, *inter alia*, that (1) the work of three men (Bingham, Francis, and Yntema) might support Pound's charge that the realists describe judicial behavior on the basis of some "current psychological dogma, *without investigation of what recorded judicial experience reveals*;" (2) that "conceivably" one realist, Jerome Frank, has done work that supports the charge that "*the rational element in law is an illusion*;" (3) that the work of one man (Frank) supports the charge that realists "conceive of the administration of justice rather as a mere aggregate of single

---

17. We had hoped to be more precise. We wrote Dean Pound to ask whom he had had in mind when he wrote his article. * * * He did mention three names specifically. Bingham and Lorenzen he had had in mind. C. E. Clark he definitely had not.

18. *The sampling of men.* * * *

(1) Bingham and Lorenzen are included as of course. (2) We add those whom we believe recognized as figures of central stimulus in the new ferment: C. E. Clark, Cook, Corbin, Moore, T. R. Powell, Oliphant. (3) We add further men peculiarly vocal in advocating new or rebellious points of view: Frank, Green, Radin. (4) We stir in all others whom we have heard

criticized as extremists on one or another point mentioned by the Dean: Hutcheson, Klaus, Sturges. (5) We fill out with as many more as time permits: Douglas, Francis, Patterson, Tulin, Yntema—chosen partly because their writing has explicitly touched points of theory, partly because their writing was either familiar to us or not too bulky. (6) We throw in Llewellyn, as both vociferous and extreme, but peculiarly because he and he alone has issued a "Call for a Realist Jurisprudence" under that peculiar label. A Realistic Jurisprudence—The Next Step (1930) 30 Col. L.Rev. 431. This gives us twenty names. There are doubtless twenty more. But half is a fair sample. * more. But half is a fair sample. * * *

determinations than as an approximation to a uniform course of behavior;" and (4) that "perhaps" one realist (Sturges) supports the charge that the realists have "an exclusive interest in the business aspects of the law." Llewellyn suggests that there is no direct support for any of Pound's other criticisms of the realist movement. The exhaustive details supporting these conclusions are given in an appendix to the original article, which is here omitted.]

Let it be conceded that we have missed men or evidence which would support these points of description on which so much of the Dean's criticism of realists is based. * * * We submit, nonetheless, that *any* description of what "realists" think, or what "most of them believe" or what "many of them write" * * * will in the light of our canvass need evidence by man and chapter and verse before it can be relied on as meaning more than: the writer has an impression that there is someone, perhaps two someones, whose writings bear this out. * * *

II

REAL REALISTS

What, then, *are* the characteristics of these new fermenters? One thing is clear. There is no school of realists. There is no likelihood that there will be such a school. There is no group with an official or accepted, or even with an emerging creed. * * *

There is, however, a *movement* in thought and work about law. * * * Individual men, then. Men more or less interstimulated— but no more than all of them have been stimulated by the orthodox tradition, or by that ferment at the opening of the century in which Dean Pound took a leading part. * * * They differ among themselves well-nigh as much as any of them differs from say, Langdell. * * *

* * *

* * * I shall endeavor to keep in mind as I go that the justification for grouping these men together lies not in that they are *alike* in belief or work, but in that from certain common points of departure they have branched into lines of work which seem to be building themselves into a whole, a whole planned by none, foreseen by none, and (it may well be) not yet adequately grasped by any.

The common points of departure are several.

(1) The conception of law in flux, of moving law, and of judicial creation of law.

(2) The conception of law as a means to social ends and not as an end in itself; so that any part needs constantly to be examined for its purpose, and for its effect, and to be judged in the light of both and of their relation to each other.

(3) The conception of society in flux, and in flux typically faster than the law, so that the probability is always given that any portion

of law needs reexamination to determine how far it fits the society it purports to serve.

(4) The *temporary* divorce of Is and Ought for purposes of study. * * * More particularly, this involves during the study of what courts are doing the effort to disregard the question what they ought to do. Such divorce of Is and Ought is, of course, not conceived as permanent. To men who begin with a suspicion that change is needed, a permanent divorce would be impossible.

(5) Distrust of traditional legal rules and concepts insofar as they purport to *describe* what either courts or people are actually doing. Hence the constant emphasis on rules as "generalized predictions of what courts will do." * * *

(6) Hand in hand with this distrust of traditional rules (on the descriptive side) goes a distrust of the theory that traditional prescriptive rule-formulations are *the* heavily operative factor in producing court decisions. This involves the tentative adoption of the theory of rationalization for the study of opinions. * * *

(7) The belief in the worthwhileness of grouping cases and legal situations into narrower categories than has been the practice in the past. This is connected with the distrust of verbally simple rules—which so often cover dissimilar and non-simple fact situations * * *

(8) An insistence on evaluation of any part of law in terms of its effects, and an insistence on the worthwhileness of trying to find these effects.

(9) Insistence on *sustained and programmatic attack* on the problems of law along any of these lines. None of the ideas set forth in this list is new. Each can be matched from somewhere; each can be matched from recent orthodox work in law. New twists and combinations do appear here and there. What is as novel as it is vital is for a goodly number of men to pick up ideas which have been expressed and dropped, used for an hour and dropped, played with from time to time and dropped—to pick up such ideas and set about *consistently, persistently, insistently to carry them through.* * * * This urge, in law, is quite new enough over the last decades to excuse a touch of frenzy among the locust-eaters.[37]

* * *

Bound, as all "innovators" are, by prior thinking, these innovating "realists" brought their batteries to bear in first instance on the work of appellate courts. * * *

(a) An early and fruitful line of attack borrowed from psychology the concept of *rationalization* already mentioned. To recanvass the

---

37. Since everyone who reads the manuscript in this sad age finds this allusion blind, but I still like it. I insert the passage: " * * * Preaching in the wilderness of Judea, And saying, Repent ye. * * * And the same John had his raiment of camel's hair, and a leathern girdle about his loins; *and his meat was locusts* and wild honey." Matthew III, 1, 2, 4.

opinions, viewing them no longer as mirroring the process of deciding cases, but rather as trained lawyers' arguments made by the judges (after the decision has been reached), intended to make the decision seem plausible, legally decent, legally right, to make it seem, indeed, legally inevitable—this was to open up new vision. * * *

But the line of inquiry via rationalization has come close to demonstrating that in any case doubtful enough to make litigation respectable the available authoritative premises—i. e., premises legitimate and impeccable under the traditional legal techniques—are at least two, and that the two are mutually contradictory as applied to the case in hand.[39] Which opens the question of what made the court select the one available premise rather than the other. * * *

(b) A second line of attack has been to discriminate among rules with reference to their relative significance. Too much is written and thought about "law" and "rules," lump-wise. Which part of law? Which rule? Iron rules of policy, and rules "in the absence of agreement"; rules which keep a case from the jury, and rules as to the etiquette of instructions necessary to make a verdict stick * * *. Such discriminations affect the traditional law curriculum, the traditional organization of law books and, above all, the orientation of study * * *.

(c) A further line of attack on the apparent conflict and uncertainty among the decisions in appellate courts has been to seek more understandable statement of them by grouping the facts in new—and typically but not always narrower—categories. The search is for correlations of fact-situation and outcome which (aided by common sense) may reveal when courts seize on one rather than another of the available competing premises. One may even stumble on the trail of *why* they do. Perhaps, e. g., third party beneficiary difficulties simply fail to get applied to promises to make provision for dependents; perhaps the pre-existing duty rule goes by the board when the agreement is one for a marriage-settlement. Perhaps, indeed, contracts in what we may broadly call family relations do not work out in general as they do in business. * * *

All of these three earliest lines of attack converge to a single conclusion: There is less possibility of accurate prediction of what courts will do than the traditional rules would lead us to suppose * * *. The particular kind of certainty that men have thus far thought to find in law is in good measure an illusion. Realistic workers have sometimes insisted on this truth so hard that they have been thought pleased with it. * * *

But announcements of fact are not appraisals of worth. The contrary holds. The immediate result of the preliminary work thus

---

39. For a series of examples, see * * * Powell, Current Conflicts Between the Commerce Clause and State Police Power, 1922–1927 (1928) 12 Minn.L.Rev. 470, 491, 607, 631.

far described has been a further, varied series of endeavors; the focusing of conscious attack on discovering the factors thus far unpredictable, in good part with a view to their control. Not wholly with a view to such elimination; part of the conscious attack is directed to finding where and when and how far uncertainty has value. * * *

(i) There is the question of the personality of the judge. * * * Some have attempted study of the particular judge [48]—a line that will certainly lead to inquiry into his social conditioning. Some have attempted to bring various psychological hypotheses to bear.[50] All that has become clear is that our government is not a government of laws, but one of laws through men.

(ii) There has been some attempt to work out the varieties of interaction between the traditional concepts * * * and the fact-pressures of the cases. * * * Closely related in substance, but wholly diverse in both method and aim, is study of the machinery by which fact-pressures can under our procedure be brought to bear upon the court.[52]

(iii) First efforts have been made to capitalize the wealth of our reported cases to make large-scale quantitative studies of facts and outcome; the hope has been that these might develop lines of prediction more sure, or at least capable of adding further certainty * * *.

(iv) Repeated effort has been made to work with the cases of single states, to see how far additional predictability might thus be gained.

(v) Study has been attempted of "substantive rules" in the particular light of the available remedial procedure; the hope being to discover in the court's unmentioned knowledge of the immediate consequences of this rule or that, in the case at hand, a motivation for decision which cuts deeper than any shown by the opinion. * * *

(vi) The set-up of men's ways and practices and ideas on the subject matter of the controversy has been studied, in the hope that this might yield a further or even final basis for prediction. The work here ranges from more or less indefinite reference to custom (the historical school), or mores (Corbin), through rough or more careful canvasses of business practice and ideology (e. g., Berle, Sturges, Isaacs, Handler, Bogert, Durfee and Duffy, Breckenridge, Turner,

---

48. E. g., * * * Commerce, Congress, and the Supreme Court, 1922–1925 (1926) 26 Col.L.Rev. 396, 521; The Judiciality of Minimum Wage Legislation (1924) 37 Harv.L.Rev. 545; * * * Brown, Police Power—Legislation for Health and Personal Safety (1929) 42 Harv.L.Rev. 866; Cushman, The Social and Economic Interpretation of the Fourteenth Amendment (1922) 20 Mich.L.Rev. 737. * * *

50. Freudian: beginnings in Frank, Law and the Modern Mind (1930). Behaviorist: an attempt in Patterson, Equitable Relief for Unilateral Mistake (1928) 28 Col.L.Rev. 859. * * *

52. The famous Brandeis brief and its successors mark the beginning. In commercial cases both Germany and England have evolved effective machinery.

Douglas, Shanks, Oliphant, and indeed Holmes) to painstaking and detailed studies in which practice is much more considered than is any prevailing set of ideas about what the practices are (Klaus) * * *. While grouped here together, under one formula, these workers show differences in degree and manner of interest * * *. Corbin's main interest is the appellate case; most of the second group mentioned rely on semi-special information and readily available material from economics, sociology, etc., with occasional careful studies of their own, and carry a strong interest into drafting or counselling work; Klaus insists on full canvass of all relevant literature, buttressed by and viewed in the light of intensive personal investigation * * *.

(vii) Another line of attack, hardly begun, is that on the effect of the lawyer on the outcome of cases, as an element in prediction. * * *

All of the above has focussed on how to tell what appellate courts will do, however far afield any new scent may have led the individual hunter. But the interest in effects on laymen of what the courts will do leads rapidly from this still respectably traditional sphere of legal discussion into a series of further inquiries whose legal decorum is more dubious. They soon extend far beyond what has in recent years been conceived (in regard to the developed state) as law at all. * * *

I. *There is first the question of what lower courts and especially trial courts are doing, and what relation their doing has to the sayings and doings of upper courts and legislatures.*

Here the question has been to begin to find out, to find some way, some ways, of getting the hitherto unavailable facts, to find some significant way or ways of classifying what business is done, how long it takes, how various parts of the procedural machinery work. * * * Another attack begins by inquiry not into records, but into the processes of trial and their effects on the outcome of cases. * * * All that is really clear to date is that until we know more here our "rules" give us no remote suggestion of what law means to persons in the lower income brackets, and give us misleading suggestions as to the whole body of cases unappealed. * * *

II. *There is the question of administrative bodies*—not merely on the side of administrative law (itself a novel concept recently enough—but including all the action which state officials take "under the law" so far as it proves to affect people. * * * [T]he trail thus broken leads into the wilds of government, and politics, and queer events in both.

III. *There is the question of legislative regulation*—in terms of what it *means in action, and to whom*, not merely in terms of what it says. And with that, the question of what goes into producing legislative change—or blocking it * * * ; legislative history on the official record; but as well the background of fact and interest and need. * * *

IV. Finally, and cutting now completely beyond the tradition-bounded area of law, there is the matter not of describing or predicting the action of officials * * * but of describing and predicting *the effects of their action on the laymen of the community.* * * * Not only what courts do instead of what courts say, but also what difference it makes to anybody that they do it. And no sooner does one begin such a study than it becomes clear that there can be no broad talk of "law" nor of "the community"; but that it is a question of reaching the particular part of the community relevant to some particular part of law. * * * There is the range of questions as to those legal "helpful devices" (corporation, contract, lease) designed to make it easier for men to get where they want and what they want. There is all the information social scientists have gathered to be explored, in its bearings on the law. * * *

Here are the matters one or another of the new fermenters is ploughing into. * * *

* * *

Is it not obvious that—if this be realism—realism is a mass of trends in legal work and thinking? * * *

* * * One will find * * * little said by realistic spokesmen that does not warrant careful pondering. Indeed, on *careful* pondering, one will find little of exaggeration in their writing. Meantime, the proof of the pudding: are there results?

* * *

Already we have a series, lengthening impressively, of the *more accurate* reformulations of what appellate courts are doing and may be expected to do. We are making headway in seeing (not just "knowing" without inquiry) what effects their doing has on some of the persons interested. We are accumulating some *knowledge* (i. e., more than guesses) on phases of our life as to which our law seems out of joint.

We have, moreover, a first attack upon the realm of the unpredictable in the actions of courts. That attack suggests strongly that one large element in the now incalculable consists in the traditional pretense or belief * * * that there is no such area of uncertainty, or that it is much smaller than it is. To *recognize* that there are limits of the certainty sought by verbalism and deduction, to seek to define those limits, is to open the door to that other and far more useful judicial procedure: *conscious* seeking, *within the limits laid down by precedent and statute*, for the wise decision. Decisions thus reached, *within those limits*, may fairly be hoped to be more certainly predictable than decisions are now * * *. And not only more certain, but what is no whit less important: more just and wise * * *.

Indeed, the most fascinating result of the realistic effort appears as one returns from trial court or the ways of laymen to the tradition-hallowed problem of appellate case-law. Criticized by those who refuse to disentangle Is and Ought because of their supposed deliberate neglect of the normative aspect of law, the realists prove the value, for the normative, of temporarily putting the normative aside. They return from their excursion into the purest description they can manage with a demonstration that the field of free play for Ought in appellate courts is vastly wider than traditional Ought-bound thinking ever had made clear. * * * Let me summarize the points of the brief:

(a) If deduction does not solve cases, but only shows the effect of a given premise; and if there is available a competing but equally authoritative premise that leads to a different conclusion—then there is a choice in the case; a choice to be justified; a choice which *can* be justified only as a question of policy—for the authoritative tradition speaks with a forked tongue.

(b) If (i) the possible inductions from one case or a series of cases—even if these cases really had each a single fixed meaning—are nonetheless not single, but many; and if (ii) the standard authoritative techniques of dealing with precedent range from limiting the case to its narrowest issue on facts and procedure * * * all the way to giving it the wildest meaning the rule expressed will allow, or even thrusting under it a principle which was not announced in the opinion at all—then the available leeway in *interpretation of precedent* is * * * nothing less than huge. * * * And—the essence of all—*stare decisis* has in the past been, now is, and must continue to be, a norm of change, and a means of change, as well as a norm of staying put, and a means of staying put. * * * Let this be recognized, and that peculiar one of the ways of working with precedent which consists in blinding the eyes to policy loses the fictitious sanctity with which it is now enveloped *some of the time*: to wit, whenever judges for any reason do not wish to look at policy.

(c) If the classification of raw facts is largely an arbitrary process, raw facts having in most doubtful cases the possibility of ready classification along a number of lines, "certainty," even under pure deductive thinking, has not the meaning that people who have wanted certainty in law are looking for. The quest of this unreal certainty, this certainty unattained in result, is the major reason for the self-denying ordinance of judges: their refusal to look beyond words to things. Let them once see that the "certainty" thus achieved is *un*certainty for the non-law-tutored layman in his living and dealing, and the way is open to reach for *layman's* certainty-through-law, by seeking for the fair or wise outcome, so far as precedent and statute make such outcome *possible*. * * *

When the matter of *program in the normative aspect* is raised, the answer is: *there is none.* A likeness of method in approaching Ought-questions is apparent. If there be, beyond that, general lines of fairly wide agreement, they are hardly specific enough to mean anything on any given issue. Partly, this derives from differences in temperament and outlook. Partly, it derives from the total lack of organization or desire to schoolify among the men concerned. But partly, it is due to the range of work involved. Business lawyers have some pet Oughts, each in the material he has become familiar with; torts lawyers have the like in torts; public lawyers in public law. * * * Yet some general points of view may be hazarded.

(1) There is fairly general agreement on the importance of personnel, and of court organization, as essential to making laws have meaning. * * * There is some tendency, too, to urge specialization of tribunals.

(2) There is very general agreement on the need for courts to face squarely the policy questions in their cases, and use the full freedom precedent affords in working toward conclusions that seem indicated. There is fairly general agreement that effects of rules, so far as known, should be taken account of in making or remaking the rules * * *.

(3) There is a strong tendency to think it wiser to narrow rather than to widen the categories in which concepts and rules *either about judging or for judging* are made.

(4) There is a strong tendency to approach most legal problems as problems in allocation of risks, and so far as possible, as problems of their reduction, and so to insist on the effects of rules on parties who not only are not in court, but are not fairly represented by the parties who are in court. To approach not only tort but business matters, in a word, as matters of *general* policy.

And so I close as I began. What is there novel here? In the ideas, nothing. In the sustained attempt to make one or another of them fruitful, much. In the narrowness of fact-category together with the wide range of fact-inquiry, much. In the technique availed of, much—for lawyers. But let this be noted—for the summary above runs so largely to the purely descriptive side: When writers of realistic inclination are writing in general, they are bound to stress the need of more accurate description, of Is and not of Ought. There lies the *common* ground of their thinking; there lies the area of new and puzzling development. * * * As to whether change is called for, on any *given* point of our law, and if so, how much change, and in what direction, there is no agreement. Why should there be? A *group* philosophy or program, a *group* credo of social welfare, these realists have not. They are not a group.

NOTES AND QUESTIONS

1. As did Frank, in 1930 Karl Llewellyn had published a controversial volume on jurisprudence, *The Bramble Bush*. That work was a series of Llewellyn's lectures to beginning law students, originally delivered to his class at Columbia, where he argued that it was necessary for law students and lawyers to pay somewhat less attention to disembodied rules, and more attention to the actions of the legal officers. Frank and Llewellyn, not unexpectedly, thus took Pound's 1931 paper as an attack principally on them, and they set about drafting a reply. Llewellyn's biographer, William Twining, reports that "At first they encountered resistance to their plan. The *Harvard Law Review* refused to grant them space for a reply until pressure was brought to bear on the Editor by members of the Harvard faculty, including Pound himself." Twining, Karl Llewellyn and the Realist Movement 73 (1973). Why might the Harvard Law Review have resisted? Why might Pound have intervened?

2. Considering the debate among Pound, Llewellyn, and Frank, Twining remarks that:

> Of all legal subjects jurisprudence is most susceptible to controversy: juristic controversies are prone to be inconclusive and unsatisfactory; of juristic controversies that surrounding realism has had more than its share of slovenly scholarship, silly misunderstandings and jejune polemics. In 1931 public discussion of "realism" got off to a bad start from which it never fully recovered.

Twining, supra, at 80. Copyright © 1973 by William L. Twining, reprinted by permission of Mr. Twining. Can you point to any "slovenly scholarship, silly misunderstandings [or] jejune polemics" in the three excerpts you have just read?

3. Pound's pique can be somewhat better understood when one considers (as Frank and Llewellyn do somewhat acknowledge) that he was the leading "legal realist" of his day. Influenced in great part by the thought of Holmes, Pound had advocated in the early years of the twentieth century something he called "sociological jurisprudence" and which he offered as an alternative to the "mechanical jurisprudence" of men like Langdell and the *Lochner* majority. Pound stressed that jurisprudence ought to be more concerned with fitting the rules of law to "human conditions," and less with deriving conclusions from "assumed first principles." Pound, Liberty of Contract, 18 Yale L.J. 454, 464 (1909). Pound believed that appropriate legal rules could be fashioned, if instead of fastening on panaceas such as freedom of contract, or *stare decisis*, or other bugaboos of nineteenth century "mechanical jurisprudence," judges would pay more attention to the insights being revealed by the emerging social and political sciences. This attitude of Pound's mirrored that of the political Progressives, who seemed to believe in "the management of government by experts," in "regulatory and welfare legislation", and in "judicial tolerance for such legislation." See generally White, From Sociological Jurisprudence to Realism: Jurisprudence and Social Change in Early Twentieth-Century America 59 Va.L.Rev. 999, 1003–1004 (1972).

The "progressivism" of the early twentieth century, as its name implies, "rested * * * on the concept of progress, a composite of the inherent perfectibility of man and the permanently dynamic quality of society." The unparallelled carnage of the First World War, and perhaps the intransigent isolationism of Americans afterwards, however, "made progress a hollow belief." White, supra, at 1013. This led to changes in jurisprudential outlook, and the changes affected Pound. By 1923, he was willing to concede that it might be best to give up the idea of reforming some doctrines in the law through social science, particularly doctrines of property and commercial law. Pound, The Theory of Judicial Decision, 36 Harv.L.Rev. 641, 952. White, supra, at 1009–1010. Do you find that it is this later aspect of Pound's work that Frank and Llewellyn seem most inclined to criticize?

4. Another recent commentator on the legal realists has written that:

It is now generally recognized that realism, both as an intellectual movement and as an effort at educational reform, was misguided in several respects. For example, it is increasingly doubted that a single "method" or "theory" can serve as an educational program for all law schools and all varieties of legal practice; similarly, the realist effort to formulate a general "scientific" approach to law is now regarded as too abstract and polemical, and the issues involved either inherently unscientific or obvious to the point of sterility.

Note, Legal Theory and Legal Education, 79 Yale L.J. 1153, 1158 (1970). Reprinted by permission of the Yale Law Journal Company and Fred B. Rothman & Company. Is there anything in the three excerpts you have just read that would lead you to similar or dissimilar conclusions? The author of this note (Professor Rand Rosenblatt of Rutgers-Camden Law School who was then a law student) suggests that the major intellectual weaknesses of the legal realists were "a failure to distinguish different levels and points of criticism, and a core ambiguity about the role of values in social and legal thought." Id., at 1159. Do you discern any weaknesses of this nature?

5. Perhaps the most disturbing aspect of the work of the legal realists is its implication for democratic theory. This is of particular relevance to us when we consider Professor White's assertion that legal realism "was the [jurisprudential] analog to the New Deal." White, supra, at 999. Professor White thus describes the governmental philosophy of the New Dealers (and by implication the legal realists):

They set out to eradicate the notions that private property was sacred and that self-help was the only way to deal with adversity. They announced that traditional bogeys such as the belief that government distribution of economic benefits was equivalent to socialism were shams: the only things the nation's citizens had to fear was fear itself. They preferred experimentation and empiricism to theorizing: it was not as important to articulate any philosophy of problem-solving as it was to try to solve problems. Despite their interest in improving the economic position of lower-income families, they were less interested in representative government than the Progressives. They preferred government experimentation conceived and executed by elites, with the primary governing institutions being administrative agencies, whose staffing and activities were not subject to a popular check.

White, supra, at 1025. Is this a vision of government that appeals to you? Is it consistent or inconsistent with the political and legal thought you have seen reflected in most of the materials we have studied?

Perhaps sensing something like these views on the part of the legal realists and the New Dealers, and considering the events in Europe in the 1930's, critics began to charge that "realism paved the way for totalitarianism by denying objective ethical standards and making law an amoral coercive force." Purcell, American Jurisprudence Between the Wars: Legal Realism and the Crisis of Democratic Theory 75 Am.Hist.Rev. 424, 438 (1969). Indeed, Pound himself joined in the critical chorus when he proclaimed that "the political and juristic preaching of today leads logically to [political] absolutism." Pound, Contemporary Juristic Theory 9 (1940), quoted in Purcell, supra, at 438. Perhaps the most extreme reaction to legal realism came from the religious legal thinkers, like Father Francis E. Lucey, one of the regents of Georgetown University School of Law, who stated in 1942 that "Godless Behaviorism and Pragmatism are the headhunters, with Democracy and popular sovereignty the victims." Quoted in Purcell, supra, at 439. Do you see any basis for these charges in the work you have read of Frank and Llewellyn? For a brilliant discussion of the general philosophical and political difficulties posed by realism in various disciplines see Edward A. Purcell, Jr. The Crisis of Democratic Theory: Scientific Naturalism and the Problem of Value (1973).

6. What, then, became of the idea of using social science discoveries to reform the law articulated first by Pound, and then by the legal realists? How were the positivistic insights of legal realism to be integrated with democratic theories of judicial review? See if you can find any answers to the first question in the case of Brown v. Board of Educ., and any answers to the second in the excerpts from Wechsler and Wright, all of which follow.

SECTION D.   BEYOND LEGAL REALISM

BROWN v. BOARD OF EDUC.

Supreme Court of the United States, 1954.
347 U.S. 483, 74 S.Ct. 686, 98 L.Ed. 873.

Mr. Chief Justice WARREN delivered the opinion of the Court.

These cases come to us from the States of Kansas, South Carolina, Virginia, and Delaware. They are premised on different facts and different local conditions, but a common legal question justifies their consideration together in this consolidated opinion.

In each of the cases, minors of the Negro race, through their legal representatives, seek the aid of the courts in obtaining admission to the public schools of their community on a nonsegregated basis. In each instance, they had been denied admission to schools attended by white children under laws requiring or permitting segregation according to race. This segregation was alleged to deprive the plaintiffs of the equal protection of the laws under the Fourteenth Amendment. In each of the cases other than the Delaware case, a three-judge federal district court denied relief to the plaintiffs on the so-called "separate but equal" doctrine announced by this Court in Plessy v. Ferguson, 163 U.S. 537. Under that doctrine, equality of treatment is accorded when the races are provided substantially equal facilities, even though these facilities be separate. In the Delaware case, the Supreme Court of Delaware adhered to that doctrine, but ordered that the plaintiffs be admitted to the white schools because of their superiority to the Negro schools.

The plaintiffs contend that segregated public schools are not "equal" and cannot be made "equal," and that hence they are deprived of the equal protection of the laws. * * * Argument was heard in the 1952 Term, and reargument was heard this Term on certain questions propounded by the Court.

Reargument was largely devoted to the circumstances surrounding the adoption of the Fourteenth Amendment in 1868. It covered exhaustively consideration of the Amendment in Congress, ratification by the states, then existing practices in racial segregation, and the views of proponents and opponents of the Amendment. This discussion and our own investigation convince us that, although these sources cast some light, it is not enough to resolve the problem with which we are faced. At best, they are inconclusive. The most avid proponents of the post-War Amendments undoubtedly intended them to remove all legal distinctions among "all persons born or naturalized in the United States." Their opponents, just as certainly, were antagonistic to both the letter and the spirit of the Amendments and wished them to have the most limited effect. What others in Congress and the state legislatures had in mind cannot be determined with any degree of certainty.

An additional reason for the inconclusive nature of the Amendment's history, with respect to segregated schools, is the status of public education at that time. In the South, the movement toward free common schools, supported by general taxation, had not yet taken hold. Education of white children was largely in the hands of private groups. Education of Negroes was almost nonexistent, and practically all of the race were illiterate. In fact, any education of Negroes was forbidden by law in some states. Today, in contrast, many Negroes have achieved outstanding success in the arts and sciences as well as in the business and professional world. It is true that public school education at the time of the Amendment had advanced further in the North, but the effect of the Amendment on Northern States was generally ignored in the congressional debates. Even in the North, the conditions of public education did not approximate those existing today. The curriculum was usually rudimentary; ungraded schools were common in rural areas; the school term was but three months a year in many states; and compulsory school attendance was virtually unknown. As a consequence, it is not surprising that there should be so little in the history of the Fourteenth Amendment relating to its intended effect on public education.

In the first cases in this Court construing the Fourteenth Amendment, decided shortly after its adoption, the Court interpreted it as proscribing all state-imposed discriminations against the Negro race.[5] The doctrine of "separate but equal" did not make its appearance in this Court until 1896 in the case of Plessy v. Ferguson, supra, involving not education but transportation. American courts have since labored with the doctrine for over half a century. In this Court, there have been six cases involving the "separate but equal" doctrine in the field of public education. * * *

In more recent cases, all on the graduate school level, inequality was found in that specific benefits enjoyed by white students were denied to Negro students of the same educational qualifications. Missouri ex rel. Gaines v. Canada, 305 U.S. 337; Sipuel v. Oklahoma, 332 U.S. 631; Sweatt v. Painter, 339 U.S. 629; McLaurin v. Oklahoma State Regents, 339 U.S. 637. In none of these cases was it necessary to re-examine the doctrine to grant relief to the Negro plaintiff. * * *

In the instant cases, that question is directly presented. Here * * * there are findings below that the Negro and white schools involved have been equalized, or are being equalized, with respect to buildings, curricula, qualifications and salaries of teachers, and other "tangible" factors. Our decision, therefore, cannot turn on merely a comparison of these tangible factors in the Negro and white schools involved in each of the cases. We must look instead to the effect of segregation itself on public education.

---

5. *Slaughter-House Cases*, 16 Wall. 36, 67–72 (1873); Strauder v. West Virginia, 100 U.S. 303, 307–308 (1880): "It ordains that no State shall deprive any person of life, liberty, or property, without due process of law, or deny to any person within its jurisdiction the equal protection of the laws. What is this but declaring that the law in the States shall be the same for the black as for the white; that all persons, whether colored or white, shall stand equal before the laws of the States, and, in regard to the colored race, for whose protection the amendment was primarily designed, that no discrimination shall be made against them by law because of their color? The words of the amendment, it is true, are prohibitory, but they contain a necessary implication of a positive immunity, or right, most valuable to the colored race,—the right to exemption from unfriendly legislation against them distinctively as colored,—exemption from legal discriminations, implying inferiority in civil society, lessening the security of their enjoyment of the rights which others enjoy, and discriminations which are steps towards reducing them to the condition of a subject race."

In approaching this problem, we cannot turn the clock back to 1868 when the Amendment was adopted, or even to 1896 when Plessy v. Ferguson was written. We must consider public education in the light of its full development and its present place in American life throughout the Nation. Only in this way can it be determined if segregation in public schools deprives these plaintiffs of the equal protection of the laws.

Today, education is perhaps the most important function of state and local governments. Compulsory school attendance laws and the great expenditures for education both demonstrate our recognition of the importance of education to our democratic society. * * * It is the very foundation of good citizenship. * * * In these days, it is doubtful that any child may reasonably be expected to succeed in life if he is denied the opportunity of an education. Such an opportunity, where the state has undertaken to provide it, is a right which must be made available to all on equal terms.

* * *

In Sweatt v. Painter, supra, in finding that a segregated law school for Negroes could not provide them equal educational opportunities, this Court relied in large part on "those qualities which are incapable of objective measurement but which make for greatness in a law school." In McLaurin v. Oklahoma State Regents, supra, the Court, in requiring that a Negro admitted to a white graduate school be treated like all other students, again resorted to intangible considerations: " * * * his ability to study, to engage in discussions and exchange views with other students, and, in general, to learn his profession." Such considerations apply with added force to children in grade and high schools. To separate them from others of similar age and qualifications solely because of their race generates a feeling of inferiority as to their status in the community that may affect their hearts and minds in a way unlikely ever to be undone. The effect of this separation on their educational opportunities was well stated by a finding in the Kansas case by a court which nevertheless felt compelled to rule against the Negro plaintiffs:

> Segregation of white and colored children in public schools has a detrimental effect upon the colored children. The impact is greater when it has the sanction of the law; for the policy of separating the races is usually interpreted as denoting the inferiority of the negro group. A sense of inferiority affects the motivation of a child to learn. Segregation with the sanction of law, therefore, has a tendency to [retard] the educational and mental development of negro children and to deprive them of some of the benefits they would receive in a racial[ly] integrated school system.

Whatever may have been the extent of psychological knowledge at the time of Plessy v. Ferguson, this finding is amply supported by modern authority.[11]   Any language in Plessy v. Ferguson contrary to this finding is rejected.

We conclude that in the field of public education the doctrine of "separate but equal" has no place.   Separate educational facilities are inherently unequal.   Therefore, we hold that the plaintiffs and others similarly situated for whom the actions have been brought are, by reason of the segregation complained of, deprived of the equal protection of the laws guaranteed by the Fourteenth Amendment.   *   *   *

*   *   *

NOTES AND QUESTIONS

1.   Brown v. Board of Educ. is probably the most important Supreme Court case concerned with race relations since *Dred Scott*.   Many articles and books have been devoted to considering the case; perhaps the best of them is the recently published Simple Justice (1976), by Richard Kluger, which gives a complete history of the case and the forces and personalties that brought it about.   As you will see in the next reading, the opinion in *Brown* is subject to severe criticism (on this point see also Alexander Bickel, The Supreme Court and the Idea of Progress (1970)).   If this is true, how do you account for the fact that there are no dissenting (or even concurring) opinions in *Brown*?   See Hutchinson, Unanimity and Desegregation: Decisionmaking in the Supreme Court, 1948–1958, 68 Geo.L.J. 1 (1979).   Is it significant that the opinion is written by the new Chief Justice, Earl Warren, a former governor of California, who had come on the court following the death of Chief Justice Vinson in 1953?

2.   Can you discern any effects of the thinking of the legal realists on Chief Justice Warren?   Take, for example, the Chief Justice's comments about the nature of the Constitutional Amendments and the relevance of legislative history.   Suppose it could be clearly demonstrated that an overwhelming majority of persons involved in the passage of the fourteenth amendment believed that there were significant differences between the races, and that while the races ought to be "equal before the law," there was no reason not to permit segregation in public facilities, even in public educational facilities.   In other words, assume that it could be proved that the legislative history of the Amendment clearly revealed that its framers would have accepted the doctrines of Plessy v. Ferguson.   Would Brown have had to be decided differently?   Of what significance is Warren's remark about not being able to "turn the clock back?"   Do you see any similarity to the views of the importance of the legislative history in the Antitrust cases?   If

11.   K. B. Clark, Effect of Prejudice and Discrimination on Personality Development (Midcentury White House Conference on Children and Youth, 1950); Witmer and Kotinsky, Personality in the Making (1952), c. VI; Deutscher and Chein, The Psychological Effects of Enforced Segregation: A Survey of Social Science Opinion, 26 J.Psychol. 259 (1948); Chein, What are the Psychological Effects of Segregation Under Conditions of Equal Facilities?, 3 Int.J. Opinion and Attitude Res. 229 (1949); Brameld, Educational Costs, in Discrimination and National Welfare (MacIver, ed., 1949), 44–48; Frazier, The Negro in the United States (1949), 674–681. And see generally Myrdal, An American Dilemma (1944).

Warren is suggesting that the meaning of Constitutional terms must change as social conditions and factors such as public educational systems change, would this notion of a variable Constitution be in accord with legal realist thinking? How might Roscoe Pound have reacted to this decision?

3. Is it the fundamental nature of public education to the American polity that dictates that *Plessy* must be overruled? How does it follow, as the court suggests, that because Black professionals in training need the opportunity to confer and discourse with their White colleagues that the same is true for Black school children? Of what significance is the psychological and sociological data referred to in the "famous footnote 11?" Suppose it could be demonstrated that Black children were more likely to be able to develop positive self-images, and would thus be able better to learn, in a segregated school environment? Suppose such an environment could be shown to be freer from the deleterious effects of racial prejudice and better calculated to the instilling of personal and racial pride? Would *Brown* then have to be reversed? One "reticent" district judge attempted, on the basis of psychological authority contrary to that in Brown, to uphold segregation. He was "promptly reversed." Friendly, In Praise of Herbert Wechsler, 78 Col.L.Rev. 974, 978 n. 40 (1978), citing Stell v. Savannah-Chatham County Bd. of Educ. 220 F.Supp. 667 (S.D.Ga.1963), rev'd., 333 F.2d 55 (5th Cir.), cert. denied, 379 U.S. 933 (1964).

HERBERT WECHSLER, TOWARD NEUTRAL PRINCIPLES OF CONSTITUTIONAL LAW *

73 Harv.L.Rev. 1 (1959).

* * *

II. THE STANDARDS OF REVIEW

* * * Are there, indeed, any criteria that both the Supreme Court and those who undertake to praise or to condemn its judgments are morally and intellectually obligated to support? * * *

* * *

* * * I mean criteria that can be framed and tested as an exercise of reason and not merely as an act of willfulness or will. Even to put the problem is, of course, to raise an issue no less old than our culture. Those who perceive in law only the element of fiat, in whose conception of the legal cosmos reason has no meaning or no place, will not join gladly in the search for standards of the kind I have in mind. * * * So too must I anticipate dissent from those more numerous among us who, vouching no philosophy to warranty, frankly or covertly make the test of virtue in interpretation whether its result in the immediate decision seems to hinder or advance the interests or the values they support. * * * The man who simply lets his judgment turn on the immediate result may not, however, realize that his position implies that the courts are free to function as a naked power organ, that it is an empty affirmation to regard them, as ambivalently he so often does, as courts of law.   *   *   *

  *   *   *   [T]his type of *ad hoc* evaluation is, as it has always been, the deepest problem of our constitutionalism, not only with respect to judgments of the courts but also in the wider realm in which conflicting constitutional positions have played a part in our politics.

Did not New England challenge the embargo that the South supported on the very ground on which the South was to resist New England's demand for a protective tariff?   Was not Jefferson in the Louisiana Purchase forced to rest on an expansive reading of the clauses granting national authority of the very kind that he had steadfastly opposed in his attacks upon the Bank?   *   *   *

To bring the matter even more directly home, what shall we think of the Harvard records of the Class of 1829, the class of Mr. Justice Curtis, which, we are told, praised at length the Justice's dissent in the *Dred Scott* case but then added, "Again, *and seemingly adverse to the above,* in October, 1862, he prepared a legal opinion and argument, which was published in Boston in pamphlet form, to the effect that President Lincoln's Proclamation of prospective emancipation of the slaves in the rebellious States is *unconstitutional.*"

*   *   *

  *   *   *   What a wealth of illustration is at hand today!   How many of the constitutional attacks upon congressional investigations of suspected Communists have their authors felt obliged to launch against the inquiries respecting the activities of Goldfine or of Hoffa or of others I might name?   How often have those who think the Smith Act, as construed, inconsistent with the first amendment made clear that they also stand for constitutional immunity for racial agitators fanning flames of prejudice and discontent?   *   *   *

All I have said, you may reply, is something no one will deny, that principles are largely instrumental as they are employed in politics   *   *   *.

  *   *   *   [W]hether you are tolerant   *   *   *   of the *ad hoc* in politics, with principle reduced to a manipulative tool, are you not also ready to agree that something else is called for from the courts? I put it to you that the main constituent of the judicial process is precisely that it must be genuinely principled, resting with respect to every step that is involved in reaching judgment on analysis and reasons quite transcending the immediate result that is achieved.   To be sure, the courts decide, or should decide, only the case they have before them.   But must they not decide on grounds of adequate neutrality and generality tested not only by the instant application but by others that the principles imply?   Is it not the very essence of judicial method to insist upon attending to such other cases, preferably

those involving an opposing interest, in evaluating any principle avowed?

Does not the special duty of the courts to judge by neutral principles addressed to all the issues make it inapposite to contend, as Judge Hand does, that no court can review the legislative choice—by any standard other than a fixed "historical meaning" of constitutional provisions—without becoming "a third legislative chamber"? Is there not, in short, a vital difference between legislative freedom to appraise the gains and losses in projected measures and the kind of principled appraisal, in respect of values that can reasonably be asserted to have constitutional dimension, that alone is in the province of the courts? * * * This must, it seems to me, have been in Mr. Justice Jackson's mind when * * * he wrote * * * "Liberty is not the mere absence of restraint, it is not a spontaneous product of majority rule, it is not achieved merely by lifting underprivileged classes to power, nor is it the inevitable by-product of technological expansion. It is achieved only by a rule of law." * * *

You will not understand my emphasis upon the role of reason and of principle in the judicial, as distinguished from the legislative or executive, appraisal of conflicting values to imply that I depreciate the duty of fidelity to the text of the Constitution, when its words may be decisive * * *. Nor will you take me to deny that history has weight in the elucidation of the text, though it is surely subtle business to appraise it as a guide. Nor will you even think that I deem precedent without importance * * *.

At all events, is not the relative compulsion of the language of the Constitution, of history and precedent—where they do not combine to make an answer clear—itself a matter to be judged, so far as possible, by neutral principles—by standards that transcend the case at hand? I know, of course, that it is common to distinguish, as Judge Hand did, clauses like "due process," cast "in such sweeping terms that their history does not elucidate their contents," from other provisions of the Bill of Rights addressed to more specific problems. But the contrast, as it seems to me, often implies an overstatement of the specificity or the immutability these other clauses really have * * *.

No one would argue, for example, that there need not be indictment and a jury trial in prosecutions for a felony in district courts. What made a question of some difficulty was the issue whether service wives charged with the murders of their husbands overseas could be tried there before a military court. * * * The right to "have the assistance of counsel" was considered, I am sure, when the sixth amendment was proposed, a right to defend by counsel if you have one, contrary to what was then the English law. That does not seem to me sufficient to avert extension of its meaning to imply a right to court-appointed counsel when the defendant is too poor to find such aid—though I admit that I once urged the point sincerely as a lawyer for the Government. * * * Nor should we, in my view, lament the fact that "the" freedom of speech or press that Congress is forbidden by the first amendment to impair is not determined only by the scope such freedom had in the late eighteenth century * * *.

* * * Equal protection could be taken as no more than an assurance that no one may be placed beyond the safeguards of the law, outlawing, as it were, the possibility of outlawry, but nothing else. Here too I cannot find it in my heart to regret that interpretation did not ground itself in ancient history but rather has perceived in these provisions a compendious affirmation of the basic values of a free society, values that must be given weight in legislation and administration at the risk of courting trouble in the courts.

So far as possible, to finish with my point, I argue that we should prefer to see the other clauses of the Bill of Rights read as an affirmation of the special values they embody rather than as statements of a finite rule of law, its limits fixed by the consensus of a century long past, with problems very different from our own. To read them in the former way is to leave room for adaptation and adjustment if and when competing values, also having constitutional dimension, enter on the scene.

* * *

The virtue or demerit of a judgment turns, therefore, entirely on the reasons that support it and their adequacy to maintain any choice of values it decrees, or, it is vital that we add, to maintain the rejection of a claim that any given choice should be decreed. * * *

III. SOME APPRAISALS OF REVIEW

[Professor Wechsler proceeds critically to apply his theory about the need for application of neutral and general principles to recent Constitutional adjudication.]

(1).—I start by noting two important fields of present interest in which the Court has been decreeing value choices in a way that makes it quite impossible to speak of principled determinations * * * since the Court has not disclosed the grounds on which its judgments rest.

[Wechsler first notes a recent group of U. S. Supreme Court decisions finding state attempts to suppress motion pictures unconstitutional because of the safeguards of the first amendment which are made applicable to the states by the fourteenth amendment. He criticizes the court for issuing per curiam opinions which made no distinctions and gave no reasoning.]

* * *

(2).—The second group of cases to which I shall call attention involves what may be called the progeny of the school-segregation ruling of 1954. Here again the Court has written on the merits of the constitutional issue posed by state segregation only once; [in Brown v. Board of Education, in 1954.] * * * The original opinion, you recall, was firmly focused on state segregation in the public schools, its reasoning accorded import to the nature of the educational process, and its conclusion was that separate educational facilities are "inherently unequal."

What shall we think then of the Court's extension of the ruling to other public facilities, such as public transportation, parks, golf courses, bath houses, and beaches, which no one is obliged to use—all by per curiam decisions? That these situations present a weaker case against state segregation is not, of course, what I am saying. I am saying that the question whether it is stronger, weaker, or of equal weight appears to me to call for principled decision. I do not know, and I submit you cannot know, whether the per curiam affirmance in the *Dawson* case, involving public bath houses and beaches, embraced the broad opinion of the circuit court that all state-enforced racial segregation is invalid or approved only its immediate result and, if the latter, on what ground. * * *

(3).—The poverty of principled articulation of the limits put on Congress as against the states before the doctrinal reversal of the Thirties was surely also true of the decisions, dealing with the very different problem of the relationship between the individual and government, which invoked due process to maintain *laissez faire*. Did not the power of the great dissents inhere precisely in their demonstrations that the Court could not present an adequate analysis, in terms of neutral principles, to support the value choices it decreed? * * *

* * *

(4).—Finally, I turn to the decisions that for me provide the hardest test of my belief in principled adjudication, those in which the Court in recent years has vindicated claims that deprivations based on race deny the equality before the law that the fourteenth amendment guarantees. The crucial cases are, of course, those involving the white primary, the enforcement of racially restrictive covenants, and the segregated schools.

* * * [S]keptical about predictions as I am, I still believe that the decisions I have mentioned—dealing with the primary, the covenant, and schools—have the best chance of making an enduring contribution to the quality of our society of any that I know in recent years. It is in this perspective that I ask how far they rest on neutral principles and are entitled to approval in the only terms that I acknowledge to be relevant to a decision of the courts.

The primary and covenant cases present two different aspects of a single problem—that it is a state alone that is forbidden by the fourteenth amendment to deny equal protection of the laws * * *. It has, of course, been held for years that the prohibition of action by the state reaches not only an explicit deprivation by a statute but also action of the courts or of subordinate officials * * *.

I deal first with the primary. So long as the Democratic Party in the South excluded Negroes from participation, in the exercise of an authority conferred by statute regulating political parties, it was entirely clear that the amendment was infringed; the exclusion involved an application of the statute. The problem became difficult only when the states, responding to these judgments, repealed the statutes, leaving parties free to define their membership as private associations * * *. In this position the Court held in 1935 that an exclusion by the party was untouched by the amendment, being action of the individuals involved, not of the state or its officialdom.

Then came the *Classic* case in 1941, which * * * involved a prosecution of election officials for depriving a voter of a right secured by the Constitution in willfully failing to count his vote as it was cast in a Louisiana Democratic primary. In holding that the right of a qualified voter to participate in choosing Representatives in Congress, a right conferred by article I, section 2, extended to participating in a primary which influenced the ultimate selection, the Court did not, of course, deal with the scope of party freedom to select its members. The victim of the fraud in *Classic* was a member of the Democratic Party, voting in a primary in which he was entitled to participate, and the only one in which he could. Yet three years later *Classic* was declared in Smith v. Allwright to have determined in effect that primaries are a part of the election, with the consequence that parties can no more defend racial exclusion from their primaries than can the state * * *. This is no doubt a settled proposition in the Court. But what it means is not, as sometimes has been thought, that a state may not escape the limitations of the Constitution merely by transferring public functions into private hands. It means rather that the constitutional guarantee against deprivation of the franchise on the ground of race or color has become a prohibition of party organization upon racial lines, at least where the party has achieved political hegemony. I ask with all sincerity if you are able to discover in the opinions thus far written in support of this result—a result I say again that I approve—neutral principles that satisfy the mind. I should suppose that a denial of the franchise on religious grounds is certainly forbidden by the Constitution. Are religious parties, therefore, to be taken as proscribed? I should regard this result too as one plainly to be desired but is there a constitutional analysis on which it can be validly decreed? Is it, indeed, not easier to project an analysis establishing that such a proscription would infringe rights protected by the first amendment?

The case of the restrictive covenant presents for me an even harder problem. Assuming that the Constitution speaks to state discrimination on the ground of race but not to such discrimination by an individual * * *, why is the enforcement of the private covenant a state discrimination rather than a legal recognition of the freedom of the individual? That the action of the state court [in enforcing the private covenant] is action of the state, the point Mr. Chief Justice Vinson emphasizes in the Court's opinion * is, of course, entirely obvious. What is not obvious, and is the crucial step, is that the state may properly be charged with the discrimination when it does no more than give effect to an agreement that the individual involved is, by hypothesis, entirely free to make. Again, one is obliged to ask: What is the principle involved? Is the state forbidden to effectuate a will that draws a racial line * * *, or is it a sufficient answer there that the discrimination was the testator's and not the state's? May not the state employ its law to vindicate the privacy of property against a trespasser, regardless of the grounds of his exclusion, or does it embrace the owner's reasons for excluding if it buttresses his power by the law? Would a declaratory judgment that a fee is determinable if a racially restrictive limitation should be violated represent discrimination by the state upon the racial ground? Would a judgment of ejectment?

None of these questions has been answered by the Court nor are the problems faced in the opinions. Philadelphia, to be sure, has been told that it may not continue to administer the school for "poor male white orphans," established by' the city as trustee under the will of Stephen Girard, in accordance with that racial limitation. All the Supreme Court said, however, was the following: "The Board which operates Girard College is an agency of the State of Pennsylvania. Therefore, even though the Board was acting as a trustee, its refusal to admit Foust and Felder to the college because they were Negroes was discrimination by the State. Such discrimination is forbidden by the Fourteenth Amendment." When the Orphans' Court thereafter dismissed the city as trustee, appointing individuals in substitution, its action was sustained in Pennsylvania. Further review by certiorari was denied.

* * *

Many understandably would like to perceive in the primary and covenant decisions a principle susceptible of broad extension, applying to the other power aggregates in our society limitations of the kind the Constitution has imposed on government. My colleague A. A. Berle, Jr., has, indeed, pointed to the large business corporation, which after all is chartered by the state and wields in many areas more power than the government, as uniquely suitable for choice as the next subject of such application. * * *

* In Shelley v. Kraemer, 334 U.S. 1, 68
S.Ct. 836, 92 L.Ed. 1161 (1948).

I do not hesitate to say that I prefer to see the issues faced through legislation, where there is room for drawing lines that courts are not equipped to draw. * * *

Lastly, I come to the school decision * * *.

The problem * * * is not that the Court departed from its earlier decisions * * *. I stand with the long tradition of the Court that previous decisions must be subject to reexamination when a case against their reasoning is made. Nor is the problem that the Court disturbed the settled patterns of a portion of the country; even that must be accepted as a lesser evil than nullification of the Constitution. Nor is it that history does not confirm that an agreed purpose of the fourteenth amendment was to forbid separate schools or that there is important evidence that many thought the contrary; the words are general and leave room for expanding content as time passes and conditions change. * * *

The problem inheres strictly in the reasoning of the opinion * *. The Court did not declare, as many wish it had, that the fourteenth amendment forbids all racial lines in legislation, though subsequent per curiam decisions may, as I have said, now go that far. Rather * * * the separate-but-equal formula was not overruled "in form" but was held to have "no place" in public education on the ground that segregated schools are "inherently unequal," with deleterious effects upon the colored children in implying their inferiority, effects which retard their educational and mental development. So, indeed, the district court had found as a fact in the Kansas case, a finding which the Supreme Court embraced, citing some further "modern authority" in its support.

Does the validity of the decision turn then on the sufficiency of evidence or of judicial notice to sustain a finding that the separation harms the Negro children who may be involved? * * * And if the harm that segregation worked was relevant, what of the benefits that it entailed: sense of security, the absence of hostility? Were they irrelevant? Moreover, was the finding in Topeka applicable without more to Clarendon County, South Carolina, with 2,799 colored students and only 295 whites? Suppose that more Negroes in a community preferred separation than opposed it? Would that be relevant to whether they were hurt or aided by segregation as opposed to integration? * * *

I find it hard to think the judgment really turned upon the facts. Rather, it seems to me, it must have rested on the view that racial segregation is, in principle, a denial of equality to the minority against whom it is directed; that is, the group that is not dominant politically and, therefore, does not make the choice involved. For many who support the Court's decision this assuredly is the decisive ground. But this position also presents problems. Does it not involve an inquiry into the motive of the legislature, which is generally foreclosed to the courts? Is it alternatively defensible to make the measure of validity of legislation the way it is interpreted by those who are affected by it? In the context of a charge that segregation *with equal facilities* is a denial of equality, is there not a point in *Plessy* in the statement that if "enforced separation stamps the colored race with a badge of inferiority" it is solely because its members choose "to put that construction upon it" ? Does enforced separation of the sexes discriminate against females merely because it may be the females who resent it and it is imposed by judgments predominantly male? Is a prohibition of miscegenation a discrimination against the colored member of the couple who would like to marry?

For me, assuming equal facilities, the question posed by state-enforced segregation is not one of discrimination at all. Its human and its constitutional dimensions lie entirely elsewhere, in the denial by the state of freedom to associate, a denial that impinges in the same way on any groups or races that may be involved. I think, and I hope not without foundation, that the Southern white also pays heavily for segregation, not only in the sense of guilt that he must carry but also in the benefits he is denied. In the days when I was joined with Charles H. Houston in a litigation in the Supreme Court, before the present building was constructed, he did not suffer more than I in knowing that we had to go to Union Station to lunch together during the recess. Does not the problem of miscegenation show most clearly that it is the freedom of association that at bottom is involved * * *?

But if the freedom of association is denied by segregation, integration forces an association upon those for whom it is unpleasant or repugnant. Is this not the heart of the issue involved, a conflict in human claims of high dimension, not unlike many others that involve the highest freedoms * * *. Given a situation where the state must practically choose between denying the association to those individuals who wish it or imposing it on those who would avoid it, is there a basis in neutral principles for holding that the Constitution demands that the claims for association should prevail? I should like to think there is, but I confess that I have not yet written the opinion. To write it is for me the challenge of the school-segregation cases.

* * *

NOTES AND QUESTIONS

1. What, exactly, does Professor Wechsler mean by "neutral principles?" We might approach this problem by first asking why "neutral principles" were needed. Wechsler points to a group of decisions which illustrate a lack of such jurisprudence, the pre-New Deal due process cases and the *Brown* case and its progeny, to repeat two of these examples. What do these cases have in common? Is Professor Wechsler advocating that the Supreme Court stay "neutral" on the great twentieth century social issues, and decline to act unless absolutely necessary? Some critics have found this meaning in this article, but it seems far more likely that Wechsler was argu-

ing exactly the opposite—that the Supreme Court should shoulder its judicial review obligations, but should reach decisions in a reasoned manner, with a logic that could be applied to govern or distinguish other factual situations. This becomes clearer when one notices that Wechsler's article was expressly intended to rebut Learned Hand's lectures from the same platform a year before (Learned Hand, The Bill of Rights (1958)). Hand had argued for judicial restraint, for the Supreme Court not to intervene by exercising judicial review except in cases of absolute necessity. See Friendly, In Praise of Herbert Wechsler, 78 Col.L.Rev. 974, 977–8 (1978).

2.   Is Professor Wechsler attempting a reply to the theories of the legal realists? This seems to be the motive attributed to him by subsequent scholars, who have called this piece the " 'inevitable reaction long overdue' to the more radical versions of legal realism." Greenawalt, The Enduring Significance of Neutral Principles, 78 Col.L.Rev. 982 (1978). Why might such a reaction be necessary? Why might the analysis of the radical legal realists (here Jerome Frank's notions in Law and the Modern Mind might be taken as example) be unacceptable to legal academics in the late fifties?

3.   Perhaps most important for our purposes is Wechsler's criticism of the decision in *Brown*. Is the *Brown* decision a failure in terms of neutral principles because the court failed to adhere to the framers' intentions when the fourteenth amendment was passed? What is the role of history in the application of neutral principles? Is the weakness in the opinion that it is based on psychological data? Is it that it is based on the fourteenth amendment? Wechsler gives up in the attempt to draft a *Brown* decision according to neutral principles. Could you draft such an opinion? Does Wechsler's condemnation of Shelley v. Kraemer, the White Primary cases, and *Brown* mean that Wechsler is insensitive to the equitable claims of minorities, or that he ultimately disagrees with the substantive result in *Brown*? Consider the comments of Judge Skelly Wright, which follow.

4.   In the meantime, pause for a moment to think about what it is that Wechsler sees as worth perpetuating in the workings of the Supreme Court. At bottom, isn't Wechsler simply suggesting adherence to the notion that we have a government of laws and not men, that American Constitutional decisions are made according to the "rule of law." How important is this? In a recent work England's leading Marxist historian wrote:

> We ought to expose the shams and inequities which may be concealed beneath this [particular] law. But the rule of law itself, the imposing of effective inhibitions upon power and the defence of the citizen from power's all-intrusive claims, seems to me to be an unqualified human good. To deny or belittle this good, is, in this dangerous century when the resources and pretensions of power continue to enlarge, a desperate error of intellectual abstraction.

E. P. Thompson, Whigs and Hunters: The Origin of the Black Act 266 (1975). One of America's leading legal historians, Morton Horwitz, seems to have been disturbed by these comments of Thompson's and wrote in a review of his book:

> Unless we are prepared to succumb to Hobbesian pessimism "in this dangerous century," I do not see how a Man of the Left

can describe the rule of law as "an unqualified human good"! It undoubtedly restrains power, but it also prevents power's benevolent exercise. It creates formal equality—a not inconsiderable virtue—but it *promotes* substantive inequality by creating a consciousness that radically separates law from politics, means from ends, processes from outcomes. By promoting procedural justice it enables the shrewd, the calculating, and the wealthy to manipulate its forms to their own advantage. And it ratifies and legitimates an adversarial, competitive, and atomistic conception of human relations.

Horwitz, The Rule of Law: An Unqualified Human Good?, 86 Yale L.J. 561, 566 (1977).* Who is right, Horwitz or Thompson? Could Horwitz's critique of Thompson also be applied to Holmes? To the legal realists? As you read the next piece, see if you can determine if Judge Wright subscribes to the "rule of law."

J. SKELLY WRIGHT, PROFESSOR BICKEL, THE SCHOLARLY TRADITION, AND THE SUPREME COURT **

84 Harv.L.Rev. 769 (1971).

[In this article Judge Wright comments on a book by the late Alexander Bickel, a Professor at Yale Law School, whose jurisprudential views were similar to those of Professor Wechsler. Judge Wright refers to those views as the "Scholarly tradition."]

* * *

* * * *The Supreme Court and the Idea of Progress* does go one step beyond the scholarly tradition. At the outset, Bickel concedes that history rarely judges the Court's work by the quality of its reasoning process. He recognizes that the scholarly praise customarily afforded the Marshall Court, despite numerous lapses in craftsmanship, is singularly result-oriented. The Justices of the Warren Court, Bickel suggests, understandably sought to emulate the Marshall Court and earn its place in history for themselves. Thoroughly result-oriented and with a broad program of social reform in mind, they made a "bet on the future," relying "on events for vindication more than on the method of reason for contemporary validation." But even accepting *arguendo* the premise of the Warren Court's supposed strategy, Bickel condemns its execution and results. Unlike his predecessors in the scholarly tradition, he does not praise the historic contribution of the Court's most important work while criticizing only the process by which it was crafted. Rather, he belittles both. In so doing he goes right for the jugular. * * * "If my probe into a near-term future is not wildly off the mark," he concludes, "the upshot is that the Warren Court's noblest enterprise—school desegregation—and its most popular enterprise—reapportionment—* * * are heading toward obsolescence, and in large measure abandonment."

Bickel's point, then, is that the Court sacrificed all on a bet which is not going to pay off. * * * Unlike his predecessors, Bickel challenges the supporters of the Warren Court on their own substantive, result-oriented ground. Yet the ultimate lesson that Bickel would have us learn still reflects the familiar teachings of the scholarly tradition. Bickel argues that it was the Warren Court's failure to heed the strict constraints of reason that headed its work for oblivion.

* * *

Bickel's new book * * * illustrates the gap between theory and practice in Wechslerian criticism. One might expect the torchbearers of neutral principles, having professed to accept significant judicial latitude in making constitutional value choices, to welcome the Court's vigorous defense of our fundamental rights and liberties. But in practice it doesn't seem to work out that way. Wechsler's scholarly followers have repeatedly demonstrated that the rule of "neutral principles" serves better as a tool of destructive criticism than as a guide to the more effective protection of constitutional values. * * *

* * * When the Court attempts to limit its holdings narrowly, the critics charge that the decisions are not sufficiently general and principled. They argue that lines have been drawn between categories of events or individuals which are more relevantly similar than different, and they conclude that the Court is surreptitiously basing its decisions either on a merely pragmatic political assessment of the consequences in the instant case or on some hidden principle it fears to state openly. * * * They commonly point to inconsistencies between the articulated principle and past Court decisions, refusing to accept the possibility that those precedents are now to be called into serious question. Alternatively, the critics do their best to extend the principle into disparate and outlying policy areas only to deplore the results it would work there. Rarely do they assist the Court in finding lines that could be drawn in future cases to limit the principle's application. * * * Just as rarely do they survey the implications of a principle and say with Professor Charles Black—not one of their number—that if the principle is right and if it would invalidate this or that precedent or common practice, then "so be it." Instead of evaluating the principle as a matter of principle, they focus on results and refuse to admit that the validity of the principle may suggest the validity of its implications. * * *

Do these scholarly critics really believe that their strictures of principled adjudication are compatible with enforcement of fundamental rights and liberties? In *The Supreme Court and the Idea of Progress* Bickel may have inadvertently provided an answer. He admits his doubt that the Court has ever fully met the Wechslerian standards and recognizes that he does not know whether the Warren Court fell any farther short than its predecessors. But, he says, such a comparison "does not matter one way or the other, for intellectual incoherence is not excusable and is no more tolerable because it has occurred before." * * * Perhaps so. But Bickel should have hesitated somewhat longer, I believe, to ask whether he is not demanding the nearly impossible. * * *

Surely it is altogether proper for legal scholars to urge the Court to strive for the rational ideal. But it is another thing to demand * * * Wechslerian "total generality" in constitutional decisions. As a matter of fact, I would argue that constitutional adjudication may properly proceed somewhat as does common law adjudication. * * * Justice Holmes believed that the great growth of the common law came about incrementally * * *. If it is proper for the Court to make fundamental value choices to protect our constitutional rights and liberties, then it is self-defeating to say that if the Justices cannot come up with a perfectly reasoned and perfectly general opinion *now,* then they should abstain from decision altogether.

* * *

* * * Wechsler's rule goes a long way toward restricting—indeed, paralyzing—the Court's enforcement of its own value choices. But by failing to provide guidance for which values are to be chosen, Wechsler's approach admits of a high degree of internal ambiguity. How are we to evaluate the "neutrality" of line-drawing except by reference to some sort of value choices? Is it proper, for example, to distinguish de jure from de facto segregation under the fourteenth amendment? Should youths under eighteen be equated with racial minorities for some purposes? Factual surveys may identify the similarities and differences which are relevant; but how are we to decide which of the two is the greater without first making value choices? * * * Wechsler and his followers seem to assume that the simple application of reason will answer the hard questions, yet they never explain how this synthesis of "value free" values comes about.

In *The Least Dangerous Branch,* Bickel characterized the Court's proper role much as Wechsler did: the Court is "predestined" to be "a voice of reason, charged with the creative function of discerning afresh and of articulating and developing impersonal and durable principles." * * * In *The Supreme Court and the Idea of Progress* he no longer seems to hold that confident belief.

Instead, Bickel now reverts to the original view of the pre-Wechsler progressive realists. The progressive realists, he says, were "skeptical * * * of claims to generality and permanence entered in behalf of social and economic principles." So, too, is he. He has now, "come to doubt in many instances the Court's capacity to develop 'durable principles,' and to doubt, therefore, that judicial supremacy can work and is tolerable in broad areas of social policy." Concepts of justice and injustice, he says, were once thought to have some stable content, but "[t]he words are used in a different sense now because they are no longer rooted in a single, well-recognized ethical precept." * * Bickel now speaks of the unruly "market of norms, values" which cannot be ordered by any institution.

Out of his profound value relativism emerges the view that the Court simply must stay out of most important policy questions. "The judicial process is too principle-prone and principle-bound—it has to be, there is no other justification or explanation for the role it plays." As a result, it is "a most unsuitable instrument for the formation of policy." Thus Bickel resists the temptation to approve judicial protection of civil rights and liberties. He would impose two central substantive rules of limitation on the Court's role: it must, as a general matter, confine itself to invalidating only totally irrational action and whimsical or arbitrary administrative measures, and it must stay out of "social policy" questions.

Bickel does not define "social policy," but * * * does, however, give the term some content by mentioning three categories of issues which do not fall within the forbidden area. He would allow the Court freedom in reforming the criminal process, agreeing with Justice Frankfurter that criminal procedure is somehow a technical matter which the public is happy to leave to the judiciary and which may be dealt with simply and without major impact on broader social goals.

* * * Bickel's two other permissible occasions for judicial value choices of more than the narrowest compass [are] * * * breakdowns in the political process, such as the *total* exclusion of an insular group from access to the process, and a "coup d'état," for example, by the military. The Professor's ideal Justices certainly would become adept at sitting on their hands * * * and the rest of us would be left to our own devices in exercising our constitutional rights and liberties.

That, Bickel says, is as it should be. Corresponding to his new skepticism about the power of reason and principle is a new faith in the pluralistic political process—and in the adequacy of reliance on that process to protect fundamental values. * * * Since he sees values as items in an undisciplined marketplace, he has only kind words for "[t]he jockeying, the bargaining, the trading, the threatening and the promising, the checking and the balancing" of the political system. Nor should the Court step in to aid minorities which have been severely disadvantaged by dominant political groups.

> In the political process, groups sometimes lose out, but so long as the process is operational and both diffuses power and allows majorities ultimately to work their will, no group that is prepared to enter into the process and combine with others need remain permanently and completely out of power.

The most conservative of post-war political scientists could not have put it better. * * *

III

* * * [Judge Wright proceeds to explain the extent of his disagreement with Wechsler, et al.] I reject not only [their] entailment of a rigidly restricted role for the courts, but also [their] fundamental axioms. The first of these axioms is that a constitutional value choice is the functional equivalent of an ordinary policy decision. Constitutional choices are in fact different from ordinary decisions. The reason is simple: the most important value choices have already been made by the framers of the Constitution.

Followers of the scholarly tradition have argued since the days of the progressive realists that the Bill of Rights and the fourteenth amendment are so vaguely worded as to provide no guidance for decision in modern times. Thus the axiom that a constitutional issue is nothing more than another policy issue. Professor Bickel, for example, stresses the infinite complexity of speech and apportionment questions * * *.

* * *

Of course, the Constitution is written in broad, majestic language. How else should it have been written? The framers were not so dim-witted as to believe that times would not change, that unforeseen problems would not arise. The reason for framing a constitution is to guarantee a general *sort* of relation between the government and its citizens. To achieve that end the Constitution must have a purposive permanence. It must serve as a "living" safeguard against certain sorts of excesses on the part of elected officials misled * * * by inflamed emotions and calculations of immediate consequences. It must, in short, be written in "vague" language. If the framers had intended only to forbid coups d'etat and clearly totalitarian measures, they could have been far more specific.

Clearly, then, constitutional protections of rights and liberties are meant to have meaning beyond what Bickel would allow. The duty of both judges and constitutional scholars is to determine what that meaning ought to be. The question really is how to do it. Here, again, Bickel is a defeatist. He is correct, of course, when he says that filling in the majestic constitutional outlines requires value choices. But the point is that those outlines provide significant and sufficient guidance; the value choices are to be made only within the parameters of the most important value choice embedded in the constitutional language. * * *

Naturally there will be differences over the purposes and underlying political theories of the various constitutional protections. But they will be reasoned differences, subject to argument. * * * An assumption of Bickel and his colleagues seems to be that if we accept this mode of constitutional interpretation, we must also accept whatever results judges who apply it may reach, be they "conservative" or "liberal." That, of course, is not the case. When the courts interpret constitutional provisions in ways which we believe wrong, we ought not to shift the focus from the merits of their position to a narrowing of their institutional function. This was the fundamental mistake made by liberal legal scholars in the 1930's. * * * Arguments over purposes and theories will be healthy, aiding both judges and the political officials who appoint them. This approach will refocus attention, spawn a new mode of judicial criticism, and allow us to get on with the business of enforcing the purposive commands of the Constitution.

Yet *The Supreme Court and the Idea of Progress* suggests that Professor Bickel would remain unconvinced by this argument. Even if he admitted that a constitutional value choice is not the functional equivalent of an ordinary policy issue, he would still say that the freely operating pluralist political process serves to protect our constitutional rights and liberties adequately. * * * His belief seems to rest on two foundations, one theoretical, one empirical, and both mistaken.

Professor Bickel appears to believe that reliance on the political process for protection of most fundamental rights and liberties is somehow inherent in democratic theory. * * * Judicial decisions are made without the form of popular consent expressed, for example, in the casting of a vote and should therefore be relatively disfavored. But * * * [a] vote for a candidate does not give him a carte blanche. Implicit in the vote is an expectation that, if elected, the candidate will conform his actions to the Constitution. Also implicit, given judicial review, is the recognition that there are courts to ensure his obedience. * * * [A voter's] power to challenge particular decisions in the courts is theoretically necessary to the claim that government officials act with his consent. The Constitution was not originally imposed on us by some court. Rather, it was adopted by the people, may be altered by the people, and must be considered by them in any authorization they give to elected officeholders. It is the people's independent check on popular democracy, and, as such, is best enforced by an independent body with power to check the actions of legislatures and executives. It is very much part of—indeed, it is at the core of—government by the consent of the governed.

* * * In this country, the majority made an original decision to protect certain minority rights, and this decision cannot be respected if these rights evaporate whenever it seems expedient to ignore them. Professor Bickel goes on to contend, however, that in fact minorities play an important though indirect role in most governmental decisions, may be presumed to consent to them, and have substantial opportunity to defend their interests without the help of the courts. No minority willing to wheel and deal with other minorities, he says,

need despair of eventually vindicating its rights. There are at least
two problems with this common position. First, from a constitutional
standpoint, is the word "eventually." The Constitution does not say
that "no law shall for an inordinately long time" or that "no state shall
in perpetuity" deny certain rights. It sets down limitations to be
made effective in the present. Nor does the Constitution say that a
minority must trade away many of its interests in order to secure
support for exercise of its fundamental rights. It does not sanction
the putting of prices on these rights. *   *   *

Bickel's empirical assertion that no minority need remain iso-
lated *   *   * is also highly doubtful. Perhaps its basic defect is
the fact that power is not distributed equally among the various
groups in our society. Bickel explicitly recognizes *   *   * the trading and pressuring that goes on *   *   *. The Professor would have
us believe that this is just fine: those groups with the most "intense" interests will be the most active in the process, and it is
proper that the more "intense" interests be more richly rewarded.
This is nonsense. The big winners in the pluralistic system are the
highly organized, wealthy, and motivated groups skilled in the art of
insider politics. They have the resources to trade *   *   * and
*   *   * to press their claims successfully. Perhaps the interest of
a great corporation in a tax break is more "intense" than that of a
political minority in its first amendment rights—that is, if intensity
is defined by how conscious of their interests they are, how articulate
and persistent they are in presenting them, and how much political
muscle they bring to bear. Intensity, so defined, however, is largely
an attribute of the already powerful elite. Unorganized, poor, unskilled minorities simply do not have the sort of "intense" interests in
their rights which the pluralistic system regularly rewards. Is this
any way to protect their constitutional rights? Under the narrowly
constricted judicial role of the scholarly tradition, it is the only way.

IV

[Judge Wright next considers Professor Bickel's substantive
attack on the Court's work.]

*   *   * Professor Bickel launches the attack by characterizing
what he believes to be the four dominant themes underlying the Justices' decisions: egalitarianism, majoritarianism, centralization, and
legalization. *   *   *

Bickel apparently feels that he must show the Warren Court to
be not simply overly activist, but consciously demonic. *   *   * Slaves
to simplistic theoretical principles, the Court in Bickel's opinion naive-
ly sought "to impose order on the market of norms, values and institutions," motivated by "[a] certain habit of command, an impatience
to take charge of unruly affairs." He depicts the Court as an over-
confident planning agency, a master builder whose "tendency was no-

ticeably to circumscribe and displace private ordering, to legalize the society, to rationalize it in the sense in which the great industrial consolidators spoke of rationalizing the economy * * *." * * *

When Bickel describes the Warren Court's themes as simplistic, zealously pursued absolutes designed to remake society on the basis of enforced mass equality, he does not attempt to hide his own sharp, single-minded disapproval. "I should say," he says, "that in my view the Court's majoritarianism is ill-conceived, egalitarianism is a worthy ideal but not in all circumstances a self-evident virtue, and centralized, unmitigatedly legalitarian government bears the seed of tyranny." * * * The inevitable result, according to Bickel, is a rigid and stifling uniformity. * * * In his own ideology, the primary value seems to be the "rich" diversity and freedom of private ordering. In any event, his view is that society is so subtle and complex an organism that it cannot be molded to any theory of man. Reason, legal or otherwise, is too blunt and unsure an instrument. * * *

It is only when the Warren Court is viewed from this profoundly conservative perspective, however, that its work appears dangerously radical and absolutist. * * * [T]he Warren Court did not bring us to Armageddon. The Court was not a grand planner or master builder, working from a blueprint of the new society. Bickel's characterization of the Justices' thematic program and approach is, in a word, inaccurate. * * * If the Court's efforts toward greater individual dignity, privacy, and more nearly fair and equal treatment for all were described appropriately in terms of degree, I have little doubt that most of us would accept whatever sacrifices of diversity and private ordering were involved. * * *

When we examine the evidence Professor Bickel himself marshals to support his approach, the radical specter begins to disappear. Take egalitarianism. * * * [W]hat indication is there that the idea ran riot through the Court's decisions? Bickel relies on two lines of cases: those ensuring equal treatment for black people, and those granting a measure of equality for the indigent. But one looks in vain through the cases cited for evidence to make out the charge that the Justices were latter-day socialist levelers. * * * Free access to the vote and to legal assistance surely does not imply a requirement that all monetary barriers fall to the ground. The Court's effort was designed to bring the poor up to a minimum standard. At most, a minimal equality of opportunity—rather than egalitarianism—would be the appropriate characterization, surely one with fewer revolutionary connotations.

"Egalitarianism" may be a more accurate description of the Court's attitude toward cases involving racial discrimination. But if it be egalitarianism, it is directed, and limited, to a very special and historic evil; surely where racial discrimination is at issue any less would be insufficient. * * *

"Majoritarianism," says Bickel, "is heady stuff. It is, in truth, a tide flowing with the swiftness of a slogan * * *. The tide is apt to sweep over all institutions, seeking its level everywhere." * * * But where is the deluge? All that Bickel can point to is the one-man, one-vote decisions and the decisions enlarging the electorate and reducing permissible qualifications for voting. * * * This emphasis on equal voting rights, according to the Professor, frustrates the true genius of our political system—the pluralist giving and taking, wheeling and dealing of myriad interest groups. But the Court has in no way banned pluralist politics. Interest groups and lobbies can operate as always; they need not secure majority support before they bring pressure to bear on the community's representatives. What the Court has actually done is considerably less dramatic than Professor Bickel's imaginings. It has insisted that when the vote—the ordinary man's one chance to play a role in the direction of public affairs—is at stake, there must be a very heavy presumption against any distinctions that would exclude or disadvantage any group substantially interested in the outcome of the election in question. * * *

The last two themes identified by Bickel are centralization and legalization. Both, he says, undermined the diversity and freedom of local and private decisionmaking. * * *

The one decision to which Bickel often refers in substantiating his centralization charge is Katzenbach v. Morgan, enlarging the power of Congress to expand and enforce the guarantees of the fourteenth amendment. That decision did allow Congress to override the "experimentation" by local governments with the rights of disadvantaged minorities. Whether or not such experiments are to be highly valued, their sacrifice to federal control is simply part of a trend in being long before the advent of the Warren Court. The only new element in this incremental step is the purpose for which central power may be exercised. At least, we may demand consistency of Professor Bickel: why is it that the cost of centralization in *Morgan* is so disturbing, while the radical enlargement of congressional commerce clause powers earns only his praise? What is at stake is not really centralization per se, but the particular "rich diversity" whereby some minorities in some localities may be systematically victimized. * * *

Legalization, too, is something of a red herring. Professor Bickel's unkind words here are reserved for the decisions "substantially loosen[ing] the definition of a lawsuit * * * open[ing] the door wider to more litigants, and * * * making the lawsuit something of a formality, still an expensive one, but within the reach of just about all who can afford it, at just about any time of their choice." * * * Of course it is true that during the Warren years the champions of racial, economic, and other disadvantaged minorities turned more and more to the lawsuit as an instrument of reform. Again, however, Bickel's opposition to these trends demonstrates his lack of perspective on the whole legal system and apparent unconcern for what freedoms and what diversity are at stake.   The lawsuit has always been a ready and effective instrument of the rich and powerful, seeking to protect their own interests.   Why, then, is it so disturbing when the lawsuit may be almost as readily employed to enforce more fully the Constitution?   *   *   *

Why is it that Bickel fails to see the possibility of a middle ground when discussing decisions of the Warren Court?   *   *   *

The best explanation for these excesses lies in the recognition that the scholarly tradition now is in fact but a part of the western conservative tradition.   At least since the French Revolution, it has been characteristic of conservatives to combat the forces of change by misrepresenting their program, by summoning up horrible disasters said to follow from liberal reform, and by depicting the liberals as extreme totalitarians.   This reaction has been particularly prevalent when the change involved would enforce for the underprivileged many the rights which have long been enjoyed by the privileged few.   The liberal tradition, on the other hand, has been based on a faith in the powers of man to adjust institutions, without making them totalitarian, in the interest of equal justice.   *   *   *

V

*   *   *   Professor Bickel   *   *   *   purports to follow a value-neutral approach.   Thus, he attacks the Court's work in the fields of racial segregation and legislative reapportionment not because the results are "wrong" but because the results will not be "historically vindicated."   *   *   *

Bickel hears

> in increasing volume notes that amount to another tune. There is in being a reaction to the steady unification and nationalization of recent years, a movement toward a decentralization and a diversity   *   *   *   A striving for diversity is not necessarily in express conflict with the goal of an egalitarian society, but it connotes a different order of priorities.   In politics, even as the Warren Court's virtually irresistible slogan—one man, one vote—may still be mouthed on all sides, the cry is for a group participation which presupposes, whether it knows it or not, the Madisonian more than the majoritarian model, and for a process calculated to heed the expression not only of desires and preferences, but of intensities that no ballot can register.

At the outset it is appropriate to ask whether Bickel's test— which he says the Court's greatest work fails—is a proper one.   He seems wholehearted in his acceptance of history as the final judge:

"If the [Warren Court's] bet [on the future trend of events] pays off, whatever their analytical failings, the Justices will have won everything." The value-neutrality of this approach must be particularly appealing to the Professor * * *.

> [Wright urges, however, that there is more to Constitutional jurisprudence than letting history be the judge. He takes as his example what might have happened had the South won the civil war.]

Should a different outcome on the Civil War battlefields really make us approve *Dred Scott*? If Taney's Court had made apartheid its overriding principle, and apartheid had actually come to pass in America, would the judicial result be any more defensible? * * * The ultimate test of the Justices' work, I suggest, must be goodness, not a cynically defined success. Since Bickel purports to believe that "justice" and "injustice" are no more than passing societal value choices of no inherent and true meaning, he is left with history and chance victories on the battlefield as his only guide * * *.

Moreover, even if we accept Bickel's historical test, we can still question its application. Perhaps the Professor ought to have taken his own advice to the Court before so confidently assessing which way the wind is blowing. Thus it may be significant that Bickel's Holmes Lectures were written to be delivered in the spring of 1969—now almost two years ago. They were probably drafted in 1968. That, indeed, was the year * * * Senators Kennedy and McCarthy (for whom Professor Bickel did campaign work) spoke eloquently of returning decisionmaking power to localities. Also in 1968, the New York City school decentralization movement had just reached its high water mark. * * * Two years later, however, Bickel's confident predictions are less convincing. With a new administration in power, the focus of attention seems to have turned. There is still much talk of decentralization, but it is more often meant as a redistribution of power to the states rather than to the local communities of which Bickel speaks. * * *

* * * Even if Professor Bickel has foreseen the trend of opinion, it is not clear that the school desegregation and voting decisions are either irrelevant to or incompatible with that trend. His technique of argument—a common one among followers of the scholarly tradition—is * * * to extend nascent principles far beyond what was intended by the Court. Yet at the same time that Bickel exhibits this failing in depicting some of the Court's greatest decisions as roadblocks to new reform, he takes far too narrow a view of the same decisions in arguing their irrelevance.

Thus, Bickel identifies two principles or ideals running through the school desegregation cases. The first is a condemnation on fourteenth amendment grounds of state-established racial segregation.

The second relates only to education, and seems to view the public school system as pursuing a great, assimilationist mission in American society. * * * Professor Bickel's argument is that if the assimilationist ideal is carried to its most extreme conclusion, it will come into direct conflict with the * * * [current trends toward Community Control in education], by requiring centralization of school districts to end de facto segregation and by outlawing tuition grant schemes and private schools. But if the assimilationist ideal is not carried all the way and mere disestablishment prevails, he says, the school desegregation decisions will become irrelevant to the burning issues of the day. It is a heads-I-win, tails-you-lose type of argument.

It is almost too obvious to point out that the extremes of mere disestablishment and total assimilation do not exhaust all possible future uses of the school desegregation cases. * * * The Court could well stop short of requiring centralized school districts, but go beyond mere disestablishment to deal with de facto segregation. Familiar and effective possibilities include judicial review of zoning and new school location decisions by local school authorities. It would not be unprincipled for the Court to recognize that city, town, or county jurisdictions are appropriate for school administration purposes and that the cost of altering these jurisdictions by judicial order would outweigh the assimilationist benefit. The Justices are not blind to the advantages of decentralization. * * * Thus the Court might well hold that when zoning and location adjustments fail to achieve acceptably integrated schools, there is a particularly heavy burden on local boards to allocate educational resources equally among all schools. * * *

The tuition grant and private school problem may be more difficult. But it might be sufficient to command simply that if tuition grants are to be made, the schools which receive the resulting public funds must encourage interracial membership or establish fair racial quotas. Such requirements would not disturb the main, legitimate goal of tuition grants: the sponsorship of diverse educational opportunities and free choice among them. Private schools, not receiving public funds, might be dealt with by forbidding racially discriminatory admission practices under the thirteenth amendment. Again, the most important free choice and diversity values to be served would remain unaffected while gross evasion of school integration would be controlled. * * *

* * * Perhaps Professor Bickel is bored with the problem, but it is still very much with us, and the line of decisions following *Brown* will continue to be applied in the South long after the executive branch has found it politically expedient to abandon the victims of racial segregation. Some day, we may hope, this horrible scar will be healed and the school desegregation decisions will be cited and applied less often. Even then, however, to call them "irrelevant" is ex-

traordinarily callous and reflects a thorough lack of historical understanding. * * *

Bickel is no more convincing when he attacks the Warren Court's voting decisions. * * *

Let us begin with irrelevance. Bickel argues, as usual, that the drawing of district lines is a highly complex and unruly problem of pluralist politics. District boundaries are drawn and can be evaluated only in terms of which minority groups gain power and which lose power thereby. The Court's past emphasis on equality in voting, Bickel says, is of no use in dealing with this distinctly pluralist, group-oriented question. It is true, of course, that one man, one vote does not provide an automatic answer to the district boundary problem. But the basic ideal underlying the reapportionment cases is by no means irrelevant. That ideal, as has been mentioned, is equality of political opportunity: every citizen should have a roughly equivalent opportunity of access to the formal levers of political power. The difficulty, of course, is devising an administrable rule whereby this ideal may be applied to the gerrymandering problem. One far-reaching solution would be to require a system of proportional representation. Such a system would seem to serve best Professor Bickel's concern with group representation. For no legislative body can catalogue the citizenry into interest groups as well as the citizens can themselves, and no malapportionment program of the sort Bickel advocates can as effectively translate the size of highly fluid interest groups into the proper degree of actual representation as a system that adjusts a group's representation to the support it actually receives in particular elections. * * *

Yet even short of required proportional representation, some judicial controls could be imposed on gerrymandering that would serve the pluralists' concerns. The rule of thumb would be largely negative. It would prohibit the most egregiously unfair forms of districting by demanding at the very least that only neutral criteria, such as existing jurisdictional or natural boundaries, be employed. An exception might be allowed for non-neutral boundaries which can be demonstrated to be plainly "benign" such as boundaries providing some representation for a minority group that would otherwise be submerged entirely.
* * *

Just as Bickel is too quick to dismiss any connection between the reapportionment cases and the district boundary problem, he too hastily assumes that a slippery doctrinal slope will frustrate experiments in federated local government. Whether school decentralization is achieved or not, he says, a federated central administrative board would be desirable. He goes on to argue that the formation of such a board would be "politically infeasible" unless it were malapportioned—giving each neighborhood school district equal representation despite unequal population. Similarly, he argues that metropolitan government of city and suburbs would be "politically infeasible" unless malapportioned, so that neither the city nor the suburbs had permanent majority control. We have reached a strange state of affairs when a spokesman for the scholarly tradition judges constitutional principles according to the "political feasibility" of achieving certain desired results in compliance with them. Nevertheless, it is not divinely ordained that the one man, one vote rule must inexorably apply to such federated administrative bodies. If Professor Bickel can see the desirability of encouraging such developments, so can the Justices. * * *

* * *

Bickel's * * * attack * * * illustrates another hidden truth about the scholarly tradition. Shifting ground from "goodness" to "success," he aspires to a neutral, scientific viewpoint; he seeks to demonstrate that the clash between himself and the Warren Court is not one of conflicting value choices, but of fundamental method. Perhaps to some extent it is. However, we may stop to wonder why Bickel chose only to attack the school desegregation and reapportionment cases on the ground of impending obsolescence, while ignoring the one body of decisions which most clearly are at odds with a discernible trend of opinion and events: the criminal procedure cases. He quite clearly provides the answer earlier in the book where he notes his satisfaction with those decisions. Yet if neutrally defined success, and not goodness, were truly at the heart of his creed, he would have to condemn them too. Instead, Bickel manifests interest only in those trends of public opinion of which he personally approves. It is useful, then, to pierce the veil of the scholarly tradition and to see its quarrel with the Warren Court for what it really is. It is, I believe, a fundamental dispute over the good society as well as over judicial method. * * * If the debate is over the true meaning and scope of particular constitutional protections, we should get on with it and avoid for a time the back roads and alleyways of theoretical methodology.

VI

* * * How is the general approach of Professor Bickel and his colleagues in the scholarly tradition likely to relate to the concerns of the new generation of lawyers?

* * * Most of their teachers had first come to see and understand the Court and the Constitution during the New Deal years— an experience which could only serve to corroborate the positions taken by the progessive realists. Thus they generally sought to school their students of the 1960's in a mode of criticism surely appropriate to the Old Court, but of doubtful relevance to the Warren Court. The students could not help but feel the tension since, for them, the Supreme Court *was* the Warren Court. For them, there was no theoretical gulf between the law and morality; and, for them, the Court was

the one institution in the society that seemed to be speaking most consistently the language of idealism which we all recited in grade school.
Just as they had not lived through the Stalin era and so could not accept the conventional wisdom of the Cold War, so their coming to
consciousness in the 1960's left them unscarred by worries of Court
packing and judicial obstructionism. Instead, they were inspired by
the dignity and moral courage of a man and an institution that was
prepared to act on the ideals to which America is theoretically and
rhetorically dedicated.

    *   *   *   [T]he new generation of lawyers—the new professors
as well as judges and practitioners, I might add—see no point in
querulous admonitions that the Court should restrain itself from com-
batting injustice now in order to preserve itself to combat a coup
later on. An institution that sits back, always emphasizing its weakness and its reasons for inaction, is unlikely to be in a fighting stance
when the tanks roll down Pennsylvania Avenue. The young lawyers
know that a country which hoards all of its moral capital in the form
of windy rhetoric is likely to die rich—and soon.

    Those of us well over thirty may grumble about naiveté and
tell ourselves that experience will make the young lawyers more cyni-
cal, more cautious, more protective of fragile institutions and tolerant
of diversity. Those are the values of the tradition we grew up in.
But if it is true that men and women form very basic attitudes, presumptions, and cognitive frameworks in their late 'teens and early
twenties, then no amount of experience will substantially dull the
inspiration of the 1960's. The students of this decade will never come
to value the "unruliness of affairs" for its own sake; for them, there
is little charm in an interminable discussion of the complexity and
subtlety of life and of how resistant it is to rational solution. They
have seen that affairs can be ordered in conformance to constitutional
ideals and that injustice—to which *they* are prepared to give powerful
meaning—can be routed. They have seen that it can be done: the
Warren Court did it and the heavens did not fall.

NOTES AND QUESTIONS

    1. Are you able to determine what, precisely, causes the passionate dis-
agreement between Wright and the adherents to the "scholarly tradition?"
You have only been exposed at first-hand to the work of Wechsler, but Wright
does an accurate job of portraying the thought of Bickel. Based on what you
have been able to determine about the thought of these men, is Wright's
point well taken that the Court's "scholarly critics" refuse to evaluate "principle as a matter of principle?" Is it true, as Judge Wright charges, that
"Wechsler and his followers" advocate a "synthesis of 'value free' values?"
Judge Wright suggests that Professor Bickel (and, by implication, Professor
Wechsler) resist "the temptation to approve judicial protection of civil rights
and liberties." Is this a "temptation" that any right-thinking person ought
to resist? Do Bickel and Wechsler really resist? Has Wright fairly characterized their jurisprudence? Judge Wright brushes aside many of the

theoretical strictures of the scholarly critics with the observation that "the most important value choices have already been made by the framers of the Constitution." Does this solve the problem? Would Wechsler and Bickel agree with the assertion?

2. Do you understand Judge Wright to be suggesting that the task of the courts is to discern the meaning that the framers put on Constitutional terms, and then to implement that meaning? In other words, is Wright suggesting that the simple task of the courts is to implement the "original understanding" of Constitutional terms? This view has been advanced, from time to time, as a means of getting around the problem of "legitimating" the inherently undemocratic institution of judicial review. Its proponents might range all the way from the framers themselves, like Alexander Hamilton, to latter-day observers, like Raoul Berger. See Berger, Government by Judiciary (1977).

3. Does Wright really feel any need to legitimate the policy-making role of the Court? Is the real issue between Wright and the "scholarly critics" joined in the penultimate section of Wright's piece (Section V), where he states that the scholarly critics subscribe to what he calls a "conservative ideology?" What does Wright mean by this term? In part of this section Judge Wright poses the question whether "If Taney's court had made apartheid its overriding principle, and apartheid had actually come to pass in America, would the judicial result be any more defensible?" Is it possible to answer that question in any manner other than negatively? Is Wright thus seeking to accuse the scholarly critics of advocating apartheid? Does he mean simply to imply that the Taney court had made apartheid an unacknowledged principle of its decision in *Dred Scott*? Would he have been correct if that was his assertion?

4. What does Wright mean when he concludes that "the ultimate test of the Justices' work, I suggest, must be goodness, not a cynically-defined success?" Are you in favor of a system of Constitutional jurisprudence with "goodness" as its touchstone? How might one determine what "goodness" was? In any event, Wright's analysis seems to have struck a somewhat responsive chord in at least some sectors of the academic community. See White, The Evolution of Reasoned Elaboration: Jurisprudential Criticism and Social Change, 59 Va.L.Rev. 279, 298–302 (1973). For a spirited defense of the jurisprudence of the Warren Court, which seems to track some of the suggestions made by White, see Archibald Cox, The Role of The Supreme Court in American Government (1976) and Cox, The Warren Court (1968). Cox (and White) suggest that it is entirely appropriate for the Supreme Court to formulate social policy in the guise of determining Constitutional law, so long as the Justices stay close to the "aspirations" that "the community is willing not only to avow but in the end to live by." Cox, The Role of the Supreme Court, at 118. Does this make sense? Or would you subscribe to the objections (to which Wechsler was responding) raised by Learned Hand:

> For myself it would be most irksome to be ruled by a bevy of Platonic Guardians, even if I knew how to choose them, which I assuredly do not. If they were in charge, I should miss the stimulus of living in a society where I have, at least theoretically, some part in the direction of public affairs. Of course, I know how illusory

would be the belief that my vote determined anything; but nevertheless when I go to the polls I have a satisfaction in the sense that we are all engaged in a common venture.

Hand, The Bill of Rights 73–74 (1959), quoted by Cox, at 116.

5.   As his final answer to the question whether the "rule of law" is an "unqualified human good", Professor Horwitz has declared that an affirmative answer is possible "Only if Hitler, Stalin, and all the other horrors of this century have forced us finally to accept the Hobbesian vision of the state and human nature on which our present conceptions of the rule of law ultimately rest.   It *is* a conservative doctrine."   Horwitz, The Rule of Law: An Unqualified Human Good?, 86 Yale L.J. 561, 566 (1977).   From what you know of American Constitutional Law in the late twentieth century, would you say that the "Hobbesian vision" and the "rule of law" predominate?   In the next Chapter we turn our attention to private law, as we did in Chapter Three, but the questions of adherence to equitable principles and/or the rule of law remain.

Chapter 7

PRIVATE LAW PRESENT AND FUTURE: TOWARDS A WELFARE STATE?

SECTION A. THE END OF CONTRACT AS WE KNEW IT?

GRANT GILMORE, THE DEATH OF CONTRACT *

6–15, 17–21, 57–72, 74–76, 87–90, 94–98, 102–103 (1974).

In a remarkable recent book, ** Professor Lawrence Freidman has contributed some novel insights into the nature of what he calls the "pure" or "classical" theory of contract, by which he refers to the theory as it developed in the nineteenth century. * * *

* * *

* * * Although we shall depart from his analysis at some points, we may retain as central ideas the concept of the general law of contract as a residual category—what is left over after all the "specialized" bodies of law have been added up—highly abstract, in close historical relationship with the free market of classical economic theory, a theoretical construct which, having little or nothing to do with the real world, would not—or could not—change as the real world changed. Professor Friedman goes on to comment on another significant aspect of the contract construct—which is that it resisted, and continues to resist, codification long after most, if not all, of the fields of law apparently most closely related to it had passed under the statutory yoke. * * *

Asked to locate the law of contract on the legal spectrum, most of us, I assume, would place it in the area usually denominated Commercial Law. It is true that our unitary contract theory has always had an uncomfortable way of spilling over into distinctly non-commercial situations and that what may be good for General Motors does not always make sense when applied to charitable subscriptions, antenuptial agreements and promises to convey the family farm provided the children will support the old people for life. But we feel instinctively that commercial law is the heart of the matter and that, the need arising, the commercial rules can be applied over * * * to fit, for example, the case of King Lear and his unruly daughters. * * *

** Lawrence Friedman, Contract Law in America (1965).

* * * In not much more than half a century the main outlines of what we call commercial law had been laid down and many of the subsidiary details worked out. That something extraordinary had occurred was apparent to observers of the time. Thus in 1837 Justice Joseph Story reported that while it was not true of all law, it was possible to codify the law of "commercial contracts."

I call your particular attention to the list of subjects which Story felt could be codified. He includes within the area of "commercial contracts," as we would not, the law of business organizations—agency and partnership although not, interestingly enough, the as yet embryonic corporation. Promissory notes and bills of exchange make their expected appearance. Financing and security transactions show up. * * * Finally there is insurance—by which he evidently meant marine insurance—and maritime or shipping law which gets the most detailed treatment of all. There is no reference to a law of "sales," as such. That, curiously, came along a generation later. The first American treatise on Sales came out in 1848, having been written by Justice Story's son, William Wetmore Story, who, after that act of filial piety, abandoned the law and spent the rest of a long life as a sculptor in Italy. The treatise on Sales is, by the way, very fine indeed and so, for all I know, the sculptures are too.

For Story, then, there was no such thing as a generalized law of—or theory of—contract. There were specialized bodies of law which had sprung up to regulate the various aspects of commercial transactions which had, with the Industrial Revolution, assumed paramount importance in our social and economic life. * * *

* * *

I have credited Dean Langdell with the almost inadvertent discovery of the general theory of Contract. The reference was to his pioneering casebook on Contracts which appeared just a hundred years ago and, even more, to the "Summary of the Law of Contracts" which he added as an appendix to the second edition of the casebook in 1880. * * *

To judge by the casebook and the Summary, Langdell was an industrious researcher of no distinction whatever. * * *

But it is with Langdell that, for the first time, we see Contract as a remote, impersonal, bloodless abstraction. The three principal chapters into which the casebook is divided are entitled: Mutual Assent, Consideration and Conditional Contracts: we are evidently at a far remove from Story's list of "commercial contracts." The casebook, according to Langdell, was to contain all the important contract cases that had ever been decided. "All the cases" turned out to be mostly English cases, arranged in historical sequence from the seventeenth century down to the date of publication; the English cases were occasionally supplemented by comparable sequences of cases from New York and Massachusetts. * * * The Summary, which

runs to a hundred and fifty pages or so, is devoted almost entirely to explaining which of the cases in the main part of the casebook are "right" and which are "wrong." The explanation, typically, is dogmatic rather than reasoned; Langdell knew right from wrong, no doubt by divine revelation, and that should suffice for the student.
* * *

* * * The [general] theory [of contract] itself was [not really Langdell's unique contribution but was] pieced together by his successors—notably Holmes, in broad philosophical outline, and Williston, in meticulous, although not always accurate, scholarly detail. At this point it is necessary to give some idea of the content of what we may call the Holmes-Williston construct. * * * Having accomplished that chore, we can return to the far more interesting business of speculating on why Langdell's idea, brilliantly reformulated by Holmes, had the fabulous success it did instead of going down the drain into oblivion as a hundred better ideas than Langdell's do every day of the week.

The theory seems to have been dedicated to the proposition that, ideally, no one should be liable to anyone for anything. Since the ideal was not attainable, the compromise solution was to restrict liability within the narrowest possible limits. Within those limits, however, liability was to be absolute. * * * Liability, although absolute—at least in theory—was nevertheless, to be severely limited. The equitable remedy of specific performance was to be avoided so far as possible. * * * Money damages for breach of contract were to be "compensatory," never punitive; Holmes explained that every man has a right "to break his contract if he chooses"—that is, a right to elect to pay damages instead of performing his contractual obligation. Therefore the wicked contract-breaker should pay no more in damages that the innocent and the pure in heart. * * *

* * *

Where did the idea for this curious—one is tempted to say, monstrous—machine come from? It is fair to say that the theory of contract represented a sharp break with the past, even the recent past. The inventors of the theory did not make it all up out of their own heads. Indeed they made industrious use of whatever bits and pieces of case law, old and new, could be made to fit the theory. Such cases were immediately promoted to "leading cases" and made to fit—in much the same way that Procrustes made his guests fit. Cases which could not be made to fit were ignored or dismissed, with Langdellian certitude, as "wrong." On the whole, however, the theory was in its origins, and continued to be during its life, an ivory tower abstraction. Its natural habitat was the law schools, not the law courts. And yet * * * the theory was an instant and spectacular success. Generations of lawyers and judges and law professors grew up believing that the theory was true * * *.

The balance-wheel of the great machine was the theory of consideration. * * * The word "consideration" has been around for a long time, but * * * until the nineteenth century the word never acquired any particular meaning or stood for any theory. * * * [Until about the turn of the eighteenth century "consideration" may have served simply as evidence that there was a serious intent to bargain present. At about that time, however, the English courts began trying to "explain" consideration.] A formula which became fashionable put it in terms of benefit and detriment. If a promisor received any benefit from a transaction, that was sufficient consideration to support his promise. On the other hand, if a promisee suffered any detriment, that, likewise, was sufficient to support the promise. Any benefit would do; any detriment would do. * * *

The new day dawned, with Holmes * * *:

* * *

It appears to me that it has not always been sufficiently borne in mind that the same thing may be a consideration or not, as it is dealt with by the parties * * *.

* * * It is hard to see the propriety of erecting any detriment which an instrument may disclose or provide for, into a consideration, unless the parties have dealt with it on that footing. * * * The detriment may be nothing but a condition precedent to performance, as where a man promises another to pay him five hundred dollars if he breaks his leg. * * * It is the essence of a consideration, that, by the terms of the agreement, it is given and accepted as the motive or inducement for furnishing the consideration. The root of the whole matter is the relation of reciprocal conventional inducement, each for the other, between consideration and promise.

Now the vulgar error that any benefit or any detriment would do has been exploded. * * * No matter how much detriment a promisee may have suffered, he has not, thereby, necessarily furnished a consideration. Nor does he have, so far as Holmes takes us, any right to redress or even any claim on our sympathies, no matter how reasonable his detrimental reliance may have been, not even if, in the course of incurring his detriment, he has conferred a benefit on the other party. Absent "consideration," the unhappy promisee has no right or claim. And nothing is "consideration" unless "the parties have dealt with it on that footing." * * *

It seems perfectly clear that Holmes was, quite consciously, proposing revolutionary doctrine * * *. His analysis of the true meaning of "consideration" comes forth almost naked of citation of authority or precedent. * * *

There is never any point in arguing with a successful revolution. * * * The "bargain" theory of consideration, proposed by Holmes, is enshrined in the definition of consideration in § 75 of the original Restatement of Contracts * * *.

With the Holmesian formulation, consideration became a tool for narrowing the range of contractual liability. "The whole doctrine of contract," he noted in this connection, "is formal and external." Unless the formalities were accomplished, there could be no contract and, consequently, no liability. The austerity of doctrine would not be tempered for the shorn lambs who might shiver in its blast.

* * *

* * * I have credited Holmes and Williston * with the design and execution of the great theory. It is tempting to set Cardozo and Corbin over against them as the engineers of its destruction. * * * Cardozo's attack was subtle, evasive, hesitant * * *. Corbin's attack was more forthright. * * * [H]is treatise on Contracts— which I will describe as the greatest law book ever written—bears the publication date: 1950. It is true that, by 1950, the ideas and the reforms which Corbin argued for were no longer particularly novel * * *. We forget that Corbin—perhaps unwisely—had spent the better part of fifty years readying the treatise for publication. * * * So resituated in time, Corbin's attack on the prevailing orthodoxy assumes revolutionary proportions.

Corbin's abiding interest was in what he called the "operative facts" of cases: * * *

> [A] sufficient reason for comparative historical study of cases in great number is the fact that such study frees the teacher and the lawyer and the judge from the illusion of certainty; and from the delusion that law is absolute and eternal, that doctrines can be used mechanically, and that there are correct and unchangeable definitions.

Evidently we have entered a universe of discourse which simply has no meeting point with the Holmesian universe in which the doctrine of contract was, and was meant to be "wholly formal and external." * * *

We must now deal with the mysterious episode of the Restatements. * * * The Restatement project [begun in the early 1920's] can be taken as the almost instinctive reaction of the legal establishment of the time to the attack of the so-called legal realists. What

---

* The author of a great multi-volume treatise on Contracts, and the chief "Reporter" of the original Restatement of Contracts, a computation of the case-law rules. Williston's ideas on Contract are much the same as those of Holmes.

the realists had principally attacked, savagely and successfully, was the essentially Langedellian idea that cases can be arranged to make sense—indeed scientific sense. * * * [I]n the 1920's there was still hope that the revolution could be put down, that unity of doctrine could be maintained and that an essentially pure case law system could be preserved from further statutory encroachment. * * * The conservative response, which, looked on as a delaying action, was remarkably successful, was the provision of Restatements of Contracts, Torts, Property and the like.

Williston and Corbin were unquestionably the dominant intellectual influences in the drafting of the *Restatement of Contracts* * * *. No doubt it was their joint participation which insured the extraordinarily high technical quality of the product * * *. No doubt it was also their joint participation—bearing in mind that Williston and Corbin held antithetical points of view on almost every conceivable point of law—that accounts for the [Restatement's fascinatingly] schizophrenic quality * * *.

* * *

* * * The first lesson will be the *Restatement's* definition of consideration (§ 75) taken in connection with its most celebrated section—§ 90, captioned Promise Reasonably Inducing Definite and Substantial Action.

First § 75:

> (1) Consideration for a promise is
>
>> (a) an act other than a promise, or
>>
>> (b) a forbearance, or
>>
>> (c) the creation, modification or destruction of a legal relation, or
>>
>> (d) a return promise,
>
> bargained for and given in exchange for the promise.

* * *

This is, of course, pure Holmes. * * * [Section 90, however, provides:]

> A promise which the promisor should reasonably expect to induce action or forbearance of a definite and substantial character on the part of the promisee and which does induce such action or forbearance is binding if injustice can be avoided only by enforcement of the promise.

And what is that all about? We have become accustomed to the idea * * * that the universe includes both matter and anti-matter. Perhaps what we have here is Restatement and anti-Restatement or Contract and anti-Contract. * * * The one thing that is clear is that these two contradictory propositions cannot live comfortably together: in the end one must swallow the other up.

* * *   When the Restaters and their advisors came to the definition of consideration, Williston proposed in substance what became § 75. Corbin submitted a quite different proposal. To understand what the Corbin proposal was about, it is necessary to backtrack somewhat. Even after the Holmesian or bargain theory of consideration had won all but universal acceptance, the New York Court of Appeals had, during the Cardozo period, pursued a line of its own. * * * Cardozo's opinions express what might be called an expansive theory of contract. Courts should make contracts wherever possible, rather than the other way around. Missing terms can be supplied. If an express promise is lacking, an implied promise can easily be found.[139] In particular Cardozo delighted in weaving gossamer spider webs of consideration. There was consideration for a father's promise to pay his engaged daughter an annuity after marriage in the fact that the engaged couple, instead of breaking off the engagement, had in fact married.[140] There was consideration for a pledge to a college endowment campaign * * * in the fact that the college, by accepting the pledge, had come under an implied duty to memorialize the donor's name * * *.[141] Evidently a judge who could find "consideration" in DeCicco v. Schweizer or in the *Allegheny College* case could, when he was so inclined, find consideration anywhere * * *. Corbin, who had been deeply influenced by Cardozo, proposed to the Restaters what might be called a Cardozoean definition of consideration—broad, vague and, essentially, meaningless * * *. In the debate Corbin and the Cardozoeans lost out to Williston and the Holmesians. * * *

* * *   Corbin returned to the attack. At the next meeting of the Restatement group, he addressed them more or less in the following manner: Gentlemen * * *, [y]ou have recently adopted a definition of consideration. I now submit to you a list of cases—hundreds, perhaps, or thousands?—in which courts have imposed contractual liability under circumstances in which, according to your definition, there would be no consideration and therefore no liability. Gentlemen, what do you intend to do about these cases?

* * *   [Indeed, g]oing back into the past, there was an indefinite number of cases which had imposed liability, in the name of consideration, where nothing like Holmes's "reciprocal conventional inducement" was anywhere in sight. Holmes's point was that these were bad cases and that the range of contractual liability should be

---

139. Wood v. Lucy, Lady Duff-Gordon, 222 N.Y. 88, 118 N.E. 214 (1917). * * *

140. De Cicco v. Schweizer, 221 N.Y. 431, 117 N.E. 807 (1917). * * *

141. Allegheny College v. National Chautauqua Bank, 246 N.Y. 369, 377, 159 N.E. 173 (1927).

confined within narrower limits. By the turn of the century, except in New York, the strict bargain theory of consideration had won general acceptance. But, unlike Holmes, many judges, it appeared, were not prepared to look with stony-eyed indifference on the plight of a plaintiff who had, to his detriment, relied on a defendant's assurances without the protection of a formal contract. However, the new doctrine precluded the judges * * * from saying * * * that the "detriment" itself was "consideration." They had to find a new solution * * *. In such a situation the word that comes instinctively to the mind of any judge is, of course, "estoppel"—which is simply a way of saying that, for reasons which the court does not care to discuss, there must be judgment for plaintiff. And [as Corbin observed,] in the contract cases after 1900 the word "estoppel," modulating into such phrases as "equitable estoppel" and "promissory estoppel," began to appear with increasing frequency.

The Restaters, honorable men, * * * instead of reopening the debate on the consideration definition, * * * elected to stand by § 75 but to add a new section—§ 90—incorporating the estoppel idea although without using the word "estoppel." The extent to which the new section § 90 was to be allowed to undercut the underlying principle of § 75 was left entirely unresolved. * * * [Indeed, concerning] the mysterious text of § 90 itself, * * * no one had any idea what the damn thing meant.

* * * The *Restatement*, we might say, ended up uneasily poised between past and future, which is no doubt the best thing that could have been done.

The future, of course, won, as it always does. During the past forty years we have seen the effective dismantling of the formal system of classical contract theory. We have witnessed what it does not seem too farfetched to describe as an explosion of liability. * * *

* * * Judge Learned Hand once suggested that § 90 * * * should be restricted to donative or gift promises. Professionals should play the game according to the professional rules. If A, in a commercial context, made what could be described as an offer to B, then A's liability to B should depend on the formal rules of offer, acceptance and consideration and on nothing else. The course of decision has, however, seen a gradual expansion of § 90 as a principle of decision in a good many types of commercial situations.

Such case law developments are reflected in an altogether fascinating manner in the provisions of the so-called *Second Restatement of Contracts*. * * * Why should there be a second series of Restatements? * * * There can be little or no doubt that the first generation of Restaters implicitly assumed that they were reducing to black letter text what we like to call the "fundamental principles of the common law." Now, we are all aware that rules of law change through time but many of us like to think that our "fundamental principles" are eternal and unchanging. * * *

* * * [N]o principles of law, or of anything else, can be guaranteed good past the next revolution. I dare say that no one will dispute the fact that, since the 1930's, there has been a world-wide revolution, scientific, social, economic and political. * * * One of the minor by-products of the revolution through which my own generation has lived will, of necessity, be the reformulation not merely of the specific "principles and rules of the common law" but of our basic attitudes toward the process of law itself. * * * We may take the second series of Restatements as [such a by-product.] * * *

* * *

Restatement (*First*) § 75 (Definition of Consideration) * * * has not been changed in substance in *Restatement* (*Second*) § 75. The accompanying Comment has, however, been revised in such a way as to leave no doubt that we are now in an antithetical universe of discourse. The § 75 Comment in *Restatement* (*First*) began with an authentically Willistonian flourish:

> No duty is generally imposed on one who makes an informal promise unless the promise is supported by sufficient consideration * * *.

The lead to the § 75 Comment in *Restatement* (*Second*) introduces us to the sound of a much less certain trumpet:

> The word "consideration" has often been used with meanings different from that given here. It is often used merely to express the legal conclusion that a promise is enforceable.

The Comment, we might say, has been Corbinized. The only recognition of the existence of § 90 in the *Restatement* (*First*) § 75 Comment was the somewhat grudging concession that "some informal promises are enforceable without the element of bargain. These fall and are placed in the category of contracts which are binding without assent or consideration (see §§ 85–94)." Furthermore, Illustration 2 to § 75 in *Restatement* (*First*) hypothesized that "A promises B $500 when B goes to college" and concluded that "If the promise * * * is reasonably to be understood as a gratuity, payable on the stated contingency, B's going to college is not consideration for A's promise." The § 75 Illustration carried no cross-reference to § 90, where one of the Illustrations was to the effect that an apparently identical "if B goes to college" promise is "binding" on A. [In the revised § 75 Comment in *Restatement* (*Second*) the "when B goes to college" illustration has been dropped and the following new illustration substituted: "A promises to make a gift of $10 to B. In reliance on the promise B buys a book from C and promises to pay C $10 for it.

There is no consideration for A's promise. As to the enforceability of such promises, see § 90."

However, the Corbinization of § 75 is insignificant quite compared to what has happened to § 90. Original § 90 * * * was exposed to the world naked of Comment and provided with four ambiguous illustrations as its sole capital. Text and illustration together took up less than a page. Revised § 90 with its Comment and Illlustrations runs to over twelve pages and the original four Illustrations have grown to seventeen. * * *

* * * The reliance principle, we are told, may have been, historically, the basis for "the enforcement of informal contracts in the action of assumpsit."

> Certainly [the Comment continues] reliance is one of the main bases for enforcement of the half-completed exchange, and the probability of reliance lends support to the enforcement of the executory exchange * * *. This Section thus states a basic principle which often renders inquiry unnecessary as to the precise scope of the policy of enforcing bargains.

Thus the unwanted stepchild of *Restatement* (*First*) has become "a basic principle" of *Restatement* (*Second*) which, the comment seems to suggest, prevails, in case of need, over the competing "bargain theory" of § 75. The Comment and the new illustrations are entirely clear that the principle of § 90 is applicable in commercial contexts as well as in noncommercial ones * * *.

Clearly enough the unresolved ambiguity in the relationship between § 75 and § 90 in the *Restatement* (*First*) has now been resolved in favor of the promissory estoppel principle of § 90 which has, in effect, swallowed up the bargain principle of § 75. * * *

* * *

[As further evidence of this trend,] a new section * * * has been added to the *Restatement* (*Second*) as § 89A (Promise for Benefit Received). * * * :

> (1) A promise made in recognition of benefit previously received by the promisor from the promisee is binding to the extent necessary to prevent injustice.

> (2) A promise is not binding under Subsection (1); (a) if the promisee conferred the benefit as a gift or for other reasons the promisor has not been unjustly enriched; or (b) to the extent that its value is disproportionate to the benefit.

This is far from going the whole hog on the unjust enrichment idea. For one thing, the ungrateful recipient may keep whatever he has received without paying for it so long as he is clever enough to avoid making a "promise" to repay. * * * For another thing what Subsection (1) giveth, Subsection (2) largely taketh away: the promise, even if made, will be "binding" only within narrow limits. * * *

Enough has been said to make the point that *Restatement* (*Second*), at least in 89A, is characterized by the same "schizophrenic quality" for which *Restatement* (*First*) was so notable. * * * The principal thing is that *Restatement* (*Second*) gives overt recognition to an important principle whose existence *Restatement* (*First*) ignored and, by implication denied. * * *

* * *

Speaking descriptively, we might say that what is happening is that "contract" is being reabsorbed into the mainstream of "tort." Until the general theory of contract was hurriedly run up late in the nineteenth century, tort had always been our residual category of civil liability. As the contract rules dissolve, it is becoming so again. * * *

* * * Classical contract theory might well be described as an attempt to stake out an enclave within the general domain of tort. The dykes which were set up to protect the enclave have, it is clear enough, been crumbling at a progressively rapid rate. With the growth of the ideas of quasi-contract and unjust enrichment,* classical consideration theory was breached on the benefit side. With the growth of the promissory estoppel idea,** it was breached on the detriment side. We are fast approaching the point where, to prevent unjust enrichment, any benefit received by a defendant must be paid for unless it was clearly meant as a gift; where any detriment reasonably incurred by a plaintiff in reliance on a defendant's assurances must be recompensed. When that point is reached, there is really no longer any viable distinction between liability in contract and liability in tort. * * * [T]he two fields, which had been artificially set apart, are gradually merging and becoming one.

* * *

We seem to be in the presence of the phenomenon which, in the history of comparative religion, is called syncretism—that is, according to Webster, "the reconciliation or union of conflicting beliefs." I have occasionally suggested to my students that a desirable reform in legal education would be to merge the first-year courses in Contracts and Torts into a single course which we could call Contorts. * * *

* * *

Let us assume, arguendo, that it is the fate of contract to be swallowed up by tort. * * * We must still provide ourselves with an

---

* E. g. § 89A of the *Restatement (Second)*.   ** E. g. § 90 of Restatements 1 and 2.

explanation of what contract—the classical or general theory of contract, as we have called it—was about in the first place and, if it is now dead or dying, what caused the fatal disease.

We started with Professor Friedman's suggestion that the "model" of classical contract theory bore a close resemblance to * * * laissez-faire—economic theory. * * * [A]s he put it, "parties could be treated as individual economic units which, in theory, enjoyed complete mobility and freedom of decision." I suppose that laissez-faire economic theory comes down to something like this: If we all do exactly as we please, no doubt everything will work out for the best. * * * [T]he lawyers and the economists, both responding to the same stimuli, produced theoretical systems which were harmonious with each other and which, in both cases, evidently responded to the felt needs of the time.

It seems apparent to the twentieth century mind, as perhaps it did not to the nineteenth century mind, that a system in which everybody is invited to do his own thing, at whatever cost to his neighbor, must work ultimately to the benefit of the rich and powerful, who are in a position to look after themselves and to act, so to say, as their own self-insurers. As we look back on the nineteenth century theories, we are struck most of all, I think, by the narrow scope of social duty which they implicitly assumed. * * * For good or ill, we have changed all that. * * * The decline and fall of the general theory of contract and, in most quarters, of laissez-faire economics may be taken as remote reflections of the transition from nineteenth century individualism to the welfare state and beyond.

* * *

The basic idea of the Langdellian revolution [consistent with the needs and beliefs of that age] seems to have been that there really is such a thing as the one true rule of law, universal and unchanging, always and everywhere the same—a sort of mystical absolute. To all of us, I dare say, the idea seems absurd. We are steeped in the idea that law is process, flux, change; our relativism admits no absolutes. * * *

For a riot of pure doctrine, nothing could have been better than Contract. Since there never had been a general theory of Contract before, there was nothing to inhibit the free play of the creative imagination * * *. Perhaps we must, after all, credit Langdell with a degree of genius for his perhaps instinctive choice of a non-existent field as the vehicle for the initial demonstration of the great theory that law is doctrine and nothing but doctrine—pure, absolute, abstract, scientific—a logician's dream of heaven. * * *

* * *

* * * We have become used to the idea that, in literature and the arts, there are alternating rhythms of classicism and romanti-

cism. During classical periods, which are, typically, of brief duration, everything is neat, tidy and logical; theorists and critics reign supreme * * *. During classical periods, which are, among other things, extremely dull, it seems that nothing interesting is ever going to happen again. But the classical aesthetic, once it has been formulated, regularly breaks down in a protracted romantic agony. The romantics * * * experiment, they improvise; they deny the existence of any rules; they churn around in an ecstacy of self-expression. At the height of a romantic period, everything is confused, sprawling, formless and chaotic—as well as, frequently, extremely interesting. Then, the romantic energy having spent itself, there is a new classical reformulation—and so the rhythms continue.

Perhaps we should admit the possibility of such alternating rhythms in the process of the law. * * * We have gone through our romantic agony—an experience peculiarly unsettling to people intellectually trained and conditioned as lawyers are. It may be that, in this centennial year, some new Langdell is already waiting in the wings * * *. Contract is dead—but who knows what unlikely resurrection the Easter-tide may bring?

NOTES AND QUESTIONS

1. Gilmore does not have much praise to lavish on Christopher Columbus Langdell. He suggests that Langdell had "no distinction," and that Langdell's version of the case method "had nothing to do with getting students to think for themselves" but instead was "a method of indoctrination through brainwashing." Is Gilmore right about Langdell's use of the case method? Does the use of it that you have seen seem different?

2. Gilmore suggests that according to Langdell, Holmes and Williston, the framers of the "classical theory" of contract, "The austerity of doctrine would not be tempered for the shorn lambs who might shiver in its blast." Does this sound like the law of contract that law students are trained in today, or that you are familiar with? Why might anyone conceive of such a law of contract? Does it bear any resemblance to the pre-New Deal Constitutional doctrines?

3. Why does Gilmore describe Corbin's treatise on contract law as "the greatest law book ever written?" Do you agree with this characterization? Where does this leave other celebrated law books, like the code of Justinian, Hammurabi's Code, or the Bible?

4. As you have seen, Gilmore suggests that Sections 75 and 90 of the *Restatement* cannot "live comfortably together," and that "in the end one must swallow the other up." Gilmore states about the framers of the Restatement who wrote Section 90 that "no one had any idea what the damn thing meant." It has been seriously maintained that many of Plato's dialogues can only be understood if they are perceived as pure farce. See, e. g., J. H. Randall, Jr., Plato: Dramatist of the Life of Reason, 124–127 (1970). Can the same be said of Grant Gilmore? What is the view of Professor Speidel, the author of the next excerpt, on this point?

5. Gilmore believes that his generation has lived through "a world-wide revolution, scientific, social, economic and political," and that the second Restatement of Contracts is the product of that Revolution. Is it correct to call what has happened in the last fifty years in America a "revolution"? Does this perhaps impart more legitimacy to the *Second Restatement* (and to the thought of Arthur Corbin?) than might be due if what has happened was *not* a "revolution?" Even if a "revolution" has come about, is it appropriate for the courts and the American Law Institute to implement its philosophy through changes in the law of contract? On the other hand, perhaps, as Professor Gilmore says in a part of this essay not reproduced here, the framers of the *Second Restatement* were merely "articulating the policy of the legislative reforms of the past thirty years or so." Would this cut for or against the legitimacy of the *Second Restatement* in the courts?

6. Would you like to be a student or Professor of "Contorts?"

RICHARD E. SPEIDEL, AN ESSAY ON THE REPORTED DEATH AND CONTINUED VITALITY OF CONTRACT*

27 Stanford Law Review 1161 (1975).

* * *

* * * To a contracts teacher who is not yet prepared to teach a course in "contorts," Professor Gilmore's gauntlet is painfully visible. So, with biases flying, let us do battle.

I. THE THESIS STATED

* * *

In the 1870's, the idea for a general theory of contract was conceived in Langdell's "casebook" laboratory at the Harvard Law School and, thereafter, was brilliantly reformulated by Holmes in his lectures on the common law and meticulously elaborated by Williston in his multivolume treatise on the law of contracts. The "balance wheel" of the new theory was consideration and the "metaphysical solvent" was the objective test. According to Gilmore, neither "wheel" nor "solvent" was rooted in case law or the real world. One has the impression of a theory conceived in the minds of East Coast magicians, supported by major surgery performed on the existing cases, and honed to a systematic and abstract construct fit only for the cloister or the classroom. And what was worse * * *, "generations of lawyers and judges and law professors grew up believing that the theory was true—and it is our beliefs, however absurd, that condition our actions."

The philosophical roots of this general contract theory lay in Holmes' basic approach to the problem of civil obligation. According to Gilmore, Holmes believed that the scope of liability should be narrow but, once imposed, liability should be absolute. However, absolute liability did not mean unlimited liability. Limitations upon the amount of liability, as well as a narrow scope of duty, were necessary so as not to deter socially useful action. The standards for liability should be "objective"—a failure to measure up to accepted community standards—and devoid of what Gilmore calls "the unnecessary and misleading overlay of moral sententiousness." * * *

* * *

Along with this construct, which narrowed the scope of legal protection, Holmes developed some ideas about damages for breach of contract. * * * Compensatory damages were the rule, specific performance the exception, and punishment to deter breach rarely, if ever, the objective. Holmes went even further. A promisor had a "right" to breach the contract and pay damages. * * *

* * * Why did the theory achieve such an emotional acceptance even though, as Gilmore aptly puts it, the courts frequently avoided doing on weekdays what they so eloquently preached on Sundays? * * *

* * * The clues * * * appear in the book as slogans: "positivism," "individualism," "laissez faire," "freedom of contract," and "certainty." * * * The combination of doctrinal analysis and these clues leads Gilmore to conclude: "The basic idea of the Langdellian revolution seems to have been that there really is such a thing as the one true rule of law, universal and unchanging, always and everywhere the same—a sort of mystical absolute." * * *

[But a]ccording to Gilmore, * * * the Holmes Williston construct was unable to survive the "transition from nineteenth century individualism to the welfare state and beyond." * * * Gilmore draws two major and almost gleeful conclusions from these developments. First, contract is dead because the bargain theory of consideration, its balance wheel, no longer rules in the formulation, performance, or adjustment of contracts. * * *

Second, instinctively and almostly unconsciously, contract is being absorbed into the mainstream of a more expansive theory of tort liability. * * *

II. THE THESIS EVALUATED

* * * I have some rather strong reactions to the method, thesis, and conclusions of this book. So I will proceed undaunted to express them, knowing full well that this is precisely what Professor Gilmore would want to happen. At the same time, I confess to an instinctive feeling that he will be amused by all of the reviewers who take him so seriously.

A. *Whatever Happened to 280 Years of American Legal and Economic History?*

* * * Using English cases, secondary sources, and impressionistic clues about the social matrix, * * * [Gilmore] has concluded that Holmes' creation of the bargain theory had little support in law or contemporary reality * * *.

A conclusion which is equally plausible is that 280 years of American economic and legal history had a strong impact upon the announcement, in 1881, of the bargain theory and upon its subsequent development. * * *

The bargain idea has enjoyed a striking persistence in American contract law. This is partially explained, no doubt, by its strong congruence with basic human behavior. * * * But the pervasiveness of this behavior does not fully explain why the concept of bargain and exchange should emerge as the primary legal technique for distinguishing between the enforceable and the unenforceable promise. The primary emphasis could have been placed upon induced reliance, formality (such as the sealed instrument), or ethical considerations rooted in expressions of the individual will.

A partial answer rests in the tangles of Anglo-American economic and legal history. According to Professor Ian Macneil, the "distinctively human" behavior of bargain and exchange flourishes when four conditions are present: (1) specialization of labor and exchange; (2) a sense by individuals of their capacity for choice and the consequences of its exercise; (3) an awareness of the continuum between past, present, and future; and (4) a social matrix which reinforces the exercise of choices made with an eye to the future.[43] * * *

From breakdowns in or excesses of this behavior, whether affecting individual interests or the broader social matrix, the need for contract law develops.

* * * Professor Macneil's four conditions apparently existed in the English trade fairs of the 12th and 13th centuries, for contract behavior flourished at that time. Also, the idea of bargain as a reason for enforcing promises was implicit in the developing common law well before the 17th century. Presumably, contract behavior persisted thereafter in England despite the procedural rigidity and ultimately preemptive quality of the common law. When English people colonized America in the 17th century, they encountered severe challenges to survival and discovered seemingly unlimited opportunities for individual expression and economic growth. In his remarkable *A History of American Law*, Professor Lawrence Friedman suggests that the colonists brought considerably less of the common law to

43. Macneil, The Many Futures of Contracts, 47 S.Cal.L.Rev. 691, 696–712 (1974).

America than is usually supposed. Instead, many turned to the bargain-oriented customs and practices of the law merchant, which had not yet been fully absorbed by the common law. * * * From the colonial period through the time of "manifest destiny" to the late 19th century, when the economic gains were being consolidated and evaluated, there occurred an explosion of contract behavior. The legal enforcement of promises represented a delegation of public force in the aid of private decisionmaking and, despite its uncertain origins, the doctrine of consideration evolved as a technique for market control. The consideration requirement "induced deliberation in the parties, limited law support to seriously intended undertakings, or refused the law's aid to unconscionable coercion." [49] In short, consideration and the objective test became very practical legal techniques used by courts to facilitate and regulate the important market transaction.

* * * Hurst and Friedman stress the practical uses of a doctrine assumed to mean "bargained for and given in exchange" * * *. As an operating principle, the "bargain" theory of consideration (1) provided a natural formality to channel human conduct and insure deliberation; (2) protected and structured the important market transaction; (3) expanded legal protection by supporting the executory exchange—a promise for a promise—and shielding the creative or idiosyncratic bargainer from later claims that the agreed exchange was disproportionate; and (4) permitted a fuller development of remedies that protected the plaintiff's expectation interest, that is, the value to the plaintiff of the agreed exchange.

It seems plausible to conclude that ideas about bargain were in the air in 1881 and that the winds from the frontier, if not the reported decisions, occasionally reached Boston. * * *

Viewed from this vantage point, although Holmes' leap from the English common law to the pages of The Common Law may be miraculous, a leap in 1880 from contemporary reality to the bargain theory was no leap at all. * * * In fact, it might be described as an intensely practical idea somewhat behind its time but sufficiently contemporary to insure quick acceptance by student, bench, and bar. At the same time, this thesis of evolution, while not salvaging Holmes's scholarship in The Common Law, is consistent with his perceived tendency "to make few affirmative proposals in the name of * * * social change" and to rely upon the "market place to produce ideas or policies for a given point in time."

* * * These factors—natural development and utility—bespeak a tradition of some durability. Traditions die hard, especially where market ideology and room for its exercise still remain. Since Professor Gilmore has slighted this dimension of the American past,

49. See J. W. Hurst, Law and the Conditions of Freedom in the Nineteenth-Century United States 11–12 (1956).

I think that he has branded the new child as illegitimate without taking all of the necessary blood tests. It remains to be seen whether the announcement of its death is exaggerated.

B. *Another Look at the Decline and Fall*

* * * Professor Gilmore is correct in concluding that something did go wrong with the bargain theory of consideration and the grand theory of which it was a part. Contract law cannot now, if it ever could, be explained by such phrases as an "objective manifestation of mutual assent to a bargain." Determining exactly what went wrong is important for understanding the forces at work during periods of rapid change and for providing a more solid platform for facing the future. * * *

* * * Professor Gilmore identifies a number of reasons for the deterioration of the bargain theory and the legal relationships it spawned. At one critical juncture he concludes that the Holmes-Williston construct could not survive the "transition from nineteenth century individualism to the welfare state and beyond." * * * What [this phrase] suggests to me is that as contract disputes reached the courts over time tension began to develop among the policies undergirding the grand theory—that is, policies associated with the maintenance and support of a free enterprise, market economy—and the perceived costs or excesses of that market system. These perceived excesses included the wasteful utilization and inefficient allocation by private parties of increasingly scarce resources, the accumulation and frequent abuse of strategic market power, and a growing disparity in wealth, capacity, and opportunity among those who used or, in some cases, were used by contract. While ill-suited for the task, courts were invited, along with other governmental agencies, to do battle with the "market gods."

Within and prompted by this tension, additional changes were in process which both help to explain why the grand theory deteriorated and provide an analytical window for viewing what lies "beyond." These changes included the development of a contextual approach to problems of contract law, the evolution of new or different forms of exchange relationships, and the steady intrusion of the legislative-administrative process into the arena once reserved for private bargainers and the courts.

The contextual approach focuses upon particular types of contracts within a relevant business or social setting rather than upon contracts in general. Instead of just contracts, there are contracts for the sale or lease of personal and real property, construction, personal and professional services, transportation, the creation of security interests, the organization of businesses, and the settlement of disputes. * * * Each context develops its own patterns, practices, and problems which, to a varying degree, influence particular exchange transactions. As the many studies of contract in context demonstrate, the pressure of reality has, among other things, influenced the courts and the legislatures to develop special rules for special problems and broad standards which are capable of particularization in each case.

From a contextual perspective, it is easier to detect and to evaluate changes in the character of the particular exchange relationship involved. According to Professor Macneil, the grand theory's emphasis upon mutual assent was based upon the assumption that the parties could or should presentiate, that is, express all of the material elements of the future exchange in the present agreement. In its extreme form, the transaction model from which this assumption derived was the "one shot deal" involving the sale of Dobbin or Blackacre. * * *

But the grand theory and its assumptions are hardly consistent with the dynamics of the long-term relationship between professor and university, husband and wife, union and corporation, supplier and middleman, government and shipbuilder, franchisor and franchisee, or two state-owned enterprises in a socialist economy. Although each relationship features contract behavior, the unwillingness or inability of the parties to "presentiate" requires, according to Macneil, the refinements of good-faith bargaining and mediation to achieve sound dispute settlement rather than the crude "either-or" approach of the common law. * * *

Within any particular context and regardless of the character of the exchange relationship, one must also determine the ever-increasing scope of preemption by the legislative-administrative process of the arena traditionally reserved for private bargainers and the courts. The regulatory intrusions—laws concerning antitrust, labor relations, consumer protection, welfare, environmental protection, licensing, land use, product safety, and insurance, to name a few—are responsive to the perceived costs or excesses of a free market system. The growing bulk of "uniform" laws, frequently in the common law tradition, stand as mute testimony to the conflict between the reality of national commerce and the decentralization of governmental power. * * *

[This] development also has long-range implications for the importance of contract law as applied by the courts. * * * To Friedman, the growth of the legislative-administrative process meant that the courts were relieved, in whole or part, of both the responsibility and the opportunity to formulate and apply broad policy through contract law. They became free to evolve doctrinal exceptions or new techniques to achieve fairness in particular cases. * * *

* * * [Bearing all of this in mind, it becomes easier to predict the future course of contract jurisprudence:] the court can play a more responsive role if it will, first, try to determine the extent to which the particular dispute is related to or a product of one or more

excesses of the market system. This determination * * * sharpens the policy issues and assists the court in deciding whether the primary task will be merely to find and implement the "intention of the parties" or to function in a regulatory mode. Equally important, the court must place the transaction from which the dispute arose into relevant context, evaluate its relational characteristics, and ascertain the extent to which the legislative process has preempted or otherwise surrounded the particular issue in dispute. When this is done, the stage is better set for resolving the dispute in the reality of the present and with an eye to the future.

C. *Whither Tort? (Or, What Happened to Consent?)*

* * * [Gilmore argues that] the future of contract is in tort, or something very much like it. This has the ring of a good idea. Unfortunately, Professor Gilmore fails to provide a systematic analysis of * * * the expanding conception of tort * * *. [Speidel argues that the only evidence of "creeping tortism" which Gilmore provides are Sections 89A and 90 of *Restatement 2nd* and related cases, and that these are not enough to substantiate contract's obituary.]

* * * Professor Gilmore's leap from the somewhat exaggerated report of the death of contract to the strong hint that tort will swallow the residue seems to rival the alleged gargantuan leap of Holmes. Something is missing. In the transition from the imperatives of the grand theory to the duties of the welfare state, what happened to freedom of contract? * * *

Individual consent is still of dominant importance in law. To illustrate from the problems discussed by Professor Gilmore, suppose that the Officious Lawn Service Company has, without invitation, mowed the shaggy lawn of Arthur, who was on vacation. Even though Arthur has no choice but to receive the "benefit" of that service, it seems highly unlikely that he will be liable to Officious in quasi-contract or anything else. His problem begins only if, for any reason, he makes a promise to pay for the service. While section 89A of the second Restatement retreats from the bargain theory, it must be activated by a promise which, in turn, is evidence that Arthur has exercised choice. * * * But without the exercise of choice, there is no hint in the cases or the Restatement that a duty to disgorge the benefit will be imposed upon Arthur * * *.

Suppose, again, that Uncle Samuel promises his favorite nephew Christopher $2,000 with which to buy a car. Relying on this promise, Christopher visits a dealer and puts down $300 of his own money, signs a contract to pay $1,200 with interest in installments, and takes delivery of a car. If Uncle then refuses to pay, it seems clear that Nephew has an appealing claim in promissory estoppel, although perhaps not for the entire $2,000. * * * But if Uncle Samuel had conditioned his promise upon Nephew Christopher's earning a grade of B or better in Professor Holmes's course in Common Law Miracles and Christopher earned a C, the framework for discussion would change. Uncle's use of promissory language would not be careless and Christopher's premature reliance would be neither foreseeable nor justified. * * *

The limitations on promissory liability discussed above are, of course, implicit in Gilmore's discussion. But the claim of "creeping tortism" is not explicitly tested against the continued efficacy of choices not to engage in contract behavior or express conditions employed by those who play the market game. * * *

This essay is too brief to venture a comprehensive answer to the question of what, if anything, remains of consent in contract law. However, it is useful to identify a few of the relevant considerations.

The issue will arise in litigation where one party engaged in contract behavior asserts some form of assent either to avoid liability or to impose it upon the other party. One form of avoidance—freedom from contract—involves the benefit conferred without request [as codified in § 89A]. The absence of any expression of assent is critical here. A variation on this theme involves an explicit refusal by one party to engage in contract behavior with another. Although freedom from contract is the rule in these situations, the antitrust laws proscribe certain concerted refusals to deal, and insurance statutes sometimes impose restraints upon the ability of an insurance company to refuse to renew a policy. * * *

The more typical form of avoidance involves the attempt by one party to withdraw without liability from an existing relationship by relying upon an express condition which has apparently failed. One example of this is the problem of Uncle Samuel and Nephew Christopher, previously discussed. More commonly, the issue is raised by the attempted withdrawal from an exchange relationship, either before or after the contract is formed [on the basis of some express condition in the contract or offer.] [T]he quality of the expressed condition determines the freedom from contract liability.

The other side of the coin involves the effort of one party to enforce (impose, if you like) terms, whether involving performance or remedy, to which the other party has apparently assented. * * *

Assuming that the issue of "freedom from or freedom to" arises beyond the scope of direct legislative or administrative regulation, by what standards will the efficacy of the critical manifestation of assent be tested? * * * If the defendant is a consumer who, without any bargaining or informed choice, has accepted terms drafted by and for the plaintiff, explaining what amounts to a unilateral imposition in terms of consent seems to be inappropriate. On the other hand, the concept of consent may be irrelevant because the parties were unable or unwilling to presentiate the critical terms to the time when performance commenced. Expressions of intent come later, where the emphasis should be upon the quality of bargaining under relational duties such as the "duty" to bargain in good faith, imposed by the court. It seems clear, then, that the standards for testing the range of freedom from and freedom to contract will develop in the undifferentiated group of transactions between the extremes of unilateral imposition and the unpresentiated relationship.

At this point in time one can perceive in the cases and law reviews a growing agitation to replace the dubious "duty to read" test with a new model of consent. The emphasis is upon the quality of the process whereby consent is manifested. Thus, the party seeking to avoid or impose liability must communicate in such a manner that the other party, considering his particular circumstances, has a realistic opportunity to read and to understand. * * * Even if the other party is more or less fully informed, he may, because of pressure from the moving party or other circumstances, have a lessened capacity to make a real choice. * * * Of course, when the moving party's manifestation is defectively or incompletely expressed, the door is open for the court to engage in purposeful interpretation, "gap filling," and the development of what might be called relational duties, such as the "duty" to disclose material facts, bargain or act in good faith, and cooperate during performance. * * *

This * * * suggests that Professor Gilmore's instincts about radically new forms of civil liability are sound. Within the large area still affected by theories about bargaining and consent, the incidence of what might be called relational rather than tort duties will be high. But these duties are part of an effort to redefine the conditions of freedom in a process where a high value is still placed upon consent. In the area where contract behavior is still valuable for attaining legitimate ends, theories about consent will remain staples in the judicial arsenal. These staples should assist in defining the principles of fairness and efficiency that ought to characterize the process of private exchange in a changing society. The effort to define and justify those principles is worthwhile, for beyond the welfare state lies a "grants" economy and, ultimately, government ownership of sources of production and supply. While there will be contract behavior in the beyond, an unthinking imposition of the new social contract may result in irreparable loss of individual freedom.

III. CONCLUSION

* * *

* * * In my heart of hearts, I do not believe that Professor Gilmore intended to equate the "death" of consideration with the death of freedom in exchange transactions or to suggest that the existence of that freedom is inconsistent with justice. But something happened on his journey from the excesses of the grand theory to the duties of the "new" tort. Although the trip was fun, the announce-

ments by the driver were not always complete and at times were less than reassuring. Perhaps pessimism is the dominant note of our times. But my preferences are for a more constructive tune, played perhaps on a Scottish bagpipe.

NOTES AND QUESTIONS

1. Professor Speidel seems to suggest that perhaps Gilmore is not meant to be taken too seriously. Why not? How is it that Speidel believes Gilmore's inaccuracies in reporting the past lead him to misconstrue the future of contract law?

2. Speidel occasionally speaks a strange language, talking of the "social matrix," of "presentiation," and of "relational characteristics." Where does this language come from, and does it have anything to do with the "constructive tune, played perhaps on a Scottish bagpipe," which Speidel prefers? Why do you suppose Speidel has no intention of becoming a Professor of "contorts?"

3. Grant Gilmore's latest word on the future of Contracts comes in Gilmore, Introduction to Havingurst's Limitations Upon Freedom of Contract, 1979 Ariz.St.L.J. 165, 166:

> In the 1970's we have entered the era of Tragic Choices—which is the title Guido Calabresi and Philip Bobbitt chose for a book, published in 1978, which they subtitled: The conflicts society confronts in the allocation of tragically scarce resources. There is not, there will not be—ever—enough to go around. The dream—if it was a noble dream—that the day will come when everyone can do exactly as he pleases without inflicting harm on his neighbor has proven to be a dream. We shall be presently rethinking our ideas about everything—including contract. Our range of choice will be progressively narrowed. It is unlikely that the nineteenth century idea of freedom of contract will have any role to play in the twenty-first century.*

Is this perspective compatible with that of Speidel? What form would a "law" of contract without "freedom of contract" take?

KIRKSEY v. KIRKSEY

Supreme Court of Alabama, 1845.
8 Ala. 131.

Assumpsit by the defendant, against the plaintiff in error. The question is presented in this Court, upon a case agreed, which shows the following facts:

The plaintiff was the wife of defendant's brother, but had for some time been a widow, and had several children. In 1840, the plaintiff resided on public land, under a contract of lease * * * and was comfortably settled, and would have attempted to secure the land she lived on. The defendant resided in Talladega county, some sixty, or seventy miles off. On the 10th October, 1840, he wrote to her the following letter:

"Dear sister Antillico—Much to my mortification, I heard, that brother Henry was dead, and one of his children. I know that your situation is one of grief, and difficulty. You had a bad chance before, but a great deal worse now. I should like to come and see you, but cannot with convenience at present. * * * I do not know whether you have a preference on the place you live on, or not. If you had, I would advise you to obtain your preference, and sell the land and quit the country, as I understand it is very unhealthy, and I know society is very bad. If you will come down and see me, I will let you have a place to raise your family, and I have more open land than I can tend; and on the account of your situation, and that of your family, I feel like I want you and the children to do well."

Within a month or two after the receipt of this letter, the plaintiff abandoned her possession, without disposing of it, and removed with her family, to the residence of the defendant, who put her in comfortable houses, and gave her land to cultivate for two years, at the end of which time he notified her to remove, and put her in a house, not comfortable, in the woods, which he afterwards required her to leave.

A verdict being found for the plaintiff, for two hundred dollars, the above facts were agreed, and if they will sustain the action, the judgment is to be affirmed, otherwise it is to be reversed.

ORMOND, J. The inclination of my mind, is, that the loss and inconvenience, which the plaintiff sustained in breaking up, and moving to the defendant's, a distance of sixty miles, is a sufficient consideration to support the promise, to furnish her with a house, and land to cultivate, until she could raise her family. My brothers, however, think that the promise on the part of the defendant, was a mere gratuity, and that an action will not lie for its breach. The judgment of the Court below must therefore be reversed * * *.

NOTES AND QUESTIONS

1. This case was decided a generation before the "Holmes-Williston construct" was conceived. Does it suggest to you that Gilmore was correct or incorrect about the "classical contract theory" being without case-law foundation?

2. How would you have decided this case? Do you believe that there was a "contract" in the case? What do you suppose the word "contract," had come to mean by 1845? How do you account for the fact that a verdict was found for the plaintiff in the trial court? Judge Ormond would be prepared to find "sufficient consideration" in Sister Antillico's "moving to the defendant's." Why do his "brothers" disagree? How would the case be decided under the *Restatement*?

3. Compare the model of "contract" that seems to exist in Kirksey v. Kirksey with that in the next case, an opinion by the apostle of the constitutional jurisprudence of "goodness," Judge J. Skelly Wright.

WILLIAMS v. WALKER–THOMAS FURNITURE CO.

United States Court of Appeals for the District of Columbia Circuit, 1965.
350 F.2d 445.

J. Skelly WRIGHT, Circuit Judge:

Appellee, Walker-Thomas Furniture Company, operates a retail furniture store in the District of Columbia. During the period from 1957 to 1962 each appellant in these cases purchased a number of household items from Walker-Thomas, for which payment was to be made in installments. The terms of each purchase were contained in a printed form contract which set forth the value of the purchased item and purported to lease the item to appellant for a stipulated monthly rent payment. The contract then provided, in substance, that title would remain in Walker-Thomas until the total of all the monthly payments made equaled the stated value of the item, at which time appellants could take title. In the event of a default in the payment of any monthly installment, Walker-Thomas could repossess the item.

The contract further provided that "the amount of each periodical installment payment to be made by [purchaser] to the Company under this present lease shall be inclusive of and not in addition to the amount of each installment payment to be made by [purchaser] under such prior leases, bills or accounts; *and all payments now and hereafter made by [purchaser] shall be credited pro rata on all outstanding leases, bills and accounts* due the Company by [purchaser] at the time each such payment is made." (Emphasis added.) The effect of this rather obscure provision was to keep a balance due on every item purchased until the balance due on all items, whenever purchased, was liquidated. As a result, the debt incurred at the time of purchase of each item was secured by the right to repossess all the items previously purchased by the same purchaser, and each new item purchased automatically became subject to a security interest arising out of the previous dealings.

* * * [O]n April 17, 1962, appellant Williams bought a stereo set of stated value of $514.95.[1] She * * * defaulted shortly thereafter, and appellee sought to replevy all the items purchased since December, 1957. The Court of General Sessions granted judgment for appellee. The District of Columbia Court of Appeals affirmed, and we granted appellants' motion for leave to appeal to this court.

1. At the time of this purchase her account showed a balance of $164 still owing from her prior purchases. The total of all the purchases made over the years in question came to $1,800. The total payments amounted to $1,400.

Appellants' principal contention, rejected by both the trial and the appellate courts below, is that these contracts, or at least some of them, are unconscionable and, hence, not enforceable. In its opinion in Williams v. Walker-Thomas Furniture Company, 198 A.2d 914, 916 (1964), the District of Columbia Court of Appeals explained its rejection of this contention as follows:

> * * * The record reveals that prior to the last purchase appellant had reduced the balance in her account to $164. The last purchase, a stereo set, raised the balance due to $678. Significantly, at the time of this and the preceding purchases, appellee was aware of appellant's financial position. The reverse side of the stereo contract listed the name of appellant's social worker and her $218 monthly stipend from the government. Nevertheless, with the full knowledge that appellant had to feed, clothe and support both herself and seven children on this amount, appellee sold her a $514 stereo set.

> We cannot condemn too strongly appellee's conduct. It raises serious questions of sharp practice and irresponsible business dealings. A review of the legislation in the District of Columbia affecting retail sales and the pertinent decisions of the highest court in this jurisdiction disclose, however, no ground upon which this court can declare the contracts in question contrary to public policy. * * * We think Congress should consider corrective legislation to protect the public from such exploitive contracts as were utilized in the case at bar.

We do not agree that the court lacked the power to refuse enforcement to contracts found to be unconscionable. In other jurisdictions, it has been held as a matter of common law that unconscionable contracts are not enforceable. While no decision of this court so holding has been found, the notion that an unconscionable bargain should not be given full enforcement is by no means novel. In Scott v. United States, 79 U.S. (12 Wall.) 443, 445, 20 L.Ed. 438 (1870), the Supreme Court stated:

> * * * If a contract be unreasonable and unconscionable, but not void for fraud, a court of law will give to the party who sues for its breach damages, not according to its letter, but only such as he is equitably entitled to. * * *

Since we have never adopted or rejected such a rule, the question here presented is actually one of first impression.

Congress has recently enacted the Uniform Commercial Code, which specifically provides that the court may refuse to enforce a contract which it finds to be unconscionable at the time it was made. 28 D.C.Code § 2–302 (Supp. IV 1965). The enactment of this section, which occurred subsequent to the contracts here in suit, does not mean that the common law of the District of Columbia was otherwise at the time of enactment, nor does it preclude the court from adopting a similar rule in the exercise of its powers to develop the common law for the District of Columbia. In fact, in view of the absence of prior authority on the point, we consider the congressional adoption of § 2–302 persuasive authority for following the rationale of the cases from which the section is explicitly derived. Accordingly, we hold that where the element of unconscionability is present at the time a contract is made, the contract should not be enforced.

Unconscionability has generally been recognized to include an absence of meaningful choice on the part of one of the parties together with contract terms which are unreasonably favorable to the other party. Whether a meaningful choice is present in a particular case can only be determined by consideration of all the circumstances surrounding the transaction. In many cases the meaningfulness of the choice is negated by a gross inequality of bargaining power. The manner in which the contract was entered is also relevant to this consideration. Did each party to the contract, considering his obvious education or lack of it, have a reasonable opportunity to understand the terms of the contract, or were the important terms hidden in a maze of fine print and minimized by deceptive sales practices? Ordinarily, one who signs an agreement without full knowledge of its terms might be held to assume the risk that he has entered a one-sided bargain. But when a party of little bargaining power, and hence little real choice, signs a commercially unreasonable contract with little or no knowledge of its terms, it is hardly likely that his consent * * * was ever given to all the terms. In such a case the usual rule that the terms of the agreement are not to be questioned should be abandoned and the court should consider whether the terms of the contract are so unfair that enforcement should be withheld.

In determining reasonableness or fairness, the primary concern must be with the terms of the contract considered in light of the circumstances existing when the contract was made. The test is not simple, nor can it be mechanically applied. The terms are to be considered "in the light of the general commercial background and the commercial needs of the particular trade or case." Corbin suggests the test as being whether the terms are "so extreme as to appear unconscionable according to the mores and business practices of the time and place." 1 Corbin, Contracts § 128 (1963). We think this formulation correctly states the test to be applied in those cases where no meaningful choice was exercised upon entering the contract.

Because the trial court and the appellate court did not feel that enforcement could be refused, no findings were made on the possible unconscionability of the contracts in these cases. Since the record is not sufficient for our deciding the issue as a matter of law, the cases must be remanded to the trial court for further proceedings.

So ordered.

DANAHER, Circuit Judge (dissenting): The District of Columbia Court of Appeals obviously was as unhappy about the situation here presented as any of us can possibly be. Its opinion * * * concludes: "We think Congress should consider corrective legislation to protect the public from such exploitive contracts as were utilized in the case at bar."

My view is thus summed up by an able court which made no finding that there had actually been sharp practice. Rather the appellant seems to have known precisely where she stood.

There are many aspects of public policy here involved. What is a luxury to some may seem an outright necessity to others. Is public oversight to be required of the expenditures of relief funds? A washing machine, e. g., in the hands of a relief client might become a fruitful source of income. Many relief clients may well need credit, and certain business establishments will take long chances on the sale of items, expecting their pricing policies will afford a degree of protection commensurate with the risk. Perhaps a remedy when necessary will be found within the provisions of the "Loan Shark" law, D.C.Code §§ 26–601 et seq. (1961).

I mention such matters only to emphasize the desirability of a cautious approach to any such problem, particularly since the law for so long has allowed parties such great latitude in making their own contracts. I dare say there must annually be thousands upon thousands of installment credit transactions in this jurisdiction, and one can only speculate as to the effect the decision in these cases will have.

I join the District of Columbia Court of Appeals in its disposition of the issues.

PATTERSON v. WALKER–THOMAS FURNITURE CO.

District of Columbia Court of Appeals, 1971.
277 A.2d 111.

KELLY, Associate Judge.

 * * * [T]he appellant, Mrs. Bernice Patterson, bought merchandise from appellee in three separate transactions during 1968. In January she bought an 18-inch Emerson portable television, with stand, for $295.95, signing an installment contract which obligated her to pay appellee $20 a month on account. In March she bought a five-piece dinette set for $119.95, increasing her monthly payments to $24. In July she purchased a set of wedding rings for $159.95 and the payments rose to $25 per month. The total price for all the goods,

including sales tax, was $597.25. Mrs. Patterson defaulted in her payments after she had paid a total of $248.40 toward the agreed purchase price.

Appellant answered Walker-Thomas' action to recover the unpaid balance on the contracts by claiming, in pertinent part, that she had paid an amount in excess of the fair value of the goods received and that the goods themselves were so grossly overpriced as to render the contract terms unconscionable and the contracts unenforceable under the Uniform Commercial Code as enacted in the District of Columbia.[3]

Objections to interrogatories addressed to appellee in an effort to establish her defense that the goods were in fact grossly overpriced were sustained, the court ruling in part that the information sought was outside the scope of discovery "because the defense of unconscionability based on price is not recognized in this jurisdiction". It ruled further "that certain information sought was readily obtainable to defendant by resort to the contracts admittedly in her possession and that certain of the interrogatories amounted to 'harassment of the business community'."

Appellant persisted in her efforts to present the defense of unconscionability by issuing a subpoena *duces tecum* for the production of appellee's records, and, alleging indigency, by moving for the appointment of a special master or expert witness to establish the value of the goods, the price Walker-Thomas paid for them, and their condition (whether new or secondhand) when she purchased them. The pretrial judge quashed the subpoena *duces tecum* on the ground that appellant was precluded from obtaining the same information by means of the subpoena that she had been denied through the use of interrogatories. The motion to appoint a special master or expert witness was also denied.

A trial judge subsequently held that the prior rulings of the motions judge and the pretrial judge established the law of the case. Inasmuch as appellant's then sole defense was that the goods were grossly overpriced and no proof on this issue was presented, the court entered judgment for appellee. We affirm.

Suggested guidelines for deciding whether or not a contract is unconscionable appear in Williams v. Walker-Thomas Furniture Co.,

---

3. D.C.Code 1967, § 28:2–302. Unconscionable contract or clause.

(1) If the court as a matter of law finds the contract or any clause of the contract to have been unconscionable at the time it was made the court may refuse to enforce the contract, or it may enforce the remainder of the contract without the unconscionable clause, or it may so limit the application of any unconscionable clause as to avoid any unconscionable result.

(2) When it is claimed or appears to the court that the contract or any clause thereof may be unconscionable the parties shall be afforded a reasonable opportunity to present evidence as to its commercial setting, purpose and effect to aid the court in making the determination.

* * *. [The court then quotes several paragraphs of Judge Wright's opinion.]

* * * [C]iting *Williams* in another context, this court said that "two elements are required to exist to prove unconscionability; i. e., 'an absence of meaningful choice on the part of one of the parties together with contract terms which are *unreasonably favorable to the other party.*'" Diamond Housing Corp. v. Robinson, D.C.App., 257 A.2d 492, 493 (1969). (Emphasis in the original.)

On the basis of these authorities we conclude that in a proper case gross overpricing may be raised in defense as an element of unconscionability. Under the test outlined in *Williams* price is necessarily an element to be examined when determining whether a contract is reasonable. The Corbin test mentioned in the opinion specifically deals with the "terms" of the contract and certainly the price one pays for an item is one of the more important terms of any contract. We emphasize, however, that price as an unreasonable contract term is only one of the elements which underpin proof of unconscionability. Specifically, therefore, in the instant case the reasonableness of the contracts is not to be gauged by an examination of the price stipulation alone or any other term of the contract without parallel consideration being given to whether or not appellant exercised a meaningful choice in entering into the contracts.

We conclude also that because excessive price-value may comprise one element of unconscionability, discovery techniques may be employed to garner information relevant to that issue for purposes of defense. By statute, upon a claim of unconscionability, the court determines as a matter of law whether a contract or any clause thereof is unconscionable *only* after the parties have been given a reasonable opportunity to present evidence as to its commercial setting, purpose and effect. Certainly, therefore, interrogatories may be used to develop evidence of the commercial setting, purpose and effect of a contract at the time it was made in order to assure an effective presentation of the defense at an evidentiary hearing.

In our judgment, however, appellant here was not erroneously precluded from developing evidence through the use of interrogatories by the ruling of the trial court.

[W]e are * * * of the opinion that a sufficient factual predicate for the defense must be alleged before wholesale discovery is allowed. An unsupported conclusory allegation in the answer that a contract is unenforceable as unconscionable is not enough. Sufficient facts surrounding the "commercial setting, purpose and effect" of a contract at the time it was made should be alleged so that the court may form a judgment as to the existence of a valid claim of unconscionability and the extent to which discovery of evidence to support that claim should be allowed.

Admittedly, appellant neither alleged nor attempted to prove the existence of any fraud, duress or coercion when she entered into the instant contracts. Her verified complaint alleges only that the goods she purchased and still retains were grossly overpriced and that she has already paid appellee a sum in excess of their fair value. These are conclusions without factual support. It cannot be said that the goods were grossly overpriced merely from an examination of the prices which appear on the face of the contracts. No other term of the contract is alleged to be unconscionable, nor is an absence of meaningful choice claimed. We hold that the two elements of which unconscionability is comprised; namely, an absence of meaningful choice and contract terms unreasonably favorable to the other party, must be particularized in some detail before a merchant is required to divulge his pricing policies through interrogatories or through the production of records in court. An answer, such as the one here, asserting the affirmative defense of unconscionability only on the basis of a stated conclusion that the price is excessive is insufficient.

Accordingly, the judgment of the trial court is

Affirmed.

NOTES AND QUESTIONS

1. Is there a different ordering of fundamental contract values in Judge Wright's opinion in *Williams* from that in Kirksey v. Kirksey? How would you describe the difference?

2. Even the District of Columbia Court of Appeals, which thought that it was without the legal power to grant relief to consumers like Mrs. Williams, condemned the conduct of Walker-Thomas as "sharp practice," "irresponsible business dealings," and the utilization of "exploitive contracts." Is this conclusion inescapable?

3. What, precisely, does Judge Wright hold in the *Williams* case? Is it that the contracts in question were unconscionable, or is the holding less specific? What do you make of the following reasoning that Judge Wright advances in support of his conclusion: " * * * in view of the absence of prior authority on the point, we consider the congressional adoption of Section 2–302 persuasive authority for following the rationale of the cases from which the section is explicitly derived." Note that the congressional act adopting the UCC was passed *after* Mrs. Williams' purchase. Is there a slip in Wright's reasoning? Why didn't Judge Danaher agree with this "persuasive authority" notion? Would Judge Ormond's "brothers" approve?

4. Applying Judge Wright's suggested tests to the facts of *Williams* as you might imagine them to be, do you think the contract was "unconscionable?"

5. Shortly after the Williams case, Congress reorganized the courts of the District of Columbia. Before the reorganization, the Federal Court of Appeals functioned more or less like a state Supreme Court for the District of Columbia in both civil and criminal matters, and, as you saw

in *Williams,* the federal appeals court took appeals from the District of Columbia inferior trial courts. After the reorganization, the federal courts were more restricted to exclusively federal matters, a new "Supreme" court was instituted in the District of Columbia system to handle appeals, and ordinary matters of civil and criminal law were, presumably, to be kept out of the federal courts to the same extent which they would be in any analogous state system. Would you have agreed or disagreed with the framers of the District of Columbia Court Reorganization Act?

6. Why do you suppose that the *Patterson* case has been called the "revenge of Walker-Thomas?" Does the District of Columbia Court of Appeals follow Judge Wright's opinion in *Williams*? Would Judge Wright have been pleased with this result?

WEISZ v. PARKE–BERNET GALLERIES, INC.

Civil Court, City of New York, 1971.
67 Misc.2d 1077, 325 N.Y.S.2d 576.

Leonard H. SANDLER, Judge.

On May 16, 1962, Dr. Arthur Weisz attended an auction conducted by the Parke-Bernet Galleries, Inc., where he ultimately bought for the sum of $3,347.50 a painting listed in the auction catalogue as the work of Raoul Dufy. Some two years later, on May 13, 1964, David and Irene Schwartz bought for $9,360.00 at a Parke-Bernet auction a painting also listed in the catalogue as the work of Raoul Dufy.

Several years after the second auction, as a result of an investigation conducted by the New York County District Attorney's office, the plaintiffs received information that the paintings were in fact forgeries. When this was called to Parke-Bernet's attention, Parke-Bernet denied any legal responsibility, asserting among other things that the Conditions of Sale for both auctions included a disclaimer of warranty as to genuineness, authorship and the like.

Following a formal demand by the plaintiffs for return of the purchase price, these two lawsuits were commenced against Parke-Bernet. * * * Juries having been waived, both cases were tried jointly.

* * * [T]he catalogue listing "Raoul Dufy" is asserted to constitute an express warranty, as that term was defined under the former Sales Act, in effect when the auctions took place. Former Personal Property Law, Sec. 93.

* * *

* * * I find that the following facts were quite clearly established by the evidence.

(1). Each of the plaintiffs bought the paintings in question in the belief that they were painted by Raoul Dufy, had formed this conclusion because Parke-Bernet so stated in the respective catalogues, and would not have bought the paintings if they were not believed to be genuine.

(2). At the time of the auctions Parke-Bernet also believed the paintings ascribed to Dufy in the catalogues were his work.

(3). Neither of the paintings was in fact painted by Dufy. Both are forgeries with negligible commercial value.

The most substantial of the defenses interposed by Parke-Bernet is that the Conditions of Sale for the auctions, appearing on a preliminary page of each catalogue, included a disclaimer of any warranty and that the plaintiffs are bound by its terms.

*   *   *

Although the auctions were separated in time by two years, the catalogues were quite similar in all legally significant respects, and the basic auction procedure was the same.

The catalogues open with several introductory pages of no direct relevance to the lawsuits. There then follows a page headed "Conditions of Sale", in large black print, under which some 15 numbered paragraphs appear, covering the side of one page and most of a second side. These provisions are in clear black print, somewhat smaller than the print used in the greater part of the catalogue.

Paragraph 2, on which Parke-Bernet relies, provides as follows:

> The Galleries has endeavored to catalogue and describe the property correctly, but all property is sold "as is" and neither the Galleries nor its consignor warrants or represents, and they shall in no event be responsible for, the correctness of description, genuineness, authorship, provenience or condition of the property, and no statement contained in the catalogue or made orally at the sale or elsewhere shall be deemed to be such a warranty or representation, or an assumption of liability.

The next page in each catalogue is headed "List of Artists", and contains in alphabetical order, one under the other, a list of the artists with a catalogue number or numbers appearing on the same line with the named artist. The implicit affirmation that the listed artists are represented in the auction and that the catalogue numbers appearing after their names represent their work could scarcely be clearer.

The name Raoul Dufy is listed in each catalogue, together with several catalogue numbers.

After the pages on which the artists are listed, over 80 pages follow in each catalogue on which the catalogue numbers appear in numerical order with descriptive material about the artist and the work.

Turning in each catalogue to the catalogue numbers for the paintings involved in the lawsuits, there appears on the top of the page a conventional black-and-white catalogue reproduction of the painting, directly under it the catalogue number in brackets, and the name RAOUL DUFY in large black print followed in smaller print by the words "French 1880–1953".

On the next line the catalogue number is repeated together with the name of the painting, a description of it, and the words, "Signed at lower right RAOUL DUFY." Finally, there appears a note that a certificate by M. Andre Pacitti will be given to the purchaser.

The procedure followed at both auctions was to announce at the beginning of the auction that it was subject to the conditions of sale, without repeating the announcement, and at no point alluding directly to the disclaimer.

As to the first auction, I am satisfied that Dr. Weisz did not in fact know of the Conditions of Sale and may not properly be charged with knowledge of its contents. I accept as entirely accurate his testimony that on his prior appearances at Parke-Bernet auctions he had not made any bids, and that on the occasion of his purchase he did not observe the Conditions of Sale and was not aware of its existence.

The test proposed for this kind of issue by Williston, quite consistent with the decided cases, is whether "the person * * * should as a reasonable man understand that it contains terms of the contract that he must read at his peril." 1 Williston on Contracts Section 90D (1937). * * *

The most obvious characteristic of the two Parke-Bernet auctions is that they attracted people on the basis of their interest in owning works of art, not on the basis of their legal experience or business sophistication. Surely it is unrealistic to assume that people who bid at such auctions will ordinarily understand that a gallery catalogue overwhelmingly devoted to descriptions of works of art also includes on its preliminary pages conditions of sale. Even less reasonable does it seem to me to expect a bidder at such an auction to appreciate the possibility that the conditions of sale would include a disclaimer of liability for the accuracy of the basic information presented throughout the catalogue in unqualified form with every appearance of certainty and reliability.

For someone in Dr. Weisz's position to be bound by conditions of sale, of which he in fact knew nothing, considerably more was required of Parke-Bernet to call those Conditions of Sale to his attention than occurred here.

The cases relied upon by Parke-Bernet where buyers were held to be bound by conditions of sale in auction catalogues are not at all apposite. For one thing, in only one of the cases does the opinion recite that the buyer flatly denied knowledge of the provision. * * * And in that case the buyer, a frequent bidder at the auction in question, acknowledged that he knew there were conditions of sale but had not undertaken to become familiar with them. More importantly, these auction cases for the most part concern business auctions, in which sellers and buyers were part of a business grouping in which a general knowledge of the governing rules and usages was reasonably to be anticipated. * * *

As to the Schwartz case, I am satisfied from the evidence that Mrs. Schwartz knew of the Conditions of Sale, and that both Schwartz plaintiffs are chargeable with that knowledge since they both participated in the purchase.

This factual conclusion leads to consideration of the extremely interesting question whether the language of disclaimer relied upon as a bar to the actions should be deemed effective for that purpose. No case has come to my attention that squarely presents the issue raised by the underlying realities of this case.

What is immediately apparent from any review of the evidence is that notwithstanding the language of disclaimer, Parke-Bernet expected that bidders at its auctions would rely upon the accuracy of its descriptions, and intended that they should. Parke-Bernet, as the evidence confirms, is an exceedingly well-known gallery, linked in the minds of people with the handling, exhibition and sale of valuable artistic works and invested with an aura of expertness and reliability. The very fact that Parke-Bernet was offering a work of art for sale would inspire confidence that it was genuine and that the listed artist in fact was the creator of the work.

The wording of the catalogue was clearly designed to emphasize the genuineness of the works to be offered. The list of artists followed by catalogue numbers, the black-and-white reproductions of the more important works, the simple listing of the name of the artist with the years of his birth and death could not have failed to impress upon the buyer that these facts could be relied on and that one could safely part with large sums of money in the confident knowledge that a genuine artistic work was being acquired.

Where one party in a contractual relationship occupies a position of superior knowledge and experience, and where that superior knowledge is relied upon and intended to be relied upon by the other, surely more is required for an effective disclaimer than appears here.

After reassuring the reader that Parke-Bernet endeavored to catalogue the works of art correctly, there follow highly technical and legalistic words of disclaimer in a situation in which plain and emphatic words are required. And this provision, in light of the critical importance to the buyer of a warning that he may not rely on the fact that a work attributed to an artist was in fact his creation, is in no way given the special prominence that it clearly requires.

The language used, the understated manner of its presentation, the failure to refer to it explicitly in the preliminary oral announcement at the auction all lead to the conclusion that Parke-Bernet did not expect the bidders to take the disclaimer too seriously or to be too concerned about it. I am convinced that the average reader of this provision would view it as some kind of technicality that should in no way derogate from the certainty that he was buying genuine artistic works, and that this was precisely the impression intended to be conveyed.

In denying legal effect to the disclaimer I am acting consistently with a whole body of law that reflects an increasing sensitivity to the requirements of fair dealing where there is a relationship between parties in which there is a basic inequality of knowledge, expertness or economic power. * * *

* * *

Judgment may be entered for the plaintiff Weisz against Parke-Bernet in the sum of $3,347.50, and for the plaintiffs David and Irene Schwartz in the sum of $9,360.00, both judgments of course with appropriate interest and costs. * * *

NOTES AND QUESTIONS

1. Professor Speidel suggests that the future course of contract law lies in refining notions about "freedom from contract," and in developing a sophisticated model of "consent," one which would seek to exclude transactions where the elements of "unfair oppression" or "unfair surprise" are present. Does the *Weisz* court help in developing such a model? Would you be prepared to write an obituary for the law of contract after reading the Weisz case?

2. The *Weisz* case, not surprisingly, was appealed. What do you make of the *Per Curiam* opinion in *Weisz* of the New York Supreme Court, Appellate Term, First Department, the text of which follows:

Plaintiffs' purchases by competitive bids, at a public auction were made in 1962 and 1964. At that time neither the statutory nor decisional law, applicable to such purchases, recognized the expressed opinion or judgment of the seller as giving rise to any implied warranty of authenticity of authorship. (See Memorandum of the State Department of Law (McKinney's 1968 Session Laws, Vol. 2, pp. 2284–2285) recommending remedial legislation (now Secs. 219 and 219–a of the General Business Law) to change the then existing law.)

Additionally defendant's auction-sale catalogue listing, describing, and illustrating these paintings, gave leading and prominent place, in its prefatory terms of sale, (explaining and regulating the conduct of the action) to a clear, unequivocal disclaimer of any express or implied warranty or representation of genuineness of any paintings as products of the ascribed artist.

One of the factors necessarily entering into the competition among bidders at the public auction was the variable value of the paintings depending upon the degree of certainty with which they could be authenticated and established as the works of the ascribed artist. (See Backus v. MacLaury, 278 App.Div. 504, 507, 106 N.Y.S.2d 401, 403). Since no element of a wilful intent to deceive is remotely suggested in the circumstances here present the purchasers assumed the risk that in judging the paintings as readily-identifiable, original works of the named artist, and scaling their bids accordingly, they might be mistaken. (Restatement, Contracts, Sec. 502, comment f., p. 964). They will not now be heard to complain that, in failing to act with the caution of one in circumstances abounding with signals of *caveat emptor*, they made a bad bargain. The judgments are reversed with $30 costs and the complaints dismissed.

Weisz v. Parke-Bernet Galleries, Inc., 77 Misc.2d 80, 351 N.Y.S.2d 911 (1974). How would you describe the nature of the disagreement between Judge Sandler and the court which reversed him? Is the disagreement over the appropriate "models" for contract law?

SECTION B.   LATE TWENTIETH–CENTURY TORTS

THOMAS v. WINCHESTER

New York Court of Appeals, 1852.
6 N.Y. 397.

RUGGLES, Ch. J. delivered the opinion of the court. This is an action brought to recover damages from the defendant for negligently putting up, labeling and selling as and for the extract of *dandelion*, which is a simple and harmless medicine, a jar of the extract of *belladonna*, which is a deadly poison; by means of which the plaintiff Mary Ann Thomas * * * was greatly injured * * *.

The facts proved were briefly these: Mrs. Thomas being in ill health, her physician prescribed for her a dose of dandelion. Her husband purchased what was believed to be the medicine prescribed, at the store of Dr. Foord * * *.

A small quantity of the medicine thus purchased was administered to Mrs. Thomas, on whom it produced very alarming effects; such as coldness of the surface and extremities, feebleness of circulation, spasms of the muscles, giddiness of the head, dilation of the pupils of the eyes, and derangement of mind. She recovered however, after some time, from its effects, although for a short time her life was thought to be in great danger. The medicine administered was *belladonna, and not dandelion*. The jar from which it was taken was labeled "*½ lb. dandelion, prepared by A. Gilbert, No. 108, John-street, N. Y. Jar 8 oz.*" It was sold for and believed by Dr. Foord to be the extract of dandelion as labeled. Dr. Foord purchased the article as the extract of dandelion from Jas. S. Aspinwall, a druggist at New York. Aspinwall bought it of the defendant as extract of dandelion, believing it to be such. The defendant was engaged at No. 108 John-street, New York, in the manufacture and sale of certain vegetable extracts for medicinal purposes, and in the purchase and sale of others. * * * The jars containing extracts manufactured by himself and those containing extracts purchased by him from others, were labeled alike. Both were labeled like the jar in question, as "prepared by A. Gilbert." Gilbert was a person employed by the defendant at a salary, as an assistant in his business. The jars were labeled in Gilbert's name because he had been previously engaged in the same business on his own account at No. 108 John-street, and probably because Gilbert's labels rendered the articles more salable. The extract contained in the jar sold to Aspinwall, and by him to Foord, was not manufactured by the defendant, but was purchased by him from another manufacturer or dealer. The extract of dandelion and the extract of belladonna resemble each other in color, consistency, smell and taste; but may on careful examination be distinguished the one from the other by those who are well acquainted with these articles. * * *

* * *

The case depends on the * * * question * * * whether the defendant, being a remote vendor of the medicine, and there being no privity or connection between him and the plaintiffs, the action can be maintained.

If, in labeling a poisonous drug with the name of a harmless medicine, for public market, no duty was violated by the defendant, excepting that which he owed to Aspinwall, his immediate vendee, in virtue of his contract of sale, this action cannot be maintained. If A. build a wagon and sell it to B., who sells it to C., and C. hires it to D., who in consequence of the gross negligence of A. in building the wagon is overturned and injured, D. cannot recover damages against A., the builder. A.'s obligation to build the wagon faithfully, arises solely out of his contract with B. The public have nothing to do with it. Misfortune to third persons, not parties to the contract, would not be a natural and necessary consequence of the builder's negligence; and such negligence is not an act imminently dangerous to human life.

So, for the same reason, if a horse be defectively shod by a smith, and a person hiring the horse from the owner is thrown and injured in consequence of the smith's negligence in shoeing; the smith is not liable for the injury. The smith's duty in such case grows exclusively out of his contract with the owner of the horse; it was a duty which the smith owed to him alone, and to no one else. * * *

This was the ground on which the case of Winterbottom v. Wright (10 Mees. & Welsb. 109,) was decided. A. contracted with the postmaster general to provide a coach to convey the mail bags along a certain line of road, and B. and others, also contracted to horse the coach along the same line.   B. and his co-contractors hired C., who was the plaintiff, to drive the coach.   The coach, in consequence of some latent defect, broke down; the plaintiff was thrown from his seat and lamed.   It was held that C. could not maintain an action against A. for the injury thus sustained.   * * *   A.'s duty to keep the coach in good condition, was a duty to the postmaster general, with whom he made his contract, and not a duty to the driver employed by the owners of the horses.

But the case in hand stands on a different ground.   The defendant was a dealer in poisonous drugs.   * * *   The death or great bodily harm of some person was the natural and almost inevitable consequence of the sale of belladonna by means of the false label.

Gilbert, the defendant's agent, would have been punishable for manslaughter if Mrs. Thomas had died in consequence of taking the falsely labeled medicine.   Every man who, by his culpable negligence, causes the death of another, although without intent to kill, is guilty of manslaughter.   (2 R.S. 662, § 19.)   A chemist who negligently sells laudanum in a phial labeled as paregoric, and thereby causes the death of a person to whom it is administered, is guilty of manslaughter. (*Tessymond's case,* 1 Lewin's Crown Cases, 169.)   * * *   And this rule applies not only where the death of one is occasioned by the negligent act of another, but where it is caused by the negligent omission of a duty of that other.   (2 Car. & Kir. 368, 371.)   Although the defendant Winchester may not be answerable criminally for the negligence of his agent, there can be no doubt of his liability in a civil action, in which the act of the agent is to be regarded as the act of the principal.

* * *   In the present case the sale of the poisonous article was made to a dealer in drugs, and not to a consumer.   The injury therefore was not likely to fall on him, or on his vendee who was also a dealer; but much more likely to be visited on a remote purchaser, as actually happened.   The defendant's negligence put human life in imminent danger.   Can it be said that there was no duty on the part of the defendant, to avoid the creation of that danger by the exercise of greater caution? or that the exercise of that caution was a duty only to his immediate vendee, whose life was not endangered?   The defendant's duty arose out of the nature of his business and the danger to others incident to its mismanagement.   Nothing but mischief like that which actually happened could have been expected from sending the poison falsely labeled into the market; and the defendant is justly responsible for the probable consequences of the act.   The duty of exercising caution in this respect did not arise out of the defendant's contract of sale to Aspinwall.   The wrong done by the defendant was in putting the poison, mislabeled, into the hands of Aspinwall as an article of merchandise to be sold and afterwards used as the extract of dandelion, by some person then unknown.   The owner of a horse and

cart who leaves them unattended in the street is liable for any damage which may result from his negligence. (Lynch v. Nurdin, 1 Ad. & Ellis, N. S. 29; Illidge v. Goodwin, 5 Car. & Payne, 190.) The owner of a loaded gun who puts it into the hands of a child by whose indiscretion it is discharged, is liable for the damage occasioned by the discharge. (5 Maule & Sel. 198.) * * *

* * *

Judgment affirmed.

BENJAMIN N. CARDOZO

MacPHERSON v. BUICK MOTOR CO.

New York Court of Appeals, 1916.
217 N.Y. 382, 111 N.E. 1050.

CARDOZO, J. The defendant is a manufacturer of automobiles. It sold an automobile to a retail dealer. The retail dealer resold to the plaintiff. While the plaintiff was in the car it suddenly collapsed. He was thrown out and injured. One of the wheels was made of defective wood, and its spokes crumbled into fragments. The wheel was not made by the defendant; it was bought from another manufacturer. There is evidence, however, that its defects could have been discovered by reasonable inspection, and that inspection was omitted. * * * The question to be determined is whether the defendant owed a duty of care and vigilance [which might include such an inspection] to any one but the immediate purchaser.

The foundations of this branch of the law, at least in this state, were laid in Thomas v. Winchester, 6 N.Y. 397, 57 Am.Dec. 455. * * "The defendant's negligence," it was said, "put human life in imminent danger." A poison, falsely labeled, is likely to injure any one who gets it. Because the danger is to be foreseen, there is a duty to avoid the injury. Cases were cited by way of illustration in which manufacturers were not subject to any duty irrespective of contract. The distinction was said to be that their conduct, though negligent, was not likely to result in injury to any one except the purchaser. We are not required to say whether the chance of injury was always as remote as the distinction assumes. Some of the illustrations might be rejected to-day. The principle of the distinction is, for present purposes, the important thing. Thomas v. Winchester became quickly a landmark of the law. * * * The chief cases are well known, yet to recall some of them will be helpful. Loop v. Litchfield, 42 N.Y. 351, 1 Am. Rep. 513, is the earliest. It was the case of a defect in a small balance wheel used on a circular saw. The manufacturer pointed out the defect to the buyer, who wished a cheap article and was ready to assume the risk. The risk can hardly have been an imminent one, for the wheel lasted five years before it broke. In the meanwhile the buyer had made a lease of the machinery. It was held that the manufacturer was not answerable to the lessee. Loop v. Litchfield was followed in Losee v. Clute, 51 N.Y. 494, 10 Am.Rep. 638, the case of the explosion of a steam boiler. That decision has been criticized (Thompson on Negligence, 233; Shearman & Redfield on Negligence [6th Ed.] § 117); but it must be confined to its special facts. It was put upon the ground that the risk of injury was too remote. The buyer in that case had not only accepted the boiler, but had tested it. The manufacturer knew that his own test was not the final one. * * *

These early cases suggest a narrow construction of the rule. Later cases, however, evince a more liberal spirit. First in importance is Devlin v. Smith, 89 N.Y. 470, 42 Am.Rep. 311. The defendant, a contractor, built a scaffold for a painter. The painter's servants were injured. The contractor was held liable. He knew that the scaffold, if improperly constructed, was a most dangerous trap. He knew that it was to be used by the workmen. He was building it for that very purpose. Building it for their use, he owed them a duty, irrespective of his contract with their master, to build it with care.

From Devlin v. Smith we pass over intermediate cases and turn to the latest case in this court in which Thomas v. Winchester was followed. That case is Statler v. Ray Mfg. Co., 195 N.Y. 478, 480, 88 N.E. 1063. The defendant manufactured a large coffee urn. It was installed in a restaurant. When heated, the urn exploded and injured the plaintiff. We held that the manufacturer was liable. We said that the urn "was of such a character inherently that, when applied to the purposes for which it was designed, it was liable to become a source of great danger to many people if not carefully and properly constructed."

It may be that Devlin v. Smith and Statler v. Ray Mfg. Co. have extended the rule of Thomas v. Winchester. If so, this court is committed to the extension. The defendant argues that things imminently dangerous to life are poisons, explosives, deadly weapons—things whose normal function it is to injure or destroy. But whatever the rule in Thomas v. Winchester may once have been, it has no longer that restricted meaning. A scaffold (Devlin v. Smith, supra) is not inherently a destructive instrument. It becomes destructive only if imperfectly constructed. A large coffee urn (Statler v. Ray Mfg. Co., supra) may have within itself, if negligently made, the potency of danger, yet no one thinks of it as an implement whose normal function is destruction. * * *

* * *

We hold, then, that the principle of Thomas v. Winchester is not limited to poisons, explosives, and things of like nature, to things which in their normal operation are implements of destruction. If the nature of a thing is such that it is reasonably certain to place life and limb in peril when negligently made, it is then a thing of danger. Its nature gives warning of the consequences to be expected. If to the element of danger there is added knowledge that the thing will be used by persons other than the purchaser, and used without new tests, then, irrespective of contract, the manufacturer of this thing of danger is under a duty to make it carefully. * * * It is possible to use almost anything in a way that will make it dangerous if defective. That is not enough to charge the manufacturer with a duty independent of his contract. Whether a given thing is dangerous may be sometimes a question for the court and sometimes a question for the jury. There must also be knowledge that in the usual course of events the danger will be shared by others than the buyer. Such knowledge may often be inferred from the nature of the transaction. But it is possible that even knowledge of the danger and of the use will not always be enough.   The proximity or remoteness of the relation is a factor to be considered. * * *

We are not required, at this time, to say that it is legitimate to go back of the manufacturer of the finished product and hold the manufacturers of the component parts.   To make their negligence a cause of imminent danger, an independent cause must often intervene; the manufacturer of the finished product must also fail in his duty of inspection.   It may be that in those circumstances the negligence of the earlier members of the series is too remote to constitute, as to the ultimate user, an actionable wrong. * * *   There is here no break in the chain of cause and effect. * * *   We have put aside the notion that the duty to safeguard life and limb, when the consequences of negligence may be foreseen, grows out of contract and nothing else. We have put the source of the obligation where it ought to be.   We have put its source in the law.

* * *   Beyond all question, the nature of an automobile gives warning of probable danger if its construction is defective.   This automobile was designed to go 50 miles an hour.   Unless its wheels were sound and strong, injury was almost certain. * * *   The defendant knew the danger.   It knew also that the car would be used by persons other than the buyer.   This was apparent * * *   from the fact that the buyer was a dealer in cars, who bought to resell. * * * The dealer was indeed the one person of whom it might be said with some approach to certainty that by him the car would not be used. Yet the defendant would have us say that he was the one person whom it was under a legal duty to protect.   The law does not lead us to so inconsequent a conclusion.   Precedents drawn from the days of travel by stagecoach do not fit the conditions of travel to-day.   The principle that the danger must be imminent does not change, but the things subject to the principle do change. They are whatever the needs of life in a developing civilization require them to be.

* * *

We think the defendant was not absolved from a duty of inspection because it bought the wheels from a reputable manufacturer.   It was not merely a dealer in automobiles.   It was a manufacturer of automobiles.   It was responsible for the finished product.   It was not at liberty to put the finished product on the market without subjecting the component parts to ordinary and simple tests. * * *   The obligation to inspect must vary with the nature of the thing to be inspected.   The more probable the danger the greater the need of caution.

* * *

The judgment should be affirmed, with costs.

Willard BARTLETT, C. J. (dissenting). * * *   The wheel was purchased by the Buick Motor Company, ready made, from the Imperial Wheel Company of Flint, Mich., a reputable manufacturer of automobile wheels which had furnished the defendant with 80,000 wheels, none of which had proved to be made of defective wood prior to the accident in the present case. The defendant relied upon the wheel manufacturer to make all necessary tests as to the strength of the material therein   *   *   *.

*   *   *

The late Chief Justice Cooley of Michigan, one of the most learned and accurate of American law writers, states the general rule thus:

> The general rule is that a contractor, manufacturer, vendor or furnisher of an article is not liable to third parties who have no contractual relations with him, for negligence in the construction, manufacture, or sale of such article. 2 Cooley on Torts (3d Ed.), 1486.

The leading English authority in support of this rule, to which all the later cases on the same subject refer, is Winterbottom v. Wright, 10 Meeson & Welsby, 109, which was an action by the driver of a stagecoach against a contractor who had agreed with the postmaster general to provide and keep the vehicle in repair for the purpose of conveying the royal mail over a prescribed route. The coach broke down and upset, injuring the driver, who sought to recover against the contractor on account of its defective construction. The Court of Exchequer denied him any right of recovery on the ground that there was no privity of contract between the parties, the agreement having been made with the postmaster general alone.

> "If the plaintiff can sue," said Lord Abinger, the Chief Baron, "every passenger or even any person passing along the road who was injured by the upsetting of the coach might bring a similar action. Unless we confine the operation of such contracts as this to the parties who enter into them the most absurd and outrageous consequences, to which I can see no limit, would ensue."

The doctrine of that decision was recognized as the law of this state by the leading New York case of Thomas v. Winchester, 6 N.Y. 397, 408, 57 Am.Dec. 455, which, however, involved an exception to the general rule.   *   *   *   Chief Judge Ruggles, who delivered the opinion of the court, distinguished between an act of negligence imminently dangerous to the lives of others and one that is not so, *   *   *

In Torgesen v. Schultz, 192 N.Y. 156, 159, 84 N.E. 956, 18 L.R.A. (N.S.) 726, 127 Am.St.Rep. 894, the defendant was the vendor of bottles of aerated water which were charged under high pressure and likely to explode unless used with precaution when exposed to sudden changes of temperature. The plaintiff, who was a servant of the purchaser, was injured by the explosion of one of these bottles. There was evidence tending to show that it had not been properly tested in order to insure users against such accidents. We held that the defendant corporation was liable notwithstanding the absence of any contract relation between it and the plaintiff—

> under the doctrine of Thomas v. Winchester, supra, and similar cases based upon the duty of the vendor of an article dangerous in its nature, or likely to become so in the course of the ordinary usage to be contemplated by the vendor, either to exercise due care to warn users of the danger or to take reasonable care to prevent the article sold from proving dangerous when subjected only to customary usage.

The character of the exception to the general rule limiting liability for negligence to the original parties to the contract of sale, was still more clearly stated * * * in Statler v. Ray Manufacturing Co., 195 N.Y. 478, 482, 88 N.E. 1063 * * * :

> In the case of an article of an inherently dangerous nature, a manufacturer may become liable for a negligent construction which, when added to the inherent character of the appliance, makes it imminently dangerous, and causes or contributes to a resulting injury not necessarily incident to the use of such an article if properly constructed, but naturally following from a defective construction.

In that case the injuries were inflicted by the explosion of a battery of steam-driven coffee urns, constituting an appliance liable to become dangerous in the course of ordinary usage.

The case of Devlin v. Smith, 89 N.Y. 470, 42 Am.Rep. 311, is cited as an authority in conflict with the view that the liability of the manufacturer and vendor extends to third parties only when the article manufactured and sold is inherently dangerous. In that case the builder of a scaffold * * * was held to be liable to the administratrix of a painter * * * . It is said that the scaffold, if properly constructed, was not inherently dangerous, and hence that this decision affirms the existence of liability in the case of an article not dangerous in itself, but made so only in consequence of negligent construction. Whatever logical force there may be in this view, it seems to me clear from the language * * * [of the opinion] of the court that the scaffold was deemed to be an inherently dangerous structure, and that the case was decided as it was because the court entertained that view. Otherwise [they would hardly have said] that the circumstances seemed to bring the case fairly within the principle of Thomas v. Winchester.

I do not see how we can uphold the judgment in the present case without overruling what has been so often said by this court and other courts of like authority in reference to the absence of any liability for negligence on the part of the original vendor of an ordinary carriage to any one except his immediate vendee. * * * In the case at bar the defective wheel on an automobile, moving only eight miles an hour, was not any more dangerous to the occupants of the car than a similarly defective wheel would be to the occupants of a carriage drawn by a horse at the same speed, and yet, unless the courts have been all wrong on this question up to the present time, there would be no liability to strangers to the original sale in the case of the horse-drawn carriage.

* * *

* * * That the federal courts still adhere to the general rule, as I have stated it, appears by the decision of the Circuit Court of Appeal in the Second Circuit, in March, 1915, in the case of Cadillac Motor Car Co. v. Johnson, 221 Fed. 801, 137 C.C.A. 279, L.R.A. 1915E, 287. That case, like this, was an action by a subvendee against a manufacturer of automobiles for negligence in failing to discover that one of its wheels was defective, the court holding that such an action could not be maintained. It is true there was a dissenting opinion in that case, but it was based chiefly upon the proposition that rules applicable to stagecoaches are archaic when applied to automobiles, and that if the law did not afford a remedy to strangers to the contract, the law should be changed. If this be true, the change should be effected by the Legislature and not by the courts. * * *

NOTES AND QUESTIONS

1. How would you phrase the holding in the Thomas v. Winchester case? What does it substitute for the restrictive doctrine requiring privity between plaintiff and defendant? Is *Thomas*, by its own language, limited in application to "inherently dangerous" products? Are you satisfied with the manner in which the *Thomas* court distinguishes Winterbottom v. Wright, the case of the stage-coach driver injured by result of negligence of the coach-maker?

2. Why does Cardozo suggest in MacPherson v. Buick that "It may be that Devlin v. Smith (the painters' scaffolding case) and Statler v. Ray Mfg. Co. (the coffee urns case) have extended the rule of Thomas v. Winchester?" Does Cardozo believe that he is extending the rule of *Thomas*? Do you? Do you agree with Cardozo's holding that there is support for the ruling that Buick was negligent?

3. Are the effects of Cardozo's holding predictable and carefully circumscribed? Why does Cardozo say that "Whether a given thing is dangerous may be sometimes a question for the court and sometimes a question for the jury?" How is the judge to decide when the question is for him and when for the jury? Does this ambiguity weaken the legitimacy of Cardozo's decision?

4. What does Cardozo mean when he rejects the idea that "the duty to safeguard life and limb * * * grows out of contract," and instead declares that "We have put its source in the law?" Is contract not "the law?"

LOVELACE v. ASTRA TRADING CORP.

United States District Court, S.D.Miss.1977.
439 F.Supp. 753.

Dan M. RUSSELL, Jr., Chief Judge [on defendants motion for summary judgment].

* * *

During November or December of 1973, Edwina Lovelace, the plaintiff's wife, purchased a compact styled hair dryer (mini-dryer). * * * at the Howard Brothers store * * *. It appears that the mini-dryer was purchased for the plaintiff's son, Terry Lovelace * * *. The record shows that the mini-dryer was exclusively used by Terry Lovelace [who] * * * was living at home * * *.

The mini-dryer apparently functioned properly until February 10, 1974. On that date, while the plaintiff and his family were at church, the family residence was severely damaged by fire. The plaintiff alleges, and seeks to prove, that the fire resulted as a direct and proximate result of the defective nature of the mini hair dryer. The dryer was left plugged in, though not in use at the time of the fire. Some 18 days after the fire in question, plaintiff was diagnosed as having extremely high blood pressure. This led to open heart surgery and a coronary bypass, resulting in plaintiff's total and permanent disability. Plaintiff alleges that this condition was brought about as a direct result of the fire. * * *

Defendant Astra is an importer of merchandise, importing various items primarily from the Far East. * * *

Astra's agent in the Far East was, for the transaction in question, the Chaun Ching Co., defendant herein. Chaun Ching is an exporter and manufacturer of sundry goods. * * * [T]he dryers were actually manufactured by the Wan Nien Electric Appliance Company of Taiwan. The record also reveals that defendant Astra furnished Chaun Ching with the design and specifications for the hair dryer it desired to import. Production samples were returned to Astra, and the two defendants reached an agreement for the products' importation into the United States.

The mini-dryers were shipped to this country in individual boxes, with each box containing one dryer enclosed in a plastic bag. The boxes containing the individual dryers prominently bore the notation "Stellar". Stellar is a registered trademark of the defendant Astra.

Depositions filed in this case disclose that upon receiving shipments, Astra would run random sample checks. This entailed a cursory visual inspection and an actual testing of the product for a period of time thought sufficient to disclose any malfunctions. * * * The product was in no way altered or enhanced by Astra. * * *

The plaintiff's suit sounds in the ever growing theory of products liability. Liability is asserted against Chaun Ching for negligence in the design and manufacture of the mini-dryer. Astra is also charged with negligence in the selection, testing and distribution of the hair dryers. Finally, plaintiff asserts that both defendants are strictly liable in tort for the property damage and personal injuries suffered by the plaintiff herein. * * *

Defendant Astra * * * [asserts] that since the plaintiff was neither a user nor a consumer of the product, that he is thereby barred from suing under a strict liability in tort theory. * * *

Since this case is premised upon diversity jurisdiction, this Court sits in essence as another court of the forum state. Therefore, the substantive law of Mississippi is to be applied. * * * The problem presented herein is that the Mississippi Supreme Court has not yet addressed the issue of whether recovery under a strict liability in tort theory should be extended to those denominated as "bystanders".

* * *

Without the benefit of any state certification process, this Court must take the "role of a prophet" and seek to forecast how this issue will ultimately be resolved by the state courts. * * * Absent definitive guidance from Mississippi decisional or statutory law, this Court may therefore look to other available resources, i. e., decisions in other states, by other federal courts " * * * and the general weight and trend of authority." Julander v. Ford Motor Co., 488 F.2d 839 (10th Cir. 1973).

Defendant Astra, in its brief and during oral argument, has stressed the point that it did not manufacture the mini-dryer that is the alleged cause of the plaintiff's damages. Defendant states that as a wholesaler, it was under no duty to inspect for latent defects, and under the authority of Shainberg v. Barlow, 258 So.2d 242 (Miss. 1972), is absolved from liability herein.

In *Shainberg*, the plaintiff sued the wholesaler and the retailer when the heel of her shoe suddenly dislodged, thereby causing her bodily injury. The manufacturer was not joined as a party-defendant. The court stated the applicable rule thusly:

> Where the wholesaler or distributor purchases an article from *a reputable and reliable manufacturer,* sells it to a retailer in its original condition, and the retailer in turn sells the article—exactly as it came from the manufacturer—to a customer in the regular course of business, *no duty devolves* on the wholesaler or retailer *to inspect and discover a latent defect.* 258 So.2d at 244 (emphasis added).

The court concluded that the co-defendants could not be held accountable, reasoning that a contrary holding would make " * * * each retail merchant an insurer or guarantor * * * " of articles sold in its capacity as a mere sales conduit. Id. at 246.

However, certain factors take the case *sub judice* out of the purview of *Shainberg*. First, on this motion for partial summary judgment, this Court is unwilling to take judicial notice and assume that Astra did in fact deal with a "reputable and reliable manufacturer". Secondly, plaintiff has raised serious factual issues as to Astra's knowledge of the defective nature and propensities of the mini-dryers. Plaintiff claims that such knowledge preceded the fire in issue here. If established, *Shainberg* would be, by its facts, inapplicable here. * * *

Additional facts mitigate in favor of plaintiff's position here. The record so far reveals that Astra was not a stereotypical wholesaler or retailer. On the contrary, Astra selected the design for the hair dryers and approved the prototype before full scale manufacturing began. * * *

Finally, the boxes containing the individual mini-dryers were distinctively emblazoned "Stellar", defendant Astra's trademark. * * *

Therefore, the markings on the individual boxes would indicate, to the average consumer, that they were purchasing a "Stellar" manufactured product. Legal support for this proposition is found in the *Restatement (Second) of Torts* § 400 (1965), which provides that one "putting out" a product as his own is subject to a manufacturer's liability even though the product in question was in fact manufactured by another. * * * The foregoing principal is soundly based in logic, and serves to meet the reasonable expectations of the consuming public. * * *

Just as motorists on the Gulf Coast soon learn that all roads lead to Vancleave, any discussion of products liability law in Mississippi will have its roots in the seminal decision of State Stove Mfg. Co. v. Hodges, 189 So.2d 113 (Miss.1966), cert. denied sub nom., Yates v. Hodges, 386 U.S. 912, 87 S.Ct. 860, 17 L.Ed.2d 784 (1967). In *State Stove*, the plaintiff homeowner sued the manufacturer of a water heater and the builder-contractor who installed it, when after installation, it subsequently exploded to plaintiff's chagrin. * * *

The court in *State Stove* explicitly adopted § 402A of the *Restatement (Second) of Torts*, * * *.

As set forth in *State Stove*, Section 402A provides:

"(1) *One who sells* any product in a defective condition unreasonably dangerous to the user or consumer or to his property *is subject to liability* for physical harm thereby caused *to the ultimate user or consumer, or to his property,* if (a) the seller is engaged in the business of selling such a product, and (b) it is expected to and does reach the user or consumer without substantial change in the condition in which it is sold.

(2) The rule stated in Subsection (1) applies although (a) the seller has exercised all possible care in the preparation and sale of

his product, and (b) the user or consumer has not bought the product from or entered into any contractual relation with the seller." (emphasis added).

It is readily apparent that the rule, by its very terms, extends liability to users and consumers. The hair dryer in question was kept in the plaintiff's house, however, only by a strained construction could plaintiff be construed as either a user or consumer. Therefore, for purposes of this motion, Mr. Lovelace will be deemed a "bystander". And, it should be noted that the Institute, by caveat, expressed no opinion on the issue of extending § 402A liability to bystanders.

As mentioned earlier, Mississippi courts have not addressed this issue yet. However, certain intimations do appear. *State Stove* expressly abrogated the requirement of privity in a suit by a consumer against a manufacturer, and stated that since liability sounds in tort, warranty concepts are irrelevant. Plaintiff's brief directs the Court to Miss.Code Ann. § 75–2–318 (1972). Section 2–318 of the U.C.C. delineates the scope of warranty protection under the code, with liability extending to include members of the purchaser's household, or guests therein. However, this Court does not perceive that plaintiff advances any warranty theory of liability. Accordingly, since strict liability in tort and breach of warranty are two different breeds of cat, this Court does not feel that the adoption of U.C.C. § 2–318 necessarily implies any legislative, or judicial, intent to extend liability to bystanders in all circumstances and under all causes of action.

More on point is the quotation from Greenman v. Yuba Power Products, Inc., 59 Cal.2d 57, 27 Cal.Rptr. 697, 377 P.2d 897 (1962), wherein the plaintiff recovered from the manufacturer for injuries from a power tool purchased by the plaintiff's wife.

> A manufacturer is strictly liable in tort when an article he places on the market, knowing that it is to be used without inspection for defects, proves to have a defect that causes injury to a human being. * * * Quoted in *State Stove*, 189 So.2d at 119.

The Mississippi Supreme Court also quoted with approval Dean Prosser's summary of the effect of MacPherson v. Buick Motor Co.:

> The conclusion is clear that the duty extends to any one who may reasonably be expected to be in the vicinity of the chattel's probable use, and to be endangered if it is defective * * *. Id. at 116.

This Court recognizes that Dean Prosser's statement refers to claims under a negligence theory, and not strict products liability. However, as discussed infra, negligence concepts are finding useful application in strict products liability cases, even though negligence itself need not be proven.

* * *

Negligence concepts found application in Walton v. Chrysler Motor Corp., 229 So.2d 568 (Miss.1970), where the plaintiff's car was struck from the rear and the resulting injuries were allegedly aggravated due to a defect in the plaintiff's car. In holding for the defendant, the Mississippi Supreme Court stated:

> * * * but this rule [strict liability] does not eliminate the requirement that, even where there is a defect in the product, that *there must be some duty owed to the plaintiff* with regard to the defect * * *. Id at 573 (emphasis added).

* * * [In Ford Motor Co. v. Cockrell, 211 So.2d 833 (Miss. 1968) the court again quoted Dean Prosser on *MacPherson* in a *strict liability* case, and thus] without explicit reference, the Mississippi Supreme Court was impliedly applying concepts of foreseeability, traditionally an element of a count in negligence, to a strict liability case. * * * Finally, as pointed out infra, other courts have used the concept of foreseeability in determining whether the umbrella of strict liability also shields bystanders.

* * *

As noted earlier, the American Law Institute, by caveat to § 402A, refused to express an opinion as to whether the theory of strict liability in tort would inure to the benefit of those who are neither users nor consumers. However, Comment C thereto sets forth the general policies underlying the strict liability concept. Seriatim, and in brief, § 402A is premised upon the assumptions that a seller assumes a special responsibility to the public; that the public has a right to expect reputable sellers to stand behind their products; that public policy demands the cost of injuries due to defective products be placed on those who market them; and, such injuries are properly treated as a cost of production and insurable risks by those in the best position to seek such protection. If the general policies and the intent of the drafters are taken as stated, it is apparent to this Court that third-party bystanders are properly protected by § 402A. * * *

In Elmore v. American Motors, 70 Cal.2d 578, 75 Cal.Rptr. 652, 451 P.2d 84, 33 A.L.R.3d 406 (1969), the plaintiff's car malfunctioned. The plaintiff lost control, crossed the roadway and struck a second plaintiff's (Waters) car. The lower court sustained nonsuits on behalf of the manufacturer and retailer. The California Supreme Court reversed, basing its holding on the general policy grounds that manufacturers should bear the cost of injuries caused by their defective products. [The court stated:]

> *If anything, bystanders should be entitled to greater protection* than the consumer or user *where injury to bystanders* from the defect *is reasonably foreseeable.* Consumers and users, at least, have the opportunity to inspect for defects * * * [but] the bystander is in greater need of protection from defective products which are dangerous * * *.

* * * Defendant relies upon Winnett v. Winnett, 57 Ill.2d 7, 310 N.E.2d 1 (1974), in support of its position. In *Winnett*, the four year old plaintiff was injured when she put her fingers in the moving screen of a farm forage wagon. The Supreme Court of Illinois denied recovery against the manufacturer on a strict products liability theory. In so doing, that court stated:

> In our judgment the *liability* of a manufacturer properly *encompasses only those individuals to whom injuries from a defective product may reasonably be foreseen* and only those situations where the product is being used for the purpose for which it was intended or for which it is reasonably foreseeable that it may be used. 310 N.E.2d at 4 (emphasis added).

The manufacturer was therefore absolved from liability because it could not reasonably foresee that a four year old child would be allowed to put her fingers in the forage screen. However, the emphasis of the court in *Winnett* was on foreseeability * * *. Therefore, the *Winnett* case is reconcilable with those allowing recovery by bystanders.

The issue has been addressed and resolved by other courts also. The court in Ciampichini v. Ring Bros., Inc., 40 A.D.2d 289, 339 N.Y. S.2d 716 (1973), without hesitation overruled a prior decision denying bystander recovery and emphatically stated:

> We resolve that issue now by laying to rest a principle which we believe outmoded and no longer adaptable to the rights of individuals in contemporary society. 339 N.Y.S.2d at 717.

* * *

The Missouri Supreme Court also extended strict liability recovery to bystanders in Giberson v. Ford Motor Co., 504 S.W.2d 8 (Mo.1974), wherein the court, quoting from Tucson Indus., Inc. v. Schwartz, 108 Ariz. 464, 501 P.2d 936, 939–40 (1972), gave the basic justification for extending liability.

> Strict liability is a public policy device to spread the risk from one to whom a defective product may be a catastrophe, to those who marketed the product, profit from its sale, and have the know-how to remove its defects before placing it in the chain of distribution.

Mississippi courts are generally in accord with the policy judgment that manufacturers should shoulder the costs of injuries resulting from their defective products. * * * Other policy reasons in support of the doctrine have been advanced * * * and accepted by the courts. "* * * The reason for extending the strict liability doctrine to innocent bystanders is the desire to minimize risks of personal injury and or property damage." Darryl v. Ford Motor Co., 440 S. W.2d 630, 633 (Tex.1969). The general consensus therefore appears to favor extension of the strict liability doctrine to provide relief to bystanders. * * *

One final case is worth noting. In West v. Caterpillar Tractor Co., Inc., 336 So.2d 80 (Fla.1976) * * *, the Florida court noted that no adequate rationale or theoretical explanation existed to deny strict liability to bystanders. That court also summed up the situation well by its quotation from Caruth v. Mariani, 11 Ariz.App. 188, 463 P.2d 83, 85 (1970), that:

> All states which have adopted the theory of strict tort liability have extended the theory to the bystander when called upon to do so * * *. 336 So.2d at 89. * * *

Part of the basis for the Florida court's holding is the notion that any restriction of the doctrine to users or consumers only " * * * would have to rest on the vestige of the disappearing privity requirement." Id. at 89. As mentioned earlier, the Mississippi Supreme Court in *State Stove* abandoned the privity requirement in suits by a consumer against a manufacturer. The court thereupon concluded:

> The obligation of the manufacturer must become what in justice it ought to be—an enterprise liability * * *. The cost of injuries or damages, *either to persons or property,* resulting from defective products, should be borne by the makers of the products who put them into the channels of trade * * * This doctrine of strict liability applies when harm befalls a *foreseeable bystander* who comes within range of the danger. 336 So.2d at 92 (emphasis added).

Based upon the foregoing, this Court holds that the plaintiff herein may avail himself of the strict liability doctrine enunciated in § 402A of the Restatement, and as adopted and construed by the Mississippi Supreme Court. Defendants' motion for partial summary judgment on this ground is therefore denied.

* * *

The court in *West*, supra, notes that 31 states have adopted § 402A in one form or another, with two federal court "predictions" in Utah and Vermont. Even a cursory perusal of the cited cases discloses that Mississippi was in the forefront in adopting § 402A. This Court has no reason to believe that the state supreme court, given the appropriate case, would not extend strict liability concepts to include "bystanders". The Mississippi court's willingness to be among judicial innovators in this area indicates a concern for consumers in general; and a sensitivity to the delicate interplay among responsible social policy, enterprise liability and the reasonable expectations of the consuming public.

* * *

[The court thus ruled that it was appropriate for the plaintiff to be allowed to bring the case to trial, and to prove his injuries resulted from a defective hair dryer.]

NOTES AND QUESTIONS

1. What changes in the rule of Thomas v. Winchester and MacPherson v. Buick are made by section 402A? Are there any similarities between *Restatement (Second) Torts* § 402A and *Restatement (Second) Contracts* §§ 89A and 90? Do you suppose Cardozo would have approved of § 402A? With regard to another analogue from the law of contract, is it true, as the *Astra* court maintains, that "strict liability in tort and breach of warranty are two different breeds of cat?" Why does the court not believe, for example, that negligence theory (*MacPherson*) and 402A are different breeds of cat? Note that the court seems to approve of the "useful application" of "negligence concepts" in "strict products liability cases."

2. The *Astra* court seems to accept the assumption of the framers of *Restatement (Second) Torts* § 402A "that public policy demands the cost of injuries due to defective products be placed on those who market them; and, such injuries are properly treated as a cost of production and insurable risks by those in the best position to seek such protection." Do you accept these assumptions? Would the judges who formulated the nineteenth century tort rules subscribe to these assumptions? Why or why not?

3. In an omitted part of the *Astra* opinion, the court quoted the Kentucky decision of Embs v. Pepsi-Cola, 528 S.W.2d 703, 705 (Ky.1975) that "[O]nce strict liability is accepted, bystander recovery is a *fait accompli*." If this is so, how can it be that the "American Law Institute, by caveat to § 402A, refused to express an opinion as to whether the theory of strict liability in tort would inure to the benefit of those who are neither users nor consumers?"

4. The court in *Astra* refers to the Mississippi state court's "sensitivity to the delicate interplay among responsible social policy, enterprise liability, and the reasonable expectations of the consuming public." Why could it be said that a holding of bystander liability under § 402A reflected that sensitivity? Why is the "interplay" here a "delicate" one?

5. We saw in Chapter Three that the nineteenth century theories of tort liability, in particular the rise of the negligence principle, seemed felicitous in the way they reduced the liability of infant industry, commerce, and transportation, which might have been unlimited under the nuisance or trespass standards. Can it be said that recent developments in tort law evince other policies? Predicting the scope of tort law in the decade just ended, Professor Marshall Shapo wrote ten years ago that:

> The New Torts will concern itself with remedies against the abuse of power—political, economic, intellectual, as well as physical. * * *
>
> * * * [T]he New Torts must be made to deal more explicitly with the question of what large enterprises and other clusters of power owe to the individual caught in their coils. The New Torts * * * will place new and vibrant emphasis on the responsibility of private and public enterprise * * *. The New Torts * * * will emphasize more sharply the question of what defendants representing significant clusters of different kinds of power owe to our civilization in the way of behaving in a civilized

manner. It will present an analogue of recent developments in constitutional law, focusing on legal checks on private groups that act with power governmental in function.

Shapo, Changing Frontiers in Torts: Vistas for the 70's, 22 Stan.L.Rev. 330, 333, 334–335 (1970). Copyright © 1970 by the Board of Trustees of the Leland Stanford Junior University, reprinted by permission of the Stanford Law Review, Fred B. Rothman & Company, and the author. See also Shapo, The Duty to Act (1977). The Constitutional law case to which Professor Shapo was making explicit reference was Monroe v. Pape, 365 U.S. 167, 81 S.Ct. 473, 5 L.Ed.2d 492 (1961). In that case, the Court held that the fourteenth amendment mandated that the prohibitions against unreasonable searches and seizures of the fourth amendment applied to the states, and thus where Chicago police officers unlawfully invaded petitioner's home, the invasion was "under color" of state law, and thus a deprivation of Constitutional rights and actionable under 42 U.S.C.A. § 1983, a federal civil rights statute. We haven't gone into this area of Constitutional law, of course, but can you relate Professor Shapo's comments to any Constitutional law cases that we have studied? If the "New Torts" is to address the problems which Professor Shapo describes, would this raise any problems of judicial legitimacy that we have seen arise in a Constitutional context?

6.   This problem has arisen in recent years as a result not only of products liability litigation, but also of other negligence developments. Perhaps the most dramatic of such cases was DILLON v. LEGG, 68 Cal.2d 728, 69 Cal. Rptr. 72, 441 P.2d 912 (1968). Mr. Legg's allegedly negligently driven automobile struck Mrs. Dillon's little girl. Mrs. Dillon, looking on, watched in horror as her child died from the collision. In the action for wrongful death of the child, Mrs. Dillon sought damages to compensate her for the "great emotional disturbance and shock and injury to her nervous system" produced by witnessing her daughter's death. Similar compensation was sought on behalf of another daughter who also saw the accident. Justice Tobriner observed that earlier American decisions had barred such recovery, based on

> the alleged absence of a required 'duty' of due care of the tortfeasor
> to the mother. Duty, in turn [these decisions] state must express
> public policy; the imposition of duty here would work disaster be-
> cause it would invite fraudulent claims and it would involve the
> courts in the hopeless task of defining the extent of the tortfeasor's
> liability. In substance, they say, definition of liability being im-
> possible, denial of liability is the only realistic alternative.

441 P.2d, at 914. Given the "natural justice upon which the mother's claim rests" however, Tobriner declared that the old rule barring recovery should not be allowed to stand, and that it was possible to provide "proper guidelines" to avoid the "fraudulent claims" and "impossible definition" of which the old decisions had warned.

Tobriner appears to have sensed that the court's undertaking was a difficult and uncertain one, but that the court's task in determining negligence was simply to assess the foreseeability of harm:

> Since the chief element in determining whether defendant owes
> a duty or an obligation to plaintiff is the foreseeability of the risk,

that factor will be of prime concern in every case. Because it is inherently intertwined with foreseeability such duty or obligation must necessarily be adjudicated only upon a case-by-case basis. We cannot now predetermine defendant's obligation in every situation by a fixed category; no immutable rule can establish the extent of that obligation for every circumstance in the future.

441 P.2d, at 920. Still, the court did give what it called "guidelines;" to wit, that three factors be taken into consideration in such cases, (1) whether the plaintiff was located near the scene of the accident, (2) whether the shock resulted from the direct emotional impact on plaintiff from sensory and contemporaneous observance of the accident, and (3) whether the plaintiff and the victim were closely related. Id. Applying these factors to the case at hand, the court held that Mrs. Dillon had made out a *prima facie* cause of action. Do you believe that the court's guidelines take care of the problems that the rule barring recovery sought to avoid?

7. Another recent negligence case that has caused concern is HELLING v. CAREY, 83 Wash.2d 514, 519 P.2d 981 (1974). Plaintiff was nearsighted, and consulted defendant opthamologists in 1959, who fitted her with contact lenses. She saw the doctors approximately ten times over the next nine years, her first visit after 1959 coming in 1963, concerning "irritation caused by the contact lenses." Her doctors apparently assumed that it was her contacts that were giving her trouble, but, when, in October 1968, for the first time, one of the defendants checked the plaintiff's eye pressure and field of vision, it was discovered that she had glaucoma. Plaintiff was then thirty-two. Plaintiff sued defendants for malpractice, alleging that she had suffered permanent visual damage due to their failure to diagnose and treat her glaucoma at an earlier stage. Defendants brought in expert witnesses whose testimony was uncontradicted, and who established that "it was the universal practice of opthamalogists not to administer glaucoma tests to patients under age 40 [as was plaintiff] because the incidence of glaucoma at younger ages was so small." Defendants argued that since it was the practice of the profession not to test for glaucoma under 40, they should not be liable for failing to catch the disease earlier. The court refused to accept this defense.

The court observed that Justice Holmes had stated in Texas & Pac. Ry. v. Behymer, 189 U.S. 468, 470, 23 S.Ct. 622, 47 L.Ed. 905 (1903) that "What usually is done may be evidence of what ought to be done, but what ought to be done is fixed by a standard of reasonable prudence, whether it usually is complied with or not. The court also referred to The T. J. Hooper, 60 F.2d 737, 740 (2d Cir. 1932), where Judge Hand had stated, in holding that the owners of tugs were negligent when they did not equip them with radios, "Courts must in the end say what is required; there are precautions so imperative that even their universal disregard will not excuse their omission."

The court proceeded to reason, from these judicial expressions, that since the tests for glaucoma were simple and harmless, and since they would have revealed the disease in time to arrest its progress, "Under the facts of this case reasonable prudence required the timely giving of the pressure test to this plaintiff." 519 P.2d, at 983. Would you have concurred in this opinion? If "reasonable prudence" as the court defines it does not mean the accepted practice among doctors of defendant's speciality, what does it mean? Can you understand why medical malpractice rates have risen dramatically in the last few years?

A concurring opinion was written in *Helling*, by Associate Justice Utter. He stated that "it seems illogical" for the court to be holding that the defendants were morally blameworthy or negligent in that they "failed to exercise a reasonable standard of care," because they "used all the precautions commonly prescribed by their profession in diagnosis and treatment." Id., at 984. "It seems to me," Justice Utter wrote, "we are, in reality, imposing liability, because, in choosing between an innocent plaintiff and a doctor, who * * * could have prevented the full effects of this disease by administering a simple, harmless test and treatment, the plaintiff should not have to bear the risk of loss." Id. Justice Utter concluded that it would be better, then, to rest liability simply on a standard of "strict liability or liability without fault." Only two of the nine justices joined in Utter's opinion, the remaining six joined in Tobriner's. Which opinion do you find the most persuasive?

8. Shapo's "New Torts" may have its counterpart in modern American property law, particularly landlord-tenant law. Probably the leading case in this regard is KLINE v. 1500 MASSACHUSETTS AVE. CORP., 141 U.S. App.D.C. 370, 439 F.2d 477 (1970). Mrs. Kline sustained serious injuries when she was assaulted by an intruder in the common hallway of her Washington, D.C. apartment house. When Mrs. Kline had first moved in, in October 1959, the entrances to the building were carefully guarded and a doorman was on duty twenty-four hours a day. By mid-1966, however, a doorman was no longer employed, and the entrances were often left unlocked and unguarded. During the years leading up to the incident there had been "an increasing number of assaults, larcenies, and robberies being perpetrated against the tenants in and from the common hallways of the apartment building." The landlord had notice of these crimes, and had even been urged by Mrs. Kline herself to "take steps to secure the building."

Judge Malcolm Richard Wilkey, writing for the majority, noted that the risk of "criminal assault and robbery" was entirely predictable if the premises were not kept secured, that no individual tenant "had it within his power" to take the steps to secure the entrances and common hallways, and that this was "a risk whose prevention or minimization was almost entirely within the power of the landlord * * *." Judge Wilkey noted that previous cases had held that the landlord had a duty to maintain "areas of common use and common danger" so that no one would be injured by physical defects of the building in those areas. The rationale of those cases "as applied to predictable criminal acts by third parties is the same," said Judge Wilkey.

The opinion noted that "As a general rule, a private person does not have a duty to protect another from a criminal attack by a third person," but that "the rationale of this very broad general rule falters when it is applied to the conditions of modern day urban apartment living * * *." In particular, the court suggested that Judge Wright's recent opinion in Javins v. First Nat. Realty Corp., 138 U.S.App.D.C. 369, 428 F.2d 1071 (1970) had rejected "the traditional analysis of a lease as being a conveyance of an interest in land—with all the medieval connotations this often brings

* * *." Under the common law analysis of a lease as a conveyance, there were few, if any, ongoing obligations of the landlord. Judge Wright's opinion in *Javins* held that "leases of urban dwelling units should be interpreted and construed like any other contract," and that this meant that the court could imply a "warrant of habitability" which included a contractual duty on the part of the landlord to maintain the premises in suitable repair where such repairs "required access to equipment in areas in the control of the landlord, and skills which no urban tenant possesses."

"[T]he duty of taking protective measures guarding the entire premises and the areas peculiarly under the landlord's control against the perpetration of criminal acts," stated Judge Wilkey, could also be placed upon the landlord, as an implied term in the lease, because the landlord was "the party to the lease contract who has the effective capacity to perform these necessary acts."

Finally, in determining the standard of care which should be applied in such cases, the court appeared to turn to the law of torts for guidance, although Judge Wilkey indicated that the landlord's obligation was the same whether considered as an obligation grounded in tort or in contract. The landlord's duty, according to the court, was to take the precautions "commonly provided in apartments of this character and type in this community." The record as to custom was "unsatisfactory," because of the limitations on evidence imposed by the trial judge as a result of objections by "defendant's counsel." Given the paucity of the record, and blaming this on "defendant's counsel and the trial judge," Judge Wilkey took the security precautions which existed at 1500 Massachusetts Avenue in 1959, when Mrs. Kline moved in, as the standard to be maintained, and held that the landlord was responsible to Mrs. Kline for the consequences of failing to keep up this standard.

Since Judge Wilkey's opinion in *Kline*, courts have held that landlord's violate an enforceable duty of protection when they fail to safeguard their tenants from foreseeable criminal acts in several other jurisdictions including Georgia, New Jersey, and New York. The rationale has apparently been rejected in Illinois and Minnesota. Note, The Duty of a Landlord to Exercise Reasonable Care in the Selection and Retention of Tenants, 30 Stan.L. Rev. 725, 728n. (1978). How might one relate the holding in *Kline* to the "death of contract" and the "New Torts?" Are these common-law developments the best means of effecting change in late twentieth century law?

9. Commenting on cases such as *Helling* and *Dillon*, Professor James A. Henderson, Jr. wrote in 1976 that:

> The reforms and changes in the law of negligence in recent years have, purportedly to advance identifiable social objectives, eliminated much of the specificity with which negligence principles traditionally have been formulated. We are rapidly approaching the day when liability will be determined routinely on a case by case, "under all the circumstances," basis, with decision makers (often juries) guided only by the broadest of general principles. When that day arrives, the retreat from the rule of law will be complete, principled decision will have been replaced with decision by whim, and the common law of negligence will have degenerated into an unjustifiably inefficient, thinly disguised lottery.

Henderson, Expanding the Negligence Concept: Retreat from the Rule of Law, 51 Ind.L.J. 467, 468 (1976).* How might Herbert Wechsler have assessed *Helling* and *Dillon*? What might have been the reaction of Morton Horwitz?

In another part of his article Professor Henderson diagnosed part of the current torts pathology as "irresponsiblility" on the part of legal academics. Only two allegedly guilty parties were named, but one of them was Marshall Shapo, for his comments quoted in note 5, supra. Stated Henderson, "These are commentaries which tend to speak of the common law torts judgment as a tool of harassment in modern political warfare, and whose disregard for judicial integrity approaches recklessness." Id., at 523. Would this diagnosis of pathology meet the standards of Helling v. Carey? From what you have seen of the modern law of torts, would you agree with Professor Henderson? What are the economic implications of these recent court decisions? Does the "New Torts" seem in accord with the notions of popular sovereignty and social mobility we saw reflected in earlier decisions? For what may be the latest comment in the *judicial integrity of process* vs. *substantive justice* debate in torts see Pedrick, The Regeneration of Tort Law, 1979 Ariz.St.L.J. 143, which returns to a position not unlike Professor Shapo's, and declares that the "crisis" caused by products liability and medical malpractice insurance seems to be over.

SECTION C. THE LAWYER AND THE PUBLIC INTEREST

RALPH NADER, LAW SCHOOLS AND LAW FIRMS **

(1969).

It was similar ritual every year. About 550 new law students would file into venerable Austin Hall at Harvard Law School on a September day and hear the no-nonsense dean, Erwin N. Griswold, orient them. The good dean had the speech down to a practiced spontaneity. He advised them that at that instant they had become members of the legal profession, that law firms were the backbone of the profession, that there were no glee clubs at the Harvard Law School and that the law was a jealous mistress. Thus was launched a process of engineering the law student into corridor thinking and largely nonnormative evaluation. It was a three-year excursus through legal minutiae, embraced by wooden logic and impervious to what Oliver Wendell Holmes once called the "felt necessities of our times." * * *

The Harvard Law pattern—honed to a perfection of brilliant myopia and superfluous rigor—became early in the century the Olympian object of mimicry for law schools throughout the country. * * * This system faithfully nourished and fundamentally upheld a developing legal order which has become more aristocratic and less responsive to the needs and strains of a complex society. In turn, the established legal order controlled the terms of entry into the profession in ways that fettered imagination, inhibited reform and made alienation the price of questioning its assumptions and proposing radical surgery.

Unreal as it may appear, the connection between the legal establishment and the spectacular increase in the breakdown of the legal system has rarely been made outside the fraternity. This is due to the functional modesty of the profession, its reluctance to parade itself as the shaper, staffer and broker for the operating legal framework in this country. What is not claimed is not attributed. This escape from responsibility for the quality and quantity of justice in the relationships of men and institutions has been a touchstone of the legal profession.

Anyone who wishes to understand the legal crises that envelop the contemporary scene—in the cities, in the environment, in the courts, in the marketplace, in public services, in the corporate-government arenas and in Washington—should come to grips with this legal flow chart that begins with the law schools and ends with the law firms, particularly the large corporate law firms of New York and Washington.

Harvard Law's most enduring contribution to legal education was the mixing of the case method of study with the Socratic method of teaching. Developed late in the nineteenth century under Dean Christopher Columbus Langdell, these techniques were tailor-made to transform intellectual arrogance into pedagogical systems that humbled the student into accepting its premises, levels of abstractions and choice of subjects. Law professors take delight in crushing egos in order to acculturate the students to what they called "legal reasoning" or "thinking like a lawyer." The process is a highly sophisticated form of mind control that trades off breadth of vision and factual inquiry for freedom to roam in an intellectual cage.

* * * Inasmuch as the Socratic method is a game at which only one (the professor) can play, the students are conditioned to react to questions and issues which they have no role in forming or stimulating. Such teaching *forms* have been crucial in perpetuating the status quo in teaching *content*. For decades, the law school curriculum reflected with remarkable fidelity the commercial demands of law firm practice. * * * What determined the curriculum was the legal interest that came with retainers. Thus, the curriculum pecking order was predictable—tax, corporate, securities and property law at the top and torts (personal injury) and criminal law, among others, at the bottom. Although in terms of the seriousness of the legal interest and the numbers of people affected, torts and criminal law would command the heights, the reverse was true, for the retain-

ers were not as certain nor as handsome. * * * Courses tracking the lucre and the prevailing ethos did not embrace any concept of professional sacrifice and service to the unrepresented poor or to public interests being crushed by private power. * * *

The generations of lawyers shaped by these law schools in turn shaped the direction and quality of the legal system. They came to this task severely unequipped except for the furtherance of their acquisitive drives. Rare was the law graduate who had the faintest knowledge of the institutionalized illegality of the cities in such areas as building and health code violations, the endemic bribing of officialdom, the illegalities in the marketplace, from moneylending to food. Fewer still were the graduates who knew anything of the institutions that should have been bathed in legal insight and compassion— hospitals, schools, probate and other courts, juvenile and mental institutions and prisons. Racialism, the gap between rich and poor, the seething slums—these conditions were brought to the attention of law firms by the illumination of city riots rather than the illumination of concerned intellects.

* * * Another failure in analysis was thematic of the entire curriculum. Normative thinking—the "shoulds" and the "oughts"— was not recognized as part and parcel of rigorous analytic skills. Although the greatest forays in past legal scholarship, from the works of Roscoe Pound to those of Judge Jerome Frank, proceeded from a cultivated sense of injustice, the nation's law schools downplayed the normative inquiry as something of an intellectual pariah. Thus the great legal challenges of access to large governmental and corporate institutions, the control of environmental pollution, the requisites of international justice suffered from the inattention of mechanized minds. * * *

Possibly the greatest failure of the law schools—a failure of the faculty—was not to articulate a theory and practice of a just deployment of legal manpower. With massive public interests deprived of effective legal representation, the law schools continued to encourage recruits for law firms whose practice militated against any such representation, even on a sideline, *pro bono* basis. Lawyers labored for polluters, not anti-polluters, for sellers, not consumers, for corporations, not citizens, for labor leaders, not rank and file, for, not against, judicial and administrative delay, for preferential business access to government and against equal citizen access to the same government, for agricultural subsidies to the rich but not food stamps for the poor, for tax and quota privileges, not for equity and free trade. None of this and much more seemed to trouble the law schools. * * *

The strains on this established legal order began to be felt with Brown v. Board of Education in 1954. *Brown* rubbed the raw nerves of the established order in public. The mounting conflict began to shake a legal order built on deception and occult oppression. The ugly scars of the land burned red. Law students began to sense, to feel, to participate, and to earn scars of their own. Then came the Kennedy era with its verbal eloquence, its Peace Corps—overseas and later here. Then came Vietnam and Watts, Newark and the perturbation became a big-league jolt. Law students began to turn away from private practice, especially at the Ivy League law schools. * * *

At the same time, more new or alternative career roles in public service began to emerge. Neighborhood Legal Services, funded by OEO, was manned by 1,800 young lawyers around the country at last count. The draft is driving many graduates into VISTA programs. There are more federal court clerkships available. * * *

Meanwhile back at the law schools, student activism has arrived. Advocacy of admission, curriculum and grading reform is occurring at Harvard and Yale. Similar currents are appearing at other law schools. New courses in environmental, consumer and poverty law are being added to the lists. The first few weeks of the present school year indicate that the activists' attention is turning to the law firms that are now coming on campus to recruit. In an unprecedented move, a number of detailed questionnaires, signed by large numbers of students, are going out to these firms. The questions range far beyond the expected areas of the firms' policies on minority and women lawyers, and *pro bono* work. They include inquiries about the firms' policies on containing their clients' ambitions, on involvement in corporate client and political activity, and on subsidizing public-interest legal activity. * * *

The responses which the firms give to these questionnaires, and whatever planned response the students envisage for those firms who choose not to reply, will further sharpen the issues and the confrontations. The students have considerable leverage. They know it is a seller's market. * * *

In recent months, there has been much soul-searching among the larger firms. * * * Some New York and San Francisco firms are considering or have instituted time off allowances ranging from a few weeks a year to a sabbatical. Piper & Marbury, a large Baltimore firm, has announced its intention to establish a branch office in the slums to service the needs of poor people, without charging fees if there is an inability to pay anything. Arnold and Porter, the second largest Washington, D.C. firm, has appointed a full time *pro bono* lawyer and is permitting all firm members to spend, if they wish, an average of 15 percent of their working hours on public service activities. Hogan and Hartson, the third largest D.C. firm, is setting up a "Community Services Department" to "take on public interest representation on a non-chargeable or, where appropriate, a discounted fee basis," according to the firm's memorandum on the subject.

The Hogan and Hartson memorandum is a fairly candid document. Like other firm memorandums on *pro bono* ventures, there is the acknowledgment that such a move "may have a favorable impact upon recruitment." * * * In its internal firm statement, the executive committee notes that it "regards the relative disfavor into which the major law firms have fallen to be attributable, at least in part, to the feeling among recent law school graduates that *these firms have failed to respond to the larger problems of contemporary society*." (Their emphasis.) Some statistics impressed the senior partners: the University of Michigan Law School reports that 26 of its 1969 graduates entered Wall Street law firms as compared with an average of 75 in preceding years. Harvard Law School reported that the percentage of its graduates entering private law practice declined from 54 percent in 1964 to 41 percent in 1968, and an even more significant decline is expected in the next few years.

* * *

Because of the enormously greater cost-benefit which attaches to the more basic *pro bono* efforts, the external and internal pressures on the firm's leaders will be in that direction. This could lead to more profound clashes between the firm's allegiance to its paying clients and its recognition of public service responsibilities. With additional law student and younger lawyer demands for cash contributions for scholarships to minority law students, for admission of more minority lawyers to firm membership, and for senior partners to pay "reparations" out of their own salaries to assist the legally deprived—all demands made or in the process of being made—the pressure may soon exceed the firms' threshold of tolerance. At that point the experiment in *pro bono* may terminate.

Whatever the outcome, the big firms will never be the same again. They will either have to dedicate substantial manpower and resources to public service, and somehow resolve the conflict of interest problem, or they will decline in status to the level of corporate house counsel or public relations firms. The polarization of the legal profession seems a more likely development. Before he left Harvard almost two years age to become U.S. Solicitor General, Dean Griswold wrote of his belief that there would be a "decline in the relative importance of private law practice as we have known it in the past." This trend is in fact occurring as far as the younger lawyers' concept of importance is concerned. However, the immense power of these firms and their tailored capacity to apply know-how, know-who and other influences remains undiminished.

Recent evidence of the resourcefulness of large corporate law firms in overwhelming the opposition on behalf of its clients comes from the firm of Wilmer, Cutler and Pickering. A firm team, headed by Lloyd Cutler, obtained last month on behalf of the domestic auto companies a feeble consent decree in return for the Justice Department's dropping its civil antitrust case charging the domestic auto companies with conspiracy to restrain the development and marketing of pollution control systems since 1953. * * * Without going into further detail, it is sufficient to state that many law students and younger lawyers see a divergence in such a case between the lawyer's commitment to the public interest and his commitment to the auto industry.

Professor Charles A. Reich of Yale Law School expressed one form of this heightened expectation of the lawyer's role as follows: "It is important to recognize explicitly that whether he is engaged publicly or privately, the lawyer will no longer be serving merely as the spokesman for others. As the law becomes more and more a determinative force in public and private affairs, the lawyer must carry the responsibility of his specialized knowledge, and formulate ideas as well as advocate them. In a society where law is a primary force, the lawyer must be a primary, not a secondary, being."

The struggle of the established law firms to portray themselves as merely legal counselors affording their corporate clients their right to legal representation is losing ground. * * *

Clearly, there is need for a new dimension to the legal profession. This need does not simply extend to those groups or individuals who cannot afford a lawyer. It extends to the immense proliferation of procedural and substantive interests which go to the essence of the kind of society we will have in the future, but which have no legal representation. The absence of remedy is tantamount to an absence of right. * * *

The yearning of more and more young lawyers and law students is to find careers as public-interest lawyers who, independent of government and industry, will work on these two major institutions to further the creative rule of law. The law, suffering recurrent and deepening breakdowns, paralysis and obsolescence, should no longer tolerate a retainer astigmatism which allocates brilliant minds to trivial or harmful interests.

NOTES AND QUESTIONS

1.   Do you agree with Mr. Nader's suggestion that law school engineers one "into corridor thinking and largely non-normative evaluation?" Even if the legal system has become "more aristocratic" does this necessarily mean that it must be "less responsive to the needs and strains of a complex society?" Mr. Nader argues that the "legal establishment" is somehow responsible for the "breakdown of the legal system." How is this, exactly? What is the "legal establishment?" How has the legal system "broken down?"

2.   Do his comments on the Socratic method (e. g. "a game that only one can play") and the determination of law school curricula have the ring of truth about them?

3.   Note that Nader, as does nearly everyone else in modern times, invokes the name of Oliver Wendell Holmes, Jr. Would Holmes have agreed

or disagreed with the main point Nader makes in this piece? For example, would Holmes agree that "the greatest failure of the law schools—a failure of the faculty—was not to articulate a theory and practice of just deployment of legal manpower?" Is there anyone else whom we have studied in the course who might subscribe to the notions articulated by Nader?

4. Nader predicts that "the big firms will never be the same again." Was he right? Nader, at the close of his piece, singles out Wilmer, Cutler & Pickering, a large Washington law firm, for criticism. In the next excerpt, a former Wilmer, Cutler & Pickering lawyer responds in kind. Your task in reading this book review and the author's response is to determine whether any of the issues Mr. Nader raises are being discussed, and how they are resolved.

DANIEL POLSBY, BOOK REVIEW (OF MARK GREEN'S THE OTHER GOVERNMENT (1975)) *

74 Mich.L.Rev. 148 (1975).

* * *

[I.]

The Other Government is about the power Washington lawyers wield over the government of the United States. Author Mark Green sets the scene for us:

> As the Washington, D.C., Tourline bus creeps along Rock Creek Parkway, the guide diligently points out the Lincoln and Jefferson memorials, * * * Congress, the Supreme Court, the White House. But a bus guide knowledgeable in the reality rather than the formality of Washington could have taken his visitors by the other government—those thirty-five large law firms, of more than twenty attorneys each, which practice powerlaw. (p. 3.)

This is a particularly felicitous beginning for The Other Government. The Tourline bus company is fictional, and none of the many Washington tour bus companies has a route that follows Rock Creek Parkway.[1] In short, Mark Green's Washington could be the capital city of Franz Kafka's Amerika. Each book, in its own way, raises genuine and difficult questions about the human condition. But in the course of dealing with these questions, each subtly shifts the relationship between truth and fantasy, the real and the unreal.

1. Commercial vehicles or common carriers are prohibited by regulation from operating on roadways in the National Capital Parks except by order of the Superintendent of National Capital Parks. 36 CFR 50.36(a) (1975).

The Other Government in essence raises two questions. First, do ethical principles require a lawyer to temper zeal for his client's interest with concern for the public good? And, second, do lawyers practicing in the national capital have any special responsibilities to the public interest? * * *

A response to the first question is found in the official posture of the American Bar Association: that a lawyer is not a mere instrumentality of his client's interests but is, above all, the guardian of our law and democratic principles. This articulates a norm that most lawyers accept: the obligation to the client is secondary to the obligation to society. But is there a conflict between this principle and the lawyer's chief function in our society, zealously to represent the interests of his client within bounds of law?

There is, I think, no real conflict between these principles. Our legal system presupposes a process dominated not by interested parties but by a disinterested decision maker who is free and competent to decide between opposing contentions. It is the existence of this neutral decision maker that harmonizes the potential dissonance between the interests of the client and the interests of society. But this proposition, of course, has a corollary: If the decision maker is incompetent or corrupt, the lawyer's moral role is drastically different. An essential but unspoken assumption of *The Other Government* is that the corollary fits the facts. But the proof Green tenders on the subject tells the opposite tale.

The second major question raised by The Other Government is whether Washington lawyers should be subject to any distinctive ethical considerations. I think the answer is clearly yes. If the Washington lawyer is involved with business decisions of large clients, if his work may affect many people and many interests, obviously his ethical considerations are broader than those of a lawyer whose work touches few. * * *

The principles, as usual, are clear enough; few are likely to quarrel with the utilitarian postulate that no lawyer can properly represent a client if the lawyer calculates that the social cost of that representation will outweigh the social benefit. The hard part is applying this principle to the facts. Lawyers may disagree on how the calculation comes out in a given case depending on (1) differing perceptions about the merits of the case; (2) differences in various lawyers' need for money, work, or other epiphenomena of representing clients; and (3) perceptions about the social value of allowing an individual to hire a lawyer to represent him * * *.

The factual thesis of The Other Government is simple: that "Washington lawyers are among the most powerful people in the country today" (p. 4); that they are "earthshakers and lawmakers" (p. 9), a shadow government of lawlords (p. 15) who function, not merely as conventional advocates, but as decision makers in their own right, actually giving orders to agency bureaucrats (p. 9). The work of these lawyers is based on "ten commandments": reputation, brains, information, interlocking interests, preferential access, lobbying, law-writing, inundation, delay, and corruption (pp. 12–15). These skills, says Green, are especially the tools of the famous law firm of Covington and Burling, and of my former associate Lloyd Cutler.[5] An examination of Green's own tale of their exploits, however, shows how tenuous is the ground upon which the thesis rests.[6]

* * * It is first retold how in 1956 Gerhard Gesell, then [Covington and Burling's] premier antitrust litigator, successfully defended du Pont in Sherman Act litigation that went to the Supreme Court (pp. 75–76). The essential question, as Green explains it, was whether there existed any economic substitutes for cellophane. Gesell convinced the Court that foil, glassine, and other packing materials did compete with cellophane. Score one for the lawlords. But there follows immediately a curious passage (p. 76) that I find difficult to reconcile with the putative theme of the book: "Government lawyers were aghast at the decision. But the Covington team * * * had won what was to be, until the 1970's, the last major antitrust victory of a private corporation against the government in the Supreme Court."[7] If Gesell in fact never won another major antitrust case in the Supreme Court [8] one would suppose an explanation to be in order. Had Gesell lost his touch?

The next bit of "evidence" also involves du Pont, this time represented by Covington's Hugh Cox. The government sought to force a divestiture of du Pont's approximately $3 billion worth of General Motors stock and at length succeeded (pp. 77–79). "Cox had lost his biggest case," Green tells us (p. 79).

Further evidence of the lawlords' mighty sway is found in Covington's representation of General Electric in the electrical industry price-fixing conspiracy trial (pp. 80–83). Gesell pleaded his client

---

5. It would be more usual in law firm parlance to say that I was Cutler's associate and he my employer, but if associateness is not a reciprocal relationship, what fun is it? It is important to stress this connection with Wilmer, Cutler, and Pickering at the outset, so that the reader can evaluate my criticisms of *The Other Government* with this possible source of bias in mind.

6. I have been content, for the most part, to rely on the facts as Green gives them; I do not mean, by repeating them, to warrant their accuracy. On the contrary, the book is filled with mistakes large and small, and I do not doubt that the facts I did not check are as snarled as the ones I did. Some of the latter I note throughout the body of this review.

7. Whether this assertion is true, I suppose, turns on what you think a major case is. See, e. g., United States v. National Dairy Prods. Corp., 372 U.S. 29, 83 S.Ct. 594, 9 L.Ed.2d 561 (1963); FTC v. National Cas. Co., 357 U.S. 560, 78 S.Ct. 1260, 2 L.Ed.2d 1540 (1958); FTC v. Standard Oil Co., 355 U.S. 396, 78 S.Ct. 369, 2 L.Ed.2d 359 (1958).

8. Gesell was appointed judge of the District Court for the District of Columbia in 1967. I have no idea what Gesell's box score was between 1956 and 1967. See note 6 supra.

guilty and fines totalling $400,000 were levied. Several executives of the corporation served thirty-day jail terms, an extremely rare occurrence in antitrust prosecutions. * * *

Then, "[i]n 1967 and 1968, the federal government brought seven anti-trust cases against [ITT's baking subsidiary], three criminal and four civil; the government won all seven" (p. 88). Green sums up: "Whatever Covington's role in these Justice Department cases, no one can doubt their significance" (p. 96). I, for one, do not doubt their significance. What they signify is that Covington and Burling's much-vaunted "power" does not appear to include the power to manipulate the outcomes of important cases. * * *

Lloyd Cutler fares little better in Green's hands. Cutler appears to hold a strange fascination for Green, who compares him to Mao Tse-Tung (p. 55) but leaves it open whether Cutler is an "evil genius" (p. 169)[9] or a "guiding genius" (p. 252).[10] * * * But does Cutler lawmake and earthshake? * * * As with Covington, the proof fails to measure up to the pleading. For example, Cutler participated on behalf of CBS in the FCC's hearings on the so-called fifty-fifty rule, proposed to prohibit networks from supplying their affiliates with more than fifty percent of regularly scheduled prime time series programming (pp. 223–24). Cutler argued, Green tells us, that there were not enough sponsors willing to assume the risk of underwriting non-network shows and that CBS was supplying the public with the programming they wanted anyway. But the Commission nevertheless went ahead with a version of the fifty-fifty rule, now called the prime time access rule, which prevents the networks from programming one of the four prime time hours nightly. * * *

Green tenders another example of Cutler's extraordinary influence: the 1970 merger plans of American and Western Airlines (pp. 200–06). To secure this result, says Green, Cutler and his client "launched a lobbying campaign impressive even for the well traveled

9. Deadpans Green: "Not surprisingly, Cutler is sensitive to such criticisms" (p. 169).

10. Green's Cutler is definitely, however, "hardworking and hustling" (p. 49), even to the point, we are told, of a bit of discreet self-promotion. In connection with the American Airlines campaign contribution scandal, for example, Cutler reportedly advised the airline, his client, to "come clean," and as part of his strategy spread the word of American's confession through the news media. According to Green, "Cutler called Washington Post executive editor Benjamin Bradlee to elaborate on American's admission and his own role in the episode. Bradlee thought this excessive self-promotion, but the Post story did laud" American's candor in the incident (p. 48). Curious about how Green could tell what Bradlee thinks, I called the Washington Post for clarification. I read Bradlee the entire paragraph in which the excerpted sentence appeared and asked him: "How does Mark Green know what you think?" "Beats the shit out of me," he explained. Elaborating, Bradlee told me that he remembers having a conversation with Green but denies the thought about Cutler that Green attributes to him. Telephone conversation, July 23, 1975.

corridors of Washington agencies" (p. 201). They visited with four of the five members of the Civil Aeronautics Board, the head of the Justice Department's Antitrust Division, officials in the White House and the Department of Transportation, and Treasury Secretary Connally; their "drumfire succeeded in inspiring transportation summitry" (p. 204). The Antitrust Division opposed the merger, however, and in the subsequent faceoff between the government and The Other Government, the former as usual, prevailed.

These tales of lost lawsuits and disappointed hopes are not meant to imply that Washington lawyers do not deliver a worthwhile service to their clients. I intend only to suggest that they cannot deliver particular results unless they can persuade The Original Government —the one I work for—to see things their clients' way. This persuasion, in my experience, has essentially involved straight lawyering— reasoned argument, on the merits, with the relevant private interests fully disclosed. Green's own showing decisively points to the conclusion that The Original Government is quite up to its task of refereeing the revenue-producing activities of business. In short, The Other Government appears to confirm the assumption that there exists a disinterested decision maker that is free and competent to choose the public interest from among opposing contentions. The verification of this assumption, in turn, has an important bearing on the morality of representing a client with whose views the lawyer does not necessarily agree.[14]

[II.]

The chief intellectual shortcoming of *The Other Government* is its many facile assumptions about the public interest. Green appears to believe that good and evil go around unmasked, equally obvious to all, and that only greed and perversity can explain differences among people about the identity of each. * * *

Safe cars and safe drugs, for example, are undeniable goods, but the question is never presented whether, *ceteris paribus*, society would rather have safe drugs and cars or unsafe drugs and cars. The question is always how much each attainable increment of safety is going to cost. The cost of producing an automobile or a drug that could not injure a human being would be so high that no one would be able to get any benefit from either. Whether one believes that an increment of benefit is worth the cost increment is a value choice about which people may differ. Society therefore needs political institutions designed to mediate differences between people in particular cases. The lawyer's special province is to administer one of the more important of these mediating institutions—the judicial system.

---

14. * * * [A]fter a year's personal experience in government, I am deeply skeptical of claims that the special access and charisma of super-lawyers exert much influence on government policy. The boring truth seems to be that for the most part policy is generated by staff bureaucrats.

But one of the necessary conditions of this trusteeship is a degree of professional detachment about which substantive policies shall be adopted in any given case. * * *

* * * [I]ntolerance of substantive policies fairly arrived at, just because they are contrary to one's own view, is inconsistent with democratic theory and is, more often than not, based on some doubtful assumptions about the nature of the public interest. * * *

The fugitive character of the public interest is illustrated by one of the examples Green uses for just the opposite purpose—the peanut butter rule-making, in which Covington and Burling participated at great and laborious length (pp. 132–40). When, in 1959, the Food and Drug Administration considered what recipe should be prescribed in the peanut butter food standard, it had no access to the Platonic Caves wherein the Idea of Peanut Butterness is kept [sic]. Green, one gathers from the book, practically lives in the Platonic Caves and could probably tell you offhand the maximum percentage of partially hardened vegetable oil that may be added to ground peanuts before the concoction stops being peanut butter and starts being something else (pp. 133–34). But the FDA was required to make its determination on the basis of record evidence compiled at a hearing. That this was no easy task can be illustrated by an experiment. Pulverize two cups of peanuts in a blender; the result will be a thick, syrupy substance like that sold in some stores as "old fashioned peanut butter." It is a good, inexpensive substitute for tahini paste if you are making *hommos*, but it tastes chalky and coats the inside of your mouth like tar. In order to make a product that most people will find acceptable as peanut butter, some hydrogenated vegetable oil must be added. Green implies that the industry had only one goal: getting FDA permission to use the smallest possible proportion of peanuts to the cheaper vegetable oil.

* * * While each manufacturer will cut costs all it can, its highest priority will be to increase its market share. This, in turn, will require that the product be formulated with continuing reference to consumer tastes. In a relatively competitive line of commerce like peanut butter, a maximum-flexibility standard would allow for widely different peanut butters, and the preferences of consumers, rather than the authoritative pronouncement of the Commissioner of Food and Drugs, would decide which was the "real" peanut butter and which were either (1) too much like tan Crisco, or (2) too much like *tahini* paste.

I do not know that the FDA standard does not, in fact, allow for sufficient variation in the product to make such competition feasible. But I have a suspicion, based on three years' experience as a group worker with children, that it does not. At least half of my former charges preferred butter or margarine on their peanut butter sandwiches. Putting margarine on peanut butter sandwiches has the same effect as increasing the percentage of vegetable oil in the peanut butter. Yet manufacturers that want to sell a product more nearly in accord with the tastes of these consumers must sell it as "peanut spread" or "imitation peanut butter." Either of these nomenclatures might present a difficult obstacle to the marketing of a new product, and, as a result, many consumers must do without a peanut spread they can enjoy without doctoring it with margarine. The great food processing conglomerates, of course, lose little: they make margarine as well as peanut butter.

Even where the public interest seems clear at one time, later events may show it is not so. One of the greatest public interest triumphs of the young Abe Fortas was persuading the United States Court of Appeals for the District of Columbia Circuit in 1954 to adopt the *Durham* rule for insanity—that a person is not responsible for criminal misconduct that is the product of a "mental disease or mental defect." At the time, it was widely considered a progressive, forward-looking rule. But almost immediately, problems began to arise. What is a "mental disease or defect" for the purposes of the test? What connection between the mental illness and the criminal act is necessary in order to characterize the latter as the "product" of the former? How can psychiatrists be permitted to testify on these matters without foreclosing the very issue the jury is supposed to decide." Finally, in 1972, the D.C. Circuit scrapped Durham for the American Law Institute's definition of insanity.[25]

Fortas probably never undertook a matter for a paying client that produced more unfortunate results. *Durham* was an unmitigated disaster for the courts and probably never eased the plight of a single insane person in the District of Columbia through its seventeen years of life. But that is precisely the point about good and evil: it is often terribly hard to tell them apart ahead of time. While careful reflection on the policy options and competing concerns may not improve outcomes in every case, it seems prudent to behave as if it would. Such reflection is best promoted by the adversary process, which in turn suggests that a party should not have to win his case before he can get a lawyer.

In other situations the alternatives and concerns are not hidden, but the morally "right" result may nevertheless be difficult to reach. Green discusses the "air bag" matter (pp. 183–85), for example, which, though he does not recognize it, involves competition between incommensurable values. In 1972, Ford Motor Company and several other automobile manufacturers went to court to overturn standard 208 of the National Highway Traffic Administration (NHTA). This standard required that automobiles, beginning with the 1974 model year, be equipped with passive occupant-restraint devices with speci-

---

25. See United States v. Brawner, 471 F.2d 969 (D.C.Cir.1972). *Brawner* re- counts the history of the insanity defense in the Circuit since *Durham*.

fied performance characteristics. As a practical matter, this standard required crash-inflated airbags. * * * John H. Pickering, Lloyd Cutler's partner, argued on behalf of Ford that, among other things, the standard's performance specifications were not sufficiently objective to allow compliance because of defects in NHTA's own testing procedures. Green saw this as "a typical public interest-private interest battle" (p. 184) in which there was no doubt where the public interest lay: he claimed that any delay in instituting the air bag standard would cause "thousands of people * * * needlessly [to] die" (p. 185). But the court saw it differently:

> * * * In the absence of objectively defined performance requirements and test procedures, a manufacturer has no assurance that his own test results will be duplicated in tests conducted by the Agency. Accordingly, such objective criteria are absolutely necessary so that "the question of whether there is compliance with the standard can be answered by objective measurement and without recourse to any subjective determination." [29]

What is the "right" result? On the one hand is the contention that manufacturers' resistance to the use of air bags will cause the loss of many lives. The competing contention is that the conduct supposedly required by the rule has not been declared with the clarity demanded by what Professor Fuller calls the "inner morality of law." [30] * * * Green, ironically, is correct in calling this case "typical": the court's conclusion is typical of what one would expect where a high value is place on regularity of government action. A similar question is before an appellate court every time a convicted defendant asks for a retrial because crucial evidence was unreasonably seized or the jury was improperly instructed. In such cases, we pretermit (or even assume) the substantive correctness of the result and ask whether the process was fair.

[III.]

The failures of *The Other Government* are not limited to intellectual ones. It also suffers from failures of the heart, and these are by far its most serious flaws. First, there is a studied evasiveness about the prose as though Green were somehow ambivalent about standing behind many of the things he wishes us to understand: "To admirers, [John W.] Davis's soaring response remains the classic explanation of the lawyer's role. But others wonder exactly what philosophy it was that required Davis to devote his professional life to the House of Morgan" (pp. 268–69). "To his admirers, [Cutler]

29. Chrysler Corp. v. Department of Transp., 472 F.2d 659, 675 (6th Cir. 1972).

30. L. Fuller, The Morality of Law 42 (1964).

is the model of the modern lawyer, but his critics would sentence him to the electric chair" (p. 45).   *   *   *   This technique might be called the Nixon euphuism: criticisms are advanced *ex nihilo* or by third persons and seldom supported with reasons. The Nixon euphuism gives an author "plausible deniability" for the things that he writes and frustrates reasoned debate. It is a technique best avoided.

Another failure of the heart is reflected in the incoherence of the book's organization; it suggests an unsettling contempt of the whole undertaking. Despite the author's assurance that the book had a gestation period of five years (p. vii), there is strong textual evidence that *The Other Government* was rushed into print.[34] Nor is the evidence of perfunctory craftsmanship formal only. Substantively, *The Other Government* wanders around in a wilderness of trivia, confusion, and malice. For example, as chapter one ends we are still awaiting evidence that Washington lawyers are "earthshakers and lawmakers." But chapter two has quite a different purpose—anthropology. Its mission is to show that Covington and Burling is "a culture as well as a law firm" (p. 31). But this is curious anthropology; rather, it is an odd ragbag of facts, nonfacts, gossip, and opinions. Thus, we start with the assertion that the firm is the city's most influential—the Everest of Washington practice (pp. 16–24). Next is a short historical sketch, beginning with the firm's origins during the Wilson Administration (pp. 20–25) and ending with the assertion that the firm is "very much an institution in flux" (p. 25.) Following this assertion are biographies of three firm lawyers, Dean Acheson, H. Thomas Austern, and Peter B. Hutt (pp. 25–31), that appear to illustrate just the opposite point.[35]   *   *   *   There follows the fact that the firm has a large support staff (p. 37) and the nonfact that associates are expected to bill eighty hours every two weeks (p. 38). We are also given some soft-core gossip: certain Covington lawyers have known drinking problems (p. 31), and a lawyer there was discovered one Saturday morning rolling on the office floor with his secretary (pp. 31–32). Finally, we come to a passage tinted with the sunset, which suggests that Covington may, in fact, be over the hill: "Great institutions come, peak and decline, from the British East India Trade Company to *Life* magazine to the New York Yankees, and it is only in retrospect that we learn that moment in time when events conspired to undo institutional inevitability" (p. 44).

---

34. In addition to many apparent proofing errors, see, e. g., pp. 37 note, 138, 166, are assorted giddy howlers like: "[Washington lawyers] are to all lawyers and citizens what the heart is to the body: by dint of central location and essential function, both are the reigning organs of their respective body politic" (p. 4) and "Is [*pro bono work*] built into the law firm's structure of merely random events?" (p. 244). Such defects, to my mind, are autoptical proof of insouciance at least.

35. From Acheson to Austern to Hutt, the firm has shown a consistent preference for graduates of the Harvard Law School who have stamina, brains, and a taste for representing business corporations.   *   *   *

Well, which is to be? Tenzings on the Everest of powerlaw, or the Yankees on their way to the cellar? Since both propositions are expounded and neither is anywhere illustrated, it presumably does not matter. Although both assertions could be false, they could not both be true.

* * *

And then there are * * * outright accusations of personally and professionally disgraceful behavior. Did you know, for example, that a certain Covington partner—Green names him, though I shall not—"does not particularly like black people"? This, according to Green, is "obvious to fellow lawyers" (p. 199). Or did you know that another (unnamed) Covington lawyer destroyed unidentified evidence of a client's criminal conduct (p. 70)? And how about H. Thomas Austern's unethical behavior in citing precedents to government officials? At least four times Austern is in effect called a knave, a bully, or worse for this offense. And what of the "ex parte" contacts Washington counsel so frequently have with public officials? Well—what about them? In his dark references to private (p. 201) or "ex parte" (p. 202) meetings between businessmen or their lawyers and government officials, Green muddles the distinction between contacts that are forbidden by agency rules and those that are not and leaves the reader who does not know better with a sinister, and inaccurate, impression. Administrative agencies, whether inside the executive branch or independent, are not courts and are not supposed to conduct their business in an ivory tower, aloof from the teeming and intricate commerce they were established to regulate. * * * Bureaucrats find many such meetings useful and constructive and are at least as available to members of the general public, including self-styled representatives of the public interest, as to businessmen and their lawyers.

[IV.]

* * *

* * * The last chapter of *The Other Government* is entitled "The Ethics of Powerlaw," and its burden is to propose "a new lawyers' ethic": that a lawyer ought in every case to "make a judgement about the likely impact [of his representation] on the public, and if the client desires tactics based on political influence or seeks a demonstrable though avoidable public harm, he should quit the account" (p. 287; italics omitted). Green quotes a Wilmer, Cutler, and Pickering recruiting memorandum that expresses the same thought: "We decline to represent clients whose objectives or tactics we find unacceptable, or who ask us to represent a position on any basis other than its merits" (p. 282). Both of these statements accord with the utilitarian calculus laid down as a truism at the beginning of this book review.

It is a comfort to know that there is at least one thing about which both Cutler and Green can agree, even if it is only a truism. Unfortunately, as Green recognizes (pp. 287–88), this truism leaves intact all the problems. Where Green and many other lawyers—I, for one—would disagree most radically is on the value to be assigned to giving even a bad client the benefit of process before deciding what should be done with him. We see the existence of process as so important to the idea of justice, both in a theoretical and in a practical sense, that we are even willing to tolerate injustice in particular cases in order to maintain the integrity of governmental processes over the long pull. For Green, however, the axis of decision is always substantive right and wrong; his conception of right is usually vivid and seldom alloyed by doubt. Accordingly, the whole idea of regular process seems senseless to him. It is worth reflecting, however, that the same logic that makes nonsense of giving General Motors the benefit of process also makes nonsense of the idea of democracy. Why give General Motors a fair trial if its guilt is self-evident? Why ask people who ought to be President if the answer is indisputable? It is a rather totalitarian world view that assumes that "true" public policy can be extracted from the raw material of experience, dialectical argument, or a leader's vision without some mediating political process.

I do not, however, accuse Green of being totalitarian. He might become so if he reasoned some of his premises through to a conclusion, but his allergy to process extends to logic as much as to law. He is a demagogue, though, and his unsystematic style hardly excuses the short shrift he gives to the very serious matters that *The Other Government* should have treated.   *   *   *

What makes his result the more embarrassing is the sound advice Green received from H. Thomas Austern. Early in chapter two, Green quotes Austern as asking whether Green had read Brandeis and Warren's famous 1890 article, "The Right to Privacy" (p. 28). No, Green replied. One wishes Green had taken the hint before The Other Government went to press. If he had—assuming Green's oft-repeated words of praise for Justice Brandeis were sincerely meant—he surely would have written a very different book. He would, among other things, have attempted to get his facts straight, collect his thoughts, marshal his arguments, and exclude from consideration the bratty, gratuitous attacks on other people that, I surmise, constitute The Other Government's chief commercial appeal.   *   *   *

Daniel D. Polsby
Legal Adviser to Commissioner Glen O. Robinson
Federal Communications Commission

MARK GREEN, THE OTHER VIEW OF THE OTHER
GOVERNMENT: A REPLY *

74 Mich.L.Rev. 1084 (1975).

The first rule of authorship is not to reply to reviews. Who is surprised that an author likes his book better than a critic does? Hence, a book should stand or fall as written. Subsequent rebuttals and explanations by authors rarely serve any redeeming social purpose.

With *The Other Government: The Unseen Power of Washington Lawyers*, it has not proven especially difficult to comply with this unwritten rule. The book has been reviewed more favorably than it probably deserves (*e. g.*, Professor John Kenneth Galbraith in *The New York Times Book Review*, Joseph Califano in *The Harvard Law Bulletin*) and less so (*The Washingtonian, The Greensboro News*). In the end, it all approximately washes out.

With one exception. Daniel Polsby's review * * * is so vituperative, one-sided and small-minded that it is a rule-breaker. * * *

The difference traces to motive. Is the writer's purpose to weigh the good and bad of a work—the usual function of honest criticism— or is it to shoehorn all observations into a preconceived form? Polsby seems to find in the system of Washington law no defects, no unfairly influential actors; in *The Other Government* he finds not a page, a thought, a punctuation that has any merit. * * * Polsby's obvious one-sidedness raises the question of his motive or perspective. That he comes from one of the two law firms discussed in the book seems not irrelevant.

To appreciate Polsby's bias, let me discuss a few of his characteristic swipes. * * * [T]he only way to understand his technique is to stitch together small examples to reveal the larger pattern of his animus.

The reviewer's itchiness for the clever sally becomes apparent in his first paragraph. After quoting my opening sentences, in which a tourist bus drives by Washington's monuments but not its law firms, Polsby writes, "This is a particularly felicitous beginning for The Other Government. The Tourline bus company is fictional, and none of the many Washington tour bus companies has a route that follows Rock Creek Parkway. In short, Mark Green's Washington could be the capital city of Franz Kafka's Amerika. Each book * * * subtly shifts the relationship between truth and fantasy, the real and the unreal." * * * All this because of one tourist bus? Incidentally, this bus did take the precise route described on that summer's day in 1974 when I saw it crawling along full of curious citizens.

Another repeated technique is his use of selective references. While Polsby did not invent this device, he deploys it with much skill. He writes, for example, that "[Lloyd] Cutler appears to hold a strange fascination for Green, who compares him to Mao Tse-Tung (p. 55) but leaves it open whether Cutler is an 'evil genius' (p. 169) or a 'guiding genius' (p. 252)." First, *The Other Government* is a book, not a courtroom brief; where is Polsby's sense of humor, his tolerance of some poetic license? I, of course, did not literally compare Mao and Lloyd. After tracing the history of Wilmer, Cutler and Pickering, I wrote, "There may not be large, brooding posters of his visage on the walls, but Lloyd Cutler dominates the firm he helped found. Like Mao Tse-Tung, once a founding father, always a founding father.* Second, it was not I but Michael Pertschuk, Senate Commerce General Counsel, who called Cutler an "evil genius" because of his work on the 1966 Traffic and Safety Act; and it was Tom Barr, of Cravath, Swaine & Moore, who called Cutler "the guiding genius of the [Violence Commission]." By compressing all this into one sentence, Polsby both trivializes and overstates my point.

*   *   *

There are also sporadic hints in the review that the book is conclusory and sloppy. "Criticisms are advanced *ex nihilo* or by third persons and seldom supported with reasons," he writes, later adding that "there is strong textual evidence that *The Other Government* was rushed into print"—the "strong" evidence being three alleged typographical errors in a 100,000 word book. I only wish the book had been rushed along. Instead, it was published nine months after the completion of the manuscript, the normal gestation period for manuscripts to reach print. Research for the book consumed healthy chunks of five years. *The Other Government's* case studies and conclusions are supported by over 300 interviews and some 600 footnotes; prior to publication the manuscript was read for errors by four attorneys, Lloyd Cutler among them, who either are or were in the two

---

* The reviewer is oddly uncharitable toward metaphors and allusions. He notes that I refer to Covington & Burling as the Everest of Washington and also later say "Great institutions come, peak and decline, from the British East India Trade Company to Life magazine to the New York Yankees, and it is only in retrospect that we learn that moment in time when events conspired to undo institutional inevitability." Polsby, predictably, then shoots his popgun. "Well, which is to be? Tenzings on the Everest of powerlaw, or the Yankees on their way to the cellar? Since both propositions are expounded and neither is anywhere illustrated, it presumably does not matter."

Not illustrated? Did he read the book? Pages 16–31 carefully explain C & B's historical rise to the acknowledged top. And material on pages 33–44, as well as throughout the entire book, explain how C & B may now be inching downhill. This hardly constitutes a contradiction, except to those who jam in one sentence two references (Everest, Yankees) which appear 28 pages and many decades apart.

major firms discussed. These things alone, of course, do not prove the book's accuracy, but they do reflect the care that went into writing and leavening the manuscript * * *.

Although Polsby conveys the impression that the book is pockmarked with errors, there are almost no examples offered to sustain his point. And one that is offered is itself wrong. [Green here quotes Polsby's comments regarding Benjamin Bradlee's opinions.] * * * Bradlee, it should be noted, did not deny the fact of his phone conversation with Cutler. More importantly, my source for the Bradlee opinion of Cutler's activity is a prominent figure associated with the Washington Post who is close to Bradlee and who personally repeated Bradlee's quoted comments about Cutler. Especially after his experience with the Woodward and Bernstein articles and books, I am sure Ben Bradlee will respect the fact that this source—who spoke to both Ralph Nader and myself—wishes to remain confidential. In this instance, Bradlee simply does not recall a brief comment he made several years ago.

These small abuses of critical technique accumulate to cripple Polsby's ability to appreciate the book's thesis and documentation. In fact, he cannot see anything wrong with the process or practice of Washington corporate law. Time and again he asserts that Washington lawyers are not particularly powerful, as he occasionally gives examples of cases they have lost. "After a year's personal experience in government," he writes, giving us a glimpse at his underwhelming data base, "I am deeply skeptical of claims that the special access and charisma of super-lawyers exert much influence on government policy." * * *

These views would not be surprising in a Covington & Burling senior partner, who would probably have difficulty rendering an objective review of this book. But it is unusual to find one so unburdened by governmental and corporate experience writing as if Washington lawyers toiled in the City of God. Even given his one-sidedness, can Polsby really be unaware of the following:

● Even in cases Washington lawyers lose, they can win. Delaying a regulatory cut-off or sanction can enable a client to profit in the interim. * * *

● Of course, Washington lawyers do prevail in many actions. The extremely low tax rates of multinational oil firms and the large number of drugs labeled as unsafe or inefficacious by the National Academy of Sciences—and still on the market—indicate that these counsel are not invariably losers.

● The adversary process often fails to operate in political forums like Congress and many regulatory agencies. Businesses can afford ample and able counsel to promote

their interests. But other than a small corps of public
interest lawyers, opposing consumer interests often lack
adequate representation. * * *

● Not only is the process of Washington lawyering institu-
tionally defective, but there are also instances of personally improper behavior. * * *

● If an average lawyer can gain an audience with Treasury
Secretary John Connally, as Lloyd Cutler did on the
American-Western Airlines merger case, or can claim
authorship of the act under question, as H. Thomas Austern does with the 1938 Food, Drug and Cosmetic Act,
then perhaps Washington lawyers do lack special influence and access. * * *

Polsby's absolutist view of the purity of Washington lawyers
predictably leads him to dismiss my conclusions. He writes, "Green
appears to believe that good and evil go around unmasked, equally
obvious to all and that only greed and perversity can explain differences among people about the identity of each. * * * For Green,
* * * the axis of decision is always substantive right and wrong;
his conception of right is usually vivid and seldom unalloyed by doubt.
Accordingly, the whole idea of regular process seems senseless to
him." This rendition is so simplistic and misstated that it raises
questions about the good faith and purpose of the reviewer. For I
argue that, precisely because the process of Washington law is flawed
by politics, favoritism, and lack of adversariness, it leads to substantive injustice. Polsby is apparently content with existing process;
I am not. This conclusion, of course, exactly contradicts the assertion that *The Other Government* was indifferent about process.

My point about what is characterized as "good and evil" was
that (a) a lawyer should recognize obligations to nonparty interests
affected by his or her advocacy and (b) he or she was free in civil or
legislative proceedings to reject retainers if, based on personal judgment, "the client desires tactics based on political influence or seeks
a demonstrable though avoidable public harm." The reviewer's
condensation fails to convey the context of this difficult issue, which
is discussed for an entire chapter. "This new ethic is no Rosetta
stone instructing all lawyers what to do in all situations," I write at
one point. "Like any ethical judgment, it is subjective and personal,
not universal, though the lawyer may wish others to follow his example. It is an ethic that throws the lawyer back on his own subjective preferences, his own view of 'the public interest'. This is
surely not new. What is the adversary process itself but a social
judgement that legal combat is in the public interest because it leads
to justice—a conclusion the author shares but one which, for example, China and Herbert Marcuse do not. Nor is it a neutral prin-

ciple that lawyers will represent those who can pay and not represent those who cannot. This means-test effectively excludes a large class of Americans from access to legal services; it is very much a value choice. So is the ethic of conscientious refusal" (pp. 287–88). This and other elaborations are omitted. Instead, Polsby parodies the point, and then attacks the parody.

Indeed, this technique runs throughout the entire review, for I did not recognize the book under discussion. Polsby's acid adjectives—"malicious * * * bratty"—say far more about himself than about his target.** It is painfully self-serving to say, as many of the lawyers in the firms discussed have privately said, that *The Other Government* is a careful and empirical analysis of the process and impact of the practice of Washington law. If you understandably discount the prior sentence as a child of bias, well, read the book. It is the best impeachment of Polsby's rantings.

What is the method to his badness? Being most charitable, one could argue that Polsby lacks *mens rea*. Former Wilmer, Cutler and Pickering attorneys have described Dan Polsby's widespread reputation as a jokester associate. It seems a fertile sense of humor would inspire him to send fictitious memoranda around the firm, of the following variety: "We have today retained Secretary of State Henry Kissinger in a libel action against Madame Chiang Kai Shek." Such humor raised a few eyebrows at the firm, but came to be accepted, even enjoyed, for its color among the greyness. So perhaps Polsby was extending his reputation as a satirist, writing a caricature of the poisonous review. In that, he succeeded. Or perhaps Polsby was engaged in his own form of primal therapy, since his review throws not a dart but a fit. In that, too, he succeeded.

> Mark Green
> Author of *The Other Government* and
> Former Director of Ralph Nader's
> Corporate Accountability Research
> Group

** About Polsby's yen for the *ad hominem*, the less said the better. It further reveals how nastiness can overwhelm judgement. Suffice it to say that while Polsby writes, "I do not, however, accuse Green of being totalitarian," he does call me "a demagogue" two sentences later. Thank goodness for implied compliments, as I would certainly prefer being a non-totalitarian demagogue to a totalitarian demagogue.

INDEX

References are to Pages

†